Legal Library
Government Employees Insurance Company

BLASHFIELD
AUTOMOBILE LAW AND PRACTICE

REVISED THIRD EDITION

VOLUME 11
Sections 416 to 434

TRIAL EVIDENCE

Author
DEAN PATRICK D. KELLY
University of Missouri—Kansas City School of Law

St. Paul, Minn.
WEST PUBLISHING COMPANY
1977

COPYRIGHT © 1968, 1970 through 1976 WEST PUBLISHING CO.

COPYRIGHT © 1977
By
WEST PUBLISHING CO.

Library of Congress Catalog Card Number: 77-78522

PREFACE

The adoption of the Federal Rules of Evidence and the many changes and developments in trial evidence since publication of Blashfield Trial Evidence volumes 11 and 12 in 1969 as a unit of the comprehensive practice oriented Third Edition have made necessary the revision of Trial Evidence volumes 11 and 12. Volume 11 as revised contains sections 416 through 434; volume 12, to be published later in 1977, will contain sections 435 through 449.

Recognizing the substantial trend toward enactment of "Codes" of Evidence, revised Trial Evidence volumes 11 and 12 incorporate citations to the Federal Rules of Evidence and to the state codes of evidence adopted to the time of revision. Other states have been deliberating on adoption of a code of evidence and some may be expected to enact codes, citations to which will be included in the annual pocket parts to the two volumes.

The material is organized according to the classical titles of Evidence law. At the same time, the emphasis in section titles and other headings is on the "words of art" of the trial lawyer.

Specifically the substantial segment on Relevancy and Materiality is organized to parallel the usual allegations of negligence and particular accident situations. The user may make easy cross reference to the substantive law sections in the "Facts of Liability" volumes of this set, and to the investigation "Checklists" in volume 1 on "Trial Preparation".

Also the law on Sufficiency of Evidence is organized principally under titles of the usual issues in automobile accident litigation. Again the lawyer may cross reference from this volume to substantive law discussion of negligence allegations and special problems of particular accidents in other volumes of this set.

These newly revised Trial Evidence volumes 11 and 12 have been prepared by Dean Patrick D. Kelly, of the UMKC School of Law. Dean Kelly was formerly a trial lawyer in Des Moines, Iowa, and has been a Professor of Evidence Law since 1961.

THE PUBLISHER

May, 1977

SUMMARY OF CONTENTS

Volume 11
TRIAL EVIDENCE

Chapter		Sections
416.	Burden of Proof	416.1–416.12
417.	Presumptions and Inferences	417.1–417.8
418.	Res Ipsa Loquitur	418.1–418.3
419.	Examination of Witnesses	419.1–419.3
420.	Cross-Examination	420.1–420.2
421.	Impeachment of Witnesses	421.1–421.6
422.	Competency of Witnesses	422.1–422.2
423.	Privileged Evidence	423.1–423.4
424.	Relevancy and Materiality—In General	424.1–424.5
425.	Relevancy and Materiality—Operation of Vehicles	425.1–425.9
426.	Relevancy and Materiality—Particular Accidents	426.1–426.7
427.	Relevancy and Materiality—Competency and Condition of Driver	427.1–427.3
428.	Relevancy and Materiality—Persons Liable	428.1–428.4
429.	Relevancy and Materiality—Damages	429.1–429.2
430.	Lay Opinion Evidence	430.1–430.2
431.	Expert Opinion Evidence	431.1–431.6
432.	Scientific Evidence	432.1–432.2
433.	Proof of Writings	433.1–433.2
434.	Hearsay	434.1–434.12

Volume 12

435.	Demonstrative Evidence	435.1–435.10
436.	Judicial Notice	436.1–436.5
437.	Sufficiency of Evidence—In General	437.1–437.6
438.	Sufficiency of Evidence—Negligence	438.1–438.6
439.	Sufficiency of Evidence—Negligence in Operation of Motor Vehicles	439.1–439.11
440.	Sufficiency of Evidence—Competency and Condition of Driver	440.1–440.3

SUMMARY OF CONTENTS

Chapter		Sections
441.	Sufficiency of Evidence—Other Particular Accidents	441.1–441.9
442.	Sufficiency of Evidence—Contributory Negligence	442.1–442.7
443.	Sufficiency of Evidence—Proximate Cause	443.1–443.3
444.	Sufficiency of Evidence—Persons Liable	444.1–444.6
445.	Sufficiency of Evidence—Damages	445.1–445.9

TABLE OF CONTENTS

Volume 11

TRIAL EVIDENCE

CHAPTER 416. BURDEN OF PROOF

Sec.
- 416.1 Burden of Proof—In General.
- 416.2 —— Negligent Operation of Vehicle.
- 416.3 —— Negligence Other than Vehicle Operation.
- 416.4 —— Gross Negligence or Wilful, Wanton or Reckless Conduct.
- 416.5 —— Persons Vicariously Liable.
- 416.6 —— Proximate Cause.
- 416.7 —— Contributory Negligence in General.
- 416.8 —— Contributory Negligence of Passengers.
- 416.9 —— Damages.
- 416.10 —— Limitation of Actions.
- 416.11 —— Venue.
- 416.12 Variance of Proof.

CHAPTER 417. PRESUMPTIONS AND INFERENCES

- 417.1 In General.
- 417.2 Exercise of Care in General.
- 417.3 Exercise of Care by Injured Party.
- 417.4 Exercise of Care by Defendant.
- 417.5 Ownership or Control.
- 417.6 Consent and Permission.
- 417.7 Agency.
- 417.8 Other Particular Matters.

CHAPTER 418. RES IPSA LOQUITUR

- 418.1 In General.
- 418.2 Situations Applicable.
- 418.3 Situations Not Applicable.

CHAPTER 419. EXAMINATION OF WITNESSES

- 419.1 In General.
- 419.2 Leading Questions.
- 419.3 Refreshing Recollection.

TABLE OF CONTENTS

CHAPTER 420. CROSS–EXAMINATION

Sec.
420.1 In General.
420.2 Permissible Scope.

CHAPTER 421. IMPEACHMENT OF WITNESSES

421.1 Impeachment—In General.
421.2 ——— Prior Inconsistent Statements.
421.3 ——— Contradiction of Facts.
421.4 ——— Bias.
421.5 ——— Character.
421.6 ——— Rehabilitation.

CHAPTER 422. COMPETENCY OF WITNESSES

422.1 Competency of Witnesses—In General.
422.2 Incompetency of Survivor of Transaction Had With Deceased.

CHAPTER 423. PRIVILEGED EVIDENCE

423.1 Privileged Evidence—In General.
423.2 Offers of Compromise.
423.3 Doctor-Patient Privilege.
423.4 Attorney-Client Privilege.

CHAPTER 424. RELEVANCY AND MATERIALITY— IN GENERAL

424.1 General Rules of Relevancy.
424.2 Proof of Legal Fault—In General.
424.3 ——— As Limited by Pleadings.
424.4 ——— Conditions Existing.
424.5 ——— Conditions Subsequent to Accident.

CHAPTER 425. RELEVANCY AND MATERIALITY— OPERATION OF VEHICLES

425.1 Operation of Vehicles—In General.
425.2 ——— Speed.
425.3 ——— Lookout.
425.4 ——— Control.
425.5 ——— Right of Way.
425.6 ——— Lights.
425.7 ——— Signals and Warnings.
425.8 ——— Stopping and Parking.
425.9 ——— Turning.

CHAPTER 426. RELEVANCY AND MATERIALITY— PARTICULAR ACCIDENTS

426.1 Proof of Legal Fault—Railroad Crossing Collisions.
426.2 ——— Favored Vehicle Accidents.

TABLE OF CONTENTS

Sec.
426.3 —— Collisions With Street Obstructions or Defects.
426.4 —— Collisions With Animals.
426.5 —— Pedestrian Accidents.
426.6 —— Injury to Passenger.
426.7 —— Defective Equipment.

CHAPTER 427. RELEVANCY AND MATERIALITY—COMPETENCY AND CONDITION OF DRIVER

427.1 Proof of Legal Fault—Competency of Driver.
427.2 —— Condition of Driver—In General.
427.3 —— —— Intoxication.

CHAPTER 428. RELEVANCY AND MATERIALITY—PERSONS LIABLE

428.1 Proof of Ownership and Control.
428.2 Proof of Agency Relationship.
428.3 Proof of Operation Within Scope of Agency.
428.4 Family Purpose Doctrine.

CHAPTER 429. RELEVANCY AND MATERIALITY—DAMAGES

429.1 Proof of Damages—Personal Injury.
429.2 —— Property Damage.

CHAPTER 430. LAY OPINION EVIDENCE

430.1 Lay Opinions—In General.
430.2 —— Speed.

CHAPTER 431. EXPERT OPINION EVIDENCE

431.1 Expert Opinion—In General.
431.2 Qualification of Expert.
431.3 Expert Opinion—Reconstruction of Occurrence.
431.4 —— Speed.
431.5 —— Bodily Injury.
431.6 —— Other Particular Matters.

CHAPTER 432. SCIENTIFIC EVIDENCE

432.1 Scientific Tests—In General.
432.2 —— Blood Tests.

CHAPTER 433. PROOF OF WRITINGS

433.1 Authentication of Writings.
433.2 "Best Evidence" Rule.

TABLE OF CONTENTS

CHAPTER 434. HEARSAY

Sec.
434.1   Hearsay—In General.
434.2   Admissions—In General.
434.3   —— As to Negligent Conduct.
434.4   —— As to Status in Vehicle.
434.5   —— As to Status of Persons Alleged to be Vicariously Liable.
434.6   Testimony at a Prior Hearing.
434.7   Dying Declarations.
434.8   Spontaneous Declarations.
434.9   Statements of Bodily Condition.
434.10 Business Records—In General.
434.11 —— Police Reports.
434.12 Other Particular Exceptions.

Volume 12

CHAPTER 435. DEMONSTRATIVE EVIDENCE

435.1   Demonstrative Evidence—In General.
435.2   Photographs—In General.
435.3   —— Of Accident Scenes.
435.4   —— Of Vehicles.
435.5   Motion Pictures.
435.6   X-Rays—In General.
435.7   —— Identification and Authentication.
435.8   Models.
435.9   Maps, Plats and Diagrams.
435.10 Courtroom Demonstrations.

CHAPTER 436. JUDICIAL NOTICE

436.1   Judicial Notice—In General.
436.2   Matters of Common Knowledge.
436.3   Matters Easily Verified.
436.4   Statutes and Regulations.
436.5   Other Particular Subjects.

CHAPTER 437. SUFFICIENCY OF EVIDENCE— IN GENERAL

437.1   General Rules as to Sufficiency of Evidence.
437.2   Credibility of Witnesses.
437.3   Effect of Admissions.
437.4   Value of "Negative" Evidence.
437.5   Use of Circumstantial Evidence.
437.6   "Physical Facts" Rule.

CHAPTER 438. SUFFICIENCY OF EVIDENCE— NEGLIGENCE

438.1   Negligence—In General.
438.2   Subsequent Negligence (Last Clear Chance and Humanitarian Doctrine).
438.3   Willful or Wanton Negligence.

TABLE OF CONTENTS

Sec.
438.4 Gross Negligence.
438.5 Habitual Negligence.
438.6 Sudden Emergency Doctrine.

CHAPTER 439. SUFFICIENCY OF EVIDENCE—NEGLIGENCE IN OPERATION OF MOTOR VEHICLES

439.1 Lookout.
439.2 Speed.
439.3 Control.
439.4 Following, Overtaking and Passing.
439.5 Being Overtaken.
439.6 Yielding, at Intersections.
439.7 Yielding, to Oncoming Vehicles.
439.8 Stopping and Parking.
439.9 Signals and Warnings.
439.10 Presence or Use of Lights.
439.11 Other Particular Conduct.

CHAPTER 440. SUFFICIENCY OF EVIDENCE—COMPETENCY AND CONDITION OF DRIVER

440.1 Competency of Driver.
440.2 Condition of Driver—In General.
440.3 —— Intoxication.

CHAPTER 441. SUFFICIENCY OF EVIDENCE—OTHER PARTICULAR ACCIDENTS

441.1 Negligence—Railroad Crossing Conditions.
441.2 —— Operation of Train.
441.3 —— Favored Vehicle Collisions.
441.4 —— Roadway Conditions.
441.5 —— Restraint of Animals.
441.6 —— Pedestrian Injuries.
441.7 —— Defective Vehicles.
441.8 Passenger Injuries—Negligence.
441.9 —— Status of Occupant.

CHAPTER 442. SUFFICIENCY OF EVIDENCE—CONTRIBUTORY NEGLIGENCE

442.1 In General.
442.2 Motor Vehicle Operation—In General.
442.3 Operation of Motor Vehicle—At Railroad Crossings.
442.4 Conduct of Pedestrians.
442.5 Conduct of Passengers.
442.6 Conduct of Bicyclist.
442.7 Conduct of Other Particular Classes of Persons.

CHAPTER 443. SUFFICIENCY OF EVIDENCE—PROXIMATE CAUSE

443.1 In General.
443.2 Motor Vehicle Accidents—In General.
443.3 Railroad Crossing Accidents.

TABLE OF CONTENTS

CHAPTER 444. SUFFICIENCY OF EVIDENCE —PERSONS LIABLE

Sec.
444.1 Identity of Driver and Vehicle.
444.2 Status as Owner or Custodian.
444.3 Consent of Owner.
444.4 Agency—Existence of Relationship.
444.5 —— Conduct Within Scope.
444.6 Partnership or Joint Adventure.

CHAPTER 445. SUFFICIENCY OF EVIDENCE— DAMAGES

445.1 Bodily Injury—In General.
445.2 —— Existence of Injury.
445.3 —— Issue of Causation.
445.4 —— Issue of Permanency.
445.5 —— Issue of Other Future Consequences.
445.6 Death Actions.
445.7 Property Damage.
445.8 Punitive Damages.
445.9 Mitigation of Damages.

†

BLASHFIELD
AUTOMOBILE LAW AND PRACTICE
REVISED THIRD EDITION

TRIAL EVIDENCE

Chapter 416

BURDEN OF PROOF

Table of Sections

Sec.
- 416.1 Burden of Proof—In General.
- 416.2 —— Negligent Operation of Vehicle.
- 416.3 —— Negligence Other than Vehicle Operation.
- 416.4 —— Gross Negligence or Wilful, Wanton or Reckless Conduct.
- 416.5 —— Persons Vicariously Liable.
- 416.6 —— Proximate Cause.
- 416.7 —— Contributory Negligence in General.
- 416.8 —— Contributory Negligence of Passengers.
- 416.9 —— Damages.
- 416.10 —— Limitation of Actions.
- 416.11 —— Venue.
- 416.12 Variance of Proof.

§ 416.1 Burden of Proof—In General

Library References:
C.J.S. Evidence § 103 et seq.; Motor Vehicles § 509 et seq.
West's Key No. Digests, Automobiles ⟲242; Evidence ⟲90 et seq.

Burden of proof means the necessity or duty of affirmatively proving a fact in dispute on an issue raised between the parties in a cause.[1] The term "burden of proof" is often used loose-

---

1. **Cal.**—Polk v. Polk, 39 Cal.Rptr. 824, 228 Cal.App.2d 763.   **N.C.**—Banks v. Shepard, 52 S.E.2d 215, 230 N.C. 86.

11 Blashfield Auto Law Revised 3rd Ed.

ly by the courts, and it is often difficult to determine whether the court meant "burden of proof" in its technical sense, or merely meant "burden of evidence." [2] There is a plain distinction between "burden of proof" and "burden of evidence." The burden of proof never shifts, while the burden of evidence or the burden of explanation may shift from one side to the other according to the testimony offered as the trial proceeds.[3]

The party on whom the burden rests to establish the right of the controversy must produce credible evidence from which persons of unbiased minds can reasonably find the necessary facts.[4] It is most often stated that the burden is to prove the

2. **Ky.**—R. L. Jeffries Truck Line v. Brown, 197 S.W.2d 904, 303 Ky. 405; Kentucky & Indiana Terminal R. Co. v. Cantrell, 184 S.W.2d 111, 298 Ky. 743.

3. **Cal.**—Allbritton v. Interstate Transit Lines, 87 P.2d 704, 31 Cal. App.2d 149.

Ga.—Lawson v. Dixie Feed & Seed Co., 145 S.E.2d 820, 112 Ga.App. 562.

Ky.—Houser v. Coursey, 221 S.W.2d 432, 310 Ky. 625.

Me.—Bushwell v. Fuller, 36 A. 1059, 89 Me. 600.

Md.—Operations Research Inc. v. Davidson & Talbird, Inc., 217 A.2d 375, 241 Md. 550.

Minn.—Lestico v. Kuehner, 283 N.W. 122, 204 Minn. 125.

Mo.—Feurt v. Ambroze, 34 Mo.App. 360.

N.Y.—Barber v. Jewel Tea Co., 300 N.Y.S. 302, 252 App.Div. 362, affirmed 16 N.E.2d 94, 278 N.Y. 540.

Pa.—Tassoni v. LeBoutillier, 196 A. 534, 130 Pa.Super. 303.

R.I.—De Arruda v. Newport Creamery, 197 A. 474, 60 R.I. 153.

Tenn.—Hansard v. Ferguson, 132 S. W.2d 221, 23 Tenn.App. 306.

Va.—Brooks v. Worthington, 143 S.E. 2d 841, 206 Va. 352.

Rule stated in guest case

In action by guest, evidence that driver fell asleep before collision places burden on driver to offer proof of circumstances in excuse or justification of his conduct. Cooper v. Kellogg, 42 P.2d 59, 2 Cal.2d 504.

4. **Alaska.**—Saxton v. Harris, 395 P. 2d 71 (must induce a belief in the minds of the jurors that asserted facts are probably true).

La.—Gassiott v. Gordey, La.App., 182 So.2d 170 (which is of greater weight or more convincing than that which is offered in opposition to it; that is, evidence which as a whole shows that fact or causation sought to be proved is more probable than not).

Me.—Wiggin v. Sanborn, 210 A.2d 38, 161 Me. 175 (as to certain issues the quality of evidence essential to proof must be of a high degree, else it will not preponderate).

N.H.—Bresnahan v. Manchester Coal & Ice Co., 188 A. 10, 88 N.H. 273 (assumed no greater burden than to make it a little more probable than otherwise that collision was caused by truck driver's negligence).

N.Y.—Motor Vehicle Acc. Indemnification Corp. v. Mahoney, 258 N.Y. S.2d 801, 46 Misc.2d 3, affirmed 270 N.Y.S.2d 831, 25 A.D.2d 821 (that existence of a fact is more probable than its nonexistence).

fact by a "preponderance or greater weight of the evidence."[5] However, the burden is variously described in different jurisdictions where the party relies upon circumstantial evidence alone.[6]

[5] **U.S.**—St. Louis Testing Laboratories, Inc. v. Mississippi Val. Structural Steel Co., D.C.Mo., 254 F.Supp. 47.

Ga.—Slater v. Dodd, 134 S.E.2d 848, 108 Ga.App. 879 (by a legal preponderance).

Ill.—Pedrick v. Peoria & E. R. Co., 211 N.E.2d 134, 63 Ill.App.2d 117.

La.—Mayon v. New Amsterdam Cas. Co., App., 191 So.2d 688; Tarbox v. Eason, App., 179 So.2d 916 (reasonable preponderance).

Minn.—Wick v. Widdell, 149 N.W.2d 20, 276 Minn. 51 (fair preponderance).

Neb.—Kolar v. Divis, 140 N.W.2d 658, 179 Neb. 756.

N.Y.—City of New York v. Benenson, 244 N.Y.S.2d 653, 41 Misc.2d 20 (by fair preponderance of credible evidence).

S.C.—Grier v. Cornelius, 148 S.E.2d 338, 247 S.C. 521.

S.D.—Weidner v. Lineback, 140 N.W. 2d 597, 82 S.D. 8 (mere preponderance of probability).

Tenn.—Crowe v. Provost, 374 S.W. 2d 645, 52 Tenn.App. 397.

Not by number of witnesses alone

U.S.—Jones v. U. S., D.C.La., 239 F. Supp. 474.

Ohio.—In re Soeder's Estate, 220 N.E. 2d 547, 7 Ohio App.2d 271.

"Preponderance" defined

U.S.—Jones v. U. S., D.C.La., 239 F. Supp. 474 (means to prove by production of such evidence as will convince trier of facts that issue asserted is more likely so than not so).

La.—Town of Slidell v. Temple, 164 So.2d 276, 246 La. 137 (means evidence which is of greater weight or more convincing than that which is offered in opposition to it).

Tex.—Fort Worth & D. Ry. Co. v. Williams, Tex., 375 S.W.2d 279 (mere scintilla of evidence is equated with "no evidence" and will support nothing more substantial than a surmise or conjecture).

Proof beyond mere scintilla

Wash.—Kurtz v. Fels, 389 P.2d 659, 63 Wash.2d 871 (means proof of facts to be assessed by senses, i. e. something seen, said, done, measured, written, or felt, in the tactile sense).

[6] **U.S.**—Kapuschinsky v. U. S., D.C. S.C., 248 F.Supp. 732 (does not mean that it must be conclusive beyond reasonable doubt).

Idaho.—Dent v. Hardware Mut. Cas. Co., 388 P.2d 89, 86 Idaho 427 (must establish circumstances of such nature and so related to each other that theory of liability is the more reasonable conclusion to be drawn).

La.—Gassiott v. Gordey, La.App., 182 So.2d 170 (by circumstantial evidence which excludes other reasonable hypotheses with a fair amount of certainty).

Mo.—Willoughby v. Safeway Stores, Inc., Mo.App., 397 S.W.2d 748 (must establish desired inference with such certainty as to cause it to be the more reasonable and probable of the conclusions to be drawn, and must rise above stature of guesswork, speculation or surmise).

Neb.—Petracek v. Haas O. K. Rubber Welders, Inc., 126 N.W.2d 466, 176 Neb. 438 (must be of such character and circumstances so related to each other that a conclusion fairly and reasonably arises that cause of action has been proved).

If all the evidence considered together leaves the case in equipoise, or evenly balanced, the party having the affirmative of the issue must fail.[7]

This rule is not relaxed merely because the facts are so veiled by reason of death of one of the drivers that no evidence of any persuasive character on the part of the plaintiff can be found,[8] because one party is disadvantaged by youth,[9] or because the plaintiff is mentally retarded or incapable of understanding what happened;[10] but the court will take a very liberal view of the testimony introduced by the plaintiff.[11]

Pa.—Fringer v. West York, Pa.Com. Pl.1965, 79 York 142, 166 (must so preponderate as to outweigh any other reasonable inferences inconsistent therewith).

Tex.—Mansell v. Hendrickson, 1967, 417 S.W.2d 908 (the burden to establish that under all circumstances in evidence the ultimate facts as found by jury on issues submitted by court probably occurred; it is not necessary to exclude that it might possibly have occurred in another manner).

7. U.S.—Diesel Tanker F. A. Verdon, Inc. v. Stakeboat No. 2, C.A. N.Y., 340 F.2d 465 (must do more than create a doubt which trier of facts is unable to resolve).

Ga.—Liberty Nat. Life Ins. Co. v. Liner, 149 S.E.2d 523, 73 Ga.App. 673.

La.—Crier v. Marquette Cas. Co., App., 159 So.2d 26, application denied 160 So.2d 229, 245 La. 644.

Minn.—Indianhead Truck Line, Inc. v. Anderson, 139 N.W.2d 271, 272 Minn. 497.

Ohio.—Hopkins v. Kissinger, 166 N. E. 916, 31 Ohio App. 229.

Tex.—Republic Nat. Life Ins. Co. v. Bullard, 399 S.W.2d 376, ref. n. r. e.

8. N.Y.—Wragge v. Lizza Asphalt Const. Co., 270 N.Y.S.2d 616, 17 N.Y.2d 313, 217 N.E.2d 666.

Wis.—Fiedler v. Kapsa, 39 N.W.2d 682, 255 Wis. 559.

9. Mo.—Graham v. Conner, App., 412 S.W.2d 193 (burden did not shift merely because pedestrian was of tender years while driver was an adult).

10. Tex.—McPhearson v. Sullivan, Civ.App.1970, 457 S.W.2d 583, reversed on other grounds 463 S.W. 2d 174.

11. N.Y.—Wartels v. County Asphalt, Inc., 1972, 328 N.Y.S.2d 410, 29 N.Y.2d 372, 278 N.E.2d 627 (highly dangerous condition of flatbed trailer blocking both lanes of expressway created by negligence in an excessive degree and posing a sudden, not to be anticipated peril, reduced burden of proof on plaintiff motorist, who sustained amnesia as a consequence of accident, almost to the vanishing point); Herbert v. W. H. Smith Paper Corporation, 1935, 276 N.Y.S. 820, 243 App.Div. 260.

S.C.—Brock v. Carolina Scenic Stages & Carolina Cas. Co. of Burlington, 65 S.E.2d 468, 219 S.C. 360.

Rule illustrated

Where automobile owned and driven by defendant administrator's intestate ran off highway into ditch while plaintiff's intestate was riding therein as guest passenger, burden was not on plaintiff to prove exactly what caused accident, but she made out prima facie case by introducing in evidence her intestate's deposition showing that automobile was

The rules of law on the subject of the burden of proof have for their purpose the establishment of the material facts in the most convenient way. In the administration of justice, it is often wise to place the ultimate burden of proof on the party best able to sustain it. It is usually possible for the party injured to prove the ownership of the car by which he was injured. On the other hand, the defendant is well able to show that the car was driven by a stranger or on an errand having no connection with the defendant's business, or that the automobile was stolen while the owner was away from home.[12]

The burden of proof is usually on the party who wishes to support the affirmative of a matter by a particular fact which lies more peculiarly within that party's knowledge, or of which the party ought to be cognizant.[13] As a general rule, where the existence of any fact is necessary for a party to make out a case or to establish a defense, the burden is on that party to show the existence of such fact.[14] Generally the burden of proof is upon

operated exclusively by defendant's intestate, whereupon burden shifted to defendant to show that accident was not due to his intestate's negligence. Threadgill v. Anderson, Okl., 303 P.2d 297.

12. Or.—West v. Kern, 171 P. 1050, 88 Or. 247.

13. U.S.—U. S. v. Hayes, C.A. Alaska, 369 F.2d 671; Erving Paper Mills v. Hudson-Sharp Machine Co., C.A.Wis., 332 F.2d 674.

Cal.—Carpenter Steel Co. v. Pellegrin, 46 Cal.Rptr. 502, 237 Cal.App. 2d 35, citing 31A C.J.S. Evidence § 113.

N.C.—Gardner v. City of Reidsville, 153 S.E.2d 139, 269 N.C. 581.

Pa.—Fazio v. Pittsburgh Rys. Co., 182 A. 696, 321 Pa. 7.

As to proof of a negative fact

Where burden of proof of negative fact normally rests on one party, but other party has peculiar knowledge or control of evidence as to such matter, burden rests on latter to produce such evidence, and failing, negative will be presumed to have been established. Allstate Finance Corp. v. Zimmerman, C.A.Fla., 330 F.2d 740, citing 31A C.J.S. Evidence § 113.

But see

That defendant necessarily was in exclusive possession of proof did not shift burden of going forward with proof from plaintiff to defendant, in view of availability to plaintiff of modern discovery. Tortora v. General Motors Corp., 130 N.W.2d 21, 373 Mich. 563.

14. Cal.—Du Frene v. Kaiser Steel Corp., 41 Cal.Rptr. 834, 231 Cal. App.2d 452.

Ind.—Decatur-Kocher Lumber, Inc. v. Ehrsam, 201 N.E.2d 568, 136 Ind. App. 397.

Iowa.—Race v. Iowa Elec. Light & Power Co., 134 N.W.2d 335, 257 Iowa 701.

La.—Levingston Supply Co. v. Basso, 164 So.2d 141.

Mont.—Stocking v. Johnson Flying Service, 387 P.2d 312, 143 Mont. 61.

Mo.—Chard v. Clarkson Const. Co., 377 S.W.2d 506.

N.C.—Powell v. Cross, 140 S.E.2d 393, 263 N.C. 764.

§ 416.1   TRIAL EVIDENCE   Ch. 416

the party who asserts the fact.[15] Included in this rule is the requirement that a party, who relies upon the law of another juris-

Okl.—Rudnicki v. Town of Valley Brook, 424 P.2d 973.

Pa.—Moyer v. Ford Motor Co., 209 A.2d 43, 205 Pa.Super. 384.

Vt.—Packard v. Quesnel, 22 A.2d 164, 112 Vt. 175.

Cross-action by one defendant against another

Where motorist and passenger in action against transit company did not amend their pleadings after coach company was made a party defendant by reason of transit company's cross-complaint, burden was upon transit company to show that the coach company was guilty of negligence which concurred with transit company's negligence. Pascal v. Burke Transit Co., 50 S.E.2d 534, 229 N.C. 435.

Where defendants in action for death resulting from automobile collision impleaded another, the burden of proof was on defendants to establish negligence of such other person. Frankland v. De Broux, 1947, 28 N.W.2d 256, 251 Wis. 210.

Defense under state indemnification plan

MVAIC, which filed application for order permanently staying arbitration of claim and which did not assert that claim was barred by limitations or that valid agreement was not made, had burden of establishing that matters it raised showed that insurance agreement had not been complied with. Hanavan v. Motor Vehicle Acc. Indemnification Corp., 1969, 303 N.Y.S.2d 117, 60 Misc.2d 407, affirmed 308 N.Y.S.2d 114, 33 A.D.2d 1100.

Fact of governmental immunity

In order to avoid, on theory of governmental immunity, liability for damages sustained by person as result of negligence of city employee, city must establish not only that department employing negligent employee was performing governmental function but also that employee was performing governmental duties at time of collision giving rise to claim for damages. City of Houston v. Edman, Tex.Civ.App.1973, 498 S.W.2d 464.

Foreign law

Question of existence of foreign law is matter of fact and person relying upon such law is under burden of going forward with proof of it at risk of nonpersuasion. Bostrom v. Seguros Tepeyac, S.A., D.C.Tex., 225 F.Supp. 222, affirmed in part, reversed in part, C.A., 347 F.2d 168 rehearing denied 360 F.2d 154.

Not as to negative averment

Burden of proof is on party who asserts affirmative, and one need not prove negative averment. Levine v. Pascal, 236 N.E.2d 425, 94 Ill.App.2d 43.

15. **U.S.**—Joseph A. Bass Co. v. U. S., to Use of Peter Kiewit Sons' Co., C.A.N.D., 340 F.2d 842; National Motor Freight Traffic Ass'n v. U. S., D.C.D.C., 242 F.Supp. 601.

Ariz.—Yeazell v. Copins, 402 P.2d 541, 98 Ariz. 109.

Ga.—Allstate Ins. Co. v. Austin, 1969, 170 S.E.2d 840, 120 Ga.App. 430, cause dismissed 172 S.E.2d 602, 226 Ga. 93.

Iowa.—Jennings v. Farmers Mut. Ins. Ass'n, 149 N.W.2d 298; Verschoor v. Miller, 143 N.W.2d 385, 259 Iowa 170.

N.M.—J. A. Silversmith, Inc. v. Marchiondo, 404 P.2d 122, 75 N.M. 290.

N.D.—Midland Oil & Royalty Co. v. Schuler, 126 N.W.2d 149, citing 31 C.J.S. Evidence § 104.

Tex.—Quarles v. Quarles, 386 S.W.2d 337, error dismissed, Sup., 388 S.W.2d 926.

diction, must prove facts which make the law of that jurisdiction applicable.[16]

However the rule is sometimes modified or limited. In suits against uninsured motorists funds, the plaintiff may have proof that the "John Doe" defendant is unknown; and the burden of producing proof of identity may then shift to the defendant.[17] Where the interest of fairness requires a party to plead a matter to avoid surprise, it may be held that the party does not assume the burden of proof.[18]

A defendant has been held to assume the burden of proof upon a certain fact which is not of itself a material issue in the case. By attempting to prove it, the defendant would be required to do so by a fair preponderance of the evidence bearing on that particular issue.[19]

The burden is always on the plaintiff to prove one's case [20] or cause of action.[21] It is incumbent on the plaintiff to prove

Plea of compensation and setoff

A plea of compensation and setoff raises special defense and burden of proof is on defendant entering plea. Ben C. Penn and Son v. Thompsons Packers, Inc., La.App., 169 So.2d 259.

16. Passing of vehicle title

Burden was on car dealer, to which car was being delivered at dealer's place of business, to show that title had not passed at time of accident in Michigan, to establish the facts that could make Ohio law applicable. Nichol v. El Par Motor Sales, 1973, 206 N.W.2d 790, 45 Mich.App. 426.

17. **Va.**—Haymore v. Brizendine, 1970, 172 S.E.2d 774, 210 Va. 578 (it was incumbent upon defendant to bring forth evidence that John Doe was known in order to justify verdict for defendant John Doe).

18. **N.Y.**—Liberty Lumber Co. v. Pye, 255 N.Y.S.2d 782, 44 Misc. 2d 950.

19. **Conn.**—Griffin v. Wood, 105 A. 354, 93 Conn. 99 (attempting to prove intoxication, because it tended to confirm his version of the accident).

20. **Fla.**—De Salvo v. Curry, 33 So. 2d 215, 160 Fla. 7.

Ga.—Clark v. Atlanta Veterans Transp., Inc., 148 S.E.2d 921, 113 Ga.App. 531.

Iowa.—Luppes v. Harrison, 32 N.W. 2d 809, 239 Iowa 88.

Mo.—Gildehaus v. Jones, 200 S.W.2d 523, 356 Mo. 8.

Okl.—Ball v. Autry, 1966, 427 P.2d 424.

Tex.—Walter E. Heller & Co. v. Allen, 412 S.W.2d 712.

Va.—Brown v. Parker, 189 S.E. 339, 167 Va. 286.

Wash.—Wappenstein v. Schrepel, 142 P.2d 897, 19 Wash.2d 371.

Wis.—Ernst v. Greenwald, 1967, 151 N.W.2d 706, 35 Wis.2d 763.

21. **Iowa.**—Cable v. Fullerton Lumber Co., 49 N.W.2d 530, 242 Iowa 1076.

La.—Fontenot v. Freudenstein, App., 199 So. 677 (action for injuries to child pedestrian).

N.Y.—Barber v. Jewel Tea Co., 300 N.Y.S. 302, 252 App.Div. 362, affirmed 16 N.E.2d 94, 278 N.Y. 540.

Tex.—G. & M. Products Corp. v. Clayton Specialties, Inc., 386 S.W. 2d 843.

§ 416.1   TRIAL EVIDENCE   Ch. 416

the material averments of the complaint (or pleading corresponding thereto),[22] and to establish the liability of the defendant,[23] a right to recover,[24] and beneficial ownership of property alleged to have been damaged.[25] However, matters admitted need not be proved.[26]

However, the plaintiff need not negate all reasonable inferences other than those supporting the claim;[27] and the plaintiff is not required to negative the existence of an emergency.[28]

22. **Ala.**—Ray v. Terry, 28 So.2d 916, 32 Ala.App. 582, certiorari dismissed, 28 So.2d 918, 248 Ala. 640.
Conn.—White v. Finch, 209 A.2d 199, 3 Conn.Cir. 138; Dunn v. Santamauro, 175 A. 913, 119 Conn. 307 (fact that truck driver was defendant's agent acting within scope of employment).
Iowa.—Wilde v. Griffel, 243 N.W. 159, 214 Iowa 1177 (guest action).
Ky.—Rodgers v. Roland, 219 S.W.2d 19, 309 Ky. 824 (that defendants were partners).
Me.—Chaisson v. Williams, 156 A. 154, 130 Me. 341 (guest action).
Mo.—Nichols v. Bresnahan, 212 S.W.2d 570, 357 Mo. 1126.
N.J.—Cohen v. Press, 105 A.2d 905, 31 N.J.Super. 45 (guest action).
Ohio.—Rossen v. Rossen, 208 N.E.2d 764, 2 Ohio App.2d 381.
Pa.—Baugh v. McCallum, 14 A.2d 364, 140 Pa.Super. 276 (averment of joint enterprise).
Tenn.—Hansard v. Ferguson, 132 S. W.2d 221, 23 Tenn.App. 306.
Tex.—Comet Motor Freight Lines v. Holmes, Civ.App., 175 S.W.2d 464, error refused.
Va.—Crabtree v. Dingus, 74 S.E.2d 54, 194 Va. 615 (guest action).
Wis.—Storlie v. Hartford Acc. & Indem. Co., 28 N.W.2d 920, 251 Wis. 340 (guest action).

23. **Ind.**—Same statement in prior edition **cited by the court** in Liberty Mut. Ins. Co. v. Stitzle, 41 N.E.2d 133, 220 Ind. 180.

Mo.—Connole v. East St. Louis & S. Ry. Co., 102 S.W.2d 581, 340 Mo. 690.

24. **Mich.**—Collar v. Maycroft, 264 N.W. 407, 274 Mich. 376.
Tex.—Wilson v. Willbanks, 393 S.W.2d 649.

25. **N.H.**—Grimes v. Labreck, 226 A.2d 787, 108 N.H. 26.

26. **Cal.**—Fuentes v. Lucker, 187 P.2d 752, 31 Cal.2d 1.
Ill.—Oran v. Kraft-Phenix Cheese Corporation, 58 N.E.2d 731, 324 Ill.App. 463.
Ind.—Oberlin v. Pyle, 49 N.E.2d 970, 114 Ind.App. 21.
Mo.—Wahlig v. Hill, App., 117 S.W.2d 706 (ownership of truck and employment of driver).
Ohio.—Cook v. Hunter, 3 N.E.2d 680, 52 Ohio App. 354.

27. **Cal.**—Erler v. Five Points Motors, 57 Cal.Rptr. 516; Lee v. Ashizawa, 37 Cal.Rptr. 71, 389 P.2d 535, 60 Cal.2d 862.

Contra where dependent upon a negative

Where negative is averred in pleading, or party's case depends upon establishment of negative, and means of proof are equally in control of each party, burden of proof is upon party averring negative. Chase Manhattan Bank v. O'Connor, 197 A.2d 706, 82 N.J.Super. 382.

28. **Iowa.**—Bletzer v. Wilson, 276 N.W. 836, 224 Iowa 884.

In some jurisdictions there are statutes under which certain allegations are taken as admitted unless denied under oath.[29] The plaintiff is not required, therefore, to offer proof of any of such allegations which are not so denied by the defendant,[30] though in some cases it seems that, as to particular allegations, it is incumbent on the plaintiff to prove them, whether denied or not.[31]

A plaintiff must prove the fact that the claimed accident actually happened,[32] and how the accident happened.[33] Where an accident is claimed to have taken place at an intersection of streets or highways, usually the burden of proving that the locus constituted an intersection rests on the plaintiff,[34] but in an action for injuries to the driver of the rear or overtaking vehicle, the defendant has the burden of establishing that the junction at that point constituted an intersection, justifying the overtaken motorist in presuming that no one would attempt to pass.[35]

Where an ordinance regulates the speed of automobiles in a business district, and provides different rates for the territory outside of such district, the burden is upon the plaintiff to show that the automobile was being operated on specific streets at a rate specially forbidden by the ordinance for that particular locality.[36]

29. See, for example, Rev.Code Ariz. 1952 Supp., § 21–430.

30. **Ariz.**—Mendez v. Moya, 91 P. 2d 870, 54 Ariz. 44.

31. **Pa.**—Fazio v. Pittsburgh Rys. Co., 182 A. 696, 321 Pa. 7 (under statute enumerating averments of statement filed in trespass action which should be taken to be admitted if not denied, plaintiff in action of trespass has burden of proving the time pleaded, even though no affidavit of defense has been filed. 12 P.S. §§ 382, 387, 412).

32. **Pa.**—Martin v. Marateck, 27 A. 2d 42, 345 Pa. 103.

33. **La.**—Lee v. Coulon, App., 180 So. 182.
N.Y.—Carp v. Wilson, 9 N.Y.S.2d 90, 256 App.Div. 165, affirmed 24 N. E.2d 992, 282 N.Y. 579.

Pa.—Martin v. Marateck, 27 A.2d 42, 345 Pa. 103.
Va.—Sanders v. Newsome, 19 S.E. 2d 883, 179 Va. 582.

34. **La.**—Vernon v. Gillham, App., 179 So. 476.
Ohio.—Campbell v. Daniels Motor Freight, Inc., 221 N.E.2d 470, 8 Ohio App.2d 244 (burden to prove that the lateral lines, real or projected, of each of the intersecting highways bounded the area).

35. **La.**—Monroe Hardware Co. v. Monroe Transfer & Warehouse Co., App., 167 So. 498.

36. **N.M.**—Floeck v. Hoover, 195 P. 2d 86, 52 N.M. 193.
Tex.—Dollar Dodge Rent Service v. McEwen, Civ.App., 273 S.W. 889.

§ 416.1   TRIAL EVIDENCE   Ch. 416

Guest actions—status of occupant

Automobile guest statutes preclude an injured guest from recovering against the host for ordinary negligence, and the occupant of a motor vehicle involved in an accident may seek to prove some status other than that contemplated by the statutes; and in this situation the burden of proof is upon the plaintiff.[37] It has been held, for example, that in an action for injuries suffered by a person when on or in a motor vehicle, it is incumbent on the plaintiff to prove status as an invitee,[38] or a passenger,[39]

---

37. **U.S.**—Jackson v. Continental Bank & Trust Co., C.A.Utah 1971, 443 F.2d 1344.

   Cal.—Tucker v. Landucci, App., 18 Cal.Rptr. 616, opinion vacated 22 Cal.Rptr. 10, 371 P.2d 754, 57 Cal. 2d 762.

   Ill.—Weinrob v. Heintz, 104 N.E.2d 534, 346 Ill.App. 30.

   Iowa.—Boge v. Jack Link Truck Line, Inc., 1972, 200 N.W.2d 544 (plaintiff must overcome rebuttable presumption of guest status); Marean v. Petersen, 144 N.W.2d 906; Clendenning v. Simerman, 263 N.W. 248, 220 Iowa 739.

   Kan.—In re Wright's Estate, 228 P. 2d 911, 170 Kan. 600.

   Ky.—Workman v. Hargadon, 345 S. W.2d 644, 92 A.L.R.2d 1123.

   Mich.—Wilcox v. Keeley, 57 N.W.2d 514, 336 Mich. 237.

   N.Y.—Naphtali v. Lafazan, 186 N.Y. S.2d 1010, 8 A.D.2d 22, appeal dismissed in part 187 N.Y.S.2d 1020, 8 A.D.2d 727, reargument denied 190 N.Y.S.2d 334, 8 A.D.2d 828, judgment affirmed 209 N.Y.S.2d 317, 171 N.E.2d 462, 8 N.Y.2d 1097 (construing Ohio guest statute).

   Or.—Smith v. Laflar, 2 P.2d 18, 137 Or. 230.

   Tex.—Autry v. Spiering, 407 S.W.2d 826.

   Contra

   Colo.—Hotchkiss v. Preble, 1974, 519 P.2d 360, 184 Colo. 157, on remand 521 P.2d 1278, 33 Colo.App. 431; Houghtaling v. Davis, 344 P. 2d 176, 140 Colo. 327 (it was not necessary for plaintiff to allege in her complaint that she was a passenger for hire, and burden was on defendant to establish that plaintiff was guest).

   Defendant must plead and prove affirmative defense

   Where defendants never pleaded Automobile Guest Statute or defense of joint venture as affirmative defenses or as an avoidance, plaintiff had no burden under pleadings to present any evidence on those issues and was required only to prove sufficient evidence of defendant driver's negligence to enable case to go to jury. Olin's Miami Rent-A-Car, Inc. v. Jorgenson, Fla.App.1970, 239 So. 2d 518.

38. **Iowa.**—Winter v. Moore, 1963, 121 N.W.2d 82, 255 Iowa 1.

   Mass.—Gallo v. Veliskakis, 1970, 259 N.E.2d 568, 357 Mass. 602 (in suit against owner, must show status as invitee of owner with evidence of driver's authority to invite).

   N.Y.—Jesselson v. Moody, 127 N.E. 2d 921, 309 N.Y. 148 (in suit against owner, must show status as invitee of owner as well as of driver).

   N.J.—Porter v. Boro Busses Corp., 68 A.2d 347, 5 N.J.Super. 6; Kluber v. Pferdeort, 199 A. 26, 120 N.J.L. 190, affirming 194 A. 154, 15 N.J. Misc. 651, reversing 188 A. 735, 15

---

39. See note 39 on page 11.

Ch. 416   BURDEN OF PROOF   § 416.1

or to show a status other than as a guest,[40] or arrangements

N.J.Misc. 17 (as an invitee of defendant employer of driver).

Pa.—Stefan v. New Process Laundry Co., 185 A. 734, 323 Pa. 373 (by invitation of owner of parked truck).

Occupant assisting driver

In action against trucking company for death of soldier who was riding in tractor-trailer, plaintiff had burden of proving that driver had express or implied authority to pick up soldier and that soldier was picked up as a helper or as an extra driver. East Coast Freight Lines v. Mayor and City Council of Baltimore, 58 A.2d 290, 190 Md. 256, 2 A.L.R.2d 386.

39. **U.S.**—Broadwater v. Coleman, C.A.Kan., 224 F.2d 186; Copp v. Van Hise, C.C.A.Mont., 119 F.2d 691.

Cal.—Benjamin v. Rutherford, 303 P. 2d 1079, 146 Cal.App.2d 561; Martinez v. Southern Pac. Co., 288 P. 2d 868, 45 Cal.2d 244.

Fla.—McDougald v. Couey, 9 So.2d 187, 150 Fla. 748.

Ill.—Miller v. Miller, 69 N.E.2d 878, 395 Ill. 273 (common carrier of property transporting plaintiff's horse permitted plaintiff to ride in the truck).

Kan.—Cope v. Radford, 383 P.2d 563, 191 Kan. 617.

Mich.—Welty's Estate v. Wolf's Estate, 76 N.W.2d 52, 345 Mich. 408.

Neb.—Sunderman v. Wardlaw, 101 N.W.2d 848, 170 Neb. 70.

N.C.—Frisbee v. West, 132 S.E.2d 609, 260 N.C. 269.

Ohio.—Birmelin v. Gist, 120 N.E.2d 711, 162 Ohio St. 98.

Utah.—Eyre v. Burdette, 330 P.2d 126, 8 Utah 2d 166.

Wash.—Nielson v. Harkoff, 287 P. 2d 95, 47 Wash.2d 205.

Owner as "passenger"

Plaintiff who was riding in automobile, which he owned, and which was being driven by defendant on a trip, which was a pleasure trip for plaintiff and a business trip for defendant, who had agreed to pay for gasoline, oil and parking, was not "guest" within Virginia statute permitting guest to recover from operator of automobile for injuries caused by operator's gross negligence or wilful and wanton disregard of safety of guest, and hence plaintiff was not required to prove more than ordinary negligence. Lorch v. Eglin, 85 A.2d 841, 369 Pa. 314.

Payment for transportation

Injured passenger had burden to prove that there was a substantial consideration and that such consideration was chief motivating cause for the carriage. Yarnall v. Gass, 217 S.W.2d 283, 240 Mo.App. 451.

Where original status was as guest

In occupant's action, if plaintiff's evidence established that she had divested herself of her status as a guest or had been divested thereof by conduct of defendant, she would not be required to establish "willful or wanton misconduct". Redis v. Lynch, 159 N.E.2d 597, 169 Ohio St. 305.

40. **Cal.**—Gosselin v. Hawkins, 1950, 214 P.2d 110, 95 Cal.App.2d 857.

Del.—DeJoseph v. Faraone, Super. 1969, 254 A.2d 257, (placing burden of proof on injured passenger, rather than deceased driver's estate, to show nonapplicability of guest statute did not, when coupled with dead man's statute, unconstitutionally deprive passenger of a cause of action, where passenger had no memory insofar as any transaction with deceased concerning his guest or nonguest status and, thus, dead man's statute was not barring anything).

11

§ 416.1   TRIAL EVIDENCE   Ch. 416

other than a joint enterprise,[41] but as one whose presence was, at least to some extent, for the benefit of the driver.[42]

Affirmative defenses

The burden of proving affirmative defenses is upon the defendant relying thereon.[43] Though a particular defense may not

---

Iowa.—Ross v. McNeal, 1969, 171 N.W.2d 515 (had to overcome the rebuttable presumption that she was a guest).

Mass.—Weida v. MacDougall, 1938, 16 N.E.2d 60, 300 Mass. 521.

Tex.—Hutcheson v. Se'Christ's Estate, Civ.App.1970, 459 S.W.2d 495, error refused n. r. e.

Rendering assistance to employee driver

Where plaintiff sought to recover from employer on ground plaintiff was rendering necessary assistance to employee who was acting within the course and scope of his employment, burden was on plaintiff to prove such facts in addition to proving wanton misconduct of employee in operation of automobile. Siemers v. Vindicator Printing Co., 32 N.E.2d 766, 66 Ohio App. 249.

41. **Ill.**—Fischer v. Ross, 223 N.E.2d 722, 79 Ill.App.2d 372.

42. **Iowa.**—Wharff v. McBride, 1971, 183 N.W.2d 700 (burden of establishing that expectation of receiving essential benefit was a substantial factor motivating the furnishing of transportation to the passenger).

Mass.—Weida v. MacDougall, 16 N.E.2d 60, 300 Mass. 521.

Mich.—Bredeweg v. Boyce, 33 N.W.2d 801, 322 Mich. 298.

Neb.—Carter v. Chicago, B. & Q. R. R. Co., 103 N.W.2d 152, 170 Neb. 438.

Ohio.—Burrow v. Porterfield, 168 N.E.2d 137, 171 Ohio St. 28.

R.I.—Kennedy v. Lenzine, 69 A.2d 231, 76 R.I. 231 (under Massachusetts law).

Wash.—Hayes v. Brower, 235 P.2d 482, 39 Wash.2d 372 (agreement to buy gasoline as consideration for transportation).

43. **U.S.**—Sheppard v. Atlantic States Gas Co. of Pa., C.C.A.Pa., 167 F.2d 841 (covenant not to sue).

Alaska.—Evans v. Buchner, 386 P.2d 836 (assumption of risk).

Ariz.—Lakin Cattle Co. v. Engelthaler, 419 P.2d 66, 101 Ariz. 282.

Cal.—Washington v. City and County of San Francisco, 266 P.2d 828, 123 Cal.App.2d 235 (emergency vehicle).

Conn.—Kakluskas v. Somers Motor Lines, 54 A.2d 592, 134 Conn. 35 (assumption of risk by occupant of cab of truck).

Fla.—Union Bus Co. v. Matthews, 192 So. 811, 141 Fla. 99.

Ill.—Pascal P. Paddock, Inc. v. Glennon, 203 N.E.2d 421, 32 Ill.2d 51; Victor v. Dehmlow, 90 N.E.2d 724, 405 Ill. 249 (defendant invoking compensation law provision for subrogation).

Iowa.—Tuttle v. Longnecker, 138 N.W.2d 851, 258 Iowa 393 (assumption of risk); In re Ditz' Estate, 125 N.W.2d 814, 255 Iowa 1272 (a special defense); Augusta v. Jensen, 42 N.W.2d 383, 241 Iowa 697 (guest's assumption of risk in riding with intoxicated driver).

La.—Fontana v. State Farm Mut. Auto. Ins. Co., 173 So.2d 284, writ denied, 175 So.2d 644, 247 La. 1027; Young v. First Nat. Life Ins. Co.,

Ch. 416 BURDEN OF PROOF § 416.1

be tantamount to a plea of contributory negligence, the burden of proof is likewise on the defendant, in the case of a defense affirmatively advanced.[44]

The burden is upon the defendant who alleges a bar to the plaintiff's claim because of a release,[45] or former judgment.[46]

La.App., 159 So.2d 395 (a special defense).

Miss.—Skelton v. Turnispeed, 1970, 235 So.2d 694 (existence of stop sign requiring stop by plaintiff).

Mo.—Mochar Sales Co. v. Meyer, 373 S.W.2d 911, citing 31 C.J.S. Evidence § 104.

N.D.—Teegarden v. Dahl, 138 N.W. 2d 668.

S.C.—McCabe v. Sloan, 191 S.E. 905, 184 S.C. 158 (allegation of motorcylist that dog ran against cycle and caused collision with pedestrian).

Va.—Moore v. Virginia Transit Co., 50 S.E.2d 268, 188 Va. 493 (that bus was parked in accordance with city ordinance).

Wash.—Gaskill v. Amadon, 38 P.2d 229, 179 Wash. 375.

Absence of safety zone

In action for injuries caused by taxicab driver's violation of ordinance prohibiting vehicles from approaching nearer than 10 feet to street cars under certain conditions, defendant taxicab company and surety had burden to plead and prove absence of properly designated safety zone. Checker Cab & Baggage Co. v. Crone, Tex.Civ.App., 117 S.W. 2d 503, affirmed Crone v. Checker Cab & Baggage Co., 135 S.W.2d 696, 134 Tex. 412.

Rule construed

In action against truck driver and his employers for death of plant foreman of paving company, who was struck by truck at company's plant when truck driver backed truck for purpose of dumping load at refuse pile, truck driver and his employers had burden of proving defense, by way of new matter, that truck driver backed his truck as directed by foreman. Murray v. Wyatt, 95 S.E.2d 541, 245 N.C. 123.

Unless plaintiff admits or establishes facts conclusively

If plaintiff admits or establishes facts constituting affirmative defense with such conclusiveness as to exclude reasonable possibility of an inference otherwise, defendant is relieved of burden of establishing defense. Rivera v. State Farm Mut. Auto. Ins. Co., 206 A.2d 338, 205 Pa. Super. 30.

44. Assumption of risk

In action for injuries to wife, riding in truck driven by her husband, burden was on defendant, claiming that plaintiff assumed risk to show that she knew of, appreciated, and deliberately and unnecessarily exposed herself to, danger. Stephenson v. Steinhauer, C.A.N.D., 188 F.2d 432.

Rule illustrated

Averment of answer that deceased negligently ran into defendant's truck held not allegation of contributory negligence, but affirmatively advanced exonerating defense, as to which burden of proof was on defendant. Guillory v. Horecky, La. App., 162 So. 89, affirmed, App., 165 So. 159, and judgment annulled on other grounds 168 So. 481, 185 La. 21.

45. N.Y.—Moses v. Carver, 298 N.Y. S. 378, 164 Misc. 204, affirmed 5 N.Y.S.2d 783, 254 App.Div. 402.

46. Mass.—Tighe v. Skillings, 9 N. E.2d 532, 297 Mass. 504.

§ 416.1   TRIAL EVIDENCE   Ch. 416

However, it has been stated that the plaintiff has the burden of showing facts justifying avoidance or cancellation of a release.[47]

In motor vehicle cases, where a license is a defense, it is a general rule that the burden of proving the license rests upon the licensee, for the possession of the license is a fact peculiarly within the licensee's knowledge.[48]

A city has the burden of establishing its affirmative defense that its driver, at the time of an accident in which the city's police automobile injured a person, was engaged in a governmental act bearing some just and true relationship to the enforcement of law and was not acting in a ministerial or corporate capacity.[49]

Where a husband is sued on the theory that the automobile causing the injury was community property, to avoid liability the burden is on him to show that the vehicle he was driving belonged exclusively to his wife.[50]

Foundation for admissibility of evidence

One offering evidence admissible under a particular doctrine or theory has the burden of proving that the evidence meets the tests or requirements imposed thereby.[51] For example, a party offering evidence as part of the res gestae has the burden of showing the element of spontaneity,[52] and party offering abandoned or superseded pleadings signed only by attorney has burden to satisfactorily show that the pleadings are those of adverse party or were approved by the party.[53]

47. **Iowa.**—Mosher v. Snyder, 276 N.W. 582, 224 Iowa 896.

Tex.—Williams v. Adams, Tex.Civ.App., 91 S.W.2d 951.

48. **Pa.**—Nevin Bus Line v. Paul R. Hostetter Co., 155 A. 872, 305 Pa. 72.

49. **Iowa.**—Jones v. Sioux City, 170 N.W. 445, 185 Iowa 1178, 10 A.L.R. 474.

50. **La.**—U. S. Fidelity & Guaranty Co. v. Moore, 119 So. 886, 9 La. App. 429.

51. **Ill.**—Johnson v. Swords Co., 3 N.E.2d 705, 286 Ill.App. 377.

Foundation for hearsay

It is burden of party seeking to offer former testimony to prove unavailability of declarant as a witness. Traxler v. Thompson, 1970, 84 Cal.Rptr. 211, 4 Cal.App.3d 278.

Qualification of witness

Burden of establishing qualifications of a witness in order to permit him to testify as an expert is on party seeking to have such evidence admitted, and it is not the burden of the adversary to prove that such witness is not qualified. McCraney v. Kuechenberg, 1969, 248 N.E.2d 171, 144 Ind.App. 629.

52. **Ill.**—Johnson v. Swords Co., 3 N.E.2d 705, 286 Ill.App. 377.

Mo.—Brautigam v. Hoffman, C.A. 1969, 444 S.W.2d 528.

Tex.—Hartford Acc. & Indem. Co. v. Hale, 389 S.W.2d 720, error granted.

53. **Ariz.**—Buehman v. Smelker, 68 P.2d 946, 50 Ariz. 18.

A party seeking to exclude evidence as privileged has been held to have the burden to show the evidence is within the class protected,[54] while, in other cases the offeror of the evidence has been required to show that the evidence was not privileged.[55]

§ 416.2 Burden of Proof—Negligent Operation of Vehicle

Library References:
C.J.S. Carriers § 764; Motor Vehicles § 509 et seq.; Railroads § 835 et seq.
West's Key No. Digests, Automobiles ⚖242; Carriers ⚖316; Railroads ⚖346.

It is elementary in motor vehicle cases, as well as in other tort actions, that the plaintiff has the burden of proving negligence of the defendant, where negligence is the gist of the action,[56] in the absence of a statute changing or modifying the rule.[57]

It is sufficient for a party to prove the material allegations of that party's pleading,[58] and immaterial matter, or surplusage, need not be proved.[59] A party is not to be penalized where the

54. U.S.—In re Bonanno, C.A.N.Y., 344 F.2d 830 (attorney-client privilege).
Cal.—Gallagher v. Boller, 41 Cal.Rptr. 880, 231 Cal.App.2d 482; D. I. Chadbourne, Inc. v. Superior Court of City and County of San Francisco, 36 Cal.Rptr. 468, 388 P.2d 700, 60 Cal.2d 723 (attorney-client privilege).
Iowa.—Allen v. Lindeman, 148 N.W.2d 610.

55. Fla.—Leithauser v. Harrison, 168 So.2d 95.

56. See section 416.1, fn. 20 et seq.

57. U.S.—Liggett & Myers Tobacco Co. v. De Parcq, C.C.A.Minn., 66 F.2d 678.
Cal.—Dewees v. Kuntz, 20 P.2d 733, 130 Cal.App. 620.
Conn.—Zint v. Wheeler, 169 A. 52, 117 Conn. 484.
Iowa.—Williams v. Cohn, 206 N.W. 823, 201 Iowa 1121.

La.—Jordan v. Ortlieb, App., 148 So. 95.
Me.—Coop v. Paradis, 157 A. 228, 130 Me. 464.
Md.—Finney v. Frevel, 37 A.2d 923, 183 Md. 355.
Mass.—Clark v. C. E. Fay Co., 183 N.E. 423, 281 Mass. 240.

58. Ind.—Brinkman v. Pacholke, 84 N.E. 762, 41 Ind.App. 662.

59. Ala.—Harper v. Griffin Lumber Co., 34 So.2d 148, 250 Ala. 339.
Ariz.—Brooks v. Neer, 47 P.2d 452, 46 Ariz. 144.
Cal.—Smith v. McLaughlin, 184 P.2d 177, 81 Cal.App.2d 460 (agency of son shown to be driving with father's consent).
Conn.—Tierney v. Correia, 180 A. 282, 120 Conn. 140.
Ind.—Schlarb v. Henderson, 4 N.E.2d 205, 211 Ind. 1 (guest's allegation that host was not negligent need not be proved in action against third person).

§ 416.2   TRIAL EVIDENCE   Ch. 416

proof fails to establish an averment which is merely descriptive.[60] Thus, the general rule is that, if the facts alleged constitute simple negligence on the part of the defendant, the mere fact that the plaintiff characterized defendant's acts as gross, wanton, wilful, and criminal negligence will not place the burden on the plaintiff of proving wilful and wanton injury.[61] However it has been held that there can be no recovery on the ground of gross negligence when the complaint charges ordinary negligence.[62]

For full discussion of rules as to variance of proof from the pleadings, see section 416.12 of this chapter.

When several specifications of negligence are charged it is not necessary for the plaintiff to prove all of them.[63] However,

Ky.—Weil v. Hagan, 179 S.W. 835, 166 Ky. 750.

Mass.—Royal Steam Heater Co. v. Hilchey, 154 N.E. 335, 257 Mass. 512 (words "agent or servant" in declaration being descriptive of driver of plaintiff's automobile, proof of agency or service was not required).

Mo.—Hathaway v. Evans, App., 235 S.W.2d 407; Nyberg v. Wells, App., 14 S.W.2d 529.

Pa.—Dougherty v. Davis, 51 Pa. Super. 229 (alleged high rate of speed, other negligence proven).

R.I.—York v. Ventilato, 94 A.2d 820, 80 R.I. 192 (truck driver alleged that motorist failed to keep his automobile on the proper side of the highway but introduced evidence that he and motorist were traveling in different directions on the same street and that he had stopped his truck and motorist, in turning left, ran into it).

Rule construed

Where petition alleged that street car company negligently permitted a switch to split which caused street car to suddenly and without warning swerve into automobile in which plaintiff was riding, the use of the words "without warning to plaintiff" did not charge a specific act of negligence, in addition to general charge of negligence in permitting the switch to split and the street car to turn into automobile so as to require the plaintiff to prove that street car company failed to warn of turning of street car, since quoted words could be treated as surplusage. Dunlap v. Kansas City Public Service Co., 130 S.W.2d 658, 234 Mo.App. 351.

60. **Ala.**—Duncan v. Robertson, 132 So. 58, 222 Ala. 131.

Ky.—Watson v. Bailey, 132 S.W.2d 53, 279 Ky. 671 (plaintiff described as a paying passenger).

Tex.—City of Corpus Christi v. Caddell, Civ.App., 98 S.W.2d 372 (location of excavation which caused accident).

Vt.—Senecal v. Bleau, 189 A. 139, 108 Vt. 486 (place of accident).

61. **Cal.**—Townsend v. Butterfield, 143 P. 760, 168 Cal. 564.

Ga.—Standard Oil Co. v. Parrish, 151 S.E. 541, 40 Ga.App. 814.

Kan.—Routh v. Weakley, 154 P. 218, 97 Kan. 74.

Wyo.—Hinton v. Wilmes, 1959, 343 P.2d 201, 80 Wyo. 360 (passenger's unnecessary allegation of gross negligence).

62. **Wis.**—Bentson v. Brown, 203 N.W. 380, 186 Wis. 629, 38 A.L.R. 1417.

63. **Ind.**—Kampo Transit, Inc. v. Powers, 211 N.E.2d 781.

one jurisdiction has held that when the plaintiff relies upon the humanitarian doctrine and avers several acts of negligence in the disjunctive, such as "failure to stop or to swerve or to warn," the plaintiff must prove all of the charges alleged in order to recover.[64]

Where two concurring acts of negligence are alleged to have been committed by the same party, from which an injury results, and which injury would not have resulted, in the absence of either one of said acts, it is necessary to prove both of the negligent acts.[65]

If the complaint contains a charge of common-law negligence and an allegation of negligence in violating a city ordinance, the fact that the latter element is not proved will not defeat a recovery on the former, if the proof supports the common-law negligence charged.[66] Similarly, a cause of action based upon a statute and upon ordinances regulating motor vehicles may be established by proof of a violation of the statute, although the ordinances alleged to have been violated are invalid.[67]

If the cause of action is based upon the violation of an ordinance, the ordinance should be proved,[68] unless the statutes of

Mo.—State ex rel. Kansas City Rys. Co. v. Trimble, Sup., 260 S.W. 746.

Or.—Pointer v. Osborne, 76 P.2d 1134, 158 Or. 573.

Alternate basis for recovery

Where defendant admitted that driver of defendant's truck was employee of defendant, plaintiff was only required to prove negligence on part of truck driver and was not required to pursue alternative remedy that defendant was negligent in selecting or retaining a truck driver who plaintiff alleged was known to be incompetent and reckless. Houlihan v. McCall, 78 A.2d 661, 197 Md. 130.

But see

Where passenger alleged that host was guilty of certain specific acts of negligence, passenger could not be permitted in her testimony to deny and disclaim such acts of negligence without forfeiting her right to recover. Wagner v. Niven, 332 S.W.2d 511, 46 Tenn.App. 581.

64. Mo.—Harrell v. Berberick, 222 S.W.2d 733, 359 Mo. 551.

65. Ind.—Southern Indiana Gas & Electric Co. v. Winstead, 175 N.E. 281, 92 Ind.App. 329.

Mo.—Daniel v. Pryor, Sup., 227 S.W. 102 (in an action by a motorist for injuries in a crossing collision, a count of the petition, based upon a statute, charged negligence in failing to "ring the bell and sound the whistle").

66. Mo.—Borah v. Zoellner Motor Car Co., App., 257 S.W. 145; Burnham v. Williams, 194 S.W. 751, 198 Mo.App. 18.

67. Mo.—Carradine v. Ford, 187 S. W. 285, 195 Mo.App. 684.

68. Ala.—Rochelle v. Lide, 180 So. 257, 235 Ala. 596.

Ga.—Tyson v. Shoemaker, 62 S.E.2d 586, 83 Ga.App. 33, reversed on other grounds 65 S.E.2d 163, 208 Ga. 28.

Mo.—Kroell v. Lutz, App., 236 S.W. 424.

§ 416.2   TRIAL EVIDENCE   Ch. 416

the particular state authorize the courts to take judicial notice thereof. Where the ordinance purports to have been approved on a date prior to the accident, it is not incumbent on the plaintiff to show, at least in the first instance, that the ordinance was still in force and effect when the accident occurred.[69]

The plaintiff must establish an element of negligence relied upon. This burden has been placed by the courts upon the plaintiff, where the negligence alleged was some common allegation of negligence, and in allegation of certain special actions or omissions.[70]

Tenn.—Central Produce Co. v. General Cab Co. of Nashville, 129 S.W. 2d 1117, 23 Tenn.App. 209.

69. Mo.—Brown v. Alton R. Co., App., 132 S.W.2d 713, record quashed, Sup., 143 S.W.2d 233.

70. U.S.—Samuel v. George Weidemann Co., C.C.A.Ky., 295 F. 314 (burden to show driver of truck saw minor on rear fender and his perilous position before starting truck).

Cal.—Wilcox v. Epstein, 1944, 151 P.2d 156, 65 Cal.App.2d 581 (failure to give signal before driving across sidewalk).

Ind.—Hancock Truck Lines v. Butcher, 94 N.E.2d 537, 229 Ind. 36 (sleeping while driving).

Mass.—Castano v. Leone, 180 N.E. 312, 278 Mass. 429 (pinching plaintiffs' finger in auto door).

Miss.—Hebert v. Lenart, 153 So.2d 658, 247 Miss. 494 (to show that bicyclist was in street sufficient time and in place within range of vision of bus driver for bus driver in exercise of ordinary care to have seen bicyclist and avoided striking him).

R.I.—Nolan v. Bacon, 216 A.2d 126 (that defendant failed to turn his tires against the curb).

Definition of burden as to negligently falling asleep

Party so claiming has burden of proving that driver fell asleep at wheel; but if evidence, whether direct or by permissible inference, tends to establish that fact, other party has burden of showing greater probability that driver's loss of consciousness was due to some other cause. Theisen v. Milwaukee Auto. Mut. Ins. Co., 118 N.W.2d 140, 18 Wis.2d 91, rehearing denied 119 N. W.2d 393, 18 Wis.2d 91.

One way lane preemption

In action arising out of collision of approaching vehicles in one way lane opposite barricaded portion of the other lane on which plaintiff had theretofore been traveling, question of preemption of one way lane was factual and plaintiff motorist had burden of proving his claim of preemption. Cardinal v. Kraft Foods Co., La.App., 86 So.2d 738.

Right of way of pedestrian

Pedestrian maintaining action to recover for injuries when struck by truck while crossing state highway at junction with unimproved road, if she sought benefit of statute imposing duty on motorist to yield right of way to pedestrian crossing within crosswalk, had burden of proving that unimproved road was publicly maintained so as to make junction an intersection in view of statute defining crosswalk as being at intersection. Carma v. Swindler, 91 S.E. 2d 254, 228 S.C. 550.

In order to enjoy the privileges of the right of way given to a pedestrian crossing the highway with any

Ch. 416   BURDEN OF PROOF   § 416.2

one jurisdiction has held that when the plaintiff relies upon the humanitarian doctrine and avers several acts of negligence in the disjunctive, such as "failure to stop or to swerve or to warn," the plaintiff must prove all of the charges alleged in order to recover.[64]

Where two concurring acts of negligence are alleged to have been committed by the same party, from which an injury results, and which injury would not have resulted, in the absence of either one of said acts, it is necessary to prove both of the negligent acts.[65]

If the complaint contains a charge of common-law negligence and an allegation of negligence in violating a city ordinance, the fact that the latter element is not proved will not defeat a recovery on the former, if the proof supports the common-law negligence charged.[66] Similarly, a cause of action based upon a statute and upon ordinances regulating motor vehicles may be established by proof of a violation of the statute, although the ordinances alleged to have been violated are invalid.[67]

If the cause of action is based upon the violation of an ordinance, the ordinance should be proved,[68] unless the statutes of

Mo.—State ex rel. Kansas City Rys. Co. v. Trimble, Sup., 260 S.W. 746.

Or.—Pointer v. Osborne, 76 P.2d 1134, 158 Or. 573.

Alternate basis for recovery

Where defendant admitted that driver of defendant's truck was employee of defendant, plaintiff was only required to prove negligence on part of truck driver and was not required to pursue alternative remedy that defendant was negligent in selecting or retaining a truck driver who plaintiff alleged was known to be incompetent and reckless. Houlihan v. McCall, 78 A.2d 661, 197 Md. 130.

But see

Where passenger alleged that host was guilty of certain specific acts of negligence, passenger could not be permitted in her testimony to deny and disclaim such acts of negligence without forfeiting her right to recover. Wagner v. Niven, 332 S.W.2d 511, 46 Tenn.App. 581.

64. Mo.—Harrell v. Berberick, 222 S.W.2d 733, 359 Mo. 551.

65. Ind.—Southern Indiana Gas & Electric Co. v. Winstead, 175 N.E. 281, 92 Ind.App. 329.

Mo.—Daniel v. Pryor, Sup., 227 S.W. 102 (in an action by a motorist for injuries in a crossing collision, a count of the petition, based upon a statute, charged negligence in failing to "ring the bell and sound the whistle").

66. Mo.—Borah v. Zoellner Motor Car Co., App., 257 S.W. 145; Burnham v. Williams, 194 S.W. 751, 198 Mo.App. 18.

67. Mo.—Carradine v. Ford, 187 S. W. 285, 195 Mo.App. 684.

68. Ala.—Rochelle v. Lide, 180 So. 257, 235 Ala. 596.

Ga.—Tyson v. Shoemaker, 62 S.E.2d 586, 83 Ga.App. 33, reversed on other grounds 65 S.E.2d 163, 208 Ga. 28.

Mo.—Kroell v. Lutz, App., 236 S.W. 424.

§ 416.2   TRIAL EVIDENCE   Ch. 416

the particular state authorize the courts to take judicial notice thereof. Where the ordinance purports to have been approved on a date prior to the accident, it is not incumbent on the plaintiff to show, at least in the first instance, that the ordinance was still in force and effect when the accident occurred.[69]

The plaintiff must establish an element of negligence relied upon. This burden has been placed by the courts upon the plaintiff, where the negligence alleged was some common allegation of negligence, and in allegation of certain special actions or omissions.[70]

Tenn.—Central Produce Co. v. General Cab Co. of Nashville, 129 S.W.2d 1117, 23 Tenn.App. 209.

69. **Mo.**—Brown v. Alton R. Co., App., 132 S.W.2d 713, record quashed, Sup., 143 S.W.2d 233.

70. **U.S.**—Samuel v. George Weidemann Co., C.C.A.Ky., 295 F. 314 (burden to show driver of truck saw minor on rear fender and his perilous position before starting truck).
Cal.—Wilcox v. Epstein, 1944, 151 P.2d 156, 65 Cal.App.2d 581 (failure to give signal before driving across sidewalk).
Ind.—Hancock Truck Lines v. Butcher, 94 N.E.2d 537, 229 Ind. 36 (sleeping while driving).
Mass.—Castano v. Leone, 180 N.E. 312, 278 Mass. 429 (pinching plaintiffs' finger in auto door).
Miss.—Hebert v. Lenart, 153 So.2d 658, 247 Miss. 494 (to show that bicyclist was in street sufficient time and in place within range of vision of bus driver for bus driver in exercise of ordinary care to have seen bicyclist and avoided striking him).
R.I.—Nolan v. Bacon, 216 A.2d 126 (that defendant failed to turn his tires against the curb).

Definition of burden as to negligently falling asleep
Party so claiming has burden of proving that driver fell asleep at wheel; but if evidence, whether direct or by permissible inference, tends to establish that fact, other party has burden of showing greater probability that driver's loss of consciousness was due to some other cause. Theisen v. Milwaukee Auto. Mut. Ins. Co., 118 N.W.2d 140, 18 Wis.2d 91, rehearing denied 119 N.W.2d 393, 18 Wis.2d 91.

One way lane preemption
In action arising out of collision of approaching vehicles in one way lane opposite barricaded portion of the other lane on which plaintiff had theretofore been traveling, question of preemption of one way lane was factual and plaintiff motorist had burden of proving his claim of preemption. Cardinal v. Kraft Foods Co., La.App., 86 So.2d 738.

Right of way of pedestrian
Pedestrian maintaining action to recover for injuries when struck by truck while crossing state highway at junction with unimproved road, if she sought benefit of statute imposing duty on motorist to yield right of way to pedestrian crossing within crosswalk, had burden of proving that unimproved road was publicly maintained so as to make junction an intersection in view of statute defining crosswalk as being at intersection. Carma v. Swindler, 91 S.E.2d 254, 228 S.C. 550.

In order to enjoy the privileges of the right of way given to a pedestrian crossing the highway with any

Since a motor vehicle may swerve or skid without negligence on the part of the driver, persons injured by reason thereof have the burden of proving that the swerving or skidding was directly due to the negligence charged.[71] Missouri modified its rule, and now does not require proof in addition to showing skidding onto the wrong side, where the collision occurs on the wrong side of the road.[72] It has been held that the circumstances of skidding may be such as to impose a burden on the driver to show absence of negligence in the operation.[73]

It has been held that the burden is on the plaintiff to prove that the injury was not the result of, nor due to, an unavoidable accident;[74] and, in some jurisdictions, the rule is not changed

clearly marked crosswalk or regular pedestrian crossing within a business or residence district, as given by statute, a pedestrian must prove that the scene of the accident was within a business or residence district as defined by statute, and such cannot be left to speculation and surmise. Conrad v. Thompson, 80 S.E.2d 561, 195 Va. 714.

71. **U.S.**—Greyhound Corp. v. Salvation Army, C.A.N.Y., 252 F.2d 331 (applying New York law).

Conn.—Amato v. Sawicki, 1970, 271 A.2d 80, 159 Conn. 490.

Ga.—Holland v. Tootle, 1971, 182 S.E.2d 898, 124 Ga.App. 186.

Ind.—Echterling v. Jack Gray Transport, Inc., 1971, 267 N.E.2d 198, 148 Ind.App. 415.

N.Y.—Lo Piccolo v. Knight of Rest Products Corp., 1959, 183 N.Y.S.2d 301, 7 A.D.2d 369, motion granted 194 N.Y.S.2d 521, 7 N.Y.2d 786, 163 N.E.2d 341.

Pa.—Lundin v. Heilman, 1953, 100 A.2d 626, 375 Pa. 315.

But see

Testimony of plaintiffs' witness, on cross-examination, that defendants' truck which had struck the automobile in which plaintiffs' decedents were riding had "slid" over to the opposite side of the road before striking the automobile did not place upon the plaintiffs the burden of establishing that the skid had resulted from the negligence of the truck driver. Campbell v. Fiorot, 191 A.2d 657, 411 Pa. 157.

72. **Mo.**—Friederich v. Chamberlain, 1970, 458 S.W.2d 360 (overruling Wray v. King, 385 S.W.2d 831).

73. **U.S.**—Nelson v. Brames, C.A. Wyo., 241 F.2d 256 (applying Wyoming law).

Ga.—Dellenback v. Dobbs, 123 S.E. 2d 565, 105 Ga.App. 159 (had burden of showing that nonnegligent skidding of automobile, before collision in oncoming traffic lane, began on own side of road, where plaintiff's witness gave testimony showing that motorist's automobile was skidding sideways as it approached witness on wrong side of road, but did not show that skidding began on motorist's side of road).

Wash.—Cook v. Rafferty, 93 P.2d 376, 200 Wash. 234.

W.Va.—Jenkins v. Chatterton, 100 S.E.2d 808, 143 W.Va. 250.

Wyo.—Butcher v. McMichael, 370 P. 2d 937.

74. **Tex.**—Sproles Motor Freight Lines v. Juge, Civ.App., 123 S.W. 2d 919, error dismissed, judgment correct.

§ 416.2   TRIAL EVIDENCE   Ch. 416

by the defendant's pleading it as a special defense.[75] In others, the issue that the accident was inevitable or unavoidable is an affirmative defense which the defendant has the burden of proving.[76]

Identity of person responsible

The burden is upon the plaintiff to prove whose machine was responsible for the accident.[77] Where ownership of a motor vehicle causing an injury is an issue, the burden of proving it is on the plaintiff.[78]

---

75. Or.—Frangos v. Edmunds, 173 P.2d 596, 179 Or. 577.

Tex.—Sullins v. Pace, Civ.App., 208 S.W.2d 583.

76. Miss.—Warren v. Pinnix, 1970, 241 So.2d 662 (attributed accident to loss of consciousness from stroke).

Okl.—Tyree v. Dunn, 315 P.2d 782.

77. Ala.—Louisville & N. R. Co. v. Nolen, 37 So.2d 912, 251 Ala. 445 (must show that defendant's train was the one involved).

Pa.—Bowling v. Roberts, 83 A. 600, 235 Pa. 89.

S.D.—Staib v. Tarbell, 273 N.W. 652, 65 S.D. 304.

Tex.—Longhorn Drilling Corporation v. Padilla, Civ.App., 138 S.W.2d 164.

Rule applied

Plea of not guilty admitted ownership of bus and agency of driver thereof and that driver was acting in scope of his employment, but such rule did not relieve plaintiffs of burden of identifying the bus. Florida Motor Lines v. Millian, 24 So.2d 710, 157 Fla. 21.

78. Ala.—Mi-Lady Cleaners v. McDaniel, 179 So. 908, 235 Ala. 469, 116 A.L.R. 639.

Cal.—Jacobs v. Bozzani Motors, 241 P.2d 642, 109 Cal.App.2d 681.

Fla.—Fletcher Motor Sales v. Cooney, 27 So.2d 289, 158 Fla. 223 (action against garage as owner of automobile in which deceased was riding).

Ill.—Watson v. Trinz, 274 Ill.App. 379.

Iowa.—Sexton v. Lauman, 57 N.W.2d 200, 244 Iowa 670, 37 A.L.R.2d 353 (action under automobile ownership liability statute).

N.Y.—Bennett v. Nazzaro, 258 N.Y.S. 828, 144 Misc. 450, affirmed Bennett v. Nazzaro, 261 N.Y.S. 1018, 237 App.Div. 866.

N.C.—Cook v. Stedman, 186 S.E. 317, 210 N.C. 345; Jeffrey v. Osage Mfg. Co., 150 S.E. 503, 197 N.C. 724, followed in Lewis v. Basketeria Stores, 161 S.E. 924, 201 N.C. 849.

Okl.—Kelly v. Employers Cas. Co., 214 P.2d 925, 202 Okl. 437 (not admitted by unverified general denials).

Pa.—Mock v. Furphy, 92 A.2d 699, 172 Pa.Super. 226.

R.I.—Dufresne v. Cooper, 1940, 11 A.2d 3, 64 R.I. 120.

Tenn.—Lawson v. Producers' & Refiners' Corporation of Tennessee, 9 S.W.2d 1026, 157 Tenn. 455.

Tex.—Longhorn Drilling Corporation v. Padilla, Civ.App., 138 S.W.2d 164.

But see

In action against truck company, where company alleged that offending truck was owned by an inde-

The burden of proving the identity of the defendant as the driver of an automobile causing an injury is on the plaintiff.[79] Where the statute makes registration in defendant's name prima facie evidence of operation under his responsibility, the burden of establishing identity and ownership may be met by proving such registration.[80]

Where an insurance company is joined as a codefendant with the owner of a motor vehicle, it is incumbent upon the plaintiff, in addition to proving the charges of negligence against the driver and owner, to prove likewise a subsisting liability on the policy of insurance at the time of the accident. This burden is met by producing the policy in evidence and proving that the codefendant was insured by the company issuing the policy, that the policy was in full force and effect on the date of the injury, and that the codefendant was the owner of a car of the registry number mentioned in the policy on that date.[81]

The plaintiff has been held to have the burden of proving the accrual of profit or corporate benefit to a defendant municipality from a particular enterprise, in the prosecution of which a motor vehicle owned by the municipality caused the injury.[82]

pendent contractor, burden was on company to prove such fact. Rogers v. Silver Fleet System of Memphis, La.App., 180 So. 445.

79. Ky.—Lee v. Tucker, 365 S.W.2d 849.

Neb.—Bushon v. Fallon, 100 N.W.2d 200, 169 Neb. 544.

S.D.—Lunde v. Dwyer, 56 N.W.2d 772, 74 S.D. 559.

Rule illustrated

Minn.—Manahan v. Jacobson, 33 N.W.2d 606, 226 Minn. 505 (in action against owner for death of occupant, burden upon plaintiff to show that son of owner was driving at time of fatal accident, and not the deceased as contended by the son).

80. Mass.—Greenburg v. Gorvine, 181 N.E. 128, 279 Mass. 339.

But see

Where defendant denied that his automobile was involved in collision, though plaintiffs identified registration number of colliding automobile as that of defendant's automobile, statutes, making evidence that colliding automobile was registered in name of defendant as owner prima facie evidence that it was being operated by and under the control of a person for whose conduct defendant was legally responsible, were not in point, and charge as to defendant's burden of proving that he was not responsible for control of colliding automobile or conduct of operator was objectionable as tending to confuse jury as to burden of proof on main issue of identity of colliding automobile. Decoteau v. Truedsson, 162 N.E.2d 772, 339 Mass. 759.

81. R.I.—Bell v. Weiner, 129 A. 339, 46 R.I. 478.

82. Mass.—Orlando v. City of Brockton, 3 N.E.2d 794, 295 Mass. 205.

§ 416.2   TRIAL EVIDENCE   Ch. 416

Last Clear Chance

A motorist has the burden, under a count charging subsequent negligence or liability under the last clear chance doctrine, of proving the charges.[83] Similar rules apply where the right of recovery is based on the humanitarian rule.[84]

Railroad crossing collisions

The rule imposing the burden of proof on the plaintiff applies also in actions based on accidents at railroad crossings, in which it is incumbent on the plaintiff to prove that the railroad was negligent.[85]

---

83. Same statement in prior edition **quoted by the court** in Schumacher v. Missouri Pac. Transp. Co., Tex.Civ.App., 116 S.W.2d 1136.

U.S.—Mast v. Illinois Cent. R. Co., D.C.Iowa, 79 F.Supp. 149, affirmed 176 F.2d 157.

Ala.—Southern Ry. Co. v. Melton, 198 So. 588, 240 Ala. 244.

Cal.—Basham v. Southern Pac. Co., 168 P. 359, 176 Cal. 320.

Conn.—Budaj v. Connecticut Co., 143 A. 527, 108 Conn. 474.

Iowa.—Kuehn v. Jenkins, 100 N.W. 2d 604, 251 Iowa 557.

Ky.—Rankin v. Green, 346 S.W.2d 477.

La.—Devall v. Chancellor, App.1974, 301 So.2d 438 (pedestrian case).

N.C.—Miller v. Southern Ry. Co., 169 S.E. 811, 205 N.C. 17.

N.H.—Couture v. Lewis, 196 A.2d 60, 105 N.H. 224.

S.D.—Haase v. Willers Truck Service, 1948, 34 N.W.2d 313, 72 S.D. 353.

Tex.—Searcy v. Sellers, Civ.App. 1971, 470 S.W.2d 103, error refused n. r. e. (facts that there was no obstruction of view in vicinity of rear-end collision and that truck driver was in a position to observe forward motorist's vehicle for a mile or so before rear-end collision were not in themselves circumstances which would permit inference that truck driver actually discovered and realized that forward motorist who had slowed down was in position of peril).

Vt.—Pooler v. Derby, 1971, 278 A.2d 732, 129 Vt. 362.

Va.—Hardiman v. Dyson, 1952, 72 S.E.2d 361, 194 Va. 116.

W.Va.—Waller v. Norfolk & W. Ry. Co., 1930, 152 S.E. 13, 108 W.Va. 576.

84. Mo.—Vietmeier v. Voss, 246 S.W.2d 785.

85. U.S.—State of N. D., for and on Behalf of N. D. Workmen's Compensation Bureau v. Northern Pac. Ry. Co., C.A.N.D., 171 F.2d 506.

Ala.—Louisville & N. R. Co. v. Griffin, 198 So. 345, 240 Ala. 213.

Fla.—Powell v. Gary, 200 So. 854, 146 Fla. 334.

Ill.—Coleman v. Chicago, B. & Q. R. Co., 5 N.E.2d 103, 287 Ill.App. 483 (blocking crossing).

Ind.—New York Cent. Ry. Co. v. Powell, 1943, 47 N.E.2d 615, 221 Ind. 321.

Iowa.—Lindquist v. Des Moines Union Ry. Co., 30 N.W.2d 120, 239 Iowa 356 (collision with freight car blocking crossing).

Mich.—McParlan v. Grand Trunk Western R. Co., 1936, 263 N.W. 734, 273 Mich. 527 (maintained statutory safeguards).

Ch. 416 BURDEN OF PROOF § 416.2

Where the negligence complained of pertains to the maintenance of a defective crossing by a railroad, the plaintiff must plead and prove that the railroad had either actual or constructive notice of the alleged defect in time to make the necessary repairs prior to the accident.[86]

Actions against carriers

The general rules developed above with reference to the burden of proof are applicable in actions by passengers injured as a result of the alleged negligence of motor carriers. In accordance with the general rule, it is incumbent on the plaintiff to

Minn.—Mlenek v. Fleming, 27 N.W. 2d 800, 224 Minn. 38 (burden of proving obstruction of crossing in violation of statute).

Miss.—New Orleans & N. E. R. Co. v. Burge, 2 So.2d 825, 191 Miss. 303.

Mont.—Sullivan v. Northern Pac. Ry. Co., 1939, 94 P.2d 651, 109 Mont. 93.

Mo.—McGrew v. Thompson, 184 S.W.2d 994, 353 Mo. 856 (burden of establishing constitutive factual issues of a defective crossing and due notice and opportunity to repair by railroad was on motorist).

Neb.—Sailors v. Lowden, 299 N.W. 510, 140 Neb. 206 (collision with freight car blocking crossing).

Okl.—Lowden v. Bowles, 105 P.2d 1061, 188 Okl. 35.

Tex.—Texas & N. O. R. Co. v. Davis, Civ.App., 210 S.W.2d 195, ref. n. r. e. (tank cars blocking crossing on dark rainy night).

Va.—Anderson v. Clinchfield R. Co., 198 S.E. 478, 171 Va. 87.

W.Va.—Parsons v. New York Cent. R. Co., 34 S.E.2d 334, 127 W.Va. 619.

Contra

Where Tennessee statute requiring that bell or whistle on a train be sounded when train is approaching or leaving a city or town was applicable in actions against railroad for wrongful deaths of automobile passengers killed in a Tennessee crossing accident, burden of showing that provisions of statute were observed was upon railroad. Williams' Code, § 2628(3). Illinois Cent. R. Co. v. Sigler, C.C.A.Tenn., 122 F.2d 279.

Held insufficient in face of striking train on crossing

In action for death of motorist who drove automobile into side of moving train on rural crossing at night, evidence that train was obscured by smoke from locomotive, and as to failure to give statutory warning signals and to maintain statutory crossing signs, was insufficient to sustain burden on plaintiff of proving railroad's negligence. M.S.A.1927, §§ 219.06, 219.17, 219.18, 616.34. Flagg v. Chicago Great Western Ry. Co., C.C.A.Minn., 143 F.2d 90.

Locomotive headlight obscuring flat cars

Where motorist suing for injuries sustained in railroad crossing collision alleged that cross rays of engine headlight deflected from tops of flat cars to ground and prevented motorist from seeing flat cars by lights of his automobile motorist had burden of establishing allegations. Wm. A. Smith Const. Co. v. Brumley, C.C.A.Okl., 88 F.2d 803.

86. Mo.—Liddle v. Thompson, 162 S.W.2d 614, 236 Mo.App. 1071.

23

§ 416.2   TRIAL EVIDENCE   Ch. 416

establish, at least prima facie,[87] the defendant's status as a "carrier," [88] and the elements of negligence.[89]

The injured passenger is not bound to point out the exact way in which the accident occurred nor to exclude the possibility that it might have happened in some way other than that claimed.[90] In fact, in actions for injuries to passengers, some

---

87. **La.**—Johnson v. City of Monroe, App., 164 So. 456.

88. **Ind.**—Bates Motor Transport Lines v. Mayer, 14 N.E.2d 91, 213 Ind. 664 (interstate commerce carrier).

Ohio.—Bolser v. Smalley, 101 N.E. 2d 147, 89 Ohio App. 161 (in absence of such proof, the rule of ordinary care would be the measure of owner's duty to passenger).

89. **U.S.**—Williams v. New Jersey-New York Transit Co., C.A.1940, 13 F.2d 649, certiorari denied 61 S.Ct. 393, 311 U.S. 712, 85 L.Ed. 463 (briefcase fell from baggage rack).

Conn.—Robinson v. Connecticut Co., 189 A. 453, 122 Conn. 300.

La.—Johnson v. City of Monroe, App., 164 So. 456.

Mass.—Johnson v. Berkshire St. Ry. Co., 198 N.E. 154, 292 Mass. 311.

N.J.—Griffin v. Hohorst, Inc., 185 A. 535, 14 N.J.Misc. 421.

N.C.—Banks v. Shepard, 52 S.E.2d 215, 230 N.C. 86.

Va.—Cleveland v. Danville Traction & Power Co., 18 S.E.2d 913, 179 Va. 256 (passenger alighting from bus and falling on curb).

Absence of arm on seat in bus
Where passenger, in action for injuries sustained when she was thrown from her seat while riding in defendant's bus, alleged that there was negligence in failing to have an arm on the seat, burden was upon passenger to produce evidence to show prima facie that defendant owed the duty of constructing seats with arms. El Paso Electric Co. v. Barker, 137 S.W.2d 17, 134 Tex. 496, reversing, Civ.App., 116 S.W. 2d 433.

Contra
Where an accident to a passenger happens through defective appliances or means of transportation, such as tracks, cars, machinery, or motive power, the burden is cast upon carrier to exculpate itself from an inference of negligence, but in all other cases the burden is upon the passenger to prove such negligence. Nebel v. Burrelli, 41 A.2d 873, 352 Pa. 70.

90. **U.S.**—Murray v. Rio Grande Motorway, C.A.Utah, 171 F.2d 82 (standing passenger injured when bus lurched).

Mass.—Koczur v. Flanagan, 27 N.E. 2d 483, 306 Mass. 121.

Mich.—Trent v. Pontiac Transp. Co., 1937, 275 N.W. 501, 281 Mich. 586.

Re proof of status as common carrier
Where one is injured by the operation of a semitrailer being operated under a certificate as a common carrier, the injured person is not required as a condition precedent to recovery to unravel and demonstrate precise arrangement which exists between the operator of the equipment and the carrier but proof of circumstances that the semitrailer was operated without the carrier's authority or under circumstances relieving him from liability is on the carrier. Brandenburg v. Buchta, 117 N.E.2d 643, 233 Ind. 221.

authorities place on the carrier the burden of showing freedom from negligence in order to overcome or rebut the presumption or prima facie case relied on by the plaintiff.[91]

In an action by a passenger for injuries resulting from something improper or unsafe in the carrier's appliances of transportation, there must be prima facie proof that the proximate cause of the injury was a want of something which as a general rule the carrier was bound to supply, or the presence of something which as a general rule the carrier was bound to keep out of the way.[92]

Burden on defendant

In some cases, however, it is said that the defendant has the burden of showing that he was free of negligence.[93] It has been

---

91. Ky.—Adams v. Louisville Taxicab & Transfer Co., 211 S.W.2d 397, 307 Ky. 405 (carrier must show that it could not have prevented the injury by the utmost skill and foresight).

La.—Etress v. Shreveport Rys. Co., App., 33 So.2d 700 (allegedly allowing passengers to rush out in disorderly manner).

N.Y.—Newell v. Brooklyn Bus Corporation, 7 N.Y.S.2d 512, 255 App. Div. 857, affirmed 20 N.E.2d 1015, 280 N.Y. 650.

Okl.—A. & A. Taxicab Co. v. Bass, 58 P.2d 567, 177 Okl. 248 (treated as presumption).

S.C.—Llewellyn v. Atlantic Greyhound Corporation, 28 S.E.2d 673, 204 S.C. 156 (delay in transportation).

W.Va.—Isabella v. West Virginia Transp. Co., 51 S.E.2d 318, 132 W. Va. 85.

Construed as shifting "burden of proof"

Ordinarily, under doctrine of res ipsa loquitur, burden of going forward, not burden of proof, shifts but, when defendant is a common carrier of passengers for hire, it is burden of proof which shifts, thereby requiring common carrier to explain the occurrence and to show that there was no negligence in operation of carrier's vehicle. Greyhound Corp. v. Brown, 113 So.2d 916, 269 Ala. 520, citing 13 C.J.S. Carriers § 764.

Ignorance of passenger

Carrier has burden of showing freedom from negligence if facts indicate that passenger had no knowledge of cause of accident. Peterson v. Louisiana Power & Light Co., La. App., 174 So. 644.

Requires evidence "to meet or balance inference"

Under California law, taxicab is a public vehicle and there is an inference of negligence on part of its operator, so that burden is on those responsible for operation of the taxicab to go forward and present evidence sufficient to meet or balance the inference of negligence. Shackelford v. Mission Taxicab Co., C.A.Cal., 224 F.2d 857.

92. Tex.—El Paso Electric Co. v. Barker, 137 S.W.2d 17, 134 Tex. 496, reversing, Civ.App., 116 S.W. 2d 433.

93. La.—McNabb v. Dugas, App., 142 So. 174 (alleged loss of control due to slickness of bridge surface).

§ 416.2 TRIAL EVIDENCE Ch. 416

held that the burden is on the defendant to establish the affirmative defense of sudden loss of consciousness,[94] or convulsive

As to products liability
Mich.—Snider v. Bob Thibodeau Ford, Inc., 1972, 202 N.W.2d 727, 42 Mich.App. 708.

Cause of brake failure
Cal.—Harris v. Irish Truck Lines, Inc., 1974, 521 P.2d 481, 113 Cal. Rptr. 489, 11 C.3d 373.

Leaving roadway
N.Y.—Warrick v. Oliver, 1971, 327 N.Y.S.2d 219, 38 A.D.2d 664 (burden of going forward with proof shifted to defendant host driver to explain that cause of the accident was due to conditions beyond her control, but on the whole case the burden of proof remained on plaintiff).

Rear-end collision
Colo.—Mather v. Holley, 1971, 483 P. 2d 992, —— Colo.App. ——.
Iowa.—Campbell v. Martin, 1965, 136 N.W.2d 508, 257 Iowa 1247.
La.—Moreau v. Safeco Ins. Co. of America, 1974, 290 So.2d 402; Vascoe v. State Farm Mut. Auto. Ins. Co., 1972, 260 So.2d 161 (except where motorist encounters an unexpected or unusual obstruction such as a stalled, unlighted vehicle in the highway).
Mich.—Petrosky v. Dzuirman, 1962, 116 N.W.2d 748, 367 Mich. 539.
N.Y.—Rogers v. Glassman Memorial Home, Inc., 1966, 275 N.Y.S.2d 228, 27 A.D.2d 542.
R.I.—Russo v. Odell, 1969, 252 A.2d 135, 105 R.I. 349.
Tex.—Pearson v. Jacob E. Decker and Sons, App.1974, 506 S.W.2d 941 (when stopped at traffic signal).

Running traffic light
Va.—Cook v. Basnight, 1966, 151 S. E.2d 408, 207 Va. 491.

Wash.—Courtright v. Youngberg, 1971, 480 P.2d 522, 4 Wash.App. 234.

Striking "innocent" party
When an innocent third party is injured as a result of a collision between two drivers, each of the drivers is deemed guilty of negligence per se, and burden of proof falls upon each to exculpate himself from negligence proximately causing injury to third party. Poche v. Frazier, La. App.1970, 232 So.2d 851, application denied 236 So.2d 36, 256 La. 266.

Where two defendants charged
As between third person injured or damaged by intersectional collision and two offending drivers, it is presumed that each of motorists was negligent, and each bears burden of exonerating or exculpating himself of fault. Travelers Ins. Co. v. Wilson, La.App.1971, 250 So.2d 463; Jordan v. Great Am. Ins. Co., App.1971, 248 So.2d 363; Sewerage and Water Bd. of New Orleans v. Phoenix Ins. Co., App.1970, 230 So. 2d 293.

94. **Ind.**—Holcomb v. Miller, 269 N. E.2d 885, 149 Ind.App. 46 (defendant's asserted epileptic seizure, in order to effectively excuse her failure to control her vehicle, must have been shown by preponderance of the evidence to have occurred without fair warning or under such circumstances as to have precluded her from taking reasonable precautions whether by pulling to the side of the street to await passage of the dizziness or faint spells, or otherwise, and burden of producing such evidence was upon person seeking to assert such defense).
La.—Dull v. Employers Liability Assur. Corp., App.1970, 233 So.2d 43 (must establish it by clear and convincing evidence).

Ch. 416　　　　BURDEN OF PROOF　　　　§ 416.2

seizure,[95] or that a third vehicle forced the defendant's vehicle against the vehicle of the plaintiff.[96] However, it also has been held that the "sudden emergency" rule is not an affirmative defense and does not place a burden of proof upon the defendant.[97]

In some jurisdictions, under statutes prescribing rules for motor vehicles on public highways and making an injury to person or property by an automobile prima facie evidence of violation of the law as to operation, and as to negligence, the burden is on the driver or owner of the automobile causing the injury in question to show the exercise of due care and the observance of the statutes.[98] Accordingly, the rule is that a motorist involved

Rule construed

Where action was brought by owner of automobile for damages to owner's automobile which was struck by motorist's vehicle as automobile was parked at curb, motorist's defense to the effect that he had "suffered a blackout" and was unconscious at time of collision, should have been pleaded in answer and burden of proof as to defense was upon motorist. Scott v. Long, 169 N.E.2d 700, 110 Ohio App. 516.

95. Ind.—Holcomb v. Miller, 1971, 269 N.E.2d 885, 149 Ind.App. 46 (must have been shown by preponderance of the evidence to have occurred without fair warning or under such circumstances as to have precluded her from taking reasonable precautions whether by pulling to the side of the street to await passage of the dizziness or faint spells, or otherwise).

96. La.—Mull v. Burkhardt, App. 1971, 252 So.2d 475, writ denied 254 So.2d 466, 259 La. 1059 (denied fault on basis of his having been struck by hit and run vehicle).

97. Mich.—Szymborski v. Slatina, 1971, 192 N.W.2d 213, 386 Mich. 339.

N.C.—Foy v. Bremson, 1974, 209 S. E.2d 439, 286 N.C. 108.

98. U.S.—Currie v. U. S., D.C.Md., 201 F.Supp. 414, judgment affirmed, C.A., 312 F.2d 1 (construing Maryland law).

Alaska.—Rogers v. Dubiel, 1962, 373 P.2d 295.

Cal.—Smith v. Wattenburg, 283 P.2d 751, 133 Cal.App.2d 193 (truck stopped on highway).

Ga.—Cruse v. Taylor, 80 S.E.2d 704, 89 Ga.App. 611.

Idaho—Bratton v. Slininger, 1969, 460 P.2d 383, 93 Idaho 248.

Ill.—Piper v. Speroni, 1943, 47 N.E.2d 120, 317 Ill.App. 540 (failure to put out flares).

La.—Jefferson v. Strickland, App. 1970, 242 So.2d 582 (burden of proving that he had complied with statute requiring that vehicle be driven as nearly as practicable entirely within single lane and not be moved from such lane until driver has first ascertained that such movement can be made with safety).

Minn.—Halloran v. Tousignant, 1950, 41 N.W.2d 874, 230 Minn. 399 (statute governing right of way).

Miss.—Flynt v. Fondren, 1920, 84 So. 188, 122 Miss. 248.

Mo.—Robinson v. Gerber, App.1970, 454 S.W.2d 933.

Ohio.—Zehe v. Falkner, 1971, 271 N. E.2d 276, 26 Ohio St.2d 258 (motorist involved in a sudden emergency situation must show that it

27

§ 416.2   TRIAL EVIDENCE   Ch. 416

in an accident while driving on the wrong side of the road has the burden of excusing or justifying presence in that place, or explaining how the accident happened without negligence.[99] The

was impossible for him to comply with the statute).

Or.—Dare v. Garrett Freightlines, Inc., 1963, 380 P.2d 119, 234 Or. 61 (left turning defendant).

Wash.—Goldfarb v. Wright, 1970, 463 P.2d 669, 1 Wash.App. 759 (motorist who collided with rear end of plaintiff's automobile while plaintiff was stopped for "red" traffic control signal was entitled to show justification or an excuse for breach of her duty to stop for traffic control signal, but had burden of going forward with evidence justifying or excusing statutory violation); Burns v. Dills, 1966, 413 P.2d 370, 68 Wash.2d 377 (prohibiting cutting corners).

Admitted brake failure

Where owner of truck admitted that defective brakes caused collision, owner assumed burden of proving that it was free from negligence in maintaining brakes. Taylor v. Buckhead Glass Co., 1969, 171 S.E.2d 779, 120 Ga.App. 663, reversed on other grounds 174 S.E.2d 568, 226 Ga. 247, conformed to 176 S.E.2d 245, 122 Ga. App. 41.

Contra by statute

The presence of statute providing that speed limitations shall not be construed to relieve plaintiff of burden of proving negligence as proximate cause of accident renders inapplicable the rule subjecting one who violates statutory speed regulation to burden of excusing the violation. Davis v. Gatlin, Tex.Civ.App. 1970, 462 S.W.2d 54, error refused n. r. e.

Held burden on defendant satisfied

In action for injuries sustained when passenger placed her foot on first step to enter bus, which had come to stop and which suddenly moved ahead when struck in rear by following automobile, bus company was not obligated to prove affirmatively that door or any other part of bus was free from defect, but discharged its obligation when it rebutted inference of negligence which arose from passenger's proof of circumstances of accident. Renzetti v. Los Angeles Motor Coach Co., 119 P.2d 164, 48 Cal.App.2d 37.

99. U.S.—Goudeau v. Christ, D.C.La. 1971, 325 F.Supp. 1154 (invading motorist must prove by clear and convincing evidence that his own negligence did not in any particular contribute to the mishap).

Alaska—Ferrell v. Baxter, 1971, 484 P.2d 250.

Cal.—Green v. Uarte, 196 P.2d 63, 87 Cal.App.2d 75.

Ga.—Griner v. Tuten, 151 S.E.2d 835, 114 Ga.App. 484 (burden of proof was on defendant to show that such action on his part was caused by act of a third party in striking rear of defendant's truck and was without negligence on his part).

Ill.—Tomlinson v. Chapman, 164 N. E.2d 240, 24 Ill.App.2d 192.

Ind.—Taylor v. Fitzpatrick, 132 N.E. 2d 919, 235 Ind. 238 (sudden peril created by child pedestrian causing swerving).

Iowa.—Schmitt v. Jenkins Truck Lines, Inc., 1969, 170 N.W.2d 632, 46 A.L.R.3d 636.

Ky.—Chittum v. Abell, C.A.1972, 485 S.W.2d 231; Mulberry v. Howard, C.A.1970, 457 S.W.2d 827.

La.—Wishom v. Ford Motor Co., App. 1971, 256 So.2d 298; Lewis v. Allstate Ins. Co., App.1971, 250 So.2d 155; Kierum v. Stonewall Ins. Co., App.1971, 247 So.2d 166; Belgard v. Aetna Cas. & Sur. Co., 1969, 227 So.2d 24, writ refused 229 So.2d

731, 255 La. 146, 229 So.2d 732, 255 La. 147; Rollins v. New York Fire & Marine Underwriters, Inc., App.1969, 225 So.2d 663, writ refused 227 So.2d 595, 254 La. 855.

Me.—Burtchell v. Willey, 1952, 87 A. 2d 658, 147 Me. 339.

Mich.—Morton v. Wibright, 1971, 187 N.W.2d 254, 31 Mich.App. 8.

Minn.—Brady v. Kroll, 1955, 70 N. W.2d 354, 244 Minn. 525.

Mo.—Middleman v. Complete Auto Transit, Inc., 1972, 486 S.W.2d 456 (burden was on owner and driver of tractor-trailer, which skidded out of control and across median strip into path of oncoming traffic, to show that plaintiff-oncoming driver could have swerved in time to avoid collision).

Neb.—McAlexander v. Lewis Estate, 1958, 93 N.W.2d 632, 167 Neb. 524, 77 A.L.R. 575.

N.M.—Paulos v. Albuquerque Nat. Bank, 1971, 487 P.2d 187, 82 N.M. 759; Paddock v. Schuelke, 1970, 413 P.2d 373, 81 N.M. 759.

Ohio.—Peters v. B. & F. Transfer Co., 219 N.E.2d 27, 7 Ohio St.2d 143; Lehman v. Haynam, 133 N.E. 2d 97, 164 Ohio St. 595 (unforeseen unconsciousness).

Or.—Gum v. Wooge, 315 P.2d 119, 211 Or. 149 (head-on collision in lane of plaintiff's decedent).

Pa.—Kralik v. Cromwell, 1969, 258 A.2d 654, 435 Pa. 613.

Tenn.—Purser v. Thompson, 219 S. W.2d 211, 31 Tenn.App. 619 (defective brakes).

Tex.—Hammer v. Dallas Transit Co., 400 S.W.2d 885.

Vt.—Frenier v. Brown, 80 A.2d 524, 116 Vt. 538.

Va.—Riley v. Harris, 1970, 177 S.E. 2d 630, 211 Va. 359; Pullen v. Fagan, 132 S.E.2d 718, 204 Va. 601.

Wash.—Wellons v. Wiley, 166 P.2d 852, 24 Wash.2d 543 (skidding to wrong side); Taylor v. Lubetich, 97 P.2d 142, 2 Wash.2d 6 (break in mechanism).

Wis.—Bunkfeldt v. Country Mut. Ins. Co., 138 N.W.2d 271, 29 Wis.2d 179.

Wyo.—Lalicker v. Halligan, 1970, 476 P.2d 737 (burden of proving that rule of road gave right-of-way).

Directed verdict for plaintiff

Where dual wheels of tractor separated, resulting in collision of trailer with oncoming vehicle in oncoming vehicle's proper lane, defendant truck driver had burden of proving that defect causing separation of wheels was not discoverable by reasonable inspection during course of maintenance, and where defendants failed to adduce any evidence on issue it was proper to grant plaintiff's motion for directed verdict. Bunkfeldt v. Country Mut. Ins. Co., 138 N.W.2d 271, 29 Wis.2d 179.

Insufficient explanation

Where salesman had forced truck driver onto shoulder, truck driver's wrongful act, after having returned to shoulder from behind salesman's automobile, in crowding salesman to salesman's left would not exculpate salesman for his unnecessary and, therefore, negligent election to invade lane of travel of oncoming automobiles, and, therefore, in action arising from resulting accident, salesman's employer did not, by establishing such facts, meet burden upon it of going forward with legally sufficient excusatory evidence. Venske v. Johnson-Lieber Co., 288 P.2d 249, 47 Wash.2d 511.

Rule limited

Rule that where collision results from one's act of driving vehicle into that part of roadway reserved exclusively for traffic proceeding in opposite direction, offending driver has burden of proving that collision was not caused by his negligence applies only where offending vehicle is

§ 416.2   TRIAL EVIDENCE   Ch. 416

person asserting the violation of statute, however, must submit evidence showing that the situation comes within the provisions of the statute.[1]

Statutory rules

In a number of instances, proof of the violation of a statute or ordinance establishes negligence per se,[2] or at least prima facie evidence of negligence.[3] Under a statute providing that no vehicle shall be driven at a greater speed than is reasonable and proper, having regard for the traffic and the use of the high-

also involved in collision in the other lane. Meskill v. Allstate Ins. Co., La.App.1971, 247 So.2d 163.

1. **Ill.**—Jones v. Illinois Iowa Power Co., 41 N.E.2d 115, 314 Ill.App. 204.

Ohio.—McFadden v. Elmer C. Breuer Transp. Co., 103 N.E.2d 385, 156 Ohio St. 430.

Okl.—Kraft Foods Co. v. Chadwell, 249 P.2d 1002, 207 Okl. 379.

Tex.—Comet Motor Freight Lines v. Holmes, Tex.Civ.App., 175 S.W.2d 464, error refused.

Rule applied

In action for death of one struck by defendant's automobile wrecker, with which an automobile collided at night while decedent was standing on highway in front of wrecker after assisting defendant's employee in charge thereof to pull truck from ditch, burden of adducing proof that truck's lighting system was disabled was on plaintiff relying on such fact to establish such employee's statutory duty to place flares on highway. Basham's Adm'x v. Witt, 159 S.W. 2d 990, 289 Ky. 639.

2. **Wash.**—Jung v. York, 1969, 449 P.2d 409, 75 Wash.2d 195 (whether or not he was able to see pedestrian, motorist had duty to stop his vehicle when he saw vehicle ahead in an adjoining lane stopped at crosswalk, and his failure to do so, in violation of ordinance, was negligence per se).

3. **U.S.**—Alford v. Blake, C.A.Fla., 1967, 385 F.2d 1010 (Florida statute requiring truck brakes to be so adjusted as to operate as equally as practicable with respect to wheels on opposit sides of vehicle); Marsden v. Patane, C.A.Fla., 1967, 380 F.2d 489; Mihalic v. Texaco, Inc., C.A.Pa., 1967, 377 F.2d 978 (Pennsylvania statute requiring that vehicle be driven on right-hand side of road).

Ariz.—Ruiz v. Faulkner, 1970, 470 P.2d 500, 12 Ariz.App. 352 (driving in excess of established speed limit).

Fla.—Holland v. Watson, 1968, 215 So.2d 498.

La.—Guillory v. Bordelon Lines, App., 1945, 23 So.2d 669 (not available on facts); Russo v. Aucoin, App., 1942, 7 So.2d 744.

Me.—Rawson v. Stiman, 1935, 176 A. 870, 133 Me. 250.

Neb.—Kuffel v. Kuncl, 1967, 150 N.W.2d 908, 181 Neb. 770.

N.C.—Reeves v. Hill, 1968, 158 S.E. 2d 529, 272 N.C. 352 (driving left of center of highway).

R.I.—Waltz v. Aycrigg, 1967, 235 A.2d 338, 103 R.I. 109.

But see

Miss.—Dr. Pepper Bottling Co. v. Gordy, 164 So. 236, 174 Miss. 392 (Code 1942, § 1742) (injured servant's action against master).

Ch. 416 BURDEN OF PROOF § 416.2

way, and specifying the rates of speed which, under specified conditions, shall be prima facie evidence of unreasonable speed, the burden is upon a motorist to show that a speed in excess of the limit so specified was reasonable.[4]

But, under the rule that the burden of proof as distinguished from the burden of evidence remains upon the party having the affirmative of an issue throughout the case, such statutes merely relieve plaintiff, on proving the forbidden conduct from establishing negligence on his opening, but do not shift the burden to the defendant after countervailing evidence has been introduced.[5]

The court of one state adopted the construction of the statute of another state in which the injury occurred, that the statute gives to the injured person a substantial substantive right and does not outline a mere rule of procedure.[6] Such a statute places the burden of proof always upon the defendant to clear itself from blame, if the plaintiff shows injury at a crossing from a moving train, and this is true, although the plaintiff may attempt to show specific negligent acts upon the part of the defendant;[7] but a statute constituting certain acts negligence per se has been held not to give to the plaintiff such a vested property right as cannot be affected by a subsequent act of the Legislature, changing the burden of proof.[8]

In some jurisdictions, under statute, it is not incumbent upon the plaintiff, in a case where the injury complained of was caused by the running of a defendant railroad's locomotive or cars, to prove allegations of negligence of the defendant.[9]

4. **Ky.**—Hornek Bros. v. Strubel, 279 S.W. 1087, 212 Ky. 631.

La.—Gulf States Utilities Co. v. Guidry, App., 183 So.2d 122.

Minn.—Olson v. Duluth, M. & I. R. Ry. Co., 5 N.W.2d 492, 213 Minn. 106.

Ohio.—Glasco v. Mendelman, 56 N.E.2d 210, 143 Ohio St. 649.

5. **Vt.**—Duprat v. Chesmore, 110 A. 305, 94 Vt. 218.

Va.—Pickett v. Cooper, 116 S.E.2d 48, 202 Va. 60.

Rule construed

When violator of traffic statute has met burden of overcoming prima facie case of negligence by reason of violation, trial proceeds as if prima facie case never existed and burden of going forward with evidence shifts to opposing litigant. Krafft v. Hirt, 110 N.W.2d 14, 260 Minn. 296.

6. **Mo.**—Hiatt v. St. Louis-San Francisco Ry. Co., 271 S.W. 806, 308 Mo. 77.

7. **Mo.**—Hiatt v. St. Louis-San Francisco Ry. Co., 271 S.W. 806, 308 Mo. 77.

8. **Cal.**—Meads v. Deener, 17 P.2d 198, 128 Cal.App. 328.

9. **Ala.**—Frierson v. Gulf, Mobile & Ohio R. Co., 48 So.2d 170, 254 Ala. 290.

Fla.—Luster v. Geneva Mills Co., 135 So. 854, 102 Fla. 350 (burden on railroad to show not negligent).

§ 416.2   TRIAL EVIDENCE   Ch. 416

The Arkansas statutes literally make all railroads responsible for all damages to persons or property caused by the running of a train, but those statutes have been construed to mean that proof of injury by a moving train only makes a prima facie case for the plaintiff, without further proof of negligence.[10]

A Tennessee statute requires railroads to perform certain specified acts to protect against a crossing accident and further provides that a railroad which fails to comply with the statute shall be civilly liable for all damage done and that the burden of proof that it has observed said precautions shall be upon the company. Where the statute is applicable, the burden of proof rests upon the railroad to show compliance with the statute, or that compliance was impossible, that it was guilty of no negligence, and that the accident was unavoidable, in order to avoid liability for damages resulting from the accident.[11]

Under some statutes, plaintiff makes out a prima facie case, growing out of a railroad collision at a crossing, by proving that the statutory signals were not given,[12] but the burden is on the injured motorist, in sustaining the burden of proof, not only to show the failure to give the statutory signals, but likewise to prove that there was a causal relation between such failure and the motorist's injury.[13]

A California statute, placing the burden of proving a motorist's negligence on the adversary, though the definite speed limit specified in the same section has been exceeded, is not unconstitutional.[14]

Where the negligence alleged is the violation of some traffic regulation, the prohibitions of which are not absolute but permit some exceptions, the injured person need only show facts constituting a violation in the absence of the exceptional conditions; it being then upon the defendant to show circumstances within the

Ga.—Lime-Cola Bottling Co. v. Atlanta & W. P. R. Co., 128 S.E. 226, 34 Ga.App. 103.

Miss.—Eastman, Gardiner & Co. v. Sumrall, 133 So. 212, 160 Miss. 792 (presumption of negligence, but ultimate burden on plaintiff, if rebutted).

10. **Ark.**—Missouri Pac. R. Co. v. Boley, 1972, 477 S.W.2d 468, 251 Ark. 964; Chicago, R. I. & P. Ry. Co. v. Thomas, 42 S.W.2d 762, 184 Ark. 457.

11. **U.S.**—Callaway v. Christison, C.C.A.Tenn., 148 F.2d 303.

Tenn.—Nashville, C. & St. L. Ry. v. Smith, 228 S.W.2d 495, 33 Tenn. App. 45.

12. **Mo.**—Rowe v. St. Louis-San Francisco Ry. Co., App., 41 S.W. 2d 631.

13. **Va.**—Norfolk & W. Ry. Co. v. Eley, 162 S.E. 3, 157 Va. 568.

14. **Cal.**—Potapoff v. Mattes, 19 P. 2d 1016, 130 Cal.App. 421.

exception;[15] as where a statute prohibits the parking of vehicles upon the highway except vehicles so disabled as to prevent moving the same.[16] Generally, a motorist violating a specific statutory requirement must show that it was due to circumstances beyond control,[17] or otherwise show an excuse for the violation.[18] A motorist may successfully explain presence on the

15. **U.S.**—Atlantic Coast Line R. Co. v. Hadlock, C.A.Fla., 180 F.2d 105.

S.C.—Maybank & Co. v. Rodgers, 82 S.E. 422, 98 S.C. 279.

Wis.—Ellison v. National Cas. Co., 35 N.W.2d 300, 254 Wis. 117 (proving that collision, which occurred outside city limits, occurred in a residential district relieving plaintiff of duty of blowing horn when attempting to pass).

Contra

In action by guest against driver for injuries sustained in collision on three lane highway, wherein evidence showed that driver had been traveling in middle lane immediately before applying his brakes and turning into right lane of traffic, guest had burden of establishing that truck driver was not within exceptions provided in statute prohibiting driving in middle lane of three lane highway. Reese v. Day, 281 P.2d 263, 131 Cal.App.2d 730.

16. **Cal.**—Rosa v. Pacific Gas & Elec. Co., 284 P.2d 844, 133 Cal. App.2d 672 (under statute providing that certain parking restrictions should not apply to vehicles owned or operated by public utility when stopped or parked at side of work involving construction, operation, removal, or repair of utility on or adjacent to street or highway, fact that vehicle was employed in one of the activities enumerated is affirmative defense which must be specially proven).

Mass.—Madden v. Berman, 88 N.E. 2d 630, 324 Mass. 699 (proviso of statute permitting an automobile to be parked without lights in a space in which unlighted parking is permitted).

Or.—Watt v. Associated Oil Co., 260 P. 1012, 123 Or. 50.

17. **Ohio.**—McFadden v. Elmer C. Breuer Transp. Co., Ohio App., 98 N.E.2d 339 (violation of assured clear distance rule); Bennett v. Sinclair Refining Co., 57 N.E.2d 776, 144 Ohio St. 139 (violation of statute requiring driver to keep to right).

Or.—Watt v. Associated Oil Co., 260 P. 1012, 123 Or. 50 (illegally parked).

R.I.—Harvey v. Corr, 160 A.2d 355, 91 R.I. 1 (due to broken steering mechanism of which he had no previous knowledge).

S.C.—Boyleston v. Baxley, 133 S.E. 2d 796, 243 S.C. 281 (suddenly stricken by fainting spell, or loses consciousness from some other unforeseen cause).

W.Va.—Keller v. Wonn, 87 S.E.2d 453, 140 W.Va. 860 (sudden attack suffered by decedent, unforeseen and unanticipated).

Order of superior military officer

In action by army private driving truck in army convoy, against operator of automobile with which truck collided at intersection, private had burden of proving that he acted in accordance with order of officer whom he was bound to obey in running through red light, but burden of proving that he did run through red light was on defendant. Neu v. McCarthy, 33 N.E.2d 570, 309 Mass. 17, 133 A.L.R. 1291.

18. **Cited by the court** in Bowen v. Baumgardner, 1972, 491 P.2d 1301, 1303, 6 Wash.App. 18.

§ 416.2 TRIAL EVIDENCE Ch. 416

wrong side of a highway by proof that the conduct measured up to the standard of common caution for the driver of a motor vehicle under like conditions and circumstances.[19]

Similarly, in actions involving vehicles used in saving life or property, or in enforcing the law, such as police vehicles [20]

Alaska.—Rogers v. Dubiel, 373 P.2d 295 (skidding to wrong side due to ice held insufficient).

Cal.—Engelman v. Consolidated House Movers, 286 P.2d 988, 135 Cal.App.2d 237 (house being towed down street); Satterlee v. Orange Glenn School Dist. of San Diego County, 177 P.2d 279, 29 Cal.2d 581 (violation of right of way statute).

Del.—Matthews v. Bryerton, 193 A.2d 83, 5 Storey 447 (burden to present evidence of any legal excuse there might be for disobeying statutes requiring motorists to yield right of way to emergency vehicles and to stop until such vehicles have passed).

Iowa.—Luppes v. Harrison, 32 N.W. 2d 809, 239 Iowa 880.

Ky.—Humphries v. Gray, 203 S.W.2d 8, 305 Ky. 205 (steering failure).

La.—Jones v. Continental Cas. Co. of Chicago, Ill., App., 159 So.2d 5, writ ref. 160 So.2d 596, 245 La. 732.

Minn.—Demmer v. Grunke, 42 N.W. 2d 1, 230 Minn. 188.

Miss.—Fink v. East Miss. Elec. Power Ass'n, 105 So.2d 548, 234 Miss. 221 ("sudden emergency" of brake failure).

N.H.—Adley Exp. Co. v. Bruzzese, 184 A.2d 564, 104 N.H. 283 (failure to comply with "flare statute" due to driver being unconscious).

Pa.—Blockinger v. Schweitzer, 214 A.2d 244, 419 Pa. 342 (passed over medial strip eight inches high and crashed head on into automobile); Hasker v. Mease, 59 Montg. 364 (failure to stop within assured clear distance ahead).

Wash.—Tutewiler v. Shannon, 111 P.2d 215, 8 Wash.2d 23 (skidding across highway).

After evidence of defective brakes

A motorist, to be relieved of liability for damage resulting from collision caused by defective brakes, must show that he had made as adequate inspection thereof as a reasonable man would recognize as necessary. Sothoron v. West, 26 A.2d 16, 180 Md. 539.

19. **Colo.**—Boyd v. Close, 257 P. 1079, 82 Colo. 150.

Iowa.—Giese v. Kimball, 169 N.W. 639, 184 Iowa 1283.

Ky.—Hunt v. Whitlocks Adm'r, 1935, 82 S.W.2d 364, 259 Ky. 286.

La.—Ford, Bacon & Davis v. Shaw, 8 La.App. 751.

Md.—Consolidated Gas, Electric Light & Power Co. of Baltimore v. O'Neill, 1938, 200 A. 359, 175 Md. 47.

Mich.—Sanderson v. Barkman, 249 N.W. 492, 264 Mich. 152.

Pa.—Chadwick v. Popadick, 159 A.2d 907, 399 Pa. 88.

Vt.—Steele v. Fuller, 158 A. 666, 104 Vt. 303 (driving without sufficient lights).

Wash.—Thomas v. Adams, 24 P.2d 432, 174 Wash. 118; Crowe v. O'Rourke, 1927, 262 P. 136, 146 Wash. 74; Segerstrom v. Lawrence, 1911, 116 P. 876, 64 Wash. 245 (showing prevailing custom of violation of regulation).

20. **Pa.**—Mashinsky v. City of Philadelphia, 3 A.2d 790, 333 Pa. 97.

Ch. 416 BURDEN OF PROOF § 416.2

and ambulances,[21] which may be entitled to disregard traffic regulations or the "rules of the road" in an emergency, the defendant owner or driver of such a vehicle has the burden of proving the existence of an emergency,[22] and status as "emergency vehicle."[23]

One who allows a motor vehicle to stand on a traveled portion of the highway has the burden of proving justification or excuse.[24] The same rule applies to one who fails to park parallel with and within a prescribed distance from the curb.[25]

As a general rule, the failure to comply with a statute regulating the equipment or operation of motor vehicles creates a prima facie case of negligence, but there may be facts which will excuse a technical violation of the statute. The burden is on the defendant to offer proof in legal excuse or avoidance of the

21. **N.C.**—Williams v. Sossoman's Funeral Home, Inc., 103 S.E.2d 714, 248 N.C. 524.

Pa.—Oakley v. Allegheny County, 193 A. 316, 128 Pa.Super. 8.

22. **Pa.**—Mashinsky v. City of Philadelphia, 3 A.2d 790, 333 Pa. 97 (police motorcycle striking pedestrian); Oakley v. Allegheny County, 193 A. 316, 128 Pa.Super. 8 (ambulance entering intersection against red light when taking patient to hospital).

23. **Ark.**—Freeman v. Reeves, 410 S.W.2d 740, 241 Ark. 867.

24. **U.S.**—Walker v. Warehouse Transp. Co., C.A.N.H., 235 F.2d 125.

Ala.—Cosby v. Flowers, 30 So.2d 694, 249 Ala. 227.

Cal.—Smith v. Wattenburg, 283 P. 2d 751, 133 Cal.App.2d 193; Woods v. Walker, 124 P.2d 844, 51 Cal. App.2d 307 (parked for temporary repairs).

Ky.—Banner Transfer Co. v. Morse, 274 S.W.2d 380.

Minn.—Martin v. Tracy, 246 N.W. 6, 187 Minn. 529 (rear lamps not lighted).

Mo.—Smith v. Producers Cold Storage Co., Mo.App., 128 S.W.2d 299.

Okl.—Roadway Express v. Baty, 114 P.2d 935, 189 Okl. 180.

Pa.—Bricker v. Gardner, 48 A.2d 209, 355 Pa. 35.

S.C.—Suber v. Smith, 134 S.E.2d 404, 243 S.C. 458.

Wash.—Berndt v. Pacific Transport Co., 231 P.2d 643, 38 Wash.2d 760.

Wis.—Henthorn v. M. G. C. Corp., 83 N.W.2d 759, 1 Wis.2d 180, 79 A. L.R.2d 142.

Rule applied

In action by widow for death of her husband from being hit by automobile allegedly due to concurrent negligence of several defendants, where parked truck had been backed up to loading dock so that truck obstructed sidewalk and extended into street obstructing one lane of traffic, burden of proving municipal permission to back into loading dock and to obstruct sidewalk and street was on defendant-owner, it being matter of defense. Anderson-McGriff Co. v. Meisel, 68 S.E.2d 377, 85 Ga.App. 58.

Me.—Coombs v. Markley, 143 A. 261, 127 Me. 335.

25. **Ind.**—Northern Ind. Transit, Inc., v. Burk, 89 N.E.2d 905, 228 Ind. 162.

§ 416.2

failure to observe the statute.[26] This is true as to a motorist who fails to comply with the statute regarding sufficient lights on the vehicle.[27]

A defendant who violates the law of the road may avoid liability by taking the burden of showing, notwithstanding such violation, having acted with ordinary care.[28] So, where a truck was parked on the highway without flares, and it was claimed there had not been sufficient time to place the flares, it was held, citing this statement of the rule from a prior edition, that the burden of proof was on defendant.[29]

After the defendant meets the burden resting of introducing evidence in opposition to the presumption or prima facie case, the burden shifts to the plaintiff to produce affirmative evidence of negligence.[30]

---

26. **Cal.**—Merry v. Knudsen Creamery Co., 211 P.2d 905, 94 Cal.App. 2d 715 (statute requiring adequate brakes).

Ga.—Allied Egg & Poultry Co. v. Jocie Motor Lines, 87 S.E.2d 172, 91 Ga.App. 725.

Mo.—Lochmoeller v. Kiel, App., 137 S.W.2d 625 (statute requiring motor vehicles to be provided at all times with two sets of adequate brakes kept in good working order).

Brakes

Ariz.—O'Donnell v. Maves, 1972, 492 P.2d 1205, 108 Ariz. 98.

La.—Holliday v. Hartford Acc. & Indem. Co., App., 38 So.2d 235 (when park truck rolled down hill and into automobile, defendant had burden of proving that truck driver effectively set brakes, which were efficient prior to and immediately after accident).

27. **Vt.**—Steele v. Fuller, 158 A. 666, 104 Vt. 303.

28. **Ark.**—Herring v. Bollinger, 29 S.W.2d 676, 181 Ark. 925.

Cal.—Barone v. Jones, 177 P.2d 30, 77 Cal.App.2d 656 (proof that defendants left truck on public highway imposed upon defendants burden of showing compliance with statute requiring operator to immediately place warning signals in advance and to the rear of disabled vehicle).

Colo.—Brothers v. Chatfield, 154 P. 2d 46, 113 Colo. 7.

Wash.—Brotherton v. Day & Night Fuel Co., 73 P.2d 788, 192 Wash. 362; Wilson v. Congdon, 37 P.2d 892, 179 Wash. 400.

Flashlight used to give warning of parked truck

In action against state of New York for death of occupant of automobile which ran into the rear of an unlighted army truck which had been parked partially on pavement at night in Ohio by national guardsmen from New York, burden was on state to show that flashlight employed by a guardsman to give warning was substantially as efficient as lights required by Ohio statute. Gibson v. State, 19 N.Y.S.2d 405, 173 Misc. 893, affirmed 21 N.Y.S.2d 362, 259 App.Div. 1104.

29. **N.H.**—MacDonald v. Appleyard, 53 A.2d 434, 94 N.H. 362.

30. **U.S.**—Delaware Coach Co. v. Savage, D.C.Del., 81 F.Supp. 293 (collision at intersection controlled by traffic lights).

§ 416.3 Burden of Proof—Negligence Other Than Vehicle Operation

Library References:
C.J.S. Motor Vehicles §§ 509 et seq., 223, 238.
West's Key No. Digests, Automobiles ⚖︎242, 304.

The rule as to the burden of proof being upon the party holding the affirmative of the issue has been applied in suits for injuries to an automobile or its occupants through the negligence of persons or travelers other than the drivers.[31]

It has been held that, where the plaintiff alleges that the defendant created or maintained a nuisance, the plaintiff may not be required to prove that the defendant was negligent. If the instrumentality causing the injury is inherently dangerous, having a natural tendency to cause injury, the nuisance is "absolute" and the plaintiff is not required to prove negligence.[32]

Defects or obstructions in highway

A traveler claiming to have been injured as a result of a defect or obstruction in the street or highway, and seeking to recover damages therefor from the defendant, has in general the same burden of proof as the plaintiff in other tort actions,[33] sub-

---

31. As to products liability

Because of technical problems involved in brake system, superior knowledge and expertise of manufacturer and close relationship between manufacturer and dealer, burden of negating individual responsibility for brake failure on truck would be placed on the manufacturer and the dealer in purchaser's products liability case. Snider v. Bob Thibodeau Ford, Inc., 1972, 202 N.W.2d 727, 42 Mich. App. 708.

32. Conn.—Warren v. City of Bridgeport, 28 A.2d 1, 129 Conn. 355.

33. Ala.—Terrell v. Alabama Water Service Co., 15 So.2d 727, 245 Ala. 68 (burst water pipes flooded highway, resulting in ice on highway).

Ariz.—Seiler v. Whiting, 84 P.2d 452, 52 Ariz. 542.

N.Y.—Roth v. Ho Penn Garage Corp., Sup., 56 N.Y.S.2d 340.

Ill.—Ebert v. City of Chicago, 58 N.E.2d 198, 324 Ill.App. 315 (unlighted safety island).

Iowa.—Harris v. Chicago, M., St. P. & P. R. Co., 278 N.W. 338, 224 Iowa 1319 (condition of railroad viaduct).

Mass.—Adams v. Town of Bolton, 9 N.E.2d 562, 297 Mass. 459, 111 A.L.R. 856 (actions against town by passengers in automobile for injuries sustained when automobile went into hollow in highway).

Minn.—Becker v. Northland Transp. Co., 275 N.W. 510, 200 Minn. 272, affirming 274 N.W. 180, 200 Minn. 272 (negligence in selecting independent contractor employed to burn brush, causing smoke over highway).

Neb.—Wittwer v. Richardson County, 43 N.W.2d 505, 153 Neb. 200.

§ 416.3 TRIAL EVIDENCE Ch. 416

ject to a few modifications due to the nature of the case,[34] and to the nature of the defendant's liability to respond in damages, which is often founded upon and limited by statute.[35] The plaintiff ordinarily must prove also that the defendant had notice, actual or constructive, of the condition allegedly giving rise to the injury,[36] and of the dangerous character thereof.[37]

N.J.—Monaco v. Comfort Bus Line, 49 A.2d 146, 134 N.J.L. 553 (motorbus unexplainably turned at an angle while crossing bridge and crashed through bridge rail).

N.Y.—Coffey v. State, 86 N.Y.S.2d 172, 193 Misc. 1060, affirmed 96 N.Y.S.2d 303, 304, (2 mems) 276 App.Div. 1049, reargument and appeal denied 97 N.Y.S.2d 918, 277 App.Div. 831 (alleged "bleeding" of asphalt in hot weather).

S.C.—Epps v. South Carolina State Highway Department, 39 S.E.2d 198, 209 S.C. 125 (automobile crashing into ravine beyond highway intersection as alleged result of failure to erect sufficient signals or warning devices).

Tenn.—Bailey v. Alloway Bros. Co., 192 S.W.2d 849, 29 Tenn.App. 1.

Tex.—Driver v. Worth Const. Co., 273 S.W.2d 603, 154 Tex. 66 (that contractor failed to give sufficient warning to travelling public that the highway was not open to travel); City of Waco v. Criswell, Tex. Civ.App., 141 S.W.2d 1046 (construction and maintenance of sewer).

Definition of burden

In action against city for death of driver who was drowned when taxicab went into creek at foot of street, administratrix was not required to exclude or eliminate every other possible cause, or to point out the particular act or omission which caused the injury. Trimble v. City of New York, 88 N.Y.S.2d 324, 275 App.Div. 169.

34. **Cal.**—Beckley v. Vezu, 73 P.2d 296, 23 Cal.App.2d 371.

Mass.—Bern v. Boston Consol. Gas Co., 39 N.E.2d 576, 310 Mass. 651.

N.Y.—Netz v. State, Ct.Cl., 46 N.Y.S. 2d 374.

Pa.—Ventura v. City of Pittsburgh, 47 A.2d 668, 159 Pa.Super. 279.

35. **Mass.**—Adams v. Town of Bolton, 9 N.E.2d 562, 297 Mass. 459, 111 A.L.R. 856.

36. **Cal.**—Briggs v. State, 1971, 92 Cal.Rptr. 433, 14 C.A.3d 489 (of large mud slide); Beckley v. Vezu, 73 P.2d 296, 23 Cal.App.2d 371.

Ky.—Evans v. Com., 1970, 459 S.W. 2d 761 (to impose liability on Department of Highways for failing to anticipate rock slide or failing to take corrective action to prevent injury when automobile ran into rock slide).

Ohio.—Neale v. Village of Tallmadge, App.1939, 35 N.E.2d 158.

Liberality of requirement

Kan.—Neiswender v. Board of Com'rs of Shawnee County, 113 P.2d 115, 153 Kan. 634, opinion supplemented 120 P.2d 218, 154 Kan. 588 (not required to prove that Chairman had five days' notice of defect at exact spot where automobile went through bridge railing).

N.Y.—Camuglia v. State, 94 N.Y.S.2d 579, 197 Misc. 180 (required only to show that the state recognized that frost upheavals existed in vicinity, without showing actual knowledge of the particular upheaval itself).

37. **Cal.**—Beckley v. Vezu, 73 P.2d 296, 23 Cal.App.2d 371 (narrowness of bridge).

Collisions with animals on highway

A plaintiff who is injured in a collision between a motor vehicle and a domestic animal of a public highway has the burden of proving that the owner of the animal was negligent in permitting the animal to roam at large on the highway.[39] However, in some cases the owner of the animal has an affirmative duty to prove the exercise of reasonable care in restraining the animal.[40]

Entrusting car to incompetent or unlicensed driver

To establish liability of an owner who lends an automobile to an incompetent driver, the burden is upon the plaintiff, not only to establish such incompetency, but also to prove the driver's negligence and that, in producing the injury, it concurred with the owner's negligence in intrusting the machine to an incompetent driver,[41] and that the lender knew or should have

---

38. N.J.—Robinson v. Township of Ocean, 9 A.2d 300, 123 N.J.L. 525 (action against municipality for injuries resulting when automobile struck gutter constructed at street intersection by municipality).

39. U.S.—Hyrum Smith Estate Co. v. Peterson, C.A.Utah, 227 F.2d 442 (motorcyclist colliding with horses).

Ill.—Guay v. Neel, 91 N.E.2d 151, 340 Ill.App. 111.

Tex.—Schrader v. Garcia, App.1974, 516 S.W.2d 690 (had to prove owner's knowledge of cattle running at large).

But see

It was not incumbent upon party injured in collision with steer on highway at night to plead or prove how steer came to be upon the highway. Burrowes v. Dean, 1970, 263 N.E.2d 416, 24 Ohio Misc. 77.

40. Idaho—Whitt v. Jarnagin, 418 P.2d 278, 9 Idaho 181.

Ill.—Fugett v. Murray, 35 N.E.2d 946, 311 Ill.App. 323 (S.H.A. c. 70, § 1 et seq.; c. 8, § 1).

La.—Audubon Ins. Co. v. Falgout, 1970, 234 So.2d 842, application denied 237 So.2d 398, 399, 256 La. 619, 621 (struck on stock law highway).

41. Ala.—Laney v. Blackburn, 144 So. 126, 25 Ala.App. 248.

Mo.—Saunders v. Prue, 151 S.W.2d 478, 235 Mo.App. 1245 (prospective purchaser using auto of dealer).

N.Y.—Beiner v. Nassau Electric R. Co., 181 N.Y.S. 628, 191 App.Div. 371 (placing physically unfit motorman in charge of street car).

Or.—Gossett v. Van Egmond, 155 P. 2d 304, 176 Or. 134 (failing to take affirmative measures to prevent use of his automobile by his incompetent son).

Tenn.—Dukes v. McGimsey, App. 1973, 500 S.W.2d 448.

Degree of proof of incompetence

Where owner was sought to be held liable for injuries caused by

§ 416.3   TRIAL EVIDENCE   Ch. 416

known that the borrower was incompetent and that injury might occur.[42]

Permitting use of defective vehicle

Where the charge made against the lender of an automobile is that its defective condition caused an injury, the plaintiff must show, not only that the automobile was defective at the time of

borrower's negligence, on ground that lender was negligent in entrusting automobile to borrower, it must be shown that reckless conduct of borrower was so constantly committed as to constitute a habit of negligence. Lix v. Gastian, Mo.App., 261 S.W.2d 497.

Issue as to fact of entrustment

Conn.—Hunt v. Richter, 1972, 302 A.2d 117, 163 Conn. 84 (evidence that son who was driving mother's automobile was married and maintained his own household precluded application of presumption established by statute relating to family automobile doctrine; plaintiffs who sustained damages as result of son's negligence were not entitled to recover from mother who was out of city at time of accident but would have let son use automobile. C.G.S.A. § 52–182).

Mass.—Leone v. Doran, 1973, 292 N.E.2d 19, 363 Mass. 1, order vacated in part on procedural matter 297 N.E.2d 493 (it is necessary for plaintiff to show, among other things, that defendant owned or controlled vehicle concerned, and that defendant gave driver permission to operate vehicle).

42. **Ala.**—Milligan v. Sparks, 1974, 286 So.2d 849, 51 Ala.App. 444.

Ind.—North Side Chevrolet v. Clark, 25 N.E.2d 1011, 107 Ind.App. 592 (entrusted to salesman employee described as "habitual drunkard").

La.—Toole v. Morris-Webb Motor Co., App., 195 So. 863 (auto dealer lending license plates to motorist).

N.C.—Cook v. Stedman, 186 S.E. 317, 210 N.C. 345.

Ohio—Gulla v. Straus, 93 N.E.2d 662, 154 Ohio St. 193; Edwards v. Benedict, 70 N.E.2d 471, 79 Ohio App. 134.

Wyo.—Finch v. Canaday, 297 P.2d 594, 75 Wyo. 472.

Knowledge of employee's prior use for personal pleasure

Where death action against owners was based on theory that driver had been not only entrusted with truck for owners' business but also for driver's own personal pleasure and entertainment and that owners knew that driver was a careless and reckless driver, owners could not be held liable in absence of showing that owners knew that driver had been using the truck after hours of service had ended for his own personal pleasure and entertainment. McGowin v. Howard, 21 So.2d 683, 246 Ala. 553.

Rule construed

Incompetency of person as a driver may not be proven by showing only one instance of negligent driving but by several instances or by reputation or by court convictions of negligence and, after proving incompetency, plaintiff must next show that owner had knowledge of such incompetence at time of entrusting vehicle to driver and that may be shown by driver's reputation for competency or by other direct or circumstantial evidence. Winchester v. Padgett, D.C.Ga., 167 F.Supp. 444.

the accident, but also that it was defective at the time of its delivery to the borrower.[43]

In similar cases, where defects in the vehicle are relied on, the plaintiff has the burden of showing that the injury resulted from some defective condition ascertainable by reasonably careful inspection.[44]

§ 416.4 Burden of Proof—Gross Negligence or Wilful, Wanton or Reckless Conduct

Library References:
C.J.S. Motor Vehicles §§ 397 et seq., 509 et seq.
West's Key No. Digests, Automobiles ⟲181, 242.

A guest's action generally must be based on more than ordinary negligence, and hence a guest must plead and prove the kind or degree of negligence required in the particular jurisdiction. In most of the jurisdictions which have adopted guest statutes, it is incumbent on the guest to prove gross negligence, heedless and reckless disregard, or wilful or wanton misconduct.[45]

---

43. **Iowa**—Gianapulos v. Saunders System, Cedar Rapids Co., 242 N.W. 53.

    N.C.—Wilcox v. Glover Motors, Inc., 153 S.E.2d 76, 269 N.C. 473 (burden of proving that dealer, a bailor, knew or in exercise of reasonable care in inspection should have known, when he allowed vehicle to leave his possession, that the brakes were defective).

44. **U.S.**—Chicago, M., St. P. & P. R. Co. v. Gilbert, C.C.A.Mont., 87 F.2d 282 (action against employer by driver whose hand was injured by fan of truck or by broken fragments therefrom).

    Vehicle driven by mechanic on test run

    In action for damages which resulted when defendant's automobile was being driven at defendant's request on highway for test purposes by a mechanic defendant employed to repair automobile during a trip after motor ceased to function properly, and defendant's automobile was struck from rear when motor again ceased to function properly after it was purportedly repaired, in order for plaintiff to recover upon theory of defendant's negligence plaintiff had to prove that defendant's automobile was defective when it went upon highway, that defendant knew or as reasonable man should have known of defect. Nawrocki v. Cole, 249 P.2d 969, 41 Wash.2d 474.

45. **Ala.**—Britton v. Doehring, 1970, 242 So.2d 666, 286 Ala. 498.

    Cal.—Caldwell v. Miller, 1943, 141 P.2d 745, 61 Cal.App.2d 1 (intoxication or wilful misconduct).

    Colo.—Carr v. Stillman, 1972, 499 P.2d 1213, —— Colo.App. —— (wilful and wanton disregard of rights of others, or intoxication).

    Ill.—Richmiller v. Reddick, 1953, 110 N.E.2d 876, 349 Ill.App. 465.

    Idaho—Hughes v. Hudelson, 169 P.2d 712, 67 Idaho 10 (that accident was intentional or caused by intoxication or reckless disregard of the rights of others).

    Mont.—Blinn v. Hatton, 1941, 114 P.2d 518, 112 Mont. 219.

§ 416.4   TRIAL EVIDENCE   Ch. 416

Gross negligence

If the statute limits the guest's right of action to gross negligence on the part of the host, the burden of proof on the plaintiff is to show that the defendant was guilty of that type of negligence.[46]

Wilful misconduct

Where wilful and wanton counts are included in the declaration or complaint, either for the purpose of obviating the defense of contributory negligence or making out a case under the statute applying to guest actions, the burden of proving wilfulness

Nev.—Downing v. Marlia, 1966, 417 P.2d 150, 82 Nev. 294 (intoxication, gross negligence or wilful conduct).

N.D.—Bjerke v. Heartso, 1971, 183 N.W.2d 496 (intoxication, wilful misconduct, or gross negligence).

Or.—Smith v. Laflar, 1931, 2 P.2d 18, 137 Or. 230 (gross negligence, intoxication, or reckless disregard).

S.C.—Kennedy v. Carter, 153 S.E.2d 312, 249 S.C. 168 (intentional or reckless misconduct of host).

Tex.—Young v. Bynum, Civ.App., 260 S.W.2d 696.

Va.—Smith v. Prater, 146 S.E.2d 179, 206 Va. 693 (utter disregard of prudence amounting to complete neglect of safety of guest).

Wash.—Taylor v. Taug, 136 P.2d 176, 17 Wash.2d 533 (guest must show that host prior to accident conceived and acted upon a premeditated intent to injure guest).

Wisconsin rule

Wis.—Heagney v. Sellen, 74 N.W.2d 745, 272 Wis. 107, rehearing denied 75 N.W.2d 801, 272 Wis. 107 (meets burden when proves that host failed to exercise ordinary care in management and control of his vehicle and this establishes prima facie that host failed to exercise such skill and judgment, and from that point burden of going forward with evidence shifts to host to adduce evidence that his skill and judgment differed from that of ordinary prudent driver).

46. Ga.—Manees v. Scicchitano, 1970, 178 S.E.2d 262, 122 Ga.App. 591.

Kan.—In re Wright's Estate, 1951, 228 P.2d 911, 170 Kan. 600.

Me.—Beaulieu v. Beaulieu, 1970, 265 A.2d 610.

Mass.—Roiko v. Aijala, 199 N.E. 484, 293 Mass. 149.

N.H.—Conant v. Collins, 10 A.2d 237, 90 N.H. 434 (running off road on a curve).

Tenn.—Olins v. Schocket, 215 S.W. 2d 18, 31 Tenn.App. 346; Richards v. Parks, 93 S.W.2d 639, 19 Tenn. App. 615 (falling asleep by driver).

Vt.—Hastings v. Murray, 20 A.2d 107, 112 Vt. 37.

Rule applied

In action against owner for death of gratuitous guest, who died when truck collided with train composed of steel gondola cars stopped across highway, on ground that driver of truck was guilty of gross negligence within Wyoming automobile guest statute, plaintiff had burden of proving that the cars were of more conspicuous color than ordinary steel cars, and not having offered any evidence to that effect, the presumption was to the contrary. Huffman v. Buckingham Transp. Co. of Colorado, C.C.A.Wyo., 98 F.2d 916.

Ch. 416　　　　　　BURDEN OF PROOF　　　　　§ **416.4**

and wantonness rests upon the plaintiff.[47] This is also the burden which as a general rule rests upon a trespasser on a motor vehicle who sues the owner or driver thereof for personal injuries,[48] though in some cases, especially where children are involved, the rule may be somewhat relaxed.[49]

Recklessness

If the statute limits the liability of a host to injuries caused by recklessness, the courts will recognize a substantial distinction between negligence and reckless operation, and recklessness will not be deemed a degree of negligence. It is incumbent on plaintiff to show heedlessness, or reckless disregard of the rights of others.[50]

---

47. **U.S.**—Swain v. American Mut. Liability Ins. Co., C.C.A.La., 134 F.2d 886 (construing Illinois law).

Ala.—Becknell v. Alabama Power Co., 143 So. 897, 225 Ala. 689.

Cal.—Mosconi v. Ryan, 210 P.2d 259, 94 Cal.App.2d 227.

Colo.—Graham v. Shilling, 291 P.2d 396, 133 Colo. 5.

Ill.—Loucks v. Pierce, 93 N.E.2d 372, 341 Ill.App. 253 (guest on motorcycle).

Ind.—Kirsch v. Harker, 89 N.E.2d 924, 120 Ind.App. 66.

Iowa—Shenkle v. Mains, 247 N.W. 635, 215 Iowa 1369.

Mass.—Harvey v. Murphy, 30 N.E.2d 854, 308 Mass. 16; Bertera v. Cuneo, 173 N.E. 427, 273 Mass. 181.

Ohio—Tighe v. Diamond, 80 N.E.2d 122, 149 Ohio St. 520; Hasbrook v. Wingate, 87 N.E.2d 87, 152 Ohio St. 50, 10 A.L.R.2d 1342.

S.C.—Martin v. Martin, 1974, 203 S.E.2d 385.

Tex.—McMillian v. Sims, Tex.Civ. App., 112 S.W.2d 793.

Va.—Woodrum v. Holland, 40 S.E.2d 169, 185 Va. 690.

Burden defined

In guest's action plaintiff has burden to prove recklessness but he need not negative every possibility that might relieve defendant from the charge of recklessness. Hebert v. Allen, 41 N.W.2d 240, 241 Iowa 684.

48. **La.**—Lipscomb v. News Star World Pub. Corp., La.App., 5 So. 2d 41.

S.C.—Nettles v. Your Ice Co., 4 S.E. 2d 797, 191 S.C. 429.

49. **Pa.**—De Francisco v. La Face, 194 A. 511, 128 Pa.Super. 538 (in action for injuries sustained by five year old boy when he allegedly fell from defendant's truck, which was parked in front of vacant lot used by children as playground, plaintiffs were required to show only lack of ordinary care of defendant, and not wilful or wanton negligence, where defendant had parked trucks at such place for several years and children had been accustomed to play on them).

50. **U.S.**—Alexander v. U. S., D.C. S.C., 98 F.Supp. 453.

Conn.—Williams v. Smith, 181 A. 622, 120 Conn. 521.

Iowa—Wright v. What Cheer Clay Products Co., 267 N.W. 92, 221 Iowa 1292 (must show, not only negligence, but a rash, heedless disregard of danger that would be apparent to or reasonably anticipated by a person exercising ordi-

§ 416.4　　　TRIAL EVIDENCE　　　Ch. 416

Where the offending vehicle is a "favored vehicle" which may have violated a traffic regulation, it is necessary to prove that the operator was reckless.[51]

§ 416.5　Burden of Proof—Persons Vicariously Liable

Library References:
C.J.S. Motor Vehicles § 511(5, 6).
West's Key No. Digests, Automobiles ⚖242(5, 6).

The burden of proving the existence of such relation between the defendant and the driver as would render the defendant liable for the driver's acts is on the plaintiff.[52]

Where the proof shows one party to be guilty of actionable negligence and another is sued on the theory that such other's negligence directly concurred in causing the injury, the burden is on the plaintiff to establish the responsibility upon the defendant charged as concurrently contributing to the injury.[53]

nary prudence and caution under existing circumstances).

Tex.—Harbin v. Seale, 1970, 461 S.W.2d 591.

51. Pa.—Roadman v. Bellone, 108 A.2d 754, 379 Pa. 483 (in order to recover against city and police officer who entered through highway from vacant lot in pursuit of racing motorists and cut diagonally across highway in the direction of plaintiff's lane of traffic, plaintiff must show recklessness or an arbitrary exercise of right-of-way by officer driving police car); Williams v. City of Pittsburgh, 37 A.2d 540, 349 Pa. 430 (fire department vehicle).

52. Fla.—McDougald v. Couey, 200 So. 391, 145 Fla. 689.

Ky.—Johnson v. Brewer, 98 S.W.2d 889, 266 Ky. 314.

Mo.—King v. Rieth, 1937, 108 S.W.2d 1, 341 Mo. 467.

N.C.—Duckworth v. Metcalf, 150 S.E.2d 485, 268 N.C. 340.

Tex.—Montfort v. Baumhardt, Civ. App., 237 S.W.2d 1004.

Wis.—Kaiser v. Streich, 26 N.W.2d 160, 249 Wis. 615.

Family purpose doctrine
Wash.—Coffman v. McFadden, 416 P.2d 99, 68 Wash.2d 954 (rests on plaintiff).

53. Mass.—Hinds v. Bowen, 167 N.E. 332, 268 Mass. 55.

N.Y.—Ackerman v. Fifth Ave. Coach Co., 162 N.Y.S. 49, 175 App.Div. 508.

Or.—West v. Kern, 171 P. 1050, 88 Or. 247.

Wash.—McCanna v. Silke, 134 P. 1063, 75 Wash. 383.

One tort-feasor released
A release given by occupant to automobile driver joined as additional defendant by bus company, placed on occupant the burden of proving that bus company was alone liable, notwithstanding that release was without consideration. Masters v. Philadelphia Transp. Co., 50 A.2d 532, 160 Pa.Super. 178.

Relationship between owner and tower
Cal.—Walton v. Donohue, 1924, 233 P. 76, 70 Cal.App. 309.

44

When the action is against the occupant of the vehicle the burden is upon the plaintiff to establish some relationship between the occupant and the driver by which the occupant becomes responsible for the negligence of the driver. This may be established by proof that the occupant was the owner of the vehicle, or that the driver was occupant's agent, or that the driver and occupant were engaged in a joint venture.[54]

The burden of proving that such a relationship exists between a husband and wife as will render the one liable for the negligence in driving the vehicle owned by the other rests upon the plaintiff.[55] But, if an action is brought against both husband and wife, for injuries caused by one in the operation of an automobile, on the theory that the one so using the car was acting for the community, in those states where community property is recognized by law, the burden of proof is on the defendant spouse to show that the other was using the car in separate affairs.[56]

Liability based upon agency

The plaintiff, if claiming that defendant is liable as owner of a vehicle involved in an accident and because the driver was acting on defendant's behalf, must plead and prove such ownership [57] and, if by an agent or servant, then that such agent or

---

54. Ill.—Kinney v. O'Flaherty, 56 N.E.2d 473, 323 Ill.App. 579 (defendant, the wife of the owner, is responsible for the negligence of the driver when defendant sat beside driver and did not complain of his driving).

Ind.—Jones v. Kasper, 33 N.E.2d 816, 109 Ind.App. 465 (all parties who go for a ride in a car belonging to another without the owner's consent are engaged in a joint venture and each are responsible for the negligence of the driver).

Wash.—McCanna v. Silke, 134 P. 1063, 75 Wash. 383.

55. Ark.—Adams v. Browning, 115 S.W.2d 868, 195 Ark. 1040 (required to prove that wife was acting as husband's agent).

Cal.—Sanfilippo v. Lesser, 210 P. 44, 59 Cal.App. 86.

Ill.—Sumner v. Griswold, 86 N.E.2d 844, 338 Ill.App. 190.

La.—Durel v. Flach, 1 La.App. 758.

56. La.—Vinson v. Picolo, App., 15 So.2d 778.

Rule applied

Where the plaintiff establishes that the accident occurred through the negligence of defendant's wife in her use of the community automobile, which she was operating with the permission and consent, actual or implied, of the husband, it then devolves upon him to show that the wife was on a mission of her own. Martin v. Brown, 124 So.2d 904, 240 La. 674.

57. Iowa.—Putnam v. Bussing, 266 N.W. 559, 221 Iowa 871.

La.—Gondolfo v. O'Berry, App., 12 So.2d 636.

Tex.—Wilhite v. Horton, Civ.App., 116 S.W.2d 807.

§ 416.5   TRIAL EVIDENCE   Ch. 416

servant was acting within the scope of authority, or in the line of duties in carrying on the owner's business.[58]

58. **U.S.**—State of Md., to Use of Bennus v. U. S., D.C.Pa., 221 F. Supp. 740; Watt v. U. S., D.C.Ark., 123 F.Supp. 906 (Federal Tort Claims Act); Hubsch v. U. S., C.A. Fla., 174 F.2d 7, (2 mems) cause remanded 70 S.Ct. 225, 338 U.S. 440, 94 L.Ed. 244 (army lieutenant driving jeep); Rutherford v. U. S., D.C.Tenn., 73 F.Supp. 867, affirmed C.A., 168 F.2d 70 (federal government's employee); Constitution Pub. Co. v. Dale, C.C.A. Ala., 164 F.2d 210; De Bord v. Proctor & Gamble Distributing Co., D.C.Ga., 58 F.Supp. 157, affirmed C.A., 146 F.2d 54; Mid-Continent Pipe Line Co. v. Whiteley, C.C.A. Okl., 116 F.2d 871.

Ala.—Schoenith, Inc. v. Forrester, 69 So.2d 454, 260 Ala. 271.

Cal.—Moeller v. De Rose, 222 P.2d 107, rehearing dismissed.

Colo.—Gibbons & Reed Co. v. Howard, 269 P.2d 701, 129 Colo. 262.

Del.—Lamanna v. Stevens, 93 A. 962, 5 Boyce 402.

Ga.—Johnson v. Webb-Crawford Co., 80 S.E.2d 63, 89 Ga.App. 524.

Ill.—McPherson v. Universal C.I.T. Credit Corp., 103 N.E.2d 677, 345 Ill.App. 476.

Ky.—Williams v. Coleman's Adm'x, 115 S.W.2d 584, 273 Ky. 122.

La.—Gondolfo v. O'Berry, App., 12 So.2d 636.

Me.—Stevens v. Frost, 32 A.2d 164, 140 Me. 1.

Md.—Wood v. H. W. Gossard Co., 103 A.2d 130, 204 Md. 177.

Mass.—Bruce v. Hanks, 178 N.E. 728, 277 Mass. 268; Wilson v. Grace, 173 N.E. 524, 273 Mass. 146.

Mich.—Holloway v. Nassar, 267 N. W. 619, 276 Mich. 212.

Minn.—Piepho v. M. Sigbert-Awes Co., 188 N.W. 998, 152 Minn. 315.

Mo.—Van Hook v. Strassberger, App., 259 S.W.2d 399.

Mont.—Ashley v. Safeway Stores, 47 P.2d 53, 100 Mont. 312.

Neb.—Watts v. Zadina, 179 Neb. 548, 139 N.W.2d 290.

N.J.—Cinque v. Crown Oil Corp., 48 A.2d 777, 135 N.J.L. 38.

N.M.—Stambaugh v. Hayes, 103 P. 2d 640, 44 N.M. 443.

N.Y.—Johnson v. R. T. K. Petroleum Co., 33 N.Y.S.2d 18, 263 App.Div. 338, reversed on other grounds 44 N.E.2d 6, 289 N.Y. 101, reargument denied 44 N.E.2d 619, 289 N.Y. 646.

N.C.—Aiken v. Sanderford, 73 S.E.2d 911, 236 N.C. 760.

N.D.—Carlson v. Hoff, 230 N.W. 294, 59 N.D. 393.

Ohio.—Senn v. Lackner, 105 N.E.2d 49, 157 Ohio St. 206, motion sustained, App., 107 N.E.2d 558 (salesman).

Okl.—Alexander v. Mayfield, 250 P. 2d 211, 207 Okl. 468 (operated by member of the family of the owner).

Or.—Jasper v. Wells, 144 P.2d 505, 173 Or. 114 (burden of showing permission to take automobile and use in owner's business).

Pa.—Mock v. Furphy, 92 A.2d 699, 172 Pa.Super. 226; Lanteigne v. Smith, 74 A.2d 116, 365 Pa. 132 (agent selling cars on commission); Gozdonovic v. Pleasant Hills Realty Co., 53 A.2d 73, 357 Pa. 23 (employee's automobile); Warman v. Craig, 184 A. 757, 321 Pa. 481 (driver was son of owner).

R.I.—McIver v. Schwartz, 145 A. 101, 50 R.I. 68.

Tenn.—Life & Casualty Ins. Co. v. Bradley, 160 S.W.2d 410, 178 Tenn. 526.

After the plaintiff has introduced evidence sufficient to raise a presumption or establish a prima facie case that the automobile

Tex.—Coca-Cola Bottling Co. v. Krueger, Civ.App., 239 S.W.2d 669; Zwernemann v. Smith, Civ.App., 175 S.W.2d 260 (truck driven by owner's son).

Wash.—Roletto v. Department Stores Garage Co., 191 P.2d 875, 30 Wash. 2d 439.

Wis.—Laughnan v. Griffiths, 73 N.W. 2d 587, 271 Wis. 247 (driven by former employee).

Boy driving automobile to place of storage

Plaintiff had burden of proving that boy was servant of storekeeper and was engaged in furtherance of storekeeper's business at time of accident. Pollock Stores Co. v. Chatwell, 90 S.W.2d 213, 192 Ark. 83.

Admission in answer

Admission by owner in answer that driver frequently drove automobile by and with consent, knowledge, and approval of owner, made out a prima facie case of agency, which would support, but did not require a verdict against owner, under doctrine of respondeat superior, for any damages assessed against driver. Hartley v. Smith, 79 S.E.2d 767, 239 N.C. 170.

But see

Plaintiffs did not have to prove that defendant's driver was acting within scope of his employment at time of the accident, but only that driver was employee of defendant at time so as to make out prima facie case. Cowles v. Erb-Restrick Lumber Co., 1970, 176 N.W.2d 412, 21 Mich. App. 642.

Defendant's control of vehicle owned by another

In action against building owner for injuries to pedestrian slipping on grease spilled on sidewalk abutting premises by building superintendent, who was greasing his truck, plaintiffs, conceding ownership of truck by superintendent, had burden to establish building owner's control of truck and of superintendent's use thereof in owner's business. Bernstein v. East 167th Street Corporation, 293 N.Y.S. 109, 161 Misc. 836.

Garage employee as agent of automobile owner

Where plaintiff alleged that garage employee, who had accompanied car owner to her place of business for purpose of driving car back to garage to be washed, was agent of car owner, burden of proof of such allegation was on plaintiff. Bailey v. Smith, 128 S.E. 423, 132 S.C. 212.

Permitting second employee to drive

Fact that restaurant manager was permitted to use employer's station wagon for his own use as well as in behalf of the company did not in itself establish that another employee was an agent of the employer when the second employee was driving the station wagon with the permission of the manager, who was also in the vehicle; it was necessary to show in addition that the manager was on the business of the company at the time and place of the accident. Oppenheimer v. Smith, Ky.1974, 512 S.W.2d 510.

Students driving school principal's car

To impose upon high school principal liability for injuries caused by students driving automobile to advertise a carnival sponsored by civic organizations to raise funds to purchase high school band uniforms, as his agents or employees, it was necessary to show that he had employed them to act for him on his personal business, and that at time of accident they were acting in his behalf and within scope of their agency or employment. Hathaway v. Siskiyou Union High School Dist., 151 P.2d 861, 66 Cal.App.2d 103.

§ 416.5   TRIAL EVIDENCE   Ch. 416

causing the injury was being operated by the defendant's agent or employee acting within the scope of employment, the burden of going forward with the evidence is upon the defendant, to show that the driver was not at the time acting within the scope of employment.[59] Similarly, the burden of going forward to establish a temporary departure is on the defendant, to show that the driver had abandoned the duties of the employment and had gone about some private purpose.[60] If the proof shows such temporary deviation, the defendant's liability is suspended and the burden shifts back to the plaintiff to prove the reestablishment of liability by showing a resumption of duties by the servant.[61]

59. **Cal.**—Robinson v. George, 105 P.2d 914, 16 Cal.2d 238 (burden shifted to defendant to prove that newspaper carrier was an independent contractor).

Conn.—Skut v. Boardman, 81 A.2d 110, 137 Conn. 675.

Ga.—West Point Pepperell, Inc. v. Knowles, 1974, 208 S.E.2d 17, 132 Ga.App. 253.

Ill.—Botich v. P. Lorillard Co., 1970, 262 N.E.2d 38, 127 Ill.App.2d 232.

Ky.—Livingston v. Fields, 225 S.W. 2d 317, 311 Ky. 714.

La.—Culver v. Toye Bros. Yellow Cab Co., App., 26 So.2d 296.

Miss.—Tullier v. Capitol Const. Co., 190 So.2d 880.

Mo.—Harris v. Mound City Yellow Cab Co., App.1963, 367 S.W.2d 43 (company's name and cab number on body of cab).

R.I.—Conant, for Use and Benefit of Indemnity Ins. Co. of North America v. Giddings, 65 R.I. 79, 13 A.2d 517.

Tex.—Broaddus v. Long, 138 S.W.2d 1057, affirming, Civ.App., 125 S.W. 2d 340 (presumption driver of taxicab within scope); Carle Oil Co. v. Owens, Civ.App., 134 S.W.2d 411.

Used car salesman

Where it was shown that driver was agent of dealer for purpose of demonstrating used cars, and that driver was driving employer's used car, and that dealer's salesmen were accustomed to take cars off lot with no express permission except to obtain gasoline, prima facie case that driver was acting within the scope of his employment was made in action for death of occupant, and burden of going forward with the evidence shifted to the dealer. Galloway Motor Co. v. Huffman's Adm'r, 137 S.W.2d 379, 281 Ky. 841.

60. **Md.**—Erdman v. Henry S. Horkheimer & Co., to Use of World Fire & Marine Ins. Co., 181 A. 221, 169 Md. 204.

Miss.—Bourgeois v. Mississippi School Supply Co., 155 So. 209, 170 Miss. 310.

61. **U.S.**—Patterson v. Kates, C.C.A. Pa., 152 F. 481.

Ill.—Stix, Baer & Fuller Co. v. Woesthaus Motor Co., 1 N.E.2d 796, 284 Ill.App. 301.

La.—Williamson v. De Soto Wholesale Grocery Co., App., 16 So.2d 739.

Miss.—Barmore v. Vicksburg, S. & P. Ry. Co., 38 So. 218, 85 Miss. 426.

N.Y.—Riley v. Standard Oil Co., 132 N.E. 97, 231 N.Y. 301.

Tex.—Placencia v. Western Union Telegraph Co., 172 S.W.2d 86, 141 Tex. 247.

In a few jurisdictions attempts have been made to afford an innocent victim more adequate protection against financial loss following an accident in case a motor vehicle is operated by a person other than the owner, by enacting statutes under which evidence that at the time of the accident the vehicle was registered in the name of the defendant as owner constitutes prima facie evidence of defendant's responsibility for the driver's conduct, and making the absence of such responsibility an affirmative defense to be pleaded and proved by the defendant.[62] Such a statute adopts the rule of evidence prevailing in some other jurisdictions without a statute.[63] The prima facie evidence created by the statute raises more than a mere presumption which would disappear on the introduction of rebutting evidence.[64]

It has been held that the burden is on the defendant to prove that the driver was an independent contractor,[65] or the employee of an independent contractor.[66] However, it has been held that,

62. **Mass.**—Arrigo v. Lindquist, 85 N.E.2d 782, 324 Mass. 278.

R.I.—Kent v. Draper Soap Co., 63 A.2d 571, 75 R.I. 30.

63. **Mass.**—Thomes v. Meyer Store, Inc., 168 N.E. 178, 268 Mass. 587, citing Potts v. Pardee, 116 N.E. 78, 220 N.Y. 431, 8 A.L.R. 785.

64. **Mass.**—Thomes v. Meyer Store, Inc., 168 N.E. 178, 268 Mass. 587.

R.I.—Kent v. Draper Soap Co., 63 A.2d 571, 75 R.I. 30.

"Prima facie evidence" defined

The effect of the statute was not merely to raise presumption requiring owner to go forward with the evidence, which presumption would be overcome upon introduction of rebutting evidence by the owner; "prima facie evidence" being such as in judgment of law is sufficient to establish a fact, and in absence of rebuttal remaining sufficient for that purpose, and not being synonymous with a "presumption." Hill v. Cabral, R.I., 2 A.2d 482, 121 A.L.R. 1072.

65. **U.S.**—Bush Bros. & Co. v. Hickey, C.A.Tenn., 223 F.2d 425.

Ark.—Ozan Lumber Co. v. McNeely, 217 S.W.2d 341, 214 Ark. 657, 8 A.L.R.2d 261.

Cal.—Phillips v. Larrabee, 1939, 90 P.2d 820, 32 Cal.App.2d 720.

La.—Taylor v. Victoria Nav. Co., App., 176 So. 519.

Mo.—Gardner v. Simmons, 1963, 370 S.W.2d 359.

N.C.—Lassiter v. Cline, 22 S.E.2d 558, 222 N.C. 271.

N.D.—La Bree v. Dakota Tractor & Equipment Co., 288 N.W. 476, 69 N.D. 561.

Or.—Mt. Hood Stages v. Dallimore, 1955, 290 P.2d 787, 206 Or. 328.

S.C.—Norris v. Bryant, 60 S.E.2d 844, 217 S.C. 389.

Wash.—Mitchell v. Maytag-Pacific-Intermountain Co., 51 P.2d 393, 184 Wash. 342.

But see

Pa.—Blakey v. Capanna, 1944, 36 A.2d 789, 349 Pa. 144.

66. **La.**—Coon v. Monroe Scrap Material Co., App., 191 So. 607.

Miss.—Mississippi Public Service Co. v. Scott, 174 So. 573, 178 Miss. 859.

§ 416.5   TRIAL EVIDENCE   Ch. 416

where the plaintiff contends that a contract engaging a third person to do certain work for the defendant as an independent contractor rather than an employee is not bona fide, but a mere sham, the burden is on the plaintiff to establish such a contention.[67] Where the defendant sustains this burden and produces evidence negativing responsibility for the driver's acts, the burden then shifts back to the plaintiff.[68]

Owner liability—when consent to use

In those states imposing liability upon the owner of an automobile for the negligence of one who is driving the vehicle with the consent of the owner, the injured person, to recover against the owner, must prove that the owner consented to the operation of the vehicle.[69] This is true where the plaintiff seeks to impose

---

67. **Tex.**—Linden Lumber Co. v. Johnston, Civ.App., 128 S.W.2d 121, error dismissed (contract engaging truck owner to haul material for lumber company).

68. **Conn.**—Skut v. Boardman, 81 A. 2d 110, 137 Conn. 675.

Ill.—Botich v. P. Lorillard Co., 1970, 262 N.E.2d 38, 127 Ill.App.2d 232.

La.—Griffin v. Yellow Cab Co. of Shreveport, App., 61 So.2d 225.

Tex.—Alfano v. International Harvester Co. of America, Civ.App., 121 S.W.2d 466 (personal use by former employee).

Presumption disappears

Conn.—Amento v. Mortensen, 37 A. 2d 231, 130 Conn. 682 (presumption ceases to be operative when trier finds proven facts which fairly put in issue the question, and burden of proving that automobile was operated by defendant's agent then rests upon plaintiff).

Tex.—Boydston v. Jones, Civ.App., 177 S.W.2d 303 (on production of such proof contrary presumption vanishes and plaintiff has burden of producing other evidence of defendant's legal responsibility).

69. **Cal.**—Irvine v. Wilson, 289 P.2d 895, 137 Cal.App.2d 843; Carroll v. Beavers, 273 P.2d 56, 126 Cal.App.2d 828, 59 A.L.R.2d 263.

Fla.—Fletcher Motor Sales v. Cooney, 1946, 27 So.2d 289, 158 Fla. 223.

Iowa—Anderson v. Lehner, 1952, 52 N.W.2d 513, 243 Iowa 851 (inference from ownership is not strong and does not change burden of proof).

La.—Abshire v. Audubon Ins. Co., App., 99 So.2d 395.

N.Y.—Atwater v. Lober, 233 N.Y.S. 309, 133 Misc. 652.

Ohio—Smith v. Smith, Com.Pl., 89 N.E.2d 588.

Wis.—Rude v. Lehman, 57 N.W.2d 393, 263 Wis. 362.

Employee allowing another to drive

Plaintiff, struck by automobile used by employee in pursuance of his employment, when driven by another, to recover from employer, must establish emergency necessitating employee's turning over wheel to such other. Corbin v. George, 162 A. 459, 308 Pa. 201.

Husband and wife as co-owners

In actions against wife for husband's negligence while driving automobile of which wife was allegedly the co-owner, burden of showing that wife gave husband permission to use vehicle was on plaintiffs. Caccamo v. Swanston, 212 P.2d 246, 94 Cal.App.2d 957.

Ch. 416　　　　BURDEN OF PROOF　　　§ 416.5

liability on a parent for the negligent operation of an automobile by a minor child.[70] The burden of proving the consent of an owner to the use by the driver whose negligence causes an injury may be fulfilled by the inference arising from proof of ownership of the offending car.[71]

Rebuttal of inference from possession

Evidence that employee was permitted to take truck home, that he was prohibited from using it for his own pleasure, that he never worked later than 6:30 p. m., and that truck collided with automobile shortly before midnight conclusively rebutted inference of employer's permission of use of truck raised by driver's possession of truck at time of accident, precluding recovery from employer for injuries to automobile occupant. Truman v. United Products Corporation, 14 N.W.2d 120, 217 Minn. 155.

Rule in guest case

Ill.—Dyreson v. Hughes, 76 N.E.2d 809, 333 Ill.App. 198.

N.J.—Cowan v. Kaminow, 26 A.2d 258, 128 N.J.L. 398 (to render owner liable for death of passenger, proof that driver had proper authority from owner to operate automobile is not sufficient, but further proof is required that driver was acting for the owner in extending the invitation to the passenger).

70.　Cal.—Sommers v. Van Der Linden, 75 P.2d 83, 24 Cal.App.2d 375.

Colo.—Kirkpatrick v. McCarty, 152 P.2d 994, 112 Colo. 588.

Tex.—Way v. Guest, Civ.App., 272 S.W. 217.

Contra—family purpose doctrine

Neb.—Jennings v. Campbell, 6 N.W. 2d 376, 142 Neb. 354 (rule does not require a plaintiff to be able to prove that driver of family purpose automobile had authority of owner to drive at the time and place).

Rule applied

Presumptions under statute that person is innocent of crime, and that law has been obeyed, held insufficient to sustain burden of proof to establish that automobile injuring him was operated by owner's son with owner's express or implied permission. Bradford v. Sargent, 27 P.2d 93, 135 Cal.App. 324.

Where mother and stepfather of driver owned truck, and driver was using truck for his own pleasure at time of collision, owners were prima facie liable for negligence of driver under family purpose doctrine, burden was upon them to overcome the presumption of agency arising from such ownership and use, and fact that driver was of legal age was immaterial. Burkhart v. Corn, 284 P. 2d 226, 59 N.M. 343.

71.　Cal.—Fountain v. Bank of America Nat. Trust & Sav. Ass'n, 240 P.2d 414, 109 Cal.App.2d 90.

Minn.—Ballman v. Brinker, 1 N.W.2d 365, 211 Minn. 322.

Ohio.—Smith v. Smith, Ohio Com. Pl., 89 N.E.2d 588 (under Michigan statute).

But see

Inference that one who admits ownership had permitted the other to drive is not strong and does not change burden of proof, under Iowa law. Webb v. Moreno, C.A.Iowa, 363 F.2d 97.

Effect of statute

Dist.Col.—Rosenberg v. Murray, 116 F.2d 552, 73 App.D.C. 67 (effect of statute making proof of ownership prima facie evidence of owner's consent to operation by another is simply to shift burden of proof and impose on owner the af-

51

§ 416.5

According to some authorities, the inference or presumption of fact arising from ownership of an automobile places on the owner the burden of showing that the automobile at the time of the accident was not used with the owner's knowledge or consent, express or implied.[72]

§ 416.6 Burden of Proof—Proximate Cause

Library References:
C.J.S. Motor Vehicles § 510.
West's Key No. Digests, Automobiles ⚖=242(7).

The burden being upon plaintiff to establish a cause of action, and proximate cause being one of the elements of such cause, the plaintiff has the burden of showing that such negligence was a proximate cause of the injury.[73] Plaintiff must show

firmative duty of proving that automobile was not operated with his express or implied consent. D. C.Code 1951, § 40–403); Conrad v. Porter, D.C.Mun.App., 79 A.2d 777, affirmed 196 F.2d 240, 90 U.S. App.D.C. 423.

72. **U.S.**—Falstaff Brewing Corporation v. Thompson, C.C.A.Neb., 101 F.2d 301, certiorari denied 59 S.Ct. 834, 307 U.S. 631, 83 L.Ed. 1514.

Ala.—Brown v. Southeastern Greyhound Lines, 51 So.2d 524, 255 Ala. 308.

D.C.—Milstead v. District of Columbia, D.C.Mun.App., 91 A.2d 93.

Ill.—Watt v. Yellow Cab. Co., 106 N. E.2d 760, 347 Ill.App. 307.

Iowa.—McCann v. Downey, 290 N. W. 690, 227 Iowa 1277.

Mass.—Fitiles v. Umlah, 77 N.E.2d 212, 322 Mass. 325.

Mich.—Roberts v. Posey, 1972, 194 N.W.2d 310, 386 Mich. 656.

R.I.—Hill v. Cabral, 2 A.2d 482, 62 R.I. 11, 121 A.L.R. 1072 (driver was owner's son).

Family purpose cases

Conn.—Perfetto v. Wesson, 86 A.2d 565, 138 Conn. 506 (where automobile was registered in wife's name and husband was operating it at time of accident, presumption that automobile was being operated as family automobile within scope of general authority from owner was raised, and imposed upon the husband and wife burden of rebutting the presumption).

Or.—Kraxberger v. Rogers, 1962, 373 P.2d 647, 231 Or. 440 (owner has burden to go forward).

Strong proof required

In case of a subpermittee minor driver, owner, in order to escape liability under Safety Responsibility Act, must make a strong showing that the subpermittee was driving without permittee's consent under conditions which approach the status of conversion or a theft. Western Nat. Mut. Ins. Co. v. Auto-Owners Ins. Co., 1974, 220 N.W.2d 362, 300 Minn. 401.

73. **Ala.**—Johnson v. Battles, 52 So. 2d 702, 255 Ala. 624.

Ariz.—Western Truck Lines v. Berry, 87 P.2d 484, 53 Ariz. 216.

Cal.—Nelson v. Black, 275 P.2d 473, 43 Cal.2d 612.

Colo.—Denver-Los Angeles Trucking Co. v. Ward, 164 P.2d 730, 114 Colo. 348 (absence of chains).

Conn.—Farquhar v. Larson, 186 A. 498, 121 Conn. 709.

that the act of the defendant complained of was the reasonable and probable cause of the accident and injury, that the accident

Del.—McGuire v. McCollum, 116 A. 2d 897, 10 Terry 359 (not affected or lessened by rule that deceased is presumed to have exercised care).

Fla.—Vasquez v. Simms, 75 So.2d 783.

Ga.—Garrett v. Royal Bros. Co., 1969, 170 S.E.2d 294, 225 Ga. 533, on remand 171 S.E.2d 870, 120 Ga.App. 686 (improperly determined that motorist's action in striking gasoline pump with bumper was negligence as a matter of law and that burden of proving any damage from ensuing fire was not proximately caused by such alleged negligence was upon motorist).

Idaho.—Matheson v. Idaho Hardware & Plumbing Co., 1954, 270 P.2d 841, 75 Idaho 171.

Ill.—Strubinger v. Coultas, 1954, 117 N.E.2d 799, 1 Ill.App.2d 424; Wolfe v. Railway Exp. Agency, 1945, 62 N.E.2d 564, 326 Ill.App. 515 (pedestrian on sidewalk struck by ring of front wheel assembly of passing truck).

Ind.—Pontiac-Chicago Motor Exp. Co. v. George Cassons & Son, 34 N.E.2d 171, 109 Ind.App. 248.

Iowa.—Clubb v. Osborn, 149 N.W.2d 318, 260 Iowa 223 (owner of stopped vehicle had burden of proving damage to vehicle was proximately caused by overtaking driver's negligence).

Kan.—Waugh v. Kansas City Public Service Co., 143 P.2d 788, 157 Kan. 690 (counterclaim by street railroad); Crowe v. Moore, 62 P.2d 846, 144 Kan. 794.

Ky.—Monroe v. Townsend, 213 S.W. 2d 803, 308 Ky. 123; Coughlin v. Mark, 191 S.W. 503, 173 Ky. 728 (approaching car frightening animal).

La.—Tallo v. Johnson, App.1971, 255 So.2d 446, writ refused 257 So.2d 157, 260 La. 704 (must show excess speed was cause in fact).

Me.—Barlow v. Lowery, 59 A.2d 702, 143 Me. 214.

Md.—Brehm v. Lorenz, 112 A.2d 475, 206 Md. 500.

Mass.—Savin v. Block, 9 N.E.2d 536, 297 Mass. 487.

Mich.—Trune v. Grahl, 60 N.W.2d 129, 337 Mich. 659 (passenger's action).

Minn.—Indianhead Truck Line, Inc. v. Anderson, 139 N.W.2d 271, 272 Minn. 497.

Miss.—New Orleans & N. E. R. Co. v. Burge, 2 So.2d 825, 191 Miss. 303; Dr. Pepper Bottling Co. v. Gordy, 164 So. 236, 174 Miss. 392 (defect in brakes).

Mo.—Graham v. Conner, 412 S.W.2d 193 (pedestrian had burden of showing a causal connection); Svehla v. Taxi Owners Ass'n, App., 157 S.W.2d 225 (unlawful turn by taxicab striking pedestrian); Schroeder v. Rawlings, 155 S.W. 2d 189, 348 Mo. 824 (three car collision when leading car made sudden stop); Saunders v. Prue, 151 S.W.2d 478, 235 Mo.App. 1245 (giving permission to drive to inexperienced driver); Madden v. Red Line Service, Inc., App., 76 S.W.2d 435 (bus passenger alighting from bus on rainy night at unsafe place).

Mont.—Cowden v. Crippen, 53 P.2d 98, 101 Mont. 187.

Neb.—Johnson v. Riecken, 1970, 173 N.W.2d 511, 185 Neb. 78 (burden on guest to show proximate cause was gross negligence); Beavers v. Christensen, 125 N.W.2d 551, 176 Neb. 162.

N.H.—Collette v. Boston & M. R. R., 140 A. 176, 83 N.H. 210.

N.J.—Wisniewski v. Weinstock, 50 A.2d 894, 135 N.J.L. 202, affirming 31 A.2d 401, 130 N.J.L. 58.

§ 416.6   TRIAL EVIDENCE   Ch. 416

and injury were such as might have been anticipated by a reasonable and prudent man from the conduct claimed to be negli-

N.M.—Pack v. Read, 419 P.2d 453, 77 N.M. 76.

N.Y.—Lewis v. Olympia Provisions & Baking Co., 122 N.Y.S.2d 193, 282 App.Div. 227; Franklin v. Marsh, 218 N.Y.S. 155, 218 App.Div. 220 (showing concurrent negligence of defendant).

N.C.—Morris v. Jenrette Transport Co., 70 S.E.2d 845, 235 N.C. 568; Love v. City of Asheville, 187 S.E. 562, 210 N.C. 476 (ice on driveway of bridge).

N.D.—Stockfeld v. Sayre, 283 N.W. 788, 69 N.D. 42.

Ohio.—Osso v. Hamilton City Lines, 89 N.E.2d 697, 86 Ohio App. 53 (motorist allegedly swerved to avoid bus crossing intersection and struck tree).

Okl.—McLeland v. Miller, 386 P.2d 181.

Or.—Copenhaver v. Tripp, 213 P.2d 450, 187 Or. 662 (attempting to pass bicyclist on bridge).

Pa.—Antonson v. Johnson, 218 A.2d 123, 420 Pa. 558; Brusis v. Henkels, 102 A.2d 146, 376 Pa. 226 (failure to warn of soft shoulder due to prior excavation).

R.I.—Randall v. Holmes, 31 A.2d 17, 69 R.I. 41.

S.C.—Epps v. South Carolina State Highway Department, 39 S.E.2d 198, 209 S.C. 125 (absence of signals or warnings as to ravine).

S.D.—Madsen v. Watertown Bottling Co., 59 N.W.2d 735, 75 S.D. 122.

Tex.—Rozner v. Harrell Drilling Co., Civ.App., 261 S.W.2d 190, ref. n. r. e.

Utah.—Alvarado v. Tucker, 268 P.2d 986, 2 Utah 2d 16.

Vt.—Leonard v. Henderson, 99 A.2d 698, 118 Vt. 29.

Va.—Tolbert v. Gillespie, 79 S.E.2d 670, 195 Va. 647.

Wash.—Johanson v. King County, 109 P.2d 307, 7 Wash.2d 111 (to establish that location of yellow line in fact deceived and misled motorist to his injury).

W.Va.—Miller v. Bolyard, 97 S.E.2d 58, 142 W.Va. 580.

Wis.—Weber v. Mayer, 63 N.W.2d 318, 266 Wis. 241; Jensen v. Jensen, 279 N.W. 628, 228 Wis. 77 (defective tires).

Wyo.—O'Mally v. Eagan, 2 P.2d 1063, 43 Wyo. 233, 77 A.L.R. 582, rehearing denied O'Malley v. Eagan, 5 P.2d 276, 43 Wyo. 350.

Death five months after accident

Plaintiff proving probable cause between automobilist's negligence and boy's death five months after accident need not prove precise organic changes. Marlow v. Dike, 168 N.E. 154, 269 Mass. 38.

Intoxication of driver

Cal.—Noble v. Key System, 51 P.2d 887, 10 Cal.App.2d 132.

Presumption foregone

Where plaintiff, a passenger in panel truck which collided with defendant's double-parked automobile, chose not to rely on rebuttable presumption that auto had been double-parked by defendant or his agent acting for him, and instead adduced evidence to effect that defendant parked his automobile next to curb, turned ignition off, kept keys on his person, and gave no one permission to move automobile, it was incumbent on plaintiff to offer evidence eliminating possible independent proximate cause of accident, and absent such evidence, case against defendant was insufficient. Roberts v. Cave, 1970, 263 A.2d 863, 257 Md. 582.

gent,[74] or that there was some causal connection between defendant's negligence and the injury, which defendant could have foreseen by the exercise of ordinary care for the safety of travelers on the highway.[75]

It is not necessary for the plaintiff to prove that the negligence of the defendant was the sole proximate cause of the injury, but the burden is satisfied by establishing that it was a contributing proximate cause of accident.[76]

Difficulty in maintaining this burden may be experienced in cases where three or more automobiles are involved in the same collision, making it necessary to prove which car actually did the damage complained of,[77] or the extent of the damage done by each defendant, and the burden of proving the causal connection is on the plaintiff.[78] It has been held, however, that, if two motorists were negligent in colliding with the plaintiff, the burden is on each to prove which damage was not caused by that defendant.[79]

Speed statute expressly preserves burden

The presence of statute providing that speed limitations shall not be construed to relieve plaintiff of burden of proving negligence as proximate cause of accident renders inapplicable the rule subjecting one who violates statutory speed regulation to burden of excusing the violation. Davis v. Gatlin, Tex.Civ.App. 1970, 462 S.W.2d 54, error refused n. r. e.

74. U.S.—Proel v. Nugent, C.C.A. N.H., 97 F.2d 353.

75. U.S.—Standard Oil Co. v. Crowl, C.A.Mo., 198 F.2d 580.

Ala.—Britt v. Daniel, 159 So. 684, 230 Ala. 79.

N.C.—Conley v. Pearce-Young-Angel Co., 29 S.E.2d 740, 224 N.C. 211.

Okl.—Schaff v. Edwards, 237 P. 620, 111 Okl. 13.

S.C.—Worrell v. South Carolina Power Co., 195 S.E. 638, 186 S.C. 306.

Tex.—Texas & N. O. R. Co. v. Young, Civ.App., 148 S.W.2d 229.

76. Cal.—Luis v. Cavin, 198 P.2d 563, 88 Cal.App.2d 107.

Mich.—Valenti v. Mayer, 4 N.W.2d 5, 301 Mich. 551.

Neb.—Miller v. Abel Const. Co., 300 N.W. 405, 140 Neb. 482.

77. La.—Jarreau v. Toye Bros. Yellow Cab Co., App., 24 So.2d 700; Romano v. Davidson, 123 So. 411, 11 La.App. 286.

Mich.—Kistler v. Wagoner, 23 N.W. 387, 315 Mich. 162 (cause of death).

78. Mo.—Daniels v. Smith, App. 1971, 471 S.W.2d 508 (that passenger was unable, short of contribution from second driver's administrator, to collect the total amount of damages would not justify departure from rule placing upon passenger the burden of proving that defendant's negligence was a proximate cause).

79. U.S.—Haddigan v. Harkins, C.A.Pa.1970, 441 F.2d 844 (to fasten liability for wrongful death of stalled automobile's occupant, who was apparently struck by two automobiles almost simultaneously,

§ 416.6   TRIAL EVIDENCE   Ch. 416

While it may be true that the violation of a statute or ordinance is prima facie negligence and the violation of a rule of the road is sometimes negligence per se, this does not change the rule that plaintiff must prove that such negligence proximately caused the injury.[80]

However, it has been held that the burden is on the defendant to demonstrate that such violation did not proximately cause the accident.[81] And it has been held that evidence that the de-

on driver of one of the automobiles which struck her, it was not necessary to prove which of the two automobiles that struck her caused the massive head injuries).

Cal.—Copley v. Putter, 207 P.2d 876, 93 Cal.App.2d 453; Cummings v. Kendall, 107 P.2d 282, 41 Cal.App. 2d 549.

La.—Jones v. Southern General Ins. Co., App., 157 So.2d 335 (each defendant is deemed guilty of negligence per se and burden of proof is upon each defendant to exculpate himself).

80. **Ala.**—Rochelle v. Lide, 180 So. 257, 235 Ala. 596.

Cal.—Carlton v. Pacific Coast Gasoline Co., 242 P.2d 391, 110 Cal. App.2d 177 (parking violation).

Colo.—Hertz Driv-Ur-Self System of Colorado v. Hendrickson, 121 P.2d 483, 109 Colo. 1.

Fla.—Jesus v. Seaboard Coast Line R. Co., 1973, 281 So.2d 198.

Iowa.—Pifer v. Chicago, M., St. P. & P. R. Co., 247 N.W. 625, 215 Iowa 1258 (failure of train to signal).

La.—Ford, Bacon & Davis v. Shaw, 8 La.App. 751 (driving on wrong side of road).

Me.—Elliott v. Montgomery, 197 A. 322, 135 Me. 372 (parking violation).

Miss.—Whatley v. Boolas, 177 So. 1, 180 Miss. 372 (speeding).

N.C.—Morris v. Jenrette Transport Co., 70 S.E.2d 845, 235 N.C. 568 (stopping on highway).

Okl.—Pittsburg County Ry. Co. v. Hasty, 233 P. 218, 106 Okl. 65.

S.C.—Chapman v. Associated Transport, 63 S.E.2d 465, 218 S.C. 554.

Tex.—Ruggles v. John Deere Plow Co., Civ.App., 146 S.W.2d 456 (parking violation); Louisiana, A. & T. Ry. Co. v. De Vance, Tex. Civ.App., 114 S.W.2d 922 (failure of train to signal).

Va.—Hamilton v. Glemming, 46 S.E. 2d 438, 187 Va. 309 (driving on wrong side of road); Barry v. Tyler, 199 S.E. 496, 171 Va. 381 (collision with truck stopped on highway, where it appeared that only part of rear lights required by statute were lighted); Virginian Ry. Co. v. Haley, 157 S.E. 776, 156 Va. 350 (failure of train to signal).

81. **La.**—Kierum v. Stonewall Ins. Co., App.1971, 247 So.2d 166 (or that there were justifiable circumstances); Meskill v. Allstate Ins. Co., App.1971, 247 So.2d 163; Savoie v. Dupuy, 1951, 50 So.2d 817, 218 La. 717 (sideswipe).

Okl.—Chicago, R. I. & P. Ry. Co. v. Richerson, 1939, 94 P.2d 934, 185 Okl. 560.

Wash.—Zurfluh v. Lewis County, 1939, 91 P.2d 1002, 199 Wash. 378.

Rear-end collision
Following motorist had burden of showing that collision was not caused by his negligence. Mather v. Holley, 1971, 483 P.2d 992, —— Colo.App. ——.

fendant motorist was under the influence of intoxicating liquors at the time of the accident raises a presumption of negligence and shifts to the defendant the burden of going forward with evidence to show that the intoxication was not a proximate cause of the collision.[82]

Nevertheless, if the testimony tends to show that both vehicles coming into collision were operated in violation of a city ordinance, the burden is not shifted to the defendant to prove that the defendant's negligence was not the proximate cause of the injury.[83]

There is a split of authority as to whether the burden of proof rests upon the defendant to establish a defense that the injury was caused solely by the negligence of some third party, or whether the burden of proof is upon the plaintiff to prove that the cause of the injury was not due solely to the negligence of another person.[84]

§ 416.7 Burden of Proof—Contributory Negligence in General

Library References:
C.J.S. Motor Vehicles §§ 512, 568.
West's Key No. Digests, Automobiles ⚖242(8).

In those jurisdictions where contributory negligence of the injured party is an affirmative defense, the burden of proving it rests upon the defendant.[85] It has been noted that it is necessary

---

82. **Cal.**—Christensen v. Harmonson, 247 P.2d 956, 113 Cal.App.2d 175.

83. **Okl.**—Pittsburg County Ry. Co. v. Hasty, 223 P. 218, 106 Okl. 65.

84. **Burden on defendant**
U.S.—Kemp v. Creston Transfer Co., D.C.Iowa, 70 F.Supp. 521.
Cal.—Schropshire v. Pickwick Stages, Northern Division, 258 P. 1107, 85 Cal.App. 216.
Iowa.—Sayre v. Andrews, 146 N.W.2d 336; Frideres v. Lowden, 17 N.W.2d 396, 235 Iowa 640 (negligence of plaintiff's host).
N.C.—Watt v. Crews, 134 S.E.2d 199, 261 N.C. 143.
Okl.—Cole v. Anderson, 304 P.2d 295.
Or.—Ross v. Willamette Valley Transfer Co., 248 P. 1088, 119 Or. 395.

Burden on plaintiff
La.—Mayon v. New Amsterdam Cas. Co., 191 So.2d 688 (burden rests upon the claimant under driver of overtaking vehicle to establish that the driver of that vehicle was free from fault).
Ohio.—Foust v. Deremberger, 173 N.E. 740, 37 Ohio App. 3.

85. **Ala.**—Allen v. Zickos, 68 So.2d 841, 37 Ala.App. 361.
Ariz.—Martinez v. Anderson, 69 P.2d 237, 50 Ariz. 95.
Cal.—McGuire v. San Diego Transit System, 299 P.2d 905, 143 Cal.App.2d 509.
Conn.—Clement v. Del Vecchio, 99 A.2d 123, 140 Conn. 274.

§ **416.7**   TRIAL EVIDENCE   Ch. 416

Del.—Baltimore & O. R. Co. v. Hawke, 143 A. 27, 4 W.W.Harr. 25.

Dist.Col.—Custom Taxicabs v. Hatch, D.C.Mun.App., 110 A.2d 690.

Fla.—Vasquez v. Simms, 75 So.2d 783.

Ga.—Kaminsky v. Blackshear, 133 S.E.2d 441, 108 Ga.App. 492.

Haw.—Anduha v. Maui County, Territory of Hawaii, 30 Haw. 44.

Idaho.—Allan v. Oregon Short Line R. Co., 90 P.2d 707, 60 Idaho 267.

Ind.—Horton v. Sater, 221 N.E.2d 452, 140 Ind.App. 1.

Iowa.—Schultz v. Gosselink, 1967, 148 N.W.2d 434, 260 Iowa 115.

Kan.—Kline v. Ash, 366 P.2d 276, 188 Kan. 745.

Ky.—Cox's Adm'r v. Cincinnati, N. O. & T. P. Ry. Co., 37 S.W.2d 859, 238 Ky. 312.

Md.—Love v. State for Use of Nelson, 142 A.2d 590, 217 Md. 290.

Mass.—Goldstein v. Gontarz, 1974, 309 N.E.2d 196, 364 Mass. 800.

Mich.—Engle v. Rawlison, 1973, 208 N.W.2d 223, 46 Mich.App. 422.

Minn.—Bielinski v. Colwell, 65 N.W. 2d 113, 242 Minn. 338.

Mo.—Hampton v. Raines, App., 334 S.W.2d 372.

Neb.—Spaulding v. Howard, 27 N.W. 2d 832, 148 Neb. 496.

Nev.—Los Angeles & S. L. R. Co. v. Umbaugh, 123 P.2d 224, 61 Nev. 214.

N.J.—Varlaro v. Schultz, 197 A.2d 16, 82 N.J.Super. 142.

N.M.—Curtis v. Schwartzman Packing Co., 299 P.2d 776, 61 N.M. 305.

N.C.—Raper v. Byrum, 144 S.E.2d 38, 265 N.C. 269 (in action for wrongful death).

N.D.—Fagerlund v. Jensen, 24 N.W. 2d 816, 74 N.D. 766 (manner of making left turn).

Ohio.—Green v. Castronova, 223 N. E.2d 641, 9 Ohio App.2d 156.

Okl.—Midland Valley R. Co. v. Pettie, 162 P.2d 543, 196 Okl. 52.

Or.—Protrka v. Alger, 307 P.2d 289, 209 Or. 479.

S.C.—Bolt v. Gibson, 83 S.E.2d 191, 225 S.C. 538.

S.D.—Staib v. Tarbell, 273 N.W. 652, 65 S.D. 304.

Tenn.—Central Produce Co. v. General Cab Co. of Nashville, 129 S. W.2d 1117, 23 Tenn.App. 209.

Tex.—Thornton v. Campise, Civ.App. 1970, 459 S.W.2d 455, error refused n. r. e. (in not seeing defendant's turn signal).

Utah.—Mecham v. Allen, 262 P.2d 285, 1 Utah 2d 79 (where presumption that decedent had used due care for own safety was eliminated by defendant's prima facie case that decedent had been guilty of contributory negligence, defendant still had burden of going forward with the evidence and of persuading jury upon issue of such contributory negligence).

Va.—Speer v. Kellam, 134 S.E.2d 300, 204 Va. 893 (pedestrian walking on right side of highway with back to traffic).

Wash.—Squires v. McLaughlin, 265 P.2d 265, 44 Wash.2d 43.

W.Va.—Lee v. Standard Oil Co., 144 S.E. 292, 105 W.Va. 579.

Wis.—Fjelstad v. Walsh, 1943, 12 N. W.2d 51, 244 Wis. 295.

Failure to use seat-belt

Burden was on defendant to show that failure of deceased to use seat belt was a factor which contributed to his fatal injury, and, in other words, defendant motorist had burden to show by substantial evidence that deceased would not have suffered terminal injuries if he had fastened his seat belt. Glover v. Daniels, D.C.Miss.1970, 310 F.Supp. 750.

to establish that the plaintiff's negligence was a proximate cause of the injury or damage;[86] but it usually is said that the negligence of the injured party need not be shown to be the sole proximate cause.[87]

Louisiana rule

U.S.—St. Paul Fire & Marine Ins. Co. v. Heath, C.A.La., 302 F.2d 326 (when left turn is made, and collision occurs, burden rests on motorist making left turn to explain how collision occurred and to show that he was free from negligence).

La.—Bernard v. Hungerford, App., 157 So.2d 246 (owner of cow struck on stock law highway had burden of proving that he was free from negligence); Desormeaux v. Continental Ins. Co., App., 153 So.2d 128 (driver desiring to make left turn must ascertain that such maneuver can be made safely and without danger or undue delay to overtaking or oncoming traffic, he must refrain from making left turn unless way is clear, and if collision occurs while he is attempting such maneuver, burden rests heavily on him to show that he was free from negligence).

Not affected by fact suit defended by state indemnification corporation

Defense that passenger was not an innocent victim within Insurance Law asserted by Motor Vehicle Accident Indemnification Corporation in wrongful death action against driver by administrator of estate of passenger who was killed was treated as affirmative defense alleging that passenger was contributorily negligent and burden of proof on that issue was on driver. Gilliam v. Lee, 1969, 303 N.Y.S.2d 966, 32 A.D.2d 1058.

Plaintiff's failure to give warning of danger

Burden was on defendant to prove that decedent or his wife was casually negligent in failing to use an electric flashlight to warn defendant's truck driver that decedent's automobile blocked the highway. Adams v. Severance, 41 A.2d 233, 93 N.H. 289.

Special rule in suit by servant

In suit against master for servant's death, plaintiff has burden of establishing due care of deceased, and all presumptions are in master's favor, where master is not railroad. Gartrell v. Russell, 180 S.E. 860, 51 Ga. App. 513.

Standing in roadway

N.Y.—Rossman v. La Grega, 1971, 321 N.Y.S.2d 588, 28 N.Y.2d 300, 270 N.E.2d 313 (driver who directed passenger to stand next to left front door of disabled automobile to waive traffic away from automobile stopped at shoulder of expressway, had burden of affirmatively showing that passenger who was killed by oncoming automobile, was guilty of contributory negligence in assuming position indicated by driver).

86. **Iowa.**—Schultz v. Gosselink, 1967, 148 N.W.2d 434, 260 Iowa 115; Schmidtt v. Jenkins Truck Lines, Inc., 1969, 170 N.W.2d 632, 46 A.L.R.3d 636.

87. 65 C.J.S., Negligence, § 129, p. 746.

Contra

Defendant has burden of proving that accident resulted solely from plaintiff's negligence, but he should receive benefit of plaintiff's evidence tending to prove such fact. Spaulding v. Howard, 27 N.W.2d 832, 148 Neb. 496.

Contra in railroad crossing case

Va.—Gregory v. Seaboard Air Line Ry. Co., 128 S.E. 272, 142 Va. 750.

§ **416.7** TRIAL EVIDENCE Ch. 416

In some jurisdictions, the majority rule, placing the burden on the defendant, has been adopted by statute.[88] In a few jurisdictions, by virtue of statute, the burden in death cases is on the defendant to prove contributory negligence, though in personal injury actions the burden is on the plaintiff to prove freedom from such negligence.[89]

In some jurisdictions the rule is that the issue of contributory negligence is not presented by the pleadings when the defendant, in addition to a general denial, pleads that plaintiff's own negligence was the sole cause of the injury.[90] However it has been held that the fact that the defendant affirmatively pleads contributory negligence, causes the burden to shift from the plaintiff to the defendant.[91] Also it has been held that, if the complaint contains allegations as to lack of contributory negligence, and the defendant denies it, the plaintiff is bound to establish the fact as alleged.[92]

The fact that the plaintiff may admit the negligence charged does not relieve the defendant from the necessity of proving that such negligence was a contributing cause of the injury.[93] Ordinarily if the contributory negligence rests upon infractions of statutes or ordinances, the defendant must prove that such infractions were a proximate cause of the injury.[94] However, it

88. **Cited by the court** in Albrecht v. Rausch, Iowa 1972, 193 N.W.2d 492, 496.

89. **N.Y.**—EPTL § 5-4.2. See generally 65 C.J.S., Negligence, pp. 972–975, § 210.

90. **Ohio.**—Hanna v. Stoll, 147 N.E. 339, 112 Ohio St. 344; Bradley v. Cleveland Ry. Co., 146 N.E. 805, 112 Ohio St. 35.

91. **U.S.**—Levine v. Shell Eastern Petroleum Products, C.C.A.N.Y., 73 F.2d 292, certiorari denied 55 S.Ct. 545, 294 U.S. 719, 79 L.Ed. 1251.

Iowa.—Taylor v. Wistey, 254 N.W. 50, 218 Iowa 785.

And see
Conn.—Squires v. Wolcott, 52 A.2d 305, 133 Conn. 449.

92. **N.Y.**—Willie v. Luczka, 184 N.Y.S. 751, 193 App.Div. 826.

Tex.—Little Rock Furniture Mfg. Co. v. Dunn, Civ.App., 218 S.W.2d 527, affirmed 222 S.W.2d 985, 148 Tex. 197; Talley Transfer Co. v. Cones, Civ.App., 216 S.W.2d 604, ref. n. r. e. (pedestrian crossing street).

93. **Or.**—Landis v. Wick, 57 P.2d 759, 154 Or. 199, rehearing denied 59 P.2d 403, 154 Or. 199.

94. **Cal.**—Chapman v. Mason, 189 P.2d 510, 83 Cal.App.2d 685.

Idaho.—Kelly v. Troy Laundry Co., 267 P. 222, 46 Idaho 214.

La.—Greenwood v. Romby, App., 51 So.2d 859 (entering intersection on red light).

N.H.—Judd v. Perkins, 138 A. 312, 83 N.H. 39.

N.J.—Kelly v. Johnson, 137 A. 849, 5 N.J.Misc. 665.

N.M.—Williams v. Neff, 326 P.2d 1073, 64 N.M. 182.

Tex.—Thurman v. Chandler, Civ. App., 52 S.W.2d 315.

has been held that, if proof of a violation by the plaintiff of such a statute is made, it prima facie establishes contributory negligence; and the burden then rests upon the plaintiff to explain or excuse that conduct.[95]

In jurisdictions where the negligence of a parent is imputable to the child, so as to bar a recovery by the child for an injury, the burden rests upon a defendant sought to be held for such an injury to show, where the child was too young to exercise care, that the parent was guilty of negligence precluding a recovery.[96]

Va.—Kinsey v. Brugh, 161 S.E. 41, 157 Va. 407.

Wash.—Perren v. Press, 81 P.2d 867, 196 Wash. 14.

95. **U.S.**—H. W. Bass Drilling Co. v. Ray, C.C.A.N.M., 101 F.2d 316.

Vt.—Steele v. Fuller, 158 A. 666, 104 Vt. 303.

Rule applied

In driver's action to recover for injuries when defendant's automobile collided with rear of driver's automobile after driver had stopped on right lane of two lane highway, driver had burden of meeting or overcoming prima facie case established against her by her violation of safety statute, by other evidence which fairly and reasonably tended to show that her negligence was not as presumed. Naylor v. Dragoon, 80 A.2d 600, 116 Vt. 552, followed in 80 A.2d 603, 116 Vt. 556.

Violation of highway "stock law"

In action filed because of death of cattleman who was struck when motorist attempted to avoid striking cattle on highway and the car jackknifed and struck decedent who was on highway right-of-way, inasmuch as the highway was a "stock" law highway, included within statute prohibiting person from permitting livestock to go at large on such highways, burden was upon plaintiffs to show that deceased had not been negligent in allowing cattle to be on highway and lower court erred in shifting burden of proof to motorist and his insurer. Richard v. Guillot, La.App.1973, 284 So.2d 127.

Wrong side of road

The presence of armored army vehicle on wrong side of road, without more being shown, gave rise to inference of negligence and cast on the United States sued for death of occupant of approaching automobile with which army vehicle collided the burden of explaining such presence. Rosenal v. U. S., D.C.Pa., 94 F.Supp. 1004, affirmed 189 F.2d 969.

There was a presumption of negligence on part of plaintiff southbound motorist when, in attempting to make left turn at intersection, a collision occurred in lane of travel of defendant northbound motorist, and plaintiff was under a burden to establish her freedom from fault which would otherwise bar her recovery. Lewis v. Allstate Ins. Co., La.App.1971, 250 So.2d 155.

96. **Mass.**—Gallagher v. Johnson, 130 N.E. 174, 237 Mass. 455, 15 A.L.R. 411 (where the child was riding in an automobile owned and driven by his father, and the child, suing by his father and next friend, and the father brought separate actions, and the father as well as the child could be deemed a "person injured" within St.1914, c. 553, providing that contributory negligence on the part of the person injured shall be an affirmative defense).

§ 416.7   TRIAL EVIDENCE   Ch. 416

And where, in a wrongful death case, it is contended that the parents were contributorily negligent, the burden of proof on the issue is on the defendant.[97]

Where the defendant alleges several acts of contributory negligence, it is not necessary to prove all of them in order to maintain the defense.[98]

Even in those states where the burden of proving the issue of plaintiff's contributory negligence rests on the defendant, it may be established by the plaintiff's own evidence, and the defendant may take advantage of such showing on motion for nonsuit.[99] So, if the plaintiff's own case presents evidence which, unexplained, makes out prima facie contributory negligence, the plaintiff cannot recover in the absence of further evidence exculpating such plaintiff.[1] The same result is reached when the

---

Child left unattended on busy street

The Massachusetts statute, which declares that contributory negligence on the part of the injured person shall be an affirmative defense, does not relieve the plaintiff, in an action by the administrator to recover for the death of a child, from the burden of showing that the mother of the child exercised due care, where it appeared that the mother left the child playing on the sidewalk on a busy street, on the opposite side from her home. Stachowicz v. Matera, 153 N.E. 547, 257 Mass. 283.

97. N.M.—Wilson v. Wylie, 1973, 518 P.2d 1213, 86 N.M. 9, certiorari denied 518 P.2d 1209, two cases, 86 N.M. 5 (allegation that minor's parents were contributorily negligent in failing to instruct minor about crossing intersection, in failing to restrict him from riding bicycle in the intersection and in failing to know of whereabouts on afternoon of the accident).

98. Tex.—Ripley v. Dozier Construction Co., Civ.App., 45 S.W.2d 661.

99. Cal.—Thomas v. Irvin, 216 P.2d 476, 96 Cal.App.2d 816; Wahrenbrock v. Los Angeles Transit Lines, 190 P.2d 272, 84 Cal.App.2d 236.

Fla.—Brandt v. Dodd, 8 So.2d 471, 150 Fla. 635.

Mo.—Everhardt v. Garner, App., 100 S.W.2d 71.

Neb.—Spaulding v. Howard, 27 N.W. 2d 832, 148 Neb. 496.

N.C.—Bundy v. Powell, 51 S.E.2d 307, 229 N.C. 707; Godarin v. Atlantic Coast Line R. Co., 17 S.E.2d 137, 220 N.C. 281.

Tex.—Hambrick v. Texas & P. Ry. Co., Civ.App., 285 S.W. 883.

Wyo.—Johnston v. Vukelic, 213 P.2d 925, 67 Wyo. 1.

1. Colo.—Aaron v. Wesebaum, 162 P.2d 232, 114 Colo. 61 (explaining negligence in taking right of way in violation of ordinance).

Fla.—Greiper v. Coburn, 190 So. 902, 139 Fla. 293.

Mont.—Rau v. Northern Pac. Ry. Co., 289 P. 580, 87 Mont. 521; Holland v. Pence Automobile Co., 234 P. 284, 72 Mont. 500.

Ohio.—Hafer v. Alex Wilson Co., 82 N.E.2d 123, 83 Ohio App. 5; Valencic v. Akron & B. B. R. Co., 13 N.E.2d 240, 133 Ohio St. 287.

Tex.—Hambrick v. Texas & P. Ry. Co., Civ.App., 285 S.W. 883.

circumstances attending the injury, as detailed by the plaintiff's evidence, raise a presumption of an absence of the exercise of due care.[2] In some jurisdictions, however, it is error to charge that the plaintiff must remove the inference or presumption of contributory negligence arising from evidence since the law requires only that the plaintiff produce evidence equaling or counterbalancing the inference or presumption so arising.[3]

In some states the defense of contributory negligence has been abolished in actions by an employee against an employer and by passengers against common carriers. However, contributory negligence may be proven in mitigation of damages, and in such cases, the burden of proof is upon the defendant.[4]

Burden on plaintiff

In a minority of jurisdictions, in some of which the plaintiff is required to negative in the complaint the contributory negligence of the injured person, the rule is firmly established that the plaintiff has the burden of showing the absence of contributory negligence, or the exercise of due care by the injured person at the time of the injury complained of.[5] However, direct and

Rule applied

Owner of preceding truck sued for death of occupant of following truck which collided with preceding truck, had burden of proving negligence proximately contributing to accident, notwithstanding that law required plaintiff to equalize or neutralize any inference of contributory negligence that might arise from his evidence. Smith v. Cushman Motor Delivery Co., 6 N.E.2d 594, 54 Ohio App. 99.

2. **Colo.**—Kracaw v. Micheletti, 276 P. 333, 85 Colo. 384.

Mont.—Rau v. Northern Pacific Ry. Co., 289 P. 580, 87 Mont. 521.

3. **Ohio.**—Osso v. Hamilton City Lines, 89 N.E.2d 697, 86 Ohio App. 53.

4. **Iowa.**—Band v. Reinke, 298 N. W. 865, 230 Iowa 515.

5. **Ark.**—Britt Trucking Co. v. Ringgold, 192 S.W.2d 532, 209 Ark. 769 (a motorist making left turn had duty to extend hand and arm and to keep the same extended during the last 100 feet traveled before turning left, and had burden of proving that he complied with such law).

Ill.—Gasperik v. Simons, 1970, 260 N. E.2d 458, 124 Ill.App.2d 360 (pedestrian); Miksatka v. Illinois Northern Ry. Co., 199 N.E.2d 74, 44 Ill.App.2d 258 (plaintiff suing railroad for crossing collision); Cook v. Boothman, 165 N.E.2d 544, 24 Ill.App.2d 552; Duffy v. Cortesi, 119 N.E.2d 241, 2 Ill.2d 511 (wrongful death).

Me.—McMann v. Reliable Furniture Co., 140 A.2d 736, 153 Me. 383; Jaeger v. Cutting, 124 A.2d 749, 152 Me. 136; cf. Sturtevant v. Ouellette, 140 A. 368, 126 Me. 558.

N.Y.—Areson v. Majek, City Ct., 65 N.Y.S.2d 474.

R.I.—McCall v. Laferriere, 86 A.2d 46, 79 R.I. 174.

§ 416.7 TRIAL EVIDENCE Ch. 416

affirmative evidence of due care is not required.[6] The plaintiff may show that the violation of a statute or traffic ordinance bore no causal relation to the injury.[7]

In such a jurisdiction, the husband, seeking to recover for the value of an automobile owned by the community and damaged while operated by the wife, must either prove that his wife was non-negligent or that the automobile was not being used on a community errand, for if on a community errand, the contributory negligence of the wife would prohibit recovery for damage to the community property.[8]

Vt.—Smith v. Grove, 119 A.2d 880, 119 Vt. 106, followed in 119 A.2d 885, 119 Vt. 115 (direct and affirmative proof of due care was not required, and all passenger had to do was to give evidence which would warrant an inference of due care); Leonard v. Henderson, 99 A.2d 698, 118 Vt. 29.

Contra where damaged auto was driven by bailee

Plaintiff suing for damages to automobile need not prove lack of contributory negligence, where automobile was driven by bailee. Bedell v. Androscoggin & K. Ry. Co., 177 A. 237, 133 Me. 268.

Contra where plaintiff relies upon wilful misconduct

In action for injuries sustained when pedestrian was struck, wherein one count charged wilful conduct of motorist and another count charged negligence, pedestrian did not have burden of proving exercise of ordinary care for his own safety in order to recover under count charging wilful conduct. Pillow v. Long, 20 N.E.2d 896, 299 Ill.App. 542.

Even when combined with wrongful death claim

Owner of vehicle, operated by deceased, who brings action for property damage to vehicle, which action is joined with action for wrongful death, must prove his freedom from contributory negligence notwithstanding statute indicating that same rule as to burden of proving contributory negligence applies when other causes of action of dead man's estate are joined with wrongful death action. Crossett v. Natali, 1969, 303 N.Y.S.2d 428, 60 Misc.2d 312.

6. **Vt.**—Higgins v. Metzger, 143 A. 394, 101 Vt. 285.

7. **Cal.**—Yates v. Morotti, 8 P.2d 519, 120 Cal.App. 710 (violation of traffic ordinance as not proximate cause of accident).

Me.—Tomlinson v. Clement Bros., 154 A. 355, 130 Me. 189.

N.Y.—Knapp v. Barrett, 1915, 110 N.E. 428, 216 N.Y. 226.

Wash.—Millspaugh v. Alert Transfer & Storage Co., 259 P. 22, 145 Wash. 111 (effect of violation of statute concerning carrying of lights); Benson v. Anderson, 223 P. 1063, 129 Wash. 19.

8. **La.**—Levy v. New Orleans & N.E. R. Co., La.App., 20 So.2d 559, rehearing denied 21 So.2d 155.

§ 416.8 Burden of Proof—Contributory Negligence of Passengers

In actions by automobile guests against their hosts for injuries, the defendant in many jurisdictions has the burden of establishing contributory negligence,[9] or contributory wilful and wanton misconduct.[10]

---

9. **Cal.**—Lindemann v. San Joaquin Cotton Oil Co., 55 P.2d 870, 5 Cal. 2d 480.

    Fla.—Welch v. Moothart, 89 So.2d 485.

    Ga.—Hanley v. Ford Motor Co., App. 1973, 196 S.E.2d 451, 128 Ga.App. 307.

    Idaho.—Willi v. Schaefer Hitchcock Co., 25 P.2d 167, 53 Idaho 367 (acquiescing to high speed of driver).

    La.—Marcotte v. Travelers Ins. Co., 1971, 249 So.2d 105, 258 La. 989 (riding with allegedly intoxicated driver).

    Md.—Lindley v. Sink, 30 N.E.2d 456, 218 Ind. 1, 2 A.L.R.2d 772 (action for death. Burns' Ann.St. § 2–1025).

    Mass.—Dinardi v. Herook, 1952, 105 N.E.2d 197, 328 Mass. 572.

    Minn.—Jasinuk v. Lombard, 250 N.W. 568, 189 Minn. 594; White v. Cochrane, 249 N.W. 328, 189 Minn. 300 (burden on automobile host to prove that guest's negligence or assumption of risk proximately caused injury).

    N.J.—Kaufman v. Pennsylvania R. Co., 66 A.2d 527, 2 N.J. 318 (burden of showing that peril was known and appreciated by deceased so that jury might determine whether deceased as a reasonably prudent person should have given a warning which would have averted the risk).

    Or.—Waller v. Hill, 190 P.2d 147, 183 Or. 53.

    Tenn.—Duvall Transfer and Delivery Service v. Beaman, 403 S.W.2d 315.

    Tex.—Louisiana Ry. & Nav. Co. of Texas v. Cotton, Civ.App., 1 S.W. 2d 393.

    Va.—Ketchmark v. Lindauer, 92 S.E. 2d 286, 198 Va. 42; Masters v. Cardi, 42 S.E.2d 203, 186 Va. 261 (under guest statute).

    Wis.—Parr v. Douglas, 34 N.W.2d 229, 253 Wis. 311.

    Directing position on roadway

    Driver who directed passenger to stand next to left front door of disabled automobile to wave traffic away from automobile stopped at shoulder of expressway, had burden of affirmatively showing that passenger, who was killed by oncoming automobile and whose administratrix brought death action, was guilty of contributory negligence in assuming position indicated by driver. Rossman v. La Grega, 1971, 321 N.Y.S.2d 588, 28 N.Y.2d 300, 270 N.E.2d 313.

    Knowledge of likelihood driver would fall asleep

    To establish affirmative defense of contributory negligence by passenger suing for injuries sustained when driver fell asleep and automobile struck bridge, driver must prove that passenger knew or should have known that driver's physical condition was such that driver was likely to fall asleep while driving. Turner v. Pfluger, C.A.Wis.1969, 407 F.2d 648.

10. **Ind.**—Ridgway v. Yenny, 57 N. E.2d 581, 223 Ind. 16.

§ 416.8 TRIAL EVIDENCE Ch. 416

In an action for injuries to an automobile guest who permitted an intoxicated driver to operate the automobile, it is not incumbent on the defendant to show that the guest had actual knowledge of the driver's intoxication.[11]

It has also been held that the burden of proof of a passenger's assumption of risk is on the defendant.[12]

Negligence of driver not imputable

The defendant cannot prevail by proving contributory negligence of the driver, unless such negligence is imputable to the guest.[13] The same rule applies where the injury is occasioned by other vehicles or agencies,[14] unless the plaintiff's pleadings or evidence disclose contributory negligence.[15] This rule has been embodied in the statutes in some jurisdictions.[16]

---

11. **Tenn.**—Hicks v. Herbert, 113 S. W.2d 1197, 173 Tenn. 1.

12. **Cal.**—Burr v. Goss, 205 P.2d 61, 91 Cal.App.2d 351.

Conn.—Kloiber v. Steinberg, 176 A. 2d 601, 23 Conn.Sup. 77 (risk of driver falling asleep and losing control); Zullo v. Zullo, 89 A.2d 216, 138 Conn. 712 (passenger's intoxication and assumption of risk).

Iowa.—Tuttle v. Longnecker, 138 N. W.2d 851, 258 Iowa 393.

N.H.—McAllister v. Maltais, 154 A. 2d 456, 102 N.H. 245.

Tex.—Schiller v. Rice, 246 S.W.2d 607, 151 Tex. 116 (passenger's intoxication and assumption of risk).

Rule applied

In actions for injuries to one passenger, and for wrongful death of another passenger in automobile which ran into side of moving freight train on foggy night, burden of establishing assumption of risk on part of deceased passenger was upon defendant; but such burden was met by establishing that she had been intoxicated. Sprague v. Hauck, 89 N. W.2d 226, 3 Wis.2d 616.

13. **Minn.**—Cokesh v. Price, 161 N. W. 715, 136 Minn. 304, 23 A.L.R.

643; La Riviere v. Pemberton, 48 N.W. 406, 46 Minn. 5.

Pa.—Lacich v. Robb, 214 A.2d 342, 419 Pa. 337.

14. **Mass.**—De Luca v. Boston, R. B. & L. R. Co., 184 N.E. 924, 282 Mass. 331 (riding in limousine).

Tex.—Dallas Ry. Co. v. Eaton, Civ. App., 222 S.W. 318.

Wis.—Paine v. Chicago & N. W. Ry. Co., 243 N.W. 205, 208 Wis. 423.

15. **Cal.**—Schurman v. Los Angeles Creamery Co., 254 P. 681, 81 Cal. App. 758.

La.—Schick v. Jenevein, 82 So. 360, 145 La. 333.

Md.—Greer Transp. Co. v. Knight, 146 A. 851, 157 Md. 528; Hopper, McGaw & Co. v. Kelly, 125 A. 779, 145 Md. 161.

Mont.—Grant v. Chicago, M. & St. P. R. Co., 252 P. 382, 78 Mont. 97.

Pa.—Anderson v. Wood, 107 A. 658, 264 Pa. 98.

16. **Cal.**—Hollowell v. Cameron, 199 P. 803, 186 Cal. 530; Howard v. Worthington, 195 P. 709, 50 Cal. App. 556.

Mass.—Levy v. Steiger, 124 N.E. 477, 233 Mass. 600; Chaplin v. Brook-

However, where the driver and the injured person are engaged in a joint enterprise on the trip, the driver's negligence may be imputed to the injured occupant, so as to defeat a recovery. But in such instance the burden of proving the joint enterprise is on the defendant.[17]

Burden on guest

In some states, the guest has the burden of proving freedom from contributory negligence, under the circumstances of the particular case.[18]

While in most states, in suits arising out of railroad crossing accidents, the plaintiff is favored with statutory provisions creating favorable presumptions, in Vermont the plaintiff has the burden of showing freedom from contributory negligence in such cases.[19]

line Taxi Co., 119 N.E. 650, 230 Mass. 155.

N.C.—Jackson v. Atlantic Coast Line R. Co., 106 S.E. 495, 181 N.C. 153.

17. Cal.—Clark v. Janss, 103 P.2d 175, 39 Cal.App.2d 523.

Minn.—Molden v. Minneapolis, St. P. & S. S. Ry. Co., 200 N.W. 740, 160 Minn. 471.

Or.—Bartholomew v. Oregonian, 216 P.2d 257, 188 Or. 407.

Pa.—Marmar v. Farrell, Super., 177 A. 224, 116 Pa.Super. 586, followed in Weiss v. Farrell, 177 A. 225, 116 Pa.Super. 591; Rogers v. Saxon, 158 A. 166, 305 Pa. 479, 80 A.L.R. 280.

Tex.—Louisiana Ry. & Navigation Co. v. Cotton, Civ.App.1927, 1 S.W.2d 393.

18. Ill.—Hanson v. Trust Co. of Chicago, 43 N.E.2d 931, 380 Ill. 194; Reed v. Alton Water Co., 22 N.E.2d 395, 301 Ill.App. 219.

Me.—Feurman v. Rourke, 180 A. 314, 133 Me. 466; Richard v. Maine Cent. R. Co., 168 A. 811, 132 Me. 197 (guest in auto colliding with train).

Mich.—White v. Huffmaster, 40 N.W.2d 87, 326 Mich. 108.

N.Y.—Knesz v. Singman, 1971, 325 N.Y.S.2d 885, 37 A.D.2d 1026.

W.Va.—Browning v. Tolley, 1932, 163 S.E. 10, 111 W.Va. 548.

But see

Me.—Richard v. Maine Central R. Co., 168 A. 811, 132 Me. 197 (riding along during fog).

19. Vt.—Bates v. Rutland R. Co., 165 A. 923, 105 Vt. 394.

§ 416.9 TRIAL EVIDENCE Ch. 416

§ 416.9 Burden of Proof—Damages

Library References:
C.J.S. Damages § 144.
West's Key No. Digests, Damages ⚖163.

In an action for personal injuries caused by the negligent operation of a motor vehicle, it is incumbent on the plaintiff to establish the injuries.[20]

The burden is on the plaintiff to prove that any physical incapacity was not caused solely by infirmities having no connection with the accident.[21]

The plaintiff seeking to recover for loss of earnings must establish a reasonable probability that the injury brought about a loss of earnings, and must afford a basis for a reasonable esti-

---

20. Ky.—Myers v. Salyer, 127 S.W. 2d 158, 277 Ky. 696.

Pa.—Rosenthal v. Carson, 27 A.2d 499, 149 Pa.Super. 428.

Contra where issue exists as to which of two autos caused injury

Where it is not known which of two automobiles caused injuries, the burden is on the operator of each individual automobile to establish the extent of injuries caused by his operation. Eramdjian v. Interstate Bakery Corp., 315 P.2d 19, 153 Cal. App.2d 590.

Multiple collisions

Plaintiff seeking to recover for death of motorist, whose automobile first collided with truck and then, while sitting on highway, was struck by a second automobile, had duty to offer at least sufficient evidence from which jury could reasonably infer that some damage flowed from the second motorist's negligence and, in absence of such evidence, the second motorist was entitled to directed verdict. Fessenden v. Roadway Exp., 1973, 208 N.W.2d 78, 46 Mich.App. 276.

21. Mo.—Franklin v. Kansas City Public Service Co., 186 S.W.2d 546, 239 Mo.App. 151 (stroke suffered by occupant of truck which had collided with streetcar ten months previously).

Ohio.—Giles v. Yellow Cab Co., 205 N.E.2d 86, 1 Ohio App.2d 404 (if injury could have resulted from any other source, it was incumbent upon plaintiff to produce evidence excluding other causes).

Tex.—Miller v. Hooper, Civ.App., 94 S.W.2d 230.

But see

Fact that plaintiff referred to prior injuries in his opening statement did not relieve defendants of burden of establishing causal relationship between prior injuries and those involved in action. Scheck v. Evanston Cab Co., 1968, 236 N.E.2d 258, 93 Ill.App.2d 220.

In action for death of plaintiff's intestate from acute gangrenous appendicitis which plaintiff claimed was due to injuries received by intestate when intestate was struck by defendant's automobile, plaintiff had burden to establish a causal connection between accident and appendicitis, but was not bound to exclude every possible cause other than accident, and plaintiff sustained such burden if evidence showed that there was greater likelihood that appendicitis resulted from accident than from some other source. O'Connor v. Griff, 29 N.E.2d 823, 307 Mass. 120.

mate of the amount of that loss,[22] and, to that end, must prove both the amount of time lost and its value.[23]

In an action for wrongful death, the administrator or other party plaintiff has the burden of showing the fact of dependency on the decedent [24] and pecuniary loss.[25]

The burden of proving any recoupment or mitigation,[26] or setoff [27] is on the one claiming it.

§ 416.10 Burden of Proof—Limitation of Actions

Library References:
C.J.S. Limitations of Actions §§ 384, 386; Motor Vehicles § 499. West's Key. No. Digests, Automobiles ⚖233; Limitation of Actions ⚖195.

It has been held that the time limited by statute for bringing an action for wrongful death is in the nature of a condition precedent, and the burden of proving compliance therewith is on the plaintiff in an action for death caused by the negligent operation of an automobile.[28]

Where it is contended that the evidence warrants a finding of fact taking the case out of the operation of the statute of limitations, the burden of proof is on the plaintiff.[29]

It also has been held that, where the defendant relies upon the doctrine of laches, the burden to show circumstances warranting application of the rule is on the defendant.[30]

22. **Mich.**—Maxwell v. Wanik, 287 N.W. 396, 290 Mich. 106.

23. **Mich.**—Maxwell v. Wanik, 287 N.W. 396, 290 Mich. 106.

24. **Ark.**—Crawford v. Center, 100 S.W.2d 83, 193 Ark. 287.

25. **Ark.**—Crawford v. Center, 100 S.W.2d 83, 193 Ark. 287.

Rule stated
In death actions, ordinarily evidence should be presented of the amount which a deceased husband had been in the habit of turning over to his wife and children for their support. De Santis v. Maddalon, 35 A.2d 72, 348 Pa. 296.

26. **Nev.**—Dinwiddie Const. Co. v. Campbell, 406 P.2d 294, 81 Nev. 469.

27. **Tenn.**—Polk v. Torrence, 405 S. W.2d 575.

28. **Mass.**—Melnik v. Perwak, 4 N. E.2d 329, 295 Mass. 512.

29. **Mass.**—Ford v. Rogovin, 194 N. E. 719, 289 Mass. 549.

30. **Or.**—Hanns v. Hanns, 423 P.2d 499, 246 Or. 282.

§ 416.11 Burden of Proof—Venue

Library References:
C.J.S. Corporations §§ 1295 et seq., 1338; Motor Vehicles §§ 498, 509 et seq.; Venue § 192.
West's Key No. Digests, Automobiles ⚖232, 242; Corporations ⚖503, 519(1); Pleading ⚖111.12.

With regard to the venue of automobile actions, where the owner of a motor vehicle residing in one county is sued in another county for injuries resulting from the owner's negligent operation of the vehicle in the county in which the suit was instituted, it has been held incumbent on the plaintiff to prove by competent evidence an affirmative negligent act in the county of the forum.[31]

When the action is brought under statutory and constitutional provisions permitting the action to be maintained in the county where plaintiff resides, plaintiff must prove residence in the county in which the action is brought.[32] In Texas, the plea of privilege statute operates to place the burden of proving the venue facts on the plaintiff, and, ordinarily, where one alleges, in a plea of privilege, that lack of residency in the county in which the suit is instituted, the fact is taken as established in the absence of proof.[33]

---

31. Tex.—McElyea v. Bowles, Civ.App., 233 S.W.2d 482; Barron v. James, 198 S.W.2d 256, 145 Tex. 283; Union Bus Lines v. Young, Civ.App., 194 S.W.2d 779; Saladiner v. Polanco, Civ.App., 160 S.W.2d 537.

32. Okl.—Southwestern Greyhound Lines v. Craig, 80 P.2d 221, 182 Okl. 610.

33. Defendants residing in different counties
A plaintiff, who seeks to obtain benefit of exception in venue statute permitting suit in any county where one of defendants resides, has burden of pleading a joint cause of action against defendants, and of proving by independent evidence that defendant alleged to reside in county where suit is pending does in fact reside in such county, and of proving further fact that plaintiff has a cause of action as alleged against the resident defendant. Kines v. Hendrickson, Civ.App., 153 S.W.2d 645.

Temporary residence
A plea of privilege alleging that defendant was not a resident of county where suit was instituted but was a resident of the state of New York, and was temporarily residing in a county other than the county in which suit was brought, did not meet requirements of plea of privilege statute, and was properly overruled, where defendant offered no proof at hearing as to where he resided or as to just how temporary his residence was in the county other than the county in which suit was brought, since the phrase "temporary residence" is not synonymous with the word "residence" as that word is used in plea of privilege statute. Nolte v. Saenz, Civ.App., 153 S.W.2d 281.

Ch. 416   BURDEN OF PROOF   § 416.12

§ 416.12 Variance of Proof

Library References:
C.J.S. Motor Vehicles § 508; Pleading § 512 et seq.
West's Key No. Digests, Automobiles ⚖️240; Pleading ⚖️370 et seq.

It is a familiar rule that the plaintiff must recover, if at all, on the theory alleged in the complaint,[34] since the case must be tried on the issues joined by the parties.[35] A "material" variance between the allegations of the cause of action or defense and the proof adduced in support thereof is fatal.[36]

---

34. **Ariz.**—City of Phoenix v. Green, 66 P.2d 1041, 49 Ariz. 376.

Conn.—Evans v. Byrolly Transp. Co., 197 A. 758, 124 Conn. 10 (where complaint alleged that, because of the negligence of driver of defendant's truck, in allowing the truck to remain stationary on traveled portion of highway without lights, words "operated and maintained" would not permit trial on theory that the truck was moving).

Ind.—Chicago & E. I. Ry. Co. v. Felling, 200 N.E. 441, 102 Ind.App. 282.

Iowa.—Luther v. Jones, 261 N.W. 817, 220 Iowa 95.

Mo.—Hein v. Chicago & E. I. R. Co., App., 209 S.W.2d 578; Browne v. Creek, 209 S.W.2d 900, 357 Mo. 576 (theory as to person responsible); Hughes v. Kiel, App., 100 S.W.2d 48.

N.C.—Hall v. Kimber, 1969, 171 S.E. 2d 99, 6 N.C.App. 669 (where plaintiff passenger alleged that median on four-lane highway was approximately 20 feet wide, and that driver drove west to intersection where she proceeded to make left turn into north-south road, but proved that median was 31 feet wide and that vehicle in which passenger was riding remained stopped in cross-over for several minutes before crossing of east-bound roadway was attempted, there was material variance between pleading and proof, precluding application of statute relating to right-of-way at intersection in manner favorable to passenger who brought action for injuries sustained when east-bound vehicle struck vehicle in which she was riding).

Tenn.—Roddy Mfg. Co. v. Dixon, 1937, 105 S.W.2d 513, 21 Tenn.App. 81.

35. **Iowa.**—Alcock v. Kearney, 288 N.W. 785, 227 Iowa 650.

Vt.—Bucklin v. Narkwich, 177 A. 198, 107 Vt. 168.

36. **Ariz.**—McClure v. Johnson, 69 P.2d 573, 50 Ariz. 76.

Cal.—Lewis v. South San Francisco Yellow Cab Co., 210 P.2d 62, 93 Cal.App.2d 849 (allegation passenger injured leaving taxicab because of fear of driver, proof in fear of other passenger).

Ga.—Eastern Carolina Service Corporation v. Robereds, 157 S.E. 916, 43 Ga.App. 87 (alleged vehicle stopped, proved did not stop before entering road).

Ill.—Buckley v. Mandel Bros., 1929, 164 N.E. 657, 333 Ill. 368 (alleged defendant drove truck against motorcycle, proved converse); Barnett v. Levy, 213 Ill.App. 129 (allegation status as guest, proof engaged in joint enterprise and sharing expenses).

Mass.—McNair v. Fraher, 146 N.E.2d 484, 336 Mass. 458 (where alleged that plaintiff was riding in automobile operated by defendant and that as the result of gross negligence of defendant she was in-

§ 416.12   TRIAL EVIDENCE   Ch. 416

jured, plaintiff was not entitled to recover when evidence showed that plaintiff, an unlicensed driver, was operating automobile at request of defendant who knew plaintiff was unlicensed); Zarski v. Creamer, 59 N.E.2d 704, 317 Mass. 744 (where plaintiffs' causes of action were restricted to negligence in operation of the truck in which plaintiffs were riding, recovery against truck owner could not be had on theory that owner was personally negligent in permitting operator to drive truck knowing that he needed sleep).

Mich.—Ritter v. Terman, 1938, 280 N.W. 136, 285 Mich. 128 (alleged pedestrian was moving, proved standing still); Gibbs v. Dayton, 1911, 131 N.W. 544, 166 Mich. 263 (directions of travel wrong, but curable by amendment of pleading).

Miss.—Sugg v. Hendrix, C.C.A.Miss., 153 F.2d 240 (allegation negligent operation by defendant's servant, proof furnished tractor with defective brakes).

Mo.—Ellis v. Wolfe-Shoemaker Motor Co., 1932, 55 S.W.2d 309, 227 Mo.App. 508; Smiley v. Kenney, App., 228 S.W. 857 (allegation failure to act to avoid striking plaintiff, proof of act of swerving into collision path).

N.Y.—Morgan v. Robinson, 159 N.Y.S.2d 639, 3 A.D.2d 216 (in action for injuries to passenger as result of falling out in attempting to rescue another passenger precipitated from automobile when door thereof opened, presentation to jury of question of defendant's negligent omission to apply brakes immediately after such other passenger was thrown from automobile as independent ground for recovery, over nine years after event, without amendment of complaint to supply omitted allegations of such negligence, was error prejudicial to defendant).

N.C.—LaVange v. Lenoir, 1969, 170 S.E.2d 622, 6 N.C.App. 603 (where plaintiff alleged that he was walking in street toward his automobile at time he was struck by defendant's automobile, plaintiff's evidence at trial that he was standing on curb at time he was struck constituted a variance which, in light of fact that defendant interposed plaintiff's contributory negligence as bar and plaintiff's evidence at trial would lessen effectiveness of defense and would require defendant to defend a cause of action completely different from cause of action alleged in complaint, was a material variance and supported granting judgment of nonsuit); Hall v. Poteat, 1962, 125 S.E.2d 924, 257 N.C. 458 (alleged operation without signal or proper lookout, proved stopped without lights); Bundy v. Belue, 116 S.E.2d 200, 253 N.C. 31 (construing plaintiff's testimony as meaning that driver of tractor-trailer which collided with oncoming automobile had negligently attempted to pass another tractor-trailer proceeding in the same direction would defeat recovery against owner and driver of either tractor-trailer because of material variance between evidence and allegations of amended complaint that tractor-trailer, parked on shoulder, was backed onto highway in front of overtaking tractor-trailer, forcing driver thereof to swerve to his left and collide with oncoming automobile, and that the driver of overtaking tractor-trailer should have known of approach of automobile and drove tractor-trailer farther into line of travel of automobile than was necessary to avoid backing tractor-trailer); Brady v. Nehi Beverage Co., 86 S.E.2d 901, 242 N.C. 32 (alleged one intersecting road to be subservient proved of equal dignity).

N.D.—Zimprich v. Coman, 234 N.W. 69, 60 N.D. 297 (alleged defendant was negligent in driving on wrong side of road at excessive speed,

Ch. 416   BURDEN OF PROOF   § 416.12

Ordinarily, however, a variance is not fatal where the defendant is not surprised or misled.[37] Thus, a variance as to the date of the accident has been held not prejudicial,[38] or of the place of the accident.[39]

Whether the proof corresponds with the allegations usually involves a construction both of the pleadings and the evidence, and, if the evidence can be reasonably construed to support the pleadings, it will not be regarded as a material variance.[40]

could not recover by proof that defendant's truck had glaring headlights).

Ohio.—Crawford v. Bohannon, 168 N.E.2d 431, 110 Ohio App. 71 (where pleadings did not charge that driver was negligent in failing to have headlights burning prior to collision with ponies, sustaining objections to such testimony was not error).

Tenn.—Woods v. Meacham, 333 S.W. 2d 567, 46 Tenn.App. 711 (where alleged defendant drove while blinded by lights, could not attempt proof driver drove without adequate sleep); Wagner v. Niven, 332 S.W.2d 511, 46 Tenn.App. 581.

Vt.—Landry v. Hubert, 137 A. 97, 100 Vt. 268 (inadequacy of brakes not ground of recovery by guest alleging negligent speed).

Wash.—Tuveson v. J. M. Colman Co., 1938, 82 P.2d 579, 196 Wash. 286.

Specific averment of negligence

A pleader undertaking to specify the particular act or omission constituting the negligence alleged must prove the more specific averment. Dallas Railway & Terminal Co. v. Bishop, Tex.Civ.App., 153 S.W.2d 298.

37. **Ariz.**—Keck v. Kelley, 1972, 492 P.2d 412, 16 Ariz.App. 163 (did not have to allege gross and wanton negligence in order to avail himself of its use to offset the defense of contributory negligence where defendants were adequately forewarned).

Ark.—Bonds v. Littrell, 1969, 446 S.W.2d 672, 247 Ark. 577.

Cal.—Wood v. Santa Cruz County, 284 P.2d 923, 133 Cal.App.2d 713.

La.—Wald v. Board of Com'rs of Port of New Orleans, 124 So. 701, 14 La.App. 337.

Miss.—Avent v. Tucker, 194 So. 596, 188 Miss. 207 (variance as to whether wife drove and husband accompanied wife as owner or vice versa).

N.C.—Broadnax v. Deloatch, 1970, 175 S.E.2d 314, 8 N.C.App. 620, appeal after remand 201 S.E.2d 525, 20 N.C.App. 430, certiorari denied 203 S.E.2d 57, 285 N.C. 85.

Tex.—Williams v. Creighton, Civ. App., 93 S.W.2d 195 (variance as to whether one or two colliding automobiles struck pedestrian).

Wyo.—Johnston v. Vukelic, 213 P.2d 925, 67 Wyo. 1 (variance as to whether wife or husband was driving).

38. **N.J.**—Auchter v. Elliott Bus Corporation, 198 A. 376, 120 N.J.L. 105.

Pa.—Fazio v. Pittsburgh Rys. Co., 182 A. 696, 321 Pa. 7.

Tenn.—Mason v. James, 89 S.W.2d 910, 19 Tenn.App. 479.

39. **Vt.**—Senecal v. Bleau, 189 A. 139, 108 Vt. 486.

40. **Ala.**—Donald v. Matheny, 158 So.2d 909, 276 Ala. 52 (no variance between averment in count that defendant permitted his "automobile to run over, upon or against said motor vehicle" and proof which showed that plaintiff's motorbike

§ 416.12   TRIAL EVIDENCE   Ch. 416

ran into the side of defendant's automobile); McMullen v. Four Wheels, Inc., 1959, 116 So.2d 611, 40 Ala.App. 408, certiorari denied 116 So.2d 615, 270 Ala. 739 (re capacity of operator); Nelson v. Johnson, 88 So.2d 358, 264 Ala. 422 (evidence that collision occurred while employee of street department of city, whose duty it was to service signal flares placed at excavations in streets of city, was returning home after extinguishing and refueling flares on a Sunday morning was not at variance with allegation that he was engaged in operation of city's truck to haul oil for purpose of refueling signal flares); Ray v. Terry, 28 So.2d 916, 32 Ala.App. 582, certiorari dismissed 28 So.2d 918, 248 Ala. 640 (allegation parked on highway, proof parked three or four feet from edge of pavement).

Cal.—Wood v. Santa Cruz County, 284 P.2d 923, 133 Cal.App.2d 713 (whether obstruction struck by motorcyclist was "pile of branches" or "one branch or stick"); Beck v. Sirota, 109 P.2d 419, 42 Cal.App. 2d 551 (variance in position auto was parked with respect to scaffold, where electric cord from scafford hooked by auto).

Conn.—Keheley v. Uhl, 26 A.2d 357, 129 Conn. 30 (discrepancy as to position of plaintiff's legs on truck prior to collision with defendant's car door).

Fla.—Gittleman v. Dixon, 4 So.2d 859, 148 Fla. 583 (allegation driver took hands off steering wheel for "protracted" period, proof driver was adjusting packages in the rear); Dunn Bus Service v. Wise, 191 So. 509, 140 Fla. 341 (where alleged that carrier's servant carelessly drove motorbus causing passenger to be thrown about in bus and injured, and passenger's evidence showed that driver continued on way without reducing speed or making investigation after he knew or should have known from sound that there was defect in bus which he stopped suddenly and violently after parts of bus fell to street, there was no variance, notwithstanding defense and evidence that injury was result of latent defect in bus).

Ga.—Stanley v. Squadrito, 131 S.E. 2d 227, 107 Ga.App. 651 (failure to prove that ambulance driver was driving at 55 miles per hour as alleged did not eliminate allegation that ambulance driver was negligent in driving at a speed greater than was reasonable and prudent); White v. Borders, 123 S.E.2d 170, 104 Ga.App. 746 (not fatal alleged self as paying passenger, where made gross negligence case); Stewart v. Wilson, 88 S.E.2d 752, 92 Ga. App. 514 (where petition alleged that left front of defendant's automobile struck the left front of plaintiff's automobile, evidence that the right front of defendant's automobile and entire front of plaintiff's automobile were damaged had the effect of amending petition to allege that the parts of automobiles thus shown to have been damaged were the parts that collided); Trawick v. Chambliss, 156 S.E. 268, 42 Ga.App. 333 (allegation that defendant operated automobile causing injury is supported by evidence that automobile was operated by defendant's servant acting within scope of employment).

Idaho.—Naccarato v. Village of Priest River, 1948, 195 P.2d 370, 68 Idaho 368 (alleged village dug a ditch in roadway, proved permitted broken water main which caused ditch); Faris v. Burroughs Adding Mach. Co., 282 P. 72, 48 Idaho 310 (alleged defendant's automobile was driven into plaintiff's automobile, showed that contrary happened).

Ill.—Hammer v. Shaffer, 86 N.E.2d 672, 338 Ill.App. 19 (allegation that collision occurred at the intersection of two highways and proof that plaintiffs were on a private road); Rich v. Albrecht, 21 N.E.2d

Ch. 416   BURDEN OF PROOF   § 416.12

633, 300 Ill.App. 493 (alleged operation by defendant, proved operation by servant); Moore v. Hines, 221 Ill.App. 589 (allegation plaintiff knocked to ground, proof sitting in debris and not actually touching ground); Kovell v. North Roseland Motor Sales, 275 Ill.App. 566 (only possession and control of the automobile by defendant need be proved, though the declaration alleges "ownership, possession and control").

Iowa.—Reynolds v. Nowotny, 1971, 189 N.W.2d 557 (although alleged that defendant was both operator and owner, failure of proof of ownership would not relieve operator from liability for negligence).

Ky.—Brady v. B. & B. Ice Co., 45 S.W.2d 1051, 242 Ky. 138 (alleged driver was drunk, and proof showed borrower of truck, who was intoxicated, had temporarily abandoned wheel to another and was in front seat directing his movements); Louisville & N. R. Co. v. Mahoney, 294 S.W. 777, 220 Ky. 30 (under complaint alleging train ran into plaintiff's automobile, plaintiff could show that his car ran into or near side of passing freight train, where automobile was struck by caboose steps).

La.—Brandon v. Texas & N. O. R. Co., App., 169 So. 254 (alleged defendant owned railroad tracks, not fatal prove was lessee).

Mo.—Browne v. Creek, 209 S.W.2d 900, 357 Mo. 576 (allegation parked near highway with blinding headlights and causing second vehicle to park on highway without lights, proof defendant skidded into muddy ditch and requested second car to stay and render assistance); Hughes v. Kiel, App., 100 S.W.2d 48 (allegation street car passenger injured in street car collision with auto, proof injured by sudden stop prior to collision); Ridenhour v. Oklahoma Contracting Co., App., 45 S.W.2d 108 (under allegations that defendant's negligence was in parking ditching machine without lights, evidence showing negligence consisted of parking it without lights at top of hill was admissible over objection of variance); Powell v. Schofield, 15 S.W.2d 876, 223 App. 1041 (petition alleged stopping of bus on pavement, while evidence showed bus stopped because of broken gas line); Underwood v. Hall, Mo.App., 3 S.W.2d 1044 (evidence as to which automobile ran against the other held immaterial); Ventimiglia v. M. A. Heiman Mfg. Co., App. 1924, 256 S.W. 139 (alleged truck ran upon sidewalk, proof pedestrian struck by overhang of truck body beyond curb).

Mont.—Kelly v. Lowney & Williams, 126 P.2d 486, 113 Mont. 385 (allegation "negligently permitted" an inexperienced driver to operate auto, proof of giving opportunity to sit behind wheel); Peabody v. Northern Pac. Ry. Co., 261 P. 261, 80 Mont. 492.

Ohio.—Ruffo v. Randall, 52 N.E.2d 750, 72 Ohio App. 396 (allegation suddenly stopped, proof slowed down before turning into driveway).

Okl.—American Fidelity & Casualty Co. v. Bennett, 76 P.2d 245, 182 Okl. 71 (where petition alleged that plaintiff's back and head had been wrenched, strained, bruised, and fractured, that internal organs around her uterus and neck had been torn and that muscles in her knee, abdomen, and neck had been torn lose, no variance was created by testimony of physician in technical terms referring to a retroflexion or sub-involution of uterus, to a sacroiliac sprain of left side and to pain along left lumbar vetebræ).

Or.—Kitchel v. Gallagher, 270 P. 488, 126 Or. 373 (alleged collision "at" intersection held not to preclude proof that collision occurred a few feet from intersection).

Pa.—Sikorski v. Philadelphia & R. Ry. Co., 103 A. 618, 260 Pa. 243

§ 416.12   TRIAL EVIDENCE   Ch. 416

A plaintiff who alleges that the negligence of the defendant was the sole cause of the injury may recover on proof that the negligence of the defendant, concurring with the negligence of another person, contributed to the injury.[41] Conversely, if the plaintiff alleges that the injury was caused by the separate but concurring acts of negligence of two or more defendants which produced a single injury, recovery may be had against either of the negligent defendants against whom negligence is proven.[42]

It has been held that, if the plaintiff undertakes in the pleadings to designate the driver of the defendant's truck by name, the failure to prove that the truck was actually driven by the named individual constituted a fatal variance between the allegations and proof.[43] However, if one asserts only that some unknown agent or servant of the defendant caused the injury, it is not necessary to establish the identity of the negligent servant.[44]

(where alleged that the plaintiff's automobile, struck at a railroad crossing, collided with the safety gates, and that the plaintiff was thrown out, proof that the gates closed down on the automobile and that plaintiff, in trying to get out, collapsed and fell to the ground and was injured, was an immaterial variance; the real cause of the injury being the negligent closing of the gates); Young v. Quaker City Cab Co., 87 Pa.Super. 294 (allegation that taxicab struck plaintiff while riding motorcycle, and proof was struck after falling from motorcycle).

R.I.—Maher v. Concannon, 185 A. 907, 56 R.I. 395 (allegation that defendant's parked truck which backed down grade into trolley car in which plaintiffs were riding was "operated" in negligent manner held not so at variance with proof that there was no one in truck as to warrant directed verdict, since truck continued to be in operation while driver, who parked it, was absent therefrom, so long as no other person or agency intervened to start or regulate movements of truck).

Tenn.—McMahan v. McMahan, 1954, 276 S.W.2d 738, 38 Tenn.App. 498 (re details of sharing trip expenses); Tennessee Coach Co. v. Young, 80 S.W.2d 107, 18 Tenn. App. 592 (averment that driver drove bus off highway and proof that bus skidded off road).

Va.—Lipscomb v. O'Brien, 25 S.E.2d 261, 181 Va. 471 (allegation failed to keep a proper lookout, proof driver fell asleep).

Wash.—Child v. Hill, 283 P. 1076, 155 Wash. 133 (that proof showed pedestrian walked into or against front wheel of car, while affirmative defense alleged that plaintiff stepped in front of defendant held not fatal); Wilbert v. Sturgeon, 1922, 204 P. 185, 118 Wash. 551 (variance in proof as to point of collision between auto and bicycle).

41. U.S.—Hower v. Roberts, C.C.A. Mo., 153 F.2d 726.

N.Y.—Daas v. Pearson, 1971, 319 N.Y.S.2d 537, 66 Misc.2d 95, affirmed 325 N.Y.S.2d 1011, 37 A.D.2d 921.

42. Mich.—Barkman v. Montague, 298 N.W. 273, 297 Mich. 588.

43. N.C.—Whichard v. Lipe, 19 S.E. 2d 14, 221 N.C. 53, 139 A.L.R. 1147.

44. S.C.—Le Gette v. Carolina Butane Gas Co., 43 S.E.2d 472, 210 S.C. 542.

76

Ch. 416 BURDEN OF PROOF § 416.12

Where plaintiff alleges damage to an owned automobile, and offers proof of ownership in another, the variance will ordinarily be fatal to a recovery.[45] However, it is not prejudicial to defendant that plaintiff alleges unconditional ownership of a damaged automobile and the proof shows possession thereof as bailee.[46]

Where the ownership of one of the defendants is not a necessary element of the cause of action, the fact that the petition alleges joint ownership in both, and the proof shows sole ownership in one, does not constitute a fatal departure.[47] Also, in an action against two defendants alleged to be copartners, evidence that the defendants were engaged in a joint venture is not a material variance and will support the judgment.[48]

Where it is manifest on the face of a petition that a certain allegation is a clerical error, it cannot be said that proof offered to show the real facts intended to be asserted constitutes a variance.[49]

Many codes provide for amendment of the pleadings to conform to the proof. Some jurisdictions have held that the pleadings will be deemed to have been amended to conform to the proof if the variance is not prejudicial to the defendant.[50] Others have held that the defendant waives the objection of variance by failure to make a timely objection to the introduction of evidence not supported by the pleading.[51]

45. Ill.—Brez Co. v. People's Gaslight & Coke Co., 209 Ill.App. 304.

46. Cal.—Harrington v. Evans, 221 P.2d 696, 99 Cal.App.2d 269.

N.J.—Bishop v. Cadman, 159 A. 536, 10 N.J.Misc. 454.

47. Mo.—Counts v. Thomas, App., 63 S.W.2d 416.

48. Cal.—Hupfeld v. Wadley, 200 P. 2d 564, 89 Cal.App.2d 171.

49. Mo.—Kroell v. Lutz, App., 210 S.W. 926.

50. Ind.—Lindley v. Skidmore, 33 N.E.2d 797, 109 Ind.App. 178 (intersection collision).

51. Ga.—Tuggle v. Waller, 87 S.E. 2d 123, 91 Ga.App. 721.

Kan.—Colin v. De Coursey Cream Co., 178 P.2d 690, 162 Kan. 683.

Affirmative defense not pleaded

Where investigating officer's testimony that there were seat belts in automobile which struck tree, resulting in death of plaintiff's decedent, and that apparently occupants had not used them, was received in wrongful death action without objection, affirmative defense of contributory negligence was properly before court even though not pleaded. Petersen v. Klos, C.A.Miss.1970, 426 F.2d 199, amended on other issues 433 F.2d 911.

Chapter 417

PRESUMPTIONS AND INFERENCES

Table of Sections

Sec.
417.1 In General.
417.2 Exercise of Care in General.
417.3 Exercise of Care by Injured Party.
417.4 Exercise of Care by Defendant.
417.5 Ownership or Control.
417.6 Consent and Permission.
417.7 Agency.
417.8 Other Particular Matters.

§ 417.1 In General

Library References:
C.J.S. Evidence §§ 114 et seq., 1044, 1018 et seq.
West's Key No. Digests, Evidence ⚖︎53, 595, 600.

A presumption and an inference are generally distinguished, the former being a deduction which the law requires a trier of facts to make, the latter being a deduction which the trier may or not make, according to the trier's own conclusions.[1] However it has been stated that a presumption of fact is merely an inference drawn from other facts and circumstances in the case.[2]

A presumption is a rule which the law makes upon a common state of facts. An inference is a conclusion which, by means of data founded upon a common experience, natural reason derives from facts which are proven.[3]

It is usually said that presumptions are not evidence.[4] However, in some jurisdictions, it is held that the presumption of due

---

1. 33 Words and Phrases, Perm.Ed., 486.

   Cal.—West's Ann.Calif.Evid.Code, § 600.

2. **Va.**—Yeary v. Holbrook, 198 S.E. 441, 171 Va. 266.

3. 33 Words and Phrases, Perm.Ed., 486.

   Kan.—Kansas Rules of Civil Procedure § 60–413.

Tex.—Strain v. Martin, Civ.App., 183 S.W.2d 246.

4. **U.S.**—Clayton v. Burston, C.A.Tex.1974, 493 F.2d 429; Slater v. Erie Lackawanna Ry. Co., D.C.Pa. 1969, 300 F.Supp. 1, affirmed, C.A., 411 F.2d 1015.

   Cal.—West's Ann.Calif.Evid.Code, § 600; Alber v. Owens, 59 Cal.Rptr. 117, 427 P.2d 781, 66 Cal.2d 790 (presumption of due care on plaintiff's part arising from evidence of

Ch. 417   PRESUMPTIONS AND INFERENCES   § **417.1**

care is a species of evidence,[5] which should control the deliberations of the jury until and unless it is overcome by satisfactory proof.[6] They determine only whether parties are required to go forward with evidence, and are often said to vanish in the presence of direct evidence as to the facts.[7] Other times it is expressed in terms that the presumption is rebuttable.[8]

his retrograde amnesia would not have the effect of evidence).

Fla.—Nationwide Mut. Ins. Co. v. Griffin, App.1969, 222 So.2d 754.

Minn.—Jensen v. City of Duluth, 130 N.W.2d 515, 269 Minn. 241.

Pa.—McElwain v. Myers, 1951, 80 A. 2d 859, 367 Pa. 346.

Tenn.—Siler v. Siler, 277 S.W. 886, 152 Tenn. 379.

Wash.—Morris v. Chicago, M., St. P. & P. R. Co., 97 P.2d 119, 1 Wash. 2d 587, opinion adhered to 100 P.2d 19, 1 Wash.2d 587.

But see

Cal.—Graybiel v. Consolidated Ass'ns, 60 P.2d 164, 16 Cal.App.2d 20.

5. **U.S.**—Shanahan v. Southern Pac. Co., C.A.Cal., 188 F.2d 564; Mast v. Illinois Cent. R. Co., D.C.Iowa, 79 F.Supp. 149, affirmed 176 F.2d 157 (under Iowa law).

Cal.—Uhl v. Baldwin, 302 P.2d 841, 145 Cal.App.2d 547 (loss of memory); Pacific Tel. & Tel. Co. v. Wellman, 219 P.2d 506, 98 Cal.App.2d 151 (sufficient to create a conflict with contrary testimony).

Idaho.—Van v. Union Pac. R. Co., 366 P.2d 837, 83 Idaho 539.

Me.—Dansky v. Kotimaki, 130 A. 871, 125 Me. 72 (will sustain burden of proving negligence in absence of other proof).

Rule illustrated

Where a pedestrian was entitled to the presumption of due care, the defendant motorist's testimony that the pedestrian failed to look as he stepped from behind a parked automobile onto the paved highway, though evidence which the jury could consider, did not of itself destroy the probative weight of the fact presumed, especially in view of testimony that the motorist stated he did not see the pedestrian until "right on him". Hoppe v. Bradshaw, 108 P.2d 947, 42 Cal.App.2d 334.

6. **U.S.**—Shanahan v. Southern Pac. Co., C.A.Cal., 188 F.2d 564; Delaware, L. & W. R. Co. v. Rebmann, C.C.A.N.Y., 285 F. 317.

Cal.—Siegell v. York, 191 P.2d 50, 84 Cal.App.2d 383; Paulsen v. Spencer, 177 P.2d 597, 78 Cal.App. 2d 268; Anthony v. Hobbie, 155 P.2d 826, 25 Cal.2d 814 (pedestrian struck on highway).

Pa.—Johnson v. Hetrick, 150 A. 477, 300 Pa. 225.

Tex.—Merritt v. Phœnix Refining Co., Civ.App., 103 S.W.2d 415.

Basis for directed verdict

If basic facts are sufficiently proven so as to give rise to presumption, and not thereafter contradicted by credible evidence, party in whose favor presumption exists becomes entitled to directed verdict. Nationwide Mut. Ins. Co. v. Griffin, App.1969, 222 So.2d 754.

7. **Cal.**—Rogers v. Interstate Transit Co., 1931, 297 P. 884, 212 Cal. 36, certiorari denied 52 S.Ct. 22, 284 U.S. 640, 76 L.Ed. 545.

Del.—McGraw v. Corrin, 1973, 303 A.2d 641 (where plaintiff did not exercise due care in crossing street

8. See note 8 on page 80.

§ 417.1   TRIAL EVIDENCE   Ch. 417

and his own act of starting to sprint across highway when defendant's automobile, which was traveling at rate of 25 miles per hour, was approximately 50 feet away was true cause of plaintiff's injuries, plaintiff's alleged amnesia, and inability to recall details of the accident did not entitle plaintiff to a presumption).

Fla.—Nationwide Mut. Ins. Co. v. Griffin, App.1969, 222 So.2d 754.

Ill.—Flynn v. Vancil, 1968, 242 N.E. 2d 237, 41 Ill.2d 236.

Kan.—Kansas Code of Civil Procedure § 60–414 (continuance of force depends upon whether base facts are probative of the existence of the presumed fact).

Mass.—Hughes v. Torregrossa, 180 N.E. 304, 278 Mass. 530.

Mich.—Hoag v. Hyzy, 63 N.W.2d 632, 339 Mich. 163.

Minn.—Steinhaus v. Adamson, 1972, 201 N.W.2d 264, 294 Minn. 387.

Mo.—Branstetter v. Gerdeman, 1955, 274 S.W.2d 240, 364 Mo. 1230.

Pa.—Snyder v. Union Paving Co., 1951, 84 A.2d 373, 170 Pa.Super. 112 (that pedestrian exercised due care).

S.D.—Peters v. Lohr, 152 N.W. 504, 35 S.D. 372.

Tenn.—Seahorn v. Karr, 1951, 242 S.W.2d 331, 35 Tenn.App. 38 (that pedestrian exercised care).

Tex.—C. L. Holder Trucking Co. v. Anthony, 1973, 499 S.W.2d 738; Rinn v. Holmstrom, Civ.App.1951, 243 S.W.2d 862 (that entered intersection in exercise of care).

Utah.—Utah Rules of Evidence § 14 (depends upon probative force of foundation facts).

Va.—Yeary v. Holbrook, 198 S.E. 441, 171 Va. 266.

Wash.—Morris v. Chicago, M., St. P. & P. R. Co., 97 P.2d 119, 1 Wash. 2d 587, opinion adhered to 100 P. 2d 19, 1 Wash.2d 587; Chadwick v. Ek, 95 P.2d 398, 1 Wash.2d 117.

Wis.—Ernst v. Greenwald, 1967, 151 N.W.2d 706, 35 Wis.2d 763 (defendant's testimony that he had green light rebutted presumption of due care of plaintiff suffering from amnesia); Booth v. Frankenstein, 245 N.W. 191, 209 Wis. 362 (plaintiff's car on wrong side of highway); Philip v. Schlager, 253 N.W. 394, 214 Wis. 370.

Admission of statutory violation

In action where defendant's truck collided with rear of truck operated by plaintiff shortly after plaintiff had stopped it alongside curb, plaintiff having admitted his truck was not equipped with rear vision mirror was not entitled to benefit of statutory presumption of due care. Gen. St.1949, § 7836. Hawley v. Rivolta, 41 A.2d 104, 131 Conn. 540.

Statutory presumption as to statement taken from injured soon after injury

Although by statute, a statement secured from an injured person is presumably fraudulent if obtained within 30 days after such injuries were sustained, where evidence is introduced showing how the statement was obtained, the rebuttable presumption disappears, and questions thereafter are whether the statement was fraudulently obtained and the weight that should be given to it. Hillesheim v. Stippel, 1969, 166 N.W. 2d 325, 283 Minn. 59.

8. U.S.—Dubrock v. Interstate Motor Freight System, C.C.A.Pa., 143 F.2d 304, certiorari denied 65 S.Ct. 119, 323 U.S. 765, 89 L.Ed. 613 (burden of coming forward with evidence to meet presumption that decedent used due care and therefore presumably gave statutory signal was on defendant).

Cal.—Fietz v. Hubbard, 138 P.2d 315, 59 Cal.App.2d 124 (presumption of due care).

Ch. 417   PRESUMPTIONS AND INFERENCES   § 417.1

The federal rule [9] is that the presumption imposes on the party against whom it is directed the burden of going forward to rebut or meet the presumption, but that it does not shift the burden of persuasion.[10] However the federal rule also allows that the effect of a presumption respecting a fact which is an element of a claim or defense as to which state law supplies the rule of decision is determined in accordance with state law.[11]

It has been held frequently that there is no room for a presumption which is inconsistent with proven facts.[12] So, where the

Idaho.—Ineas v. Union Pac. R. Co., 241 P.2d 1178, 72 Idaho 390 (presumption of due care).

Iowa.—Webster v. Luckow, 258 N.W. 685, 219 Iowa 1048 (presumption of due care).

Mich.—Billingsley v. Gulick, 233 N.W. 225, 252 Mich. 235 (presumption of due care).

Minn.—Hack v. Johnson, 275 N.W. 381, 201 Minn. 9 (presumption of due care).

Pa.—Griffith v. Weiner, 95 A.2d 517, 373 Pa. 184 (presumption of due care).

Wash.—Sweazey v. Valley Transport, 107 P.2d 567, 6 Wash.2d 324, adhered to on rehearing 111 P.2d 1010, 6 Wash.2d 324, 140 A.L.R. 20 (testimony sufficient to rebut presumption of due care).

Wis.—Greene v. Farmers Mut. Auto. Ins. Co., 93 N.W.2d 431, 5 Wis.2d 551.

9. Federal Rules of Evidence § 301, 28 U.S.C.A.

10. Federal Rules of Evidence § 301, 28 U.S.C.A.

11. Federal Rules of Evidence § 302, 28 U.S.C.A.

12. **Cal.**—Ringo v. Johnson, 221 P. 2d 267, 99 Cal.App.2d 124 (where pedestrian's own testimony, though confused, showed that pedestrian was crossing street outside crosswalk, presumption of due care could not be invoked); Barry v. Maddalena, 146 P.2d 974, 63 Cal. App.2d 302 (uncontradicted facts outweighed the presumption that pedestrian was exercising ordinary care).

Ill.—Flynn v. Vancil, 242 N.E.2d 237, 41 Ill.2d 236 (rebuttable presumptions may be disputed and eliminated if they do not correspond with circumstances actually proved); Rzeszewski v. Barth, App. 1944, 58 N.E.2d 269, 324 Ill.App. 345.

Iowa.—Shannahan v. Borden Produce Co., 263 N.W. 39, 220 Iowa 702; Van Gorden v. City of Fort Dodge, 245 N.W. 736, 216 Iowa 209.

Kan.—Goodloe v. Jo-Mar Dairies Co., 185 P.2d 158, 163 Kan. 611 (pedestrian crossing between intersections).

Md.—Baltimore Transit Co. v. Swindell, 103 A. 566, 132 Md. 274 (evidence lamp not lighted as required overcomes presumption traffic officers performed their duty).

Mass.—Austin v. Eastern Massachusetts St. Ry. Co., 169 N.E. 484, 269 Mass. 420.

Mich.—O'Brien v. Loeb, 201 N.W. 488, 229 Mich. 405.

Miss.—Natchez Coca-Cola Bottling Co. v. Watson, 133 So. 677, 160 Miss. 173.

Neb.—Eden v. Klaas, 89 N.W.2d 74, 166 Neb. 354 (loss of memory of defendant); Anderson v. Nincehelser, 44 N.W.2d 518, 153 Neb. 329.

Pa.—Perry v. Ryback, 153 A. 770, 302 Pa. 559; Frank v. Reading Co.,

§ 417.1   TRIAL EVIDENCE   Ch. 417

circumstances of an automobile collision are fully testified to, the testimony controls, rather than a presumption deduced from such circumstances.[13] And it has been held that the presumption of due care does not apply in an automobile collision case where the driver or other person whose negligence is in issue testifies as to that person's actions at the time.[14]

However, presumptions are not overcome, as a matter of law, by evidence which is of a suspicious nature or is impeached to any extent, or by evidence which is contradictory or reasonably subject to contrary interpretation.[15] And it has also been stated

146 A. 598, 297 Pa. 233 (presumption opposed to physical facts); Lessig v. Reading Transit & Light Co., 113 A. 381, 270 Pa. 299.

Utah.—Tuttle v. Pacific Intermountain Exp. Co., 242 P.2d 764, 121 Utah 420 (where jury could reasonably find that decedent was driving his automobile in same direction as tractor-trailer and turned his automobile suddenly without warning into course of tractor-trailer when it was too late to avoid an accident and in so doing he did not use reasonable care for his own safety, presumption of due care on part of decedent was thereby destroyed and instructing jury thereon could only confuse rather than enlighten them, but that was not prejudicial in view of fact that court instructed that there was a presumption in absence of evidence to contrary and the defendant had burden of persuading them decedent was guilty of contributory negligence).

Wis.—Dekeyser v. Milwaukee Automobile Ins. Co., 1941, 295 N.W. 755, 236 Wis. 419.

13. **U.S.**—Clayton v. Burston, C.A. Tex.1974, 493 F.2d 429 (defendant, who adduced evidence that he had proceeded safely through stop sign, only to collide with plaintiff's blacked out vehicle, met Texas statutory presumption of failure to yield right-of-way, and, under Texas law, the presumption had vanished from case).

Cal.—Tyson v. Burton, 294 P. 750, 110 Cal.App. 428.

Conn.—Reetz v. Mansfield, 178 A. 53, 119 Conn. 563 (presumption that person behind steering wheel of automobile is controlling automobile not conclusive).

La.—Coffey v. Baham, App., 29 So. 2d 494 (where evidence established negligence of truck driver in veering to left of center of highway as overtaking automobile was about to pass truck, statutory provision imposing prima facie responsibility upon driver of overtaking automobile did not relieve truck owner of liability).

Mich.—Cebulak v. Lewis, 32 N.W.2d 21, 320 Mich. 710, 5 A.L.R.2d 186.

14. **Cal.**—Powley v. Appleby, 318 P.2d 712, 155 Cal.App.2d 727.

Ill.—Flynn v. Vancil, 1968, 242 N.E. 2d 237, 41 Ill.2d 236 (presumption is essentially inference as to existence of one fact from existence of some other basic fact established by the proof).

N.M.—Flanary v. Transport Trucking Stop, 1968, 438 P.2d 637, 78 N.M. 797 (inference is logical deduction from facts proven).

15. **Ky.**—Dixie-Ohio Exp. Co. v. Webb, 184 S.W.2d 361, 299 Ky. 201.

Evidence not overcoming presumption

The defendant's testimony that he saw no vehicle approaching intersec-

Ch. 417 PRESUMPTIONS AND INFERENCES § 417.1

that, before the presumption is so rebutted, the evidence of physical facts must be uncontroverted and wholly irreconcilable with the presumption of due care.[16]

A presumption, even if created by statute cannot overcome positive evidence to the contrary.[17]

From failure to produce evidence

Presumptions or inferences may be drawn against a party because of failure to produce evidence,[18] when such evidence is

tion when he was approximately at intersection of the curb lines did not overcome presumption of lawful operation by driver of other automobile involved in collision which had the right of way. General Exchange Ins. Co. v. Elizer, Ohio App., 31 N.E. 2d 147.

Rebuttal as jury issue

Presumption of following driver's negligence created by rear-end collision can be rebutted by evidence which is less than clear, positive and credible; and if the evidence is less than clear, positive and credible, question of whether such presumption has been overcome should be settled, on proper instructions, by the jury. Szymborski v. Slatina, 1970, 182 N.W.2d 723, 26 Mich.App. 538, affirmed 192 N.W.2d 213, 386 Mich. 339.

16. **U.S.**—U. S. v. Fotopulos, C.A. Cal., 180 F.2d 631.

Pa.—Fisher v. Hill, 66 A.2d 275, 362 Pa. 286.

17. **Colo.**—Sauers v. Stolz, 218 P. 2d 741, 121 Colo. 456 (presumption of simultaneous death of husband and wife overcome by lay witness testimony of body condition of both).

18. **U.S.**—Georgia Southern & F. Ry. Co. v. Perry, C.A.Fla., 326 F. 2d 921 (inference, which is subject to comment by court and counsel); Chicago, M., St. P. & P. R. Co. v. Slowik, C.A.Minn., 184 F.2d 920 (driver of plaintiff's automobile).

Conn.—Secondino v. New Haven Gas Co., 165 A.2d 598, 147 Conn. 672 (own doctor).

Ga.—Johnson v. Rooks, C.A.1967, 157 S.E.2d 527, 116 Ga.App. 394 (medical witness).

La.—Moore v. Skidmore, App.1974, 301 So.2d 428 (own passenger); Perigoni v. McNiece, App.1972, 262 So.2d 407 (where driver of following vehicle knew of pending action against him for injuries sustained by driver of forward vehicle when following driver's daughter struck him with pliers during altercation at intersection but did nothing to secure presence or testimony of other occupant of following vehicle even though her testimony might have been material, it would be assumed that her testimony would have been adverse); Wells v. Aguillard, App.1971, 244 So.2d 689 (where insurance adjuster was not called by defendant automobile liability insurer which asserted that one plaintiff had entered into compromise releasing insurer from all liability insofar as plaintiff was concerned, legal presumption was that adjuster's testimony would have been adverse to insurer); Jordon v. Travelers Ins. Co., App. 1970, 231 So.2d 678, writ issued 235 So.2d 95, 256 La. 65, 235 So. 2d 96, 256 La. 68; decree amended on other grounds, 245 So.2d 151, 257 La. 995 (doctors who treated, examined or diagnosed his condition); Marshall v. Southern Farm Bureau Cas. Co., 204 So.2d 665, writ refused 206 So.2d 711, 251 La.

860, certiorari denied 89 S.Ct. 189, 393 U.S. 883, 21 L.Ed.2d 158 (in wrongful death action brought by parents of deceased eight-year-old boy who was struck and killed by a motor vehicle, failure of parents to utilize testimony of deceased boy's companions who witnessed fatal accident or to explain absence of such companions).

Mo.—McInnis v. St. Louis-Southern, 1937, 108 S.W.2d 113, 341 Mo. 677 (own doctor).

Nev.—N.R.S. § 47.250(3) (if willfully suppressed).

N.Y.—Rice v. Ninacs, 1970, 312 N.Y. S.2d 246, 34 A.D.2d 388 (doctor who examined plaintiff on behalf of defendant was not called to testify).

S.C.—Canady v. Martschink Beer Distributors, Inc., 1970, 177 S.E.2d 475, 255 S.C. 119 (brother).

Tenn.—Bennett v. Duffle, 1947, 198 S.W.2d 287, 29 Tenn.App. 526.

Tex.—Douglas v. Vaughn, Civ.App., 416 S.W.2d 438 (where testimony of any interested witness is uncontradicted, is clear and positive, and there are no circumstances in evidence tending to discredit or impeach such testimony, conclusive effect may be given thereto and this rule is further strengthened where testimony of interested witness is corroborated by other witnesses and opposite party had means and opportunity of disproving testimony, if it were not true, and failed to do so).

Vt.—Choiniere v. Sulikowski, 229 A. 2d 305, 126 Vt. 274 (relatives of party are not considered to be equally available to his opponent even though relatives are present in court).

Wyo.—Marvel v. Pursel, 202 P.2d 656, 65 Wyo. 395 (patrolman who investigated accident).

Application of "availability" test

U.S.—Kean v. C. I. R., C.A.1972, 469 F.2d 1183 (determination of question of equal availability depends on all the facts and circumstances bearing on the witness' relation to the parties and not merely on his physical presence at trial or accessability for service of subpoena; the potential witness must be equally available both legally and practically); Tann v. Service Distributors, Inc., D.C.Pa.1972, 56 F.R.D. 593, affirmed C.A.3, 1973, 481 F.2d 1399 (could not be drawn from failure of defendant's expert to appear and testify in negligence action arising from collision, in view of fact that expert had been stricken with a grave illness and could not appear to testify).

La.—Fidelity & Cas. Co. of New York v. Employers Liability Assur. Corp., App.1967, 205 So.2d 623 (one police officer out of country, other no longer employed by city and whereabouts unknown).

Md.—Levin v. Arrabal, 1971, 272 A. 2d 818, 11 Md.App. 89 (principle that jury could infer that testimony of two physicians who were not called as witnesses by plaintiff would not be favorable toward plaintiff's case was not applicable where plaintiff explained that one physician had told him he was retired and would not be available for trial and that second physician had examined plaintiff some months before trial but not for the purpose of coming to court).

Pa.—Fenstermaker v. Bodamer, 171 A.2d 641, 195 Pa.Super. 436 (did not err in failing to instruct jury that it could draw inference where plaintiff introduced a letter from the doctor explaining that because of physical disability he would be unable to attend the trial, and court instructed that absence of witnesses was for jury based upon evidence it had heard on the matter).

R.I.—Benevides v. Canario, 1973, 301 A.2d 75, 111 R.I. 204 (where defendant testified that her husband who was passenger in her automobile was at place of trial Monday because they thought there was going to be trial that day but that he had to go back to Maryland Monday night before trial opened, it was for jury to determine whether such witness was available to his wife at time of trial).

Wis.—Schemenauer v. Traveler's Indem. Co., 149 N.W.2d 644, 34 Wis.2d 299 (witness' "availability" means within control, or power of, such party).

Conduct of other party defeating presumption

La.—White v. Employers Liability Assur. Corp., App.1968, 210 So.2d 580 (summoned by adverse attorney); Trahan v. Travelers Ins. Co., App.1970, 241 So.2d 609, writ refused 243 So.2d 274, 257 La. 607 (advised of intention to call the witness).

Rule limited

La.—Gauthier v. Henry, App.1971, 255 So.2d 378 (where suit was filed August 28, 1963, trial did not begin until June 24, 1969 and on that day plaintiff put on her case and called one officer who investigated accident but not second officer who had been subpoenaed and who also signed the report and case was recessed and did not begin again until May 12, 1970 and defendant put on all of her case, passage of time made second officer equally available to defendant and presumption that second officer would testify contrary to other officer would not lie); Feehan v. Travelers Ins. Co., App.1971, 251 So.2d 534 (where investigating officer came upon scene after vehicles had been moved and obtained statements only from drivers involved, officer was not a witness possessed of definite knowledge of material facts such that plaintiff's failure to call officer as witness might raise adverse presumption); Hebert v. Farrington, App.1968, 207 So.2d 789 (failure of defendants to request continuance for purpose of taking testimony of missing defense witness, whose testimony was not considered necessary by counsel to defendants' case, did not raise presumption); Aguillard v. Home Ins. Co., App. 1967, 203 So.2d 746, application denied 205 So.2d 440, 251 La. 672 (party must have known that the witness possessed useful information); Williams-McWilliams Industries, Inc. v. Bankers Fire & Marine Ins. Co., App., 121 So.2d 253 (in action by corporate owner of pickup truck against driver of automobile and her insurer for damage to pickup truck resulting from intersectional collision, where it was shown that driver of tractor van, which approached from automobile driver's left, resided in another state, and attorneys for defendants were advised as to name and address of driver, owner of truck was under no greater duty to produce van driver as witness than was owner of automobile or her insurer).

Md.—Jacobson v. Julian, 1967, 229 A.2d 108, 246 Md. 549 (not obligated to call persons listed as being "at or near the scene" in response to opponent's interrogatory).

Rule specially defined

Inference which may be drawn when a party fails to call a witness under his control is that the evidence already in may be taken most strongly against him, but jury may not infer that such a witness would, if called, testify unfavorably to the party who fails to call him. Gill v. Anderson, 1972, 333 N.Y.S.2d 49, 39 A.D.2d 941.

Sufficient presented deposition

Conn.—Sileo v. Curran, 1971, 290 A. 2d 325, 161 Conn. 572 (son was working in another state).

§ **417.1** TRIAL EVIDENCE Ch. 417

available to be produced,[19] and especially so when deemed to be under the control of the party.[20] In like manner the unexplained

19. **La.**—Sonnier v. Broussard, App. 1950, 44 So.2d 339 (witness in courtroom).

20. **La.**—U. S. Fidelity & Guaranty Co. v. Dixie Parking Service, Inc., App.1971, 248 So.2d 377, writ issued 252 So.2d 453, 259 La. 752, reversed on other grounds 262 So. 2d 365, 262 La. 45 (failure of parking attendant to appear as witness in suit against parking garage arising out of alleged oral contract of deposit made by the attendant for storage of mink stole which was stolen from automobile); Fackrell v. Gulley, App.1971, 246 So.2d 368 (that truck driver was operating within the course and scope of employment); Robinson v. Melton Truck Lines, Inc., App.1971, 244 So.2d 705 (failure of lessee of truck and lessee's insurer to call driver of truck); Sun Ins. Office, Limited v. Batiste, 1968, 205 So.2d 71, writ refused 206 So.2d 712, 251 La. 862 (relative of party).

Minn.—Fonda v. St. Paul City Ry. Co., 74 N.W. 166, 71 Minn. 438, 70 Am.St.Rep. 341 (failure to produce employee).

S.C.—Padgett v. Southern Ry. Co., 58 S.E.2d 895, 216 S.C. 487 (railroad's failure to call train crew); Robinson v. Duke Power Co., 48 S.E.2d 808, 213 S.C. 185 (defendant's bus driver).

Burden to show control

Minn.—Malik v. Johnson, 219 N.W.2d 631 (burden was on plaintiffs, who sought to have jury draw adverse inference from failure of defendant to call any of eight friends in attendance at party which defendant attended prior to time he was involved in accident, to show that witnesses were so close to defendant, who testified that he had consumed only 1½ cans of beer at party, as to fall into the "natural witness" category).

Deemed not under control

La.—Wolfe v. Employers Commercial Union Ins. Co., App.1973, 272 So. 2d 714 (where pedestrian in suit to recover against liability insurer of automobile which struck him had no control over or close relationship to the automobile driver, who was equally available as a witness to both plaintiff and defendant, plaintiff's failure to call the driver as a witness did not create a presumption that her testimony would have been unfavorable to plaintiff).

N.Y.—Potomac Ins. Co. v. Donovan, 112 N.Y.S.2d 714, 279 App.Div. 1135 (where events involved occurred six years before trial when employee was about fifteen).

Pa.—Bentivoglio v. Ralston, 1972, 288 A.2d 745, 447 Pa. 24 (plaintiff's doctors, known to defendant, not peculiarly within plaintiff's reach).

Wis.—Dawson v. Jost, 1967, 151 N.W. 2d 717, 35 Wis.2d 644 (daughter of party).

Not when equally accessible to both parties

Colo.—Oglesby v. Conger, 1972, 507 P.2d 883, 31 Colo.App. 504 (in view of fact that plaintiff could have called physician, who had examined her at request of defendant-motorist and who had been listed as possible witness for defendant-motorist, if she thought it would have been of benefit to her, presumption did not arise that, due to failure of defendant-motorist to call the physician, evidence from physician would have been unfavorable to defendant-motorist).

Conn.—Grillo v. Howe, 1967, 239 A. 2d 59, 4 Conn.Cir. 649 (where defendants did not produce one of defendants as witness after plaintiff had made out prima facie case and defendant was equally available to plaintiff and could have

failure of a party to testify may warrant an inference against that party.[21]

However, before failure to testify on one's own behalf may be held to establish the negative inference, there must be a duty to refute the evidence of the adversary.[22] Also, when a party has no knowledge or information concerning the subject matter, the failure to refute may not be considered as creating the inference.[23]

been compelled to testify and could have been examined to same extent as an adverse witness no inference was permissible).

Ill.—French v. City of Springfield, 1972, 283 N.E.2d 18, 5 Ill.App.3d 368 (jury could not infer from failure to call all police officers or agents of city who examined scene that their testimony would have been adverse to city as to street obstruction, especially since police officers and city employees were public officials who were equally available to both parties); Maradeo v. Chicago Transit Authority, 1950, 90 N.E.2d 795, 339 Ill.App. 646.

Plaintiff's wife

Where it appeared that plaintiff's wife was in peculiarly advantageous position to observe and testify as to plaintiff's disability earnings and effects of his prior disability and to dissociate his previous ailments from injuries sued on, it was not incumbent on defendant to show that plaintiff's wife was available to testify but duty of explaining her failure to testify rested on plaintiff. Lombardo v. Simko, 1965, 214 A.2d 911, 3 Conn.Cir. 363, certiorari denied 213 A.2d 526, 153 Conn. 724.

21. **Me.**—Berry v. Adams, 1950, 75 A.2d 461, 145 Me. 291.

Mich.—Dauer's Estate v. Zahel, 1969, 172 N.W.2d 701, 19 Mich.App. 198.

Pa.—Schwegel v. Goldberg, 1967, 228 A.2d 405, 209 Pa.Super. 280.

22. **Conn.**—Grillo v. Howe, 1967, 239 A.2d 59, 4 Conn.Cir. 649; Seney v. Trowbridge, 16 A.2d 573, 127 Conn. 284.

Ohio.—Hubbard v. Cleveland, Columbus & Cincinnati Highway, 76 N.E. 2d 721, 81 Ohio App. 445.

Pa.—Raffaele v. Andrews, 178 A.2d 847, 197 Pa.Super. 368 (no presumption or inference could arise against corporate defendant because of corporate defendant's failure to call its witnesses, where corporate defendant was satisfied that plaintiff had not met burden of proof and that therefore corporate defendant had no burden to meet).

R.I.—Enos v. W. T. Grant Co., 1972, 294 A.2d 201, 110 R.I. 523.

Tex.—Comet Motor Freight Lines v. Holmes, Civ.App.1947, 203 S.W.2d 233, (did not arise until after the party upon whom rests the burden of proof had made a prima facie case).

23. **U.S.**—Grady v. Kenny Ross Chevrolet Co., D.C.Pa.1972, 332 F. Supp. 689 (in action, based on theory of strict liability, by administrator of estate of passenger who died from monoxide poisoning in automobile almost year after such vehicle was sold by defendant dealer, adverse inference did not arise from refusal of dealer to call its expert witness where issue of case pertained to whether defects continued over period of year after vehicle was sold by dealer and expert, who had found defects in vehicle, had no knowledge with respect to such issue).

§ 417.1   TRIAL EVIDENCE   Ch. 417

Also, the failure of a party to the action to testify may not be considered against that party when evidence of other witnesses refutes the evidence.[24]

There also may be a presumption from a party's handling of potential physical evidence.[25]

Ga.—Maloy v. Dixon, 1972, 193 S.E. 2d 19, 127 Ga.App. 151 (statutory presumption was not applicable by reason of defendant's alleged failure to call a certain named witness where there was nothing in the record to reveal that such a witness existed or that any such witness knew anything of the matters in issue or was within the control or even in the employment of defendant).

Pa.—Shedlock v. Wyoming Valley Autobus Co., 17 A.2d 384, 340 Pa. 377.

24. U.S.—Kean v. C. I. R., C.A.9, 1972, 469 F.2d 1183.

La.—Saulter v. Cousin, 294 So.2d 251 (failure of plaintiff in reconvention to call his treating physicians did not raise presumptions that his injuries were not accident related and that such physicians would testify adversely to his interests, where he testified that his rib and dental injuries resulted from the accident, he was hospitalized for eight days, and the medical bills adequately corroborated the fact of his injury); Vicknair v. Home Indem., App.1973, 273 So.2d 542 (where there was nothing in the record to suggest that the injuries did not result from the accident, and where physician whose reports appeared in the record treated plaintiff for those injuries for over two years, so that it was not apparent how testimony or reports of first physician would have added anything to the record in the case); Jordan v. Kansas City Southern Ry. Co., App.1972, 260 So.2d 115 (where from facts indicated in record train engineer took all precautions necessary on approach to the cattle on railroad's right-of-way, court improperly inferred that railroad would have been hurt by testimony of nonappearing fireman, who was riding in locomotive with the engineer, since even if fireman testified that cattle in question were spotted a mile before collision duty of engineer would not have been appreciably changed); Harvey v. Kountz, App.1969, 218 So.2d 913, writ refused 221 So.2d 521, 253 La. 1093; Bagley v. Commercial Union Ins. Co. of New York, 1968, 216 So.2d 102.

Mass.—Murphy v. Moore, 51 N.E.2d 305, 314 Mass. 731.

25. U.S.—Cardullo v. General Motors Corp., D.C.Pa., 378 F.Supp. 890 (in action against automobile manufacturer, arising out of accident which allegedly resulted from defective manufacture, it was properly left to jury, under proper instructions, whether husband plaintiff was justified in disposing of damaged vehicle in order to collect insurance and whether he had offered satisfactory explanation for failure to preserve material evidence, notwithstanding contention that there was no showing that the evidence was under control of plaintiffs at time of trial).

Ga.—Glynn Plymouth, Inc. v. Davis, 1969, 170 S.E.2d 848, 120 Ga.App. 475, affirmed 173 S.E.2d 691, 226 Ga. 221, supplemented on other issue 175 S.E.2d 410, 121 Ga.App. 717 (fact that plaintiff suing manufacturer and retailer for death of purchaser of automobile was in possession of automobile after accident and disposed of automobile in another state prior to trial gave rise to presumption that examina-

Ch. 417 PRESUMPTIONS AND INFERENCES § 417.1

Presumption upon a presumption

Another general rule is that a presumption may not be based upon another presumption;[26] and it also is said that an inference may not be based upon a presumption,[27] or another inference.[28]

tion or tests upon automobile would have been negative, and question whether presumption had been rebutted was for jury).

N.J.—Scanlon v. General Motors Corp., Chevrolet Motor Division, 326 A.2d 673, 65 N.J. 582 (where plaintiff in products liability case failed to produce product or to offer any explanation or otherwise justify his failure to have done so, and product was produced by defendant manufacturer, trier of fact was free to draw inference, adverse to plaintiff, as to existence of defect).

Owned by another

U.S.—Sowicz v. U. S., D.C.Pa.1973, 368 F.Supp. 1165 (failure to produce or identify military serviceman's privately owned automobile, which, due to defective brakes, struck longshoreman when it was shoved into container for purposes of shipment and was subsequently shipped overseas, did not raise inference, in action by longshoreman to recover against Government under Federal Tort Claims Act, that data which could be obtained if automobile would have been available would have been detrimental to Government).

26. **Ala.**—Johnson v. Louisville & N. R. Co., 198 So. 350, 240 Ala. 219.

Ill.—Globe Acc. Ins. v. Gerisch, 45 N.E. 563, 163 Ill. 625, 54 Am.St. Rep. 486.

Kan.—Emigh v. Andrews, 191 P.2d 901, 164 Kan. 732.

Ohio.—New York, C. & St. L. R. Co. v. Bowles, 171 N.E. 844, 35 Ohio App. 145.

Okl.—Highway Const. Co. v. Shue, 49 P.2d 203, 173 Okl. 456; Star v. Brumley, 263 P. 1086, 129 Okl. 134.

Tenn.—Edenton v. McKelvey, 212 S. W.2d 616, 186 Tenn. 655; Gulf Refining Co. v. Frazier, 83 S.W.2d 285, 19 Tenn.App. 76.

Tex.—Carroll v. Ford Motor Co., Civ. App.1970, 462 S.W.2d 57; Polasek v. Quinius, 1969, 438 S.W.2d 828, error refused n. r. e.; Hamilton v. Newbury, Civ.App., 412 S.W.2d 801.

Vt.—Merrihew v. Goodspeed, 147 A. 346, 102 Vt. 206, 66 A.L.R. 1109.

Va.—Yeary v. Holbrook, 198 S.E. 441, 171 Va. 266.

27. **Minn.**—Jensen v. City of Duluth, 130 N.W.2d 515, 269 Minn. 241.

Pa.—Wenhold v. O'Dea, 1940, 12 A. 2d 115, 338 Pa. 33.

28. **U.S.**—Hall v. Atchison, T. & S. F. Ry. Co., D.C.Kan.1972, 349 F. Supp. 326.

Ariz.—Gipson v. E. D. Babbitt Motor Co., 1970, 478 P.2d 117, 13 Ariz. App. 502.

Fla.—Byrd v. Leach, App.1969, 226 So.2d 866 (no requirement existed, in relation to collision between minor pedestrian and truck, for driver to sound horn or veer his truck out of his traffic lane since it would be first necessary to infer that child was not aware of truck and danger, and that she would step into side of truck following its passage, and that driver knew or should have known this, after which second inference would have to be made to effect that blowing horn or veering truck

§ 417.2 Exercise of Care in General

Library References:
C.J.S. Evidence § 135; Motor Vehicles § 509 et seq.; Negligence §§ 204, 207.
West's Key No. Digests, Automobiles ⚖242; Evidence ⚖59; Negligence ⚖121.

In negligence cases, there ordinarily is no presumption that either party was or was not negligent.[29] Negligence will not be

would have been successful in preventing the accident; such proposition was barred by rule against pyramided inferences where first inference could not be said to have been established to exclusion of any other reasonable inference).

Ky.—Briner v. General Motors Corp., 1970, 461 S.W.2d 99.

N.Y.—David v. Granger, 1970, 312 N.Y.S.2d 963, 35 A.D.2d 636.

Tex.—Hamilton v. Newbury, Civ. App., 412 S.W.2d 801.

Vt.—Wellman v. Wales, 129 A. 317, 98 Vt. 437.

Va.—Johnson v. Richmond, F. & P. R. Co., 169 S.E. 603, 160 Va. 766 (inference of speed of train attempted from inference of sudden stop when thrown forward in seat).

29. **U.S.**—Van Wie v. U. S., D.C. Iowa, 77 F.Supp. 22.

Ark.—Arkmo Lumber Co. v. Luckett, 143 S.W.2d 1107, 201 Ark. 140.

Ariz.—Hall v. Wallace, 130 P.2d 36, 59 Ariz. 503.

Cal.—Nevarov v. Caldwell, 327 P.2d 111, 161 Cal.App.2d 762; Voorheis v. Hawthorne-Michaels Co., 312 P. 2d 51, 151 Cal.App.2d 688; Mosconi v. Ryan, 210 P.2d 259, 94 Cal. App. 227 (also no presumption of willful misconduct).

Colo.—Boulder Val. Coal Co. v. Jernberg, 197 P.2d 155, 118 Colo. 486.

Fla.—Johnson v. City of Jacksonville, 24 So.2d 717, 157 Fla. 14.

Ga.—Augusta Coach Co. v. Lee, 1967, 154 S.E.2d 689, 115 Ga.App. 511

(no presumption traffic does not stop when traffic light is green).

Ill.—Ulrich v. Rickert, 149 N.E.2d 341, 17 Ill.App.2d 185.

Ind.—Pennsylvania R. Co. v. Lytle, 34 N.E.2d 939, 109 Ind.App. 318.

Ky.—Herrin's Adm'x v. Jackson, 265 S.W.2d 775.

La.—Morales v. Employers' Liability Assur. Corporation, 12 So.2d 804, 202 La. 755.

Md.—Traish v. Hasan, 226 A.2d 573, 245 Md. 489 (where it appears that driver brought automobile to sudden stop because of some emergency, without giving warning to driver following at a reasonable distance, there is no presumption that rear driver was negligent unless he had the chance to stop after the necessity of stopping became apparent).

Neb.—Floyd v. Edwards, 1948, 33 N.W.2d 555, 150 Neb. 41 (as to pedestrian walking along street without sidewalk).

N.J.—Vanderbeek v. Conlon, 1956, 125 A.2d 531, 41 N.J.Super. 574 (no presumption officers at scene acted to provide adequate warning to public, so as to relieve one who caused dangerous condition).

N.Y.—Brown v. Klein, 245 N.Y.S. 654, 230 App.Div. 681 (finding of taxicab at the bottom of viaduct, where no showing is made that the deceased was a passenger and no showing that accident could not have happened without driver's negligence, did not raise an

Ch. 417 PRESUMPTIONS AND INFERENCES § 417.2

inferred or presumed from the mere fact that an accident has happened.[30]

inference that the fall was caused by the driver's negligence).

N.C.—Harward v. General Motors Corp., 68 S.E.2d 855, 235 N.C. 88.

N.D.—Durick v. Winters, 296 N.W. 744, 70 N.D. 592.

Ohio—Robinson v. Ferguson, 149 N.E.2d 152, 105 Ohio App. 311, reconsideration denied 152 N.E.2d 157, 105 Ohio App. 311.

Okl.—Barger v. Mizel, 424 P.2d 41 (cannot be inferred from owner's failure to advise another individual concerning a presumed inherent danger involved in casual operation of a particular type of automobile).

Pa.—Knox v. Simmerman, 151 A. 678, 301 Pa. 1.

Tex.—Parks v. Airline Motor Coaches, 193 S.W.2d 967, 145 Tex. 44 (would not be presumed that driver was guilty of violating the principles of the doctrine of discovered peril).

But see

In an action by a passenger, who is the guest of the host driver, it will be presumed that the host driver exercised the skill and judgment which he possessed in the management of his automobile. Saxby v. Cadigen, 63 N.W.2d 820, 266 Wis. 391.

30. See section 418.1 et seq. for discussion of exceptions under the rule of res ipsa loquitur.

Same statement in prior edition **cited by the court** in Kaatz v. State, Alaska, 1975, 540 P.2d 1037, 1045.

U.S.—Demers v. Railway Express Agency, C.C.A.Mass., 108 F.2d 107 (starting truck struck child who had been bending over and looking at ground in front of truck).

Cal.—Frediani v. Ota, 29 Cal.Rptr. 912, 215 Cal.App.2d 127 (intersection); Burnett v. Reyes, 256 P.2d 91, 118 Cal.App.2d Supp. 878 (re conduct of owner of animal upon the highway); Safirstein v. Nunes, 50 Cal.Rptr. 642, 241 Cal.App.2d 416 (even against unfavored driver at controlled intersection).

Conn.—Chasse v. Albert, 166 A.2d 148, 147 Conn. 680.

Del.—Lynch v. Lynch, 195 A. 799, 9 W.W.Harr. 1.

Fla.—Tackett v. Hartack, App., 98 So.2d 896; Mathers v. Botsford, 90 So. 375, 82 Fla. 497 (pedestrian knocked down in public highway).

Ga.—Hines v. Pair, 83 S.E.2d 857, 90 Ga.App. 653.

Ill.—Coulson v. Discerns, 66 N.E.2d 728, 329 Ill.App. 28 (seven year old boy killed while crossing road at point where there was no crosswalk); Roberts v. City of Rockford, 16 N.E.2d 568, 296 Ill.App. 469 (running across street in front of approaching traffic).

Ind.—La Noux v. Hagar, 1974, 308 N.E.2d 873 (struck bicycle).

Iowa—Barton v. Armstrong, 23 N.W. 2d 912, 237 Iowa 734.

Kan.—Abbott v. Howard, 219 P.2d 696, 169 Kan. 305 (re conduct of owner of animal on highway).

Ky.—F. H. Sammons Coal Co. v. Stamper, 356 S.W.2d 35.

La.—Larkin v. State Farm Mut. Auto. Ins. Co., 97 So.2d 389, 233 La. 544.

Me.—Bickford v. Berry, 196 A.2d 752, 160 Me. 9, opinion amended 199 A.2d 566, 160 Me. 132; Adams v. Richardson, 182 A. 11, 134 Me. 109 (striking animal); King v. Wolf Grocery Co., 137 A. 62, 126 Me. 202 (pedestrian struck by rear

91

§ 417.2   TRIAL EVIDENCE   Ch. 417

end of truck skidding when driver turned sharply).

Md.—Nicholson v. Kreczmer, 13 A.2d 596, 178 Md. 680 (pedestrian crossing at proper place, on foggy night).

Mass.—Spano v. Wilson Tisdale Co., 1972, 279 N.E.2d 725, 361 Mass. 209 (pedestrian case); Cousins v. Cummings, 127 N.E.2d 180, 332 Mass. 649 (collision with horse); Baker v. Davis, 12 N.E.2d 816, 299 Mass. 345 (stumbling and falling into path of automobile).

Mich.—Nagy v. Balogh, 61 N.W.2d 47, 337 Mich. 691 (minor pedestrian was run over by automobile).

Minn.—Hagsten v. Simberg, 44 N.W.2d 611, 232 Minn. 160.

Mo.—Pitts v. Garner, 321 S.W.2d 509; Herr v. Ruprecht, 331 S.W.2d 642.

Mont.—Nissen v. Johnson, 339 P.2d 651, 135 Mont. 329.

Neb.—Pongruber v. Patrick, 61 N.W.2d 578, 157 Neb. 799.

N.J.—Murphy v. Terzako, 82 A.2d 1, 14 N.J.Super. 254; Crisciotti v. Greatrex, 74 A.2d 611, 9 N.J.Super. 26.

N.Y.—Cole v. Swagler, 125 N.E.2d 592, 308 N.Y. 325.

N.C.—Winters v. Burch, 1973, 200 S.E.2d 55, 284 N.C. 205 (struck darting child); Lane v. Dorney, 113 S.E.2d 33, 252 N.C. 90 (failed to negotiate a curve); Gardner v. Black, 9 S.E.2d 10, 217 N.C. 573 (re conduct of owner of animal on highway).

N.D.—Vannett v. Cole, 170 N.W. 663, 41 N.D. 260.

Ohio.—Woodworth v. New York Cent. R. Co., 80 N.E.2d 142, 149 Ohio St. 543 (motorist, killed at railroad crossing, allegedly misled by flood lights at defendant manufacturer's plant).

Okl.—Agee v. Gant, 412 P.2d 155 (speed issue); Green v. Thompson, 344 P.2d 272 (speed issue); Champlin Refining Co. v. Cooper, 86 P.2d 61, 184 Okl. 153 (re conduct of owner of animal on highway).

Or.—Johnson v. Bennett, 357 P.2d 527, 225 Or. 213; Simpson v. Hillman, 97 P.2d 527, 163 Or. 357 (crossing at point other than pedestrian lane).

Pa.—Gist v. Allentown Wholesale Distributors, Inc., 158 A.2d 777, 398 Pa. 428 (driving on the wrong side of the street); Rennie v. Schepps, 146 A. 261, 297 Pa. 39 (re conduct of owner of animal on highway); Bloom v. Bailey, 141 A. 150, 292 Pa. 348, 57 A.L.R. 585 (head-on collision while rounding curve); Sgier v. Philadelphia & R. Ry. Co., 103 A. 730, 260 Pa. 343 (safety gate lowered at crossing).

S.C.—Turner v. Elrod, 148 S.E. 701, 151 S.C. 131 (striking animal).

S.D.—Larson v. Loucks, 6 N.W.2d 436, 69 S.D. 60.

Tenn.—Delaney v. Turner, 237 S.W.2d 965, 34 Tenn.App. 380.

Tex.—Renfroe v. Ramsey, Civ.App. 1972, 477 S.W.2d 648 (collision at intersection of paved and unpaved roads); Comet Motor Freight Lines v. Holmes, Civ.App., 175 S.W.2d 464, error refused (death of person claimed to have been struck by truck).

Va.—Grasty v. Tanner, 146 S.E.2d 252, 206 Va. 723 (gross negligence issue); Newton v. Carpenter, 117 S.E.2d 109, 202 Va. 347 (injuries sustained by seven-year-old boy on bicycle); Arnold v. Wood, 3 S.E.2d 374, 173 Va. 18 (decedent, according to truck driver, lunged beneath wheels of truck).

Wash.—Gaylord v. Schwartz, 281 P.2d 247, 46 Wash.2d 315 (boy toppling from bicycle).

Wis.—Klinzing v. Huck, 1970, 173 N.W.2d 159, 45 Wis.2d 458.

Ch. 417 PRESUMPTIONS AND INFERENCES § 417.2

It is often stated that the mere fact that an automobile skidded does not give rise to a presumption of negligence.[31] The

But see

Mass.—Olofson v. Kilgallon, 1973, 291 N.E.2d 600, 362 Mass. 803 (does not establish negligence on part of the defendant, even in a case where the defendant's vehicle strikes the plaintiff's vehicle in the rear, but a finding of negligence in such a case may be warranted on slight evidence of the circumstances).

Tex.—Miller v. Harrison, Civ.App. 1969, 446 S.W.2d 372 (on issue of whether defendant's automobile, which collided with plaintiff's motorcycle, was within or so close to intersection as to constitute immediate hazard, at time defendant undertook left turn, in absence of circumstances from which it could reasonably be concluded that cause of collision was something other than close proximity of vehicles, fact of collision would be conclusive of presence of danger of collision at that time).

31. U.S.—Miller v. Brazel, C.A. Colo., 300 F.2d 283; Halprin v. Mora, C.A.Pa., 231 F.2d 197 (Pennsylvania law).

Conn.—Grillo v. Bonauito, 193 A. 730, 123 Conn. 226 (intersectional collision); James v. Von Schuckman, 162 A. 3, 115 Conn. 490 (30 miles per hour on curve).

Ky.—Rose v. Vasseur, 320 S.W.2d 608; O'Neil & Hearne v. Bray's Adm'x, 90 S.W.2d 353, 262 Ky. 377 (ambulance skidded into parked automobile).

La.—Cosse v. Henley, App., 193 So. 206 (collision on a hill having slippery pavement); Leitz v. Rosenthal, App., 166 So. 651 (depends upon circumstances).

Md.—Wolfe v. State, for Use of Brown, 194 A. 832, 173 Md. 103 (head-on collision).

Mass.—Goyette v. Amor, 2 N.E.2d 219, 294 Mass. 355; Folan v. Price, 199 N.E. 320, 293 Mass. 76 (automobile skidded into tree).

Minn.—Hammond v. Minneapolis St. Ry. Co., 101 N.W.2d 441, 257 Minn. 330; Cohen v. Hirsch, 42 N.W.2d 51, 230 Minn. 512.

Mo.—Triplett v. Beeler, 268 S.W.2d 814; Annin v. Jackson, 100 S.W.2d 872, 340 Mo. 331 (automobile skidded into telephone pole).

N.M.—Zanolini v. Ferguson-Steere Motor Co., 265 P.2d 983, 58 N.M. 96 (on icy pavement).

N.Y.—Povol v. Storch, 196 N.Y.S.2d 309, 19 Misc.2d 559; Neumann v. Metropolitan Tobacco Co., 189 N.Y.S.2d 600, 20 Misc.2d 1013.

N.C.—Picklesimer v. Robbins, 1973, 198 S.E.2d 443, 19 N.C.App. 280.

Ohio.—Elfers v. Bright, 162 N.E.2d 535, 108 Ohio App. 495; Corriveau v. Defenbaugh, App., 91 N.E.2d 39.

Okl.—Keiffer v. Strbac, 349 P.2d 6.

Pa.—Cirquitella v. C. C. Callaghan, Inc., 200 A. 588, 331 Pa. 465 (rear-end collision); Wertz v. Shade, 182 A. 789, 121 Pa.Super. 4 (collision with parked truck).

R.I.—Luiz v. Ingram, 190 A. 439, 57 R.I. 428 (truck skidded into pedestrian); Peters v. United Electric Rys. Co., 189 A. 901, 57 R.I. 311 (bus skidded into pedestrian).

S.D.—Vaughn v. Payne, 63 N.W.2d 798, 75 S.D. 292; Zeigler v. Ryan, 271 N.W. 767, 65 S.D. 110 (automobile struck telephone pole).

Vt.—Johnson v. Burke, 183 A. 495, 108 Vt. 164 (automobile struck telephone pole).

Wash.—Cook v. Rafferty, 93 P.2d 376, 200 Wash. 234 (collision with oncoming vehicle); Gayson v. Daugherty, 66 P.2d 1148, 190

§ 417.2   TRIAL EVIDENCE   Ch. 417

same rule has had a limited application upon mere evidence of a tire blowout.[32] Although, an automobile sometimes stalls, the proof of such an event does not give rise to the inference that it would have been avoidable by the exercise of reasonable care.[33]

It will not be presumed that a person failed to keep a proper lookout;[34] and, in the absence of evidence of such failure, it will be presumed that a motorist exercised ordinary care to keep a proper lookout.[35] However, it is also frequently stated that one is presumed to have seen that which could and should have been

Wash. 133 (automobile struck signpost, which struck girl).

W.Va.—Boury v. Hamm, 1972, 190 S.E.2d 13, — W.Va. —.

Wis.—Olson v. Milwaukee Auto. Ins. Co., 62 N.W.2d 549, 266 Wis. 106, mandate modified on rehearing 63 N.W.2d 740, 266 Wis. 106 (driving on the wrong side of the street).

Contra

Where injured plaintiff, not a guest in defendant's automobile, has shown proof of "skidding and nothing more" under extraordinary conditions known to defendant, plaintiff would be deemed to have done enough to shift to defendant burden of proffering such evidence as is reasonably available to him, and if defendant fails to do this plaintiff goes to jury not simply on his own evidence of skid, but with added help of inference from defendant's failure to produce available evidence, and the combination meets plaintiff's burden of persuasion. Evans v. S. J. Groves & Sons Co., C.A.N.Y., 315 F.2d 335.

32. **Mich.**—Bobich v. Rogers, 241 N.W. 854, 258 Mich. 343.

Rule elaborated

Mo.—Kitchen v. Pratt, App., 324 S.W.2d 144 (rule that mere blowout of tire does not of itself constitute negligence applies only where evidence shows that skidding is sole factual cause of occurrence).

33. **Colo.**—Clune v. Mercereau, 1 P.2d 101, 89 Colo. 227.

34. **Ky.**—King's Adm'r v. Matthews, 257 S.W.2d 898; Cook v. Gillespie, 82 S.W.2d 347, 259 Ky. 281.

La.—Beckendorf v. Armour & Co., App., 56 So.2d 262.

Okl.—Green v. Thompson, 344 P.2d 272 (no presumption that a driver colliding at night with an unlighted object parked in his lane of traffic is guilty of negligence, regardless of the facts).

Tex.—Groendyke Transport Co. v. Dye, Civ.App., 259 S.W.2d 747.

35. **Cal.**—Reed v. Simpson, App., 189 P.2d 776, subsequent opinion 196 P.2d 895, 32 Cal.2d 444 (may be overcome by physical facts).

Mo.—Allen v. Kessler, 64 S.W.2d 630 (struck a pedestrian).

Ohio—McDonald v. Kelly, 134 N.E.2d 396, 101 Ohio App. 46.

Or.—Spence v. Rasmussen, 226 P.2d 819, 190 Or. 662 (bicyclist).

Va.—Hoffman v. Stuart, 59 S.E.2d 94, 190 Va. 880 (motorist killed in collision at "T" intersection).

Wis.—Ray v. Milwaukee Automobile Ins. Co., Limited Mutual, 283 N.W. 799, 230 Wis. 323.

Ch. 417　　PRESUMPTIONS AND INFERENCES　　§ 417.2

seen.[36] However, this rule has been held not applicable as to the view to the rear.[37]

36. U.S.—Kiner v. Northcutt, C.A. Colo.1970, 424 F.2d 222.

Cal.—Cucuk v. Payne, 1956, 296 P. 2d 7, 140 Cal.App.2d 881.

Colo.—Hernandez v. Ratliff, 1970, 470 P.2d 579, 172 Colo. 129 (motorist who looks but fails to see what is plainly visible is guilty of negligence, but to properly apply such rule, as matter of law, approaching vehicle must be plainly visible and view of it must be unobstructed).

Fla.—Central Truck Lines, Inc. v. Rogers, App.1962, 140 So.2d 130; Budgen v. Brady, App.1958, 103 So.2d 672.

Kan.—Morris v. Hoesch, 1970, 466 P.2d 272, 204 Kan. 735; Bottenberg Implement Co. v. Sheffield, 1951, 229 P.2d 1004, 171 Kan. 67 (conclusively presumed).

La.—Landry v. Meligan, App.1971, 245 So.2d 782 (charged with duty of seeing an obstruction in lane); Mabile v. Thibaut Farms, App. 1971, 244 So.2d 66; Wilhite v. Beavers, 1969, 227 So.2d 919; Reynolds v. Transamerica Ins. Co., App.1969, 221 So.2d 889; Naquin v. Callais, 1966, 191 So.2d 885 (that saw pedestrian); Carter v. Connecticut Fire Ins. Co., 1966, 189 So.2d 724 (that 12-yr. old saw oncoming traffic).

Mich.—Heckler v. Laing, 1 N.W.2d 484, 300 Mich. 139; Gallagher v. Walter, 299 N.W. 811, 299 Mich. 69.

Miss.—Pullin v. Nabors, 1961, 128 So. 2d 117, 240 Miss. 864 (presumed to perceive that red lights indicted a dangerous situation); Lee v. Reynolds, 1 So.2d 487, 190 Miss. 692 (nighttime with headlight beam of 500 feet).

N.Y.—New York Cent. R. Co. v. Campbell, 117 N.Y.S.2d 370, 203 Misc. 387 (railroad warning sign).

N.C.—Roberson v. City Coach Lines, 1970, 176 S.E.2d 359, 9 N.C.App. 450.

N.D.—Schuh v. Allery, 1973, 210 N. W.2d 96.

Ohio.—Laws v. Vance, 136 N.E.2d 134, 100 Ohio App. 255 (driver having statutory right of way at an intersection failed to observe vehicle approaching such intersection from driver's left).

S.D.—Cowan v. Dean, 137 N.W.2d 337, 81 S.D. 486 (pedestrian).

Tenn.—DeRossett v. Malone, 239 S. W.2d 366, 34 Tenn.App. 451 (pedestrian); Harbor v. Wallace, 211 S.W.2d 172, 31 Tenn.App. 1 (pedestrian).

Tex.—Berlanga v. Elizondo, Civ.App. 1971, 463 S.W.2d 757, error refused n. r. e. (not entitled to close eyes to what is visible); Turner v. Texas Co., 159 S.W.2d 112, 138 Tex. 380 (inference warranted).

Vt.—Hastings v. Soule, 100 A.2d 577, 118 Vt. 105 (backing onto highway); Smith v. Grove, 119 A.2d 880, 119 Vt. 106, followed in 119 A.2d 885, 119 Vt. 115.

Va.—Cook v. Shoulder, 105 S.E.2d 860, 200 Va. 281.

Wash.—Bleiler v. Wolff, 161 P.2d 145, 23 Wash.2d 368.

Wis.—Hafemann v. Milwaukee Auto. Ins. Co., 34 N.W.2d 809, 253 Wis. 540 (driver backing onto arterial highway would be presumed not to have looked, or to have heedlessly submitted himself to the danger).

37. U.S.—Sigman v. Van Gilder, D. C.Pa., 115 F.Supp. 366, affirmed, C.A., 207 F.2d 414 (rule cannot be applied with same result in case of

§ 417.2 TRIAL EVIDENCE Ch. 417

In the absence of evidence on the question, freedom from negligence will be presumed.[38] Especially it may be presumed that minors of tender age are free from negligence.[39]

a driver looking into rear view mirror to see what is on the road behind him).

38. U.S.—Todd County, Minn. v. Loegering, C.A.Minn.1961, 297 F. 2d 470; Dennler v. Dodge Transfer Corp., D.C.Conn., 201 F.Supp. 431; White v. State of Maryland, to Use of Anderson, C.C.A.Md., 106 F.2d 392; Abood v. Turner, C.C.A. Pa., 72 F.2d 880; Railway Express Agency v. Little, C.C.A.Pa., 50 F. 2d 59, 75 A.L.R. 963 (pedestrian crossing street).

Cal.—Tarasco v. Moyers, 1947, 185 P.2d 86, 81 Cal.App.2d 804 (that employee exercised care); Ribble v. Cook, 245 P.2d 593, 111 Cal.App. 2d 903 (bicyclist); Brooks v. E. J. Willig Truck Transp. Co., 243 P.2d 84, 110 Cal.App.2d 571, subsequent opinion 255 P.2d 802, 40 Cal.2d 669 (pedestrian hit at intersection); Duvall v. T. W. A., 219 P.2d 463, 98 Cal.App.2d 106 (inability of injured person to testify due to brain injury); Dennis v. Gonzales, 205 P. 2d 55, 91 Cal.App.2d 203 (pedestrian unable to remember); Sparrer v. Kersgard, 85 P.2d 449; Lowell v. Harris, 74 P.2d 551, 24 Cal. App.2d 70 (pedestrian); White v. Barker Bros., 55 P.2d 248, 12 Cal. App.2d 164 (guest); Swigert v. Pacific Electric Ry. Co., 47 P.2d 353, 7 Cal.App.2d 661 (presumed that all men are ordinarily careful in protecting themselves); Eastman v. Rabbeth, 17 P.2d 1009, 128 Cal. App. 534 (pedestrian used ordinary care for his safety and that in so doing he looked); Hauskins v. Buck Co., 298 P. 137, 113 Cal.App. 176 (injury to bicycle rider).

Conn.—Thomas v. Commerford, 1970, 268 A.2d 413, 28 Conn.Sup. 506.

Del.—Odgers v. Clark, 19 A.2d 724, 2 Terry 232.

Ill.—Goldstein v. Hertz Corp., 1974, 305 N.E.2d 617, 16 Ill.App.3d 89; Anderson v. Launer, 142 N.E.2d 838, 13 Ill.App.2d 530 (guest); Gillan v. Chicago, N. S. & M. R. Co., 117 N.E.2d 833, 1 Ill.App.2d 466 (guest who did nothing inferred exercising due care); Budek v. City of Chicago, 279 Ill.App. 410 (guest).

Iowa.—Lindloff v. Duecker, 251 N.W. 698, 217 Iowa 326.

Ky.—Illinois Cent. R. Co. v. Applegate's Adm'x, 105 S.W.2d 153, 268 Ky. 458.

Mass.—Herlihy v. Kane, 38 N.E.2d 620, 310 Mass. 457; Brown v. Henderson, 189 N.E. 41, 285 Mass. 192.

Mich.—Billingsley v. Gulick, 233 N. W. 225, 252 Mich. 235; Jenks v. Ingham County, 286 N.W. 93, 288 Mich. 600 (guest).

Mo.—Arnold v. Manzella, App., 186 S.W.2d 882; Borrson v. Missouri-Kansas-Texas R. Co., Sup., 161 S. W.2d 227 (presumption of fact, not of law); Thompson v. St. Louis-San Francisco Ry. Co., 69 S.W.2d 936, 334 Mo. 958.

Neb.—Costello v. Hild, 40 N.W.2d 228, 152 Neb. 1 (guest); Nichols v. Hablat, 1 N.W.2d 829, 140 Neb. 723, opinion set aside in part on other grounds 7 N.W.2d 84, 142 Neb. 534.

N.J.—Murphy v. Terzako, 1951, 82 A.2d 1, 14 N.J.Super. 254; McConachy v. Skalerew, 171 A. 817, 113 N.J.L. 17.

N.C.—Etheridge v. Etheridge, 24 S.E. 2d 477, 222 N.C. 616.

Ohio.—Shapiro v. Kilgore Cleaning & Storage Co., 156 N.E.2d 866, 108 Ohio App. 402; Bohnenkamp v. Hibberd, 41 N.E.2d 259, 70 Ohio

39. See note 39 on page 97.

App. 278 (alighting bus passenger struck by taxicab).

Or.—Evans v. General S. S. Corp., 349 P.2d 269, 220 Or. 476 (in action for injuries sustained by motorcycle policeman when he collided with taxicab door opened by passenger of taxicab which had stopped in traffic lane next to line of parked automobiles along side of street, in absence of evidence that there was sufficient space between the taxicab and the line of parked automobiles to have permitted taxicab passenger to depart on curb side of taxicab, court must assume that taxicab driver was obedient to demands of due care and stopped in such manner that passenger could have departed from curb side of taxicab); Waller v. Hill, 190 P.2d 147, 183 Or. 53 (guest passenger); Greenslitt v. Three Bros. Baking Co., 133 P.2d 597, 170 Or. 345.

Pa.—Grgona v. Rushton, 101 A.2d 768, 174 Pa.Super. 417 (pedestrian); Rutovitsky v. Magliocco, 147 A.2d 153, 394 Pa. 387 (pedestrian); Perry v. Ryback, 153 A. 770, 302 Pa. 559 (guest).

S.D.—Stratton v. Sioux Falls Traction System, 226 N.W. 644, 55 S.D. 464.

Tex.—Polasek v. Quinius, 1969, 438 S.W.2d 828, error refused n. r. e.; Lynch v. Ricketts, Civ.App., 306 S.W.2d 410, reformed 314 S.W.2d 273, 158 Tex. 487; Blunt v. H. G. Berning, Inc., Civ.App., 211 S.W.2d 773, writ of error refused n. r. e.

Va.—Yeary v. Holbrook, 1938, 198 S.E. 441, 171 Va. 266.

Wash.—Spokane County v. Great Northern Ry. Co., 35 P.2d 1, 178 Wash. 389; Geer v. Gellerman, 4 P.2d 641, 165 Wash. 10; Hirst v. Standard Oil Co. of California, 261 P. 405, 145 Wash. 597 (keeping within speed limit).

Wis.—Kreft v. Charles, 66 N.W.2d 618, 268 Wis. 44; Parr v. Douglas, 34 N.W.2d 229, 253 Wis. 311 (guest); Bohren v. Lautenschlager, 1 N.W.2d 792, 239 Wis. 400 (deceased driver); Ledvina v. Ebert, 296 N.W. 110, 237 Wis. 358 (death resulting from collision between automobile and truck).

As to absence of willful misconduct

A motorist driving with a friend would be presumed not to have been taking a chance of seriously injuring the friend or himself, as respects whether motorist was guilty of willful misconduct so as to be liable under guest statute. Sparrer v. Kersgard, Cal.Sup., 85 P.2d 449.

Assured clear distance statute

Okl.—Kraft Foods Co. v. Chadwell, 249 P.2d 1002, 207 Okl. 379.

But see

Ind.—Pennsylvania R. Co. v. Lytle, 34 N.E.2d 939, 109 Ind.App. 318 (no presumption that either party was or was not negligent); Atkinson v. Davis, 13 N.E.2d 355, 105 Ind.App. 375.

Pa.—Sadowski v. Eazor Exp., Inc., 1968, 249 A.2d 842, 213 Pa.Super. 471 (where dying driver of truck-tractor stated that he had to leave road to avoid being hit by defendant's vehicle, presumption that deceased driver exercised due care did not furnish proof as to where driver was on road when he observed defendant's vehicle).

Observance of law

Colo.—Thorpe v. City and County of Denver, 1971, 494 P.2d 129, 30 Colo.App. 284 (rebuttable presumption that deceased motorist, who entered intersection while traffic signals facing him were not illuminated and collided with a tractor-trailer vehicle proceeding across intersection with a green light, observed ordinance relating to entrance to intersection when traffic control signal is inoperative).

39. **U.S.**—Dulansky v. Iowa-Illinois Gas & Elec. Co., D.C.Iowa, 10 F.

§ 417.2 TRIAL EVIDENCE Ch. 417

In the absence of evidence to the contrary, it may be presumed that a motorist has complied with the traffic laws.[40]

R.D. 566 (in action for death of ten year old bicyclist, presumption against contributory negligence of a minor cast on company burden of producing evidence of capacity).

Ala.—Reaves v. Hoffman, 1938, 180 So. 600, 28 Ala.App. 188 (bicyclist).

Cal.—McCallum v. Howe, 243 P.2d 894, 110 Cal.App.2d 792.

Del.—Beggs v. Wilson, Del.1971, 272 A.2d 713 (facts which showed that 4½-year-old infant struck by defendant motorist was a typical child served only to buttress presumption that child of that age lacked capacity for contributory negligence, and in order to submit contributory negligence question to jury defendant would have had to introduce sufficient evidence from which jury could conclude that the child possessed perceptive abilities, development and judgment far greater than that of most children his age).

Fla.—Swindell v. Hellkamp, 1970, 242 So.2d 708 (four year, 7-month-old girl).

Iowa.—Hampton v. Burrell, 17 N.W. 2d 110, 236 Iowa 79 (six-year old boy).

Mass.—Friedman v. Berthiaume, 21 N.E.2d 261, 303 Mass. 159; Birch v. Strout, 20 N.E.2d 429, 303 Mass. 28 (girl crossing street); Capano v. Melchionno, 7 N.E.2d 593, 297 Mass. 1 (truck started off after driver saw pair of hands on tailboard, killing boy).

N.C.—Champion v. Waller, 1966, 150 S.E.2d 783, 268 N.C. 426 (13 yr.-old bicyclist).

Pa.—Moore v. Zimmerman, 1972, 292 A.2d 458, 221 Pa.Super. 359 (child struck while crossing street was unable to recall accident because of injuries sustained); Middleton v. Glenn, 143 A.2d 14, 393 Pa. 360 (bicyclist).

S.C.—Matthews v. Porter, 124 S.E.2d 321, 239 S.C. 620.

Tex.—Jennison v. Darnielle, Civ.App., 146 S.W.2d 788, error dismissed (child bicyclist).

Va.—Read v. Daniel, 91 S.E.2d 400, 197 Va. 853 (eight year old boy); American Tobacco Co. v. Harrison, 27 S.E.2d 181, 181 Va. 800 (evidence did not overcome presumption that 9 year old plaintiff could not be negligent).

Wis.—Straub v. Schadeberg, 10 N.W. 2d 146, 243 Wis. 257, 147 A.L.R. 476 (bicyclist).

40. **La.**—Hamilton v. Lee, App., 144 So. 249; Guinn v. Kemp, 136 So. 764, 18 La.App. 3; Willis v. Standard Oil Co. of Louisiana, 135 So. 777, 17 La.App. 217.

Neb.—Ripp v. Riesland, 104 N.W.2d 246, 170 Neb. 631; Nichols v. McArdle, 102 N.W.2d 848, 170 Neb. 382; Bell v. Crook, 97 N.W.2d 352, 168 Neb. 685, 74 A.L.R.2d 223.

N.D.—Austinson v. Kilpatrick, 105 N. W.2d 258.

Ohio.—General Exchange Ins. Co. v. Elizer, App., 31 N.E.2d 147.

Va.—Temple v. Ellington, 12 S.E.2d 826, 177 Va. 134.

As to giving of signal

Cal.—Renzetti v. Los Angeles Motor Coach Co., 119 P.2d 164, 48 Cal. App.2d 37.

Va.—Scott v. Cunningham, 171 S.E. 104, 161 Va. 367.

As to lawful speed

Ariz.—McCarthy v. Kenosha Auto Transport Corp., 411 P.2d 58, 2 Ariz.App. 620 (where there was testimony that speed of truck was under 50 miles per hour and witnesses gave credible reasons for their conclusions regarding speed, in absence of evidence regarding posted

Ch. 417 PRESUMPTIONS AND INFERENCES § 417.2

In the absence of evidence to the contrary, in a suit based upon negligent operation of an automobile, it will be presumed that the automobile was not in any respect defective.[41]

speed limit at point of accident on open highway it would be assumed that speed of truck was within lawful limits).

Cal.—Garrison v. Williams, 17 P.2d 1072, 128 Cal.App. 598.

N.D.—Norgart v. Hoselton, 39 N.W. 2d 427, 77 N.D. 1 (speed of 50 miles per hour on highway in open country was presumptively lawful).

Pa.—Ferne v. Chadderton, 30 West. 131.

Wis.—Olk v. Marquardt, 234 N.W. 723, 203 Wis. 479; Hamus v. Weber, 226 N.W. 392, 199 Wis. 320 (within posted limit).

41. **Cal.**—George v. Kleinbrodt, 23 Cal.Rptr. 822, 206 Cal.App.2d 224 (turn signal device issue).

La.—Giglio v. Toups, App.1939, 192 So. 553.

Mo.—Comstock v. Ingles, 296 S.W. 2d 68 (width of vehicle legal); Allen v. Kessler, Sup.1933, 64 S.W.2d 630.

Ohio.—Feiss v. Hensch, 162 N.E. 456, 28 Ohio App. 42.

Vt.—Ellison v. Colby, 8 A.2d 637, 110 Vt. 431.

Contra

Where defendant, driving for the first time, while descending a hill was unable to stop by reason of defective brakes and collided with plaintiff's automobile which was waiting for a traffic signal to change, and defendant offered no evidence of any inspection of the brakes, defendant could not rely on a presumption that the machine was safe and was liable for all damage proximately resulting. Sothoron v. West, 26 A.2d 16, 180 Md. 539.

Efficient brakes

Cal.—Hickambottom v. Cooper Transp. Co., 9 Cal.Rptr. 276, 186 Cal.App.2d 479 (presumed that equipment complied with the code requirements).

Colo.—Denver-Los Angeles Trucking Co. v. Ward, 164 P.2d 730, 114 Colo. 348 (that driver of truck-trailer stalled on icy hill kept his foot on brake pedal to prevent truck from rolling backward, did not give rise to inference that brakes were defective).

Lights adequate

Ga.—Rogers v. Johnson, 96 S.E.2d 285, 94 Ga. 666; Sumner v. Thomas, 33 S.E.2d 825, 72 Ga.App. 351.

Mo.—Cox v. Moore, 394 S.W.2d 65; Brown v. Wooderson, 362 S.W.2d 525.

Or.—Spence v. Rasmussen, 226 P.2d 819, 190 Or. 662 (reflectors on bicycle).

Tex.—Manning v. Block, Civ.App., 322 S.W.2d 651, writ of error refused n. r. e.

Vt.—Ellison v. Colby, 8 A.2d 637, 110 Vt. 431.

Wash.—Ebling v. Nielsen, 186 P. 887, 109 Wash. 355.

Contra

Conn.—Miles v. Sherman, 166 A. 250, 116 Conn. 678 (there is no presumption of law that vehicle is equipped with lights complying with statutory requirement).

Lights operative

U.S.—Reilly v. Dunnavant, C.A.Va., 200 F.2d 213.

Pa.—Newman v. Reinish, 163 A. 58, 106 Pa.Super. 351.

§ 417.2 TRIAL EVIDENCE Ch. 417

Also it has been presumed that a deceased did not commit suicide,[42] and that a motorist would not deliberately run into another vehicle.[43]

Nor will proximate cause be presumed from the fact of an injury alone.[44] However, one exception to this general rule

Vt.—Emerson v. Hickens, 164 A. 381, 105 Vt. 197.

Wash.—Hauswirth v. Pom-Arleau, 119 P.2d 674, 11 Wash.2d 354 (no presumption not burning).

But see

Police officer's testimony was insufficient to raise presumption that tail light on disabled truck-tractor was lit at any time. Parr v. Douglas, 34 N.W.2d 229, 253 Wis. 311.

Rule construed

If person is looking and does not see, a reasonable inference follows that signal lights on preceding automobile did not turn on, but the contrary is true when person who would have seen had he been looking testifies that he was not in fact looking. Turner v. McGee, 360 P.2d 383, 68 N.M. 191.

42. U.S.—Miller v. American Cas. Co. of Reading, Pa., C.A.Tenn.1967, 377 F.2d 479 (Tennessee law).

Ga.—Seaboard Coast Line R. Co. v. Clark, 1970, 176 S.E.2d 596, 122 Ga.App. 237 (presumed that deceased, who was lying near railroad tracks, and who was killed by train, did not assume his position near tracks voluntarily).

La.—Bunch v. Frezier, App.1970, 239 So.2d 680.

Miss.—State for Use and Benefit of Richardson v. Edgeworth, 1968, 214 So.2d 579 (is rebuttable).

Mo.—Zickefoose v. Thompson, 148 S.W.2d 784, 347 Mo. 579.

N.Y.—Rooney v. S. A. Healy Co., 1967, 281 N.Y.S.2d 321, 20 N.Y.2d 42, 228 N.E.2d 383.

N.D.—Trihub v. City of Minot, 23 N.W.2d 753, 74 N.D. 582.

Ohio.—Birmelin v. Gist, 120 N.E.2d 711, 162 Ohio St. 98.

S.C.—Smith v. Blackwell, 1967, 156 S.E.2d 867, 250 S.C. 170.

Does not disappear

Presumption against suicide is not evidence, but it does have probative or evidentiary value and does not just disappear when evidence is offered in opposition thereto. Life & Cas. Ins. Co. of Tenn. v. Daniel, 1968, 163 S.E.2d 577, 209 Va. 332.

43. Iowa.—Pazen v. Des Moines Transp. Co., 272 N.W. 126, 223 Iowa 23.

Wis.—Fitzpatrick v. Rice, 77 N.W.2d 515, 273 Wis. 201.

44. Mo.—Callanan v. United Rys. Co. of St. Louis, Sup., 232 S.W. 213; Battles v. United Rys. Co. of St. Louis, 161 S.W. 614, 178 Mo. App. 596.

N.C.—Whitson v. Frances, 83 S.E.2d 879, 240 N.C. 733.

S.C.—Lawrence v. Southern Ry.—Carolina Division, 1933, 167 S.E. 839, 169 S.C. 1.

Tex.—Rozner v. Harrell Drilling Co., Civ.App., 261 S.W.2d 190, ref. n. r. e.; Comet Motor Freight Lines v. Holmes, Civ.App., 175 S.W.2d 464, error refused (death of person claimed to have been struck by truck).

But see

If train was moving at excessive speed for that time and place, such fact may afford an inference of negligence as proximate cause of collision and consequent liability, where no question of contributory negligence of motorist is involved. Alabama Great Southern R. Co. v. Moundville Motor Co., 4 So.2d 305, 241 Ala. 633.

arises where a railroad fails to give the statutory signals at a crossing, the presumption being that this failure is the proximate cause of a collision with an automobile.[45] Statutes creating such a presumption of proximate cause of injury merely permit a plaintiff to establish a prima facie case by proof of failure to give such signals, which may be overcome by other evidence.[46]

If a collision occurs between the motor vehicle of a person driving on the wrong side of a highway, in violation of a statute, and that of one traveling in the opposite direction, the presumption might reasonably arise that the accident was proximately caused by the violation of the statute.[47]

It also has been held that evidence that the defendant motorist was under the influence of intoxicating liquors at the time of the accident raises a presumption of negligence and shifts to the defendant the burden of going forward with evidence to show that the intoxication was not a proximate cause.[48]

When presumption of negligence does arise

It must be presumed that every person knows and is aware of surroundings,[49] and of the condition of the vehicle.[50] One would be presumed to have known of the present visibility.[51]

A party's intent, knowledge, understanding, and consciousness are frequently important in determining fault or freedom

---

45. U.S.—Atlantic Coast Line R. Co. v. Ford, 1933, 53 S.Ct. 249, 287 U. S. 502, 77 L.Ed. 457.

S.C.—Cammer v. Atlantic Coast Line R. Co., 51 S.E.2d 174, 214 S.C. 71; Mishoe v. Atlantic Coast Line R. Co., 197 S.E. 97, 186 S.C. 402; Truett v. Atlantic Coast Line R. Co., 33 S.E.2d 396, 206 S.C. 114; Whitehead v. Atlantic Coast Line R. Co., 150 S.E. 769, 153 S.C. 339; McBride v. Atlantic Coast Line R. Co., 138 S.E. 803, 140 S.C. 260.

46. Mo.—Dobson v. St. Louis-San Francisco R. Co., 10 S.W.2d 528, 223 Mo.App. 812; Gann v. Chicago, R. I. & P. R. Co., 6 S.W.2d 39, 319 Mo. 214; Malone v. St. Louis-San Francisco R. Co., 285 S.W. 123, 220 Mo.App. 9.

47. U.S.—Willmore v. Hertz Corp., C.A.Mich.1971, 437 F.2d 357; Maxworthy v. Horn Elec. Service, Inc., D.C.Md.1970, 314 F.Supp. 899, affirmed C.A., 452 F.2d 1141.

S.C.—Tinsley v. Parris, 178 S.E. 496, 174 S.C. 412; Bowers v. Carolina Public Service Co., 145 S.E. 790, 148 S.C. 161.

48. Cal.—Christensen v. Harmonson, 247 P.2d 956, 113 Cal.App.2d 175.

49. Ga.—Stephens v. Tatum, 1955, 88 S.E.2d 456, 92 Ga.App. 256 (presumed familiar with the road).

Pa.—Stewart v. McGarvey, 1944, 34 A.2d 901, 348 Pa. 221.

50. N.M.—Ferran v. Jacquez, 362 P.2d 519, 68 N.M. 367 (owner presumed to know defective condition of brakes).

51. N.H.—L'Heureux v. Desmarais, 197 A. 327, 89 N.H. 237 (as lessened on rainy evening).

§ 417.2   TRIAL EVIDENCE   Ch. 417

from fault. One who performs an act which is known likely to produce a particular result is presumed to have intended that result,[52] and a motorist is presumed to have been conscious and aware of the reasonable and probable consequences of the particular conduct, until overturning the presumption with proof to the contrary.[53] However, there is no inference or presumption that one knew facts which are not of common knowledge, or are not determined by observation.[54]

A party will be presumed to know the law.[55] However it also has been held that the presumption that one knows the law could not be charged against a child.[56]

---

52. **Vt.**—Benway v. Hooper, 8 A.2d 658, 110 Vt. 497.

But see

Inference that motorist intentionally drove off highway at high speed, causing injury to himself and his two passengers, could not be reached on the basis of expert testimony alone relating to the physical facts of the accident; thus, the motorist's insurer's offer of proof, tending to show that the automobile was traveling at 40 to 45 miles per hour when it left highway, that it traveled at a speed of up to 100 miles per hour thereafter, and that it pursued an unswerving path until it came to rest, was properly excluded, and the question of motorist's intent was properly refused submission to the jury. McDonnell v. Hestnes, 1970, 177 N.W. 2d 845, 47 Wis.2d 553.

53. **Ill.**—McKinney v. Evans, 164 N. E.2d 822, 24 Ill.App.2d 447 (farmer was fatally injured when crushed against barn door by truck being backed up by defendant who raced his motor and backed up with his wheels spinning, defendant was presumed to know that when the wheels got traction the vehicle would suddenly move backward).

Mass.—McKnight v. Red Cab Co., 64 N.E.2d 433, 319 Mass. 64 (taxicab operator presumed to know the danger of an insecurely fastened door).

Tenn.—Richards v. Parks, 93 S.W.2d 639, 19 Tenn.App. 615.

Owner knew of intended use of vehicle on highway

It would be presumed that owner knew that automobile was going to be used on public highway when he loaned it to his son unless, as a matter of defense, it was shown affirmatively that some different use was contemplated. Ferran v. Jacquez, 362 P.2d 519, 68 N.M. 367.

54. **Cal.**—Katz v. Kuppin, 112 P.2d 681, 44 Cal.App.2d 406 (plaintiffs' testimony that defendant became angry when requested by plaintiffs to decelerate speed did not justify inference that she acted with knowledge that such speed would probably lead to injuries to plaintiffs and herself under circumstances, the presumption being otherwise).

Tenn.—J. Avery Bryan, Inc. v. Hubbard, 225 S.W.2d 282, 32 Tenn. App. 648 (custom of pedestrians to cross only at intersections).

55. **Tex.**—Travelers Ins. Co. v. Warren, 1969, 447 S.W.2d 698, error refused n. r. e. (that a claim must be filed within six months after accident).

As to authority over highway closing

Operator of tractor trailer who did not see sign posted by highway commissioner and sustained injuries as

---

56. See note 56 on page 103.

However, negligence has been presumed in cases involving violations of law.[57] This rule has been held applicable to viola-

result of defective highway was presumed to know the law and that the state could invoke statute relating to closing highways for construction or repairs whenever state finds it necessary to reconstruct or repair highway. Rodgers v. Cox, 36 A.2d 373, 130 Conn. 616.

Including law of another state

Where insurer issued commercial type truck policy, with unlimited trip radius, on truck, which was owned by Minnesota corporation, insurer was on notice that truck might be operated in Kentucky and was presumed to have knowledge of Kentucky's state laws relating to registration and licensing. Cotner v. Grissley, Ky.1969, 447 S.W.2d 603.

56. N.Y.—Dugan v. Dieber, 1969, 302 N.Y.S.2d 423, 32 A.D.2d 815 (although an adult is presumed to know the law, 5½-year-old child could not be charged, as matter of law, with such knowledge and understanding of New York City Traffic Regulations and be held to comply with them, so that charge was not merely confusing to jury but also contained prejudicial error where such instruction charged the contents of these regulations to the jury and submitted to them an issue whether the child knew and understood the regulations and nevertheless violated them).

57. U.S.—Shulins v. New England Ins. Co., C.A.Vt., 360 F.2d 781 (under Vermont law, the violation of a highway safety statute may be considered as prima facie evidence of negligence); Texas Mut. Ins. Co. v. Curtin, C.A.La., 197 F.2d 617 (pedestrian crossing as light changed).

Cal.—De Ruiz v. Jack Rudy Trucking Co., 341 P.2d 388, 171 Cal.App. 2d 609.

Fla.—Booth v. Mary Carter Paint Co., 182 So.2d 292.

Ind.—Pitts v. Stewart, 186 N.E.2d 800, 138 Ind.App. 102, rehearing 201 N.E.2d 833, cause remanded 208 N.E.2d 468, on remand 211 N.E. 2d 781.

La.—Ard v. Fidelity & Cas. Co. of New York, App., 148 So.2d 905; Codifer v. Occhipinti, App., 57 So. 2d 697 (left-hand turn).

Me.—Gamache v. Cosco, 87 A.2d 509, 147 Me. 333 (left-turn at intersection); Bennett v. Lufkin, 85 A.2d 922, 147 Me. 216 (passing at intersection); Collins v. Kelley, 179 A. 65, 133 Me. 410 (right of way); Fitts v. Marquis, 140 A. 909, 127 Me. 75 (right of way statute).

Minn.—Lynghaug v. Payte, 76 N.W. 2d 660, 247 Minn. 186, 56 A.L.R.2d 1090; Landeen v. De Jung, 17 N.W. 2d 648, 219 Minn. 287 (violation of statute requiring motorist to give appropriate signal of intention to stop).

Ohio.—McLain v. Ford, 184 N.E.2d 530, 115 Ohio App. 69; Moody v. Vickers, 72 N.E.2d 280, 79 Ohio App. 218 (pedestrian crossing street elsewhere than at crossway).

Or.—Barnum v. Williams, 1972, 504 P.2d 122, 264 Or. 71.

Vt.—Purington v. Newton, 49 A.2d 98, 114 Vt. 490; Palmer v. Marceille, 175 A. 31, 106 Vt. 500.

Only creates inference

Fla.—Bryant v. Swarts, 1969, 227 So. 2d 715 (violation of traffic statute or ordinance is prima facie evidence of negligence that may be overcome by other facts and circumstances, but it does not create presumption of negligence).

§ 417.2 TRIAL EVIDENCE Ch. 417

tions of regulations relating to the law of the road,[58] right of

58. **U.S.**—Ward v. McDan Dav Leasing Corp., D.C.Pa.1972, 340 F.Supp. 86 (rebutted by evidence that tire blew out due to striking a piece of steel on roadway); Maxworthy v. Horn Elec. Service, Inc., D.C.Md. 1970, 314 F.Supp. 899, affirmed C. A., 452 F.2d 1141 (under Maryland law).

Cal.—Scott v. Mackey, 324 P.2d 703, 159 Cal.App.2d 690; Temple v. De Mirjian, 125 P.2d 544, 51 Cal.App. 2d 559 (presumption remained as evidence).

Colo.—Ankeny v. Talbot, 250 P.2d 1019, 126 Colo. 313; Drake v. Hodges, 161 P.2d 338, 114 Colo. 10.

Ill.—Calvetti v. Seipp, 216 N.E.2d 497, 70 Ill.App.2d 58.

Ky.—Gross v. Barrett, 350 S.W.2d 457; Smith v. Sizemore, 300 S.W. 2d 225.

La.—Mistich v. Matthaei, App.1973, 277 So.2d 239 (crossed neutral ground and struck automobile proceeding inbound in inbound lane); Rollins v. New York Fire & Marine Underwriters, Inc., App.1969, 225 So.2d 663, writ refused 227 So.2d 595, 254 La. 855; United Services Automobile Ass'n v. Sullen, 1969, 224 So.2d 849; Stewart v. Bixler, App.1969, 222 So.2d 653 (where automobile of defendant driver was in its proper lane of travel at moment of headon collision, a presumption of fault was imposed on plaintiffs); Pittman v. Fowler, App., 191 So.2d 172 (necessitated decision under legal presumption that defendant driver of vehicle crosswise in lane of traffic occupied by plaintiff was the one at fault); Lambert v. U. S. Fire Ins. Co., App., 148 So.2d 406, writ refused 150 So.2d 588, 244 La. 127 (14-year-old boy who rides his bicycle into opposite lane of highway in face of approaching traffic).

Me.—Atherton v. Crandlemire, 33 A. 2d 303, 140 Me. 28; Coombs v. Markley, 143 A. 261, 127 Me. 335 (but his presence on that side may be explained or justified).

Md.—Miller v. Mullenix, 176 A.2d 203, 227 Md. 229 (ordinarily, mere violation of rule of road is not negligence per se, but driver who fails to comply with statute requiring drivers to keep to right is prima facie negligent when violation directly and proximately causes collision, and driver then has burden to overcome presumption of negligence by showing justification); Sun Cab Co. v. Cusick, 121 A.2d 188, 209 Md. 354; Campbell v. State, to Use of Dix, 100 A.2d 798, 203 Md. 338 (is strong evidence of negligence, where such violation proximately caused collision with another vehicle, and burden is on him to show that condition of road or a traffic emergency caused him to be rightfully on left side of road).

Mass.—Goodale v. Morrison, 180 N. E.2d 67, 343 Mass. 607 (in actions by guests against host for injuries suffered in collision in New Hampshire, that in absence of evidence explaining host's action, crossing of yellow line was only some evidence of host's negligence).

Mo.—Berry v. Harmon, 323 S.W.2d 691; Evans v. Colombo, App., 311 S.W.2d 141, appeal transferred to 319 S.W.2d 549.

Neb.—Becks v. Schuster, 48 N.W.2d 67, 154 Neb. 360.

N.Y.—Betts v. Queens Farms Dairy Co., 295 N.Y.S. 78, 162 Misc. 583 (tractor and trailer swerved into approaching automobile which was approximately three feet from curb of boulevard to right of automobile).

N.C.—Anderson v. Webb, 148 S.E.2d 846, 267 N.C. 745 (may rebut infer-

way,[59] speed,[60] parking,[61] inadequate brakes,[62] and lights.[63]

ence by evidence of cause other than negligence).

Okl.—Clark v. Hawkins, 321 P.2d 648; Garner v. Myers, 318 P.2d 410.

Pa.—Keba v. Pickett, 1969, 252 A.2d 675, 434 Pa. 148; Smail v. Flock, 180 A.2d 59, 407 Pa. 148; Benner v. Weaver, 147 A.2d 388, 394 Pa. 503; Kotal v. Goldberg, 100 A.2d 630, 375 Pa. 397.

Tenn.—American Trust & Banking Co. v. Parsons, 108 S.W.2d 187, 21 Tenn.App. 202.

Utah.—Wood v. Strevell-Paterson Hardware Co., 313 P.2d 800, 6 Utah 2d 340.

Vt.—Larmay v. VanEtten, 1971, 278 A.2d 736, 129 Vt. 368 (and upon failure of defendant to offer any countervailing evidence or to explain her manner of operating her vehicle, it was proper to grant plaintiff's motion for a directed verdict as to liability).

Va.—Spiegelman v. Birch, 129 S.E.2d 119, 204 Va. 96 (hit pedestrian); Early v. Mathena, 124 S.E.2d 183, 203 Va. 330; Bedget v. Lewin, 118 S.E.2d 650, 202 Va. 535 (after plaintiff makes prima face case of negligence in being on wrong side of road and defendant produces explanation, plaintiff has ultimate burden to prove negligence.

Wash.—Wilson v. Wright, 329 P.2d 461, 52 Wash.2d 805; Lee & Eastes v. Continental Carriers, 265 P.2d 257, 44 Wash.2d 28; Weaver v. Windust, 80 P.2d 766, 195 Wash. 240 (due to skidding).

Wis.—Geis v. Hirth, 146 N.W.2d 459, 32 Wis.2d 580 (inference of negligence unless it was shown that such was beyond her control); Voigt v. Voigt, 126 N.W.2d 543, 22 Wis.2d 573 (overcomes presumption that deceased driver exercised due care for own safety); Zeinemann v. Gasser, 29 N.W.2d 49, 251 Wis. 238 (unless it is shown that presence there was beyond driver's control).

Wyo.—Wallis v. Nauman, 157 P.2d 285, 61 Wyo. 231 (where automobile skids across center line of road to left side thereof and collides with another automobile, the skidding in itself is not ordinarily evidence of negligence, but burden is upon driver on the wrong side of road to excuse or justify such violation).

Contra where swerved to avoid hazard

Pa.—Wolf v. Needleman, 218 A.2d 321, 421 Pa. 113 (swerved to avoid plaintiff infant who ran into street).

Vehicle using center lane

In action by guest of automobile driver against truck driver, who just prior to collision was driving in center lane which was not allocated exclusively to traffic moving in his direction and from which lane he could not make a left turn, for injuries sustained in collision on a three lane highway, evidence was sufficient to give rise to an inference of negligence on part of truck driver proximately contributing to happening of accident, and granting of nonsuit was erroneous. Reese v. Day, 281 P.2d 263, 131 Cal.App.2d 730.

59. **Cal.**—Ornales v. Wigger, 218 P. 2d 531, 35 Cal.2d 474 (right of way of pedestrian at crosswalk).

Me.—Gregware v. Poliquin, 190 A. 811, 135 Me. 139.

Vt.—Dashnow v. Myers, 155 A.2d 859, 121 Vt. 273.

60. **U.S.**—Petersen v. Klos, C.A. Miss.1970, 426 F.2d 199, amended

61. See note 61 on page 106.
62. See note 62 on page 107.
63. See note 63 on page 107.

§ 417.2 TRIAL EVIDENCE Ch. 417

on other issues 433 F.2d 911 (negligence per se under Mississippi law).

Ala.—Whittaker v. Walker, 135 So. 185, 223 Ala. 167 (that defendant was driving automobile at fifty miles per hour held prima facie negligence only).

Ariz.—Ruiz v. Faulkner, 1970, 470 P.2d 500, 12 Ariz.App. 352.

Cal.—Faselli v. Southern Pac. Co., 310 P.2d 698, 150 Cal.App.2d 644 (party charging negligence has burden of proving negligence even though there is proof of speed in excess of statutory prima facie limit); Lowery v. Hallett, 287 P. 110, 105 Cal.App. 84 (held presumption strengthened by silence of defendant at trial).

Conn.—Radwick v. Goldstein, 98 A. 583, 90 Conn. 701.

Fla.—Bessett v. Hackett, 66 So.2d 694; Florida Motor Lines, Inc., v. Ward, 137 So. 163, 102 Fla. 1105.

Idaho.—Dawson v. Salt Lake Hardware Co., 136 P.2d 733, 64 Idaho 666 (speed at an obstructed intersection); Brixey v. Craig, 288 P. 152, 49 Idaho 319.

Ind.—Miles v. State, 129 N.E. 10, 189 Ind. 691.

Ky.—Thompson v. Shutz, 217 S.W.2d 315, 309 Ky. 253; Knecht v. Buckshorn, 25 S.W.2d 727, 233 Ky. 329.

La.—McDaniel v. Walker, App., 111 So.2d 208 (driving at grossly excessive rate of speed created presumption of fault and responsibility).

Minn.—Butler v. Engel, 68 N.W.2d 226, 243 Minn. 317; Hustvet v. Kuusinen, 238 N.W. 330, 184 Minn. 222 (rebuttable character of presumption).

Miss.—Walker v. Dickerson, 184 So. 438, 183 Miss. 642 (driving with one light).

Mo.—Leek v. Dillard, App., 304 S.W. 2d 60.

N.Y.—Gibson v. State, 19 N.Y.S.2d 405, 173 Misc. 893, affirmed 21 N.Y.S.2d 362, 259 App.Div. 1104.

Ohio.—Solomon v. Mote, App., 49 N.E.2d 703.

Or.—Elliott v. Callan, 1970, 466 P.2d 600, 255 Or. 256 (driver of automobile which struck child at school crossing was entitled to show that in spite of fact that he was traveling in excess of designated speed he was nevertheless exercising due care under particular circumstances); Mercer v. Risberg, 188 P.2d 632, 182 Or. 526.

S.D.—Frager v. Tomlinson, 57 N.W. 2d 618, 74 S.D. 607.

Vt.—Le Clair v. Bruley, 122 A.2d 742, 119 Vt. 164, 67 A.L.R.2d 89; Labrecque v. American News Co., 58 A.2d 873, 115 Vt. 305 (tractor towing hay baler extending laterally beyond lights).

61. Cal.—Kline v. Barkett, 158 P.2d 51, 68 Cal.App.2d 765 (that defendant's tractor-trailer angled onto four-lane highway, blocking most of outer lane, established prima facie case of violation of parking statute, and burden was on defendant to prove that it was not practicable to park off highway); Barry v. Bruce, 19 Cal.Rptr. 518, 200 Cal.App.2d 335 (stopped automobile on main traveled portion of road at night without lights).

La.—Odom v. Texas Farm Products Co., 1969, 229 So.2d 118 (on the traveled portion of a highway); Smith v. Henry, App., 147 So.2d 416, application not considered 149 So.2d 766, 243 La. 1013.

Me.—Baker v. McGary Transp. Co., 36 A.2d 6, 140 Me. 190 (car parked partly on highway without lights).

Neb.—Huston v. Robinson, 13 N.W. 2d 885, 144 Neb. 553.

Ch. 417   PRESUMPTIONS AND INFERENCES   § 417.2

In some cases it has been held that, so far as excessive speed is concerned, it does *presumptively* show that a motor vehicle was being driven at an unreasonable and an improper rate of speed; and, in the absence of other evidence to overcome it, the presumption is accepted as a fact established,[64] and becomes conclusive in absence of other evidence to contradict and overcome it.[65] However, it also has been held that a state law or ordinance which limits a motorist's speed to a reasonable and proper rate, having regard to the traffic, the use of the way, etc., presents a rule of evidence only, and that excess speed is not presumptive negligence.[66]

The rule, creating prima facie negligence or a presumption of negligence, has been applied against a motorist who executes a turn,[67] suddenly turns to the left side of the road while being passed,[68] and against a motorist who overtakes and rearends the

N.C.—Melton v. Crotts, 125 S.E.2d 396, 257 N.C. 121.

Vt.—Le Clair v. Bruley, 122 A.2d 742, 119 Vt. 164, 67 A.L.R.2d 89; Farren v. McMahon, 1 A.2d 726, 110 Vt. 55; Hall v. Royce, 192 A. 193, 109 Vt. 99.

62. **U.S.**—Mills v. U. S., D.C.D.C. 1969, 297 F.Supp. 972 (showing that brakes of defendant's vehicle collapsed and failed is sufficient to justify inference of negligence on defendant's part and burden shifts to him to go forward).

Cal.—Dutcher v. Weber, 1969, 80 Cal. Rptr. 378, 275 Cal.App.2d 961; Alcorn v. Davies, 1959, 343 P.2d 621, 173 Cal.App.2d 569 (instruction mere happening not negligence was error).

Conn.—Eddy v. McAninch, 347 P.2d 499, 141 Colo. 223 (presumption arises that failure of brakes to operate resulted from want of due care, and in absence of evidence sufficient to overcome such presumption, injured party is entitled to recover).

Ind.—Smith v. Glesing, 1969, 248 N.E.2d 366, 145 Ind.App. 11.

63. **U.S.**—Sweeney v. Bonacci, C.A. Pa., 173 F.2d 541.

64. **Conn.**—Radwick v. Goldstein, 98 A. 583, 90 Conn. 701.

Idaho.—Hughes v. Hudelson, 169 P. 2d 712, 67 Idaho 10.

Ky.—Knecht v. Buckshorn, 25 S.W. 2d 727, 233 Ky. 329.

65. **Cal.**—Lowery v. Hallett, 287 P. 110, 105 Cal.App. 84.

66. **Ohio.**—Allen v. Leavick, 182 N. E. 139, 43 Ohio App. 100.

67. **La.**—Bourque v. Haycock, App. 1971, 243 So.2d 108 (could not remember signalling).

68. **La.**—Grinnel Mut. Reinsurance Co. v. Rich, App.1971, 251 So.2d 450, application denied 253 So.2d 222, 259 La. 898 (changing lanes abruptly, then rear-ended).

Neb.—Bixby v. Ayers, 298 N.W. 533, 139 Neb. 652.

§ **417.2** TRIAL EVIDENCE Ch. 417

vehicle ahead,[69] leaves the roadway,[70] strikes a parked vehicle,[71]

69. **U.S.**—Allstate Ins. Co. v. Alterman Transport Lines, Inc., C.A.Fla. 1972, 465 F.2d 710 (under Florida law); DiGregorio v. Industrial Supply Corp. of Orlando, C.A.Fla. 1971, 438 F.2d 303 (but such presumption is not evidence and has no probative value and is not to be charged to jury); Goudeau v. Christ, D.C.La.1971, 325 F.Supp. 1154.

Cal.—Merry v. Knudsen Creamer Co., 1949, 211 P.2d 905, 94 Cal.App.2d 715 (stopped for traffic light).

Colo.—Lesondak v. O'Hara, 483 P.2d 417, —— Colo.App. —— (where driver is without fault and is struck in rear by following automobile); Oldham v. Roman, 1970, 474 P.2d 169, —— Colo.App. —— (that following motorist began to slow down when he first saw an unidentifiable object without lights before him and attempted a panic stop when he determined that the object was an automobile stopped in center of right lane of 70-mile per hour highway in darkness and without lights, all of which occurred within a span of two to three seconds, overcame any presumption of negligence for violation of statute regarding passing on left).

Fla.—Lincoln v. Miggins, App.1971, 249 So.2d 88; Holden v. Dye, App. 1969, 224 So.2d 350; Busbee v. Quarrier, App., 172 So.2d 17 (where there is no direct testimony available and facts are such as to raise reasonable inference that operator of leading vehicle was exercising due care); Rianhard v. Rice, App., 119 So.2d 730 (is dissipated upon the introduction of the evidence reflecting due care on the part of the driver of the overtaking vehicle).

Ill.—Nielsen v. Pyles, 54 N.E.2d 753, 322 Ill.App. 574 (stopped at traffic signal).

Iowa.—Harvey v. Borg, 257 N.W. 190, 218 Iowa 1228 (inference arises that careful driver would not rearend vehicle ahead).

La.—Welch v. Thomas, App.1972, 263 So.2d 427, writ denied 266 So.2d 434, 262 La. 1132, and 266 So.2d 436, 262 La. 1137, and 266 So.2d 438, 262 La. 1143 (on the theory that either he has failed in responsibility to maintain a sharp lookout to events taking place before him, or that he was following at an insufficient distance from the preceding vehicle to allow him to safely stop under normal conditions); Hightower v. Dixie Auto Ins. Co., App.1971, 247 So.2d 912; Strother v. State Farm Mut. Auto. Ins. Co., 1970, 238 So.2d 774; Coates v. Marcello, App.1970, 235 So.2d 162.

Mich.—Spillers v. Simons, 1972, 201 N.W.2d 374, 42 Mich.App. 101; Corbin v. Yellow Cab Co., 84 N.W. 2d 775, 349 Mich. 434 (negligence of overtaking vehicle was not open to question); Gordon v. Hartwick, 39 N.W.2d 61, 325 Mich. 534.

Minn.—Bowe v. Fredlund, 1972, 203 N.W.2d 327, 295 Minn. 103 (may suggest negligence as matter of law).

Mo.—Boresow v. Manzella, 330 S.W. 2d 827; Jones v. Austin, App., 154 S.W.2d 378 (stopped for traffic signal); Hollensbe v. Pevely Dairy Co., App., 38 S.W.2d 273 (inference of excessive speed or insufficient effort to control).

Ohio.—Beauchamp v. B. & L. Motor Freight, Inc., 152 N.E.2d 334, 106 Ohio App. 530 (vehicle ahead was proceeding in a careful manner along public highway).

R.I.—Maklar v. Greene, 1970, 261 A. 2d 15, 106 R.I. 405; Heath v. Cook,

70. See note 70 on page 110.

71. See note 71 on page 110.

68 A. 427 (came up behind plaintiff on a bicycle).

Tex.—Boddy v. Canteau, Civ.App. 1969, 441 S.W.2d 906, error refused n. r. e.; Manning v. Block, Civ. App., 322 S.W.2d 651, writ of error refused n. r. e. (collision itself is some evidence of negligence).

But see

Mere occurrence of a rear-end collision does not constitute negligence as a matter of law, nor is any particular act of negligence attributable to a driver who drives into the rear of another vehicle, and specific acts of negligence must be proved. O'Neill v. Craig, Tex.Civ.App.1973, 493 S.W. 2d 898, certiorari denied 94 S.Ct. 1418, 415 U.S. 919, 39 L.Ed.2d 474.

Contra

U.S.—Zink v. Radewald, C.A.Ind., 369 F.2d 253.

Mass.—Buda v. Foley, 19 N.E.2d 537, 302 Mass. 411.

Pa.—Meek v. Allen, 58 A.2d 370, 162 Pa.Super. 495; Cirquitella v. C. C. Callaghan, Inc., 200 A. 588, 331 Pa. 465.

Contra where leading vehicle stopped suddenly

La.—Porter v. Barron, App., 185 So. 2d 304.

Md.—Brehm v. Lorenz, 112 A.2d 475, 206 Md. 500 (where driver suddenly stopped because of emergency, without giving any warning to driver following at reasonable distance, there is no presumption that rear driver was negligent, unless he had chance to stop after necessity of stopping became apparent).

Even where also rear-ended by third vehicle

Evidence that defendant's truck hit plaintiffs' automobile from behind after truck had been hit from behind by a light automobile was not sufficient, as matter of law, to rebut presumption of negligence which arises against operator of overtaking vehicle in rear-end collision with vehicle properly stopped at intersection or traffic light. Bell's Fish & Poultry Co. v. Jenkins, Fla.App.1969, 227 So. 2d 512.

Rebuttable

Fla.—Railway Exp. Agency, Inc. v. Garland, App.1972, 269 So.2d 708 (that bus was improperly stopped in center lane of expressway in order to pick up box which had fallen from truck was sufficient to overcome presumption that driver of second truck which struck bus in rear was negligent); Keyser v. Brunette, App., 188 So.2d 840 (evidence indicated that automobile in which plaintiff had been guest passenger had passed defendant's automobile and then slowed or completely stopped when driver became apprehensive about colliding with third automobile which had pulled onto highway).

Mich.—Lucas v. Carson, 1972, 196 N. W.2d 819, 38 Mich.App. 552 (evidence required to rebut as matter of law the statutory presumption that a motorist who collides with the rear end of another vehicle traveling ahead and in the same direction is negligent should be positive, unequivocal, strong and credible).

Relevant factors

Time and distance available to overtaking driver are necessary factors in determining whether fact of rear-end collision gives rise to an inference of negligence on his part. Lichtenberg v. Hug, Mo.App.1972, 481 S.W.2d 527.

Rule held inapplicable

U.S.—Mikolajczyk v. Allcutt, C.C.A. Pa., 102 F.2d 82 (inapplicable in absence of evidence showing whether truck was, when struck, moving forward, standing still or moving backward).

Colo.—Mahoney v. Crow, App.1974, 516 P.2d 658 (where there was un-

§ 417.2   TRIAL EVIDENCE   Ch. 417

drives while under the influence of liquor,[72] or who falls asleep.[73]

contradicted evidence that defendant crossed only after proper signal in order to pass and that accident occurred only after plaintiff also crossed into northbound lane).

Ind.—Dimmick v. Follis, App., 111 N.E.2d 486.

La.—Bailey v. Moore, App.1973, 276 So.2d 708 (where forward vehicle is struck from rear as result of making sudden, unsignaled lane change); Grinnell Mut. Reinsurance Co. v. Rich, App.1971, 251 So. 2d 450, application denied 253 So. 2d 222, 259 La. 898; Anthony v. State Farm Mut. Ins. Co., App. 1969, 227 So.2d 180 (driver of forward automobile attempted a change of traffic lanes at time when it was unsafe to do so).

Rule limited

Mass.—Warren v. Howe, 124 N.E.2d 250, 332 Mass. 213 (rear end collision without evidence of attending circumstances is not proof of negligence of operator of either vehicle, but slight evidence of the circumstances may place the fault); Glennon v. Boston Elevated Ry. Co., 146 N.E. 250, 251 Mass. 103 (restricted to when squarely in front).

70. Ky.—Haragan v. American Federation of Grain Millers Intern., AFL–CIO, 1969, 445 S.W.2d 131 (when motorist runs off road, he is called on to demonstrate that his action in doing so was not brought about through his negligence).

La.—Ardoin v. State Farm Mut. Auto. Ins. Co., App.1974, 302 So.2d 372.

N.Y.—Cromwell v. Rodriguez, 1971, 319 N.Y.S.2d 1014, 66 Misc.2d 243 (if unanswered, was sufficient to support motion for accelerated judgment in favor of pedestrian); Schwartz v. Sar Corp., 195 N.Y.S. 2d 496, 19 Misc.2d 660, reversed 195 N.Y.S.2d 819, 9 A.D.2d 910 (backing onto sidewalk and against pedestrian).

71. La.—Keystone Auto. Club Cas. Co. v. Indemnity Ins. Co. of North America, App., 117 So.2d 308.

72. U.S.—McConville v. U. S., C.A. N.Y., 197 F.2d 680, certiorari denied 73 S.Ct. 172, 344 U.S. 877, 97 L.Ed. 679.

Cal.—Christensen v. Harmonson, 247 P.2d 956, 113 Cal.App.2d 175.

La.—Bourg v. Aetna Cas. & Sur. Co., App., 77 So.2d 131 (where driver and passenger embarked on prearranged party and drank continuously for over ten hours, and driver remembered nothing from time shortly after leaving saloon until after fatal accident, inference was compelling that driver was under influence of liquor to extent that his ability was impaired).

Statutory presumption limited to criminal prosecution

U.S.—Bach v. Penn Central Transp. Co., C.A.Ohio 1974, 502 F.2d 1117.

Ariz.—Mattingly v. Eisenberg, 285 P. 2d 174, 79 Ariz. 135 (statutory presumption that a driver is under influence if there is .15% or more alcohol in his blood creates a rule of evidence in criminal prosecution of persons charged with driving while under influence of intoxicating liquor, but does not apply to civil cases, and instruction on this statute, in civil automobile accident case, was reversible error as a comment upon evidence).

La.—Brown v. Collins, 1969, 223 So. 2d 453.

N.J.—Raponotti v. Burnt-Mill Arms Inc., 1971, 273 A.2d 372, 113 N.J. Super. 173.

73. Del.—Diamond State Tel. Co. v. Hunter, 21 A.2d 286, 2 Terry 336.

Ch. 417 PRESUMPTIONS AND INFERENCES § 417.2

And it has been held that a presumption or prima facie negligence arises against a motorist in a variety of other factual instances.[74]

Unexplained occasion of a runaway vehicle raises an inference or presumption of negligence.[75]

An inference or presumption of negligence by an owner or custodian of an animal may arise from the fact it is unattended

Me.—Gendron v. Gendron, 69 A.2d 668, 144 Me. 347.

N.Y.—Stanley v. Burnside, 192 N.Y. S.2d 452, 20 Misc.2d 932.

74. U.S.—James v. U. S., Service Fire Ins. Co. of N. Y., Intervenor, D.C.La., 151 F.Supp. 404, affirmed, C.A., 252 F.2d 687 (running into object blocking highway).

Cal.—Owens v. Carmichael's U-Drive Autos, Inc., 2 P.2d 580, 116 Cal. App. 348 (permitting unlicensed person to drive).

Ga.—English v. Georgia Power Co., 17 S.E.2d 891, 66 Ga.App. 363 (driving on the wrong side of the street).

Iowa.—Kuehn v. Jenkins, 100 N.W.2d 610, 251 Iowa 718 (if a motorist drives on left-hand side of roadway, a fair inference arises that he has not been properly watchful).

Me.—Rouse v. Scott, 164 A. 872, 132 Me. 22 (passing to left of the intersection of the medial lines of the ways).

Md.—Longenecker v. Zanghi, 2 A.2d 20, 175 Md. 307 (aproaching intersection at 35 to 40 miles per hour).

Ohio.—Washabaugh v. Kaiser, 120 N. E.2d 325, —— Ohio App. —— (backing auto without sounding warning).

Pa.—Dougherty v. O'Connell, 4 Chest. 143 (where injured in broad daylight by a defect in the highway which is easily observable).

Vt.—Furgat v. Brooks, 1970, 272 A.2d 125, 129 Vt. 98 (violation of statute relating to signals upon changing direction or speed).

75. U.S.—Endler v. U. S., D.C.Pa., 101 F.Supp. 332 (unless driver produces evidence which is believed by the trier of fact that explains the accident the trier of fact has a right to believe that the driver was negligent).

Cal.—Fedler v. Hygelund, 235 P.2d 247, 106 Cal.App.2d 480.

Mass.—McFarlane v. McCourt, 2 N.E. 2d 1017, 295 Mass. 85 (automobile rolled from driveway at side of house into street after having been parked in garage).

N.J.—Barbanes v. Brown, 163 A. 148, 110 N.J.L. 6 (tended to show that defendant left in the car two small, mischievous and irresponsible children who, seated on the front seat, played and meddled with the machine and jumped out before the car started to run down the hill); Sheridan v. Arrow Sanitary Laundry Co., 146 A. 191, 105 N.J.L. 608.

Indicates wheels not turned to curb

N.C.—Watts v. Watts, 113 S.E.2d 720, 252 N.C. 352; Arnett v. Yeago, 100 S.E.2d 855, 247 N.C. 356 (when automobile started downhill with three year old child in front seat sitting under steering wheel with feet hanging out of open left hand front door automobile went straight down the street three or four car lengths before it turned to left into another yard permitted reasonable inference that motorist when parking automobile did not turn its front wheels to curb or side, in violation of statute, constituting negligence per se).

111

§ 417.2   TRIAL EVIDENCE   Ch. 417

on the highway.[76] The rule is more applicable when the proof shows that the condition in which an unattended animal was left constituted a violation of a statute.[77]

No-eyewitness rule

In the absence of any evidence as to the conduct of one deceased, in most jurisdictions, in view of the instinct of self-preservation, there is a presumption that such person was in the exercise of ordinary care at the time of an automobile accident.[78]

---

76. Cal.—Kenney v. Antonetti, 295 P. 341, 211 Cal. 336.

Ky.—Sparks v. Doe, 379 S.W.2d 252 (jury question of negligence).

La.—Primeaux v. Kinney, App.1971, 256 So.2d 140, writ not considered 258 So.2d 87, 260 La. 1065 (defendant successfully rebutted statutory presumption of fault).

N.J.—Pincus v. Sublett, 97 A.2d 712, 26 N.J.Super. 188; Sheridan v. Arrow Sanitary Laundry Co., 146 A. 191, 105 N.J.L. 608.

N.Y.—Doherty v. Sweetser, 31 N.Y. S. 649, 82 Hun. 556.

Tex.—Dorman v. Cook, Civ.App., 262 S.W.2d 744, writ of error dismissed.

Vt.—Wright v. Shedd, 177 A.2d 240, 122 Vt. 475 (inference that horses had made their way onto highway from open gate at point along highway where accident took place was entitled to stand against horse owner until evidence that horses were stabled or pastured elsewhere was forthcoming).

77. La.—Salvant v. Estate of Frank Newfield, Inc., 128 So. 320, 13 La. App. 410.

78. U.S.—Gebhardt v. Wilson Freight Forwarding Co., C.A.Pa., 348 F.2d 129 (under Pennsylvania law); Northern Pac. Ry. Co. v. Haugan, C.A.Minn., 184 F.2d 472; Chicago Rock Island & Pacific R. Co. v. Consumers Cooperative Association, C.A.Kan., 180 F.2d 900, certiorari denied 71 S.Ct. 42, 340 U.S. 813, 95 L.Ed. 598 (Kansas law); Peterson v. Sheridan, C.C.A. Iowa, 115 F.2d 121; Bell v. Shoff, C.C.A.Pa., 89 F.2d 339 (pedestrian crossing highway); Kriesak v. Crowe, D.C.Pa., 44 F.Supp. 636, affirmed 131 F.2d 1023 (pedestrian, without explanation, lying on highway when struck and killed).

Ala.—Griffin Lumber Co. v. Harper, 39 So.2d 399, 252 Ala. 93.

Ariz.—Robledo v. Kopp, 409 P.2d 288, 99 Ariz. 367.

Cal.—Orbach v. Zern, 291 P.2d 120, 138 Cal.App.2d 178 (to be assumed that pedestrian in crossing highway looked in the direction in which danger was to be apprehended and that having such an unobstructed view she saw the defendant's automobile and no others approaching, and that after having observed the distance and speed, judged that she had a safe interval for crossing); Chambers v. Spada, 283 P.2d 1067, 133 Cal.App. 2d 231 (operative unless dispelled by uncontradicted testimony which is wholly irreconcilable with presumption); Blackwell v. American Film Co., 209 P. 999, 189 Cal. 689 (conduct of passenger); Rios v. Bennett, 200 P.2d 73, 88 Cal.App. 2d 919 (presumed that pedestrian looked before stepping into street); Wright v. Sniffin, 181 P.2d 675, 80 Cal.App.2d 358 (despite evidence that infant bicyclist failed to give warning of intention to cross highway); Duehren v. Stewart, 102 P.2d 784, 39 Cal.App.2d 201 (pedestrian struck at intersection);

Cannon v. Kemper, 73 P.2d 268, 23 Cal.App.2d 239 (pedestrian walking along highway).

Del.—Vietri v. Ruggerio, 194 A.2d 46, 6 Storey 511; Gray v. Pennsylvania R. Co., 139 A. 66, 3 W.W. Harr. 450.

Fla.—Ritter v. Brengle, 185 So.2d 7.

Idaho.—Larsen v. Jerome Co-op. Creamery, 283 P.2d 1096, 76 Idaho 439.

Ill.—National Bank of Mattoon v. Hanley, 155 N.E.2d 318, 20 Ill.App. 2d 191; Campbell v. Ragel, 129 N.E.2d 451, 7 Ill.App.2d 301.

Iowa.—Weppler v. Smith, 108 N.W. 2d 247, 252 Iowa 679; Turbot v. Repp, 72 N.W.2d 565, 247 Iowa 69; Ruble v. Carr, 59 N.W.2d 228, 244 Iowa 990.

Kan.—Townsend v. Jones, 331 P.2d 890, 183 Kan. 543; Finch v. Phillips, 326 P.2d 763, 183 Kan. 219; Thummel v. Kansas State Highway Commission, 164 P.2d 72, 160 Kan. 532 (death from washout in highway).

Ky.—Downing v. Baucom's Adm'x, 287 S.W. 362, 216 Ky. 108.

Me.—Ward v. Cumberland County Power & Light Co., 187 A. 527, 134 Me. 430 (collision with trolley car); Stone v. Roger, 154 A. 73, 130 Me. 512; Sturtevant v. Ouellette, 140 A. 368, 126 Me. 558.

Md.—Gresham v. Commissioner of Motor Vehicles, 1970, 260 A.2d 649, 256 Md. 500 (that pedestrian was in crosswalk and had favorable light); Sheriff Motor Co. v. State for Use of Parker, 179 A. 508, 169 Md. 79 (pedestrian crossing street).

Mass.—Lucier v. Norcross, 37 N.E.2d 498, 310 Mass. 213, 137 A.L.R. 749; Wanamaker v. Shaw, 2 N.E.2d 209, 294 Mass. 416.

Mich.—Kohl v. Marin, 78 N.W.2d 621, 346 Mich. 693; Holtz v. L. J. Beal & Son, Inc., 63 N.W.2d 627, 339 Mich. 235 (presumption held immaterial).

Minn.—Steinhaus v. Adamson, 1972, 201 N.W.2d 264, 294 Minn. 387; Aubin v. Duluth St. R. Co., 211 N.W. 580, 169 Minn. 342.

Mo.—Ruby v. Clark, 208 S.W.2d 251, 358 Mo. 318 (death of pedestrian); Sanford v. Gideon-Anderson Co., App., 31 S.W.2d 580 (riding on running board).

Neb.—Price v. King, 72 N.W.2d 603, 161 Neb. 123; Anderson v. Nincehelser, 43 N.W.2d 182, 152 Neb. 857 (person assisting sheriff in setting up road block).

N.J.—Joyce v. Englehart, 153 A. 96, 9 N.J.Misc. 168; Klein v. Offen, 136 A. 419, 5 N.J.Misc. 357.

N.M.—Griego v. Conwell, 222 P.2d 606, 54 N.M. 287.

N.D.—Quam v. Wengert, 86 N.W.2d 741.

Ohio.—Leach v. Nanna, 135 N.E.2d 451, 100 Ohio App. 26 (pedestrian); Bush v. Harvey Transfer Co., 67 N.E.2d 851, 146 Ohio St. 657 (guest killed in rear-end collision); Meier v. Joseph R. Peebles Sons Co., 11 N.E.2d 707, 57 Ohio App. 80 (pedestrian crossing street).

Pa.—Lear v. Shirk's Motor Exp. Corp., 152 A.2d 883, 397 Pa. 144 (rebuttable); Schofield v. King, 130 A.2d 93, 388 Pa. 132 (rebuttable); Pantazis v. Follweiler, 73 A.2d 410, 364 Pa. 553 (pedestrian crossing highway in front of home at night); Scholl v. Philadelphia Suburban Transp. Co., 51 A.2d 732, 356 Pa. 217 (railroad crossing collision); Atkinson v. Coskey, 47 A.2d 156, 354 Pa. 297 (presumed pedestrian looked before crossing street); Di Gregorio v. Skinner, 41 A.2d 649, 351 Pa. 441 (though decedent crossed street between intersections); De Santis v. Maddalon, 35 A.2d 72, 348 Pa. 296 (pedestrian struck by taxicab at night).

§ 417.2 TRIAL EVIDENCE Ch. 417

S.D.—Vaughn v. Payne, 63 N.W.2d 798, 75 S.D. 292 (presumption not overcome).

Tex.—North Tex. Producers Ass'n v. Stringer, Civ.App., 346 S.W.2d 500; Groendyke Transport Co. v. Dye, Civ.App., 259 S.W.2d 747, writ of error dismissed by agreement.

Utah.—Mecham v. Allen, 262 P.2d 285, 1 Utah 2d 79; Clark v. Union Pac. R. Co., 257 P. 1050, 70 Utah 29.

Va.—Stratton v. Bergman, 192 S.E. 813, 169 Va. 249 (motorcyclist).

Wash.—McCoy v. Courtney, 172 P.2d 596, 25 Wash.2d 956; Lyle v. Fiorito, 60 P.2d 709, 187 Wash. 537 (intersectional collision due to absence of warning and stop signs).

Wis.—Stoll v. Andro, 26 N.W.2d 162, 250 Wis. 26 (deceased driver of car with which plaintiffs collided); Guderyon v. Wisconsin Tel. Co., 2 N.W.2d 242, 240 Wis. 215 (lookout); Potter v. Potter, 272 N.W. 34, 224 Wis. 251 (guest); Smith v. City of Green Bay, 271 N.W. 28, 223 Wis. 427 (street in dangerous condition).

Wyo.—Gish v. Colson, 1970, 475 P.2d 717; Wilhelm v. Cukr, 230 P.2d 507, 69 Wyo. 1.

Created by statute

Mass.—Calderone v. Wright, 1971, 274 N.E.2d 588, 360 Mass. 174; Wanamaker v. Shaw, 2 N.E.2d 209, 294 Mass. 416 (providing that person killed shall be presumed to have been in exercise of due care, and contributory negligence shall be affirmative defense, held applicable in action for death of pedestrian).

Obscured by instructions to jury

In action against contractor for wrongful death of passenger in collision at night with defendant's grader, where trial court instructed jury that passenger, being deceased, was presumed to have exercised ordinary care and to have obeyed law, but did not withdraw statement made to jury at beginning of trial that defendant relied upon a claim of contributory negligence of deceased and did not advise jury that instructions on subject of contributory negligence had been refused, question of contributory negligence of deceased was not entirely eliminated from the case and giving an instruction reflecting defendant's theory of such issue was not improper. Royko v. Griffith Co., 306 P.2d 36, 147 Cal. App.2d 770.

Rule available to employer of deceased driver

In action for damage to corporation's tractor and trailer, driven by plaintiff's employee in course of his employment, jury being authorized to consider presumption that such employee exercised due care for his own safety in action, consolidated with employer's action, by employee's widow and children for his wrongful death as result of collision, was authorized to consider such presumption from same facts in employer's action. Wells Truckways v. Cebrian, 265 P.2d 557, 122 Cal.App.2d 666.

Where survivor disqualified by deadman's statute

Because there were no eyewitnesses to actions of decedent prior to time he was struck in intersection by automobile of defendant who was not permitted to testify because of the Dead Man's statute, court properly admitted evidence that decedent was man of careful habits when crossing streets. Zeller v. Durham, 179 N.E.2d 34, 33 Ill.App.2d 273.

Whether adult or minor

U.S.—Stephenson v. Grand Trunk Western R. Co., C.C.A.Ill., 110 F.2d 401, certiorari granted Grand Trunk Western R. Co. v. Stephenson, 60 S.Ct. 1101, 310 U.S. 623, 84 L.Ed. 1395, and 60 S.Ct. 1102, 310 U.S. 623, 84 L.Ed. 1395, cer-

Ch. 417   PRESUMPTIONS AND INFERENCES   § 417.2

This includes the presumption of prior due observance of the traffic laws by the deceased.[79]

The same presumption of due care as presumed for a deceased person prevails where the party's version is unavailable due to disability or loss of memory.[80]

tiorari dismissed, 60 S.Ct. 1107 (2 cases).

79. Cal.—Meyer v. Blackman, 31 Cal.Rptr. 36, 381 P.2d 916, 59 Cal. 2d 668 (that plaintiff was passenger and not driver where lacked operator's license); Rice v. Southern Pac. Co., 55 Cal.Rptr. 840, 247 Cal.App.2d 701 (that decedent had complied with statute relating to drivers' duties when approaching crossing where signal device is operating); Brooks v. E. J. Willig Truck Transp. Co., 243 P.2d 84, 110 Cal.App.2d 571, subsequent opinion 255 P.2d 802, 40 Cal.2d 669 (pedestrian yielding right of way).

Me.—Field v. Webber, 169 A. 732, 132 Me. 236.

Ohio.—Miller v. City of Dayton, 41 N.E.2d 728, 70 Ohio App. 173.

Wis.—Odya v. Quade, 90 N.W.2d 96, 4 Wis.2d 63.

80. Cited by the court in Merritt v. Reed, 1971, 185 N.W.2d 261, 186 Neb. 561.

U.S.—U. S. v. Reichel, C.A.Cal., 220 F.2d 869.

Cal.—Brumley v. Barney O'Hern Trucking Co., 314 P.2d 200, 152 Cal. App.2d 514 (that a witness testified that driver of a tractor with semitrailer attached had stated that driver remembered some of the details of a collision with another trucking rig, although driver allegedly did not remember details of accident did not deprive driver of presumption); Gardner v. City of San Jose, 57 Cal.Rptr. 176, 248 Cal.App.2d 798; Gadbury v. Ray, 340 P.2d 66, 171 Cal.App.2d 150 (instruction on contributory negligence should not be given); Masterson v. Ward, 320 P.2d 613, 157 Cal.App.2d 142; Eramdjian v. Interstate Bakery Corp., 315 P.2d 19, 153 Cal.App.2d 590; Napoli v. Hunt, 297 P.2d 653, 141 Cal.App.2d 782; Zollars v. Barber, 295 P.2d 561, 140 Cal.App.2d 502 (was unconscious and therefore could not testify to what happened during certain period in which could have been negligent).

Del.—McGahey v. Swinehart, Super. 1970, 267 A.2d 469; Wagner v. Shanks, 194 A.2d 701, 6 Storey 555.

Iowa.—Plumb v. Minneapolis & St. L. Ry. Co., 91 N.W.2d 380, 249 Iowa 1187; Ruble v. Carr, 59 N.W.2d 228, 244 Iowa 990.

La.—Lowenburg v. Labor Pool of America, Inc., App.1974, 296 So. 2d 846.

Md.—Nizer v. Phelps, 1969, 249 A.2d 112, 252 Md. 185.

Mich.—Breker v. Rosema, 4 N.W.2d 57, 301 Mich. 685, 141 A.L.R. 867.

Pa.—Gregorich v. Pepsi-Cola Metropolitan Bottling Co., Inc., Super. 1974, 327 A.2d 171; Moore v. Zimmerman, 1972, 292 A.2d 458, 221 Pa.Super. 359.

Tex.—Little Rock Furniture Mfg. Co. v. Dunn, Civ.App., 218 S.W.2d 527, affirmed 222 S.W.2d 985, 148 Tex. 197.

Wis.—Walter v. Shemon, 66 N.W.2d 160, 267 Wis. 424; Vogel v. Vetting, 60 N.W.2d 399, 265 Wis. 19.

Foundation required

Where motorist had no recollection of events which occurred during and immediately prior to the accident, inference of due care could not arise

§ 417.2 TRIAL EVIDENCE Ch. 417

On occasion both parties are deceased, are disabled, or lack memory, creating offsetting presumptions of due care.[81]

This "eyewitness rule" is subject to reasonable limitations.[82] The presumption of the exercise of due care merely negatives contributory negligence, and does not compel the conclusion that the other person involved in the accident was negligent.[83] The presumption disappears when there is direct evidence of lack of due care,[84] and mathematical tests may be resorted to in determining the true situation.[85]

in absence of showing of the cause for his loss of memory, such as a head injury or unconsciousness. Nevarov v. Caldwell, 327 P.2d 111, 161 Cal.App.2d 762.

Statutory presumption

Cal.—Lopez v. Knight, 263 P.2d 452, 121 Cal.App.2d 387.

81. Cal.—Laird v. Moss, 342 P.2d 463, 173 Cal.App.2d 48 (where driver was killed in collision with truck at blind street intersection and automobile passenger and truck driver suffered injuries resulting in complete loss of memory as to circumstances surrounding collision, statutory presumption was applicable to conduct of truck driver, automobile passenger, and deceased automobile driver).

Conn.—Sigel v. Gordon, 167 A. 719, 117 Conn. 271.

Iowa.—In re Goretska's Estate, 13 N. W.2d 432, 234 Iowa 1080 (all occupants of both automobiles were killed); In re Hill's Estate, 208 N. W. 334, 202 Iowa 1038, modified 210 N.W. 241, 202 Iowa 1038.

N.Y.—Cole v. Swagler, 125 N.E.2d 592, 308 N.Y. 325.

82. Ill.—Lauer v. Elgin, J. & E. Ry. Co., 27 N.E.2d 315, 305 Ill.App. 200.

83. U.S.—Riess v. Pennsylvania R. Co., C.C.A.N.Y., 107 F.2d 385; Mast v. Illinois Cent. R. Co., D.C.Iowa, 79 F.Supp. 149, affirmed 176 F.2d 157.

Cal.—Gigliotti v. Nunes, 286 P.2d 809, 45 Cal.2d 85.

N.C.—Yost v. Hall, 64 S.E.2d 554, 233 N.C. 463.

Pa.—Ebersole v. Beistline, 82 A.2d 11, 368 Pa. 12; Moore v. Esso Standard Oil Co., 72 A.2d 117, 364 Pa. 343.

84. Prior edition **cited by the court** in McGahey v. Swinehart, Del.Super.1970, 267 A.2d 469, 471.

U.S.—Luther v. Maple, C.A.N.D., 250 F.2d 916 (under Nebraska law); Bastian v. Baltimore & O. R. Co., C.C.A.Pa., 144 F.2d 120 (physical facts excluding presumption); Mast v. Illinois Cent. R. Co., D.C.Iowa, 79 F.Supp. 149, affirmed 176 F.2d 157.

Del.—McGahey v. Swinehart, Super. 1970, 267 A.2d 469 (went through flashing light at 40 mph., in wrong lane).

Iowa.—Weppler v. Smith, 108 N.W. 2d 247, 252 Iowa 679 (administratrix was not entitled to benefit of the "no eyewitness rule", where driver of other automobile testified to what allegedly happened, and administratrix failed to pursue rumor of existence of another eyewitness, even though driver's testimony was negatived by physical facts); Lingle v. Minneapolis & St. L. Ry. Co., 104 N.W.2d 467, 251 Iowa 1183 (as to approach to cross-

85. See note 85 on page 118.

Ch. 417   PRESUMPTIONS AND INFERENCES   § 417.2

ing); Ruble v. Carr, 59 N.W.2d 228, 244 Iowa 990 (substantial evidence that motorist had been driving without lights, at unreasonable speed, and partly on defendant's half of highway at time of accident).

Kan.—Long v. Foley, 299 P.2d 63, 180 Kan. 83.

La.—McCraine v. T. L. James & Co., App., 95 So.2d 156.

Me.—Greene v. Willey, 86 A.2d 82, 147 Me. 227 (child darting into street).

Mass.—Hall v. Shain, 197 N.E. 437, 291 Mass. 506 (evidence that deceased crossed street and that was last he remembered insufficient to show as matter of law that motorist sustained burden of proving contributory negligence of deceased).

Mich.—Rushford-Surine v. Grand Trunk R. Co., 214 N.W. 168, 239 Mich. 19.

Neb.—Bush v. James, 40 N.W.2d 667, 152 Neb. 189 (intersectional collision).

N.M.—Teeter v. Miller, Smith & Jones, 342 P.2d 864, 66 N.M. 49; Morrison v. Rodey, 340 P.2d 409, 65 N.M. 474.

Or.—Blanchette v. Arrow Towing Co., 410 P.2d 1010, 242 Or. 590.

Pa.—Heath v. Klosterman, 23 A.2d 209, 343 Pa. 501 (evidence established that deceased did not look for approaching traffic before alighting from the automobile); Grimes v. Pennsylvania Ry. Co., 137 A. 451, 289 Pa. 320.

S.D.—Dehnert v. Garrett Feed Co., 1969, 169 N.W.2d 719, 84 S.D. 233 (where, notwithstanding fact that feed company's truck was visible for at least one-half mile prior to accident, decedents' vehicle nevertheless engaged in hazardous maneuver of driving on wrong side of road and into path of oncoming truck, presumption of due care as to decedent driver was dispelled, and he was chargeable with contributory negligence, more than slight, as matter of law).

Va.—Martin v. Carrington, 70 S.E.2d 313, 193 Va. 627.

Wash.—Bellantonio v. Warner, 288 P.2d 459, 47 Wash.2d 550 (driver, failing to yield right of way at street intersection to automobile approaching from his right, was not entitled to presumption); Allen v. Porter, 143 P.2d 328, 19 Wash. 2d 503 (motorcycle rider); Trainor v. Interstate Const. Co., 60 P.2d 7, 187 Wash. 142 (in failing to stop automobile when visibility of road was completely destroyed).

Wis.—Ernst v. Greenwald, 1967, 151 N.W.2d 706, 35 Wis. 763 (if evidence which would support finding contrary to presumption is introduced, presumption is eliminated and drops out of case entirely and no instruction upon that subject should be given to jury); Odya v. Quade, 90 N.W.2d 96, 4 Wis.2d 63 (position of automobiles after collision was evidence from which it could be inferred was over centerline); Ackley v. Farmers Mut. Auto. Ins. Co., 78 N.W.2d 744, 273 Wis. 422 (driving over centerline toward crest of hill).

But see

Bove v. Beckman, 46 Cal.Rptr. 164, 236 Cal.App.2d 555 (acts of deceased pedestrian, who looked first to left and, being partially behind two men and of shorter stature, and because of low beam of approaching automobile's lights, saw no vehicle coming, looked to right and, seeing no danger approaching, stepped into highway lane and was immediately struck and killed by defendant's automobile traveling at high speed in that lane and with lights on low bean were within presumption that pedestrian did whatever careful person would have done in her situation); Scalf v. Eicher, 53 P.2d 368, 11 Cal.App.

§ 417.2   TRIAL EVIDENCE   Ch. 417

The party is not entitled to such a presumption where there was an eyewitness to the accident, who is able to testify as to the conduct of the deceased.[86] "Eyewitnesses," in such cases, are

2d 44 (violation of statute prohibiting pedestrian from walking along highway outside of business or residence district otherwise than close to his left-hand edge of highway did not overcome presumption that decedent took ordinary care of his own concerns, unless there was evidence that violation proximately contributed to accident).

Wash.—Knutson v. McMahan, 58 P. 2d 1033, 186 Wash. 518 (pedestrian who died shortly after being struck by automobile presumably was exercising due care in crossing street, notwithstanding pedestrian was crossing street between intersections in violation of ordinance).

Not rebutted

Cal.—Hom v. Clark, 35 Cal.Rptr. 11, 221 Cal.App.2d 622 (that pedestrian might have been familiar with intersection was merely evidence which could be weighed against presumption of due care arising from loss of memory, and which would not dispel presumption as a matter of law).

Va.—Powell v. Nichols, 1969, 166 S. E.2d 243, 209 Va. 654 (testimony of defendant who collided with truck that entered highway without stopping, was not sufficient to overcome presumption that truck driver had obeyed the law where defendant testified at other points that truck was coming out in the road when he first saw it, and defendant admitted that he did not know whether truck driver was stopped at stop sign or not).

85.   **U.S.**—Perucca v. Baltimore & O. R. Co., C.C.A.Pa., 35 F.2d 113, certiorari denied Baltimore & O. R. Co. v. Perucca, 50 S.Ct. 236, 281 U.S. 721, 74 L.Ed. 1139.

Pa.—Weber v. Pittsburgh & W. V. Ry. Co., 150 A. 624, 300 Pa. 351;

O'Neill v. Reading Co., 145 A. 840, 296 Pa. 319; Grimes v. Pennsylvania R. Co., 137 A. 451, 289 Pa. 320.

86. **U.S.**—Mast v. Illinois Cent. R. Co., D.C.Iowa, 79 F.Supp. 149, affirmed 176 F.2d 157.

Cal.—Downing v. Southern Pac. Co., 59 P.2d 578, 15 Cal.App.2d 246.

Idaho.—Lallatin v. Terry, 340 P.2d 112, 81 Idaho 238.

Ill.—Wilkerson v. Cummings, 58 N.E. 2d 280, 324 Ill.App. 331.

Iowa.—Andrew v. Clements, 45 N.W. 2d 861, 242 Iowa 144; Tegtmeyer v. Byram, 216 N.W. 613, 204 Iowa 1169; Brown v. McAdoo, 188 N.W. 7, 195 Iowa 286.

Md.—Britton v. Samuelson, 23 N.W. 2d 267, 147 Neb. 318 (riding on load of loose hay).

Mich.—Marchlewicz v. Morrisette, 50 N.W.2d 849, 332 Mich. 271 (pedestrian crossing at place other than crosswalk); Schillinger v. Wyman, 49 N.W.2d 119, 331 Mich. 160 (even though eyewitness was defendant, and defendant saw deceased only an instant before impact; Mercure v. Popig, 40 N.W.2d 95, 326 Mich. 140 (even though eyewitness is the adverse party); Conrad v. Krause, 37 N.W.2d 906, 325 Mich. 175 (injured child with no recollection of accident); Swartz v. Dahlquist, 30 N.W.2d 809, 320 Mich. 135 (death of pedestrian); Molitor v. Burns, 28 N.W. 2d 106, 318 Mich. 261 (where decedent, when he was struck by truck, was standing by open door of police car talking to officers who were eyewitnesses).

Mo.—State ex rel. Alton R. Co. v. Shain, 143 S.W.2d 233, 346 Mo. 681.

those who have knowledge of some fact or circumstance which throws light upon the question as to whether or not the deceased did those things which, under the circumstances, constituted exercise of due care.[87]

Pa.—Weber v. Pittsburgh & W. V. Ry. Co., 150 A. 624, 300 Pa. 351; Tull v. Baltimore & O. R. Co., 141 A. 263, 292 Pa. 458.

Utah.—Mingus v. Olsson, 201 P.2d 495, 114 Utah 505.

Wash.—Allen v. Hart, 201 P.2d 145, 32 Wash.2d 173; Sweazey v. Valley Transport, 107 P.2d 567, 6 Wash.2d 324, adhered to on rehearing 111 P.2d 1010, 6 Wash.2d 324, 140 A.L.R. 20; Morris v. Chicago, M., St. P. & P. R. Co., 97 P.2d 119, 1 Wash.2d 587, opinion adhered to 100 P.2d 19, 1 Wash.2d 587.

But see

Fact that witnesses produced by plaintiff gave detailed evidence of happening of accident did not bar reliance on presumption of due care by plaintiff, who had no memory of the accident, when evidence was in conflict as to whether plaintiff was standing on paved portion of roadway when struck by automobile driven by defendant. Lovett v. Hitchcock, 14 Cal.Rptr. 117, 192 Cal.App.2d 806.

[87] **U.S.**—MacHale v. U. S., D.C. Wash., 81 F.Supp. 372 (occupant of jeep saw deceased pedestrian only 10 feet away); Mast v. Illinois Cent. R. Co., D.C.Iowa, 79 F.Supp. 149, affirmed 176 F.2d 157.

Iowa.—Vandello v. Allied Gas & Chemical Co., 110 N.W.2d 232, 252 Iowa 1313 (one who saw decedent's auto only for an instant not an "eyewitness"); Hamilton v. Becker, 1957, 86 N.W.2d 142, 249 Iowa 516 (fleeting glimpse not enough); Turbot v. Repp, 1955, 72 N.W.2d 565, 247 Iowa 69 (eyewitness though couldn't say whether deceased stopped at intersection); Ruble v. Carr, 59 N.W.2d 228, 244 Iowa 990; Prewitt v. Rutherford, 30 N.W.2d 141, 238 Iowa 1321 (one who did not see plaintiff's actions during material moments just before collision was not an "eyewitness"); Graby v. Danner, 18 N.W.2d 595, 236 Iowa 700 (testimony of witnesses who did not see deceased during all the material time does not exclude inference).

Mich.—Fairchild v. Detroit, G. H. & M. Ry. Co., 230 N.W. 167, 250 Mich. 252.

Wash.—Byerley v. Northern Pac. Ry. Co., 120 P.2d 453, 11 Wash.2d 604.

Interested witness

In action for wrongful deaths against owner and against driver of the truck, the driver was an "interested witness" whose testimony would not be considered in determining whether presumption of due care on part of driver of automobile had been overcome. Sweazey v. Valley Transport, 107 P.2d 567, 6 Wash.2d 324, adhered to on rehearing 111 P.2d 1010, 6 Wash.2d 324, 140 A.L.R. 20.

Party to collision as eyewitness

Plaintiff was not entitled to benefit of "no eyewitness rule" on issue of decedent's freedom from contributory negligence, where driver of semitrailer observed and testified concerning decedent's conduct at and immediately before collision. Smith v. Darling & Co., 56 N.W.2d 47, 244 Iowa 133.

§ 417.3 Exercise of Care by Injured Party

Library References:
C.J.S. Motor Vehicles §§ 512, 568; Negligence §§ 205, 210; Railroads § 955 et seq.
West's Key No. Digests, Automobiles ⚷242(8); Negligence ⚷122; Railroads ⚷396.

As a rule, there is no presumption that the injured person was contributorily negligent.[88] The general rule is that, in the absence of evidence as to the circumstances attending an accident, one who is injured through the negligence of another in the operation of a motor vehicle upon the highway or of a vehicle moving upon tracks, will be presumed to have used due care.[89] Such presumption disappears in the presence of evidence on the issue of due care.[90]

However, circumstances shown may create prima facie evidence of negligence or a presumption of plaintiff's contributory negligence.[91]

Railroad crossing collisions

In the absence of evidence to the contrary, a motorist while crossing or upon railroad tracks may be presumed to have been

---

88. See § 417.2 at fn. 29.

89. See § 417.2 at fn. 38.

90. See § 471.1 at fn. 12 et seq. for discussion of disappearance of presumption upon introduction of proof.

91. See also general discussion of inferences or presumptions of lack of care in § 417.2, fn. 49 et seq.

Cal.—Servito v. Lynch & Sons Van & Storage Co., 13 Cal.Rptr. 313, 191 Cal.App.2d 799 (pedestrian crossing at other than marked crosswalk).

Ky.—Riley v. Hornbuckle, 366 S.W. 2d 304 (where ordinance prohibited, subject to exceptions, presence of pedestrians on expressway, there was no presumption that pedestrian's presence on expressway was unlawful, but his unexplained presence was evidence of negligence, and in absence of further evidence tending to bring it within exceptions of ordinance was conclusive evidence of negligence).

Ohio.—Flannery v. Tessaromatis, 108 N.E.2d 146, 91 Ohio App. 215 (failure to stop or look to left at intersection).

Riding with intoxicated driver

Cal.—Taylor v. Rosiak, 45 Cal.Rptr. 759, 236 Cal.App.2d 68 (no conclusive presumption that decedent passenger knew or should have known that driver was intoxicated while driving automobile or that decedent knew or should have known that he was exposing himself to consequences of dangerous and wanton misconduct by remaining in automobile).

Ky.—Smith's Adm'r v. Smith, 269 S. W.2d 260 (danger of riding in an automobile operated by an intoxicated driver is a matter of such common knowledge that it will be conclusively presumed that injured person appreciated the danger if he was aware of driver's intoxication and fact that his ability to operate automobile was thereby impaired).

exercising due care in approaching and going upon the tracks.[92]

[92]. **U.S.**—Delaware, L. & W. R. Co. v. Rebmann, C.C.A.N.Y., 285 F. 317 (not overcome in obstructed view situation by testimony of engineer that he did not see motorist looking toward train); Beckham v. Hines, C.C.A.Ky., 279 F. 241; Begert v. Payne, C.C.A.Ohio, 274 F. 784; Hines v. Hoover, C.C.A.Ga., 271 F. 645.

Ariz.—Davis v. Boggs, 199 P. 116, 22 Ariz. 497.

Ark.—Bussell v. Missouri Pac. R. Co., 376 S.W.2d 545, 237 Ark. 812.

Cal.—Brewer v. Southern Pac. Co., 84 P.2d 230, 29 Cal.App.2d 251 (collision with train blocking crossing); Lahey v. Southern Pac. Co., 61 P.2d 461, 16 Cal.App.2d 652, certiorari denied Southern Pac. Co. v. Lahey, 57 S.Ct. 508, 300 U.S. 665, 81 L.Ed. 873 (collision on foggy day); Whitney v. Northwestern Pac. R. Co., 178 P. 326, 39 Cal.App. 139.

Idaho.—Van v. Union Pac. R. Co., 366 P.2d 837, 83 Idaho 539 (where plaintiff had suffered loss of memory of events surrounding accident, presumption arose).

Ind.—Pennsylvaia R. Co. v. Lytle, 34 N.E.2d 939, 109 Ind.App. 318.

Ky.—Cincinnati, N. O. & T. P. Ry. Co. v. Hare's Adm'x, 1944, 178 S. W.2d 835, 297 Ky. 5; Illinois Cent. R. Co. v. Applegate's Adm'x, 105 S.W.2d 153, 268 Ky. 458 (private crossing); Louisville & N. R. Co. v. Ratliff's Adm'r, 85 S.W.2d 1006, 260 Ky. 380 (failure to exercise reasonable care to discover train and stop charged); Stephenson's Adm'x v. Sharp's Ex'rs, 1 S.W.2d 957, 222 Ky. 496.

Mass.—Emery v. New York, N. H. & H. R. Co., 20 N.E.2d 563, 302 Mass. 578 (failure to proceed cautiously charged); Brown v. Boston & M. R. R., 18 N.E.2d 440, 302 Mass. 90.

Mo.—Zickefoose v. Thompson, 148 S.W.2d 784, 347 Mo. 579 (in determining whether truck driver colliding with freight train at crossing was contributorily negligent, presumption could be indulged that driver did not intentionally drive headlong into train for purpose of killing or injuring himself, but presumption that driver exercised due care could be indulged only in absence of evidence to contrary); Grotjan v. Thompson, App., 140 S.W.2d 706 (driver remained in stalled automobile); Mundy v. St. Louis-San Francisco Ry. Co., App., 45 S.W.2d 941.

Ohio.—Smith v. Pennsylvania R. Co., App., 40 N.E.2d 445, 35 O.L.A. 237, motion overruled.

Pa.—Thomas v. Pennsylvania R. Co., 119 A. 717, 275 Pa. 579; Miller v. Delaware, L. & W. R. Co., 67 Pa. Super. 249.

Tex.—Texas & P. Ry. Co. v. Midkiff, Civ.App., 275 S.W.2d 841 (was presumed that motorist killed in crossing accident was doing whatever was reasonably necessary for his own safety, and railroad, in order to relieve itself of consequences of its negligent acts, was required to prove conclusively that deceased motorist was not so doing); Henwood v. Gilliam, Civ.App., 207 S. W.2d 904, writ of error refused; International-Great Northern R. Co. v. Acker, Civ.App., 128 S.W.2d 506, error dismissed, judgment correct (motorist's failure to stop charged).

Wash.—Smith v. City of Seattle, 19 P.2d 652, 172 Wash. 66; Mattingley v. Oregon-Washington R. & Nav. Co., 280 P. 46, 153 Wash. 514.

Wis.—Waitkus v. Chicago & N. W. Ry. Co., 237 N.W. 259, 204 Wis. 566; Waitkus v. Chicago & N. W. Ry. Co., 236 N.W. 531, 204 Wis. 566.

§ 417.3   TRIAL EVIDENCE   Ch. 417

Similarly, an occupant in a vehicle which collided with a train at a crossing may be presumed to have been exercising care.[93]

But see

Wilbur Motors, Inc., v. Eastern Massachusetts St. Ry. Co., 170 N.E. 922, 271 Mass. 31.

Utah.—Clark v. Los Angeles & Salt Lake R. Co., 275 P. 582, 73 Utah 486.

Contra

Me.—Plante v. Canadian Nat. Rys., 23 A.2d 814, 138 Me. 215; Hesseltine v. Maine Cent. R. Co., 154 A. 264, 130 Me. 196.

Person assisting motorist with stalled vehicle

In action for wrongful death of decedent who was killed by defendants' train while he was lawfully attempting to assist driver in getting stalled cement mixer truck across railway tracks, there was no reversible error in giving instruction that law presumed that decedent took due care for his own concern, where plaintiffs produced no direct evidence as to conduct of decedent immediately prior to or at precise time of accident and testimony of driver indicated that he did not see the train approaching and that he was not watching decedent for an appreciable time before accident. Henley v. Atchison, T. & S. F. R. Co., 333 P.2d 388, 166 Cal. App.2d 554.

Rule limited

Under Iowa law, a presumption that driver killed in railroad crossing accident was exercising due care is applicable only where no eyewitness' testimony has been produced by either party as to driver's conduct or movements of his vehicle during material moments preceding collision, and only where physical facts of situation do not give rise to existence of contributory negligence on driver's part. Chicago, R. I. & P. R. Co. v. Lovejoy, C.A.Iowa, 206 F.2d 77.

Signals not heard by others

In action for death of motorist, where witnesses watching train heard no signals, motorist cannot be presumed to have heard signals nor held to such accuracy of judgment as if he had heard them. Illinois Cent. R. Co. v. Applegate's Adm'x, 105 S.W. 2d 153, 268 Ky. 458.

93. U.S.—Conner v. Pennsylvania R. Co., D.C.Pa., 163 F.Supp. 718, affirmed C.A., 263 F.2d 944; Baltimore & O. R. Co. v. Green, C.C.A. W.Va., 136 F.2d 88; Garrett v. Pennsylvania R. Co., C.C.A.Ill., 47 F.2d 10.

Cal.—Smellie v. Southern Pac. Co., 299 P. 529, 212 Cal. 540; Carpenter v. Atchison, T. & S. F. Ry. Co., 195 P. 1073, 51 Cal.App. 60.

Ga.—Georgia R. & Banking Co. v. Stanley, 145 S.E. 530, 38 Ga.App. 773.

Ill.—Lauer v. Elgin, J. & E. Ry. Co., 27 N.E.2d 315, 305 Ill.App. 200 (six-track crossing).

Iowa.—Jensvold v. Chicago Great Western R. Co., 12 N.W.2d 293, 234 Iowa 627.

Ky.—Illinois Cent. R. Co. v. Applegate's Adm'x, 105 S.W.2d 153, 268 Ky. 458.

Mo.—Fair v. Thompson, 212 S.W.2d 923, 240 Mo.App. 664 (where the vehicle was stalled on grade crossing, it was to be presumed that occupants would have made an effort to escape from the track had they known of train's approach in absence of evidence to indicate they intended to commit suicide); Benton v. Thompson, 156 S.W.2d 739, 236 Mo.App. 1000, certiorari quashed State ex rel. Thompson v. Shain, 163 S.W.2d 967, 349 Mo. 1075; Borrson v. Missouri-Kansas-Texas R. Co., Sup., 161 S.W.2d 227 (driver and wife both killed); Brown

Ch. 417 PRESUMPTIONS AND INFERENCES § 417.3

This presumption arises from the instinct for self-preservation,[94] and, as respects a driver, from the natural tendency to protect others riding in the vehicle.[95]

By the weight of authority, it is presumed, in the absence of contrary evidence, that one injured or killed at a railroad crossing carefully looked and listened.[96] This presumption yields, however, to evidence that the injured or deceased person did not, in fact, exercise ordinary care.[97] So, where the undisputed evi-

v. Alton R. Co., App., 132 S.W.2d 713, record quashed, Sup., 143 S. W.2d 233 (speed of truck allegedly excessive); Dirickson v. Thompson, App., 120 S.W.2d 198 (guest and driver both killed); Cunningham v. St. Louis & S. F. R. Co., App., 9 S.W.2d 166.

Pa.—Suchy v. Buffalo & Lake Erie Traction Co., 129 A. 571, 283 Pa. 533; Jerko v. Buffalo, R. & P. R. Co., 119 A. 543, 275 Pa. 459.

Tenn.—Morgan v. Tennessee Cent. Ry. Co., 216 S.W.2d 32, 31 Tenn. 409.

W.Va.—McClaugherty v. Tri-City Traction Co., 14 S.E.2d 432, 123 W.Va. 112 (driver and guest both killed in collision with interurban trolley car).

But see

Wash.—Byerley v. Northern Pac. Ry. Co., 120 P.2d 453, 11 Wash.2d 604 (presumed knew that operative crossing signal required vehicle to stop).

94. Mo.—Wolf v. New York, C. & St. L. R. Co., 148 S.W.2d 1032, 347 Mo. 622.

Va.—Virginian Ry. Co. v. Bacon, 157 S.E. 789, 156 Va. 337.

Wis.—Sweeo v. Chicago & N. W. R. Co., 197 N.W. 805, 183 Wis. 234.

95. Tex.—Gulf, C. & S. F. Ry. Co. v. Bouchillon, Civ.App., 186 S.W.2d 1006, writ of error refused w. m.; International-Great Northern R. Co. v. Acker, Civ.App., 128 S.W.2d 506, error dismissed, judgment correct.

96. U.S.—Garrett v. Pennsylvania R. Co., C.C.A.Ill., 47 F.2d 10; Rebmann v. Delaware, L. & W. R. Co., D.C.N.Y., 275 F. 1009.

Ga.—Collier v. Pollard, 2 S.E.2d 821, 60 Ga.App. 105; Georgia R. & Banking Co. v. Stanley, 145 S.E. 530, 38 Ga.App. 773.

Mich.—Fairchild v. Detroit, G. H. & M. Ry. Co., 230 N.W. 167, 250 Mich. 252.

Mo.—Ledkins v. Missouri-Kansas-Texas R. Co., 316 S.W.2d 564.

Ohio.—Woodworth v. New York Cent. R. Co., 80 N.E.2d 142, 149 Ohio St. 543 (motorist, killed at railroad crossing, allegedly misled by flood lights at defendant manufacturer's plant).

Pa.—Tomlinson v. Northwestern Electric Service Co. of Pennsylvania, 151 A. 680, 301 Pa. 72; Frank v. Reading Co., 146 A. 598, 297 Pa. 233; Rice v. Erie R. Co., 114 A. 640, 271 Pa. 180.

Utah.—Ludlow v. Los Angeles & Salt Lake R. Co., 275 P. 592, 73 Utah 513.

Wis.—Sprague v. Hauck, 89 N.W.2d 226, 3 Wis.2d 616; Prunty v. Vandenberg, 44 N.W.2d 246, 257 Wis. 469.

Presumption did listen sufficient to take that question to the jury

Pa.—Knobeloch v. Pittsburgh, H. B. & N. C. R. Co., 109 A. 619, 266 Pa. 140.

97. U.S.—Chicago, Rock Island & Pacific R. Co. v. Consumers Cooperative Association, C.A.Kan.,

§ 417.3   TRIAL EVIDENCE   Ch. 417

dence shows that a deceased motorist had an unobstructed view of the train at a crossing, the presumption of proper care for self-preservation does not arise.[98] If by the exercise of ordinary care and prudence, the approach of a train could have been seen by looking in time to have avoided the injury, the presumption is that there was a failure to look or to heed what was seen.[99]

180 F.2d 900, certiorari denied 71 S.Ct. 42, 340 U.S. 813, 95 L.Ed. 598 (Kansas law); Garrett v. Pennsylvania R. Co., C.C.A.Ill., 47 F.2d 10.

Cal.—Durkee v. Atchison, T. & S. F. Ry., 324 P.2d 91, 159 Cal.App. 2d 615 (benefit of the presumption of due care by a decedent is available if the testimony of plaintiff's witnesses respecting decedent's acts and conduct at the time involved is not wholly irreconcilable with such presumption); Noble v. Key System, 51 P.2d 887, 10 Cal. App.2d 132 (guest's participation with defendant in drinking liquor held insufficient to overcome presumption that deceased guest exercised ordinary care for own safety).

Mich.—Mallory v. Pitcairn, 11 N.W. 2d 318, 307 Mich. 40 (claim of loss of memory); Barnett v. New York Cent. R. Co., 295 N.W. 255, 295 Mich. 536.

Minn.—Luce v. Great Northern Ry. Co., 281 N.W. 812, 203 Minn. 470.

Mo.—Oxford v. St. Louis-San Francisco Ry. Co., 52 S.W.2d 983, 331 Mo. 53; Sullivan v. Atchison, T. & S. F. R. Co., 297 S.W. 945, 317 Mo. 996.

Pa.—Leaman Transp. Corp. v. Philadelphia Transp. Co., 57 A.2d 889, 358 Pa. 625; Ray v. Lehigh Valley R. Co., 184 A. 445, 321 Pa. 538.

Va.—Norfolk & W. Ry. Co. v. Wellons' Adm'r, 154 S.E. 575, 155 Va. 218.

Wis.—Ligman v. Bitker, 72 N.W.2d 340, 270 Wis. 556; Prunty v. Vandenberg, 44 N.W.2d 246, 257 Wis. 469; Sweeo v. Chicago & N. W. R. Co., 197 N.W. 805, 183 Wis. 234.

98. Cal.—Heintz v. Southern Pac. Co., 147 P.2d 621, 63 Cal.App.2d 699; Dull v. Atchison, Topeka & S. F. Ry. Co., 81 P.2d 158, 27 Cal. App.2d 473; Hughes v. Atchison, T. & S. F. Ry. Co., 8 P.2d 853, 121 Cal.App. 271.

Mich.—Tomczyk v. Detroit, G. H. & M. Ry., 255 N.W. 230, 267 Mich. 474 (unobstructed view for one mile).

99. Ariz.—Morenci Southern R. Co. v. Monsour, 185 P. 938, 21 Ariz. 148.

Cal.—McCarthy v. Pacific Electric R. Co., 255 P. 868, 82 Cal.App. 503.

Mo.—Stillman v. St. Louis-San Francisco R. Co., App., 266 S.W. 1005.

Tex.—Edmiston v. Texas & N. O. R. Co., Civ.App., 111 S.W.2d 848, reversed on other grounds, Com. App., 138 S.W.2d 526.

Utah.—Nuttall v. Denver & R. G. W. R. Co., 99 P.2d 15, 98 Utah 383.

But see

Whether driver of bus which was struck by train at street crossing was guilty of contributory negligence was not to be determined by application of alleged presumption that he did not look or if he did look that he did not heed what he saw but was to be determined from the evidence, and it was the right solely of jury to weigh and determine the evidence. Pennsylvania R. Co. v. Lytle, 34 N.E.2d 939, 109 Ind.App. 318.

Guest's duty

Where, although view is unobstructed, an accident results, the

Ch. 417   PRESUMPTIONS AND INFERENCES   § 417.3

If there are indisputable physical conditions, indicated by actual measurements, maps, and photographs in addition to oral testimony, the existence of the fact ordinarily presumed is negatived.[1]

Even though the evidence to the contrary is uncontradicted, where it is oral testimony, there is still a jury question.[2]

In a crossing accident case in which the evidence shows that the railroad employees did not sound the statutory signals, the presumption arises that the automobile driver would have stopped before reaching the tracks, had such signals been given.[3]

As bearing on the question of the exercise of due care, an automobile driver who had traveled over a railroad crossing customarily for a long period of time would be presumed to have known of the dangers connected with the crossing, of the location of the tracks, and of the manner of the operation of the gates.[4]

It will not be presumed that a decedent was guilty of wanton negligence from proof showing an attempt to cross ahead of a train.[5]

guest must satisfactorily account for failure to see or hear the approaching train, since it is presumed that collision resulted from failure of guest to exercise due care, especially where guest admits looking ahead only. Edmiston v. Texas & N. O. R. Co., Tex.Civ.App., 111 S.W.2d 848, reversed on other grounds, Com. App., 138 S.W.2d 526.

1. **U.S.**—Riess v. Pennsylvania R. Co., C.C.A.N.Y., 107 F.2d 385.

Cal.—Brewer v. Southern Pac. Co., 84 P.2d 230, 29 Cal.App.2d 251.

Ohio.—Ballmer v. Pennsylvania R. Co., 17 N.E.2d 435, 59 Ohio App. 221.

Pa.—Lamp v. Pennsylvania R. Co., 158 A. 269, 305 Pa. 520, 84 A.L.R. 1217.

Facts not irreconcilable with presumption

The physical facts and circumstances surrounding collision which occurred during early morning at a time when visibility was not good, between truck and railroad gondola car which blocked highway crossing, and which car was lighted only by two red lights, were not irreconcilable with the presumption that truck driver was in exercise of ordinary care at the time of the collision, which presumption was sufficient to require submission to jury, of question of contributory negligence of truck driver. Brewer v. Southern Pac. Co., 84 P.2d 230, 29 Cal.App.2d 251.

2. **Pa.**—Lamp v. Pennsylvania R. Co., 158 A. 269, 305 Pa. 520, 84 A.L.R. 1217.

3. **Mo.**—Pierson v. Missouri Pac. R. Co., App., 275 S.W. 561.

4. **Wis.**—Sweeo v. Chicago & N. W. Ry. Co., 197 N.W. 805, 183 Wis. 234.

5. **Tex.**—Galveston, H. & H. R. Co. v. Sloman, Civ.App., 195 S.W. 321.

§ 417.4 Exercise of Care by Defendant

Library References:
C.J.S. Motor Vehicles § 509 et seq.; Negligence §§ 204, 207; Railroads § 955 et seq.
West's Key No. Digests, Automobiles ⚖242; Negligence ⚖121; Railroads ⚖396.

As a rule, there is no presumption that the defendant was negligent, but, in fact, the presumption is to the contrary.[6]

Railroads

However, in some jurisdictions it is held, often by statutory provision, that proof of the happening of an accident at a street or railway crossing prima facie establishes negligence or raises a presumption thereof.[7] The statute is not decisive, however, in a case where a motor vehicle is driven into a locomotive, car, or train which is not "running," but is standing on a crossing.[8]

There is a presumption of negligence arising out of the railroad's violation of statute requiring a proper and conspicuous sign indicating a crossing.[9]

The presumption that a railroad company complied with a statute by ringing the bell at a crossing will not prevail against testimony showing all the facts and circumstances connected with the injury, where there is conflict in the evidence on that question.[10]

---

6. For discussion generally of presumptions of negligence, or the absence thereof, see § 417.2 et seq.

7. Ark.—Missouri Pac. R. Co. v. Hood, 135 S.W.2d 329, 199 Ark. 520.

Fla.—Powell v. Gary, 200 So. 854, 146 Fla. 334; Atlantic Coast Line R. Co. v. Voss, 186 So. 199, 136 Fla. 32; Powell v. Jackson Grain Co., 184 So. 492, 134 Fla. 596, followed in 184 So. 498, 134 Fla. 609.

Ga.—Central of Georgia Ry. Co. v. Hester, 94 S.E.2d 124, 94 Ga.App. 226; Atlantic Coast Line R. Co. v. Parker, 82 S.E.2d 706, 90 Ga.App. 251; Eason v. Crews, 77 S.E.2d 245, 88 Ga.App. 602; Collier v. Pollard, 2 S.E.2d 821, 60 Ga.App. 105.

Miss.—Columbus & G. R. Co. v. Lee, 115 So. 782, 149 Miss. 543; Columbia & G. Ry. Co. v. Fondren, 110 So. 365, 145 Miss. 679; Krebs v. Pascagoula St. Ry. & Power Co., 78 So. 753, 117 Miss. 771.

Mo.—Brist v. Kurn, 189 S.W.2d 419, 238 Mo.App. 913 (applying Arkansas statute); McGlothin v. Thompson, 148 S.W.2d 558, 347 Mo. 708.

Contra

The doctrine of res ipsa loquitur does not apply to a collision at a crossing any more than at other points on the highway. Ebersole v. Beistline, 82 A.2d 11, 368 Pa. 12.

8. U.S.—Good v. Atlantic Coast Line R. Co., C.C.A.Fla., 142 F.2d 46.

9. U.S.—Slowik v. Chicago, M., St. P. & P. R. Co., D.C.Minn., 89 F. Supp. 590, reversed on other grounds 184 F.2d 920.

Conn.—Hunt v. Central Vermont Ry. Co., 122 A. 563, 99 Conn. 657.

10. Miss.—Granthan v. Gulf & S. I. R. Co., 103 So. 131, 138 Miss. 360.

§ 417.5 Ownership or Control

Library References:
C.J.S. Motor Vehicles § 511(5).
West's Key No. Digests, Automobiles ⚙︎242(5).

Evidence that a party's name was inscribed in some manner on the vehicle is prima facie evidence of ownership or raises a presumption of ownership.[11]

Registration evidence

Proof that a motor vehicle was registered in the name of a person, as owner, creates a presumption which makes out a prima facie case of ownership of the vehicle.[12] It also has been

---

11. **U.S.**—Harlem Taxicab Ass'n v. Nemesh, 191 F.2d 459, 89 U.S.App. D.C. 123; Marchetti v. Olyowski, 181 F.2d 285, 86 U.S.App.D.C. 125 (presumption rebuttable); Callas v. Independent Taxi Owners' Ass'n, 66 F.2d 192, 62 App.D.C. 212, certiorari denied 54 S.Ct. 89, 290 U.S. 669, 78 L.Ed. 578.

Ill.—Robeson v. Greyhound Lines, Inc., 257 Ill.App. 278 (prima facie evidence of ownership); Bosco v. Boston Store of Chicago, 195 Ill. App. 133 (name on truck).

Ky.—Webb v. Dixie-Ohio Express Co., 165 S.W.2d 539, 291 Ky. 692.

Pa.—Fullerton v. Motor Exp. Inc., 100 A.2d 73, 375 Pa. 173; Vance v. Freedom Oil Works Co., 173 A. 496, 113 Pa.Super. 280; Talarico v. Baker Office Furniture Co., 149 A. 883, 298 Pa. 211.

Rebutted only by uncontradicted proof

U.S.—Silent Automatic Sales Corporation v. Stayton, C.C.A.Mo., 45 F. 2d 471.

12. **Ala.**—Thompson v. Havard, 1970, 235 So.2d 853, 285 Ala. 718.

Fla.—Powell v. Henry, App.1969, 224 So.2d 730, certiorari dismissed 231 So.2d 518.

Idaho.—Maier v. Minidoka County Motor Co., 105 P.2d 1076, 61 Idaho 642.

Iowa.—Bash v. Hade, 62 N.W.2d 180, 245 Iowa 332.

La.—Brunning v. Brock, App., 191 So. 551.

N.Y.—United Services Auto. Ass'n v. Spyres, 1970, 310 N.Y.S.2d 798, 34 A.D.2d 181, affirmed 320 N.Y.S.2d 245, 28 N.Y.2d 631, 269 N.E.2d 35; Gerard v. Simpson, 299 N.Y.S. 348, 252 App.Div. 340.

R.I.—Hartley v. Johnson, 175 A. 653, 54 R.I. 477.

Wash.—Coffman v. McFadden, 416 P. 2d 99, 68 Wash.2d 954; Gams v. Oberholtzer, 310 P.2d 240, 50 Wash.2d 174.

Contra

Proof of registration of motor vehicle in name of specified person creates no presumption of ownership of the vehicle and does not shift burden of issue from plaintiff, who proves registration, to defendant to rebut the presumption. Chappell v. Dean, 128 S.E.2d 830, 258 N.C. 412.

Rule limited

Rule that the registered owner must be presumed to have been owner and will not be permitted to deny such ownership applies as matter of policy only in an action by an injured party against record owner. Aetna Cas. & Sur. Co. v. Garrett, 1971, 323 N.Y.S.2d 465, 37 A.D.2d 750.

held permissible to prove ownership by showing that the license number or dealer's license tag on the machine is the same as that issued to the person sought to be charged or credited with the ownership.[13]

The presumption of ownership, in the absence of any statute to the contrary, may be rebutted;[14] and, where any evidence is offered in rebuttal, a jury question is presented.[15]

13. **Iowa.**—King v. Mack International Motor Truck Corp., 60 N.W. 2d 792, 245 Iowa 48 (at best be a rebuttable presumption).

Ky.—Lever Bros. Co. v. Stapleton, 233 S.W.2d 1002, 313 Ky. 837.

Mich.—Jones v. Detroit Taxicab & Transfer Co., 188 N.W. 394, 218 Mich. 673; Wald v. Packard Motorcar Co., 169 N.W. 957, 204 Mich. 147; Hatter v. Dodge Bros., 167 N. W. 935, 202 Mich. 97.

N.Y.—Morgan v. Termine, 149 N.Y. S.2d 42, 2 Misc.2d 109 (even prior to enactment of Vehicle and Traffic Law provision prohibiting any one from knowingly permitting number plate issued for motor vehicle owned and registered by him to be displayed on any other motor vehicle, display of another's license plate created a common-law presumption of ownership of the automobile on part of owner of plate, but affirmative proof of non-ownership would overcome the presumption); Buono v. Stewart Motor Trucks, 26 N.Y.S.2d 986, 261 App.Div. 1095.

Okl.—Norton v. Harmon, 133 P.2d 206, 192 Okl. 36.

Pa.—Frew v. Barto, 52 Dauph. 147, affirmed 26 A.2d 905, 345 Pa. 217 (dealers tags are issued for restricted purpose and therefore the vehicle bearing such tags is presumed to be driven in the business of the person to whom the tags are issued); Coates v. Commercial Credit Co., 165 A. 377, 310 Pa. 330.

Tex.—Longhorn Drilling Corp. v. Padilla, Civ.App., 138 S.W.2d 164.

Wash.—Peters v. Casualty Co. of America, 172 P. 220, 101 Wash. 208.

Wis.—Kruse v. Weigand, 235 N.W. 426, 204 Wis. 195, followed 235 N. W. 431, 204 Wis. 206.

Jury question though rebutted by uncontradicted testimony

Where license plates issued to defendant as a dealer were on automobile at time of accident, that alone created a rebuttable presumption that automobile belonged to defendant, and, without more, required submission of that question to the jury, even though rebutted by uncontradicted oral testimony of defendant's witnesses. Frew v. Barto, 26 A.2d 905, 345 Pa. 217.

14. **Ala.**—Ford v. Hankins, 96 So. 349, 209 Ala. 202.

Iowa.—Waldman v. Sanders Motor Co., 243 N.W. 555, 214 Iowa 1139.

N.Y.—Nemzer v. Newkirk Ave. Automobile Co., 154 N.Y.S. 117, 91 Misc. 13.

S.D.—Lunde v. Dwyer, 56 N.W.2d 772, 74 S.D. 559.

Wash.—Gams v. Oberholtzer, 310 P. 2d 240, 50 Wash.2d 174 (where third party furnished purchase price of automobile, and defendant signed registration papers only because automobile dealers were unwilling to enter into contract with third party because of his minority, and third party took possession of the automobile after the purchase

15. See note 15 on page 129.

Ch. 417   PRESUMPTIONS AND INFERENCES   § 417.5

In some states, statutes have made registration evidence of ownership.[16] Such statutes are in derogation of the common law and must be strictly construed.[17] It is not intended that the statutory provision should make a jury question in every case. If the testimony as to ownership is conflicting, the statutes war-

and exercised dominion over it up to time of accident, presumption that defendant, as registered owner, was actual owner for purpose of vicarious liability was rebutted).

Wis.—Kruse v. Weigand, 235 N.W. 426, 204 Wis. 195, followed in 235 N.W. 431, 204 Wis. 206, Smith v. Weigand, 235 N.W. 431, 204 Wis. 207, 208 (two cases), and Woodard v. Weigand, 235 N.W. 432, 204 Wis. 209.

Conclusively rebutted

Iowa.—King v. Mack International Motor Truck Corp., 60 N.W.2d 792, 245 Iowa 48 (where evidence was that dealer and truck driver had entered into conditional sales contract entitling driver to immediate possession of unit, presumption, if any, of ownership of vehicle in dealer created by presence of plates on vehicle, was conclusively rebutted).

15. **Ala.**—Ford v. Hankins, 96 So. 349, 209 Ala. 202.

Ark.—Terry Dairy Co. v. Parker, 223 S.W. 6, 144 Ark. 401.

Idaho.—Maier v. Minidoka County Motor Co., 105 P.2d 1076, 61 Idaho 642.

N.J.—Le Strange v. Krivit, 158 A. 117, 10 N.J.Misc. 146.

Question for court

Where uncontradicted testimony rebutted presumption of law arising from ownership of automobile that car was in owner's control at time of accident, liability is question of law for court. Le Strange v. Krivit, 158 A. 117, 10 N.J.Misc. 146.

16. **U.S.**—Davis v. Slocomb, C.C.A. Wash., 288 F. 352, certiorari denied 44 S.Ct. 6, 263 U.S. 700, 68 L.Ed. 513, and error dismissed 44 S.Ct. 59, 263 U.S. 158, 68 L.Ed. 226 (not conclusive where father gave vehicle to son but did not remove the plates).

Ala.—Cox v. Roberts, 27 So.2d 617, 248 Ala. 372.

Cal.—Cook v. Mehlberg, 294 P.2d 746, 140 Cal.App.2d 10 (presumption); Hammond v. Hazard, 180 P. 46, 40 Cal.App. 45.

Ind.—Greaf v. Breitenstein, 187 N.E. 347, 97 Ind.App. 525.

Iowa.—Hartman v. Norman, 112 N.W. 2d 274, 253 Iowa 694.

Ky.—Vansant v. Holbrook's Adm'r, 146 S.W.2d 337, 285 Ky. 88 (partnership as owner).

Minn.—Uphoff v. McCormick, 166 N.W. 788, 139 Minn. 392.

N.Y.—Elfeld v. Burkham Auto Renting Co., 87 N.E.2d 285, 299 N.Y. 336, 13 A.L.R.2d 370; Scholick v. Fifth Ave. Coach Co., 68 N.Y.S.2d 208, 188 Misc. 476.

N.C.—Hartley v. Smith, 79 S.E.2d 767, 239 N.C. 170 (rule of evidence only).

Tenn.—English v. George Cole Motor Co., 111 S.W.2d 386, 21 Tenn.App. 408.

Tex.—Empire Gas & Fuel Co. v. Muegge, 143 S.W.2d 763, 135 Tex. 520.

17. **Tenn.**—English v. George Cole Motor Co., 111 S.W.2d 386, 21 Tenn.App. 408 (may be limited to instances where no evidence of agency is adduced).

§ 417.5   TRIAL EVIDENCE   Ch. 417

rant a finding by the jury that the person in whose name the automobile is registered is in fact the rightful owner.[18]

Likewise the statute cannot be invoked to fix ownership conclusively for the purpose of the law of imputed negligence in such a case.[19]

This presumption, being an administrative presumption of law, is rebuttable by parol evidence,[20] and may be entirely overcome by countervailing testimony.[21]

18. **Cal.**—Hammond v. Hazard, 180 P. 46, 40 Cal.App. 45.

Minn.—Uphoff v. McCormick, 166 N.W. 788, 139 Minn. 392.

Tenn.—Jetton v. Polk, 68 S.W.2d 127, 17 Tenn.App. 395.

19. **U.S.**—Davis v. Slocomb, C.C.A.Wash., 288 F. 352, certiorari denied 44 S.Ct. 6, 263 U.S. 700, 68 L.Ed. 513, and error dismissed 44 S.Ct. 59, 263 U.S. 158, 68 L.Ed. 226.

20. For general discussion of overcoming presumptions, see section 417.1, at fn. 7 et seq.

U.S.—American Emp. Ins. Co. v. Zablosky, C.A.Tex., 292 F.2d 412, certiorari denied 82 S.Ct. 387, 368 U.S. 946, 7 L.Ed.2d 343.

Ind.—Greaf v. Breitenstein, 187 N.E. 347, 97 Ind.App. 525.

Iowa.—Hartman v. Norman, 112 N.W.2d 374, 253 Iowa 694.

Ky.—Siler v. Williford, 350 S.W.2d 704 (mere statements of driver and his wife, whom he had picked up from her work before collision, that automobile "belonged to" their son was insufficient to refute presumption arising from documentary records of ownership by the wife, and contributory negligence instruction should have been predicated upon ownership of the automobile by the wife, and not upon agency relationship between driver and wife).

Tex.—Insurance Co. of Tex. v. Stratton, Civ.App., 287 S.W.2d 320.

21. **Ala.**—Peoples v. Seamon, 31 So.2d 88, 249 Ala. 284; Shipp v. State, 141 So. 366, 25 Ala.App. 104 (driver as donee colliding with another car); Ford v. Hankins, 96 So. 349, 209 Ala. 202.

Cal.—Dorsey v. Barba, App., 226 P.2d 677, subsequent opinion 240 P.2d 604, 38 Cal.2d 350.

Iowa.—Waldman v. Sanders Motor Co., 243 N.W. 555, 214 Iowa 1139.

N.Y.—Nemzer v. Newkirk Ave. Automobile Co., 154 N.Y.S. 117, 91 Misc. 13.

Or.—Henry v. Condit, 53 P.2d 722, 152 Or. 348, 103 A.L.R. 131.

Pa.—Preston v. Schroeder, 27 Del. 350.

Tenn.—Ross v. Griggs, 296 S.W.2d 641, 41 Tenn.App. 491 (by positive credible evidence on subject); Long v. Tomlin, 125 S.W.2d 171, 22 Tenn.App. 607.

Tex.—Knops v. Ordorica, Civ.App., 242 S.W.2d 454; Pioneer Mut. Compensation Co. v. Diaz, 177 S.W.2d 202, 142 Tex. 184; Empire Gas & Fuel Co. v. Muegge, 143 S.W.2d 763, 135 Tex. 520.

Wis.—Kruse v. Weigand, 235 N.W. 426, 204 Wis. 195, followed in 235 N.W. 431, 204 Wis. 206, Smith v. Weigand, 235 N.W. 431, 204 Wis. 207, 208 (two cases), and Woodard v. Weigand, 235 N.W. 432, 204 Wis. 209.

Other evidence of ownership

The presumption of ownership also may arise from evidence that the defendant paid the purchase price and cost of all repairs, maintenance and operation of the automobile.[22]

Where a statute merely provides that the owner shall file a statement of his name and address, with a description of the vehicle, and shall obtain from the secretary of state a numbered certificate, the certificate is prima facie proof of ownership.[23]

In the absence of contrary evidence, it will be presumed, where a transfer of the ownership of an automobile is proved, that statutes regulating such transfers have been fully complied with.[24]

Where it is shown that an automobile once belonged to a certain party, a rebuttable presumption arises that the ownership continues.[25]

Owner in vehicle as driver

Evidence that the owner was riding in the vehicle creates a presumption that the owner was the driver.[26]

---

22. **N.Y.**—Scholick v. Fifth Ave. Coach Co., 68 N.Y.S.2d 208, 188 Misc. 476 (but such presumption inferior to one arising from registration).

23. **Wash.**—Delano v. La Bounty, 114 P. 434, 62 Wash. 595.

24. **Cal.**—Collard v. Love, 61 P.2d 458, 17 Cal.App.2d 72 (presumption existed that new certificate of registration had been issued).

    Tex.—Harper v. Highway Motor Freight Lines, Civ.App., 89 S.W.2d 448 (presumed that bill of sale for truck was in defendant's possession).

25. **Tex.**—Longhorn Drilling Corporation v. Padilla, Civ.App., 138 S.W.2d 164.

    But see

    Where liability of one of defendants depended upon alleged existence of partnership with other defendant, and defendants offered evidence that partnership was dissolved in January of year in which collision occurred in October, the fact that a partnership existed during the three preceding years did not raise a presumption that the partnership continued on through year in which collision occurred. Elmore v. Peavy, Tex.Civ.App., 143 S.W.2d 983.

26. **Ala.**—Gladwell v. Searborough, 1971, 252 So.2d 325, 47 Ala.App. 208 (or under his control); Taylor v. Bass, 187 So.2d 560, 279 Ala. 518 (under owner's control or was being driven by him).

    Conn.—State v. Jordan, 1969, 258 A.2d 552, 5 Conn.Cir. 561.

    Iowa—Marean v. Petersen, 144 N.W.2d 906, 259 Iowa 557 (rebuttably presumed to be driver in absence of direct testimony as to identity of driver).

    Mich.—Grinstead v. Anscer, 92 N.W.2d 42, 353 Mich. 542.

    Minn.—Sprader v. Mueller, 121 N.W.2d 176, 265 Minn. 111 (owner has the burden of overcoming presumption that he was in control at the time of the accident, and

§ 417.5

Presumptions of control

Evidence of ownership may raise a presumption of control of the vehicle at the time in question.[27]

The fact that the owner of an automobile is riding therein raises a presumption or inference that the driver was under the owner's control,[28] especially where the driver is a member of the

in the absence of direct evidence, because of death or amnesia, or wholly inconclusive circumstantial evidence, court has duty to hold that owner of the automobile was the driver).

Pa.—Rodney v. Staman, 89 A.2d 313, 371 Pa. 1, 32 A.L.R.2d 976 (presumption that deceased was driving); Limes v. Keller, 74 A. 2d 131, 365 Pa. 258 (both occupants killed).

Tenn.—Lawing v. Johnson, App., 355 S.W.2d 465, 49 Tenn.App. 403 (did not overcome presumption the defendant was the driver of his own automobile where his testimony was impeached by cross-examination and contradicted by circumstantial evidence and inferences); Moore v. Watkins, 293 S. W.2d 185, 41 Tenn.App. 246.

Contra

Mo.—Campbell v. Fry, App.1969, 439 S.W.2d 545.

N.C.—Stegall v. Sledge, 102 S.E.2d 115, 247 N.C. 718.

Not rebutted by fact owner found outside of vehicle

In action for death of guest against administrator of owner of automobile which left highway and struck tree, killing both owner and guest, fact that owner was found outside automobile was not sufficient to rebut statutory presumption. Ross v. Griggs, 296 S.W.2d 641, 41 Tenn.App. 491.

27. Ill.—McElroy v. Force, 220 N.E. 2d 761, 75 Ill.App.2d 441.

Not countermanded by presumption of innocence

Oklahoma City ordinance providing that proof that vehicle was parked in violation of law or regulation shall constitute prima facie presumption that registered owner of vehicle was person who parked it places burden upon owner to offer proof that he was not in possession or control of the vehicle but does not change law as to presumption of innocence and is not unconstitutional on that theory. Cantrell v. Oklahoma City, Okl.Cr.1969, 454 P.2d 676, certiorari denied 90 S.Ct. 568, 396 U.S. 1010, 24 L.Ed.2d 501.

28. U.S.—Jackson v. Continental Bank & Trust Co., C.A.Utah 1971, 443 F.2d 1344; Myles v. Philadelphia Transp. Co., C.A.Pa.1951, 189 F.2d 1014.

Ala.—Gladwell v. Scarbrough, 1971, 252 So.2d 325, 47 Ala.App. 208 (or that it was being operated by him).

Cal.—Ray v. Hanisch, 306 P.2d 30, 147 Cal.App.2d 742.

Ga.—Central of Georgia Ry. Co. v. Luther, 1973, 196 S.E.2d 149, 128 Ga.App. 178 (but such inference applies only where nothing else appears); Blount v. Sutton, 152 S.E.2d 777, 114 Ga.App. 767.

Ill.—Anderson v. Launer, 142 N.E.2d 838, 13 Ill.App.2d 530.

Md.—Merritt v. Darden, 176 A.2d 205, 227 Md. 589; Powers v. State, for Use and Benefit of Reynolds, 11 A.2d 909, 178 Md. 23.

Ohio—Clauss v. Fields, 1971, 278 N.E.2d 677, 29 Ohio App.2d 93; Blake v. Stauffer, 175 N.E.2d 194,

owner's family;[29] and similarly the presence of joint owners in an automobile gives rise to a presumption of joint possession and therefore of joint control.[30]

A husband who is head of the family may be presumed to be in control of a family vehicle, even though it is registered in the name of another.[31]

These presumptions are rebuttable.[32]

112 Ohio App. 59; Ross v. Burgan, 126 N.E.2d 592, 163 Ohio St. 211, 50 A.L.R.2d 1275.

Pa.—Santore v. Reading Co., 84 A. 2d 375, 170 Pa.Super. 57; Beam v. Pittsburgh Rys. Co., 77 A.2d 634, 366 Pa. 360, certiorari denied 71 S.Ct. 851, 341 U.S. 936, 95 L.Ed. 1364.

Tex.—Whistler's Estate v. Shoemaker, 1973, 502 S.W.2d 237, judgment affirmed 513 S.W.2d 10 (but such theory is not applicable where driver and passenger are coowners).

Utah.—Hall v. Blackham, 417 P.2d 664, 18 Utah 2d 164; Morley v. Rodberg, 323 P.2d 717, 7 Utah 2d 299; Fox v. Lavender, 56 P.2d 1049, 89 Utah 115, 109 A.L.R. 105.

Wis.—Strupp v. Farmers Mut. Auto. Ins. Co., 109 N.W.2d 660, 14 Wis. 2d 158.

29. **Mass.**—Levangie v. Gutterson, 194 N.E. 79, 289 Mass. 287 (son).

Ohio.—General Exchange Ins. Co. v. Elizer, App., 31 N.E.2d 147, 32 O. L.A. 579 (son).

Pa.—Spegele v. Blumfield, 182 A. 149, 120 Pa.Super. 231 (son).

But see

N.D.—Pearson v. Erb, 82 N.W.2d 818 (rebuttable presumption or inference arises that owner has control over it and that the driver is acting as his agent in operating vehicle; but such presumption is not strengthened merely by reason of fact that owner and driver are husband and wife).

30. **U.S.**—W. W. Clyde & Co. v. Dyess, C.C.A.Utah, 126 F.2d 719, certiorari denied 63 S.Ct. 29, 317 U.S. 638, 87 L.Ed. 514.

Utah.—Nielsen v. Watanabe, 62 P.2d 117, 90 Utah 401; Fox v. Lavender, 56 P.2d 1049, 89 Utah 115, 109 A. L.R. 105.

31. **Ky.**—Gray v. Golden, 192 S.W. 2d 371, 301 Ky. 477 (family purpose doctrine is applicable, though legal title to automobile is in some one else).

N.D.—Jasper v. Freitag, 145 N.W.2d 879 (when he is driving his wife's automobile, even with her riding in the automobile, there is a rebuttable presumption that he is in control).

Contra

Where automobile was in name of 18-year-old infant and his mother, presumption was that they alone had control and, in absence of anything to rebut that presumption, infant's father could not be held liable for injuries sustained while infant was driving. Dortman v. Lester, 143 N.W.2d 130, 3 Mich.App. 600.

32. For discussion on rebutting presumptions generally, see section 417.1 at fn. 7 et seq.

U.S.—Hansen v. Nicholas Moving & Storage, Inc., C.A.Utah 1971, 451 F.2d 319 (presumption of control by owner-passenger was overcome by evidence relating to driver's customary use of car and purpose of trip); Rose v. Ruan Transport Corp., C.A.Ill., 214 F.2d 583.

§ 417.5 TRIAL EVIDENCE

Where it is conceded that the defendant did not own the vehicle causing the injuries, the plaintiff has the burden of rebutting the presumption that the owner was in control and of establishing the fact that the owner had surrendered control to the defendant.[33]

§ 417.6 Consent and Permission

Library References:
C.J.S. Motor Vehicles § 511(6).
West's Key No. Digests, Automobiles ⛬242(6).

The general rule is that there is an inference or presumption to be drawn from the use of another's automobile that such use is by and with the owner's consent.[34]

Ga.—Lash v. State, 103 S.E.2d 653, 97 Ga.App. 622.

Ill.—McElroy v. Force, 220 N.E.2d 761, 75 Ill.App.2d 441 (presumption of control by owner is not rebutted by a mere countervailing presumption, only by clear and convincing evidence to the contrary); Hilyard v. Duncan, 158 N.E.2d 438, 21 Ill. App.2d 514; Sutherland v. Guccione, 131 N.E.2d 130, 8 Ill.App.2d 201 (presumption owner parked vehicle not overcome by his uncontradicted denial).

Ky.—Broadway Motors v. Bass, 67 S.W.2d 955, 252 Ky. 628.

N.Y.—Orlando v. Pioneer Barber Towel Supply Co., 146 N.E. 621, 239 N.Y. 342 (not overcome by mere denial).

Ohio.—Clauss v. Fields, 1971, 278 N. E.2d 677, 29 Ohio App.2d 93.

Pa.—Kaplan Trucking Co. v. Coshocton Cartage, Inc., 215 A.2d 320, 207 Pa.Super. 43 (lessee's evidence of lease and voucher rebutted presumption that lessee whose name appeared on signs attached to truck was in exclusive control of truck); Huster v. Continental Cas. Co., 37 D. & C.2d 197, Pa.Com.Pl., 10 Lycoming 33 (the presumption arising where a commercial vehicle bears legend indicating its ownership, that the vehicle is owned by such party and that the driver of the vehicle was the servant of the owner acting within the scope of his employment, does not apply where plaintiff offers evidence that the vehicle was not owned by defendant and that the master-servant relationship did not exist).

S.D.—Lunde v. Dwyer, 56 N.W.2d 772, 74 S.D. 559.

Tenn.—Lawing v. Johnson, 355 S.W. 2d 465, 49 Tenn.App. 403; Thompson v. Malone & Hyde, 65 S.W.2d 1079, 16 Tenn.App. 152.

Utah.—Fox v. Lavender, 56 P.2d 1049, 89 Utah 115, 109 A.L.R. 105.

Wis.—Schweidler v. Caruso, 69 N.W. 2d 611, 269 Wis. 438.

33. N.Y.—Richter v. Merola Bros., 277 N.Y.S. 288, 243 App.Div. 392.

34. U.S.—Royal Indem. Co. v. Wingate, D.C.Md.1973, 353 F.Supp. 1002, affirmed C.A.4, 1973, 487 F. 2d 1398; Webb v. Moreno, C.A.8, 1966, 363 F.2d 97; Lukehart v. Gleason, C.A.Iowa, 207 F.2d 529 (under Iowa law, a rebuttable presumption).

Cal.—Bruce v. Ullery, 25 Cal.Rptr. 841, 375 P.2d 833, 58 Cal.2d 702; Anderson v. Wagnon, 242 P.2d 915, 110 Cal.App.2d 362; Blank v. Coffin, App.1941, 117 P.2d 53, subsequent opinion 126 P.2d 868, 20 Cal. 2d 457 (rebuttal only makes jury question on issue).

Ch. 417   PRESUMPTIONS AND INFERENCES   § **417.6**

Continued and customary use of an automobile by one other than the owner prior to an accident gives rise to a permissible inference that such use was with the consent of the owner.[35]

Fla.—Dowling v. Nicholson, 135 So. 288, 101 Fla. 672.

Iowa.—Tuttle v. Longnecker, 138 N. W.2d 851, 258 Iowa 393. Sexton v. Lauman, 57 N.W.2d 200, 244 Iowa 670, 37 A.L.R.2d 353.

Mich.—Cowles v. Erb-Restrick Lumber Co., 1970, 176 N.W.2d 412, 21 Mich.App. 642; Rabaut v. Venable, 280 N.W. 129, 285 Mich. 111 (loaned to customer by sales company).

Minn.—Schultz v. Swift & Co., 299 N.W. 7, 210 Minn. 533.

N.Y.—Lovetere v. Stackhouse, 267 N.Y.S.2d 758, 25 A.D.2d 628 (Canadian resident's admission of ownership of vehicle used in New York); Lozada v. Copeland, 138 N. Y.S.2d 521, 207 Misc. 382.

Tenn.—Green v. Powell, 124 S.W.2d 269, 22 Tenn.App. 481.

Wis.—Christiansen v. Schenkenberg, 236 N.W. 109, 204 Wis. 323.

But see

Cal.—Engstrom v. Auburn Automobile Sales Corporation, 77 P.2d 1059, 11 Cal.2d 64; Di Rebaylio v. Herndon, 44 P.2d 581, 6 Cal.App. 2d 567; Bradford v. Sargent, 27 P. 2d 93, 135 Cal.App. 324.

Leased vehicle

Mich.—Michigan Mut. Liability Co. v. Staal Buick, Inc., 1972, 200 N.W.2d 726, 41 Mich.App. 625 (has been extended to include owners of vehicles which have been rented or leased).

N.Y.—Kenneth v. Gardner, 1971, 317 N.Y.S.2d 798, 36 A.D.2d 575; Platt v. Hertz Corp., 1970, 315 N.Y.S.2d 780, reversed on other grounds 321 N.Y.S.2d 613, 66 Misc.2d 505 (fact that employee, as ultimate driver, was unlicensed did not in and of itself break chain of presumptive permission created by statute); Lorippo v. Chrysler Leasing Corp., 1969, 299 N.Y.S.2d 672, 59 Misc.2d 534.

Not rental agency vehicle

Statutory presumption vehicle being driven with knowledge and consent did not apply in absence of evidence that driver was a member of the "immediate family" of owner, an automobile rental agency. Lahey v. Sharp, 1970, 179 N.W.2d 195, 23 Mich.App. 556.

Rule applicable against owner defendant or plaintiff

Under Maryland law, if automobile is negligently operated, it is presumed that owner consented to negligence and in absence of proof that owner abandoned right of control, he is liable and no different rule applies in respect to imputing driver's negligence when owner-passenger is not being sued but is suing a third person. Capital Transit Co. v. Simpson, 235 F.2d 525, 98 U.S.App D.C. 298, certiorari denied 77 S.Ct. 103, 352 U.S. 882, 1 L.Ed.2d 81.

Use by co-owner

Where husband and wife were admittedly co-owners, an inference of consent to wife's driving arose. Bruce v. Ullery, 21 Cal.Rptr. 310, opinion vacated 25 Cal.Rptr. 841, 375 P.2d 833, 58 Cal.2d 702.

35. Iowa.—Bridges v. Welzien, 300 N.W. 659, 231 Iowa 6.

Or.—Steele v. Hemmers, 40 P.2d 1022, 149 Or. 381 (relative of owner).

Wis.—Main v. Cameron, 108 N.W.2d 142, 13 Wis.2d 15; Christiansen v. Schenkenberg, 236 N.W. 109, 204 Wis. 323 (relative of owner).

A presumption of consent may arise in the form of a presumption of compliance with the law, as where a statute makes temporary use of an automobile without the owner's consent a misdemeanor.[36] However, a penal statute making it a misdemeanor to drive the automobile of another without consent, and providing that consent will not be implied by prior conduct, does not preclude the application of the doctrine of implied consent in civil actions against the owner for the negligent acts of the owner's son.[37]

Some statutes provide that the owner of a motor vehicle shall be liable for any injury occasioned by the negligent operation of it when it is being driven with express or implied consent or knowledge of the owner, and that it shall be presumed that such motor vehicle is being driven with the knowledge and consent of the owner if it is driven at the time of an injury by any immediate member of the family.[38]

Some statutes have provided that proof of ownership of the vehicle shall be prima facie evidence that the driver operated the vehicle with the owner's consent, and it has been held that the statutory presumption continues until there is credible evidence to the contrary and only ceases when there is uncontradicted proof that the vehicle was not at the time being used with the owner's permission.[39]

36. **Cal.**—Lanfried v. Bosworth, 114 P.2d 406, 45 Cal.App.2d 408; Prickett v. Whapples, 52 P.2d 972, 10 Cal.App.2d 701.

Minn.—Schultz v. Swift & Co., 299 N.W. 7, 210 Minn. 533.

37. Idaho.—Abbs v. Redmond, 132 P.2d 1044, 64 Idaho 369.

38. Mich.—Pulford v. Mouw, 272 N.W. 713, 279 Mich. 376; Transcontinental Ins. Co. v. Berens, 236 N.W. 887, 254 Mich. 613.

Stronger than ordinary presumption

Presumption that member of owner's family was driving with knowledge and consent of owner is a stronger presumption than the ordinary rebuttable presumption because of the dangerous instrumentality involved, difficulty of showing actual consent, and because of high likelihood that those in the intimate family relationship are aware of each other's movements. Krisher v. Duff, 50 N.W.2d 332, 331 Mich. 699 (though legislature removed word "conclusively").

39. U.S.—Hudson v. Lazarus, 217 F.2d 344, 95 U.S.App.D.C. 16; Hiscox v. Jackson, 127 F.2d 160, 75 U.S.App.D.C. 293.

Dist.Col.—District of Columbia v. Abramson, D.C.Mun.App., 148 A.2d 578; Sawyer v. Miseli, D.C.Mun.App., 156 A.2d 141; Rice v. Simmons, D.C.Mun.App., 53 A.2d 587.

Fla.—Newcomb v. Harding, 181 So. 2d 573 (did not prevail in face of testimony that on the night in question the owner said "no" when driver asked to use the automobile).

Minn.—Eicher v. Universal Underwriters, 83 N.W.2d 895, 250 Minn. 7 (employee driver).

N.Y.—Deyo v. Belotte, 27 N.Y.S.2d 1, 261 App.Div. 1119, reargument

The presumption of a motor vehicle owner's consent to the use of the vehicle is rebuttable,[40] but the rebutting evidence must

denied 29 N.Y.S.2d 910, 262 App. Div. 921, appeal denied.

Tenn.—Teague v. Pritchard, 279 S.W. 2d 706, 38 Tenn.App. 686 (prima facie evidence).

40. For general discussion of rebuttable presumptions, see section 417.1 at fn. 7 et seq.

U.S.—Conrad v. Porter, 196 F.2d 240, 90 U.S.App.D.C. 423, affirming, D.C.Mun.App., 79 A.2d 777.

Ala.—Thompson v. Havard, 1970, 235 So.2d 853, 285 Ala. 718.

Cal.—Hicks v. Reis, 134 P.2d 788, 21 Cal.2d 654.

Dist.Col.—Lancaster v. Canuel, D.C. Mun.App., 193 A.2d 555 (rebutted by denial by owner); District of Columbia v. Abramson, Mun.App., 148 A.2d 578 (evidence, consisting of regulation of district commissioners requiring that government-owned vehicles be used exclusively for official purposes and testimony of employee's superiors in the department that employee did not have permission to use truck to go home for lunch, was sufficient to overcome such presumption).

Iowa.—Hunter v. Irwin, 263 N.W. 34, 220 Iowa 693 (inference that automobile is being operated with consent of owner has no evidential weight after it has been overcome by undisputed evidence).

Mich.—Ensign v. Crater, 1972, 200 N. W.2d 341, 41 Mich.App. 477 (that owner instructed daughter that car was to be home by midnight and that no one else was to drive it and that daughter's boyfriend who was driving car when it left road after 2:00 a. m. causing injury to passenger was not operating car with knowledge of owner was sufficient to rebut presumption of consent and knowledge); Muma v. Brown, 148 N.W.2d 760, 378 Mich. 637 (operation by son of owner); Christiansen v. Hilber, 276 N.W. 495, 282 Mich. 403; Union Trust Co. v. American Commercial Car Co., 189 N.W. 23, 219 Mich. 557 (where proof shows loaned vehicle was not returned in time stipulated, no question for the jury remains).

N.Y.—Peemoller v. Viscarra, 1971, 321 N.Y.S.2d 809, 36 A.D.2d 1971; Febraro v. Hertz Corp., 1970, 315 N.Y.S.2d 702, 64 Misc.2d 794; Nickens v. City of New York, Sup., 71 N.Y.S.2d 877 (nullified by proof of non-consent); Houlihan v. Selengut, 25 N.Y.S.2d 371, 175 Misc. 854, reversed on other grounds 31 N.Y. S.2d 560, 263 App.Div. 811.

Tenn.—Teague v. Pritchard, 279 S.W. 2d 706, 38 Tenn.App. 686 (established use by employee without knowledge or permission); Card v. Commercial Casualty Ins. Co., 95 S.W.2d 1281, 20 Tenn.App. 132.

Rebutted by denial of owner

Iowa.—Harms v. Ridgeway, 64 N.W. 2d 286, 245 Iowa 810 (prima facie case is overcome by a denial of owner that such operation was by his consent, and the burden of proof remains with the complainant to prove that vehicle was being driven with owner's consent).

Unlicensed co-owner

Although use by co-owner gave rise to presumption of consent by the absent co-owner, circumstances that co-owner who used automobile was an unlicensed driver and was using automobile without absent co-owner's consent when automobile struck plaintiff served to rebut the presumption. Payne v. Payne, 1971, 322 N.Y. S.2d 238, 28 N.Y.2d 399, 271 N.E.2d 220.

§ 417.6   TRIAL EVIDENCE   Ch. 417

be direct, positive, and credible.[41] The presumption continues until there is substantial evidence to the contrary.[42]

41. **U.S.**—Rosenberg v. Murray, 116 F.2d 552, 73 App.D.C. 67.

Dist.Col.—Alsbrooks v. Washington Deliveries, Inc., App.1971, 281 A.2d 220 (uncontradicted proof entitles owner to directed verdict); Conrad v. Porter, Mun.App., 79 A.2d 777, affirmed 196 F.2d 240, 90 U.S. App.D.C. 423; Senator Cab Co. v. Rothberg, Mun.App., 42 A.2d 245.

Iowa.—Schneberger v. Glenn, 1970, 176 N.W.2d 782; Bridges v. Welzien, 300 N.W. 659, 231 Iowa 6.

Mich.—Michigan Mut. Liability Co. v. Staal Buick, Inc., 1972, 200 N.W. 2d 726, 41 Mich.App. 625 (has been extended to include owners of vehicles which have been rented or leased); Ensign v. Crater, 1972, 200 N.W.2d 341, 41 Mich.App. 477 (evidence that owner instructed daughter that car was to be home by midnight and that no one else was to drive it and that daughter's boyfriend who was driving car when it left road after 2:00 a. m. causing injury to passenger was not operating car with knowledge of owner was sufficient to rebut presumption); Lahey v. Sharp, 1970, 179 N.W.2d 195, 23 Mich.App. 556; Detroit Auto. Inter-Insurance Exchange v. Gordon, 1968, 165 N.W. 2d 923, 15 Mich.App. 41; Krisher v. Duff, 50 N.W.2d 332, 331 Mich. 699 (testimony of plaintiff's witness that he had seen brother driving automobile five days a week and also on Saturday, thereby specifically contradicting owner's testimony that brother had not driven the automobile during that time, cast at least some doubt upon owner's testimony that brother drove without knowledge and consent of owner and was not customarily given permission to drive, thereby casting burden on owner to refute by clear, positive and credible proof, prima facie case made out by plaintiff); Christiansen v. Hilber, 276 N.W. 495, 282 Mich. 403 (defendant's logging truck being driven by his son, statutory presumption that truck was being driven with defendant's consent was overcome by uncontradicted testimony, that truck was used only for business purposes, that defendant never gave any one permission to use it for pleasure purposes, and that at time of accident it was being used for pleasure purposes without defendant's consent).

Minn.—Eicher v. Universal Underwriters, 83 N.W.2d 895, 250 Minn. 7 (presumption may not always be overcome by uncontradicted testimony of owner that his consent had not been given therefor, and if other evidence makes the issue inconclusive, or if different inferences may be drawn therefrom, or if the credibility of such testimony may be in question, the issue is for the finders of fact).

N.Y.—Platt v. Hertz Corp., 1971, 321 N.Y.S.2d 613, 66 Misc.2d 505 (terms of rental agreement limited extension of secondary permission); Beach v. Richtmyer, 90 N.Y.S.2d 332, 275 App.Div. 466.

42. **U.S.**—Tomack v. U. S., C.A.N. Y., 369 F.2d 350.

Fla.—Alred v. Jones, 189 So.2d 226 (where uncontradicted evidence shows that driver was operating truck without owner's consent the presumption vanishes); Leonetti v. Boone, 74 So.2d 551.

Iowa.—Schneberger v. Glenn, 1970, 176 N.W.2d 782 (that owner gave another permission to use the vehicle while the other's automobile was being repaired and left a note with keys stating that owner would prefer that no one else use the automobile, owner, as a matter of law, had successfully overcome presumption of consent to operation of automobile by a second per-

Ch. 417 PRESUMPTIONS AND INFERENCES § 417.7

The fact that an automobile, at the time of an accident, was being driven by some one other than the person to whom the owner entrusted it does not necessarily preclude the presumption of consent.[43]

§ 417.7 Agency

Library References:
C.J.S. Motor Vehicles § 511(6).
West's Key No. Digests, Automobiles ⚖242(6).

In most jurisdictions, proof of ownership has been held to create a presumption or to justify an inference that the driver mittee who was driving automobile with consent of first permittee).

Mo.—Campbell v. Fry, App.1969, 439 S.W.2d 545 (where deputy sheriff, who investigated scene where defendant's automobile ran off the road and struck plaintiff's tractor and trailer, testified on direct examination that defendant stated to him that he had been kidnapped and that automobile was being operated by kidnappers over his protest, against his will and without his consent, and all other evidence introduced on issue was consistent therewith, there was substantial evidence on question of agency and scope thereof, so that presumption that automobile was being driven with acquiescence of defendant was not applicable).

N.Y.—Woods v. Britt, 1974, 361 N.Y. S.2d 678, 46 A.D.2d 865; Casiano v. Weinstein & Son Floor Covering Corp., 1971, 322 N.Y.S.2d 497, 37 A.D.2d 564; Rivera v. W. & R. Service Station, Inc., 1970, 309 N.Y.S. 2d 274, 34 A.D.2d 115.

Michigan rule
Presumption that motor vehicle, taken with permission of its owner, is thereafter being driven with his express or implied consent or knowledge is not overcome by evidence that driver has violated terms of original permission or by evidence of good faith efforts by owner to get vehicle returned voluntarily by driver; overruling Merritt v. Huron Motor Sales, Inc., 1937, 282 Mich. 322, 276 N.W. 464. Roberts v. Posey, 1972, 194 N.W.2d 310, 386 Mich. 656.

43. Cal.—Randolph v. Hunt, 183 P. 358, 41 Cal.App. 739.

Iowa.—Tuttle v. Longnecker, 138 N. W.2d 851, 258 Iowa 393 (evidence including owner's testimony that he had never told his daughter not to allow anyone else to drive automobile and evidence that owner's daughter had entrusted vehicle to driver, was sufficient to take to jury issue as to whether vehicle was driven with owner's consent); Sexton v. Lauman, 57 N.W.2d 200, 244 Iowa 670, 37 A.L.R.2d 353 (evidence was insufficient to overcome such presumption or inference, in view of fact that driver was driving under direction of such person's nephew who had lawful possession of the automobile).

N.Y.—Sternberg v. Liberty Mut. Ins. Co., 1972, 340 N.Y.S.2d 550, 72 Misc.2d 655 (where lessee gave permission to son to drive leased automobile, it would be presumed that driver had implied permission from lessor); Aarons v. Standard Varnish Works, 296 N.Y.S. 312, 163 Misc. 84, affirmed 3 N.Y.S.2d 910, 254 App.Div. 560.

§ 417.7 TRIAL EVIDENCE Ch. 417

was the agent or servant of the owner and an inference of operation in pursuit of the owner's business and within the scope of the driver's employment.[44] The presumption shifts upon the owner the burden of going forward with the evidence.[45]

---

44. Cited by the court in Palmer v. Van Petten Lumber Co., 1972, 509 P.2d 420, 428, 265 Or. 347.

U.S.—Jack Cole Co. v. Hudson, C.A. Miss.1969, 409 F.2d 188; Guthrie v. U. S., D.C.Wis., 260 F.Supp. 289 (under Wisconsin law, there is a prima facie presumption); Baker v. U. S., D.C.D.C., 159 F.Supp. 925, affirmed 265 F.2d 123, 105 U.S. App.D.C. 139 (soldier in army truck); Holland v. Cooper, C.A. Ga., 192 F.2d 214 (rebutted by evidence); Martin v. Burgess, C.C.A. Ala., 82 F.2d 321 (administrative presumption raised); Simon v. City Cab Co., 78 F.2d 506, 64 App.D.C. 364, certiorari denied 56 S.Ct. 173, 296 U.S. 640, 80 L.Ed. 455 (taxicab driver).

Ala.—Goggins v. Miller Transporters, Inc., 1973, 276 So.2d 571, 290 Ala. 326; Thompson v. Curry, 56 So.2d 359, 36 Ala.App. 334, certiorari denied 56 So.2d 362, 256 Ala. 564 (raises administrative presumption only); Lowry v. Nobles, 44 So.2d 20, 35 Ala.App. 99 (defendant's son); Scott v. Birmingham Elec. Co., 33 So.2d 344, 250 Ala. 61 (administrative rebuttable presumption); Craft v. Koonce, 187 So. 730, 237 Ala. 552 (presumption distinguished from "inference of fact"); Grimes v. Fulmer, 180 So. 321, 235 Ala. 645, followed in 180 So. 323, 235 Ala. 664 and 183 So. 924, 28 Ala. 630 (owner riding in automobile driven by another); United Wholesale Grocery Co. v. Minge Floral Co., 142 So. 586, 25 Ala.App. 153, certiorari denied 142 So. 587, 225 Ala. 160 (salesman who had completed his day's work and was on an indirect route home); Jefferson County Burial Soc. v. Cotton, 133 So. 256, 222 Ala. 578 (automobile ambulance).

Ariz.—Hatchimonji v. Homes, 3 P.2d 271, 38 Ariz. 535 (servant taking car to have it washed).

Ark.—Adkins v. L. L. Cole & Son, 211 S.W.2d 885, 213 Ark. 585 (temporary presumption); Ford & Son Sanitary Co. v. Ransom, 210 S.W. 2d 508, 213 Ark. 390 (temporary presumption).

Cal.—Smith v. Johe, 316 P.2d 688, 154 Cal.App.2d 508; Ceranski v. Muensch, 141 P.2d 750, 60 Cal.App. 2d 751 (proof of use with owner's permission); Shields v. Oxnard Harbor Dist., 116 P.2d 121, 46 Cal. App.2d 477; Malmstrom v. Bridges, 47 P.2d 336, 8 Cal.App.2d 5 (may draw inference); Kanananakoa v. Badalamente, 6 P.2d 338, 119 Cal. App. 231 (incompetent driver); Wilson v. Droege, 294 P. 726, 110 Cal.App. 578 (no inference arises from proof of ownership alone that the machine was being operated by an agent within the scope of his employment); McWhirter v. Fuller, 170 P. 417, 35 Cal.App. 288 (wife driving with express consent of husband).

Dist.Col.—McMickle v. Nickens, Mun. App., 104 A.2d 409 (based upon Financial Responsibility Law); Gasque v. Saidman, Mun.App., 44 A.2d 537 (taxicab).

Fla.—Dowling v. Nicholson, 135 So. 288, 101 Fla. 672.

Ga.—Veal v. Paulk, 1970, 174 S.E.2d 465, 121 Ga.App. 575; F. E. Fortenberry & Sons, Inc. v. Malmberg, 102 S.E.2d 667, 97 Ga.App. 162; Swift & Co. v. Lawson, 97 S. E.2d 168, 95 Ga.App. 35.

Ill.—State Farm Mut. Auto Ins. Co. v. Short, 1970, 260 N.E.2d 415, 125

---

45. See note 45 on page 144.

140

Ill.App.2d 97 (driver was brother of owner); Watts v. Staunton Lumber Co., 116 N.E.2d 908, 1 Ill.App.2d 224 (could be rebutted by self-serving testimony of the defendant's manager).

Ind.—Frick v. Bickel, 1944, 54 N.E.2d 436, 115 Ind.App. 114, motion denied 57 N.E.2d 62, 222 Ind. 610 (used truck all day, then drove it away from place of business after 5:00 p. m.).

Iowa.—Hunter v. Irwin, 263 N.W. 34, 220 Iowa 693 (prima facie case made).

Ky.—Farrell v. Pinson Transfer Co., 293 S.W.2d 170; Wagner v. Emmett, 280 S.W.2d 210 (commercial vehicle); Union Transfer & Storage Co. v. Fryman's Adm'r, 200 S.W.2d 953, 304 Ky. 422; Rawlings v. Clay Motor Co., 154 S.W.2d 711, 287 Ky. 604.

La.—Leson Chevrolet Co. v. Phoenix Ins. Co. of Hartford, 195 So.2d 444; Cofield v. Burgdorf, App., 111 So.2d 845, reversed 115 So.2d 357, 238 La. 297, on remand, App., 117 So.2d 663 (rebuttable presumption); Simms v. Lawrence Bros., App., 72 So.2d 538 (rebuttable inference of responsibility arises from proof of ownership, and when proof supporting such inference goes far towards establishing that the operator of the vehicle was on mission for owner, inference takes on a status nearly equal to conviction, to overcome which evidence of unusually strong and convincing character must be adduced).

Md.—Hoerr v. Hanline, 149 A.2d 378, 219 Md. 413; Fowser Fast Freight v. Simmont, 78 A.2d 178, 196 Md. 584; Gutheridge, On Behalf and to Use of Ring Engineering Co. v. Gorsuch, 8 A.2d 885, 177 Md. 109 (failure to deny ownership).

Mass.—Morton v. Dobson, 30 N.E.2d 231, 307 Mass. 394.

Mich.—Morrow v. Trathen, 284 N.W. 687, 288 Mich. 172 (general rule stated, but employee found to be driving truck for own pleasure).

Minn.—Lausche v. Denison-Harding Chevrolet Co., 243 N.W. 52, 185 Minn. 635 (automobile salesman); Martin v. Schiska, 236 N.W. 312, 183 Minn. 256.

Miss.—Pennebaker v. Parker, 100 So.2d 363, 232 Miss. 725.

Mo.—Fidelity & Cas. Co. of N. Y. v. Western Cas. & Sur. Co., App., 337 S.W.2d 566 (owner in vehicle); Steele v. Thomas, 101 S.W.2d 499, 231 Mo. 865 (vehicle used for business purposes, accident during business hours); Nagle v. Alberter, App., 53 S.W.2d 289.

Neb.—Ebers v. Whitmore, 241 N.W. 126, 122 Neb. 653; Finegold v. Union Outfitting Co., 193 N.W. 331, 110 Neb. 202.

N.J.—Eule v. Eule Motor Sales, 170 A.2d 241, 34 N.J. 537 (partnership); Tinsman v. Parsekian, 167 A.2d 407, 65 N.J.Super. 217; Cowan v. Kaminow, 26 A.2d 258, 128 N.J.L. 398; Coopersmith v. Kalt, 196 A. 649, 119 N.J.L. 474 (rule stated but presumption held overcome).

N.Y.—Traub v. Blum, 31 N.Y.S.2d 735, 263 App.Div. 92 (involving law of New Jersey); Duffy v. Ascher, 181 N.Y.S. 934, 191 A.D. 918 (driving with express consent).

N.C.—Randall Ins., Inc. v. O'Neill, 128 S.E.2d 239, 258 N.C. 169; Williamson v. Varner, 114 S.E.2d 92, 252 N.C. 446; Hartley v. Smith, 79 S.E.2d 767, 239 N.C. 170 (statutory).

Ohio.—Griffith v. Rutledge, 169 N.E.2d 464, 110 Ohio App. 301 (owner present in vehicle); Paduchik v. Mikoff, 112 N.E.2d 69, Com.Pl., affirmed 110 N.E.2d 562, 158 Ohio St. 533 (owner present in auto); Brooks v. Sentle, 58 N.E.2d 234, 74 Ohio App. 231 (owner in car).

Or.—Blevins v. Phillips, 343 P.2d 1110, 218 Or. 121; Ellenberger v. Fremont Land Co., 107 P.2d 837, 165 Or. 375 (inference driver was

§ 417.7   TRIAL EVIDENCE   Ch. 417

the defendant's servant, and that vehicle was being used for defendant's purposes); Kantola v. Lovell Auto Co., 72 P.2d 61, 157 Or. 534 (inference raised in absence of contrary evidence).

Pa.—Waters v. New Amsterdam Cas. Co., 144 A.2d 354, 393 Pa. 247; Preston v. Schroeder, 27 Pa.Del. Co. 350 (used for business purposes, accident during business hours).

R.I.—Hill v. Cabral, 18 A.2d 145, 66 R.I. 145 (owner's son).

Tenn.—Sadler v. Draper, 326 S.W.2d 148, 46 Tenn.App. 1; Moore v. Union Chevrolet Co., 1959, 326 S.W.2d 855, 46 Tenn.App. 206 (by statute); Mofield v. Haynes, 230 S.W.2d 200, 33 Tenn.App. 127; Maysay v. Hickman, 97 S.W.2d 662, 20 Tenn.App. 262.

Tex.—Henderson Drilling Corp. v. Perez, Civ.App., 304 S.W.2d 172; Austin Road Co. v. Willman, Civ. App., 303 S.W.2d 878; Poe Motor Co. v. Martin, Civ.App., 201 S.W. 2d 102 (question of fact though no rebuttal testimony introduced); Alfano v. International Harvester Co. of America, Civ.App., 121 S. W.2d 466 (truck used by salesman); Hudson v. Ernest Allen Motor Co., Civ.App., 115 S.W.2d 1167 (rule stated but presumption held overcome); Harper v. Highway Motor Freight Lines, Civ.App., 89 S.W.2d 448 (prima facie case made).

Vt.—Young v. Lamson, 160 A.2d 873, 121 Vt. 474; Cappello v. Aero Mayflower Transit Co., 68 A.2d 913, 116 Vt. 64.

Va.—McNeill v. Spindler, 62 S.E.2d 13, 191 Va. 685; Ercole v. Daniel, 141 S.E. 631, 105 W.Va. 118.

Wash.—Callen v. Coca-Cola Bottling Inc., 310 P.2d 236, 50 Wash.2d 180; McMullen v. Warren Motor Co., 25 P.2d 99, 174 Wash. 454.

W.Va.—Stevens v. Frump, 52 S.E. 2d 181, 132 W.Va. 66; Malcolm v. American Service Co., 191 S.E. 527, 118 W.Va. 637 (rule stated but presumption held overcome); Shahan v. Jones, 177 S.E. 774, 115 W.Va. 749 (traveling salesman); Ercole v. Daniel, 141 S.E. 631, 105 W.Va. 118 (owner's son).

Wis.—Edwards v. Gross, 90 N.W.2d 142, 4 Wis.2d 90 (wife driving husband's auto); Topel v. Correz, 89 N.W.2d 295, 3 Wis.2d 495 (wife driving owner husband home); Burant v. Studzinski, 1940, 291 N. W. 390, 234 Wis. 385 (presumption of fact, not law).

But see

Ga.—Durden v. Maddox, 37 S.E.2d 219, 73 Ga.App. 491 (agency will not be presumed from mere ownership).

Conclusive in absence of rebuttal

U.S.—Department of Water and Power of City of Los Angeles v. Anderson, C.C.A.Nev., 95 F.2d 577, certiorari denied 59 S.Ct. 67, 305 U.S. 607, 83 L.Ed. 386.

Defendant corporation engaged in interstate commerce

Evidence that bus was common carrier owned by defendant corporation engaged in interstate commerce warranted inference that bus driver was defendant's agent. Midland Trail Bus Lines v. Martin, 194 N.E. 862, 100 Ind.App. 206.

Family purpose doctrine

N.M.—Le Doux v. Peters, 1971, 486 P.2d 70, 82 N.M. 661, affirmed in part 491 P.2d 524, 83 N.M. 307 (child).

N.Y.—Traub v. Blum, 31 N.Y.S.2d 735, 263 App.Div. 92 (presumption that was an "agent" in driving husband's automobile, particularly in view of fact that she had purchased provisions for the household while traveling to their home accompanied by the plaintiff niece as a guest of the family).

No presumption agent of joint owner

N.M.—Pavlos v. Albuquerque Nat. Bank, 1971, 487 P.2d 187, 82 N.M. 759 (joint owner present).

Not affected by title in name of employer's wife

Ala.—Mobile Pure Milk Co. v. Coleman, 161 So. 826, 26 Ala.App. 402, certiorari denied 161 So. 829, 230 Ala. 432 (where automobile was generally used by employee in business of employer, with knowledge of employee's wife, whether title to automobile was in wife or employer did not affect employer's liability).

Not applicable for accident on private premises

R.I.—Pescosolido v. Crugnale, 171 A. 2d 443, 93 R.I. 82 (pedestrian struck on service station premises had burden of proving that driver, who operated truck with owner's consent, was agent of owner and could not rely on statute providing that where motor vehicle is operated on public highway with owner's consent, operator shall be deemed agent of owner).

Not as to vehicle being towed

Pa.—Fuller v. Palazzolo, 197 A. 225, 329 Pa. 93 (driver of towing vehicle not deemed servant of owner of towed vehicle).

Operating under common carrier certificate

Where defendant held a certificate to operate a semitrailer as a common carrier and to operate it on the highways himself or to his servant and he was not authorized to loan it or contract it out or otherwise permit it to be driven by an unauthorized person, semitrailer when found operating upon the highway was presumably being operated under defendant's certificate for his benefit and by one whom he had lawfully authorized to use it. Brandenburg v. Buchta, 117 N.E.2d 643, 233 Ind. 221.

Permitting woman companion to drive

There was a presumption, from a defendant's ownership, that his woman companion, whom he had permitted to drive automobile prior to time it was involved in accident, was driving automobile as defendant's agent, and such presumption required some evidence on part of defendant reasonably tending to rebut it. Sevey v. Jones, 292 N.W. 436, 235 Wis. 109.

Presumption that driver is agent "or" the owner

N.J.—Nicosia v. Marangi, 81 A.2d 20, 13 N.J.Super. 550.

Proof employee in vehicle inadequate, unless controlling driver

Presumption that, where employee was in employer's truck, vehicle was being used in course of employer's business, even though it was being driven by third party, could not arise in absence of showing that vehicle at time of accident was in charge of employee. Hubbard v. Dooley, Ky., 324 S.W.2d 818.

Prospective buyer driving, dealer in auto

The presence in an automobile of dealer, while the automobile was driven by a prospective buyer of the automobile at the dealer's invitation, created a rebuttable presumption that the prospective buyer was the dealer's agent. Dahnke v. Meggitt, 26 N.E.2d 223, 63 Ohio App. 252.

State owned vehicle

Concession that automobile was owned by the state and had been legally assigned to a state official for his use raised presumption that person operating automobile was engaged in service of official to whom automobile had been assigned and that it was being used with his permission and such presumption continued until there was substantial evidence to the contrary. Hukey v. Massachusetts Bonding & Ins. Co., 100 N.Y.S.2d 643, 277 App.Div. 411.

§ 417.7

The presumption of a driver's agency and operation in the scope of employment arises from evidence of registration in the name of the defendant, where there is no notice of transfer of defendant's interest, as required by law.[46]

It has been said that such a deduction is an inference and not a presumption.[47]

Where an automobile, although not owned by a master, is repeatedly used in the master's business with the master's knowledge and consent, there arises an implied assent and authority to use it in the master's business, rendering the master liable for the driver's negligent acts.[48]

45. For general discussion of the force of presumptions, see section 417.1 at fn. 7 et seq.

Conn.—Bogart v. Tucker, 1973, 320 A.2d 803, 164 Conn. 277.

Ill.—Botich v. P. Lorillard Co., 1970, 262 N.E.2d 38, 127 Ill.App.2d 232.

Utah.—Saltas v. Affleck, 102 P.2d 493, 99 Utah 381; Fox v. Lavender, 1936, 56 P.2d 1049, 89 Utah 115, 109 A.L.R. 105.

Wis.—Burant v. Studzinski, 291 N.W. 390, 234 Wis. 385.

46. Pa.—Preston v. Schroeder, 27 Pa.Del.Co. 350.

R.I.—Giblin v. Dudley Hardware Co., 117 A. 418, 44 R.I. 371.

Tenn.—Bell Cab & U-Drive-It Co. v. Sloan, 246 S.W.2d 41, 193 Tenn. 352 (rebutted as to taxicabs); English v. George Cole Motor Co., 111 S.W.2d 386, 21 Tenn.App. 408; Maysay v. Hickman, 97 S.W.2d 662, 20 Tenn.App. 262.

47. Similar statement in prior edition **cited by the court** in Walker v. Johnston, Tex.Civ.App., 236 S. W.2d 534, 537, error dismissed.

Cal.—Pozzobon v. O'Donnell, 36 P. 2d 236, 1 Cal.App.2d 151.

Conn.—Middletown Trust Co. v. Bregman, 174 A. 67, 118 Conn. 651.

Ga.—Ficklen v. Heichelheim, 176 S. E. 540, 49 Ga.App. 777.

Or.—Jasper v. Wells, 144 P.2d 505, 173 Or. 114 (inference that operator of borrowed car is owner's agent).

Rule stated

The Massachusetts statute does not create presumption that operator was agent of registered owner which would disappear upon showing of facts, but rather statute made fact of registration prima facie proof of such agency. Tirone v. Tirone, 222 N.Y.S.2d 986, 32 Misc.2d 962, order affirmed 222 N.Y.S.2d 1016, 14 A.D. 2d 992.

48. Ala.—Mobile Pure Milk Co. v. Coleman, 161 So. 826, 26 Ala.App. 402, certiorari denied 161 So. 829, 230 Ala. 432 (where generally used by employee in business of employer, with knowledge of employee's wife, whether title to automobile was in wife or employer did not affect employer's liability).

But see

U.S.—Fidelity & Cas. Co. of N. Y. v. Carpenter, C.A.La., 234 F.2d 528 (where salesman uses his own privately owned automobile at will for his business, and is not paid any allowance for expenses on mileage or any other basis, more must be shown by plaintiff, to recover against salesman's employer, than fact that salesman is employee and that he is in automobile which he uses for his work).

Ch. 417   PRESUMPTIONS AND INFERENCES   § 417.7

Possession of a vehicle as bailee is not sufficient basis to establish a presumption that the driver was an employee, agent or representative of the bailee.[49]

If ownership is in the employee, no inference of agency arises from proof in itself of ownership and it is incumbent upon the plaintiff to show that the employee was driving the automobile at the time of the accident with the actual or implied consent of the employer and in the furtherance of the latter's business.[50]

An automobile or truck driver may be in the general service of one employer and, with respect to particular work, may be transferred to the service of another, so as to become, by agreement or by force of circumstances, the servant of the latter, thereby visiting upon the latter the legal consequences of the new relation.[51] From the evidence, it may be determined whether the driver was merely a bailee, an independent contractor, or a servant. As a rule, a general employer is not freed from responsibility for the negligent acts of an employee merely because the employee has been hired out by the employer to a third person to be used by the latter in the performance of the third person's work.[52] So, in the absence of an agreement, the presumption is that the driver, as respects the manner and method of operating

Dist.Col.—Lancaster v. Canuel, Mun. App., 193 A.2d 555 (lending of automobile to pharmacy as matter of courtesy for making small deliveries by pharmacy employees did not make pharmacy a co-owner within statutory presumption that driver is owner's agent).

Not from single occasion
Idaho.—Hayward v. Yost, 242 P.2d 971, 72 Idaho 415.

Mo.—McCaughen v. Missouri Pac. R. Co., App., 274 S.W. 97.

Tenn.—National Life & Accident Ins. Co. v. Morrison, 162 S.W.2d 501, 179 Tenn. 29.

Va.—Barber v. Textile Machine Works, 17 S.E.2d 359, 178 Va. 435.

49. La.—Palmer v. Turner, App. 1971, 252 So.2d 700 (garage).

Contra
N.J.—Bartell v. Razzano, 1972, 291 A.2d 22, 119 N.J.Super. 243 (where trucking company had leased tractor from its owner by written instrument, presumption arose that the driver of tractor was operating the vehicle as an agent of such lessee, and when presumption was unrebutted a jury question was presented as to agency between trucking company defendant, owner of trailer, and driver who also owned tractor).

50. Ala.—Jessup v. Shaddix, 154 So. 2d 39, 275 Ala. 281.

Miss.—Humes v. Young, 69 So.2d 245, 219 Miss. 417.

Or.—Larkins v. Utah Copper Co., 127 P.2d 354, 169 Or. 499.

51. Cal.—Billig v. Southern Pac. Co., 209 P. 241, 189 Cal. 477.

52. Cal.—Billig v. Southern Pac. Co., 209 P. 241, 189 Cal. 477; Stewart v. California Improvement Co., 63 P. 177, 724, 131 Cal. 125, 52 L.R.A. 205.

§ 417.7   TRIAL EVIDENCE   Ch. 417

the machine and the negligence of the driver, was the servant of the owner and not the servant of the hirer.[53]

This presumption of agency has been held also to pertain to co-employees accompanying an employee driver.[54]

When an automobile is found unattended, it is presumed to have been so left by the owner or a servant acting within the servant's authority.[55]

There is a presumption that an automobile dealer, in the use and operation of cars and trucks on the highways with dealer's plates, will obey the law, as respects the question of whether its vehicle, while operated by a third person with the dealer's plates on it, was used in fact on the dealer's business.[56]

---

53. **Cal.**—Billig v. Southern Pac. Co., 209 P. 241, 189 Cal. 477.

    N.Y.—Neuschaefer v. Colonial Sand & Stone Co., Sup., 180 N.Y.S. 413.

54. **Ala.**—Barber Pure Milk Co. v. Holmes, 84 So.2d 345, 264 Ala. 45 (in action by pedestrian when struck by suddenly opened door of truck blocking the sidewalk, presumption of agency in driver of a vehicle injuring a person because of movement thereof was applicable to helper in control of the rear door of the truck causing the injury).

55. **Ala.**—Southeastern Const. Co. v. Robbins, 27 So.2d 703, 32 Ala.App. 532, followed in 27 So.2d 708, 32 Ala.App. 535, 27 So.2d 709, 248 Ala. 371, 372. Certiorari denied 27 So. 2d 705, 248 Ala. 367; Newell Contracting Co. v. Berry, 134 So. 870, 223 Ala. 109.

    N.Y.—Peemoller v. Viscarra, 1971, 321 N.Y.S.2d 809, 36 A.D.2d 971.

Advantage waived by plaintiff

Where plaintiff, a passenger in panel truck which collided with defendant's double-parked automobile, chose not to rely on rebuttable presumption that automobile had been double-parked by defendant or his agent acting for him, and instead adduced evidence to effect that defendant parked his automobile next to curb, turned ignition off, kept keys on his person, and gave no one permission to move automobile, it was incumbent on plaintiff to offer evidence eliminating possible independent proximate cause of accident, and absent such evidence, case against defendant was insufficient. Roberts v. Cave, 1970, 263 A.2d 863, 257 Md. 582.

56. **Ohio.**—Fredericks v. Birkett L. Williams Co., 40 N.E.2d 162, 68 Ohio App. 217.

    Or.—Miller v. Service & Sales, 38 P. 2d 995, 149 Or. 11, 96 A.L.R. 628.

    Pa.—Frew v. Barto, 26 A.2d 905, 345 Pa. 217; Reed v. Bennett, 119 A. 827, 276 Pa. 107.

    Wis.—Borkenhagen v. Baertschi, 300 N.W. 742, 239 Wis. 21.

But see

Where dealers possessing dealers plates agreed to sell secondhand car to employé if he would repair it and he took it home for that purpose and then paid something on account, put it in shape, and obtained from them set of their license plates so he could make test trip to see whether it was in good operating condition, but employers refused consent to his operating it himself and sent along another employee to drive the car while he rode as passenger, and these two were injured while driving at midnight, dealers' plates, while possibly raising presumption of ownership,

Ch. 417   PRESUMPTIONS AND INFERENCES   § 417.7

Such presumptions do not have the effect of shifting the burden of proof to the defendant to prove by a preponderance of the evidence that the automobile causing the injury was not being used in the defendant's business, but only shifts the burden of presenting or going forward with the evidence.[57]

In some jurisdictions, the presumption of agency upon proof of ownership is statutory.[58] A statute establishing prima facie a

raised no presumption of course of employment. Reed v. Bennett, 119 A. 827, 276 Pa. 107.

57. For discussion generally of force of presumption in shifting the burden to go forward with evidence, see section 417.1 at fn. 7 et seq.

U.S.—Terminal Transport Co. v. Foster, C.C.A.Ala., 164 F.2d 248.

Cal.—Fahey v. Madden, 206 P. 128, 56 Cal.App. 593.

Colo.—American Ins. Co. v. Naylor, 70 P.2d 349, 101 Colo. 34.

Conn.—Scalora v. Shaughnessy, 196 A.2d 763, 151 Conn. 252; Koops v. Gregg, 32 A.2d 653, 130 Conn. 185.

Idaho.—Magee v. Hargrove Motor Co., 296 P. 774, 50 Idaho 442.

N.C.—Freeman v. Dalton, 111 S.E. 863, 183 N.C. 538.

Ohio.—Arthurs v. Citizens' Coal Co., App., 47 N.E.2d 654.

Tenn.—Southern Motors v. Morton, 154 S.W.2d 801, 25 Tenn.App. 204.

Tex.—Hudiburgh v. Palvic, Civ.App., 274 S.W.2d 94, writ of error refused n. r. e.; Merryman v. Zeleny, Civ.App., 143 S.W.2d 410 (provisions of the 1941 edition of this work similar to the provisions of this section were quoted).

Wash.—Bradley v. S. L. Savidge, Inc., 123 P.2d 780, 13 Wash.2d 28.

W.Va.—Lacewell v. Lampkin, 13 S.E. 2d 583, 123 W.Va. 138 (court said that presumption "merely shifts burden of proof," but did not define meaning of term "burden of proof").

58. **Conn.**—Scalora v. Shaughnessy, 196 A.2d 763, 151 Conn. 252.

D.C.—Joyner v. Holland, Mun.App., 212 A.2d 541 (vehicle jointly owned by driver).

Mass.—Dineasoff v. Casey, 29 N.E.2d 25, 206 Mass. 555 (but is not evidence of permission to invite a guest to ride along); Thomas v. Meyer Store Inc., 168 N.E. 178, 268 Mass. 587.

N.Y.—Tirone v. Tirone, 222 N.Y.S.2d 986, 32 Misc.2d 962, order affirmed 222 N.Y.S.2d 1016, 14 A.D.2d 992 (presumption arises from proof of registration).

R.I.—Gemma v. Rotondo, 5 A.2d 297, 62 R.I. 293, 122 A.L.R. 223 (from registration in defendant's name).

Tenn.—Haggard v. Jim Clayton Motors, Inc., 393 S.W.2d 292, 216 Tenn. 625.

Conclusive if not rebutted

Under Financial Responsibility Act providing that proof of ownership shall be "prima facie evidence" that driver operated automobile with owner's consent, with proof that defendant owned automobile involved and with no evidence on behalf of defendant, a plaintiff who has otherwise established liability is entitled to a directed verdict. Hiscox v. Jackson, 127 F.2d 160, 75 U.S.App.D.C. 293.

If no evidence relevant to issue as to whether was operating automobile as defendant's agent is produced, or if countervailing evidence is produced but trier does not believe it, statutory presumption that driver is automobile owner's agent applies and plaintiff is entitled to have issue

§ 417.7   TRIAL EVIDENCE   Ch. 417

driver's agency for the registered owner of an automobile is in derogation of the common law and must be strictly construed.[59] It has been held to be applicable only where there is proof of registration and no proof of agency.[60]

Some opinions have used the terms that proof of ownership alone makes a prima facie case of agency.[61] It has also been

found in his favor. Amento v. Mortenson, 37 A.2d 231, 130 Conn. 682.

Not applicable to plaintiff owner

Such statute is inapplicable to action in which owner is plaintiff, the statute in terms applying to a defendant. Thompson v. Sides, 176 N.E. 623, 275 Mass. 568.

Not superseded by I.C.C. regulation re leased vehicles

Ruling of Bureau of Motor Carriers of Interstate Commerce Commission that a carrier hiring motor vehicle should do so by lease providing for transfer to lessee of exclusive control over vehicle and operator, did not supersede statute making registration in name of owner prima facie evidence that vehicle is being operated under control of a person for whose conduct registered owner is legally responsible. Garfield v. Smith, 59 N.E.2d 287, 317 Mass. 674, certiorari denied 65 S.Ct. 1568, 1569, 325 U.S. 879, 89 L.Ed. 1995.

59. Tenn.—English v. George Cole Motor Co., 111 S.W.2d 386, 21 Tenn.App. 408.

60. Tenn.—Southern Motors v. Morton, 154 S.W.2d 801, 25 Tenn.App. 204; English v. George Cole Motor Co., 111 S.W.2d 386, 21 Tenn.App. 408.

61. U.S.—Shulins v. New England Ins. Co., C.A.Vt., 360 F.2d 781; Louisville & N. R. Co. v. Byrd, C.A.Ala., 298 F.2d 586; Siebrand v. Gossnell, C.A.Ariz., 234 F.2d 81; Hawthorne v. Eckerson Co., C.C.A. Vt., 77 F.2d 844; State of Md. to Use and Benefit of Gaegler v. Thomas, D.C.Md., 173 F.Supp. 568; Watson v. U. S., D.C.Alaska, 90 F.Supp. 900; Clemens v. U. S., D.C. Minn., 88 F.Supp. 971 (M.S.A. § 170.54).

Ala.—Schoenith, Inc. v. Forrester, 69 So.2d 454, 260 Ala. 271; Slaughter v. Murphy, 194 So. 649, 239 Ala. 260 (plaintiff entitled to affirmative charge in absence of countervailing evidence); Craft v. Koonce, 187 So. 730, 237 Ala. 552 (plaintiff need not offer further proof until defendant offers contrary proof); Cruse-Crawford Mfg. Co. v. Rucker, 123 So. 897, 220 Ala. 101 (administrative presumption).

Cal.—Montanya v. Brown, 88 P.2d 745, 31 Cal.App.2d 642; Bushnell v. Yoshika Tashiro, 2 P.2d 550, 115 Cal.App. 563; Mathe v. White Auto Co., 291 P. 599, 108 Cal.App. 286; Perry v. A. Paladini, Inc., 264 P. 580, 89 Cal.App. 275; Sanfilippo v. Lesser, 210 P. 44, 59 Cal.App. 86 (directed verdict for owner upon proof husband not present, wife drove to her mother's home, and had taken mother shopping).

Dist.Col.—Miller v. Imperial Ins. Inc., Mun.App., 189 A.2d 359 (statutory).

Ga.—Lee v. Queen, 46 S.E.2d 509, 76 Ga.App. 513 (testimony to contrary conflicting).

Idaho.—Maier v. Minidoka County Motor Co., 105 P.2d 1076, 61 Idaho 642.

Ill.—McCarty v. O. H. Yates & Co., 14 N.E.2d 254, 294 Ill.App. 474 (admission of ownership makes prima facie case).

Ind.—Frick v. Bickel, 54 N.E.2d 436, 115 Ind.App. 436, motion denied 57 N.E.2d 62, 222 Ind. 610.

148

Ch. 417   PRESUMPTIONS AND INFERENCES   § 417.7

held that, before the inference of the relationship of master and servant can be drawn from proof creating a presumption of ownership of a vehicle causing an injury, such presumption must be

Iowa.—Olinger v. Tiefenthaler, 285 N.W. 137, 226 Iowa 847; Mitchell v. Automobile Underwriters of Des Moines, 281 N.W. 832, 225 Iowa 906.

Ky.—Galloway Motor Co. v. Huffman's Adm'r, 137 S.W.2d 379, 281 Ky. 841; W. T. Liter Co. v. Graham, 136 S.W.2d 1059, 281 Ky. 634 (owner's duty to bring forth clear and convincing proof to the contrary).

Md.—Taylor v. Wesley Freeman, Inc., 47 A.2d 500, 186 Md. 474; Pennsylvania R. Co. v. Lord, 151 A. 400, 159 Md. 518; Louis v. Johnson, 125 A. 895, 146 Md. 115.

Mass.—Dineasoff v. Casey, 29 N.E. 2d 25, 306 Mass. 555.

Mich.—Rabaut v. Venable, 280 N.W. 129, 285 Mich. 111.

Minn.—Foster v. Bock, 39 N.W.2d 862, 229 Minn. 428 (M.S.A. § 170.-54); Truman v. United Products Corporation, 14 N.W.2d 120, 217 Minn. 155.

Miss.—West v. Aetna Ins. Co. of Hartford, Conn., 45 So.2d 585, 208 Miss. 776.

Mo.—Berry v. Emery, Bird, Thayer Dry Goods Co., 211 S.W.2d 35, 357 Mo. 808; Spellmeyer v. Theo. Hiertz Metal Co., App., 272 S.W. 1068; Rockwell v. Standard Stamping Co., 241 S.W. 979, 210 Mo.App. 168.

N.J.—Pugliese v. McCarthy, 160 A. 81, 10 N.J.Misc. 601; Le Strange v. Krivit, 158 A. 117, 10 N.J.Misc. 146.

N.Y.—St. Andrassy v. Mooney, 186 N.E. 867, 262 N.Y. 368; Benevento v. Poertner Motor Car Co., 139 N.E. 213, 235 N.Y. 125; Rose v. Balfe, 119 N.E. 842, 223 N.Y. 481.

N.C.—Morris v. Bigham, 1969, 170 S.E.2d 534, 6 N.C.App. 490 (statutory).

Okl.—Norton v. Harmon, 133 P.2d 206, 192 Okl. 36.

Or.—Milwaukee Mechanics Ins. Co. v. Childs, 270 P.2d 139, 201 Or. 347; White v. Keller, 215 P.2d 986, 188 Or. 378; Judson v. Bee Hive Auto Service Co., 297 P. 1050, 136 Or. 1, 74 A.L.R. 944.

R.I.—Gemma v. Rotondo, 5 A.2d 297, 62 R.I. 293, 122 A.L.R. 223; Smith v. Tompkins, 161 A. 221, 52 R.I. 434.

S.C.—Watson v. Kennedy, 186 S.E. 549, 180 S.C. 543 (prevails until rebutted by owner).

Tex.—Broaddus v. Long, 138 S.W.2d 1057, 135 Tex. 353, affirming Civ. App., 125 S.W.2d 340; Carle Oil Co. v. Owens, Civ.App., 134 S.W. 2d 411.

Va.—Kavanaugh v. Wheeling, 7 S.E. 2d 125, 175 Va. 105; Sydnor & Hundley v. Bonifant, 164 S.E. 403, 158 Va. 703.

Wash.—McGinn v. Kimmel, 221 P.2d 467, 36 Wash.2d 786 (testimony must be uncontradicted, unimpeached, clear and convincing); Hanford v. Goehry, 167 P.2d 678, 24 Wash.2d 859; Davis v. Browne, 147 P.2d 263, 20 Wash.2d 219.

W.Va.—Lacewell v. Lampkin, 13 S.E. 2d 583, 123 W.Va. 138.

Wis.—Hanson v. Engebretson, 294 N.W. 817, 237 Wis. 126 (rule recognized but held inapplicable); Sevey v. Jones, 292 N.W. 436, 235 Wis. 109.

Discussion of rule

"It is argued that, if proof of ownership alone be considered sufficient to make out a prima facie case, one must presume (1) that the operator

§ 417.7   TRIAL EVIDENCE   Ch. 417

supplemented by other proof.[62] Such supplemental proof may be of various types.[63]

was the agent of the owner, and (2) that the agent was acting within the scope of his employment. It is insisted that such cannot be done for the reason that an inference cannot be based upon an inference. This contention, in our opinion, is untenable, although there is authority to support it, because it involves the splitting of one inference into two. Ownership implies the right of possession and control. It is a statutory presumption (section 9–807, subdivision 12, Oregon Code 1930) 'that a person is the owner of property from exercising acts of ownership over it. * * *' We think, therefore, that when a person is found in possession of a car and is operating it, it is not an unreasonable deduction that he is the agent of the owner and is using the automobile for the latter's benefit. Experience teaches that when automobiles are involved in accidents they are ordinarily being operated by the owner or by some one for whose negligence he will be responsible." Judson v. Bee Hive Auto Service Co., 297 P. 1050, 1052, 136 Or. 1, 74 A.L.R. 944.

Even when not a business agency

"In this state it has been held that the ownership of an automobile operated by another constitutes a prima facie case for the jury of the principal's liability for injuries negligently inflicted by the agent in driving a machine of which he had general charge, although for purposes of his own, and that these facts make a prima facie case, even though the agency is not a business agency." Foster v. Farra, 243 P. 778, 782, 117 Or. 286.

62. **U.S.**—Kas v. Gilkerson, 199 F. 2d 398, 91 U.S.App.D.C. 153.

Cal.—Duff v. Schaefer Ambulance Service, 283 P.2d 91, 132 Cal.App. 2d 655; Stewart v. Norsigian, 1944, 149 P.2d 46, 64 Cal.App.2d 540, rehearing denied 150 P.2d 554, 64 Cal.App.2d 540 (auto dealer's employee, repossessing vehicle on behalf of finance company, held not employee of finance company).

Conn.—Smith v. Firestone Tire & Rubber Co., 177 A. 524, 119 Conn. 483 (even where used at other times on defendant's business); Middletown Trust Co. v. Bregman, 174 A. 67, 118 Conn. 651 (proof employed in capacity as driver).

Del.—Lamanna v. Stevens, 93 A. 962, 5 Boyce 402.

Ind.—Bojrab v. B. & B. Sand & Gravel Co., 156 N.E. 519, 86 Ind.App. 556; Fame Laundry Co. of Indiana v. Henry, 144 N.E. 545, 195 Ind. 453.

Kan.—Tice v. Crowder, 240 P. 964, 119 Kan. 494, 42 A.L.R. 893.

Ky.—Coleman v. Blackburn, 265 S. W.2d 781 (must be employee also); Galloway Motor Co. v. Huffman's Adm'r, 1940, 137 S.W.2d 379, 281 Ky. 841; Consolidated Coach Corporation v. Bryant, 86 S.W.2d 88, 260 Ky. 452.

Mass.—DuBois v. Powdrell, 171 N.E. 474, 271 Mass. 394 (evidence was that defendant was the owner, that the driver was in the habit of using it to do errands for her and he had used it on an errand for her at noon on the day of the accident, although both denied that he was using it for her when the plaintiff was injured).

N.H.—Caswell v. Maplewood Garage, 149 A. 746, 84 N.H. 241, 73 A.L.R. 433.

N.D.—Carlson v. Hoff, 230 N.W. 294, 59 N.D. 393; Clark v. Feldman, 224 N.W. 167, 57 N.D. 741.

Ohio.—Goodyear Tire & Rubber Co. v. Marhofer, 176 N.E. 120, 38 Ohio App. 143; Fach v. Canton Yellow

63. See note 63 on page 151.

Ch. 417   PRESUMPTIONS AND INFERENCES   § 417.7

In applying the above-mentioned presumption from proof of ownership, no distinction is made between pleasure and business

Cab Co., 173 N.E. 245, 36 Ohio App. 247; White Oak Coal Co. v. Rivoux, 102 N.E. 302, 88 Ohio St. 18.

Okl.—Randolph v. Schuth, 90 P.2d 880, 185 Okl. 204 (rule stated and evidence found insufficient to establish agency of father); Jamar v. Brightwell, 19 P.2d 366, 162 Okl. 124; Stumpf v. Montgomery, 226 P. 65, 101 Okl. 257, 32 A.L.R. 1490, distinguishing Boling v. Asbridge, 203 P. 894, 84 Okl. 280 (on the ground that in the latter case the facts were not sufficient to overcome the presumption, but were sufficient to go to the jury).

Pa.—Capozi v. Hearst Pub. Co., 92 A.2d 177, 171 Pa. 503; Buck v. Quaker City Cab Co., 1921, 75 Pa.Super. 440 (still insufficient if shown driver wore chauffeur's uniform).

S.C.—Craig v. Clearwater Mfg. Co., 200 S.E. 765, 189 S.C. 176 (trucks bore license plates issued in name of corporation).

S.D.—Hauge v. Tiffany Laundry & Dry-Cleaning Co., 1925, 203 N.W. 998, 48 S.D. 275.

Tenn.—East Tennessee & Western North Carolina Motor Transp. Co. v. Brooks, 121 S.W.2d 559, 173 Tenn. 542 (do not make bare proof of ownership presumptive evidence that a vehicle involved was being used in the owner's business at such time without proof of registration in owner's name).

Tex.—Tinney v. Williams, Civ.App., 144 S.W.2d 344.

Utah.—Fox v. Lavender, 56 P.2d 1049, 89 Utah 115, 109 A.L.R. 105 (no presumption that driver is agent of owner where owner not present); Ferguson v. Reynolds, 176 P. 267, 52 Utah 583.

Evidence necessary to establish presumption

In addition to permissive use of automobile, either employment of operator by owner or that operator was member of family group of owner or was operating automobile under control of or for a member of family group of owner must be established to justify inference of agency. Stewart v. Norsigian, 150 P.2d 554, 64 Cal.App.2d 540.

Owner in vehicle

Where owner of vehicle is riding as passenger, there arises a rebuttable presumption that driver is acting as agent for the owner and, under such circumstances, negligence is imputed to owner. Gervais v. Kostin, 1970, 179 N.W.2d 828, 48 Wis.2d 190.

Where presumption of control based upon presumption of ownership

Where complaint alleged that automobile was owned by defendant and was operated by him or by someone under his control or that he interfered with its operation, and alleged that death of occupant when automobile overturned was proximate result of defendant's negligence but did not allege agency and negligence of any other person, plaintiff suing for death of occupant could not supply deficiency in his proof as to defendant's operation of automobile by invoking statute making automobile registration evidence of ownership and ownership evidence of owner's responsibility for conduct of operation. Osborne v. Gilreath, 86 S.E.2d 462, 241 N.C. 685.

63.   **U.S.**—Benn v. Forrest, R.I., 213 F. 763, 130 C.C.A. 277 (employment as chauffeur).

Cal.—Duff v. Schaefer Ambulance Service, 283 P.2d 91, 132 Cal.App. 2d 655 (must show that servant

151

§ 417.7 TRIAL EVIDENCE Ch. 417

vehicles, in some states,[64] but in others such a distinction is observed. In the case of cars employed for business, the operation is presumed to be in the owner's service, and the burden rests upon the owner to show the contrary.[65] But, in the case of an automobile used for pleasure, it may be necessary to affirmatively establish that the driver was engaged upon the owner's work.[66]

was engaged in performing a service for employer or some act incidental thereto); Market St. Ry. Co. v. George, 3 P.2d 41, 116 Cal. App. 572 (driven by one employed to drive it); Frierson v. Pacific Gas & Electric Co., 203 P. 788, 55 Cal.App. 397 (exercise of control over driver's services, and payment for services).

Del.—Roach v. Parker, 107 A.2d 798, 9 Terry 519 (owner present in vehicle).

Ky.—Webb v. Dixie-Ohio Express Co., 165 S.W.2d 539, 291 Ky. 692 (holding franchise over designated route).

Mich.—Hatter v. Dodge Bros., 167 N.W. 935, 202 Mich. 97 (defendant's name on vehicle and admissions of employee).

Minn.—Behrens v. Hawkeye Oil Co., 187 N.W. 605, 151 Minn. 478 (customary usage by customary driver, and vehicle loaded as customary).

Mo.—Brucker v. Gambaro, Sup., 9 S.W.2d 918 (defendant personally present on occasion and admitting ownership); McCarter v. Burger, App., 6 S.W.2d 979 (owner present in vehicle); Edwards v. Rubin, 2 S.W.2d 205, 221 Mo.App. 246 (owner present in vehicle).

N.D.—Clark v. Feldman, 224 N.W. 167, 57 N.D. 741 (if employed for the special purpose of operating the automobile at the time).

Ohio.—Riley v. Speraw, 181 N.E. 915, 42 Ohio App. 207 (owner present in vehicle); Fach v. Canton Yellow Cab Co., 173 N.E. 245, 36 Ohio App. 247 (operation of his employer's car, which the chauffeur was employed to operate); Schmidt & Schmidt v. Schwab, 17 Ohio App. 127 (in charge of a servant whose duty it was to operate it, and who was regularly in the possession and use of same, with consent, knowledge, and authority of owner).

Tex.—Commercial Credit Co. v. Groseclose, Civ.App., 66 S.W.2d 709, error dismissed (performing services expressly authorized).

Ordinary indicia of agency apply

Where owner's wife is operating vehicle as his servant or agent, he is liable for her negligence, and in determining whether agency relationship exists, ordinary rules of agency apply, and relationship of agency of wife or husband may be shown by express creation or may be implied from proof of conduct or circumstances reasonably creating the agency. McKamey v. Andrews, 289 S.W. 2d 704, 40 Tenn.App. 112.

64. **Mo.**—Hampe v. Versen, 32 S.W. 2d 793, 224 Mo.App. 1144; McCarter v. Burger, App., 6 S.W.2d 979; Edwards v. Rubin, 2 S.W.2d 205, 221 Mo.App. 246; Jacobson v. Beffa, App., 282 S.W. 161.

65. **U.S.**—Liberty Baking Co. v. Kellum, C.C.A.Pa., 79 F.2d 931 (defendant's name on truck).

Pa.—Kline v. Kachmar, 61 A.2d 825, 360 Pa. 396; Marach v. Kooistra, 198 A. 66, 329 Pa. 324; Martin v. Lipschitz, 149 A. 168, 169, 299 Pa. 211.

66. **Pa.**—Martin v. Lipschitz, 149 A. 168, 299 Pa. 211; Laubach v. Colley, 129 A. 88, 283 Pa. 366.

§ 417.7 PRESUMPTIONS AND INFERENCES Ch. 417

A number of decisions, however, have held that no presumption of agency arises from mere proof of ownership.[67]

It has been held that, in the absence of a statute making it so, and in the absence of the application of the family purpose doctrine, agency for the other in the use of an automobile belonging to a spouse is not inferred merely from the marital relation, and that one spouse may make personal use of the other's automobile without being presumed to be the other's agent in the use of it.[68] The converse presumption has even been held, where it is stated that it is presumed a member of the family driving the family auto drives the auto for personal benefit and not for the benefit of the community.[69]

67. **Conn.**—Middletown Trust Co. v. Bregman, 174 A. 67, 118 Conn. 651 (mere physical possession insufficient).

Ga.—Durden v. Maddox, 1946, 37 S.E.2d 219, 73 Ga.App. 491 (ownership alone does not invoke family purpose doctrine).

Ky.—Spencer's Adm'r v. Fisel, 71 S.W.2d 955, 254 Ky. 503, and cases cited therein.

Okl.—Gilbert v. Walker, 1960, 356 P.2d 346 (even when know of use).

Tenn.—East Tennessee & Western North Carolina Motor Transp. Co. v. Brooks, 121 S.W.2d 559, 173 Tenn. 542.

Tex.—Moreland v. Hawley Independent School Dist., Civ.App., 163 S.W.2d 892, supplemented as to other questions, Civ.App., 169 S.W. 2d 227.

Utah.—Galarowicz v. Ward, 230 P.2d 576, 119 Utah 611; Galarowicz v. Ward, 230 P.2d 576, 119 Utah 611 (rule ownership by one and use by another raises no presumption of agency is applicable both as to strangers and as to family members).

Even with owner in vehicle

Okl.—Deskins v. Woodward, 1971, 483 P.2d 1134.

Pa.—Smalich v. Westfall, 1970, 269 A.2d 476, 440 Pa. 409 (mere presence of owner does not necessarily make owner liable or impute to him the driver's negligence, nor will it create presumption of master-servant relationship).

R I.—Darman v. Zilch, 1936, 186 A. 21, 51 R.I. 413, 110 A.L.R. 826 (no presumption of contributory negligence as to chauffeur's driving).

No presumption agent of joint owner

Nev.—Zimmerman v. First Judicial Dist. Court, 1958, 332 P.2d 654, 74 Nev. 344.

N.M.—Pavlos v. Albuquerque Nat. Bank, 1971, 487 P.2d 187, 82 N.M. 759 (presence of co-owner husband as passenger when automobile was driven by co-owner wife did not raise presumption that wife was agent of husband).

N.C.—Rushing v. Polk, 128 S.E.2d 675, 258 N.C. 256 (evidence of agency or proof of joint enterprise is necessary to impose liability on absent joint owner, and mere fact of marital relationship between joint owners does not raise presumption that husband or wife is acting as agent of other).

68. **Md.**—Charles v. Mayor and City Council of City of Baltimore, 114 A. 565, 138 Md. 523.

69. **U.S.**—Huddleston v. Angeles Cooperative Creamery, D.C.Wash. 1970, 315 F.Supp. 307 (but such presumption is overcome when husband is a passenger, and his

§ 417.7 TRIAL EVIDENCE Ch. 417

The presumption, arising from ownership of an automobile, that it was in the owner's possession, personally or through the driver as a servant, and that the driver was acting within the scope of employment, is a rebuttable one,[70] in the absence of any statute to the contrary.[71]

wife's negligence would have to be imputed to him under doctrine of imputed negligence).

70. For general discussion of rebuttable presumptions, see section 417.1 at fn. 7 et seq.

Ala.—Thompson v. Havard, 1970, 235 So.2d 853, 285 Ala. 718; Red's Elec. Co. v. Beasley, 129 So.2d 676, 272 Ala. 200; Barber Pure Milk Co. v. Holmes, 84 So.2d 345, 264 Ala. 45; Nehi Bottling Co. of Boaz v. Templeton, 1949, 38 So.2d 606, 34 Ala.App. 266 (on personal mission).

Ariz.—Peters v. Pima Mercantile Co., 27 P.2d 143, 42 Ariz. 454 (deviated from work route); Lutfy v. Lockhart, 295 P. 975, 37 Ariz. 488.

Ark.—Page Lumber Co. v. Carman, 217 S.W.2d 930, 214 Ark. 784; Casteel v. Yantis-Harper Tire Co., 39 S.W.2d 306, 183 Ark. 912.

Cal.—Ceranski v. Muensch, 141 P.2d 750, 60 Cal.App.2d 751 (driver serving another person); Hanchett v. Wiseley, 290 P. 311, 107 Cal.App. 230 (left state without permission to acquire liquor); Hathaway v. Mathews, 258 P. 712, 85 Cal.App. 31.

Conn.—Scalora v. Shaughnessy, 196 A.2d 763, 151 Conn. 252; Leitzes v. F. L. Caulkins Auto Co., 196 A. 145, 123 Conn. 459 (presumption effective until true facts are ascertained).

Fla.—Johnson v. Mills, 37 So.2d 906.

Ga.—Brennan v. National NuGrape Co., 128 S.E.2d 81, 106 Ga.App. 709.

Idaho.—Litalien v. Tuthill, 272 P.2d 311, 75 Idaho 335; Manion v. Waybright, 86 P.2d 181, 59 Idaho 643 (may be rebutted by testimony of parties).

Ill.—Nelson v. Stutz Chicago Factory Branch, 173 N.E. 394, 341 Ill. 387.

Ind.—Frick v. Bickel, 54 N.E.2d 436, 115 Ind.App. 114, motion denied 57 N.E.2d 62, 222 Ind. 610 (driving after working hours without permission).

Ky.—Hickman v. Strunk, 197 S.W.2d 442, 303 Ky. 397 (driver serving another person); Galloway Motor Co. v. Huffman's Adm'r, 137 S.W.2d 379, 281 Ky. 841 (on personal pleasure deviation).

La.—Cofield v. Burgdorf, App., 111 So.2d 845, reversed 115 So.2d 357, 238 La. 297, on remand, App., 117 So.2d 663; Antoine v. Louisiana Highway Commission, App., 188 So. 443 (not rebutted that accident occurred between 6:30 and 7:00 a. m. and employee usually went to work at 7:00 a. m.); Mancuso v. Hurwitz-Mintz Furniture Co., App., 183 So. 461, denying rehearing App., 181 So. 814 (on personal mission of own); Hunt v. Chisholm, La.App., 183 So. 132 (proof that accident occurred at night, after employee's duties of delivering clothes in automobile were over and employee had been given automobile to store, with distinct understanding that it would not be used on personal business, and that at time of accident employee had intention of going to beauty parlor and of leaving automobile at garage to have defective lights repaired, rebutted presumption that employee was acting within scope of employment and required denial of recovery).

71. See note 71 on page 156.

154

Md.—State, Use of Shipley v. Walker, 186 A.2d 472, 230 Md. 133; Scott v. James Gibbons Co., 64 A.2d 117, 192 Md. 319; Maryland Cas. Co. v. Sause, 57 A.2d 801, 190 Md. 135 (where hauling contractor hires driver to drive truck for third party with whom contractor has a contract, presumption of agency arising from ownership is rebuttable); State, for Use of Mitchell, v. Jones, 46 A.2d 623, 186 Md. 270 (took truck to go home to sleep); National Trucking & Storage v. Durkin, 39 A.2d 687, 183 Md. 584.

Mich.—Wehling v. Linder, 226 N.W. 880, 248 Mich. 241.

Mo.—State ex rel. Waters v. Hostetter, 126 S.W.2d 1164, 344 Mo. 443, quashing record Waters v. Hays, App., 118 S.W.2d 39, conforming to State ex rel. Steinbruegge v. Hostetter, 115 S.W.2d 802, 342 Mo. 341, quashing Waters v. Hays, App., 103 S.W.2d 498. Mandate conformed to App., 130 S.W.2d 220.

Mont.—Monaghan v. Standard Motor Co., 29 P.2d 378, 96 Mont. 165.

Neb.—Philleo v. Hefnider, 2 N.W.2d 31, 140 Neb. 808; Harrell v. People's City Mission Home, 267 N.W. 344, 131 Neb. 138 (rebutted where the evidence shows employee was engaged in his personal affairs).

N.J.—Harvey v. Craw, 1970, 264 A.2d 448, 110 N.J.Super. 68; Onufer v. Strout, 183 A. 215, 116 N.J.L. 274; Kirrer v. Bromberg, 172 A. 498, 113 N.J.L. 98.

N.M.—Morris v. Cartwright, 258 P.2d 719, 57 N.M. 328.

N.Y.—Berry v. Employers' Liability Assur. Corporation, 5 N.Y.S.2d 887, 254 App.Div. 424 (presumption overcome); Schwartz v. Lawrence, 1926, 212 N.Y.S. 494, 214 App.Div. 559 (chauffeur use without consent); Frankel v. C. & E. Chapal Fréres & Cie, Sup., 165 N.Y.S. 441 (jury question upon uncontradicted testimony of interested witnesses that driver took vehicle without permission).

N.D.—Bryan v. Schatz, 39 N.W.2d 435, 77 N.D. 9.

Ohio.—Griffith v. Rutledge, 169 N.E. 2d 464, 110 Ohio App. 301.

Okl.—Claxton v. Page, 124 P.2d 977, 190 Okl. 422.

Or.—Bunnell v. Parelius, 111 P.2d 88, 166 Or. 174; Judson v. Bee Hive Auto Service Co., 297 P. 1050, 136 Or. 1, 74 A.L.R. 944.

Pa.—Kline v. Kachmar, 61 A.2d 825, 360 Pa. 396; Grossman v. Kniess, 193 A. 369, 127 Pa.Super. 310 (dealer car used in violation of statute concerning license plates).

R.I.—Smith v. Tompkins, 161 A. 221, 52 R.I. 434 (master introduced evidence showing chauffeur was unauthorized to use automobile for own purposes).

Tenn.—Caldwell v. Adams, 367 S.W. 2d 804, 51 Tenn.App. 373 (stopped at cafe and became intoxicated); Walters v. Kee, 366 S.W.2d 534, 51 Tenn.App. 261 (prospective buyer was using it to take himself and others to a lake for motor boating and water skiing); Sadler v. Draper, 326 S.W.2d 148, 46 Tenn.App. 1; Long v. Tomlin, 125 S.W.2d 171, 22 Tenn.App. 607.

Tex.—Mitchell v. Ellis, Civ.App., 374 S.W.2d 333, error ref. n. r. e. (uncontradicted admission of driver had abandoned employer's mission); Merryman v. Zeleny, Civ. App., 143 S.W.2d 410; Alfano v. International Harvester Co. of America, Civ.App., 121 S.W.2d 466 (evidence that driver had been furnished the truck by owner for use as a salesman but that driver had left owner's employ a week preceding accident, that use of truck at time of accident was not known or authorized by owner, and that use was on a personal mission of driver, was sufficient to rebut prima facie liability).

§ **417.7** TRIAL EVIDENCE Ch. 417

In some jurisdictions, the presumption is deemed to exist only so long as there is no substantial or positive or undisputed testimony to the contrary.[72] The presumption is rebutted by un-

Wash.—Williams v. Andresen, 388 P. 2d 725, 63 Wash.2d 645; Sullivan v. Associated Dealers, 103 P.2d 489, 4 Wash.2d 352 (use by employees and relatives at 1 a. m. on Sunday); Murray v. Kauffman Buick Co., 85 P.2d 1061, 197 Wash. 469.

W.Va.—Hollen v. Reynolds, 1941, 15 S.E.2d 163, 123 W.Va. 360; Lacewell v. Lampkin, 1941, 13 S.E.2d 583, 123 W.Va. 138 (personal mission).

Wis.—Philip v. Schlager, 1934, 253 N.W. 394, 214 Wis. 370 (does not survive explicit denial); Edwards v. Kohn, 241 N.W. 331, 207 Wis. 381 (held not rebutted); Kruse v. Weigand, 235 N.W. 426, 204 Wis. 195, followed in 235 N.W. 431, 204 Wis. 206, Smith v. Weigand, 235 N.W. 431, 204 Wis. 207, 208 (two cases), and Woodard v. Weigand, 235 N.W. 432, 204 Wis. 209.

Effect after rebuttal

"It is well settled that those presumptions do arise from proof of the defendant's ownership of the vehicle; but it is well settled also that they are prima facie presumptions merely, or, as they are sometimes called, administrative presumptions, based upon considerations of fairness and convenience in placing the burden of proof. They are not in themselves evidence, and in practice their effect is merely to impose upon the defendant the burden of showing that the driver was not his agent, or that, if he was, he was not acting within the scope of his authority or in the course of his employment. If the evidence thereon is in conflict, or leads to doubtful inference only, the issue should go to the jury. If, however, the evidence, without dispute, rebuts the facts thus presumed, there is no issue for the jury, and the general affirmative charge should be given for the defendant on request." Tullis v. Blue, 114 So. 185, 187, 216 Ala. 577.

Although presumption that driver was acting in scope of employment, arising from proof of ownership by defendant and that driver was in defendant's general employ, may be overcome upon appearance in evidence of the facts themselves, evidence which gave rise to such presumption remains in the case for consideration of trial court on demurrer. State ex rel. Waters v. Hostetter, 126 S.W.2d 1164, 344 Mo. 443, quashing record Waters v. Hays, App., 118 S. W.2d 39, conforming to State ex rel. Steinbruegge v. Hostetter, 115 S.W. 2d 802, 342 Mo. 341, quashing judgment Waters v. Hays, App., 103 S. W.2d 498. Mandate conformed to, App., 130 S.W.2d 220.

Where defendant admitted ownership and that alleged agent was in his employ, presumption obtained that automobile was being operated in and about the defendant's business, but presumption was not "evidence" and would serve in the place of evidence only until prima facie evidence had been adduced by plaintiff. Sullivan v. Associated Dealers, Wash., 103 P.2d 489, 4 Wash.2d 352.

Rebutted as a matter of law

N.J.—Onufer v. Strout, 183 A. 215, 116 N.J.L. 274.

Stronger inference when owner in car

Or.—White v. Keller, 215 P.2d 986, 188 Or. 378.

71. **Cal.**—Hanchett v. Wiseley, 290 P. 311, 107 Cal.App. 230.

72. **U.S.**—Jones v. Halun, 296 F.2d 597, 111 U.S.App.D.C. 340, certiorari denied 82 S.Ct. 1249, 370 U.S. 904, 8 L.Ed.2d 401; Mandelbaum

Ch. 417   PRESUMPTIONS AND INFERENCES   § 417.7

v. U. S., C.A.N.Y., 251 F.2d 748; Walsh v. Rosenberg, 81 F.2d 559, 65 App.D.C. 157, certiorari denied 56 S.Ct. 747, 298 U.S. 663, 80 L.Ed. 1388; Pariso v. Towse, C.C.A.N.Y., 45 F.2d 962.

Ala.—Grimes v. Fulmer, 180 So. 321, 235 Ala. 645, followed in 180 So. 323, 235 Ala. 664, and 183 So. 924, 28 Ala. 630.

Ariz.—Silva v. Traver, 162 P.2d 615, 63 Ariz. 364 (even though contradictory evidence consists solely of testimony of an interested party).

Ark.—Ford & Son Sanitary Co. v. Ransom, 210 S.W.2d 508, 213 Ark. 390 (presumption disappeared, unless there were substantial contradictions in defendant's evidence or it was substantially contradicted by plaintiffs' proof).

Cal.—Montanya v. Brown, 88 P.2d 745, 31 Cal.App.2d 642; Rock v. Orlando, 280 P. 377, 100 Cal.App. 498; Ransford v. Ainsworth, 237 P. 747, 196 Cal. 279.

Conn.—Dibble v. Wolff, 65 A.2d 479, 135 Conn. 428; Koops v. Gregg, 32 A.2d 653, 130 Conn. 185.

Fla.—Hudson v. Smith, App., 135 So. 2d 450.

Ga.—Royal Undertaking Co. v. Duffin, 196 S.E. 208, 57 Ga.App. 760 (presumption cannot prevail against positive and uncontradicted testimony of unimpeached witnesses).

Ill.—Dean v. Ketter, 65 N.E.2d 572, 328 Ill.App. 206.

Iowa.—Mitchell v. Automobile Underwriters of Des Moines, 281 N.W. 832, 225 Iowa 906.

Kan.—Halverson v. Blosser, 168 P. 863, 101 Kan. 683, L.R.A.1918B, 498.

Ky.—Rawlings v. Clay Motor Co., 154 S.W.2d 711, 287 Ky. 604; Home Laundry Co. v. Cook, 125 S.W.2d 763, 277 Ky. 8 (presumption may be overcome by uncontradicated and unimpeached testimony).

La.—Coon v. Monroe Scrap Material Co., App., 191 So. 607; Brown v. Indemnity Ins. Co. of North America, App., 178 So. 768 (may be rebutted by positive proof).

Md.—Phipps v. Milligan, 199 A. 498, 174 Md. 438 (presumption will support verdict for plaintiff in absence of contrary evidence).

Mich.—Christiansen v. Hilber, 276 N.W. 495, 282 Mich. 403.

Mo.—Terminal Warehouses of St. Joseph, Inc. v. Reiners, 371 S.W.2d 311; Dennis v. Creek, App., 211 S.W.2d 59; Mauzy v. J. D. Carson Co., App., 189 S.W.2d 829 (though such evidence comes entirely from witnesses testifying on owner's behalf); Sowers v. Howard, 139 S.W. 2d 897, 346 Mo. 10 (presumption disappears on substantial proof to the contrary); Ross v. St. Louis Dairy Co., 98 S.W.2d 717, 339 Mo. 928 (presumption that truck, on which dairy company's name was printed, was being operated by its servant, acting within scope of employment, disappeared when defendants introduced positive and unequivocal contrary evidence).

Neb.—Witthauer v. Paxton-Mitchell Co., 19 N.W.2d 865, 146 Neb. 436.

N.J.—Nicosia v. Marangi, 81 A.2d 20, 13 N.J.Super. 550; Gluck v. Castles Ice Cream Co., 140 A. 419, 104 N.J.L. 397.

N.Y.—Rose v. Balfe, 119 N.E. 842, 223 N.Y. 481; Healy v. Moss, Sup., 104 N.Y.S.2d 694, affirmed 111 N.Y.S.2d 762, 279 App.Div. 926, appeal denied 113 N.Y.S.2d 447, 279 App.Div. 1077; Wilson v. Harrington, 56 N.Y.S.2d 157, 269 App.Div. 891, affirmed 65 N.E.2d 101, 295 N.Y. 667 (stolen auto).

Ohio.—Senn v. Lackner, App., 100 N.E.2d 419, rehearing denied 100 N.E.2d 432, 91 Ohio App. 83, affirmed 105 N.E.2d 49, 157 Ohio St. 206.

Or.—Lehl v. Hull, 54 P.2d 290, 152 Or. 470, denying rehearing 53 P.2d

§ 417.7   TRIAL EVIDENCE   Ch. 417

contradicted proof to the contrary,[73] though not by mere counter-

48, 152 Or. 470 (inference of agency is without effect).

Pa.—Waters v. New Amsterdam Cas. Co., 140 A.2d 844, 186 Pa.Super. 425; Kunkel v. Vogt, 47 A.2d 195, 354 Pa. 279 (presumption lost when plaintiff called defendant's driver as witness for plaintiff, and driver testified that he was not on defendant's business).

R.I.—Kent v. Draper Soap Co., 63 A.2d 571, 75 R.I. 30; Callahan v. Weybosset Pure Food Market, 133 A. 442, 47 R.I. 361.

Tenn.—Cutshaw v. Randles, 357 S.W. 2d 628, 49 Tenn.App. 592; McMahan v. Tucker, 216 S.W.2d 356, 31 Tenn.App. 429; Pratt v. Duck, 191 S.W.2d 562, 28 Tenn.App. 502; Southern Motors v. Morton, 154 S.W.2d 801, 25 Tenn.App. 204.

Tex.—Poe Motor Co. v. Martin, Civ. App., 201 S.W.2d 102; Crabb v. Zanes Freight Agency, Civ.App., 123 S.W.2d 752, error dismissed, judgment correct (plaintiffs, whose testimony extended into details of relation between owner and employee, could not employ further the presumption).

Utah.—Saltas v. Affleck, 102 P.2d 493, 99 Utah 381 (testimony that truck was being driven by employee on an errand of his own).

Wash.—Bradley v. S. L. Savidge, Inc., 123 P.2d 780, 13 Wash.2d 28; Sullivan v. Associated Dealers, 103 P. 2d 489, 4 Wash.2d 352; Savage v. Donovan, 204 P. 805, 118 Wash. 692.

W.Va.—Laslo v. Griffith, 102 S.E.2d 894, 143 W.Va. 469; Weismantle v. Petros, 19 S.E.2d 594, 124 W.Va. 180; Jenkins v. Spitler, 199 S.E. 368, 120 W.Va. 514 (if credible evidence to contrary is offered, the presumption loses its legal force, and only the facts remain to be considered by the jury).

Wis.—Kowalsky v. Whipkey, 2 N.W. 2d 704, 240 Wis. 59; Sevey v. Jones, 292 N.W. 436, 235 Wis. 109; Laurent v. Plain, 281 N.W. 660, 229 Wis. 75 (presumption must yield to undisputed credible evidence to the contrary).

73. Similar statement in prior edition **cited by the court** in Baltimore Transit Co. v. State to Use of Schriefer, 40 A.2d 678, 686, 184 Md. 250.

U.S.—Erwin v. U. S., C.A.Okl.1971, 445 F.2d 1035, certiorari denied 92 S.Ct. 536, 404 U.S. 992, 30 L.Ed. 2d 543 (on way to catch airplane for vacation trip).

Ariz.—Davis v. Vumore Cable Co., 1971, 484 P.2d 23, 14 Ariz.App. 411.

D.C.—Eastern Aquatics, Inc. v. Washington, Mun.App., 213 A.2d 293.

Ga.—Red Top Cab Co., Inc. v. Hyder, 1974, 204 S.E.2d 814, 130 Ga. App. 870.

Ill.—Botich v. P. Lorillard Co., 1970, 262 N.E.2d 38, 127 Ill.App.2d 232; State Farm Mut. Ins. Co. v. Short, 1970, 260 N.E.2d 415, 125 Ill.App. 2d 97.

Ky.—Hubbard v. Dooley, 324 S.W.2d 818.

Md.—Hoerr v. Hanline, 1959, 149 A. 2d 378, 219 Md. 413 (must be uncontradicted and conclusive); Fowser Fast Freight v. Simmont, 78 A.2d 178, 196 Md. 584; Goldman v. Johnson Motor Lines, 63 A.2d 622, 192 Md. 24.

Mo.—Barz v. Fleischmann Yeast Co., 271 S.W. 361, 308 Mo. 288; Guthrie v. Holmes, 198 S.W. 854, 272 Mo. 215, Ann.Cas.1918D, 1123.

Mont.—Monaghan v. Standard Motor Co., 29 P.2d 378, 96 Mont. 165.

N.J.—Wallace v. A. R. Perine Co., 172 A. 499, 113 N.J.L. 20.

§ 417.7 PRESUMPTIONS AND INFERENCES

vailing evidence.[74] In other jurisdictions, it has been said that the rebutting evidence must be undisputed, clear, and convincing.[75] Before a court will take a case from the jury and direct a

Pa.—Hunter v. Rossi, 172 Pa.Super. 301, 93 A.2d 912; Felski v. Zeidman, 126 A. 794, 281 Pa. 419.

Tenn.—Haggard v. Jim Clayton Motors, Inc., 393 S.W.2d 292, 216 Tenn. 625.

Tex.—Texas Motors, Inc. v. McBee, Civ.App.1971, 465 S.W.2d 234 (unchallenged recitation of facts and record that driver of moving vehicle which struck parked vehicle at 4:00 a. m. and which was owned by driver's employer was on a personal mission of his own and that employee who had loaned automobile to driver had no authority to loan vehicles after working hours for any purpose nullified presumption that driver was engaged in the course of his employment).

Va.—McNeill v. Spindler, 1950, 62 S.E.2d 13, 191 Va. 685.

Wash.—Matthews v. Ruddy, 1971, 491 P.2d 261, 5 Wash.App. 879; Murray v. Corson Corp., 1960, 350 P.2d 468, 55 Wash.2d 733.

Wis.—Gervais v. Kostin, 1970, 179 N.W.2d 828, 48 Wis.2d 190 (where one plaintiff drove motorcycle owned by the other plaintiff solely for pleasure of trying out the newly-purchased motorcycle, purpose of trip was purely social, and owner who was passenger derived no benefit and served no purpose of his own by letting driver drive motorcycle, presumption that driver was acting as agent of owner was dispelled); Laurent v. Plain, 1938, 281 N.W. 660, 229 Wis. 75 ("undisputed credible evidence"); Hahn v. Smith, 1934, 254 N.W. 750, 215 Wis. 277.

74. U.S.—Indemnity Ins. Co. of North America v. Kellas, C.A. Mass., 173 F.2d 120.

Conn.—Lockwood v. Helfant, 1940, 13 A.2d 136, 126 Conn. 584.

Evidence insufficient to overcome prima facie case

Evidence of witnesses called by plaintiff that the automobile had been at a garage for repairs, and after these were completed was being driven by the garage keeper to the owner's place of business, with the intent of leaving it there when the accident occurred, did not overcome the effect of prima facie evidence of defendant's responsibility established by virtue of registration as owner, so as to warrant a direction of verdict for defendant. Haun v. Le Grand, 168 N.E. 180, 268 Mass. 582.

75. U.S.—Standard Coffee Co. v. Trippet, C.C.A.Tex., 108 F.2d 161 (may be rebutted by clear, positive, and unequivocal evidence); Murphey v. U. S., D.C.Cal., 79 F.Supp. 925 affirmed 179 F.2d 743.

Ala.—Rogers v. Hughes, 39 So.2d 578, 252 Ala. 72 (evidence that defendant, as owner, knew nothing about truck being disabled on public street and that he knew nothing of efforts to tow it in without brakes was not so clear and convincing as to entitle defendant to general affirmative charge); Cox v. Roberts, 27 So.2d 617, 248 Ala. 372; Perfection Mattress & Spring Co. v. Windham, 182 So. 6, 236 Ala. 239 (may be overcome by clear evidence).

Cal.—Huddy v. Chronicle Pub. Co., 103 P.2d 421, 15 Cal.2d 554, superseding App., 94 P.2d 56; Tsirlis v. Standard Oil Co. of California, 90 P.2d 128, 32 Cal.App.2d 469 (clear, positive and uncontradicted evidence required); Montanya v. Brown, 88 P.2d 745, 31 Cal.App.2d 642; Bourne v. Northern Counties Title Ins. Co., 40 P.2d 583, 4 Cal. App.2d 69 (inference cannot stand in face of clear, positive, and convincing testimony to the contrary).

§ 417.7   TRIAL EVIDENCE   Ch. 417

verdict in opposition to the presumption, the evidence to the contrary must be of a conclusive or unimpeached character,[76] and

Ky.—W. T. Liter Co. v. Graham, 136 S.W.2d 1059, 281 Ky. 634 (owner's duty to bring forth clear and convincing proof).

La.—Fackrell v. Gulley, App.1971, 246 So.2d 368; Cofield v. Burgdorf, 1959, 115 So.2d 357, 238 La. 297, on remand, App., 117 So.2d 663 ("strong and convincing"); Simms v. Lawrence Bros., App.1954, 72 So.2d 538 (status nearly equal to conviction, to overcome which "unusually strong and convincing" evidence must be adduced).

Mo.—Robb v. Bartels, App.1924, 263 S.W. 1013 (must be positive, unequivocal and unimpeached).

N.J.—Efstathopoulos v. Federal Tea Co., 196 A. 470, 119 N.J.L. 408 (can be overcome as a matter of law only by uncontradicted proof).

Neb.—Ebers v. Whitmore, 241 N.W. 126, 122 Neb. 653.

Okl.—Pollard v. Grimes, 210 P.2d 778, 202 Okl. 118; Claxton v. Page, 124 P.2d 977, 190 Okl. 422.

Tex.—Hudiburgh v. Palvic, Civ.App., 274 S.W.2d 94, writ of error refused n. r. e. (statement by employee); Boydston v. Jones, Civ. App., 177 S.W.2d 303 (proof must be positive, free of equivocations, and such as jury has right to believe and defendant's uncorroborated testimony is not sufficient); Alfano v. International Harvester Co. of America, Civ.App., 121 S.W. 2d 466.

Wash.—Davis v. Browne, 147 P.2d 263, 20 Wash.2d 219; Carlson v. Wolski, 147 P.2d 291, 20 Wash.2d 323; Bradley v. S. L. Savidge, Inc., 123 P.2d 780, 13 Wash.2d 28.

Wis.—Buchholz v. Kastner, 213 N.W. 329, 193 Wis. 224 (clear and satisfactory).

Also "not open to doubt"

In action against newspaper company, to dispel the inference of employment at time and place of accident which inference was established by plaintiff, it was necessary for evidence produced by company, not only to be clear, positive, and uncontradicted, but also not open to doubt. Huddy v. Chronicle Pub. Co., 103 P. 2d 421, 15 Cal.2d 554, superseding, App., 94 P.2d 56.

76. U.S.—Silent Automatic Sales Corporation v. Stayton, C.C.A.Mo., 45 F.2d 471.

Ky.—Galloway Motor Co. v. Huffman's Adm'r, 137 S.W.2d 379, 281 Ky. 841 (where evidence is contradictory, question whether presumption is overcome, is for the jury, but if undisputed, it is a question of law).

Mo.—Staley v. Lawler, 27 S.W.2d 1039, 224 Mo.App. 884; Robb v. Bartels, App., 263 S.W. 1013 (evidence must be positive, unequivocal and unimpeached to overthrow the presumption).

N.J.—Spelde v. Galtieri, 130 A. 526, 102 N.J.L. 203.

N.Y.—Schultze v. McGuire, 150 N.E. 516, 241 N.Y. 460; Orlando v. Pioneer Barber Towel Supply Co., 146 N.E. 621, 239 N.Y. 342; Fiocco v. Carver, 137 N.E. 309, 234 N.Y. 219; Ferris v. Sterling, 108 N.E. 406, 214 N.Y. 249, Ann.Cas.1916D, 1161; Banker v. Haynes Stellite Co., 238 N.Y.S. 587, 135 Misc. 452.

Wash.—Griffin v. Smith, 232 P. 929, 132 Wash. 624; Vernarelli v. Sweikert, 213 P. 482, 123 Wash. 694; Burger v. Taxicab Motor Co., 120 P. 519, 66 Wash. 676.

Destroying all inferences

Under Financial Responsibility Act providing that proof of ownership of automobile shall be prima facie evi-

must not be contradictory or reasonably subject to contradictory interpretations;[77] but, if the evidence is well-nigh conclusive that an automobile was not being operated in the business of the defendant, although the record shows a mere possibility that defendant's business might have been involved, a judgment for plaintiff may be reversed.[78]

It has been held that it is for the court to say whether evidence introduced in opposition to the presumption is of such a conclusive character as to overcome it.[79] In most jurisdictions

dence that driver was operating automobile with owner's consent, to justify a directed verdict for defendant, shown to be owner of automobile involved, evidence must destroy all inferences and presumptions supporting plaintiff and must raise no doubts against defendant. Hiscox v. Jackson, 127 F.2d 160, 75 U.S.App. D.C. 293.

Insufficient impeachment of denial

Delay in pleading defense that defendant's chauffeur had departed from course of employment until seven months after complaint was served, and withdrawal of testimony of defendant's manager that salesmen had written orders not to leave their territory, held not to throw suspicion on uncontradicted testimony that chauffeur was using car for his own pleasure, so as to require submission to jury. Rich v. American Tobacco Co., 204 N.Y.S. 538, 209 App. Div. 439.

Rule fully stated

The character of evidence necessary to overcome the presumption that an employee was engaged in the employer's business must be of a conclusive or unimpeached character, or must be undisputed, clear, and convincing, and such presumption is not overcome as a matter of law by evidence presented on behalf of the employer by interested witnesses, or by evidence which is of a suspicious nature, or which is impeached to any extent, or by evidence which is contradictory or reasonably subject to contradictory interpretations. Rawlings v. Clay Motor Co., 154 S.W.2d 711, 287 Ky. 604 (citing Blashfield).

77. **Ga.**—Eason v. Joy Floral Co., 130 S.E. 352, 34 Ga.App. 501 (where impeaching evidence went wholly to immaterial issues).

Md.—International Co. v. Clark, 127 A. 647, 147 Md. 34.

N.J.—Tischler v. Steinholtz, 122 A. 880, 99 N.J.L. 149.

Rule illustrated

Where car was driven with dealer's license, raising presumption, testimony that the dealer had loaned it to a third person for the latter to drive into the country, to get produce for the latter's own personal use and that the injury occurred during the return trip, held not to justify direction of verdict for defendant as evidence is not so persuasive or of such indubitable verity and probative force as to nullify the presumption created by using dealer's plates. Theil v. Wolfe, 77 Pa.Super. 312.

78. **N.Y.**—Audubon Taxicab Co. v. Marlin-Rockwell Corporation, Sup., 184 N.Y.S. 485.

79. **Md.**—Wagner v. Page, 20 A.2d 164, 179 Md. 465; International Co. v. Clark, 127 A. 647, 147 Md. 34; Salowitch v. Kres, 127 A. 643, 147 Md. 23.

N.J.—Harvey v. Craw, 1970, 264 A. 2d 448, 110 N.J.Super. 68 (trial judge was still required to determine whether minds of reasonable men could differ as to existence or

§ 417.7   TRIAL EVIDENCE   Ch. 417

the rule is recognized that, if the uncontradicted evidence introduced by either party shows that the injury complained of was caused by some independent agency over which defendant had no control, or that the negligent driver was not acting within the scope of employment, it becomes the duty of the court to declare, as a matter of law, that the plaintiff cannot recover.[80] Other

nonexistence of presumed fact of agency).

Wash.—Bradley v. S. L. Savidge, Inc., 123 P.2d 780, 13 Wash.2d 28 (if trial court finds that defendant's evidence has not attained the degree and character required for purpose of directed verdict, case should be submitted to jury).

80. Same sentence in prior edition **cited by the court** in Manion v. Waybright, 86 P.2d 181, 59 Idaho 643, in connection with the holdings that, where rebutting evidence is contradictory, jury question is presented, that, where evidence is undisputed, question is for court, and that, where evidence leaves court in doubt, question is for jury.

U.S.—Caldwell v. Wilson Freight Forwarding Co., D.C.Pa.1971, 322 F.Supp. 43; Curry v. Stevenson, 26 F.2d 534, 58 App.D.C. 162; Manning v. State Farm Mut. Auto. Ins. Co., D.C.N.C., 243 F.Supp. 619.

Ala.—Lowry v. Nobles, 44 So.2d 20, 35 Ala.App. 99; Grimes v. Fulmer, 180 So. 321, 235 Ala. 645, followed in 180 So. 323, 235 Ala. 664 and 183 So. 924, 28 Ala. 630.

Ariz.—Davis v. Vumore Cable Co., 1971, 484 P.2d 23, 14 Ariz.App. 411; Otero v. Soto, 267 P. 947, 34 Ariz. 87.

Cal.—McCammon v. Edmunds, 299 P. 551, 114 Cal.App. 36; Lemka v. Nauman, 284 P. 1062, 103 Cal.App. 757; Musachia v. Jones, 223 P. 1006, 65 Cal.App. 283; Fahey v. Madden, 206 P. 128, 56 Cal.App. 593.

Idaho.—Magee v. Hargrove Motor Co., 296 P. 774, 50 Idaho 442.

Iowa.—Mitchell v. Automobile Underwriters of Des Moines, 1938, 281 N.W. 832, 225 Iowa 906; Curry v. Bickley, 195 N.W. 617, 196 Iowa 827.

Ky.—Mullen & Haynes Co. v. Crisp, 268 S.W. 576, 207 Ky. 31 (presumption met by defendant's evidence in harmony with that of plaintiff).

Md.—Forbstein v. General Tire Co., 175 A. 445, 167 Md. 686; Wells v. Hecht Bros. & Co., 142 A. 258, 155 Md. 618; Nattans v. Cotton, 133 A. 270, 150 Md. 466; Butt v. Smith, 129 A. 352, 148 Md. 340 (accident on Sunday, and intoxicated driver not authorized use on that day); Salowitch v. Kres, 127 A. 643, 147 Md. 23 (owner loaned truck and driver for other's business).

Mich.—Morrow v. Trathen, 284 N.W. 687, 288 Mich. 172; Wehling v. Linder, 226 N.W. 880, 248 Mich. 241.

Minn.—Menton v. L. Patterson Mercantile Co., 176 N.W. 991, 145 Minn. 310.

Mo.—Guthrie v. Holmes, 198 S.W. 854, 272 Mo. 215, Ann.Cas.1918D, 1123; Glassman v. Harry, 170 S.W. 403, 182 Mo.App. 304; Whimster v. Holmes, 164 S.W. 236, 177 Mo.App. 130.

N.J.—Krolak v. Chicago Exp., 76 A. 2d 266, 10 N.J.Super. 60; Fullmer v. Scott-Powell Dairies, 166 A. 129, 111 N.J.L. 44.

N.Y.—Reilly v. Connable, 108 N.E. 853, 214 N.Y. 586, L.R.A.1916A, 954, Ann.Cas.1916A, 656; Wilson v. Harrington, 56 N.Y.S.2d 157, 269 App.Div. 891, affirmed 65 N.E.2d 101, 295 N.Y. 667 (stolen auto).

N.D.—Erickson v. Foley, 262 N.W. 177, 65 N.D. 737.

cases have stated that whether or not the presumption has been rebutted is generally a question for the jury.[81] The jury is not

Okl.—De Camp v. Comerford, 272 P. 475, 134 Okl. 145; Carder v. Martin, 250 P. 906, 120 Okl. 179 (effect of evidence brought out on cross-examination of plaintiff's witnesses).

Pa.—Kunkel v. Vogt, 47 A.2d 195, 354 Pa. 279 (only evidence was defendant's driver called by plaintiff).

Tex.—Pyle v. Phillips, Civ.App., 164 S.W.2d 569 (evidence that employee before work hours was driving the truck to a store to pay a personal bill); Empire Gas & Fuel Co. v. Muegge, 143 S.W.2d 763, 135 Tex. 520.

Wash.—Mitchell v. Nalley's Inc., 300 P. 526, 163 Wash. 183, followed in Cypert v. Nalley's Inc., 300 P. 528, 163 Wash. 703, and Parker v. Nalley's, Inc., 300 P. 529, 163 Wash. 703.

Wis.—Buchholz v. Kastner, 213 N.W. 329, 193 Wis. 224.

Unauthorized passenger

Where invitee of defendant's truck driver testified that he had not previously seen any driver carrying a passenger, in absence of other evidence, knowledge and consent of defendant to driver's habit of carrying passengers could not be implied to support an inference that driver was acting within ostensible authority in carrying invitee. Russell v. Cutshall, 26 S.E.2d 866, 223 N.C. 353.

81. **U.S.**—Pariso v. Towse, C.C.A.N. Y., 45 F.2d 962 (despite denial of owner and driver).

Ala.—Massey v. Pentecost, 90 So. 866, 206 Ala. 411.

Cal.—Randolph v. Hunt, 183 P. 358, 41 Cal.App. 739.

Ky.—Dixie-Ohio Exp. Co. v. Webb, 1944, 184 S.W.2d 361, 299 Ky. 201.

Md.—Hooper v. Brawner, 129 A. 672, 148 Md. 417, 42 A.L.R. 1437 (owner loaned chauffeur to another); Jordan Stabler Co. of Baltimore City v. Tankersly, 126 A. 65, 146 Md. 454 (single fact not on most direct route).

Mo.—Mauzy v. J. D. Carson Co., App., 189 S.W.2d 829; Brucker v. Gambaro, Sup., 9 S.W.2d 918 (regardless of contrary proof); Barz v. Fleischmann Yeast Co., 271 S.W. 361, 308 Mo. 288.

N.J.—De Bello v. Reep & Blackford, 127 A. 522, 101 N.J.L. 218, 2 N.J. Misc. 456 (deviation from direct course); Crowell v. Padolsky, 120 A. 23, 98 N.J.L. 552.

N.Y.—Moore v. Rosenmond, 144 N. E. 639, 238 N.Y. 356 (on return from master's business, picked up friend and became intoxicated); Ferris v. Sterling, 108 N.E. 406, 214 N.Y. 249, Ann.Cas.1916D, 1161; Crawford v. Nilan, 35 N.Y.S.2d 33, 264 App.Div. 46, reversed on other grounds 46 N.E.2d 512, 289 N.Y. 444; Lorenzo v. Manhattan Steam Bakery, Inc., 1917, 165 N.Y.S. 847, 178 A.D. 706 (notwithstanding formal lease of vehicle to another).

Okl.—Claxton v. Page, 124 P.2d 977, 190 Okl. 422.

Or.—Clark v. Shea, 279 P. 539, 130 Or. 195; Kahn v. Home Telephone & Telegraph Co., 152 P. 240, 78 Or. 308.

Pa.—Kunkel v. Vogt, 47 A.2d 195, 354 Pa. 279; Frew v. Barto, 26 A. 2d 905, 345 Pa. 217; Dugan v. McGara's, Inc., 25 A.2d 718, 344 Pa. 460; Gojkovic v. Wageley, 1924, 123 A. 466, 278 Pa. 488 (despite oral testimony on personal pleasure mission).

W.Va.—Weismantle v. Petros, 19 S.E. 2d 594, 124 W.Va. 180.

Despite uncontradicted testimony of driver

Presumption raised by proof of ownership by the defendant and of

§ **417.7** TRIAL EVIDENCE Ch. 417

required to believe the rebuttal testimony,[82] but it cannot arbitrarily or capriciously disregard the testimony of credible witnesses introduced to obviate the effect of the presumption.[83] Some decisions have recognized the presumption as evidence which may be weighed against the positive testimony of witnesses against it; the jury being at liberty to accept or reject the evidence or the presumption.[84]

Proof of ownership and driver in general employment

In some jurisdictions, proof of ownership or control by the defendant of the automobile causing an accident, together with the added proof that the negligent driver was in the general employment of the defendant, raises a presumption that the driver

employment by the defendant of the driver for the special purpose of operating the car is sufficient to take the case to the jury as to whether the driver was acting within the scope of employment, notwithstanding the undisputed evidence of the driver that he was engaged upon an errand of his own. Clark v. Feldman, 224 N.W. 167, 57 N.D. 741.

82. U.S.—Mandelbaum v. U. S., C. A.N.Y., 251 F.2d 748.

Cal.—Phillips v. Cuccio, 42 P.2d 1050, 5 Cal.App.2d 520.

Mo.—Wrightsman v. Glidewell, 239 S.W. 574, 210 Mo.App. 367 (notwithstanding the uncontradicted testimony of the servant and two other witnesses that the servant was then on his way to take a witness to his work and intended to return for the other witness before going to his own work, there being evidence that on other occasions the servant had transported the first witness along the same route and left him at the street nearest his place of employment while the servant proceeded to his own place of employment).

Tenn.—McMahan v. Tucker, 1948, 216 S.W.2d 356, 31 Tenn.App. 429.

Wash.—Van Court v. Lodge Cab Co., 1939, 89 P.2d 206, 198 Wash. 530.

83. Ark.—Langston v. Harper, 227 S.W.2d 973, 216 Ark. 778.

Tenn.—Green v. Powell, 124 S.W.2d 269, 22 Tenn.App. 481.

84. U.S.—Montgomery v. Hutchins, C.C.A.Cal., 118 F.2d 661.

Cal.—Shields v. Oxnard Harbor Dist., 116 P.2d 121, 46 Cal.App.2d 477; Montanya v. Brown, 88 P.2d 745, 31 Cal.App.2d 642; Bushnell v. Yoshika Tashiro, 2 P.2d 550, 115 Cal.App. 563 (rebutting testimony uncontradicted).

R.I.—Kent v. Draper Soap Co., 63 A. 2d 571, 75 R.I. 30.

Tenn.—McMahan v. Tucker, 216 S.W. 2d 356, 31 Tenn.App. 429 (the statutory presumption remains notwithstanding explanatory evidence if there is any substantial evidence upon which jury could discredit witness and there is no other credible evidence).

Supports verdict

If jury should disregard evidence that automobile owner instructed driver who was owner's employee not to carry passengers, presumption of responsibility would remain and would justify a finding against owner. Hartstein v. U. S. Trucking Corporation, 23 N.Y.S.2d 251, 260 App. Div. 643, reargument denied 25 N.Y. S.2d 398, 260 App.Div. 1006, and 25 N.Y.S.2d 400, 260 App.Div. 1006.

Ch. 417 PRESUMPTIONS AND INFERENCES § **417.7**

was acting within the scope of employment,[85] or raises an inference of agency.[86]

85. Same statement in prior edition **cited by the court** in Frick v. Bickel, 54 N.E.2d 436, 437, 115 Ind.App. 114, motion denied 57 N.E.2d 62, 222 Ind. 610.

U.S.—Pacheco v. U. S., C.A.Virgin Islands 1969, 409 F.2d 1234, (coast guardsman driving truck at night, wearing fatigues); Capital Transp. Co. v. Armour & Co., C.A.Ark., 200 F.2d 722 (presumption rebutted); R. J. Reynolds Tobacco Co. v. Newby, C.C.A.Idaho, 145 F.2d 768 (rebuttable); Standard Coffee Co. v. Trippet, C.C.A.Tex., 108 F.2d 161 (rule stated and evidence held not to overcome presumption); Hawthorne v. Eckerson Co., C.C.A.Vt., 77 F.2d 844 traveling salesman); Rakowsky v. U. S., D.C.Ill., 201 F.Supp. 74 (post-office truck).

Ala.—General Foods Corp. v. Coney, 48 So.2d 781, 35 Ala.App. 492; Chandler v. Owens, 179 So. 256, 235 Ala. 356 (making delivery for employer); Luquire Funeral Homes Ins. Co. v. Turner, 178 So. 536, 235 Ala. 305 (general field manager of insurance company).

Ark.—Curtis Circulation Co. v. Henderson, 342 S.W.2d 89, 232 Ark. 1029; Bullock v. Miner, 286 S.W.2d 328, 225 Ark. 897; Langston v. Harper, 227 S.W.2d 973, 216 Ark. 778; Brooks v. Bale Chevrolet Co., 127 S.W.2d 135, 198 Ark. 17 (automobile dealer's employee); Ball v. Hail, 118 S.W.2d 668, 196 Ark. 491 (automobile salesman on way home from salesmen's meeting); Mullins v. Ritchie Grocer Co., 35 S.W.2d 1010, 183 Ark. 218 (salesman).

Cal.—Nash v. Wright, 186 P.2d 686, 82 Cal.App.2d 467; Shields v. Oxnard Harbor Dist., 116 P.2d 121, 46 Cal.App.2d 477 (port director); Tsirlis v. Standard Oil Co. of California, 90 P.2d 128, 32 Cal.App.2d 469 (salesman); Malmstrom v. Bridges, 47 P.2d 336, 8 Cal.App.2d 5 (testing automobile after making repairs for employer); Hutson v. Gerson, 23 P.2d 816, 132 Cal.App. 665 (taxicab).

Colo.—Ward v. Teller Reservoir & Irrigation Co., 1915, 153 P. 219, 60 Colo. 47.

Ga.—Cravey v. J. S. Gainer Pulpwood Co., Inc., 1973, 197 S.E.2d 171, 128 Ga.App. 465 (noted defendant paid for damage to vehicle of plaintiff's husband); Early v. Ramey, 1969, 168 S.E.2d 629, 119 Ga.App. 621; Price v. Star Service & Petroleum Corp., 1969, 166 S.E.2d 593, 119 Ga.App. 171 (overcome by positive uncontradicted evidence of personal mission); Clark v. Atlanta Veterans Transp., Inc., 148 S.E.2d 921, 113 Ga.App. 531; Ayers v. Barney A. Smith Motors, Inc., 145 S.E.2d 753, 112 Ga.App. 581; Pratt v. Melton, 129 S.E.2d 346, 107 Ga.App. 127; Yellow Cab Co. of Savannah v. Cohen, 82 S.E.2d 27, 90 Ga.App. 104; Southern Gas Corp. v. Cowan, 81 S.E.2d 488, 89 Ga.App. 810; J. W. Starr & Sons Lumber Co. v. York, 78 S.E.2d 429, 89 Ga.App. 22.

Idaho.—Manion v. Waybright, 86 P.2d 181, 59 Idaho 643 (rule stated and question held for jury).

Ill.—Sutherland v. Guccione, 131 N.E.2d 130, 8 Ill.App.2d 201.

Ky.—Bowling v. Lewis, 287 S.W.2d 629; Higgans v. Deskins, 263 S.W.2d 108, 52 A.L.R.2d 1346; Mullen & Haynes Co. v. Crisp, 268 S.W. 576, 207 Ky. 31 (manager of owner's business deemed to have implied authority); Livingston v. Fields, 225 S.W.2d 317, 311 Ky. 714; Hickman v. Strunk, 197 S.W.2d 442, 303 Ky. 397; Galloway Motor Co. v. Huffman's Adm'r,

---

86. See note 86 on page 168.

§ 417.7   TRIAL EVIDENCE   Ch. 417

137 S.W.2d 379, 281 Ky. 841 (auto salesman); Davis v. Bennett's Adm'r, 132 S.W.2d 334, 279 Ky. 799 (rule stated, but evidence found insufficient); Home Laundry Co. v. Cook, 125 S.W.2d 763, 277 Ky. 8 (laundry truck); Hinternisch v. Brewsaugh, 87 S.W.2d 934, 261 Ky. 432 (rule stated and recovery upheld); Keeling v. Nall, 87 S.W.2d 370, 261 Ky. 232 (taxicab).

La.—Gonzales v. Beaumont Cement Sales Co., App., 125 So.2d 785; Harding v. Christiana, App., 103 So.2d 301; Futch v. W. Horace Williams Co., App., 26 So.2d 776, rehearing refused 27 So.2d 184 (employee permitted to use truck to go to and from work); Antoine v. Louisiana Highway Commission, App., 188 So. 443 (highway commission's truck); Hunt v. Chisholm, App., 183 So. 132 (automobile used to deliver and pick up clothes for cleaning); Mancuso v. Hurwitz-Mintz Furniture Co., App., 181 So. 814, rehearing denied, App , 183 So. 461 (employee returning to employer's garage after completing mission of his own); Brown v. Indemnity Ins. Co. of North America, App., 178 So. 768 (used car salesman); Middleton v. Humble, App., 172 So. 542 (owner's tenant by sufferance permitted to use car).

Md.—Tregellas v. American Oil Co., 188 A.2d 691, 231 Md. 95; Salowitch v. Kres, 127 A. 643, 147 Md. 23.

Miss.—Riverside Industries of Philadelphia v. Watkins, 195 So.2d 844.

Mich.—Rabaut v. Venable, 280 N.W. 129, 285 Mich. 111 (automobile loaned to chauffeur's employer).

Minn.—Ewer v. Coppe, 271 N.W. 101, 199 Minn. 78 (employee used car for personal pleasure).

Miss.—Colotta v. Phillips, 85 So.2d 574, 226 Miss. 870; Eagle Motor Lines v. Mitchell, 78 So.2d 482, 223 Miss. 398 (was regular driver);

Merchants Co. v. Tracy, 166 So. 340, 175 Miss. 49 (rule stated and question held for jury); Slaughter v. Holsomback, 147 So. 318, 166 Miss. 643 (permitting owner's son to drive).

Mont.—Gagnon v. Jones, 62 P.2d 683, 103 Mont. 365; Monaghan v. Standard Motor Co., 1934, 29 P.2d 378, 96 Mont. 165.

Neb.—Ebers v. Whitmore, 241 N.W. 126, 122 Neb. 653; Berggren v. Hannan, Odell & Van Brunt, 215 N.W. 556, 116 Neb. 18.

N.J.—Schultz v. Hinz, 90 A.2d 19, 20 N.J.Super. 346 (presumption rebuttable); Trojan v. Brennan, 187 A. 138, 117 N.J.L. 110 (rule stated and question held for jury).

N.Y.—Fisher v. New York Good Humor, 39 N.Y.S.2d 28, 265 App. Div. 967, appeal dismissed 50 N.E. 2d 305, 290 N.Y. 921 (presumption overcome); Katz v. Wolff & Reinheimer, 221 N.Y.S. 476, 129 Misc. 384 (taxicab driver, having general control of car, without instructions, presumed to have authority to do things he considers essential).

N.C.—Clark v. Sweaney, 95 S.E. 568, 175 N.C. 280.

Okl.—Pollard v. Grimes, 210 P.2d 778, 202 Okl. 118; Claxton v. Page, 124 P.2d 977, 190 Okl. 422.

Or.—Foster v. Farra, 243 P. 778, 782, 117 Or. 286.

Pa.—Hunter v. Rossi, 172 Pa.Super. 301, 93 A.2d 912 (shifts burden of proof); Thatcher v. Pierce, 125 A. 302, 281 Pa. 16.

R.I.—Haining v. Turner Centre System, 149 A. 376, 50 R.I. 481; McIver v. Schwartz, 145 A. 101, 50 R.I. 68; Callahan v. Weybosset Pure Food Market, 133 A. 442, 47 R.I. 361.

Tenn.—Delaney v. Turner, 237 S.W. 2d 965, 34 Tenn.App. 380; D. S. Etheridge Co. v. Peterson, 90 S.W.

2d 957, 19 Tenn.App. 530 (under conditions resembling normal use by agent of dealer).

Tex.—Creekmore v. Horton & Horton, Inc., Civ.App.1972, 487 S.W. 2d 148, error refused n. r. e. (subject to being rebutted by showing that the motorist was engaged on a mission which was purely personal to him); Robertson Tank Lines, Inc. v. Van Cleave, 1971, 468 S.W.2d 354; Czikora v. Hutcheson, 1969, 443 S.W.2d 871, error dismissed (upon contrary evidence being introduced, presumption vanished); Younger Bros. v. Moore, Civ.App., 135 S.W.2d 780, error dismissed, judgment correct (rule stated and evidence found sufficient to show liability); Broaddus v. Long, Civ.App., 125 S.W.2d 340, affirmed 138 S.W.2d 1057, 135 Tex. 353 (taxicab driver); Guitar v. Wheeler, Civ.App., 36 S.W.2d 325, error dismissed (holding that mere proof that the driver was his servant was insufficient; proof of scope of employment being necessary); Robert Oil Corporation v. Garrett, Civ.App., 22 S.W.2d 508, affirmed, Com.App., 37 S.W. 2d 135 (driver having authority to drive); Robertson v. Holden, Civ. App., 297 S.W. 327, reversed on other grounds, Com.App., 1 S.W. 2d 570 (ambulance driver).

Vt.—Hawthorne v. Eckerson Co., C. C.A.Vt., 77 F.2d. 844 (traveling salesman accustomed to using auto).

Va.—Crowell v. Duncan, 134 S.E. 576, 145 Va. 489, 50 A.L.R. 1425.

Wash.—Handley v. Anacortes Ice Co., 105 P.2d 505, 5 Wash.2d 384; Murray v. Kauffman Buick Co., 85 P. 2d 1061, 197 Wash. 469 (rule stated, and question held for jury); Templin v. Doan, 59 P.2d 1110, 187 Wash. 68 (motorcycle used as delivery car).

W.Va.—Alloy v. Hennis Freight Lines, Inc., 80 S.E.2d 514, 139 W. Va. 480; Ercole v. Daniel, 1928, 141 S.E. 631, 105 W.Va. 118.

But see

Mo.—Chandler v. New Moon Homes, Inc., Sup.1967, 418 S.W.2d 130.

Contra as to driver's own vehicle

Proof that general relationship of master and servant existed between power company and motorist was insufficient in itself to raise rebuttable presumption that at time of collision, motorist, who was driving his own automobile, was engaged in course of employment and in furtherance of company's business. Mississippi Power & Light Co. v. Laney, 154 So. 2d 128, 247 Miss. 71.

Especially where owner's wife is passenger

The natural presumption is that one employed in operating an automobile is doing so in the service of the owner, especially where the passenger is the owner's wife. Clark v. Sweaney, 95 S.E. 568, 175 N.C. 280.

Vehicle furnished for personal transportation to work

Evidence that, as a part of the consideration of his employment, employee was furnished automobile to be used in going to and from work raised presumption that employee was operating employer's automobile within scope of his employment. Pest Masters, Inc. v. Callaway, 1974, 210 S.E.2d 243, 133 Ga.App. 123.

Vehicle rented with driver

Where one is engaged in business of renting out vehicles and furnishes driver or operator as part of hiring, there is factual presumption that operator remains in employ of his original employer, since he is engaged in very occupation for which he was originally so employed, and so long as employee is furthering business of his general employer by services rendered to another, fact that employee is carrying out instruction of hirer as to specific de-

§ 417.7   TRIAL EVIDENCE   Ch. 417

But in other cases it has been held that general employment alone is not enough to show prima facie that the driver was engaged in the defendant's business.[87]

tails of work does not warrant inference that there has been a change of employer in sense of relieving general employer of liability for operator's negligence. Viggiano v. William C. Reppenhagen, Inc., 150 A.2d 40, 55 N.J.Super. 114.

Where lessor of truck was engaged in business of renting trucks and furnishing drivers as part of hiring, the fact that truck bore name of both lessor and lessee did not equalize presumption that driver remained in lessor's employ. Franceschino v. Mack, 102 A.2d 217, 174 Pa.Super. 518.

When supported by other evidence

Proof of ownership coupled with existence of master-servant relationship, when supported by evidence concerning nature of relationship and scope of employment, raises presumption that commercial vehicle was being used within scope of driver's employment. Howell v. Olson, Okl.1969, 452 P.2d 768.

On showing that truck was owned by defendant and was being driven by defendant's employee and that none of defendant's trucks were being operated by unauthorized persons on day of accident, presumption arose that driver was operating truck for defendant within scope of employment and burden shifted to defendant to offer evidence that driver was not acting within scope. Id.

86. **Guam.**—San Nicolas v. Lizama, 361 F.Supp. 595.

87. **U.S.**—Standard Accident Ins. Co. v. Rivet, C.C.A.La., 89 F.2d 74.

Conn.—Matulis v. Gans, 141 A. 870, 107 Conn. 562; Lane v. Ajax Rubber Co., 120 A. 724, 99 Conn. 16.

Ga.—Ruff v. Gazaway, 60 S.E.2d 467, 82 Ga.App. 151 (hunting trip, plus visit to prospective employee); Beard v. Oliver, 182 S.E. 921, 52 Ga.App. 229.

Mass.—Thompson v. Sides, 176 N.E. 623, 275 Mass. 568; Karpowicz v. Manasas, 176 N.E. 497, 275 Mass. 413; Ferreira v. Franco, 173 N.E. 529, 273 Mass. 272; Wilson v. Grace, 173 N.E. 524, 273 Mass. 146 (rule in absence of statute); Simmons v. Rabinowitz, 164 N.E. 806, 266 Mass. 109 (decided before 1928 statute).

Mo.—Humphrey v. Hogan, App., 104 S.W.2d 767.

Okl.—Neilan Co. v. Miller, 52 P.2d 783, 175 Okl. 104.

Pa.—Henry v. Beck, 36 A.2d 734, 154 Pa.Super. 585 (insufficient even with evidence of presence in vehicle of briefcases bearing employer's name).

Tenn.—Maysay v. Hickman, 97 S.W.2d 662, 20 Tenn.App. 262 (truck used to transport fellow employee's furniture).

Vt.—Ronan v. J. G. Turnbull Co., 131 A. 788, 99 Vt. 280.

Evidence insufficient to establish presumption

Fact that employee is driving automobile with dealer's tag does not authorize presumption that employee is acting within scope of his employment. Lanteigne v. Smith, 74 A.2d 116, 365 Pa. 132.

Master out of the country

Where the only proof was that the servant was driving with two young ladies, the jury could not reasonably hold that he was about his master's business, particularly when the master was in Europe. Mutulis v. Gans, 141 A. 870, 107 Conn. 562.

In jurisdictions where this presumption arises, it may be deemed stronger than that arising from mere proof of ownership.[88]

Under the Federal Torts Claims Act there is no express presumption arising out of ownership of the vehicle by the Federal government that the operator thereof was acting within the scope of the employee's office at the time of the injury. That part of the Act reading: " * * * caused by the negligent or wrongful act or omission of any employee of the Government while acting within the scope of his office or employment * * *" has been construed as to impose upon the plaintiff the affirmative duty to establish that the employee was acting within the scope of employment without aid of presumptions.[89] However, it has also been held that it will be presumed that a driver of a military vehicle was driving with authority.[90]

This presumption, too, is rebuttable.[91]

Proof defendant's name inscribed on vehicle

The weight of authority is that the fact that the name of the defendant was painted or inscribed in some manner on the motor vehicle which inflicted the injury raises a presumption, or is prima facie evidence, that the defendant owned such vehicle, and

---

88. Ala.—Chandler v. Owens, 179 So. 256, 235 Ala. 356.

89. U.S.—Friedman v. U. S., D.C. Ill., 139 F.Supp. 600; Hubsch v. U. S., C.A.Fla., 174 F.2d 7, cause remanded 70 S.Ct. 225, 338 U.S. 440, 94 L.Ed. 244.

90. U.S.—Pacheco v. U. S., C.A. Virgin Islands 1969, 409 F.2d 1234 (coast guardsman); Cox v. U. S., 73 F.Supp. 1022, 109 Ct.Cl. 470.

91. For general discussion of rebuttable presumptions, see section 417.1 at fn. 7 et seq.

Colo.—Horst v. Smith, App.1973, 510 P.2d 1379 (that employee, who had been given permission to use one of employers' cars to drive directly home in evening and back to work the following morning, was not working on day of accident and that he had completed his trip from job site, where he picked up a vehicle in order to have transportation to work the following morning, to his home before accident occurred rebutted presumption).

Ga.—Georgia Power Co. v. Mozingo, 1974, 209 S.E.2d 66, 132 Ga.App. 666 (should be clear, positive and uncontradicted).

Ill.—Gilpin v. Lev, 1966, 217 N.E.2d 477, 70 Ill.App.2d 66.

Mo.—Snead v. Sentlinger, 1959, 327 S.W.2d 202 (presumption disappears).

Tex.—Gifford-Hill & Co. v. Moore, Civ.App.1972, 479 S.W.2d 711 (was rebutted or dispelled by testimony, even though supplied by a party at interest, which was clear, positive and uncontradicted to effect that employee had abandoned his master's mission and was engaged in one exclusively his own when the accident occurred); Whittle v. Saunders, Civ.App.1965, 396 S.W. 2d 155 (disappears).

§ 417.7   TRIAL EVIDENCE   Ch. 417

that the driver was using it in defendant's behalf.[92] It has been

---

92. **U.S.**—Newell v. Harold Shaffer Leasing Co., Inc., C.A.Miss.1974, 489 F.2d 103 (under Mississippi law); Montague v. Goolsby, 237 F.2d 776, 99 U.S.App.D.C. 148 (taxicab); Liberty Baking Co. v. Kellum, C.C.A.Pa., 79 F.2d 931 (truck used for business purposes).

Ala.—Barber Pure Milk Co. v. Holmes, 84 So.2d 345, 264 Ala. 45; Hancock v. Liggett & Myers Tobacco Co., 42 So.2d 632, 253 Ala. 63.

Cal.—Similar statement in prior edition **cited by the court** in Brown-Forman Distillers Corp. v. Walkup Drayage & Warehouse Co., 163 P.2d 878, 880, 71 Cal.App.2d 795, and Tieman v. Red Top Cab Co., 3 P.2d 381, 117 Cal.App. 40; Harrington v. Evans, 221 P.2d 696, 99 Cal.App.2d 269; Nash v. Wright, 186 P.2d 686, 82 Cal.App 2d 467.

Fla.—Florida Motor Lines v. Millian, 24 So.2d 710, 21 Fla. 157.

Ga.—West End Cab Co. v. Stovall, 106 S.E.2d 810, 98 Ga.App. 724 (taxicab).

Ill.—Sutherland v. Guccione, 131 N.E.2d 130, 8 Ill.App.2d 201; Hartley v. Red Ball Transit Co., 176 N.E. 751, 344 Ill. 534.

Neb.—Myers v. McMaken, 276 N.W. 167, 133 Neb. 524; Weber v. Thompson-Belden & Co., 181 N.W. 649, 105 Neb. 606.

N.J.—Kelley v. Hicks, 76 A.2d 23, 9 N.J.Super. 266.

N.Y.—Lawson v. Wells, Fargo & Co., Sup., 113 N.Y.S. 647.

Ohio.—McDougall v. Glenn Cartage Co., 160 N.E.2d 266, 169 Ohio St. 522 (overruling Sobolovitz v. Lubric Oil Co., 107 Ohio St. 204, 140 N.E. 634).

Pa.—Lindenmuth v. Steffy, 98 A.2d 242, 173 Pa.Super. 509; Capozi v. Hearst Pub. Co., 1952, 92 A.2d 177, 371 Pa. 503; Sweeney v. City of Pittsburgh, 34 A.2d 67, 348 Pa. 80; Nalevanko v. Marie, 195 A. 49, 328 Pa. 586 (trade name on business automobile); Sieber v. Russ Bros. Ice Cream Co., 120 A. 272, 276 Pa. 340 (truck loaded with ice cream cans and bearing the name of the defendant, a manufacturer and vendor of ice cream).

Tenn.—McAmis v. Carlisle, 1956, 300 S.W.2d 59, 42 Tenn.App. 195.

Tex.—Henderson Drilling Corp. v. Perez, Civ.App., 304 S.W.2d 172; Strickland Transportation Co. v. Carmona, Civ.App., 303 S.W.2d 851. Austin Road Co. v. Willman, Civ.App., 303 S.W.2d 878; J. A. & E. D. Transport Co. v. Rusin, Civ.App., 202 S.W.2d 693, set aside on other grounds on rehearing 206 S.W.2d 95 (insignia).

Vt.—Cappello v. Aero Mayflower Transit Co., 68 A.2d 913, 116 Vt. 64.

Wash.—Bennett v. King County Cab Co., 27 P.2d 125, 175 Wash. 216 (taxicab).

Exactness of name

In order to raise presumption of ownership, it is not necessary that there should be an exact correspondence between designation on vehicle and actual name of alleged owner. Midora v. Alfieri, 17 A.2d 873, 341 Pa. 27.

The words "Farmers Dairy" on truck did not create presumption that "Farmers Dairy Association" of another state owned the truck, since quoted words seem to be a generic term designating a type of establishment rather than name of a particular concern, especially where legend on truck indicated that truck was owned and operated by an individual not connected with the association. Id.

Proof that truck is business vehicle and bears trade-mark of defendant displayed on truck in usual manner

held by a Texas court, citing this section in a prior edition, that the rule is not limited to corporations, but applies to vehicles bearing the insignia of a business, whether the business is incorporated, or one operated by partners or individuals.[93]

However, it has been held that, because modern case discovery should enable the plaintiff to ascertain the facts as to agency, no presumption should be accorded from mere proof of ownership.[94]

This presumption is also rebuttable.[95]

establishes rebuttable presumption that truck is owned by person whose name appears thereon and is being used in such person's business, notwithstanding that name of truck is given without abbreviation "Inc.," which is part of defendant's true name. Reed v. Horn's Motor Express, 187 A. 275, 123 Pa.Super. 411.

Not from presence of business papers in vehicle

"The presence of these papers in the car does not give rise to the presumption that the car at the time of the accident was engaged in the defendant's business. That presumption arises where the car is a business car with the business sign of the defendant displayed thereon." Deater v. Penn Mach. Co., 166 A. 846, 847, 311 Pa. 291.

93. **Tex.**—J. A. & E. D. Transport Co. v. Rusin, Civ.App., 202 S.W.2d 693, set aside on other grounds on rehearing 206 S.W.2d 95.

94. **Mo.**—Chandler v. New Moon Homes, Inc., Sup.1967, 418 S.W.2d 130 (showed fact of name on doors, and opinion, without objection, of ownership in defendant).

95. For discussion of rebuttable presumptions generally, see section 417.1 at fn. 7 et seq.

U.S.—Molinaro v. Scott Bros., Inc., 229 F.2d 773, 97 U.S.App.D.C. 199; Harlem Taxicab Ass'n v. Nemesh, 191 F.2d 459, 89 U.S.App.D.C. 123; Constitution Pub. Co. v. Dale, C.C.A.Ala., 164 F.2d 210 (under Alabama law); Domarek v. Bates Motor Transport Lines, C.C.A.Ill., 93 F.2d 522; Simon v. City Cab Co., 78 F.2d 506, 64 App.D.C. 364, certiorari denied 56 S.Ct. 173, 296 U. S. 640, 80 L.Ed. 455 (taxicab); Young v. Wilky Carrier Corporation, D.C.Pa., 54 F.Supp. 912, affirmed 150 F.2d 764, certiorari denied 66 S.Ct. 470, 326 U.S. 786, 90 L.Ed. 477 (evidence was insufficient to rebut presumption arising under Pennsylvania law that tractor was being used in defendant's business at time of accident).

Ala.—Sears Roebuck & Co. v. Hamm, 81 So.2d 915, 38 Ala.App. 258 (evidence of corporation that trucks bearing name of corporation were owned by third party, which garaged and serviced the trucks while not being used by the corporation, was insufficient to rebut administrative presumption).

Fla.—Mercury Cab Owners' Ass'n v. Jones, 79 So.2d 782 (insignia on taxicab).

Ill.—Hartley v. Red Ball Transit Co., 176 N.E. 751, 344 Ill. 534 (may be overcome as a matter of law); Bosco v. Boston Store of Chicago, 195 Ill.App. 133 (proof owned and operated by another under contract with defendant).

Mont.—Ashley v. Safeway Stores, 47 P.2d 53, 100 Mont. 312 (freight being carried to defendant in truck bearing defendant's name).

Neb.—Myers v. McMaken, 276 N.W. 167, 133 Neb. 524 (driver found to be the owner).

§ 417.8 Other Particular Matters

Library References:
C.J.S. Evidence § 114 et seq.; Motor Vehicles § 509 et seq.
West's Key No. Digests, Automobiles ⇒242; Evidence ⇒53 et seq.

There is no presumption one way or the other as to the skill or want of skill of the driver of a vehicle.[96]

However, if a statute fixes the age at which a child may drive an automobile, a rebuttable presumption of the incompetency of those under the age fixed arises.[97]

Pa.—Henry v. Beck, 36 A.2d 734, 154 Pa.Super. 585.

Tex.—Creekmore v. Horton & Horton, Inc., Civ.App.1972, 487 S.W.2d 148, error refused n. r. e.; Gifford-Hill & Co. v. Moore, Civ.App.1972, 479 S.W.2d 711 (was rebutted or dispelled by testimony, even though supplied by a party at interest, which was clear, positive and uncontradicted to effect that employee had abandoned his master's mission and was engaged in one exclusively his own); McGee v. Phillips Petroleum Co., Civ.App. 1963, 373 S.W.2d 773, error ref. n. r. e.; Rodgers v. Jackson Brewing Co., Civ.App.1956, 289 S.W.2d 307; Lewis v. J. P. Word Transfer Co., Civ.App.1938, 119 S.W.2d 106 (driver found to be the owner).

Jury question

Pa.—Sefton v. Valley Dairy Co., 28 A.2d 313, 345 Pa. 324 (such presumption is sufficient to take case to jury even though defendant produces uncontradicted evidence that driver was not its employee or produces evidence that defendant did not own vehicle in question); Holzheimer v. Lit Bros., 105 A. 73, 262 Pa. 150 (fact that this presumption is rebuttable does not mean that it has any less probative force than it would have if it rested on direct evidence; defendant's evidence that the driver at the time of the collision had taken the machine for his own use during a brief absence of the regular driver, who had left it in charge of a delivery helper who had nothing to do with its control, would not justify instruction directing a verdict for the defendant).

96. Ill.—Devine v. Brunswick-Balke-Collender Co., 110 N.E. 780, 270 Ill. 504.

Contra

Wash.—Vikelis v. Jaundalderis, 348 P.2d 649, 55 Wash.2d 565 (held evidence was insufficient to overcome presumption that operator who held valid license was competent and qualified).

Effect of license

Fact that chauffeur's license of truck driver authorized him to operate motor vehicle of not over 6,000 pounds unladen weight would not give rise to presumption that Motor Vehicle Department had determined that driver was not competent to drive heavy truck nor would evidence of such opinion constitute evidence of negligence on part of driver. Armenta v. Churchill, Cal.App., 258 P.2d 861, subsequent opinion 267 P. 2d 303, 42 Cal.2d 448.

97. N.Y.—Edwards v. Pickens, 1971, 320 N.Y.S.2d 857, 66 Misc.2d 352.

Wis.—Canzoneri v. Heckert, 1936, 269 N.W. 716, 223 Wis. 25.

Inference of negligence of owner

Negligence may be inferred by reason of defendant's violation of statute prohibiting any person from al-

Involvement in a single collision will not raise an inference of an automobile driver's incompetency so as to establish the liability of one who had control of the automobile and permitted such driver to operate it.[98]

A rebuttable presumption has been held to exist that a teen-age party was capable of exercising the same degree of care as an adult.[99]

Licensed motorists are presumed to understand the significance of painted lines used to denote the division of a highway into one-way lanes;[1] and when an arterial highway has been duly established and a stop sign erected on a street crossing it, any one approaching it on the intersecting street is presumed to know that the highway is arterial.[2]

Traffic control signs will be presumed to have been lawfully erected and maintained.[3]

lowing a motor vehicle owned by him or under his control to be operated by any person who has no legal right to do so. Leone v. Doran, 1973, 292 N.E.2d 19, 363 Mass. 1, order vacated in part as to other matter 297 N.E.2d 493.

98. Ky.—Wilhelmi v. Berns, 119 S.W.2d 625, 274 Ky. 618.

99. Ga.—Sheetz v. Welch, 81 S.E.2d 319, 89 Ga.App. 749 (sixteen year old plaintiff).

1. N.H.—Himmel v. Finkelstein, 4 A.2d 657, 90 N.H. 78.

2. N.M.—Bunton v. Hull, 177 P.2d 168, 51 N.M. 5.

Wash.—Metzger v. Moran, 96 P.2d 580, 1 Wash.2d 657.

3. Ala.—Gilbert v. Gwin-McCollum Funeral Home, Inc., 106 So.2d 646, 268 Ala. 372.

Ga.—Munday v. Brissette, 1966, 148 S.E.2d 55, 113 Ga. 147, reversed on other grounds, 149 S.E.2d 110, 222 Ga. 162, on remand 149 S.E.2d 829, 113 Ga.App. 849; Fields v. Jackson, 115 S.E.2d 877, 102 Ga.App. 117.

Idaho.—Howard v. Missman, 337 P.2d 592, 81 Idaho 82.

Ind.—Stull v. Davidson, 127 N.E.2d 130, 125 Ind.App. 565.

N.J.—Davidson v. Fornicola, 118 A.2d 838, 38 N.J.Super. 365.

N.Y.—Bailey v. Herrmann, 1 N.Y.S.2d 404, 253 App.Div. 125, followed in 1 N.Y.S.2d 405, 253 App.Div. 126.

Ohio.—McDonald v. Kelly, 134 N.E.2d 396, 101 Ohio App. 46; Shapiro v. Butts, 1950, 102 N.E.2d 270, 89 Ohio App. 377, affirmed 99 N.E.2d 173, 155 Ohio St. 407.

Or.—Schoenborn v. Broderick, 277 P.2d 787, 202 Or. 634.

Tenn.—Trimble v. Bridges, 180 S.W.2d 590, 27 Tenn.App. 320.

Wash.—Hanson v. Anderson, 335 P.2d 581, 53 Wash.2d 601; Warner v. Ambrose, 332 P.2d 941, 53 Wash.2d 231 ("Yield" sign).

Contra

Me.—Hill v. Janson, 31 A.2d 236, 139 Me. 344 (cannot be assumed without evidence that one of the ways was a through way and that the stop sign was erected under authority of the highway commission).

Pa.—Kowalsky's Exp. Service v. Haverford Tp., 85 A.2d 884, 170 Pa.

§ 417.8   TRIAL EVIDENCE   Ch. 417

It has been presumed that the accident occurred outside the business district in absence of evidence to the contrary.[4]

It has been presumed that the road was straight,[5] and that the weather was clear.[6]

There may be a presumption that a rider in an automobile is a guest, and not a passenger for hire, unless there is proof of an express arrangement to the contrary.[7] It is also presumed that the guest had no right to control the vehicle or its manner of operation.[8]

Super. 229 (no presumption that stop sign erected on private property on private road leading from highway is a legally erected sign).

Purpose of signs

In claims against State where plaintiffs' automobile skidded on recently oiled highway which had become wet with rain, but which was marked with signs warning of the oil, it would be presumed, in absence of evidence of the erection of signs on morning when accident occurred, that signs were placed in anticipation of application of oil two days earlier. Gamjian v. State, 119 N.Y.S.2d 596, 281 App.Div. 923.

4. **Cal.**—Johnson v. Williams, 223 P.2d 266, 100 Cal.App.2d 294 (street was conclusively presumed to have been outside of a business or residential district in absence of evidence that it was sign-posted); Kline v. Barkett, 158 P.2d 51, 68 Cal.App.2d 765 (statutory); Blanchard v. Norton, 1942, 122 P.2d 349, 49 Cal.App.2d 730 (signs limiting speed in one direction did not establish limit for traffic going in opposite direction); Cavalli v. Luckett, 104 P.2d 708, 40 Cal.App.2d 250 (provision that highway shall be conclusively presumed to be outside of business or residence district unless its existence within business or residence district is established by clear and competent evidence as to nature of district, and unless district is duly signposted, was not applicable only to criminal cases); Gayton v. Pacific Fruit Express Co., 15 P.2d 217, 127 Cal.App. 50.

5. **Ga.**—Rogers v. Johnson, 96 S.E. 2d 285, 94 Ga.App. 666.

6. **Ga.**—Rogers v. Johnson, 96 S.E. 2d 285, 94 Ga.App. 666.

7. **Del.**—DeJoseph v. Faraone, Super.1969, 254 A.2d 257.

Iowa.—Sauer v. Scott, 1970, 176 N. W.2d 140; Johnson v. Johnson, 1970, 174 N.W.2d 444; Marean v. Petersen, 1966, 144 N.W.2d 906, 259 Iowa 557.

Ohio.—Hasbrook v. Wingate, 87 N. E.2d 87, 152 Ohio St. 50, 10 A.L.R. 2d 1342.

Ohio statutory rule as to wife

Under Ohio law, a wife may not only be a guest of her husband when riding in his automobile, but in such circumstances, there arises a presumption precluding wife from claiming the status of a person who has paid for her transportation unless there is proof of an express arrangement or proof of circumstances which indicate that parties intended and understood otherwise. Naphtali v. Lafazan, 165 N.Y.S.2d 395, 7 Misc.2d 1057, affirmed in part and reversed in part 186 N.Y.S.2d 1010, 8 A.D.2d 22, appeal dismissed in part 187 N. Y.S.2d 1020, 8 A.D.2d 727, and in which reargument is denied 190 N. Y.S.2d 334, 8 A.D.2d 828, judgment affirmed 209 N.Y.S.2d 317, 171 N.E. 2d 462, 8 N.Y.2d 1097.

8. **La.**—Russo v. Aucoin, App., 7 So.2d 744.

Ch. 417   PRESUMPTIONS AND INFERENCES   § 417.8

It has been presumed one previously seen driving a vehicle was the driver at the time of the accident.[9]

There is no presumption that other occupants of the car are invitees of the owner.[10]

In a joint action by a husband and wife, presumptions may arise as to the legality of the marriage,[11] and as to whether the damages sought would constitute community property.[12]

Proof of the existence of a present condition does not raise a presumption of the existence of such condition at a prior time.[13] However, it has been presumed that a defect found in a

9. **Ill.**—Hall v. Kirk, 1973, 300 N.E.2d 600, 13 Ill.App.3d 656 (collision killed both occupants).

La.—Ehrhard v. State Farm Mut. Auto. Ins. Co., 1973, 274 So.2d 911, application denied 279 So.2d 202 (where father lent automobile to his son and son was last seen driving when he left his home to meet his friend, and son and friend were both found outside automobile after one-car accident fatal to both, there was rebuttable presumption that son was driver).

10. **Md.**—East Coast Freight Lines v. Mayor and City Council of Baltimore, 58 A.2d 290, 190 Md. 256, 2 A.L.R.2d 386 (there is no presumption, where driver is forbidden to pick up hitchhiker but does have authority to pick up an extra driver or helper at his own expense, that one on vehicle at time of accident is extra driver or helper, particularly when that person is a member of the armed forces).

N.J.—Cowan v. Kaminow, 26 A.2d 258, 128 N.J.L. 398 (in an action for wrongful death of occupant of car, which was owned by the husband and operated by his wife, there was no presumption that occupant, who was mother of wife, was invitee of owner).

11. **Cal.**—Hamburgh v. Hys, 71 P.2d 301, 22 Cal.App.2d 508.

Ga.—Atlanta, B. & C. R. Co. v. Thomas, 12 S.E.2d 494, 64 Ga.App. 253 (in action by decedent's second wife for wrongful death of decedent wherein Florida divorce decree obtained by first wife was before the court, and second wife proved ceremonial marriage, the jury was authorized to find that evidence was insufficient to overcome presumption of legality of Florida divorce decree and legality of marriage between decedent and second wife).

Effect of license and certificate

Introduction of marriage license and certificate, with oral testimony showing that plaintiffs had been married by a minister and had thereafter deported themselves as husband and wife, created a presumption that plaintiffs were lawfully married and would sustain a joint judgment for plaintiffs. Record showing that no decree of divorce had been obtained by wife in her proceedings for divorce from her former husband was insufficient to overcome presumption that plaintiffs were lawfully married. Hamburgh v. Hys, 71 P.2d 301, 22 Cal.App.2d 508.

12. **Tex.**—Urban v. Field, Civ.App., 137 S.W.2d 137 (presumed that the damages sought constituted community property).

13. **Ark.**—Eudoro Motor Co. v. Womack, 111 S.W.2d 530, 195 Ark. 74.

But see

Conditions once shown to exist are presumed to continue, and presump-

§ **417.8** TRIAL EVIDENCE Ch. 417

vehicle was present at the time of the accident.[14]

Ownership of vehicles engaged in road construction creates a presumption that the construction was being performed by the owner.[15]

It has been presumed that a woman of child bearing age had the capacity to bear children before receiving injuries in an automobile accident.[16]

Presumption of mailing has been found from certain proven facts.[17]

An insured was presumed to know the terms of an insurance policy.[18]

Knowledge of the law at the time of certain conduct may be charged to a party.[19]

tion may be applied backwards in time from subsequent condition. Larsen Baking Co. v. City of New York, 1968, 292 N.Y.S.2d 145, 30 A.D.2d 400, judgment affirmed 303 N.Y.S.2d 80, 24 N.Y.2d 1036, 250 N.E.2d 356.

14. Kan.—Lenhart v. Owens, 1973, 507 P.2d 318, 211 Kan. 534 (it would be presumed that defective piston cup found in brake cyclinder had not been substituted for a nondefective piston cup after the accident to make false case against manufacturer for implied warranty and manufacturer had burden of producing evidence that defective piston cup, which expert testified had caused power brake failure had been substituted for a nondefective one).

15. Ky.—Robert Beedle & Sons, Inc. v. Stone, 1969, 441 S.W.2d 121 (equipment being used in road construction bore name of company).

16. Ill.—Enloe v. Kirkwood, 1970, 256 N.E.2d 459, 120 Ill.App.2d 117 (in absence of evidence to contrary).

17. U.S.—Richardson v. Brown, C.A.Okl.1971, 443 F.2d 926 (post office receipt obtained by insurer upon mailing cancellation notice with respect to automobile liability policy created presumption of mailing).

Presumed received

Ala.—Harrell v. Alabama Farm Bureau Mut. Ins. Co., 1971, 251 So.2d 220, 287 Ala. 259 (presumption of law is that a letter, properly addressed with sufficient postage, and unreturned to the sender whose address is shown on the envelope, was received by the addressee).

W.Va.—National Grange Mut. Ins. Co. v. Wyoming County Ins. Agency, Inc., 1973, 195 S.E.2d 151, —— W.Va. —— (where insurer placed cancellation notice in the mail, a presumption was created that insured received the notice, but such presumption was not conclusive and could be rebutted).

18. Mich.—Russell v. State Farm Mut. Auto. Ins. Co., 1973, 209 N.W.2d 815, 47 Mich.App. 677 (knowledge of terms and conditions contained in policy, even though may not have read it).

19. Colo.—Vigil v. Motor Vehicle Division of Dept. of Revenue, 1974, 519 P.2d 332, 184 Colo. 142 (licensee to operate motor vehicle on highways is presumed to know law regarding his use of public highways).

It will be presumed that the law of another state is the same as that of the forum, in the absence of proof to the contrary.[20] It has been presumed that a witness is testifying from personal knowledge, in the absence of evidence to the contrary.[21]

Tex.—Travelers Ins. Co. v. Warren, 1969, 447 S.W.2d 698, error refused n. r. e. (that a claim must be filed within six months after accident).

Doctrine of case law

Tort-feasor who enters into settlement agreement subsequent to March 22, 1972 decision providing for apportionment of liability of tort-feasors is chargeable with knowledge of doctrine of that decision so that permitting claim for indemnity to be asserted against tort-feasor who has entered into agreement absolving him of any possible future liability would not result in unfairness. Valentino v. State, 1974, 355 N.Y.S.2d 212, 44 A.D.2d 338.

20. **Ga.**—Kersh v. Life & Cas. Ins. Co. of Tenn., 137 S.E.2d 493, 109 Ga.App. 793.

Ill.—Mitchell v. Burnett, 1971, 272 N.E. 393, 1 Ill.App.3d 24.

But see

There is no presumption that either statutes or common law of another state are similar to statutes of forum, but common law of other state is presumed to be same. Schiavi's Mobile Homes, Inc. v. Johnson, 1968, Me., 244 A.2d 72.

Deemed "procedural" rule

Under Nebraska law, unless laws of other states are pleaded and proved, such laws are presumed to be the same as law of forum, but that rule is merely one of pleading and not one of substantive law and therefore not subject to Erie doctrine. Simmons v. Continental Cas. Co., 1968, D.C.Neb., 285 F.Supp. 997, affirmed C.A. 410 F.2d 881.

Special rule

Where law of a sister state is not pleaded or proved, statutes of Georgia will control if the sister state was not one of the thirteen original colonies. Capital Auto. Co. v. Continental Credit Corp., 1968, 160 S.E. 2d 836, 117 Ga.App. 451.

21. **Ga.**—Gazaway v. Secured Ins. Co., 136 S.E.2d 531, 109 Ga.App. 428.

Chapter 418

RES IPSA LOQUITUR

Table of Sections

Sec.
418.1 In General.
418.2 Situations Applicable.
418.3 Situations Not Applicable.

§ 418.1 In General

Library References:
C.J.S. Motor Vehicles §§ 508, 511(3); Negligence §§ 200 et seq., 220.1 et seq.; Pleading §§ 41, 88, 90.
West's Key No. Digests, Automobiles ⟐240, 242(2); Negligence ⟐119, 121(2); Pleading ⟐20, 53(2).

Generally, a defendant's negligence will not be presumed from the mere happening of an accident.[1] The most important exception to this rule arises under the res ipsa loquitur doctrine, though the rule is not available in some jurisdictions.[2]

Confusion has frequently arisen, in applying the maxim, from failure to observe the distinction between circumstantial evidence and the technical definition of res ipsa loquitur. The principle is imbedded, not in the relation existing between the parties, but in the inherent nature of the act causing the injuries.[3]

It is also said to be invoked because of defendant's superior or exclusive knowledge of what caused the injury.[4]

---

1. See section 417.2, fn. 30 et seq.

2. **Fla.**—Abrams v. Nolan Brown Cadillac Co., App.1969, 228 So.2d 131; Smith's Bakery, Inc. v. Jernigan, App.1961, 134 So.2d 519 (pebbles thrown up from tire); Babcock v. Flowers, 1940, 198 So. 326, 144 Fla. 479; O'Reilly v. Satler, 1940, 193 So. 817, 141 Fla. 770 (rearend collision).

   Mich.—Spiers v. Martin, 58 N.W.2d 821, 336 Mich. 613; Trafamczak v. Anys, 31 N.W.2d 832, 320 Mich. 653.

3. **N.C.**—Howard v. Texas Co., 169 S.E. 832, 205 N.C. 20 (explosion at filling station damaging auto parked nearby).

4. **Ark.**—Lambert v. Markley, 1974, 503 S.W.2d 162, 255 Ark. 851 (where plaintiff railroad employee was working on siding and was struck by right rear dual wheels which became detached from defendant's truck and rolled across ground).

   Cal.—Kenney v. Antonetti, 1931, 295 P. 341, 211 Cal. 336.

   But not necessary to the rule
   In action by building owners against city for damage to building by tractor and trailer owned by city,

Ch. 418 RES IPSA LOQUITUR § 418.1

A distinction also has been made between the res ipsa loquitur rule and a legal inference of a material fact connected with the accident.[5] It has been held to be an evidential inference which, under like circumstances, may be drawn by the court when the court is the trier of the facts.[6] So, while it may be true

death of operator of truck for city would not deprive plaintiffs of right to invoke doctrine of res ipsa loquitur, on ground that city was without superior knowledge as to cause of accident due to death of operator. Lasek v. Jaroschak, 162 A.2d 25, 192 Pa.Super. 350.

Not applicable with equal knowledge

La.—Flowers v. Travelers Indem. Co., App., 136 So.2d 492 (not applicable when motorist drove into a ditch to avoid collision with defendants' stalled truck, in view of fact nature of the accident was not such that knowledge of the cause was exclusively with defendants, defendants were free from negligence, and sole proximate cause of the accident was negligence of motorist as to lookout); Bryant v. Ouachita Coca-Cola Bottling Co., App., 99 So.2d 152, reversed 117 So.2d 919, 239 La. 83 (was inapplicable, where passenger was seated to right of her driver and from her position was afforded an opportunity to observe all relevant factors leading up to and causing collision).

Minn.—Klingman v. Loew's Inc., 296 N.W. 528, 209 Minn. 449 (where there was evidence that road was of tarvia construction and as such would absorb much of the light rays from the lights of the automobile, that occupant sat in the front seat with the driver and as such could and did see as well as the driver, that occupant was acquainted with the road, that accident happened at night, and that occupant knew of the speed at which the automobile was being driven, doctrine was inapplicable).

Wash.—Hughes v. Jolliffe, 313 P.2d 678, 50 Wash.2d 554 (where motorist, when he parked automobile on grade in private driveway, placed automatic gear shift in "park" position, serving as an effective brake, but did not set hand brake or lock doors, and after the automobile rolled backwards and crushed an infant to death, it was discovered then that the gear shift was in neutral position, since motorist and his wife were no better able to know how gear shift was moved than were parents of deceased infant, res ipsa loquitur doctrine was not available to parents in their death action against motorist and his wife).

W.Va.—Ellis v. Henderson, 95 S.E. 2d 801, decision on rehearing recalled 98 S.E.2d 719, 142 W.Va. 824.

5. **Iowa.**—Hebert v. Allen, 41 N.W. 2d 240, 241 Iowa 684 (in an action where the defendant's car suddenly left the road and struck a pole, injuring the plaintiffs who were riding on the fender, res ipsa loquitur was not applicable, but the jury could infer a wanton disregard of the safety of the plaintiffs from the nature of the defendant's conduct).

6. **Me.**—Sylvia v. Etscovitz, 189 A. 419, 135 Me. 80.

Md.—Hickory Transfer Co. v. Nezbed, 96 A.2d 241, 202 Md. 253; Frenkil v. Johnson, to Use of National Retailers Mut. Ins. Co., 3 A.2d 479, 175 Md. 592.

Mo.—Moehle v. St. Louis Public Service Co., App., 229 S.W.2d 285.

N.J.—Murphy v. Terzako, 82 A.2d 1, 14 N.J.Super. 254.

Ohio.—Scovanner v. Toelke, 163 N.E. 493, 119 Ohio St. 256.

§ 418.1　　　TRIAL EVIDENCE　　　Ch. 418

that mere skidding is not, under all circumstances, evidence of negligence, the skidding may be one of the incidents in the occurrence [7] from which an inference may be drawn. The weight of the inference, as well as the weight of the explanation offered to meet it, is for the jury in a jury trial or for the court when the court is trying the facts.[8]

When both the apparatus and the operation of it are in the exclusive control of the defendant, and the accident is one which ordinarily could not happen except by reason of defects in the apparatus or negligence in its operation, a presumption of one or the other arises from the happening of the accident.[9]

7. **Cal.**—Smith v. Hollander, App., 257 P. 577.

N.Y.—Rosenberg v. American Ry. Express Co., Sup., 198 N.Y.S. 224.

Wash.—Kiessling v. Northwest Greyhound Lines, 229 P.2d 335, 38 Wash.2d 289.

8. **Ohio.**—Scovanner v. Toelke, 163 N.E. 493, 119 Ohio St. 256.

Rule further defined

Inquiry as to whether doctrine applies to make a jury question is initially made by trial judge who, based on understanding of how accidents of kind in question happen, determines where probabilities lie, and if he decides that probabilities of nonnegligent causes are as great or greater than probability of negligent cause attributable to defendant he withdraws case from jury. Kaufman v. Fisher, 371 P.2d 948, 230 Or. 626.

Rule illustrated

In action for damage inflicted on house when automobile crashed into it, inference of defendant's negligence arising out of application of doctrine did not disappear on introduction of defendant's exculpatory evidence that she "blanked out" but abided to end of trial and warranted, although it did not require, finding of defendant's negligence. Wells v. Asher, Mo.App., 286 S.W.2d 567.

Statutory exception on railroad damage in Florida

U.S.—Seaboard Air Line R. Co. v. Bailey, C.A.Fla., 190 F.2d 812.

9. This sentence in prior edition **quoted by the court** in U. S. v. Johnson, C.A.Cal., 181 F.2d 577.

Cal.—Finnegan v. Giffen, 265 P. 496, 89 Cal.App. 702 (boy riding as guest on motorcycle); Morris v. Morris, 258 P. 616, 84 Cal.App. 599; Brown v. Davis, 257 P. 877, 84 Cal.App. 180 (automobile overturning and injuring guest).

Del.—Delaware Coach Co. v. Reynolds 71 A.2d 69, 6 Terry 226.

Ga.—Minkovitz v. Fine, 19 S.E.2d 561, 67 Ga.App. 176 (the rule applies only where plaintiff does not know what caused accident, and the accident, though unexplained, would not have happened according to the common experience of man if due care had been exercised, and the general circumstances, thus unexplained, justify inference of negligence).

Ill.—Krueger v. Richardson, 61 N.E. 2d 399, 326 Ill.App. 205 (explosion and fire following collision between street car and automobile); Roberts v. Economy Cabs, 2 N.E.2d 128, 285 Ill.App. 424.

Ky.—Lewis v. Wolk, 228 S.W.2d 432, 312 Ky. 536, 16 A.L.R.2d 974; Thompson v. Kost, 181 S.W.2d 445, 298 Ky. 32 (sufficient evidence under doctrine that it was caused by

Md.—Brehm v. Lorenz, 112 A.2d 475, 206 Md. 500.

Mass.—Bryne v. Great Atlantic & Pacific Tea Co., 168 N.E. 540, 269 Mass. 130.

Minn.—Hector Const. Co. v. Butler, 260 N.W. 496, 194 Minn. 310.

Mo.—Powell v. St. Joseph Ry., Light Heat & Power Co., 81 S.W.2d 957, 336 Mo. 1016.

N.J.—Doryk v. Perth Amboy Bottling Co., 139 A. 419, 104 N.J.L. 87 (brakes locking, causing jerk throwing plaintiff out); Rapp v. Butler-Newark Bus Line, 138 A. 377, 103 N.J.L. 512 (injury to bus passenger through alleged negligence in not keeping bus in proper repair).

N.C.—Etheridge v. Etheridge, 24 S.E. 2d 477, 222 N.C. 616.

Okl.—Creswell v. Temple Mill Co., 1972, 499 P.2d 421, — Colo. — (at speed of 20 m. p. h. or less, on straight road, with no approaching traffic, vehicle does not ordinarily leave the road without negligence).

Ohio.—Scovanner v. Toelke, 163 N.E. 493, 119 Ohio St. 256.

Or.—Francisco v. Circle Tours Sight-Seeing Co., 265 P. 801, 125 Or. 80.

Pa.—Shedloch v. Wyoming Valley Autobus Co., 17 A.2d 384, 340 Pa. 377.

Wis.—Klein v. Beeten, 172 N.W. 736, 169 Wis. 385, 5 A.L.R. 1237.

Could happen without negligence

Absence of evidence, or inference to be drawn therefrom, that accident resulting when road grader went out of control was kind which ordinarily does not occur in absence of someone's negligence defeated application of doctrine. Renfro v. J. D. Coggins Co., 378 P.2d 130, 71 N.M. 310.

In suit brought against owner and against operator of bulldozer to recover for death of pipelayer who was injured when stone snapped from under wheel of bulldozer and hit pipelayer in the head, where it appeared that bulldozer operator had not known at time of accident that stone had been hurled or the cause of pipelayer's injury, case was not one for application of doctrine. Rockey v. Ernest, 80 A.2d 783, 367 Pa. 538.

Expert testimony to show likely caused by negligence

Plaintiff may strengthen inference of negligence under doctrine through use of expert testimony showing that accidents of kind in question do not commonly happen in absence of negligence by persons in defendant's position. Mayor v. Dowsett, 400 P.2d 234, 240 Or. 196.

Necessity of showing defendant's control

Cal.—Cordova v. Ford, 54 Cal.Rptr. 508, 246 Cal.App.2d 180 (since injured motorist who was driving south when she collided with defendant's automobile about to turn north from intersection was in exclusive control of her own automobile, requisite exclusive control in defendant of instrumentality causing accident was not established for purposes of application of doctrine).

Ill.—Crowley v. A-North Shore Driving School, 1974, 313 N.E.2d 200, 19 Ill.App.3d 1035 (inapplicable in action for injuries incurred by state driver's license examiner in course of administering driving test to student of defendant driving school, in absence of showing that defendant's control of immediate cause of injury was exclusive and that injury complained of was caused by someone under defendant's control).

La.—Ardoin v. Millers Mut. Fire Ins. Co. of Tex., App., 92 So.2d 123 (in action against driver for death of decedent who fell from the rear seat thereof when the rear door

§ 418.1 TRIAL EVIDENCE Ch. 418

Where the injured person and the alleged wrongdoer were both in the exercise of an equal right and were chargeable with the same degree of care, the rule is not applicable.[10]

It has been held that the doctrine is inapplicable under proof that the accident might have happened as a result of one or more causes,[11] or where either the defendant's negligence or that of

flew open while the automobile was being driven at a speed of 45 miles an hour along a black top road where the accident might have happened as the result of one or two causes and the rear portion of the automobile was not in exclusive control of the driver, evidence was insufficient to authorize the recovery).

Minn.—Hector Const. Co. v. Butler, 260 N.W. 496, 194 Minn. 310 (it must be shown, among other things, that agency causing injury was under control and management).

Rule limited

Rule will only be invoked where circumstances of accident leave no room for a presumption other than negligence on part of defendant. Minton v. Continental Ins. Co., La.App., 110 So.2d 789.

10. **Cal.**—Gonzalez v. Nichols, 294 P. 758, 110 Cal.App. 738; Sauer v. Eagle Brewing Co., 84 P. 425, 3 Cal.App. 127.

Ill.—Halowatsky v. Central Greyhound Lines, 35 N.E.2d 541, 311 Ill.App. 127 (highway collapsed due to defective sewer pipe).

N.C.—Swainey v. Great Atlantic & Pacific Tea Co., 162 S.E. 557, 202 N.C. 272.

Ohio.—Kelcik v. Cleveland Ry. Co., 156 N.E. 248, 24 Ohio App. 82 (collision between street car and automobile).

Rule illustrated

Where cattle escaped from meat packing establishment of employer and were at large on city streets, and employer directed employee to round up the cattle, and employee, who was familiar with custom of running down and disabling escaped cattle with an automobile, went in pursuit of a cow with his automobile, and cow damaged the automobile, employee could not recover from employer for damage to automobile. Jos. N. Rice Co. v. Grayson, Ky., 341 S.W.2d 238.

11. Statement in prior edition **quoted by the court** in Estes v. Estes, Mo.App., 127 S.W.2d 78.

Cal.—Gonsalves v. Petaluma Bldg. Materials Co., 5 Cal.Rptr. 332, 181 Cal.App.2d 320 (assuming that doctrine may be applied in favor of innocent third party injured by collision between two vehicles, its application to action by bystander victim of collision between trucks traveling in same direction was not warranted, where it could not be said that it was more probable than not that both drivers had been negligent or that one had been at fault to exclusion of other).

Mo.—State ex rel. and to Use of Brancato v. Trimble, 18 S.W.2d 4, 322 Mo. 318.

Or.—Wilbur v. Home Lumber & Coal Co., 282 P. 236, 131 Or. 180.

Pa.—McElwain v. Myers, 80 A.2d 859, 367 Pa. 346.

Wis.—Klein v. Beeten, 172 N.W. 736, 169 Wis. 385, 5 A.L.R. 1237.

Equally probable causes

Cal.—Stanford v. Richmond Chase Co., App., 263 P.2d 108, subsequent opinion 272 P.2d 764, 43 Cal.App. 2d 287 (in action where truck was being loaded by defendant's employees through the use of two

another might have caused the injury.[12] And it has been held that the rule will not be applied where the evidence discloses that

mechanized fork-lifters, wherein there was no direct evidence as to exactly how injuries to truck driver occurred, but circumstances indicated that he might have been struck by one of the lifters, or that he might have fallen from truck, it was for jury to determine whether the two possibilities were equally probable, thus barring application of the doctrine).

La.—Elliott v. General Motors Corp., 1970, 232 So.2d 907 (not applicable in suit against automobile manufacturer and dealer when automobile left road and collided with tree as alleged result of brakes locking, in view of evidence that accident might as easily have occurred through negligence of plaintiff driver, who applied his brakes while traveling at 50 to 60 miles an hour on slick blacktop road when he saw hog at side of the road).

12. Same statement in prior edition **cited by the court** in Cavaretta v. Universal Film Exchange, La.App., 182 So. 135, in connection with the statement that the doctrine is inapplicable where the injury might have occurred by reason of the concurrent negligence of two or more persons or causes, one of which was not under defendant's control; and **quoted by the court** in Estes v. Estes, Mo.App., 127 S.W.2d 78, 81.

Ariz.—Alexander v. Pacific Greyhound Lines, 177 P.2d 229, 65 Ariz. 187 (injury to bus passenger from collision with automobile).

Ark.—Saunders v. Lambert, 188 S.W. 2d 633, 208 Ark. 990.

Cal.—Cordova v. Ford, 54 Cal.Rptr. 508, 246 Cal.App.2d 180 (it was incumbent upon injured motorist to produce evidence permitting conclusion that it was more likely than not that defendant was responsible for accident); McDonald v. Cantley, 3 P.2d 552, 214 Cal. 40; Keller v. Cushman, 285 P. 399, 104 Cal.App. 186; Carlsen v. Diehl, 208 P. 150, 57 Cal.App. 731.

Colo.—Zimmerman v. Franzen, 220 P.2d 344, 121 Colo. 574.

Del.—Mackey v. O'Neal, 101 A.2d 337, 9 Terry 233.

Ill.—Hatowatsky v. Central Greyhound Lines, 35 N.E.2d 541, 311 Ill.App. 127 (not applicable against bus company when defective sewer pipe under highway collapsed under bus).

La.—Scarborough v. St. Paul Mercury Indemnity Co., La.App., 11 So.2d 52.

Md.—Klan v. Security Motors, 164 A. 235, 164 Md. 198; Cumberland & Westernport Transit Co. v. Metz, 149 A. 4, 158 Md. 424, reargument denied 149 A. 565, 158 Md. 424, and appeal dismissed American Oil Co. v. Metz, 51 S.Ct. 40, 282 U.S. 801, 75 L.Ed. 720.

Mo.—Niklas v. Metz, 222 S.W.2d 795, 359 Mo. 601; State ex rel. and to Use of Brancato v. Trimble, 18 S. W.2d 4, 322 Mo. 318.

N.J.—Warshawsky v. Nevins Bus Co., 153 A. 114, 9 N.J.Misc. 227.

Okl.—Cosden v. Wright, 211 P.2d 523, 202 Okl. 211 (explosion while unloading natural gasoline at refinery).

Wash.—Morner v. Union Pac. R. Co., 196 P.2d 744, 31 Wash 2d 262.

Carbon monoxide inhaled while in tunnel

Where passenger on bus took sick when riding through tunnel, illness being of such character as to be attributable to inhalation of carbon monoxide gas, but there being nothing to show that gas was produced by bus instead of that accumulated in tunnel as result of traffic generally

§ 418.1   TRIAL EVIDENCE   Ch. 418

the injury might have occurred by reason of the concurrent negligence of two or more persons or causes, one of which was not under the management and control of the defendant.[13]   However

through it, rule held not applicable to raise inference of negligence. Warshawsky v. Nevins Bus Co., 153 A. 114, 9 N.J.Misc. 227.

13. Similar statement in prior edition **quoted by the court** in Joynes v. Valloft & Dreaux, La.App., 1 So. 2d 108; Dunaway v. Maroun, La. App., 178 So. 710; Estes v. Estes, Mo.App., 127 S.W.2d 78.

U.S.—Sanderson v. Chapman, C.A. Ariz.1974, 487 F.2d 264; Merritt v. Interstate Transit Lines, C.A. Iowa 1948, 171 F.2d 605 (did not load baggage which fell).

Colo.—Yellow Cab Co. v. Hodgson, 14 P.2d 1081, 91 Colo. 365, 83 A.L. R. 1156.

Iowa.—Welch v. Greenberg, 14 N.W. 2d 266, 235 Iowa 159.

Kan.—Emigh v. Andrews, 191 P.2d 901, 164 Kan. 732.

Ky.—Louisville Taxicab & Transfer Co. v. Jackson, Ky., 251 S.W.2d 874 (in action against owner of taxicab for injury to pedestrian when struck by a bottle allegedly thrown by passenger from window of cab, doctrine was inapplicable, since bottle was in the possession of passenger and not in the control or custody of cab driver).

Md.—Frenkil v. Johnson, to Use of National Retailers Mut. Ins. Co., 3 A.2d 479, 175 Md. 592 (not applicable when due to act of God or an unavoidable accident).

Miss.—Denman v. Denman, 1961, 134 So.2d 457, 242 Miss. 59 (in guest case, driver of other car negligent).

Mo.—Hall v. Lewis, 272 S.W.2d 260, 364 Mo. 1096 (was not applicable since driver was required to surrender control over his automobile at entrance to car wash, and driver was not liable to employee for injuries sustained when automobile suddenly lurched forward while driver's guest, who was occupying right side of front seat, was attempting to get out on driver's side at request of another employee).

N.J.—State, by Abbott v. Powell, 83 A.2d 636, 15 N.J.Super. 423 (after a two-car collision, one of the cars struck the State's highway directional signs, but there was no evidence that it was the defendant's vehicle).

Or.—Snodgrass v. Risley, 1952, 250 P.2d 392, 196 Or. 506 (part of load fell off truck).

Va.—Vaughn v. Huff, 41 S.E.2d 482, 186 Va. 144.

Wash.—Morner v. Union Pac. R. Co., 196 P.2d 744, 31 Wash.2d 262.

Intermittent control

Doctrine did not permit recovery of damage to radiator of automobile which plaintiff had illegally parked on street and which had been towed by defendant city to one of its automobile pounds, where there were intervals of time during which city did not possess exclusive control. Leman & Co. v. City of New Orleans, La.App.1970, 230 So.2d 461.

Plaintiff had role in incident

Plaintiff who was struck by a jeep which careened downhill after chain anchoring jeep to crane, which belonged to plaintiff's employer, snapped while defendant's jeep was being used as an anchor to keep tractor, attached to house trailer, from sliding farther downhill failed to show that instrumentality which caused injury was within exclusive control of defendant who was responsible for operation of winch in response to hand signals from plaintiff, and basic condition prerequisite

Ch. 418 RES IPSA LOQUITUR § 418.1

it has also been held that the mere fact that the injury might have been caused by some other agency than defendant does not prevent the application of the doctrine.[14]

The word "exclusive," as used above, does not require that control be several and defendant be singular, but that control be exclusive as against all who do not have a concurrent joint control in fact as joint users, or by representation.[15] Therefore, the doctrine may be applicable against all defendants charged with concurrent negligence.[16]

to application of doctrine was not present. Hilzer v. MacDonald, 1969, 454 P.2d 928, 169 Colo. 230.

Rule explained

There may be situations in which doctrine may be applied, but doctrine should seldom be applied where two automobiles participate and where driver of either or both may have been at fault, since rule ordinarily should be invoked only where all of agencies which may have been involved were under control of one defendant. Guiteau v. Southern Parking Co., La.App., 49 So.2d 880.

Skidding of another on sand spread by defendant

In action where automobile skidded into parked truck when brakes were suddenly applied while proceeding at a speed of 10 to 15 miles per hour over thin film of sand which had been scattered by street railway's employee, the fact that street railway did not have complete control over the situation precluded application of doctrine. Koch v. Cincinnati St. R. Co., 37 N.E.2d 222, 68 Ohio App. 33.

Under direction of driving instructor

Va.—Smith v. Tatum, 1957, 97 S.E.2d 820, 199 Va. 85.

14. Ark.—Prickett v. Farrell, 1970, 455 S.W.2d 74, 248 Ark. 996 (evidence clearly showed that grandfather never exercised requisite exclusive control over horse).

Cal.—Strock v. Pickwick Stages System, 290 P. 482, 107 Cal.App. 298; Brown v. Davis, 257 P. 877, 84 Cal.App. 180.

15. Kan.—Pierce v. Schroeder, 232 P.2d 460, 171 Kan. 259.

Md.—Frenkil v. Johnson to Use of National Retailers Mut. Ins. Co., 3 A.2d 479, 175 Md. 592.

N.Y.—Covey v. State, 106 N.Y.S.2d 18, 200 Misc 340.

Wash.—Morner v. Union Pac. R. Co., 196 P.2d 744, 31 Wash.2d 262.

16. Cal.—Tobler v. Chapman, 1973, 107 Cal.Rptr. 614, 31 Cal.App.3d 568 (conditional res ipsa loquitur instruction would have been proper in action by southbound motorist and passengers in her automobile to recover from preceding and following northbound motorists and others for injuries sustained when following motorist attempted to pass preceding motorist at turn out area and was forced into southbound lane, notwithstanding that preceding motorist had been dismissed from action on fourth day of trial, since plaintiffs, as admittedly innocent bystanders, were entitled to benefit of having all of the actors explain their conduct; however, refusal to give such instruction was not prejudicial where other instructions shifted to remaining defendants the burden of proving, by a preponderance of the evidence, justification for their vehicle being on wrong side of road at time of collision); Stark v. Yellow Cab Co., 202 P.2d 802, 90 Cal.App.2d 217 (a passenger is not deprived of benefits of doctrine

§ 418.1   TRIAL EVIDENCE   Ch. 418

However, the rule is generally not applicable to two car collisions involving the plaintiff and defendant, in absence of evidence of lack of fault on the part of the plaintiff, because the inference of negligence arising from the occurrence of the accident would be as equally applicable to the plaintiff as to the defendant.[17]

It is not necessary that the defendant have control of the instrumentality at the time the injury occurred. It is sufficient that there was the means of preventing the injury while the instrumentality was under the defendant's control.[18]

merely because accident involved another vehicle not under control of carrier); Armstrong v. Pacific Greyhound Lines, 168 P.2d 457, 74 Cal.App.2d 367.

Colo.—La Rocco v. Fernandez, 277 P.2d 232, 130 Colo. 523.

La.—Gauthreaux v. Hogan, App.1966, 185 So.2d 44.

17. **Iowa.**—Jordan v. Schantz, 264 N.W. 259, 220 Iowa 1251.

La.—Chapman v. Travelers Indem. Co., App., 45 So.2d 557 (left turn); Nuss v. MacKenzie, La.App., 4 So. 2d 845.

Md.—Brehm v. Lorenz, 112 A.2d 475, 206 Md. 500; Gloyd v. Wills, 23 A.2d 665, 180 Md. 161.

Mass.—Bryne v. Great A. & P. Tea Co., 168 N.E. 540, 269 Mass. 130; Reardon v. Boston Elevated Ry., 141 N.E. 857, 247 Mass. 124.

N.J.—Bettes v. Scott, 192 A. 433, 15 N.J.Misc. 487 (collision with oncoming vehicle on rainy night).

Ohio.—Collins v. Zimmermann, App., 57 N.E.2d 245, 40 O.L.A. 240. Pitt v. Nichols, 37 N.E.2d 379, 138 Ohio St. 555.

Or.—Kiddle v. Schnitzer, 117 P.2d 983, 167 Or. 316.

Pa.—Grimes v. Yellow Cab Co., 25 A.2d 294, 344 Pa. 298; Master v. Goldstein's Fruit & Produce, 23 A.2d 443, 344 Pa. 1.

18. **U.S.**—Kurdziel v. Pittsburgh Tube Co., D.C.Ohio 1968, 305 F. Supp. 953, affirmed 416 F.2d 881 (not applicable where bundle of steel tubes fell from truck, where loaded steel was out of control of defendant and not an unusual occurrence during unloading operation).

Fla.—Yarbrough v. Ball U-Drive System, 48 So.2d 82.

Tire manufacture

Where tire manufacturer's chief design engineer testified that storage procedures followed by plaintiff's employer would not normally have adverse effect on tire and there was testimony that nothing unusual was observed about tire either when it was received by employer or at time of mounting, for purpose of doctrine, there was sufficient evidence, if believed, to meet requirement that injuries sustained when attempting to mount tire on wheel were caused by agency or instrumentality within exclusive control of tire manufacturer. Ewer v. Goodyear Tire & Rubber Co., 1971, 480 P.2d 260, 4 Wash.App. 152.

Vehicle manufacturer

Doctrine could properly be applied in action against truck manufacturer for injuries sustained in single vehicle accident allegedly resulting from failure of bearing on left rear axle, notwithstanding that manufacturer was not in control of instrumentality at time of accident. Nelson v. Ford Motor Co., C.A.Fla. 1972, 469 F.2d 261.

The doctrine of res ipsa loquitur does not have the effect, when applied, of cutting off defenses.[19] It simply establishes a prima facie case,[20] and calls upon the defendant to meet the same.[21] The burden is still on the plaintiff to make out a case by a preponderance of the evidence; the burden of proof, as distinguished from the burden of going forward with the evidence, still being upon the plaintiff.[22]

19. **Cal.**—Raymer v. Vandenbergh, 51 P.2d 104, 10 Cal.App.2d 193.

20. **Cal.**—Raymer v. Vandenbergh, 51 P.2d 104, 10 Cal.App.2d 193.

Ga.—Gay v. Sylvania Cent. R. Co., 53 S.E.2d 713, 79 Ga.App. 362.

Kan.—Pierce v. Schroeder, 232 P.2d 460, 171 Kan. 259 (negligence is never presumed but must be established by proof, and where direct proof is lacking circumstances may be proved, and if they leave no conclusion to be drawn other than that defendant is at fault, they may be shown to make prima facie case warranting application of doctrine).

La.—Anderson v. City of Monroe, La.App., 2 So.2d 499.

W.Va.—Laphew v. Consolidated Bus Lines, 55 S.E.2d 881, 133 W.Va. 291.

Summary judgment denied
In action for injuries sustained when passenger attempted to leave defendant's parked automobile by rear door and automobile suddenly shot forward and struck wall, defendant's pretrial testimony that his brother, capable of driving automobile, remained in front seat when defendant got out and that automobile had hydromatic shift and that defendant did not remember whether ignition was turned off but that automobile was out of gear and in "park" position and that brakes were pulled on and that automobile pulled away and went through building raised doubt as to whether automobile remained under control of defendant, in which event doctrine would apply as asserted by plaintiff, and defendant's explanation required plaintiff to establish lack of reasonable care, and consequently plaintiff was not entitled to summary judgment. Bishop v. Bishop, 193 N.Y.S.2d 911, 20 Misc.2d 407.

21. **Ala.**—Sinclair v. Taylor, 173 So. 878, 27 Ala.App. 418.

Kan.—Misner v. Hawthorne, 212 P.2d 336, 168 Kan. 279.

La.—Anderson v. London Guarantee & Accident Co., App , 36 So.2d 741.

Mo.—Tabler v. Perry, 85 S.W.2d 471, 337 Mo. 154 (burden of proof remains with plaintiff, but need not prove defendant's negligence beyond reasonable doubt).

Nev.—Nyberg v. Kirby, 188 P.2d 1006, 65 Nev. 42, rehearing denied, 193 P.2d 850, 65 Nev. 42 (when doctrine was applied to overturning of truck and no explanation was offered by defendant, injured occupant was entitled to recover).

Tenn.—Oliver v. Union Transfer Co , 71 S.W.2d 478, 17 Tenn.App. 694.

Tex.—Sims v. Dallas Ry. & Terminal Co., Civ.App., 135 S.W.2d 142.

Va.—Virginia Transit Co. v. Durham, 59 S.E.2d 58, 190 Va. 979 (bus ran upon sidewalk).

Wash.—Covey v. Western Tank Lines, 218 P.2d 322, 36 Wash.2d 381.

Wyo.—Corson v. Wilson, 108 P.2d 260, 56 Wyo. 218 (striking parked automobile).

22. **Ala.**—Langley Bus Co. v. Messer, 133 So. 287, 222 Ala. 533.

§ 418.1   TRIAL EVIDENCE   Ch. 418

No inference of negligence arises from the failure of the defendant to explain an accident where there is no proof of surrounding circumstances or events leading up to the accident to justify the application of the doctrine of res ipsa loquitur.[23]

A defendant may rebut the presumption of negligence by proving circumstances excusing the complaint of conduct,[24] but

Ariz.—Pickwick Stages Corp. v. Messinger, 36 P.2d 168, 44 Ariz. 174.

Cal.—Allbritton v. Interstate Transit Lines, 87 P.2d 704, 31 Cal.App.2d 149.

La.—Wolfe v. Baumer Food Products Co., App., 171 So. 155.

Md.—Finney v. Frevel, 37 A.2d 923, 183 Md. 355.

Mo.—Belding v. St. Louis Public Service Co., App., 205 S.W.2d 866, reversed on other grounds 215 S.W.2d 506, 358 Mo. 491.

N.J.—Spill v. Stoeckert, 15 A.2d 773, 125 N.J.L. 382.

N.Y.—Judd v. Sams, 62 N.Y.S.2d 678, 270 App.Div. 981, affirmed 71 N.E.2d 772, 296 N.Y. 801.

Tex.—Sims v. Dallas Ry. & Terminal Co., Civ.App., 135 S.W.2d 142.

Va.—Virginia Transit Co. v. Durham, 59 S.E.2d 58, 190 Va. 979.

W.Va.—Fleming v. Hartrick, 131 S.E. 558, 100 W.Va. 714.

23. N.Y.—Brown v. Klein, 245 N.Y.S. 654, 230 App.Div. 681 (where taxicab crashed through railing of viaduct and plunged to street below, the bodies of the driver and of plaintiff's decedent were found in the wreckage, and there was no evidence of decedent's status with reference to taxicab company, of the causes or surrounding conditions of the accident, etc., nothing existed to justify application to case of doctrine); Salomone v. Yellow Taxi Corporation, 151 N.E. 442, 242 N.Y. 251, reargument denied 152 N.E. 445, 242 N.Y. 602.

Pa.—McElwain v. Myers, 80 A.2d 859, 367 Pa. 346.

24. Cal.—Binns v. Standen, 5 P.2d 637, 118 Cal.App. 625 (held unavailable to guest where caused by motorist being momentarily blinded by sun).

Fla.—Greyhound Corp. v. Ford, App., 157 So.2d 427.

Ill.—Roberts v. Economy Cabs, 2 N.E.2d 128, 285 Ill.App. 424.

Ky.—Thomas v. Platt, 282 S.W.2d 354; Brock v. Pillion, 1955, 277 S.W.2d 27 (guest grabbed steering wheel); Gilreath v. Blue & Gray Transp. Co., 108 S.W.2d 1002, 269 Ky. 787, followed in 108 S.W.2d 1004, 269 Ky. 791 (condition of street as cause of accident).

Md.—Smith v. Blue Ridge Transp. Co., 191 A. 66, 172 Md. 42.

Tenn.—Sloan v. Nevil, 229 S.W.2d 350, 33 Tenn.App. 100 (not applicable when front end of car suddenly collapsed while car was in motion, and defendant presented evidence of due care in the inspection and maintenance of car).

Tex.—Sims v. Dallas Ry. & Terminal Co., Civ.App., 135 S.W.2d 142.

Vt.—Labrecque v. American News Co., 58 A.2d 873, 115 Vt. 305 (where automobile sideswiped hay baler being towed by tractor with spotlights focused straight ahead, baler extended into road ebyon baler extended into road beyond tractor lights, another spotlight shown on projecting part but there was no evidence that illumination of baler was adequate to disclose its presence to one facing tractor headlights, presumption of negligence was not rebutted).

Wis.—Meyer v. Niedhoefer & Co., 251 N.W. 237, 213 Wis. 389.

the explanation must be reasonable, with as much probative force as the presumption itself.[25] The prima facie case may be met by offering evidence tending to show an unavoidable accident,[26] or by showing that surrounding circumstances permit a different presumption than that arising under the res ipsa loquitur doctrine.[27]

The defendant meets and overcomes plaintiff's prima facie case when the case is balanced evenly, without proving absence of negligence by a preponderance of the evidence.[28] However, in the absence of evidence sufficient to meet the prima facie case made out by the res ipsa loquitur doctrine, such prima facie case cannot be disregarded by the jury.[29]

Caused by act of third party

Del.—Mackey v. O'Neal, 101 A.2d 337, 9 Terry 233 (in action by paying passenger in Maryland when defendants' bus allegedly made a sudden stop, propelling passenger from seat, defendants may move at close of plaintiffs' case for judgment on count based on doctrine, if plaintiffs' evidence shows circumstances indicating that sudden stop which caused injury was the result of negligent operation of some other vehicle).

La.—Cinquemano v. O'Quinn, App., 180 So.2d 873, writ refused 183 So. 2d 650, 248 La. 1026 (not applicable against following driver who was forced off road because preceding driver in inside lane turned into following driver's outside lane when the vehicles were in very close proximity and who immediately applied brakes, swerved to right, and was unable to avoid telephone pole).

Mo.—Hall v. Rager, 357 S.W.2d 83 (driving off road and striking bank at Kansas intersection did not create res ipsa situation where evidence on both sides indicated that accident resulted from efforts to avoid collision at intersection).

Slippery condition of road

Cal.—Turner v. Mannon, 45 Cal.Rptr. 831, 236 Cal.App.2d 134 (did not apply to accident occurring during heavy rainstorm and due in part to existence of slick mud on highway).

Ky.—Whitt v. Farley, 275 S.W.2d 906, 50 A.L.R.2d 990 (when automobile skidded from road and overturned, evidence that accident resulted from slippery condition of road caused by rain and that driver exercised due care was sufficient to overcome any presumption of negligence).

25. **Ala.**—Sinclair v. Taylor, 173 So. 878, 27 Ala.App. 418 (vehicle properly equipped and managed).

Me.—Sylvia v. Etscovitz, 189 A. 419, 135 Me. 80.

26. **Cal.**—Smith v. Hollander, App., 257 P. 577.

27. **Ill.**—Roberts v. Economy Cabs, 2 N.E.2d 128, 285 Ill.App. 424.

28. **Cal.**—Faulk v. Soberanes, 14 Cal.Rptr. 545, 363 P.2d 593, 56 Cal. 2d 466; Allbritton v. Interstate Transit Lines, 87 P.2d 704, 31 Cal. App.2d 149; Smith v. Hollander, App., 257 P. 577.

Utah.—Morrison v. Perry, 140 P.2d 772, 104 Utah 151.

29. **Cal.**—Morris v. Morris, 258 P. 616, 84 Cal.App. 599; Seney v. Pickwick Stages Northern Division, 255 P. 279, 82 Cal.App. 226.

§ 418.1   TRIAL EVIDENCE   Ch. 418

It has been held that the presumption does not vanish as a matter of law when contradicted by evidence of the party against whom it is invoked.[30]

Limitations on application of doctrine

The application of the rule of res ipsa loquitur may be affected by the state of the pleadings,[31] as where the plaintiff relies upon alleged specific acts of negligence.[32] In such a case, it is generally held that the plaintiff will be required to prove the specific acts alleged and cannot rely upon the presumption of negligence under the res ipsa loquitur rule.[33]

Ky.—Schechter v. Hann, 205 S.W.2d 690, 305 Ky. 794.

Mo.—Gibbons v. Wells, App., 293 S.W. 89.

30. Ark.—Missouri Pac. R. Co. v. Creekmore, 102 S.W.2d 553, 193 Ark. 722.

Cal.—Bushnell v. Yoshika Tashiro, 2 P.2d 550, 115 Cal.App. 563.

La.—Weddle v. Phelan, App., 177 So. 407.

Md.—Potomac Edison Co. v. Johnson, 152 A. 633, 160 Md. 33.

31. Iowa.—Savery v. Kist, 11 N.W.2d 23, 234 Iowa 98 (in action for injuries to patron of cafe, into which defendant's truck crashed, allegation that defendant permitted truck to operate without driver was sufficiently general to warrant application); Peterson v. De Luxe Cab Co., 281 N.W. 737, 225 Iowa 809 (general allegation of negligence in operation and control of taxicab door).

Mo.—Mulanix v. Reeves, 112 S.W.2d 100, 233 Mo.App. 143, certiorari quashed, State ex rel. and to Use of Reeves v. Shain, 122 S.W.2d 885, 343 Mo. 550 (charge of general negligence permitted application of doctrine if available on the facts); Powell v. St. Joseph Ry., Light, Heat & Power Co., 81 S.W.2d 957, 336 Mo. 1016; Kaiser v. Butler County R. Co., App., 217 S.W. 535.

32. Kan.—Pierce v. Schroeder, 232 P.2d 460, 171 Kan. 259.

Mo.—Bommer v. Stedelin, App., 237 S.W.2d 225.

Ohio.—Shadwick v. Hills, 69 N.E.2d 197, 79 Ohio App. 143.

Utah.—Nelson v. Lott, 17 P.2d 272, 81 Utah 265.

W.Va.—Griffith v. Wood, 149 S.E.2d 205, 150 W.Va. 678 (claim was not based upon general charge of negligence but specified manner in which driver operated truck and alleged defective condition of door).

33. Cal.—Jianou v. Pickwick Stages System, 296 P. 108, 111 Cal.App. 754; Horney v. Dillingham, 253 P. 970, 81 Cal.App. 443.

Iowa.—Armbruster v. Gray, 282 N.W. 342, 225 Iowa 1226; Luther v. Jones, 261 N.W. 817, 220 Iowa 95; Bauer v. Reavell, 260 N.W. 39, 219 Iowa 1212.

Ky.—Wallace v. Norris, 220 S.W.2d 967, 310 Ky. 424.

La.—Weddle v. Phelan. App., 177 So. 407.

Mo.—Hughes v. East St. Louis City Lines, App., 149 S.W.2d 440; Powell v. St. Joseph Ry., Light, Heat & Power Co., 81 S.W.2d 957, 336 Mo. 1016; Kaiser v. Butler County R. Co., App., 217 S.W. 535.

N.J.—Hartpence v. Grouleff, 105 A.2d 514, 15 N.J. 545.

Ohio.—Corriveau v. Defenbaugh, App., 91 N.E.2d 39, 56 O.L.A. 57. Kaltenbach v. Cleveland, Columbus

However, there are authorities to the effect that the plaintiff will not be prevented from relying upon the doctrine by alleging specific negligent acts in addition to general averments of negligence,[34] or by alleging in the alternative,[35] or where the specific acts averred are the same as those which the doctrine tends to establish.[36] The limitation is imposed on the theory

& Cincinnati Highway, 80 N.E.2d 640, 82 Ohio App. 10; Winslow v. Ohio Bus Line Co., 73 N.E.2d 504, 148 Ohio St. 101 (petition alleged that collision between busses resulted from negligence in respect to control, lookout, operation, and failure to stop within assured clear distance ahead).

Tex.—Reberger v. Reed, Civ.App., 278 S.W.2d 591, writ of error refused n. r. e.; Smith v. Houston Transit Co., Civ.App., 215 S.W.2d 187, ref. n. r. e.; Sims v. Dallas Ry. & Terminal Co., Civ.App., 135 S.W.2d 142; Ortiz v. El Paso Electric Co., Civ.App., 126 S.W.2d 515; National Union Fire Ins. Co. v. Wallace, Civ.App., 118 S.W.2d 609 (improper speed and lookout and failure to fasten trailer securely specifically charged).

Wash.—Anderson v. Harrison, 103 P. 2d 320, 4 Wash.2d 265.

34. **U.S.**—Remer v. Flying Eagle Whiteway Lines, C.A.Conn., 172 F. 2d 831. McCarty v. Hosang, D.C. Mo., 154 F.Supp. 852; Hampton v. U. S., D.C.Nev., 121 F.Supp. 303.

Ariz.—Tenney v. Enkeball, 158 P.2d 519, 62 Ariz. 416.

Cal.—Ellis v. Jewett, 64 P.2d 432, 18 Cal.App.2d 629; Cookson v. Fitch, 3 P.2d 27, 116 Cal.App. 544 (in guest's action when automobile overturned, allegation that it was negligently constructed from old parts did not preclude application); Burke v. Dillingham, 258 P. 627, 84 Cal.App. 736; Seney v. Pickwick Stages Northern Division, 255 P. 279, 82 Cal.App. 226.

Kan.—Clarke v. Cardinal Stage Lines, 31 P.2d 1, 139 Kan. 280.

La.—Hamiter v. Duncan, App.1955, 78 So.2d 80.

Ohio.—Motorists Mut. Ins. Co. v. Calland, 1952, 114 N.E.2d 162, 93 Ohio App. 543.

Okl.—Creswell v. Temple Mill. Co., 1972, 499 P.2d 421 (allegation that driver allowed the truck to run off the road and overturn when he looked away from direction of travel did not preclude relying on doctrine and it was unnecessary to amend petition to allege the doctrine).

Or.—Francisco v. Circle Tours Sightseeing Co., 265 P. 801, 125 Or. 80.

Tenn.—McCloud v. City of LaFollette, 1954, 276 S.W.2d 763, 38 Tenn.App. 553 (not affected by allegation vehicle left unattended, was surplusage); Oliver v. Union Transfer Co., 71 S.W.2d 478, 17 Tenn.App. 694.

Wash.—Vogreg v. Shepard Ambulance Co., 289 P.2d 350, 47 Wash. 2d 659; Morner v. Union Pac. R. Co., 196 P.2d 744, 31 Wash.2d 262.

35. **Me.**—Shea v. Hern, 171 A. 248, 132 Me. 361.

Mo.—Morris v. Israel Bros., Inc., 1974, 510 S.W.2d 437 (not error to submit suit by passenger against driver on theory of res ipsa and to submit passenger's suit against highway contractor based on specific negligence).

36. **Cal.**—Strock v. Pickwick Stages System, 290 P. 482, 107 Cal.App. 298.

Me.—Chaisson v. Williams, 156 A. 154, 130 Me. 341.

§ 418.1   TRIAL EVIDENCE   Ch. 418

that, by pleading specific acts, the plaintiff admits knowing the specific acts being relied upon, and therefore the reason for the application of the res ipsa loquitur rule fails.[37]

The Supreme Court of Iowa [38] also has given as the reason for the limitation the conclusion that the allegation of specific negligent acts "is equivalent to saying that there are no other acts of negligence which caused or contributed to the injury, and * * * there is no occasion for relying upon presumption."

A determination is required as to whether the allegations amount to general or specific averments.[39]

The furnishing of a bill of particulars, in compliance with defendant's demand, cannot be invoked as an abandonment of the benefit of the doctrine.[40]

The application of the doctrine may be altered or abolished by statute in specific cases. Thus, the provision of the Agricultural Code that in an action by the owner, driver or occupant of a motor vehicle for damages resulting from collision with do-

---

37. Cal.—Kenney v. Antonetti, 295 P. 341, 211 Cal. 336.

La.—B & B Cut Stone Co. v. Uhler, App., 1 So.2d 149 (allegations did not make rule inapplicable).

Mo.—Roscoe v. Metropolitan St. Ry. Co., 101 S.W. 32, 202 Mo. 576.

38. Iowa.—Luther v. Jones, 261 N.W. 817, 220 Iowa 95.

39. Mo.—Hall v. St. Louis Public Service Co., 259 S.W.2d 88, appeal transferred 266 S.W.2d 597; Motsch v. Standard Oil Co. of Indiana, App., 223 S.W. 677 (doctrine refused); Hennekes v. Beetz, 217 S.W. 533, 203 Mo.App. 63 (doctrine refused where alleged turned vehicle completely around).

Complaint held not to allege specific acts of negligence within rule

Cal.—Jianou v. Pickwick Stages System, 296 P. 108, 111 Cal.App. 754 (allegation of complaint that defendant carelessly and negligently operated and conducted its automobile stage so that a wheel broke or collapsed constituted mere general averment that negligent conduct of defendant caused the wheel to break, and warranted inference from language employed that plaintiff was ignorant of specific acts of negligence).

Dist.Col.—Lindsey v. D. C. Transit Co., Mun.App., 140 A.2d 306 (pleadings nor proof revealed particular conditions which may have been inducing cause of sudden stop of bus, and no attempt was made by passenger to account for the stop or to explain its cause, and no specific act of negligence on part of driver to maintain a proper lookout was mentioned).

Mo.—Bone v. General Motors Corp., 322 S.W.2d 916, 71 A.L.R.2d 361 (in action for injuries sustained by switchman when he was struck, while guarding crossing, by swinging right rear door of truck, doctrine was not rendered inapplicable by alleged facts that it was obligation of owner of truck leased by defendant to make material alterations or repairs and that it was duty of railroad to maintain crossing).

40. N.J.—Rapp v. Butler-Newark Bus Line, 138 A. 377, 103 N.J.L. 512.

mestic animal on a highway, there is no presumption that the collision was due to the negligence of the owner of livestock does no more than abolish the effect of the doctrine of res ipsa loquitur.[41]

It has been held not necessary to plead the doctrine of res ipsa loquitur to give it the force of presumptive evidence.[42]

In the same sense that the plaintiff may preclude the application of the doctrine by the pleadings, the plaintiff cannot rely on the doctrine where the evidence is an attempt to explain how the accident happened and in what respect the defendant was negligent,[43] unless the acts shown by the evidence would

41. **U.S.**—Galeppi Bros. v. Bartlett, C.C.A.Cal., 120 F.2d 208.

42. **Cal.**—Bennett v. Phelps, 1955, 289 P.2d 36, 136 Cal.App.2d 645.

43. **Miss.**—Landrum v. Smith, 1970, 233 So.2d 217 (facts sufficiently developed to resolve question of negligence without resort to doctrine).

Mo.—Hill v. Hill, 401 S.W.2d 438 (fall from automobile).

R.I.—Dufresne v. Theroux, 32 A.2d 609, 69 R.I. 280.

But see

Tenney v. Enkeball, 158 P.2d 519, 62 Ariz. 416 (in action by minor who fell from the fender of defendant's truck where he had been riding, applicable even though specific acts of negligence were alleged and proved as an aid to the proofs of those specific acts).

Calling defendant as witness

Mere fact that passenger suing driver called driver as a witness and driver offered testimony did not destroy the application of doctrine. Hudson v. Stepp, 393 S.W.2d 301, 54 Tenn.App. 640.

Doctrine held available

Idaho.—Shaffer v. Adams, 378 P.2d 816, 85 Idaho 258 (westbound driver's introduction of evidence tending to show that cause of collision with hay conveyor being towed by eastbound truck was separation of draw bar from conveyor did not preclude application).

Mo.—Burr v. Kansas City Public Service Co., 276 S.W.2d 120, 365 Mo. 115 (facts and circumstances testified to by passenger did not directly and definitely show precise and specific negligent act); Van Volkinburgh v. Kansas City Public Service Co., App., 254 S.W.2d 287 (testimony by plaintiff and her witnesses, to effect that bus had come to sudden, unexpected stop which threw the passengers about, made case for submission, and further testimony by plaintiff and her witnesses to effect that they did not know what caused accident or that they heard others say truck had caused accident but had no independent knowledge did not so clearly show the specific cause of the accident as to preclude submission).

Wash.—Vogreg v. Shepard Ambulance Co., 1955, 289 P.2d 350, 47 Wash.2d 659.

Not defeated by conclusory evidence

In action by passenger for injuries sustained when company's driver allegedly caused bus to jerk forward while passenger was boarding bus, evidence was sufficient to sustain submission of cause under doctrine in view of fact that passenger had testified to conclusions and results and not to specific facts, acts, or conduct of bus driver in causing movement in

§ 418.1 TRIAL EVIDENCE Ch. 418

be within the rule under a complaint containing only a general allegation of negligence.[44] Similarly, one cannot rely upon the doctrine where that party's own evidence repels any inference of negligence.[45]

Where all the conditions attendant upon an injury are fully testified to by witnesses, so that the case depends upon whether the version presented by the plaintiff or the version presented by the defendant should prevail, the doctrine is not available.[46]

question. White v. St. Louis Public Service Co., 259 S.W.2d 795, 364 Mo. 111.

Rule limited

A plaintiff does not lose benefit of doctrine by introducing evidence which does not establish clearly and definitely cause of injury. Missile Cab Ass'n v. Rogers, Mun.App., 184 A.2d 845.

Use of defendant's deposition

A plaintiff who used defendant's deposition as part of his case was not bound by the deposition testimony unless it was uncontradicted by plaintiff's other evidence, and thus even though the deposition contained direct evidence of defendant's precise negligence causing plaintiff's injury, when plaintiff's other evidence contradicted such testimony, plaintiff could rely on the doctrine. Browne v. Heeter, Mo., 267 S.W.2d 666.

44. **Ariz.**—Pickwick Stages Corporation v. Messinger, 36 P.2d 168, 44 Ariz. 174.

Cal.—Fedler v. Hygelund, 235 P.2d 247, 106 Cal.App.2d 480 (where plaintiff passenger pleaded negligence of truck driver in general terms and offered evidence suggesting definite negligent acts and omissions, he did not thereby waive right to rely upon inference of negligence arising under doctrine from fact that truck ran away and proceeded out of control down grade when truck was in exclusive control of driver).

45. **Md.**—Hickory Transfer Co. v. Nezbed, 96 A.2d 241, 202 Md. 253.

Mo.—Long v. St. Louis Public Service Co., 288 S.W.2d 417.

Doctrine not defeated

Passenger's testimony that while she was stepping down the bus started to roll "as if" driver had released the brake and then suddenly it gave a jerk "as though" driver applied the brake again did not show cause of the accident. Moehle v. St. Louis Public Service Co., Mo.App., 229 S. W.2d 285.

46. **Cal.**—Johnson v. Ostrom, 16 P. 2d 794, 128 Cal.App. 38.

Ill.—Turner v. Wallace, 217 N.E.2d 11, 71 Ill.App.2d 160.

La.—Williams v. Barton, App., 81 So. 2d 22.

Md.—Armstrong v. Johnson Motor Lines, Inc., 1971, 280 A.2d 24, 12 Md.App. 492.

Minn.—Heffter v. Northern States Power Co., 217 N.W. 102, 173 Minn. 215.

N.C.—Lewis v. Piggott, 1972, 192 S. E.2d 128, 16 N.C.App. 395 (skidded due to water on road, left roadway); Baldwin v. Smitherman, 88 S.E. 854, 171 N.C. 772 (where automobile struck and injured mule, rider's contention being that automobilist negligently drove into mule, also that he failed to have brakes in proper condition, while driver's testimony was that mule, which had given no indications of fright, backed into and against automobile, despite driver's efforts to avoid him, doctrine had no place).

194

Ch. 418   RES IPSA LOQUITUR   § 418.1

It does not apply in any case where there is direct testimony as to the cause of the accident.[47]

Wash.—Morner v. Union Pac. R. Co., 1948, 196 P.2d 744, 31 Wash.2d 262.

47. Statement in prior edition **quoted by the court,** with the statement that comparable sections carry a correct and cogent discussion of the doctrine in all of its phases, in Dunaway v. Maroun, La.App., 178 So. 710.

U.S.—Kraklau v. Bayman, C.A.Ind., 318 F.2d 400 (conflicting evidence).

Ala.—DeBardeleben v. Tynes, 1973, 276 So.2d 126, 290 Ala. 263 (where plaintiff was fully aware of defendant's postaccident account of accident in which she stated that when she stopped runaway automobile in her driveway, she placed shift lever in "park," and put on foot brake, and turned front wheels to right, and such account did not vary in any real material aspect from account given by defendant in her testimony at trial, there was no necessity for application of doctrine).

Alaska.—Evans v. Buchner, 1963, 386 P.2d 836.

Cal.—Pollard v. Foster, 1942, 129 P.2d 448, 54 Cal.App.2d 502 (evidence clear); Edwards v. Gullick, 1931, 1 P.2d 11, 213 Cal. 86 (instruction erroneous, but harmless).

Ga.—Collis v. Ashe, 1956, 95 S.E.2d 654, 212 Ga. 746; Kimberly v. Reed, 1949, 53 S.E.2d 208, 79 Ga.App. 137.

Ind.—Taylor v. Fitzpatrick, 1955, 126 N.E.2d 248, superseded 132 N.E.2d 919, 235 Ind. 238 (from defendant's testimony).

La.—Palmer v. Turner, App.1971, 252 So.2d 700 (where full facts attending accident resulting when automobile overtaking plaintiff's automobile collided with defendant's unlighted and stopped or slow moving vehicle were known); Layfield v. Bourgeois, App.1962, 142 So.2d 799 (established that 5 yr. old boy leaped from ditch and onto roadway); Peranio v. Superior Ins. Co., App.1954, 76 So.2d 315; Aden v. Allen, App.1941, 3 So.2d 905 (guest case); Dunaway v. Maroun, App., 178 So. 710.

Md.—Coastal Tank Lines v. Carroll, 106 A.2d 98, 205 Md. 137 (vehicle left highway and struck plaintiffs' house); Frenkil v. Johnson, to Use of National Retailers Mut. Ins. Co., 3 A.2d 479, 175 Md. 592.

Mich.—Noonan v. Volek, 224 N.W. 657, 246 Mich. 377 (automobile striking wagon).

Minn.—Heffter v. Northern States Power Co., 217 N.W. 102, 173 Minn. 215.

Miss.—Eastman, Gardiner & Co. v. Sumrall, 133 So. 212, 160 Miss. 792; Columbus & G. Ry. Co. v. Fondren, 110 So. 365, 145 Miss. 679.

Mo.—Venditti v. St. Louis Public Service Co., 226 S.W.2d 599, 360 Mo. 42 (action against carrier); Gibbons v. Wells, App., 293 S.W. 89.

N.C.—Springs v. Doll, 148 S.E. 251, 197 N.C. 240.

Ohio.—Allen v. Leavick, 182 N.E. 139, 43 Ohio App. 100 (guest injured in bouncing vehicle, cause was condition of street).

Tenn.—Schindler v. Southern Coach Lines, 217 S.W.2d 775, 188 Tenn. 169 (opening door of bus).

Tex.—Whitehead v. Montgomery, Civ.App., 228 S.W.2d 196, writ of error refused n. r. e.

Va.—Darden v. Murphy, 11 S.E.2d 579, 176 Va. 511.

Wash.—Anderson v. Harrison, 103 P.2d 320, 4 Wash.2d 265; Anderson v. McCarthy Drygoods Co., 49 Wash. 398, 95 P. 325.

Wis.—Brunner v. Van Hoof, 90 N.W.2d 551, 4 Wis.2d 459 (when a trail-

§ 418.1

There may be evidence tending to show specific acts of negligence, but, unless that evidence clearly shows what did cause the accident, it will not defeat the plaintiff's right to rely upon the doctrine.[48]

§ 418.2 Situations Applicable

Library References:
C.J.S. Motor Vehicles § 511(3); Negligence § 220.2 et seq.
West's Key No. Digests, Automobiles ⊜242(2); Negligence ⊜121(3).

The res ipsa loquitur doctrine has been applied where an automobile ran into the rear of the vehicle ahead,[49] or struck another vehicle or other object standing on the highway,[50] or a

er hitched to defendant-driver's automobile disengaged and invaded decedent's lane of travel and collided with decedent's truck, evidence that hitch was defective because its safety lock was missing, and that socket on trailer did not match ball on defendant-driver's hitch, was sufficient evidence to preclude application).

48. Cal.—Kilgore v. Brown, 266 P. 297, 90 Cal.App. 555 (that plaintiff hits on circumstance which constituted the cause of the accident, in giving a general account with reference to what happened at that time, does not preclude reliance on res ipsa); Seney v. Pickwick Stages Northern Division, 255 P. 279, 82 Cal.App. 226 (doctrine not inapplicable where although plaintiff goes further than necessary and shows more than mere happening of accident, precise cause of accident still remains unknown).

Mo.—Venditti v. St. Louis Public Service Co., 226 S.W.2d 599, 360 Mo. 42 (evidence must make a submissible issue of the specific negligence); Hill v. St. Louis Public Service Co., 221 S.W.2d 130, 359 Mo. 220 (injuries to minor bus passenger); Timmons v. Kurn, 100 S. W.2d 952, 231 Mo.App. 421; Powell v. St. Joseph Ry., Light, Heat & Power Co., 81 S.W.2d 957, 336 Mo. 1016 (evidence does not make doctrine inapplicable if cause of accident, under evidence, is doubtful).

49. For many cases discussing "presumptions" and "inferences" of negligence arising where vehicle strikes the rear end of a vehicle ahead, see section 417.2 at fn. 69.

Ariz.—Conner v. Brkich, 1971, 481 P. 2d 894, 14 Ariz.App. 208.

Cal.—Villa v. Shaffer, 51 Cal.Rptr. 856, 242 Cal.App.2d 815; Ponce v. Black, 36 Cal.Rptr. 419, 224 Cal. App.2d 159 (stopped for red light); Persike v. Gray, 30 Cal.Rptr. 603, 215 Cal.App.2d 816 (stopped for red light).

Dist.Col.—Andrews v. Forness, 1971, 272 A.2d 672 (testified brakes failed, when preceding vehicle stopped at intersection).

Iowa.—Ruud v. Grimm, 110 N.W.2d 321, 252 Iowa 1266.

La.—Dominique v. Insurance Co. of North America, 195 So.2d 312; Steadman v. American Fidelity & Cas. Co., App., 113 So.2d 489.

N.Y.—Schwartzberg v. Norotsky, 194 N.Y.S.2d 26, 20 Misc.2d 638 (stopped at red signal).

50. U.S.—Rivers v. Bauer, D.C.Pa., 79 F.Supp. 403, affirmed 175 F.2d 774 (even though an overtaking truck first came into contact with defendant's truck).

Ch. 418 RES IPSA LOQUITUR § 418.2

pedestrian on the sidewalk,[51] or on or near the highway.[52]

Cal.—Pittman v. Boiven, Cal.App., 57 Cal.Rptr. 319; Slappey v. Schiller, 2 P.2d 577, 116 Cal.App. 274.

Colo.—Iacino v. Brown, 217 P.2d 266, 121 Colo. 450.

Del.—Cannon v. Delaware Electric Power Co., 24 A.2d 325, 2 Terry 415 (bus backed into parked automobile).

Dist.Col.—Bonbrest v. Lewis, Mun. App., 54 A.2d 751; Schwartzbach v. Thompson, Mun.App., 33 A.2d 624.

Ill.—Pearlman v. W. O. King Lumber Co., 1939, 23 N.E.2d 826, 302 Ill. App. 190.

La.—O'Reilly v. State Farm Mut. Auto. Ins. Co., 1970, 230 So.2d 630 (where first driver's automobile, after he applied brakes and attempted lane change, went into skid and became entangled in fence just over crest of overpass and second driver collided with entangled vehicle stopped on interstate highway when there was neither time, distance nor opportunity for second driver to take any effective evasive action to prevent collision); Plotkin v. Martino, 192 So.2d 381; Asen v. Taxicab Bonding Ass'n, 184 So. 2d 90; Frey v. DiMaggio, App., 153 So.2d 571; Adams v. Spellman, App., 130 So.2d 460.

Md.—Shirks Motor Exp. v. Oxenham, 106 A.2d 46, 204 Md. 626.

Mass.—Bryne v. Great Atlantic & Pacific Tea Co., 168 N.E. 540, 269 Mass. 130.

Mo.—Boresow v. Manzella, 1959, 330 S.W.2d 827; Hollensbe v. Pevely Dairy Co., App., 38 S.W.2d 273.

N.Y.—Bondar v. Ar Jay Paint Co., 191 N.Y.S.2d 767, 20 Misc.2d 643 (parked at curb); Rosenberg v. American Ry. Express Co., Sup., 198 N.Y.S. 224.

Tenn.—Burkett v. Johnston, 282 S.W. 2d 647, 39 Tenn.App. 276 (properly applied to action for death of husband, who was found on right front seat of automobile owned by defendant's decedent, who was found under steering wheel of vehicle under circumstances indicating that the two people had met death as result of collision with some object).

Wash.—Hardman v. Younkers, 131 P.2d 177, 15 Wash.2d 483, 151 A. L.R. 868.

Wyo.—Corson v. Wilson, 108 P.2d 260, 56 Wyo. 218 (striking parked automobile).

Limited to "no-witness" occurrence

In the event of a "no-witness" occurrence involving a single vehicle which left its proper lane of travel and struck a stationary object, the plaintiff could invoke the doctrine. Van Dyke v. Merchants Indem. Corp. of New York, D.C.Wis., 215 F.Supp. 428.

51. **Cal.**—Brandes v. Rucker-Fuller Desk Co., 282 P. 1009, 102 Cal. App. 221; Smith v. Hollander, 259 P. 958, 85 Cal.App. 535; Smith v. Hollander, App., 257 P. 577.

La.—Tymon v. Toye Bros. Yellow Cab Co., App., 10 So.2d 599; Bonner v. Boudreaux, App., 8 So.2d 309 (after intersectional collision of two vehicles); Tymon v. Toye Bros. Yellow Cab Co., App., 180 So. 839; Scott v. Checker Cab Co., 126 So. 241, 12 La.App. 598.

Mo.—Murray v. St. Louis Public Service Co., App., 201 S.W.2d 775.

N.J.—Sheridan v. Arrow Sanitary Laundry Co., 146 A. 191, 105 N.J. L. 608 (runaway truck).

N.Y.—Green v. Baltuch, Sup., 191 N. Y.S. 70 (another auto turned in ahead of defendant in passing).

Pa.—Matzasoszki v. Jacobson, 186 A. 227, 122 Pa.Super. 180; Griffith v.

52. See note 52 on page 198.

§ 418.2 TRIAL EVIDENCE Ch. 418

The doctrine has been applied where an automobile collided with a stray animal.[53]

It has also been applied where a motor vehicle left the road and ran into an object;[54] and where a car left the road and

V. A. Simrell & Son Co., 155 A. 299, 304 Pa. 165.

Va.—Virginia Transit Co. v. Durham, 59 S.E.2d 58, 190 Va. 979; L. Bromm Baking Co. v. West, 186 S.E. 289, 166 Va. 357.

Presumption irrespective of speed

Irrespective of speed, presumption of negligence arises where driver permits automobile to deflect from its course and skid across highway and injure person on sidewalk. Matzasoszki v. Jacobson, 186 A. 227, 122 Pa.Super. 180.

52. **U.S.**—Andruss v. Nieto, C.C.A.Cal., 112 F.2d 250.

Cal.—Alcorn v. Davies, 343 P.2d 621, 173 Cal.App.2d 569.

Iowa.—Peterson v. De Luxe Cab Co., 281 N.W. 737, 225 Iowa 809 (prospective passenger struck by door of taxicab).

La.—Antoine v. Louisiana Highway Commission, App., 188 So. 443 (striking of a pedestrian on graveled strip alongside of traveled highway in broad daylight by motorist coming from behind without warning).

Pa.—Glover v. Struble, 48 A.2d 50, 159 Pa.Super. 305 (ran over motionless boy on unobstructed highway in broad daylight); Urbanick v. Croneweth Dairy Co., 1943, 35 A.2d 83, 154 Pa.Super. 44 (to run down a child in an unobstructed street in daylight is evidence of negligence, unless child suddenly darts out into pathway); Smith v. Shatz, 200 A. 620, 331 Pa. 453 (standing upon a highway in plain view for sufficient length of time to have been seen and avoided); O'Leary v. Willis, 200 A. 125, 131 Pa.Super. 578 (who is in full view and does not suddenly change his course).

53. **U.S.**—Nuclear Corp. of America v. Lang, D.C.Neb.1972, 337 F.Supp. 914, affirmed C.A.8, 1973, 480 F.2d 990 (during 12-hour period farmer had left premises unattended and had left open gate on lane leading to enclosed area, to which area heifer could have had access).

Cal.—Anderson v. I. M. Jameson Corporation, 59 P.2d 962, 7 Cal.2d 60 (stray cow upon highway in nighttime).

La.—Boudreau v. Louviere, App., 178 So. 173 (defect in cattle guard presumed).

Mo.—Moss v. Bonne Terre Farming & Cattle Co., 10 S.W.2d 338, 222 Mo.App. 808 (damage to automobile by animals running at large).

Pa.—Bender v. Welsh, 25 A.2d 182, 344 Pa. 392 (unattended horse on highway).

Applied against animal owner

U.S.—Mercer v. Byrons, C.A.Mass., 200 F.2d 284 (unexplained appearance of horse, admittedly owned by defendant's minor sons and quartered in barn on defendant's premises, galloping on heavily traveled public highway at night).

Cal.—Kenney v. Antonetti, 295 P. 341, 211 Cal. 336 (that defendant's horses were unattended upon the highway at night and other facts adduced by the evidence, considered in the light of statutory provisions against permitting livestock to remain unaccompanied upon a public highway).

Idaho.—Shepard v. Smith, 1953, 263 P.2d 985, 74 Idaho 459.

54. **U.S.**—Machanic v. Storey, 1963, 115 U.S.App.D.C. 87, 317 F.2d 151 (Pennsylvania law).

La.—Emmco Ins. Co. v. Alexander, App.1969, 224 So.2d 114 (crossed highway and hit embankment and fence).

Bridge

Kan.—Misner v. Hawthorne, 1950, 212 P.2d 336, 168 Kan. 279.

Ky.—Grigsby v. Smith, 1940, 146 S. W.2d 719, 285 Ky. 48 (taxi).

La.—Bourg v. Aetna Cas. & Sur. Co., App.1955, 77 So.2d 131 (been drinking for 10 hours); Gomer v. Anding, App.1933, 146 So. 704, rehearing denied 147 So. 545.

Building

La.—Gauthreaux v. Hogan, App., 185 So.2d 44.

N.J.—Iannuzzi v. Bishop, 151 A. 477, 8 N.J.Misc. 609.

Ohio.—Scovanner v. Toelke, 163 N. E. 493, 119 Ohio St. 256.

Pa.—Lasek v. Jaroschak, 162 A.2d 25, 192 Pa.Super. 350.

Tenn.—McCloud v. City of La Follette, 276 S.W.2d 763, 38 Tenn.App. 553.

Fence

U.S.—Ramsel v. Ring, C.A.Mo., 173 F.2d 41 (motorist could recover for injuries received in collision with horse which escaped from pasture through gap made in fence by defendant's truck which left highway and broke down fence).

Conn.—Rindge v. Holbrook, 149 A. 231, 111 Conn. 72.

Pole

Cal.—Taylor v. Pacific Gas & Electric Co., 134 P.2d 12, 57 Cal.App. 2d 11 (light pole); Goss v. Pacific Motor Co., 259 P. 455, 85 Cal.App. 455 (struck lamp post, injuring a pedestrian); Morris v. Morris, 258 P. 616, 84 Cal.App. 599 (collision with electric light pole).

Iowa.—Brown v. Des Moines Bottling Works, 156 N.W. 829, 174 Iowa 715, 1 A.L.R. 835 (struck a lamp post, injuring a pedestrian).

La.—Gulf States Utilities Co. v. Guidry, App., 183 So.2d 122.

N.Y.—Kinary v. Taylor, 276 N.Y.S. 688, 243 App.Div. 651; Spreen v. McCann, 263 N.Y.S. 46, 147 Misc. 41, affirmed 264 N.Y.S. 1008, 240 App.Div. 709, affirmed 191 N.E. 558, 264 N.Y. 546.

Ohio—Morrow v. Hume, 3 N.E.2d 39, 131 Ohio St. 319; Zwick v. Zwick, 163 N.E. 917, 29 Ohio App. 522, error dismissed 166 N.E. 202, 119 Ohio St. 644.

Tenn.—Hudson v. Stepp, 393 S.W.2d 301, 54 Tenn.App. 640.

Wis.—Wisconsin Tel. Co. v. Matson, 41 N.W.2d 268, 256 Wis. 304 (truck sideswiped pole).

Tree

Cal.—Fiske v. Wilkie, 154 P.2d 725, 67 Cal.App.2d 440 (fifteen feet from pavement).

Ill.—Masten v. Cousins, 216 Ill.App. 268.

Ky.—Vernon v. Gentry, 334 S.W.2d 266.

Mass.—Cook v. Cole, 174 N.E. 271, 273 Mass. 557.

Mo.—Lindsey v. Williams, 260 S.W. 2d 472, certiorari denied 74 S.Ct. 428, 347 U.S. 904, 98 L.Ed. 1063.

N.J.—Smith v. Kirby, 178 A. 739, 115 N.J.L. 225 (automobile, traveling 25 to 30 miles per hour, left highway).

Ohio—Manker v. Shaffer, 121 N.E.2d 908, 96 Ohio App. 350, affirmed 118 N.E.2d 641, 161 Ohio St. 285 (slippery spot in highway).

Wis.—Novakofski v. State Farm Mut. Auto. Ins. Co. of Bloomington, Ill., 148 N.W.2d 714.

Wall

N.J.—Sibley v. City Service Transit Co., 63 A.2d 708, 1 N.J.Super. 199, affirmed 66 A.2d 864, 2 N.J. 458

§ 418.2　　　　TRIAL EVIDENCE　　　　Ch. 418

turned into a ditch,[55] or a creek.[56]

The doctrine has been applied where a vehicle was driven to the edge of the road and overturned,[57] and where a vehicle overturned upon the road.[58]

(bus suddenly left road and crashed into a wall).

55. U.S.—Worsham v. Duke, C.A.Ky.1955, 220 F.2d 506; Alexander v. Corey, 1951, 98 F.Supp. 1013, 13 Alaska 382.

Ariz.—Lewis v. Cooley, 1971, 480 P.2d 370, 14 Ariz.App. 33 (arising out of accident which occurred when automobile in which plaintiff was a sleeping passenger left road in early morning hours, killing driver, permissible jury inference was that driver fell asleep).

Cal.—Scott v. Burke, 247 P.2d 313, 39 Cal.2d 388; Mansfield v. Pickwick Stages, Northern Division, 229 P. 890, 68 Cal.App. 507; Lawrence v. Pickwick Stages, Northern Division, 229 P. 885, 68 Cal.App. 494.

Ky.—Wireman v. Salyer, 336 S.W.2d 349; Reibert v. Thompson, 194 S.W.2d 974, 302 Ky. 688.

La.—Ehrhard v. State Farm Mut. Auto Ins. Co., 1973, 274 So.2d 911, application denied 279 So.2d 202; Levy v. Indemnity Ins. Co. of North America, App., 8 So.2d 774; Galbraith v. Dreyfus, App., 162 So. 246 (proof that driver, after losing control of automobile on level portion of graveled road, traveled zigzagging from one side of road to other for 700 feet without slowing down until turned over in ditch, made out prima facie case).

Mo.—Dodson v. Maddox, 223 S.W.2d 434, 359 Mo. 742 (plaintiff injured while extricating driver from burning truck after truck left the highway and collided with embankment); Adams v. Le Bow, 160 S.W.2d 826, 236 Mo.App. 899; Mackler v. Barnert, App., 49 S.W.2d 244.

N.Y.—Bennett v. Edward, 267 N.Y.S. 417, 239 App.Div. 157 (car apparently in good order, operated at moderate speed, suddenly turned by driver out of heavy line of traffic, ran across road into ditch, injuring plaintiff, held to establish prima facie case).

N.C.—Etheridge v. Etheridge, 24 S.E.2d 477, 222 N.C. 616.

Ohio.—Sprenger v. Braker, 49 N.E.2d 958, 71 Ohio App. 349 (skidded off road).

Okl.—Threadgill v. Anderson, 303 P.2d 297.

Or.—Francisco v. Circle Tours Sight-Seeing Co., 265 P. 801, 125 Or. 80.

Tenn.—Sullivan v. Crabtree, 258 S.W.2d 782, 36 Tenn.App. 469.

Tex.—Bower Auto Rent Co. v. Young, Civ.App., 274 S.W. 295, error refused.

Wis.—Modl v. National Farmers Union Property & Cas. Co., 76 N.W.2d 599, 272 Wis. 650, rehearing denied 77 N.W.2d 607, 272 Wis. 650.

Bus passenger injured

Doctrine held applicable where bus was run off main highway along embankment, causing passenger to be violently thrown against side of car. Francisco v. Circle Tours Sight-Seeing Co., 265 P. 801, 125 Or. 80.

56. N.C.—Lassiter v. Jones, 1970, 174 S.E.2d 630, 8 N.C.App. 506 (pond).

Ohio.—Nassar v. Interstate Motor Freight System, 16 N.E.2d 832, 58 Ohio App. 443.

57. U.S.—Frisby v. Olin Mathieson Chemical Corp., C.A.Ark., 279 F.2d 939.

58. See note 58 on page 201.

Ch. 418 RES IPSA LOQUITUR § **418.2**

It may also be applied to head-on collisions, but only after the plaintiff has established that the collision occurred on the plaintiff's side of the road.[59]

It has been applied where an intersectional collision occurred.[60]

Cal.—Druzanich v. Criley, 122 P.2d 53, 19 Cal.2d 439; Queirolo v. Pacific Gas & Electric Co., 300 P. 487, 114 Cal.App. 610.

Ky.—V. T. C. Lines v. Taylor, 134 S.W.2d 991, 281 Ky. 83.

La.—Pearce v. U. S. Fidelity & Guaranty Co., App., 8 So.2d 743 (applicable in one car accident case in which car, on a straight road, suddenly swerved from side to side and overturned); Hamburger v. Katz, 120 So. 391, 10 La.App. 215.

Md.—Hanes v. State, Use of Lamm, 202 A.2d 364, 236 Md. 28.

Minn.—Nicol v. Geitler, 247 N.W. 8, 188 Minn. 69 (overturning at curve).

Mo.—Tabler v. Perry, 85 S.W.2d 471, 337 Mo. 154 (went off pavement, into embankment, and overturned).

Ohio.—Weller v. Worstall, 196 N.E. 637, 120 Ohio St. 596, affirming 197 N.E. 410, 50 Ohio App. 11 (passenger injured).

Okl.—Creswell v. Temple Mill Co., Okl.1972, 499 P.2d 421 (20 mph. or less on straight road).

Tenn.—Sullivan v. Crabtree, 258 S. W.2d 782, 36 Tenn.App. 469; Oliver v. Union Transfer Co., 71 S.W.2d 478, 17 Tenn.App. 694.

W.Va.—Isabella v. West Virginia Transp. Co., 51 S.E.2d 318, 132 W. Va. 85.

58. U.S.—Hartsell v. Hickman, D.C. Ark., 148 F.Supp. 782.

Ala.—Baker v. Baker, 124 So. 740, 220 Ala. 201 (on a curve).

Cal.—Fenstermacher v. Johnson, 32 P.2d 1106, 138 Cal.App. 691 (straight, level, and dry highway); Seney v. Pickwick Stages, Northern Division, 255 P. 279, 82 Cal. App. 226.

Ky.—Supplee v. Webster, 320 S.W. 2d 615; Ralston v. Dossey, 157 S. W.2d 739, 289 Ky. 40.

La.—Harris v. Varnado, App., 94 So. 2d 74, 79 A.L.R.2d 204.

Nev.—Nyberg v. Kirby, 188 P.2d 1006, 65 Nev. 42, rehearing denied 193 P.2d 850, 65 Nev. 42 (truck being driven at 50 miles an hour on a straight, level road in the daytime with no obstruction swerved and overturned).

N.Y.—Russo v. State, 2 N.Y.S.2d 350, 166 Misc. 316.

59. U.S.—Bologach v. U. S., D.C. Pa., 122 F.Supp. 502; Hopper v. U. S., D.C.Tenn., 122 F.Supp. 181, affirmed C.A., 214 F.2d 129.

Ariz.—Throop v. F. E. Young & Co., 1963, 382 P.2d 560, 94 Ariz. 146 (even though driver had heart condition and it was alleged had heart attack).

Ark.—Penny v. Gulf Refining Co., 233 S.W.2d 372, 217 Ark. 805.

Cal.—Amar v. Union Oil Co. of Cal., 333 P.2d 449, 166 Cal.App.2d 424.

La.—Travelers Fire Ins. Co. v. Meadows, App., 13 So.2d 537; Giglio v. Toups, App.1939, 192 So. 553.

Pa.—Central Greyhound Lines of N. Y. v. George, 108 A.2d 746, 379 Pa. 221.

Wash.—Wentz v. T. E. Connolly, Inc., 273 P.2d 485, 45 Wash.2d 127; Purdie v. Brunswick, 146 P.2d 809, 20 Wash.2d 292.

60. Fla.—Orr v. Avon Florida Citrus Corporation, 177 So. 612, 130 Fla. 306 (straight 18 ft. highway).

§ 418.2   TRIAL EVIDENCE   Ch. 418

Likewise the rule has been applied where an automobile, after being left unattended, moved and inflicted injuries.[61]

Minn.—Jefferis v. Baumann, 221 N. W. 680, 175 Minn. 623.

Ohio.—Flook v. Kemp, App., 125 N. E.2d 739 (driver of westbound automobile was proceeding in lawful manner with right-of-way, and was struck by instrumentality in exclusive control of driver of southbound automobile).

61. Ariz.—Clint v. Northern Assur. Co., 223 P.2d 401, 71 Ariz. 44.

Cal.—Towers v. Massey-Harris Co., 302 P.2d 77, 145 Cal.App.2d 210 (self-propelled combine rolled backwards off of ramp); Nungaray v. Pleasant Val. Lima Bean Growers & Warehouse Ass'n, 300 P.2d 285, 142 Cal.App.2d 653 (truck, which had been tilted for unloading, rolled backwards despite presence of blocks); Prager v. Isreal, 98 P.2d 729, 15 Cal.2d 89.

Ga.—Kroger Co. v. Perpall, 125 S.E. 2d 511, 105 Ga.App. 682.

Kan.—Lamb v. Hartford Acc. & Indem. Co., 300 P.2d 387, 180 Kan. 157.

Ky.—Lewis v. Wolk, 228 S.W.2d 432, 312 Ky. 536, 16 A.L.R.2d 974.

La.—Speight v. Southern Farm Bureau Ins. Co., App.1971, 254 So. 2d 485 (rolled from hill and hit house, driver not sure in "park" or brake set); Hamiter v. Duncan, App., 78 So.2d 80; Yates v. Williams, App., 32 So.2d 505 (person standing at bus stop when struck by automobile rolling from parking lot).

Mass.—Pelland v. D'Allesandro, 73 N.E.2d 590, 321 Mass. 387; Glaser v. Schroeder, 168 N.E. 809, 269 Mass. 337.

Minn.—Holten v. Parker, 1974, 224 N.W.2d 139, —— Minn. —— (except where defendant offers evidence establishing is not solely responsible for any negligence connected with the loss of the wheel); Borg & Powers Furniture Co. v. Clark, 260 N.W. 316, 194 Minn. 305 (taxicab rolled backwards down hill).

Mo.—Bobbitt v. Salamander, 221 S. W.2d 971, 240 Mo.App. 902.

Okl.—Hill v. Thompson, 1971, 484 P.2d 513 (though lapse of 4 hours between parking and roll down slope).

Pa.—Wallace v. Keystone Automobile Co., 86 A. 699, 239 Pa. 110.

Tenn.—Bullington v. Whitson, 1969, 444 S.W.2d 152, 223 Tenn. 315; Roberts v. Ray, 322 S.W.2d 435, 45 Tenn.App. 280.

Tex.—Ketchum v. Gillespie, Civ. App., 145 S.W.2d 215.

Wash.—Kolbe v. Public Market Delivery & Transfer, 226 P. 1021, 130 Wash. 302.

Wis.—Colla v. Mandella, 1955, 72 N. W.2d 755, 271 Wis. 145 (though children present in parked vehicle).

Contra:
Globe Indemnity Co. v. Quesenberry, 1 La.App. 364.

Vehicle rolling off of sales lot

Evidence that dealer owned and operated vehicle auction lot for automobiles consigned to dealer for sale, and that it was dealer's practice, when parking automobiles on lot, to apply brakes and leave automobiles in gear with ignition keys in automobiles, and that dealer accorded prospective purchasers privilege of starting motors and driving automobiles parked on lot, and that during sale parked automobile, which had no driver, rolled down slanting driveway from lot into highway and collided with automobile being driven on highway, justified application of rule. Hudson v. Bennett, 115 N.E.2d 20, 94 Ohio App. 329.

The doctrine has been held to apply when an accident is caused by a wheel becoming detached;[62] or where objects fell from the defendant's vehicle,[63] or from some other defect in the vehicle.[64]

62. **Cal.**—McLaughlin v. Lasater, 1954, 277 P.2d 41, 129 Cal.App.2d 432, 46 A.L.R.2d 106.

Conn.—Gates v. Crane, 1928, 139 A. 782, 107 Conn. 201 (wheel struck pedestrian).

La.—Theriot v. Transit Cas. Co., App.1972, 265 So.2d 845, writ denied 267 So.2d 211, 263 La. 106 (in absence of presentation of broken wheel lugs or testimony to indicate why lugs may have sheared and caused accident and in view of driver's admission that he failed to inspect lugs before driving tractor trailer truck, driver of tractor trailer did not overcome inference of negligence from detachment of wheel); Ross v. Tynes, La.App., 14 So.2d 80 (wheel struck pedestrian).

Miss.—Peerless Supply Co. v. Jeter, 65 So.2d 240, 218 Miss. 61 (outside rear dual wheel of tractor-trailer became detached from trailer and struck front of oncoming automobile).

Mo.—Hanson v. Dalton Coal & Materials Co., 264 S.W.2d 897; Sakowski v. Baird, 69 S.W.2d 649, 334 Mo. 951.

63. **Cal.**—Williams v. Field Transp. Co., App., 166 P.2d 884, subsequent opinion 171 P.2d 722, 28 Cal.2d 696.

La.—State Farm Mut. Auto. Ins. Co. v. Herrin Transp. Co., App., 136 So.2d 272.

N.J.—Forsch v. Liebhardt, 68 A.2d 416, 5 N.J.Super. 75.

N.Y.—Cunningham v. Exposition Greyhound, 22 N.Y.S.2d 79, 174 Misc. 865.

64. **Dist.Col.**—Missile Cab Ass'n v. Rogers, Mun.App., 184 A.2d 845 (wheel of taxicab collapsed).

Fla.—Tamiami Trail Tours v. Locke, 75 So.2d 586 (failure of trailer coupling).

Ill.—Roberts v. Economy Cabs, 2 N. E.2d 128, 285 Ill.App. 424 (taxicab door opened).

Kan.—Clarke v. Cardinal Stage Lines, 31 P.2d 1, 139 Kan. 280 (front axle of bus broke, injuring passenger).

Ky.—Schechter v. Hann, 205 S.W.2d 690, 305 Ky. 794 (collision with pole allegedly caused by breaking of spring).

La.—Morales v. Employers' Liability Assur. Corporation, App., 7 So. 2d 660, affirmed 12 So.2d 804, 202 La. 755 (door on ambulance opened); Jones v. Baton Rouge Electric Co., App., 192 So. 539 (against carrier of passengers).

Md.—Smith v. Blue Ridge Transp. Co., 191 A. 66, 172 Md. 42 (folding aisle seat dropped and tripped bus passenger).

Mass.—Liberatore v. Town of Framingham, 53 N.E.2d 561, 315 Mass. 538 (dump truck dumped, injuring laborers riding in bed of truck).

Mo.—Adams v. Le Bow, 172 S.W.2d 874, 237 Mo.App. 1191 (guest fell from seat when door opened suddenly without any apparent reason).

Wash.—Vogreg v. Shepard Ambulance Service, 268 P.2d 642, 44 Wash.2d 528 (door on ambulance opened).

Brakes

Fla.—Holman v. Ford Motor Co., 1970, 239 So.2d 40, appeal after remand 254 So.2d 812 (sufficient for inference that manufacturer's defective tailstock caused booster unit to malfunction and result in

§ **418.2** TRIAL EVIDENCE Ch. 418

It has been applied in a variety of other situations involving the operation of vehicles,[65] and trains.[66]

loss of use of even ordinary, non-power brakes).

Tire

Wash.—Ewer v. Goodyear Tire & Rubber Co., 1970, 480 P.2d 260, 4 Wash.App. 152 (mishap while mounting tire).

65. U.S.—Siebrand v. Gossnell, C.A. Ariz., 234 F.2d 81 (struck by trailer which became disconnected from defendants' pick-up truck traveling in opposite direction).

Ariz.—Tenney v. Enkeball, 158 P.2d 519, 62 Ariz. 416 (minor fell from fender of truck).

Cal.—Mart v. Riley, 49 Cal.Rptr. 6 (truck suddenly jerked, bed of truck suddenly elevated, end tail gate failed to hold with result that lessee's employee avalanched with load of sand down onto roadway); Isaacs v. City and County of San Francisco, 167 P.2d 221, 73 Cal. App.2d 621 (failure of fire apparatus to sound siren when traveling against red stop sign); Prunty v. Allred, 165 P.2d 935, 73 Cal.App. 2d 67 (baggage fell from overhead rack); Juchert v. California Water Service Co., 106 P.2d 886, 16 Cal. 2d 500, prior opinion, App., 97 P.2d 259 (motorcyclist struck hole in road, applied against water company responsible for broken water pipe); Weddle v. Loges, 125 P.2d 914, 52 Cal.App.2d 115 (tow rope broke and towed vehicle struck tree).

Iowa.—Breeding v. Reed, 110 N.W.2d 552, 253 Iowa 129 (truck driver failed to close a truck door so it would latch, and such failure was proximate cause of injury to running board passenger).

Kan.—Lackey v. Price, 378 P.2d 19, 190 Kan. 648 (explosion of liquified petroleum gas from truck which was being washed); Hohmann v. Jones, 72 P.2d 971, 146 Kan. 578 (winch chain broke striking nearby person).

Mo.—Gibbons v. Wells, App., 293 S. W. 89 (injury to passenger by coming in contact with insulator at end of street railway guy wire).

Ohio.—Barnes v. Kirk Bros. Auto Co., 32 Ohio Cir.Ct.R. 233 (motion of car while being inspected by prospective purchaser in garage).

Okl.—Furr v. McGrath, 340 P.2d 243 (plaintiff struck by jack placed under automobile by defendant).

Or.—Powell v. Moore, 364 P.2d 1094, 228 Or. 255 (ramp placed between moving van and porch of plaintiff's house slid with plaintiff on it).

Tex.—Coastal Coaches v. Ball, 234 S.W.2d 474, 22 A.L.R.2d 955, ref. n. r. e. (bus passenger gassed by exhaust fumes from the bus).

W.Va.—Ellis v. Henderson, 98 S.E. 2d 719, 142 W.Va. 824 (gratuitous rider in bucket of tractor-loader when bucket tipped and dumped rider on ground).

Wis.—Henthorn v. M. G. C. Corp., 83 N.W.2d 759, 1 Wis.2d 180, 79 A.L.R.2d 142 (tractor-trailer unit, stopped across highway); Dunham v. Wisconsin Gas & Electric Co., 280 N.W. 291, 228 Wis. 250 (trailing wire wrapped around leg of pedestrian).

Combined with claim against manufacturer for defect in vehicle

Pedestrian who was injured when struck while standing on a public sidewalk could sue manufacturer of allegedly defective tire with which automobile was equipped and still retain applicability of res ipsa loquitur as against driver. Merriman v. Kraft, 1969, 249 N.E.2d 485, 253 Ind. 58.

66. See note 66 on page 205.

Guest actions

If a guest's action is grounded upon a charge of ordinary negligence, it is inaccurate to say generally that the res ipsa loquitur doctrine does or does not apply. Since the unexplained conditions surrounding the accident, the exclusive control of the machine in the defendant, and the state of the pleadings, rather than the relation of the parties, constitutes the test,[67] the same rules are followed in determining its application in a guest's action as in other tort actions. Applying the usual test, courts have given effect to the doctrine in such cases when the pleadings and surrounding circumstances justified it.[68]

When the operation of an automobile is exclusively within a host's control, and it is not reasonably within the power of the injured guest to prove the cause of the accident, which is one not commonly incident to the operation of the automobile, the occurrence itself, although unexplained, is prima facie evidence of the host's negligence.[69]

Entitled to have doctrine applied, by showing that automobile was under exclusive control of driver, that accident was result of driver's lack of reasonable care, and that pedestrian was without information as to exact cause of accident, and fact that pedestrian later plead and introduced evidence of a tire blowout did not destroy his right to have doctrine applied, where there was evidence that blowout would not have caused driver to lose control of vehicle. Id.

66. U.S.—Brown v. Lowden, D.C. Mo., 3 F.R.D. 173 (derailment).

Md.—Potomac Edison Co. v. Johnson, 152 A. 633, 160 Md. 33 (derailment).

67. Me.—Chaisson v. Williams, 156 A. 154, 130 Me. 341.

68. U.S.—Alexander v. Corey, D.C. Alaska, 98 F.Supp. 1013.

Cal.—Doggett v. Lacey, 9 P.2d 257, 121 Cal.App. 395 (car overturned); Kenney v. Antonetti, 295 P. 341, 211 Cal. 336; Curry v. Williams, 293 P. 623, 109 Cal.App. 649 (presumption does not arise from speed of 30 mph. on 18 foot road unless driver was warned of danger);

Ireland v. Marsden, 291 P. 912, 108 Cal.App. 632 (sudden bounce threw guest to top of automobile).

La.—Harrelson v. McCook, App., 198 So. 532.

Mo.—Tabler v. Perry, 85 S.W.2d 471, 337 Mo. 154.

N.J.—Spill v. Stoeckert, 15 A.2d 773, 125 N.J.L. 382.

69. Cal.—Ellis v. Jewett, 64 P.2d 432, 18 Cal.App.2d 629.

Kan.—Rupe v. Smith, 313 P.2d 293, 181 Kan. 606.

Ky.—Smith v. Hamm, 235 S.W.2d 437, 314 Ky. 334.

La.—Gomer v. Anding, App., 146 So. 704, rehearing denied 147 So. 545.

Me.—Gendron v. Gendron, 69 A.2d 668, 144 Me. 347; Chaisson v. Williams, 156 A. 154, 130 Me. 341.

Mo.—Vesper v. Ashton, 118 S.W.2d 84, 233 Mo.App. 204; Mackler v. Barnert, App., 49 S.W.2d 244.

N.J.—Bevilacqua v. Sutter, 98 A 2d 60, 26 N.J.Super. 394.

Wis.—Wood v. Indemnity Ins. Co. of North America, 76 N.W.2d 610, 273 Wis. 93 (wife a sleeping passenger).

§ 418.2　　　　　TRIAL EVIDENCE　　　　　Ch. 418

Carrier passenger actions

The doctrine may be available for passengers of a carrier.[70]

§ 418.3　Situations Not Applicable [71]

Library References:
 C.J.S. Carriers § 764; Motor Vehicles § 511(3); Railroads § 669; Street Railroads § 306.
 West's Key No. Digests, Automobiles ⚖242(2); Carriers ⚖316; Railroads ⚖320(3); Street Railroads ⚖346.

That the rule is not available in some jurisdictions is noted in section 418.1 at fn. 2.

The application of the doctrine has been denied in automobile accident cases resulting from collisions between pedes-

---

70. U.S.—Slaughter v. D. C. Transit System, Inc., 261 F.2d 741, 104 U.S.App.D.C. 275 (injuries sustained by infant when bus door, automatically controlled by treadle step, closed on her foot as she was leaving bus).

Cal.—Hardin v. San Jose City Lines, 260 P.2d 63, 41 Cal.2d 432; Stark v. Yellow Cab Co., 202 P.2d 802, 90 Cal.App.2d 217; Renzetti v. Los Angeles Motor Coach Co., 119 P.2d 164, 48 Cal.App.2d 37 (proof that bus came to complete stop for purpose of discharging and receiving passengers, and that plaintiff placed her foot on first step to enter bus, and that bus suddenly moved ahead when rear end thereof was hit by following automobile, raised an inference that bus company was negligent).

Ill.—Brock v. Vancil, 1950, 92 N.E.2d 526, 340 Ill.App. 432 (incubator in ambulance caught fire).

Mo.—McSkimming v. St. Louis Service Co., App., 257 S.W.2d 176 (door closed upon departing passenger); Van Volkinburgh v. Kansas City Public Service Co., App., 254 S.W.2d 287; Smith v. Creve Coeur Drayage & Motorbus Co., 296 S.W. 457, 220 Mo.App. 1122.

N.Y.—Richter v. Trailways of New England, Inc., 1967, 282 N.Y.S.2d 148, 28 A.D.2d 737 (raised prima facie case of negligence of driver of bus which passed over construction site and allegedly caused passenger in washroom to receive a "terrible jolt", lose her balance, and fracture the coccyx).

Ohio.—Hall v. Redifer, Ohio Mun., 79 N.E.2d 237 (passenger became ill after riding in wet bus seat).

Va.—Cleveland v. Danville Traction & Power Co., 18 S.E.2d 913, 179 Va. 256 (passenger alighting from bus and falling on curb).

When due to agency or instrumentality of carrier

Presumption of negligence on part of carrier arises on proof of injury to passenger sustained as result of some agency or instrumentality of the carrier, some act of omission or commission of the servants of the carrier, or some defect in the instrumentalities of transportation. Poliakoff v. Shelton, 8 S.E.2d 494, 193 S.C. 398.

71. This section in prior edition **cited by the court** in Larkin v. State Farm Mut. Auto. Ins. Co., 97 So.2d 389, 392, 233 La. 544; De Witt v. Rissman, 346 P.2d 104, 109, 218 Or. 549; Day v. National U. S. Radiator Corp., 128 So.2d 660, 665, 241 La. 288; Denman v. Denman, 134 So.2d 457, 461, 242 Miss. 59; Pilie v. National Food Stores of La., Inc., La.App., 148 So.2d 391, 395, writ issued 150 So.2d 586, 244

Ch. 418   RES IPSA LOQUITUR   § 418.3

trians and motor vehicles;[72] bicycles and vehicles,[73] unattended animals and vehicles,[74] and to a collision between a vehicle and a horseback rider.[75]

Its application has been denied in cases involving the skidding of a vehicle.[76] The doctrine has also been held inapplicable

La. 122, judgment affirmed 158 So. 2d 162, 245 La. 276; Blakeman v. Lofland, 252 P.2d 852, 856, 173 Kan. 725; Storey v. Parker, La. App., 13 So.2d 88, 95; Charlton v. Lovelace, 173 S.W.2d 13, 16, 18, 351 Mo. 364.

This section in prior edition **quoted by the court** in Joynes v. Valloft & Dreaux, La.App., 1 So.2d 108.

72. U.S.—Reaver v. Walch, 3 F.2d 204, 55 App.D.C. 159.

Cal.—Sheller v. Blue Diamond Corp., 220 P.2d 26, 98 Cal.App.2d 400 (large tractor trailer turning and struck pedestrian on curb); Blanton v. Curry, App., 121 P.2d 125, affirmed and supplemented 129 P. 2d 1, 20 Cal.2d 793; Zulim v. Van Ness, 38 P.2d 820, 3 Cal.App.2d 82 (doctrine inapplicable to afford presumption of negligence from mere fact ran over a child).

Md.—Thompson v. Sun Cab Co., 184 A. 576, 170 Md. 299.

Mass.—Clark v. C. E. Fay Co., 183 N.E. 423, 281 Mass. 240 (dark rainy evening); O'Keefe v. United Motors Service, 149 N.E. 599, 253 Mass. 603; Whalen v. Mutrie, 142 N.E. 45, 247 Mass. 316.

N.Y.—Wank v. Ambrosino, 121 N.E. 2d 246, 307 N.Y. 321; Rothfeld v. Clerkin, 162 N.Y.S. 1056, 98 Misc. 192 (elderly woman saw vehicle before entering street).

N.C.—Lane v. Bryan, 97 S.E.2d 411, 246 N.C. 108 (lying on highway at time that he was struck).

N.D.—Vannett v. Cole, 170 N.W. 663, 41 N.D. 260.

Pa.—Brooks v. Morgan, 200 A. 81, 331 Pa. 235 (pedestrian with artificial leg); Rhoads v. Herbert, 148 A. 693, 298 Pa. 522.

Tenn.—Nichols v. Smith, 111 S.W.2d 911, 21 Tenn.App. 478.

Unattended vehicle

La.—Taylor v. Travelers Indem. Co., App.1970, 241 So.2d 564 (unattended automobile rolled down inclined driveway).

73. Mass.—Ellis v. Ellison, 175 N.E. 502, 275 Mass. 272 (bicyclist passing parked vehicle, struck oncoming vehicle).

74. U.S.—Rodgers v. Webb, D.C. D.C.Tenn.1971, 335 F.Supp. 584.

Cal.—Jackson v. Hardy, 1945, 160 P.2d 161, 70 Cal.App.2d 6 (due to Agricultural Code provision).

Colo.—Barnes v. Frank, 1970, 472 P. 2d 745, 28 Colo.App. 389 (cattle may have entered highway because of any number of factors, including acts of third persons).

Miss.—Hughes v. W & S Const. Co., 196 So.2d 339.

N.M.—Tapia v. McKenzie, 1971, 489 P.2d 181, 83 N.M. 116 (collided with defendant's cow on interstate highway after dark, was not entitled to go to the jury upon showing that defendant's cow escaped through highway department cattle guard); Akin v. Berkshire, 1973, 512 P.2d 1261, 85 N.M. 425 (was insufficient to show that accident was of kind which ordinarily does not occur in absence of someone's negligence).

75. Ariz.—Sawyer v. People's Freight Lines, 22 P.2d 1080, 42 Ariz. 145.

76. Ga.—Jackson v. Martin, 79 S.E. 2d 406, 89 Ga.App. 344 (in action

§ 418.3   TRIAL EVIDENCE   Ch. 418

in actions involving vehicles parked,[77] vehicles rearending cars

against driver of first automobile to recover for death of guest passenger in second automobile as result of head-on collision when driver of first automobile drove over onto wrong side of highway, wherein evidence was that first automobile, which was not being operated at high rate of speed, for some unexplained reason slipped or skidded across center line of slippery highway and collided with second automobile); Minkovitz v. Fine, 19 S.E.2d 561, 67 Ga.App. 176.

Ky.—Thurmond v. Chumbler's Adm'x, 287 S.W.2d 908; Head v. Lucas, 231 S.W.2d 81, 313 Ky. 356.

La.—Schaubhut v. Liberty Mut. Ins. Co., App., 157 So.2d 346.

Md.—Glass v. Bair, 195 A.2d 680, 233 Md. 194; Christ v. Wempe, 150 A.2d 918, 219 Md. 627 (slid a few inches off hard surface of road and onto shoulder); Billmeyer v. State, for Use of Whiteman, 64 A.2d 755, 192 Md. 419 (fact that automobile, not equipped with chains, skidded on an icy surface would not alone be evidence of negligence, but would only be significant in connection with antecedent conduct).

Mass.—Sherwood v. Radovsky, 57 N. E.2d 912, 317 Mass. 307.

Minn.—Marsh v. Henriksen, 7 N.W. 2d 387, 213 Minn. 500.

Mo.—Bear v. Devore, App., 176 S.W. 2d 862 (skidding alone is no evidence of excessive speed thereof, but may be considered with other circumstances and conditions). Polokoff v. Sanell, App., 52 S.W. 2d 443.

N.Y.—Lo Piccolo v. Knight of Rest Products Corp., 183 N.Y.S.2d 301, 7 A.D.2d 369, motion granted 194 N.Y.S.2d 521, 7 N.Y.2d 786, 163 N.E.2d 341, affirmed 212 N.Y.S.2d 75, 9 N.Y.2d 662, 173 N.E.2d 51 (slippery bridge surface); Coffey v. State, 86 N.Y.S.2d 172, 193 Misc. 1060, affirmed 96 N.Y.S.2d 303, 304 (2 mems.) 276 App.Div. 1049, reargument and appeal denied 97 N.Y.S.2d 918, 277 App.Div. 831; Brush v. State, 75 N.Y.S.2d 758, 190 Misc. 909.

N.C.—Lewis v. Piggott, 1972, 192 S. E.2d 128, 16 N.C.App. 395 (due to water on roadway); Mitchell v. Melts, 18 S.E.2d 406, 220 N.C. 793; Butner v. Whitlow, 161 S.E. 389, 201 N.C. 749 (35 miles per hour on curve in drizzling rain); Springs v. Doll, 148 S.E. 251, 197 N.C. 240 (where host driver pulled out to avoid collision with approaching truck following center line of highway, and, the hazard having passed, attempted to straighten out course and automobile skidded on wet road and slid into embankment).

Pa.—Miller v. Measmer, 44 A.2d 284, 353 Pa. 18; Johnson v. American Reduction Co., 158 A. 153, 305 Pa. 537.

S.D.—Jacobson v. Coady, 84 N.W.2d 1, 77 S.D. 1.

Tenn.—Shepherd v. Ball, 337 S.W.2d 243, 47 Tenn.App. 189.

Vt.—Johnson v. Burke, 183 A. 495, 108 Vt. 164 (skidded on icy road after passing another automobile traveling in same direction, causing injury to guest); Williamson v. Clark, 153 A. 448, 103 Vt. 288.

Wash.—Wellons v. Wiley, 166 P.2d 852, 24 Wash.2d 543; Cartwright v. Boyce, 8 P.2d 968, 167 Wash. 175.

Wis.—Churchill v. Brock, 58 N.W.2d 290, 264 Wis. 23.

77. Ark.—Sauter v. Atchinson, 1971, 466 S.W.2d 475, 250 Ark. 697 (placed gearshift lever in park and set handbrake before going to front of car to shoot cans with shotgun and plaintiff's minor was struck when car suddenly rolled forward

ahead,[78] vehicles suddenly swerving,[79] vehicles intersecting,[80]

when he took his position in front of car to shoot).

Cal.—Gonzalez v. Nichols, 1930, 294 P. 758, 110 Cal.App. 738.

La.—Palmer v. Turner, App.1971, 252 So.2d 700 (where full facts attending accident resulting when automobile overtaking plaintiff's automobile collided with defendant's unlighted vehicle were known, and negligence of driver of defendant's automobile was the sole proximate cause of accident, owner of the unlighted vehicle could not invoke doctrine); Craker v. Allstate Ins. Co., 1971, 250 So.2d 746, 259 La. 578 (when host's automobile collided with truck that had been parked on dark country road without lights at 4 o'clock on a rainy morning).

Md.—Johnson v. Jackson, 226 A.2d 883, 245 Md. 589 (produced no witnesses other than himself and presented no proof as to the manner in which defendants' automobile was parked or with respect to the length of time it was parked before it began to roll, but acknowledged in his testimony presence of third person at scene of accident).

Va.—Gilmer v. Southern Ry. Co., 1961, 120 S.E.2d 294, 202 Va. 826 (left in gear and remained as parked for several days prior to rolling from parking lot); Barry v. Tyler, 199 S.E. 496, 171 Va. 381 (collision with a truck which had been stopped at side of highway at night when it ran out of gasoline).

Wash.—Joseph v. Schwartz, 224 P. 5, 128 Wash. 634 (after standing five or six hours).

78. **Cal.**—Steuer v. Phelps, 1974, 116 Cal.Rptr. 61, 41 C.A.3d 468 (where both vehicles were moving in the same direction and in different traffic lanes, and where sudden movement of oncoming car over double line forced lead automobile to swerve and come to a sudden stop upon impact, doctrine did not apply to action brought by driver and passengers of lead automobile against driver of following automobile); Pittman v. Boiven, Cal. App., 57 Cal.Rptr. 319 (car ahead abruptly slowed or stopped just prior to impact for purpose of making a left turn without giving signal as required by law).

Ind.—Hoesel v. Cain, 53 N.E.2d 165, 222 Ind. 330, rehearing denied 53 N.E.2d 769, 222 Ind. 330 (when plaintiff's car started to pass the car ahead, but could not do so and pulled back into the right hand lane, fact of collision with car approaching from plaintiff's rear did not justify inference that following car was traveling at excessive speed, was following too closely, or that brakes were faulty).

Iowa.—Humphrey v. Happy, 1969, 169 N.W.2d 565 (where change of movement of plaintiff's vehicle immediately before collision from rear negated defendant's exclusive or sole control of instrumentality causing accident); Mickelson v. Forney, 143 N.W.2d 390.

Md.—Brehm v. Lorenz, 112 A.2d 475, 206 Md. 500 (front automobile was stopped unexpectedly and very suddenly when driver saw a cat running in front of it).

Mass.—Reardon v. Boston Elevated Ry. Co., 141 N.E. 857, 247 Mass. 124 (defendant trolley car).

Tex.—Thomason v. Ulmer, Civ.App., 274 S.W.2d 103.

79. **Mass.**—Bartlett v. Town Taxi, 160 N.E. 797, 263 Mass. 215.

N.C.—Ivey v. Rollins, 108 S.E.2d 63, 250 N.C. 89, rehearing dismissed 118 S.E.2d 194, 251 N.C. 345 (struck bridge).

80. **Cal.**—Cordova v. Ford, 54 Cal. Rptr. 508, 246 Cal.App.2d 180.

§ 418.3 TRIAL EVIDENCE Ch. 418

vehicles leaving the highway,[81] vehicles backing,[82] and in an action for injuries sustained when an automobile overturned on a highway.[83]

The res ipsa loquitur doctrine has been held inapplicable where, after an accident, a tire was found to have blown out;[84] where a wheel came off and caused an injury,[85] where brakes failed,[86] or for other defects in a vehicle.[87]

81. **La.**—Scott v. Many Motor Co., App.1962, 140 So.2d 778.

Md.—Armstrong v. Johnson Motor Lines, Inc., 1971, 280 A.2d 24, 12 Md.App. 492 (where everything relative to case was known concerning swerving due to lane obstruction and striking vehicle parked on median strip).

N.C.—Lewis v. Piggott, 1972, 192 S.E.2d 128, 16 N.C.App. 395 (skidded on water); Peoples Bank & Trust Co. v. Snowden, 148 S.E.2d 833, 267 N.C. 749; Lane v. Dorney, 108 S.E.2d 55, 250 N.C. 15, rehearing 113 S.E.2d 33, 252 N.C. 90 (on curve).

Va.—Boggs v. Plybon, 160 S.E. 77, 157 Va. 30 (left roadway and struck telephone pole).

82. **U.S.**—Lewis v. Super Valu Stores, Inc., C.A.Iowa, 364 F.2d 555 (in action against employer of truck driver for death of driver's 11-year-old son, who was crushed when driver backed truck at loading dock of store after warning son to stand back).

Cal.—Turnipseed v. Hoffman, App., 136 P.2d 355, subsequent opinion 144 P.2d 797, 23 Cal.2d 532; Hanson v. Weckerle, 1936, 63 P.2d 322, 18 Cal.App.2d 214 (backed against plaintiff trying to chock stalled truck on steep incline).

83. **Tenn.**—Sloan v. Nevil, 229 S.W.2d 350, 33 Tenn.App. 100 (driver explained cause as falling down of the front of the automobile onto the pavement); Granert v. Bauer, 67 S.W.2d 748, 17 Tenn.App. 370.

84. **Conn.**—Giddings v. Honan, 159 A. 271, 114 Conn. 473, 79 A.L.R. 1215.

Ky.—Knop v. Atcher, 308 S.W.2d 287.

Me.—Dostie v. Lewiston Crushed Stone Co., 8 A.2d 393, 136 Me. 284.

Wis.—Pawlowski v. Eskofski, 244 N.W. 611, 209 Wis. 189; Klein v. Beeten, 172 N.W. 736, 169 Wis. 385, 5 A.L.R. 1237.

85. **Mass.**—Sennett v. Nonamtum Coal Co., 187 N.E. 758, 284 Mass. 390.

86. **U.S.**—Mills v. U. S., D.C.D.C. 1969, 297 F.Supp. 972 (could not recover under Federal Tort Claims Act since government's evidence, which affirmatively established that brakes were properly inspected and operating properly until immediately before accident, met government's burden).

As against dealer

N.C.—Wilcox v. Glover Motors, Inc., 153 S.E.2d 76, 269 N.C. 473 (alleged brake failure occurring several hours and many miles after delivery of the vehicle to a prospective buyer, a bailee).

87. **U.S.**—Union Pac. R. Co. v. Ward, C.A.Colo.1956, 230 F.2d 287 (battery failure resulting in stall on railroad crossing).

La.—Estill v. Hanover Ins. Co., App. 1968, 209 So.2d 542 (in action by service station attendant against owner of tractor tire and rim, when exploded while being inflated).

Ch. 418 RES IPSA LOQUITUR § 418.3

And it has been held inapplicable in actions involving defects in a bridge,[88] or a railroad crossing.[89]

It has also been held inapplicable in a variety of other instances involving the operation of vehicles.[90]

N.J.—Griffin v. Hohorst, Inc., 1936, 185 A. 535, 14 N.J.Misc. 421 (ice on bus step).

Or.—Pattle v. Wildish Const. Co., 1974, 529 P.2d 924, 270 Or. 792 (evidence in suit by plaintiff who was injured when vehicle was struck by truck which went out of control because idler arm shaft in steering mechanism broke was insufficient to warrant application of doctrine so as to impose liability on owner of truck which was approximately five years old, had been driven in excess of 100,000 miles, and had been regularly serviced during six months preceding accident).

Tex.—El Paso Electric Co. v. Barker, 137 S.W.2d 17, 134 Tex. 496, reversing Civ.App., 116 S.W.2d 433 (absence of seat arm on bus).

As against manufacturer

Doctrine was inapplicable to wrongful death action against manufacturer of automobile which had been carried by commercial carrier and had been in possession of owner and victim of accident for 19 months. Lashley v. Ford Motor Co., D.C.Ga. 1973, 359 F.Supp. 363, judgment affirmed C.A., 480 F.2d 158, certiorari denied 94 S.Ct. 585, 414 U.S. 1072, 38 L.Ed.2d 478.

Ill.—Garofalo v. General Motors Corp., 243 N.E.2d 691, 103 Ill.App. 2d 389 (not applicable in action by motorist seeking to recover from manufacturer and dealer damages for personal injuries sustained when motorist was allegedly rendered unconscious by carbon monoxide or gasoline fumes allegedly due to defect in automobile and automobile left road and overturned).

N.C.—Williams v. General Motors Corp., 1973, 198 S.E.2d 766, 19 N.C.App. 337, certiorari denied Sup., 200 S.E.2d 659, 284 N.C. 258 (in action against manufacturer and seller for injuries suffered by motorist in Virginia accident which allegedly was caused by defective carburetor in automobile driven by motorist, where motorist had access to knowledge of cause of accident and presented evidence as to cause, accident was not unexplainable event and doctrine would not apply under Virginia law.)

88. **Conn.**—Shirlock v. MacDonald, 186 A. 562, 121 Conn. 611.

89. **Cal.**—Adams v. Southern Pac. Co., 53 P.2d 121, 4 Cal.2d 731.

90. **U.S.**—Louisiana & A. R. Co. v. Fireman's Fund Ins. Co., C.A.La. 1967, 380 F.2d 541 (that defendant's laundry truck stalled on plaintiff's railroad tracks and was struck by train and inconclusive evidence as to whether driver flooded engine through improper manipulation of accelerator or whether defective fuel pump caused truck to stall would not support giving of instruction); Hall v. National Supply Co., C.A.Tex., 270 F.2d 379 (driver was blinded by lights of approaching truck and when attempting to get back onto highway he swerved into left lane and struck truck).

Cal.—Gonzalez v. Nichols, 294 P. 758, 110 Cal.App. 738 (hit rear of vehicle with small rear light, the occupants of which were engaged in picking up and replacing part of its cargo which had fallen to road); Carlsen v. Diehl, 208 P. 150, 57 Cal.App. 731 (plaintiff was loading truck standing beside

211

§ 418.3 TRIAL EVIDENCE Ch. 418

driveway leading from scales to boat slip at ferryboat dock).

Colo.—Clune v. Mercereau, 1 P.2d 101, 89 Colo. 227 (host attempted to shift gears on a steep road).

Iowa.—Shinofield v. Curtis, 66 N.W. 2d 465, 245 Iowa 1352, 50 A.L.R.2d 964 (woman had alighted safely from the truck at foot of steps up to sidewalk, but had been injured before she reached sidewalk).

Ky.—Randall v. Shelton, 1956, 293 S. W.2d 559 (stone thrown up by passing truck).

La.—New Orleans Shrimp Co., Inc. v. Duplantis Truck Lines, Inc., App. 1973, 283 So.2d 521 (marshbuggy, loaded on trailer, struck conveyor extending over highway); Clark v. Cit Con Oil Corp., App., 150 So. 2d 784, writ refused 152 So.2d 62, 244 La. 395 (not applicable to truck driver's suit for injuries sustained when he drove truck and trailer underneath defendant's canopy which had plainly marked thereon its clearance height which was too low for trailer's passage thereunder); Thomas v. Lumbermen's Mut. Cas. Co., App., 146 So. 2d 275 (doctrine was not applicable to establish liability of driver of overtaking vehicle or his liability insurer for damages sustained by truck driver when overtaking vehicle collided with rear of truck, where negligence in operating truck on highway at night without tail light in violation of statutes was a proximate cause of collision); McClain v. Missouri Pac. R. Co., App.1941, 200 So. 57 (collision with train).

Mass.—Bartlett v. Town Taxi, Inc. 160 N.E. 797, 263 Mass. 215 (taxicab turned around abruptly, injuring passenger).

N.M.—Pack v. Read, 419 P.2d 453, 77 N.M. 76 (for damage to parked automobile struck when a bolt broke and farm machine, which was known as a "land leveler" and which was being towed by a pickup truck driven by defendant, swerved from side to side).

N.Y.—Clark v. City of Rochester, 270 N.Y.S.2d 173, 25 A.D.2d 713 (action against city for damage to automobile and injuries to occupant when manhole cover allegedly "flipped" off striking automobile).

N.C.—Johnson v. Libby Hill Seafood Restaurants, Inc., 125 S.E.2d 324, 257 N.C. 115 (customer in fall from defendant's truck).

Tenn.—Heaton v. Kagley, 281 S.W.2d 385, 198 Tenn. 530 (boy came onto adjoining farm on which haying was being carried on and climbed onto tractor fender and was knocked therefrom by a falling bale of hay and run over by tractor); Gray v. Brown, 217 S.W.2d 769, 188 Tenn. 152 (under undisputed evidence that right door of taxicab was not mechanically defective, that driver securely closed door at start of trip with passenger, and no one touched it thereafter until passenger was injured by fall from taxicab in attempt to close door, unexplained opening of door raised no presumption of negligence against either driver or owner of taxicab).

Tex.—Whitehead v. Montgomery, Civ.App., 228 S.W.2d 196, writ of error refused n. r. e. (tow chain broke, damaging towed vehicle).

Wash.—Capen v. Wester, 365 P.2d 326, 58 Wash.2d 900 (automobiles collided at intersection, and one automobile left street and struck house).

Load unsecure

Ind.—Farmer v. Werner Transp. Co., 1972, 284 N.E.2d 861, 152 Ind.App. 609 (air-conditioning unit alleged to have fallen from defendant's truck).

Striking parked vehicle

Res ipsa loquitur did not apply in suit by guest against host driver's liability insurer for injuries sustained

212

It has been held that the doctrine does not apply in guest actions [91] including cases where the attempt is to establish gross

when host's automobile collided with truck that had been parked on dark country road without lights at 4 o'clock on a rainy morning. Craker v. Allstate Ins. Co., 1971, 250 So.2d 746, 259 La. 578.

Unloading vehicle

La.—Woodall v. Kent Enterprises, Inc., App.1971, 250 So.2d 254 (timbers fell while truck was being unloaded from other side by forklift operator, where all facts and circumstances surrounding accident were presented).

Vehicles meeting

La.—Nuss v. MacKenzie, La.App., 4 So.2d 845 (not applicable in two car, head-on collision in absence of proof as to which side of the highway the collision occurred, because the inference, if any, would be equally applicable to both drivers).

Mo.—Dwyer v. Moss, 1971, 462 S.W. 2d 645.

91. U.S.—Liggett & Myers Tobacco Co. v. De Parcq, C.C.A.Minn., 66 F.2d 678 (overturned after struck loose gravel).

Cal.—Binns v. Standen, 5 P.2d 637, 118 Cal.App. 625 (motorist blinded by sun); Curry v. Williams, 293 P. 623, 109 Cal.App. 649 (head-on collision).

Fla.—Brooks v. Plant, 1974, 296 So. 2d 71 (boy fell from rear of pickup truck).

Iowa.—Gianopulos v. Saunders System, Cedar Rapids Co., 242 N.W. 53.

La.—Jenkins v. Travelers Indem. Co., App.1971, 245 So.2d 503 (host vehicle struck in chain collision); Coffey v. Ouachita River Lumber Co., App., 191 So. 561 (steering mechanism locked).

Mo.—Polokoff v. Sanell, App., 52 S. W.2d 443 (skidding into ditch); State ex rel. and to Use of Brancato v. Trimble, 18 S.W.2d 4, 322 Mo. 318 (collision with bus).

N.H.—Conant v. Collins, 10 A.2d 237, 90 N.H. 434 (leaving road and striking wall and tree).

N.Y.—Haddix v. Tomich, 280 N.Y.S. 56, 245 App.Div. 727 (collision with tree).

Ohio.—Allen v. Leavick, 182 N.E. 139, 43 Ohio App. 100 (guest thrown from seat when automobile bounced).

Pa.—Ebey v. Schwartz, 158 A. 291, 104 Pa.Super. 181 (automobile upset after passing truck at high speed and after wheel broke).

Tenn.—Lively v. Atchley, 256 S.W. 2d 58, 36 Tenn.App. 399; Granert v. Bauer, 67 S.W.2d 748, 17 Tenn. App. 370 (automobile overturned).

Va.—Jones v. Nugent, 180 S.E. 161, 164 Va. 378 (skidding off road because of drop-off between pavement and shoulder on hill); Boggs v. Plybon, 160 S.E. 77, 157 Va. 30 (collision with telephone pole).

Wash.—Cartwright v. Boyce, 8 P.2d 968, 167 Wash. 175 (skidding and colliding with overtaken vehicle).

Wis.—Tracy v. Malmstadt, 296 N.W. 87, 236 Wis. 642 (mere fact was head-on collision not proof that host was negligent as to lookout).

Falling from vehicle

La.—Favalora v. Travelers Ins. Co., App.1969, 223 So.2d 702 (did not apply to action for injuries to child who fell from automobile when door opened).

N.C.—Johnson v. Johnson, 1970, 174 S.E.2d 85, 8 N.C.App. 274 (almost five-year-old daughter fell out of cab of moving pickup truck, conjecture as to why door opened).

§ 418.3 TRIAL EVIDENCE Ch. 418

negligence or recklessness of a host, in absence of direct proof.[92]

The doctrine may not be relied on to prove plaintiff's contributory negligence.[93]

The doctrine of res ipsa loquitur has been held not to apply as between master and servant.[94]

Vehicle moved as plaintiff entered

Fact that automobile rolled when plaintiff entered it was not evidence of any negligence on part of owner who parked vehicle. Smith v. Perkins, 1969, 168 S.E.2d 14, 5 N.C.App. 120.

92. Similar comment in prior edition **cited by the court** in Minkovitz v. Fine, 19 S.E.2d 561, 566, 67 Ga.App. 176.

U.S.—Russell v. Turner, D.C.Iowa, 56 F.Supp. 455, affirmed 148 F.2d 562 (not applicable under Iowa automobile guest statute).

Cal.—Phillips v. Noble, 323 P.2d 385, 50 Cal.2d 163; Fiske v. Wilkie, 154 P.2d 725, 67 Cal.App.2d 440.

Ga.—Minkovitz v. Fine, 19 S.E.2d 561, 67 Ga.App. 176 (though doctrine may be applicable to make out prima facie case of negligence, can not be relied on to make out prima facie case of gross negligence).

Iowa.—Johnson v. Johnson, 1970, 174 N.W.2d 444; Harvey v. Clark, 1942, 6 N.W.2d 144, 232 Iowa 729, 143 A.L.R. 1141; Phillips v. Briggs, 245 N.W. 720, 215 Iowa 461.

Ky.—Carter v. Driver, 316 S.W.2d 378 (Illinois law).

Nev.—Garland v. Greenspan, 323 P.2d 27, 74 Nev. 88; Nyberg v. Kirby, 188 P.2d 1006, 65 Nev. 42, rehearing denied 193 P.2d 850, 65 Nev. 42 (applicable only in cases of ordinary negligence and cannot be invoked to establish gross negligence or willful misconduct).

Tenn.—Sloan v. Nevil, 229 S.W.2d 350, 33 Tenn.App. 100 (not applicable under Illinois guest statute).

Ambulance rider

La.—Rushing v. Mulhearn Funeral Home, App., 200 So. 52 (plaintiff with consent of ambulance driver entered ambulance to administer to sick man during course of trip, and plaintiff while ambulance was moving fell out of side door of ambulance, and plaintiff alleged that door opened because of pressure of plaintiff's body against it or because of plaintiff's knee resting against inside door lever or handle).

Inherently inconsistent

"In our opinion, the use of this doctrine for such a purpose * * * would be inconsistent with the doctrine itself. It applies only where the plaintiff does not know what caused the accident and negligence may be presumed from the fact that an accident occurred, in view of the general circumstances. But, where a plaintiff is required to prove not only negligence, but gross negligence, this very requirement would seem to imply the necessity of proving how the accident occurred and that certain facts exist which in themselves disclose the presence of gross negligence as distinguished from ordinary negligence." Lincoln v. Quick, 24 P.2d 245, 133 Cal.App. 433.

93. **Cal.**—Hert v. Firestone Tire & Rubber Co. of California, 41 P.2d 369, 4 Cal.App.2d 598.

Tex.—Schumacher Co. v. Shooter, 124 S.W.2d 857, 132 Tex. 560 (passenger's negligence).

94. **Okl.**—Sanders v. McMichael, 197 P.2d 280, 200 Okl. 501.

Chapter 419

EXAMINATION OF WITNESSES

Table of Sections

Sec.
419.1 In General.
419.2 Leading Questions.
419.3 Refreshing Recollection.

§ 419.1 In General

Library References:
C.J.S. Witnesses § 315 et seq.
West's Key No. Digests, Witnesses ⟐224 et seq.

A witness' examination should be controlled by exercise of the trial court's discretion to limit proof so as to develop the issues involved and aid the search for the truth.[1] The questions to witnesses should be required to be definite as to the intended meaning.[2]

1. **Cal.**—West's Ann.Calif.Evid. Code, § 765.
Colo.—Ager v. Adams, 395 P.2d 735, 155 Colo. 544.
Conn.—Fahey v. Clark, 3 A.2d 313, 125 Conn. 44, 120 A.L.R. 517.
Fla.—Florida Evidence Code § 90.-612(1).
Me.—Maine Rules of Evidence § 611(a).
Neb.—Nebraska Rules of Evidence § 611(1).
Nev.—N.R.S. § 50.115(1).
N.M.—New Mexico Rules of Evidence § 611(a).
Utah.—In re Baxter's Estate, 1965, 399 P.2d 442, 16 Utah 2d 284.
Wis.—Wisconsin Rules of Evidence § 906.11(1).

Should prevent inference party wrongfully inhibited on its proof
Trial judge should prevent interrogation which hints at existence of facts being withheld from jury by judge and implies that if the truth were known to jury facts withheld by judge would settle case in favor of party who is unable to present facts. Tippit v. Hunter, Miss., 1967, 205 So. 2d 267.

2. **U.S.**—New Orleans & N. E. R. Co. v. Weary, Miss., 1969, 217 So. 2d 274 (question on direct examination of plaintiff "just try to tell what you remember" was not improper as being too general in view of prior testimony that plaintiff had suffered damage to brain in collision with train which impaired his ability to comprehend).
Or.—Groce v. Fidelity General Ins. Co., 1968, 448 P.2d 554, 252 Or. 296 (can ask opposing attorney to define questionable or misleading or undefined terms used in question).

§ 419.1 TRIAL EVIDENCE Ch. 419

Testimony should be limited to first-hand knowledge,[3] but which may be as to facts learned subsequent to the event in question.[4]

Questions may not be argumentative,[5] and the court has broad discretion to permit or refuse repetitious questioning in the direct examination.[6] The question may not erroneously

---

3. **U.S.**—Federal Rules of Evidence, § 602, 28 U.S.C.A.; Hing Lee v. Gray, C.A.N.J.1972, 456 F.2d 1276 (defendant motorist who asserted defense of mechanical defect was competent to testify that car acted in given manner and about his attempts to control car).

Ariz.—Dobbertin v. Johnson, 390 P. 2d 849, 95 Ariz. 356 (may testify only to such subsidiary or extrinsic facts as are reasonably subject to objective and accurate perception by observers).

Cal.—West's Ann.Calif.Evid.Code, § 702.

Fla.—Florida Rules of Evidence § 90.604.

Kan.—Kansas Rules of Civil Procedure § 60–419.

Me.—Maine Rules of Evidence § 602.

Mo.—Nutz v. Sheperd, App.1973, 490 S.W.2d 366 (not one's "understanding").

Neb.—Nebraska Rules of Evidence § 602.

Nev.—N.R.S. 50.025(1)(a).

N.J.—New Jersey Evidence Rule 19.

N.M.—New Mexico Rules of Evidence § 602.

Tex.—Strickland Transp. Co. v. Ingram, 1966, 403 S.W.2d 192 (as to ownership).

Utah.—Utah Rules of Evidence, § 19.

Wis.—Wisconsin Rules of Evidence § 906.02.

Disqualified self

Refusal to allow plaintiff's counsel to further examine his witness in effort to establish the weight of plaintiff's employer's truck and its load at time of collision was not error where the witness had already testified that he did not know that fact. Braswell v. Owen of Georgia, Inc., 1973, 197 S.E.2d 463, 128 Ga.App. 528.

Insufficient knowledge as to street condition

Proffered testimony of man who, nine months before motor scooter accident allegedly caused by depression in street, excavated and refilled the area prior to its being paved by city, which testimony was needed as a predicate for the testimony of an expert who said that he could not give an opinion as to how long the depression existed without knowing nature of soil removed and replaced, its depth, whether there was a temporary or final surface placed over fill, whether it was compacted and the street's vehicular traffic, was properly excluded, since, even if the man could recall the nature and depth of replaced soil, there was no suggestion that he re-examined the surfacing after city put it down, or knew whether the fill had been compacted, or could supply information concerning traffic. Tangney v. City of New York, 1973, 341 N.Y.S.2d 116, 41 A.D.2d 621.

4. **Tex.**—Strickland Transp. Co. v. Ingram, Civ.App., 403 S.W.2d 192.

5. **Wash.**—Glazer v. Adams, 391 P. 2d 195, 64 Wash.2d 144.

6. **Ga.**—Sullivan v. State, 152 S.E. 2d 382, 222 Ga. 691 (sustaining objections was not abuse of discretion).

Ill.—Hann v. Milla, 237 N.E.2d 753, 95 Ill.App. 447 (where various questions had been asked four, five

assume that a material fact has been proved.[7]

Examination on documents should be limited to those in evidence.[8]

The answers must be responsive to the questions, but an improper answer may not constitute reversible error if the answer is merely irrelevant or immaterial, or if the issues are covered in other testimony.[9] Voluntary statements not responsive to the question, should be stricken on motion of examining counsel.[10]

and six times, trial court did not abuse its discretion by limiting further questioning); Barrett v. Wallenberg, 1965, 210 N.E.2d 782, 62 Ill.App.2d 478.

Ky.—Com., Dept. of Highways v. Smith, 1965, 390 S.W.2d 194.

Mass.—Hebert v. Massachusetts Bay Transp. Authority, App.1974, 305 N.E.2d 869.

Mich.—People v. Lloyd, 147 N.W.2d 740, 5 Mich.App. 717.

N.D.—Haugen v. Mid-State Aviation, Inc., 144 N.W.2d 692.

7. **Ala.**—Cherry v. Hill, 1968, 214 So.2d 427, 283 Ala. 74 (in action by father against motorist under the Homicide Act to recover for death of child who was struck while crossing a highway, on ground that motorist knew that pedestrians were accustomed to cross highway at point of accident and should have been driving in more prudent manner, objection to question asked witness how long witness had seen pedestrians use the place as a crossing was properly sustained, because question assumed, without more, that pedestrians had been using place as a crossing).

Wyo.—DeBaca v. State, 404 P.2d 738.

8. **Conn.**—State v. Sullivan, 199 A. 2d 709, 2 Conn.Cir. 412, certification and appeal denied 199 A.2d 705, 151 Conn. 737.

9. **Cal.**—West's Ann.Calif.Evid.Code § 766.

R.I.—Perry v. New England Transp. Co., 45 A.2d 481, 71 R.I. 352.

10. **Ill.**—Felton v. Coyle, 1968, 238 N.E.2d 191, 95 Ill.App.2d 202 (officer's answer to question as to what he observed about defendant's manner of speech, that officer did not think he could be judge of that but that it seemed that defendant had been drinking, was improper as volunteering information not responsive to question, and answer was properly stricken, there being no question pending as to whether defendant had been drinking).

Neb.—Cardenas v. Peterson Bean Co., 1966, 144 N.W.2d 154, 180 Neb. 605.

But see

Where plaintiff's answer to defendant's inquiry on cross-examination was relevant to issue of contributory negligence, it was within discretion of trial judge to allow answer to stand even though unresponsive. Brown v. Wong Gow Sue, 1968, 241 N.E.2d 919, 354 Mass. 646.

Requires motion

Cross-examination question whether driver had pleaded guilty to driving over center line was proper and permitting nonresponsive answer, that he had forfeited bond, to stand was not error where court was not called on by driver to make any ruling on the voluntary answer given, to give any admonition to the jury, or to do anything at all. Midwest Bus Lines, Inc. v. Williams, 1968, 422 S.W.2d 869, 243 Ark. 854.

§ 419.1

Calling adverse witness

In federal court, one is permitted to call a hostile witness, an adverse party, or a witness identified with an adverse party; and the interrogation may be by leading questions.[11] In some state jurisdictions, often by rule or statute, one is permitted to call an adverse party[12] or the agent of an adverse party[13] for

---

11. Federal Rules of Evidence § 611 (c), 28 U.S.C.A.

12. Cal.—West's Ann.Calif.Evid. Code, § 776.

Ill.—Hann v. Milla, 1968, 237 N.E.2d 753, 95 Ill.App.2d 447 (court's permitting defendant's counsel to question plaintiff, under statute permitting examination of adverse party, as to matters which had already been given in plaintiff's prior testimony was not error where purpose of later examination was in conjunction with admission of exhibits as part of defendant's case in chief); Lantz v. Dortman, 58 N.E.2d 992, 324 Ill.App. 564 (right denied as to one who was not adverse party as to one count).

Kan.—Riley v. Holcomb, 1961, 359 P.2d 849, 187 Kan. 711.

Me.—Maine Rules of Evidence § 611 (c).

Minn.—Bylund v. Carroll, 281 N.W. 873, 203 Minn. 484.

Neb.—Nebraska Rules of Evidence § § 611(3).

Nev.—N.R.S. 50.115(4).

N.M.—New Mexico Rules of Evidence § 611(c).

Ohio.—Murray v. Landenberger, 1966, 215 N.E.2d 412, 5 Ohio App. 2d 294.

Wis.—Wisconsin Rules of Evidence § 906.11(3).

Decedent's employer called in action against third party

Permitting wife in action against third-party tortfeasor for death of husband to call one of husband's employers and to examine him as though he had been called under statute was not abuse of discretion. Benwell v. Dean, 57 Cal.Rptr. 394, 249 Cal.App.2d 345.

Even where adverse party's insurer also a defendant

In wrongful death suit arising from accident in which automobile struck decedent as decedent was pouring gasoline into vehicle parked on shoulder, plaintiff had right under statute to cross examine defendant motorist on issue of negligence, though plaintiff had also named as defendant an alleged insurer of defendant motorist and such insurer had denied liability. Silva v. Allen, La.App.1972, 256 So.2d 447.

Workmen's compensation carrier representative

Workmen's compensation carrier which paid benefits to injured workman was "person for whose immediate benefit" the personal injury action by workman was prosecuted and was subject to have its officers, agents and employees called adversely by alleged tort-feasor. Skornia v. Highway Pavers, Inc., 148 N.W.2d 678, 34 Wis.2d 160.

13. Cal.—West's Ann.Calif.Evid. Code, § 776.

Ga.—Huell v. Southeastern Stages, 50 S.E.2d 745, 78 Ga.App. 311 (bus driver is "agent" within meaning of statute).

La.—Walters v. Seven Up Bottling Co. of Alexandria, 1968, 212 So.2d 443, writ refused 215 So.2d 124, 252 La. 948 (driver of truck); Liberty Mut. Ins. Co. v. Bryant, App., 191 So.2d 747 (under statute permitting cross-examination of any party or his representative by adverse party and defining representatives as agent having knowledge of matter in controversy, juveniles who allegedly damaged automobile of insured were subject to being called as representatives of their defendant fathers in insurer's action as subrogee even though juveniles were not joined with their fathers as parties defendant).

Me.—Maine Rules of Evidence § 611(c).

Mich.—Ruhaia v. Roby, 1966, 140 N.W.2d 785, 2 Mich.App. 557, affirmed 150 N.W.2d 146, 379 Mich. 102 (should announce intent to cross-examine).

Neb.—Nebraska Rules of Evidence § 611(3).

Nev.—N.R.S. 50.115(4)(b).

N.M.—New Mexico Rules of Evidence § 611(c).

Wis.—Wisconsin Rules of Evidence § 906.11(3).

Contra

In passenger's action, where bus driver was called as a witness by plaintiff for cross-examination under the statute, refusal to permit cross-examination of bus driver was not error where passenger, if she wished to bring the driver within the rule, could have joined him as a defendant and cross-examined him under the statute. S.H.A. c. 110, § 184. Olsen v. Evanston Bus Co., 30 N.E.2d 947, 307 Ill.App. 669.

Driver of independent company as agent

Where truck driver of independent business performing local pickup and delivery service of less than carload quantities of freight for railroad was agent of railroad within meaning of provision of Federal Employers' Liability Act rendering railroad liable for negligence of other's employees, driver was "agent" within rule providing that either party may call as an adverse witness any person who at time of happening of transaction was employee or agent of opposite party. Salvail v. Great Northern Ry. Co., 1970, 473 P.2d 549, 156 Mont. 12.

Erroneous instruction to jury

Refusal, in action by pedestrian struck by bus, and which was brought against bus company, its insurer and city, to grant plaintiffs' request to call city's special investigator adversely, and statement by trial judge, in presence of jury, that such police officer, whose testimony tended to show that pedestrian was negligent as to lookout, was "an independent witness" was error, though his testimony related directly only to negligence as between pedestrian and bus company, in view of applicability of comparative negligence law. Schueler v. City of Madison, 1971, 183 N.W.2d 116, 49 Wis.2d 695.

Insured not agent of insurer

Wife suing husband's insurer, but not husband who was driving vehicle in which she was injured, had no right to call husband for cross-examination as adverse witness; overruling Hunter v. United Services Automobile Ass'n, La.App., 129 So. 2d 908. LSA–C.C.P. art. 1634. Soprano v. State Farm Mut. Auto. Ins. Co., 165 So.2d 308, 246 La. 524. Automobile driver was not "representative", "officer", "agent", or "employee" of his automobile liability insurer within statute permitting a party or the party's officer, agent, representative, or employee to be called and cross-examined as an adverse witness. Id.

Must be officer or managing agent type

Allowing plaintiff to cross-examine truck driver under statute providing for examination of adverse party or agent of adverse party was error because truck driver was not included in types of persons who may be called as adverse witnesses under that statute since truck driver was not shown to have been an officer, director, managing agent, or foreman of the defendant truck owner.

§ 419.1   TRIAL EVIDENCE   Ch. 419

cross-examination. Such rules or statutes will be liberally construed and applied.[14] One who is named as a party, but who is in fact neither a necessary nor a proper party, may not be called as an adverse witness under such a rule or statute.[15]

Following plaintiff's cross-examination of a witness called as an adverse witness, the scope of further examination by the defendant is largely in the discretion of the court.[16]

S.H.A. ch. 110, § 60. Lamberes v. Northern Cartage Co., 1967, 229 N.E. 2d 901, 86 Ill.App.2d 311.

In automobile passenger's action against driver's insurer to set aside release of claim, insurance adjuster who was not shown to be either a party or a managing agent of insurer was not an adverse witness when called by passenger. Lambert v. State Farm Mut. Auto. Ins. Co., 1970, 467 P.2d 214, 2 Wash.App. 136.

Question is agency at time of trial

A witness called for cross-examination as an agent of opposite party must be the party's agent at time of trial and it is not sufficient that he was the party's agent at time of occurrence, and thus it was reversible error for trial judge to allow plaintiff to call a witness for cross-examination who was not agent of defendant at time of trial. Code, § 38–1801. Mullis v. Chaika, 1968, 162 S.E.2d 448, 118 Ga.App. 11.

14. Minn.—Bylund v. Carroll, 281 N.W. 873, 203 Minn. 484.

Ohio.—Bates v. Flath, 78 N.E.2d 56, 81 Ohio App. 188 (where plaintiff called the defendant for cross-examination, sustaining objection to all questions asked defendant concerning what happened or what he did immediately before collision was prejudicial error. Gen.Code, § 11497).

Pa.—Rudella v. Lofland, 1968, 247 A.2d 792, 213 Pa.Super. 305 (insured's interest in litigation was adverse to that of automobile liability insurer, in garnishment proceeding by insured's judgment creditors wherein insurer claimed that policy had been cancelled before accident, and insurer was entitled to call insured as on cross-examination).

15. Cal.—Gerhard v. Stephens, 1968, 442 P.2d 692, 69 Cal.Rptr. 612, 68 Cal.2d 864 (former Code of Civil Procedure permitting cross-examination of an adverse party gave no absolute right to examine a witness claiming adversely).

Pa.—Suckling v. Pennsylvania Threshermen & Farmers Mut. Cas. Ins. Co., 1967, 233 A.2d 279, 426 Pa. 503 (where driver of owner's automobile was insolvent and financially unable to pay judgment rendered against him in prior trespass action, and unpaid trespass judgment would be obstacle in his path toward any possible future solvency, and if assumpsit judgment were to be paid by automobile owner's insurer, driver would have vital interest, driver's interest was "adverse" to owner's insurer and insurer should have been permitted to call driver as on cross-examination).

Wis.—Locke v. General Accident Fire & Life Assur. Corporation, Limited, of Perth, Scotland, 279 N.W. 55, 227 Wis. 489 (owner of vehicle operated by secondary permittee).

16. Ill.—Darling v. Charleston Community Memorial Hospital, 200 N.E.2d 149, 50 Ill.App.2d 253, affirmed, 211 N.E.2d 253, 33 Ill.2d 326, certiorari denied 86 S.Ct. 1204, 383 U.S. 946, 16 L.Ed. 209 (should not be so extended as to interject defense into plaintiff's case at that stage of the trial).

Redirect examination

Upon redirect examination, a witness may explain matters brought out on cross-examination,[17] including the development of

Limited to subject of prior examination

Colo.—Burr v. Green Bros. Sheet Metal, Inc., 409 P.2d 511, 159 Colo. 25 (also by leading questions).

Ill.—La Prise v. Carr-Leasing, Inc., 62 N.E.2d 26, 326 Ill.App. 514.

Iowa.—Womochil v. Peters, 285 N.W. 151, 226 Iowa 924 (in passenger's action, where plaintiff called defendant taxicab driver as witness, witness' cross-examination was properly limited to matters brought out on direct examination, since witness might be regarded as hostile to plaintiff's cause).

N.J.—Vargo v. P. Ballantine & Sons, 197 A. 52, 119 N.J.L. 561 (in bus passenger's action for injuries sustained in collision between bus and truck, truck owner's cross-examination of truck driver and his assistant as to what bus driver said after the collision was properly excluded where direct examination was limited to matters occurring before the collision and the vehicles' positions afterwards and cross-examination was not intended to affect credibility of witnesses or of bus driver who had not yet testified).

Pa.—Tolomeo v. Harmony Short Line Motor Transp. Co., 37 A.2d 511, 349 Pa. 420 (where plaintiffs were compelled to summon bus driver in order to establish that he was driving bus as defendant's agent, it was error to permit defendant to cross-examine driver, over plaintiffs' objection, on subject of negligence generally, and prejudicial where witnesses' testimony was educed by leading questions and court's charge intensified the error).

17. **Cal.**—West's Ann.Calif.Evid. Code, § 774; Myers v. Rose, 80 P.2d 527, 27 Cal.App.2d 87.

Conn.—Kucza v. Stone, 1967, 230 A.2d 559, 155 Conn. 194.

Ill.—Rzeszewski v. Barth, 58 N.E.2d 269, 324 Ill.App. 345; Wist v. Pitcairn, 26 N.E.2d 998, 305 Ill.App. 167.

Mich.—Hammock v. Sims, 21 N.W.2d 118, 313 Mich. 248 (speed of truck).

Mo.—James v. LaMear, App., 189 S.W.2d 131 (contra where cross-examination only developed suggestion of existence of other information, and not the content).

N.Y.—People v. Regina, 277 N.Y.S.2d 683, 19 N.Y.2d 65, 224 N.E.2d 108 (prosecution's question, on redirect examination of police officer who had testified on cross-examination that he had made no notes on night that he had allegedly seen defendant riding as passenger in automobile, whether officer had ever made notes of such occurrence and his answer that he had done so three days later).

Pa.—Quartz v. City of Pittsburgh, 16 A.2d 400, 340 Pa. 277 (where plaintiff was confronted on cross-examination with fact that in prior action she had claimed impairment of nervous system, refusal to allow plaintiff's counsel to examine her concerning actual extent of her injuries in the former accident was error).

Tex.—Lockley v. Page, 180 S.W.2d 616, 142 Tex. 594 (driver's testimony on redirect that he could have seen plaintiff's car had it had lights was entitled to consideration to explain driver's previous testimony that he was blinded by lights of approaching automobile).

§ 419.1   TRIAL EVIDENCE   Ch. 419

the balance of a prior statement referred to on cross-examination.[18] Evidence relevant to the issues should be elicited on

But see

Refusal to allow plaintiffs to rehabilitate police officer witness by showing on redirect that officer left scene of accident immediately to give breathalyzer test to defendant to explain to jury the reason for officer's failure to make more detailed investigation of accident was not an abuse of discretion, where defendant admitted that he had been drinking prior to accident and had entered guilty plea to charge of driving while intoxicated on day of accident and such evidence could have been offered on direct testimony of officer. Jensen v. Walker, Mo.App.1973, 496 S.W.2d 317.

Contra where prior testimony inconsequential

Testimony of police officer, or cross-examination by plaintiff, as to what witnesses he had interviewed and what notes he had taken at scene of accident did not raise any unfavorable implications which entitled defendant to counter or correct on redirect examination where officer did not testify as to content of his notes or conversations he had with witnesses. Day v. Goodwin, 1970, 478 P.2d 774, 3 Wash.App. 940.

Good character evidence held proper rebuttal

Permitting line of questioning of defendant as to defendant's teaching of Sunday school and affiliation with scouting was not such an abuse of discretion as to deny plaintiffs a fair and impartial trial where defendant's testimony was brought out in supplementation and explanation of testimony solicited by plaintiffs' counsel. Murnigham v. Dark, 1970, 268 A.2d 274, 107 R.I. 457.

Limitation not prejudicial

N.C.—Key v. Merritt-Holland Welding Supplies, Inc., 1969, 169 S.E.2d 27, 5 N.C.App. 654 (officer had already exhaustively described marks on highway).

Right to see document referred to in cross-examination

Failure of defendant's counsel to obey court's order to allow plaintiff's counsel to see disputed statement of plaintiff's witness before redirect examination constituted prejudicial error where testimony of the witness who saw the accident was undoubtedly important, witness was a disinterested party, and limited use of witness' previous statement during cross-examination weakened the testimony given by him on direct examination. Arnovitz v. Wozar, 222 N.E.2d 660, 9 Ohio App.2d 16.

Rule illustrated

Admission of explanation by witness on redirect examination that she noticed whistles of trains because about a month prior to accident involved in litigation she had almost been hit at same crossing because no whistle was sounded by train was not error where witness had testified on direct examination that up to particular time train had not whistled or rung bell, and on cross-examination had been asked whether she like most people that live around railroad crossing wouldn't pay any attention to trains' whistles. St. Louis-San Francisco Ry. Co. v. Kilgore, Okl., 366 P.2d 936.

18. See section 421.6 for discussion generally as to rehabilitation after impeachment.

Cal.—Hawkinson v. Oesdean, 1944, 143 P.2d 967, 61 Cal.App.2d 712.

Ill.—People v. Ray, 1966, 222 N.E. 2d 176, 77 Ill.App.2d 166.

Ind.—Elgin, J. & E. Ry. Co. v. Collins, 1970, 260 N.E.2d 810, 147 Ind. App. 343.

Ch. 419　　EXAMINATION OF WITNESSES　　§ 419.1

direct examination, and it may not be error for the court to refuse the right to recall the witness at a later stage in the trial.[19]

Examination by court

The court may examine a witness [20] when the examination is conducted fairly and impartially and elicits material facts

Neb.—Marquardt v. Nehawka Farmers Co-op Co., 1971, 184 N.W. 2d 617, 186 Neb. 494.

N.H.—Williams v. Williams, 1935, 182 A. 172, 87 N.H. 430 (as to other statements in deposition).

N.Y.—Friedman v. N. Y. City Omnibus Corp., 1947, 70 N.Y.S.2d 628, 272 App.Div. 265.

Tex.—Acker v. Thompson, Civ.App. 1939, 128 S.W.2d 852, reversed by agreement.

Denied right while still on cross-examination

Where, when plaintiff was cross-examining defendant's witness and plaintiff read paragraph of letter witness had written to defendant's attorney and asked witness if he agreed with it, the witness said that he did, refusal of defendant's request to read entire letter into evidence at that point was not an abuse of discretion as one party cannot interrupt another party's cross-examination for purpose of starting its redirect examination and if defendant desired to introduce letter in its entirety he should have done so at close of plaintiff's cross-examination. Van Welden v. Ramsay's Inc., 1967, 430 P.2d 298, 199 Kan. 417.

Reference to prior statement as to photograph mentioned in cross-examination

Where defense cross-examined plaintiff driver as to whether she had at any time testified or pointed out on photograph that her automobile had been 15 or 20 feet ahead of stop sign after collision with defendant's truck at intersection, plaintiffs' redirect examination of plaintiff driver regarding the photograph, which was not produced at the second trial but had been introduced at first trial, was within scope of defendant's cross-examination and was not improper. Rose v. B. L. Cartage Co., 1969, 249 N.E.2d 199, 110 Ill. App.2d 260.

19. **Pa.**—Stively v. Rineer, 59 Lanc. Rev. 129.

20. **U.S.**—Federal Rules of Evidence § 614, 28 U.S.C.A.; Atlantic Greyhound Corp. v. Eddins, C.A.S.C., 177 F.2d 954.

Cal.—Schonberg v. Perry, 55 Cal. Rptr. 579, 247 Cal.App.2d 436.

Fla.—Florida Rules of Evidence § 90.-615(2).

Ga.—Atlanta Stove Works, Inc. v. Hollon, 146 S.E.2d 358, 112 Ga. App. 862 (asked witness whether either vehicle ran a red light).

Ill.—People v. King, 200 N.E.2d 411, 50 Ill.App.2d 421.

Me.—Maine Rules of Evidence § 614.

Neb.—Nebraska Rules of Evidence § 614.

Nev.—N.R.S. 50.145.

N.M.—New Mexico Rules of Evidence § 614.

Or.—Frangos v. Edmunds, 1946, 173 P.2d 596, 179 Or. 577.

Wis.—Wisconsin Rules of Evidence § 906.14.

Held improper

N.Y.—Siefring v. Marion, 1964, 253 N.Y.S.2d 619, 22 A.D.2d 765 (should not have interrupted frequently, particularly during cross-examination of medical expert).

§ 419.1   TRIAL EVIDENCE   Ch. 419

which aid the jury in understanding the issues to be decided.[21] However, the court must be careful not to give, either by intonation of voice or the character of the question, the impression to the jury of leaning to one side or the other.[22] The court may also call a witness initially,[23] after which both parties have a right of cross-examination.[24]

"Right and duty"

District judge has right and duty to elicit facts from witnesses in order to obtain clear presentation of issues. Spindler v. U. S., C.A.Cal., 336 F.2d 678.

Witness confused

Where cross-examination concerning former testimony confused witness, it was not improper for court to read the former testimony and ask witness to explain it. Montifue v. American Mut. Liability Ins. Co., La.App., 26 So.2d 407.

21. **U.S.**—Jackson v. U. S., 329 F.2d 893, 117 U.S.App.D.C. 325 (may intercede with caution because of seeming inadequacy of examination of witnesses by counsel, and to draw more information from reluctant witnesses or experts who are either inarticulate, less than candid or not adequately interrogated).

Ariz.—Ruth v. Rhodes, 185 P.2d 304, 66 Ariz. 129.

Cal.—Burns v. California Transport, 200 P.2d 43, 89 Cal.App.2d 70.

Ill.—People v. Crouch, 222 N.E.2d 46, 77 Ill.App.2d 290 (with restraint and circumspection).

22. **U.S.**—DiBello v. Rederi A/B Svenska Lloyd, C.A.N.Y., 371 F.2d 559 (should exercise self-restraint and preserve an atmosphere of impartiality and detachment); U. S. v. Hill, C.A.Ill., 332 F.2d 105.

Ariz.—Ruth v. Rhodes, 185 P.2d 304, 66 Ariz. 129.

N.C.—Southwire Co. v. Long Mfg. Co., 1971, 183 S.E.2d 253, 12 N.C. App. 335 (went beyond the clarification stage).

S.C.—Williams v. South Carolina Farm Bureau Mut. Ins., 1968, 163 S.E.2d 212, 251 S.C. 464, appeal after remand 164 S.E.2d 794, 253 S.C. 53 (discretion of trial judge is not controlled except where it appears that manner in which judge exercised right tended to unduly impress jury with importance of testimony elicited, or would be likely to lead jury to suppose judge was of opinion that one party rather than other was correct upon particular issue of fact).

Held prejudicial

Where judge asked plaintiff's medical witness as to cause of plaintiff's injuries, and fact of injury and relation of plaintiff's condition to accident were contested by defendants, and plaintiff's case consisted of only three witnesses, judge's questions, which assumed fact of injury and which by trial judge's admission had material and substantial influence upon jury, were prejudicial and required new trial. Risley v. Moberg, 419 P.2d 151, 69 Wash. 2d 560.

23. **U.S.**—Federal Rules of Evidence § 614(a), 28 U.S.C.A.; Smith v. U. S., C.A.Iowa 1964, 331 F.2d 265.

Cal.—West's Ann.Calif.Evid.Code, § 775.

Fla.—Florida Rules of Evidence § 90.615(1).

Me.—Maine Rules of Evidence § 614.

Neb.—Nebraska Rules of Evidence § 614.

Nev.—N.R.S. 50.145.

24. See note 24 on page 225.

§ 419.2 Leading Questions

Library References:
C.J.S. Witnesses § 329 et seq.
West's Key No. Digests, Witnesses ⌾239 et seq.

Whether counsel should be permitted to ask leading questions of one's own witness is within the discretion of the trial court;[25] stated in the federal rule and in some state rules to be proper when "necessary" to develop testimony.[26]

N.M.—New Mexico Rules of Evidence § 614.

Wis.—Wisconsin Rules of Evidence § 906.14.

Court's refusal upon request

Where defendant, seeking to have a witness called as a court's witness, failed to show that he was caught by surprise or by a showing of hostility from that witness, trial court properly denied defendant's motion to call the witness as a court's witness. People v. Davis, 223 N.E.2d 214, 78 Ill.App.2d 86.

Witness once a party-defendant

Where plaintiff sued two defendants for damages sustained when automobiles of defendants collided, and first defendant's automobile veered out of control and collided with plaintiff's automobile, and first defendant stated that she intended to call second defendant as adverse party until second defendant was dismissed out of the suit shortly before trial, when second defendant paid plaintiff $2,000, and plaintiff executed covenant not to sue second defendant, trial court did not abuse its discretion in calling second defendant as its own witness over objection of plaintiff. Green v. Smith, 207 N.E.2d 169, 59 Ill.App.2d 279.

Witness recalled by court to perfect record

Basis for objecting to calling witness back to stand as court's witness is effect such action may have on jury; and appellant could not have been harmed where court heard evidence without jury and purpose of recalling witness was to obtain testimony which had been erroneously rejected when offered earlier by appellant. Wabash Life Ins. Co. v. Cadillac Associates, Inc., 219 N.E.2d 639, 72 Ill.App.2d 413.

24. **U.S.**—Smith v. U. S., C.A.Iowa, 331 F.2d 265.

25. **U.S.**—Esco Corp. v. U. S., C.A. Or., 340 F.2d 1000; U. S. v. Barrow, D.C.Pa., 229 F.Supp. 722.

Alaska.—Groseth v. Ness, 421 P.2d 624 (refusal to permit pedestrian's counsel to ask leading questions of pedestrian as to why he had not obtained an attorney was not abuse of discretion in action to determine whether defendant was estopped by its adjuster's conduct from asserting defense of statute of limitations).

Ariz.—State v. Hunter, 423 P.2d 727, 5 Ariz.App. 112, modified on other grounds 433 P.2d 22, 102 Ariz. 472 (not every question that is capable of being answered with simple yes or no answer is subject to valid objection).

Ill.—People v. Ferrara, 221 N.E.2d 144, 75 Ill.App.2d 346.

Mass.—Com. v. Subilosky, 224 N.E. 2d 197, 352 Mass. 153 (narrow exclusions unnecessarily delay and interrupt the course of trial and should be avoided).

Me.—Towle v. Aube, 1973, 310 A. 2d 259.

26. See note 26 on page 226.

§ 419.2

Miss.—New Orleans & N. E. R. Co. v. Weary, 1969, 217 So.2d 274 (permitting question on direct examination of plaintiff "did you get well from that operation" was within discretion in view of prior testimony that plaintiff had suffered damage to brain impairing ability to comprehend).

Mo.—Sheets v. Kurth, 1968, 426 S.W.2d 103 (will not constitute reversible error unless discretion is abused).

N.H.—Atherton v. Rowe, 195 A. 676, 89 N.H. 196.

N.J.—Williams v. Guerreri, 54 A.2d 198, 136 N.J.L. 60.

Pa.—Rozik v. Heilman, 45 Wash.Co. 189 (where he is liberal as to both sides, where the accident is eight years old, and where counsel is inexperienced, no error is committed in a liberal construction of the rule).

Tex.—American Sur. Co. v. McCarty, 395 S.W.2d 665 (asking witness if he had same control over pickup assigned to him as he would have over his own private vehicle was leading question, but allowing question was not an abuse of discretion in case tried to court.)

Wis.—Rausch v. Buisse, 146 N.W.2d 801, 33 Wis.2d 154 (question may suggest a subject but not an answer).

Contra

Fla.—Florida Rules of Evidence § 90.612(3)(a).

Definition of leading

Suggestive question is "leading" and hence improper only if it so suggests to the witness the specific tenor of the reply desired by counsel that such reply is likely to be given irrespective of an actual memory. Urbani v. Razza, 1968, 238 A.2d 383, 103 R.I. 445.

Held error to allow

Allowing defense counsel to lead defendant truck driver into stating while testifying in his own behalf that he first saw plaintiff's automobile as it was just entering the intersection, whereas he had stated while testifying as an adverse witness for plaintiff that he had first seen the automobile when it was about half way through the intersection, and allowing driver to explain that contradiction was due to nervousness as an adverse witness, a subjective conclusion the record failed to disclose, was reversible error. Matthews v. Ballard, Miss., 1969, 217 So.2d 518.

Multiple status of party

Where same taxicab driver was defendant in wrongful death and personal injury actions and plaintiff in action against the Unsatisfied Claim and Judgment Fund Board, he could not be bifurcated to permit counsel representing him as defendant to ask leading questions and to cross-examine him after he was examined on direct by counsel who represented him as plaintiff; the attorneys could divide their areas of participation as they chose, but they had the rights of one. Sun Cab Co. v. Walston, 1972, 289 A.2d 804, 15 Md.App. 113, affirmed 298 A.2d 391, 267 Md. 559.

Neither as to own party called by opponent

When a party is called as a witness by the adverse party, the witness is adverse, thus permitting the calling party the leeway of leading questions on direct examination; conversely, on cross-examination of that witness by his own counsel, the witness remains adverse to the calling party and leading questions are not permitted. Zukowsky v. Brown, 1971, 488 P.2d 269, 79 Wash.2d 586.

26. **U.S.**—Federal Rules of Evidence § 611(c), 28 U.S.C.A.

Me.—Maine Rules of Evidence § 611(c).

Neb.—Nebraska Rules of Evidence § 611(3).

Various questions have been held to be leading;[27] and others not to have been leading.[28]

If proper questions are erroneously excluded as leading, but the subject is completely covered in subsequent questions, the error may be deemed harmless.[29]

N.M.—New Mexico Rules of Evidence § 611(c).

Wis.—Wisconsin Rules of Evidence § 906.11(3).

27. **Ala.**—Yeager v. Miller, 1970, 240 So.2d 221, 286 Ala. 38 (question, "was it a strong odor?" directed to plaintiff by plaintiff's counsel in attempt to elicit whether defendant had strong odor of whiskey on his breath following collision, was leading).

Cal.—Gladstone v. Fortier, 70 P.2d 255, 22 Cal.App.2d 1 (whether vehicle was not 20 to 25 feet from curve when other vehicle first appeared).

Fla.—Jack v. State, 183 So.2d 296 (questions put to defendant by his attorney as to whether a lot of his friends knew where he kept keys to his automobile and whether any of his friends had ever had opportunity to see where defendant left keys when he left the vehicle).

Mass.—Carney v. Bereault, 204 N.E. 2d 448, 348 Mass. 502 ("and they [the brakes] needed adjustment, as you knew, to hold the car in place?").

Could not be cured by instruction

La.—Lefevre v. Allstate Ins. Co., App.1972, 258 So.2d 397 (question of defense counsel on direct examination of defendant wife as to whether defendants' daughter had told defendant wife that plaintiff's son had climbed into husband's automobile with defendants' daughter and moved lever of transmission was improper and contained suggested answer which was not admissible, and instruction to disregard question could not have erased from minds of jurors the impression that plaintiff's son, injured when automobile parked by defendant wife rolled down incline and into street, may have climbed into vehicle and moved transmission lever).

28. **Ga.**—Lowe v. Athens Marble & Granite Co., 1961, 122 S.E.2d 483, 104 Ga.App. 642 (question as to length of a second, after driver testified that impact occurred "just a matter of a second" after he stopped truck).

La.—Franklin v. New Orleans Public Service, App.1939, 187 So. 126 ("from the time that it stopped and from the time that you heard someone say: 'Don't move the bus', did the bus move forward any?").

Me.—Towle v. Aube, 1973, 310 A. 2d 259 (inquiry as to whether there had been anything about plaintiff's driving that seemed to be affected by his drinking did not constitute a "leading question" subject to exclusion).

Ohio.—Netzley v. Nationwide Mut. Ins. Co., 1973, 296 N.E.2d 550, 34 Ohio App.2d 65 (whether questions could be answered "yes" or "no" was not correct criteria for determining if they were leading).

N.J.—Rider v. Lynch, 201 A.2d 561, 42 N.J. 465 (questions "Did you explain how you happened to have the car?" and "Do you recall what was said about how you happened to get the car?", were not offensively leading, but at most called attention to topic of subject about which testimony was desired).

29. **Cal.**—Germ v. City and County of San Francisco, 222 P.2d 122, 99 Cal.App.2d 404.

§ 419.2   TRIAL EVIDENCE   Ch. 419

A party may ask leading questions of a witness called by that party where the witness is "hostile",[30] and where the party is surprised by the witness' testimony.[31] However, where the

30. **U.S.**—U. S. v. Barrow, D.C.Pa., 229 F.Supp. 722 (known recalcitrant and hostile witness).

Ill.—Turnbull v. Porter, 206 N.E.2d 97, 55 Ill.App.2d 374 (held refusal not abuse of discretion).

Minn.—Holmboe v. Cook, 1970, 179 N.W.2d 276, 288 Minn. 222 (friend of opponent, and court stated was sarcastic and answering with wisecracks).

N.Y.—Cornwell v. Cleveland, 1974, 355 N.Y.S.2d 679, 44 A.D.2d 891 (improperly limited).

Ohio.—Oleksiw v. Weidener, 207 N. E.2d 375, 2 Ohio St.2d 147.

Tex.—Bryant v. Trinity Universal Ins. Co., 411 S.W.2d 945 (where witness was brought into court under attachment after he ignored two subpoenas and when interrogated the witness repeatedly stated that he could not remember what had happened).

Definition of hostile

A "hostile witness" who may be interrogated by leading questions is one who demonstrates by his demeanor that he is hostile. Lambert v. State Farm Mut. Auto. Ins. Co., 1970, 467 P.2d 214, 2 Wash.App. 136.

Definition of "managing agent"

A "managing agent," within rule authorizing a party to call a managing agent of a public or private corporation which is an adverse party and to interrogate such agent by leading questions, is one who, as to particular subject matter of litigation, acts with superior authority and is invested with general control to exercise his discretion on behalf of his principal on an overall or partial basis and can be expected to identify himself with interests of his principal rather than those of other party.

Hodgins v. Oles, 1973, 505 P.2d 825, 8 Wash.App. 279.

Limited as to certain issues

Where driver defendant's interests were only adverse to those of plaintiff on issue of liability, but not on issue of whether driver defendant was employed by another defendant, trial court did not err in refusing to permit plaintiff to examine driver defendant adversely as to question of his employment. West v. Aipperspach, 1974, 221 N.W.2d 1, —— S.D. ——.

Not defendant's employee driver

Pa.—Kauffman v. Carlisle Cement Products Co., Inc., 1974, 323 A.2d 750, 227 Pa.Super. 320 (driver had no pecuniary interest, direct or otherwise, in the outcome of the case).

Test of "adverse"

U.S.—Chumbler v. Alabama Power Co., C.A.Ala., 362 F.2d 161 (whether party sought to be called could have been sued either instead of named defendant or as codefendant; if so, and if witness is alleged tort-feasor and if standard for recovery would be same whichever was sued, he is adverse party within meaning of rule).

31. **Cal.**—Gladstone v. Fortier, 70 P. 2d 255, 22 Cal.App.2d 1 (not permitted where testified of inability to estimate a distance, and where in deposition "imagined" it was a certain distance).

Ill.—Tarasuik v. Russell, 199 N.E.2d 629, 49 Ill.App.2d 418 (defendant, who had talked to witness before trial then called him as a witness, vouched for his witness and could not claim surprise and could not cross-examine him or have him made a court witness).

basis is surprise, the right to lead is limited to inquiry as to the subject of the prior inconsistent statement.[32]

§ 419.3   Refreshing Recollection

Library References:
C.J.S. Witnesses § 357 et seq.
West's Key No. Digests, Witnesses ☞253 et seq.

A witness may gain refreshment of memory, either before or during trial, by referring to memoranda, reports or other documents;[33] except, as in some states, it may be required that the

Kan.—Riley v. Holcomb, 359 P.2d 849, 187 Kan. 711 (should have been permitted to cross-examine highway patrolman called as their witness as to whether he had studied manual supplied to troopers of State Highway Patrol and, if he had, whether he applied physical facts obtained at scene of accident to scientific findings contained in manual, after he gave his opinion that defendant was not driving more than 70 miles an hour).

Tenn.—Sanders v. McNatt, 1968, 430 S.W.2d 797, 58 Tenn.App. 385 (where defense counsel called as defense witness the driver of automobile in which plaintiff was passenger, trial court's refusal to permit defense counsel to cross-examine witness after her testimony on cross-examination by plaintiff's counsel allegedly surprised defense counsel was not an abuse of discretion).

32. Ill.—Schoolfield v. Witkowski, 203 N.E.2d 460, 54 Ill.App.2d 111 (to specifically call attention of witness to former statements made by him for purpose of refreshing his memory or awakening his conscience, but may go no further, and under no circumstances may show, either by written statement of witness or by other witnesses, that witness did, in fact, make those statements).

33. U.S.—Sayen v. Rydzewski, C.A. Wis.1967, 387 F.2d 815 (no error in failing to strike testimony of public health service physician regarding his examination and treatment of plaintiff over years on behalf of the Coast Guard from which plaintiff had been forced to retire following accident, although physician referred from time to time to notes which had been typed by his wife from his original hand written notations which were not produced for examination, despite objection that physician was relying entirely on typed notes and had no present recollection, since it appeared that physician may have relied on notes for dates but did have a recollection as to other matters).

Ala.—McCright v. State, 189 So.2d 581, 43 Ala.App. 292, certiorari denied 189 So.2d 583.

Cal.—People v. Seiterle, 54 Cal.Rptr. 745, 420 P.2d 217 (prior testimony of party's own witness may be used).

Dist.Col.—Fistere, Inc. v. Helz, Mun. App., 226 A.2d 578 (is largely within discretion of trial judge).

Fla.—King v. Califano, Fla.App., 183 So.2d 719 (refusal to permit officer who investigated collision to refresh his recollection from notes copied from and identical to notes he made at the scene was error).

Ga.—Stubbs v. Daughtry, 153 S.E.2d 633, 115 Ga.App. 22 (police officer who investigated collision could use his report).

Idaho.—Bell in O'Connor Transport Limited, 1971, 489 P.2d 439, 94 Idaho 406 (officer used his accident report).

Ill.—Kerz v. Arkin, 1971, 278 N.E. 2d 124, 2 Ill.App.3d 1057 (police officer to whom plaintiff reported accident had no independent recollection of his conversation with plaintiff); Tuskey v. Callos, 1969, 250 N.E.2d 524, 112 Ill.App.2d 213 (allowing officer who had investigated automobile-pedestrian accident to refresh his recollection from report which he made shortly after accident as to language used by pedestrian at time of investigation); Hall v. Checker Taxi Co., 1969, 248 N.E.2d 721, 109 Ill.App. 2d 445 (testimony of police officer, who did not observe accident, as to weather and road conditions and speed and distance that automobiles traveled before and after impact, after refreshing his memory from accident report); Frank v. Davies, 1966, 214 N.E.2d 297, 66 Ill.App.2d 271; Adamaitis v. Hesser, 206 N.E. 2d 311, 56 Ill.App.2d 349 (allowing doctor to refresh his recollection from report was not error because testimony indicated that he saw report for the first time on day of trial, he had no copy of it in his files and he was never asked whether notations had been made by him, or, if so, when, where records for period involved had been destroyed, and only plausible inference was that he dictated the letter and caused it to be mailed, and he unequivocally asserted that it did refresh his recollection).

Minn.—Ackerman v. Theis, 1968, 160 N.W.2d 583, 281 Minn. 82 (always proper to use an accident report to refresh witness' memory whether it is received in evidence or not).

Mo.—Dudeck v. Ellis, 399 S.W.2d 80; Davis v. Werremeyer, 377 S.W.2d 319 (witness testified that defendant had said that collision was defendant's fault but did not add defendant's admission that defendant had not had time to stop, permitted to refresh memory of witness from witness' written statement and to elicit the additional admission); Smith v. Bergmann, 377 S.W.2d 519 (paper which he had prepared the night before testifying to refresh his recollection as to how much time he had lost from work as result of accident); Voyles v. Columbia Terminals Co., App., 223 S.W.2d 870 (where police officers who testified for defendant had no part in the preparation of accident report, permitting plaintiff, on pretext of refreshing recollections of police officers, to discredit their testimony was reversible error).

Neb.—Anderson v. State, 33 N.W.2d 362, 150 Neb. 116.

Or.—Waterway Terminals Co. v. P. S. Lord Mechanical Contractors, 406 P.2d 556, 242 Or. 1 (by calling to attention of witness his earlier oral statements or by memorandum not made by witness).

Pa.—Kofalt, Inc. v. Massachusetts Bonding & Ins. Co., Com.Pl., 77 York 121 (any writing).

Tex.—J. A. Robinson Sons, Inc. v. Wigart, Civ.App.1967, 420 S.W.2d 474, reversed on other grounds, 431 S.W.2d 327 (generally, any writing may be used).

Wis.—Kenwood Equipment, Inc. v. Aetna Ins. Co., 1970, 180 N.W.2d 750, 48 Wis.2d 472, rehearing 182 N.W.2d 241, 48 Wis.2d 472.

Actual refreshment challenged

Permitting highway patrolman, who wrote accident report, to testify from report as a refreshing of recollection was not error on theory that he had no independent recollection without the report and that proper foundation had not been laid where, though officer testified that "The only thing I have to go on as far as memory is concerned is from my report, as far as actually getting it down on my own, I can't do it"

writing have been prepared by the witness or have been once verified by the witness.[34] Both parties may seek to refresh a witness' memory.[35]

Memory may not be refreshed from a statement which is inadmissible under a statute restricting use of certain statements taken from injured persons.[36]

and that "I am telling you what is in the report after I studied it * * *" he also testified, inter alia, that he remembered certain particulars about which he testified independently of the report. Massee v. State Farm Mut. Auto. Ins. Co., 1973, 197 S.E.2d 459, 128 Ga.App. 439.

But see

N.H.—Bartis v. Warrington, 20 A.2d 642, 91 N.H. 415 (where witness' testimony was positive, on both direct and cross-examination, that speed was 15 to 20 m. p. h., could not be refreshed as to deposition statement that it "flashed" across the street).

Rule limited

Where witness was not specifically asked to refresh his recollection, moving party failed to lay proper foundation and thus could not rely on rule permitting witness to refresh his recollection. Katz v. Exclusive Auto Leasing, Inc., Del.Super.1971, 282 A.2d 866.

34. **Ga.**—Wallis v. Odom, 1973, 203 S.E.2d 613, 130 Ga.App. 437 (did not err in refusing to allow police officer to refresh his memory from police reports prepared by another, where, although officer had participated in investigation and in writing pen and ink police report, the document submitted was typewritten by another).

Made or verified at reasonably contemporaneous time

A writing to be used for the purpose of refreshing the recollection of a witness must be made reasonably contemporaneously with the matter recorded by the witness himself or made by another under his supervision or verified by him. Jackson v. Feather, 112 P.L.J. 27.

35. **Ill.**—Barrett v. Wallenberg, 210 N.E.2d 782, 62 Ill.App.2d 478.

Mass.—Leonard v. Taylor, 53 N.E.2d 705, 315 Mass. 580, 151 A.L.R. 1002.

N.J.—Hess v. Hess, 200 A.2d 627, 83 N.J.Super. 583 (entitled to inspect and use on cross-examination notes of witness for adverse party even though witness had not used them to refresh his recollection); Echtermacht v. Cohen, 265 N.Y.S.2d 422, 24 A.D.2d 968 (was error to refuse to permit defendants' counsel to test police officer's testimony, favorable to plaintiff, by examining him with respect to memorandum book which officer had with him when he testified, although he did not refer to it while testifying).

Or.—Waterway Terminals Co. v. P. S. Lord Mechanical Contractors, 406 P.2d 556, 242 Or. 1.

Wash.—McCoy v. Courtney, 190 P.2d 732, 30 Wash.2d 125.

36. **Minn.**—Hillesheim v. Stippel, 1969, 166 N.W.2d 325, 283 Minn. 59 (if a statement taken from an injured person is inadmissible under statute because a copy of it was not furnished to the person from whom the statement was taken, it would be improper to admit its contents by permitting one who prepared it to refresh his memory by reading the statement and then testifying as to its contents).

§ 419.3 TRIAL EVIDENCE Ch. 419

In federal court (except as to Jencks statute matters in criminal cases), the writing must be presented for inspection and use in cross-examination by the adverse party whenever the witness uses the writing for refreshment while testifying and also when used before testifying when the court should determine that the interests of justice require production.[37]

In state courts, the rule usually was that a memorandum used for refreshment before testifying need not be produced to the opposing party.[38] However, some states have followed the federal rule, and require its production in such instances.[39]

However where used during trial, it must be given to the opposite party for examination and use in further examination of the witness.[40]

Normally, such memoranda and other writings are used only to refresh the memory of the witness, and may not be introduced as evidence.[41]

---

37. Federal Rules of Evidence § 612, 28 U.S.C.A.

38. **Or.**—Marsh v. Davidson, 1973, 510 P.2d 558, 265 Or. 532 (where notes of interview which were in possession of claimant's representative when he testified were not referred to by him and were not introduced into evidence, plaintiff was not entitled to recross-examine witness concerning notes).

39. **Cal.**—West's Ann.Calif.Evid. Code, § 771.

Me.—Maine Rules of Evidence § 612 (b).

Neb.—Nebraska Rules of Evidence § 612.

Nev.—NRS 50.125.

N.M.—New Mexico Rules of Evidence § 612.

Wis.—Wisconsin Rules of Evidence § 906.12.

And see

In action against taxicab owner by passenger, it was error to refuse to direct owner to produce at trial written statement made by taxicab driver immediately following accident, and since such statement was relevant to plaintiff's case and could have proved useful to plaintiff's attorney for purpose of impeachment or testing driver's credibility, error would require reversal of judgment for taxicab owner. Cox v. Yellow Cab Co., 1974, 16 Ill.App. 665, 306 N.E.2d 738.

40. **Fla.**—Florida Rules of Evidence § 90.613.

Kan.—State v. Oswald, 417 P.2d 261, 197 Kan. 251 (if actually used for that purpose).

Mich.—Miles v. Clairmont Transfer Co., 1971, 192 N.W.2d 619, 35 Mich. App. 319; Papajesk v. C & O R Co., 1968, 166 N.W.2d 46, 14 Mich.App. 550 (immediate right to see any memoranda used by witness to refresh his memory and to use such memoranda in cross-examination).

41. **Ill.**—Rigor v. Howard Liquors, Inc., 1973, 295 N.E.2d 491, 10 Ill. App.3d 1004 (admitted on cross-examination that he could testify only as to facts in report).

Ky.—Payne v. Zapp, 1968, 431 S.W. 2d 890 (allowing pretrial statement of a witness to be read and introduced in evidence under the guise of refreshing recollection of the witness, or of impeaching him, or of leading him as a hostile witness, is error since, for purpose of refreshing his recollection, the party doing the examining, whether direct or cross, may show to witness a pretrial statement, but may not for that purpose introduce it in evidence or read it to jury).

N.C.—Goldston v. Lynch, 1968, 163 S.E.2d 26, 2 N.C.App. 291 (books which had been furnished to plaintiffs by counsel for purpose of maintaining daily record of how they felt after collision were properly excluded, since use of books was limited to refreshing recollection of plaintiffs).

R.I.—Jurgiewicz v. Adams, 43 A.2d 310, 71 R.I. 239.

But see

Cal.—Vogelsang v. Wolpert, 38 Cal. Rptr. 440, 227 Cal.App.2d 628 (opposing counsel may read notes to jury).

Ind.—Elgin, J. & E. Ry. Co. v. Collins, 1970, 260 N.E.2d 810, 147 Ind. App. 343 (one exception to hearsay rule is that when witness testifies in chief from memorandum used to refresh his recollection, memorandum is admissible on cross-examination).

N.H.—McCarthy v. Boston & M. R. R., 27 A.2d 97, 92 N.H. 149.

Wis.—Zweifel v. Milwaukee Auto. Mut. Ins. Co., 1965, 137 N.W.2d 6, 28 Wis.2d 249.

Limitation on introduction of memorandum

It is permissible for testifying police officer to use accident report made out by him to refresh his recollection and, in turn, be cross-examined upon basis of report and in event there appears to be conflict between his testimony at trial and his accident report, such portion of accident report relating solely to police investigation may be offered in evidence in contradiction, but, if officer does not deny inconsistency, then there is no occasion for introduction of report. 21 Del.C. § 318 and subd. (b). Halko v. State, Del., 204 A.2d 628.

Chapter 420

CROSS–EXAMINATION

Table of Sections

Sec.
420.1 In General.
420.2 Permissible Scope.

---

§ 420.1 In General

Library References:

C.J.S. Witnesses § 368 et seq.
West's Key No. Digests, Witnesses ⚖︎266 et seq.

It is said that a fair and full cross-examination is an absolute right, rather than a mere privilege.[1] A party, however, may waive the right of cross-examination.[2]

---

1. **U.S.**—Parker v. Gladden, 87 S. Ct. 468, 385 U.S. 363, 17 L.Ed.2d 420; DiBello v. Rederi A/B Svenska Lloyd, C.A.N.Y., 371 F.2d 559 (a third-party defendant has right to examine and cross-examine witnesses on trial of the plaintiff's claim against defendant).

    Ala.—Coward v. McKinney, 1965, 172 So.2d 538, 277 Ala. 513.

    Ariz.—Chavez v. Pima County, 1971, 488 P.2d 978, 107 Ariz. 358 (where Uniform Traffic-Control Device Manual had already been admitted in evidence in motorist's action against county for injuries sustained when his automobile collided with concrete abutment erected and maintained by county on a county highway, motorist's attorney should have been allowed to fully cross-examine witnesses as to any relevant portions thereof).

    Cal.—Board of Trustees of Mount San Antonio Jr. College Dist. of Los Angeles County v. Hartman, 55 Cal.Rptr. 144, 246 Cal.App.2d 756.

    Conn.—Fahey v. Clark, 3 A.2d 313, 125 Conn. 44, 120 A.L.R. 517.

    Ga.—Salisbury v. State, 1966, 150 S. E.2d 819, 222 Ga. 549; Owens v. Shugart, 1939, 6 S.E.2d 121, 61 Ga.App. 177.

    Ill.—DuPree v. Terry, 1971, 273 N.E. 2d 630, 1 Ill.App.3d 169 (fact that physician of plaintiff may have recorded notes of his conversation with plaintiff concerning accident and prepared a history therefrom did not foreclose inquiry as to any independent recollection physician may have had of events referred to in notes and restriction of defense cross-examination of physician to mere reading of notes without elaboration was error).

    Iowa.—Barnard v. Cedar Rapids City Cab Co., 133 N.W.2d 884, 257 Iowa 734.

    Md.—Ridgeway Shopping Center, Inc. v. Seidman, 1966, 221 A.2d 393, 243 Md. 358.

2. See note 2 on page 235.

Ch. 420 CROSS–EXAMINATION § 420.1

It is uniformly held that the extent of cross-examination rests in the sound discretion of the trial judge,[3] and the ruling

Mo.—Bartlett v. Kansas City Public Service Co., 160 S.W.2d 740, 349 Mo. 13, 142 A.L.R. 666.

N.Y.—Ziehm v. State, 61 N.Y.S.2d 99, 270 App.Div. 876 (denial of cross-examination of officer as to knowledge of previous accidents).

N.C.—Brewer v. Garner, 141 S.E.2d 806, 264 N.C. 384.

Pa.—Kaplan v. Loev, 194 A. 653, 327 Pa. 465, certiorari denied 58 S.Ct. 477, 302 U.S. 766, 82 L.Ed. 595 (the right of cross-examination cannot be denied by trial judge where fairly conducted).

Tex.—Alpine Telephone Corp. v. McCall, Civ.App., 195 S.W.2d 585, ref. n. r. e.

Alleged impartial medical witness

Although both sides agreed that plaintiff would submit to examination by doctor who could be called by either side as witness and doctor stated in various ways that he was impartial witness when called by defendant, plaintiff had right to vigorously cross-examine doctor on his findings and conclusions. City of Philadelphia v. Shapiro, 206 A.2d 308, 416 Pa. 308.

But see

Where suit of northbound motorist against approaching left turning motorist was consolidated with suit of left turning motorist against northbound motorist and witness to collision, and in left turning motorist's action northbound motorist and his insurer were represented by attorney who was given full opportunity to cross-examine witness to collision but declined to do so, refusal to permit northbound motorist's attorney in northbound motorist's action to cross-examine witness to collision was not abuse of discretion. Neider v. Spoehr, 1969, 165 N.W.2d 171, 41 Wis.2d 610.

Deprival as denial of due process

U.S.—Derewecki v. Pennsylvania R. Co., C.A.Pa., 353 F.2d 436.

Cal.—Polk v. Polk, 39 Cal.Rptr. 824, 228 Cal.App.2d 763 (results in denial of a fair hearing).

Not by counsel for co-plaintiff

Where cases involving two plaintiffs were consolidated for trial, and counsel for plaintiff Keller, in chambers and in his opening to the jury, agreed to adopt as his witnesses, the witnesses and testimony produced for trial by counsel for plaintiff Bartholomew, counsel for plaintiff Keller may not cross-examine a witness called by counsel for plaintiff Bartholomew because there is no adversity of interest between plaintiffs Keller and Bartholomew. Bartholomew v. Peoples Cab Co., Pa.Com.Pl., 113 P.L.J. 22.

2. **Pa.**—Yurechko v. Allegheny County, 1968, 243 A.2d 372, 430 Pa. 325 (not denied right to cross-examine witness in negligence action against county arising from pot hole in county highway when witness allegedly changed her testimony that "the only hole she saw was in the middle of the curve", where witness did not so testify but spoke of many pot holes, and county's counsel had talked of one hole and tried to get witness to give its exact location and then agreed to abide by court's request that subject be dropped and failed to object to trial court's ruling).

3. **U.S.**—Federal Rules of Evidence § 611(a) (court to control mode of interrogation); U. S. v. Chase, C.A. Va., 372 F.2d 453; Grant v. U. S., C.A.Ga., 368 F.2d 658 (only after a party has had opportunity to exercise that right does discretion become operative); Dixon v. U. S.,

§ 420.1 TRIAL EVIDENCE Ch. 420

C.A.Ala., 333 F.2d 348 (after opportunity substantially to exercise right).

Ala.—Mobile Cab & Baggage Co. v. Busby, 169 So.2d 314, 277 Ala. 292.

Alaska.—Pedersen v. State, 420 P.2d 327.

Ariz.—Zier v. Shamrock Dairy of Phoenix, Inc., 420 P.2d 954, 4 Ariz. App. 382 (a wide latitude is allowed).

Cal.—Marshall v. Marshall, 42 Cal. Rptr. 686, 232 Cal.App.2d 232; Germ v. City and County of San Francisco, 222 P.2d 122, 99 Cal. App.2d 404 (could limit examination as to matters already covered).

Colo.—Burr v. Green Bros. Sheet Metal, Inc., 409 P.2d 511, 159 Colo. 25.

Conn.—Fahey v. Clark, 3 A.2d 313, 125 Conn. 44, 120 A.L.R. 517 (entitled to substantial and fair exercise of right).

Dist.Col.—Jackson v. District of Columbia, Mun.App., 200 A.2d 199 (once right freely exercised).

Ga.—Elliott v. Georgia Power Co., 197 S.E. 914, 58 Ga.App. 151.

Ill.—Young v. Miller, 223 N.E.2d 854, 79 Ill.App.2d 463.

Ind.—Kavanagh v. Butorac, 221 N.E.2d 824, 140 Ind.App. 139 (in matters of knowledge, intent, and the like, as general rule, cross-examiner is given wide latitude).

Iowa.—Barnard v. Cedar Rapids City Cab Co., 133 N.W.2d 884, 257 Iowa 734 (after right substantially and fairly exercised).

Ky.—Com., Dept. of Highways v. Smith, 390 S.W.2d 194.

La.—State v. Johnson, 192 So.2d 135, 249 La. 950 (has full authority to prevent needless questioning).

Me.—Maine Rules of Evidence § 611 (a) (court to control mode of interrogation).

Md.—Ridgeway Shopping Center, Inc. v. Seidman, 221 A.2d 393, 243 Md. 358.

Mass.—Com. v. Nunes, 221 N.E.2d 752, 351 Mass. 401.

Mich.—Gonzalez v. Hoffman, 1968, 157 N.W.2d 475, 9 Mich.App. 522 (if there is anything suspicious in the testimony, may be subjected to rigid cross-examination).

Mo.—Olsten v. Susman, 391 S.W.2d 328.

Neb.—Nebraska Rules of Evidence § 611(a) (court to control mode of interrogation); Chicago Lumber Co. of Kearney v. Gibson, 138 N. W.2d 832, 179 Neb. 461.

Nev.—N.R.S. 50.115(a) (court to control mode of interrogation).

N.J.—Derowski v. Zaremba, 1968, 241 A.2d 670, 100 N.J.Super. 284 (may take wider range when witness is a party); State v. Steele, 224 A.2d 132, 92 N.J.Super. 498.

N.M.—New Mexico Rules of Evidence § 611(a) (court to control mode of interrogation).

N.Y.—Tirschwell v. Dolan, 251 N.Y. S.2d 91, 21 A.D.2d 923 (wide discretion as to a cross-examination bearing on credibility).

Ohio.—Gest v. Piketon Lanes, Inc., 212 N.E.2d 922, 5 Ohio App.2d 1.

Pa.—Williams v. Philadelphia Transp. Co., 203 A.2d 665, 415 Pa. 370.

R.I.—State v. Frazier, 221 A.2d 468, 101 R.I. 156 (reasonable guidelines must be established to regulate such latitude in order to insure an orderly, as well as a fair, trial).

S.C.—Shockley v. Cox Circus Co., 29 S.E.2d 491, 204 S.C. 353.

Tenn.—Monts v. State, 379 S.W.2d 34, 214 Tenn. 171.

Tex.—Merrifield v. Seyferth, Civ. App., 408 S.W.2d 558.

Wash.—Glazer v. Adams, 391 P.2d 195, 64 Wash.2d 144, citing 98 C. J.S. Witnesses § 404.

on the question will not be disturbed in absence of a manifest abuse of discretion.[4]

In a variety of situations the court has held no abuse of discretion occurred;[5] and, in others, that the discretion exercised created prejudicial error.[6]

Wis.—Wisconsin Rules of Evidence § 906.11(1) (court to control mode of interrogation); Abbott v. Truck Ins. Exchange Co., 148 N.W.2d 116, 33 Wis.2d 671.

Rule further defined

So far as cross-examination relates either to facts at issue or relevant facts, it is a matter of right, but when its object is to ascertain accuracy or credibility, method and duration of cross-examination are subject to discretion of trial judge. Schwartz v. Triff, 139 N.W.2d 907, 2 Mich.App. 379.

"Discretion" of judge in limitation of cross-examination means legal discretion in exercise of which judge must take account of law applicable to particular circumstances of case and be governed accordingly. State v. Steel, 224 A.2d 132, 92 N.J.Super. 498.

4. **U.S.**—Burns v. Travelers Ins. Co., C.A.La., 344 F.2d 70; Leavitt v. Scott, C.A.Utah, 338 F.2d 749 (wide latitude proper where injury severe and uncommon).

Ariz.—State v. Baca, 425 P.2d 108, 102 Ariz. 83.

Cal.—Marshall v. Marshall, 42 Cal. Rptr. 686, 232 Cal.App.2d 232.

Fla.—Alvarez v. Mauney, 175 So.2d 57.

Ga.—Mitchell v. Gay, 143 S.E.2d 568, 111 Ga.App. 867.

Ill.—Piechalak v. Liberty Trucking Co., 208 N.E.2d 379, 58 Ill.App.2d 289.

Ind.—Vanosdol v. Henderson, 22 N. E.2d 812, 216 Ind. 240.

Kan.—State v. Greenwood, 421 P.2d 24, 197 Kan. 676.

Mass.—Caron v. Hazlett, 75 N.E.2d 233, 321 Mass. 671.

Minn.—Nelson v. Austin Transit, Inc., 135 N.W.2d 886, 271 Minn. 377.

Mo.—Hungate v. Hudson, 185 S.W. 2d 646, 353 Mo. 944, 157 A.L.R. 598.

N.J.—Lawlor v. Kolarsick, 223 A.2d 281, 92 N.J.Super. 309.

Wyo.—Cederburg v. Carter, 1968, 448 P.2d 608 (even though objection that question whether motorist could make a certain turn while travelling 60 miles an hour improperly called for conclusion was sustained, record did not support contention that cross-examination of motorist as to speed of automobile when it turned corner had been foreclosed).

5. **U.S.**—Leonteos v. Haase, C.A.Ill. 1969, 410 F.2d 633 (inquiries permitted of police officer, who on direct examination described physical features of scene of accident including place on pavement where plaintiff was then lying, as to contents of police accident report, which was put in issue by plaintiff's identification and officer's reference to it, and on officer's oral testimony were within rules of proper cross-examination).

Colo.—Shellabarger v. Atencio, 1971, 482 P.2d 415, —— Colo.App. —— (sustaining of objections to questions by defendants' counsel concerning plaintiff's apprehension over movement of defendants' automobile before vehicles collided at intersection did not restrict the cross-examination and was not er-

6. See note 6 on page 240.

§ 420.1   TRIAL EVIDENCE   Ch. 420

ror where objections were to the form of the question and not the substance and where court suggested that question be rephrased, but no effort was made to do so).

Cal.—Payette v. Sterle, 21 Cal.Rptr. 22, 202 Cal.App.2d 372 (where refused questioning re mental illness, in absence of evidence witness had such information).

Ga.—Gunnells v. Cotton States Mut. Ins. Co., 159 S.E.2d 730, 117 Ga. App. 123 (in crossing collision case, wherein wrongful death and other actions were filed to recover for death and injuries of automobile passengers and there was a dispute as to who had been driving automobile at time of collision, permitting attorneys for various parties to cross-examine witnesses for other parties was not error); Cox v. Norris, 1944, 28 S.E.2d 888, 70 Ga.App. 580 (trial court's refusal to require defendant to answer question as to whether he had before entered highway without looking and later regretted such failure).

Ill.—Hann v. Milla, 1968, 237 N.E.2d 753, 95 Ill.App.2d 447 (actions in permitting cross-examination of plaintiff as to width of street on which he was driving, whether there was man in uniform at scene of accident, length of plaintiff's car, position of cars before and after impact, and in asking both attorneys out of presence of jury if they would stipulate as to certain questions and answers having been given at deposition because court reporter had lost his notes were proper).

Iowa.—Oakes v. Peter Pan Bakers, Inc., 138 N.W.2d 93, 258 Iowa 447, 10 A.L.R.3d 247 (where oil transport driver testified that after he saw van in front of him he was able to turn steering wheel three complete turns to right and thus move transport onto right shoulder but that he had no idea how long it took to do so, sustaining of defendant van owner's objection to next question propounded on cross-examination by plaintiff owner of automobile struck in rear by van as to whether transport driver would say it took more than a second was not an abuse of discretion); Spry v. Lamont, 132 N.W. 2d 446, 257 Iowa 321 (limiting defendant's cross-examination of witness who visited scene of head-on collision, as to whether witness had observed any debris or had seen officer taking photographs at scene).

Kan.—Tucker v. Lower, 1967, 434 P. 2d 320, 200 Kan. 1 (where income tax returns of 62-year-old plaintiff were introduced, doctors and others testified that, after the accident and to time of trial, plaintiff was unable to work because of his injuries, denying defendant right to cross-examine plaintiff on number of days he spent in jail during previous year was not an abuse of discretion, even if such evidence might have indicated lack of earning capacity, especially where conviction of crimes had been properly excluded from evidence).

Md.—Maged v. Yellow Cab Co., 1965, 206 A.2d 257, 237 Md. 340 (sustained objection to inquiry as to whether claim manager recalled that driver had denied passenger's version of accident).

Mich.—York v. James, 1973, 208 N. W.2d 185, 46 Mich.App. 498 (refusal to permit plaintiff to cross-examine defendant, whose deposition contained inconsistent statements as to whether his automobile was stopped or moving when he first observed plaintiff, concerning inconsistency was not error, since deposition already established inconsistency and further cross-examination would be cumulative).

Mo.—Krez v. Mickel, 1968, 431 S.W. 2d 213 (cross-examination of plaintiff, who sustained fractures of

238

pelvic bone in fall resulting when defendant ran into her on public sidewalk, as to injury to ribs in fall six months before fall on sidewalk and as to injury to wrist in fall five years previous to fall on sidewalk was not abuse of discretion, and in any event cross-examination as to previous falls was not prejudicial on theory that jury was indoctrinated with idea that plaintiff was accident prone).

N.J.—Ettin v. Ava Truck Leasing, Inc., 1968, 242 A.2d 663, 100 N.J. Super. 515, affirmed in part, reversed in part on other grounds, 251 A.2d 278, 53 N.J. 463 (trial court did not abuse discretion in limiting scope of cross-examination of plaintiff truck lessee, suing truck lessor and another defendant for damages arising out of collision, on issue of how far lessee was from tractor-trailer into which he crashed when he first saw vehicle, since discrepancy between lessee's pre-trial depositions and trial testimony had been fully explored by lessor's counsel).

N.Y.—Middleton v. Levy, 1970, 308 N.Y.S.2d 212, 33 A.D.2d 1015, affirmed 315 N.Y.S.2d 852, 27 N.Y. 2d 788, 264 N.E.2d 346.

Ohio.—Hershovics v. Mindlin, 1973, 320 N.E.2d 702, 40 Ohio App.2d 551 (in action by pedestrian struck by motorist backing from private driveway, even if testimony as to whether it was foreseeable that someone would be standing in driveway between sidewalk and curb, sought to be elicited during cross-examination of defendant was relevant, limitation of the cross-examination was within discretion); Johnson v. English, 214 N. E.2d 254, 5 Ohio App.2d 109 (in refusing to permit cross-examination of plaintiff as to whether he had had a source of income since accident).

Pa.—Grzywacz v. Meszaros, 208 A. 2d 237, 417 Pa. 51 (refusing cross-examination of plaintiff regarding alleged prior inconsistent statements with regard to a back ailment allegedly suffered by plaintiff from childhood where defendant in cross-examination did not ask plaintiff about any ailment existing prior to accident so that there was nothing to impeach); Phillips v. Pickell, 57 Berks 107 (cross-examination of defendant regarding his conduct prior to the accident was proper where the evidence related to defendant's intoxication at the time of the accident).

Va.—Rakes v. Fulcher, 1970, 172 S. E.2d 751, 210 Va. 542 (refusal to permit counsel to cross-examine witness through use of questions which began "do you recall telling me," "didn't you also tell me," "didn't you tell me," "why didn't you tell me," was not abuse of discretion, since to permit questions in proposed form would, in effect, have permitted counsel to testify against witness without becoming a witness and would have amounted to unwarranted and improper attempt to discredit witness).

Wash.—State v. Johnson, 1964, 393 P.2d 284, 64 Wash.2d 613 (no error in refusal of request to recall witness already cross-examined extensively).

Attempt to mislead

Refusal to permit cross-examination of motorist as to "did I understand you to testify that as you reached the fog that you said you ran into you were driving 30 miles an hour" was proper where question pertained to testimony given on previous day and motorist had not testified on such day. Lawlyes v. Torpy, 1973, 300 N.E. 2d 898, —— Ind.App. ——.

Ill health precluded further attendance in court

Plaintiffs who claimed deprivation of right to cross-examine witness as an adverse party failed to show that court, which during plaintiffs' case

§ 420.1 TRIAL EVIDENCE Ch. 420

As in the case of direct examination, the trial court has broad discretion to refuse repetitious questioning.[7] Likewise, cross-examination may not be argumentative,[8] or assume facts.[9]

in chief, ruled that testimony sought could more appropriately be presented during plaintiffs' rebuttal and then refused to order witness to reappear due to ill health, had abused its discretion by failing to allow questioning of witness in his own home, where permission to prepare questions for submission by court reporter was given. Gerhard v. Stephens, 1968, 442 P.2d 692, 69 Cal.Rptr. 612, 68 Cal.2d 864.

Subject abandoned by counsel

Record in wrongful death action did not sustain contention that defendant had been restricted in cross-examination of plaintiff widow as to her premarital pregnancy, but disclosed rather that cross-examination was restricted by defendant's choice. Cherrigan v. City and County of San Francisco, 1968, 69 Cal.Rptr. 42, 262 Cal.App.2d 643.

6. **Mo.**—Hungate v. Hudson, 185 S. W.2d 646, 353 Mo. 944, 157 A.L.R. 598 (where plaintiff motorist was within his legal rights in instituting action in Missouri where defendant resided, rather than in Illinois where cause of action accrued and plaintiff resided, permitting cross-examination of plaintiff as to why action had not been brought where he lived and among his friends, was an abuse of discretion).

Nev.—Henry v. Baber, 334 P.2d 839, 75 Nev. 59 (wife, who was called by defendants as an adverse witness and who on cross-examination testified that for a period of about two years before accident she earned $140 a month, question asked of wife as to whether she reported that amount to government on her income tax returns was relevant and material and sustaining of objection to question was prejudicial error when jury found specially for wife in the precise amount claimed).

N.Y.—Womble v. Michelson, 254 N. Y.S.2d 861, 22 A.D.2d 815 (to foreclose cross-examination by defendant as to whether plaintiff in fact lost wages she claimed to have lost because of accident, absent proof whether wages were gratuitously paid by plaintiff's employer or were some kind of sick pay extended as fringe benefit or as some part of pension plan).

7. **U.S.**—Clonce v. U. S., C.A.Okl. 1966, 356 F.2d 912.

Cal.—Badorek v. General Motors Corp., 1970, 90 Cal.Rptr. 305, 12 C.A.3d 447, hearing granted (was error, but examination of record disclosed no miscarriage of justice).

Ga.—Mitchell v. Gay, 143 S.E.2d 568, 111 Ga.App. 867.

Ill.—Hann v. Milla, 1968, 237 N.E. 2d 753, 95 Ill.App.2d 447; People v. Brown, 222 N.E.2d 227, 76 Ill. App.2d 362; Rennie v. Jacoel, 1966, 217 N.E.3d 105, 70 Ill.App.2d 201 (another question on very same point).

Iowa.—Castner v. Wright, 127 N.W. 2d 583, 256 Iowa 638, opinion supplemented 128 N.W.2d 885.

Mich.—People v. Lloyd, 147 N.W.2d 740, 5 Mich.App. 717.

Mo.—Smith v. Thompson, 142 S.W. 2d 70, 346 Mo. 502.

Neb.—Chicago Lumber Co. of Kearney v. Gibson, 138 N.W.2d 832, 179 Neb. 461 (counsel was either confused or misunderstood witness' testimony); Holtz v. Plumer, 277 N.W. 589, 133 Neb. 878.

Permitting repetition held error

Cross-examination of defendants' witness implying that truck driver

---

8. See note 8 on page 241.

9. See note 9 on page 241.

and his associates had been drinking liquor before accident, and repetition of such questions and trial court's conduct in permitting such cross-examination over repeated objections was prejudicial to defendants, where there was no evidence that defendants had been drinking. Pierce v. Heusinkveld, 14 N.W.2d 275, 234 Iowa 1348.

8. **Ark.**—Self v. Dye, 1974, 516 S. W.2d 397, 257 Ark. 360 (trial court did not abuse discretion in sustaining objection to defense cross-examination of investigating police officer as to whether defendant motorist's statement that he did not know what happened was unusual when man was driving down highway and light was green and someone ran into him).

Cal.—Newsom v. Smiley, 1943, 135 P.2d 24, 57 Cal.App.2d 627 (objection properly sustained to question, "It never occurred to you, did it, Mr. Smiley to make any effort to determine whether there were any other boys running along the sidewalk?").

Mich.—People v. Lloyd, 147 N.W.2d 740, 5 Mich.App. 717.

Minn.—LeClair v. Sickler, 146 N.W. 2d 853, 275 Minn. 320.

Mo.—State v. Jackson, 412 S.W.2d 428; Eddings v. Keller, 400 S.W.2d 164 (where plaintiff was permitted to inquire as to which of defendant's two inconsistent statements was correct and defendant gave his answer, statement that "This prior statement is not correct then" was argumentative, and objection thereto was properly sustained).

N.M.—Francis v. Johnson, 1970, 471 P.2d 682, 81 N.M. 648 (question put by owner's counsel to passenger on cross-examination as to how long it would have taken to open door to get out of the automobile after he learned that race was to take place and if five seconds would have afforded sufficient time in which to do so was argumentative and exclusion of evidence was proper).

Wis.—Pagel v. Kees, 1964, 127 N.W. 2d 816, 23 Wis.2d 462.

9. **Ark.**—Self v. Dye, 1974, 516 S. W.2d 397, 257 Ark. 360 (after driver of automobile involved in intersectional collision gave negative answers in cross-examination as to whether she had examined the other vehicle and knew which part of that vehicle had been struck, the court properly sustained objection to further inquiry, "You don't know that his extreme right front . . .." inasmuch as cross-examiner in effect made a statement of fact).

Mo.—State v. Jackson, 412 S.W.2d 428; Eddings v. Keller, 400 S.W. 2d 164.

But see

Refusal, in consolidated actions by operator of railroad track car and fellow employees to recover from motorist for personal injuries sustained in collision between track car and motorist's vehicle at railroad crossing, to permit cross-examination of motorist as to whether statement was correct "that you made in a sworn statement yesterday that you may have been traveling 30 miles an hour at the time of impact" was proper where motorist had not made such a statement. Lawlyes v. Torpy, 1973, 300 N.E.2d 898, —— Ind.App. ——.

Ind.—LaNoux v. Hagar, 1974, 308 N.E.2d 873, —— Ind.App. —— (cross-examination of bicyclist's mother as to whether bicyclist had received training concerning stopping for stop signs and looking in either direction for traffic before crossing a preferential street was not improper on theory that the questions assumed that bicyclist had not stopped and looked both ways before attempting to cross street).

§ 420.1 TRIAL EVIDENCE Ch. 420

Cross-examination must be confined to matters which are relevant and material and otherwise competent.[10] However, the

10. **U.S.**—Mann v. Anderson, C.A. Ind.1971, 447 F.2d 533 (in action for injuries sustained by six-year-old plaintiff-pedestrian, court properly refused to allow defense attorney to cross-examine plaintiff as to whether immediately before accident he had asked his mother to take him across the street and she had told him to go by himself); Harris v. U. S., C.A.Nev.1967, 371 F.2d 365.

Ala.—Bradley v. Jones, 211 So.2d 465, 282 Ala. 331 (question in explanation or rebuttal of statements made by witness on direct examination is proper even if facts elicited may not have been admissible as independent evidence).

Ariz.—Zier v. Shamrock Dairy of Phoenix, Inc., 1967, 420 P.2d 954, 4 Ariz.App. 382.

Cal.—Marshall v. Marshall, 1965, 42 Cal.Rptr. 686, 232 Cal.App.2d 232.

Conn.—Robinson v. Faulkner, 1973 306 A.2d 857, 163 Conn. 365 (refusal to permit cross-examination of defendant concerning contents of document, which was marked for identification but which was not an exhibit in evidence, was not error where trial court was not apprised that any ground of admissibility was being relied on other than claimed right to attack credibility of defendant by questions concerning contents of such document); Anderson v. Burgess Express Co., 1946, 45 A.2d 825, 132 Conn. 545.

Fla.—Seaboard Coast Line R. Co. v. Zufelt, App.1973, 280 So.2d 723 (correctly rejected photograph of bottle of whiskey found in wrecked automobile shortly after accident with the seal broken and portion of contents missing on ground that proper predicate had not been laid, over contention that photograph was admissible for purpose of impeaching testimony of witness).

Ga.—Millhollan v. Watkins Motor Lines, Inc., 1967, 157 S.E.2d 901, 116 Ga.App. 452; Langdale Co. v. Day, 1967, 153 S.E.2d 671, 115 Ga. App. 30.

Ill.—Esderts v. Chicago, R. I. & P. R. Co., 222 N.E.2d 117, 76 Ill.App.2d 210 (cross-examination on immaterial matters for purpose of contradicting answers is improper); Marut v. Costello, 214 N.E.2d 768, 34 Ill.2d 125.

Ind.—Kavanagh v. Butorac, 221 N.E. 2d 824, 140 Ind.App. 139 (where it appeared that if failure of passenger to use seat belts could prevent his recovery it would be equally so whether he knew and appreciated danger or not, there was no legal significance to his knowledge and no error was committed in sustaining objections to questions designed to show awareness that danger could be lessened by using seat belts); Brindle v. Harter, 211 N.E. 2d 513, 138 Ind.App. 692, citing I.L.E. Witnesses § 122.

Ky.—Shirley v. Com., 378 S.W.2d 816.

Mich.—Henson v. Veteran's Cab Co. of Flint, 1971, 185 N.W.2d 383, 384 Mich. 486 (may not be cross-examined as to contents of specially excluded portion of hospital record).

N.J.—State v. Pollack, 1964, 202 A. 2d 433, 43 N.J. 34 (should be allowed to show improbability of direct).

Pa.—Brodie v. Philadelphia Transp. Co., 1964, 203 A.2d 657, 415 Pa. 296).

R.I.—Handy v. Geary, 1969, 252 A. 2d 435, 105 R.I. 419 (what one of the passengers would have done on the next day if no accident had occurred).

242

S.C.—Shockley v. Cox Circus Co., 29 S.E.2d 491, 204 S.C. 353 (cannot ask groundless questions for purpose and with result of prejudicing a party who is testifying by nature of the questions, but such rule must be harmonized with the ordinarily wide range which cross-examination may properly take).

Tex.—Austin Road Co. v. Ferris, Civ. App.1973, 492 S.W.2d 64 (refusal to permit defendant to cross-examine dentist, after he had testified that his dental charge for dental work performed on plaintiff as result of accident was $2,650, if it was not true that professional committee of dental association had not suggested to him that he resubmit a fee and that the new fee be realistic and that he should compare his fees with the Texas Dental Journal was not improper); Johnston Testers v. Rangel, 1969, 435 S.W.2d 927, error refused n. r. e. (under record, court's refusal to admit certain of plaintiff's income tax returns, offered by defendant, did not restrict right of cross-examination of defendant whose counsel did not question plaintiff as to existence of drug bills and work expenses connected with income tax returns); Continental Bus System, Inc. v. Toombs, Civ.App.1959, 325 S.W. 2d 153, writ of error ref. n. r. e. (as to prior statement of "fault"); Grocers Supply Co. v. Stuckey, Civ.App., 152 S.W.2d 911, error refused for want of merit (only limitation is that of relevancy, and even that limitation is not applied with the same strictness in a cross-examination as in examination in chief).

Wash.—Glazer v. Adams, 1964, 391 P.2d 195, 64 Wash.2d 144 (may not degrade, humiliate or disgrace witness).

Burden to show relevancy

Conn.—Fahey v. Clark, 3 A.2d 313, 125 Conn. 44, 120 A.L.R. 517 (where it does not reasonably appear that evidence sought to be elicited may be relevant and material, court, in its discretion, may require of counsel sufficient intimation of purpose thereof, but nothing further than bare intimation should generally be required).

Mont.—O'Brien v. Great Northern Ry. Co., 400 P.2d 634, 145 Mont. 13 (sustaining objection was not undue restriction of cross-examination where intention was to establish that railroad engine movement mentioned by witness involved a different engine than that involved in fatal collision, but at time of the cross-examination evidence that would show such relevancy had not been introduced).

But see

U.S.—U. S. v. Spatuzza, 1964, C.A. Ill., 331 F.2d 214, certiorari denied 85 S.Ct. 58, 379 U.S. 829, 13 L.Ed. 2d 38 (may permit cross-examination on collateral matters, within discretion).

Mo.—Chism v. Cowan, 1967, 425 S.W.2d 942 (a witness may be asked any questions which tend to test his accuracy, veracity, or credibility, or shake his credit by injuring his character and he may be compelled to answer any such question, however irrelevant it may be to the facts in issue, and however disgraceful the answer may be to himself, except where the answer might expose him to a criminal charge).

N.J.—Mazza v. Winters, 1967, 230 A.2d 139, 95 N.J.Super. 71 (where it involves collateral matters should be measured by trial judge in light of effect of such examination upon substantial justice).

Not as to privileged matter

Defendant's use of police report in cross-examination of police officers to present to jury matter contained in report which could not itself be

§ 420.1 TRIAL EVIDENCE Ch. 420

opposing party may have "opened the door" for otherwise incompetent matter because of matters raised in the direct examination.[11]

admitted was improper. Anderson v. Universal Delta, 1968, 234 N.E.2d 21, 90 Ill.App.2d 105.

Any statement made concerning automobile accident to investigating patrolman, embodied in his filed report, was privileged although overheard and reduced to writing by sheriff who did not file report, and sheriff, who used his copy to refresh his memory, was not subject to cross-examination as to statements by parties involved. Meyer v. Schumacher, Iowa 1968, 160 N.W.2d 433.

Preliminary hearing in absence of jury

Defendant, who claimed that pedestrian was under influence of alcohol and that such was contributing cause of his injuries, would be required to produce sufficient testimony at opening of trial to be heard by court outside hearing of jury to determine if jury could reasonably reach finding of intoxication and, if so, defendant would be permitted to inquire into such issue on cross-examination, otherwise defendant would be barred from introducing issue on cross-examination but not from producing affirmative evidence in her own case, providing court first examined proposed testimony for its sufficiency as basis for such finding. Young v. Bentley, D.C.Pa. 1969, 299 F.Supp. 356.

Reference to publications

In action against county for damage from accident allegedly resulting from dangerous condition of public property, plaintiff was properly permitted to cross-examine county's traffic engineer concerning two State Department of Public Works' publications which contained standards admittedly used by such traffic engineer as guides in posting traffic signs on county highways. Bakity v. Riverside County, 1970, 90 Cal. Rptr. 541, 12 Cal.App.3d 24.

11. **U.S.**—Hinkle v. Hampton, C.A. Okl.1968, 388 F.2d 141 (receiving in evidence the details of a prior accident in which plaintiff was involved was proper where plaintiff opened the door to such evidence in her direct examination, in which she sought to minimize the extent of her injuries and underestimated the amount of the settlement, where in fact her injuries had been relatively serious and were shown to be continuing, and in addition, court had discretionary authority to allow defendant to meet such evidence on an equally broad front by allowing development of the true facts); Gladden v. P. Henderson & Co., C.A.Pa.1967, 385 F.2d 480, certiorari denied 88 S.Ct. 1262, 390 U.S. 1013, 20 L.Ed.2d 162 (collateral benefit rule of Pennsylvania cannot be made a springboard from which a plaintiff may go forward with affirmative evidence that he returned to work while still ailing because of financial need and then seek immunity from cross-examination regarding this).

Ill.—Biel v. Wolff, 1970, 261 N.E.2d 474, 126 Ill.App.2d 209 (where pedestrian's counsel had inquired about statements allegedly made to officer by motorist at accident scene, motorist's counsel had right to inquire into further aspects of conversation and despite self-serving nature of motorist's statements); Hendler v. Wolozin, 1969, 245 N.E.2d 74, 105 Ill.App.2d 132, certiorari denied 90 S.Ct. 264, 396 U.S. 929, 24 L.Ed.2d 227 (since conversation between operator of automobile that struck children and investigating police officer was brought out in direct exami-

Ch. 420 CROSS–EXAMINATION § 420.1

In a variety of situations the cross-examination has been held to be relevant and material,[12] and in other situations held not proper.[13]

nation of officer, cross-examination as to that conversation was proper although it brought out certain self-serving statements).

Ind.—Shelby Nat. Bank v. Miller, 1970, 259 N.E.2d 450, 147 Ind.App. 203 ("opened door" by asking investigating police officer about his conversation with defendant, permitting cross-examination which elicited from officer that he told defendant that officer thought accident was unavoidable and that defendant had done everything he could do to avoid it).

Mich.—LaForest v. Grunow, 1972, 204 N.W.2d 355, 43 Mich.App. 254 (in action by husband and wife against Motor Vehicle Accident Claims Fund, did not abuse its discretion in permitting Fund, in cross-examining plaintiffs, to use, for purpose of impeachment, pleadings alleging nonsupport in divorce case between plaintiffs, where it was plaintiffs who interjected cause of divorce into case); Buckeye Union Ins. Co. v. Hallman, 1969, 172 N.W.2d 203, 19 Mich. App. 12 (allowing cross-examination as to whether motorist, who had testified that he tried to be a good driver, had ever been convicted of any moving violation did not constitute abuse of discretion).

And see

In action arising out of collision between plaintiff's automobile and locomotive at crossings, defendants could interrogate officer as to whether plaintiff was charged with any traffic violations on evening of wreck, where plaintiff had cross-examined officer as to whether plaintiff was arrested for alcoholic matters on such evening. Jameson v. McCaffry, 1973, 300 N.E.2d 889, —— Ind.App. ——.

Use of intoxicants

Where plaintiff testified that he was in complete control of his faculties, and defendants' attorneys attempted through cross-examination to elicit testimony from plaintiff concerning intoxication, ruling which eliminated any further testimony as to plaintiff's drinking of intoxicants resulted in an undue restriction and limitation of defendants' rights to cross-examination. Crosby v. Sande, N.D.1970, 180 N.W.2d 164.

12. U.S.—McSparran v. Ford Motor Co., D.C.Pa., 238 F.Supp. 329 (where plaintiff's expert in field of automotive maintenance testified on direct that he was an expert on driving procedure, it was not irrelevant to elicit his testimony on cross-examination that it would be negligent to operate truck for 29,500 miles without adjusting brakes).

Ark.—Ben M. Hogan Co., Inc. v. Nichols, 1973, 496 S.W.2d 404, 254 Ark. 771 (where a person who perhaps was driver of allegedly offending vehicle was important witness in support of injured employee's theory that such witness was employee of general contractor and had apparently changed his mind about such relationship after discovery depositions were taken, general contractor in cross-examining him should have been allowed to inquire as to understanding he had with truck owner and general contractor, or both, as to source of his pay and as to whether witness' cashing of general contractor's check rather than turning it over to truck owner was not unusual and contrary to understanding among parties); Livingston v.

13. See note 13 on page 249.

§ 420.1   TRIAL EVIDENCE   Ch. 420

Fuel, 1968, 433 S.W.2d 380, 245 Ark. 618 (in view of testimony that chief of police, sued for damages as a result of killing of horse while driving his personal automobile, had been driving automobile within city limits at 65 miles per hour in a direction away from home and office and toward a particular club, trial court erred in refusing to allow cross-examination of police chief, who claimed he was acting in scope of employment at time of accident, as to his frequent visits to the particular club and his indulgence in intoxicants and in gambling there as well as why police chief failed to claim workmen's compensation benefits as result of accident); Midwest Bus Lines, Inc. v. Williams, 1968, 422 S.W.2d 869, 243 Ark. 854 (driver's plea of guilty to charge of driving his automobile over center mark would have been declaration against interest, and interrogation of driver about the plea was permissible); Interurban Transp. Co. v. Reeves, 1937, 108 S.W.2d 594, 194 Ark. 321 (re who suggested plaintiff hire attorney).

Cal.—Dillenbeck v. City of Los Angeles, 1968, 446 P.2d 129, 72 Cal. Rptr. 321, 69 Cal.2d 472 (court should have permitted, because of potential relevance to issue of negligence in action for wrongful death of motorist whose automobile had collided with police car on emergency run at intersection, cross-examination of police officer as to his knowledge of safety rules contained in city police department bulletins and factual matters contained therein to establish his training and current familiarity with such matters); Wade v. Todd, 20 Cal.Rptr. 245, 201 Cal.App.2d 594 (by testifying that she was married and that back injuries suffered in accident had interfered with their sexual relations, plaintiff made her marital status a material issue on question of damages, and defendant was justified in cross-examining on that subject in an attempt to establish that relationship of husband and wife did not in fact exist between plaintiff and the man in question).

Dist.Col.—Evans v. Greyhound Corp., Mun.App., 200 A.2d 194 (that she had history of two previous claims for which she had received payments in settlement).

Fla.—Shalley v. Fiore, App., 161 So. 2d 18 (plaintiff having testified that she had sustained no earlier back injury was subject to cross-examination concerning statements made in divorce proceeding indicating earlier back injury).

Ga.—Gahring v. Barron, 133 S.E.2d 389, 108 Ga.App. 530 (to determine what part of injuries resulted from defendant's alleged tort and what part from other causes); Brock v. Cato, 42 S.E.2d 174, 75 Ga.App. 79 (refusal to permit defendants to cross-examine plaintiff as to whether he had an accident and health insurance policy and as to whether he made any claim thereunder for injury forming basis of present action, for purpose of attempting to show that plaintiff had made no claim under policy due to inconsequential nature of the injury sustained, was error); Sewell v. Goodman, 189 S.E. 857, 55 Ga.App. 247 (in head-on collision case, allowing cross-examination of defendant disclosing defect in vision of defendant's right eye held not error, notwithstanding no allegation of negligence was based on such defect, since its admitted existence was relevant in determining conflict in testimony as to which automobile was on wrong side).

Ill.—DuPree v. Terry, 1971, 273 N.E. 2d 630, 1 Ill.App.3d 169 (restriction of cross-examination of plaintiff as to manner in which cab was being operated immediately before and at precise point of impact was error); Geaschel v. Rokita, 1967, 232

N.E.2d 204, 89 Ill.App.2d 161 (court properly permitted defendant, being sued by plaintiff for injuries resulting from collision on August 16, 1963, to cross-examine plaintiff and his physician with respect to plaintiff's fall on August 7, 1964, in view of fact that plaintiff was claiming injury to intervertebral disc in the lumbar area and the testimony of physician who treated him after the fall showed injury to area in close proximity to the lumbar area); Froman v. Day, 1967, 231 N.E.2d 10, 87 Ill.App.2d 250 (defense counsel's cross-examination of plaintiff, a married woman, regarding identity and whereabouts of hitch-hiker in her husband's automobile at time of collision did not constitute error and any innuendo was created by facts in case and not by improper innuendo deliberately injected into case by defendant); Pushauer v. Demers, 1967, 229 N.E.2d 908, 86 Ill.App.2d 251 (in view of repeated emotional outbursts which appeared to trial court to have been histrionic on part of defendant, plaintiff's attorney was properly allowed to question defendant as to her background as an actress); Greenberg v. Karris, 1967, 225 N.E.2d 490, 80 Ill.App.2d 270 (where contributory wilful and wanton misconduct was alleged as a defense in action by guest passenger, restricting cross-examination of witness in regard to the drinking of the guest was error); Hoffman v. Wilson, 1965, 208 N.E.2d 607, 60 Ill.App.2d 396 (as to earlier matters which may have caused injury); Tarasuik v. Russell, 1964, 199 N.E.2d 629, 49 Ill.App.2d 418 (to further develop marks and debris at the scene).

Iowa.—Gaskill v. Gahman, 1963, 124 N.W.2d 533, 255 Iowa 891 (as to former residence and occupation, though may show in jail).

Ky.—Daniels v. Tackett, 1967, 416 S.W.2d 749 (should allow questions as to drinking by passenger and driver, as to contributory negligence of passenger).

Mich.—Dudek v. Popp, 129 N.W.2d 393, 373 Mich. 300 (defendant in case wherein officer testified to his opinion that defendant's vehicle had been on wrong side of road was entitled to cross-examine officer as to whether he had issued traffic violation ticket to defendant, and if not, why not).

Minn.—Souden v. Johnson, 1967, 151 N.W.2d 767, 277 Minn. 87 (where plaintiff claimed extensive injury attributable to collision which seemed relatively minor at time of its occurrence, defense counsel was properly permitted to ask what defendant driver told plaintiff at scene of collision with respect to collision, so that jury could consider defendant driver's statement in attempting to determine whether impact so slight was or could have been proximate cause of injury so severe as that claimed by plaintiff, even though, by virtue of prior decision of Supreme Court, liability of defendant was established as a matter of law); Nelson v. Austin Transit, Inc., 1965, 135 N.W.2d 886, 271 Minn. 377 (as to prior injury, where established full history not given plaintiff's medical witness).

Miss.—Young v. Cameron, 1967, 203 So.2d 315 (charge that defendant failed to keep his truck under proper control was broad enough to encompass his speed at time of accident; and speed was proper subject of cross-examination of defendant); Pickering v. Continental Southern Lines, Inc., 168 So.2d 43 (reference to another incident in which was injured in an automobile accident subsequent to occurrence of bus accident).

Mo.—Krudwig v. Fowler, 394 S.W.2d 290 (where plaintiffs' counsel asked plaintiff motorcyclist what time he had arrived at service station where automobile and motorcycle collided and then asked whether he had started his trip from home and motorcyclist gave affirmative answer, on cross-examination defendant was entitled to develop that motorcyclist's activities had not started with trip from home to service station and to inquire fully into those activities); Kuehn v. Hahn, 380 S.W.2d 445 (driver of bus from which pedestrian alighted prior to accident was properly cross-examined as to whether he had not stated that, when passengers left bus, he was glad to get rid of them, since such cross-examination tended to test his opportunity and interest to observe pedestrian).

N.H.—Dane v. MacGregor, 1947, 52 A.2d 290, 94 N.H. 294 (as to statements about collateral matters).

N.Y.—Miller v. City of New York, 145 N.Y.S.2d 295, 286 App.Div. 1033 (where plaintiff testified that prior to accident he had been in very good health and that he had headaches after the accident, it was proper in absence of claim of privilege, to receive in evidence records of county hospital relating to treatment of plaintiff for chronic alcoholism, and to cross-examine him regarding such treatment).

N.C.—State v. Brooks, 1968, 162 S.E. 2d 45, 1 N.C.App. 590 (defense witness in prosecution for, inter alia, driving while intoxicated witness having accompanied defendant on occasion, could be cross-examined as to whether he had been "stoned"); Potts v. Howser, 1968, 161 S.E.2d 737, 274 N.C. 49 (cross-examination of injured party concerning drinking habits which could affect earning capacity, as to disability benefits previously received by plaintiff, and whether he had not complained about tenseness in his wrists to his fifth wife who was employed in his office prior to accident in suit merely identified wife to which complaints were allegedly made, and was not objectionable as evidence of bad character).

Or.—Twilleager v. Modin, 1965, 398 P.2d 181, 240 Or. 69 (as to prior injury and testimony related thereto in prior litigation).

Pa.—Atene v. Lawrence, 1968, 239 A.2d 346, 428 Pa. 424 (after defendant's introduction of hospital records of plaintiff which predated accident involved in suit by 11 years, plaintiff should have been given an opportunity to cross-examine on the records).

R.I.—Bedrosian v. O'Keefe, 215 A.2d 423, 100 R.I. 331 (cross-examination inquiry concerning involvement in prior automobile accident where such inquiry was intended to relate back to testimony given by motorist in direct examination concerning injuries he claimed resulted from collision which present case involved).

Tex.—Robertson v. Southwestern Bell Tel. Co., Civ.App., 403 S.W. 2d 459 (as to previous injuries, physical conditions, claims and actions for purpose of showing that his present physical condition is not result of injury presently sued for, but was caused in whole or in part by earlier or subsequent injury or pre-existing condition).

Wis.—Schmit v. Sekach, 139 N.W.2d 88, 29 Wis.2d 281 (cross-examination of passenger concerning earlier operation for intestinal disorder and permitting admission of hospital records concerning operation where passenger affirmatively asserted absence of any prior abdominal difficulty and where there was physical proximity between injured portion of anatomy in instant case and that involved in past operation).

Against whom absent passengers made claim

S.C.—Gainer v. Tyner, 1972, 193 S.E.2d 525, 259 S.C. 629 (failure of plaintiff driver to call as witnesses three relatives who were occupants of her automobile was a relevant circumstance; since cross-examination of plaintiff as to whether relatives had made a claim against her and not against other driver involved in collision tended to suggest a concrete reason for their absence, trial judge did not exceed his discretion in allowing such an examination; in view of fact that witness' response to question was negative, any error in asking of question was not prejudicial).

Showing collateral benefits

Tex.—Royal v. Cameron, Civ.App. 1964, 382 S.W.2d 335 (that had health and accident insurance was admissible for limited purpose of impeachment where had testified on direct that he had not earlier sought medical attention because of financial inability).

Wash.—Fleming v. Mulligan, 1970, 478 P.2d 754, 3 Wash.App. 951 (permitting questioning of plaintiff as to sick leave benefits received from his employer for purpose of testing accuracy of his testimony on direct examination as to time he had lost from work was proper where court offered to give limiting instruction to effect that collateral benefit would not mitigate damages).

13. Ala.—Cobb-Kirkland Motor Co. v. Rivers, 1971, 248 So.2d 725, 46 Ala.App. 686, certiorari denied 248 So.2d 730, 287 Ala. 727 (in action brought by automobile buyer against seller for failure to obtain collision policy after voluntarily assuming duty to do so, seller's questions propounded to buyer on cross-examination asking "Did that lady have insurance?" "Did you make a claim against this lady?" and "As result of their investigation, did they charge anyone in that accident with any violation?" were not proper for purpose of securing information as to whether damage to buyer's automobile had been previously paid for by a third-party tort-feasor); Dean v. Johnston, 206 So.2d 610, 281 Ala. 602 (even if questions put to tractor truck driver on cross-examination in action by owner for property damage against driver of automobile with which tractor truck had collided had been properly framed to elicit testimony of his convictions, rather than his arrest, for speeding, error would have ensued had objections to such line of questions been overruled regardless of whether testimony had been sought to be introduced for impeachment of credibility of witness or on issue of contributory negligence by employment of incompetent servant).

Cal.—Kolaric v. Kaufman, 1968, 67 Cal.Rptr. 729, 261 Cal.App.2d 20 (cross-examination of plaintiff as to whether or not she had ever been in concentration camp and defense counsel's comments bringing into question her citizenship were improper); Dean v. Feld, 175 P.2d 278, 77 Cal.App.2d 327 (cross-examination of child's mother, if she was in habit of letting child play around sidewalk unattended); Cordi v. Garcia, 102 P.2d 820, 39 Cal.App.2d 189 (cross-examination of mother of driver, whether her boy had previously caused her trouble by "getting into other automobiles," was improper).

Conn.—Eamiello v. Piscitelli, 51 A.2d 912, 133 Conn. 360 (cross-examination of defendant as to whether police officers' investigation of defendant's driving at time of accident was anything new to him was properly denied).

Ga.—Johnson v. Myers, 1968, 165 S.E.2d 739, 118 Ga.App. 773, 33 A.L.R.3d 1047 (evidence in negligence actions of similar acts or omissions on part of defendant on other and different occasions is not admissible, even on cross-examination, if such is used simply as ve-

§ 420.1 TRIAL EVIDENCE Ch. 420

hicle to place before jury irrelevant and prejudicial matter violative of "other transactions" rule); Millhollan v. Watkins Motor Lines, Inc., 1967, 157 S.E.2d 901, 116 Ga. App. 452 (intrastate regulations concerning length of compulsory rest stops did not apply to defendant truck driver who was engaged in interstate commerce, and it was not error to refuse to permit cross-examination as to whether he had knowledge of such regulations); Gahring v. Barron, 133 S.E.2d 389, 108 Ga.App. 530 (lengthy cross-examination of plaintiff as to his subsequent collisions, to place before jury evidence of plaintiff's negligence in unrelated situations, ceased to perform its original function of determining what part of his injuries resulted from defendant's alleged tort and what part from other causes and became irrelevant and prejudicial under "other transactions" rule); Elliott v. Georgia Power Co., 197 S.E. 914, 58 Ga.App. 151 (re refusal on deposition to answer, on advice of counsel, whether he had been instructed how to answer a question).

Ill.—Cobean v. Richardson, 4 N.E.2d 769, 287 Ill.App. 618 (re injection of workmen's compensation benefits).

Ind.—Lengyel v. Hecht, 1969, 242 N.E.2d 135, 143 Ind.App. 660 (in action for injuries sustained by plaintiff when struck by electric golf cart operated by defendant, refusal to permit plaintiff to cross-examine defendant as to what intoxicating beverages he had drunk was not improper in that, despite any probative value, such evidence would have unfairly prejudiced defendant).

Minn.—Souden v. Johnson, 1963, 125 N.W.2d 742, 267 Minn. 151 (as to plea of guilty of driving while intoxicated and leaving scene on a prior occasion).

Mo.—Steele v. Yacovelli, 1967, 419 S.W.2d 477 (proper exclude as to discussion with plaintiff as to prior back injury where no present back injury alleged); State ex rel. State Highway Commission v. Eilers, 406 S.W.2d 567 (points of differences between what a photograph shows and what is contended to be actual facts may be the basis for cross-examination, thus enabling jury to give proper weight).

N.H.—Winslow v. Dietlin, 121 A.2d 573, 100 N.H. 147 (cross-examination of mother on whether son was mistaken in testifying that she took down names of witnesses after accident, merely sought opinion on accuracy of another's testimony which would have presented contradiction to a collateral issue, and was properly disallowed).

N.Y.—Hartley v. Szadkowski, 1969, 300 N.Y.S.2d 82, 32 A.D.2d 550 (prejudicial error to permit cross-examination of plaintiff concerning a prior accident since, if such evidence was offered to show that plaintiff was generally careless, it was incompetent, and if such evidence were admissible to establish plaintiff's knowledge of allegedly dangerous condition of highway at point of impact, it was incumbent upon defendants to prove that prior accident occurred under similar conditions at approximately the same point, which defendants did not show to be the case); Jensen v. Casale, 254 N.Y.S.2d 880, 22 A.D.2d 994 (defendants sued in connection with rear-end collision were entitled to prove that plaintiff had previously claimed injuries caused by other accidents, but protracted cross-examination of her husband, not as to such injuries but as to litigation concerning them, was improper); Womble v. Michelson, 254 N.Y.S.2d 861, 22 A.D.2d 815 (for trial judge to permit and participate in cross-examination of defendant with respect to policemen's visit to his place of business a week after accident); Kirkpatrick v. Fesinger, 239 N.Y.S.2d 395, 18 A.D.2d 1132 (cross-examination of defendant to bring out the fact that there was special equipment upon his automobile was relevant as bearing upon ability of defendant to bring his automobile to a stop in time to avoid accident, but his cross-examination as to use of automobile in racing and as to drag racing done by defendant shortly before trial but more than two years after the accident went beyond the fair limits of cross-examination); Phass v. MacClenathen, 85 N.Y.S.2d 643, 274 App.Div. 535 (re revocation of driver's license).

N.C.—Potts v. Howser, 1968, 161 S.E.2d 737, 274 N.C. 49 (questions asked of injured party on cross-examination concerning delinquency nature of income tax returns, and whether he got a Mexican divorce after accident in suit tended to prejudice him in eyes of jury without rational basis as affecting his credibility and were improper).

N.D.—Thornburg v. Perleberg, 1968, 158 N.W.2d 188 (improper for plaintiff to ask defendant whether he did not have record of accidents and traffic violations, but there was no prejudicial error, in view of cautionary instruction).

Okl.—Parker v. Washington, 421 P. 2d 861 (permitting cross-examination of driver relating to her involvement in prior accidents was improper).

Pa.—Hess v. Bahoric, 84 Dauph. 11 (may not be cross-examined at length on details as to the happening of an accident, where he has already testified that he has no recollection of such details, and further questions would only elicit hypothetical answers).

Tex.—Osterloh v. San Antonio Public Service Co., Civ.App.1934, 77 S.W. 2d 290 (re knowledge of street defects, where no evidence showed presence of defects).

Vt.—Mitchell v. Amadon, 1969, 260 A.2d 213, 128 Vt. 169 (where at time defendant was asked question on cross-examination there was no evidence that alleged oncoming truck from behind which minor plaintiff appeared on roadway was not in fact there at all, trial judge did not err in excluding question inquiring whether defendant could have avoided accident if no truck existed).

Wash.—State v. Hudson, 1970, 463 P.2d 786, 1 Wash.App. 813 (in prosecution for taking and riding in automobile without permission of owner, even if defendant's testimony put his prior conduct in issue, questions whether on prior occasion a friend had loaned automobile to defendant and such automobile had been stolen were not permissible to impeach defendant on such issue).

W.Va.—Lilly v. Taylor, 1967, 155 S.E.2d 579, 151 W.Va. 730 (permitting counsel for defendant, over objection, to inquire on cross-examination whether tires being transported in plaintiff's automobile at time of collision were "racing car slicks" and whether plaintiff was en route to certain home "to work on a racing car" was error).

Wis.—Knight v. Hasler, 128 N.W.2d 407, 24 Wis.2d 128 (allowing defendants' counsel to cross-examine plaintiff to show that she had, at other times, made claims against third persons for injuries sustained by her on other occasions).

Familiarity with law

Court properly sustained an objection to question on cross-examination whether driver of automobile occupied by plaintiff was familiar with the rule that gave motorist approaching from the right the right of way, since it was immaterial whether driver knew the law, and witness'

§ 420.1 TRIAL EVIDENCE Ch. 420

The court also may determine the order of cross-examination by multiple parties.[14]

When one of several co-defendants is called as a witness by the plaintiff, the other co-defendants have the right of cross-examination.[15]

If a party to the action refuses to answer a proper question upon cross-examination, the entire testimony of that witness may be stricken, and the refusal of the court to reopen the case to permit further testimony is discretionary.[16]

knowledge could not affect rights, duties and obligations of occupant who was suing owner of the other automobile involved in the collision. Watt v. Feuerlicht, Ohio App., 41 N.E.2d 719, 35 O.L.A. 509.

Inquiry of statement stenographer as to identity of investigator

Where insurance adjuster who, with public stenographer, took statements from injured plaintiffs at hospital did not testify, his credibility or possible interest or bias was not relevant, and question on cross-examination to stenographer as to adjuster's occupation was improper as potentially serving no purpose except to inject irrelevant matter, i. e., that defendant carried insurance. Ikerd v. Lapworth, C.A.Ind.1970, 435 F.2d 197.

Remarriage by widow plaintiff

Cal.—Benwell v. Dean, 1967, 57 Cal. Rptr. 394, 249 Cal.App.2d 345 (refusal proper).

Ohio.—Helmick v. Netzley, 229 N.E. 2d 476, 12 Ohio Misc. 97 (remarried widow suing for wrongful death was not subject to cross-examination to show that her name was not that of her deceased husband).

Showing collateral benefits

S.C.—Powers v. Temple, 1967, 156 S.E.2d 759, 250 S.C. 149 (that had been paid salary by employer).

14. **N.C.**—Yelton v. Dobbins, 1969, 170 S.E.2d 552, 6 N.C.App. 483.

15. **Pa.**—Peters v. Shear, 1945, 41 A.2d 556, 351 Pa. 521 (husband of plaintiff made party defendant).

But see

U.S.—Grunenthal v. Long Island R. Co., 1967, D.C.N.Y., 292 F.Supp. 813, affirmed in part, remanded in part, 388 F.2d 480, reversed on other grounds 89 S.Ct. 331, 393 U.S. 156, 21 L.Ed.2d 309 (third-party defendant had no right to cross-examine witness as to signed statement of witness where interests of both third-party defendant and third-party plaintiff with respect to contents of statement were identical).

Miss.—Bigelow v. Sports Cars, Limited, 1969, 221 So.2d 108 (because interests of the two defendants were so close one defendant should not be permitted to cross-examine or ask leading questions of witnesses of other defendant).

Contra

Where one defendant was called by plaintiff in plaintiff's case in chief under the Civil Practice Act for cross-examination, the defendants were entitled, after cross-examination was completed, to examine that defendant for the purpose of clarifying or explaining evidence brought out in the cross-examination, but were not entitled to cross-examine defendant. Wist v. Pitcairn, 26 N.E. 2d 998, 305 Ill.App. 167.

16. **Wash.**—Rutger v. Walken, 143 P.2d 866, 19 Wash.2d 681.

As to cross-examination on the issue of credibility, see Chapter 421, Impeachment.

§ 420.2 Permissible Scope

Library References:
C.J.S. Witnesses § 377 et seq.
West's Key No. Digests, Witnesses ⇐268 et seq.

The federal court rule is stated in the terms that cross-examination "should be limited to the subject matter of the direct examination" (except as to credibility matter); but the court "may, in the exercise of discretion, permit inquiry into additional matter as if on direct examination." [17] The same rule has been enacted in certain states.[18]

In many other state jurisdictions, except on the issue of credibility, the rule has been that cross-examination must be confined to matters brought out on direct examination.[19]

17. Federal Rules of Evidence § 611 (b), 28 U.S.C.A.

18. **Fla.**—Florida Rules of Evidence § 90.612(2).

Neb.—Nebraska Rules of Evidence § 611(2).

Nev.—N.R.S. 50.115(2).

19. **Cal.**—West's Ann.Calif.Evid. Code, § 773(a); People v. Butler, 55 Cal.Rptr. 511, 421 P.2d 703, 65 Cal.2d 569 (to elicit any information that may tend to overcome, qualify or explain testimony given by witness on direct examination).

Conn.—State v. Fisher, 201 A.2d 200, 2 Conn.Cir. 446.

Ga.—Granger v. National Convoy & Trucking Co., 7 S.E.2d 915, 62 Ga.App. 294.

Idaho—Rosenberg v. Toetly, 1971, 489 P.2d 446, 94 Idaho 413 (cross-examination of attorney, who had represented defendant in suit against garage which worked on his automobile, as to extent he aided defendant in answering interrogatories propounded by plaintiff-passengers, was beyond scope of direct examination wherein attorney was only questioned as to origin of expert's report on brakes of automobile).

Ill.—Young v. Miller, 1967, 223 N.E.2d 854, 79 Ill.App.2d 463; Rennie v. Jacoel, 1966, 217 N.E.2d 105, 70 Ill.App.2d 201.

Ind.—Brindle v. Harter, 211 N.E.2d 513, 138 Ind.App. 692, citing I.L.E. Witnesses § 113 (may go into any phase of that subject which tends to modify, explain, or rebut witness' statements on direct).

Iowa.—Castner v. Wright, 1964, 127 N.W.2d 583, opinion supplemented 128 N.W.2d 885, 256 Iowa 638 (no direct testimony as to conversation being inquired about); Hope v. Ted McGrevey, Inc., 1950, 44 N.W.2d 369, 241 Iowa 1022 (limitation not abuse of discretion).

Kan.—Frame v. Bauman, 1969, 449 P.2d 525, 202 Kan. 461 (not restricted to identical details).

Mich.—Socony Vacuum Oil Co. v. Marvin, 21 N.W.2d 841, 313 Mich. 528 (absence of insurance).

Mont.—Garrison v. Trowbridge, 177 P.2d 464, 119 Mont. 505.

N.J.—Vargo v. P. Ballantine & Sons, 197 A. 52, 119 N.J.L. 561.

§ 420.1 TRIAL EVIDENCE Ch. 420

In a variety of situations the court has held the cross-examination to have been within the scope of the direct examination;[20] and, in others, to have been beyond the scope of the direct.[21]

N.Y.—Cavalier v. Bittner, 60 N.Y.S. 2d 355, 186 Misc. 848 (becomes witness of cross-examining party as to matters not inquired about in direct examination).

Okl.—Frierson v. Hines, 1967, 426 P.2d 362 (may be asked any question which reasonably tends to explain, contradict, or discredit his testimony); Rapp v. State, 1966, 418 P.2d 357 (anything which tends to elucidate, modify, explain, contradict or rebut).

Or.—Still v. Benton, 1968, 445 P.2d 492, 251 Or. 463 (court did not abuse its discretion in limiting scope of recross-examination to specific matters brought out in redirect).

Pa.—Brodie v. Philadelphia Transp. Co., 203 A.2d 657, 415 Pa. 296.

Wash.—Harrington v. Goe, Pa.Com. Pl., 45 Wash.Co. 177 (inquiry on direct examination strictly limited to one independent part of a conversation between the witness and another does not open the door to cross-examination on all unrelated matters embraced by the conversation).

Rule qualifed as to party

Ill.—Roewe v. Lombardo, 221 N.E. 2d 521, 76 Ill.App.2d 164 (generally broader than scope permitted in cross-examination of other witnesses).

N.J.—Derowski v. Zaremba, 1968, 241 A.2d 670, 100 N.J.Super. 284 (may take wider range, even though subject matter was not touched on direct).

20. **U.S.**—Kemnitz v. U. S., C.A.Ill., 369 F.2d 389 (where witness testified on direct as to certain details observed at accident scene, inquiry on cross-examination relating to observation of additional relevant details); Podolsky v. La Forge, C.

C.A.Mass., 92 F.2d 954 (where nearby resident testified on direct concerning locus of accident and what he saw there immediately after accident but did not testify about tire marks on street, resident's testimony on cross-examination that he did see tire marks was competent).

Ala.—Bradley v. Jones, 1968, 211 So. 2d 465, 282 Ala. 331 (where general contractor's witness on direct made reference to state highway specifications with respect to standards governing subdivision street grading, permitting subcontractor to use specifications for cross-examination of general contractor's witnesses was not abuse of discretion).

Ark.—Henry v. Landreth, 1973, 494 S.W.2d 114, 254 Ark. 483 (in action by woman who, on direct, testified that before the accident her medical condition was good, that she was planning to go to work and that, during hospitalization subsequent to automobile injury, she was bedfast and confined to her room, defendants should have been permitted to cross-examine plaintiff concerning self-inflicted gunshot wound sustained two months before automobile accident, concerning her asserted instructions to hospital personnel not to let anyone see her hospital records relative to the self-inflicted injury and concerning whether she was ambulatory and visited in another room on another floor during her hospitalization subsequent to the automobile injury).

Ga.—Elliott v. Georgia Power Co., 1938, 197 S.E. 914, 58 Ga.App. 151 (refusal to permit cross-examination of motorman as to whether motorman had "proceeded on that

21. See note 21 on page 256.

outbound track up to the point where this accident occurred" was not error, where motorman testified in direct that collision had not occurred).

Ill.—Rose v. B. L. Cartage Co., 1969, 249 N.E.2d 199, 110 Ill.App.2d 260 (in view of importance and materiality of testimony of plaintiff's witness, who had been defendant truck owner's manager, that color of plaintiffs' automobile was identical with paint he saw on saddle tank of defendant's truck after intersectional collision, cross-examination of witness by defendant on that point was properly permitted over objection that it was beyond scope); Rylko v. Katz, 228 N.E.2d 135, 84 Ill.App.2d 93 (defendant's questions pertaining to plaintiff's income after accident were not improper in view of plaintiff's testimony that he had not worked after accident).

Md.—Williams v. Graff, 71 A.2d 450, 194 Md. 516, 23 A.L.R.2d 106 (where police officer, called by plaintiff in action against owner of taxicab, testified on direct as to his observations at scene, including a pool of blood, owner of taxicab could cross-examine as to location of skid marks).

Mo.—Bader v. Hylarides, App., 374 S.W.2d 616 (admission of testimony of highway patrolman on cross-examination as to what plaintiff had told him at scene was not error where he had testified on direct as to what defendant had told him at scene).

Neb.—Clark v. Smith, 149 N.W.2d 425, 181 Neb. 461 (where testimony of sole primary witness necessarily involves questions of speed of vhicles involved in collision, he may be required on cross-examination to answer direct inquiries as to speed even though no such inquiry is made in course of his direct); In re Potts' Estate, 14 N.W.2d 323, 144 Neb. 729 (where witness, on direct, was interrogated about his knowledge of collision and as to speed of one automobile but not of other, permitting, on cross-examination, of interrogation as to speed of the other automobile was not an abuse of discretion).

N.J.—Murray v. Boston & M. R. R., 1966, 224 A.2d 66, 107 N.H. 367 (where plaintiff claimed loss of salary because of need to stay home to care for injured wife, cross-examination showing husband could afford to employ maid was proper).

Ohio.—Giles v. Yellow Cab Co., 205 N.E.2d 86, 1 Ohio App.2d 404 (where plaintiff's medical witness testified on direct that plaintiff's headaches and pain were proximately caused by collision and that examination of plaintiff disclosed degenerative arthritis of spine, defendant's question, on cross-examination, as to whether such type of pain could be coming from the arthritis was proper).

Tenn.—Sanders v. McNatt, 1968, 430 S.W.2d 797, 58 Tenn.App. 385 (where direct developed identity of claims representative, proper to cross-examine as to information received from the insured).

Wash.—State v. Hayes, 1968, 439 P.2d 978, 73 Wash.2d 568 (cross-examination of police officer, who had observed defendant and had conducted tests to determine his degree of intoxication, as to chemical tests administered to defendant was proper where defendant, on direct, elicited testimony from officer as to physical tests administered to defendant).

Wis.—Boller v. Cofrances, 1969, 166 N.W.2d 129, 42 Wis.2d 170 (in action in which plaintiff's husband and his passenger were killed, where widow sought to recover damages for loss of society and companionship and testified that she and her husband had a close relationship and were very happily

§ 420.2 TRIAL EVIDENCE Ch. 420

Other state court cases hold that cross-examination may be as broad as the whole case.[22] The rule of several states authorizes the court to restrict the otherwise broad rule, in the interest of justice.[23]

married, cross-examination of plaintiff as to whether she was aware of affair that her husband was having with passenger was within scope); Seitz v. Seitz, 1967, 151 N.W.2d 86, 35 Wis.2d 282 (cross-examination of plaintiff's driver, who testified for plaintiff on direct examination only as to his conduct and observations up to time of accident, as to what he did after accident, was permissible where plaintiff's opening statement referred to driver's conduct after accident).

Balance of impeachment statement

Where defendant elicited from witness on direct examination facts relating to taking of statement of plaintiff at hospital by representative of defendant cab company and then elicited only the desired question and answer, permitting plaintiff's attorney to elicit plaintiff's answers to remainder of questions in the statement was not error, in that area covered by defendant was the entire circumstance of the statement and not merely one question and one answer, and having opened the subject, it was precluded from objecting to the plaintiff's further inquiry. Siciunas v. Checker Cab Co., Inc., 1974, 217 N.W.2d 824, 191 Neb. 766.

N.J.—Lieberman v. Saley, 227 A.2d 339, 94 N.J.Super. 156 (where Acting Director of Division of Motor Vehicles introduced portion of statement made by plaintiff at hospital indicating that she had been traveling about 40–45 miles per hour before her automobile left road, plaintiff had right on cross-examination to elicit from officer the rest of statement made at that time to effect that accident had been caused by unknown driver in going across center line of highway and into lane of plaintiff's vehicle).

21. **Ill.**—Watson v. Fishbach, 1973, 301 N.E.2d 303, 54 Ill.2d 498 (in dramshop action for wrongful death of husband, where cross-examination of plaintiff widow regarding her remarriage clearly exceeded scope of direct and emphasized remarriage and disclosed to jury that plaintiff had child by new husband and that she and her family were living in home formerly occupied by plaintiff and her deceased husband).

Iowa.—Hayungs v. Falk, 27 N.W.2d 15, 238 Iowa 285 (did not open door for cross-examination on whether she had been paid workmen's compensation insurance).

Pa.—Harrington v. Goe, 45 Wash. Co. 177 (an inquiry on direct strictly limited to one independent part of a conversation between the witness and another does not open the door to cross-examination on all unrelated matters embraced by the conversation).

22. **Ala.**—Riddle v. Dorough, 187 So.2d 568, 279 Ala. 527. Coward v. McKinney, 172 So.2d 538, 277 Ala. 513.

La.—State v. Williams, 193 So.2d 787, 250 La. 64.

Miss.—Saxon v. Harvey, 1966, 190 So.2d 901.

Mo.—Arnold v. Manzella, App., 186 S.W.2d 882.

23. **Me.**—Maine Rules of Evidence § 611(b).

N.M.—New Mexico Rules of Evidence § 611(b).

Wis.—Wisconsin Rules of Evidence § 906.11(2).

If, in a state court action, the testimony of a witness called by one party is desired by the opposite party as to matters which could not properly be brought out on cross-examination, the witness must be made the party's own witness.[24] It is discretionary with the court as to whether it will permit one to make the adversary's witness the party's own upon cross-examination.[25]

24. Md.—Williams v. Graff, 71 A. 2d 450, 194 Md. 516, 23 A.L.R.2d 106.

Minn.—Jones v. Peterson, 1968, 156 N.W.2d 733, 279 Minn. 241 (in suit for death of occupant of automobile which was driven either by occupant who was wearing a green dress or by her companion who was clothed in white, permitting plaintiff's witness, who had observed automobile prior to collision and who had testified on direct as to speed, direction, and distances traveled but not with respect to attire of driver, to testify upon cross-examination that she noticed arm of driver and that it was covered by sleeve of a colored dress was not improper, as defendants had made plaintiff's witness their witness as to that fact question).

N.J.—Vargo v. P. Ballantine & Sons, 1938, 197 A. 52, 119 N.J.L. 561.

25. Cal.—Germ v. City and County of San Francisco, 222 P.2d 122, 99 Cal.App.2d 404.

Chapter 421

IMPEACHMENT OF WITNESSES

Table of Sections

Sec.
421.1 Impeachment—In General.
421.2 —— Prior Inconsistent Statements.
421.3 —— Contradiction of Facts.
421.4 —— Bias.
421.5 —— Character.
421.6 —— Rehabilitation.

---

§ 421.1 Impeachment—In General

Library References:
C.J.S. Evidence §§ 571, 575; Witnesses § 458 et seq.
West's Key No. Digests, Evidence ⚖560; Witnesses ⚖311 et seq.

The court, within its discretion, should permit interrogation designed to impeach the credibility of an adversary witness.[1]

1. **U.S.**—Harris v. U. S., C.A.Nev., 371 F.2d 365 (ought to be given largest possible scope).

   Ill.—Sweeney v. Matthews, 1968, 236 N.E.2d 439, 94 Ill.App.2d 6, affirmed 264 N.E.2d 170, 146 Ill.2d 64; Roewe v. Lombardo, 221 N.E.2d 521, 76 Ill.App.2d 164 (permitting some testing by cross-examination of correctness of defendant's statement of place of residence).

   Ky.—Bolin v. Com., 407 S.W.2d 431 (although jury was likely to be prejudiced against defendant by introduction of evidence tending to show he was shiftless bum, nevertheless, cross-examination of defendant regarding his employment was proper, since certain amount of background information is relevant, proper and admissible).

   Mich.—Hes v. Haviland Products Co., 148 N.W.2d 509, 6 Mich.App. 163

   N.C.—Potts v. Howser, 161 S.E.2d 737, 274 N.C. 49 (may not be used to take unfair advantage nor to discredit by questions tending merely to prejudice him in eyes of jury without rational basis as affecting credibility).

   R.I.—Bedrosian v. O'Keefe, 1965, 215 A.2d 423.

   Tex.—Walker v. Missouri Pac. R. Co., 425 S.W.2d 462, error refused n. r. e. (anything may be shown which might affect credibility, such as bias, interest and prejudice, and a wide latitude is allowed in such matters).

   Confinement in mental institution
   Admission, for testing credibility, in action by owner to recover from manufacturer for injury sustained when automobile, in which owner was passenger, overturned, on theories of negligence and breach of implied warranties, of evidence that driver had been treated for nervous breakdown in mental institution for two three-month periods in consecu-

Prior conduct inconsistent with a witness' testimony may be shown,[2] but this rule may not be abused in order to show a highly prejudicial circumstance which could not otherwise be shown.[3]

tive years about eight years prior to accident was not abuse of discretion. Ramseyer v. General Motors Corp., C.A.Neb.1969, 417 F.2d 859.

May not inquire in bad faith

Record showing that only one question was asked and answered without objection failed to show that defense counsel committed error by asking question under guise of laying basis for impeachment and upon eliciting a denial failed to follow up with impeaching evidence. Littlefield v. Alton and Southern R. R., 1968, 239 N.E.2d 147, 96 Ill.App.2d 470.

Statutory methods not exclusive

Fact that statute prescribed three methods of impeachment does not mean that witness cannot be discredited for other reasons. Lewis v. American Road Ins. Co., 1969, 167 S. E.2d 729, 119 Ga.App. 507.

2. Pa.—Kaplan v. Loev, 194 A. 653, 327 Pa. 465, certiorari denied 58 S.Ct. 477, 302 U.S. 766, 82 L.Ed. 595.

Choice of defendant for own claim

S.C.—Gainer v. Tyner, 1972, 193 S. E.2d 525, 259 S.C. 629 (cross-examination as to whether he had made a claim against his wife and whether he had made any claim against driver of the other involved car was proper since it had a bearing on credibility).

Fact of prior claims

N.J.—Graf v. Folarno, 1968, 239 A.2d 15, 99 N.J.Super. 173 (cross-examination of driver, who sought recovery for injuries sustained in rear-end collision, concerning prior workmen's compensation cases went to driver's credibility and was proper).

Failure to identify self at scene as a witness

Fact that plaintiffs' witnesses failed to identify themselves as such to policeman who made investigation of accident, notwithstanding queries by officer of crowd that had gathered, threw shadow on credibility of their testimony. McBride v. Raidt, 1968, La.App., 206 So.2d 299.

3. Pa.—Kaplan v. Loev, 194 A. 653, 327 Pa. 465, certiorari denied 58 S.Ct. 477, 302 U.S. 766, 82 L.Ed. 595.

Va.—Diamond Cab Co. v. Jones, 174 S.E. 675, 162 Va. 412 (failure to report accident, in violation of statute, not admissible).

Driving history as distorting own speed opinion

Evidence that motorist, alleged to have been speeding at time of accident, was convicted of speeding on three occasions subsquent to date of accident and before trial was not admissible to show that motorist's habit or custom was to speed and that she was not, for that reason, competent judge of her own speed at time of accident. Dimond v. Kling, N.D.1974, 221 N.W.2d 86.

Failure to issue ticket alleged to impeach officer

Under facts of actions arising out of three-vehicle collision, evidence as to whether the patrolman had charged truck driver with any traffic violation was not competent to impeach such officer. Beanblossom v. Thomas, N.C., 146 S.E.2d 36, 266 N.C. 181.

Prior lawsuits alleged to show litigious

N.Y.—Bowers v. Johnson, 271 N.Y.S. 2d 106, 26 A.D.2d 552.

§ 421.1 TRIAL EVIDENCE Ch. 421

Evidence that the witness was intoxicated at the time of an accident, is admissible as bearing upon the credibility of the testimony.[4]

While psychiatric testimony may be used to attack the credibility of a witness,[5] the technique is sharply limited.[6]

Prior driving record

Refusal to permit cross-examination of plaintiff motorist as to his driving history and driving record was not improper, where plaintiff suffered from amnesia and was not able to testify as to any of the events surrounding the accident, where defendants were thus attempting to introduce plaintiff's driving record as positive evidence of negligence, and where the accidents contained in plaintiff's record lacked any logical relevance to plaintiff's behavior in the collision in question; further, even if logically relevant, plaintiff's driving record was inadmissible because of the substantial danger of prejudice. Willmore v. Hertz Corp., D.C.Mich.1969, 322 F.Supp. 444, affirmed C.A.6th, 1971, 437 F.2d 357.

Unrelated prior injury

Mo.—Senter v. Ferguson, App.1972, 486 S.W.2d 644 (evidence, elicited from plaintiff on cross-examination, of plaintiff's prior injuries or conditions which were unrelated to injuries complained of, was inadmissible to impeach plaintiff who had testified on direct examination that she had been in good health prior to accident upon which her action was based).

4. **Cal.**—Ketchum v. Massa, 266 P. 352, 90 Cal.App. 762.
Iowa.—Maland v. Tesdall, 5 N.W.2d 327, 232 Iowa 959.
N.D.—State v. Glavkee, 138 N.W.2d 663, citing 98 C.J.S. Witnesses § 461h (however, the fact that witness was arrested for being drunk is wholly immaterial and sheds no light on credibility of his testimony).
Ohio.—Johnson v. Knipp, 1974, 304 N.E.2d 914, 36 Ohio App.2d 218.

Va.—Lambach v. Bailey, 119 S.E.2d 305, 202 Va. 620.

Not history of intoxication

Evidence of long history of intoxication is inadmissible for impeaching credibility unless it is clearly shown that intoxication occurred contemporaneously with events about which witness is testifying. Springer v. Reimers, 1970, 84 Cal.Rptr. 486, 4 Cal.App.3d 325.

Rule limited

U.S.—Miles v. Ryan, C.A.Pa.1973, 484 F.2d 1255 (not admissible unless proof reasonably establishes a degree of intoxication which affected the capacity of the witness to observe and remember).
Ill.—Ballard v. Jones, 1974, 316 N.E.2d 281, 21 Ill.App.3d 496 (refusal to allow defense counsel to cross-examine host driver as to whether he had consumed intoxicants prior to accident was not improper, notwithstanding claim that such ruling prevented defendant from introducing evidence that had a direct bearing on credibility of host driver's testimony, where there was no evidence that the host motorist was intoxicated).
Ohio.—Camerlin v. Starr, App.1964, 200 N.E.2d 817 (where admitted negligence, and testimony did not contradict plaintiff's proof, held inadmissible).

5. **Cal.**—Ballard v. Superior Court of San Diego County, 49 Cal.Rptr. 302, 401 P.2d 838.

6. **Cal.**—Ballard v. Superior Court of San Diego County, 49 Cal.Rptr. 302, 410 P.2d 838 (not admissible if witness has been declared com-

§ 421.1 IMPEACHMENT OF WITNESSES

A witness may be impeached by inquiry on cross-examination even as to collateral matters referred to on direct examination.[7] However, a party who elicits collateral matters on cross-examination cannot attempt to introduce extrinsic evidence to impeach the witness on those matters.[8]

The court may refuse cross-examination intended to make a witness testify upon an incompetent matter in the hope of creating a contradiction.[9]

petent or if no objection is urged to his competency).

Ill.—Adams v. Ford Motor Co., 1968, 243 N.E.2d 843, 103 Ill.App.2d 356 (evidence of need for mental treatment of witness who had been ordered confined for mental treatment but had been given absolute discharge from confinement was not admissible to affect his credibility, notwithstanding contention that mental weakness not rendering witness incompetent may nevertheless affect his credibility).

7. U.S.—U. S. v. Barash, C.A.N.Y., 365 F.2d 395.

Pa.—Bruno v. Brown, 200 A.2d 405, 414 Pa. 361.

Testimony as to subsequent precautions

Generally, evidence of precautions taken and repairs made after happening of accident is not admissible to show negligent condition at time of accident, but such evidence may be admitted to impeach testimony of witness who has testified that condition prior to accident was not a dangerous one. Love v. Wolf, 1967, 58 Cal.Rptr. 42, 249 Cal.App.2d 822.

8. Ky.—Baker Pool Co. v. Bennett, 411 S.W.2d 335.

Mass.—Leone v. Doran, 1973, 292 N.E.2d 19, 363 Mass. 1, order vacated in part 297 N.E.2d 493 (rule that if a party cross-examines a witness on a collateral matter, he must take answer as it is given was applicable to situation where it was obvious that sole purpose of plaintiff's counsel in calling an insurance investigator to stand was to establish collateral matter, and, prior to asking investigator whether defendant had stated that "he would sue the company for one million dollars if they didn't properly represent him").

Mich.—Oppenheim v. Rattner, 1967, 149 N.W.2d 881, 6 Mich.App. 554.

Okl.—Montgomery v. Nance, 425 P. 2d 470.

Pa.—Harrison v. Nichols, 1971, 281 A.2d 696, 219 Pa.Super. 428 (where on direct examination plaintiff testified that he was living with his wife and children at time of trial which occurred more than a year after accident, on cross-examination it was brought out that he was living with another woman at time of accident, and in response to question asking plaintiff when he began living with his wife again, plaintiff answered that he had resumed living with her about two weeks after he got out of hospital, it was improper for defense counsel to atttempt to impeach plaintiff's credibility by further cross-examining plaintiff on his deposition where he had indicated that he resumed living with his wife about three months after he left hospital).

Vt.—Macauley v. Hyde, 42 A.2d 482, 114 Vt. 198.

9. U.S.—Stevens v. Consolidated Mut. Ins. Co., C.A.Puerto Rico, 352 F.2d 41.

Cal.—Marocco v. Ford Motor Co., 1970, 86 Cal.Rptr. 526, 7 Cal.App.

§ 421.1   TRIAL EVIDENCE   Ch. 421

Party's own witness

Except in federal court,[10] and in certain state jurisdictions,[11] a party may not impeach a witness called by that party unless surprised by the witness' testimony,[12] and the surprise must be

3d 84 (elimination of "collateral matter" limitation on attacking credibility of witness does not give party license to secure admission of otherwise inadmissible evidence for purpose of subsequently impeaching it).

Mo.—Wiesemann v. Pavlat, 1967, 413 S.W.2d 23 (when defendant abandoned claim for medical expense, it became collateral matter and court did not err in refusing to permit cross-examination of defendant, on his abandoned counterclaim, to show original claim of medical treatment which was inconsistent with defendant's testimony of no medical treatment).

10. Federal Rules of Evidence § 607, 28 U.S.C.A.

11. **Cal.**—West's Ann.Calif.Evid. Code, § 785.

Ill.—Ill.Rev.Stats.1967, c. 110, § 60 (selected instances).

Kan.—Kansas Code of Civil Procedure § 60–420.

Me.—Maine Rules of Evidence § 607.

Mass.—Mass.Laws Annot. 1959, c. 233, § 23 (selected instances).

Neb.—Nebraska Rules of Evidence 607.

Nev.—N.R.S. 50.075.

N.J.—New Jersey Evidence Rule 20 (except by proof of prior inconsistent statement).

N.M.—New Mexico Rules of Evidence § 607.

N.Y.—N.Y. CPLR 4514 (McKinney 1963) (selected instances).

Utah.—Utah Rules of Evidence § 20.

Vt.—12 Vt.Stats.Annot.1959, §§ 1641a, 1642 (selected instances).

Wis.—Wisconsin Rules of Evidence § 906.07.

12. **Conn.**—Sosnowski v. Lenox, 53 A.2d 388, 133 Conn. 624.

Ill.—Paul v. Carroll, 1974, 305 N.E.2d 588, 16 Ill.App.3d 173; Rose v. B. L. Cartage Co., 1969, 249 N.E.2d 199, 110 Ill.App.2d 260 (redirect examination of witness by plaintiffs as to when he had first mentioned matter and whether he had mentioned it at previous trial was properly permitted on basis of surprise); Closterides v. Dalton, 1964, 200 N.E.2d 29, 49 Ill.App.2d 286; Tarasuik v. Russell, 1964, 199 N.E.2d 629, 49 Ill.App.2d 418 (not where had talked to counsel); Moran v. Gatz, 1946, 64 N.E.2d 564, 327 Ill.App. 480.

Mich.—Haynes v. Seiler, 1969, 167 N.W.2d 819, 16 Mich.App. 98; Cohen v. McGregor, 164 N.W.2d 682, 13 Mich.App. 519 (where witness who was called by defendants was close associate of plaintiff and witness did not answer defendants' question concerning condition of plaintiff's hearing prior to accident in manner expected and trial court charged jury that it could consider witness' prior contradictory affidavit only for impeachment, trial court did not abuse its discretion in permitting defendants to refer to witness' pretrial statement).

Miss.—Clark v. Lansford, 191 So.2d 123 (when he proves to be hostile, and when his testimony differs from that on a former hearing); Hall v. State, 165 So.2d 345, 250 Miss. 253 (when they prove to be hostile).

N.Y.—Cavalier v. Bittner, 60 N.Y.S. 2d 355, 186 Misc. 848 (rule applied though witness cross-examined as to matter not inquired about in direct examination).

N.C.—Morris v. Beaty Service Co., 199 S.E. 922, 214 N.C. 562 (where plaintiff called defendant's driver as witness, could not impeach by prior conviction).

Available even where grounds to believe witness intends to testify contrary to statement

Although counsel may have good ground for believing that a witness intends to testify in a manner contrary to a statement he has previously given, counsel may still call the witness under the belief that, when confronted by the prior statement the witness will abandon efforts to deviate materially therefrom, and under such circumstances, if the witness fails to testify in substantial accord with his prior statement, admission of his inconsistent statement is discretionary. Liebman v. Society of Our Lady of Mount St. Carmel, Inc., Conn., 200 A.2d 721, 151 Conn. 582.

But see

Hostility of party's own witnss and absence of other prior statements are not prerequisites to admission of a statement under prior inconsistent statements statute. Goodney v. Smith, 1968, 242 N.E.2d 413, 354 Mass. 734, appeal after remand 269 N.E.2d 707, 359 Mass. 749; Under statute permitting a party to contradict his own witness, a signed statement of a witness introduced by the party calling him was admissible only in so far as it tended to contradict the witness' testimony at trial. G.L., Ter.Ed., c. 233, § 23. Kavanaugh v. Colombo, 24 N.E.2d 14, 304 Mass. 379.

General rule that a party who calls a witness represents him as being worthy of belief and cannot impeach him has been considerably relaxed to prevent injustice, and tendency of courts is to permit parties to show the truth without strict regard to technicalities. Com. v. Smith, 227 A.2d 653, 424 Pa. 544.

Called as "adverse witness"

In action brought by guest passenger against host driver and other motorist, host driver could be impeached where he had been called as an adverse witness by other motorist. Perkins v. Culver, 1971, 269 N.E.2d 333, 131 Ill.App.2d 881.

Refusal to admit prior contradictory statement, which was offered for purpose of impeaching testimony given by defendant as adverse witness, was error; overruling Chandler v. Fleeman, 50 Mo. 239. Wells v. Goforth, Mo.1969, 443 S.W.2d 155.

Change of testimony known

Where witness for plaintiff changed depositions plaintiff took several weeks before trial before notary before witness signed depositions, plaintiff could not introduce depositions made by witness in first instance to affect his credibility where witness testified in trial court in accordance with changed depositions and plaintiff was not taken by surprise. Gosney v. May Lumber & Coal Co., 179 S.W.2d 51, 352 Mo. 693.

Held not "entrapment"

In action by insured against insurer to recover for loss of automobile, circumstances that insurer's witness who had been found guilty of arson in connection with burning of automobile invoked privilege against self-incrimination and contradicted or repudiated certain details of written confession he had given to sheriff did not constitute entrapment entitling insurer to impeach witness by use of his statement. Lewis v. American Road Ins. Co., 1969, 167 S.E.2d 729, 119 Ga.App. 507.

Limited when on redirect

Where reason why party called witness was sufficiently explained by direct examination, favorable to party, party was properly not allowed to impeach the witness on redirect on basis of surprise and inconsistent pretrial statement when the witness

§ 421.1   TRIAL EVIDENCE   Ch. 421

substantial and founded on the fact that the witness' testimony is not only at variance with what the party had reason to believe it would be, but that it is also prejudicial or detrimental.[13] For on cross-examination gave answers unsatisfactory to the party. Sun Cab Co. v. Walston, 1972, 289 A.2d 804, 15 Md.App. 113, affirmed 298 A.2d 391, 267 Md. 559.

No claim of surprise

Refusal to allow defendant to impeach brother of plaintiff in action for death of plaintiff's son by introducing a claimed inconsistent written statement when defendant had called brother as his own witness was not error where there was no showing of surprise by defendant at brother's testimony. Gabel v. Koba, 1969, 463 P.2d 237, 1 Wash. App. 684.

Prior knowledge of character of witness

A litigant who knew or had means of knowing, before he offered a witness, the general character of the witness and has neither been deceived nor misled by this should not be allowed to impeach the witness by evidence of witness' general bad character when witness made contradictory statements. Kitchens v. Hall, 1967, 156 S.E.2d 920, 116 Ga.App. 41.

Proper as "contradiction"

Permitting plaintiff to question witness as to how he had answered certain questions at a previous hearing was not error, as against contention that such constituted improper impeachment by plaintiff of plaintiff's own witness, where it appeared that plaintiff was attempting to contradict the witness rather than impeach him. Jordan v. Williams, 1969, 171 S.E.2d 110, 7 N.C.App.2d 33.

Refreshing recollection

Even though defendant could not impeach a witness called by him, he had the right to appeal to the witness' conscience and refresh his memory, and accordingly, in reminding the witness, after the witness gave unsatisfactory reply to question asked, of a deposition taken earlier in the case and of a different reply by the witness to a similar question, defendant was not impeaching his own witness. Vancil v. Fletcher, 1967, 232 N.E.2d 789, 90 Ill. App.2d 277.

A party surprised by testimony of his witness may call his attention to conflicting statements made at another time, not for purpose of laying foundation for impeachment, but to test and quicken his recollection, and give him an opportunity to correct his testimony, if it is erroneous, and to show that it has surprised the party who called him. Breeding v. Reed, 110 N.W.2d 552, 253 Iowa 129.

Requisite be signed or under oath

A party may impeach his own witness pursuant to statutory authority by showing that witness made prior contradictory written statement, provided that it was subscribed by witness or made under oath. CPLR Rule 4514. Brown v. W. U. Tel. Co., 274 N.Y.S.2d 52, 26 A.D.2d 316.

Rule limited

Fla.—Florida Evidence Code § 90.608 (2) (if own witness "proves adverse", may impeach by proof of prior inconsistent statement without regard to surprise).

13.   Fla.—Gibbs v. State, 193 So.2d 460 (cannot impeach such a witness unless he not only fails to give beneficial testimony but also becomes adverse by giving evidence that is prejudicial to party producing him).

Ill.—Hall v. Baum Corp., 1973, 299 N.E.2d 156, 12 Ill.App.3d 755 (only testimonial reluctance was their

264

discussion of a party's right to ask leading questions of that party's own witness, see section 419.2, at footnote 25 et seq.

However, it is generally held that a party may contradict the testimony of that party's own witness by subsequent testimony.[14]

§ 421.2 Impeachment—Prior Inconsistent Statements

Library References:
C.J.S. Witnesses § 573 et seq.
West's Key No. Digests, Witnesses ⟶379 et seq.

Evidence of a witness' prior statement which is contradictory to the witness' testimony is generally admissible for impeachment purposes,[15] provided a proper foundation or "predi-

unwillingness to say what the defendant wanted them to).

Va.—Virginia Elec. & Power Co. v. Hall, 1945, 34 S.E.2d 382, 184 Va. 102 (not when merely negative in character and not injurious).

14. U.S.—Northern Pac. Ry. Co. v. Everett, C.A.Wash., 232 F.2d 488; Smith v. Central Linen Service Co., D.C.Md., 39 F.R.D. 15.

Ga.—Lewis v. American Road Ins. Co., 1969, 167 S.E.2d 729, 119 Ga. App. 507.

Ind.—Voorhees-Jontz Lumber Co. v. Bezek, 209 N.E.2d 380.

La.—Thibodeaux v. Hebert, 1967, 204 So.2d 419.

Mo.—Jones v. Chicago, R. S. & P. Ry. Co., 108 S.W.2d 94, 341 Mo. 640.

Neb.—Guyette v. Schmer, 35 N.W. 2d 689, 150 Neb. 659.

N.C.—Alexander Funeral Home, Inc. v. Pride, 136 S.E.2d 120, 261 N.C. 723.

Okl.—Glens Falls Ins. Co. v. Johnson, 403 P.2d 229.

Tenn.—Haggard v. Jim Clayton Motors, Inc., 393 S.W.2d 292, 216 Tenn. 625.

15. U.S.—Pollard v. Fennell, C.A. N.C., 400 F.2d 421 (about apparent inconsistencies between testimony in court and testimony on deposition); Joynor v. Berman Leasing Co., 398 F.2d 875 (properly permitted to read from deposition of plaintiff truck driver in previous workmen's compensation proceedings); Lewis v. Owen, 1968, C.A. Okl., 395 F.2d 537; Salsberg v. Modern Transfer Co., C.A.N.Y., 324 F.2d 737 (accident investigation report prepared by police officer at scene was properly admitted even though, on night before trial, officer had drawn additional lines on report diagram, where adequate charge on limitations upon jury's consideration of diagram was given).

Ala.—Johnson v. State, 187 So.2d 281, 43 Ala.App. 224 (prior testimony).

Alaska.—Menard v. Acevedo, 418 P. 2d 766 (report of investigating police officer).

Ariz.—Ruth v. Rhodes, 185 P.2d 304, 66 Ariz. 129 (condition of brakes).

Cal.—Hazel v. McGrath, 27 Cal. Rptr. 713, 212 Cal.App.2d 18 (testimony given at former trial).

Colo.—Schafer v. National Tea Co., 1973, 511 P.2d 949, 32 Colo.App. 372 (where plaintiff testified that truck was the only vehicle involved in the accident, impeaching

§ 421.2   TRIAL EVIDENCE   Ch. 421

plaintiff's credibility on cross-examination by showing that she had made prior inconsistent statements in a deposition indicating presence of a third vehicle and describing its action was not error as to third party from whom defendant sought indemnity, where deposition was employed for limited purpose of impeachment following proper foundation, and trial court carefully instructed jury).

Conn.—State v. Keating, 1964, 200 A.2d 724, 151 Conn. 592.

Dist.Col.—Weaver v. Irani, Minn. App.1966, 222 A.2d 846 (contradictory estimate of speed stated to treating doctor).

Fla.—Hicks v. Daymude, 1966, 190 So.2d 6; Shalley v. Fiore, 1964, 161 So.2d 18 (divorce proceedings statement indicating earlier injury).

Ga.—Gandy v. Griffin, 1969, 169 S.E.2d 651, 120 Ga.App. 100 (testimony of plaintiff's father that defendant's wife had told father that defendant was driving too fast was admissible to impeach wife, who had testified that defendant was driving 45 to 50 miles when approaching the intersection); Stubbs v. Daughtry, 153 S.E.2d 633, 115 Ga.App. 22 (testimony that driver stated that dust generated by his having driven down highway at speed of 75 miles per hour might have caused collision involving following automobile was admissible for purpose of impeaching driver's statement at trial that he had been traveling from 50 to 55 miles per hour); McKinney v. Pitts, 137 S.E.2d 571, 109 Ga.App. 866 (statement to examining physician); Phillips v. Howard, 136 S.E.2d 473, 109 Ga.App. 404 (deposition); Henry v. Hoch, 47 S.E.2d 159, 76 Ga.App. 819 (prior testimony).

Idaho.—Hodge v. Borden, 1966, 417 P.2d 75, 91 Idaho 125 (deposition).

Ill.—Johnson v. Cunningham, 1969, 244 N.E.2d 205, 104 Ill.App.2d 406; Vander Veen v. Yellow Cab Co., 1968, 233 N.E.2d 68, 89 Ill.App.2d 91 (transcript of prior hearing); Hendler v. Wolozin, 1969, 245 N.E.2d 74, 105 Ill.App.2d 132, certiorari denied 90 S.Ct. 264, 396 U.S. 929, 24 L.Ed.2d 227 (where, in action for injuries sustained by school children when they were struck after alighting from and crossing in front of bus, police officer who investigated accident testified for plaintiffs and stated on direct examination that it was his original opinion that transit authority was involved, counsel for transit authority could cross-examine officer as to whether there was anything in his report to show that the authority was involved in accident); Black v. DeWitt, 204 N.E.2d 820, 55 Ill.App.2d 220 (police report); Johnson v. Nevenhoven, 100 N.E.2d 60, 344 Ill.App. 125 (child witness); Huyler v. City of Chicago, 62 N.E.2d 574, 326 Ill.App. 555 (plan for intersection approved by witness); Fickerle v. Herman Seekamp, Inc., 274 Ill.App. 310 (prior statement made at coroner's inquest).

Ind.—Kilmer v. Galbreth, 218 N.E.2d 361.

Iowa.—Chandler v. Harger, 113 N.W.2d 250, 253 Iowa 565; State v. De Bont, 273 N.W. 873, 223 Iowa 721 (grand jury minutes).

Kan.—McGrath v. Mance, 400 P.2d 1013, 194 Kan. 640.

Ky.—Barker v. Danville Const. Co., 1965, 389 S.W.2d 931 (with proper admonition by court); Applegate v. Johnson, 1948, 208 S.W.2d 77, 306 Ky. 358 (deposition).

La.—April v. Millers Mut. Fire Ins. Co. of Texas, App.1973, 273 So.2d 50 (insured's prior statement that hit-and-run motorist's vehicle did not make contact, where testified to contact).

266

Mass.—Posner v. Minsky, 234 N.E. 2d 287, 353 Mass. 656; Langan v. Pianowski, 1940, 29 N.E.2d 700, 307 Mass. 149.

Mich.—Gonzalez v. Hoffman, 157 N.W.2d 475, 9 Mich.App. 522 (plaintiff's answers to questions on employment application was proper subject matter for cross-examination); Ruhala v. Roby, 150 N.W.2d 146, 379 Mich. 102 (portion of deposition containing prior inconsistent statements); Conlon v. Dean, 1968, 165 N.W.2d 623, 14 Mich.App. 415 (motorist's statement given to assistant prosecuting attorney within a few hours of accident while assistant prosecuting attorney was questioning her in his official role as prosecutor for people was not privileged, and the exclusion of such statement, which was inconsistent with trial testimony, constituted reversible error).

Minn.—Hillesheim v. Stippel, 1969, 166 N.W.2d 325, 283 Minn. 59.

Miss.—Jones v. Welford, 215 So.2d 240 (permitting highway patrolman to contradict defendant-driver with reference to conversation officer had with defendant-driver); Kelly v. King, 1967, 196 So.2d 525 (alleged involuntary confession); Boyd v. Donald, 1964, 167 So.2d 661, 250 Miss. 618 (officer's report as to location of debris).

Mo.—Freeman v. Kansas City Power & Light Co., 1974, 502 S.W.2d 277 (what plaintiff's eyewitness stated another person said at time of accident, as contained in accident report, was admissible to impeach what witness testified in court such other person said); State v. Alexander, 1973, 499 S.W. 2d 439 (where key issue in prosecution on charge of operating a motor vehicle without consent of owner was whether defendant actually drove the automobile as opposed to being a passenger in it, proffered testimony by qualified stenographer as to inconsistent statements by identifying officer at preliminary hearing as to year and color of automobile under observation and as to amount of time defendant was under surveillance should have been admitted); Neavill v. Klemp, 1968, 427 S.W.2d 446 (permitting police officer to read into record portions of statement taken from crosswalk crossing guard outside presence of plaintiff was not error).

Neb.—Bartek v. Glasers Provisions Co., 71 N.W.2d 466, 160 Neb. 794; Havlik v. Anderson, 264 N.W. 146, 130 Neb. 94 (prior testimony).

Nev.—Jefferes v. Cannon, 397 P.2d 1, 80 Nev. 551.

N.M.—Selgado v. Commercial Warehouse Co., 1974, 526 P.2d 430, 86 N.M. 633 (insurance claim attributing certain injuries to subsequent accident).

N.Y.—Burns v. Dixon, 1974, 362 N.Y. S.2d 245, 46 A.D.2d 943 (statement given one day later); Grassie v. Brown, 1971, 318 N.Y.S.2d 812, 36 A.D.2d 720 (signed report to Dept. of Motor Vehicles); Detzker v. City of New York, 47 N.Y.S.2d 203, 267 App.Div. 912, appeal denied 48 N. Y.S.2d 807, 267 App.Div. 1001 (alleged statement by motorman that trolley struck rear of automobile); Babecki v. Charles Kurzon, Inc., 46 N.Y.S.2d 573, 181 Misc. 11 (testimony at prior trial).

N.C.—Brewer v. Garner, 141 S.E.2d 806, 264 N.C. 384.

Ohio.—Al McCullough Transfer Co. v. Pizzulo, 5 N.E.2d 796, 53 Ohio App. 470 (unfiled deposition).

Or.—Osborne v. Bessonette, 1973, 508 P.2d 185, 265 Or. 224 (deposition available to party joined after taking); Black v. Nelson, 424 P.2d 251, 246 Or. 161 (defendant's pretrial written statement that saw plaintiff's automobile when it was two car lengths from intersection which conflicted with direct testimony that saw plaintiff's automobile ten car lengths away).

Pa.—Curran v. B. & P. Motor Express, Inc., 113 P.L.J. 567 (concerning similar facts or opinions); Bruno v. Brown, 200 A.2d 405, 414 Pa. 361; Knies v. Kraftson, 40 A.2d 122, 156 Pa.Super. 296 (signed statement given to police officer).

R.I.—State v. Colavecchio, 1973, 303 A.2d 760, 111 R.I. 428 (in reckless driving prosecution, wherein the explanation proffered by defendant at trial for driving north in southbound lane of state highway was that left front wheel of his automobile had locked causing him to jump median divider, hit his head against door, come to rest in southbound lane and then pass out, "Alcoholic Influence Report Form" filled out by the police on night of accident and signed by defendant, which report indicated, inter alia, that defendant had negatively answered a question as to whether he had hit his head, was clearly relevant for impeachment purposes, and the trial justice did not abuse his discretion in admitting the report, with certain prejudicial portions excluded and covered); Allen v. D'Ercole Const. Co., 1968, 244 A.2d 864, 104 R.I. 362 (use of doctor's prior inconsistent statements to discredit the testimony he gave).

S.C.—Squires v. Henderson, 1946, 36 S.E.2d 738, 208 S.C. 58.

Tex.—Smith v. Red Arrow Freight Lines, Inc., Tex.Civ.App.1970, 460 S.W.2d 257, error refused n. r. e. (contradictory declarations contained in written statements); Gonzalez v. Layton, 1968, 429 S.W.2d 215 (testimony of witness that defendant had stated that he did not see the blinker light was properly admitted for impeachment purposes, where defendant denied making any such statement); McEntire v. Baygent, Civ.App., 229 S.W.2d 866, 20 A.L.R.2d 300 (statement to patrolman); Acker v. Thompson, Civ.App., 128 S.W.2d 852, reversed by agreement (prior testimony); St. Louis, S. F. & T. Ry. Co. v. Williams, Civ.App.1937, 104 S.W.2d 103, error dismissed (unsigned deposition).

Va.—Goodwin v. Gilman, 1967, 157 S.E.2d 912, 208 Va. 422; Neblett v. Hunter, 150 S.E.2d 115, 207 Va. 335.

Wash.—Burien Motors, Inc. v. Balch, 1973, 513 P.2d 582, 9 Wash.App. 573 (in unpublished deposition).

Wis.—Abbott v. Truck Ins. Exchange Co., 1967, 148 N.W.2d 116, 33 Wis. 2d 671 (statement in hospital, under sedation, but believed sufficiently aware to protect own rights).

Contra as to abandoned pleading

Tex.—Harms Marine Service, Inc. v. Swiere, Civ.App., 1967, 411 S.W.2d 602.

Discretion of court

N.Y.—Scarborough v. Schenck Transp. Co., Inc., 1974, 352 N.Y.S. 2d 825, 76 Misc.2d 1074 (may weigh degree of inconsistency and probative force of statement on issue of credibility against prejudice that would result if jury considered it as evidence in chief).

Expression of opinion

U.S.—Atlantic Greyhound Corp. v. Eddins, C.A.S.C., 177 F.2d 954 (where expression of opinion inconsistent with testimony was made before discovery of all the material facts, refusal to permit evidence as to prior inconsistent statement was within the discretion of the trial court).

Ill.—Harris v. Minardi, 220 N.E.2d 39, 74 Ill.App.2d 262 (driver's affirmative answer to discovery deposition question, "You failed to yield the right-of-way?", was a conclusion and not an admission and was not admissible); Allen v. Yancy, 206 N.E.2d 452, 57 Ill.App. 2d 50 (statements of plaintiff's witness to effect that witness believed that motorist was not responsible for injuries received by minor plaintiff were inadmissible as improper expressions of opinion on ultimate issue in the case and could not be received to impeach).

Minn.—Carpenter v. Mattison, 1974, 219 N.W.2d 625, 300 Minn. 273 (opinions as to fault normally inadmissible).

Mo.—Ford v. Dahl, 228 S.W.2d 800, 360 Mo. 437 (rule that a broad statement of opinion which contains an implied assertion of fact inconsistent with an assertion of fact made by a witness is admissible for impeachment purposes, is not applicable in Missouri).

Mont.—Tigh v. College Park Realty Co., 1967, 427 P.2d 57, 149 Mont. 358 (father's prior inconsistent statement that his son, prior to injuries giving rise to present suit, had a 75% permanently disabled left leg).

N.J.—Weilbacher v. Rudlin, 17 A.2d 538, 125 N.J.L. 631 (statement made by driver at police station, that accident was his fault, admitted).

N.Y.—Wolfe v. Madison Ave. Coach Co., 1939, 13 N.Y.S.2d 741, 171 Misc. 707 (should be received).

Ohio.—Dorsten v. Lawrence, 1969, 253 N.E.2d 804, 20 Ohio App.2d 297 (witness could not be discredited by prior expression of opinion as to which driver was at fault).

R.I.—Major v. Grieg, 1967, 230 A.2d 846, 102 R.I. 379 (conclusions concerning fault in police report held admissible).

Tex.—Snyder v. Schill, Civ.App., 388 S.W.2d 208 (that admission made by party is conclusion or opinion does not prevent its use for impeachment or as substantive evidence).

Inquiry must be pursued

Ill.—Rigor v. Howard Liquors, Inc., 1973, 295 N.E.2d 491, 10 Ill.App. 3d 1004 (interrogation of fact of prior statement raises burden to prove same upon denial or answers less than acknowledgement); Schoolfield v. Witkowski, 1964, 203 N.E.2d 460, 54 Ill.App. 2d 111.

Limitation on prior pleadings

Ill.—Schusler v. Fletcher, 1966, 219 N.E.2d 588, 74 Ill.App.2d 249 (not unverified alternative pleadings).

N.Y.—Arestivo v. Matusewitz, 1969, 303 N.Y.S.2d 139, 60 Misc.2d 236 (bill of particulars verified by a parent in representative capacity is not prior inconsistent statement of infant who happens to be the adversary witness sought to be impeached).

Tex.—Spring Branch Bank v. Wright, Civ.App., 404 S.W.2d 659 (it must be shown that they were made with knowledge, authority or acquiescence of the party).

Limitation on use of statements

Conn.—Lombardo v. Simko, 214 A. 2d 911, 3 Conn.Cir. 363, certiorari denied 213 A.2d 526 (where copy of purported statement had not been delivered at time statement was given to liability insurer of defendant or within 30 days thereafter, statement was inadmissible against plaintiff claiming injury but was admissible against plaintiff claiming only property damage).

Va.—Harris v. Harrington, 22 S.E.2d 13, 180 Va. 210 (statute intended to prohibit proof of ex parte written statements prepared by an interested party. Code 1950, § 8–293).

Limited to contradiction of damaging testimony

Contradictory statements by witness, admissible for impeachment, must be confined to contradictions of testimony of witness which are injurious to party seeking to im-

§ 421.2   TRIAL EVIDENCE   Ch. 421

peach him. Hicks v. M. K. & O. Transit Lines, Inc., Okl., 368 P.2d 236.

Need not offer irrelevant portion

Mich.—Socony Vacuum Oil Co. v. Marvin, 21 N.W.2d 841, 313 Mich. 528 (not bound to prove whole conversation, including irrelevant matters, and defendant could not prove such matters).

N.M.—Franklin's Earthmoving, Inc. v. Loma Linda Park, Inc., 395 P.2d 454, 74 N.M. 531 (properly limited portion received in evidence to that applicable to impeaching question, and it was not required to admit entire deposition).

Not prior recitation of another's declaration

Plaintiff motorist's written statement that "the sheriff said to me that I skidded about 75 feet" was mere admission of what she had heard without adoption or endorsement, was not prior inconsistent statement and properly excluded. Sherwood v. Fleming, 1969, 307 N.Y.S.2d 800, 33 A.D.2d 800.

Omission of fact in prior statement

Hawaii—Asato v. Furtado, 1970, 474 P.2d 288, 52 Haw. 284 (where defendant in his prosecution for careless driving testified that he had been blinded and hit something and subsequently testified at civil trial of negligence action against him that he heard crash, was blinded and hit something, plaintiffs in negligence action should have been allowed to show that defendant had omitted at prior trial to mention that he heard crash before he was blinded and hit something).

Ill.—Rose v. B. L. Cartage Co., 1969, 249 N.E.2d 199, 110 Ill.App.2d 260; Rice v. Gulf, Mobile & Ohio R. Co., 1967, 228 N.E.2d 162, 84 Ill.App. 163 (witness who testified that he saw trainmen on one side of track which plaintiff was attempting to cross when struck by train was properly shown transcript of testimony of prior trial of case, requested to review it, and cross-examined as to whether he had made any reference at prior trial to seeing such trainmen; especially since defendant was then permitted to bring out on redirect examination that no one had inquired at prior trial as to whether witness had seen such trainmen); Esderts v. Chicago, R. I. & P. R. Co., Ill.App., 222 N.E.2d 117, 76 Ill.App.2d 210 (if a witness fails to mention facts under circumstances which make it reasonably probable that he would mention them if true, the omission may be shown for impeachment purposes as an indirect inconsistency); Barrett v. Wallenberg, 210 N.E.2d 782, 62 Ill.App.2d 478 (cross-examination of plaintiff as to fact that plaintiff had failed to state in discovery deposition that his left leg hit accelerator during accident causing car to pick up speed was within rule permitting party to be discredited by failure to state a fact when it is incumbent to state such a fact, if it is true).

N.Y.—Guido v. Kuster, 1971, 320 N.Y.S.2d 261, 36 A.D.2d 727 (photostat of police accident report of accident involving bicycle and automobile that was based on version of accident by bicyclist's father, who was not eyewitness to accident, was inadmissible for purpose of impeaching father on ground that absence of any statement in accident report to effect that father, who testified that defendant motorist made liability admissions to him after accident, claimed that such admissions, which allegedly were made before father gave his version of accident to officer, were made indicated that such admissions had not been made).

Prior pleadings admissible

U.S.—Walker v. International Harvester Co., D.C.Okl.1969, 294 F.

Supp. 1095 (where testified to the effect that the entire blame for injury should be placed on truck manufacturer because of defective door latch, petition filed in prior action against truck manufacturer and other defendants and containing allegations which were generally contradictory to assertion that truck manufacturer was solely at fault was admissible).

Ariz.—Buehman v. Smelker, 1937, 68 P.2d 946, 50 Ariz. 18.

Cal.—Cseri v. D'Amore, 1965, 43 Cal.Rptr. 36, 232 Cal.App. 622.

Conn.—Frye v. Krasicky, 1968, 247 A.2d 439, 5 Conn.Cir. 164; Kucza v. Stone, 230 A.2d 559, 155 Conn. 194 (so far as allegations therein relative to a 1955 permanent injury to his back were inconsistent with plaintiff's testimony that 1959 accident was sole cause of his back injuries).

Ga.—Krasner v. Lester, 1973, 202 S.E.2d 693, 130 Ga.App. 234.

La.—Mack Trucks, Inc. v. Capitano, 1967, 204 So.2d 710 (statements of fact offered in original and amending answers).

Mich.—Hanik v. Wilczynski, 1971, 189 N.W.2d 815, 33 Mich.App. 268. Schwartz v. Triff, 139 N.W.2d 907, 2 Mich.App. 379 (unverified Canadian pleading which had not been signed by plaintiff suing for personal injuries but had been authenticated in conformity with Michigan statute).

Minn.—Johnson v. Lorraine Park Apts. Inc., 128 N.W.2d 758, 268 Minn. 273.

Mo.—Jimenez v. Broadway Motors, Inc., 1969, 445 S.W.2d 315 (abandoned pleadings may be used); Littell v. Bi-State Transit Development Agency, 1967, 423 S.W.2d 34 (abandoned pleadings or pleadings in another lawsuit); Turner v. Cowart, Mo.1969, 450 S.W.2d 441 (in head-on collision case, exhibit, consisting of petition for damages which defendant's passenger filed against him in another lawsuit, and which alleged that defendant had failed to operate his northbound automobile on right half of roadway, was admissible to impeach that passenger's testimony that he had not told his lawyer that defendant had driven at a high speed, on wrong side of road, without keeping a lookout).

N.Y.—People v. Barton, 1968, 291 N.Y.S.2d 577, 30 A.D.2d 726; Capone v. New York City Housing Authority, 1968, 289 N.Y.S.2d 239, 29 A.D.2d 951, order amended 307 N.Y.S.2d 828, 33 A.D.2d 776 (cross-examination of plaintiff in subsequent action with regard to bill of particulars which he had verified in prior action arising out of a prior accident was proper where bill set forth injuries to plaintiff similar to those claimed as basis for subsequent action).

Or.—Moore v. Drennan, 1974, 523 P.2d 1250, 269 Or. 189 (properly admitted plaintiff's original complaint, first amended complaint and second amended complaint in action arising from automobile accident inasmuch as each subsequent complaint alleged substantially greater damages and more severe injuries and inasmuch as the superseded pleadings were inconsistent with plaintiff's pleading and testimony).

S.C.—Poulos v. James, 1970, 174 S.E.2d 152, 254 S.C. 156 (where plaintiff's answers to questions as to what injuries he had claimed in previous action arising out of earlier automobile collision were equivocal, complaint in prior action was properly admitted as prior verified statement on his part contrary to testimony he was then giving); Young v. Martin, 1970, 173 S.E.2d 361, 254 S.C. 50 (complaint filed in previous action arising from earlier automobile collision should have been admitted and motorist's counsel should

§ 421.2   TRIAL EVIDENCE   Ch. 421

cate" has been laid by calling the witness' attention to the statement and offering an opportunity to deny or explain it.[16] The

have been permitted to cross-examine relative to the previous complaint as it might have been inconsistent with her testimony).

Tex.—Davis v. Breithaupt, 1968, 427 S.W.2d 666, error refused n. r. e.

Unfounded opinion

In action for death of child killed by automobile, admission of impeaching evidence as to statements made by witness to effect that accident was unavoidable was prejudicial error, where witness admittedly could not have seen child or surface of highway at time of accident, or have had knowledge of circumstances surrounding the accident until he reached the scene thereof, notwithstanding instruction that such evidence could be considered only as affecting credibility of witness. Kennedy v. Aron, 176 So. 127, 179 Miss. 458.

Unsworn interrogatory answers

Answers to interrogatories need not be under oath to be admissible as prior inconsistent or consistent statements. LeGrand v. Yellow Cab Co. of San Gabriel Valley, 1970, 87 Cal. Rptr. 292, 8 Cal.App.3d 125.

16.   **U.S.**—Federal Rules of Evidence § 613(b), 28 U.S.C.A.; Troublefield v. U. S., 1966, 372 F.2d 912, 125 U.S.App.D.C. 339; Osborne v. McEwan, D.C.D.C.1961, 194 F.Supp. 117.

Ala.—Chambers v. Culver, 1973, 272 So.2d 236, 289 Ala. 724 (referred to occasion of alleged statement, but not fact of declaration).

Ariz.—Miller v. Schafer, 1967, 432 P.2d 585, 102 Ariz. 457 (physician's report in hospital records).

Ark.—Industrial Farm Home Gas Co. v. McDonald, 355 S.W.2d 174, 234 Ark. 744.

Fla.—Florida Evidence Code § 90.614 (2).

Ga.—Stubbs v. Daughtry, 153 S.E.2d 633, 115 Ga.App. 22.

Idaho.—Hodge v. Borden, 417 P.2d 75, 91 Idaho 125.

Ill.—Sidwell v. Sidwell, 1966, 220 N.E. 479, 75 Ill.App.2d 133; Healy v. New York Cent. R. Co., 1945, 62 N.E.2d 707, 326 Ill.App. 556 (held sufficient); Little v. Gogotz, 1944, 58 N.E.2d 336, 324 Ill.App. 516 (admission of signature is sufficient).

Iowa.—Mead v. Scott, 1964, 130 N.W.2d 641, 256 Iowa 1285.

Kan.—Kansas Code of Civil Procedure § 60–422; Thompson v. Norman, 1967, 424 P.2d 593, 198 Kan. 436.

Mass.—Goodney v. Smith, 242 N.E. 2d 413, 354 Mass. 734, appeal after remand 269 N.E.2d 707, 359 Mass. 749 (where time, place and content of insurer's witness' prior statement, which contained no reference of permission to operate automobile, were mentioned to witness after she testified she had received permission of owner's son, and she was shown statement, which she identified and was given opportunity to explain the statement, insurer was entitled to have statement admitted).

Miss.—Kelly v. King, 1967, 196 So.2d 525.

Mo.—Aboussie v. McBroom, 1967, 421 S.W.2d 805 (allegations in prior pleadings).

Neb.—Nebraska Rules of Evidence § 613(2).

Nev.—N.R.S. § 50.135(2)(b).

N.J.—New Jersey Evidence Rule 22 (b); Schneider v. Preis, 191 A.2d 770, 79 N.J.Super. 400 (insufficient foundation).

N.M.—New Mexico Rules of Evidence § 613(b).

N.Y.—Wolfe v. Madison Ave. Coach Co., 13 N.Y.S.2d 741, 171 Misc. 707.

Ohio.—Kunkel v. Cincinnati St. Ry. Co., 80 N.E.2d 442, 82 Ohio App. 341.

Pa.—Giles v. Valentic, 49 A.2d 384, 355 Pa. 108 (discretionary with court to exclude pleading in conflict with testimony when foundation not laid).

Tex.—Smith v. Red Arrow Freight Lines, Inc., Civ.App.1970, 460 S.W. 2d 257 error refused n. r. e. (insufficiency not reversible error); Bayshore Bus Lines v. Cooper, Civ. App., 223 S.W.2d 77, ref. n. r. e.

Utah.—Utah Rules of Evidence § 22 (b).

Wash.—Brown v. Cannon, 1972, 495 P.2d 705, 6 Wash.App. 653; McCall v. Washington Coop. Farmers Ass'n, 212 P.2d 813, 35 Wash.2d 337.

Wis.—Wisconsin Rules of Evidence § 906.13(2).

But see

Court properly refused to strike testimony of witnesses as to party's admissions which were inconsistent with her testimony regarding her speed even though such party was subsequently dismissed from action and no foundation had been laid for impeachment. Goodwin v. Gilman, 1967, 157 S.E.2d 912, 208 Va. 422.

Foundation required

U.S.—Sylvester v. Meditz, 1968, D.C. Wis., 278 F.Supp. 810 (proper procedure for laying a foundation for impeachment by prior inconsistent statements made orally is to call attention of witness to particular time and occasion when witness purportedly made statement, and witness should be informed what statements were and conditions and circumstances under which they were made).

Cal.—Shallenberger v. Duncan, 1966, 53 Cal.Rptr. 77, 244 Cal.App.2d 197 (must relate statement, with circumstances of time, place, and persons present, and ask whether said).

Ill.—Vancil v. Fletcher, 1967, 232 N. E.2d 789, 90 Ill.App.2d 277 (where witness on cross-examination was not asked if he had made a particular statement at a particular time in the past but was simply handed a document and asked if the document refreshed his recollection, and where previous question addressed to the witness was then repeated, the procedure followed by the cross-examiner did not amount to laying foundation); People v. Irish, 222 N.E.2d 114, 77 Ill.App.2d 67 (may direct attention of witness to time, place and substance of alleged inconsistent statement and ask witness if he made such statement).

Md.—Campbell v. Patton, 175 A.2d 761, 227 Md. 125 (properly permitted where the witness was fully apprised as to time, place, and circumstances under which he made statement in question, admitted reading account of his story as he told it to the reporter, stated that the reporter's account was incorrect, denied parts of the statement, and had opportunity to further explain inconsistencies between published story and his testimony).

Miss.—Hall v. State, 1964, 165 So.2d 345, 250 Miss. 253 (the times, places, and circumstances being described in detail).

Mo.—Moore v. Kopp, Mo., 400 S.W. 2d 176 (where plaintiff was asked, on cross-examination, about her former testimony and she gave equivocal and indecisive answers, it was not error to permit reading of testimony given by her at previous trial, notwithstanding contention that no proper foundation had been laid).

Neb.—Havlik v. Anderson, 264 N.W. 146, 130 Neb. 94 (after plaintiff

§ 421.2 TRIAL EVIDENCE Ch. 421

federal rule,[17] and the rule of certain states,[18] however, expressly allow that the "statement need not be shown nor its contents

was asked on cross-examination if he remembered testifying in police court regarding case and objection to question was sustained, excluding evidence of plaintiff's statement during testimony in police court as to how accident happened held error).

N.J.—Miller v. Henderson, 124 A.2d 23, 41 N.J.Super. 15 (when a witness acknowledges his signature on a paper, cross-examination as to the facts set forth therein is proper and not dependent upon the representation of counsel that he intends to produce person who took the statement in the event that witness denied any of the matters contained therein).

N.Y.—Wolfe v. Madison Ave. Coach Co., 13 N.Y.S.2d 741, 171 Misc. 707 (where bus driver denied having had conversation with witness shortly after accident, but was not asked specifically whether he said to her at that time that accident was his fault, admission of witness' testimony that driver admitted accident was his fault, if proper objection had been made, would have been error).

Tex.—Acker v. Thompson, Tex.Civ. App., 128 S.W.2d 852, reversed by agreement (consists of asking witness whether he made certain contradictory statements, the name of persons to whom he is supposed to have made them, and the time and place, and if the particular words, names, time or place cannot be related, such matters substantially must be called to attention of witness so that he may either affirm, deny, or explain them or indicate that he does not know).

Wash.—Shaw v. Sjoberg, 1973, 517 P.2d 622, 10 Wash.App. 328 (cross-examination of defense witness by plaintiffs' counsel concerning whether witness recalled having testified under oath about facts of accident on a prior occasion adequately alerted witness, who responded in the affirmative, and established proper foundation for introduction of an alleged prior inconsistent statement given by the witness at traffic court trial).

Foundation too restricted

Ruling that defense was required to read exact questions and answers made in preliminary hearing to state's witness in order to lay proper foundation for admission of witness' statement which was allegedly made during preliminary hearing and which was inconsistent with witness' trial testimony was erroneous and unduly restricted cross-examination of witness. People v. Irish, 222 N.E. 2d 114, 77 Ill.App.2d 67.

17. Federal Rules of Evidence § 613 (a), 28 U.S.C.A.

18. **Kan.**—Kansas Rules of Civil Procedure § 60–422.

Me.—Maine Rules of Evidence § 613.

Neb.—Nebraska Rules of Evidence § 613(1).

N.J.—New Jersey Evidence Rule 22.

N.M.—New Mexico Rules of Evidence § 613(a).

Ohio.—Bluestein v. Thompson, 139 N.E.2d 668, 102 Ohio App. 157 (where defendant's counsel, in cross-examination of material witness for plaintiffs, asked witness, for purpose of impeachment, if she had not stated in signed written statement, which she had given to adjuster of defendant's insurer, and which defendant's counsel held in his hand, that defendant was only 30 feet away when driver of automobile of one of the plaintiffs saw defendant's automobile and applied brakes, instead of 90 or 100 feet away as witness had testified, and wherein witness did not categorically admit that she

§ 421.2   IMPEACHMENT OF WITNESSES   Ch. 421

disclosed to the witness at that time", though it must be disclosed to opposing counsel upon request.

Completion of the impeachment must be with impeaching evidence offered in the proper manner.[19]

had so stated to adjuster, denial of plaintiffs' request for examination of the written statement was prejudicial error).

Utah.—Utah Rules of Evidence § 22.

Wis.—Wisconsin Rules of Evidence § 906.13(1).

Contra by rule

Fla.—Florida Evidence Code § 90.614.

19. **Ill.**—Anderson v. Universal Delta, 1967, 234 N.E.2d 21, 90 Ill.App. 2d 105 (proper to show that a police report is contradictory to a witness' testimony but improper to bring contents of report before jury where document itself cannot be admitted).

Mich.—White v. Dirks, 1968, 155 N.W.2d 165, 380 Mich. 1 (where driver of first westbound automobile stopped while waiting to make left turn into club, and driver of second westbound automobile struck rear of first and caused it to collide with oncoming first eastbound automobile, it was error for driver of second westbound automobile to use for impeachment of driver of second eastbound automobile a deposition taken from driver of second eastbound automobile by driver of second westbound automobile without notice to driver of first westbound automobile, and driver of first westbound automobile was entitled to retrial not only as to cross-claim against driver of second westbound automobile but also as to principal case of driver of first eastbound automobile).

Mo.—Kern v. Danbury, App.1971, 471 S.W.2d 489 (not where signature not identified and not confronted with statement).

Neb.—Costello v. Hild, 1949, 40 N.W. 2d 228, 152 Neb. 1 (failure to call one who prepared signed statement).

All relevant portion of statement to be received

Where plaintiff's counsel cross-examined witness relative to statement which witness had made in deposition taken prior to trial for purpose of showing conflict in testimony, defendant was entitled to require that all of the witness' statement on deposition relative to statement about which he was cross-examined be introduced for purpose of explaining or reconciling statements. Wells v. Alderman, 1968, 162 S.E.2d 18, 117 Ga.App. 724.

Authorship of prior statement not established

When litigant denied that she gave her attorney the information from which attorney made answers to interrogatories submitted to litigant in another action, the answers, which conflicted with litigant's testimony at trial, were not admissible for impeachment purposes. Kesmarki v. Kisling, 1968, C.A.Ohio, 400 F.2d 97.

Diagram not part of deposition

Diagram of wreck was not "part of deposition" to which it was attached and could not be used to impeach or contradict deponent who drew another diagram in court, where diagram was drawn before deposition was taken at another time and place, and parties did not agree to make diagram part of deposition. Allen v. Pearson, C.A.La.1969, 415 F.2d 499.

Improper proof of prior statement

Testimony of police officer that he had been told by an insurance investigator that defendant had stated that "he would sue the company for one million dollars if they didn't properly represent him" was hearsay

§ 421.2   TRIAL EVIDENCE   Ch. 421

as to issue whether defendant had made statement and was not admissible for purpose of impeaching credibility of testimony of insurance investigator denying that statement was made, where there was no evidence to show that defendant had made statement inasmuch as testimony of insurance investigator did not establish that fact. Leone v. Doran, 1973, 292 N.E.2d 19, 363 Mass. 1, order vacated in part on procedural matter 297 N.E.2d 493.

Irregularity in deposition procedure

Rule excluding deposition taken in disregard of substantial rights extends not only to use of deposition in proceedings for testimonial purposes but to use for purpose of impeaching witness. White v. Dirks, 1967, 146 N.W.2d 845, 5 Mich.App. 437.

Issue whether witness still available to rebut extrinsic proof

Prior inconsistent statement was not inadmissible on theory that defense witness who allegedly had made the statement had been excused and was, therefore, deprived of opportunity to rebut or explain it, where the statement of facts revealed only court reporter's notation "witness excused" at conclusion of plaintiffs' cross-examination of the witness and did not indicate that witness had been excused by trial court. Shaw v. Sjoberg, 1974, 517 P.2d 622, 10 Wash.App. 328.

Not privileged statement

Even in absence of eventual lawsuit against plaintiff, statement given by plaintiff to her liability insurer was made in "preparation for litigation," within statute providing that writing by party in preparation for litigation shall not be obtainable unless withholding will result in injustice or undue hardship, and statement was inadmissible on cross-examination of plaintiff. Cunningham v. Cook, 1968, 290 N.Y.S.2d 79, 56 Misc.2d 771.

Not surreptitiously taped telephone conversation

Under statute proscribing eavesdropping, tape recorded conversations between defendants and plaintiff's mother were not admissible to refresh recollections of defendants who denied having had conversations, even though the tape recordings were of conversations held over plaintiff's telephone, upon arrangement of plaintiff. Penal Law, §§ 738–740. Plotkin v. Rabinowitz, 1967, 283 N.Y.S.2d 156, 54 Misc.2d 550.

Prior written statement is best evidence of prior declaration

Where witness had testified on direct examination that defendant's automobile had been traveling at 60 to 90 miles per hour before accident and on cross-examination admitted initialing statement which was admitted in evidence and which recited that the speed was over 40 miles per hour, objection to subsequent question asking if witness had not admitted in statement that he could not estimate speed except that it was more than 40 miles per hour was properly sustained since statement was best evidence and question was repetitious. Hanks v. LaQuey, 1968, Tex.Civ.App., 425 S.W.2d 396, error refused n. r. e.

Recording

Jackman v. Montgomery, 1974, 320 N.E.2d 770, —— Ind.App. —— (voicewriter recording of a telephone conversation between plaintiff's witness and an insurance adjuster was admissible to impeach witness, despite claim that opposing counsel did not lay a proper foundation showing that statement of speaker on recording was voluntarily given, where speaker knew that person to whom he was speaking was an insurance adjuster, was aware that conversation was being recorded, and was free to hang up at any time, and no evi-

276

Some jurisdictions preclude impeachment by prior inconsistent statements as to irrelevant matter.[20]

dence was presented which tended to show duress or coercion).

Requisite show copy given declarant

Where plaintiff driver could neither read nor write, he admitted giving written statement to insurance adjuster, and he identified his signature but he could not recall making any of crucial statements contained therein inconsistent with his trial testimony and he denied that he had ever received copy, and defendant's offer of proof did not assert that the adjuster would testify that plaintiff driver could in fact read or write or that copy had in fact been furnished as required, statement was inadmissible and motion for adjournment to obtain the adjuster as a witness to provide foundation for admission of statement was properly denied. Ford v. Kline Oldsmobile, Inc., 143 N.W.2d 209, 274 Minn. 284.

Transcript of prior testimony not required

Even if transcript of prior trial was available, questions relating to testimony witness gave in such prior trial in the district court should have been permitted for purpose of showing that witness had made prior inconsistent statements. D & P Equipment Corp. v. White Spot Const. Corp., 1969, 243 N.E.2d 922, 355 Mass. 787.

Whole pleading admissible

Admission of entire pleading in prior automobile accident case, in which plaintiff in instant action was also a plaintiff, was proper in instant action also arising out of automobile accident, since it was all one single document and could not be split into parts and still give jury an adequate understanding of the significance of plaintiff's statement of his injuries. Kucza v. Stone, 1967, 230 A.2d 559, 155 Conn. 194.

Written statement inadmissible only in part

Where a plaintiff sought to contradict his own witness by the introduction of a statement signed by witness which contained one sentence contradicting witness' testimony, it was not error to exclude statement which was offered as a whole where statement contained many matters not tending to contradict testimony of witness and which were inadmissible. Kavanaugh v. Colombo, 24 N.E.2d 14, 304 Mass. 379.

Where police report containing statement attributed to three witnesses was offered to impeach credibility of only one witness and bolstered testimony of other two, and portion so bolstering could not be separated from other part and where officer could have been called to testify to prior inconsistent statement of particular witness, it was error to receive portion of report containing statement attributed to three witnesses, but error did not require reversal. Kaczmarskij v. Mattil, 258 N.Y.S.2d 205, 23 A.D.2d 804.

20. U.S.—Rogers v. U. S., C.A.Okl. 1966, 369 F.2d 944.

Ill.—Rose v. B. L. Cartage Co., 1969, 249 N.E.2d 199, 110 Ill.App.2d 260 (objections to cross-examination of plaintiff driver about shape of stop sign and how long highway on which she had been driving had been paved east of intersection and to cross-examination of plaintiff passenger as to where automobile had been when she came to after accident and what she saw immediately before the collision were properly sustained on ground that questions were not impeaching, even if inconsistent with prior statements, since they concerned irrelevant matters).

A prior statement may be introduced to complete the impeachment where the witness, on cross-examination, testifies as to lack of memory concerning making of prior statement.[21]

If the witness admits the fact of and the content of the prior statement, the impeachment has been completed and the statement need not be admitted.[22] It has also been held that the im-

Minn.—Jackson v. Wyatt Bros. Cement Co., 1972, 203 N.W.2d 360, 295 Minn. 145 (out-of-court opinion cannot be introduced for impeachment if opinion would be inadmissible as direct evidence, and statement which was made by witness who was bicycling with minor plaintiff to effect that it was dangerous to go alongside truck was inadmissible for impeachment purposes after witness testified there was no reason for his not going alongside truck).

Pa.—Com. v. Kubacki, 1966, 224 A.2d 80, 208 Pa.Super. 523 (closeness of relation to be required depends on importance of subject matter).

Tex.—Spring Branch Bank v. Wright, 1966, 404 S.W.2d 659.

But see
Where plaintiff motorist testified on direct examination and on cross-examination that he was using crutches because of hip injury sustained after falling down stairs at cocktail party and that use of crutches was not directly related to accident on which his suit against county was based, county had right to call witnesses who had been at the party and thereby discredit plaintiff's story by showing that plaintiff became embroiled in a heated argument and was knocked to floor after being hit, notwithstanding claim that such testimony introduced collateral issues. Chavez v. Pima County, 1971, 488 P.2d 978, 107 Ariz. 358.

21. **Ill.**—Jenkins v. Hechtman, 1967, 226 N.E.2d 383, 83 Ill.App.2d 72 (motorist sued for injury to minor pedestrian was properly permitted to show that policeman's report, based on information received from motorist about an hour after the accident, showed there were vehicles parked along the street, in order to impeach the officer after he denied noticing condition of parked vehicles along the street).

Mich.—Osberry v. Watters, 1967, 151 N.W.2d 372, 7 Mich.App. 258 (that plaintiff had admitted a prior accident after first denying it and later testifying that she did not remember it did not preclude admission for impeachment purposes of hospital record containing extrajudicial admissions by plaintiff of the prior accident).

Utah.—Morton v. Hood, 143 P.2d 434, 105 Utah 484.

22. **Alaska.**—Patterson v. Cushman, 394 P.2d 657 (exclusion of written statement not error).

Miss.—Hall v. State, 165 So.2d 345, 250 Miss. 253.

N.J.—Gall v. New York & New Brunswick Auto Express Co., 36 A.2d 403, 131 N.J.L. 346, reversed on other grounds 40 A.2d 643, 132 N.J.L. 466 (refusal of admission of statement not error).

Admission not prejudicial error
It was error to permit defendant, over plaintiff's objection, to introduce a portion of prior inconsistent written statement of one of plaintiff's witnesses where witness had admitted making such prior inconsistent statements, but error was not prejudicial. Smith v. Red Arrow Freight Lines, Inc., Tex.Civ.App.1970, 460 S.W.2d 257, error refused n. r. e.

peachment has been completed if the witness just admits the signature on the statement.[23]

Evidence of witnesses' prior statements, offered for impeachment purposes, have been held inadmissible on various grounds,[24]

Held error to exclude

In action for injuries sustained, at night, when automobile which plaintiff was driving collided with rear of defendant's automobile which defendant had stopped on highway to let approaching vehicles pass in order that defendant might make left turn, wherein police officer testified that he had made inspection of defendant's automobile after accident and that there were no taillight bulbs in sockets of taillights and he found no fragments of any white light bulbs, trial court committed error prejudicial to defendant in excluding such officer's contemporaneous written report in which he had made statement that defendant's automobile had no defects, even though, on cross-examination, officer admitted making such statement. Thompson v. Princeton, 76 N.W.2d 273, 272 Wis. 589.

Prior statement inadmissible

U.S.—Dilley v. Chesapeake & O. Ry. Co., C.A.Ohio, 327 F.2d 249, certiorari denied, 379 U.S. 824, 85 S.Ct. 47, 13 L.Ed.2d 34, citing 98 C.J.S. Witnesses § 610 (exhibit containing witness' opinion as to how accident happened could not be introduced for purpose of contradicting or impeaching witness' testimony, where witness testified that he had made statement contained in exhibit).

Ga.—Pethel v. Waters, 140 S.E.2d 252, 220 Ga. 543 (where witness is read transcript of his testimony given at previous hearing and admits that he testified as shown by transcript, transcript of previous hearing is not admissible).

Tex.—Richter's Bakery, Inc. v. Verden, Civ.App., 394 S.W.2d 230 (diagram which was attached to litigant's deposition and placed vehicles in different position from that in which litigant placed them at trial was inadmissible for purpose of impeachment in view of litigant's admission at trial of every fact which the diagram and related testimony could establish).

23. Ga.—Hodges v. Haverty, 154 S.E.2d 276, 115 Ga.App. 199.

Ill.—Vancil v. Fletcher, 232 N.E.2d 789, 90 Ill.App.2d 277; Rogers v. Gehrke, 1966, 222 N.E.2d 351, 77 Ill.App.2d 343.

N.H.—Moran v. Carignan, 1968, 238 A.2d 735, 108 N.H. 487.

Tenn.—Puckett v. Laster, App., 405 S.W.2d 35 (it was not indispensable that defendant introduce testimony of one to whom written statement was allegedly given or trace possession of such statement into hands of defendant's attorney, although failure to introduce such evidence was a factor to be considered by jury in weighing plaintiff's testimony).

Wis.—Mack v. Decker, 128 N.W.2d 455, 24 Wis.2d 219 (testimony that two signatures on a statement containing an admission contrary to her trial testimony were signatures of the witness constituted sufficient authentication to entitle the statement to be admitted).

24. See this section at fn. 15 for cases deciding admissibility of prior statements which were "expressions of opinions."

Conn.—Frye v. Krasicky, 1968, 247 A.2d 439, 5 Conn.Cir. 164 (excluding from evidence plaintiff's complaint in prior action for injuries which were different from injuries allegedly sustained as a result of collision with defendant's motor vehicle in intersection was within court's discretion where introduction of pleadings would have offered nothing new on question of plaintiff's credibility).

Mo.—Cash v. Bolle, 1968, 423 S.W. 2d 743 (refusal, in northbound motorist's action wherein southbound motorist cross-claimed against motorist passing plaintiff, to permit impeachment of plaintiff's testimony that when he first saw cross-claimant's automobile it was two-thirds across center line by plaintiff's deposition testimony that when he first saw cross-complainant's automobile it was in center northbound lane was not abuse of discretion).

N.Y.—Peck v. Saltzman, 296 N.Y.S. 299, 163 Misc. 50 (not a "statement in an inquiry" within terms of statute).

Pa.—Curran v. B. & P. Motor Express, Inc., 113 P.L.J. 567 (must be a direct contradiction as opposed to a qualified contradiction).

Alleged alteration of signed statement

Where plaintiff offered a signed statement to contradict testimony of his witness and witness stated that one sentence in statement which contradicted his testimony had been altered without his knowledge, statement was not admissible in order to enable jury to determine whether it had been altered, where appearance of statement, the body of which was written by some one other than witness, did not indicate that anything had been changed or added. Kavanaugh v. Colombo, 24 N.E.2d 14, 304 Mass. 379.

Document not in evidence

It was improper and prejudicial to permit plaintiff's counsel, in cross-examining defendant driver, to impeach driver by use of police officer's report and report to department of motor vehicles which was signed by defendant but neither of which were in evidence. Rodriguez v. Zampella, 1973, 346 N.Y.S.2d 558, 42 A.D.2d 805.

Expression of opinion on ultimate issue

Ill.—Ballard v. Jones, 1974, 316 N.E. 2d 281, 21 Ill.App.3d 496 (where police officer testified for defendant city that he did not observe anything obstructing stop sign on corner of intersection and further testified that he had never made an examination of any foliage to determine its relative position with respect to the stop sign, officer's previous statement that driver could not see stop sign because of foliage and darkness improperly allowed into evidence an opinion of the witness on an ultimate issue).

Injected insurance coverage on loss

In action arising out of collision of plaintiff's truck with defendant's train, trial court properly refused to permit jury to hear information that there was a suit in which plaintiff recovered judgment against his insurer for total loss of truck, and trial court did not err in refusing to permit plaintiff to impeach testimony of plaintiff by referring to his prior testimony, in his suit with his insurer for property damage, where questions unnecessarily referred to recovery for total loss. Atchison, T. & S. F. Ry. Co. v. Acosta, 1969, Tex. Civ.App., 435 S.W.2d 539, error refused n. r. e.

Not statement of counsel for alleged declarant

Evidence of certain statement made by spouses' counsel at 1969 pretrial conference, viz., that wife-motorist could not recall accident, was properly excluded as impeachment evidence at the trial, at which wife testified she did recall the accident and had begun remembering "things" in 1968, since wife was not present at the conference and since

including the ground that offered statements were not inconsistent,[25] or not sufficiently inconsistent,[26] with the testimony of the witnesses in question.

counsel's statement could have been made as a result of inconclusive communications with wife; moreover, as counsel's statement was not transcribed, evidence thereof would have necessitated trial judge's own clarification and explanation; lastly, such evidence would have been cumulative. Eldridge v. Melcher, 1974, 313 A.2d 750, 226 Pa.Super. 381.

Not sufficiently attributed to witness

Cal.—LeGrand v. Yellow Cab. Co. of San Gabriel Valley, 1970, 87 Cal. Rptr. 292, 8 Cal.App.3d 125 (any presumption that witness had knowledge of contents of document purporting to be his answers to interrogatories and that he adopted statement therein as his own, claimed to arise from act of signing the document, was dispelled by witness' denial and prompt but thorough explanation of manner in which document was presented to him for signature, and thus, where plaintiffs, who were seeking to introduce the document as prior inconsistent statement, though having ample opportunity to produce additional evidence, produced no evidence tending to contradict the explanation of the witness, the document was properly excluded).

N.H.—Eckhart v. Linaberry, 1973, 312 A.2d 704, 113 N.H. 652 (police report of prior statement claimed to have been made by one of two hitchhikers who had alighted from left-turning vehicle just prior to turn was inadmissible as a prior inconsistent statement affecting credibility of one hitchhiker's testimony where that hitchhiker did not acknowledge that he had made the statement in question and the report did not indicate as to which hitchhiker statement was to be attributed).

Offer not timely

Fla.—Curtiss Nat. Bank of Miami Springs v. Street, App.1970, 233 So.2d 453 (judge did not abuse his discretion in refusing to permit introduction of deposition during rebuttal for impeachment purposes on ground that counsel had had innumerable opportunities to impeach the witness on cross-examination prior to proffered deposition).

Where testimony is lack of recollection

U.S.—Taylor v. Baltimore & O. R. Co., C.A.N.Y., 344 F.2d 281, certiorari denied 382 U.S. 831, 86 S. Ct. 72, 15 L.Ed.2d 75 (held prior favorable statement not available).

Cal.—Anthony v. Hobbie, 193 P.2d 748, 85 Cal.App.2d 798 (where a witness merely states that he does not remember he cannot be impeached by showing of former statements regarding facts which he claims not to have remembered).

Mo.—Offenbacker v. Sodowsky, 1973, 499 S.W.2d 421 (where tractor-trailer driver had testified that he did not recollect seeing northbound truck strike automobile, tractor-trailer driver's prior statement that he had seen such collision was admissible).

25. Conn.—Altiere v. Peattie Motors, 1936, 185 A. 75, 121 Conn. 316 (statement that was employee of owner did not contradict testimony of use without permission).

Ga.—Berry v. Dinsmore, 1967, 154 S.E.2d 653, 115 Ga.App. 256 (where witness for plaintiff allegedly struck by defendant's automobile testified that defendant after ac-

---

26. See note 26 on page 283.

cident had stated "he was sorry that it happened, he said he didn't see her because the sun was in his eyes," testimony by defendant's witness that ten minutes after accident defendant had stated "he didn't think he had hit her" was not contradictory and testimony by defendant's witness was not admissible).

Ill.—Rogall v. Kischer, 1971, 273 N. E.2d 681, 1 Ill.App.3d 227 (properly sustained objection to cross-examination question whether witness had told police that accident occurred when three minor pedestrians attempted to "beat traffic across North Avenue" where witness had made no contrary statements); Kelly v. Reynolds, 1971, 271 N.E.2d 370, 132 Ill.App.2d 1098 (statements that his car "stopped" at or "pretty close" to point of impact, made on deposition, did not contradict and were not inconsistent with trial testimony that he did not know whether car stopped or continued after impact and thus should not have been admitted on cross-examination, but error was harmless); Garrett v. S. N. Nielson Co., 200 N.E.2d 81, 49 Ill.App.2d 422.

Kan.—McGrath v. Mance, 400 P.2d 1013, 194 Kan. 640.

Ky.—Marshall v. Merrifield, 1971, 474 S.W.2d 99 (where motorist and his witness had given written statements which contained nothing to contradict what they said in their testimony there was no necessity for reception of statements in evidence even though counsel for pedestrian wanted to demonstrate that statements contained no mention of pedestrian running at time of accident, while motorist and his witness so testified at trial).

Minn.—O'Neill v. Minneapolis St. Ry. Co., 1942, 7 N.W.2d 665, 213 Minn. 514.

Mo.—Howell v. Dowell, 1967, 419 S.W.2d 257 (since no real inconsistency existed between host driver's plea of contributory negligence on part of guest and host driver's position on trial that host had not been negligent, host driver's plea of contributory negligence was not admissible for impeachment purposes); Conlon v. Roeder, 418 S.W. 2d 152 (mother's statement to doctor that her daughter had been rendered unconscious for approximately 5 minutes following collision was not impeached by the mother's admission that she did not remember telling any doctor at hospital that plaintiff had been unconscious since contact with the testifying doctor was in his office).

N.H.—Calley v. Boston & M. R. R., 42 A.2d 329, 93 N.H. 359, 159 A. L.R. 115 (writ in witness' separate action against railroad wherein negligent construction was alleged was not admissible on issue of credibility of witness who testified concerning operation of automobile and not as to the condition of bridge, since claim that railroad was guilty of negligence contributing to accident was not inconsistent with claim that driver of automobile was also negligent).

N.Y.—Dallas v. Lahl, 59 N.Y.S.2d 886, 270 App.Div. 819, appeal denied 61 N.Y.S.2d 521, 270 App.Div. 852.

Ohio.—Netzley v. Nationwide Mut. Ins. Co., 1971, 296 N.E.2d 550, 34 Ohio App.2d 65 (although in action by insured against insurer based on alleged failure of insurer to properly negotiate a settlement in a prior negligence action, counsel for insurer and for insured in negligence action asserted on direct examination that he had informed insured of an offer of settlement, whereas answer of insurer admitted that insured had not been so informed, refusal to permit insured to use testimony of trial counsel for purposes of impeachment was not error, where counsel testified that there had been two answers filed in negligence action and that answer pursuant to which case went to trial had not been prepared by him).

Pa.—Kaplan v. Loev, 194 A. 653, 327 Pa. 465 certiorari denied 58 S.Ct. 477, 302 U.S. 766, 82 L.Ed. 595.

26. Cal.—Marocco v. Ford Motor Co., 1970, 86 Cal.Rptr. 526, 7 Cal. App.3d 84 (in action against manufacturer for injuries allegedly resulting from defects in transmission selector mechanism, evidence from record of congressional hearing, of manufacturer's admission of other defects in the model of automobile in question was inadmissible to impeach manufacturer's negative answers to interrogatories inquiring whether manufacturer was aware of "any defect" in the model in question, as if "defect" within interrogatories, when read in context, referred to mechanism in question, alleged impeaching evidence was not impeaching, and as, if "defect" were literally interpreted, question and answer were inadmissible, and thus there was properly no statement to be impeached); Fibreboard Paper Products Corp. v. East Bay Union of Machinists, Local 1304, United Steelworkers of America, AFL–CIO, Cal.App., 39 Cal.Rptr. 64, vacated for retrial on damages issue only 227 Cal.App.2d 675, 36 Cal. Rptr. 497 (prior statement must be clearly inconsistent, and inconsistency in effect rather than contradiction in express terms is the test).

Del.—Halko v. State, 1964, 204 A.2d 628.

Ill.—Goldstein v. Hertz Corp., 1973, 305 N.E.2d 617, 16 Ill.App.3d 89 (in the single instance, in intersectional collision case, set forth by defendants in which witness for plaintiffs recalled an allegedly inconsistent prior question and answer, both the question and answer were so confusing that it was difficult to discern whether the prior statement was in fact contradictory to the witness' trial testimony; accordingly, there was no abuse of discretion on the part of the court in directing the jury to disregard such a highly confusing and at best marginally probative aspect of the witness' testimony); Spiotta v. Hamilton, 1970, 256 N.E.2d 649, 120 Ill.App.2d 387 (where plaintiff testified that he "heard something" at moment of impact, quote from deposition that he heard sound of brakes was not impeaching material); Taylor v. Carborundum Co., 1969, 246 N. E.2d 898, 107 Ill.App.2d 12; Greim v. Sharpe Motor Lines, 1968, 242 N.E.2d 282, 101 Ill.App.2d 142 (where plaintiff on direct examination testified that he had received prior whiplash injury to neck and that he had fully recovered from prior injury, but did not testify that neck injury was only injury received, excluded evidence as to whether prior complaint had alleged that plaintiff had received severe injuries to neck, etc., and that plaintiff had been compelled to expend large sums for medical evidence and as to name of attorney who then represented plaintiff but whose name was on prior complaint would not have served to impeach plaintiff).

Iowa.—Ceretti v. Des Moines Ry. Co., 293 N.W. 45, 228 Iowa 548 (a written statement wherein defendant's witness stated that defendant's trolley struck automobile was not sufficiently inconsistent with witness' testimony, on direct examination that automobile struck trolley).

Ky.—Ford Motor Co. v. Zipper, 1973, 502 S.W.2d 74 (where subsequent deposition of treating physician showed that as result of 1967 accident there was aggravation of plaintiff's preexisting, permanent injuries and some additional injury to ligaments, and defendant was

§ 421.2   TRIAL EVIDENCE   Ch. 421

In various other cases, sufficient inconsistency has been found.[27]

permitted to develop its claim that plaintiff's injuries were not attributable to the 1967 accident giving rise to lawsuit, treating physician's prior deposition, which was given in prior personal injury case, that plaintiff received permanent disability, in the 1965 accident, consisting of intermittent neck and back pain and stiffness with radiating pain in her arms and legs was noncontradictory and essentially cumulative and refusal to permit introduction thereof was not an abuse).

La.—Jones v. Dozier, 160 So.2d 395.

Mich.—Thompson v. Essex Wire Co., 1970, 183 N.W.2d 818, 27 Mich. App. 516.

Pa.—Kopar v. Mamone, 215 A.2d 641, 419 Pa. 601 (testimony in pretrial deposition of passenger in automobile, which collided with taxicab, that she could not estimate the speed of the taxicab, over objection should have been allowed because she subsequently testified that taxicab was going faster than automobile which was traveling at 25 to 30 miles per hour).

Tex.—Spring Branch Bank v. Wright, 404 S.W.2d 659 (exclusion of testimony given by husband at trial of another law suit some years before that he was the "head of the concern" which was offered to impeach his testimony at the trial that his wife was the "backbone of the business" and that he was "only a helper" was not error, where it was obvious that when using the phrase "head of the concern" husband had reference to both himself and his wife, and it was undisputed that both were active in the florist business).

Wash.—Weber v. Biddle, 1967, 431 P.2d 705, 72 Wash.2d 22 (refusal to permit defendants to cross-examine plaintiff relative to earlier judgment which she had secured against another for same injury and which then had been vacated on her motion was not error where defendants made no offer to prove that plaintiff had, while a witness at the time judgment was secured in the first action or at any time, made any statement or allegation which was in any way inconsistent with her testimony in the case against them).

Refusal to respond at deposition

Refusal to respond to questions in discovery proceedings is not tantamount to making statement or giving testimony contradictory to testimony on trial. Lewis v. American Road Ins., 1969, 167 S.E.2d 729, 119 Ga. App. 507.

Too remote

Conn.—Lombardo v. Simko, 3 Conn. Cir. 363, 214 A.2d 911, certiorari denied 213 A.2d 526 (although plaintiff stated that in March 1962, when he allegedly sustained permanent injuries resulting from severe strain of muscles and tendons of his neck, he was suffering from no other injury or disability, exclusion of files of court in unrelated 1957 and 1958 negligence actions, in which plaintiff had sought damages for injuries to the neck, in one of which plaintiff had stated in 1960 that he had never fully recovered and which defendant contended were in nature of prior inconsistent statements and would tend to affect credibility of plaintiff's testimony, on basis that evidence in such files was too remote was discretionary).

27. **U.S.**—Pollard v. Fennell, 1968, C.A.N.C., 400 F.2d 421; Bowman v. Kaufman, C.A.N.Y., 387 F.2d 582 (where witness denied having heard driver state that he had no brakes and to attack witnesses'

Ch. 421 IMPEACHMENT OF WITNESSES § 421.2

Declaration of non-testifying witness

The testimony sought to be impeached may be a declaration of another person, which has been received as an exception to the

credibility plaintiff offered in evidence statements signed by witness shortly after accident indicating that driver had stated that brakes did not work, court's refusal to admit such statement was error but was not under circumstances, prejudicial); Slatinsky v. Bailey, C.A.1964, Iowa, 330 F.2d 136 (testified deceased was in proper lane, tape recorded statement that didn't know position).

Ark.—St. Louis Southwestern Ry. Co. v. Jackson, 1967, 416 S.W.2d 273, 242 Ark. 858, appeal after remand 438 S.W.2d 41, 246 Ark. 268 (interoffice memorandum prepared by highway department employees, referring to observations of danger at crossing, proposed measures, and additional observations to study measures that might be taken by railroad, was admissible to impeach testimony of employees that signal lights were visible at considerable distance and that they had made no recommendations).

Fla.—Wingate v. New Deal Cab Co., 1969, 217 So.2d 612 (where witness for taxicab company testified at trial that plaintiff was traveling 75 miles per hour on expressway prior to intersection collision with taxicab in which witness was passenger, refusal to permit plaintiff to introduce prior statement of witness that she could not correctly estimate speed of plaintiff's vehicle was prejudicial error); Rosenfeld v. Johnson, 161 So.2d 703 (where officer testified that if operator had been driving properly she would not have lost control of automobile merely because automobile hit board about one foot wide and a half inch thick, court erred in refusing to permit testimony that officer had previously told operator that officer concluded accident was unavoidable).

Iowa—Parks v. Firgard, 1968, 163 N.W.2d 385 (as to hospital statement).

Kan.—Southard v. Lira, 1973, 512 P.2d 409, 212 Kan. 763 (in passenger's action against driver of second vehicle, it would have been proper for passenger to have been cross-examined on whether or not she had ever stated or contended that her own driver was to blame for the accident, and if she denied such fact, to show briefly that she had made claim on theory that her own driver was responsible for her injuries).

Ky.—Tri-City Van & Storage, Inc. v. Slone, 1969, 437 S.W.2d 211, appeal after remand 485 S.W.2d 889 (testimony did not see vehicle over centerline, signed statement to that fact).

La.—Guerra v. W. J. Young Const. Co., 165 So.2d 882 (erred in treating plaintiff's testimony, that his treating physician had said he "didn't know" whether plaintiff's condition was caused by accident, as excludable hearsay, since such testimony was admissible as affecting credibility of doctor's testimony at trial relating plaintiff's condition to the accident).

Mass.—Wasserman v. Wasserman, 221 N.E.2d 467, 351 Mass. 700 (cross-examination to effect that son had been confined for two and one-half years in four penal institutions during five-year period was admissible as being contradictory to or inconsistent with fair import of his direct testimony to effect that he had been in service of armed forces and thereafter had "bummed around country for couple of years", during the period under

§ 421.2   TRIAL EVIDENCE   Ch. 421

hearsay rule, and the credibility of such a declaration may be attacked by proof of an inconsistent declaration of the other per-

inquiry); Kavanaugh v. Colombo, 24 N.E.2d 14, 304 Mass. 379 (where plaintiff's witness testified that all he heard defendant say after accident was that he wasn't traveling very fast, a sentence in a written statement signed by witness that defendant stated after accident that he caught plaintiff in his rear right wheel, and sent him spinning).

Mich.—Osberry v. Watters, 1967, 151 N.W.2d 372, 7 Mich.App. 258 (hospital record which contained extrajudicial admissions of a prior accident and complaint of injury and which recorded those admissions in ordinary course of business of the outpatient department at time of the event related to matter in issue—plaintiff's prior state of health—and was admissible to impeach plaintiff who had originally denied the prior accident in her action for injuries sustained in subsequent accident and whose health before the second accident was in question).

Miss.—Boyd v. Donald, 167 So.2d 661, 250 Miss. 618 (report made by highway patrolman who had investigated accident and who had testified at trial that most of the debris was in the west lane of traffic was admissible for purpose of impeachment of officer's testimony indicating that accident happened in defendant's lane of travel).

N.Y.—Blakney v. Gleam Cab Corp., 1973, 349 N.Y.S.2d 77, 43 A.D.2d 520 (it was reversible error to exclude signed statement of witness taxicab passenger which was given on the day of accident and which was apparently contrary to such passenger's testimony in wrongful death action, against owner and driver of taxicab, on issue of whether fatal injuries to other passenger resulted from the short stop made by taxicab or the subsequent impact to rear of taxicab by driver of following automobile with whom passenger witness had settled); Peters v. Gersch, 1970, 311 N.Y.S.2d 20, 26 N.Y.2d 976, 259 N.E.2d 488 (curtailment of his cross-examination was prejudicial error).

Pa.—DeJohn v. Orell, 1968, 240 A.2d 472, 429 Pa. 359 (refusal to permit cross-examination on differentiation in testimony of witness who testified on direct examination that motorist was in line of traffic that was moving from 50 to 60 miles per hour and who had testified at coroner's inquest that most of automobiles were traveling from 60 to 70 miles an hour was reversible error).

R.I.—Major v. Grieg, 1967, 230 A.2d 846, 102 R.I. 379 (paper on which pedestrian, injured while crossing street, wrote her name and address and words "my own fault", was admissible for impeachment purposes).

Tex.—Birch v. Howard, 1969, 435 S.W.2d 945, error refused n. r. e. (testimony of patrolman concerning statements by witness to accident, in which automobile driver hit highway flagman standing in center of four-lane highway when flagman stepped three or four feet backward into path of defendant's automobile, that driver could not help it was admissible to impeach witness who had testified that accident could have been avoided if driver had been driving 20 miles per hour in outside lane of four-lane highway); Allen v. Riedel, 1968, 425 S.W.2d 665 (in action by doctor's widow and children for doctor's wrongful death, testimony of psychiatrist treating widow that, during doctor's lifetime, doctor and widow had accused each other of infidelity was admissible as ad-

son.[28] Where practiced, the rule expressly allows such impeachment without any foundation requirement that the declarant first have been confronted with the statement.[29]

mission contradictory of her testimony that doctor and she wanted their marriage to work and that their marriage was happy and normal).

Careless driving plea contradictory to claim of vehicle defect

Mo.—McIntosh v. Ford Motor Co., 1973, 505 S.W.2d 155 (in action against manufacturer and dealer for injuries sustained when pickup truck went off road allegedly because of defective drive shaft, trial court properly allowed defendants to cross-examine plaintiff's father, driver of truck, with regard to his plea of guilty to charge of careless and imprudent driving arising out of accident for purpose of showing prior inconsistent statement, particularly where plaintiff's father was permitted explanation of his actions).

28. **U.S.**—Federal Rules of Evidence § 806, 28 U.S.C.A. (where received as a vicarious admission of a party, under § 801(d)(2), (C), (D), or (E)).

Fla.—Florida Evidence Code § 90.-806.

Kan.—Kansas Rules of Civil Procedure § 60–462 (any declaration received under § 60–460).

Me.—Maine Rules of Evidence § 806.

Neb.—Nebraska Rules of Evidence § 806 (where received as a vicarious admission of a party, under 801 (4)(b)(iii), (iv), or (v)).

Nev.—N.R.S. 51.375(1).

N.J.—New Jersey Evidence Rule 65.

N.M.—New Mexico Rules of Evidence § 806.

Utah—Utah Rules of Evidence § 65.

Wis.—Wisconsin Rules of Evidence § 908.06.

Prior or subsequent inconsistent statement

Cal.—Am-Cal Inv. Co. v. Sharlyn Estates, Inc., 1967, 63 Cal.Rptr. 518, 255 Cal.App.2d 526 (where a witness in court testifies to admissible extrajudicial statements of a third-party declarant, the prior or subsequent inconsistent statements of the declarant may be received).

29. **U.S.**—Federal Rules of Evidence § 806, 28 U.S.C.A.

Fla.—Florida Evidence Code § 90.-806.

Kan.—Kansas Rules of Civil Procedure § 60–462.

Me.—Maine Rules of Evidence § 806.

Neb.—Nebraska Rules of Evidence § 806.

Nev.—N.R.S. 51.375(2).

N.J.—New Jersey Evidence Rule 65.

N.M.—New Mexico Rules of Evidence § 806.

Utah—Utah Rules of Evidence § 65.

Wis.—Wisconsin Rules of Evidence § 908.06.

§ 421.3 Impeachment—Contradiction of Facts

Library References:
C.J.S. Witnesses § 629 et seq.
West's Key No. Digests, Witnesses ⚖︎398 et seq.

Generally speaking, any evidence which tends to contradict or discredit the testimony of a witness may be introduced for

§ 421.3   TRIAL EVIDENCE   Ch. 421

consideration by the jury.[30] However, impeachment of a witness by introduction of extrinsic evidence on collateral [31] or irrelevant [32] matter is not proper.

---

30. **U.S.**—Kirkendoll v. Neustrom, C.A.Kan., 1967, 379 F.2d 694 (in action arising out of collision of front of plaintiff's automobile with rear of defendant's truck, permitting impeachment of plaintiff by his own witness' deposition which contained testimony that plaintiff's automobile had a Thunderbird engine and a 4-speed transmission was not error as issue was relevant as to speed and power of plaintiff's automobile and, therefore, could have been independently admitted to show capacity of plaintiff's automobile); Atlantic Greyhound Lines v. Isabelle, 1946, 157 F.2d 260, 81 U.S.App.D.C. 221 (that signed name to document, though void, contradicted claim was unable to write on day after accident); Mintz v. Premier Cab Ass'n, 1942, 127 F.2d 744, 75 U.S. App.D.C. 389 (that plaintiff filed two prior claims as showing "claim-minded").

Ark.—St. Louis Southwestern Ry. Co. v. Jackson, 1967, 416 S.W.2d 273, 242 Ark. 858, appeal after remand 438 S.W.2d 41, 246 Ark. 268 (interoffice memorandum prepared by highway department employees, referring to observations of danger at crossing, proposed measures, and additional observations to study measures that might be taken by railroad, was admissible to impeach testimony of employees that signal lights were visible at considerable distance and that they had made no recommendations); Missouri Pacific Transp. Co. v. Sharp, 108 S.W.2d 579, 194 Ark. 405 (proof of dates of certain events disputing witness' testimony on bus on date of plaintiff's alleged injury).

Cal.—Pritchard v. Veterans Cab Co., 1965, 47 Cal.Rptr. 904, 408 P.2d 360 (proof of use of prior accident settlement proceeds, to refute claim took job to earn money to enable college study).

Colo.—Alcorn v. Erasmus, 1971, 484 P.2d 813, —— Colo.App. —— (patrolman's testimony, offered in wrongful death action to rebut defendant's testimony that an eyewitness told defendant that accident occurred when plaintiffs' decedent struck defendant on the head with a flashlight, concerning conversation in which accident witness allegedly told patrolman that he did not know what happened).

Ga.—Kapplin v. Selden, 1964, 137 S. E.2d 55, 109 Ga.App. 586; Elliott v. Georgia Power Co., 1938, 197 S. E. 914, 58 Ga.App. 151 (testified witnessed accident while walking around seeking employment, proof had regular employment).

Hawaii—Barretto v. Akau, 1969, 463 P.2d 917, 51 Haw. 461 (where mother of plaintiff-passenger had testified that her postaccident statement that defendant-driver, who had picked up plaintiff shortly before accident, was obviously drunk was based on a police report, such report was admissible over hearsay objection to show that no mention was made of intoxication of defendant in it, except for statement that defendant had been drinking).

Idaho—Rosenberg v. Toetly, 1971, 489 P.2d 446, 94 Idaho 413 (where contributory negligence of driver of automobile containing plaintiff-passengers was issue at time of introduction of photograph of ice chest which contained beer and whiskey bottles and which was in trunk of such automobile, photograph was probative of accuracy of observations of driver and one passenger-plaintiff and was relevant in attempted impeachment of testimony of such driver and pas-

---

31. See note 31 on page 291.

32. See note 32 on page 293.

senger as to quantity of liquor actually consumed in hours preceding collision).

Ill.—Freehill v. DeWitt County Service Co., 1970, 261 N.E.2d 52, 125 Ill.App.2d 306 (use of joint income tax returns of decedent and his spouse either to refresh spouse's recollection or to impeach her in connection with decedent's earnings); Castle v. Searles, 28 N.E. 2d 619, 306 Ill.App. 304 (where plaintiff testified that he was making trip from home to farm owned by him in Missouri, cross-examination showing that plaintiff operated farm within county where trial was had was not error).

Mass.—Langan v. Pianowski, 29 N.E. 2d 700, 307 Mass. 149 (when fairly tend to control or qualify testimony).

Mont.—Seder v. Peter Kiewit Sons' Co., 1971, 479 P.2d 448, 156 Mont. 322 (that witness had seen decedent's truck earlier in the afternoon being driven at speed between 65 and 70 was admissible for impeachment of testimony of decedent's employer that truck driven by decedent had maximum speed in third gear of 35 and 38 miles an hour and while in fourth gear would have to go between 45 and 50 miles per hour to pull load).

Okl.—Perry v. City of Oklahoma City, 1970, 470 P.2d 974 (blood sample taken from body of passenger's deceased driver was admissible in view of conflicting testimony of passengers as to whether the group had been drinking).

Pa.—Downey v. Weston, 1973, 301 A.2d 635, 451 Pa. 259 (it was open to defendant to contradict impression of perfect health given, and no error was committed in permitting defendants to show that in six-year period preceding date of accident, plaintiff made various complaints to his doctor, and, though it was true that a sizeable portion of doctor's testimony related to "various and sundry colds and respiratory infections" it could not be said as a matter of law that verity of plaintiff's sweeping statement that he had "no [health] problems whatsoever" was not affected by proof that person making it had in fact been afflicted with the "various and sundry colds" of the ordinary person).

S.C.—Rhodes v. Spartanburg County, 1974, 207 S.E.2d 85, 262 S.C. 644 (that plaintiff, who earned $145 per week by working on Saturdays, who was disabled by her injuries from performing any work for a period of 26 weeks, received semi-monthly payments of $125 from her employer, with at least three of the payments by check being identified on their faces as being "for labor", was admissible as bearing upon the credibility of plaintiff's testimony that she performed no services for which she received pay for period of 26 weeks following her injury, notwithstanding contention it violated the collateral source rule).

Tenn.—Wood v. Craig, 1967, 424 S. W.2d 561, 57 Tenn.App. 685 (where it was defendant's theory that plaintiff was not seriously injured in collision but that her complaints antedated collision, and plaintiff testified as to previous good health, hospital records showing that plaintiff had been hospitalized seven times since 1960 for various complaints or operations was properly admitted in trial court's discretion).

Tex.—Hix v. Wirt, Civ.App.1949, 220 S.W.2d 530, ref. n. r. e. (where officer testified to highway marks, proper inquire of another officer whether first officer showed him any marks).

Wash.—Parris v. Johnson, 1970, 479 P.2d 91, 3 Wash.App. 853 (defendant who had testified that he had spent the previous night at his apartment could be impeached by evidence that he had stayed up all night with party, where it appeared that accident occurred on bright, clear afternoon and that defendant's truck had veered into wrong lane, so that any evidence explaining lack of alertness or momentary inattention was relevant).

Wis.—Vinicky v. Midland Mut. Cas. Ins. Co., 1967, 151 N.W.2d 77, 35 Wis.2d 246 (whenever it becomes apparent that a medical expert relies on other physician's or expert's reports not in evidence, those reports may, in their relevant and competent portions, be introduced by the adverse party into evidence for purpose of impeachment and in the interest of verbal completeness).

Actions at a later time

Where defendant's employee denied he turned left into center lane but investigators who watched him after collision confirmed that employee in traversing his route changed lanes in manner charged, such testimony by investigators as to route traveled by employee several months after accident was admissible as circumstantially impeaching employee. Newspapers, Inc. v. Love, Tex.Civ.App., 367 S.W.2d 185, error granted 380 S.W.2d 582.

Contradiction not found

U.S.—Culp v. Repper, 78 F.2d 221, 64 App.D.C. 337 (testified couldn't afford to call non-resident passengers as witnesses, offered proof of existence of liability insurance).

Cal.—Henninger v. Southern Pac. Co., 1967, 59 Cal.Rptr. 76, 250 Cal. App.2d 872 (motion picture film purporting to show double amputee walking on hydrocadence legs without aid of either canes or crutches did not contradict physician's expert opinion that former conductor-brakeman who lost both legs in an accident could never wear functional type of prosthesis and be ambulatory and did not contradict physician's experience; hence, film was not admissible to impeach physician's testimony).

Fla.—Powell v. Horne, 5 So.2d 451, 149 Fla. 240 (where engineer did not contend he never passed over crossing involved in accident without blowing whistle, fireman and brakeman merely testified that engine was required to go slow in yard limits and nearby resident testified that at time of accident the whistle was sounded like it always had been, testimony that three or four days after the accident a train approached the crossing without signalling until the cowcatcher had reached the crossing and that about 15 months after the accident a train on schedule of train involved approached the crossing at a speed in excess of that permitted by ordinance was not admissible to impeach the engineer and the other witnesses).

Tex.—Kainer v. Walker, 377 S.W.2d 613 (testimony concerning plaintiff's receipt of disability payments from Veterans Administration which had not given him a physical examination in the last 20 years was not admissible either generally or for purpose of impeaching plaintiff who had testified as to his good physical condition before accident).

Not in hearsay form

In action arising out of head-on collision, wherein one plaintiff passenger testified that before collision she saw lights of oncoming automobile coming at an angle toward automobile in which she was riding, statement made to police detective by another passenger that he had been necking with plaintiff passenger at time of collision was properly excluded on grounds that it was not material, since he testified he did not know how accident occurred, the issue involved, that, although it might have impeached plaintiff passenger, it was hearsay as to her, and that any probative value of statement was outweighed by its potentially prejudicial effect on jury. Felde v. Kohnke, 1971, 184 N.W.2d 433, 50 Wis.2d 168.

Not to rebut claimed lack of memory

Where record did not disclose that minor plaintiff had made any statement as to who was driver of automobile in which he was injured, information appearing in hospital report indicating that he had been driver was not admissible to contradict his claimed lack of memory of events surrounding collision or as an admission that he had been driving the automobile, in action by plaintiff, wherein there was disputed issue as to whether plaintiff or the other occupant had been driving. Kelly v. Sheehan, 1969, 259 A.2d 605, 158 Conn. 281.

Rebutting testimony elicited on cross-examination

Admitting testimony concerning drinking habits of plaintiff pedestrian, who was struck while walking on right shoulder of roadway, was not error, where testimony was offered to impeach testimony elicited from pedestrian on cross-examination that he did not habitually use intoxicating beverages. Kovacs v. Sturgeon, 1969, 79 Cal.Rptr. 426, 274 Cal.App.2d 478.

Scope of contradiction limited

Where plaintiff testified that he lost his job as result of personal injuries, defendant was within proper bounds in presenting evidence that plaintiff allegedly did not leave his job because of injuries but defendant had no right to go beyond that and show that plaintiff was allegedly discharged for dishonesty. Jordan v. Morrissey, 1970, 264 N.E.2d 734, 130 Ill.App.2d 418.

31. U.S.—Walker v. Firestone Tire & Rubber Co., C.A.Vt.1969, 412 F.2d 60 (copy of unrelated proceedings, offered by defendant to show that plaintiff's expert witness had made misstatements as to his qualifications, was inadmissible); Gaynor v. Atlantic Greyhound Corp., C.A.Pa.1950, 183 F.2d 482.

Cal.—Rousseau v. West Coast House Movers, 1968, 64 Cal.Rptr. 655, 256 Cal.App.2d 878 (even though plaintiff claimed to suffer from traumatic epilepsy and, in cross-examination of plaintiff, defendant raised question of plaintiff's driving automobile, records as to plaintiff's convictions for drunk driving and resulting implication of loss of driver's license were inadmissible to rebut plaintiff's claim that he no longer drove automobile because of injuries sustained).

Idaho.—Mundy v. Johnson, 1962, 373 P.2d 755, 84 Idaho 438.

Ill.—Rodriguez v. City of Chicago, 1974, 316 N.E.2d 88, 21 Ill.App.3d 623 (properly excluded testimony offered by plaintiff to impeach defense witness' statement that he had not told plaintiff's counsel that he could not speak with them without first obtaining permission from defense counsel).

Md.—Howard v. State, 1964, 199 A.2d 611, 234 Md. 410.

Mich.—Skiff v. Dickens, 1972, 196 N.W.2d 481, 38 Mich.App. 357 (bound by defendant's testimony had only passed intersection 6 times).

Mo.—Frechin v. Thornton, 326 S.W. 2d 122, quoting 98 C.J.S. Witnesses § 633(b) (in action for injuries sustained while a passenger in automobile which was allegedly forced off highway when defendant's preceding truck stopped suddenly before making left turn, evidence that a new stop light had been installed on truck after accident would not have been admissible as part of plaintiff's case in chief on issue as to whether stop light had

§ 421.3 TRIAL EVIDENCE Ch. 421

been operating at time of accident and, therefore, such evidence related to a collateral matter, and when defendant testified on cross-examination that truck had not been taken to garage to have taillight fixed, plaintiff was bound thereby, and could not impeach defendant on such collateral matter by introducing invoice tending to prove that new switch had been installed); State v. Miles, 412 S.W. 2d 473.

Mont.—Garrison v. Trowbridge, 177 P.2d 464, 119 Mont. 505.

N.M.—Empire Fire & Marine Ins. Co. v. Lee, 1974, 527 P.2d 502, 86 N.M. 739 (bound by answer had no prior accident).

Or.—Davis v. Dean, 350 P.2d 910, 221 Or. 110 (evidence of particular collateral wrongful acts).

Pa.—McGoldrick v. Pennsylvania R. Co., 1968, 241 A.2d 90, 430 Pa. 597 (testimony of plaintiff's witness on direct examination that he had not seen any whiskey and had seen only two bottles of beer at picnic he had attended with plaintiff prior to collision at crossing should not have been admitted unless and until evidence of drinking by plaintiff raised issue of contributory negligence and therefore impeaching testimony of pathologist as to indications of drinking found in autopsy of body of one of riders in plaintiff's automobile concerned collateral matter and should have been excluded).

Vt.—State v. Jackson, 1967, 227 A.2d 280, 126 Vt. 250.

But see

Evidence of mailing to insured and his testimony as to nonreceipt of notices from department of public safety that his insurance certificate would expire or be cancelled on a certain date and copy of notice of license suspension and notice from insurer that liability insurance policy was cancelled effective 10 days after service of notice were admissible in action by insurer seeking determination that it was not liable under policy, on issue of credibility of insured's story that he had not received notice of cancellation. Hartsfield v. Carolina Cas. Ins. Co., Alaska 1969, 451 P.2d 576.

Where doctor's testimony on direct examination, that he had not kept a record or billed plaintiff for many visits because of her inability to pay for them, made issue of payment of doctor's bills a vital one in regard to doctor's credibility, defendants were entitled to show on cross-examination that plaintiff's bills had in fact been paid and would continue to be paid under workmen's compensation, to cast doubt on doctor's testimony though such evidence would otherwise have been inadmissible under collateral source rule. Acampora v. Ledwitz, 1970, 269 A.2d 288, 159 Conn. 377.

Evidence that plaintiff had been reimbursed for medical expenses by insurer was properly admitted, for impeachment, over objection that compensation payments would have to be paid back out of any recovery in tort, where plaintiff on direct examination specifically testified that he had paid medical bills. Fahler v. Freeman, 1968, 241 N.E.2d 394, 143 Ind.App. 493.

Evidence that plaintiff's employer paid benefits for two and one-half week period that plaintiff was absent from work because of accident and that plaintiff submitted a doctor bill to his own insurer was not inadmissible in action to recover for injuries sustained as a result of accident because of collateral source rule, but was rather admissible for purposes of impeachment, under circumstances, including fact that plaintiff had testified that he went back to work because he needed money for support of his family. Hack v. State Farm Mut. Auto. Ins. Co., 1967, 154 N.W.2d 320, 37 Wis. 2d 1.

Ch. 421 IMPEACHMENT OF WITNESSES § 421.3

Discretion of court

U.S.—State of Md. for Use of Geils v. Baltimore Transit Co., C.A.Md., 329 F.2d 738 (evidence discrediting witness' claim he had opportunity to observe accident could be said to be collateral).

Pa.—Curran v. B. & P. Motor Express, Inc., Pa.Com.Pl., 113 P.L.J. 567 (trial court has broad discretion in determining whether or not such impeaching tactics' value is outweighed by the trial delay which inevitably results, and the added confusion the jury may suffer).

Limitation held proper

It was not error to terminate questioning of repairman who had deviated from closest route in returning automobile to owner as to location of traffic signals and stop signs for purpose of impeaching repairman's statement that he had chosen quickest route after repairman had manifested uncertainty as to location of stop signs. Harnage v. Hall, 1969, 169 S.E.2d 345, 120 Ga.App. 12.

Test of collateral

Mich.—Hall v. Iosco County Bd. of Road Com'rs, 140 N.W.2d 761, 2 Mich.App. 511 (depends on whether direct evidence to establish matter could be introduced).

Okl.—Montgomery v. Nance, 425 P. 2d 470 (cannot be used where not be admissible if offered in evidence independent of the impeachment).

Tex.—Hanover Ins. Co. v. Johnson, Civ.App., 397 S.W.2d 904, citing C.J.S. Witnesses § 633, ref. n. r. e. (is whether party seeking to introduce it would be entitled to prove it as part of his own case).

32. U.S.—Livergood v. S. J. Groves & Sons Co., D.C.Pa., 254 F.Supp. 879.

Cal.—Gladstone v. Fortier, 70 P.2d 255, 22 Cal.App.2d 1.

Colo.—Allstate Ins. Co. v. Miller, 381 P.2d 255, 152 Colo. 249 (divorce complaint, motion for temporary restraining order, order directing husband not to molest wife, citation issued pursuant to order, summons, order vacating restraining citation, and divorce decree were matters entirely foreign to issue whether wife's back trouble was caused by accident, as claimed by husband suing under medical payments provision of his policy).

Ill.—Sullivan v. Fawver, 206 N.E.2d 492, 58 Ill.App.2d 37.

N.H.—Valliere v. Filfalt, 1970, 266 A.2d 843, 110 N.H. 331 (testimony that no limitation would be placed on social security benefits after age 72, evidence of eligibility for retirement benefits at 70 was not admissible as rebuttal).

Pa.—Curran v. B. & P. Motor Express, Inc., 113 P.L.J. 567 (held that the prior statement was not admissible since a proper foundation would require the introduction of many collateral facts showing the particular injuries involved in the former trial, and the introduction of these qualified circumstances and collateral facts would have little, if any, effect on the doctor's testimony as opposed to the confusion that would have been created in the minds of the jury).

Tex.—Grocers Supply Co. v. Stuckey, Civ.App., 152 S.W.2d 911, error refused for want of merit.

But see

Cal.—Garfield v. Russell, 1967, 59 Cal.Rptr. 379, 251 Cal.App.2d 275 (evidence that a plaintiff is being wholly or partially compensated for medical expenses or perhaps even making money every time he sees doctor may be relevant on his motives in seeking medical help and on his credibility as witness, even if only remotely).

§ 421.4 Impeachment—Bias

Library References:
C.J.S. Witnesses § 538 et seq.
West's Key No. Digests, Witnesses ⚖️363 et seq.

It is the general rule that a witness' bias or interest may be shown on the issue of credibility.[33] A wide range is allowed

Mich.—Buckeye Union Ins. Co. v. Hallman, 1969, 172 N.W.2d 203, 19 Mich.App. 12 (permitted cross-examination as to witness' own opinion of self as careful driver, then further cross-examination as to prior driving record).

Nev.—Whittlesea Blue Cab Co. v. McIntosh, 1970, 472 P.2d 356, 86 Nev. 609 (refusal to admit pleadings and other preliminary documents from action formerly filed by plaintiff, which action had been dismissed on motion of plaintiff's own counsel, was prejudicial error where jury in instant action had been told by plaintiff's counsel about the former case, and where plaintiff's counsel sought to leave a strong impression with jury that filing of that case upon totally different factual occurrence of negligence was a lawyer's error and in no way attributable to or admissible against plaintiff, where such pleadings were offered by defendant to impeach plaintiff's testimony as to how her injuries occurred).

Door opened by opponent

In action for injuries suffered by plaintiff who had been involved in a later accident with another party, inasmuch as plaintiff's counsel brought to issue the matter of the lawsuit arising out of the later accident, trial court did not err in permitting defendants' counsel to use allegations from pleadings of that action to impeach plaintiff's credibility in the instant case. Selph v. Evanoff, 1970, 184 N.W.2d 282, 28 Mich.App. 201.

Exclusion of failure to issue ticket

Exclusion of testimony by highway patrolman on cross-examination for impeachment as to whether he had preferred traffic charge against driver, to whose speeding before accident he had testified, was not error, although driver's automobile had collided with one driven by another patrolman, inasmuch as his opinion of speed was based on physical facts found at scene of accident. Rosen v. Lawson, 1967, 202 So.2d 716, 281 Ala. 351.

33. **Ala.**—Insurance Co. of North America v. Mays, 174 So.2d 700, 278 Ala. 20; Alaga Coach Line v. McCarroll, 151 So. 834, 227 Ala. 686, 92 A.L.R. 470 (cross-examination).

Cal.—Gladstone v. Fortier, 70 P.2d 255, 22 Cal.App.2d 1 (the state of mind of a witness with respect to bias or prejudice, interest in outcome of case, and friendship or hostility toward parties, are always proper matters for investigation).

Ga.—Freedman v. Housing Authority of City of Atlanta, 136 S.E.2d 544, 108 Ga.App. 418 (feelings or bias of witness as to subject matter of controversy or as to any party).

Ill.—Sidwell v. Sidwell, 220 N.E.2d 479, 75 Ill.App.2d 133.

Kan.—Long v. Shafer, 174 P.2d 88, 162 Kan. 21.

Ky.—Bowling Green-Hopkinsville Bus Co. v. Montgomery, 129 S.W. 2d 535, 278 Ky. 837 (it is competent to show interest or motive of witnesses or circumstances which

Ch. 421   IMPEACHMENT OF WITNESSES   § 421.4

in cross-examination intended to show bias or interest,[34] and much discretion is accorded to trial court.[35]

may influence witnesses); Hedger v. Davis, 33 S.W.2d 310, 236 Ky. 432 (cross-examination).

La.—Howze v. Hollandsworth, App., 26 So.2d 381.

N.Y.—Goldstein v. Albany Yellow Cab Co., 291 N.Y.S. 328, 249 App. Div. 701.

Okl.—Frierson v. Hines, 1967, 426 P.2d 362 (right not abridged because discloses insurance).

Pa.—Anderson v. Pittsburgh Railways Co., 225 A.2d 548, 423 Pa. 550.

S.D.—Plank v. Heirigs, 1968, 156 N. W.2d 193, 83 S.D. 173 (benefits from litigation).

Tex.—Southern Truck Leasing Co. v. Manieri, Civ.App., 325 S.W.2d 912, writ of error refused, n. r. e.

Even by inquiry into collateral matters

Cal.—Goody v. City of El Cajon, 35 Cal.Rptr. 896, 223 Cal.App.2d 259.

Rule limited

Ala.—Rosen v. Lawson, 1967, 202 So.2d 716, 281 Ala. 351 (on cross-examination any but the briefest inquiry into a supposed bias is improper if witness' testimony is of a character not readily responsive to bias or merely cumulative to that of witnesses whose statements are clear, reasonable, and undiscredited).

Ariz.—Vegodsky v. City of Tucson, 399 P.2d 723, 1 Ariz.App. 102 (proper on cross-examination to bring forth prior connection between witness and party to show bias, but rule is not inflexible and court must always consider danger of injecting collateral issues).

Minn.—Bosell v. Rannestad, 33 N.W. 2d 40, 226 Minn. 413 (properly refused to permit plaintiff to show, on cross-examination of defendant's witness, who was riding with defendant at time of collision, that witness had made and settled a claim against defendant for injuries received therein, in absence of any inconsistency between offered proof and witness' testimony).

Re compensation of witness

Ky.—Current v. Columbia Gas of Ky., Inc., 383 S.W.2d 139 (inquiries into compensation of witnesses rests largely within discretion of trial court, and limitation of such questioning is not reversible error absent abuse).

34. **Ky.**—Chesapeake & O. Ry. Co. v. Pittman, 138 S.W.2d 962, 283 Ky. 63.

Pa.—Duffy v. Griffith, 4 A.2d 170, 134 Pa.Super. 447 (whatever tends to show interest or feeling of a witness in a cause is competent by way of cross-examination).

Tex.—Consolidated Underwriters v. Foster, 383 S.W.2d 829.

Error to exclude

N.C.—Redmon v. U. S. Fidelity & Guaranty Co., 1974, 206 S.E.2d 298, 21 N.C.App. 704 (committed prejudicial error in not permitting alleged insured to answer question, "you would like to see [plaintiff] recover from this insurance company, wouldn't you?" where record disclosed that witness' answer would have been "Yes,").

35. **U.S.**—Abeyta v. U. S., C.A.N.M. 1966, 368 F.2d 544; U. S. v. Higgins, C.A.Ill.1966, 362 F.2d 462, certiorari denied 385 U.S. 945, 87 S.Ct. 316, 17 L.Ed.2d 224 (even as to use of collateral matter).

Cal.—Granville v. Parsons, 1968, 66 Cal.Rptr. 149, 259 Cal.App.2d 298 (even if it appears that witness

§ 421.4   TRIAL EVIDENCE   Ch. 421

It may be that a foundation must be shown to introduce extrinsic evidence of bias.[36]

Various types of evidence have been found to be proper proof of bias,[37] and other types inadmissible.[38]

could have been influenced in his testimony by payment of money to plaintiff to have negligence action dismissed as to him or by obtaining of the dismissal, party resisting admission of evidence of settlement, tendered to affect witness' credibility, may appeal to trial court's discretion to exclude such evidence).

Mich.—King v. Daly, 138 N.W.2d 548, 2 Mich.App. 120 (cross-examination of defense witness, who was shown to have practiced law for 31½ years and whose specialty was representation of insurance companies, had not been improperly limited by termination thereof upon making of argumentative charge that witness gave talents to the defendant).

Mo.—Pfefer v. Bachman, 386 S.W.2d 680.

Tex.—City of Corpus Christi v. Polasek, 404 S.W.2d 826.

Bias obvious

Mont.—Stephens v. Brown, 1972, 503 P.2d 667, 160 Mont. 453 (exclusion of decedent's will proper where "interest" of widow obvious).

36. **Ill.**—People v. Payton, 218 N.E. 2d 518, 72 Ill.App.2d 240.

37. **U.S.**—Luna v. Beto, C.A.Tex. 1968, 395 F.2d 35, certiorari denied 89 S.Ct. 1310, 394 U.S. 966, 22 L.Ed.2d 568 (evidence of pending charges is admissible in Texas for limited purpose of showing bias, prejudice and motive of a witness); U. S. v. Dardi, C.A.N.Y., 330 F.2d 316 (an arrest alone is not normally admissible to impair the credibility of a witness, but the fact that it might have embittered him so as to motivate him to testify as he has may be relevant).

Fla.—Mitchell v. Gillespie, 1964, 164 So.2d 867 (witnesses were paid investigators).

Ill.—Runge v. Smith, 1968, 244 N.E. 2d 391, 104 Ill.App.2d 270 (refusal of plaintiff's witness to give statement to defense counsel concerning accident after he had given such statement to plaintiff's counsel was proper material for cross-examination); Pfaelzer v. Kostner, 1967, 231 N.E.2d 668, 87 Ill.App. 2d 315 (sustaining of objection to question asked of plaintiff as to whether witness whose deposition testimony was read at trial was related by blood or marriage to either plaintiff's wife or himself was error).

Ind.—Pickett v. Kolb, 1968, 237 N.E. 2d 105, 250 Ind. 449 (may properly be cross-examined with respect to his interest in litigation in question; he may be cross-examined with reference to his motives, his feelings, friendly or unfriendly, toward parties or other witnesses involved, his employment by either of parties or some third party, and contractual relationship with reference to his interest in litigation and any financial considerations that might have influenced him).

Ky.—Chesapeake & O. Ry. Co. v. Pittman, Civ.App., 138 S.W.2d 962 (pendency of criminal proceedings against witness, where one of commonwealth's attorneys represented a party in civil case).

Mass.—Ford v. Kremer, 1972, 277 N. E.2d 679, 360 Mass. 870 (where

38. See note 38 on page 299.

witness, whose testimony appeared to be the mainstay of plaintiff's claim for injuries to plaintiff who was struck by defendant's motor vehicle in 1962, admitted without objection that he had been found guilty in 1965 of drunkenness, and stated over objection that on night of the arrest he was in company of plaintiff, and a prior question, which was excluded, attempted to extract admission that witness was arrested for drunkenness at time that plaintiff was arrested, the admission of the questions and answers was not abuse of discretion since defendant was attempting to show a relationship between witness and plaintiff which could have colored witness' testimony on behalf of plaintiff).

Mo.—Thornton v. Vonallmon, App. 1970, 456 S.W.2d 795 (the existence of past or present sexual relations between witness and party for whom he or she was called may be shown as a circumstance tending to affect credibility of witness, though specific occasions or particular acts may not be inquired into); Pfefer v. Bachman, 386 S.W.2d 680 (permitted to ask witness whether he was connected with one of the defendants in certain "ill-fated" venture); Harris v. Goggins, 374 S.W.2d 6 (permitted to show that witness, the decedent's widower, was heir to decedent's estate and thus had financial interest in the case).

Neb.—Johnson v. Griepenstroh, 33 N.W.2d 549, 150 Neb. 126 (threat of witness to obtain revenge against plaintiff).

N.J.—Lawlor v. Kolarsick, 223 A.2d 281, 92 N.J.Super. 309 (doctor who had testified as expert that he devoted his time primarily to general medical work and research and was essentially a full time practicing doctor could be cross-examined on his extensive writings and publications, including those on non-medical subjects and those susceptible of inference that doctor exhibited bias against medical profession generally, particularly in view of indication of evasiveness).

Tex.—Barrios v. Davis, Civ.App. 1967, 415 S.W.2d 714 (allowing cross-examination of doctor as to number of cases he had testified in, amount collected by him in one year from lawyers in cases referred to him by lawyers, and that he was well known as doctor who testified on behalf of injured people was not error).

Va.—Doe v. Simmers, 1967, 154 S.E. 2d 146, 207 Va. 956 (in insured's action against insurer for damages caused by unknown operator of another vehicle, where insurer's adjuster testified insured told him name of vehicle involved in accident but insured denied making statement, testimony of adjuster as to nature of coverage was admissible to show adjuster's bias or interest in outcome of case and bore upon his credibility).

Employment status

U.S.—Ridgeway Nat. Bank v. North Am. Van Lines, Inc., C.A.Pa.1964, 326 F.2d 934; Majestic v. Louisville & N. R. Co., C.A.Tenn.1945, 147 F.2d 621.

Mo.—Turner v. Cowart, 1969, 450 S.W.2d 441 (investigating patrolman also employee of defendant's insurer).

Financial interest

U.S.—Harris v. U. S., C.A.Nev.1967, 371 F.2d 365.

Tex.—Dixie Motor Coach Corporation v. Shivers, Civ.App., 131 S.W. 2d 677 (agreement among claimants to share litigation proceeds).

Insurance representative

U.S.—Brown v. Edwards, D.C.Pa. 1966, 258 F.Supp. 696.

Ill.—Yelm v. Masters, 1967, 225 N.E. 2d 152, 81 Ill.App.2d 186 (identity of representative taking impeachment statement).

Miss.—Skelton v. Turnispeed, 1970, 235 So.2d 694.

N.Y.—Wood v. New York State Electric & Gas Corporation, 1939, 12 N.Y.S.2d 947, 257 App.Div. 172, affirmed 24 N.E.2d 480, 281 N.Y. 797.

Pa.—O'Donnell v. Bachelor, 1968, 240 A.2d 484, 429 Pa. 498 (refusing to permit plaintiff to show that witness, who testified about what plaintiff allegedly admitted during course of witness' unilaterally imposed visit to plaintiff's hospital room after serious accident, was employed by insurance company which was responsible for any verdict against the defendant, so that jury could determine whether such employment-relationship predisposed the witness toward favoring defendant's side of case in his recollection, constituted reversible error).

Tex.—Hammond v. Stricklen, Civ. App.1973, 498 S.W.2d 356 (entitled to cross-examine defendant's witness to show that witness, who testified in regard to certain measurements of skid marks he had made at scene and as to distances ascertained from such measurements, was employed by defendant's insurance carrier).

Pending suit against a party

Ga.—Elliott v. Georgia Power Co., 1938, 197 S.E. 914, 58 Ga.App. 151.

Mo.—Olsten v. Susman, 1965, 391 S.W.2d 328 (and to show amount sued for).

Or.—Schmitz v. Yant, 1965, 409 P.2d 346, 242 Or. 308, citing C.J.S. Witnesses § 546 (fact husband of plaintiff sued, but deleting amount asked).

Prior claim against both parties

Where on cross-examination, testimony was elicited that plaintiff's witness, a passenger in plaintiff's automobile, had settled claim against plaintiff, plaintiff was entitled to prove that witness had similarly settled her claim, arising out of same accident, against defendant. Ryan v. Dwyer, 1969, 307 N.Y.S.2d 565, 33 A.D.2d 878.

Prior settlement received from party calling

U.S.—Geehan v. Monahan, C.A.Wis. 1967, 382 F.2d 111.

Ark.—Missouri Pac. Transp. Co. v. Norwood, 1936, 90 S.W.2d 480, 192 Ark. 170.

Cal.—Sheperd v. Walley, 1972, 105 Cal.Rptr. 387, 28 Cal.App.3d 1079.

Ill.—Reese v. Chicago, Burlington & Q. R. Co., 1973, 303 N.E.2d 382, 55 Ill.2d 356 (evidence of loan receipt agreement between plaintiff and one defendant in tort action, whereby plaintiff agreed to repay to defendant amount of "loan" from any judgment plaintiff was legally entitled to collect from codefendant and further agreed to pursue any reasonable and legal means available to collect any judgment obtained against codefendant, could be considered solely on issue of motive and credibility of lender-defendant's witnesses and not on liability or damage issues).

La.—Belanger v. Employers Mut. Liability Ins. Co. of Wis., 1964, 159 So.2d 500.

Mo.—Stevens v. Waldman, App., 375 S.W.2d 633 (right to question defendant's witness as to whether she had made claim against defendant for damage to her automobile and, if so, whether it had been paid); Merk v. St. Louis Public Service Co., Mo., 299 S.W. 2d 446 (reversible error to refuse passenger right to ask and have answered, under proper limitations, question whether bus company had paid driver of third automobile, who was bus company's witness).

N.Y.—Geddes v. Red Star Exp. Lines, Inc., 1968, 291 N.Y.S.2d 885, 30 A.D.2d 761; Goldstein v. Albany Yellow Cab Co., 291 N.Y.S. 328, 249 App.Div. 701 (where cab company offered as witnesses two passengers who were riding in cab and stated on direct examination that cab company had settled their claim for injuries, evidence as to amounts paid on such settlements brought out on cross-examination held admissible).

Okl.—Frierson v. Hines, 426 P.2d 362.

Tex.—Robertson Tank Lines, Inc. v. Watson, Civ.App.1973, 491 S.W.2d 706, error refused n. r. e. (even if transaction were a compromise settlement agreement).

Re compensation of witness

Va.—Slayton v. Weinberger, 1973, 194 S.E.2d 703, 213 Va. 690 (agreement to pay witness for lost time and expenses incurred, in excess of statutory fees, may be shown as affecting the weight and credibility).

38. Ariz.—Keck v. Kelley, 1972, 492 P.2d 412, 16 Ariz.App. 163 (trial court, in action where truck driven by plaintiff collided with defendants' semitrailer which was parked on highway allegedly in emergency lane, erred in permitting plaintiff to question investigating officer as to after-the-accident criticisms he allegedly received for not moving the trailer from the highway prior to the accident, in an effort to show that the officer was defensive and biased, where no foundation was laid as to the time, place and questions relating to the prospective testimony as to criticism, and there were no admissions by the officer that he was aware of such criticisms).

Ga.—Atlantic Coast Line R. Co. v. Grover, 1968, 164 S.E.2d 356, 118 Ga.App. 547, citing 98 C.J.S. Witnesses § 556 (fact that witness, suing for mother's death, was plaintiff established his interest in case and that his position was adverse to defendant, so that refusal to permit cross-examination as to whether witness and brother had another suit pending for death of father was not harmful, and refusal to permit questioning to show further witness' bias, interest, or feeling was not abuse of discretion).

Ill.—Deeke v. Steffke Freight Co., 199 N.E.2d 442, 50 Ill.App.2d 1 (refusal to talk to the plaintiffs' counsel did not reveal hostility toward child plaintiff); Shanowat v. Checker Taxi Co., 198 N.E.2d 573, 48 Ill.App.2d 81 (witness for plaintiff had formerly been codefendant and had been discharged from suit under covenant of plaintiff not to sue).

Minn.—Esser v. Brophey, 3 N.W.2d 3, 212 Minn. 194 (that a witness for plaintiff settled an action brought against him by defendant arising out of same accident).

N.J.—Nesta v. Meyer, 1968, 242 A.2d 386, 100 N.J.Super. 434 (that defendant was issued summons for careless driving not admissible to show interest in outcome).

N.Y.—Doyle v. Dapolito, 247 N.Y.S. 2d 340, 20 A.D.2d 318 (where retired court reporter was called to read from original notes the answers which a witness had previously given at interview but denied at trial, it was proper to establish interest and possible bias of reporter by cross-examination showing he was hired by company, but allowing further cross-examination as to insurance company's agent and fact that particular defendant was insured was error).

Tex.—Austin Road Co. v. Ferris, Civ. App.1973, 492 S.W.2d 64 (did not abuse discretion in refusing to permit defendant to cross-examine physician who testified on plaintiff's behalf concerning a case and nature of such case that plaintiff, as an attorney, had tried in physi-

§ 421.5   TRIAL EVIDENCE   Ch. 421

§ 421.5 Impeachment—Character

Library References:
C.J.S. Witnesses § 491 et seq.
West's Key No. Digests, Witnesses ⟬333 et seq.

Usually general evidence of immoral conduct is not admissible on the issue of credibility.[39] In federal court [40] and in some

cian's behalf); Merrifield v. Seyferth, 408 S.W.2d 558 (exclusion of cross-examination testimony that doctor testifying as witness for plaintiffs had known defendants' counsel, who had been employed by his liability insurer to defend malpractice suit against the doctor, and who had recommended to insurer that case be settled for limits of policy, thus resulting in cancelling of doctor's insurance, was not error in that testimony did not show bias or prejudice on part of doctor to defendants' counsel and in that it was not relevant to any issue in the case, and in any event no harm resulted to defendants by exclusion of such testimony).

Wash.—Dods v. Harrison, 319 P.2d 558, 51 Wash.2d 446 (not error to refuse to permit plaintiff to elicit from defendants' principal witness an admission that witness had refused at time of accident to make statement to police).

Bias against counsel only

U.S.—Lee Way Motor Freight v. True, C.C.A.Okl., 165 F.2d 38 (cross-examination of driver of tractor-trailer regarding his union affiliations and activities, as part of examination designed to show animosity toward counsel because of other pending controversy in which counsel's firm represented party against union was improper).

Proof of compensation benefits as evidence of common employer of witness

Even though defendant in wrongful death action arising out of death of invitee on gravel pit premises who was struck by truck driven by pit owner's employee claimed that evidence as to employer's payment of compensation benefits was admissible to show that decedent's fellow employees who testified were not wholly disinterested witnesses, exclusion of such evidence was not error. Vanden Berg v. Grand Rapids Gravel Co., 1972, 202 N.W.2d 694, 42 Mich.App. 722.

39.   **U.S.**—Federal Rules of Evidence § 608(a), 28 U.S.C.A.

Cal.—West's Ann.Calif.Evid.Code § 786.

Fla.—Florida Evidence Code § 90.609 (1).

Ill.—McWethy v. Lee, 1971, 272 N.E.2d 663, 1 Ill.App.3d 80 (permitting cross-examination of surviving passengers as to presence of beer was improper); Rose v. B. L. Cartage Co., 1969, 249 N.E.2d 199, 110 Ill.App.2d 260 (that former police officer, who testified for plaintiffs, had left police force rather than face charges of drinking in uniform, filing false report and committing perjury under oath at an inquest concerning another occurrence was properly excluded); People v. Brown, 1966, 222 N.E.2d 227, 76 Ill.App.2d 362 (as to drug addiction).

Kan.—Kansas Code of Civil Procedure § 60–422(c); Standinger v. Sooner Pipe & Supply Co., 1971, 490 P.2d 619, 208 Kan. 100 (as to alleged adulterous conduct).

La.—State v. Perkins, 178 So.2d 255, 248 La. 293.

40.   See note 40 on page 301.

Ch. 421   IMPEACHMENT OF WITNESSES   § 421.5

Me.—Maine Rules of Evidence § 608(a).

Minn.—Clifford v. Peterson, 1967, 149 N.W.2d 75, 276 Minn. 142 (evidence that defendant concealed blindness in one eye when applied for driver's license not admissible).

Mo.—Benfield v. Thompson, App. 1940, 139 S.W.2d 1009 (not proper show lack of apearance in divorce proceedings wherein charged with immoral conduct).

Neb.—Nebraska Rules of Evidence § 608(1)(a).

Nev.—N.R.S. 50.085(1)(a).

N.J.—New Jersey Evidence Rule 22(c).

N.M.—New Mexico Rules of Evidence § 608(a)(1).

N.C.—Ingle v. Roy Stone Transfer Corp., 1967, 156 S.E.2d 265, 271 N.C. 276; Pearce v. Barham, 1966, 149 S.E.2d 22, 222 N.C. 707, appeal after remand 156 S.E.2d 290, 271 N.C. 285 (error to show that married passenger was intimate with deceased driver).

Pa.—Com. v. Jones, 36 North. 92 (not evidence of reputation for lack of chastity).

Utah.—Utah Rules of Evidence § 22(c).

Wis.—Wisconsin Rules of Evidence § 906.08(1)(a).

But see

Ala.—J. Truett Payne Co. v. Jackson, 1967, 203 So.2d 443, 281 Ala. 426 (in action against dealer for fraud and deceit in sale of used automobile which dealer had allegedly represented as new, testimony as to conversation which was between dealer's salesman and another dealer from whom salesman purchased automobile as a used demonstrator and in which salesman lied with respect to person for whom purchase was being made was admissible as affecting salesman's credibility).

Ga.—Kapplin v. Seiden, 1964, 137 S.E.2d 55, 109 Ga.App. 586.

Mich.—Lucas v. Carson, 1972, 196 N.W.2d 819, 38 Mich.App. 552 (that a party to civil action was issued a traffic ticket is not barred from evidence as it rebuts testimony of the party that he drove with care and therefore impeaches).

Pa.—Downey v. Weston, 1973, 301 A. 2d 635, 451 Pa. 259 (some misconduct or some past events throwing light on human character is admissible on cross-examination, but such evidence is restricted to evidence which bears directly on witness' character for truth).

Prior false testimony

On cross-examination, defendant should have been permitted to attempt to impeach plaintiff's expert by showing that expert had testified incorrectly with respect to his qualifications in another unrelated case, and, inasmuch as virtually whole of plaintiff's case was based on that witness' testimony, exclusion of impeaching questions was prejudicial. Walker v. Firestone Tire & Rubber Co., C.A.Vt.1969, 412 F.2d 60.

Plaintiff's withdrawal of loss of income claim made immaterial question whether plaintiff had sustained loss of earnings but not question whether he had testified falsely at adverse examination, and, therefore, cross-examination as to whether plaintiff had told truth in answers given at adverse examination on issue of loss of earnings was properly admissible on issue of plaintiff's credibility. Hunter v. Kuether, 1968, 156 N.W.2d 353, 38 Wis.2d 140.

40. Federal Rules of Evidence § 608(b), 28 U.S.C.A.

§ 421.5 TRIAL EVIDENCE Ch. 421

state jurisdictions,[41] a witness may be asked on cross-examination about specific instances of misconduct, but the answer cannot be rebutted by extrinsic proof. When admissible such conduct must be directly relevant to the trait of truth and veracity.[42]

Conviction of crimes

A special type of character evidence exists whereby conviction of crimes may be shown.[43] However, specific limitations to

---

41. **Me.**—Maine Rules of Evidence § 608(b).
Neb.—Nebraska Rules of Evidence § 608(2).
Nev.—N.R.S. 50.085(3).
N.M.—New Mexico Rules of Evidence 608(b); Martinez v. Avila, 1966, 415 P.2d 59, 76 N.M. 372.
Pa.—Com. v. Boggio, 205 A.2d 694, 204 Pa.Super. 434.
Wis.—Wisconsin Rules of Evidence § 906.08(2).

Contra by rule
Cal.—West's Ann.Calif.Evid. Code § 787.
Kan.—Kansas Code of Civil Procedure § 60–422(d).
N.J.—New Jersey Evidence Rule 22 (d).
Utah.—Utah Rules of Evidence § 22 (d).

Discretion of court
Plaintiff lacked absolute right to pursue collateral credibility cross-examination of defendant based on defendant's prior employment and specific reasons for its termination, decision to exclude cross-examination by which plaintiff sought to show that defendant had been discharged for stealing and had lied during investigation was within trial court's discretion, and exclusion was not an abuse of discretion, but receipt of such testimony would not have been error. Lehr v. Rogers, 1969, 168 N.W.2d 636, 16 Mich.App. 585.

42. **U.S.**—Federal Rules of Evidence 608(b), 28 U.S.C.A.
Conn.—Heating Acceptance Corp. v. Patterson, 208 A.2d 341, 152 Conn. 467.

Ky.—Dix v. Gross, 111 S.W.2d 673, 271 Ky. 231 (that two women were with two men in a parked automobile at night was not such conduct as would make them unworthy of belief).
Me.—Maine Rules of Evidence § 608 (b)(1).
Neb.—Nebraska Rules of Evidence § 608(2)(a).
Nev.—N.R.S. 50.085(3).
N.M.—New Mexico Rules of Evidence § 608(b).
N.Y.—Tirschwell v. Dolan, 1964, 251 N.Y.S.2d 91, 21 A.D.2d 923 (any immoral, vicious or criminal act showing unworthy of belief). Batease v. Dion, 1949, 90 N.Y.S.2d 851, 275 App. 451 (suspension from law practice).
Wis.—Wisconsin Rules of Evidence § 906.08(2).

But see
Showing on cross-examination of plaintiff driver that he had no operator's license for many months before and at time of accident was proper as bearing on issue of his credibility, since operation of motor vehicle on public highway without license is misdemeanor, unless operator's license expired within 30 days before such operation. Phass v. MacClenathen, 85 N.Y.S.2d 643, 274 App.Div. 535.

43. **Fla.**—Florida Evidence Code § 90.610 (limited to those crimes involving dishonesty).
Ill.—Krantz v. O'Neil, 240 N.E.2d 180, 99 Ill.App.2d 179 (may be attacked by showing that witness or

party has been convicted of an infamous crime, and one of methods of proving conviction is by witness himself); People v. Rowland, 1967, 223 N.E.2d 113, 36 Ill.2d 311 (judge's affidavit of fact of plea and sentence supported transcript where record lost).

Ind.—Andrews v. McNaughton, 1967, 226 N.E.2d 167, 141 Ind.App. 1 (15 traffic offenses).

Kan.—Kansas Rules of Civil Procedure, § 60–421 (must involve dishonesty or false statement).

Md.—Nelson v. Seiler, 1927, 139 A. 564, 154 Md. 63.

Mass.—Morrissey v. Powell, 1939, 23 N.E.2d 411, 304 Mass. 268, 124 A.L.R. 1522.

Mich.—Cobb v. Harris, 1973, 209 N.W.2d 741, 47 Mich.App. 617 (refusal to allow to cross-examine the driver concerning a drunk driving conviction was error, notwithstanding contention that trial court allowed the passenger to question the driver concerning certain aspects of his past driving record and merely exercised its discretion when it refused to allow questioning on the drunk driving charge); Taylor v. Walter, 1971, 189 N.W.2d 309, 385 Mich. 599 (erred reversibly in refusing to uphold plaintiff's right to cross examine defendant as to whether he had been arrested and convicted of crime of prohibited left turn); Sting v. Davis, 1971, 185 N.W.2d 360, 384 Mich. 608 (no discretion to exclude cross-examination with regard to defendant driver's driving history); Taylor v. Walter, 1970, 180 N.W.2d 24, 384 Mich. 114, opinion adhered to 189 N.W.2d 309, 385 Mich. 599 (discretionary as to traffic convictions); Williams v. Fiedlar, 1970, 177 N.W.2d 461, 22 Mich.App. 179 (prior driving violations); Zimmerman v. Goldberg, 268 N.W. 837, 277 Mich. 134 (reckless driving).

Minn.—Kvanli v. Village of Watson, 139 N.W.2d 275, 272 Minn. 481 (guilty plea in criminal proceedings against village's employee involving a charge arising out of illegal sale of liquor).

Miss.—Murphree v. Hudnall, 1973, 278 So.2d 427 (requires final judgment).

Mo.—Kansas City v. Roberts, 411 S.W.2d 847 (statute allowing cross-examination to show that defendant has been convicted of crime must be strictly construed).

N.Y.—Geiger v. Weiss, 281 N.Y.S. 154, 245 App.Div. 817 (drunken driving).

N.C.—Ingle v. Roy Stone Transfer Corp., 1967, 156 S.E.2d 265, 271 N.C. 276 (any sort of offense).

Ohio.—Garland v. Standard Oil Co., 1963, 196 N.E.2d 810, 119 Ohio App. 291.

Or.—Otten v. Gladden, 1966, 417 P.2d 1017, 244 Or. 327.

R.I.—Mercurio v. Fascitelli, 1970, 268 A.2d 427, 107 R.I. 511 (not limited to offenses involving dishonesty).

Tex.—Columbus v. State, 409 S.W.2d 400 (defendant's negative answer to inquiry as to whether he was pretty upstanding citizen was no bar to cross-examination of defendant concerning prior felony and misdemeanor theft convictions).

Utah.—Utah Rules of Evidence § 21 (not admissible unless involves dishonesty or false statement).

Wash.—State v. Johnson, 1969, 463 P.2d 205, 1 Wash.App. 553 (in prosecution for driving under influence of alcohol, to inquire about defendant's convictions for a similar misdemeanor was not error); City of Mercer Island v. Walker, 1969, 458 P.2d 274, 76 Wash.2d 607 (in prosecution for operating automobile under influence of intoxicants or drugs, in violation of ordinance, there was no error in allowing cross-examination of defendant with regard to three prior convictions for the same offense); Conklin v. City of Seattle, 1961, 361 P.2d 578, 58 Wash.2d 189 (disorderly conduct).

W.Va.—Moore v. Skyline Cab, 1950, 59 S.E.2d 437, 134 W.Va. 121.

Contra by statute as to driving record

Excluding from evidence plaintiff's prior driving record was mandated by statute providing that "[s]uch record shall not be admissible as evidence in any action, civil or criminal, arising out of a motor vehicle accident"; moreover, since plaintiff could not testify about the accident because of amnesia, even if the statute permitted, the record could not have been employed to impeach him. Willmore v. Hertz Corp., C.A.Mich. 1971, 437 F.2d 357.

Discretion of court

Tex.—Travelers Ins. Co. v. Dunn, Civ.App., 383 S.W.2d 197 (exclusion of evidence of conviction of crime involving moral turpitude rests largely on discretion of trial court which must take into consideration all facts and circumstances present at time testimony is proffered, and decision to admit or exclude the testimony because of remoteness will not be disturbed unless it is evident trial judge abused discretion).

Not a conviction

A traffic ticket issued to defendant for failure to yield at stop sign and attached form which had been signed by defendant and which authorized entry of guilty plea and waiver of trial and voluntary payment of fine could not be used as proof of prior conviction of crime or as proof of prior inconsistent statement for purpose of impeachment of defendant, or as independent evidence of a material fact by admission of defendant. Hannah v. Ike Topper Structural Steel Co., 201 N. E.2d 63, 120 Ohio App. 44, citing 98 C.J.S. Witnesses § 593.

In action for collision in Massachusetts, court did not err in excluding from evidence a copy of Massachusetts court record containing a complaint against driver of defendant's truck for having driven, on the occasion of collision, "so that lives and safety of the public might be endangered," and which indicated defendant pleaded guilty and that case was "filed," since under Massachusetts law there was no "conviction," as against contention that the record was admissible under Rhode Island statute providing that conviction of witness of a crime may be shown to affect credibility. Solomon v. Shepard Co., 200 A. 993, 61 R. I. 332.

Not violation of municipal regulation

A defendant convicted of dangerous driving in violation of regulations for control of traffic in the City of New York was not convicted of a "crime", and evidence thereof could not be used to discredit defendant as a witness. Walther v. News Syndicate Co., 93 N.Y.S.2d 537, 276 App.Div. 169.

Limitation on crime arising out of same occurrence

Ordinarily witness may be cross-examined with respect to his previous conviction of crime; but to admit such evidence in damage action growing out of same accident as that responsible for conviction would cause jury to give undue weight to conviction. Beanblossom v. Thomas, 146 S.E.2d 36, 266 N.C. 181.

Not indictment

U.S.—Jenkins v. General Motors Corp., C.A.Ga.1971, 446 F.2d 377, certiorari denied 92 S.Ct. 959, 405 U.S. 922, 30 L.Ed.2d 793 (under Georgia law, and in the federal courts, it is improper for purposes of impeachment to show the accusation, arrest or indictment for

Ch. 421 IMPEACHMENT OF WITNESSES § 421.5

the general rule may preclude such proof. There may be a problem of remoteness in time,[44] as under the federal rule where a

a crime to use against a witness in a civil or criminal case).

Ohio.—James v. Franks, 1968, 240 N.E.2d 508, 15 Ohio App.2d 215.

Questioning re nature of crime

U.S.—Magnuson v. Fairmont Foods Co., C.A.Wis.1971, 442 F.2d 95 (under Wisconsin law, if witness admits conviction, nature of offense may not be shown by adversary, but if witness denies conviction, cross-examiner may specify particular offense in proving that witness was, in fact, convicted).

Ohio—James v. Franks, 1968, 240 N.E.2d 508, 15 Ohio App.2d 215 (cross-examination of defendant as to whether he had been convicted of aggravated assault from a charge of rape and sodomy was improper, but new trial was not required, where defendant had juggled truth when responding to previous questions concerning prior conviction, and trial court had instructed jury as to limited purpose of such testimony).

S.D.—Jeitz v. Fleming, 1974, 217 N.W.2d 868, —— S.D. —— (refusal to permit defendants to question driver concerning precise nature of felonies of which he had been convicted was within trial court's discretion).

Wis.—Rausch v. Buisse, 146 N.W.2d 801, 33 Wis.2d 154 (plaintiff who, on cross-examination, denied ever having been convicted of crime, could be questioned as to whether he had ever been convicted, as he had, of specific offense of contributing to delinquency of minor).

44. **Fla.**—Florida Evidence Code § 90.610(1)(a).

Me.—Maine Rules of Evidence § 609(b) (not conviction of over 15 years, or where incarceration was more than 10 years before).

Neb.—Nebraska Rules of Evidence, § 609(2) (not if more than 10 years elapsed from time of conviction or release from confinement, whichever is later).

Nev.—N.R.S. 50.095(2) (not if over 10 years elapsed from date of release from confinement or expiration of parole, probation or sentence, whichever is later).

N.M.—New Mexico Rules of Evidence § 609(b) (not if over 10 years elapsed since release from confinement for most recent conviction or the expiration of the period of parole, probation or sentence or most recent conviction).

Pa.—McIntosh v. Pittsburgh Railways Co., 1968, 247 A.2d 467, 432 Pa. 123 (admission of evidence that motorist had been convicted of the felony of pandering 12 years before accident for purpose of impeaching credibility of motorist's testimony was reversible error).

R.I.—Mercurio v. Fascitelli, 1970, 268 A.2d 427, 107 R.I. 511 (would be clear abuse of discretion to exclude because of remoteness prior traffice convictions which occurred within three years of time at which they were offered).

S.D.—Allen v. McLain, 1955, 69 N.W.2d 390, 75 S.D. 520 (four years not too remote).

Tex.—Missouri Pac. Ry. Co. v. Miller, Civ.App.1968, 426 S.W.2d 569.

Absolute right to prove

Plaintiff had absolute right, regardless of remoteness of speeding and passing in no passing zone convictions of driver of one of vehicles which struck plaintiff's decedent's vehicle, to cross-examine driver as to such prior convictions for purpose of impeaching his credibility. Forbis v. Associated Wholesale Grocers, Inc., Mo.App.1974, 513 S.W.2d 760.

§ 421.5   TRIAL EVIDENCE   Ch. 421

period of ten years or more has elapsed since the later of the conviction or the release from confinement, unless the court finds that the probative value for impeachment outweighs the prejudice and the offeror gave "sufficient advance written notice" to provide a fair opportunity to contest the evidence.[45]

Juvenile adjudications are generally inadmissible,[46] as they are under the federal rule.[47]

And, there may be limitations on the admission, as where the court finds that the probative value for impeachment is outweighed by its prejudicial effect.[48] In some state jurisdictions the crime must involve moral turpitude [49] or have been a felony,[50]

45. Federal Rules of Evidence § 609(b), 28 U.S.C.A.

46. **Fla.**—Florida Evidence Code § 90.610(1)(c).

Ky.—Coleman v. Staples, Ky.1969, 446 S.W.2d 557 (that witness, when he was 15 years old, was involved in theft and removal of aumobile across state line and received two-year suspended sentence in federal court was inadmissible as such proceeding was juvenile delinquency proceeding resulting in adjudication of status rather than conviction of crime).

Me.—Maine Rules of Evidence § 609(d).

Neb.—Nebraska Rules of Evidence § 609(4).

Nev.—N.R.S. 50.095(4).

N.M.—New Mexico Rules of Evidence § 609(d).

Wis.—Wisconsin Rules of Evidence § 906.09(4).

But see

Ala.—Crenshaw v. Alabama Freight, Inc., 1971, 252 So.2d 33, 287 Ala. 372 (conviction at age 13).

Mo.—Ward v. Goodwin, 345 S.W.2d 215 (allowing of cross-examination of plaintiff's juvenile witness as to witness' confinement at home for boys and reasons for such confinement did not violate rule that juvenile may not be impeached by showing criminal conviction, where witness was not asked and did not state that he had been convicted of crime, but merely stated that he was on probation at one time and had accepted some stolen money).

47. Federal Rules of Evidence § 609(d), 28 U.S.C.A.

48. Federal Rules of Evidence § 609(a), 28 U.S.C.A. (unless the crime involved dishonesty or false statement).

Wis.—Wisconsin Rules of Evidence § 906.09.

Contra

Or.—Marshall v. Martinson, 1974, 518 P.2d 1312, 268 Or. 46 (that one of the defendants had previously been convicted of driving while under the influence of intoxicating liquor was admissible and trial court had no discretion to reject such evidence on ground that undue prejudice would result).

49. **Ala.**—Dean v. Johnston, 1968, 206 So.2d 610, 281 Ala. 602 (conviction for speeding does not involve moral turpitude and consequently may not be shown as going to credibility of witness); Ramsey v. City of Huntsville, 1965, 172 So.2d 812, 42 Ala.App. 603 (not for selling whiskey in violation of city ordinance).

50. See note 50 on page 307.

as is a requirement under the federal rule unless the crime involved dishonesty or false statement.[51] The method of proof may be constricted by the rule of the jurisdiction.[52]

Ga.—Kaminsky v. Blackshear, 133 S.E.2d 441, 108 Ga.App. 492.

Hawaii—Asato v. Furtado, 1970, 474 P.2d 288, 52 Haw. 284 (careless driving bore no rational relation to witness' credibility and was properly excluded).

Ill.—People v. Smith, 221 N.E.2d 68, 74 Ill.App.2d 458 (witness can be required to testify only as to convictions of infamous crimes and it is error to inquire as to prior arrests or indictments).

N.Y.—Hamby v. Bonventre, 1971, 318 N.Y.S.2d 178, 36 A.D.2d 648 (whether he was familiar with college rule forbidding freshmen to operate a motor vehicle on campus).

Tex.—Nutter v. Dearing, 1966, 400 S.W.2d 346, ref. n. r. e. (not "carnal knowledge of a female"); Gibbs v. State, 1964, 385 S.W.2d 258 (neither drunkenness or drunken driving).

Vt.—Pond v. Carter, 1967, 229 A.2d 248, 126 Vt. 299 (after trial court's preliminary ruling that defendant could not cross-examine plaintiff concerning plaintiff's conviction of tax evasion, it was incumbent upon defendant to produce record of conviction so that it could be determined whether crime involved moral turpitude and defendant's failure to produce record of such conviction so that court could determine whether the crime involved moral turpitude rendered court's ruling proper).

Wash.—Breimon v. General Motors Corp., 1973, 509 P.2d 398, 8 Wash. App. 747 (for reckless driving inadmissible).

50. Ariz.—State v. Owen, 416 P.2d 589, 101 Ariz. 156.

Cal.—West's Ann.Calif.Evid.Code, § 788; People v. Washington, 57 Cal. Rptr. 487.

Colo.—Hawkins v. People, 423 P.2d 581, 161 Colo. 556.

Ky.—Shirley v. Com., 378 S.W.2d 816.

Minn.—State v. Currie, 126 N.W.2d 389, 267 Minn. 294.

Neb.—Nebraska Rules of Evidence § 609(1) (unless crime involved dishonesty or false statement).

Nev.—N.R.S. 50.095(1).

N.M.—New Mexico Rules of Evidence § 609(a) (unless involved dishonesty or false statement).

51. Federal Rules of Evidence § 609 (a), 28 U.S.C.A.

52. Fla.—Robinson v. Citrus Council of Girl Scouts, Inc., App.1966, 193 So.2d 42 (should ask straightforward question whether convicted of a crime, and inquiry ends unless the conviction is denied).

Ill.—People v. Osborne, 223 N.E.2d 243, 78 Ill.App.2d 132 (introduction of record of conviction is proper method of impeaching testimony of a defendant and such fact cannot be established by cross-examination).

Ky.—Cowan v. Com., Ky., 407 S.W. 2d 695 (statute will henceforth be so construed that a witness may be asked if he has been convicted of a felony, but if he answers in the affirmative no more questions will be allowed, with the usual admonition that such can be considered only as affecting witness' credibility, but if he answers in the negative refutation by the record will be limited to one previous conviction, again with the admonition).

Mich.—Lucas v. Carson, 1972, 196 N.W.2d 819, 38 Mich.App. 552

§ 421.5 TRIAL EVIDENCE Ch. 421

It has been held that a conviction for a crime arising out of the same transaction or occurrence which is the basis for the lawsuit may be shown,[53] but in other cases that it may not be shown.[54]

Religious belief

A witness may not be examined as to religious beliefs for the purpose of impeachment.[55]

(may not be extrinsically proven, but may be referred to on cross-examination of a driver who has testified generally to having exercised care); Kuhnee v. Miller, 1972, 195 N.W.2d 299, 37 Mich.App. 649 (where plaintiff testified that he could not remember any circumstances of accident due to amnesia, lack of testimony as to circumstances surrounding accident did not render his driving record admissible to impeach his credibility with regard to exercise of due care).

Miss.—Emily v. State, 1966, 191 So. 2d 925 (details of previous offense are not admissible).

Wis.—Underwood v. Strasser, 1970, 180 N.W.2d 631, 48 Wis.2d 568 (may be asked whether he has been convicted of criminal offense, and how many times he has been convicted; given responses and accurate responses to such questions, no further questions may be asked).

Not via cross-examination

Exclusion of questions put to defendant concerning certain convictions was not error where plaintiff did not introduce records of the convictions and convictions cannot be proved by oral cross-examination. Ford v. Kremer, 1972, 277 N.E.2d 679, 360 Mass. 870.

53. **Md.**—Nelson v. Seiler, 139 A. 564, 154 Md. 63.

Mich.—Socony Vacuum Oil Co. v. Marvin, 21 N.W.2d 841, 313 Mich. 528 (cross-examination).

54. **N.C.**—Freeman v. Hamilton, 1972, 187 S.E.2d 485, 14 N.C.App. 142, certiorari denied 188 S.E.2d 897, 281 N.C. 314 (properly excluded cross-examination of motorist as to whether motorist had been convicted of an offense growing out of accident, since question called for incompetent testimony; had cross-examiner elected to do so, he could have rephrased his question and deleted any reference to a conviction based on the acts giving rise to the civil action being tried).

N.Y.—Reitano v. Dobbs, 1968, 295 N.Y.S.2d 573, 31 A.D.2d 104, order affirmed 306 N.Y.S.2d 3, 254 N.E. 2d 222, 25 N.Y.2d 612 (sustaining of objection to question asked of defendant on cross-examination as to whether he had ever been convicted of a crime was not improper where crime inquired about was leaving scene of the accident in question).

N.D.—Thornburg v. Perleberg, 1968, 158 N.W.2d 188 (it was prejudicial error to permit plaintiff to question defendant regarding latter's conviction for aggravated reckless driving, where conviction arose out of same accident as guest's civil case, though question was permitted on theory that defendant's answer went to his credibility as witness).

Okl.—Haynes v. Rollins, 1967, 434 P.2d 234.

55. **U.S.**—Federal Rules of Evidence § 610.

Cal.—West's Ann.Calif.Evid.Code, § 789.

Ch. 421　　IMPEACHMENT OF WITNESSES　　§ 421.5

Reputation for truth telling

A witness' character trait for truth and veracity may be shown by evidence of reputation in the community.[56] Under the federal rule,[57] and under certain state rules,[58] such proof may be in the form of the personal opinion of the testifying witness as to the truthfulness of the other witness.

Fla.—Florida Evidence Code § 90.611.

Me.—Maine Rules of Evidence § 610.

Neb.—Nebraska Rules of Evidence § 610.

Nev.—N.R.S. 50.105.

N.M.—New Mexico Rules of Evidence § 610.

Pa.—McKim v. Philadelphia Transp. Co., 72 A.2d 122, 364 Pa. 237.

Wis.—Wisconsin Rules of Evidence § 906.10.

56.　**U.S.**—Federal Rules of Evidence § 608(a), 28 U.S.C.A.

Ala.—Pugh v. State, 169 So.2d 27, 42 Ala.App. 499.

Me.—Maine Rules of Evidence § 608(a).

N.C.—Wells v. Bissette, 147 S.E.2d 210, 266 N.C. 774.

Pa.—Com. v. Jones, 36 North. 92.

Tex.—Compton v. Jay, 389 S.W.2d 639.

Utah.—LeGrand Johnson Corp. v. Peterson, 420 P.2d 615, 18 Utah 2d 260 (where there is conflict in testimony of opposing witnesses).

Vt.—State v. Jackson, 227 A.2d 280, 126 Vt. 250.

Contra by statute

Nev.—N.R.S. 50.085(z).

Definition of community

U.S.—U. S. v. Harris, C.A.N.C., 331 F.2d 185 (if defendant testifies as witness in his own behalf, his general reputation for truth and veracity in community where he resides, among his friends, neighbors and acquaintances and people with whom he transacts business, may be shown).

S.C.—In re Greenfield's Estate, S. C., 141 S.E.2d 916, 245 S.C. 595 (does not mean that testimony thereabout must necessarily reflect opinion of all people, or even of great number of people, throughout large area; for "community" in such context is composed of those persons who have had opportunity, through social or business contact, to form opinion of character of person, or of relationship, under inquiry).

Limitation on number

Imposition of reasonable limitations on number of witnesses who will be permitted to give testimony about another's reputation for truth and veracity is proper. Redd v. Ingram, 1967, 154 S.E.2d 149, 207 Va. 939.

Not single untruthfulness

While it is proper to reflect upon credibility of witness by showing that his reputation for truth and veracity in neighborhood where he lives is bad, it is not permissible to reflect upon his credibility by establishing that on former occasion he lied about an entirely unrelated matter. Rose v. B. L. Cartgage Co., 1969, 249 N.E.2d 199, 110 Ill.App.2d 260.

57.　Federal Rules of Evidence § 608 (a), 28 U.S.C.A.

58.　**Fla.**—Florida Evidence Code § 90.609.

Neb.—Nebraska Rules of Evidence § 608(1).

Nev.—N.R.S. 50.085(1).

N.M.—New Mexico Rules of Evidence § 608(a).

§ 421.5 TRIAL EVIDENCE Ch. 421

In some instances, the character witness may then testify whether he would believe the other witness on his oath.[59]

§ 421.6 Impeachment—Rehabilitation

Library References:
C.J.S. Witnesses §§ 472, 473, 490, 532 et seq., 569, 571, 620 et seq., 641 et seq.
West's Key No. Digests, Witnesses ⇆318, 360, 361, 376, 377, 394–396, 407 et seq.

A witness, once impeached, may be rehabilitated with evidence supporting credibility.[60] Evidence of the good reputation

---

Wis.—Wisconsin Rules of Evidence § 906.08(1).

Contra

Tex.—Sherrill v. Phillips, Civ.App. 1966, 405 S.W.2d 627.

59. Ga.—Banks v. State, 149 S.E.2d 415, 113 Ga.App. 661.

60. For discussion of rehabilitation by redirect examination, which explains matter brought out in cross-examination, see section 419.1, at footnote 17, et seq.

Mich.—People v. Gardineer, 139 N.W.2d 890, 2 Mich.App. 337 (proof of consistent statement at a time prior to existence of a fact said to indicate bias, interest, or corruption of the witness).

Mo.—Rotundo v. Fischlowitz, 1968, 428 S.W.2d 581 (where police officer testified on direct examination for driver of automobile which struck pedestrian that there was nothing unusual about driver's manner at time of accident, but was impeached on cross-examination by being made to acknowledge that he had made a signed statement containing information that driver was evasive, evidence extracted by use of statement on redirect that a witness to accident had, as officer testified on direct, told officer that pedestrian stepped back into driver's path prior to being struck was not objection-

able as improper rehabilitation); Aboussie v. McBroom, 421 S.W.2d 805 (where plaintiff had previously impeached defendant's witness, who had been passenger in defendant's automobile, by showing that he had sued defendant in a separate action and plaintiff had cast witness in unfavorable light by questions about inconsistent allegations in witness' petition filed in the separate action, permitting witness' lawyer in the separate suit to testify that he felt it was his duty to client to file suit against both parties and let jury decide who caused the accident was not error).

N.Y.—Abrams v. Gerold, 1971, 326 N.Y.S.2d 1, 37 A.D.2d 391 (cross-examination of defendant's witness in intersection accident case, inquiring whether defense counsel had told witness which vehicle went through red light and whether counsel promised to pay witness, it appearing that counsel had promised to compensate her for expenses and lost earnings, constituted an attack on her testimony as recent fabrication); Ryan v. Dwyer, 1969, 307 N.Y.S.2d 565, 33 A.D.2d 878 (may produce evidence in denial or explanation of impeaching statements); Albrecht v. Karbiner, 1968, 290 N.Y.S.2d 654, 30 A.D.2d 545 (where attorney for defendants on opening charged that plaintiff's discontinuance of action against son-in-law had been pursuant to agreement by which son-in-law would testify in attempt to establish negligence of remaining defendants, and cross-examination of plaintiff and son-in-law established fact of discontinuance and role played by son-in-law in retention of plaintiff's attorney, plaintiff should have been permitted to testify as to factual basis for discontinuance so as to render innocuous prejudicial inference of dishonest arrangement); Flatow v. International Terminal Operating Co., 1968, 289 N.Y.S.2d 257, 29 A. D.2d 952 (exclusion of police officer's memorandum book from evidence in negligence action in which verdict was for plaintiff was prejudicial error, where book was offered to rebut inference, raised by plaintiff's cross-examination, that officer's testimony, which was favorable to one defendant and based on plaintiff's alleged admissions, was a recent fabrication, plaintiff's version of accident was supported only by his testimony, and issue of liability was close).

Pa.—Com. v. Cohen, 1964, 199 A.2d 139, 203 Pa.Super. 34, certiorari denied 379 U.S. 902, 85 S.Ct. 191, 13 L.Ed.2d 176 (prior consistent statement admissible where attacked on cross-examination for bias and for recent fabrication).

Limitation on rule

Where cross-examination was directed toward showing witness' possible bias and not toward establishing that his testimony was a recent fabrication, trial judge properly refused to allow prior consistent statements of the witness to be admitted to corroborate his testimony. Sesterhenn v. Saxe, 1967, 232 N.E.2d 277, 88 Ill.App.2d 2.

Not by proof of good deeds

Evidence in chief relating to plaintiff's good works in church and school was inadmissible although later, in cross-examining plaintiff and his medical witnesses, defendant questioned validity of plaintiff's claims of constant pain. Ratliff v. Line, Ky.1970, 451 S.W.2d 391.

Only when impeached

Ind.—Faulkner v. Waterman, 1972, 288 N.E.2d 269, 153 Ind.App. 573 (should not have been permitted to testify on redirect examination that he had never been arrested and convicted of anything, and court should not have suggested that such testimony might have had bearing on credibility of defendant, but errors were not shown to have affected fairness of trial or determination of merits).

Reading balance of deposition

Fla.—King v. Califano, App., 183 So. 2d 719 (where plaintiff's attorney read portions of defendant's deposition in order to discredit her testimony, prohibiting defendant's attorney from reading relevant sections of the deposition which explained portions read by plaintiff's attorney was error).

Showing memory restored by drugs

Testimony of psychiatrist as to use of sodium pentothal and sodium amytal and that administering of such drugs to and subjecting to psychiatric interview person who two years previously had been involved in accident in which he suffered mild head concussion and was thereafter unable to remember events immediately prior thereto could result in recovered memory was properly admitted to rehabilitate person, whose testimony at postinterview trial that passenger was operating automobile was sought to be impeached by introduction of statement and deposition which were taken prior to psychiatric interview and in which person stated he could not remember events prior to accident, and as such was relevant to sole issue of who was operating automobile at time of accident. Sallee v. Ashlock, Ky., 1969, 438 S.W.2d 538.

§ 421.6   TRIAL EVIDENCE   Ch. 421

of a witness for truth and veracity is admissible if the witness' character is attacked;[61] and, under the federal rule,[62] and the rule of certain states,[63] the rehabilitation proof may be by personal opinion of the supporting witness.

After impeachment by proof or admission of a prior inconsistent statement, rehabilitation by proof of a prior consistent statement upon the same issue is usually proper.[64] And, under

---

61. Me.—Main Rules of Evidence § 608(a).

Mo.—State ex rel. Thym v. Shain, 104 S.W.2d 237, 340 Mo. 927, quashing certiorari Drake v. Thym, 97 S.W.2d 128, 231 Mo.App. 383.

N.C.—Wells v. Bissette, 147 S.E.2d 210, 266 N.C. 774 (number of persons that testifying party may call to testify to his general reputation as bearing on his credibility is matter which rests in large measure in sound discretion of trial judge).

Va.—Redd v. Ingram, 1967, 154 S.E. 2d 149, 207 Va. 939 (where driver of automobile had introduced testimony contradicting guest's testimony, guest was properly permitted to introduce evidence of his reputation for truth and veracity).

Contra by statute

Nev.—N.R.S. 50.085(2).

62. Federal Rules of Evidence § 608(a), 28 U.S.C.A.

63. Fla.—Florida Evidence Code § 90.609.

Neb.—Nebraska Rules of Evidence § 608(1).

N.M.—New Mexico Rules of Evidence § 609(a).

Wis.—Wisconsin Rules of Evidence § 906.08(1).

64. U.S.—Dagley v. Armstrong Rubber Co., C.A.Ind., 344 F.2d 245 (without necessity of showing recent fabrication or motive to falsify); Mosson v. Liberty Fast Freight Co., C.C.A.N.Y., 124 F.2d 448.

Cal.—West's Ann.Calif.Evid.Code, § 791; Bickford v. Mauser, 128 P.2d 79, 53 Cal.App.2d 680; Jayne, Occidental Indemnity Co., Intervener, v. Morck, 111 P.2d 696, 43 Cal.App. 2d 743.

Idaho.—Oppenshaw v. Adams, Idaho, 1968, 445 P.2d 663, 92 Idaho 488 (when a statement made by witness before trial is inconsistent with statement made at trial and indicates witness has faulty memory, consistent statements made before inconsistent statement and near in time to occurrence spoken about should be admitted to indicate witness' true belief).

Md.—Virginia Freight Lines, Inc. v. Montgomery, 1969, 260 A.2d 59, 256 Md. 221.

Mass.—Guy v. Union St. Ry., 1935, 193 N.E. 740, 289 Mass. 225.

Mo.—Galovich v. Hertz Corp., 1974, 513 S.W.2d 325 (even if the witness admitted having made the statement used to impeach him).

N.C.—Reeves v. Hill, 1968, 158 S.E.2d 529, 272 N.C. 352 (subject to judge's duty to control course and conduct of trial; Humphries v. Queen City Coach Co., 45 S.E.2d 546, 228 N.C. 399.

Okl.—Kurn v. Thompson, 105 P.2d 422, 187 Okl. 664.

Or.—Hale v. Smith, 1969, 460 P.2d 351, 254 Or. 300.

Tex.—Connally v. Culver, Civ.App., 150 S.W.2d 126, error dismissed, judgment correct.

But see

Cal.—Weisbart v. Flohr, 1968, 67 Cal.Rptr. 114, 260 Cal.App.2d 281 (admission of former written statement made to investigator for defendants by witness for purpose of rebutting inferential charge that witness had made a recent fabrication did not authorize admission of tape-recorded interview of witness taken before trial by one of plaintiff's attorneys).

Ga.—Douglas v. Herringdine, 1968, 159 S.E.2d 711, 117 Ga.App. 72 (witness attempted to be impeached by proof of prior contradictory statements is properly sustained by proof of good character and may not ordinarily be sustained by proof that he made prior statements consistent with his testimony, even though the consistent statements were made under oath on a previous trial of the same case).

Ind.—Beard v. Dodd, 1973, 296 N.E.2d 442, —— Ind.App. —— (where passenger testified that, in her opinion, host was driving approximately 70 miles an hour when he entered intersection and host then offered witness who testified that passenger had previously told witness that host's automobile was traveling 30 or 35 miles an hour, passenger could not then offer rebuttal witnesses to show prior consistent statements made by her to support her original statement on speed; passenger's 30 to 35 mile an hour admission was direct, original evidence of manner in which accident occurred and evidence thereof was not offered or received as impeaching evidence).

Contra

Ill.—Littlefield v. Alton and Southern R. R., 1968, 239 N.E.2d 147, 96 Ill.App.2d 470 (claim that cross-examination by plaintiff's counsel tended to impute that witness was testifying under influence of motive to make a false statement or that her testimony was a fabrication of recent date did not furnish authority to admit witness' prior consistent statement which was in defendant's possession, lest defendant suffer consequences of presumption that evidence which it failed to produce was unfavorable); Sesterhenn v. Saxe, 1967, 232 N.E.2d 277, 88 Ill.App.2d 2.

Neb.—Siciunas v. Checker Cab Co., Inc., 1974, 217 N.W.2d 824, 191 Neb. 766.

Limitation on rule

Fla.—Kellam v. Thomas, App.1974, 287 So.2d 733 (only where there is an issue as to whether witness did, in fact, utter the self-contradiction).

Ga.—Douglas v. Herringdine, 1968, 159 S.E.2d 711, 117 Ga.App. 72 (when a motive for falsification did not exist at time consistent statements were made).

N.Y.—Cornwell v. Cleveland, 1974, 355 N.Y.S.2d 679, 44 A.D.2d 891 (unsigned statement of police officer which gave officer's opinion respecting fault should not have been received on redirect examination to bolster direct testimony of officer, even though plaintiff had made reference on cross-examination to portions of statement).

Only when prior consistent statement was made before inconsistent statement

Idaho.—Oppenshaw v. Adams, 1968, 445 P.2d 663, 92 Idaho 488 (where plaintiff motorist testified at trial that defendant truck driver had said at scene that his wife, also a defendant, who had been driving an automobile, had been honking her horn before accident and defense sought to impeach plaintiff by showing that her statement made to insurance adjuster less than a month after accident had not referred to such statement by

§ 421.6   TRIAL EVIDENCE   Ch. 421

the federal rule,[65] and under the rule of certain states,[66] the prior statement also constitutes substantive evidence of the fact asserted.

defendant, plaintiff was not entitled to testify on redirect that when her attorney took her deposition some nine months after accident she had told him about the honking incident).

Mo.—Nielsen v. Dierking, Mo.1967, 418 S.W.2d 146.

N.D.—Wall v. Zeeb, 1967, 153 N.W. 2d 779.

Only where charge of recent fabrication

Fla.—Wofford Beach Hotel, Inc. v. Glass, App.1965, 170 So.2d 62.

N.J.—Sas v. Strelecki, 1970, 264 A.2d 247, 110 N.J.Super. 14.

N.Y.—Romanchuk v. Westchester County, 1972, 337 N.Y.S.2d 926 (history portions of hospital admission records which indicated that infant had been struck by a moving vehicle were admissible for purpose of rebutting defendants' implication, when cross-examining plaintiff father, that father's version of accident that boy was hit by defendant's pickup truck was a recent fabrication); Beltrone v. New York City Transit Authority, 1969, 307 N.Y.S.2d 520, 33 A.D.2d 907 (written report prepared for defendant transit authority by its allegedly negligent employee (bus driver) was inadmissible as a prior consistent statement, where, as a witness at trial, employee was charged only with mistake or confusion, not recent fabrication and, in any event, since report was prepared as "attorney's work product and material prepared for litigation," report was not made at a time when there was no motive to falsify); Lichtrule v. City Sav. Bank of Brooklyn, 1967, 286 N.Y.S.2d 307, 29 A.D.2d 565.

Wis.—Johnson v. Smitz, 1956, 79 N.W.2d 337, 274 Wis. 96 (where bystander was permitted to testify that he overheard one plaintiff tell deceased investigating officer one story as to the cause of the accident, and plaintiffs attempted in rebuttal to introduce in evidence a statement made by such plaintiff, to another investigating officer and reduced to writing, consistent with plaintiffs' present testimony as to the cause of the accident, in absence of charge by defendant that plaintiffs' present testimony was recent fabrication, trial court did not abuse its discretion in excluding rebuttal evidence.)

Proof of absence of statement similar to alleged inconsistent statement

Testimony of wife who was with her husband a great deal of time he was in hospital after accident that as long as he lived he never told her that the accident was his fault was competent evidence admissible to refute testimony of physician that while husband was in hospital he admitted to physician that accident was his fault. Rosen v. Lawson, 1967, 202 So.2d 716, 281 Ala. 351.

65. Federal Rules of Evidence § 801(d)(1), 28 U.S.C.A.

66. **Cal.**—West's Ann.Calif.Evid. Code, § 1236.

Me.—Maine Rules of Evidence § 801(d)(1).

Neb.—Nebraska Rules of Evidence § 801(4)(a)(ii).

Nev.—N.R.S. 51.035(2)(b).

N.M.—New Mexico Rules of Evidence § 801(d)(1)(B).

Wis.—Wisconsin Rules of Evidence § 908.01(4)(a)(3).

Ch. 421　　IMPEACHMENT OF WITNESSES　　§ 421.6

Proof of prior consistent statements is not proper rehabilitation after impeachment by contradiction,[67] or after mere cross-examination.[68]

Where plaintiff's prior inconsistent statement was introduced as part of the cross-examination, it was proper to explain, on redirect examination, the circumstances surrounding the making of the statement.[69] A witness who, on cross-examination, ad-

---

67. U.S.—U. S. v. Adams, C.A.N.Y. 1967, 385 F.2d 548.

68. Ill.—Littlefield v. Alton and Southern R.R., 1968, 239 N.E.2d 147, 96 Ill.App.2d 470 (admission of memorandum made by witness for railroad shortly after conversation with switch foreman, a memorandum which was cumulative of witness' testimony and also referred to other matter outside her testimony in foreman's suit against railroad, was improper where there had been only cross-examination of witness without other impeaching evidence).

But see

Where pedestrian, who was struck by truck, which allegedly did not stop, was vigorously cross-examined in effort to affect her credibility and raise inference that accident did not occur as she had testified, and there was no corroborating testimony so that jury could well have been dubious as to her veracity, police report, which tended to substantially support that phase of her testimony, was properly admitted in her suit under hit and run provisions of Unsatisfied Claim and Judgment Fund Act. Schneiderman v. Strelecki, 1969, 257 A.2d 130, 1969, 107 N.J.Super. 113.

69. U.S.—Berry v. Monongahela Connecting R. Co., C.A.Pa.1968, 397 F.2d 181 (where witness seeks to explain away his prior statement, contradictory of his trial testimony, on grounds that it was obtained by improper conduct of one to whom it was given, or under circumstances which establish that witness was incompetent at the time, rebuttal testimony is admissible as to circumstances attending execution of the statement); Pattison v. Standard Oil Co. of Ohio, C.A.Ohio, 1967, 375 F.2d 643 (where investigating officer was only witness, other than plaintiff motorist and defendant's truck driver, to testify as to rear-end collision of automobile and truck, officer testified that motorist stated that accident was his fault and plaintiff brought out that officer had inserted words "no improper action" next to plaintiff's name on accident report, refusal to admit officer's explanation that he had inserted the words because motorist had told him that his wife's mother had died was prejudicial error).

Ala.—Powell v. Goforth, 1966, 188 So.2d 766, 279 Ala. 601 (extent in discretion of court).

Conn.—Kucza v. Stone, 1967, 230 A.2d 559, 155 Conn. 194 (plaintiff in rear-end collision case, who had also been a plaintiff in a prior rear-end collision case arising out of another accident, should have been permitted to testify and offer any explanation which he might have for apparent inconsistencies between his pleading in the prior case and his present testimony, in which he stated that he had completely recovered from back injury sustained in previous accident).

Ill.—Schusler v. Fletcher, 1966, 219 N.E.2d 588, 74 Ill.App.2d 249; Brennan v. Leshyn, 1964, 201 N.E. 2d 167, 51 Ill.App.2d 132.

§ 421.6   TRIAL EVIDENCE   Ch. 421

mits having made a statement inconsistent with testimony on direct examination can, on redirect examination, relate any un-

Mo.—Freeman v. Kansas City Power & Light Co., 1973, 502 S.W.2d 277 (even if plaintiffs' witness as a deposition witness had waived reading and signing of his deposition, such witness, whose answers during deposition were used against him at trial, would not be prevented from explaining inconsistencies between his deposition and his trial testimony); Aboussie v. McBroom, 1967, 421 S.W.2d 805 (if defense witness, passenger in defendant's automobile, had been impeached on basis that he had sued defendant in separate action, on redirect examination it would have been proper to allow him to say why he had sued both plaintiff and defendant drivers).

N.D.—Munro v. Privratsky, 1973, 209 N.W.2d 745 (in action, wherein plaintiff's postaccident application for health insurance was introduced in evidence as part of cross-examination to impeach credibility of plaintiff in regard to his testimony of lingering injury resulting from the accident, plaintiff could show all the surrounding circumstances on redirect examination to effect that plaintiff had told insurer's agent that "My neck bothered me and I had headaches" and that agent replied "It didn't matter.").

But see

Ga.—Daugherty v. Vick, 1972, 195 S.E.2d 208, 127 Ga.App. 767 (within discretion to exclude evidence intended to show witness had been pressured).

Disclosing identity of taker of statement

Ala.—Powell v. Goforth, 188 So.2d 766, 279 Ala. 601 (by representative of defendant's insurance carrier).

Ill.—Guardado v. Navarro, 197 N.E.2d 469, 47 Ill.App.2d 92 (when written statement or transcript has been utilized in impeachment of witness for plaintiff, it is open to plaintiff to show that person taking statement had interest in defense of litigation, but right to establish adverse interest must not be used as screen for introduction of prejudicial fact entirely outside issues of case).

N.M.—Wood v. Dwyer, 1973, 515 P.2d 1291, 85 N.M. 687 (where defendant brought out on plaintiff's cross-examination that she made statement concerning accident and asked plaintiff if she said her automobile "fishtailed" but plaintiff replied negatively and said that such words were used by another person and plaintiff's counsel on redirect examination brought out that certain portions of plaintiff's statement were not written by plaintiff, question on redirect examination if plaintiff knew who took the statement to which plaintiff replied that defendant's insurance man took the statement was proper).

S.C.—Powers v. Temple, 1967, 156 S.E.2d 759, 250 S.C. 149 (should have been allowed to prove full circumstances surrounding taking of statement, including identity of taker and his connection with case).

S.D.—Stygles v. Ellis, 123 N.W.2d 348, 80 S.D. 346, quoting C.J.S. Witnesses § 422 (plaintiff should have been permitted to ascertain identity of the taker of the statement and his interest in the litigation, and plaintiff's reference to the adjuster as a person who was required to remain anonymous was not misconduct).

Wyo.—Hawkins v. B. F. Walker, Inc., 1967, 426 P.2d 427 (but refusal not error).

disclosed intent, motive, or other mental state as an explanation for having made the inconsistent statement.[70]

If impeached by showing of conviction of a crime, the witness is permitted some explanation testimony,[71] though he may not introduce extrinsic evidence to disprove guilt.

However, the uncontradicted testimony of a witness may not be corroborated.[72]

Interlineations in signed statement

Where plaintiffs' witness admitted that he had signed written statement which was then introduced by defendant for purpose of impeaching witness, questions as to whether witness had made statement appearing in writing or whether there were any interlineations were proper subjects for examination by plaintiffs' counsel. Little v. Gogotz, 58 N.E.2d 336, 324 Ill.App. 516.

Refusal not error

Where attorney, who in fact represented automobile insurer, offered proof that statement given by plaintiff to insurance adjuster was silent concerning plaintiff's assertion at trial that defendant truck driver at scene had stated that his wife, also a defendant, who had been driving an automobile had honked at him shortly before his truck collided with plaintiff's automobile, attorney opened up subject and authorized plaintiff to relate all pertinent circumstances explaining omission, but refusal to permit plaintiff's testimony did not require reversal, in view of fact that it did not appear that even totally unexplained silence would seriously damage credibility of plaintiff's trial testimony. Openshaw v. Adams, 1968, 445 P.2d 663, 92 Idaho 488.

Allowing defense counsel to lead defendant truck driver into stating while testifying on his own behalf that he first saw plaintiff's automobile as it was just entering the intersection, whereas he had stated while testifying as an adverse witness for plaintiff that he had first seen the automobile when it was about half way through the intersection, and allowing driver to explain that contradiction was due to nervousness as an adverse witness, a subjective conclusion the record failed to disclose, was reversible error. Matthews v. Ballard, Miss.1969, 217 So. 2d 518.

70. **Ala.**—Louisville & N. R. Co. v. Self, 1970, 233 So.2d 90, 45 Ala. App. 530; Ross Neely Motor Express, Inc. v. Robinson, 48 So.2d 252, 35 Ala.App. 431, certiorari denied 48 So.2d 254, 254 Ala. 293; Pollard v. Rogers, 173 So. 881, 234 Ala. 92.

71. **Ga.**—Utzman v. Srochi, 1972, 193 S.E.2d 195, 127 Ga.App. 294 (should have been permitted to state reasons why pleaded guilty).

Mich.—Taylor v. Klahm, 1967, 154 N.W.2d 529, 8 Mich.App. 516, appeal after remand 198 N.W.2d 715, 40 Mich.App. 255; Perin v. Peuler, 130 N.W.2d 4, 373 Mich. 531 (scope within trial court's discretion).

Contra

Where credibility of witness is sought to be affected by showing conviction of crime, the record is conclusive evidence of the conviction and must be left unexplained. Morrissey v. Powell, 23 N.E.2d 411, 304 Mass. 268, 124 A.L.R. 1522.

72. **U.S.**—Chestnut v. Ford Motor Co., C.A.Va.1971, 445 F.2d 967 (where plaintiff called father to testify before he called daughter, and thus daughter's credibility was not yet under attack, father's testimony of a prior consistent state-

ment made by daughter to father was inappropriate time-wise); U. S. v. Adams, C.A.N.Y.1967, 385 F.2d 548.

Ala.—Kilcrease v. Harris, 1972, 259 So.2d 797, 288 Ala. 245.

Conn.—Mei v. Alterman Transport Lines, Inc., 1970, 268 A.2d 639, 159 Conn. 307.

Dist.Col.—May v. Washington Coach Co., Mun.App.1964, 197 A.2d 267.

Fla.—Yanzito v. Wagner, App.1971, 244 So.2d 761.

Ga.—Seaboard Coast Line R. Co. v. Duncan, 1971, 181 S.E.2d 535, 123 Ga.App. 479.

Idaho.—Martin v. Argonaut Ins. Co., 1967, 434 P.2d 103, 91 Idaho 885.

Ill.—Hickey v. Chicago Transit Authority, 1964, 201 N.E.2d 742, 52 Ill.App.2d 132.

N.J.—State v. Parsons, 1964, 200 A. 2d 340, 83 N.J.Super. 430.

N.C.—Miller v. Kennedy, 1974, 205 S.E.2d 741, 22 N.C.App. 163, certiorari denied 207 S.E.2d 755, 285 N.C. 661 (construction of rule as to use of depositions).

N.D.—Wall v. Zeeb, 1967, 153 N.W. 2d 779.

Va.—Graham v. Danko, 129 S.E.2d 825, 204 Va. 135 (where there was no charge that defendant's testimony as to presence of another vehicle at scene was fabrication and no one testified that defendant had previously failed to make such claim, there was no occasion to support his credibility by proof that defendant had, at scene, told driver of vehicle with which he collided of presence of unlighted automobile ahead of him just before collision, and such statement was properly excluded).

Wash.—Choate v. Robertson, 195 P. 2d 630, 31 Wash.2d 118 (hospital record to corroborate uncontradicted statement that witness was rendered unconscious at time of collision and did not remember anything about what occurred, properly refused).

Not from mere inconsistencies

Mere fact that cross-examination of plaintiff exposed inconsistencies in his testimony given on direct examination was not a sufficient predicate upon which to permit him to offer character witnesses. Royal v. Cameron, Tex.Civ.App., 382 S.W.2d 335.

Testimony as to consistent nature of own observations

Permitting plaintiff's counsel to ask his witness if what he observed at scene was consistent with what he saw through his rear-view mirror at moment of collision was improper as calling for answer bolstering credibility of witness, but the error was harmless under circumstances of case. Jordan v. Taylor, 1968, 161 S.E.2d 790, 209 Va. 43.

Chapter 422

COMPETENCY OF WITNESSES

Table of Sections

Sec.
422.1 Competency of Witnesses—In General.
422.2 Incompetency of Survivor of Transaction Had With Deceased.

---

§ 422.1 Competency of Witnesses—In General [1]

Library References:
C.J.S. Witnesses § 49 et seq.
West's Key No. Digests, Witnesses ⟜35 et seq.

Determination whether one is competent to testify is within the discretion of the trial court,[2] except that, under federal rule,

1. **Cited by the court**, as § 6325 of prior edition (now included in §§ 422.1 and 422.2 of this edition), in Threadgill v. Anderson, Okl., 303 P.2d 297, 300.

2. **U.S.**—U. S. v. McFarland, C.A. N.Y., 371 F.2d 701 (that witness had been mental hospital patient did not render her incompetent as matter of law); U. S. v. Barnes, C.A.S.C., 368 F.2d 567 (is for the court rather than the jury).

   Ala.—Orton v. Gay, 1970, 231 So.2d 305, 285 Ala. 270 (mental disorder rendering incapable of managing affairs, or even that confined in a hospital, does not disqualify).

   Ariz.—State v. Brown, 425 P.2d 112, 102 Ariz. 87 (permitting witness who had never been adjudged insane but who had been committed to state hospital for examination and treatment to testify was proper absent a showing that witness was not capable of understanding nature of oath or perceiving incidents in question and properly relating them to the court); State v. Reyes, 408 P.2d 400, 99 Ariz. 257.

   Colo.—Alcorn v. Erasmus, 1971, 484 P.2d 813, —— Colo.App. —— (20 yr. old, with I.Q. of 50 to 80, properly disqualified).

   Conn.—State v. Vars, 224 A.2d 744, 154 Conn. 255 (ruling will not be disturbed in absence of clear case of abuse).

   Ga.—Dawn Memorial Park v. DeKalb County, 142 S.E.2d 72, 111 Ga.App. 429.

   Ill.—People v. Nash, 222 N.E.2d 473, 36 Ill.2d 275 (a psychopath has the capacity to observe, recollect and communicate and is therefore a competent witness).

   Ind.—Barbee v. McKay, 1968, 238 N. E.2d 690, 143 Ind.App. 205 (14-yr. old, 11 at time of accident, properly allowed to testify as to speed); Plummer v. Ulsh, 211 N.E.2d 312, —— Ind.App. ——.

   Mass.—Com. v. Welcome, 201 N.E. 2d 827, 348 Mass. 68 (permitting juvenile witness, who knew that it was wrong to tell a lie, but didn't know what would happen if she did, to testify was not error).

§ 422.1   TRIAL EVIDENCE   Ch. 422

Wash.—State v. Wyse, 1967, 429 P. 2d 121, 71 Wash.2d 434 (though attending school for retarded, not of unsound mind).

Child of 6

Fla.—Radiant Oil Co. v. Herring, Fla., 200 So. 376 (for determination of trial court and there was no abuse of discretion in permitting a child of six to testify).

N.Y.—Jensen v. Shady Pines, Inc., 1969, 300 N.Y.S.2d 746, 32 A.D.2d 648 (not incompetent as matter of law).

N.C.—McCurdy v. Ashley, 131 S.E. 2d 321, 259 N.C. 619 (permitting boy to testify not an abuse of discretion, in view of boy's testimony as to religious background and penalties for wrongdoing, and knowledge of difference between telling the truth and telling stories).

Child of 8

Ga.—Thurmond v. State, 1964, 138 S.E.2d 372, 220 Ga. 277.

Md.—Perlin Packing Co. v. Price, 231 A.2d 702, 247 Md. 475 (striking of testimony of passenger on school bus, where it appeared passenger did not understand questions asked or know what she was saying when she attempted to answer them, was exercise of sound discretion and in any event testimony was of no probative value).

Or.—Elliott v. Callan, 1970, 466 P.2d 600, 255 Or. 256.

Child of 11

S.D.—Finch v. Christensen, 1969, 172 N.W.2d 571, 84 S.D. 420.

Child of 4 at time of accident

Ill.—Hollaris v. Jankowski, 42 N.E.2d 859, 315 Ill.App. 154 (not a competent witness to testify to an accident that happened to him when he was between four and five years of age, where testimony showed he was not a smart, precocious child and that he had little, if any, independent recollection as to the facts).

Pa.—De Lio v. Hamilton, 1973, 308 A.2d 607, 227 Pa.Super. 581; Rosche v. McCoy, 156 A.2d 307, 397 Pa. 615 (child called as witness when four years of age would have been incompetent to testify, and even though her capacity to communicate in terms of words had improved in intervening years, her memory of event and details could not have improved as time went on, and she was not competent, at age of seven, to testify as to striking of another child by automobile when witness was only four years old.)

Definition of "unsound mind"

Statute providing that persons of "unsound mind" are not competent to testify applies only to those persons who are commonly called "insane", i. e., those suffering from some derangement of mind rendering them incapable of distinguishing right from wrong. RCWA 5.60.050. State v. Wyse, 1967, 429 P.2d 121, 71 Wash.2d 434.

Statute declaring that person of "unsound mind" is not competent to testify does not apply to persons who are merely ignorant or uneducated, or even to those who are incapable of receiving all of impressions within comprehension of those more commonly gifted. RCWA 5.60.050. Id.

Not question of religious belief

U.S.—U. S. v. Rabb, 1968, C.A.N.J., 394 F.2d 230 (where defendant is follower of minority religion which is unpopular with many persons in community, it is better practice to permit him to affirm and have any questions on subject of his religion asked out of presence of jury).

Alaska.—Flores v. State, 1968, Alaska, 443 P.2d 73 (not rendered incompetent by statement did not believe in God).

the court is obligated to apply the state rule of competency in civil cases, with respect to an element of a claim or defense as to which state law supplies the rule of decision.[3]

The test of one's competency is as of the date offered as a witness, and not as of the time of occurrence in question.[4]

At certain ages in different jurisdictions a child may be presumed competent as a witness.[5] Below the prescribed age, there should be a preliminary examination, on the record, to determine competency.[6] A child's competency as a witness depends on

Ill.—People v. Ballinger, 1967, 225 N. E.2d 10, 36 Ill.2d 620, certiorari denied 87 S.Ct. 2141, 388 U.S. 920, 18 L.Ed.2d 1366 (child's infrequent church attendance was of no consequence since a religious opinion or belief is no longer required).

Not question of "sanity"

U.S.—In re Loughran, 1967, D.C.Cal., 276 F.Supp. 393 (lunatic, or a person affected with insanity, is a competent witness if he has sufficient understanding to apprehend the obligation of an oath, and to be capable of giving a correct account of the matters which he has seen or heard in reference to questions at issue).

Ill.—People v. Cox, 1967, 230 N.E.2d 900, 87 Ill.App.2d 243, appeal after remand 255 N.E.2d 208, 119 Ill. App.2d 163 (an insane person may be acceptable as a witness if he has the capacity to observe, recollect and communicate, and a feeble-minded person or an idiot may be competent as a witness).

Prior mental illness

Okl.—Tilford v. State, 1967, Okl.Cr., 437 P.2d 261 (when a court finds that at time a person is produced as a witness, such person is of sound mind, fully understands the obligations of an oath, and is capable of giving correct accounts of matters at issue, such person is not an incompetent witness because previously he had been adjudged incompetent).

R.I.—State v. Franklin, 1968, 241 A. 2d 219, 103 R.I. 715 (that key state witness may have been hospitalized for mental illness ten years prior to his appearance on witness stand was not enough standing alone to make him incompetent).

Va.—Helge v. Carr, 1971, 184 S.E.2d 794, 212 Va. 485 (supported ruling that witness, who psychiatrist stated was suffering from severe psychiatric illness and was psychotic and schizophrenic in years preceding and following taking of witness' deposition was not a competent witness).

3. Federal Rules of Evidence § 601, 28 U.S.C.A.

4. **Ill.**—Knab v. Alden's Irving Park, Inc., 199 N.E.2d 815, 49 Ill. App.2d 371.

Ky.—Boehm v. Hishmeh, 1967, 421 S. W.2d 836.

5. **Ind.**—Jones v. State, 1968, 240 N. E.2d 809, 251 Ind. 256 (over ten years of age).

Pa.—Rosche v. McCoy, 156 A.2d 307, 397 Pa. 615 (age 14).

6. **Ill.**—Knab v. Alden's Irving Park, Inc., 199 N.E.2d 815, 49 Ill.App.2d 37 (should consider degree of necessity for use of child's testimony).

Nev.—Martin v. State, 393 P.2d 141, 80 Nev. 307 (under 10 years of age).

Ohio.—Huprich v. Paul W. Varga & Sons, Inc., 209 N.E.2d 390, 3 Ohio

§ 422.1   TRIAL EVIDENCE   Ch. 422

capacity and intelligence and appreciation of the difference between truth and falsehood.[7] The preliminary examination to

St.2d 87 (4 years old at time of accident, 13 years old at trial).

Wash.—State v. Allen, 424 P.2d 1021, 70 Wash.2d 690 (lies within sound discretion of trial judge and will not be disturbed on appeal in absence of proof of manifest abuse of discretion).

But see

Allowing a ten-year-old child to testify without questioning her as to her competence was not an abuse of discretion where the same witness was questioned as to competency by the same judge at a prior trial and was found competent, and only change which would have affected her competency at the second trial was that she was approximately one year older. Boehm v. Hishmeh, 1967, Ky., 421 S.W.2d 836.

Determination premature

Trial court acted prematurely in determining, as a matter of law, that plaintiff, who was a ten-year-old fourth grader at time of suit and who was nine years old at time of accident, was not competent to give evidence as to speed of vehicle in which she was a passenger; trial judge should have permitted plaintiff's counsel an opportunity to examine her on her intelligence, experience and powers of observation in determining her knowledge concerning speed. Kauffman v. Carlisle Cement Products Co., Inc., 1974, 323 A.2d 750, 227 Pa.Super. 320.

Waiver

Cal.—People v. Berry, 1968, 67 Cal. Rptr. 312, 260 Cal.App.2d 649 (where defense counsel did not request further inquiry into compunction of six- and nine-year-old girls to tell truth before commencement of their testimony in chief, any objection was waived).

7. **Cal.**—People v. McIntyre, 1967, 64 Cal.Rptr. 530, 256 Cal.App.2d 894 (should have understanding and ability to receive and fairly accurately recount impressions, and understanding of nature of oath and moral sensibility of obligation to tell truth, and appreciate be punished for falsehood).

Fla.—Oliva v. Baum, App.1967, 194 So.2d 319 (refusal proper, as to 5 yr.-old, age 3 at time of accident, who did not know where or with whom he lived, or where he went to church).

Ill.—People v. Ballinger, 1967, 225 N.E.2d 10, 36 Ill.2d 620, certiorari denied 87 S.Ct. 2141, 388 U.S. 920, 18 L.Ed.2d 1366 (determination of trial judge that nine-year-old boy, who did not know how to spell his last name, who did not know the address of place where he lived with his grandmother and who went to church infrequently but who stated that he knew what it meant to tell the truth, was a competent witness was not an abuse of discretion); Dallas v. Granite City Steel Co., 211 N.E.2d 907, 64 Ill. App.2d 409 (requirements are capacity for recollection, ability to understand questions and frame intelligent answers, and consciousness of duty to speak truth); Knab v. Alden's Irving Park, Inc., 199 N.E.2d 815, 49 Ill.App.2d 371 (should inquire into whether child was able to receive accurate impressions of facts to which its testimony related and to tell truly the impressions received).

Ky.—Whitehead v. Stith, 1937, 105 S.W.2d 834, 268 Ky. 703 (not competent, and abuse of discretion, where did not know what was side of or fender on auto, and did not know meaning of truth).

Me.—State v. Hodgkins, 1968, 238 A.2d 41 (should know difference

Ch. 422 COMPETENCY OF WITNESSES § 422.1

determine competency should be more searching in proportion to chronological immaturity.[8]

In most jurisdictions statutes exist which make spouses competent to testify in all civil actions, though they were incompetent to do so under common law.[9]

---

between truth and falsehood, be able to receive accurate impressions of facts, be able to relate truly impressions received, and should have sufficient capacity to understand, in some measure, obligation of an oath or to realize it is wrong to falsify and that he is likely to be punished if he does tell an untruth).

Mass.—Malchanoff v. Truehart, 1968, 236 N.E.2d 89, 354 Mass. 118 (8½ yr.-old, in third grade, attended church often, and knew meaning of truth and consequences of not telling truth).

Minn.—State ex rel. Dugal v. Tahash, 1967, 153 N.W.2d 232, 278 Minn. 175.

Neb.—Rueger v. Hawks, 36 N.W.2d 236, 150 Neb. 834 (no abuse of discretion to permit a child who was six at time of accident, and seven at time of trial to testify).

Ohio.—Jennings v. Ebie, 143 N.E.2d 744, 105 Ohio App. 51 (did not abuse discretion in not permitting the boy to testify in view of boy's testimony that he was in the first grade for the second time and that he did not know about God); Huprich v. Paul W. Varga & Sons, Inc., 209 N.E.2d 390, 3 Ohio St.2d 87 (where plaintiff sought to introduce testimony of minor plaintiff who was four years of age at time of accident and 13 years of age at time of trial and who was the only eyewitness to accident, it was duty of trial court to conduct an examination and to determine whether he was capable of receiving just impressions of "facts and transactions").

S.D.—Moser v. Moser, 143 N.W.2d 369, 82 S.D. 149 (there is no arbitrary age which prohibits child from testifying as witness, but witness should have sufficient mental capacity to observe, recollect and communicate and sense of moral responsibility).

Wash.—State v. Allen, 424 P.2d 1021, 70 Wash.2d — (test of young child as witness consists of understanding of obligation to speak truth on witness stand, mental capacity at time of occurrence concerning which child is to testify, to receive accurate impression of occurrence, a memory sufficient to retain independent recollection of occurrence, capacity to express in words child's memory of occurrence, and capacity to understand simple questions about occurrence).

8. **Pa.**—Rosche v. McCoy, 156 A.2d 307, 397 Pa. 615, 81 A.L.R.2d 377.

9. **Ark.**—Southwestern Greyhound Lines v. Wisdom, 95 S.W.2d 904, 192 Ark. 903 (in wife's action against bus carrier for breach of transportation contract, husband, who purchased ticket for wife and procured particular routing and schedule, was competent to testify for wife as to transportation contract, since husband acted as wife's agent in making contract).

Ky.—Brooks v. New Albany & L. Electric Ry. Corporation, 132 S.W.2d 777, 280 Ky. 157.

Mich.—Cain v. Enyon, 49 N.W.2d 72, 331 Mich. 81 (competent witness as to matters concerning accident, which did not involve privileged communications between herself and deceased husband, and exclusion of all of the testimony of the wife was erroneous).

§ 422.1 TRIAL EVIDENCE Ch. 422

A wife is generally permitted, by statutory authority, to testify for herself in her tort action against her husband.[10]

Also, most jurisdictions have statutes which remove the common law disqualification of persons convicted of crimes,[11] though such convictions may be admissible for impeachment of such a witness.[12]

Neb.—Forman v. Andersen, 149 N.W. 2d 525, 181 Neb. 528 (husband's allegations as to loss of consortium and loss of services placed in issue alleged tortious destruction and interference with an essential part of his marital relationship, and therefore his wife was a competent witness and neither she nor her husband could claim statutory privilege of marital disqualification and refuse to testify on taking of wife's deposition).

But see

Ohio.—Community Traction Co. v. Neorr, 1936, 3 N.E.2d 638, 52 Ohio App. 190.

Does not preclude certain questions by deposition

Privilege of defendant not to have defendant's wife testify against defendant did not entitle defendant to have plaintiff precluded from asking defendant's wife by deposition whether she was a defendant in the action, whether she was served with summons and complaint, what her name was and where she resided and whether she owned automobile which allegedly struck plaintiff, since defendant's liability depended on whether defendant's negligence proximately caused injury to plaintiff, and whether defendant's wife owned the automobile had no relation to defendant's liability. Dean v. Superior Court, 230 P.2d 362, 103 Cal.App.2d 892.

Statute requires consent of spouse

In consolidated actions by occupants of automobile against owner of truck for injuries sustained by occupants of automobile when automobile struck rear of truck after truck came out of driveway, testimony of truck driver's estranged wife in favor of occupants of automobile was properly excluded as incompetent under statute preventing a wife from testifying against her husband without his consent, though the two occupants of the automobile who complained of the exclusion of such testimony had not joined the truck driver as a defendant, and though wife's testimony would allegedly have been admissible if truck driver had not been made a defendant, where truck driver was clearly identified and designated as a party defendant in the action by terms of pretrial conference order, and the complaints of all occupants named the truck driver and stated primary causes of action against him, and in two of the complaints he was joined as a defendant. De Stackelberg v. Lamb Transp. Co., 335 P.2d 522, 168 Cal.App.2d 174.

10. **Okl.**—Courtney v. Courtney, 87 P.2d 660, 184 Okl. 395.

11. **Mo.**—State v. Washington, 383 S.W.2d 518.

Contra as to perjury

Conviction of perjury disqualifies person in absence of reversal or pardon from testifying as witness. State v. Shaffer, 1967, 434 P.2d 591, 72 Wash.2d 630.

Even when perjury

Witness was not disqualified as witness in proceeding in Oklahoma Supreme Court because of his alleged conviction of perjury in federal district court in Oklahoma. Marshall v. Amos, 1968, Okl., 442 P.2d 500.

12. See section 421.5, at footnote 43 et seq., for impeachment by proof of crimes.

Counsel for a party are not disqualified as witnesses, but the practice is generally disfavored.[13]

In Ohio, a statute disqualifies an arresting officer as a witness when using an unmarked vehicle for the purpose of enforcing traffic laws.[14]

That a witness appears in the uniform of a police officer does not constitute grounds for exclusion from the witness stand

---

13. U.S.—U. S. v. Fiorillo, 1967, 376 F.2d 180 (an interested attorney's testimony is not always incompetent but an attorney should not deliberately put himself in a position where he becomes a relevant witness and then testify when other witnesses are available).

Cal.—Romeo v. Jumbo Market, 56 Cal.Rptr. 26, 247 Cal.App.2d 817.

Del.—Phillips v. Liberty Mut. Ins. Co., Del., 235 A.2d 835, citing C.J.S. Witnesses § 71 (aside from privilege question, there is no evidentiary rule against calling an attorney to stand, although better practice is that it should not be done except in cases of real necessity).

Idaho—Barthel v. Johnston, 437 P.2d 366, 99 Idaho 94, citing 97 C.J.S. Witnesses § 71.

Ill.—Kanter v. Truehart, 241 N.E.2d 521, 100 Ill.App.2d 316 (that witness had been defendant's attorney in the past went only to the credibility of the witness and not to his competency).

Md.—Bris Realty Co. v. Phoenix Sav. & Loan Ass'n., 1965, 208 A.2d 68, 238 Md. 84.

Minn.—Schwartz v. Wenger, 1963, 124 N.W.2d 489, 267 Minn. 40 (generally may not testify, unless circumstances could not be anticipated).

Discretion to exclude

Court did not abuse its discretion either in refusing to allow defendant's co-counsel, who participated throughout trial by assisting principal defense counsel, to testify in an attempt to impeach one of plaintiff's witnesses, or in refusing to permit defendant to introduce expert testimony pertaining to time and motion studies where name of the witness had not been listed in pretrial order within prescribed time. Travelers Ins. Co. v. Dykes, C.A.La., 395 F.2d 747.

14. Ohio—Milnark v. City of Eastlake, 1968, 237 N.E.2d 921, 14 Ohio Misc. 185 (where prosecution did not show in prosecution of motorist for driving while intoxicated that arresting officers were qualified to testify under statutes requiring a marked police automobile and a distinctive uniform for officer to be a competent witness, motorist could have offered evidence during his own case or could have asked for permission to recall officers for further cross-examination to show that arresting officers were not competent to testify because police automobile was not a marked vehicle or because arresting officers were not wearing a distinctive uniform); City of Dayton v. Adams, 223 N.E.2d 822, 9 Ohio St.2d 89 (municipal police officer who was operating radar device in unmarked automobile in effort to detect speeders was incompetent to testify as a witness in prosecution of an alleged speeder detected by use of the radar, where officer's automobile was not distinctively marked as required by statute).

where it was contended the jury would give officer's testimony undue weight.[15]

§ 422.2 Incompetency of Survivor of Transaction Had With Deceased

Library References:
C.J.S. Witnesses § 132 et seq.
West's Key No. Digests, Witnesses ⚿125 et seq.

Under the statutory rule of many states, in an action against a decedent's estate or the personal representative, the survivor may not testify as to a transaction with decedent;[16] and, under

---

15. **Iowa**—Dougherty v. Boyken, 1968, 155 N.W.2d 488, 261 Iowa 602 (otherwise admissible opinion testimony of highway patrolman was not rendered inadmissible because of patrolman's official position or because he would have testified in uniform, on theory that jury would blindly follow opinion and accord to it greater veracity than it deserved).

16. **Ark.**—Rankin v. Morgan, 102 S.W.2d 552, 193 Ark. 751.

Cal.—Miller v. Du Bois, 314 P.2d 27, 153 Cal.App.2d 310.

Colo.—Gushurst v. Benham, 417 P.2d 777, — Colo. —.

Fla.—Florida Evidence Code § 90.602; Laragione v. Hagan, App., 195 So.2d 246.

Ill.—Logue v. Williams, 1969, 250 N.E.2d 159, 111 Ill.App.2d 327; Clifford v. Schaefer, 1969, 245 N.E.2d 49, 105 Ill.App.2d 233 (guest passenger and operator and owner of oncoming automobile were, in absence of waiver, incompetent to testify as to any conversation or transaction had with host motorist); Clifford v. Schaefer, 1969, 245 N.E.2d 49, 105 Ill.App.2d 233 (police officer's testimony); Gillson v. Gulf, M. & O. R. Co., 236 N.E.2d 113, 94 Ill.App.2d 170, reversed on other grounds 246 N.E.2d 269, 42 Ill.2d 193 (where railroad fireman, who was an eyewitness, was himself a party defendant in wrongful death action, he was statutorily barred from testifying with respect to movement of the automobile before the collision, and administrator's evidence with respect to decedent automobile passenger's careful habits was admissible); Garb v. Harris, 232 N.E.2d 83, 87 Ill.App.2d 437 (fact that amount sued for did not exceed amount of insurance coverage did not render insurer the real party in interest or render inapplicable provisions of "Dead Man's Act" with respect to testimony offered by plaintiff regarding incidents relating to defendant administrator's deceased on theory that purpose of Act is to protect estate of deceased person from being depleted); Compton v. Frank, 1970, 261 N.E.2d 727, 126 Ill.App.2d 356.

Mich.—Brooks v. Haack, 1965, 132 N.W.2d 13, 374 Mich. 261.

Miss.—Watts v. Kelly, 171 So.2d 869, 251 Miss. 826.

Mo.—Robertson v. Weinheimer, 411 S.W.2d 197.

N.Y.—Northrop v. Kay, 171 N.Y.S.2d 660, 5 A.D.2d 957 (defendant could not testify as to conversations between himself and plaintiff's intestate from which it appeared that plaintiff's intestate instigated and encouraged an automobile race which resulted in the latter's death).

N.C.—Stegall v. Sledge, 102 S.E.2d 115, 247 N.C. 718.

Pa.—Tomasek v. Monongahela Ry. Co., 1967, 235 A.2d 359, 427 Pa. 371.

Tex.—Grant v. Griffin, 390 S.W.2d 746.

Wis.—Kading v. Roark, 97 N.W.2d 187, 7 Wis.2d 483.

Certain evidence excepted

Refusal, in action arising out of rear-end collision in which principal issue related to whether plaintiff motorist, in preparing to make left turn, had stopped her vehicle on main traveled portion of highway or on shoulder or berm, to admit written interrogatories and answers thereto by defendant motorist, who thereafter died from unrelated causes, in which he apparently stated that he had no version of accident other than that of plaintiff was reversible error, notwithstanding contention that deadman's statute precluded admission. Rockwell v. Vandenbosch, 1970, 183 N.W.2d 900, 27 Mich.App. 583; Sworn answer to written interrogatory falls within terminology "all entries, memoranda and declarations by the individual so incapable of testifying" within portion of deadman's statute to effect that all entries, memoranda and declarations by individual so incapable of testifying, relevant to matter, as well as evidence of his acts and habits of dealing tending to prove or show improbability of claims of adverse party, may be received in evidence. M.C.L.A. § 600.2166. Id.

Construed in favor of competency

Miss.—Rosetti v. Stein, 1973, 272 So.2d 633.

Even where estate suffers no loss

Ill.—Engstrom v. Edgar, 1970, 261 N.E.2d 788, 126 Ill.App.2d 369 (that estate of decedent would not be depleted because an insurer would pay judgment did not affect applicability); Garb v. Harris, 1967, 232 N.E.2d 83, 87 Ill.App.2d 437 (not significant insured for loss).

Tex.—Hutcheson v. Se'Christ's Estate, Civ.App.1970, 459 S.W.2d 495, error refused n. r. e. (size and extent of decedent's estate was not material factor in determining availability of dead man's statute, and plaintiff's testimony in regard to actions and conduct of deceased automobile driver was properly excluded, even if decedent had liability insurance and left no assets).

Limited application

Ala.—Stanley v. Hayes, Ala., 165 So. 2d 84, 276 Ala. 532 (if plaintiff who sued estate of deceased owner had been only guest, had not exercised any supervision over what driver did and had been free from any active fault, she should be permitted to testify that deceased had been driving and to facts and circumstances of accident, but not to statements by or conversations with deceased, but if plaintiff exercised supervision or was not free from fault such evidence should be excluded).

Fla.—Allstate Ins. Co. v. Doody, App.1967, 193 So.2d 687 (business records not excluded).

Ill.—Cunningham v. Central & Southern Truck Lines, Inc., 1968, 244 N.E.2d 412, 104 Ill.App.2d 247 (where administratrix in first count sought to recover in her representative capacity for death of husband in truck collision and in second count sought to recover for damage individually sustained in payment of funeral expenses, as to latter count defendant driver of truck which collided with decedent's truck was competent).

Iowa.—Vipond v. Jergensen, 1967, 148 N.W.2d 598, 260 Iowa 646 (owner of auto used with consent cannot object to evidence of warnings to deceased driver).

§ 422.2   TRIAL EVIDENCE   Ch. 422

the federal rule, the court is obligated to apply the state rule of competency, with respect to any element of a claim or defense as to which state law supplies the rule of decision.[17]

The usual statutory provision expressly defines the class of persons disqualified [18] and the class of persons or parties intended

Ohio.—Canary v. Wallace, 1971, 267 N.E.2d 784, 25 Ohio St.2d 244 (where action arising out of three-car accident was one in which one defendant driver and defendant administratrix of estate of deceased driver were subject to joint and several liability and jury could have reached different conclusions as to liability of each defendant, even though dead man's statute prevented plaintiff motorist from testifying against administratrix as to matters which occurred prior to death of administratrix' decedent, plaintiff was entitled to testify in that regard against defendant driver and call the defendant driver as upon cross-examination).

Not unconstitutional

Dead Man's Act, in wrongful death action, precluded defendant motorist and his wife from testifying to facts of the collision and, so interpreted, was not unconstitutional. Murphy v. Hook, 1974, 316 N.E.2d 146, 21 Ill. App.3d 1006.

Only where estate suffers loss

Since recovery by guest passenger against deceased host driver's estate could not affect the distribution of estate assets since the estate had been fully administered, distribution made, and the estate finally closed before suit was filed, the Dead Man Statute, whose application in part depends on it appearing that "the allowance to be made, or the judgment to be rendered, may either directly or indirectly affect the estate of the decedent," was inapplicable and did not preclude passenger's testimony about driver's turning left across raised median despite passenger's repeated warnings and fact that the fast approaching oncoming traffic was open and obvious. Jenkins v. Nachand, 1972, 290 N.E.2d 763, 154 Ind.App. 672.

17. Federal Rules of Evidence § 601, 28 U.S.C.A.

18. **Ga.**—Travelers Indem. Co. v. State Farm Mut. Ins. Co., 1973, 202 S.E.2d 260, 130 Ga.App. 51 (widow of corporation's employee was not a personal representative of the employee's estate, and widow and corporation's insurer were not "opposite parties," and corporation's insurer, seeking declaratory judgment as to coverage with respect to two wrongful death actions, should have been permitted to present testimony of corporation's sales manager to the effect that, in turning the corporation's automobile over to corporation's employee, certain restrictions had been placed on its use).

Ill.—Mernick v. Chiodini, 139 N.E. 2d 784, 12 Ill.App.2d 249 (in action for damages sustained by persons in southbound truck which collided with a northbound truck which swerved into the opposite lane because of sudden slowing down of automobile ahead without warning, where to have deceased owner of southbound truck attached with responsibility for collision would be to advantage of both driver of northbound truck and owner of preceding automobile and such parties were called as adverse witnesses under statute by plaintiffs, such parties were directly and adversely interested as to the administrator and their testimony was properly disregarded).

Ohio.—Parker v. Parker, 203 N.E.2d 513, 2 Ohio Misc. 93 (refers to adverse character of parties at

to be protected.[19] In some statutes, the survivors who are disqualified include only persons "interested" in the outcome of the suit.[20]

time of trial rather than at time of the transaction).

Okl.—City Nat. Bank & Trust Co. v. Conrad, Okl., 416 P.2d 942 (concerns itself with party asserting cause of action, title to which was acquired immediately from deceased, and not against party only seeking to defend against cause of action asserted against him).

Pa.—Leader v. Gillespie, Com.Pl., 36 Northumb.L.J. 63 (three conditions must exist before any such witness is disqualified: (1) the deceased must have had an active right or interest in the matter at issue, i. e., an interest in the immediate result of the suit; (2) the interest of the witness—not simply the testimony—must be adverse; (3) a right of the deceased must have passed to a party of record who represents the deceased's interest).

19. Ala.—Baggett v. Sellers, 1968, 210 So.2d 796, 282 Ala. 235 (defendant in administrator's action for death of decedent could testify to color of light at intersection, because estate was not interested in result of suit).

Del.—Connor v. Lyness, Sup.1971, 284 A.2d 473 (vehicular negligence action against corporate defendant did not constitute action or proceeding "by or against executors, administrators or guardians in which judgment could be rendered for or against them.").

Ohio.—Canary v. Wallace, 1971, 267 N.E.2d 784, 25 Ohio St.2d 244 (where action arising out of three-car accident was one in which one defendant driver and defendant administratrix of estate of deceased driver were subject to joint and several liability and jury could have reached different conclusions as to liability of each defendant, even though dead man's statute prevented plaintiff motorist from testifying against administratrix as to matters which occurred prior to death of administratrix' decedent, plaintiff was entitled to testify in that regard against defendant driver and call the defendant driver as upon cross-examination).

Pa.—In re Donsavage's Estate, 1966, 218 A.2d 112, 420 Pa. 587 (party claiming disqualification must claim through the decedent).

20. Ala.—Stanley v. Hayes, 1964, 165 So.2d 84, 276 Ala. 532 (and, where deceased acted in representative relation to party against whom offered).

Colo.—Gushurst v. Benham, 1966, 417 P.2d 777, 160 Colo. 428.

Del.—State Highway Dept. v. Buzzuto, Del.1970, 264 A.2d 347 (testimony of doctor, who dispatched ambulance which collided with truck killing ambulance driver, as to instructions which he gave ambulance crew did not violate deadman's statute in wrongful death action brought by driver's wife).

Ga.—Sumter County v. Pritchett, 1971, 186 S.E.2d 798, 125 Ga.App. 222 (means one having pecuniary interest, one who stands to gain or to lose, as result of the litigation and a mere personal interest or bias does not render witness incompetent to testify).

Minn.—Pautz v. American Ins. Co., 128 N.W.2d 731, 268 Minn. 241 (in view of direct and beneficial interest of decedent's parents in outcome of action against liability insurer on two alleged contracts to settle decedent's action pending

§ 422.2   TRIAL EVIDENCE   Ch. 422

Normally witnesses who are not parties to an action against a decedent's estate arising out of an automobile accident may testify therein.[21]

against insureds at decedent's death, proffered testimony of parents relative to purported oral communication to them by decedent that he accepted alleged settlement offer of insurer was inadmissible).

N.C.—Brown v. Whitley, 1971, 183 S.E.2d 258, 12 N.C.App. 306 (even if testimony of driver of tractor-trailer as to how collision with decedent's automobile occurred was inadmissible as to personal injury counterclaim of driver of tractor-trailer because of the "personal transaction" portion of the dead man's statute, the driver of the tractor-trailer, employed by the owner of the tractor-trailer, was not "interested in the event" to the extent that he was disqualified to testify in support of owner's counterclaim).

Pa.—Fedun v. Mike's Cafe, Inc., 204 A.2d 776, 204 Pa.Super. 356, affirmed 213 A.2d 638, 419 Pa. 607 (only an interest on which judgment in case will operate).

S.C.—Long v. Conroy, 143 S.E.2d 459, 246 S.C. 225 (if he is a party or person having interest which may be affected by outcome or person who has had such interest which has been transferred to party, or assignor of thing in controversy).

Tex.—Monger v. Monger, Civ.App. 1965, 390 S.W.2d 815.

21. Fla.—Allstate Ins. Co. v. Doody, 193 So.2d 687 (an agent of an insurer who was not a party to a suit between insurer and policy claimant was not barred from being examined as a witness in regard to any transaction or communication with deceased named insured).

Ill.—Sankey v. Interstate Dispatch, 90 N.E.2d 265, 339 Ill.App. 420 (driver of defendant's truck, who was named as a defendant but was never served).

Mo.—Brautigam v. Hoffman, 1969, 444 S.W.2d 528 (officer, who did scene investigation, testified to statement of decedent as to having skidded). Hunter v. Norton, 412 S.W.2d 163 (where witness, the driver of automobile in which plaintiff was riding as passenger when collision with another automobile occurred, was not party to action and testified neither in his own favor nor in favor of any party to the action claiming under him, witness' testimony as to statement of other driver who died before action was filed and whose estate was sued was properly admitted).

Nev.—Zeigler v. Moore, 335 P.2d 425, 75 Nev. 91 (testimony of sheriff who took report).

Pa.—Alinkoff v. McDonald, 33 D. & C.2d 715, 15 Fiduciary 44, 54 Luz.L.Reg. 272.

Wash.—Zenith Transport, Limited v. Bellingham Nat. Bank, 395 P.2d 498, 64 Wash.2d 967 (driver of plaintiff's truck).

Even potential plaintiff

Where neither of eyewitnesses was a party to action against motorist's administrator arising out of accident and there was no valid reason in record for joining them, fact that plaintiff might have sued one witness or that witnesses could have sued motorist did not provide the direct, certain and immediate interest required to bar their testimony, and allowing such witnesses to testify for plaintiff was not error. Gilberto v. Nordtvedt, 1971, 274 N.E.2d 139, 1 Ill.App.3d 677.

In wrongful death cases where the plaintiff has a statutory action as a statutory beneficiary, and is not claiming as an heir, the plaintiff is not disqualified as such person personally did not have a transaction with the deceased.[22]

In some jurisdictions, testimony as to transactions with a deceased agent is barred by statutory provisions;[23] but, in others, the testimony is admissible.[24]

Mich.—Pietrantonio v. Tonn's Estate, 1936, 270 N.W. 777, 278 Mich. 535 (even though intends suit).

22. Ga.—Lawrence v. Edwards, 1973, 195 S.E.2d 244, 128 Ga.App. 1; Sumter County v. Pritchett, 1971, 186 S.E.2d 798, 125 Ga.App. 222 (action against county by father and mother for death of their son while passenger in automobile driven by principal of high school operated by county board of education as agency of county did not come within ambit of statute).

Tenn.—Newark Ins. Co. v. Seyfert, 392 S.W.2d 336, 54 Tenn.App. 459, citing 97 C.J.S. Witnesses § 137 (statute did not render inadmissible wife's testimony as to husband's declarations of his intentions shortly before he set out on trip which ended in his death, where the action was on group travel accident policy, recovery would not go to the estate but to statutorily designated beneficiaries, and the judgment would not be for or against the wife as personal representative).

Tex.—Airline Motor Coaches v. Curry, Civ.App., 191 S.W.2d 98, ref. w. m.

And see

Deadman's statute applies only where one of actual parties to action on trial is deceased and a wrongful death action is separate and distinct from any cause of action a decedent might have had. Myers v. Griffith, Mo.1973, 495 S.W.2d 447.

23. N.C.—Tharpe v. Newman, 125 S.E.2d 315, 257 N.C. 71.

Partner as agent

In suit against surviving partner for injuries suffered by prospective purchaser of automobile which deceased partner was demonstrating on behalf of partnership, deceased partner was partnership's "agent" within meaning of statute prohibiting testimony by a surviving party in his own favor concerning transactions or communications with a deceased "agent under circumstances where such witness would be incompetent if deceased agent had been principal." Rogers v. Carmichael, 198 S.E. 318, 58 Ga.App. 343, certiorari dismissed 200 S.E. 800, 187 Ga. 432.

24. U.S.—M. F. A. Mut. Ins. Co. v. Dixon, D.C.Ark.1965, 243 F.Supp. 806 (Arkansas rule).

Ill.—Hudson v. Augustine's Inc., 1966, 218 N.E.2d 510, 72 Ill.App. 2d 225 (incompetent as against deceased truck driver, but not as to driver's employer).

Miss.—City of Bay St. Louis v. Johnston, Miss.1969, 222 So.2d 841 (admission of plaintiff's testimony was not error, though city truck driver was deceased at time of trial and city might have claim for indemnity against driver's estate if city were found liable for plaintiff's injury, where deceased's estate was not a party).

Or.—Bush v. Johnson, 390 P.2d 932, 237 Or. 173 (even though owners of a truck were sued jointly with the administrator of their deceased agent-driver, they were not entitled to benefit of statute, and such limitation on the cause of action against their agent did not

§ 422.2   TRIAL EVIDENCE   Ch. 422

In many jurisdictions it has been held that an automobile accident is a "transaction" within this rule.[25] But the contrary result has been reached elsewhere.[26]

limit their respondeat superior liability).

Wash.—Johns v. Hake, 131 P.2d 933, 15 Wash.2d 651 (in action against owners of truck for damages allegedly caused by negligence of truck driver whose death occurred before the trial, statute did not preclude motorist from testifying concerning circumstances of the accident, since no representative of decedent was a party to the action and owners in defending action derived no right through truck driver).

25. **U.S.**—Pritchard v. Nelson, C.A.Vt., 228 F.2d 878 (Vermont law); Wright v. Wilson, C.C.A.Pa., 154 F.2d 616, 170 A.L.R. 1237, certiorari denied 67 S.Ct. 50, 329 U.S. 743, 91 L.Ed. 640 (applying Pa. statute); Rehm v. Interstate Motor Freight System, C.C.A.Mich., 133 F.2d 154 (applying Michigan statute).

Del.—Kaufmann v. McKeown, 193 A.2d 81, 6 Storey 217.

Ill.—Countryman v. Sullivan, 100 N.E.2d 799, 344 Ill.App. 371; Secrist v. Raffleson, 62 N.E.2d 36, 326 Ill.App. 489 (therefore failure of plaintiff to testify cannot be considered as an attempt to conceal true facts concerning accident); Mondin v. Decatur Cartage Co., 60 N.E.2d 38, 325 Ill.App. 332 (guest cannot testify as to warning deceased host and other occurrences prior to accident).

Mich.—Blair v. Consolidated Freight Co., 41 N.W.2d 512, 327 Mich. 167 (jury should disregard any part of plaintiff's testimony found to be on a matter equally within the knowledge of decedent).

Nev.—Zeigler v. Moore, 335 P.2d 425, 75 Nev. 91.

N.C.—Tharpe v. Newman, 125 S.E.2d 315, 257 N.C. 71 (and surviving occupant, in action against estate of decedent, is incompetent to testify as to identity of driver immediately preceding and at time of wreck).

Ohio.—Grass v. Ake, 93 N.E.2d 590, 154 Ohio St. 84.

But not events preceding accident

Testimony of surviving passenger, seeking to recover from estate of deceased owner and driver, as to seating arrangement when automobile left Colorado, that owner was driving when automobile left Colorado, that another passenger paid for gas in Utah town, that suing passenger paid for breakfast in Utah town, that when automobile left Utah town owner was in right front seat and suing passenger was in back seat and that when automobile left city suing passenger went to sleep and had no memory of anything after that for about a month following Utah accident was properly admitted and was not shielded by the Utah deadman's statute. U.C.A.1953, 78–24–2. Jackson v. Continental Bank & Trust Co., C.A.Utah 1971, 443 F.2d 1344.

26. **Ala.**—Gibson v. McDonald, 91 So.2d 679, 265 Ala. 426.

Ark.—Eisele v. Beaudoin, 398 S.W.2d 676, 240 Ark. 227.

Del.—Connor v. Lyness, Sup.1971, 284 A.2d 473 (where deceased and surviving drivers, who were involved in vehicular accident, were strangers and had no prior relationship, Dead Man Statute did not bar testimony by survivor, in negligence case which arose out of such accident and in which no contemporaneous utterance by deceased was involved).

§ 422.2 COMPETENCY OF WITNESSES Ch. 422

The survivor is only disqualified on those subjects which the deceased could have controverted if living.[27] And a plaintiff may testify as to facts occurring after the death of the defendant.[28]

Fla.—Farley v. Collins, 1962, 146 So.2d 366, on remand 147 So.2d 593.

Ga.—Simmons v. Larry, 1964, 136 S.E.2d 502, 109 Ga.App. 424 (passenger could report observation of vehicle's speed).

Iowa.—In re Fisher's Estate, 1970, 176 N.W.2d 801 (that deceased took over the wheel at last stop before accident was not as to a "transaction" within meaning of Dead Man's Statute and was admissible).

Minn.—Spafford v. Hahn, 143 N.W. 2d 81, 274 Minn. 180 (testimony of defendant, in wrongful death action, that just prior to his driving onto the frozen lake one of the decedents had gone ahead and waved him on in his approach to the lake did not constitute testimony as to conversation with a deceased person, but merely described his conduct and actions just prior to entry onto lake).

Mo.—Fellows v. Farmer, App., 379 S.W.2d 842.

N.D.—Knoepfle v. Suko, 1961, 108 N.W.2d 456.

S.C.—Hicks v. Battey, 1972, 192 S.E.2d 477, 259 S.C. 426 (plaintiff hit by boat trailer being towed).

Tex.—Grant v. Griffin, Civ.App.1964, 383 S.W.2d 643, affirmed 390 S.W.2d 746 (not applicable when strangers collide on highway). Harper v. Johnson, 1961, 345 S.W. 2d 277, 162 Tex. 117.

Circumstances as to auto purchase not deemed a transaction

Evidence, in action regarding ownership of automobile, showing that decedent's stepson made down payment on automobile which had certificate of title reflecting decedent as owner, that automobile was financed in name of decedent due to stepson's minority and that stepson made monthly payments did not constitute transactions or communications with a deceased person and was not inadmissible. Frazier v. Willis, 1973, 197 S.E.2d 831, 128 Ga.App. 762.

Not to "personally" unknown party

In statute prohibiting a party to any transaction had personally with the decedent from testifying in an action against a decedent's estate, the word "personally" imports more than unilateral observations of a survivor as to the operation of a vehicle by a decedent who was personally unknown to the survivor. Shaneybrook v. Blizzard, 121 A.2d 218, 209 Md. 304.

27. **Ky.**—Williams v. Balmut, 1944, 182 S.W.2d 779, 298 Ky. 249.

Mich.—Skiff v. Dickens, 1972, 196 N.W.2d 481, 38 Mich.App. 357 (matters testified to by defendant, i. e., her speed, her visibility, her evasive action, and her distance from intersection at time she saw vehicle belonging to plaintiff's decedent, were not of the type which necessarily must have been equally within knowledge of deceased, and testimony was admissible where defendant never testified to what she saw and how she reacted, and there was no way of knowing whether deceased at any time even knew he was going to be in an accident let alone whether he observed all of things testified to by defendant); Benaway v. Pere Marquette R. Co., 295 N.W. 536, 296 Mich. 1.

28. **Ill.**—Heil v. Kastengren, 65 N. E.2d 579, 328 Ill.App. 301.

Pa.—In re McLane's Estate, 34 D. & C.2d 574, 14 Fiduciary 631.

§ 422.2   TRIAL EVIDENCE   Ch. 422

In some jurisdictions, the witness is not disqualified when there is corroboration of the survivor's testimony.[29]

Waiver of disqualification

The protection of the dead man statute provisions may be waived in a number of ways,[30] including failure to make timely objection to otherwise forbidden testimony,[31] examination of a survivor on forbidden subject,[32] introduction of proof on the for-

---

29. **Or.**—De Witt v. Rissman, 346 P.2d 104, 218 Or. 549 (guest must establish gross negligence).
Va.—Whitmer v. Marcum, 1973, 196 S.E.2d 907, 214 Va. 64.

30. **Cal.**—Bruce v. Ullery, 25 Cal. Rptr. 841, 375 P.2d 833, 58 Cal. 2d 702 (statute does not prevent cross-defendant from testifying as to fact preceding death of original cross-complainant in case in which estate presses cross-complaint, but, in such case, there is waiver of statute which attaches to testimony of all witnesses defending against cross-complaint).

Inadequate objection

Ga.—Sumter County v. Pritchett, 1971, 186 S.E.2d 798, 125 Ga.App. 222 (objection that evidence seeks to go into transactions with a deceased person is not sufficient to raise issue of incompetency of witness).

31. **Mo.**—Prentzler v. Schneider, 411 S.W.2d 135; Fellows v. Farmer, 379 S.W.2d 842.

32. **Ill.**—Clifford v. Schaefer, 1969, 245 N.E.2d 49, 105 Ill.App.2d 233 (host motorist's executor, by calling guest passenger as witness, under statute permitting examination of adverse party and in action by guest passenger against executor and operator and owner of other automobile involved in collision from which action arose, to testify as to nature of host motorist's action while executing left turn prior to collision waived incompetency of operator and owner of oncoming automobile to testify as to the entire accident); Clarke v. Storchak, 1944, 52 N.E.2d 229, 384 Ill. 564, appeal dismissed 64 S.Ct. 1270, 322 U.S. 713, 88 L.Ed. 1555.

Miss.—Coney v. Coney, 163 So.2d 692, 249 Miss. 561.

Mo.—Prentzler v. Schneider, 411 S. W.2d 135 (by introducing testimony which plaintiff had given, in another action arising out of same collision, pertaining to facts of collision).

Vt.—Shearer v. Welch, 223 A.2d 552, 126 Vt. 106 (either by calling the witness or by permitting the witness to testify about the issues in the suit or in some antecedent proceeding).

But see

Ill.—De Young v. Ralley, 67 N.E.2d 221, 329 Ill.App. 1.

Contra as to Interrogatory admission

Defendant bus driver's answer "on Clark, between Wacker and Lake." to interrogatory which requested driver to state "where the occurrence specified in the Complaint occurred." was an admission against interest, in view of defendant's allegation that bus was not moving, but was stopped, and thus answer's introduction into evidence at trial did not make driver plaintiff administrator's witness, and plaintiff did not, by its introduction, waive his right to assert bar of Dead Man's Act. Premack v. Chicago Transit Authority, 1971, 276 N.E.2d 77, 2 Ill.App.3d 127.

Cross-examination

N.C.—Smith v. Dean, 1968, 163 S.E. 2d 551, 2 N.C.App. 553.

bidden subject from other witnesses,[33] and the exercise of pretrial discovery.[34]

Cross-examination after objection overruled

Where the timely objection of counsel for administratrix of decedent's estate to testimony of plaintiff and plaintiff's wife on ground that such testimony was barred was overruled, cross-examination of plaintiff and plaintiff's wife within the scope of direct examination concerning an alleged agreement between plaintiff and deceased did not constitute a waiver of the protection of the statute. McGugart v. Brumback, 1969, 463 P.2d 140, 77 Wash.2d 441.

33. **Ill.**—Tarasuik v. Russell, 199 N.E.2d 629, 49 Ill.App.2d 418.

Nev.—Weaks v. Mounter, 1972, 493 P.2d 1307, 88 Nev. 118.

N.C.—Bowen v. Jones, 1974, 203 S.E.2d 669, 21 N.C.App. 224 (plaintiff having offered evidence on material question of sobriety of the parties, waived such right as he might have had under statute to object to rebuttal testimony on same question from defendant, who alleged contributory negligence and claimed that decedent participated in drinking party with defendant and rode as passenger with defendant while knowing that defendant was intoxicated); Bryant v. Ballance, 1971, 185 S.E.2d 315, 13 N.C.App. 181, certiorari denied 186 S.E.2d 513, 280 N.C. 495 (testimony of third person as to condition of driver); Smith v. Dean, 1968, 163 S.E.2d 551, 2 N.C.App. 553 (where administrator of estate in order to establish identity of driver offered evidence of highway patrolman as to statement made by defendant that he was driver, plaintiff opened door to defendant to present evidence that he was not driver of vehicle); Pearce v. Barham, 149 S.E.2d 22, 222 N.C. 707 (where deceased driver's administratrix introduced statement of third party, who had been present in automobile, concerning conduct of driver and passenger up to and including accident, passenger was entitled to testify concerning her version of what took place).

Ohio.—Ferrebee v. Boggs, 1970, 263 N.E.2d 574, 24 Ohio App.2d 18 (plaintiff administratrix who presented herself as witness on her own behalf in proving causes of action for wrongful death and for pain, suffering and expenses prior to death, and who testified as to facts occurring before death of her decedent, waived objection to defendant's testimony as to statement by deceased allegedly acknowledging responsibility for collision).

Pa.—Perlis v. Kuhns, 1963, 195 A.2d 156, 202 Pa.Super. 80.

Held no waiver

Where employee of decedent, passenger in truck driven by decedent, testified as to collision between truck and truck driven by defendant, but did not testify to any conversation he had with defendant, employee's testimony did not render defendant competent witness to testify to transaction between defendant and plaintiff's decedent. Cunningham v. Central & Southern Truck Lines, Inc., 244 N.E.2d 412, 104 Ill.App.2d 247.

Not testimony by doctor as to declaration of deceased

It was doubtful that doctor was "agent," within section providing that when, in action by administrator of a deceased person, any agent of deceased person shall testify to any conversation or transaction between such agent and opposite party, such opposite party may testify concerning the same conversation or

---

34. See note 34 on page 336.

transaction, but in any event admission of decedent's doctor's testimony that decedent informed him that on previous day he had boarded a bus at a certain place, and that as he was walking toward his seat, the bus started off with a violent jerk, causing him to be thrown against the post and to the floor did not make bus driver a competent witness. Premack v. Chicago Transit Authority, 1971, 276 N.E.2d 77, 2 Ill.App.3d 127.

34. U.S.—Trehorne v. Callahan, D.C.Pa.1968, 288 F.Supp. 131 (filing interrogatories).

Ind.—Plummer v. Ulsh, 211 N.E.2d 312, —— Ind.App. ——.

Pa.—Brown v. Saladoff, 1967, 228 A.2d 205, 209 Pa.Super. 263, 35 A.L.R.3d 952; Perlis v. Kuhns, 195 A.2d 156, 202 Pa.Super. 80 (even if interrogatories were not used and disclosed nothing as to liability of parties); Anderson v. Hughes, Pa.Com.Pl., 12 Chest. 168 (dictum).

But see

U.S.—Wittbrot v. Anderson, D.C.Mich., 262 F.Supp. 10 (discovery before trial is not, by itself, fatal to right or privilege under Michigan dead man's statute).

Mich.—Kirban v. Johnston, 145 N.W.2d 851, 5 Mich.App. 85 (permitting defendant as administratrix of her husband's estate to take discovery depositions of plaintiffs without waiving plaintiffs' disqualifications was not error where decedent had committed suicide, defendant's children remembered nothing about accident because of their tender ages and there were no other witnesses to accident other than occupants of plaintiffs' automobile); Koenig v. Lake Shore, Inc., 136 N.W.2d 9, 376 Mich. 131 (by interrogating plaintiff on deposition before trial regarding matters equally within knowledge of defendant's deceased president did not thereby waive its right to object at trial in event plaintiff offered such evidence).

Contra as to deposition taking

U.S.—Hortman v. Henderson, C.A.Ill.1970, 434 F.2d 77.

Ill.—Premack v. Chicago Transit Authority, 1971, 276 N.E.2d 77, 2 Ill.App.3d 127.

Ind.—Wilhoite v. Beck, 1967, 230 N.E.2d 616, 141 Ind.App. 543; Plummer v. Ulsh, 1967, 229 N.E.2d 799, 248 Ind. 462, 23 A.L.R.3d 385 (overruling Oleska, Administrator v. Kotur, 1943, 113 Ind.App. 428, 48 N.E.2d 88).

N.Y.—Phillips v. Joseph Kantor & Co., 1972, 291 N.E.2d 129, 338 N.Y.S.2d 882, 31 N.Y.2d 307.

Rule limited

Interrogatories and answers thereto filed in proceeding in probate court for purpose of discovery of assets constitute the pleadings and frame issues to be tried, and, therefore, such interrogatories and answers do not constitute a waiver of incompetency. Rogers' Estate v. Courier, Mo.1968, 429 S.W.2d 258.

Former administrator, during his lifetime, was incompetent to testify as to facts occurring prior to his appointment as administrator, and, therefore, exclusion of his testimony was proper in action by administratrix de bonis non against former administrator and, subsequently, against his estate to discover concealed or embezzled assets, even though interrogatories had been propounded to former administrator, where interrogatories were relevant and necessary to frame the issues. Id.

Use of deposition for summary judgment motion

Fla.—Barber v. Adams, Fla.App., 1968, 208 So.2d 869 (use of a deposition in support of a motion for summary decree may be the basis for waiving the protection).

Chapter 423

PRIVILEGED EVIDENCE

Table of Sections

Sec.
423.1 Privileged Evidence—In General.
423.2 Offers of Compromise.
423.3 Doctor-Patient Privilege.
423.4 Attorney-Client Privilege.

§ 423.1 Privileged Evidence—In General

Library References:
C.J.S. Witnesses § 252 et seq.
West's Key No. Digests, Witnesses ⌾184 et seq.

For discussion as to which party bears the burden of establishing the admissibility or inadmissibility of evidence claimed to be privileged, see section 416.1, at footnote 54 et seq.

Under the federal rule, in civil cases, the court is obligated to determine the privilege of a person or governmental party in accordance with State law with respect to an element of a claim or defense as to which State law provides the rule of decision.[1]

As a general rule, statutory privileges are strictly construed against the party claiming the benefit of the privilege.[2]

In addition to Doctor-Patient privilege, discussed in § 423.3, and Attorney-Client privilege, discussed in § 423.4, some statutes create an Accountant-Client privilege.[3]

Husband and wife communications

Communications between husband and wife may be privileged as confidential communications.[4]

1. Federal Rules of Evidence § 501, 28 U.S.C.A.

2. **Minn.**—Larson v. Montpetit, 147 N.W.2d 580, 275 Minn. 394.

Ohio—Arnovitz v. Wozar, 222 N.E. 2d 660, 9 Ohio App.2d 16.

3. **Colo.**—Pattie Lea, Inc. v. District Court of City and County of Denver, 423 P.2d 27, 161 Colo. 493 (whether or not communications were made for purpose of preparing "certified" reports).

Nev.—N.R.S. 49.125 et seq.

4. **Cal.**—West's Ann.Calif.Evid. Code, § 980; Hixson v. International Harvester Co., 32 Cal.Rptr. 905, 219 Cal.App.2d 88 (remark of truck driver to his wife prior to accident in which he was killed when truck overturned that he had been

§ 423.1 TRIAL EVIDENCE Ch. 423

Precautions subsequent to accident

Evidence of one's taking safety measures subsequent to the happening of an accident have been held to be inadmissible as evidence of prior negligence, sometimes on the grounds of privilege.[5] For more elaborate discussion of the admissibility of such proof, see Chapter 424, Relevancy and Materiality—In General, § 424.2, at fn. 57, et seq.

Limitation on use of investigation statement

Some jurisdictions have statutes which may preclude use of statements taken from injured persons within a certain number of hours or days after the injury.[6] The limitation does not apply

having trouble with the brakes on the truck was privileged).

Fla.—Florida Evidence Code § 90.-504.

Kan.—Kansas Code of Civil Procedure § 60–428.

Me.—Maine Rules of Evidence § 504.

Miss.—Graham v. State, 168 So.2d 496, 250 Miss. 816.

Neb.—Nebraska Rules of Evidence § 505.

Nev.—N.R.S. 49.295.

N.J.—New Jersey Evidence Rule 28.

N.Y.—People v. Sullivan, 249 N.Y.S. 2d 589, 42 Misc.2d 1014.

Pa.—Com. v. Wilkes, 199 A.2d 411, 414 Pa. 246 (if knowledge of facts is not gained through marital relationship and in confidence which that relationship inspires, it is not privileged).

Utah.—Utah Rules of Evidence § 28.

Wis.—Wisconsin Rules of Evidence § 905.05.

Not when overheard by third person

Statements made by a spouse to a third party or statements between spouses that are overheard by a third party are not within the privilege covering communications between husband and wife. Matlock v. State, Tex.Cr.App., 373 S.W.2d 237.

Wyoming rule

Under statute, one spouse is rendered incompetent to testify against the other (with certain exceptions), irrespective of whether testimony relates to confidential communication, but duration of bar against matters not confidential does not (as in case of confidential communications) continue after termination of relationship. Fox v. Fox, 296 P.2d 252, 75 Wyo. 390.

5. **Ark.**—Johns v. Pomtree, 398 S. W.2d 674, 240 Ark. 234, citing C.J.S. Evidence § 291.

6. **Conn.**—C.G.S.A. § 52–147.

Minn.—M.S.A. § 602.01.

Any form of statement

Minn.—Price v. Grieger, 1955, 70 N. W.2d 421, 244 Minn. 466 (extends prohibition to any written statement or memorandum, signed or otherwise, and whether taken in shorthand, longhand, typed or recorded by tape or wire).

Contra as to statement to officer

Wis.—Hack v. State Farm Mut. Auto Ins. Co., 1967, 154 N.W.2d 320, 37 Wis.2d 1.

Rebuttable presumption fraudulent

Minn.—Hillesheim v. Stippel, 1969, 166 N.W.2d 325, 283 Minn. 59 (although presumably fraudulent if obtained within 30 days after in-

if the person is given a copy of the statement within a certain number of days,[7] or where the litigation is other than a claim for such injury.[8]

Another jurisdiction by statute, precludes use of written post-accident statements for impeachment purposes.[9]

Statutory accident reports

Some states have enacted rules or statutes which provide that accident reports filed with designated officials are privileged.[10]

juries were sustained, where evidence is introduced showing how the statement was obtained, the rebuttable presumption disappears, and questions thereafter are whether the statement was fraudulently obtained and the weight that should be given to it).

Rule limited

The statute providing that no statement made by injured person within 72 hours after injury happened shall be received in evidence in action for resulting damages, unless admissible as part of res gestae, held inapplicable to statements made by party injured in automobile accident to traffic officer at scene of accident between 45 minutes and one hour thereafter and statements made and diagram exhibited by such party to disinterested acquaintance within 72 hours after accident. Kirsch v. Pomisal, 294 N.W. 865, 236 Wis. 264.

7. **Minn.**—Ford v. Kline Oldsmobile, Inc., 1966, 143 N.W.2d 209, 274 Minn. 284.

8. **Conn.**—Lombardo v. Simko, 1965, 214 A.2d 911, 3 Conn.Cir. 363, certiorari denied 213 A.2d 526, 153 Conn. 724.

Minn.—Hillesheim v. Stippel, 1969, 166 N.W.2d 325, 283 Minn. 59; Dike v. American Family Mut. Ins. Co., 1969, 170 N.W.2d 563, 284 Minn. 412 (third-party declaratory judgment action to establish automobile liability insurance coverage); Edeler v. O'Brien, 1968, 158 N.W.2d 301, 38 Wis.2d 691 (statement of defendant admissible, though also injured).

9. **Va.**—Harris v. Harrington, 1942, 22 S.E.2d 13, 180 Va. 210 (may impeach with proof of oral statements).

10. Section 16 of the Uniform Act.

U.S.—Stephenson v. Millers Mut. Fire Ins. Co., D.C.Ariz., 236 F. Supp. 420.

Alaska—Menard v. Acevedo, 418 P. 2d 766 (not limited to reports of accidents made by drivers but made inadmissible reports submitted by investigating police officers).

Ariz.—Krek v. Briel, 412 P.2d 301, 3 Ariz.App. 126 (accident report prepared by investigating officer is generally inadmissible in evidence over objection).

Cal.—Morales v. Thompson, 340 P.2d 700, 171 Cal.App.2d 405 (a police report, offered in evidence by plaintiff to rehabilitate the testimony of injured child's mother, was properly excluded under statute prohibiting use of required accident reports as evidence); Zollars v. Barber, 295 P.2d 561, 140 Cal.App.2d 502 (where operator made written report to police concerning facts of accident immediately following accident, report, though not made on approved form, and though operator testified differently from report in sub-

§ 423.1 TRIAL EVIDENCE Ch. 423

sequent action, was properly excluded from evidence).

Del.—Halko v. State, 204 A.2d 628, 8 Storey 47 (prohibits admission into evidence of portion of report relating solely to facts and circumstances of accident itself but privileged classification is given only to such facts and circumstances and not to other information contained in such report and obtained as result of police investigation).

Fla.—Southern Life & Health Ins. Co. v. Medley, 161 So.2d 19; Nash Miami Motors, Inc. v. Ellsworth, App., 129 So.2d 704, certiorari discharged, Sup., 142 So.2d 733 (statement, to special accident investigator of police, by motorist who was told that he was not required to answer but that his answers could be used against him and who had given to another officer information from which to prepare required accident report, was privileged as "accident report", although the information was not used in the required report); Stevens v. Duke, 42 So.2d 361.

Ill.—Kelly v. Chicago Transit Authority, 217 N.E.2d 560, 69 Ill.App. 2d 316.

Mich.—People v. Gilbert, 1967, 154 N.W.2d 800, 8 Mich.App. 393 (testimony of officer as to responses to questions on report form inadmissible in manslaughter prosecution).

Minn.—Lowen v. Pates, 18 N.W.2d 455, 219 Minn. 566 (officer's report based on memoranda taken as basis of report is inadmissible when report itself is made confidential by statute).

Nev.—N.R.S. 49.025.

N.M.—New Mexico Rules of Evidence § 502.

N.Y.—Malanify v. Pauls Trucking Co., 275 N.Y.S.2d 948, 27 A.D.2d 622 (state trooper's memorandum was properly excluded in passengers' actions against owners of truck for injuries and death sustained in automobile-truck collision); Bothner v. Keegan, 89 N.Y. S.2d 288, 275 App.Div. 470 (police record inadmissible).

Tenn.—McBee v. Williams, App., 405 S.W.2d 668 (portion of investigating officer's accident report which indicated that no improper driving was involved in death of boy who was struck by defendant's automobile was properly excluded, under statute providing that no reports or information mentioned in section dealing with accidents, arrests, crimes, and penalties should be used as evidence in any trial, civil or criminal).

Tex.—Martin v. Jenkins, 381 S.W.2d 115, ref. n. r. e.

Va.—Phillips v. Schools, 1970, 175 S.E.2d 279, 211 Va. 19 (could not be used for cross-examination, even though testimony differed from report); Lee v. Artis, 136 S. E.2d 868, 205 Va. 343 (use of accident report made by policeman who died prior to trial).

Wash.—Gooldy v. Golden Grain Trucking Co., 419 P.2d 582, 69 Wash.2d 610.

Wis.—Wisconsin Rules of Evidence § 905.02.

Wyo.—Wyoming Farm Bureau Mut. Ins. Co. v. May, 1967, 434 P.2d 507 (applicable in declaratory judgment action under liability policy).

Available to one not a party to report

Prohibition against use in civil cases of accident report prepared by police officers is available to one not a party to the report. Martin v. Cafer, Iowa, 138 N.W.2d 71.

Blood test held privileged

Where police officer, at time of requesting blood sample from defendant, allegedly warned her that results of blood-alcohol test could be used against her but did not tell her that he was through with his investigation for purpose of making accident reports, fact that blood sample was obtained for purpose of such privileged report rendered the results of blood test also privileged and admission of evidence thereof was reversible error. Cooper v. State, Fla.App., 183 So.2d 269.

Blood test of pedestrian was confidential to the Department of Public Safety. Hamilton v. Becker, 1957, 86 N.W.2d 142, 249 Iowa 516.

Blood test held not privileged

Fla.—Mitchell v. State, 1971, 245 So. 2d 618 (sample which was used in report of accident to Department of Public Safety and which was taken involuntarily at hospital immediately after accident from defendant who was not arrested for any criminal offense at hospital or told that he would be so arrested or even investigated was not privileged under statute, where the test was not taken for and did not constitute the basis for the accident report); Cannon v. Giddens, 1968, 210 So.2d 714 (in absence of showing that investigating officer directly or indirectly required, obtained or utilized blood alcohol test of blood taken from plaintiff involved in automobile accident, results of test were not inadmissible).

Wis.—Luedtke v. Shedivy, 1971, 186 N.W.2d 220, 51 Wis.2d 110 (coroner had already determined cause of death prior to taking sample).

Not an "accident report"

Fla.—Wise v. W. U. Tel. Co., App., 177 So.2d 765 (statement made by defendant's representative, who came to scene, to effect that messenger had been working for defendant and was engaged in that work at time of accident was not inadmissible under statute making accident report confidential, where representative had no firsthand knowledge of any matter affecting circumstances of the accident and statement attributed to him did not concern cause of accident or circumstances under which accident occurred); Goodis v. Finkelstein, App., 174 So.2d 600 (statement of host driver at scene to police officer to the effect that driver must have passed out, before losing control and that she had thought this would happen was not an "accident report" within meaning of statute).

Mich.—Conlon v. Dean, 1968, 165 N. W.2d 623, 14 Mich.App. 415 (statement given voluntarily to assistant prosecuting attorney).

Not privileged in criminal case

Iowa.—State v. Flack, 101 N.W.2d 535, 251 Iowa 529 (written accident report and evidence of oral admissions by a defendant which may be included in such report are not rendered inadmissible in a criminal case).

Not waived by partial disclosure

Iowa.—Martin v. Cafer, Iowa, 138 N. W.2d 71 (where, on cross-examination of police officer, defendant host asked officer if he had prepared accident report and on receiving affirmative answer he asked officer if he had stated speed of defendant's automobile on report at 30 to 35 miles per hour and received affirmative answer, defendant did not thereby waive statute except as permitted by statute to effect that when part of writing is given in evidence by one party whole of subject matter may be inquired into by the other, and defendant's objection to admission of whole report was properly sustained).

Pedestrian's statement

Fla.—Williams v. Scott, App., 153 So. 2d 18 (pedestrian's statements come within statute making accident reports confidential and inadmissible).

§ 423.1 TRIAL EVIDENCE Ch. 423

In some jurisdictions the investigating officers may not testify to statements made as part of the official investigation,[11] while in others it is permitted.[12] The officer, however, may be

Mich.—Duncan v. Starting, 99 N.W. 2d 559, 357 Mich. 654 (notes, which deputy sheriff made concerning statements made to him by pedestrian and his wife at scene, were not subject to exclusion under section of the Motor Vehicle Code declaring that report made by investigating police officers concerning vehicles involved in accident shall not be available for use in any court action).

Rule limited

U.S.—Jacobsen v. International Transport, Inc., C.A.Iowa, 1968, 391 F.2d 49, certiorari denied 89 S.Ct. 105, 393 U.S. 833, 21 L.Ed.2d 104 (medical examiner's report was not a "privileged communication" under statute dealing with required reports to be filed with Department of Public Safety).

Conn.—Jacobs v. Connecticut Co., 1950, 75 A.2d 427, 137 Conn. 189 (admissible against motorist, but not admissible against, or in favor of, codefendant).

N.Y.—Spielman v. Fields, 28 N.Y.S. 2d 536, 262 App.Div. 885, reargument denied, 29 N.Y.S.2d 723, 262 App.Div. 891 (excluding report to Motor Vehicle Bureau was error but not prejudicial against defendant).

Pa.—Panik v. Didra, 88 A.2d 730, 370 Pa. 488 (a report of accident to city police by driver, as required by city ordinance enacted pursuant to statutory authority, is not privileged from use as evidence in trial arising from reported accident, as is required report of accident to state revenue department).

Tex.—Brown & Root v. Haddad, 180 S.W.2d 339, 142 Tex. 624 (portions admissible for purpose of impeaching patrolman).

11. U.S.—Glens Falls Ins. Co. v. Gray, C.A.Fla.1967, 386 F.2d 520 (excluding from jury's consideration testimony of officer that he had interviewed insured at hospital a few days after accident and had been told by insured that he did not know whether his automobile was covered by insurance was not error under Florida statute providing, inter alia, that all accident reports made by persons involved in an accident shall be without prejudice to the individual so reporting, and that no such report could be used as evidence in any trial arising out of an accident).

Fla.—Hall v. Haldane, App.1972, 268 So.2d 403 (erred in permitting plaintiff's attorney to use for impeachment purposes a written statement made by one defendant to an investigating officer from highway patrol shortly after highway accident which gave rise to litigation, but such error was harmless where similar written statement which had been given by defendant to his own employer shortly after the accident was properly admitted in evidence); Ippolito v. Brener, 89 So.2d 650 (such admission was not admissible to impeach testimony of driver, even if driver on cross-examination denied having made such admission); St. Germain v. Carpenter, 84 So.2d 556 (statement made by decedent while in hospital to police officer was in nature of accident report).

Or.—Henry v. Condit, 53 P.2d 722, 152 Or. 348, 103 A.L.R. 131 (report to officer that auto dealer owned auto driven by salesman).

12. Cal.—People v. Misner, 285 P.2d 938, 134 Cal.App.2d 377 (in prosecution for leaving the scene without complying with requirements

permitted to testify to personal observations,[13] or may be permitted to give testimony based on statements or memoranda taken for the purpose of preparing the report.[14]

Government records

Certain governmental records are privileged by statute and governmental regulations.[15]

of law, evidence of statements of accused made to officer at time accused filed accident report were admissible, although report itself was not admissible; Carpenter v. Gibson, 181 P.2d 953, 80 Cal.App. 2d 269 (testimony of traffic officer relating to statement made by motorist to officer relative to how collision occurred was not confidential under statutes prohibiting use of statements as evidence which were made in required written report of accident to police where testimony was not shown to be an oral statement of motorist's report or part of it).

Ill.—Ritter v. Nieman, 67 N.E.2d 417, 329 Ill.App. 163.

Iowa.—Grocers Wholesale Co-op., Inc. v. Nussberger Trucking Co., 1971, 192 N.W.2d 753.

13. **Iowa**—Soreide v. Vilas & Co., 78 N.W.2d 41, 247 Iowa 1139 (patrolman's testimony as to his observations and measurements at scene); Goodman v. Gonse, 76 N.W.2d 873, 247 Iowa 1091.

Minn.—Ackerman v. Theis, 1968, 160 N.W.2d 583, 281 Minn. 82 (proper for an officer to testify to facts which are within his knowledge, and statute relating to accident reports did not bar use of those portions of report prepared by officer who was testifying where they were based on information derived from his own observations); Larson v. Montpetit, 1966, 147 N.W. 2d 580, 275 Minn. 394.

14. **Fla.**—Rosenfeld v. Johnson, App., 161 So.2d 703 (statute mak-

ing motor vehicle accident reports confidential does not extend privilege to statements by investigating officer which do not form part of his report).

Minn.—Garey v. Michelsen, 35 N.W. 2d 750, 227 Minn. 468 ("all that is rendered privileged * * * [by the statute as amended] is the report itself or information gained directly therefrom"); Hickok v. Margolis, 22 N.W.2d 850, 221 Minn. 480.

Va.—Moore v. Warren, 122 S.E.2d 879, 203 Va. 117 (exhibit, made by police officer investigating accident, and identical to one filed with officer's official report to State Division of Motor Vehicles, was not "report" in violation of statutory provision prohibiting use of confidential official reports in trials arising from actions).

But see

Iowa.—Chandler v. Harger, 113 N.W. 2d 250, 253 Iowa 565 (evidence consisting of a paper prepared by patrolman containing drawing and notations was not admissible to explain exhibit offered by plaintiff consisting of a department of public safety memorandum form showing the highway and location of the vehicles after the collision and some distances).

Minn.—Op.Atty.Gen., Sept. 14, 1945, No. 989–A–1, interpreting Lowen v. Pates, 18 N.W.2d 455, 219 Minn. 566.

15. **U.S.**—State of N. C. v. Carr, D.C.N.C., 264 F.Supp. 75 (order of

§ 423.1   TRIAL EVIDENCE   Ch. 423

Privilege against self-incrimination

The privilege against self-incrimination may be asserted in a civil action to protect the witness from creating evidence against that person in separate criminal proceedings.[16] And it has been held that a prior assertion of the privilege cannot be shown in a later civil action.[17]

attorney general, issued pursuant to statute authorizing department heads to issue regulations, prohibiting disclosure of information in official files or discovered in course of official investigation by officer or employee of Department of Justice was a lawful order authorized by law).

Alaska.—Mace v. Jung, 386 P.2d 579 (State Division of Welfare records).

Cal.—Payette v. Sterle, 21 Cal.Rptr. 22, 202 Cal.App.2d 372 (veterans' administration records).

But see

Minn.—Sprader v. Mueller, 130 N.W. 2d 147, 269 Minn. 25 (statute providing that public officer may not disclose confidential communications when public interests would suffer did not afford privilege to plaintiff's statement which was delivered to county attorney's office by plaintiff's attorney, where it was disclosed to defendant, where it did not appear that public interest suffered except insofar as public might hesitate to extend cooperation to county attorney in future investigations).

Not income tax returns

Fla.—Fryd Const. Corp. v. Freeman, App., 191 So.2d 487.

Ga.—Willis v. Hill, 1967, 159 S.E.2d 145, 116 Ga.App. 848, reversed on other grounds 161 S.E.2d 281, 224 Ga. 263, conformed to 162 S.E.2d 299, 117 Ga.App. 855, quoting 28 C.J.S. Druggists § 6c (that income tax returns had been made jointly by decedent and his widow before decedent was killed did not entitle widow to avoid production of the returns pursuant to notice in her wrongful death action).

16. U.S.—de Antonio v. Solomon, D.C.Mass., 41 F.R.D. 447.

Cal.—West's Ann.Calif.Evid.Code, § 940.

Del.—Ratsep v. Mrs. Smith's Pie Co., Super., 221 A.2d 598.

Kan.—Kansas Code of Civil Procedure § 60–425.

N.J.—New Jersey Evidence Rule 25.

N.Y.—People ex rel. Catherwood v. Purvis, 265 N.Y.S.2d 865, 48 Misc. 2d 848.

Pa.—Shor v. Redden, Pa.Com.Pl., 14 Bucks 26 (where defendant was asked questions at oral depositions which she, on advice of counsel, refused to answer because the answers might tend to incriminate her, the fact that this is a civil action and that the statute of limitations had run on a criminal prosecution in no way compelled defendant to answer said questions).

Utah—Utah Rules of Evidence § 25.

17. Ky.—Hovious v. Riley, 403 S.W. 2d 17 (testimony that motorist refused to submit to blood test to determine alcoholic content of blood violated statutory and constitutional rule of immunity from self-incrimination).

344

Waivers

The right to object to the introduction of testimony on the ground of privilege may be waived,[18] as by failing to object,[19] or by calling the recipient of the communication.[20]

18. **U.S.**—Laughner v. U. S., C.A. Fla., 373 F.2d 326 (attorney and his client); Bishop Clarkson Memorial Hospital v. Reserve Life Ins. Co., C.A.Neb., 350 F.2d 1006 (physician-patient privilege); Chore-Time Equipment, Inc. v. Big Dutchman, Inc., D.C.Mich., 258 F.Supp. 233 (waiver of attorney-client privilege need not be expressed in writing nor in any particular form, but the intent to waive must be expressed either by word or act or omission to speak and act).

Ariz.—Throop v. F. E. Young & Co., 382 P.2d 560, 94 Ariz. 146 (where defendant declined to claim privilege as to any individual question or make a record thereon and insisted that all questions and answers in the deposition be read and not all questions asked of the doctor were within the privilege).

Colo.—Weck v. District Court of Second Judicial District, 1967, 422 P.2d 46, 161 Colo. 384 (trustee in bankruptcy, like corporate officers, had power to waive accountant-client privilege).

Fla.—Soler v. Kukula, 1974, 297 So. 2d 600 (by allowing disclosure in direct examination of own witness).

Minn.—Halloran v. Tousignant, 41 N.W.2d 874, 230 Minn. 399 (arrangement between insurers of vehicles to exchange statements of their respective insureds waived any privilege that might otherwise have been invoked on ground of communication between attorney and client).

Mo.—Wells v. City of Jefferson, 132 S.W.2d 1006, 345 Mo. 239.

N.Y.—Cote v. Knickerbocker Ice Co., 290 N.Y.S. 483, 160 Misc. 658.

Ohio—Parisky v. Pierstorff, 27 N.E. 2d 254, 63 Ohio App. 503.

Okl.—Lazzell v. Harvey, 49 P.2d 519, 174 Okl. 86.

Tex.—Dobbins v. Gardner, 377 S.W. 2d 665, ref. n. r. e. (attorney-client privilege).

Wash.—State ex rel. Sowers v. Olwell, 394 P.2d 681, 64 Wash.2d 828, 16 A.L.R.3d 1021 (attorney-client privilege).

Wis.—Alexander v. Farmers Mut. Auto. Ins. Co., 131 N.W.2d 373, 25 Wis.2d 623 (by her consent to doctor to allow investigation of all X-ray photographs, hospital and medical records and other medical information of documentary nature concerning her injuries, and also by her consent to examination of records of other physician who had examined her); Schwartz v. Schneuriger, 69 N.W.2d 756, 269 Wis. 535 (motorist, who had freely permitted taking of sample of his blood to test it for alcoholic content, waived, if he knew purpose of such taking, privilege granted him by statute providing that doctor shall not be permitted to disclose any information).

Conduct evincing intention

If waiver of physician-patient privilege cannot be implied from filing of personal injury suit, it can be implied from conduct of plaintiff which indicates a plain intention to abandon the privilege, and also by conduct which, though not evincing that intention, places plaintiff in such position with reference to the evi-

---

19. See note 19 on page 346.
20. See note 20 on page 346.

§ 423.1   TRIAL EVIDENCE   Ch. 423

In some jurisdictions the right is waived as respects a statement to a physician, when the patient commences an action,[21]

dence that it would be unfair and inconsistent to permit the retention of the privlege. Lambdin v. Leopard, 1968, 251 N.E.2d 165, 20 Ohio Misc. 189.

Not by consent for disclosure of medical information to insurance company

Iowa.—Rutten v. Investors Life Ins. Co. of Iowa, 140 N.W.2d 101, 258 Iowa 749 (consent of assured or beneficiary that doctor may reveal condition of assured to insurance company for purpose of satisfying company rules does not constitute waiver).

19. Cal.—Romeo v. Jumbo Market, 56 Cal.Rptr. 26, 247 Cal.App.2d 817; Stearns v. Los Angeles City School Dist., 53 Cal.Rptr. 482, 244 Cal.App.2d 696 (attorney-client).

Iowa—Shepherd v. McGinnis, 131 N.W.2d 475, 257 Iowa 35 (physician-patient privilege).

N.Y.—Cote v. Knickerbocker Ice Co., 290 N.Y.S. 483, 160 Misc. 658 (statement to insurer).

Tex.—Hudson v. Smith, 391 S.W.2d 441 (attorney-client).

Not by failing to object at deposition

That plaintiffs had taken deposition of defendant's wife prior to trial without objection by defendants did not constitute waiver by defendants of protection afforded by statute prohibiting wife from testifying without husband's consent. Roche v. Schartz, 419 P.2d 779, 82 Nev. 409.

20. U.S.—Boyd v. Wrisley, D.C. Mich., 228 F.Supp. 9 (not waived unless or until plaintiff elected to submit his attending physicians as witnesses in the trial).

Cal.—People v. Dubrin, App., 43 Cal. Rptr. 60.

Minn.—Maas v. Laursen, 18 N.W.2d 233, 219 Minn. 461, 158 A.L.R. 215.

Mo.—Wells v. City of Jefferson, 132 S.W.2d 1006, 345 Mo. 239 (physician).

Attorney may be called by client though previously urged the privilege

Although defendant's attorney asserted attorney-client privilege when subpoenaed by plaintiffs for pretrial deposition, the attorney could not be barred from later testifying, at the request of his client, after waiver of the attorney-client privilege by his client. Hunter v. Kenney, 422 P.2d 623, 77 N.M. 336.

Listing as court witness

Plaintiff was deemed to have waived physician-patient privilege as to any doctor whom plaintiff had indicated would be called at trial. Mattson v. Pennsylvania R. Co., D.C. Ohio 1967, 43 F.R.D. 523.

21. U.S.—Lind v. Canada Dry Corp., D.C.Minn.1968, 283 F.Supp. 861 (under Minnesota law).

Ind.—Collins v. Bair, 1971, 268 N.E. 2d 95, 256 Ind. 230, superseding 252 N.E.2d 448 (overruling Warsaw v. Fisher, 1899, 55 N.E. 42) 24 Ind.App. 46.

Mo.—State ex rel. McNutt v. Keet, 1968, 432 S.W.2d 597.

Contra

U.S.—Boyd v. Wrisley, D.C.Mich., 228 F.Supp. 9 (physician-patient privilege is a continuing one).

Issue not tendered

Cal.—Carlton v. Superior Court for Los Angeles County, 1968, 67 Cal. Rptr. 568, 261 Cal.App.2d 282, rehearing denied 68 Cal.Rptr. 469, 261 Cal.App.2d 282 (defendant's denial of allegation in complaint that defendant was intoxicated at time of accident did not amount to "tender" of issue concerning his condition within purview of statute governing exceptions to patient-

Ch. 423   PRIVILEGED EVIDENCE   § **423.1**

and in others by testifying about the condition or producing other proof as to the condition.[22] A waiver by calling as a wit-

physician privilege and providing that there is no privilege as to communication relevant to issue concerning condition of patient if such issue has been tendered by patient).

N.Y.—Koump v. Smith, 1968, 303 N.Y.S.2d 858, 25 N.Y.2d 287, 250 N.E.2d 857 (such pretrial waiver as far as defendant is concerned is limited to cases in which defendant affirmatively asserts condition either by way of counterclaim or to excuse conduct complained of by plaintiff and where defendant simply denies allegation of complaint, privilege should be recognized).

Waiver limited to conditions alleged

Ill.—Tylitzki v. Triple X Service, Inc., 1970, 261 N.E.2d 533, 126 Ill.App. 2d 144 (did not place her mental condition in issue by claiming past and future pain and suffering as one element of damages).

22. **Ariz.**—Patania v. Silverstone, 415 P.2d 139, 3 Ariz.App. 424.

Colo.—Mauro v. Tracy, 380 P.2d 570, 152 Colo. 106.

Iowa.—Barnard v. Cedar Rapids City Cab Co., 133 N.W.2d 884, 257 Iowa 34 (but not as to any other condition).

Miss.—Dennis v. Prisock, 181 So.2d 125, 254 Miss. 574 (by exhibiting to jury surgical scar on her back, and by testifying in some detail as to her injuries and communications from and to physicians and treatments of her by them); City of Laurel v. Upton, 175 So.2d 621, 253 Miss. 380 (where plaintiff's physician was basing his opinion in part on reports and letters of another of plaintiff's physicians who did not testify, defendants had right to cross-examine witness relative to those reports and mat-

ters and to introduce them in evidence if they so desired).

Mo.—Wells v. City of Jefferson, 132 S.W.2d 1006, 345 Mo. 239.

N.Y.—Beeler v. Hildan Crown Container Corp., 271 N.Y.S.2d 373, 26 A.D.2d 163.

Ohio—Ramey v. Mets, 210 N.E.2d 449, 3 Ohio App.2d 329.

Okl.—Robinson v. Lane, 1971, 480 P.2d 620 (overruling Hudson v. Blanchard, 294 P.2d 554).

Not by involuntary testimony at deposition

Okl.—Avery v. Nelson, 1969, 455 P.2d 75 (testifying in response to questions of opposing counsel pertaining to communications plaintiff had with her doctors and to extent of plaintiff's physical disability on occasion of taking plaintiff's deposition did not amount to voluntary offering of plaintiff as witness and did not waive statutory privilege).

Or.—Nielson v. Bryson, 1970, 477 P.2d 714, 257 Or. 179 (not from verifying a written complaint in such an action or testifying involuntarily).

Wash.—Phipps v. Sasser, 1968, 445 P.2d 624, 74 Wash.2d 439 (not where the testimony is in response to defendant's pretrial subpoena and the plaintiff is examined as an adverse witness in compliance with subpoena and rules of court governing discovery).

Limited to physician called

Iowa.—Brown v. Guiter, 128 N.W.2d 896, 256 Iowa 671 (calling of one of a number of physicians acting independently and successively on the same injury or illness does not waive privilege as to others).

Miss.—Hill v. Stewart, 1968, 209 So. 2d 809.

§ 423.1   TRIAL EVIDENCE   Ch. 423

ness an attending physician also waives any privilege as to all other physicians who treated the patient.[23]

The right of waiver does not pass to a patient's personal representative or heirs.[24]

§ 423.2   Offers of Compromise

Library References:
C.J.S. Evidence § 285 et seq.
West's Key No. Digests, Evidence ⟐212 et seq.

An offer of compromise is not to be regarded as an admission that anything is due, and is not admissible in evidence;[25]

Not by testimony on cross-examination

In order to make applicable waiver provision of statute to the effect that if the patient voluntarily testifies the physician may be compelled to testify on the same subject, patient's testimony in a negligence action must be voluntary, and such waiver was therefore not applicable where patient's testimony was upon cross-examination. Black v. Port, Inc., 202 N.E.2d 638, 120 Ohio App. 369.

Not from mere testimony as to treatment prescribed

Mere testimony as to treatment prescribed by physician did not constitute express or implied waiver of doctor-patient privilege and instruction that privilege had been waived was erroneous. Bryan Bros. Packing Co. v. Grubbs, 168 So. 2d 289, 251 Miss. 52.

23. Colo.—Kelley v. Holmes, 1970, 470 P.2d 590, 28 Colo.App. 79.

Mo.—Wells v. City of Jefferson, 132 S.W.2d 1006, 345 Mo. 239.

Waiver limited to a treating physician

Where defendant sought to question physician, who had given plaintiff a physical examination, to establish that the plaintiff did not complain to the physician about back and neck problems at examination, examination was not "treatment for such injury" within statute providing that if plaintiff produces physician as witness who has treated plaintiff for his injury, plaintiff is deemed to waive the privilege as to all other physicians who may have treated him for such injury, and trial court did not err in refusing to permit defendant to examine physician concerning the examination. Orlich v. Buxton, 1970, 177 N.W.2d 184, 22 Mich.App. 96.

24. Ohio.—Parisky v. Pierstorff, 27 N.E.2d 254, 63 Ohio App. 503 (it was incompetent for administrator in wrongful death action to offer testimony of physician of a decedent as to communications made to physician in his capacity as a physician).

25. U.S.—Federal Rules of Evidence § 408, 28 U.S.C.A.; Maulding v. Louisville & N. R. Co., C.C.A.Ill., 168 F.2d 880.

Ark.—Smith v. Ramsey, 1974, 513 S.W.2d 501, 256 Ark. 1098; Conway v. Hudspeth, 318 S.W.2d 137, 229 Ark. 735 (statement after suit was filed that he did not want to get in a lawsuit over the matter and that he was willing to sell the salvage and pay on the claim if he could get it stopped was inadmissible); Folsom v. Watson, 228 S.W.2d 1006, 217 Ark. 158.

Cal.—West's Ann.Calif.Evid.Code, § 1152; Grant v. Hipsher, 64 Cal.

Rptr. 892, 257 Cal.App.2d 375 (offer of compromise and negotiations in relation thereto are not admissible).

Conn.—Danahy v. Cuneo, 1943, 33 A.2d 132, 130 Conn. 213.

Fla.—Florida Rules of Evidence § 90.408.

Ill.—Adkins v. Blue Bird Coach Lines, Inc., 169 N.E.2d 368, 27 Ill.App.2d 34.

Iowa.—Sandman v. Hagan, 1967, 154 N.W.2d 113, 261 Iowa 560.

Kan.—Kansas Rules of Civil Procedure § 60–452.

Ky.—Smith v. Blue Ribbon Lines, Inc., 227 S.W.2d 185, 12 Ky. 246 (offer by plaintiff).

La.—Belanger v. Employers Mut. Liability Ins. Co. of Wis., App., 159 So.2d 500.

Me.—Maine Rules of Evidence § 408.

Mich.—Thirlby v. Mandeloff, 90 N. W.2d 476, 352 Mich. 501.

Mo.—Kelsey v. Kelsey, App., 329 S. W.2d 272 (remark of counsel for plaintiff that a small offer had been made in settlement of the plaintiff's claim which the plaintiff had rejected was improper).

Neb.—Nebraska Rules of Evidence § 408.

Nev.—N.R.S. 48.105.

N.H.—Alexander v. Todd, 1938, 199 A. 82, 89 N.H. 365.

N.J.—New Jersey Evidence Rule 52.

N.M.—New Mexico Rules of Evidence § 408.

Tex.—McGuire v. Commercial Union Ins. Co. of New York, 431 S.W. 2d 347 (settlement agreement with respect to wrongful death action would not be admissible in suit on counterclaim for injuries on issues of liability or as an admission against interest, where it was made in settlement of disputed claims and expressly disclaimed any liability on part of counter-claimant and his codefendant); Graham v. San Antonio Mach. & Supply Corp., 418 S.W.2d 303, error refused n. r. e. (excluded as irrelevant); Skyline Cab Co. v. Bradley, Civ.App.1959, 325 S.W.2d 176, writ of error refused n. r. e.

Utah.—Utah Rules of Evidence § 52.

W.Va.—Shaffer v. Burton, 155 S.E. 2d 884, 151 W.Va. 761 (unaccepted offer to compromise a disputed claim does not constitute an "admission" on part of person making it, whether the offer was made orally or in writing, or whether it was made directly to the opposing party or through his agent).

Wis.—Wisconsin Rules of Evidence § 904.08.

But see

Dist.Col.—Firestone Tire & Rubber Co. v. Hillow, to Use of American Auto Ins. Co., Mun.App.1949, 65 A.2d 338.

Ohio.—Elgin v. Heaton, App.1949, 84 N.E.2d 299, 54 OLA 321.

Not an admission of agency

In absence of independent admission as to existence of agency relationship or as to liability generally, alleged assurance that defendant automobile owner would contact plaintiff to see that plaintiff's automobile would be repaired constituted inadmissible offer of settlement and was not admissible to prove agency relationship between defendant owner and driver. Prewitt v. Hall, 1969, 252 N.E.2d 43, 113 Ill.App.2d 198.

Not available to alleged joint tortfeasor

Consent judgment entered for automobile passenger riding in automobile which collided with city fire department truck pursuant to stipulation which reserved the defendant city's rights against third-party automobile driver was a compromise agreement and was therefore inadmissible in third party action. Hent-

§ 423.2 TRIAL EVIDENCE Ch. 423

and, as under the federal rule,[26] furnishing or offering or promising to pay medical, hospital, or similar expenses is not admissible to prove liability.[27]

However, except under the federal rule and in certain states,[28] admissions of particular facts, though made in negotiations for compromise, may be admissible.[29]

schel v. Smith, 1967, 153 N.W.2d 199, 278 Minn. 86.

Partial payment of claim not privileged

Where there was no proof that compromise had been attempted or was pending and court charged that measure of damages was fair value of automobile, less amount received from sale after accident, letter from defendant's claim agent inclosing draft for what wrecked automobile had sold for, and stating that such amount was to be credited to defendant when final settlement should be made, was not inadmissible as an offer of compromise, and its admission was not prejudicial to defendant. Maulding v. Louisville & N. R. Co., C.C.A.Ill., 168 F.2d 880.

Settlement of claim of adverse party

In action for damages to plaintiff's ambulance struck by truck driven by one defendant and owned by the other defendant, compromise settlement agreement in defendants' justice court cases against plaintiff was not an admission of plaintiff's liability and was properly excluded from evidence, where settlement recited that such compromise should not be offered or admitted in evidence in any lawsuit pending or thereafter brought and should not be construed as an admission of liability, and where judgment of dismissal was without prejudice. Caswell v. Satterwhite, Tex.Civ.App., 277 S.W.2d 237, ref. n. r. e.

26. Federal Rules of Evidence § 409, 28 U.S.C.A.

27. **Fla.**—Florida Evidence Code § 90.409.

La.—Young v. Creegan, La.App., 23 So.2d 820.

Me.—Maine Rules of Evidence § 409.

Mo.—Smith v. Fine, 175 S.W.2d 761, 351 Mo. 1179.

Neb.—Nebraska Rules of Evidence § 409.

N.M.—New Mexico Rules of Evidence § 409.

Ohio.—Quiel v. Wilson, App., 34 N.E. 2d 590 (otherwise, "the Good Samaritan would have furnished evidence thus against himself for the injuries to the wayfarer who fell among thieves and robbers").

Wis.—Wisconsin Rules of Evidence § 904.09.

But see

Ga.—Rentz v. Collins, 1935, 181 S.E. 678, 51 Ga.App. 782.

28. Federal Rules of Evidence § 408, 28 U.S.C.A.

Cal.—West's Ann.Calif.Evid.Code, § 1152.

Fla.—Florida Evidence Code § 90.408.

Me.—Maine Rules of Evidence § 408.

Neb.—Nebraska Rules of Evidence § 408.

Nev.—N.R.S. 48.105(1)(b).

N.M.—New Mexico Rules of Evidence § 408.

Wis.—Wisconsin Rules of Evidence § 904.08.

29. **Or.**—Dunning v. Northwestern Elec. Co., 199 P.2d 648, 186 Or. 379, reversed on other grounds 206 P.2d 1177, 186 Or. 379.

Although it has been held that evidence of settlement with injured persons other than plaintiff is admissible,[30] such evidence is generally held inadmissible.[31]

§ 423.3 Doctor-Patient Privilege [32]

Library References:
C.J.S. Witnesses § 293 et seq.
West's Key No. Digests, Witnesses ⟲207 et seq.

Communications between a patient and physician are generally privileged,[33] though not under some statutes.[34]

---

30. **Tenn.**—Tennessee Coach Co. v. Young, 80 S.W.2d 107, 18 Tenn. App. 592 (bus passenger could prove that bus company had paid claims of other passengers injured in same accident).

31. **U.S.**—Jackson v. Shell Oil Co., C.A.Tenn.1968, 401 F.2d 639.
    Cal.—Brown v. Pacific Elec. Ry. Co., 180 P.2d 424, 79 Cal.App.2d 613.
    Iowa.—Jones v. Krambeck, 290 N.W. 56, 228 Iowa 138.
    La.—Broussard v. State Farm Mut. Auto Ins. Co., App.1966, 188 So. 2d 111, writ refused 190 So.2d 233, 249 La. 713, certiorari denied 386 U.S. 909, 87 S.Ct. 855, 17 L.Ed.2d 783.
    Md.—Tregellas v. American Oil Co., 188 A.2d 691, 231 Md. 95.
    Minn.—Dornberg v. St. Paul City Ry. Co., 91 N.W.2d 178, 253 Minn. 52 (except for impeachment of third party who becomes witness).
    N.Y.—Schenker v. Bourne, 102 N.Y. S.2d 928, 278 App.Div. 699; Fitzgerald v. State, 96 N.Y.S.2d 452, 198 Misc. 39 (settlement by claimant's insurer).
    Okl.—Dallas v. Malernee, 71 P.2d 492, 180 Okl. 532.
    Tex.—Otwell v. Scott, 1968, 425 S. W.2d 9.

    But see
    Tex.—McEntire v. Baygent, Civ.App. 1949, 229 S.W.2d 866, 20 A.L.R. 2d 300.

32. See section 423.1, at fn. 1, for federal rule imposition of state law as to privilege.

33. **U.S.**—Franklin Life Ins. Co. v. William J. Champion & Co., C.A. Mich., 353 F.2d 919 (intern); Taylor v. Reo Motors, Inc., C.A.Kan., 275 F.2d 699 (pertains to matters germane to the physician's diagnosis and treatment of patient); Hammonds v. Aetna Cas. & Sur. Co., D.C.Ohio, 243 F.Supp. 793.
    Cal.—West's Ann.Calif.Evid.Code, § 990 et seq.; and § 1010 et seq. (as to psychotherapist).
    Colo.—Riss & Co. v. Galloway, 114 P.2d 550, 108 Colo. 93, 135 A.L.R. 878.
    Fla.—Florida Evidence Code § 90.503.
    Ind.—Aspy v. Botkins, 66 N.E. 462, 160 Ind. 170 (including X-rays).
    Iowa.—Newman v. Blom, 89 N.W.2d 349, 249 Iowa 836 (exhibit identified as plaintiff's medical record and as having been made by doctor who attended plaintiff at hospital).
    Kan.—Kansas Code of Civil Procedure § 60–427.
    Me.—Maine Rules of Evidence § 503.
    Mich.—Knoper v. Burton, 1968, 163 N.W.2d 453, 12 Mich.App. 644, judgment reversed on other grounds 173 N.W.2d 202, 383 Mich.

34. See note 34 on page 353.

62 (where plaintiff exercised physician-patient privilege with respect to treating physicians and sought to support personal injury claim by means of hypothetical questions to nontreating doctors, x-rays taken at request of treating physician were privileged and hypothetical question relying in part upon the x-rays taken at request of treating physician was objectionable).

Miss.—Gulf Refining Co. v. Myrick, 71 So.2d 217, 220 Miss. 429 (refusal to permit counsel for defendant, over plaintiff's plea of privilege, to examine doctor who had treated plaintiff's injuries for stated purpose of showing that doctor was available as a witness).

Neb.—Nebraska Rules of Evidence § 504.

Nev.—N.R.S. 49.215 et seq.

N.J.—New Jersey Evidence Rule 28.

N.M.—New Mexico Rules of Evidence § 504.

Ohio.—Kassow v. Robertson, Ohio Com.Pl., 143 N.E.2d 926 (Veterans Administration's records of plaintiff would be admissible into evidence upon condition precedent that defendant, who claimed that alleged injuries existed before accident involved, obtain permission from the Administrator but subject to the qualification that portions of records which included communications between plaintiff and his physician were privileged and not admissible).

Utah.—Utah Rules of Evidence § 27.

Wis.—Wisconsin Rules of Evidence § 905.04.

Applicable to doctor provided by adverse party

Wash.—Ballard v. Yellow Cab Co., 145 P.2d 1019, 20 Wash.2d 67 (where person injured by taxicab and taken to public hospital submitted to examination by physician on hospital staff without knowing examination was being made for taxicab company, relation of "physician and patient" was created by implication so as to preclude physician from testifying without patient's consent).

Blood alcohol test findings

Ark.—Ragsdale v. State, 1968, 432 S. W.2d 11, 245 Ark. 296 (test run on defendant for purpose of prescribing and treating his injuries and not at request of police officer or prosecuting attorney was privileged).

Limited protection

U.S.—Woods v. National Life & Acc. Ins. Co., C.A.Pa., 347 F.2d 760 (inadmissible only if they tended to blacken character of patient).

N.C.—Lockwood v. McCaskill, 136 S.E.2d 67, 261 N.C. 754 (proviso permitting presiding judge of superior court to compel disclosure when necessary to proper administration of justice was intended to refer to exceptional rather than ordinary factual situations).

Medical records

U.S.—Bishop Clarkson Memorial Hospital v. Reserve Life Ins. Co., C.A.Neb., 350 F.2d 1006 (hospital records even though they may be quasi-public are deemed to be privileged within statutes such as physician-patient privilege statute).

Ohio.—Heinemann v. Mitchell, Ohio Com.Pl., 220 N.E.2d 616 (where hospital records contained communications between physician and patient which have been reduced to writing and incorporated in records, such portions of records are privileged).

Wis.—Leusink v. O'Donnell, 39 N.W. 2d 675, 255 Wis. 627 (hospital records and nurses' and technician's notes and records concerning treatment of injured plaintiff were not privileged, but privilege, if appli-

A doctor-patient professional relationship for curative treatment must have existed;[35] and there may be an issue whether

cable, would be to the medical reports of the attending physicians).

Not as to fact of relationship

Md.—Shaneff v. Sabo, 237 N.E.2d 277, 143 Ind.App. 1, superseded on other grounds 240 N.E.2d 820, 251 Ind. 229.

Pa.—Sweeney v. Green, 1935, 176 A. 849, 116 Pa.Super. 190.

To be claimed by doctor in absence of patient

Where patients of a doctor about whom he was cross-examined were not parties and were not present at trial, their failure to claim patient-physician privilege could not be deemed a waiver thereof, and doctor had a duty to claim the privilege in regard to such patients. Shepherd v. McGinnis, 131 N.W.2d 475, 257 Iowa 35.

34. Ga.—Elliott v. Georgia Power Co., 197 S.E. 914, 58 Ga.App. 151.

Discretion of court

Statute making communication between patient and physician privileged but providing that judge may compel such disclosure if in his opinion it is necessary to proper administration of justice was not violated in manslaughter prosecutions of motorist in admitting testimony of physician and laboratory technicians that motorist was intoxicated. State v. Bryant, 1969, 167 S.E.2d 841, 5 N.C. App. 21.

35. U.S.—Gardner v. Meyers, C.A. Neb., 1973, 491 F.2d 1184 (no physician-patient relationship existed between passenger who was fatally injured in collision and physician who was summoned by sheriff's office which requested that he perform the services of a coroner's physician); Elliott v. Watkins Trucking Co., C.A.Ind.1969, 406 F. 2d 90 (under Illinois law, communication to psychologist at rehabilitation institute who interviewed plaintiff for purpose of grouping was not privileged).

Ill.—People v. English, 1964, 201 N. E.2d 455, 31 Ill.2d 301 (not as to court appointed physician).

Ind.—Grossnickle v. Avery, 152 N.E. 288, 96 Ind.App. 479 (statement to motorist who was also doctor, and attended injured bicyclist not privileged).

Neb.—Garska v. Harris, 109 N.W.2d 529, 172 Neb. 339.

Wash.—State v. Kuljis, 422 P.2d 480, 70 Wash.2d 168 (where doctor makes particular examination other than for purpose of treating the patient, it is not within doctor-patient privilege rule, even though the doctor had previously or subsequently treated the patient, provided patient was not misled as to purpose of such examination).

Blood alcohol test

Colo.—Hanlon v. Woodhouse, 160 P. 2d 998, 113 Colo. 504 (where sample was taken from unconscious driver at request of officer, and test was not needed for treatment, test results were admissible).

Kan.—Williams v. Hendrickson, 371 P.2d 188, 189 Kan. 673 (doctor who had withdrawn motorist's blood for blood alcohol test was not incompetent where motorist had given sheriff his written consent to submit to test, where sheriff had called in doctor to withdraw sample, and where doctor was not motorist's regular physician).

N.H.—State v. Davis, 226 A.2d 873, 108 N.H. 45 (as to test inadmissible in prosecution for operating motor vehicle while intoxicated).

N.C.—State v. Bryant, 1969, 167 S.E. 2d 841, 5 N.C.App. 21 (not prejudicial error in manslaughter prose-

§ 423.3   TRIAL EVIDENCE   Ch. 423

the person to whom the party communicated was a "physician" within the rule of privilege.[36] It has been held that the extent of the privilege is limited to information gained which was germane to the diagnosis or treatment.[37]

In some cases, the information is not protected when gained by a third person;[38] and, in others, it has been held privileged.[39]

It has been held that no unfavorable inference may be drawn because a patient makes a claim of privilege with regard to disclosures to a physician or surgeon.[40]

---

cutions for laboratory technician to testify that she took some blood from body of motorist after accident).

36. Chiropractor

"Physician" as used in statute granting physician-patient privilege encompasses a doctor of chiropractic. Collins v. Bair, Ind.App.1969, 252 N. E.2d 448, opinion superseded on other issues 268 N.E.2d 95, 256 Ind. 230.

Psychologist

Under Indiana law, a psychologist is not a "physician" within statute rendering physicians incompetent to testify as to matters communicated to them by patients in course of their professional business. Elliott v. Watkins Trucking Co., C.A.Ind.1969, 406 F.2d 90.

37. U.S.—Taylor v. Reo Motors, Inc., C.A.Kan., 275 F.2d 699 (Kansas statute).

Iowa—Shepherd v. McGinnis, 131 N. W.2d 475, 257 Iowa 35; Newman v. Blom, 89 N.W.2d 349, 249 Iowa 836 (could have had a definite relation to doctor's treatment or possible treatment, of plaintiff).

N.Y.—Munson v. Model Taxi Corp., 78 N.Y.S.2d 629, 273 App.Div. 1039, appeal denied 85 N.Y.S. 323, 274 App.Div. 1016 (admission was driver of vehicle not privileged).

Opposing party may call doctor as witness for unprivileged matter

Defendant had right to call as a witness plaintiff's attending physician to testify on matters not within realm of privileged communication, even though plaintiff had not waived physician-patient privilege, and even though plaintiff might thereby be put in position of appearing to hide some evidence prejudicial to his case by being forced to assert his privilege only after physician had been called as a witness. Vincenzo v. Newhart, 219 N.E.2d 212, 7 Ohio App.2d 97.

38. Ind.—General Accident, Fire & Life Assur. Co., Limited, of Scotland v. Tibbs, 2 N.E.2d 229, 102 Ind.App. 262 (nurse not a "physician" within statute).

39. N.Y.—People v. Decina, 157 N. Y.S.2d 558, 2 N.Y.2d 133, 138 N.E. 2d 799, 63 A.L.R.2d 970 (taken to county hospital by police after his arrest and was examined by house physician and a police guard was standing close enough to overhear statements given by defendant).

40. Iowa—Howard v. Porter, 35 N. W.2d 837, 240 Iowa 153.

Wash.—Sumpter v. National Grocery Co., 78 P.2d 1087, 194 Wash. 598, 116 A.L.R. 1166.

§ 423.4 Attorney-Client Privilege [41]

Library References:
C.J.S. Witnesses § 276 et seq.
West's Key No. Digests, Witnesses ⚷197 et seq.

Generally, an attorney cannot, without the client's consent, testify as to matters communicated to the attorney by the client in the course of the attorney's employment,[42] nor can the attor-

---

41. See section 423.1, at fn. 1, for federal rule imposition of state law as to privilege.

42. **U.S.**—Grummons v. Zollinger, D.C.Ind., 240 F.Supp. 63, affirmed 341 F.2d 464; Chore-Time Equipment, Inc. v. Big Dutchman, Inc., D.C.Mich., 255 F.Supp. 1020; Tillotson v. Boughner, D.C.Ill., 238 F.Supp. 621 (is personal to client and may only be asserted by client); In re Bretto, D.C.Minn., 231 F.Supp. 529 (prevents disclosure by attorney or employee).

Ariz.—Buell v. Superior Court of Maricopa County, 391 P.2d 919, 96 Ariz. 62 (one which attorney is bound to assert unless authorized to testify by client or client's legal representative).

Cal.—West's Ann.Calif.Evid.Code, § 950 et seq.; Stearns v. Los Angeles City School Dist., 53 Cal.Rptr. 482, 244 Cal.App.2d 696 (generally, attorney should claim privilege on behalf of client unless attorney has been otherwise instructed, and if attorney fails to assert privilege when he should, judge may exclude information that is subject to claim of privilege on judge's own motion); People By and Through Dept. of Public Works v. Glen Arms Estate, Inc., 41 Cal.Rptr. 303, 230 Cal.App.2d 841 (available to corporation client); D. I. Chadbourne, Inc. v. Superior Court of City and County of San Francisco, 36 Cal.Rptr. 468, 388 P.2d 700 (client, not attorney, may claim attorney-client privilege).

Fla.—Florida Evidence Code § 90.502.

Ga.—Weatherbee v. Hutcheson, 152 S.E.2d 715, 114 Ga.App. 761 (rule is applicable with reference to attorney's knowledge concerning insurance which his client may have carried); Smith v. Smith, 152 S.E.2d 560, 222 Ga. 694; Atlantic Coast Line R. Co. v. Daugherty, 141 S.E.2d 112, 111 Ga.App. 144.

Kan.—Kansas Code of Civil Procedure § 60–426; Olney v. Hobble, 396 P.2d 367, 193 Kan. 692.

Me.—Maine Rules of Evidence § 502.

Neb.—Nebraska Rules of Evidence § 503.

Nev.—N.R.S. 49.035 et seq.

N.H.—Riddle Spring Realty Co. v. State, 220 A.2d 751, 107 N.H. 271.

N.J.—New Jersey Evidence Rule 26.

N.M.—New Mexico Rules of Evidence § 503; Hunter v. Kenney, 422 P.2d 623, 77 N.M. 336 (attorney has no option to waive the privilege but has affirmative duty to assert the privilege until client has waived it).

N.Y.—Cote v. Knickerbocker Ice Co., 290 N.Y.S. 483, 160 Misc. 658.

R.I.—Lapan v. Lapan, 217 A.2d 242, 100 R.I. 498.

S.D.—State Highway Commission v. Earl, 143 N.W.2d 88, 82 S.D. 139.

Utah—Utah Rules of Evidence § 26.

Wash.—State ex rel. Sowers v. Olwell, 394 P.2d 681, 64 Wash.2d 828, 16 A.L.R.3d 1021.

Wis.—Wisconsin Rules of Evidence § 905.03.

Confidentiality waived
Trial testimony of attorney who talked with defendant while he was

ney be compelled to produce confidential documents received from the client for use in judicial proceedings.[43]

under arrest on drunken driving charge before being charged with murder, was not violative of defendant's statutory rights where attorney's testimony indicated that client had waived privilege by stating that he wanted communication made to a third party. State v. Dombrowski, 1969, 171 N.W.2d 349, 44 Wis.2d 486.

Employee of client

Cal.—Sierra Vista Hospital v. Superior Court for San Luis Obispo County, 56 Cal.Rptr. 387, 248 Cal. App.2d 359 (when an employee of corporation is not a codefendant or person who may be charged with liability his communication should not be privileged unless, under all circumstances of case, he is the natural person to be speaking for corporation, that is, the privilege will not attach unless communication constitutes information which emanates from corporation as distinguished from nonlitigant employee and communicating employee is such person who would ordinarily be utilized for communication to corporation's attorney).

Mass.—Ellingsgard v. Silver, 223 N. E.2d 813, 352 Mass. 34 (may extend to communications from client's agent or employee).

Not as to the fact of relationship

U.S.—U. S. v. Kendrick, C.A.N.C., 331 F.2d 110; Tillotson v. Boughner, D.C.Ill., 238 F.Supp. 621.

Ga.—Smith v. Smith, 152 S.E.2d 560, 222 Ga. 694.

Not for consultation to commit fraud

Cal.—Stearns v. Los Angeles City School Dist., 53 Cal.Rptr. 482, 244 Cal.App.2d 696.

Not in action between insured and insurer

U.S.—La Rocca v. State Farm Mut. Auto. Ins. Co., D.C.Pa.1969, 47 F.

R.D. 278 (as to disclosure of letters from counsel to insurer).

Ala.—Nationwide Mut. Ins. Co. v. Smith, 194 So.2d 505, 280 Ala. 343 (pre-trial status report written by law firm, with respect to action against operator of insured's automobile, and forwarded to insurer, was admissible in excess verdict suit brought by operator of insured's automobile against insurer on theory that law firm representing insurer at time report was made was also representing operator of insured's automobile).

Privilege lost by attorney's disclosure

Within limits of professional propriety, an attorney has implied authority to divulge to third persons a client's confidential communications if he deems it advantageous to his client's cause, but the communication thus divulged loses its privileged character and, if otherwise admissible, its exclusion from evidence constitutes error. Sprader v. Mueller, 121 N.W.2d 176, 265 Minn. 111. Attorney had implied authority to give his client's statement to a county attorney in order to obtain from the attorney fingerprints taken from automobile steering wheel and to spare his client an interview, and the disclosure served to waive the attorney-client privilege protecting the statement. M.S.A. § 595.02, subds. 2, 5. Id.

Unprivileged matter passed to attorney

Verbal reports made by insurance adjuster to insurers' attorney and communicated by him in writing to insurers acquired no privileged status simply because unprivileged reports were communicated by way of attorney. Fratto v. Northern Ins. Co. of New York, D.C.Pa., 242 F.Supp. 262.

43. **Cal.**—New York Casualty Co. v. Superior Court in and for City and

The privilege is restricted to statements intended to be "confidential communications".[44]

Even if the information was delivered to an attorney's clerk or representative, the rule of privilege would apply.[45]

County of San Francisco, 85 P.2d 965, 30 Cal.App.2d 130.

44. **U.S.**—Wirtz v. Fowler, C.A.Fla., 372 F.2d 315; U. S. v. Kendrick, C.A.N.C., 331 F.2d 110 (such things as physical characteristics of client, which are observable by anyone who talked with client, are not within privilege).

Del.—Johns v. City of Wilmington, Super., 227 A.2d 571 (the facts of each case must be considered separately to determine when privilege should be applied).

Ill.—Monier v. Chamberlain, 213 N. E.2d 425, 66 Ill.App.2d 472.

Minn.—Schwartz v. Wenger, 124 N. W.2d 489, 267 Minn. 40.

N.M.—State ex rel. State Highway Commission v. Steinkraus, 417 P. 2d 431, 76 N.M. 617 (should only be applied to protect communications and not facts).

N.Y.—Kew Gardens Sanitarium, Inc. v. Trussell, 255 N.Y.S.2d 742, 45 Misc.2d 104.

N.C.—Brown v. Green, 1969, 165 S. E.2d 534, 3 N.C.App. 506, appeal after remand 175 S.E.2d 379, 9 N. C.App. 12.

Tenn.—Trice v. Hewgley, 1964, 381 S.W.2d 589, 53 Tenn.App. 259 (third parties present).

Knowledge gained by third party

Under privilege, third person whom privileged communication reaches is required to testify concerning it. Dobbins v. Gardner, Tex. Civ.App., 377 S.W.2d 665, ref. n. r. e.

Not as between co-clients

U.S.—Shapiro v. Allstate Ins. Co., D. C.Pa.1968, 44 F.R.D. 429 (with respect to all matters from beginning of litigation against assured covered by liability policy until termination of attorney-client relationship between assured and attorney retained by insurer to defend claim, there can be no privilege); Chitty v. State Farm Mut. Auto. Ins. Co., D.C.S.C., 1965, 38 F.R.D. 37.

La.—Brasseaux v. Girouard, App., 1968, 214 So.2d 401, writ refused 216 So.2d 307, 253 La. 60 (in suits between insurer and the insured, communications made by the insured to the insurer's counsel during a period of simultaneous representation are not privileged as against the co-client, at least where the issue to which the communications relate concern matters of the legal representation of the insured).

N.Y.—Finn v. Morgan, 1974, 362 N. Y.S.2d 292, 46 A.D.2d 229 (where one attorney represented both passenger and driver, court could assume that the attorney's retainer followed a full disclosure to his clients of the effects of his multiple representation, and the clients could not have intended that their disclosures would be confidential as to each other, and an account of the accident given by the passenger to the attorney was not privileged from disclosure in subsequent action by the passenger against the driver); Liberty Mutual Ins. Co. v. Engels, 1963, 244 N.Y.S.2d 983, 41 Misc.2d 49, order affirmed 250 N.Y.S.2d 851, 21 A.D.2d 808.

N.C.—Brown v. Green, 1969, 165 S. E.2d 534, 3 N.C.App. 506, appeal after remand 175 S.E.2d 379, 9 N. C.App. 12.

45. **N.Y.**—Cote v. Knickerbocker Ice Co., 290 N.Y.S. 483, 160 Misc. 658.

§ 423.4 TRIAL EVIDENCE Ch. 423

The rule would be inapplicable, however, if the attorney-client relationship did not exist at the time of the delivery of the statement.[46]

It has been held that the relationship of insured and insurer does not make the rule of privilege applicable;[47] but, in other instances the privilege is recognized.[48]

Ohio.—In re Hyde, 79 N.E.2d 224, 149 Ohio St. 407.

Unless statement given for transmittal to legal counsel not privileged

Where original report of street car motorman regarding collision was made on day of accident and immediately thereafter on printed form and two days later it was supplemented by statements from motorman to adjuster, and there was no evidence that either original or supplemental statement was taken for bona fide purpose of being later transmitted to trial counsel for street railroad company for his advice thereon or to be used in connection with pending or threatened litigation, the report was not a "privileged communication" which the counsel could not be compelled to produce. Robertson v. Commonwealth, 25 S.E.2d 352, 181 Va. 520, 146 A.L.R. 966.

46. **U.S.**—In re Bonanno, C.A.N.Y., 344 F.2d 830; U. S. v. Barrow, D.C.Pa., 229 F.Supp. 722.

Mo.—State ex rel. Headrick v. Bailey, 278 S.W.2d 737, 365 Mo. 160 (statements made in the presence of others to an attorney, who was not at the time acting as attorney for persons making such statements, were not privileged).

N.Y.—Cote v. Knickerbocker Ice Co., 290 N.Y.S. 483, 160 Misc. 658.

Wis.—Foryan v. Firemen's Fund Ins. Co., 133 N.W.2d 724, 27 Wis.2d 133 (automobile owners' attorney did not stand in attorney-client relationship to operator's parents and parents' liability insurer, sought to be held under non-owned automobile coverage, and owed them no duty of statutory confidence concerning owners' alleged statement to attorney that owners' daughter, who gave operator permission to drive automobile, had owners' permission to use automobile at time of accident giving rise to negligence action against insurer, one owner, and others).

47. **Ga.**—Sweet v. Awtrey, 28 S.E.2d 154, 70 Ga.App. 334 (statement made by husband of insured to insurer not privileged).

N.Y.—Cote v. Knickerbocker Ice Co., 290 N.Y.S. 483, 160 Misc. 658.

Wis.—Jacobi v. Podevels, 127 N.W.2d 73, 23 Wis.2d 152 (overruling Wojciechowski v. Baron, 274 Wis. 364, 80 N.W.2d 434).

48. **Cal.**—D. I. Chadbourne, Inc. v. Superior Court of City and County of San Francisco, 36 Cal.Rptr. 468, 388 P.2d 700.

Ill.—Monier v. Chamberlain, 213 N.E.2d 425, 66 Ill.App.2d 472; People v. Ryan, 197 N.E.2d 15, 30 Ill. App. 456.

Minn.—Sprader v. Mueller, 130 N.W.2d 147, 269 Minn. 25 (waived by attorney's voluntary disclosure).

N.Y.—Liberty Mutual Ins. Co. v. Engels, 244 N.Y.S.2d 983, 41 Misc. 2d 49, order affirmed 250 N.Y.S.2d 851, 21 A.D.2d 808 (dictum).

Tex.—Gass v. Baggerly, Civ.App., 332 S.W.2d 426 (written statement which was made by defendant-driver of truck-trailer to adjuster for a claims service employed by driver's insurer); Lantex Const. Co. v. Lejsal, Civ.App., 315 S.W.

2d 177, writ of error refused n. r. e. (where compensation carrier's representative prepared unsigned, typewritten statement purportedly made by injured employee while employee was in hospital, under sedatives, and unable to use his arms, such statements were privileged communications and, therefore, were properly excluded).

Wis.—Jacobi v. Podevels, 127 N.W. 2d 73, 23 Wis.2d 152.

Chapter 424

RELEVANCY AND MATERIALITY—IN GENERAL

Table of Sections

Sec.
424.1 General Rules of Relevancy.
424.2 Proof of Legal Fault—In General.
424.3 —— As Limited by Pleadings.
424.4 —— Conditions Existing.
424.5 —— Conditions Subsequent to Accident.

---

§ 424.1 General Rules of Relevancy

Library References:

C.J.S. Evidence § 158 et seq.; Trial § 150.
West's Key No. Digests, Evidence ⚖️99 et seq.; Trial ⚖️105.

Relevancy is generally defined as whether the evidence tends to make existence of a material fact more probable or less probable than it would be without the evidence,[1] as is the definition stated under the federal rule.[2]

1. **Ala.**—Cherry v. Hill, 1968, 214 So.2d 427, 283 Ala. 74 (tends to shed light, and does not inject matters which are foreign, or of questionable pertinency).

   Cal.—West's Ann.Calif.Evid.Code, § 210; Taylor v. Centennial Bowl, Inc., 1966, 52 Cal.Rptr. 561, 416 P.2d 793, 65 C.2d 114 (tends logically, naturally and by reasonable inference to prove material issue).

   Fla.—Florida Evidence Code § 90.401.

   Ga.—Hardwick v. Price, 152 S.E.2d 905, 114 Ga.App. 817 (which in connection with other evidence tends, however slightly, to prove, explain or illustrate a fact, even though it is not sufficient standing alone to sustain finding of such fact).

   Ill.—Marut v. Costello, 214 N.E.2d 768, 34 Ill.2d 125 (tends to prove a fact in controversy or renders a matter in issue more or less probable; to be probable, it must be tested in light of logic, experience, and accepted assumptions as to human behavior).

   Ind.—Kavanagh v. Butorac, 221 N. E.2d 824, 140 Ind.App. 139 (naturally and logically tends to establish a fact in issue).

   Kan.—Kansas Code of Civil Procedure § 60–401(b).

   Me.—Maine Rules of Evidence § 401.

   Minn.—Boland v. Morrill, 1965, 132 N.W.2d 711, 270 Minn. 86 (logically tends to prove or disprove a material fact in issue).

   Neb.—Nebraska Rules of Evidence § 401.

   Nev.—N.R.S. 48.015.

   N.J.—New Jersey Evidence Rule 1(2).

   N.M.—New Mexico Rules of Evidence § 401.

2. See note 2 on page 361.

Ch. 424   RELEVANCY AND MATERIALITY   § 424.1

Evidence has been held to be subject to objection where it is immaterial,[3] has the danger of undue consumption of trial time,[4] raises consideration of collateral matters,[5] tends to confuse the

Okl.—Iven v. Roder, 431 P.2d 321 (legally tends to prove some matter in issue or tends to make a proposition in issue more or less probable).

S.C.—Gause v. Livingston, 159 S.E.2d 604, 251 S.C. 8 (must be a logical or rational connection between fact sought to be presented and matter of fact which has been made an issue).

Tex.—Herfurth v. City of Dallas, Civ. App.1966, 410 S.W.2d 453, ref. n. r. e.

Utah.—Utah Rules of Evidence § 1 (2).

Wash.—Ladley v. Saint Paul Fire & Marine Ins. Co., 1968, 442 P.2d 983, 73 Wash.2d 928 (reasonably tends to establish theory of party or to qualify or disprove testimony of adversary).

Wis.—Wisconsin Rules of Evidence § 904.01.

2. Federal Rules of Evidence § 401, 28 U.S.C.A.

3. Ala.—Stegall v. Wylie, 1973, 277 So.2d 85, 291 Ala. 1 (defense objection to a question propounded by plaintiff's counsel, to-wit, "Would you state whether or not he [the boy] appeared to be dead?" was properly sustained since the question sought evidence relating to an undisputed fact, i. e., that the boy was not dead, and therefore sought evidence of no probative value).

Cal.—Gallo v. Southern Pac. Co., 110 P.2d 1062, 43 Cal.App.2d 339 (in action for wrongful death, refusal to allow defendants, on cross-examination of decedent's widow, to ask her whether she contemplated remarriage in the near future was not error).

Colo.—Powell v. Brady, 1972, 496 P. 2d 328, 30 Colo.App. 406, affirmed 508 P.2d 1254, 181 Colo. 218 (asserted negligence in plaintiff's treatment).

Ga.—McDaniel v. Richards, 13 S.E. 2d 710, 64 Ga.App. 612 (did not err in not requiring plaintiff to answer question whether, after prior suit by plaintiff against third persons was over, plaintiff asked attorney about bringing action against defendant); Elliott v. Georgia Power Co., 197 S.E. 914, 58 Ga.App. 151 (witness' testimony that he suggested that the plaintiff be taken to a physician after he crossed the street to the scene of the accident).

Ill.—Kooyumjian v. Stevens, 135 N. E.2d 146, 10 Ill.App.2d 378 (evidence referring to ownership of various automobiles, to number of tenants she had, and to her ownership of property was improper and prejudicial).

Ky.—Bowling Green-Hopkinsville Bus Co. v. Adams, 261 S.W.2d 14 (error to admit evidence showing that defendant knew revival was in progress at church and that a number of vehicles was around church); Wright v. Kinslow, Ky., 264 S.W. 2d 673 (partial indemnity to plaintiff driver and passenger by driver's insurance).

Md.—York Ice Machinery Corporation v. Sachs, 173 A. 240, 167 Md. 113 (whether or not driver reported accident to commissioner of motor vehicles).

Mich.—Haynes v. Clark, 233 N.W. 321, 252 Mich. 295 (testimony that woman, who drove automobile involved in accident, was pregnant held properly excluded).

---

4. See note 4 on page 362.

5. See note 5 on page 362.

§ 424.1   TRIAL EVIDENCE   Ch. 424

N.Y.—Neill v. Jodum Cab Corp., 1971, 328 N.Y.S.2d 540, 38 A.D.2d 562 (cross-examination of infant's mother regarding instructions to the infant on street crossing was irrelevant and prejudicial).

N.C.—Riddle v. Whisnant, 1941, 16 S.E.2d 698, 220 N.C. 131 (agreement of negligent driver to inspect car of third party).

Okl.—Deskins v. Woodward, 1971, 483 P.2d 1134 (where no one had questioned presence of witnesses at scene, evidence showing manner in which witnesses were found by newspaper ad was properly excluded, but the abortive attempt to introduce such evidence did not require mistrial on theory that it prejudiced jury or unjustly aroused sympathy or passion).

Or.—Henry v. Condit, 53 P.2d 722, 152 Or. 348, 103 A.L.R. 131 (testimony of automobile salesman who allegedly owned automobile at time of accident as to whether dealer had repurchased automobile held properly excluded).

Wash.—Worthington v. Caldwell, 396 P.2d 797, 65 Wash.2d 269 (testimony by physician that plaintiff had been awarded $4,000 damages for injuries sustained in prior automobile accident); Thomas v. Inland Motor Freight, 68 P.2d 603, 190 Wash. 428 (truck carrying load greater than licensed to carry).

Wis.—Boden v. Transit Cas. Co., 1972, 193 N.W.2d 839, 53 Wis.2d 803 (that plaintiff would lose his job if he lost the case).

Obligations upon road contractor

Project contract between state and defendant contractor sued for injuries sustained when truck doing work on highway construction project struck plaintiff's automobile, performance bond, plans and specifications on contract project and state manual on Standard Specifications for Road and Bridge Construction were inadmissible. Shira v. Wood, 1967, 432 P.2d 243, 164 Colo. 49.

Only a portion admissible

Del.—Sammons v. Ridgeway, 1972, 293 A.2d 547 (where most of the regulations promulgated by State Board of Education to govern operation of school buses were irrelevant, court's refusal to admit into evidence the entire set of regulations, two of which plaintiffs claimed school bus owner and operator had violated, was not error).

Justified as rebuttal

Trial judge properly permitted plaintiff motorist to testify on cross-examination as to her reason for waiting two and a half years to file suit for personal injuries although her testimony referred to statement of her doctor that her bones would not improve any further and would likely deteriorate, where there was inference from earlier interrogation that she had waited because someone had paid her $5,000 and that she brought suit when no more money was paid. Tippit v. Hunter, Miss. 1967, 205 So.2d 267.

4.   Federal Rules of Evidence § 403, 28 U.S.C.A.

Cal.—West's Ann.Calif.Evid.Code, § 352.

Fla.—Florida Evidence Code § 90.403.

Me.—Maine Rules of Evidence § 403.

Neb.—Nebraska Rules of Evidence § 403.

Nev.—N.R.S. 48.035(2).

N.J.—DiNizio v. Burzynski, 195 A.2d 470, 81 N.J.Super. 267.

N.M.—New Mexico Rules of Evidence § 403.

Wis.—Wisconsin Rules of Evidence § 904.03.

5.   Federal Rules of Evidence § 403, 28 U.S.C.A. (misleading the jury).

issues,[6] is only remotely connected with the issues or the accident,[7] is merely cumulative,[8] or where its inflammatory nature outweighs its probative value.[9]

Conn.—Frye v. Krasicky, 1968, 247 A. 2d 439, 5 Conn.Cir. 164; Lombardo v. Simko, 214 A.2d 911, 3 Conn. Cir. 363, certiorari denied 213 A.2d 526, 153 Conn. 724.

Ill.—Messina v. City of Chicago, 212 N.E.2d 320, 64 Ill.App.2d 171 (admission over objection of testimony pertaining to injuries to plaintiff from accidents other than that for which action was brought was improper where defendant failed to connect up testimony with accident sued on and testimony was not shown to have been elicited for impeachment purposes).

Mo.—Matta v. Welcher, 387 S.W.2d 265; Johnson v. Sandweg, 378 S.W.2d 454 (admission of notes of treating physician as to personal history of plaintiff, including fact that he had been thrice married and twice divorced).

Pa.—Bruno v. Brown, 200 A.2d 405, 414 Pa. 361.

Discretion of court

Mo.—Boehmer v. Boggiano, 412 S.W. 2d 103 (large discretion in determining admissibility of evidence on collateral matter).

6. Federal Rules of Evidence § 403, 28 U.S.C.A.

Ala.—Crotwell v. Cowan, 184 So. 195, 236 Ala. 578 (erred in overruling defendant's objection to question asking witness whose name one of defendants had her business in).

Cal.—West's Ann.Calif.Evid.Code, § 352; People By and Through Dept. of Public Works v. Miller, 41 Cal.Rptr. 645, 231 Cal.App.2d 130.

Conn.—Ianni v. Daily, 217 A.2d 707, 153 Conn. 445 (admission of 1959 hospital record containing many notes and entries bearing no relation to questions for jury in action arising out of 1958 automobile collision).

Fla.—Florida Code of Evidence § 90.403.

Ill.—Kitchell v. Chicago & I. M. Ry. Co., 2 N.E.2d 164, 285 Ill.App. 368.

Me.—Maine Rules of Evidence § 403.

Neb.—Nebraska Rules of Evidence § 403.

Nev.—N.R.S. 48.035(1).

N.J.—DiNizio v. Burzynski, Super A.D., 195 A.2d 470, 81 N.J.Super. 267.

N.M.—New Mexico Rules of Evidence § 403.

Pa.—Bruno v. Brown, 82 Montg. 298.

Wash.—Coleman v. Dennis, 1969, 461 P.2d 552, 1 Wash.App. 299.

Wis.—Wiscosin Rules of Evidence § 904.03.

7. **Cal.**—Nelson v. Southern Pac. Co., 67 P.2d 682, 8 Cal.2d 648 (railroad's time-table excluded in crossing collision case).

Colo.—Campbell v. Trate, 149 P.2d 380, 112 Colo. 265 (excluding remarks made by host indicating a state of mind which would have caused him later to drive into borrow pit along highway was not error since such remarks were too remote).

Suggestion of suppression of evidence

Fla.—Dixie-Bell Oil Co., Inc. v. Gold, App., 1973, 275 So.2d 19 (letter from plaintiff's attorney advising examining doctor to destroy or hide enclosed medical reports on

8. See note 8 on page 364.

9. See note 9 on page 364.

§ 424.1 TRIAL EVIDENCE Ch. 424

Generally wealth of a party,[10] and domestic relationship,[11] are not admissible.

plaintiff after reviewing them was not relevant and material and was properly denied admission into evidence, since the letter per se had no bearing on plaintiff's medical condition and there was no reason why the examining doctor could not read the reports enclosed therein).

8. Federal Rules of Evidence § 403, 28 U.S.C.A.

Fla.—Florida Evidence Code § 90.403.

Ill.—Shellabarger v. Nattier, 7 N.E. 2d 365, 289 Ill.App. 473.

Me.—Maine Rules of Evidence § 403.

Neb.—Nebraska Rules of Evidence § 403.

Nev.—N.R.S. 48.035(2).

N.M.—New Mexico Rules of Evidence § 403.

N.C.—Caldwell v. Southern Ry. Co., 10 S.E.2d 680, 218 N.C. 63.

Wis.—Wisconsin Rules of Evidence § 904.03.

Held admissible

In action for injuries by guest against owner of automobile who had rented the automobile to driver, testimony of owner to establish existence of a custom of having his employees test brakes of an automobile before renting it, was admissible, though employee of owner had previously testified that he tested brakes of the automobile in question before renting it. Buxton v. Langan, 3 A.2d 647, 90 N.H. 13.

9. Federal Rules of Evidence § 403, 28 U.S.C.A.

Cal.—West's Ann.Calif.Evid.Code § 352; Atwood v. Villa, 1972, 101 Cal.Rptr. 508, 25 Cal.App.3d 145 (where defedant was not driving in improper manner as he approached intersection defendant's state of mind was irrelevant, and allowing, allegedly for purpose of showing state of mind on question of willful and wanton misconduct, testimony as to defendant's alleged indecent exposure shortly before accident was abuse of discretion).

Fla.—Florida Evidence Code § 90.403.

Ill.—Anthony v. New York Cent. R. R., 1965, 209 N.E.2d 686, 61 Ill. App.2d 466.

Me.—Maine Rules of Evidence § 403.

Mo.—Brown v. Parker, App.1964, 375 S.W.2d 594 (family status); Donze v. Swofford, App.1963, 368 S.W.2d 917 (number of children).

Neb.—Nebraska Rules of Evidence § 403.

Nev.—N.R.S. 48.035(1).

N.M.—New Mexico Rules of Evidence § 403.

Tex.—Armstrong Tire & Rubber Co. v. Shearer, Civ.App.1956, 290 S.W. 2d 294, ref. n. r. e. (proof of wife's wheelchair disability in attempt to show plaintiff's changed disposition).

Wis.—Wisconsin Rules of Evidence § 904.03.

Abandonment by father held admissible

In mother's action for medical expenses, incurred as result of injuries sustained by minor child, evidence that child's father had abandoned him and that plaintiff was the only and real party in interest looking after child's welfare, and that she did in fact support and maintain child, was admissible under allegations of complaint. Pokeda v. Nash, Sup., 47 N.Y.S.2d 954.

10. **Ga.**—Brackin v. Brackin, 149 S. E.2d 485, 222 Ga. 226.

---

11. See note 11 on page 365.

§ 424.1   RELEVANCY AND MATERIALITY   Ch. 424

Waiver of objection

A party must make timely objections that the evidence is not supported by the pleadings, and failure to object may be taken as an implied consent to the submission of the issues and they will be treated as though they were properly pleaded;[12]

N.D.—Intlehouse v. Rose, 1967, 153 N.W.2d 810 (automobile owner's testimony to effect that since he was unable to make a reasonable trade-in of damaged automobile for a new one and he could not afford to buy a new one, he was required to submit automobile for attempted repair was not objectionable as attempting to interject owner's financial condition in his suit for damages to automobile).

But see

Plaintiff's financial condition should be shown if he asserts it as reason for avoidance of surgery which allegedly will mitigate damage and his testimony should be subject to cross-examination. Colton v. Benes, 126 N.W.2d 652, 176 Neb. 483.

11. **U.S.**—Nichols v. Marshall, C.A. Kan.1973, 486 F.2d 791 (in consolidated suit by wife for personal injuries suffered in accident in which husband was killed, and for wrongful death of the husband, court properly excluded evidence that wife had remarried almost three years after accident occurred).

Ill.—McKasson v. Zimmer Mfg. Co., 1973, 299 N.E.2d 38, 12 Ill.App.3d 429 (marriage and number of dependents is irrelevant); Payne v. Noles, 1972, 283 N.E.2d 329, 5 Ill. App.3d 433; Hedge v. Midwest Contractors Equipment Co., 202 N. E.2d 869, 53 Ill.App.2d 365.

Mo.—Cardello v. Bauer, App.1968, 433 S.W.2d 81 (refusing to allow plaintiff to show death of husband, as explanation for going to work while allegedly disabled).

Matter opened up by adversary

Alaska.—Jakoski v. Holland, 1974, 520 P.2d 569 (testimony of plaintiff accident victim pertaining to her home and family life and her children invited further inquiry into her home and family life on cross-examination).

Tex.—Franco v. Graham, Civ.App. 1971, 470 S.W.2d 429, reformed 488 S.W.2d 390 (where plaintiffs injected their family life into evidence by answering questions intended to impress upon jury that their home and family life was happy, gay, and free from any extraordinary circumstances and events that would indicate any marital trouble or discord, defendants were authorized to show that plaintiffs' family life may not have been so ideal by introducing evidence of a criminal complaint against husband by wife and by cross-examining husband concerning troubles that led to filing of wife's petition for divorce).

Remarriage of plaintiff widow

N.Y.—Rodak v. Fury, 1969, 298 N.Y. S.2d 50, 31 A.D.2d 816 (requiring swearing as witness under remarried name was error).

12. **Cal.**—Brandes v. Rucker-Fuller Desk Co., 282 P. 1009, 102 Cal.App. 221.

Tex.—Northern Texas Traction Co. v. Smith, Civ.App., 223 S.W. 1013; Bigelow v. Rupp, Civ.App., 192 S. W.2d 791, ref. n. r. e. (plaintiff, making no objection to evidence respecting legal relationship between them and driver of their automobile at time of collision with defendant's automobile, impliedly consented to trial of issue whether such driver's negligence should be imputed to plaintiff, even if such issue was not properly raised by

§ 424.1 TRIAL EVIDENCE Ch. 424

and all other objections as to relevancy and materiality must be timely,[13] and proper.[14]

pleading); Thomas v. Southern Lumber Co., Civ.App., 181 S.W.2d 111 (where plaintiff alleged that corporate defendant and individual defendant owned and jointly operated truck for their mutual benefit, but did not expressly plead partnership, and objected to evidence that truck belonged to and was controlled by individual only on ground that it was not raised by pleading, without urging that partnership had to be denied under oath, issue of corporation's relations to individual and to truck driver was tried by implied consent of parties, and should be treated as having been properly raised by pleadings).

13. U.S.—Vogrin v. Hedstrom, C.A. Mo., 220 F.2d 863, certiorari denied 76 S.Ct. 86, 350 U.S. 845, 100 L. Ed. 753 (in action by passenger, wherein driver's counsel in opening statement stated he believed evidence would show passenger was a guest, and he made other references to passenger as a guest, and passenger offered proof which she contended made her a compensating guest, issue was raised as to whether passenger was guest under California guest statute, and contention that no such issue was raised would not be considered when urged for the first time on appeal).

Cal.—Hastings v. Serleto, 143 P.2d 956, 61 Cal.App.2d 672.

Ill.—Murray v. Pennsylvania R. Co., 106 N.E.2d 819, 347 Ill.App. 218 (evidence of habits of care of deceased).

Mass.—Bachand v. Vidal, 101 N.E. 2d 884, 328 Mass. 97 (where trial judge asked one of codefendants whether liability insurance in partnership's name was in force at time of the accident and witness answered in affirmative and no complaint was made by defense counsel at time of question that he had no opportunity to object before answer, motion made following day to dismiss jury because it had received improper evidence as to insurance was properly denied).

N.J.—Puorro v. Kaskenas, 1933, 167 A. 737, 11 N.J.Misc. 630 (insurance injected).

Tenn.—Logwood v. Nelson, 1952, 250 S.W.2d 582, 35 Tenn.App. 639 (insurance injected).

Absence of objection to prior testimony

Statement of nurse from hospital at which plaintiff was confined to effect that visiting doctor had commented that he was from insurance company was not prejudicial where prior witness had testified without objection that defendant had told witness he was traveling approximately 60 miles an hour at time of accident but was going to say around 45 because of his insurance. Packard v. Moore, 71 P.2d 922, 9 Cal.2d 571.

14. Alaska.—Ahlstrom v. Cummings, 388 P.2d 261 (bringing out that the action was a friendly action and was designed to effect a recovery only from liability insurer formed no basis for appeal where appellants' counsel had made no objection when testimony had been given and had even conducted a cross-examination on the subject of insurance).

Cal.—Mullanix v. Basich, 155 P.2d 130, 67 Cal.App.2d 675 (evidence of insurance).

Ga.—Henry Chavin Corporation v. Dumas, 16 S.E.2d 603, 65 Ga.App. 820 (evidence of insurance).

A general objection to the admission of an entire statement, part of which is admissible, is not sufficient. The objection should be made to the admission of the part of the statement which is objectionable.[15]

§ 424.2 Proof of Legal Fault—In General

Library References:
C.J.S. Evidence § 586 et seq.; Motor Vehicles § 514 et seq.
West's Key No. Digests, Automobiles ⊂⊃243; Evidence ⊂⊃150.

The conduct of the alleged negligent driver after the accident is not material, except so far as it is part of the res gestae and tends to explain the act claimed to be negligence.[16] Evidence

Kan.—Olsen v. Lambert, 145 P.2d 159, 158 Kan. 94 (evidence of insurance).

Ohio.—Tighe v. Diamond, 82 N.E.2d 99, 82 Ohio App. 487, affirmed 80 N.E.2d 122, 149 Ohio St. 520 (evidence of insurance).

S.C.—McLeod v. Rose, 97 S.E.2d 899, 231 S.C. 209 (evidence of insurance).

No request to admonish jury

Injection of subject of insurance into case was not reversible error, where employer's counsel made no request that court admonish jury that testimony was improper and stated to court that any admonition which court might make would be more prejudicial than prejudice already existing, since counsel thereby impliedly invited court not to admonish jury. Neely v. Goldberg, 114 S.W.2d 455, 195 Ark. 790.

15. **N.H.**—McCurdy v. Flibotte, 139 A. 367, 83 N.H. 143 (reference to insurance).

16. **Colo.**—Carsell v. Edwards, 1968, 439 P.2d 33, 165 Colo. 335 (testimony concerning defendant operator's concern over possibility of losing points and losing operator's license was irrelevant and prejudicial).

Fla.—Lynch v. McGovern, App., 1972, 270 So.2d 770 (there was no error in disallowing evidence of ordinances dealing with leaving the scene and failing to render aid, on ground that they were irrelevant and immaterial).

Wash.—Minor v. Stevens, 118 P. 313, 65 Wash. 423, 42 L.R.A.,N.S. 1178.

Driver crying

Fact that defendant was crying at scene of collision with 65-year-old plaintiff on sidewalk, brought out on cross-examination of plaintiff, was immaterial and irrelevant, but improper admission of testimony into evidence was not sufficient to convict trial court of abuse of discretion requiring reversal. Krez v. Mickel, 1968, Mo., 431 S.W.2d 213.

Fault inferred from flight from scene

Conn.—Gaul v. Noiva, 1967, 230 A.2d 591, 155 Conn. 218 (admissible on issue of whether defendant or plaintiff was driving at time of accident as an admission, by conduct, of consciousness of liability, but its weight might be affected by defendant's mental condition at time and other circumstances).

N.J.—Jones v. Strelecki, 1967, 231 A.2d 558, 49 N.J. 513 (failure of a motorist to stop after an accident permits an inference of consciousness of lack of care and of liability for the occurrence).

§ 424.2   TRIAL EVIDENCE   Ch. 424

of a truck driver's nervousness after an accident has been held inadmissible.[17]

Evidence of defendant's refusal to assist an injured party has been held admissible,[18] while evidence of defendant's failure to make any inquiry concerning an injured party has been held inadmissible.[19]

While, ordinarily, witnesses will not be permitted to testify to conclusions, a driver may testify to the assumption that another driver would obey the law.[20]

It has been held proper to exclude testimony by a party as to what that party would have done under certain conditions, which did not then and there exist.[21] However, a motorist's general views for meeting traffic likely to come suddenly in that motorist's path are a proper matter of inquiry on the issue of whether, under all the circumstances, what was done was careless, and may be shown by example and illustration.[22] Questions propounded to obtain such views and for illustrative purposes have a bearing on a defendant's state of mind which might account for the actual conduct, and such an illustration would not necessarily be too remote to aid such purpose.[23] However, the refusal to permit a witness who had testified that a motorist drove into an intersection at a rapid rate of speed while a truck was in the intersection to state what the witness would have done at the intersection has been approved, on the ground that the issue was what a reasonably prudent person would have done under similar circumstances.[24]

Providing transportation for medical attention

Fact that party picks someone up and takes him to hospital and is solicitous for his welfare cannot be construed as admission of liability. Lyons v. Levine, 1967, 225 N.E.2d 593, 352 Mass. 769.

17. N.H.—Christie v. New England Telephone & Telegraph Co., 177 A. 300, 87 N.H. 236.

18. Mo.—Pogue v. Rosegrant, Sup., 98 S.W.2d 528.

Contra

Fla.—Lynch v. McGovern, App.1972, 270 So.2d 770.

19. Ky.—Field v. Collins, 92 S.W. 2d 793, 263 Ky. 474.

Defendant's failure to visit injured party

Cal.—Hastings v. Serleto, 143 P.2d 956, 61 Cal.App.2d 672 (permitting guest to show that none of the defendants visited her after the accident was error).

20. Ohio.—Szabo v. Tabor Ice Cream Co., 174 N.E. 18, 37 Ohio App. 42.

21. N.C.—Plyler v. Southern Ry. Co., 117 S.E. 297, 185 N.C. 357.

22. N.H.—Lapolice v. Austin, 157 A. 73, 85 N.H. 244.

23. N.H.—Lapolice v. Austin, 157 A. 73, 85 N.H. 244.

24. Md.—Bode v. Carroll-Independent Coal Co., 191 A. 685, 172 Md. 406.

Evidence of plaintiff's negligence may be admissible, as affecting defendant's duty to use due care, though plaintiff's negligence would not be a defense in the particular case.[25]

Failure to use protective gear has been held inadmissible on the issue of contributory negligence.[26]

Habits of due care [27]

There is a conflict among the cases as to whether evidence of the habits of persons involved in accidents is admissible. In perhaps the majority of state jurisdictions, the rule is that, where the driver of an automobile or an employee of a railroad is alleged to have been negligent in a traffic accident case, and where there were eyewitnesses, evidence that on former occasions such driver or employee had been in the habit of being a careful and cautious driver, or had pursued a certain line of conduct, is ordinarily not admissible to show that the person was acting with care and caution or otherwise, or was following the same method when the accident in question happened.[28] Also generally inadmissible is evidence of prior reckless conduct.[29]

25. **Me.**—Bedell v. Androscoggin & K. Ry. Co., 177 A. 237, 133 Me. 268.

26. **Colo.**—Fischer v. Moore, 1973, 517 P.2d 458, 183 Colo. 392 (prior to comparative negligence statute, as to driver's non-use of seat belt).

Ind.—Kavanagh v. Butorac, 221 N.E. 2d 824, 140 Ind.App. 139 (where there was no showing that contents of three magazines containing articles with respect to use of seat belts in automobiles were known to passenger who failed to use available seat belts in automobile and was injured in collision, or that documents had wide circulation which of itself might constitute some proof that use of seat belts was so normal, natural, safety oriented, and generally accepted that reasonably prudent men would never fail to use them, exclusion of exhibits was not error).

27. See section 427.1 for discussion of relevancy of proof of past driving habits on issue of competency of driver.

28. Same statement in prior edition **quoted by the court** in Jackson v. Chesapeake & O. Ry. Co., 20 S.E. 2d 489, 491, 179 Va. 642.

Ala.—Poole v. Evergreen Livestock Co., 77 So.2d 475, 262 Ala. 131; Stoudemire v. Davis, 94 So. 498, 208 Ala. 495; Jackson v. Vaughn, 86 So. 469, 204 Ala. 543 (testimony that defendant always blew his horn in turning around corners is inadmissible).

Ga.—Willis v. Hill, 1967, 159 S.E.2d 145, 116 Ga.App. 848, reversed on other grounds 161 S.E.2d 281, 224 Ga. 263, conformed to 162 S.E.2d 299, 117 Ga.App. 855 (driver's driving record was not admissible); Grannemann v. Salley, 99 S.E.2d 338, 95 Ga.App. 778; Hawkins v. Benton Rapid Exp., 62 S.E.2d 612, 82 Ga.App. 819.

Ill.—Elliott v. Elgin, J. & E. Ry. Co., 59 N.E.2d 486, 325 Ill.App. 161 (evidence of careful habits of occupants of automobile); Todd v. Chicago City Ry. Co., 197 Ill.App. 544.

Iowa.—Rickabaugh v. Wabash R. Co., 1950, 44 N.W.2d 659, 242 Iowa 76

29. See note 29 on page 371.

§ 424.2   TRIAL EVIDENCE   Ch. 424

(railroad crossing accident); Hamilton v. Boyd, 256 N.W. 290, 218 Iowa 885; Nyswander v. Gonser, 253 N.W. 829, 218 Iowa 136.

Ky.—Price v. Bates, 320 S.W.2d 786; Ice Delivery Co. v. Thomas, 160 S.W.2d 605, 290 Ky. 230 (driver of ice truck from which boy fell); Siler v. Renfro Supply Co., 26 S. W.2d 12, 233 Ky. 487; Dawson v. Shannon, 9 S.W.2d 998, 225 Ky. 635 (habit of drinking).

Mass.—Luiz v. Falvey, 117 N.E. 308, 228 Mass. 253; O'Hare v. Gloag, 108 N.E. 566, 221 Mass. 24.

Mich.—Hinderer v. Ann Arbor R. Co., 211 N.W. 734, 237 Mich. 232.

Minn.—Sauke v. Bird, 125 N.W.2d 421, 267 Minn. 129 (driving in careful manner not exceeding 50 miles per hour on day of fatal head-on collision); Ryan v. International Harvester Co. of America, 283 N.W. 129, 204 Minn. 177; Young v. Avery Co., 170 N.W. 693, 141 Minn. 483.

Mo.—Gerhard v. Terminal R. Ass'n of St. Louis, 299 S.W.2d 866; Rhineberger v. Thompson, 202 S. W.2d 64, 356 Mo. 520 (general reputation for sobriety).

N.D.—Thornburg v. Perleberg, 1968, 158 N.W.2d 188.

Okl.—Barger v. Mizel, 424 P.2d 41; Gillette Motor Transport, Inc. v. Kirby, 1952, 253 P.2d 139, 208 Okl. 68.

S.C.—Westbrook v. Jefferies, 175 S. E. 433, 173 S.C. 178 (but proper on issue of wilfulness).

Tex.—Hudson v. Hightower, 394 S. W.2d 46, ref. n. r. e. (testimony as to usual manner in which he drove automobile through intersection); M. K. Hall Co. v. Caballero, Civ. App., 358 S.W.2d 179, writ of error n. r. e. (exclusion of testimony as to the intemperate habits of plaintiff, was not error where defendants did not contend plaintiff was intoxicated at time of accident); Hearn v. Mrs. Baird's Bread Co., Civ.App., 295 S.W.2d 689, reversed on other grounds 300 S.W.2d 646, 157 Tex. 159 ("About how fast did he ordinarily run passing down at end of that alley?"); Missouri-Kansas-Texas R. Co. v. McFerrin, 291 S.W.2d 931, 156 Tex. 69 (even though the eyewitness be an employee of the opposite party, no eyewitness rule did not apply).

Va.—Jackson v. Chesapeake & O. Ry. Co., 20 S.E.2d 489, 179 Va. 642 (eyewitnesses present); Crowell v. Duncan, 134 S.E. 576, 145 Va. 489, 50 A.L.R. 1425; Southern Ry. Co. v. Mason, 89 S.E. 225, 119 Va. 256.

Vt.—Loomis v. Abelson, 144 A. 378, 101 Vt. 459 (excessive speed on former occasion).

Wash.—Breimon v. General Motors Corp., 1973, 509 P.2d 398, 8 Wash. App. 747 (previous habit of speed is not admissible to prove conduct at a later time inasmuch as such an inquiry would raise a collateral issue); Chilberg v. Parsons, 1920, 186 P. 272, 109 Wash. 90.

Contra

Ark.—Arkansas Power & Light Co. v. Cummins, 28 S.W.2d 1077, 181 Ark. 1145; Bush v. Brewer, 206 S.W. 322, 136 Ark. 246.

N.H.—Whipple v. Boston & Maine R. R., 7 A.2d 239, 20 N.H. 261; Davis v. Concord & M. R. R., 44 A. 388, 68 N.H. 247.

N.D.—Glatt v. Feist, 1968, 156 N.W. 2d 819 (where issue whether pedestrian while returning from church had been struck on pedestrian crosswalk or at a point east of the crosswalk was critical and there was direct conflicting evidence by pedestrian and defendant motorist, evidence as to alleged habit of plaintiff of crossing at point east of crosswalk in returning from church was admissible).

Evidence of conduct to show mental state

Ohio.—Kennard v. Palmer, Ohio App., 53 N.E.2d 652, reversed on other

Ch. 424 RELEVANCY AND MATERIALITY § 424.2

Under the federal rule and the rules of certain states, "habit of a person" or "routine practice of an organization" is relevant to prove that the conduct of the person or organization conformed with the habit or routine practice;[30] but evidence of a person's character or a trait of character, is not admissible to prove that the person acted in conformity therewith on a particular occasion.[31]

Even in the absence of a rule or statute in state jurisdictions, evidence of a driver's habits has been held admissible under some circumstances.[32] Where there is no direct proof of the driver's

grounds 53 N.E.2d 908, 143 Ohio St. 1 (where conduct of defendant host immediately before collision was identical in character with what it had been throughout the entire trip, evidence of defendant's conduct before collision occurred was properly admitted to show defendant's mental state); Clark v. Stewart, 1933, 185 N.E. 71, 126 Ohio St. 263.

Tex.—Allen v. Bland, Civ.App.1914, 168 S.W. 35, error refused.

29. Miss.—Murphy v. Burney, 27 So.2d 773.

N.C.—Heath v. Kirkman, 82 S.E.2d 104, 240 N.C. 303 (reputation for negligence not competent).

Okl.—McCarley v. Durham, 266 P.2d 629 (properly admitted against father although such evidence was not admisible against son).

30. Federal Rules of Evidence § 406, 28 U.S.C.A.; Frase v. Henry, C.A.Kan.1971, 444 F.2d 1228.

Cal.—West's Ann.Calif.Evid.Code, § 1105.

Fla.—Florida Evidence Code § 90.406 (only as to routine practice of an organization).

Kan.—Kansas Code of Civil Procedure § 60–449.

Me.—Maine Rules of Evidence § 406.

Neb.—Nebraska Rules of Evidence § 406.

Nev.—N.R.S. 48.059.

N.J.—New Jersey Evidence Rule 49.

N.M.—New Mexico Rules of Evidence § 406.

Utah.—Utah Rules of Evidence § 49.

Wis.—Wisconsin Rules of Evidence § 904.06.

31. Federal Rules of Evidence § 404 (a), 28 U.S.C.A.

Cal.—West's Ann.Calif.Evid.Code, § 1101.

Fla.—Florida Evidence Code § 90.-404.

Kan.—Kansas Code of Civil Procedure § 60–448.

Me.—Maine Rules of Evidence § 404 (a).

Neb.—Nebraska Rules of Evidence § 404.

Nev.—N.R.S. 48.045.

N.J.—New Jersey Evidence Rule 48.

N.M.—New Mexico Rules of Evidence 404.

Utah.—Utah Rules of Evidence § 48.

Wis.—Wisconsin Rules of Evidence § 904.04.

32. Ind.—Pennsylvania R. Co. v. Patesel, 76 N.E.2d 595, 118 Ind. App. 233 (testimony as to habitual and customary speed of defendant's trains over crossing was ad-

§ 424.2 TRIAL EVIDENCE Ch. 424

missible as tending to prove speed of train).

Iowa.—Barrick v. Smith, 80 N.W.2d 326, 248 Iowa 195 (testimony of a school bus driver that he habitually turned on flashing stop lights and put out the stop arm although he did not remember for sure but that on the particular occasion he handled them the same as always).

Mass.—O'Hare v. Gloag, 108 N.E. 566, 221 Mass. 24.

Mich.—Stinson v. Payne, 203 N.W. 831, 231 Mich. 158 (habitual violation of ordinance).

N.H.—Abbott v. Hayes, 26 A.2d 842, 92 N.H. 126.

Vt.—Abel v. Salebra, 61 A.2d 605, 115 Vt. 336 (testimony of previous prudent driving of the defendant on the question of speed in an action based on guest statute for motorist's gross negligence).

Wash.—Jaquith v. Worden, 132 P.2d 33, 73 Wash. 349 (evidence that the defendant habitually left his car standing unlighted in the street in front of his house after dark was admissible as tending to prove that he personally left the car there on the night in question, and to show an invitation to the driver to do so also; those questions being in issue).

Door opened by cross-examination

In action for death of plaintiffs' decedent whose truck collided with defendants' truck when the latter vehicle pulled onto highway from shoulder in front of decedent's truck, defendants put decedent's competency and skill as truck driver in issue when they developed, upon cross-examination, fact that decedent had been driving smallest truck in convoy and by inquiring whether he "had not yet been promoted" to larger truck, by inquiring whether he had worked irregularly for employer during last four years and "moved around from company to company" and by eliciting from witness that shortly before fatal accident decedent had had another accident; and it was therefore not error to permit decedent's fellow employee, who had been qualified truck driver for 30 years, to testify that decedent was as good a driver as the witness ever saw. Bolstad v. Egleson, Tex.Civ. App., 326 S.W.2d 506, ref. n. r. e.

On issue of identity of driver

Testimony as to the careful habits of plaintiff's decedent, who died instantly, along with a companion, was properly admitted for the purpose of showing that plaintiff's decedent was not the driver of the automobile, where there was no direct evidence as to who was driving at the time of the accident. Hall v. Kirk, 1973, 300 N.E.2d 600, —— Ill.App. ——.

Rebutting inference of physical unfitness

Where the declaration alleged that the injuries were due to the defendant's negligent operation of the car, as well as to his physical unfitness to operate the machine, and there was evidence that the defendant wore an artificial leg, his leg having been amputated two or three inches above the knee, and that his other leg was withered, evidence to show the manner in which defendant operated his car within a reasonable time before and after the accident was admissible to rebut the inference that he was physically unfit to safely operate the car. O'Hare v. Gloag, 108 N.E. 566, 221 Mass. 24.

Where deadman statute applicable

Trial court properly admitted evidence of plaintiff's habits of care where plaintiff had the burden of proving that he had exercised proper degree of care for his own safety and was not allowed under the Evidence Act to testify against defendant, who was administratrix of deceased's estate, that he exercised the proper degree of care. McElroy v. Force, 1968, 232 N.E.2d 708, 38 Ill. 2d 528.

Ch. 424   RELEVANCY AND MATERIALITY   § 424.2

behavior on the particular occasion,[33] or where the eyewitnesses had no time to view the situation clearly and opposite inferences may reasonably be drawn from their testimony.[34] And such evidence is relevant in support of other proof of negligence and on the question of wilfulness.[35]

Under the federal rule and the rule in certain states character traits may, in those cases in which the trait is in issue, be proven by testimony as to reputation or by testimony in the form of the opinion of the testifying witness; and, in cases in which the trait is an essential element of a charge, claim or defense, proof may be made by testimony as to specific instances

33. **Ill.**—Logue v. Williams, 1969, 250 N.E.2d 159, 111 Ill.App.2d 327; McElroy v. Force, 220 N.E.2d 761, 75 Ill.App.2d 441; Barana v. James A. Hannah, Inc., 140 N.E.2d 301, 12 Ill.App.2d 364; Wilson v. Peters, 99 N.E.2d 150, 343 Ill.App. 354; Hughes v. Wabash R. Co., 95 N.E.2d 735, 342 Ill.App. 159; Wilson v. Decatur Cartage Co., 39 N.E.2d 379, 313 Ill.App. 148; Zimmer v. Hill, 1939, 20 N.E.2d 811, 30 Ill.App. 613 (not evidence of stopping at intersection on 5 or 6 occasions).

Mich.—Hoffman v. Rengo Oil Co., 1969, 174 N.W.2d 155, 20 Mich. App. 575 (deceased's habitual manner of crossing highway).

N.H.—Barton v. Plaisted, 1969, 256 A.2d 642, 109 N.H. 428, 38 A.L.R. 3d 799 (testimony concerning decedent's customary driving speed over a period of years, along the "flat" leading southerly into curve where accident occurred, was competent and properly received); Judd v. Perkins, 1958, 138 A. 312, 83 N.H. 39.

Contra

Ohio.—Ashdown v. Tresise, 1928, 160 N.E. 502, 26 Ohio App. 575, affirmed 160 N.E. 898, 118 Ohio St. 307, 58 A.L.R. 1476.

Defendant must tender name of eyewitness to exclude habit proof

Ill.—Moore v. Bloomington D. & C. R. Co., 128 N.E. 721, 295 Ill. 63.

"Eyewitness" described

Where witness whose automobile was about 100 feet behind defendant's automobile saw pedestrian near middle of 50-foot street about 100 feet from defendant's automobile, and after glancing at dashboard looked up and saw defendant's automobile swerve and then stop in 40 or 50 feet, and saw person lying in street but did not see defendant's automobile come in contact with anything, he was not "eyewitness" of fatal accident, and hence testimony of pedestrian's careful habits was properly admitted. Szalacha v. Landsman, 60 N.E.2d 643, 325 Ill. App. 691.

34. **N.H.**—Judd v. Perkins, 138 A. 312, 83 N.H. 39.

Not applicable

Direct affirmative testimony of plaintiff's eyewitness that decedent was proceeding with due care just prior to collision did not raise issue of decedent's generally careful driving, and decedent's driving records, being irrelevant to issue of due care at time of accident and dealing with a collateral matter, were not admissible to rebut such direct testimony. Burnett v. Mitchell, 1973, 210 N.W.2d 457, 48 Mich.App. 393.

35. **S.C.**—Westbrook v. Jefferies, 175 S.E. 433, 173 S.C. 178; Jennings v. Northwestern R. Co. of South Carolina, 136 S.E. 639, 138 S.C. 385.

§ 424.2   TRIAL EVIDENCE   Ch. 424

of conduct.[36] And, under the federal rule and under the rule in certain states, proof of "habit of a person" or "routine practice of an organization" may be proven by either opinion or specific instances of conduct.[37]

In state jurisdictions, except by express rule, habits may be provable by general reputation but not by isolated instances.[38]

When admissible, evidence of specific instances of conduct offered to prove a motorist's habits must be limited to places similar to the one involved in the accident.[39]

Custom and practice

Although customary methods or conduct do not furnish a conclusive test of negligence,[40] evidence thereof is generally admissible for consideration, with other evidence, on the issue of

36. Federal Rules of Evidence § 405, 28 U.S.C.A.

Cal.—West's Ann.Calif.Evid.Code, § 1100.

Fla.—Florida Evidence Code § 90.405.

Kan.—Kansas Code of Civil Procedure § 60–446.

Neb.—Nebraska Rules of Evidence § 405.

Nev.—N.R.S. 48.055.

N.J.—New Jersey Evidence Rules 46, 47 (specific instances not admissible).

N.M.—New Mexico Rules of Evidence § 405.

Utah.—Utah Rules of Evidence § 46.

Wis.—Wisconsin Rules of Evidence § 904.05.

Not by opinion

Me.—Maine Rules of Evidence § 405.

37. Federal Rules of Evidence § 406, 28 U.S.C.A. (see comment in Report of House Committee on the Judiciary for reserved approval of opinion evidence).

Kan.—Kansas Code of Civil Procedure § 60–450.

Neb.—Nebraska Rules of Evidence § 406.

Nev.—N.R.S. 48.059.

N.M.—New Mexico Rules of Evidence § 406(b).

Utah.—Utah Rules of Evidence § 50.

Wis.—Wisconsin Rules of Evidence § 904.06.

Not by opinion

Me.—Maine Rules of Evidence § 406(b).

38. Tex.—Southern Traction Co. v. Kirksey, Civ.App., 222 S.W. 702 (proof of habit of getting drunk and driving recklessly while in such condition, as tending to show whether or not driver was intoxicated at time of accident).

39. Cal.—Lindsey v. Pacific Electric Ry. Co., 296 P. 131, 111 Cal.App. 482 (habit as to stopping, looking, and listening at a railroad crossing).

40. Tex.—J. A. Robinson Sons, Inc. v. Wigart, 1968, 420 S.W.2d 474, reversed on other grounds 431 S.W.2d 327; El Paso Electric Co. v. Barker, Civ.App., 116 S.W.2d 433, reversed on other grounds 137 S.W.2d 17, 134 Tex. 496.

Ch. 424 RELEVANCY AND MATERIALITY § 424.2

due care.[41] Such evidence may also be admissible on other issues.[42]

41. **U.S.**—Napolitano v. Eastern Motor Exp., Inc., C.A.N.J., 246 F.2d 249.

Ala.—Allred v. Dobbs, 190 So.2d 712, 280 Ala. 159 (whether automobiles customarily used that area for driving).

Ariz.—American Smelting & Refining Co. v. Wusich, 375 P.2d 364, 92 Ariz. 159 (truck driver's knowledge, if any, that motorists on east-west highways habitually passed intersections without yielding right of way to motorists on north-south highways).

Cal.—Martin, Continental Casualty Co., Intervener, v. Clinton Const. Co., 105 P.2d 1029, 41 Cal.App.2d 35, rehearing denied 106 P.2d 629, 41 Cal.App. 35; Perumean v. Wills, 67 P.2d 96, 8 Cal.2d 578 (that schools in other cities and garages customarily did not block wheels when starting motors was competent on question of care and diligence).

Iowa.—Langner v. Caviness, 28 N.W.2d 421, 238 Iowa 774, 172 A.L.R. 1135 (custom between truckers when working upon public works to yield right of way to loaded truck in narrow or defective place in highway).

Ky.—Barnes v. F. C. Gorrell & Sons, 177 S.W.2d 395, 296 Ky. 583 (placing by highway contractors of steel beams along edge of newly constructed apron to prevent vehicular travel on the apron).

Md.—Pennsylvania R. Co. v. State, 53 A.2d 562, 188 Md. 646 (custom of having flagman at crossing during switching operations); Holler v. Miller, 9 A.2d 250, 177 Md. 204 (frequency of turning and passing on both sides when road was crowded with factory employees).

Minn.—Thelen v. Spilman, 86 N.W.2d 700, 251 Minn. 89, 77 A.L.R.2d 1315.

Mo.—Schlegel v. Knoll, 1968, 427 S.W.2d 480 (police officer who was driving motorcycle west on eastbound lane of street when defendant's automobile, which was traveling west, turned left and was struck by motorcycle was entitled to show justification or excuse that traffic was clogged or stopped in westbound lanes, that he had to reach a second traffic control assignment quickly, that eastbound lanes were clear, or practically clear, of traffic, and that other officers had preceded west using eastbound lanes).

N.J.—Mathis v. Fantozzi, 1969, 251 A.2d 469, 105 N.J.Super. 181 (where both plaintiff and defendant acknowledged that drivers using boulevard on which accident occurred would stop at nearest corner when lights on boulevard were red against them, a practice which both said they followed, that practice was appropriately a factor to be considered by jury in determining issue of negligence and it was not error to admit testimony as to such custom and usage).

N.M.—Irwin v. Graham, 1956, 304 P.2d 875, 62 N.M. 72 (yielding to loaded trucks, on private road).

Or.—Barnes v. Davidson, 1951, 226 P.2d 289, 190 Or. 508.

Tex.—Turner v. General Motors Corp., Civ.App.1974, 514 S.W.2d 497 (while conformance to industry custom of automobile design or structure is admissible on the question of negligence of manufacturer, the custom itself may be shown to be negligent); El Paso Electric Co. v. Barker, Civ.App. 1938, 116 S.W.2d 433, reversed on other grounds, 137 S.W.2d 17, 134 Tex. 496.

42. See note 42 on page 377.

§ 424.2   TRIAL EVIDENCE   Ch. 424

But see

Ky.—Lee v. Dutli, 403 S.W.2d 703 (evidence as to allege custom of parking automobiles in private parking lot at rear of store in shopping center was inadmissible as bearing on question of negligence in collision which occurred when one parked automobile backed into another parked automobile).

Mich.—Hoag v. Hyzy, 63 N.W.2d 632, 339 Mich. 163 (in action against highway construction company, which had removed stop sign, admission of testimony as to practices in the county regarding removal and placement of stop signs was error).

Mo.—Davis v. Illinois Terminal R. Co., 326 S.W.2d 78 (court would not be deemed to have erred in excluding an offer of proof that there was a general practice and custom of motorists traveling over highway in question to drive with their headlights depressed because of the volume of traffic passing over the highway, in view of fact such evidence would have had slight probative value on question of whether lights on decedent's automobile were on high beam or low beam).

But see, as to use of headgear

Md.—Rogers v. Frush, 1970, 262 A.2d 549, 257 Md. 233, 40 A.L.R.3d 847 (proffered testimony of motorcycle dealer, who did not relate that he had attempted to sell motorcyclist helmet, that it was commonly accepted that motorcycle purchasers would also buy helmets and that dealers recommended their purchase was not indicative of failure of motorcyclist to anticipate danger or injury, thus admission of testimony was properly denied).

Discretion of court

Exclusion of plaintiff's tabulations of speeds at which motorists crossed railroad tracks at which decedent was fatally injured was within trial court's sound judgment where decedent was under duty to yield to the train and plaintiff sought to introduce the evidence as bearing on railroad's knowledge of speeds at which motorists crossed the tracks. White v. Seaboard Coast Line R. Co., Fla. App.1969, 227 So.2d 227.

Driving on wrong side of road

Wyo.—McVicker v. Kuronen, 256 P.2d 111, 71 Wyo. 222 (testimony that it was custom among truck drivers to permit driver of loaded truck to drive on his wrong side of the road to avoid dangerous spots in road, was properly admitted, not in derogation of right of way statute or to prove that a right of way was established by custom contrary to statutory right of way, but as a circumstance having direct bearing on question of negligence).

Elbow on door

Ga.—Harper v. Williams, 80 S.E.2d 722, 89 Ga.App. 645 (court did not err in admitting testimony that, where three ride in one seat, the one riding on the right customarily rides with his elbow in the window, and custom testified to was not so obviously dangerous as to preclude it from being considered on question of whether plaintiff was negligent).

Position on vehicle

Ala.—City of Birmingham v. Latham, 162 So. 675, 230 Ala. 601 (in suit against city for death of person standing guard over prisoners in moving truck with face to rear and killed when head collided with viaduct having only eight-foot clearance over city street, testimony that it was customary for guard to so stand in proper discharge of his duties held properly admitted).

Practices of bus passengers

Ga.—Co-op Cab Co. v. Preston, 21 S.E.2d 251, 67 Ga.App. 580 (testimony of bus passengers' custom of standing in aisle to reach for garments on upper rack was admissible on question of passenger's alleged negligence).

Mo.—Sullivan v. Kansas City Public Service Co., 231 S.W.2d 822, 241 Mo.App. 56, opinion quashed in part 248 S.W.2d 605, 363 Mo. 68 (testimony that at transfer point passengers habitually passed in front of, behind and between busses was relevant and admissible on question of defendant's negligence and injured passenger's contributory negligence).

Practices of one other person

Ga.—Crafton v. Livingston, 150 S.E.2d 371, 114 Ga.App. 161 (did not err in admitting testimony of witness, who in his employment had for eight years read water meter at which plaintiff was working when automobile backed into him, that in reading the meter he never used any signs or safety measures, over defendant's objection that what safety measures some particular person used was irrelevant and immaterial).

Product manufacturing practice

Tex.—Sharp v. Chrysler Corp., Civ. App.1968, 432 S.W.2d 131, error refused n. r. e. (ordinarily, testimony from qualified witness as to what other manufacturers have done would be admissible in products liability case against manufacturer, not as establishing standard of care, but to be considered along with other evidence to determine whether automobile was defectively designed).

42. Cal.—Mace v. Watanabe, 87 P.2d 893, 31 Cal.App.2d 321 (permitting traffic officer who was familiar with intersection to testify that it was general custom and habit of motorists to travel the roadway along each leg of "Y" rather than to use soft gravel covering portion between the two legs for purpose of showing that there were two intersections).

Defendant's own custom as proof of knowledge of danger

Iowa.—Lindquist v. Des Moines Union Ry. Co., 30 N.W.2d 120, 239 Iowa 356 (testimony of witness that he had repeatedly seen trainmen station a flagman with lighted lantern at the crossing to warn oncoming automobiles, was admissible to show recognition by railroad of a dangerous condition due to obstruction of crossing).

Location of unmarked crosswalk

Tenn.—Lemons v. Memphis Transit Management Co., 1966, 413 S.W.2d 88, 56 Tenn.App. 737 (testimony by mail carrier who had crossed intersection many times in vicinity where pedestrian was struck by bus, tending to locate unmarked crosswalk across unusual intersection as established by public custom and offered for purpose of showing compliance by pedestrian with definition of "unmarked crosswalk" as defined in ordinance and to show that pedestrian had exercised ordinary care in her effort to cross intersection, was competent and its exclusion was prejudicial).

Pedestrians' common usage

Ala.—Cherry v. Hill, 1968, 214 So.2d 427, 283 Ala. 74 (in action by father against motorist to recover for death of child who was struck by automobile while crossing a highway, on ground that motorist knew that pedestrians were accustomed to cross highway at point of accident and should have been driving automobile in more prudent manner, sustaining of motorist's objection to question asked of disinterested witness if place of accident had been used as a

§ 424.2   TRIAL EVIDENCE   Ch. 424

However, before evidence of conduct may be introduced as "custom", the evidence must show that the acts extended over some period of time and were not just isolated acts.[43]

pedestrian crossing by people in the community was prejudicial error).

Fla.—Lambeth v. Kapp, App.1967, 197 So.2d 313 (in absence of showing whether street on which pedestrian was attempting to cross at point between intersections when she was struck by automobile being backed from a parked position was through street, evidence that it was customary for pedestrians to cross at that point was admissible).

Similarity of happening as relevant to ambulance driver's belief of existence of emergency

Cal.—Gallup v. Sparks-Mundo Engineering Co., 271 P.2d 34, 43 Cal.2d 1 (where question arose whether driver of ambulance reasonably believed that he was responding to an emergency call, so that he was entitled to ignore traffic signals, and wherein there was evidence that restraint straps and three-man crew were in the ambulance when the collision occurred, testimony that restraint straps and three-man crew were taken in an ambulance whenever an emergency was involved was properly admitted).

To show knowledge of party relevant to question of conduct being negligent

Ark.—King v. Cardin, 319 S.W.2d 214, 229 Ark. 929 (in action for wrongful death of highway worker who was killed when he attempted to avoid approaching automobile and stepped into path of dump truck which was being operated by fellow worker, which was carrying hot asphalt used for repairing highways and which was being backed to asphalt spreader while motor of spreader was shut off, evidence that all the crew understood that dump trucks were not to be backed to spreader while its motor was shut off was admissible even though practice was adopted to prevent damage to newly laid asphalt and not adopted as a safety measure).

Cal.—Muir v. Grier, 325 P.2d 664, 160 Cal.App.2d 671 (did not err in admitting testimony to the effect that the average speed at which vehicles travelled on street was 55 miles per hour for the express limited purpose of informing jury as to facts and circumstances existing at time and place of accident and which facts were known to deceased so as to permit jury to pass on question whether deceased conducted herself as an ordinary and reasonable person would have in light of all the circumstances).

43.   **U.S.**—Norfolk Southern Ry. Co. v. Davis Frozen Foods, C.A.N.C., 195 F.2d 662 (placing clearance signs on trestles of underpasses).

Mass.—Liberatore v. Town of Framingham, 53 N.E.2d 561, 315 Mass. 538 (in action against town and truck operator for injuries to laborers employed by Works Progress Administration under contract between WPA and town, question asked of WPA official as to custom in other towns respecting transporting WPA workers was properly excluded, in absence of showing what contract existed between WPA and other towns or how general any custom was).

Practice of defendant only

Wis.—Marolla v. American Family Mut. Ins. Co., 1968, 157 N.W.2d 674, 38 Wis.2d 539 (in action by motorized railroad track car operator against automobile liability

378

Ch. 424 RELEVANCY AND MATERIALITY § **424.2**

Evidence of customs contrary to law has been held inadmissible,[44] nor is evidence of custom which is manifestly negligent

insurer for injuries sustained in crossing collision, proof as to custom of employees of the particular railroad to stop at highway crossings when automobile was approaching would not be admissible, but proof of custom of sustantially all operators of such cars would be admissible).

44. U.S.—Klas v. Yellow Cab Co., C.C.A.Ill., 106 F.2d 935 (although sign on post located on corner of intersection contained words "No left turn," evidence that it was common practice for automobiles to make left turns at the intersection was inadmissible).

Cal.—Beaird v. Bryan, 53 Cal.Rptr. 428, 244 Cal.App.2d 836 (in making left hand turn at intersection); Hom v. Clark, 35 Cal.Rptr. 11, 221 Cal.App.2d 622; Ortega v. Garner, 1963, 32 Cal.Rptr. 632, 218 Cal. App.2d 823 (as to lane of travel on highway by motorcyclists, where controlled by statute); Haerdter v. Johnson, 207 P.2d 855, 92 Cal.App.2d 547 (pedestrian crossing street at place other than crosswalk); Muir v. Cheney Bros., 148 P.2d 138, 64 Cal.App.2d 55 (that most of traffic on highway where defendant's truck was traveling followed the curve to the south and that not more than two or three out of 10 automobiles proceeded across intersection); Hurtel v. Albert Cohn, Inc., 52 P.2d 922, 5 Cal.2d 145 (evidence of local custom of pedestrians of starting across street intersection after ringing of first traffic signal bell and before ringing of second).

Ga.—Etheridge v. Hooper, 121 S.E.2d 323, 104 Ga.App. 227 (evidence that pedestrians, including children, customarily cross street at points other than crosswalks or intersections, in violation of city ordinance); Arnold v. Chupp, 92 S.E.2d 239, 93 Ga.App. 583.

Ind.—Indianapolis Rys. v. Boyd, 53 N.E.2d 762, 222 Ind. 481, rehearing denied 54 N.E.2d 272, 222 Ind. 481; Town of Remington v. Hesler, 41 N.E.2d 657, 112 Ind.App. 34 (parking on the left side of the street).

Kan.—Wood v. Melton, 293 P.2d 252, 179 Kan. 128.

N.Y.—Murphy v. Long Island R. Co., 77 N.Y.S.2d 435, 273 App.Div. 913 (crossing railroad while warning flashing).

Okl.—Smith v. Cox, 301 P.2d 649 (crossing at place other than pedestrian crossing designated).

Or.—Elliott v. Callan, 1970, 466 P.2d 600, 255 Or. 256 (practices of traveling approx. 40 mph. in 20 mph. zone); Frame v. Arrow Towing Service, 64 P.2d 1312, 155 Or. 522 (evidence of custom in conflict with statutory duty of operator of tow car to place signal on roadway warning on-coming traffic of obstruction of highway held not admissible).

Pa.—Allen v. Mack, 28 A.2d 783, 345 Pa. 407.

Tex.—Huey & Philp Hardware Co. v. McNeil, Civ.App., 111 S.W.2d 1205, error dismissed (admission of testimony that point at which pedestrian was attempting to cross was used as crossing when such use was prohibited by ordinance).

Wash.—Mathias v. Eichelberger, 45 P.2d 619, 182 Wash. 185 (city patrolman's testimony that he had driven past one-way signs on such street without seeing them and seen other cars go in wrong direction thereon held inadmissible).

W.Va.—Elswick v. Charleston Transit Co., 36 S.E.2d 419, 128 W.Va. 241.

§ 424.2　　　　　　TRIAL EVIDENCE　　　　　　Ch. 424

admissible, for custom cannot make due care out of negligent conduct.[45]

Custom is not admissible unless the person alleged to have been negligent for failure to comply with the custom is shown to have knowledge of the custom, or at least should have known of it.[46]

Practices expressed in rules of an employer may be relevant.[47]

But see

U.S.—Dugan v. Fry, C.C.A.N.J., 34 F.2d 723 (action for striking bicycle rider).

Pa.—McMillen v. Strathmann, 107 A. 332, 264 Pa. 13.

Contra

Cal.—Fowler v. Key System Transit Lines, 230 P.2d 339, 37 Cal.2d 65 (committed prejudicial error in rejecting evidence relating to custom, whereby bus usually stopped at cross-walk at intersection in question in order that passengers alighting from bus would not have to step into gutter, notwithstanding fact that such evidence would also have tended to establish violation of statute preventing bus from stopping at cross-walks).

Status as "through highway" requires legislation

Court's suppression of evidence of custom and usage for purpose of establishing that highway was through highway at time of collision was not error. Lemke v. Mueller, Iowa 1969, 166 N.W.2d 860.

45. Cal.—Milton v. Los Angeles Motor Coach Co., 128 P.2d 178, 53 Cal.App.2d 566 (in action by commercial photographer struck by bus while standing in street to take a picture, evidence of custom to place camera in street to take picture is inadmissible).

Utah.—Caperon v. Tuttle, 116 P.2d 402, 100 Utah 476, 135 A.L.R. 1399 (where automobile struck defendant's sheep on highway, evidence of defendant that it had been his custom to graze sheep on side of highway for several years and that this was the first accident is inadmissible).

46. Conn.—Eamiello v. Piscitelli, 51 A.2d 912, 133 Conn. 360 (testimony that place where pedestrian was walking when struck was commonly used by pedestrians is inadmissible, in absence of showing that motorist knew or was chargeable with knowledge).

Ga.—Taylor v. Crawford, 1969, 167 S.E.2d 404, 119 Ga.App. 262 (as to alleged custom of pedestrians to cross street at point other than crosswalk).

Ind.—Indianapolis Rys. v. Boyd, 53 N.E.2d 762, 222 Ind. 481, rehearing denied 54 N.E.2d 272, 222 Ind. 481 (evidence of custom to give street cars making left hand turn right of way is inadmissible, in absence of showing that motorist had notice of alleged custom).

Md.—Stafford v. Zake, 20 A.2d 144, 179 Md. 460 (that children played in the alley at all times was "relevant" to the issue of knowledge of conditions by driver who used the alley frequently).

N.H.—Desautelle v. Fletcher, 167 A. 2d 685, 103 N.H. 177 (whether he had ever seen pedestrian struck by automobile walk in that direction before).

47. Dist.Col.—Garrison v. D. C. Transit System, Inc., Mun.App., 196 A.2d 924 (error in exclusion of company rule held not prejudicial).

380

§ 424.2

Results of experiments

Evidence of the results of experiments, made for the purpose of verifying or disproving particular theories as to how the accident occurred, may be admissible, if the conditions under which the experiments were conducted correspond substantially to those surrounding the accident.[48] Evidence of experiments

---

Fla.—Fowler v. City of Gainesville, 1968, 213 So.2d 38 (training manual).

Safety manual written by individual defendant

Safety manual, which was written by defendant prior to time he acted as supervisor of salvage operation on overturned truck in vicinity of collision wherein plaintiff was injured, was properly excluded, notwithstanding that it was offered to show that defendant had superior knowledge and judgment and that he was personally aware that motorists sometimes make mistakes or act recklessly or absentmindedly, where it might have created doubts in minds of jury as to which standard of care was applicable to defendant, and plaintiff was permitted a wide latitude in proving defendant's expertise in highway safety, including his familiarity with truck safety literature, and his responsibility in connection with safety operations for a large fleet of trucks, and with accident salvage operations and investigations. Jones v. Mitchell Bros. Truck Lines, 1973, 511 P.2d 347, 266 Or. 513, rehearing denied 514 P.2d 350, 266 Or. 513.

48. U.S.—Weaver v. Ford Motor Co., D.C.Pa.1974, 382 F.Supp. 1068 (in products liability suit against manufacturer, exclusion of evidence, which pertained to experiment conducted on another van and which was offered to disprove plaintiffs' allegations as to cause of accident, was not abuse of discretion, in view of determination that conditions of experiment were not substantially similar to conditions at time of accident and in light of fact that pretrial order did not refer to any experiment and that results of tests and photos were not made available to plaintiff before day in which trial commenced); Glick v. White Motor Co., C.A.Pa.1971, 458 F.2d 1287 (where tests were not conducted in same manner as testimony showed accident happened, allegedly defective part on vehicle involved in test was not same as similar part on test vehicle, test vehicle had 51,000 miles on it and was convertible while vehicle involved in collision had 8,000 miles and was sports coupe, test car had new part placed on it which was necessary part of steering system, and track used for test was made of concrete construction whereas area where accident occurred was of blacktop construction, trial court did not abuse its discretion in refusing to admit tests); Ramseyer v. General Motors Corp., C.A.Neb. 1969, 417 F.2d 859 (where there was substantial similarity between plaintiff owner's automobile's gear, softness of which was alleged by owner to have precipitated mechanical failure of steering assembly and accident, and kinds of gears tested by manufacturer's expert witness as to hardness of gears and, generally, in wear factors applied in experiments as compared to normal driving wear in light of automobile, and trial court instructed that gears should be considered in connection with testimony describing experiment, admission of results of test experiments was not abuse of discretion); Giffin v. Ensign, C.A. Pa., 234 F.2d 307 (demonstration, which involved axle assembly not

§ 424.2   TRIAL EVIDENCE   Ch. 424

made by supplier, was incompetent and properly disallowed in absence of showing that the assembly had same spacing as assembly made by supplier for the truck); Navajo Freight Lines v. Mahaffy, C.A.N.M., 174 F.2d 305 (similarity not shown).

Cal.—Poggetto v. Owen, 9 Cal.Rptr. 395, 187 Cal.App.2d 128 (where there were conflicting claims as to whether policeman had his red warning lights on, court did not err in permitting witness for defendant to conduct an experiment to show that if the red light was on and bulb was broken in collision, tungsten oxide would have formed on the filament); Zollars v. Barber, 295 P.2d 561, 140 Cal. App.2d 502 (experiments which defendant made day after accident and which tended to prove that defendant could not, under circumstances, have struck pedestrian); Chambers v. Silver, 230 P.2d 146, 103 Cal.App.2d 633 (where auto had veered onto wrong side of road and sole defense was that main leaf in spring at front wheel had broken when wheel crossed two-inch deposit of soil on road and vehicle had thereby been rendered impossible to control, and mechanic testified for defendant that it was physically impossible to drive automobile with this type suspension in such condition, it was prejudicial error to refuse plaintiffs' rebuttal evidence as to an experiment in which automobile with same suspension system was driven without loss of control over 2 x 4 boards at a speed of 45 to 50 miles per hour).

Colo.—Kling v. City and County of Denver, 1959, 335 P.2d 876, 138 Colo. 567 (trial runs three or four days later, in auto other than one involved, at faster and slower speeds).

Kan.—Torgeson v. Missouri-Kansas-Texas R. Co., 262 P. 564, 124 Kan. 798, 55 A.L.R. 1335 (tests made to show safest way to traverse railroad crossing).

La.—Shaw v. New Orleans Public Service, App., 188 So. 187 (in passenger's action against bus company for injuries allegedly received when caught between automatic doors while departing from bus, experiments in presence of jury with a bus similar to those used on line on which plaintiff claimed to have been injured).

Mont.—McGuire v. Nelson, 1973, 508 P.2d 558, 162 Mont. 37, appeal after remand 536 P.2d 768 (where no similarity of conditions was shown between amount of force applied by clamp in furniture clamp demonstration and pressure actually exerted by two persons riding a motorcycle and there was no showing that clamp pressure was not significantly greater than pressure of two riders, demonstration should not have been admitted).

N.M.—Alford v. Drum, 361 P.2d 451, 68 N.M. 298 (experiments to determine speed of automobile).

N.D.—Larson v. Meyer, 135 N.W.2d 145, citing 32 C.J.S. Evidence § 587 (trial court did not abuse discretion in wrongful death action in denying admission of evidence respecting an experiment in which tractor pulled milk truck on hard surfaced street where fatal accident occurred, as tractor was pulling milk truck on soft ground in farmyard).

Ohio.—Streit v. Kestel, 161 N.E.2d 409, 108 Ohio App. 241 (motion pictures of experimental turns at same intersection).

Okl.—Drake v. Tims, 287 P.2d 215 (test of siren inadmissible).

Tex.—Sanchez v. Billings, Civ.App. 1972, 481 S.W.2d 911, error refused n. r. e. (turning experiments at intersection); Pittman v. Baladez, 312 S.W.2d 210, 158 Tex. 372 (testimony of constable that he had observed 15 or 20 similar trucks as they came around curve and approached scene and that most of them crossed center line of highway was inadmissible, where tests were not made under circumstances substantially the same).

Utah.—Coon v. Utah Const. Co., 1951, 228 P.2d 997, 119 Utah 446 (test of vibrations from operation of heavy trucks).

Wash.—Bichl v. Poinier, 1967, 429 P.2d 228, 71 Wash.2d 492 (test to show brake hose could quickly develop hole); Truva v. Goodyear Tire & Rubber Co., 1923, 214 P. 818, 124 Wash. 445.

Availability of subject tire required

In action arising out of alleged blowout of tire recapped by one defendant and sold and installed by another, court properly excluded evidence as to experiment by witness who pushed his pencil through tire sidewall four days after accident, in view of fact that tire was not available at trial and could not be located. Johnson v. Newell, 1970, 278 A.2d 776, 260 Conn. 269.

Coefficient of friction experiment

Ark.—St. Louis Southwestern Ry. Co. v. Jackson, 1967, 416 S.W.2d 273, 242 Ark. 858, appeal after remand 438 S.W.2d 41, 246 Ark. 268.

Conditions need not be identical

U.S.—Ramseyer v. General Motors Corp., C.A.Neb.1969, 417 F.2d 859.

Cal.—Ortega v. Pacific Greyhound Lines, 67 P.2d 702, 20 Cal.App.2d 596 (conditions surrounding test or experiment, such as an experiment to determine visibility of reflector at night).

La.—Leathem v. Moore, App.1972, 265 So.2d 270 (tests conducted by plaintiff's expert to determine effect the presence or absence of dust shields on brakes had on braking efficiency under conditions involving saturation of brake mechanism with water, mud and muck, was admissible, even though tests had been conducted on a dry surface).

Tex.—Hullum v. St. Louis Southwestern Ry. Co., Civ.App., 384 S.W.2d 163; Standard Motor Co. v. Blood, Civ.App., 380 S.W.2d 651 (where the dissimilarity is minor or is made abundantly clear by explanation, admissibility of evidence of experiment is discretionary); Fort Worth & D. Ry. Co. v. Williams, 375 S.W.2d 279 (as to simulation of curtain of light from locomotive).

Definition of "substantially similar"

Conditions under which experiments are made are not substantially similar to those out of which disputed fact arose if the conditions under which experiments are made vary to such a degree that results of the experiments will be altered. Holling v. Chandler, 50 Cal.Rptr. 219, 241 Cal.App.2d 19.

Limitation when proof by motion picture

In action against manufacturer based on alleged defect in steering system of automobile which left road, admission of motion pictures of experiment allegedly confirming contention of defendant's expert that automobile was still steerable despite alleged defect was reversible error where, inter alia, it appeared plaintiffs had no knowledge of experiments and films despite order requiring defendants to submit to plaintiffs copies of their expert's reports, though defendant contended, inter alia, that movies were not "reports" covered by the pre-trial order and that defendants were not aware before trial of the precise theory upon which plaintiffs were proceeding. Balian v. General Motors, 1972, 296 A.2d 317, 121 N.J.Super. 118. Cross-examination alone will not ordinarily provide a sufficient avenue of rebuttal with respect to motion picture evidence; rather, fundamental fair-

§ 424.2   TRIAL EVIDENCE   Ch. 424

to demonstrate lines of sight and visibility,[49] and experiments in stopping an automobile [50] have been held admissible; but evi-

ness dictates that party proposing to introduce into evidence motion pictures of a reconstructed event or a posed demonstration give notice thereof and opportunity to his adversary to monitor the experiment and the taking of the film. Id.

Admission of moving pictures taken of experiment conducted by defendants was prejudicial, where pictures were taken at different time of day than when accident occurred and they were taken at stationary positions instead of from moving vehicle so that they did not reflect fair representation of what plaintiff driver may, or may not, have observed as he approached intersection. Gray v. Pistoresi, 390 P.2d 697, 64 Wash.2d 106.

Objections as to dissimilarity waived

In prosecution for manslaughter and for drunken driving, wherein deputy district attorney submitted to experiment to determine effect of bathing skin with alcoholic solution and covering needle with alcohol-filled cotton on withdrawing blood to determine its alcoholic content, defendant's general objection that insufficient foundation was laid for evidence of results of the experiment was insufficient to preserve an objection that size of needle and strength of solution might be different than those used on defendant, and such specific objections were thereby waived. People v. Modell, 300 P.2d 204, 143 Cal.App.2d 724.

Tire inflation

Ill.—Schofield v. Crandall, Inc., 1974, 319 N.E.2d 585, 24 Ill.App.3d 101 (in action by service station owner against tire manufacturer for injuries sustained when tire he was inflating blew off changer, allowing jury to watch film of experiment by tire manufacturer in which same tire on similar rim was inflated to 45 pounds without leaving rim was not abuse of discretion, in that variables of temperature, amount of lubrication, and speed of inflation, alleged to be different, were within control of service station owner, and did not operate against probative value of experiment as to issue of whether tire was so defective it could not sustain normal inflation without leaving rim).

Mich.—Thorp v. Dayton Tire & Rubber Co., 1974, 215 N.W.2d 600, 51 Mich.App. 514 (in action arising out of tire explosion occurring when tire bead wire broke and blew over rim as plaintiff was inflating tubeless snow tire after inserting inner tube, testimony as to test performed on tires, which had been selected at random, had not been manufactured or sold by defendants and had had bead bundles similar to bundle on exploding tire, was admissible though test beads were broken by mechanical force, to show that wires would break only when subjected to extremely high pressure when inflated, or inflated when bead was in improper position or when tube was pinched).

49. **U.S.**—Gregory v. Hardgrove, C.A.Vt.1969, 419 F.2d 589 (not fatal road had been widened, as to visibility over hill ahead).

Ala.—Atlantic Coast Line R. Co. v. Jackson, 144 So. 813, 225 Ala. 652 (admitting evidence of demonstration, on question of point at which vision of engineer to scene of accident became unobstructed by reason of curve in cut, held not reversible error notwithstanding embankment had been lowered somewhat).

Cal.—Ortega v. Pacific Greyhound Lines, 67 P.2d 702, 20 Cal.App.2d 596 (visibility of red reflex mirrors on a bicycle).

50. See footnote 50 on page 387.

Ga.—Patton v. Smith, 1969, 168 S.E. 2d 627, 119 Ga.App. 664 (testimony of witness for the plaintiff as to his ability to see, at night, at distance of 260 feet and 180 feet, a man on the street at the scene of a fatal collision on which plaintiff's suit was based).

Iowa.—Galbraith v. George, 1974, 217 N.W.2d 598 (even though subsequent to collision involving westbound milk truck and northbound automobile, but before experts observed intersection and prior to taking of photographs, the east approach to the intersection was regraded and raised approximately four feet, stop signs were erected inhibiting east and west traffic, and vegetation along roadways had undergone feasible changes, admission of expert's testimony relating to experiments and observations made at intersection and of photographs of the intersection did not constitute an abuse of discretion, where all changes in the intersection and the effect of those changes on expert's experiments were pointed out).

Md.—Beckner v. Chalkley, 1973, 310 A.2d 569, 19 Md.App. 239 (observations made by expert witness in order to determine when northbound and eastbound motorists first had ability to see each other prior to collision constituted an "experiment").

Miss.—Elliott v. Massey, 134 So.2d 478, 242 Miss. 159 (receipt of testimony of police officer that a short while before trial, approximately two and one-half years after an intersectional accident, he had gone to the scene and made experiments to see how far an automobile moving in a certain direction on one of the streets could be seen as it approached the intersection, was discretionary, even though there was testimony that some of the trees near the intersection had been trimmed about a month before the trial, where such testimony was considered in connection with pictures fairly representing appearance of the intersection on day of the accident).

Mo.—Hall v. Hannibal-Quincy Truck Line, Sup., 211 S.W.2d 723 (how far lights of an automobile would reveal object on highway); Balman v. H. A. Lueking Teaming Co., 219 S.W. 603, 281 Mo. 342 (test of visibility of sign painted on truck).

Mont.—Hurly v. Star Transfer Co., 376 P.2d 504, 141 Mont. 176 (in action for death of motorist killed when his vehicle struck the rear end of defendant's tractor-trailer which, because of a backing maneuver negotiated by truck driver, extended partly into motorist's lane, it was not error to admit evidence of an experiment conducted several hours later by police determining that a motorist in decedent's position would have to come to within approximately 50 feet of trailer before seeing its lights).

N.Y.—Thomas v. Central Greyhound Lines, Inc., 180 N.Y.S.2d 461, 6 A.D.2d 649 (it was improper to exclude testimony of an experiment conducted with bus involved establishing incapacity on part of a passenger in the bus by reason of physical circumstances to see a line 6 to 12 inches from and parallel with left side of the bus, in view of fact that passenger testified that shortly before the accident he observed the center line of the highway 6 to 12 inches left of the left side of the bus, but that he lost sight of the center line immediately prior to the collision, since evidence as to experiment under the circumstances was relevant on bus company and its driver's theory that approaching truck entered the lane in which bus was traveling).

S.C.—Hankins v. Foye, 1974, 210 S.E. 2d 305, 263 S.C. 310 (simply to show that an automobile would disappear from view of left-turning motorist in a depression within 300 feet of the intersection, without

§ 424.2 TRIAL EVIDENCE Ch. 424

showing at what point it would reappear into view, would be of doubtful aid to jury in deciding whether left-turning motorist should have seen oncoming vehicle when she started to make the turn, so that testimony to the effect that the oncoming vehicle would disappear was of little, if any, relevancy).

Tex.—Kirk v. Bennett, Civ.App.1970, 456 S.W.2d 191, error refused n. r. e. (where experiment was conducted at scene, using same road and same hill as involved in accident, and defendant placed her automobile in substantially same position over crest of hill where plaintiffs' automobile was located prior to the collision and walked down to level where her automobile would be, thereby giving her same view of hill as immediately before accident, evidence of experiment was admissible to show limited visibility).

Va.—Doss v. Martin, 136 S.E.2d 854, 205 Va. 306 (results of visibility test made by parking an automobile in approximate position of plaintiff's automobile, turning its tail lights on, and then driving another automobile toward the parked automobile).

Contra

Ala.—Helton v. Easter, 148 So.2d 486, 41 Ala. 648 (refusal to allow a witness to testify as to whether or not a person could see over hill which plaintiff was ascending just before he collided with defendant's left-turning automobile was proper where predicate for such testimony based on an experiment had not been laid); Robinson v. Morrison, 1961, 133 So.2d 230, 272 Ala. 552 (proper to exclude test of visibility of mailboxes where different vantage point, time of day, and weather conditions).

Iowa—Cunningham v. Court, 82 N. W.2d 292, 248 Iowa 654 (where visibility was unobstructed for 500 feet westward from intersection at which defendant's following automobile collided with plaintiff's automobile which was making left turn and each motorist was in view of the other a sufficient time prior to collision, refusal of trial court to admit testimony concerning an experiment and observation made by witness as to depressions and rises in the highway west of intersection was not an abuse of discretion).

Mich.—Taylor v. Murphy, 149 N.W. 2d 210, 6 Mich.App. 398 (refusal to allow test of defendant motorist's view through rear window of his automobile was not error where plaintiff wanted to make test in the afternoon, although accident had occurred at 1:00 a. m. on rainy, misty night).

Mont.—Bernhard v. Lincoln County, 1968, 437 P.2d 377, 150 Mont. 557 (as to lighting conditions at scene).

S.C.—Peagler v. Atlantic Coast Line R. Co., 107 S.E.2d 15, 234 S.C. 140, 84 A.L.R.2d 794 (in action for injuries sustained when motorist collided with an empty black pulpwood flatcar blocking a railroad crossing at night, refusing to admit photograph taken in the nighttime of an experiment conducted at the crossing to show conditions of visibility and the appearance of objects at the crossing at the time of accident, was not error).

Va.—Habers v. Madigan, 1973, 193 S.E.2d 653, 213 Va. 485 (in action arising out of collision with rear of defendant's truck at night, wherein issue was visibility of truck taillight, experiment at scene a year later in which taillight was placed on road on child's highchair, covered with disk with aperture approximately same size as clean portion of taillight at time of accident, and connected to 12-volt battery, was inadmissible on account of difference in circumstances, since power source and background were different, light

Ch. 424   RELEVANCY AND MATERIALITY   § 424.2

and viewer were stationary, and viewer knew of light, and admission of evidence was prejudicial).

50. U.S.—Chicago & N. W. Ry. Co. v. Golay, C.A.Wyo.1946, 155 F.2d 842.

Ga.—McBrayer v. Ballenger, 1956, 95 S.E.2d 718, 94 Ga.App. 620 (same make and model auto, on same stretch of road, comparable weather).

Idaho—Hansen v. Howard O. Miller, Inc., 1969, 460 P.2d 739, 93 Idaho 314 (not abuse of discretion, though automobile employed in experiment differed in make, year, weight, and tire size from vehicle involved).

Iowa—Althof v. Benson, 147 N.W.2d 875, 259 Iowa 1254 (admission of testimony of a police officer that after his investigation of an accident he made an experimental stop with his vehicle at the same intersection was not an abuse of discretion, and in view of testimony that defendant's vehicle was a 1951 Chevrolet and the police vehicle a 1963 Ford, and that both vehicles were equipped with snow tires, a sufficient foundation was laid to support admission of such experimental evidence).

Mo.—Faught v. Washam, 329 S.W. 2d 588 (though made on dry concrete pavement, which was not littered with debris as was scene of collision, and though experiments were made in daytime rather than in nighttime when collision occurred, and though witnesses knew that they were to be called on to make emergency stop).

Neb.—State ex rel. Finigan v. Norfolk Line Stock Sales Co., 128 N. W.2d 130, 177 Neb. 31 (permitting jury to view motion pictures of certain experimental tests in braking automobile similar to that involved was not abuse of discretion in view of minor differences in conditions at time of accident and tests and differences were easily explained).

N.H.—Hanson v. N. H. Pre-Mix Concrete, Inc., 1970, 268 A.2d 841, 110 N.H. 377 (cement mixer of same model).

S.C.—Weaks v. South Carolina Highway Dept., 159 S.E.2d 234, 250 S.C. 535 (evidence of braking and reaction time shown by experiment in which conditions were substantially similar to those existing at time automobile collided with highway maintenance truck was properly excluded, in action by motorist against highway department, on ground that motorist did not have knowledge of obstruction in the highway which patrolman possessed in driving automobile during experiment, that he had been subjected to a sudden emergency to which patrolman had not been subjected, and had been required to react to additional factor of approaching vehicle not present in experiment).

Va.—Saunders v. Bulluck, 159 S.E.2d 820, 208 Va. 551.

Wash.—Truva v. Goodyear Tire & Rubber Co., 1923, 214 P. 818, 124 Wash. 445.

Contra

Idaho—Jones v. Talbot, 394 P.2d 316, 87 Idaho 498 (exclusion of rebuttal evidence of skid mark test made with motorcycle of plaintiff's kind and of test as to defendant driver's automobile did not constitute abuse of discretion where at scene the automobile had left no skid marks, those of the motorcycle had been interrupted by the collision and there was no testimony as to how the measurements had been taken).

Ill.—Jenkins v. Hechtman, 1967, 226 N.E.2d 383, 83 Ill.App.2d 72 (conducted by officer, showing brakes in good condition).

N.D.—Armstrong v. Miller, N.D.1971, 189 N.W.2d 688 (refusal not an

§ 424.2

dence of the results of tests made with reference to the noise made by trains approaching a crossing has been held inadmissible.[51]

The admission of evidence of the result of a test or experiment is largely discretionary with the trial court, and the test or experiment is merely a circumstance to be considered in connection with other evidence.[52]

abuse of discretion where defendant, in attempting to lay a foundation for introduction of results of braking and stopping test with truck which was similar to truck he was driving at time of accident, did not show whether milk tank at time of test was loaded or empty, did not show whether tires were old or new or whether they were inflated to approximately the same pressure as that of tires of truck at time of the accident, and where defendant did not attempt to show that highway on which test was conducted was of the same smoothness as was the surface of highway where the accident occurred).

Wis.—Keplin v. Hardware Mut. Cas. Co., 129 N.W.2d 321, 24 Wis.2d 319, rehearing denied 130 N.W.2d 3, 24 Wis.2d 319 (tests performed by expert assertedly relating to physical facts of accident and particularly to braking ability and stopping distance were not admissible where automobile he used was different from that driven by party and tires, braking apparatus and its working conditions were not testified to as being similar).

Not stopping distance chart
Chart of stopping distances does not qualify as an "experiment" as that term is ordinarily understood in law of evidence. Hughes v. Vestal, 142 S.E.2d 361, 264 N.C. 500.

51. Mo.—Bretall v. Missouri Pac. R. Co., App., 239 S.W. 597.

N.M.—Dahl v. Turner, 1969, 458 P.2d 816, 80 N.M. 564, 39 A.L.R.3d 207, certiorari denied 458 P.2d 860, 80 N.M. 564.

52. Cal.—Ortega v. Pacific Greyhound Lines, 1937, 67 P.2d 702, 20 Cal.App.2d 596.

Idaho—Stuchbery v. Harper, 1964, 390 P.2d 303, 87 Idaho 12.

Mich.—Pohlod v. General Motors Corp., 1972, 199 N.W.2d 277, 40 Mich.App. 583.

Mo.—Wilcox v. St. Louis-Southwestern R. Co., 1967, 418 S.W.2d 15 (where test railroad engine and accident engine were shown to be same model and type of locomotive and were purchased at about same time, and where evidence was presented from which it reasonably could have been found that engines were in substantially the same condition, trial court did not abuse its discretion in admitting into evidence results of experiments with test engine); Calvert v. Super Propane Corp., 400 S.W.2d 133 (although conditions of test were shown to be substantially the same as those existing at time of head-on, automobile-truck collision on icy county road, court's refusal to admit evidence of a re-enactment, ostensibly for timing purposes, of movements of person who was in nearby house at time of accident was not an abuse of discretion, in view of testimony of such person that she made six or seven steps and that six or seven seconds elapsed from time she saw truck in road until she heard crash).

N.D.—Larson v. Meyer, 1968, 161 N.W.2d 165 (that experiment was

The test or experiments must not be too remote with respect to time.[53]

Testimony based on experiments made after an accident should not be excluded on the ground that photographs are in evidence tending to show the same matters.[54]

Even in absence of proof that the experiment was conducted under conditions similar to those surrounding the accident, and therefore not admissible as substantive evidence, the results of the experiment may be admissible for other purposes. Thus, evidence of the conduct of the defendant during a demonstration of how the driver had driven at the time of the accident may be admissible as an "admission against interest", to impeach the testimony of the driver given at the trial which was inconsistent with that driver's conduct during the demonstration.[55]

conducted at same time of year, but 4 years later, approximately 60 miles from scene and that there were minor variations in soil conditions, truck and its weight, the tractor, tires, slope of ground and method of hooking chain to truck and tractor from those which existed at the time a farm tractor, being used in an attempt to pull a milk truck up an incline, tipped over backwards did not affect the admissibility of, but only the weight to be attached to, results of the experiment).

Tex.—Kirk v. Bennett, Civ.App.1970, 456 S.W.2d 191, error refused n. r. e. (discretionary whenever dissimilarity between occurrence conditions and circumstances of experiment is minor, or can be made abundantly clear by explanation).

Wash.—Breimon v. General Motors Corp., 1973, 509 P.2d 398, 8 Wash. App. 747 (sufficient similarity in conditions to justify allowance of a demonstration by an expert witness concerning experiments conducted with respect to a steering column on an automobile similar to that being driven by plaintiff at time of accident).

Performance of safety belt

Refusal, in action alleging defect in safety belt, to allow proof of results of simulated reenactment of accident was not abuse of discretion. Price v. Buckingham Mfg. Co., 1970, 266 A.2d 140, 110 N.J.Super. 462.

53. Cal.—Schauf v. Southern California Edison Co., 52 Cal.Rptr. 518, 243 Cal.App.2d 436 (refusal to allow father of plaintiff, injured in collision after plaintiff drove through stop sign, allegedly obscured by power pole, to testify as to how stop sign and power pole appeared to him was not error where such testimony was based on experiment one week after accident).

La.—Elder v. Travelers Indem. Co., App., 125 So.2d 694 (tests of a particular driver's reaction time and the condition of the brakes of his vehicle were made more than six months after the collision in question).

Wash.—Washington v. City of Seattle, 16 P.2d 597, 170 Wash. 371, 86 A.L.R. 113 (excluding experiments disclosing speed of bus on entering same street intersection 15 months after accident held not abuse of discretion).

54. N.Y.—Havecker v. Weiss, 261 N.Y.S. 494, 237 App.Div. 856, resettled 262 N.Y.S. 907.

55. Conn.—Cashman v. Terminal Taxi Co., 37 A.2d 613, 131 Conn. 31.

§ 424.2   TRIAL EVIDENCE   Ch. 424

Subsequent precautions taken [56]

Where the known changes in conditions or practices constitute precautions taken by the other party, the evidence of such change is not admissible as evidence of negligence in maintenance of the prior condition or practice.[57]

Re issue accident unavoidable

Tex.—Keith v. Silver, Civ.App.1971, 476 S.W.2d 335, ref. n. r. e.

[56]. For treatment of such evidence as privileged matter, see discussion in Chapter 423, Privileged Evidence, § 423.1 at fn. 5.

[57]. **U.S.**—Federal Rules of Evidence § 407, 28 U.S.C.A.; Russell v. Page Aircraft Maintenance, Inc., C.A.Ala.1972, 455 F.2d 188 (in action against contractor for injuries received when army-owned ground vehicle driven by contractor's employee struck civilian employee at night when vehicle was unlighted, contractor's later safety bulletins forbidding vehicles to be operated without lights did not rebut position that Army had prohibited use of lights on vehicle at time of accident and bulletins were not admissible on issue of whether contractor had had authority to operate the army vehicle with lights at time of accident); Esposito v. Emery, 1967, D.C.Pa., 266 F.Supp. 219, affirmed C.A., 402 F.2d 878.

Ariz.—Fitzgerald v. Maricopa County, 1971, 480 P.2d 385, 14 Ariz.App. 48 (when automobile went through "T" intersection and plunged into canal bank as alleged result of failure of county to place any warning signs at intersection, rejection of plaintiff's offered evidence to show specific number of signs were erected in area subsequent to accident was not error).

Ark.—Livingston v. Fuel, 1968, 433 S.W.2d 380, 245 Ark. 618 (erred in permitting testimony as to repairs to pasture fence after accident for purpose of showing that fence holding horse was inadequate).

Cal.—West's Ann.Calif.Evid.Code § 1151.

Fla.—Florida Evidence Code § 90.407.

Ga.—Georgia Southern & F. R. Co. v. Cartledge, 42 S.E. 405, 116 Ga. 164, 59 L.R.A. 118.

Ill.—Howe v. Medaris, 55 N.E. 724, 183 Ill. 288.

Kan.—Kansas Code of Civil Procedure § 60–451.

Ky.—Cox v. City of Louisville, 1969, 439 S.W.2d 51 (exclusion of that part of deposition which pertained to photographs showing alterations and repairs made to intersection after accident was proper); Herrin's Adm'x v. Jackson, 1954, 265 S.W.2d 775; City of Catlettsburg v. Sutherland's Adm'r, 1933, 57 S.W.2d 512, 247 Ky. 540 (city repaired holes in street).

La.—McDaniel v. Welsh, 1970, 234 So.2d 833, writ refused 237 So.2d 397, 256 La. 616 (showing that traffic signal was repaired on morning following accident was not admissible in action against parish arising from intersectional collision allegedly occasioned by malfunctioning of the signal, but no prejudicial error resulted from its admission, where other evidence was sufficient).

Mass.—National Laundry Co. v. City of Newton, 14 N.E.2d 108, 300 Mass. 126 (sanding slippery avenue).

Minn.—Lally v. Crookston Lumber Co., 1957, 85 N.W. 157, 82 Minn. 407; Hammargren v. St. Paul, 1896, 69 N.W. 470, 67 Minn. 6; Morse v. Minneapolis & St. L. Ry. Co., 1883, 16 N.W. 358, 30 Minn. 465.

Mo.—Frechin v. Thornton, 326 S.W. 2d 122 (dictum).

Neb.—Nebraska Rules of Evidence § 407.

Nev.—N.R.S. 48.095(1).

N.H.—Ware v. Boston & M. R. R., 1943, 31 A.2d 58, 92 N.H. 373.

N.J.—New Jersey Evidence Rule 51.

N.M.—New Mexico Rules of Evidence § 407.

N.Y.—Weiner v. Serps Auto Wreckers, Inc., 1969, 300 N.Y.S.2d 852, 24 N.Y.2d 845, 248 N.E.2d 601 (in action against city by infant for injuries sustained when towed automobile broke away from towing automobile because of alleged defect in street and struck infant, proof of repairs of street by city after accident at site of purported defect referred to in court testimony was inadmissible and did not become so on basis of photograph offered by city of part of the street specified in the notice of claim); Howell v. Dearling, 85 N.Y.S.2d 620, 274 App.Div. 1069 (defendant had changed windshield).

N.C.—Bailey v. North Carolina R. Co., 25 S.E.2d 833, 223 N.C. 244; Farrall v. Universal Garage Co., 102 S.E. 617, 179 N.C. 389.

Okl.—City of Muskogee v. Magee, 57 P.2d 252, 177 Okl. 39 (in action against city for injuries to street sweeper riding on footboard of city truck, who was thrown therefrom when door came open after he grabbed for handle, evidence that handhold was placed on top of cab after injury).

Pa.—Elias v. Lancaster City, 1902, 53 A. 507, 203 Pa. 638; Baron v. Reading Iron Co., 1902; 51 A. 979, 202 Pa. 274.

Tex.—Bowman v. Texas & N. O. R. Co., Civ.App.1953, 254 S.W.2d 167, writ of error refused n. r. e.

Utah.—Utah Rules of Evidence § 51.

Wis.—Wisconsin Rules of Evidence § 904.07.

But see

In action against city, testimony of a traffic signal mechanic regarding when city received notice of malfunction and when it was repaired was relevant to issue as to whether city had notice of defect and timely corrected it and admission of testimony was not error, where malfunction was admitted by city, thereby removing any danger that jury would infer negligence from fact of repair. Thorpe v. City and County of Denver, 1971, 494 P.2d 129, 30 Colo. App. 284.

Admission of evidence of subsequent repairs to roadway in passenger's suit against state for injuries suffered when automobile in which she was riding left a state highway due to slippery condition of roadway was not error, notwithstanding that question of feasibility or practicality of repair allegedly had not been raised by state. Meabon v. State, 1970, 463 P.2d 789, 1 Wash. App. 824.

Contra as to proof of defect in strict liability case

Statute providing that when, after occurrence of an event, remedial measures are taken which, if taken previously, would have tended to make event less likely to occur, evidence of such subsequent measures is inadmissible to prove negligence or culpable conduct in connection with the event, was not intended to apply to cases in which a manufacturer is alleged to be strictly liable for placing a defective product on the market, so that, in action by passenger against motor vehicle manufacturer for injuries sustained in 1964 when vehicle abruptly left road because of alleged failure of aluminum steering gearbox, evidence that manufacturer began utilizing malleable iron instead of aluminum in its gearboxes in 1967 was admissible. Ault v. International Harvester Co., 1974, 528 P.2d 1148, 117 Cal.Rptr. 812.

§ 424.2 TRIAL EVIDENCE Ch. 424

Following the general rule, evidence that, after an accident allegedly caused by the negligent operation of an automobile by a servant of the owner, the owner discharged the driver,[58] or that, after an accident, the defendant drove differently and in a safer manner,[59] is inadmissible to show previous negligence.

In an action for injuries caused by a collision between a train and an automobile, evidence of subsequent changes in defendant's signals and warnings is inadmissible to prove negligence.[60]

Evidence as to what persons other than the parties to the action did after the accident to prevent a reoccurrence is also inadmissible.[61]

Evidence of the repairs or alterations made after an accident is admissible for some purposes, if offered and received for the proper limited purpose.[62]

Contra by rule

Me.—Maine Rules of Evidence § 407.

Including request to vehicle owner to alter, prior to accident

Cal.—Burch v. Levy Bros. Box Co., 1941, 117 P.2d 435, 47 Cal.App.2d 104 (where backed against pedestrian, inquiry about adding rear view mirror and driver's request for same prior to accident).

58. Ala.—Coleman v. Hamilton Storage Co., 180 So. 553, 235 Ala. 553.

Cal.—Webster v. Orr, 163 P. 361, 174 Cal.Sup. 426.

N.Y.—New York Polyclinic Medical School and Hospital v. Mason-Seaman Transp. Co., Sup., 155 N. Y.S. 200.

Pa.—Buchanan v. Flinn, 51 Pa.Super. 145.

59. Vt.—Desmarchier v. Frost, 99 A. 782, 91 Vt. 138.

60. **Cited by the court** in Leuck v. Goetz, 1972, 280 N.E.2d 847, 853, 151 Ind.App. 528.

Ill.—Grubb v. Illinois Terminal Co., 8 N.E.2d 934, 366 Ill. 330, reversing 3 N.E.2d 948, 286 Ill.App. 499 (testimony that original flash signal was replaced after accident by another).

N.C.—Atlantic Coast Line R. Co. v. McLean Trucking Co., 78 S.E.2d 159, 238 N.C. 422 (subsequent installation of gates at crossing); McMillan v. Atlanta & C. Air Line Ry. Co., 90 S.E. 683, 172 N.C. 853.

61. Md.—Belle Isle Cab Co. v. Trammell, 177 A.2d 404, 227 Md. 438.

Tex.—Dallas Ry. & Terminal Co. v. Orr, Civ.App., 210 S.W.2d 863, affirmed 215 S.W.2d 862.

62. U.S.—Federal Rules of Evidence § 407, 28 U.S.C.A.; Jennings v. U. S., D.C.Md., 207 F.Supp. 143 (evidence that deepening of inadequate drainage ditch for highway, which United States was charged with maintaining, alleviated drainage problem that had caused icy patch on which automobile skidded).

Cal.—People v. Lang Transp. Corporation, 110 P.2d 464, 43 Cal.App. 2d 134 (in action by state for damage to bridge by one of defendant's trucks, defendant was properly permitted to show that long timers were installed as wheel guards on bridge after accident in order to offset inference from plaintiff's previous evidence as to safe use of bridge by defendant's trucks after accident).

Neb.—Nebraska Rules of Evidence § 407.

Nev.—N.R.S. 48.095(2).

N.J.—Ryan v. Port of New York Authority, 1971, 281 A.2d 539, 116 N.J.Super. 211 (that bridge on which accident occurred was closed 50 minutes after the accident was properly admitted in action for damages against Port of New York Authority and others arising out of collision with van-type vehicle on George Washington Bridge, over objection that such closing was a normal reaction on part of those in charge of the bridge taken as result of the accident, where the Authority called no witnesses and offered no testimony to show that the closing was anything other than a closing taken under memorandum of party in charge of the bridge, written nearly one year prior to the accident, setting forth guidelines for determining when certain type vehicles, such as that involved in the accident, should be barred from using the bridge).

N.M.—New Mexico Rules of Evidence § 407.

Pa.—Leghart v. Montour R. Co., 150 A.2d 836, 395 Pa. 469 (in action arising out of a train-automobile collision which occurred when right front wheel of automobile dropped into a hole that was about two and one half feet beyond rails and automobile was struck by train while it was stalled in such position, testimony and pictures showing that hole was repaired after the accident were properly admitted).

Wis.—Wisconsin Rules of Evidence § 904.07.

To explain exhibit which includes change

Ind.—Montgomery v. Gerteisen, 195 N.E.2d 868, 135 Ind.App. 633.

N.H.—Lovett v. Manchester St. Ry., 159 A. 132, 85 N.H. 345 (removal of a center trolley pole after it was struck by an automobile was competent to be shown in explanation of a view which showed the absence of the pole, but for no other purpose).

Tex.—Rash v. Ross, Civ.App., 371 S.W.2d 109, ref. n. r. e. (photograph which portrayed scene on day after fatal collision and which showed that center stripe not present when collision occurred had been painted was admissible, over objection that post-accident safety precautions may not be proved with instructions to disregard alterations).

To rebut contention alteration existed earlier

Ga.—Seaboard Air Line Ry. Co. v. Young, 148 S.E. 757, 40 Ga.App. 4.

Ky.—Golubic v. Rasnich, 60 S.W.2d 616, 249 Ky. 266.

To rebut contention condition inevitable

Mo.—Lang v. J. C. Nichols Inv. Co., 59 S.W.2d 63, 227 Mo.App. 1123 (contended dirt from newly graded area would flow to street because of rainfall, but later had placed mud barriers).

To rebut contention condition proper

Cal.—Westbrooks v. Gordon H. Ball, Inc., 56 Cal.Rptr. 422, 248 Cal.App. 2d 209 (if one in charge of installing safety measures were to testify that, in his opinion, construction which was questioned was proper and it should develop that he himself ordered performance of additional safety measures, it would be legitimate in cross-examination to ask him whether he had not adopted new measures at variance with his statement of previous safety).

Wash.—Ewer v. Goodyear Tire & Rubber Co., 1970, 480 P.2d 260, 4

§ 424.2   Evidence of existence of insurance coverage

Under the federal rule,[63] and the general state court rule of almost uniform enforcement in motor vehicle accident cases, the jury should not be informed of the fact that the defendant is protected by liability or indemnity insurance, as such evidence is generally irrelevant and injects prejudicial collateral matter.[64] Similarly a party may not show that he is uninsured.[65]

Wash.App. 152 (manufacturer's change in specifications order).

To show feasibility of earlier action

Wash.—Wheeler v. Portland-Tacoma Auto Freight Co., 9 P.2d 101, 167 Wash. 218 (availability of warning flares).

63. Federal Rules of Evidence § 411, 28 U.S.C.A.

64. **Ala.**—Thorne v. Parrish, 90 So. 2d 781, 265 Ala. 193 (where defendant was required on cross-examination to answer question "Have you ever given another statement in regard to this accident?" and answered "It was an insurance company, I don't know his name", and counsel for plaintiff stated during argument "after they collect $30,000" defendant "and I will still be friends", reference to fact of indemnification of defendant by insurance was prejudicial, especially in absence of attempt by trial judge to cure or eradicate effect).

Ariz.—Dunipace v. Martin, 242 P.2d 543, 73 Ariz. 415.

Ark.—Derrick v. Rock, 236 S.W.2d 726, 218 Ark. 339 (one defendant uninsured).

Cal.—West's Ann.Calif.Evid.Code, § 1155; Crawford v. Alioto, 1951, 233 P.2d 148, 105 Cal.App.2d 45 (cross-examination of defendant as to identity of person investigating accident in his behalf); King v. Kaplan, 211 P.2d 578, 94 Cal.App. 2d 697.

Colo.—Phelps v. Loustalet, 14 P.2d 1011, 91 Colo. 350.

Dist.Col.—Wisdom v. Armstrong, Mun.App., 196 A.2d 88.

Ga.—Shapiro Packing Co. v. Landrum, 136 S.E.2d 446, 109 Ga.App. 519; Huell v. Southeastern Stages, 50 S.E.2d 745, 78 Ga.App. 311.

Ill.—Humkey v. Hueslmann Quarry, 99 N.E.2d 351, 343 Ill.App. 377.

Ind.—Taggart v. Keebler, 154 N.E. 485, 198 Ind. 633 (admitted over objection).

Iowa.—Miller v. Kooker, 224 N.W. 46, 208 Iowa 687, rehearing denied and opinion corrected 225 N.W. 868.

Kan.—Kansas Code of Civil Procedure § 60–454; Powell v. Kansas Yellow Cab Co., 131 P.2d 686, 156 Kan. 150, opinion supplemented 133 P.2d 755, 156 Kan. 406.

Ky.—Sellers v. Cayce Mill Supply Co., 349 S.W.2d 677 (agreement between insurance adjusters for one to furnish the other with a copy of a witness' statement was not relevant); Hall v. Ratliff, 312 S.W.2d 473; Howard v. Adams, Ky., 246 S.W.2d 1002 (testimony concerning negotiations with insurance agent and defendants' attorneys for a settlement was not admissible as showing cause for five months delay in having automobile repaired).

Me.—Maine Rules of Evidence § 411; Downs v. Poulin, 216 A.2d 29.

Mich.—Deffenbaugh v. Inter-State Motor Freight Corporation, 235 N. W. 896, 254 Mich. 180.

Miss.—Lancaster v. Lancaster, 1952, 57 So.2d 302, 213 Miss. 536.

65. See footnote 65 on page 396.

Ch. 424 RELEVANCE AND MATERIALITY § 424.2

Mo.—Whitman v. Carver, 88 S.W.2d 885, 337 Mo. 1247.

Neb.—Nebraska Rules of Evidence § 411.

Nev.—N.R.S. 48.135(1).

N.H.—Hutchins v. John Hancock Mut. Life Ins. Co., 192 A. 498, 89 N.H. 79.

N.J.—New Jersey Evidence Rule 54; Decker v. Everson, 187 A. 783, 14 N.J.Misc. 860.

N.M.—New Mexico Rules of Evidence § 411.

N.C.—Spivey v. Babcock & Wilcox Co., 141 S.E.2d 808, 264 N.C. 387; Scott v. Bryan, 187 S.E. 756, 210 N.C. 478.

N.D.—Bischoff v. Koenig, 1959, 100 N.W.2d 159.

Okl.—Million v. Rahhal, 417 P.2d 298 (whether accomplished by inadvertence or intentionally); Bratten v. White, 75 P.2d 474, 181 Okl. 543 (testimony that insurance man had talked with witness concerning case); Beatrice Creamery Co. v. Goldman, 52 P.2d 1033, 175 Okl. 300 (plaintiff was seeking to set aside release on ground of fraud, but there was no cause for acquainting jury with nature of interest party actually perpetrating fraud might have had).

Or.—Skeeters v. Skeeters, 1963, 389 P.2d 313, 237 Or. 204, rehearing denied 391 P.2d 386, 237 Or. 204 (even indirect reference).

Pa.—Trimble v. Merloe, 197 A.2d 457, 413 Pa. 408; Kaplan v. Loev, 194 A. 653, 327 Pa. 465, certiorari denied 58 S.Ct. 477, 302 U.S. 766, 82 L.Ed. 595.

R.I.—Lavigne v. Ballantyne, 1941, 17 A.2d 845, 66 R.I. 123.

Tenn.—Marshall v. North Branch Transfer Co., 59 S.W.2d 520, 166 Tenn. 96.

Tex.—Alexander Schroeder Lumber Co. v. Merritt, Civ.App., 323 S.W. 2d 163 (defendant's failure to request that jury be admonished to disregard testimony did not waive the error); Lubbock Bus Co. v. Pearson, Civ.App., 266 S.W.2d 439, ref. n. r. e. (extended examination of bus driver, who testified in favor of plaintiff and who was not a party, as to his personal liability to repair damaged automobile could be expected to elicit from driver response that it was insurance company's duty to repair the automobile, and such response, along with repeated mentioning of insurance adjuster's name by plaintiff's counsel, required mistrial, though plaintiff's counsel had requested an instruction that defendant's witnesses be ordered not to mention insurance); Continental Oil Co. v. Barnes, Civ.App., 97 S.W.2d 494 (testimony of plaintiff's witness, in direct response to question asked by plaintiff's counsel at a time when counsel knew insurance company was defending suit and procuring witnesses, that insurance company would pay witness' expense).

Utah.—Utah Rules of Evidence § 54; Saltas v. Affleck, 105 P.2d 176, 99 Utah 381.

Vt.—Glass v. Bosworth, 1943, 34 A. 2d 113, 113 Vt. 303.

Va.—Lanham v. Bond, 160 S.E. 89, 157 Va. 167.

W.Va.—Leftwich v. Wesco Corp., 119 S.E.2d 401, 146 W.Va. 196 (regardless of instructions that jury should not consider insurance and fact that objection was not made immediately).

Wis.—Wisconsin Rules of Evidence § 904.11.

Wyo.—Eagan v. O'Malley, 1933, 21 P.2d 821, 45 Wyo. 505.

Agent at trial table

Trial court properly refused, after jury was impaneled, to direct counsel for defendant to disclose name of insurance agent sitting at defendant's

§ 424.2   TRIAL EVIDENCE   Ch. 424

trial table, where in accord with Supreme Court's decision which had not then been modified. Lacey v. Heisey, 5 N.E.2d 699, 53 Ohio App. 451.

As against public carrier required by law to be insured

It is not the law in Pennsylvania that because defendant was a public utility carrier and, therefore, required to have protection against liability, no prejudice could result from disclosure that he had insurance because jury would be presumed to have knowledge of it. Nicholson v. Garris, 210 A.2d 164, 418 Pa. 146.

But see

Cal.—Douglass v. Webb, 26 Cal.Rptr. 60, 209 C.A.2d 290 (where plaintiff's counsel mentioned insurance company in his effort to refresh witness' recollection before counsel had exhausted other normal inquiry concerning identity of third party who prepared a statement for witness to sign, and before witness testified he could remember neither his name nor who he was, counsel's reference to named insurance company was improper, but in view of circumstances was not prejudicial).

Iowa.—Connelly v. Nolte, 21 N.W.2d 311, 237 Iowa 114.

Okl.—Fixico v. Harmon, 70 P.2d 114, 180 Okl. 412 (testimony of witness, who had signed statement at request of defendant's attorney, that she had been told that statement was some kind of insurance or referred to insurance, held not to require mistrial).

Contra where insurance company active in case

Mo.—State ex rel. Tramill v. Shain, 161 S.W.2d 974, 349 Mo. 82, quashing certiorari Tramill v. Prater, 152 S.W.2d 684, 236 Mo.App. 757.

Wis.—Sheehan v. Lewis, 1935, 260 N.W. 633, 218 Wis. 588 (joined as defendant).

Discretion in court

Ariz.—Muehlebach v. Mercer Mortuary & Chapel, Inc., 378 P.2d 741, 93 Ariz. 60 (must not allow bare mention of word "insurance" to cause mistrial; must use discretion).

Cal.—Mart v. Riley, 1966, 49 Cal. Rptr. 6, 239 Cal.App.2d 649.

Ill.—Clarke v. Rochford, 224 N.E.2d 679, 79 Ill.App.2d 336.

Iowa.—Stewart v. Hilton, 77 N.W.2d 637, 247 Iowa 988 (plaintiff, during cross-examination, stated that an insurance man had come to see her in hospital and reference made in argument).

Mich.—Gegan v. Kemp, 4 N.W.2d 525, 302 Mich. 218 (rule excluding evidence should not be employed to set aside judgments except in cases of flagrant violations).

Notation on hospital records

Where hospital records contained statement that they had been examined by an insurance company, the records should not have been admitted with such notation. Babecki v. Charles Kurzon, Inc., 46 N.Y.S.2d 573, 181 Misc. 11.

65. Ala.—Mobile Cab & Baggage Co. v. Busby, 169 So.2d 314, 277 Ala. 292.

Fla.—Daniel v. Rogers, 72 So.2d 391.

Ind.—Miller v. Alvey, 207 N.E.2d 633, 246 Ind. 560.

Mo.—Guiley v. Lowe, 314 S.W.2d 232.

N.H.—Graves v. Boston & M. R. R., 149 A. 70, 84 N.H. 225; Piechuck v. Magusiak, 135 A. 534, 82 N.H. 429.

N.D.—Kuntz v. Stelmachuk, 136 N.W.2d 810.

Tex.—Gilmer v. Griffin, Civ.App., 265 S.W.2d 252 (notwithstanding that witness had previously vol-

Ch. 424   RELEVANCE AND MATERIALITY   § 424.2

The conduct of defendant in placing information relating to insurance coverage before the jury has also been held prejudicial to the plaintiff.[66]

In a variety of circumstances, however, it has been found that the fact of insurance was not injected.[67]

unteered statement that plaintiff had collision insurance); Rojas v. Vuocolo, 177 S.W.2d 962, 142 Tex. 152 (permitting truck driver to reply to juror's question, over objection of other defendants, that truck was not insured, was improper and prejudicial to other defendants).

Exception noted

Under circumstances, while effect of evidence was probably to show that motorist had no insurance, it was material because of truck owner's contention that plaintiffs had given a complete release to motorist whereas they had merely executed a covenant not to sue, and hence reference to financial responsibility was not improper as informing jury that motorist had no insurance and that truck owner did. Palestine Contractors, Inc. v. Perkins, Tex.Civ.App., 375 S.W.2d 751.

66. Fla.—Crowell v. Fink, App., 135 So.2d 766 (that plaintiff's own insurance carrier had investigated facts and reached conclusion that plaintiff was guilty of negligence and had paid damages suffered by defendant resulting from collision, was prejudicial).

Vt.—Wilbur v. Tourangeau, 71 A.2d 565, 116 Vt. 199.

Contra

Disclosure by defendant's counsel that defendant was insured could not be considered to have prejudiced plaintiff who disclosed the fact that he had collision insurance and had collected for the loss sustained, less the deductible amount stated in his policy. Senecal v. Hovey, 253 N.Y. S.2d 698, 44 Misc.2d 409.

67. Ill.—Johnson v. Stotts, 101 N.E.2d 880, 344 Ill.App. 614 (statement made by witness that he was interviewed in the presence of a representative of the Chicago Motor Club, was not reversible error, where court ordered the statement stricken, since it is not common knowledge that the Chicago Motor Club is an insurer for automobile drivers); Rossman v. Solway, 84 N.E.2d 857, 337 Ill.App. 105 (testimony of plaintiff and her husband that plaintiff was examined by certain doctor at request of "representatives" of defendant, was not error, on ground that it intimated that an insurance was involved).

Me.—Collins v. Dunbar, 162 A. 897, 131 Me. 337.

Mo.—Eaves v. Wampler, App., 390 S.W.2d 922 (use of word investigator by plaintiff's counsel in objecting to question did not improperly inject fact that defendant had insurance or compel reversal and new trial where, under circumstances, it would seem reasonable that jury might conclude that the investigator was an investigator for the defendant); Moss v. Nehman, App.1952, 247 S.W.2d 305.

Nev.—Henry v. Baber, 334 P.2d 839, 75 Nev. 59 (where husband on direct examination answered in response to question of whether he had any conversation with one of defendants that he went to get her name and her insurance company so he could fill in his report, answer could not be characterized as a statement of inference that such defendant was covered by insurance).

S.C.—Matthews v. Porter, 124 S.E.2d 321, 239 S.C. 620 (testimony

§ 424.2　　　　　TRIAL EVIDENCE　　　　　Ch. 424

An exception to the general rule that the plaintiff may not show that the defendant carried liability insurance arises where it is shown that an occupant admonished a driver to be more careful in the operation of the motor vehicle and the driver replied by reference to the insurance carried. In such a case, the driver's statement may be shown as indicating lack of concern because of being protected by insurance, and as indicating consciously taking of chances in operating the vehicle.[68]

The fact that the defendant was insured may, however, incidentally and unavoidably appear.[69] Where the subject of insur-

elicited on cross-examination of defendant that his wife had made a claim against him was not improper on theory it created an inference that husband had liability insurance, but such evidence was proper rebuttal of testimony by defendant explaining that his wife's absence as a witness was due to her lack of knowledge of facts).

Tex.—Green v. Rudsenske, Civ.App., 320 S.W.2d 228 (where witness related attending banquet with the plaintiff, and plaintiff's counsel asked her whether or not it was a "Blue Cross" banquet to which she replied that it was, motion for mistrial on ground of injection of insurance was properly denied in view of failure to show how use of term "Blue Cross", wholly disconnected with defendant or any relevant issue in the case, could be an intimation that defendant was covered by insurance); Stein v. Boehme, Civ.App.1957, 302 S.W.2d 663 (testimony of plaintiff's witness that "two adjusters came out" after he brought plaintiff's wrecked automobile to shop for repairs, showed no reversible error in trial court's denial of defendant's motion for mistrial, as witness' statement concerning adjusters did not indicate that they represented insurance company carrying indemnity insurance for defendant and was inadvertently made and not responsive to any question asked witness by plaintiff's attorney); Montgomery v. Vinzant, Civ.App., 297 S.W.2d 350 (where plaintiff's counsel made reference to fact that a "representative" of defendant came to talk to plaintiff about case and plaintiff made a voluntary and unresponsive answer concerning defendant's "representative," there was no vice in use made of term "representative" requiring reversal); H. J. Heinz Co. v. Ashley, Civ.App., 291 S.W.2d 427 (plaintiff's testimony that he had reported collision to his insurance agent was not prejudicial to defendants as suggesting to jury that defendants were protected by insurance, and refusal to declare a mistrial because of such testimony was not reversible error, where any prejudice to plaintiff's insurer as intervenor was waived by attorney for insurer and trial court instructed jury not to consider such testimony for any purpose).

68. **N.H.**—Herschensohn v. Weisman, 119 A. 705, 80 N.H. 557, 28 A.L.R. 514.

69. **Ala.**—Burnett v. Bledsoe, 1964, 159 So.2d 841, 276 Ala. 139 (so interwoven as to be inseparable).

Cal.—Luis v. Cavin, App., 191 P.2d 527, subsequent opinion 198 P.2d 563, 88 Cal.App.2d 107; Rannard v. Harris, 8 P.2d 864, 121 Cal.App. 281; Elsey v. Domeco, 299 P. 794, 114 Cal.App. 42; McKinney v. Red Top Cab Co., 299 P. 113, 113 Cal. App. 637; Rowe v. Rennick, 297 P. 603, 112 Cal.App. 576.

Ch. 424 RELEVANCY AND MATERIALITY § 424.2

ance has not been wilfully injected into a case [70] as where a witness makes an unsolicited statement,[71] where it was legitimately

Iowa.—Remer v. Takin Bros. Freight Lines, 297 N.W. 297, 230 Iowa 290; Ryan v. Simeons, 229 N.W. 667, 209 Iowa 1090.

N.H.—Piechuck v. Magusiak, 135 A. 534, 82 N.H. 429.

N.Y.—Gelfond v. Kirschenbaum, 292 N.Y.S. 568, 249 App.Div. 894.

Or.—Webb v. Hoover-Guernsey Dairy Co., 4 P.2d 631, 138 Or. 24.

Tex.—Pattison v. Highway Ins. Underwriters, Civ.App., 278 S.W.2d 207, ref. n. r. e. (ordinarily reversible error for plaintiff to get before the jury information that defendant is protected by insurance, unless such information is produced as an incident to the vindication of injured person's legal rights).

70. Ala.—Hargett v. Rhoads, 1954, 70 So.2d 820, 37 Ala.App. 507.

Cal.—Corral v. Sager, 77 P.2d 303, 25 Cal.App.2d 322 (where the reference is merely incidental, or where point is debatable and offers open field for legitimate argument, misconduct will not be found).

Fla.—Acme Radio & Television, Inc. v. Childers, 183 So.2d 42; Wall v. Little, 136 So. 676, 102 Fla. 1015.

Kan.—Thompson v. Barnette, 227 P. 2d 120, 170 Kan. 384 (inadvertent mention).

Ky.—Bowling Green-Hopkinsville Bus Co. v. Montgomery, 129 S.W. 2d 535, 278 Ky. 837 (where witness, upon being asked who had measurements of truck, replied that he did not know unless insurance company might have them, whereupon court admonished jury not to consider answer); Marsee v. Johnson, 86 S.W.2d 299, 260 Ky. 615 (inadvertently brought out).

Mich.—Samuelson v. Olson Transp. Co., 36 N.W.2d 917, 324 Mich. 278; Deffenbaugh v. Inter-State Motor Freight Corp., 235 N.W. 896, 254 Mich. 180.

Or.—Jones v. Imperial Garages, 145 P.2d 469, 174 Or. 49 (related examined by "insurance companies doctors" in response to question as to what physicians were consulted).

Tex.—Texas Textile Mills v. Gregory, 177 S.W.2d 938, 142 Tex. 308 (reference was made suddenly and inadvertently by witness and plaintiff's counsel was without fault in the matter).

Vt.—Bressett v. O'Hara, 70 A.2d 238, 116 Vt. 118.

Va.—Carter v. Butler, 42 S.E.2d 201, 186 Va. 186.

Wash.—Lyster v. Metzger, 412 P.2d 340, 68 Wash.2d 216; Nicholson v. Brado, 297 P. 1093, 162 Wash. 146.

71. Cal.—Packard v. Moore, 71 P.2d 922, 9 Cal.2d 571; Hughes v. Duncan, 300 P. 147, 114 Cal.App. 576 (asking a witness, while testifying in his own behalf, if he had reported such facts to his attorney or to anyone else is not reversible as tending to bring before the jury improper evidence of defendant's insurance).

Ill.—Sphatt v. Tulley, 1962, 186 N.E. 2d 670, 38 Ill.App.2d 229 (unresponsive remark of disinterested witness); Hoffman v. Jenard, 78 N.E.2d 322, 334 Ill.App. 74 (unresponsive answer); Cooper v. Safeway Lines, 26 N.E.2d 632, 304 Ill. App. 302.

Ky.—Nichols v. Luster's Adm'r, 82 S.W.2d 498, 259 Ky. 379 (where plaintiff's attorney in good faith asked driver, a defendant, whether on night of accident he had anything showing ownership of truck and expected witness to testify that there was a certificate of ownership in the truck, that witness stated he had an insurance

§ 424.2 TRIAL EVIDENCE Ch. 424

developed in cross-examination,[72] or on redirect examination to meet a subject opened up by cross-examination,[73] or where objections to questions calculated to bring out such information are promptly sustained,[74] the disclosure may be harmless. The proof

card); Hedger v. Davis, 1930, 33 S.W.2d 310, 236 Ky. 432 (merely asked medical witness if he made report, and replied he filed it with insurance company).

Miss.—Petermann v. Gary, 49 So.2d 828, 210 Miss. 438 (question by defendants' own attorney).

Ohio.—Morse v. Wise, Ohio Com.Pl., 77 N.E.2d 105.

Okl.—John W. Simmons Trucking Co. v. Briscoe, 373 P.2d 49 (unsolicited testimony of one of defendants that after truck of one of defendants collided with automobile of plaintiff such defendant called insurance agent).

Or.—Melcher v. Connell, 250 P. 742, 119 Or. 626.

Pa.—Deeney v. Krauss, 147 A.2d 369, 394 Pa. 380.

Tex.—Harrin Transp. Co. v. Peterson, Civ.App., 216 S.W.2d 245, error refused.

72. **Ariz.**—Muehlebach v. Mercer Mortuary & Chapel, Inc., 378 P.2d 741, 93 Ariz. 60 (defendant's reference to insurance was not ground for new trial where defense counsel knew that plaintiff's counsel had in his possession a statement given by defendant to insurance adjuster and knew the statement was to be used to impeach defendant's testimony and knew that the statement would have to be identified by defendant, plaintiff's counsel inquired whether defendant had made a statement with regard to the accident, and the defendant replied that he had made a statement to an insurance agent).

Cal.—Corral v. Sager, 77 P.2d 303, 25 Cal.App.2d 322; Elsey v. Domeco, 299 P. 794, 114 Cal.App. 42;

Bluemel v. Kroizy, 299 P. 756, 114 Cal.App. 205.

Ill.—Isenhart v. Seibert, 127 N.E.2d 469, 6 Ill.App.2d 220 (where pedestrian's witness was asked on cross-examination if he had ever talked to any one about this case, and witness answered that one lawyer from insurance company came over, although answer was not responsive, the reference to insurance was general and did not inform the jury that defendant was protected by insurance, and trial court's ruling that statement did not prejudice defendant was not an abuse of discretion); Hemphill v. Miller, 84 N.E.2d 660, 336 Ill. App. 601.

Ky.—Gayheart v. Smith, 42 S.W.2d 877, 240 Ky. 596; Hedger v. Davis, 33 S.W.2d 310, 236 Ky. 432.

Miss.—Mississippi Ice & Utilities Co. v. Pearce, 134 So. 164, 161 Miss. 252.

Mo.—Todd v. Libby, McNeill & Libby, App., 110 S.W.2d 830.

Or.—Jones v. Sinsheimer, 214 P. 375, 107 Or. 491.

Tex.—Finck Cigar Co. v. Campbell, 133 S.W.2d 759, 134 Tex. 250, affirming, Civ.App., 114 S.W.2d 348 (when asked whether he had talked to people other than defendant's counsel about the case); Finck Cigar Co. v. Campbell, Civ. App., 114 S.W.2d 348, affirmed 133 S.W.2d 759, 134 Tex. 250; Amberson v. Woodul, Civ.App., 108 S.W.2d 852, error dismissed.

73. **Mo.**—Mahowald v. Garrison, 397 S.W.2d 713.

74. **Conn.**—Baptist v. Shanen, 145 A.2d 592, 145 Conn. 605 (statement "don't worry, I'm insured, all our cars are insured so you'll get paid

400

Ch. 424   RELEVANCY AND MATERIALITY   § 424.2

may not be prejudicial error where the defendant or the defendant's attorney, has made the particular disclosure complained of,[75] or a similar disclosure.[76]

The action of the court may render harmless any disclosure of the fact of defendant's insurance protection, as where the court admonishes the jury to disregard the disclosure.[77] However,

anyhow", and court instructed jury to disregard reference to insurance and no objection to instruction was made).

Ind.—Renner v. Jones, 85 N.E.2d 266, 119 Ind.App. 267.

Tex.—Engler v. Hatton, Civ.App., 2 S.W.2d 519, affirmed, Com.App., 12 S.W.2d 990.

75. Md.—Snowhite v. State, Use of Tennant, 221 A.2d 342, 243 Md. 291.

Miss.—Chilcutt v. Keating, 71 So.2d 472, 220 Miss. 545.

Mo.—Fisher v. Duster, App., 245 S.W. 2d 172 (where jury knew that insurance was in the case because of defendant's statement to that effect made in questions propounded by his own counsel, the subsequent questioning by plaintiff's counsel injecting insurance into the case during cross-examination of defendant was not prejudicial error).

Tex.—Finck Cigar Co. v. Campbell, 1939, 133 S.W.2d 759, 134 Tex. 250, affirming 114 S.W.2d 348.

Instigated by defense counsel

Tenn.—Goodall v. Doss, 312 S.W.2d 875, 44 Tenn.App. 145 (asked plaintiff who had testified about signing a statement, "Who was there?" and plaintiff answered "Two men. Two insurance adjusters," but no further reference to insurance was made, court sustained exception and it did not appear that plaintiff or his counsel tried to improperly influence jury).

76. Cal.—Baker v. Rodriguez, 105 P.2d 1018, 41 Cal.App.2d 58.

Ga.—Essig v. Cheves, 44 S.E.2d 712, 75 Ga.App. 870.

Ill.—Cooper v. Safeway Lines, 26 N. E.2d 632, 304 Ill.App. 302 (question of insurance was brought out in the first instance by defendants' counsel and in the second instance by an unresponsive answer of one of defendants' witnesses to a question asked by trial court).

Iowa.—Bauer v. Reavell, 260 N.W. 39, 219 Iowa 1212 (direct examination of one of plaintiff's witnesses disclosed that insurance had been mentioned in certain conversation heard by two other witnesses, and defendant cross-examined one of such other witnesses as to conversation, again disclosing that insurance had been mentioned).

77. Ark.—Vineyard v. Storm, 51 S. W.2d 860, 185 Ark. 1148.

Cal.—Kroplin v. Huston, 179 P.2d 575, 79 Cal.App.2d 332 (did not constitute reversible error where the evidence called for was merely cumulative and the court had repeatedly instructed the jury to disregard); Weiner v. Mizuta, 44 P.2d 421, 6 Cal.App.2d 142.

Fla.—Rosenberg v. Coman, 1938, 184 So. 238, 134 Fla. 768.

Ill.—Williams v. Matlin, 1946, 66 N.E. 2d 719, 328 Ill.App. 645.

Md.—Kirsch v. Ford, 183 A. 240, 170 Md. 90 (trial judge cautioned jury to entirely disregard insurer).

Mass.—Gartland v. Freeman, 1931, 178 N.E. 732, 277 Mass. 520.

Mich.—Trafamczak v. Anys, 31 N.W. 2d 832, 320 Mich. 653.

Mont.—Adams v. Misener, 131 P.2d 472, 113 Mont. 559.

401

§ 424.2   TRIAL EVIDENCE   Ch. 424

under some circumstances, the disclosure has been held prejudicial notwithstanding that the court admonished the jury to disregard the disclosure,[78] or instructed that there was no evidence of insurance coverage,[79] or polled the jurors to determine whether the disclosure would prejudice them.[80]

The determination of reviewing courts as to when the giving of such information to the jury is reversible error and when it is harmless depends largely upon the facts and circumstances in a particular case, and they will especially be influenced by the tendency of counsel to inject improperly this immaterial matter for the purpose of prejudicing the jury.[81] The closeness of the

Okl.—Wagner v. McKernan, 1947, 177 P.2d 511, 198 Okl. 425.

Pa.—Bortz v. Henne, 1964, 204 A.2d 52, 415 Pa. 150, Harriett v. Ballas, 1955, 117 A.2d 693, 383 Pa. 124.

R.I.—Romano v. Caldarone, 79 A.2d 763, 78 R.I. 107 (denial of motion for mistrial was not an abuse of discretion on the part of the trial justice in view of fact that trial justice's offer to instruct jury to disregard reference was refused).

Tenn.—Ingolsby v. Burnett, 40 S.W. 2d 1013, 163 Tenn. 173.

But see

Wis.—Georgeson v. Nielsen, 260 N. W. 461, 218 Wis. 180 (reprimand of offending counsel does not cure wrong done to litigants by prejudicial remarks).

78. **Iowa**—Floy v. Hibbard, 289 N. W. 905, 227 Iowa 154.

Mo.—Boyne v. Schulte, App., 222 S. W.2d 503; Lindsey v. Rogers, App., 220 S.W.2d 937.

N.Y.—Burgess v. Essler, 25 N.Y.S.2d 814, 261 App.Div. 1042.

S.D.—Zeller v. Pikovsky, 268 N.W. 729, 64 S.D. 544.

Tex.—M. J. Const. Co. v. Deatherage, Civ.App., 231 S.W.2d 501 (closely contested case and substantial verdict).

79. **N.Y.**—Tacktill v. Eastern Capitol Lines, 21 N.Y.S.2d 14, 260 App.Div. 58.

80. **N.Y.**—Tacktill v. Eastern Capitol Lines, 21 N.Y.S.2d 14, 260 App.Div. 58.

81. **Ariz.**—Butane Corp. v. Kirby, 187 P.2d 325, 66 Ariz. 272.

Ky.—Stott v. Hinkle, 150 S.W.2d 655, 286 Ky. 143.

Mo.—Kaiser v. Jaccard, Mo.App., 52 S.W.2d 18 (absence of showing lack of good faith).

Mont.—Francis v. Heidel, 68 P.2d 583, 104 Mont. 580.

N.J.—Puorro v. Kaskenas, 167 A. 737, 11 N.J.Misc. 630.

Okl.—Fixico v. Harmon, 70 P.2d 114, 180 Okl. 412.

Tex.—Finck Cigar Co. v. Campbell, Civ.App., 114 S.W.2d 348, affirmed 133 S.W.2d 759, 134 Tex. 250.

"Diligent suggestion" of insurance

Iowa—Ryan v. Simeons, 229 N.W. 667, 209 Iowa 1090 (continued course of "diligent suggestion" that the defendant was protected by insurance).

S.D.—O'Connor v. Sioux Falls Motor Co., 232 N.W. 904, 57 S.D. 397 (by examination of jurors and otherwise that the action was a mere method of collecting insurance seems to be a growing practice of trial stratagem, not calculated to secure a fair trial, and which incurs the increasing disfavor of the courts).

Ch. 424   RELEVANCE AND MATERIALITY   § 424.2

case is important on the issue of whether such a disclosure is prejudicial,[82] as is, also, the effect of the disclosure on the verdict.[83]

If the jury voluntarily inquires into insurance, without suggestion by counsel or witnesses, the error may be cured by proper instructions of the judge in absence of other evidence tending to show bias or prejudice.[84]

Under the federal rule,[85] and in some state jurisdictions, if evidence as to the defendant's insurance coverage tends to prove any issue in the case, it should not be excluded on the ground that it may tend to prejudice the defendant.[86] Evidence of in-

Persistent reference after first disclosure

Where plaintiff motorist on cross-examination denied that he told defendant that he had tried to beat defendant's truck driver across intersection, plaintiff was not entitled to bring out other parts of same conversation relating to insurance, and admission of such evidence was reversible error, especially where plaintiff persistently referred to insurance thereafter. Jeddeloh v. Hockenhull, 18 N.W.2d 582, 219 Minn. 541.

82. **Ill.**—Galek v. Winters, 92 N.E. 2d 360, 340 Ill.App. 635.

83. **Fla.**—Southern Liquor Distributors v. Kaiser, 7 So.2d 600, 150 Fla. 434 (jury not influenced); Morton v. Holaday, 164 So. 514, 121 Fla. 813 (new trial required in view of excessive verdict notwithstanding that immediately following the statement trial judge instructed jury that they should not consider testimony).

Ga.—Babb v. Kirk, 195 S.E. 452, 57 Ga.App. 299 (verdict less than evidence authorized).

Kan.—Witt v. Roper, 96 P.2d 643, 150 Kan. 722 (excessive verdict appeared traceable in part to plaintiff's tactics).

Ky.—Howard v. Adams, 246 S.W.2d 1002 (excessive damages).

N.Y.—Hager v. Bushman, 8 N.Y.S.2d 725, 255 App.Div. 934, reargument denied 10 N.Y.S.2d 217, 256 App. Div. 895 (refusal to declare mistrial or set aside verdict because evidence that defendant was insured was admitted and jury was not instructed to disregard it proper, where such evidence clearly did not influence verdict).

Tenn.—Ingolsky v. Burnett, 40 S.W. 2d 1013, 163 Tenn. 173 (verdict not affected).

Tex.—Eichelberger v. Rankin, Civ. App., 278 S.W.2d 278, ref. n. r. e. (where damages awarded went to limit of pleadings).

Utah—Robinson v. Hreinson, 409 P. 2d 121, 17 Utah 2d 261.

84. **Ind.**—Rust v. Watson, 215 N.E. 2d 42, —— Ind.App. ——, rehearing denied 217 N.E.2d 859.

Mo.—McComb v. Vaughn, 218 S.W. 2d 548, 358 Mo. 951.

85. Federal Rules of Evidence § 411, 28 U.S.C.A.

86. **Ala.**—Moore-Handley Hardware Co. v. Williams, 189 So. 757, 238 Ala. 189.

Cal.—Turner v. Mannon, 1965, 45 Cal.Rptr. 831, 236 Cal.App.2d 134 (shown in connection with proof of payment under medical pay provision of policy; Packard v. Moore, 71 P.2d 922, 9 Cal.2d 571.

Iowa—Wolfe v. Decker, 266 N.W. 4, 221 Iowa 600.

§ 424.2   TRIAL EVIDENCE   Ch. 424

surance coverage may be admissible to show who owns the vehicle in question,[87] or the relationship between defendant and the driver of the vehicle or defendant's responsibility for the negligence charged.[88] However, a defendant's testimony that certain

Ky.—Gayheart v. Smith, 42 S.W.2d 877, 240 Ky. 596.

Md.—Snowhite v. State, Use of Tennant, 221 A.2d 342, 243 Md. 291 (reference, in deposition of truck operator, to insurance, to effect that truck operator's employer had expressed concern over ability to obtain insurance if truck operator had another accident, was relevant to one of principal issues of case, that is, employer's knowledge of truck operator's incompetence as driver, and hence was within exception to general rule).

Mo.—Muckenthaler v. Ehinger, 1966, 409 S.W.2d 625; Steinman v. Brownfield, App.1929, 18 S.W.2d 528; Paepke v. Stadelman, 1927, 300 S.W. 845, 222 Mo.App. 346.

Neb.—Nebraska Rules of Evidence § 411.

Nev.—N.R.S. 48.135(2).

N.M.—New Mexico Rules of Evidence § 411.

N.Y.—Oltarsh v. Aetna Ins. Co., 256 N.Y.S.2d 577, 15 N.Y.2d 111, 204 N.E.2d 622; Rashall v. Morra, 294 N.Y.S. 630, 250 App.Div. 474.

Ohio—Taylor v. Ross, App., 78 N.E. 2d 395, reversed on other grounds 83 N.E.2d 222, 150 Ohio St. 448, 10 A.L.R.2d 377; Booth v. Coldiron, 9 N.E.2d 161, 55 Ohio App. 144; Cushman Motor Delivery Co. v. Bernick, 8 N.E.2d 446, 55 Ohio App. 31; Hoover v. Turner, 182 N. E. 598, 42 Ohio App. 528.

Wash.—Carlson v. P. F. Collier & Son Corporation, 67 P.2d 842, 190 Wash. 301.

Wis.—Wisconsin Rules of Evidence § 904.11.

Release as exhibit

Where defendant had taken a release for some of plaintiff's claim, release was relevant evidence to be submitted to jury for its consideration in determining how much defendant should pay, even though release brought out fact that plaintiff was insured. Jury v. New York Cent. R. Co., 74 A.2d 531, 167 Pa. Super. 244.

87. **U.S.**—Federal Rules of Evidence § 411, 28 U.S.C.A.

Fla.—Carlton v. Johns, 194 So.2d 670.

Md.—Rhinehart v. Lemmon, 29 A.2d 279, 181 Md. 663.

Neb.—Nebraska Rules of Evidence § 411.

Nev.—N.R.S. 48.135(2).

N.M.—New Mexico Rules of Evidence § 411.

Wash.—Coffman v. McFadden, 416 P.2d 99, 68 Wash.2d 954; Jerdal v. Sinclair, 342 P.2d 585, 54 Wash.2d 565.

Wis.—Wisconsin Rules of Evidence § 904.11.

88. **U.S.**—Federal Rules of Evidence § 411, 28 U.S.C.A.

Ind.—Snider v. Truex, 51 N.E.2d 477, 222 Ind. 18.

Md.—Snowhite v. State, Use of Tennant, 221 A.2d 342, 243 Md. 291.

Neb.—Nebraska Rules of Evidence § 411.

Nev.—N.R.S. 48.135(2).

N.M.—New Mexico Rules of Evidence § 411.

Wis.—Wisconsin Rules of Evidence § 904.11.

Ohio.—Cushman Motor Delivery Co. v. Smith, 1 N.E.2d 628, 51 Ohio App. 421.

witnesses were not produced because of the expense did not render admissible evidence as to existence of liability insurance coverage.[89]

A statement relating to insurance which is an inseparable part of a material admission of liability made by a party may be proved,[90] but if a declarant acknowledges liability and then continues by reference to being insured, a limitation admitting only the acknowledgment would seem generally to be practicable. The court should receive only the essential and material part of the statement, when the two parts are separable.[91] If such evi-

---

89. **U.S.**—Culp v. Repper, 78 F.2d 221, 64 App.D.C. 337.

90. **Cal.**—Anderson v. Mothershead, 64 P.2d 995, 19 Cal.App.2d 97; Weiner v. Mizuta, 44 P.2d 421, 6 Cal.App.2d 142 (defendant told plaintiff he saw him too late, and then directed plaintiff to go to doctor with injured wife and stated that "we are insured"); King v. Wilson, 2 P.2d 833, 116 Cal.App. 191 (defendant stated to injured party that he was sorry but that he had insurance to pay for everything).

Iowa—Wolfe v. Decker, 266 N.W. 4, 221 Iowa 600 (refusal to strike testimony of witnesses relating that defendant in admitting liability informed witnesses that he carried insurance held not error, where there was no deliberate attempt to inject into trial fact that defendant carried insurance); Bauer v. Reavell, 260 N.W. 39, 219 Iowa 1212 (motorist stated that he had insurance and would see that injured pedestrian was taken care of); Ryan v. Simeons, 229 N.W. 667, 209 Iowa 1090.

S.D.—O'Connor v. Sioux Falls Motor Co., 232 N.W. 904, 57 S.D. 397 (owner's report to insurer containing admissions that driver was negligent and acting within scope of employment).

Tenn.—Seals v. Sharp, 212 S.W.2d 620, 31 Tenn.App. 75.

Vt.—Joslin v. Griffith, 211 A.2d 249, 125 Vt. 104.

Wash.—Rich v. Campbell, 2 P.2d 886, 164 Wash. 393 (application for insurance offered as exhibit to rebut certain evidence and to show statements made by party contradictory to his testimony).

Proof of loss made to insurer
Admission over objection of statement of proof of loss as to amount of damages made by insured to insurer was admissible as declaration against interest even though it disclosed fact that owners were insured. Moore v. Dallas Ry. & Terminal Co., Tex.Civ.App., 238 S.W.2d 741.

91. **N.H.**—McCurdy v. Flibotte, 139 A. 367, 83 N.H. 143.

Or.—Cameron v. Columbia Builders, Inc., 1957, 320 P.2d 251, 212 Or. 388 (trial court did not err in excluding testimony to the effect that individual defendant had stated that he would do all in his means to have case settled with his insurance company, and that he was cancelling his insurance with them because he did not feel they had done him justice, in view of fact such testimony would have added nothing to many unequivocal admissions of responsibility already in evidence).

Vt.—Wilbur v. Tourangeau, 71 A.2d 565, 116 Vt. 199.

But see

Ga.—Owens v. Shugart, 6 S.E.2d 121, 61 Ga.App. 177 (party given right to show "entire conversation").

§ 424.2   TRIAL EVIDENCE   Ch. 424

dence is admissible as showing an admission, a request for the limitation of its use is as much called for as a request for the limitation of its form and extent.[92]

A contract which is otherwise admissible as bearing upon a material issue involved in the litigation is not rendered inadmissible merely because it incidentally discloses that the defendant is insured.[93]

Under proper circumstances evidence of insurance coverage may be admissible for the purpose of impeachment.[94]

92. **N.H.**—McCurdy v. Flibotte, 139 A. 367, 83 N.H. 143.

N.Y.—Akin v. Lee, 99 N.E. 85, 206 N.Y. 20, Ann.Cas.1914A, 947.

93. **Cal.**—Taylor v. Oakland Scavenger Co., 110 P.2d 1044, 17 Cal. 2d 594.

Pa.—Jury v. New York Cent. R. Co., 74 A.2d 531, 167 Pa.Super. 244.

94. **U.S.**—Federal Rules of Evidence § 411, 28 U.S.C.A.

Ark.—Industrial Farm Home Gas Co. v. McDonald, 1962, 355 S.W.2d 174, 234 Ark. 744.

Cal.—Kroplin v. Huston, 179 P.2d 575, 79 Cal.App.2d 332 (asking witness, for purpose of impeaching defendant, whether defendant had said he was insured and would take care of plaintiff's expenses, was not prejudicial misconduct).

Md.—Grossnickle v. Avery, 152 N.E. 288, 96 Ind.App. 479 (where one of defendant's lawyers testified concerning certain statements by plaintiff's witnesses, it was proper, on cross-examination, to show that he was representing defendant's insurance carrier when he procured such statements).

Ky.—Reddy Cab Co. v. Harris, 90 S. W.2d 1004, 262 Ky. 661 (statement of driver of cab that inconsistent statement which he had signed after accident had been written by insurance man held not prejudicial error, where evidence showed that statement had been prepared by official of cab company).

Miss.—Skelton v. Turnispeed, 1970, 235 So.2d 694.

Mo.—Wren v. St. Louis Public Service Co., App., 355 S.W.2d 365 (where authenticity and accuracy of movies taken of plaintiff by defendant's witness were material to issue of extent and nature of plaintiff's injuries and damages, plaintiff was entitled to show that witness was an employee of insurance company which was financially interested in outcome of litigation).

Nev.—N.R.S. 48.135(2) (bias).

N.M.—New Mexico Rules of Evidence § 411 (bias).

Okl.—Beatrice Creamery Co. v. Goldman, 52 P.2d 1033, 175 Okl. 300.

Tex.—Barton Plumbing Co. v. Johnson, Civ.App., 285 S.W.2d 780, writ of error refused; Pattison v. Highway Ins. Underwriters, Tex.Civ. App., 278 S.W.2d 207, ref. n. r. e. (that such witness wrote liability policy covering defendant's automobile, for the purpose of showing bias).

Vt.—Joslin v. Griffith, 1965, 211 A. 2d 249, 125 Vt. 104, citing C.J.S. Trial § 53a.

Wis.—Wisconsin Rules of Evidence § 904.11 (bias).

Excluding identification of statement taker

Me.—Poland v. Dunbar, 157 A. 381, 130 Me. 447 (on cross-examination of plaintiff, defendant having been

Where a physician called by a defendant admitted having testified for and against the defendant's attorney in other cases, plaintiff's interrogation as to whether the physician's associate had frequently testified for such attorney's "company" did not require a mistrial.[95]

§ 424.3 Proof of Legal Fault—As Limited by Pleadings

Library References:
C.J.S. Motor Vehicles § 508; Pleading § 512 et seq.
West's Key No. Digests, Automobiles ⚖240; Pleading ⚖370 et seq.

The universally accepted rule of evidence is that evidence not confined to the issues presented by the pleadings is inadmissible.[96] The federal rule and the rule of certain states define

allowed to introduce in evidence a statement signed by plaintiff to the effect that defendant drove her automobile in a careful manner, at a moderate rate of speed, and that witness thought that defendant was not at fault, plaintiff's testimony that the man who got the statement from her represented the insurance company, being without probative value, was prejudicial hearsay).

Okl.—Hankins v. Hall, 54 P.2d 609, 176 Okl. 79 (where plaintiff's witness, asked on redirect examination where person who came to get statements from witness was from, stated that person said he was from an insurance company, held reversible error, since answer was responsive and not inadvertent).

Utah—Ivie v. Richardson, 336 P.2d 781, 9 Utah 2d 5 (where defendant's attorney found it necessary in cross-examining plaintiff to use a statement taken from plaintiff by a man some time after the accident, and although plaintiff's counsel were well aware that such man was an insurance company investigator, plaintiff's counsel persisted in inquiring about identification of such man in presence of jury, such conduct was improper since his inquiry lent itself to thinly veiled ulterior design of getting fact of insurance before the jury, especially in view of fact that the jury award seemed out of proportion to plaintiff's injury).

Witness as employee of party

U.S.—Lipshutz v. Ullman, D.C.Pa. 1969, 313 F.Supp. 320, affirmed C. A.3d, 1970, 426 F.2d 1298 (where counsel for defendant attempted to impeach non-party eyewitness by questioning him about a prior inconsistent statement given to a man described by counsel as "my investigator", it was proper to permit opposing counsel in cross-examination to clear up any misapprehension which may have been created in minds of jury as to relationship of scrivener to the litigation, notwithstanding defendant's claim that jury was improperly made aware of fact that defendant was insured).

Ill.—Guardado v. Navarro, 1964, 197 N.E.2d 469, 47 Ill.App.2d 92; Williams v. Matlin, 1946, 66 N.E.2d 719, 328 Ill.App. 645.

95. Or.—Hahn v. Dewey, 72 P.2d 593, 157 Or. 433.

96. U.S.—Sugg v. Hendrix, C.C.A. Miss., 153 F.2d 240 (could not re-

§ 424.3   TRIAL EVIDENCE   Ch. 424

cover for injuries on ground that defendant failed to keep premises in a reasonably safe condition, in absence of allegation of negligence based on unsafe premises).

Ala.—Berry v. Dannelly, 145 So. 663, 226 Ala. 151 (contributory negligence not made an issue).

Ark.—Coca-Cola Bottling Co. v. Shipp, 297 S.W. 856, 174 Ark. 130.

Cal.—Duggan v. Forderer, 249 P. 533, 79 Cal.App. 339 (ordinance prohibiting parking in certain district).

Conn.—Kenneson v. City of Bridgeport, 33 A.2d 313, 130 Conn. 298.

Ga.—Madaris v. Madaris, 1968, 163 S.E.2d 745, 224 Ga. 577; Stewart v. Avery, 144 S.E. 218, 38 Ga.App. 431 (ordinance regulating conduct of persons alighting from vehicles).

Idaho.—Riggs v. Roberts, 264 P.2d 698, 74 Idaho 473.

Ill.—Dina v. Passaglia, 23 N.E.2d 773, 302 Ill.App. 159 (ordinance designating street as through street).

Iowa.—Miller v. Illinois Cent. R. Co., 272 N.W. 96, 223 Iowa 316 (ordinance required railroad to keep a watchman at crossing from 7 a. m. to 7 p. m. and collision took place at 8 p. m.); Martinek v. Swift & Co., 98 N.W. 477, 122 Iowa 611.

La.—Driefus v. Levy, App., 140 So. 259 (admission of ordinance not pleaded).

Md.—Huber v. State, 1967, 234 A.2d 264, 2 Md.App. 245; Nelson v. Seiler, 139 A. 564, 154 Md. 63 (evidence of incompetence of driver).

Miss.—Dixie Greyhound Lines v. Everett, 187 So. 508.

Mo.—Gurwell v. Jefferson City Lines, 192 S.W.2d 683, 239 Mo.App. 305 (contributory negligence under ordinance immaterial because case decided under humanitarian doctrine); Christman v. Reichholdt, App., 150 S.W.2d 527 (where desire to establish duty beyond statutory requirement, as by custom, the custom or special circumstances had to be plead); Cunningham v. Kansas City Public Service Co., 77 S.W.2d 161, 229 Mo.App. 174 (ordinance requiring stopping for through street inadmissible when action based on humanitarian rule); Chawkley v. Wabash R. Co., 297 S.W. 20, 317 Mo. 782 (evidence of incompetence of driver).

N.J.—Perth Amboy Garage Co. v. National Fire Ins. Co. of Hartford, 164 A. 285, 110 N.J.L. 131 (re evidence of a particular defense).

Ohio.—Kilgore v. U-Drive It Co., App., 79 N.E.2d 785, affirmed 79 N.E.2d 908, 149 Ohio St. 505 (evidence of willful misconduct not admissible under allegation of ordinary negligence).

Okl.—Barger v. Mizel, 424 P.2d 41 (in action against automobile owner by injured guest, brought on theory of owner's negligence in permitting it to be driven by incompetent driver, wherein pleadings made no issue that steering mechanism was defective or made the vehicle inherently dangerous, evidence comparing steering ratio of such automobile with another vehicle was properly excluded).

Or.—Persons v. Raven, 1949, 207 P. 2d 1051, 187 Or. 1 (dangerous character of road not pleaded); Hamilton v. Finch, 111 P.2d 81, 166 Or. 156 (evidence of statute requiring driving close to curb not admissible on allegation of failure to swerve right after danger of collision arose); Hanna v. Royce, 1926, 249 P. 173, 119 Or. 450 (ordinance re through streets).

Pa.—Emanuel v. Ketner, 1970, 269 A. 2d 759, 440 Pa. 141 (that at time of accident one driver was not licensed was immaterial to issues involved under pleadings and proof and was unduly prejudicial where

408

Ch. 424   RELEVANCY AND MATERIALITY   § 424.3

"relevant evidence" as that which makes more probable or less probable a fact "that is of consequence to the determination of the action." [97]

issue of liability resolved itself into a pure question of negligence on part of either or both drivers while proceeding through intersection).

R.I.—Commonwealth of Massachusetts v. Martin, Sup., 125 A. 219 (statute of another state).

Tex.—Dallas Ry. & Terminal Co. v. Rogers, 218 S.W.2d 456, 147 Tex. 617; City of Wichita Falls v. Phillips, Civ.App., 87 S.W.2d 544 (fellow servant doctrine).

Utah.—Industrial Commission of Utah v. Wasatch Grading Co., 14 P.2d 988, 80 Utah 223 (complaint failed to allege sufficient acts to charge negligence respecting defective brakes).

Vt.—Porter v. Fleming, 156 A. 903, 104 Vt. 76 (ordinance regulating traffic at intersections).

Wash.—Knight v. Pang, 201 P.2d 198, 32 Wash.2d 217 (pedestrian's testimony that automobile was farther than it ordinarily would have been toward center line was insufficient to raise issue of driver's negligence in violating ordinance requiring motorist to proceed as closely as practicable to right hand curb, in absence of specific allegations that driver was negligent in that respect); Lubliner v. Ruge, 153 P.2d 694, 21 Wash.2d 881 (evidence that motorist had been drinking intoxicating liquor); Wright v. Zido, 276 P. 542, 151 Wash. 486 (the custom of traffic officers in signaling traffic).

Existence of pedestrian crossing

In pedestrian's action for injuries sustained when crossing street at point not dedicated as crossing, admission of testimony that point at which pedestrian was attempting to cross was used as crossing, in absence of pleading showing usage, was error, since custom not being generally known was a "special custom" which must be pleaded if relied upon. Huey & Philp Hardware Co. v. McNeil, Tex.Civ.App., 111 S.W.2d 1205.

Necessity to plead park district speed regulation

Ill.—Laux v. Kummer, 96 N.E.2d 828, 342 Ill.App. 448 (properly refused to admit offered evidence of regulation by park district as to speed and existence of posted signs where complaint failed to cite statute authorizing local authorities to regulate speed of vehicles in public parks, and to cite regulation relied upon by plaintiff, and failed to allege violation of statute or regulation).

Not matters admitted in pleadings

Generally, evidence should be excluded as to matters about which there is no dispute and the record should not be burdened by proof of facts admitted. Willis v. Hill, 1967, 159 S.E.2d 145, 116 Ga.App. 848, reversed on other grounds 161 S.E.2d 281, 224 Ga. 263, conformed to 162 S.E.2d 299, 117 Ga.App. 855.

97. Federal Rules of Evidence § 401, 28 U.S.C.A.

Cal.—West's Ann.Calif.Evid.Code, § 210.

Me.—Maine Rules of Evidence § 401.

Neb.—Nebraska Rules of Evidence § 401.

Nev.—N.R.S. 48.015.

N.M.—New Mexico Rules of Evidence § 401.

Wis.—Wisconsin Rules of Evidence § 904.01.

§ 424.3   TRIAL EVIDENCE   Ch. 424

However, specific factual allegations do not prevent proof varying in detail but bearing upon the same issue.[98] A party need not have alleged the detailed facts to be offered, so long as the ultimate issuable fact is alleged.[99]

---

98. For discussion of fatal variances of proof, see § 416.12.

Ind.—Terre Haute Union Transfer & Storage Co. v. Pickett, 15 N.E.2d 765, 106 Ind.App. 82, rehearing denied 16 N.E.2d 778, 106 Ind.App. 82 (allegation that "at about seven o'clock p. m." defendant's truck loaded with steel beams projecting 8 feet from rear of truck was parked on street, without lights required by statute, sufficiently charged violation of statutes relating to maintenance of lights on rear of motor vehicles to permit proof that accident occurred later than one-half hour after sunset).

La.—Webb v. Dunn, App., 15 So. 2d 129; Masaracchia v. Inter-City Express Lines, App., 162 So. 221 (that left rear wheels of truck were on edge of paved portion of highway at time, not so substantially different from plaintiff's allegations that truck was completely off road as to render such testimony inadmissible).

Mo.—Brown v. Alton R. Co., 151 S. W.2d 727, 236 Mo.App. 26 (where alleged speed in stated miles per hour).

Neb.—Tate v. Borgman, 92 N.W.2d 697, 167 Neb. 299 (specific allegation as to rate of speed).

Ohio.—Smith v. Pennsylvania R. Co., Ohio App., 40 N.E.2d 445, 35 O.L. A. 257, motion overruled (under the allegation that no signal was given by train, it could be shown that no seasonable signal was given).

Or.—Lindekugel v. Spokane, P. & S. Ry. Co., 42 P.2d 907, 149 Or. 634, 99 A.L.R. 721 (where alleged speed in stated miles per hour).

Tex.—Rosenthal Dry Goods Co. v. Hillebrandt, Civ.App., 299 S.W. 665, reversed on other grounds, Com.App., 7 S.W.2d 521 (where alleged lane of travel); Debes v. Greenstone, Civ.App., 260 S.W. 211 (where alleged speed in stated miles per hour).

Va.—Simmers v. Depoy, 1971, 184 S.E.2d 776, 212 Va. 447 (variance between allegation, in motion for judgment, that pedestrian had been struck south of intersection and investigating officer's testimony that she had been struck north of intersection was not a fatal variance).

99. U.S.—Knight v. Baltimore & O. R. Co., D.C.N.Y., 8 F.R.D. 256 (may prove prior accidents, at railroad crossing, and obstruction of vision by buildings).

Mo.—Pfeiffer v. Schee, Mo.App., 107 S.W.2d 170 (allegations of petition of existence of rule and custom, of which defendant was aware, that persons should not stop automobiles on concrete portion of highway, authorized plaintiff's testimony that Highway Department had erected signs warning against parking on highways); Kourik v. English, 100 S.W.2d 901, 340 Mo. 367 (under petition alleging automobile accident occurred when automobile struck elevated portion of highway causing injuries to guest, proof that at place in question there was dip of 8 or 10 inches in highway and gradual rise from bottom of dip held within pleadings).

Tex.—Northern Texas Traction Co. v. Smith, Civ.App., 223 S.W. 1013 (on issue of speed, may prove distance vehicle was dragged, marks on the street, and stopping distance after collision).

A party may be aided by the adversary's pleadings in offer of testimony otherwise inadmissible under the party's own pleadings.[1]

Nature and extent of injuries

Colo.—Westfall v. Kern, 43 P.2d 392, 96 Colo. 383 (allegations of injuries to female held sufficient to admit testimony respecting effect of injuries on passenger's ability to bear children).

Iowa.—Keller v. Dodds, 277 N.W. 467, 224 Iowa 935 (when the allegations are in effect that the injury is permanent and future pain is reasonably certain, a general allegation of damages will be a sufficient basis for allowing compensation for these elements, as they are the natural result of the act complained of).

Mo.—Ziervogel v. Royal Packing Co., App.1949, 225 S.W.2d 798 (where no special damages pleaded, evidence of increased blood pressure inadmissible); Carson v. Thompson, App., 161 S.W.2d 995 (petition alleging that plaintiff suffered great physical pain and "anguish", warranted examination of physician testifying for plaintiff, as to whether injury to throat or vocal cords, resulting in inability to speak above a whisper, would depress a person mentally); Granberg v. King Candy Co, App., 81 S.W.2d 981 (admissible if it relates to such results of injury pleaded as defendant might reasonably take notice of and expect from general allegations).

N.D.—Myers v. Hagert Const. Co., 23 N.W.2d 29, 74 N.D. 435 (evidence of dislocation of wrist and traumatic arthritis was admissible under allegation of broken bones).

Ohio.—Major v. Liggett, 50 N.E.2d 795, 72 Ohio App. 71 (that while plaintiff was confined to hospital her hair began to fall out, and that she received a severe blow upon her forehead causing an indentation in skull and severe headaches properly admitted under allegations was seriously and permanently injured and became nervous).

Pa.—Durdella v. Trenton-Philadelphia Coach Co., 37 A.2d 481, 349 Pa. 482 (where statement enumerated "injuries to the back and dorso-lumbar junction", court properly overruled motion to strike out expert testimony relating to injury to vertebrae and intervening cartilages); Lynch v. Bornot, Inc., 182 A. 49, 120 Pa.Super. 242 (averment that plaintiff suffered severe shock to nervous system is sufficient notice that testimony will be offered of severity and character of shock as manifested by effect upon plaintiff's health, directly traceable to injured nervous system); Lynch v. Bornot, Inc., 182 A. 49, 120 Pa.Super. 242 (evidence of mother that child suffered from abdominal disorders on evening of accident for which he was treated for almost seven months thereafter held admissible under statement that plaintiff had been injured in nerves and nervous system, especially where judge did not refer to or discuss alleged abdominal injuries in charge, and, from moderate verdict rendered, jury apparently did not consider such injuries).

Wash.—West v. Airth, 120 P.2d 536, 12 Wash.2d 77 (evidence that the tremor in plaintiff's right arm was caused by an injury to the motor nerves of that arm at the point where they center in the brain, and that such injury to motor nerve or nerve nuclei was caused by the accident, was admissible).

1. **Fla.**—Atlantic Greyhound Lines v. Lovett, 184 So. 133, 134 Fla. 505.

Md.—Longenecker v. Zanghi, 2 A.2d 20, 175 Md. 307.

§ 424.3   TRIAL EVIDENCE   Ch. 424

A further rule recognized by the courts and textwriters is that under a general allegation of negligence the plaintiff may prove any act of negligence of the defendant.[2] A general charge of negligence has been held broad enough to include negligence in driving while intoxicated.[3] However, it has been held that if

Tex.—Northern Texas Traction Co. v. Smith, Civ.App., 223 S.W. 1013.

Relevant to charge of contributory negligence

Iowa—Haines v. Mahaska Bottling Works, 288 N.W. 70, 227 Iowa 228 (plaintiff's testimony that lights on defendant's truck were not burning was admissible as relevant and material on issue of plaintiff's contributory negligence in failing to maintain proper lookout and see truck approaching, though he did not allege failure to have such lights on as ground of defendants' negligence).

2. U.S.—Southern Pac. Co. v. Stephens, C.C.A.Cal., 24 F.2d 182 (speed of locomotive).

Ark.—Rogers v. Woods, 42 S.W.2d 390, 184 Ark. 392 (violation of statute).

Cal.—Brooks v. E. J. Willig Truck Transp. Co., 255 P.2d 802, 40 Cal. 2d 669 (not limited to proof of breach of common law standards of care but had right to show statutory violations amounting to negligence); Hernandez v. Murphy, 115 P.2d 565, 46 Cal.App.2d 201 (inadequacy of equipment); Latky v. Wolfe, 259 P. 470, 85 Cal.App. 332 (defective brakes).

Conn.—Doerr v. Woodland Transp. Co., 136 A. 693, 105 Conn. 689 (proof of speed and failure to keep lookout); Butler v. Hyperion Theater Co., 124 A. 220, 100 Conn. 551; Mezzi v. Taylor, 120 A. 871, 99 Conn. 1 (failure to have proper lights).

Ill.—Scally v. Flannery, 11 N.E.2d 123, 292 Ill.App. 349 (violation of statute).

Ind.—Taylor v. Fitzpatrick, App., 126 N.E.2d 248, superseded 132 N.E.2d 919, 235 Ind. 238 (under allegation negligently failed to keep car under proper control so as to avoid collision would be proper to prove that driver's inability to stop was due to excessive speed, defective brakes, or inattention); Jones v. Cary, 37 N.E.2d 944, 219 Ind. 268 (complaint alleging that defendants carelessly and negligently failed to keep automobile under control would authorize evidence that defendants were driving too fast, were inattentive to driving, or were driving while under influence of intoxicating liquor).

Ky.—Jones v. Miller, 1951, 243 S.W. 2d 933.

Md.—Miller v. Hall, 155 A. 327, 161 Md. 111 (charge of negligence in collision at intersection brings up question of yielding right of way).

Mo.—Miller v. W. E. Callahan Const. Co., App., 46 S.W.2d 948; Alley v. Wall, App., 272 S.W. 999.

Or.—Fiebiger v. Rambo, 284 P. 565, 132 Or. 115.

Pa.—Altsman v. Kelly, 9 A.2d 423, 336 Pa. 481 (disregard of traffic signal).

But see

In action against receiver of street railway company, wherein passenger pleaded general negligence in collision between street car and automobile, evidence of negligence in sudden and abrupt stopping of street car held inadmissible. Hughes v. Kiel, Mo. App., 100 S.W.2d 48.

3. See section 427.3 for discussion of the relevancy of such evidence on the issue of negligence. Cases at this point in text are cited to

the general charge of negligence is restricted to acts of negligence in the operation of the vehicle evidence of faulty equipment is inadmissible.[4]

But where a party alleges specific acts of negligence, or where the petition contains a charge of general negligence coupled with specific acts of negligence, the party is confined to the specific acts,[5] unless the allegations of specific acts were intended

the question of admissibility under the pleadings.

Ala.—Kingry v. McCardle, 98 So.2d 44, 266 Ala. 533; Wise v. Schneider, 88 So. 662, 205 Ala. 537.

Ill.—Fox v. Hopkins, 99 N.E.2d 363, 343 Ill.App. 404, 26 A.L.R.2d 352.

N.C.—Rick v. Murphy, 110 S.E.2d 815, 251 N.C. 162.

Or.—Abel v. Cone, 1974, 520 P.2d 899, 268 Or. 339 (where alleged lack of control); Hall v. Tams, 346 P.2d 1115, 219 Or. 263; Walker v. Penner, 227 P.2d 316, 190 Or. 542.

S.C.—Milhouse v. Stroud, 131 S.E. 619, 134 S.C. 17.

Wash.—Shephard v. Smith, 88 P.2d 601, 198 Wash. 395.

Contra

Ga.—Southern Gas Corp. v. Cowan, 81 S.E.2d 488, 89 Ga.App. 810 (drunkenness must be alleged specifically in pleading before evidence of that fact can be introduced over objection).

Tex.—Surkey v. Smith, Civ.App., 136 S.W.2d 893, error refused (properly refused to permit plaintiff to ask defendant while on witness stand if he was not a drinking man, where there was no allegation of negligence based on intoxication, and plaintiff's own witnesses testified that defendant was not drunk at time of accident).

4. Ky.—Clifton v. McMakin, 157 S.W.2d 85, 288 Ky. 806.

5. Ariz.—Marcione v. Marcione, 289 P.2d 689, 79 Ariz. 336 (under specific allegation that defendant drove automobile in such a careless and negligent manner as to cause it to overturn, thereby injuring passenger, evidence as to any defect in mechanism of automobile, such as steering gear, which might probably cause it to overturn, and that defendant drove automobile with knowledge of such defect without warning passenger thereof was inadmissible).

Conn.—Nazionale v. Hutchinson, 1930, 152 A. 579, 112 Conn. 686.

Ga.—Smith v. Hodges, 161 S.E. 284, 44 Ga.App. 318.

Ky.—Couch's Adm'r v. Black, 1945, 190 S.W.2d 681, 301 Ky. 24; V. T. C. Lines v. Taylor, 134 S.W.2d 991, 281 Ky. 83; Lang v. Cooper, 1936, 90 S.W.2d 382, 262 Ky. 407.

Minn.—Baufield v. Warburton, 233 N.W. 237, 181 Minn. 506.

Mo.—Hoffman v. People's Motorbus Co. of St. Louis, App., 288 S.W. 948 (petition held to charge violation of speed ordinance by bus operator as specific act of negligence); Priebe v. Crandall, App. 1916, 187 S.W. 605.

Mont.—West v. Wilson, 4 P.2d 469, 90 Mont. 522 (plaintiff's allegation that defendant motorist neglected to keep lookout held narrowed by allegation of negligence in having windshield obscured).

N.D.—Peterson v. Bober, 56 N.W.2d 331, 79 N.D. 300.

Or.—Gano v. Zidell, 10 P.2d 365, 140 Or. 11, rehearing denied 12 P.2d 1118, 140 Or. 11.

§ 424.3   TRIAL EVIDENCE   Ch. 424

as an addition to, rather than a limitation of, the general charge of negligence.[6] Where a general allegation of negligence is followed by an explanatory charge of specific acts, the plaintiff is likewise confined to the specific acts, in some jurisdictions.[7] The rule has been extended to an amended petition containing specific acts of negligence, where the original petition contained allegations of general negligence.[8] This rule, however, does not preclude the admission of evidence which emphasizes the negligent character of the particular act charged, but which does not tend to establish an independent ground of negligence.[9]

Tex.—Yanowski v. Fort Worth Transit Co., Civ.App.1947, 204 S.W.2d 1001, ref. n. r. e.; Northern Texas Traction Co. v. Singer, Civ.App., 34 S.W.2d 920; Robert Oil Corporation v. Garrett, Civ.App.1929, 22 S.W.2d 508, affirmed, Com.App., 37 S.W.2d 135.

But see

Evidence that truck driver did not have license and that truck owner knew such fact was admissible where the plaintiff, in addition to alleging negligence of defendant in knowingly permitting driver to drive the truck, alleged many specific acts of negligence on the part of the driver, including the allegation that driver drove at an excessive rate of speed on icy pavement and that driver drove down center of highway. Garner v. Prescott, Tex.Civ.App., 234 S.W.2d 704.

6. **Cal.**—Jackson v. Hardy, 160 P.2d 161, 70 Cal.App.2d 6.

Colo.—Drumright v. Goldberg, 19 P.2d 764, 92 Colo. 271 (alleged "negligently and recklessly turned * * * without giving signal," proof not limited to failure to signal).

Ky.—Carpenter v. Page Bros. Motor Co., 242 S.W.2d 993 (where basic assertion in petition of motorist, who collided with rear of wrecking truck, was that wrecker had been stopped negligently upon traveled portion of highway, fact that he alleged negligence in that wrecker had been stopped on right side of highway at night without flares being placed on the highway did not preclude motorist from offering proof of other alleged acts of negligence); Diamond Taxicab Co. v. McDaniel, 1935, 80 S.W.2d 562, 258 Ky. 478; Coach Corporation v. Phillips, 1931, 34 S.W.2d 722, 236 Ky. 823.

Minn.—Baufield v. Warburton, 1930, 233 N.W. 237, 181 Minn. 506.

7. **U.S.**—Cherry v. Dealers Transport Co., D.C.Mo., 64 F.Supp. 682.

But see

Where petition in passenger's action against bus company when bus ran off highway contained an allegation of general negligence of bus driver, a subsequent allegation that accident was due wholly to driver's negligence and defective mechanism, brakes, and other mechanical parts of bus was not an allegation of specific negligence qualifying previous allegation of general negligence, and subsequent allegation did not limit passenger to proof of specific negligence. V. T. C. Lines v. Taylor, 134 S.W.2d 991, 281 Ky. 83.

8. **Ky.**—American Savings Life Ins. Co. v. Riplinger, 60 S.W.2d 115, 249 Ky. 8.

9. **U.S.**—St. Louis-San Francisco Ry. Co. v. Thompson, C.C.A.Miss., 30 F.2d 586; Boston & M. R. R. v. Card, C.C.A.Mass., 7 F.2d 428.

Conn.—De Antonio v. New Haven Dairy Co., 136 A. 567, 105 Conn.

Ch. 424   RELEVANCE AND MATERIALITY   § 424.3

If the plaintiff pleads alternate theories of recovery in separate counts, evidence in support of any of the various counts is properly admitted, even though the plaintiff may thereafter abandon the count under which the evidence was admissible.[10]

It has been held that pleading of wilful and wanton negligence does not commit the plaintiff to a theory of guest status, but rather the plaintiff may prove a status as a passenger other than a guest.[11]

Multiple defendant actions

A plaintiff who elects to sue two or more tort-feasors jointly, such joint liability not being predicated upon previous concert of action, is not bound to prove a joint wrong in order to re-

663 (may show violation of statute requiring slowing and turning to right upon meeting within allegation of illegal operation on left side).

Ga.—Steinmetz v. Chambley, 83 S.E. 2d 318, 90 Ga.App. 519 (evidence relating to white center line was admissible as illustrating character and condition of highway at place of collision although truck driver was not charged with passing where white line indicated passing was unsafe).

Minn.—Saylor v. Motor Inn, 162 N. W. 71, 136 Minn. 466.

Mo.—Floyd v. St. Louis Public Service Co., 280 S.W.2d 74 (where alleged both common-law negligence and violation of city ordinance regulating the parking of vehicles and requiring operator of vehicle overtaking and desiring to pass another to sound signaling device, and defendants contended that bicyclist was contributorily negligent, such provisions of ordinance were admissible in evidence, though plaintiffs did not intend to submit case to jury on issue of negligence based on violation of ordinance); Nash v. People's Motorbus Co. of St. Louis, App., 20 S.W.2d 570; Rettlia v. Salomon, 274 S.W. 366, 308 Mo. 673 (may show absence of skid chains).

Ohio.—Kronenberg v. Whale, 153 N.E. 302, 21 Ohio App. 322 (may show absence of lights on issue of inadequate warning).

Or.—McCarty v. Hedges, 321 P.2d 285, 212 Or. 497 (may show defective brakes on issues of negligent rate of speed and lack of control).

Vt.—Milligan v. Clogston, 138 A. 739, 100 Vt. 455 (may show condition of lights on issues of speed or lookout); Landry v. Hubert, 137 A. 97, 100 Vt. 268 (defective brakes may be shown under allegations of driving at a negligent rate of speed and lack of control).

W.Va.—Frampton v. Consolidated Bus Lines, 62 S.E.2d 126, 134 W. Va. 815 (may prove lack of lights on allegation of absence of warning).

But see

In action for death of guest, evidence as to indulgence by defendant and the deceased in intoxicants should not have been admitted where the complaint did not charge and the evidence did not show that defendant's indulgence affected his conduct or proximately contributed to the accident. La Fevre v. Bear, Fla.App., 113 So.2d 390.

10. **Mo.**—Borrson v. Missouri-Kansas-Texas R. Co., Sup., 161 S.W.2d 227.

11. **Ark.**—Dieter v. Byrd, 360 S.W. 2d 495, 235 Ark. 435.

415

§ 424.3   TRIAL EVIDENCE   Ch. 424

cover separately against a particular defendant, and is not confined to evidence admissible as against both.[12]

Evidence admissible under general denial

The occupation, ownership, or operation of a vehicle, set out as connected with or as the cause of the injuries of which the complaint is made, and the character in which the parties appear in the litigation are not put in issue by a plea of general denial.[13] Under the general issue, the defendant may show absence of the negligence charged;[14] that the driver was not the agent of the defendant;[15] or that the driver of defendant's automobile was the servant of an independent contractor,[16] or was acting beyond the scope of employment.[17]

Where the defendant adds certain specific denials to a general denial, it may be held that the defendant has not put in issue any question not specifically denied.[18]

12. Iowa.—McDonald v. Robinson, 224 N.W. 820, 207 Iowa 1293, 62 A.L.R. 1419.

Mo.—Brown v. Alton R. Co., 151 S. W.2d 727, 236 Mo.App. 26.

13. Fla.—Dowling v. Nicholson, 135 So. 288, 101 Fla. 672.

Ill.—Foreman Bros. Banking Co. v. Dudeck, 233 Ill.App. 364.

14. Ala.—Government Street Lumber Co. v. Ollinger, 94 So. 177, 18 Ala.App. 518, certiorari denied Ex parte Ollinger, 94 So. 922, 208 Ala. 699.

Iowa.—Kuehn v. Jenkins, 100 N.W. 2d 610, 251 Iowa 718.

Ky.—Mann v. Woodward, 290 S.W. 333, 217 Ky. 491 (that the defendant had the right of way).

Mo.—Virgil v. Riss & Co., App., 241 S.W.2d 96.

Intoxication of plaintiff

Ill.—Moore v. Daydif, 130 N.E.2d 119, 7 Ill.App.2d 534 (intoxication of pedestrian prior to accident).

Mo.—Boehm v. St. Louis Public Service Co., 368 S.W.2d 361 (evidence that motor scooter driver was not in full possession of his faculties or that his faculties were impaired by use of alcohol would be admissible under the general issue for injuries sustained by motor scooter passenger, and statement in hospital record pertaining to treatment of motor scooter driver that he had alcoholic breath was relevant and material and properly admitted).

15. Ill.—Dennehy v. W. A. Wood Co., 2 N.E.2d 586, 285 Ill.App. 598.

16. Okl.—Texas Pipe Line Co. of Oklahoma v. Willis, 45 P.2d 138, 172 Okl. 148.

17. La.—James v. J. S. Williams & Son, 150 So. 9, 177 La. 1033.

Tex.—Shrader v. Roberts, Civ.App., 255 S.W. 469.

Unauthorized use of car

Evidence that possession of automobile had been secured from garage by discharged chauffeur by misrepresentation, and was being driven by another at time of accident, not incompetent as proof of unpleaded defense. Kimbles v. Kelly, 43 P.2d 871, 6 Cal.App.2d 91.

18. Ohio.—Hermanies v. Standard Oil Co., 131 N.E.2d 233, 102 Ohio App. 143.

Evidence in support of the defense that the defendant was confronted with a sudden emergency is admissible under the general denial since such defense is neither an affirmative one nor one of confession and avoidance requiring it to be specially pleaded.[19] Also the defendant may be permitted to show a legal excuse for violation of a traffic law under the plea of general denial.[20]

It has been held that matters as to mitigation of damages must be pleaded to entitle the defendant to introduce such proof.[21]

Evidence admissible under plea of contributory negligence

Under a plea of contributory negligence, the defendant may be limited to proving only those specifications of negligence pleaded.[22] However, a general averment of contributory negligence may permit any proof constituting negligence,[23] and that

---

19. **Iowa**—Koob v. Schmolt, 1950, 45 N.W.2d 216, 241 Iowa 1294.

Mo.—Coffel v. Spradley, App.1973, 495 S.W.2d 735 (sudden brake failure); Payne v. Stott, App., 181 S.W.2d 161 (in passenger's action against taxicab operator when thrown to floor by sudden stop, evidence that driver was forced to make emergency stop when another car pulled from the curb without warning was available under general denial, because it tends to show driver was not negligent).

Va.—Southern Passenger Motor Lines v. Burks, 46 S.E.2d 26, 187 Va. 53.

But see

La.—Shell v. Nelson, App., 161 So. 639 (in action against driver of truck, crashing into automobile parked before filling station at night, that defendant was blinded by lights of automobile approaching from opposite direction held inadmissible, where such excuse was not pleaded).

Okl.—Yellow Taxicab & Baggage Co. v. Alsup, 52 P.2d 724, 175 Okl. 332.

20. **Utah.**—White v. Shipley, 160 P. 441, 48 Utah 496 (on wrong side of street due to excavation).

21. **Iowa.**—Morse v. Century Cab Co., 297 N.W. 877, 230 Iowa 443, 134 A.L.R. 635.

22. **La.**—Service Fire Ins. Co. of N. Y. v. Indiana Lumbermans Mut. Ins. Co., App., 111 So.2d 358 (court could not consider whether overtaking motorist was or was not guilty of contributory negligence in endeavoring to pass truck at intersection, where answer failed to charge attempt to pass at an intersection).

Plea of "gross intoxication"

Allegation of "gross intoxication", as set forth in defendant's answer that sole proximate cause of automobile accident was the carelessness and gross intoxication of the plaintiff, although not a model of draftsmanship, was sufficient to raise the issue of intoxication and therefore it was improper to exclude evidence of plaintiff's alleged intoxication. Crosby v. Sande, N.D.1970, 180 N.W.2d 164.

23. **Mass.**—Herman v. Sladofsky, 1938, 17 N.E.2d 879, 301 Mass. 534 (violation of statute).

Mo.—Rickman v. Sauerwein, 1971, 470 S.W.2d 487 (evidence tending to give support to negligence of pedestrian in permitting his automobile to be driven onto highway

§ 424.3   TRIAL EVIDENCE   Ch. 424

such negligence was a contributing cause of the injury.[24]

§ 424.4   Proof of Legal Fault—Conditions Existing

Library References:
    C.J.S. Motor Vehicles § 514 et seq.; Railroads § 842 et seq.
    West's Key No. Digests, Automobiles ⇒243; Railroads ⇒347.

Generally, any evidence of conditions leading up to or surrounding an automobile accident, which will throw light on the question of whether a traveler was in the exercise of due care at the time of the accident, is admissible.[25]

knowing it to be in defective condition, and in having his automobile stopped partially on the highway at night without lights was material and relevant, even though only contributory negligence of pedestrian submitted by motorist was that of alleged failure to keep careful lookout, where, in answering, motorist asserted general affirmative defense of contributory negligence, he submitted interrogatories which required pedestrian to state how he had left his automobile on the highway, and he was not, prior to submission, requested to specify acts to which he attributed pedestrian's negligence); Merritt v. Wilkerson, App.1962, 360 S.W.2d 283.

Tex.—St. Louis Southwestern Ry. Co. of Texas v. Daniel, Civ.App., 151 S.W.2d 877 (inadequate brakes).

But see

La.—Service Fire Ins. Co. of N. Y. v. Indiana Lumbermans Mut. Ins. Co., App., 111 So.2d 358 (general averments in defendant's plea that overtaking motorist failed "to take proper action to avoid the accident", and that he was "operating his vehicle in a careless and reckless manner without due regard to the property and safety of others," were insufficient to permit showing to be made that, contrary to statute, overtaking motorist endeavored to pass at intersection, or that he failed to sound horn).

24. **Iowa**—Hogan v. Nesbitt, 246 N.W. 270, 216 Iowa 75.

    Tex.—St. Louis Southwestern Ry. Co. of Texas v. Daniel, Civ.App., 151 S.W.2d 877.

25. For discussion of use of demonstrative models representing conditions that existed, see section 435.8, infra.

    U.S.—Horowitz v. Solomon, C.A.N. Y., 283 F.2d 759 (testimony of local traffic policeman that traffic on street that defendants' automobile was traveling upon was five to six times as heavy as that on street which plaintiffs' automobile was traveling upon); Wabash Ry. Co. v. Glass, C.C.A.Ohio, 32 F.2d 697.

    Ala.—Towney v. Thornton, 118 So. 230, 22 Ala.App. 598.

    Ark.—Kittrell v. Wilkerson, 9 S.W. 2d 788, 177 Ark. 1174.

    Colo.—Oliver v. Weaver, 212 P. 978, 72 Colo. 540.

    Ill.—Robbins v. Illinois Power & Light Corporation, 255 Ill.App. 106.

    Ind.—Whitaker v. Borntrager, 122 N. E.2d 734, 233 Ind. 678.

    Iowa.—Faatz v. Sullivan, 200 N.W. 321, 199 Iowa 875 (location of school buildings in an action for injuries to a boy while on his way to school).

    Ky.—Louisville & N. R. Co. v. Mahoney, 294 S.W. 777, 220 Ky. 30 (showing defective condition of

Ch. 424   RELEVANCE AND MATERIALITY   § 424.4

wig-wag bell some hours before crossing accident).

Me.—Fernald v. French, 115 A. 420, 121 Me. 4.

Mass.—Reardon v. Marston, 38 N.E. 2d 644, 310 Mass. 461.

Mich.—Buchel v. Williams, 262 N.W. 759, 273 Mich. 132.

Mo.—Rettlia v. Salomon, 274 S.W. 366, 308 Mo. 673.

Mont.—Koppang v. Sevier, 75 P.2d 790, 106 Mont. 79 (cautionary card received by driver as he entered upon part of highway being oiled).

N.H.—Wentworth Bus Lines v. Sanborn, 104 A.2d 392, 99 N.H. 5 (evidence as to room available to pass when defendant collided from rear); Putnam v. Bowman, 195 A. 865, 89 N.H. 200; Reed v. Nashua Buick Co., 147 A. 898, 84 N.H. 156 (justifying place of parking).

N.J.—Jones v. Lahn, 63 A.2d 804, 1 N.J. 358 (testimony that other vehicles passed parked vehicle before collision was admissible to show clearance between it and safety aisle in center of highway, though inadmissible to show dangerous character of situation).

N.M.—Miller v. Marsh, 201 P.2d 341, 53 N.M. 5.

N.Y.—Holder v. Abramson, 67 N.Y.S.2d 224, 271 App.Div. 649 (absence of any condition precluding keeping to right); O'Neil v. Kopke, 156 N.Y.S. 664, 170 App.Div. 601.

N.C.—Gaffney v. Phelps, 178 S.E. 231, 207 N.C. 553 (presence of hedge near intersection); Eaves v. Coxe, 165 S.E. 345, 203 N.C. 173 (dusty condition of road); Goss v. Williams, 145 S.E. 169, 196 N.C. 213; Plyler v. Southern Ry. Co., 117 S.E. 297, 185 N.C. 357.

Ohio.—Johnson v. Eastern Ohio Transport Corporation, 50 N.E.2d 1003, 72 Ohio App. 172 (width of bridge, as shown on scaled map).

Or.—West v. Jaloff, 232 P. 642, 113 Or. 184, 36 A.L.R. 1391.

Pa.—Fitzpatrick v. Pralon Cleaners & Dyers, 195 A. 644, 129 Pa.Super. 437.

R.I.—Town of Barrington v. De Stefano, R.I., 142 A. 164 (showing that vehicle was unusually noisy).

Tenn.—Coca-Cola Bottling Works v. Brown, 202 S.W. 926, 139 Tenn. 640.

Tex.—Richardson v. Impey, Civ.App., 94 S.W.2d 490, error dismissed (trailer out of line with truck two and one-half miles away).

Va.—Reid v. Boward, 26 S.E.2d 27, 181 Va. 718.

Wash.—Edwards v. Washkuhn, 119 P.2d 905, 11 Wash.2d 425 (testimony of operator of cafe that on night of accident plaintiffs stopped at her restaurant, and that the plaintiffs appeared tired and sleepy); Reamer v. Walter H. C. Griffiths, Inc., 291 P. 714, 158 Wash. 665 (amount of traffic at place of accident).

Wis.—Hefele v. Rotter, 222 N.W. 220, 197 Wis. 300 (sleepiness of driver prior to accident).

Wyo.—Merback v. Blanchard, 109 P. 2d 49, 56 Wyo. 286 (in action for death of truck driver as result of colliding with rear end of truck which stopped on highway because of defective lights, testimony as to dimming of rear warning lights on defendant's truck just before collision was relevant as tending to show conditions affecting visibility at time and place of collision, as against contention that, if rear lights were burning at all, their dimness was immaterial).

But see

Ill.—Padilla v. Walker, 91 N.E.2d 158, 340 Ill.App. 222 (distance parked from curb held immaterial where struck while standing behind parked car).

Mich.—Nordman v. Mechem, 198 N.W. 586, 227 Mich. 86 (evidence

419

§ 424.4   TRIAL EVIDENCE   Ch. 424

that area of pedestrian accident was populous inadmissible in absence of use by others at time in question).

Wash.—Burns v. Dills, 413 P.2d 370, 68 Wash.2d 377 (officer's solicited testimony in action for injuries sustained by surveyor who was working in unmarked crosswalk when he was hit by defendant's automobile which was making left turn and cutting corner, as to difficulty in making turn at intersection without cutting corner, was inadmissible as immaterial and as invading jury's province).

Circumstantial evidence of notice of defect in bridge

In action against county for injuries sustained when bridge collapsed, evidence as to necessity of frequent inspections of bridge structure was admissible for purpose of charging county with notice of defect. Turner County, S. D. v. Miller, C.A.S.D., 170 F.2d 820, certiorari denied 69 S.Ct. 656, 336 U.S. 925, 93 L.Ed. 1087.

Condition of electric line equipment

In motorist's action against electric company for injuries sustained when he came in contact with charged wire which, together with insulator, had fallen onto highway when pole was struck as result of automobile collision, wooden pin on which insulator was allegedly fastened prior to collision held properly admitted in evidence, in view of evidence justifying conclusion that pin was part of pin which had held wire, and was decayed and unsound. Robbins v. Thies, 189 A. 67, 117 N.J.L. 389.

Contra re school and school children in vicinity

In action for injuries sustained in a collision at an intersection, where the court ruled out all evidence with reference to schools and school children at the intersection and confined its ruling to allowing the plaintiff to show who was at the scene of the accident, and whether they were grown people and children, the ruling was proper. Smith v. Lawson, 88 So.2d 322, 264 Ala. 389.

Evidence of available inexpensive tests to predetermine defects

In action for death from electric wire broken when truck collided with pole, evidence that inexpensive tests before turning on current would have shown that wire was down was admissible. Edgarton v. H. P. Welch Co., 74 N.E.2d 674, 321 Mass. 603, 174 A.L.R. 462.

Eye condition of driver

Where action for death of guest was based on theory that defendant's automobile was being operated on wrong side of highway, jury had right to take into consideration condition of eyes of driver of defendant's automobile in determining whether he was on wrong side of highway. Campbell v. Trate, 149 P.2d 380, 112 Colo. 265.

Facts causing first collision which led to second

In action for injuries sustained when automobile in which plaintiff was riding at night collided with truck which had collided with another truck forming obstruction in highway, testimony of one truck driver that other truck driver drove his truck upon wrong side of pavement and head-on against other truck was improperly excluded on ground that collision between trucks had no causal connection with plaintiff's injuries. Johnson v. Sunshine Creamery Co., 274 N.W. 404, 200 Minn. 428.

Foundation required

Testimony of witness that from examining photograph of intersection and from his knowledge of the scene there were double yellow lines marking pavement at point where plaintiff made left turn was improperly admitted in view of other testimony of witness that he did not know whether pavement markings were in existence at time of collision. Boatner v. Sims, 1967, 154 S.E.2d 282, 115 Ga.App. 284.

Whenever condition of particular place or thing at certain time is in question, evidence of its condition at prior or subsequent time is inadmissible unless there is accompanying proof that it had not changed in the meantime. Murray v. Siegal, 195 A. 2d 790, 413 Pa. 23.

Other available route

In action for injuries sustained when plaintiff's automobile collided with rear of bakery truck while it was making a left turn between street intersections to reach entrance to bakery, testimony concerning back entrance to bakery was admissible, and its admission could not be prejudicial, since truck driver was under no compulsion to make left turn between intersections even to reach front entrance. Phoenix Baking Co. v. Vaught, 156 P.2d 725, 62 Ariz. 222.

Evidence that other automobiles at scene of fatal accident, occurring when decedent's vehicle crashed into the rear of defendant's log loader being operated on public highway, were being detoured around the scene on alternate route merely showed that automobiles could use the alternate route but did not prove that such route was available to the log loader or that he proceeded on highway in face of great danger, and trial court did not err in refusing to allow further evidence or argument to jury regarding alternate routes, a claim of negligence which trial court had properly stricken from pleading. Cutsforth v. Kinzua Corp., 1973, 517 P.2d 640, 267 Or. 423.

Place for parking disabled vehicle off highway

Evidence of location of driveways to service stations and other similar areas adjacent to highway into which plaintiff could have driven to park automobile entirely off pavement while changing tire was relevant to issue of possibility for plaintiff to have parked vehicle off of road or improved main traveled portion of highway. Ralston v. Vessey, 260 P. 2d 324, 43 Wash.2d 76.

Prior conduct evidencing relationship

Evidence that plaintiff's minor and defendants had been headlighting rabbits from car hood prior to time car suddenly rolled forward from parked position and struck plaintiff's minor who had taken position in front of car to shoot cans was admissible to show the relationship among the parties and trial court did not err in refusing plaintiff's motion in limine. Sauter v. Atchinson, 1971, 466 S.W.2d 475, 250 Ark. 697.

State manual re three-lane road

In action for injuries sustained in accident occurring in center or "passing" lane of three-lane highway, portions of state manual on uniform highway control devices containing instructions for design of three-lane highways and instructions for various lines and other traffic control devices placed on such highways were material to issue of whether defendant or plaintiff violated any statute in driving in center lane and were properly admitted over objection that information contained in document was immaterial. Konnerup v. Baker, 1971, 488 P.2d 241, —— Colo.App. ——.

Time interval after vehicle breakdown

Evidence as to whether driver of parked truck had time, after putting out fire in brake drum, to put out fusees, was material to issue of his negligence in not having put out fusees, and trial judge's comment, when admitting such evidence, that it was immaterial, was prejudicial. Grounds v. Roth, C.A.Okl., 210 F.2d 239.

§ 424.4 TRIAL EVIDENCE Ch. 424

However, before such evidence is admissible, it must be shown that it has some probative value in explaining the cause of the injury or the conduct of the parties, and is not a mere collateral search into immaterial matters.[26]

In proving the surrounding conditions at the time and place of various accidents, evidence has been admissible to show the weather conditions at the place of the accident;[27] and of the conditions of the roadway, including the shoulder.[28]

The existence of stop or warning signs where an automobile collision occurred may be shown on the question of negligence;[29]

26. See general discussion of limitation in section 424.1, at fn. 1 et seq.

27. **Ill.**—Guffey v. Gale, 74 N.E.2d 730, 332 Ill.App. 207 (where there is direct evidence as to weather conditions, testimony as to manner in which another motorist drove shortly before the accident tending to establish weather conditions at time and place of accident, was properly excluded and as not establishing a standard of care required to be exercised by motorist involved).

Ind.—Rodinelli v. Bowden, 1973, 293 N.E.2d 812, — Ind.App. — (8 to 10 miles from scene).

Md.—York Motor Exp. Co. v. State, for Use of Hawk, 74 A.2d 12, 195 Md. 525 (fog).

Mass.—Crowe v. Ward, 1973, 292 N. E.2d 716, 363 Mass. 85 (weather 7¼ miles away admissible, and expert could state chances of like weather at scene).

Okl.—Kellogg Sales Co. v. Holroyd, 73 P.2d 139, 181 Okl. 82 (wind).

Contra 25 miles distant
Weather Bureau reports of rainfall 25 miles from the property in question are not admissible to contradict testimony as to the rainfall at the place in question. Sunshine Packing Corp. v. Com., Pa.Com.Pl., 45 Erie 231, motion denied 45 Erie 237.

28. **Cal.**—Perry v. McLaughlin, 1931, 297 P. 554, 212 Cal. 1.

Colo.—Leonard v. Bauer, 149 P.2d 376, 112 Colo. 247 (evidence of dip on hay truck's right side of road 200 feet from point of collision was admissible as tending to show that there was a reason for the hay truck's not being on right side of road wholly unconnected with the oncoming truck).

Ga.—Scott v. Torrance, 25 S.E.2d 120, 69 Ga.App. 309.

Ky.—Lally v. Cochran, 1929, 21 S. W.2d 272, 231 Ky. 211.

Mich.—Parker v. Kettinger, 1932, 241 N.W. 226, 257 Mich. 385.

Tex.—John F. Buckner & Sons v. Allen, Civ.App.1956, 289 S.W.2d 387 (slickness of road).

29. **Ala.**—Harris v. Blythe, 130 So. 548, 222 Ala. 48 (stop signal).

Cal.—Anderson v. Newkirch, 1950, 225 P.2d 247, 101 Cal.App.2d 171.

Ill.—Hamann v. Lawrence, 188 N.E. 333, 354 Ill. 197.

Iowa.—Rogers v. Jefferson, 272 N. W. 532, 223 Iowa 718.

Mass.—Salvato v. Di Silva Transp. Co., 108 N.E.2d 51, 329 Mass. 305.

Miss.—Graves v. Johnson, 176 So. 256, 179 Miss. 465, followed in Graves v. Hamilton, 177 So. 360 (signs and objects indicating approach to end of usable part of highway).

Mo.—Arditi v. Brooks Erection Co., 1954, 266 S.W.2d 556 (stop sign at

§ 424.4

as may be evidence of the absence of warning signs.[30]

intersection); Scaggs v. Uetrecht, 1951, 244 S.W.2d 17 (presence of children); Pfeiffer v. Schee, App., 107 S.W.2d 170 (warning against stopping on pavement).

Ohio.—Willaman v. Graber, 1936, 11 N.E.2d 710, 57 Ohio App. 39.

Okl.—Burton v. Harn, 1945, 156 P.2d 618, 195 Okl. 232 (ordinance creating slow zone).

Or.—Harrison v. Avedovech, 1968, 439 P.2d 877, 249 Or. 584 ("deer" signs).

But see

Testimony of pedestrian hit while attempting to cross road that signs indicating 15-mile speed limit had been posted lacked evidential value in absence as to proof of location of the signs, authority for locating them, and location of those signs where motorist would or could have seen them. Fowler v. Smith, 213 A. 2d 549, 240 Md. 240.

Contra where not then applicable

In action arising out of collision at intersection where a school "slow" sign had been erected, evidence relative to the authority to erect the sign and the speed restriction established thereby was properly excluded as irrelevant where collision occurred at midnight. De Pace v. O'Neal, Del., 54 A.2d 854, 5 Terry 34.

Even in absence of evidence of public authority

Del.—Malcom v. Dempsey, 184 A.2d 474, 5 Storey 93.

Ohio.—McDonald v. Kelly, 134 N.E. 2d 396, 101 Ohio App. 46 (existence of "slow sign", short distance before intersection).

Tenn.—McMahan v. McMahan, 1954, 276 S.W.2d 738, 38 Tenn.App. 498 (admitting testimony concerning road warning signs approaching

traffic on the curve where the accident occured, and pictures of the road signs, on ground of failure to show they were erected by proper state authority, was not error, where signs appeared to be of the type used generally, were so located as to give warning of the curve and since it would be presumed in absence of a contrary showing that the signs were placed by lawful authority).

Status of sign as advisory only

In view of testimony indicating existence of 15-mile-per-hour speed sign north of intersection, highway department's regulation denoting sign of type involved as merely advisory was admissible to rebut any inference that commissioner of highways had determined that speed limit otherwise established was greater than that reasonable or safe under conditions found to exist. Swanson v. Thill, 1967, 152 N.W.2d 85, 277 Minn. 122.

Yellow lines on roadway

Presence and crossing of yellow line on highway were evidential details in totality of circumstances involved in accident causing injury to passenger when operator lost control of automobile as it began to skid on wet blacktop while operator was passing another vehicle or vehicles, and, therefore, admission of evidence as to crossing of yellow lines was not error. Rushing v. Polk, 128 S.E.2d 675, 258 N.C. 256.

30. **Ark.**—McGeorge Contracting Co. v. Mizell, 226 S.W.2d 566, 216 Ark. 509 (as to fact highway and bridge under repair).

Wash.—Sage v. Northern Pac. Ry. Co., 380 P.2d 856, 62 Wash.2d 6 (lack of signs requiring chains on mountain pass, where such signs are customarily posted by highway department).

§ 424.4 　　　　TRIAL EVIDENCE　　　　Ch. 424

Evidence of conditions remote in time and distance from the time and place of the accident in question is inadmissible.[31] Evi-

---

[31] **Cal.**—Formosa v. Yellow Cab Co., 87 P.2d 716, 31 Cal.App.2d 77 (markers at other intersections); Perry v. McLaughlin, 297 P. 554, 212 Cal. 1 (character of road).

Idaho.—Hoffman v. Barker, 330 P. 2d 978, 80 Idaho 372 (condition of highway one week before accident was properly excluded); Jakeman v. Oregon Short Line R. Co., 256 P. 88, 43 Idaho 505.

Iowa.—Tobin v. Van Orsdol, 45 N.W. 2d 239, 241 Iowa 1331; Strand v. Grinnell Automobile Garage Co., 113 N.W. 488, 136 Iowa 68 (condition of highway 300 feet away from place of accident).

Mich.—Janse v. Haywood, 259 N.W. 347, 270 Mich. 632.

Mo.—Fenton v. Missouri Motor Distributing Corporation, App., 52 S.W.2d 213 (testimony of highway engineer as to visibility at other points).

N.J.—Williamson v. Berger, 95 A.2d 150, 11 N.J. 500.

Ohio.—Winters v. Pence, 123 N.E.2d 669, 97 Ohio App. 59 (in absence of evidence that intersecting street that child bicyclist was traveling on was a stop street, admission of evidence that some streets intersecting street were stop streets, was prejudicial error).

Pa.—Becker v. Saylor, 177 A. 804, 317 Pa. 573.

Wash.—Rutherford v. Deur, 282 P. 2d 281, 46 Wash.2d 435 (evidence, submitted upon issue whether defendant had had his lights on, as to street lights in parts of city other than at scene of collision, was irrelevant and inadmissible, but its admission was not prejudicial error).

Condition of highway at prior time held proper

Or.—Clement v. Cummings, 317 P.2d 579, 212 Or. 161 (condition of highway when observed approximately 45 minutes prior to the accident).

Condition of highway elsewhere

N.Y.—Hurst v. City of New York, 279 N.Y.S. 64, 244 App.Div. 737 (proper to show absence of ice elsewhere).

Distant warning sign

Exclusion of testimony by state policeman as to signs warning of gusty winds was not abuse of discretion where nearest such sign was 25 miles from scene and there was no showing as to relevancy of signs at such distances. Pavlos v. Albuquerque Nat. Bank, 1971, 487 P.2d 187, 82 N.M. 759.

Knowledge of status as through highway at point fifty miles away

N.D.—Austinson v. Kilpatrick, 105 N.W.2d 258 (where collision occurred with automobile proceeding on inferior highway from which stop sign had been removed by repair crew, testimony sought to be elicited from motorist's wife that he knew that intersecting highway was a through highway at an intersection approximately 50 miles south of the intersection at which collision occurred was properly excluded).

Weather conditions at distant location

Where defendant contended that fog obscured his view, testimony of meteorologist at airport weather bureau 15 miles from point of accident concerning weather and fog conditions at airport was incompetent. Harding v. Hoffman, 62 N.W. 2d 333, 158 Neb. 86.

Wind conditions earlier

Or.—Marshall v. Martinson, 1973, 518 P.2d 1312, 268 Or. 46 (though existence or nonexistence of strong winds at time and place of accident

dence of such conditions is regarded as not too remote if traced almost to the scene of the accident.[32]

Railroad crossing collisions

In an action arising out of a collision at a railroad crossing, the jury may be informed of the whole area covered by the acts attending the collision.[33] The erection and maintenance of build-

was in issue due to defendants' contention that action of wind against side of "camper" or "canopy" body on plaintiff's empty pickup truck could have caused it to strike automobile, evidence of certified copies of official weather records showing wind velocity at various times during day of accident at specified weather stations was inadmissible where lapse of four hours existed between recording of the data and time of the accident).

32. **Idaho.**—Jakeman v. Oregon Short Line R. Co., 256 P. 88, 43 Idaho 505.

Mo.—McCrary v. Ogden, Sup., 267 S.W.2d 670 (testimony that thirteen miles from point of collision witness observed a log protruding approximately two feet beyond left front side of truck bed was relevant in view of direct testimony that same condition as to protruding log existed at time of collision and testimony as to manner in which logs were loaded and that truck had not stopped between loading and collision points).

Va.—Nelson v. Dayton, 36 S.E.2d 535, 184 Va. 754 (pedestrian's evidence relating to congestion of area immediately adjacent to point of collision was admissible).

33. **Ala.**—Atlantic Coast Line R. Co. v. McLendon, 94 So. 193, 18 Ala. App. 669 (location of pile of crossties); Alabama Great Southern R. Co. v. Molette, 93 So. 644, 207 Ala. 624 (rail sticking up).

Cal.—Mallett v. Southern Pac. Co., 68 P.2d 281, 20 Cal.App.2d 500.

Ill.—Campbell v. Chicago, B. & Q. R. Co., 27 N.E.2d 327, 305 Ill.App. 264.

Miss.—Magers v. Okolona, Houston & Calhoun City R. Co., 165 So. 416, 174 Miss. 860 (absence of street light at crossing).

Mo.—McKerall v. St. Louis-San Francisco Ry. Co., App., 257 S.W. 166.

N.C.—Caldwell v. Southern Ry. Co., 10 S.E.2d 680, 218 N.C. 63.

Ohio.—Franklin v. Nowak, 1935, 4 N.E.2d 232, 53 Ohio App. 44; Strayer v. New York Cent. R. Co., 179 N.E. 424, 41 Ohio App. 19.

Or.—Case v. Northern Pac. Terminal Co., 1945, 160 P.2d 313, 176 Or. 643 (absence of automatic signal).

S.C.—Moore v. Atlantic Coast Line R. Co., 7 S.E.2d 4, 192 S.C. 406.

Condition of bridge at point other than where vehicle went off

Testimony relating to condition of guard rail on south side of overhead railroad bridge, though automobile went off from the north side, was admissible to show general defective condition of bridge. Central of Georgia Ry. Co. v. Keating, 165 S.E. 873, 45 Ga.App. 811, reversed on other grounds 170 S.E. 493, 177 Ga. 345, conformed to 170 S.E. 497, 47 Ga. App. 336.

Contra as to distant crossing

Pictures of crossing one block distant from crossing in question were inadmissible for purpose of showing contrast between warning devices. Missouri Pac. R. Co. v. Emberton, 327 S.W.2d 726, 230 Ark. 865.

§ 424.4   TRIAL EVIDENCE   Ch. 424

ings near railroad tracks may be shown on the questions of negligence in the operation of a train and the contributory negligence of a motorist.[34] However, evidence of the location of objects a considerable distance from the crossing is inadmissible.[35]

Generally, however, evidence of the existence of objects which allegedly obstruct the view of a crossing is admissible.[36] Likewise, other proof relevant to the question of visibility at the crossing are properly shown.[37]

§ 424.5   Proof of Legal Fault—Conditions Subsequent to Accident

Library References:
   C.J.S. Motor Vehicles § 516.
   West's Key No. Digests, Automobiles ⚖=243(14).

Evidence as to conditions at the place of the accident at a time thereafter is admissible upon a proper showing that the conditions had not been changed in the meantime.[38]

Similar crossings at other locations

Evidence as to conditions existing at similar railroad grade crossings in the same general area may be admissible in an action arising out of an accident at another railroad grade crossing if a showing is made as to similarity and relevancy. Martindale v. City of Mountain View, 25 Cal.Rptr. 148, 208 Cal.App.2d 109.

34. **U.S.**—Knight v. Baltimore & O. R. Co., D.C.N.Y., 8 F.R.D. 256.

   Tex.—Texas & P. Ry. Co. v. Eddleman, Civ.App., 175 S.W. 775.

35. **Ohio.**—Franklin v. Nowak, 4 N. E.2d 232, 53 Ohio App. 44 (coal yard and other objects over 75 feet away).

36. **Ala.**—Callaway v. Adams, 40 So.2d 73, 252 Ala. 136.

   N.C.—Williams v. Randolph & C. Ry. Co., 108 S.E. 915, 182 N.C. 267 (undergrowth obstructing view).

   Tex.—Wichita Falls & S. R. Co. v. Hesson, Civ.App., 151 S.W.2d 270, error dismissed, judgment correct.

37. **Ala.**—Alabama Great Southern R. Co. v. Molette, 93 So. 644, 207 Ala. 624 (height of a fill on which tracks approached the crossing).

   Ill.—Johnson v. Chicago & N. W. Ry. Co., 132 N.E.2d 678, 9 Ill.App.2d 340 (on ground testimony was evidence of tests or experiments).

Difficulty experienced by others in seeing approaching locomotives

Testimony of other motorists as to difficulty of seeing approaching locomotives at the crossing and near accidents resulting from such difficulty was admissible. Texas Mexican R. Co. v. Bunn, Tex.Civ.App., 264 S.W. 2d 518.

Objects deepening shadows

Color of object on highway on a dark night and presence of other objects which might deepen the shadows in that vicinity must be considered in determining how clearly standing train car might be seen by means of standard automobile headlights. Mallett v. Southern Pac. Co., 68 P.2d 281, 20 Cal.App.2d 500.

38. **U.S.**—Padgett v. Buxton-Smith Mercantile Co., C.A.N.M., 262 F.2d 39; Richter v. Hoglund, C.C.A.Wis., 132 F.2d 748; Evansville Container

Ch. 424   RELEVANCE AND MATERIALITY   § 424.5

Corporation v. McDonald, C.C.A. Tenn., 132 F.2d 80; American Film Co. v. Moye, C.C.A.Cal., 267 F. 419 (witnesses testified as to condition of road and marks thereon immediately following accident, which authorized jury to draw proper inference as to whether the condition of the road was the same at the time another witness saw it as it was at the time of the accident).

Ala.—Holley v. Josey, 82 So.2d 328, 263 Ala. 349 (testimony as to objects found at scene about six hours after accident, but defendants would be entitled on cross-examination to show all facts surrounding witnesses' observations, including lapse of time, fact that many people had gathered around scene of accident, and fact that there was much travel over highway); Davis v. Radney, 38 So.2d 867, 251 Ala. 629.

Ark.—McGeorge Contracting Co. v. Mizell, 226 S.W.2d 566, 216 Ark. 509 (absence of warning signs indicating that the road was under repair or that bridge was out, three or four days later); Floyd v. Johnston, 100 S.W.2d 975, 193 Ark. 518 (measurements of road made about 8 months later).

Ill.—Meade v. Robinson, 100 N.E.2d 400, 344 Ill.App. 189 (photographs several months later); Thomas v. Buchanan, 277 Ill.App. 393 (existence and visibility of "stop" signs on night of day following occurrence).

Iowa.—Baysinger v. Haney, 1968, 155 N.W.2d 496, 261 Iowa 577; Brower v. Quick, 88 N.W.2d 120, 249 Iowa 569; Soreide v. Vilas & Co., 78 N.W.2d 41, 247 Iowa 1139; Meier v. Town of Cushing, 68 N.W.2d 74, 246 Iowa 441 (testimony of driver, based on investigation made two days after accident, that automobile struck a ridge and hole in graveled street); Hackman v. Beckwith, 64 N.W.2d 275, 245 Iowa 791; Hayes v. Stunkard, 10 N.W.2d 19, 233 Iowa 582 (testimony as to where a squash, which deceased was carrying when struck, was found).

Ky.—Shewmaker v. Richeson, 344 S.W.2d 802; Arnett v. Dalton, 257 S.W.2d 585; Emerine v. Ford, 254 S.W.2d 938; Whitney v. Louisville & N. R. Co., 138 S.W.2d 503, 282 Ky. 392 (manner electric railroad crossing signal operated during afternoon following the morning of collision).

La.—Massicot v. Nolan, App., 65 So. 2d 648.

Me.—Masse v. Wing, 149 A. 385, 129 Me. 33.

Mass.—Lilien v. Bibby, 167 N.E.2d 863, 341 Mass. 206 (permitting police officer, who arrived at scene approximately 15 minutes later, to testify that automobiles had been moved, that lights on plaintiffs' automobile were not then lighted, that he had a diagram on which he had made reference to lights on plaintiffs' automobile, and that he saw mud and dirt on easterly lane for 40 feet beginning five feet beyond street intersection, at which defendant allegedly was making a left turn, was not error).

Mich.—Delfosse v. Bresnahan, 9 N.W.2d 866, 305 Mich. 621.

Minn.—Martinco v. Hastings, 122 N.W.2d 631, 265 Minn. 490; Raths v. Sherwood, 262 N.W. 563, 195 Minn. 225 (in action for pedestrian's death caused when automobile collided with deceased, or with horses which deceased and another were leading by halters on right shoulder of highway at night, evidence as to tracks of horses and skid marks of automobile observed next morning at place of accident); Quinn v. Zimmer, 239 N.W. 902, 184 Minn. 589 (day after accident).

Neb.—Spani v. Whitney, 110 N.W.2d 103, 172 Neb. 550 (condition of accident site when he arrived

427

§ 424.5   TRIAL EVIDENCE   Ch. 424

some 17 minutes after accident); Tate v. Borgman, 92 N.W.2d 697, 167 Neb. 299; Styskal v. Brickey, 62 N.W.2d 854, 158 Neb. 208 (testimony of police officers who arrived at scene shortly after accident, before automobiles were moved); Ficke v. Gibson, 45 N.W.2d 436, 153 Neb. 478.

N.H.—Bennett v. Bennett, 31 A.2d 374, 92 N.H. 379.

N.J.—Girdwood v. Balder, 140 A. 894, 6 N.J.Misc. 302 (more than one witness may be used to show that conditions testified to remained the same as at time of accident).

N.Y.—Hickey v. City of New York, 1967, 284 N.Y.S.2d 7, 28 A.D.2d 1008; Broderick v. City of New York, 7 N.Y.S.2d 809, 255 App.Div. 875 (lights at scene where automobile ran into excavation).

N.C.—Hatcher v. Clayton, 88 S.E.2d 104, 242 N.C. 450 (testimony by witness who, several hours after accident, visited scene and saw footprints and tire marks on shoulder, was admissible as corroborative of pedestrian's testimony, even though the footprints were not identified as those of pedestrian nor the wheel tracks identified as those of defendants' truck); Lambert v. Caronna, 175 S.E. 303, 206 N.C. 616.

Ohio.—Schaller v. Chapman, App., 66 N.E.2d 266, 44 O.L.A. 631; Bailey v. Parker, 170 N.E. 607, 34 Ohio App. 207 (wheel marks after application of brake, showing distance traveled after blow-out).

Okl.—Maples v. Bryce, 1967, 434 P.2d 214 (highway patrolman, who arrived at scene a short time after the occurrence, could testify with respect to physical facts at place of accident); Groninger & King, Inc. v. T. I. M. E. Freight, Inc., 1963, 384 P.2d 39.

Or.—Burnham v. Eshleman, 1971, 479 P.2d 501, 257 Or. 400 (testified that road was same as nearly as he could see); Myhre v. Peterson, 378 P.2d 1002, 233 Or. 470 (position of pedestrian in street after he was hit by automobile); Clark v. Fazio, 230 P.2d 553, 191 Or. 522; West v. Marion County, 188 P. 184, 95 Or. 529 (testimony as to width of road and height of grade competent).

Pa.—Mantz v. Rufft, 170 A.2d 101, 403 Pa. 436.

Tenn.—Colwell v. Jones, 346 S.W.2d 450, 48 Tenn.App. 353 (condition of road a few days before trial at and near scene).

Tex.—Chesshir v. Nall, Tex.Civ.App., 218 S.W.2d 248, ref. n. r. e.; Lone Star Gas Co. v. Haire, Civ.App., 41 S.W.2d 424 (testimony that immediately after accident truck was on left-hand side of road is admissible on the issue whether the truck driver swerved to left, as testified by a motorist attempting to pass).

Va.—Mosley v. Chenault, 125 S.E.2d 832, 203 Va. 648; Richardson v. Lovorn, 101 S.E.2d 511, 199 Va. 688.

Wis.—Carstensen v. Faber, 1962, 116 N.W.2d 161, 17 Wis.2d 242; Atkinson v. Huber, 1955, 68 N.W.2d 447, 268 Wis. 615.

Addition of stop sign

Testimony of photographer on cross-examination that since the date of the accident a stop sign had been placed to control traffic proceeding in the lane in which plaintiffs were traveling at time of intersectional collision was irrelevant and inadmissible. Leuck v. Goetz, 1972, 280 N.E.2d 847, 151 Ind.App. 528.

Inconsequential variance

Testimony of highway maintenance foreman as to width of shoulder at location of accident was admissible, even though high weeds or grass existed on shoulder at time

Ch. 424   RELEVANCE AND MATERIALITY   § 424.5

Wheel marks and tracks,[39] skid marks,[40] and other marks

of collision and not at time foreman made his measurements, where foreman did not testify as to weeds or grass on shoulder at time of collision. Gerler v. Cooley, 190 N.E.2d 488, 41 Ill.App. 233.

No error in exclusion

In action by driver for injuries sustained when automobile overturned during freeway lane-changing maneuver, court did not abuse its discretion in excluding expert evidence that paint scrapings taken from median rail matched paint of driver's car, where scrapings were taken some three years after accident in question. Culpepper v. Volkswagen of America, Inc., 1973, 109 Cal.Rptr. 110, 33 Cal.App.3d 510.

In action arising out of collision of plaintiff's automobile with rear end of defendants' tractor-trailer parked on road, where all witnesses other than plaintiff testified that lights were burning on rear of trailer at time of accident, evidence as to condition of truck's electrical system and lights on morning following accident had little, if any, probative value on issues whether lights were burning at time of collision or were so covered with road dirt as to be not readily visible, and hence exclusion of evidence was proper exercise of discretion. Johnson v. Lee Way Motor Freight, Inc., Mo., 261 S.W.2d 95.

Exclusion of owner's proffered evidence showing that subsequent to collision between calf and his automobile on highway a cow was seen on same side of highway within 50 yards of scene was not abuse of discretion. Hartford Ins. Group v. Massey, Miss., 1968, 216 So.2d 415.

Operation of traffic signals

Okl.—Short v. Unsell, 1972, 497 P.2d 1060 (exclusion of proffered testimony of police officer who investigated accident that after the accident the traffic light was showing green for both eastbound and southbound traffic was reversible error).

39. Ala.—McPherson v. Martin, 174 So. 791, 234 Ala. 244 (automobile tracks); McWhorter Transfer Co. v. Peek, 167 So. 291, 232 Ala. 143 (automobile tracks).

Ark.—Jewel Tea Co. v. McCrary, 122 S.W.2d 534, 197 Ark. 294 (testimony of witness who viewed scene about 12 hours after it occurred, that tracks at the scene indicated that motorist's automobile had passed the truck before the accident, and that the other automobile had turned to the left just before the collision).

Cal.—Hughes v. Hartman, 273 P. 560, 206 Cal. 199 (testimony as to automobile tracks going over highway embankment given by witness at scene 2½ hours after accident occurred).

Iowa.—Stutzman v. Younkerman, 216 N.W. 627, 204 Iowa 1162 (wheel tracks in mud and marks on curb observed about five hours after accident and again twelve hours after).

Kan.—Thomas v. Meyer, 95 P.2d 267, 150 Kan. 587 (proper to permit a witness who arrived a few minutes after it occurred, and before either the automobile or truck had been moved, to testify that tracks of truck started at certain point on shoulder of highway and as to the path followed by the tracks from the point where he first observed them to the point where the truck was when he arrived).

Ky.—Whitehead v. Stith, 131 S.W.2d 455, 279 Ky. 556 (evidence of eyewitness about 100 feet from the scene that he went to the scene immediately after the acci-

---

40. See note 40 on page 430.

§ 424.5 TRIAL EVIDENCE Ch. 424

dent and observed fresh sliding tracks on pavement extending about 21 feet back from defendant's automobile was competent, especially where there was other testimony to same effect, and that defendant had applied brakes).

Md.—Gloyd v. Wills, 23 A.2d 665, 180 Md. 161 (testimony of marks on the road clearly shown to have been made by one of the automobiles); Opecello v. Meads, 135 A. 488, 152 Md. 29, 50 A.L.R. 1385 (testimony as to wheel marks seen half hour after pedestrian's injury held admissible).

Mich.—Wilhelm v. Skiffington, 103 N.W.2d 451, 360 Mich. 348 (even though police officer testifying could not positively connect the marks with automobile's tires); Pearce v. Rodell, 276 N.W. 883, 283 Mich. 19 (automobile tracks on berm).

Miss.—Arnold v. Reece, 92 So.2d 237, 229 Miss. 862 (that on Monday after Saturday night when accident happened, witness saw heavy tracks leading from point of impact onto shoulder of road and that, if truck's right dual wheels were off highway at place of contact, they would not have lined up with such tracks).

N.H.—Abbott v. Hayes, 26 A.2d 842, 92 N.H. 126 (admission of testimony of plaintiff's witness, in response to question concerning where left rear wheels of truck would have been if certain marks on the highway were made by the right rear wheels, was not error).

N.Y.—Coffin v. Cunningham, 206 N. Y.S.2d 353, 11 A.D.2d 1082 (observations of tire marks in newly fallen snow on highway and running to vehicle).

N.D.—Attleson v. Boomgarden, 73 N. W.2d 448.

Wash.—McCreedy v. Fournier, 194 P. 398, 113 Wash. 351 (witness may testify that, on the morning after an accident, he noticed zigzag tracks leading to the immediate scene of the accident, where the plaintiff's contention is that the defendants were driving on the left side of the road, notwithstanding defendants' claim that other cars might have passed in the meantime, where the witness testifies that there had been a slight rain, settling the dust, and that he did not see any other tracks, but noticed the tracks in question, leading to the place of the accident, where plaintiff's car was on its side).

Wis.—Rausch v. Buisse, 146 N.W.2d 801, 33 Wis.2d 154.

40. **U.S.**—D. C. Transit System, Inc. v. Acors, D.C.App., 1972, 293 A.2d 871 (in light of directly conflicting testimony concerning speed at which plaintiff's automobile and defendant's bus were traveling prior to collision, concerning view toward top of hill, and concerning which vehicle first entered intersection, photographs of scene, which contained skid marks, were relevant to issues of negligence and contributory negligence, it was an abuse of discretion to deny admission of the photographs); Elek v. Boyce, D.C.S.C.1970, 308 F.Supp. 26.

Ariz.—Mattingly v. Eisenberg, 285 P.2d 174, 79 Ariz. 135 (testimony by witnesses who saw accident, heard screeching of brakes, saw location of automobile when brakes were applied, observed its course and later watched police officer's measurement of skid marks, warranted permitting officer to testify to measurement of skid marks, even though he had not been present when marks were made).

Cal.—Bowker v. Illinois Electric Co., 297 P. 615, 112 Cal.App. 740 (marks apparently made by tires when brakes were applied); Flach v. Fikes, 267 P. 1079, 204 Cal. 329.

Ill.—Conway v. Tamborini, 215 N.E. 2d 303, 68 Ill.App.2d 190 (admission of testimony as to his measurements of skid marks, some five hours after accident, did not constitute reversible error as such evidence was cumulative in nature, where other witnesses had also testified as to length of skid marks); Mondin v. Decatur Cartage Co., 60 N.E.2d 38, 325 Ill.App. 332; Hann v. Brooks, 73 N.E.2d 624, 331 Ill.App. 535 (and photographs of vehicles); Johnson v. McKnight, 39 N.E.2d 700, 313 Ill. App. 260 (testimony of witnesses that the next morning they examined the pavement and found skid marks extending to a place where motorist's automobile was stopped, was admissible over objection that it was incompetent because other automobiles had passed over the highway, where such automobiles could not have made the marks concerning which the witnesses testified).

Ind.—Grossnickle v. Avery, 152 N. E. 288, 96 Ind.App. 479.

Iowa—Weilbrenner v. Owens, 68 N. W.2d 293, 246 Iowa 580; Thornbury v. Maley, 45 N.W.2d 576, 242 Iowa 70 (skid marks near scene and just off highway pavement); Brady v. McQuown, 40 N.W.2d 25, 241 Iowa 34 (testimony of highway patrolman that tire marks led to defendants' car).

Ky.—Adrian v. McGillivray, 243 S. W.2d 895 (observed by witnesses about an hour and a half after accident); Lever Bros. Co. v. Stapleton, 233 S.W.2d 1002, 313 Ky. 837 (skid or tire marks on highway and blood spots as being 54 feet from truck); Bybee Bros. v. Imes, 155 S.W.2d 492, 288 Ky. 1 (testimony of witness who arrived at scene within a few minutes and saw skid marks that ran from the truck's right side of the road to the left and to the place where the accident occurred).

La.—Moore v. Johnson, 1972, 262 So.2d 105.

Md.—Fowler v. Smith, 213 A.2d 549, 240 Md. 240 (not admissible unless there is sufficient showing either from time of observation, from relative location of marks and vehicle, or other convincing facts to support reasonable inference that the marks had been made by vehicle involved); Williams v. Graff, 71 A.2d 450, 194 Md. 516, 23 A.L.R.2d 106 (skid marks on highway in proximity to pool of blood); Sheer v. Rathje, 197 A. 613, 174 Md. 79 (testimony about location of skid marks, indicating that accident occurred in pedestrians' crossing, though witness testified that actual identification was difficult and that he identified marks "by the logic of the thing.")

Mass.—Mernagh v. Lillie, 1942, 45 N.E.2d 473, 312 Mass. 697.

Minn.—Raths v. Sherwood, 1935, 262 N.W. 563, 195 Minn. 225 (observed following day).

Mo.—Neavill v. Klemp, 1968, 427 S.W.2d 446 (by officer who arrived about five minutes later); Clark v. Reising, 107 S.W.2d 33, 341 Mo. 282 (testimony as to skid marks observed by automobile repairman not over hour after accident).

N.Y.—Boyer v. Scripter, 102 N.Y.S. 2d 2, 278 App.Div. 601; Lazar v. Westchester Street Transp. Co., 51 N.Y.S.2d 533, 268 App.Div. 387 (position of cars and skid marks 10 or 20 minutes after accident).

Ohio—Brewer v. Crupper, 173 N.E. 2d 178.

Pa.—Kissell v. Motor Age Transit Lines, 1947, 53 A.2d 593, 359 Pa. 204 (and gouges, which led directly to one vehicle).

Tex.—Vandel v. Seitz, Civ.App., 396 S.W.2d 227.

Va.—Stevens v. Summers, 150 S.E.2d 83, 207 Va. 320 (although witness

§ 424.5   TRIAL EVIDENCE   Ch. 424

on the roadway [41] at the scene are generally admissible.

stated he did not know when they were made or who made them, since it could be inferred that the marks which were the only ones present on highway after accident had been left by one of the two vehicles involved); Venable v. Stockner, 1959, 108 S.E.2d 380, 200 Va. 900.

W.Va.—Bragg v. C. I. Whitten Transfer Co., 26 S.E.2d 217, 125 W.Va. 722.

Wis.—Zinda v. Pavloski, Wis., 139 N.W.2d 563, 29 Wis.2d 640 (if evidence is not so remote in time and is located so as to be reasonably attributable to particular automobile involved, trial court in its discretion may permit); Beyer v. Schuett, 1953, 57 N.W.2d 701, 263 Wis. 498.

No error in exclusion

Md.—Kirsch v. Ford, 183 A. 240, 170 Md. 90 (on issue of which of colliding automobiles was partly on wrong side of road, excluding evidence of skid mark measurements made by officer who arrived an hour and a half after accident held not reversible error, where measurements were made in necessary reliance upon identification by witnesses whose observations were made immediately after collision and who testified as to length and direction of marks, and position rather than extent of skid marks was important); Marine v. Stewart, 168 A. 891, 165 Md. 698 (in absence of proof that conditions three days after collision were same as at time of collision, and that no other automobile had been there, evidence concerning skid marks on concrete in front of road machine collided with held properly excluded, where testimony of defendant's employee concerning skid marks of plaintiff's automobile immediately after accident was uncontradicted).

Neb.—Egenberger v. National Alfalfa Dehydrating & Milling Co., 83 N.W.2d 523, 164 Neb. 704 (evidence as to skidding tracks around curve near which accident occurred was properly excluded in absence of proof that such tracks were made by automobile in which passenger was riding).

Or.—Brice v. Danisch, 1966, 419 P. 2d 18, 244 Or. 505.

41. U.S.—Wilkins v. Hogan, C.A. Kan.1970, 425 F.2d 1022 (gouge).

Cal.—Whitfield v. Debrincat, 1942, 123 P.2d 591, 50 Cal.App.2d 389 (where gouge commenced).

Conn.—Engelke v. Wheatley, 171 A. 2d 402, 148 Conn. 398 (testimony of police officer regarding scratches found in concrete on morning following collision); Tomasko v. Raucci, 155 A. 64, 113 Conn. 274.

Idaho—McKee v. Chase, 253 P.2d 787, 73 Idaho 491 (where impact allegedly dislodged drive shaft of truck and drive shaft caused gouges in road permanent in nature, witnesses' testimony as to their observation of such gouges from one to four days after accident was not too remote).

Ky.—Southern Oxygen Co. v. Martin, 1942, 163 S.W.2d 459, 291 Ky. 238 (observed day following).

Miss.—Wallace v. Billups, 1948, 33 So.2d 819, 203 Miss. 853 (grease spots, scratches and skid marks, observed following day).

Or.—Davis v. Lavenik, 1946, 165 P.2d 277, 178 Or. 90 (scrape mark made by bicycle); Peters v. Consolidated Freight Lines, 1937, 73 P.2d 713, 157 Or. 605 (indentations observed 3–4 months later).

Pa.—Kissell v. Motor Age Transit Lines, 1947, 53 A.2d 593, 357 Pa. 204 (skid marks and gouges which led directly to one vehicle).

Ch. 424   RELEVANCE AND MATERIALITY   § **424.5**

Evidence of the location of broken glass and other debris on a highway after an accident is admissible.[42] The same is true as to the location of [43] or the condition [44] of a vehicle involved in

Va.—Venable v. Stockner, 1959, 108 S.E.2d 380, 200 Va. 900 (cuts on pavement, and tire marks).

42. U.S.—Elek v. Boyce, D.C.S.C. 1970, 308 F.Supp. 26.

Ga.—Kirkland v. Wheeler, 1951, 66 S.E.2d 348, 84 Ga.App. 352.

Ill.—Goodwin v. Lamb, 1951, 101 N.E.2d 207, 344 Ill.App. 449 (oil mark).

Ind.—Spears v. Aylor, 1974, 319 N. E.2d 639, —— Ind.App. ——.

Ky.—Bowling Green - Hopkinsville Bus Co. v. Montgomery, 129 S. W.2d 535, 278 Ky. 837 (location of broken glass was competent in determining exact location of vehicles at time of collision).

La.—Moore v. Johnson, 1972, 262 So.2d 105.

Mich.—Winter v. Perz, 56 N.W.2d 276, 335 Mich. 575 (in administrator's action for death of bicyclist who was struck from behind by automobile, testimony of officer as to position of a newspaper bag which decedent was carrying was properly admitted).

Mo.—McCrary v. Ogden, 267 S.W. 2d 670 (in action for death of motorist when log protruding from side of truck struck windshield of deceased's oncoming automobile, lapse of 2½ hours before witness arrived at scene affected the weight but not the materiality of testimony that witness observed skid marks, glass and dirt on side of pavement on which deceased should have been traveling, and, in ditch on that side of highway, a log from the end of which bark had been peeled back approximately two feet).

Vt.—Healy v. Moore, 187 A. 679, 108 Vt. 324, followed in 187 A. 692, 108 Vt. 324 (location of parts of auto emblem).

Wis.—Anderson v. Eggert, 291 N.W. 365, 234 Wis. 348 (glass came from fog lights of certain automobile).

But see

Where there was no direct tieup between reflector glass found at scene where automobile allegedly collided with semitrailer and reflector glass missing from left rear of the same semitrailer, no error was committed in excluding the reflector glass. Wilson v. Don LaCost, Inc., 1974, 314 N.E.2d 27, 20 Ill.App.3d 624.

Refusal not prejudicial

Md.—Reid v. Humphreys, 122 A.2d 756, 210 Md. 178 (refusal to permit a police officer to testify as to what debris on highway indicated as to point of impact in his opinion was not error prejudicial to administratrix, in view of officer's testimony that only debris consisted of glass from headlight and pieces of chrome and casting in front of truck and uncontradicted testimony that automobile struck left from corner of truck and that vehicles were traveling toward each other, not in same direction).

43. U.S.—Elek v. Boyce, D.C.S.C. 1970, 308 F.Supp. 26.

La.—Nuss v. MacKenzie, App.1942, 4 So.2d 845.

44. For discussion of condition of lights, see § 425.6.

U.S.—Ginns v. Towle, C.A.Conn., 361 F.2d 798 (description of manner in which defendants' automobile broke into two sections and was scattered over the roadside, where there was dispute concerning proximate cause of some claimed inju-

§ 424.5   TRIAL EVIDENCE   Ch. 424

ries in a case in which liability was admitted and only question was as to damages); Shenko v. Jack Cole Co., C.C.A.Pa., 147 F. 2d 361, certiorari denied 65 S.Ct. 1199, 325 U.S. 860, 89 L.Ed. 1981 (finger marks on rear of truck on question whether child was in front of truck); Boyle v. Ward, D.C.Pa., 39 F.Supp. 545, affirmed C.C.A., 125 F.2d 672 (photographs of defendant's automobile immediately after the accident and of testimony concerning the condition of the automobile and of corroborating evidence on such points).

Ala.—Davis v. Smitherman, 1923, 96 So. 208, 209 Ala. 244.

Ark.—Mallet v. Brannon, 1968, 423 S.W.2d 880, 243 Ark. 898, appeal after remand 439 S.W.2d 32, 246 Ark. 541 (blinker light blinking).

Colo.—West v. Torbuc Corp., 1973, 517 P.2d 485, —— Colo.App. —— (admission of expert testimony on behalf of plaintiff, suing motorcycle dealer for injuries sustained because of allegedly defective throttle mechanism on motorcycle he was taking for a test drive, that the cable was defective based on examination of cable at time of trial three years after the accident and the admission of the cable itself were both improper in absence of any evidence that the cable was in a condition similar to that at the time of accident).

Conn.—Johnson v. Newell, 1970, 278 A.2d 776, 160 Conn. 269 (in action arising out of alleged blowout of tire recapped by one defendant and sold and installed by another, court erred in refusing evidence that, on inspection of tire after accident, witness saw lines or cracks showing on sidewall, but not as to exclusion of evidence tire was flat four days later).

Ill.—Cribbs v. Daily, 214 N.E.2d 588, 67 Ill.App.2d 441 (where tire was properly identified as left front tire by driver, witness testified that it was in same condition at trial as it had been when he saw it on morning following accident, lapse of time between accident and time witness saw it was adequately explained); Gass v. Carducci, 185 N.E.2d 285, 37 Ill.App.2d 181 (in action for injuries to passenger who fell from front seat of automobile, testimony of mechanic regarding examination and repair of door two weeks subsequent to accident, at which time he found a weak latch spring which caused the door to open when pressure was exerted against it).

Ky.—Young v. De Bord, 351 S.W.2d 502 (state troopers, who reached scene one or two hours after collision, were properly permitted to testify concerning positions of vehicles, condition of each as result of collision, and location on highway of ridges or mounds of slack coal from truck); Randle v. Mitchell, 142 S.W.2d 124, 283 Ky. 501; Crampton v. Daime, 6 S.W.2d 686, 224 Ky. 507 (splinters from running board and other pieces knocked from the cars seen in the road at scene while cars were still there).

La.—Moore v. Johnson, 1972, 262 So.2d 105 (location of damage).

Md.—Kelly v. Huber Baking Co., 125 A. 782, 145 Md. 321 (condition of steering gear).

Mass.—Curtin v. Benjamin, Mass., 26 N.E.2d 354, 305 Mass. 489, 129 A.L.R. 433 (permitting testimony concerning condition of tires on date of examination several months after the accident was not reversible error, where there was some evidence from garage owner that condition of tires was the same on that date as on evening of the collision).

Mich.—Delfosse v. Bresnahan, 9 N. W.2d 866, 305 Mich. 621.

Minn.—Carpenter v. Birkholm, 65 N. W.2d 250, 242 Minn. 379; Nolan

Ch. 424   RELEVANCY AND MATERIALITY   § 424.5

v. Newfert, 229 N.W. 97, 179 Minn. 293.

Miss.—Bryan Bros. Packing Co. v. Grubbs, 168 So.2d 289, 251 Miss. 52 (what parts of the several vehicles were damaged).

Mo.—Adams v. Le Bow, 172 S.W.2d 874, 237 Mo.App. 1191.

Mont.—Dieruf v. Gollaher, 1971, 481 P.2d 322, 156 Mont. 440 (photographs of plaintiff's automobile which merely showed that automobiles collided at an angle were relevant in reconstruction of the accident).

N.C.—Little v. Poole, 1971, 182 S.E. 2d 206, 11 N.C.App. 597 (location on defendant's vehicle of damage sustained in head-on collision was competent as tending to show the location of the vehicles when they came together); Miller v. Lucas, 1966, 147 S.E.2d 537, 267 N.C. 1 (of trailer hitch, after trailer broke loose); Mitchell v. Atkins, 1926, 135 S.E. 28, 192 N.C. 376 (before either vehicle moved).

N.D.—Olson v. Wetzstein, 1929, 225 N.W. 459, 58 N.D. 263 (condition of bus tire carrier).

Ohio—Bailey v. Parker, 1930, 170 N.E. 607, 34 Ohio App. 207.

Or.—Goodale v. Hathaway, 39 P.2d 678, 149 Or. 237; Hayes v. Uglow, 3 P.2d 126, 137 Or. 373; Holman v. Uglow, 3 P.2d 120, 137 Or. 358; Ragan v. MacGill, 292 P. 1094, 134 Or. 408, 72 A.L.R. 860 (test of brakes).

Pa.—Andrews v. Jackson, 1967, 235 A.2d 452, 211 Pa.Super. 116 (brakes); Topelski v. Universal South Side Autos, Inc., 180 A.2d 414, 407 Pa. 339 (testimony concerning inspection of condition of brakes approximately 20 days thereafter); Nicholson v. Feagley, 14 A.2d 122, 339 Pa. 313 (admitting testimony of patrolman who arrived an hour and a half after accident regarding position of the automobiles, over objection that sufficient time had elapsed before patrolman's arrival for automobiles to have been moved from their original position, was not error, where patrolman expressed opinion that their position had not been altered, basing his conclusion in part upon tire marks leading to the vehicles).

Vt.—O'Connor v. Vermont Transit Co., 68 A.2d 699, 116 Vt. 6 (to show responsibility for accident).

Va.—Staples v. Spence, 19 S.E.2d 69, 179 Va. 359, 140 A.L.R. 527 (condition of automobiles after accident).

Wash.—Henderson v. Bahlman, 310 P.2d 1077, 50 Wash.2d 259.

Wis.—Krueger v. Steffen, 141 N.W. 2d 200, 30 Wis.2d 445 (condition of damaged automobile six months after accident).

Foundation required for "Tactograph"

Ark.—Bell v. Kroger Co., 1959, 323 S.W.2d 424, 230 Ark. 384, 73 A.L.R.2d 1019 (admission of a "Tactograph", which is an instrument containing a clock with a paper dial attached which is fastened onto motor of a truck in such manner that a needle will indicate on the paper dial the speed of truck at any given time and also each truck stop and time thereof, was error where there was insufficient proof of accuracy of such Tactograph which had been placed on truck some three years prior to collision).

Presence of features relevant to identification

In action against owner and driver of truck and others for wrongful death of automobile driver, fact that photographs of vehicle other than truck which allegedly had struck deceased's automobile and knocked it into path of southbound tractor-trailer did not show hexagon shaped

§ 424.5   TRIAL EVIDENCE   Ch. 424

an accident. A different rule applies, however, where there is no showing that the conditions have not been changed since the accident.[45]

bolts on front bumper was material to issue of whether truck or the other vehicle had caused indentations which had been made on deceased's automobile by hexagon shaped object, and admission of witness' testimony concerning absence of such bolts after witness had been shown the photographs was not improper. Offenbacker v. Sodowsky, Mo.1973, 499 S.W.2d 421.

45. Same statement in prior printing **cited by the court** in Leuck v. Goetz, 1972, 280 N.E.2d 847, 853, 151 Ind.App. 528.

U.S.—Hook v. National Brick Co., C.C.A.Ind.1945, 150 F.2d 184 (condition of cables of crane used in loading truck).

Ga.—Finley v. Franklin Aluminum Co., 1974, 207 S.E.2d 543, 132 Ga.App. 70 (did not abuse discretion in excluding for remoteness testimony of expert witness who had conducted chemical analysis of skid marks taken from highway pavement more than 90 days after the accident, where record established that thousands of vehicles traversed highway daily). Atlanta Metallic Casket Co. v. Hollingsworth, 131 S.E.2d 61, 107 Ga.App. 594 (that at time of trial there was at scene a sign showing speed limit where accident occurred about 4½ years earlier).

Ill.—Redmond v. Huppertz, 217 N.E.2d 85, 71 Ill.App.2d 254 (absence of showing that reason for sticking of accelerator after accident was not some malfunction or defect caused by the accident); Maxwell v. Franklin, 172 N.E.2d 393, 29 Ill.App.2d 33.

Ky.—Lowe v. McMurray, 412 S.W.2d 571 (trial court properly rejected testimony relating to skid marks near scene of intersectional collision, where witnesses, who were to give such testimony, did not inspect scene of collision until some four to six hours after collision, and they were not able to trace skid marks to tractor-trailer and could not say that skid marks had not been laid down by some other vehicle, and it was shown that much traffic used roadway at site between time of collision and time of inspection by witnesses); Mountain Petroleum Co. v. Howard, Ky., 351 S.W.2d 178; Beasley v. Evans' Adm'x, Ky., 311 S.W.2d 195 (testimony of witnesses who did not see skid marks until day after collision as to estimated length of skid marks made by automobile was inadmissible); Powell v. Commercial Standard Ins. Co., 170 S.W.2d 857, 294 Ky. 7; Girtman's Adm'r v. Akins, 120 S.W.2d 660, 275 Ky. 2 (evidence of witnesses concerning marks they saw on highway near scene on following day was properly excluded where witnesses who saw marks shortly after accident testified concerning them, and highway was a heavily travelled road, and no proof was offered to show that conditions at scene had remained the same); Appalachian Stave Co. v. Pickard, 86 S.W.2d 685, 260 Ky. 720.

Md.—Marine v. Stewart, 168 A. 891, 165 Md. 698 (skid marks).

Mass.—Blodgett v. Springfield St. Ry. Co., 158 N.E. 660, 261 Mass. 333 (obstruction of view of railroad crossing by brush); Trask v. Boston & M. R. R., 106 N.E. 1022, 219 Mass. 410.

Mich.—Van Gilder v. C. & E. Trucking Corp., 90 N.W.2d 828, 352 Mich. 672 (where highway was well traveled and where there was undisputed testimony that there

Ch. 424 RELEVANCY AND MATERIALITY § 424.5

was no debris consisting of pieces of glass and chrome on center line of highway or in motorist's lane of traffic immediately following accident and that, a short time later, at direction of police officers, debris was removed and pavement swept at scene of accident, testimony of one who visited scene five or six hours after its occurrence, to effect that there was debris on center line of highway and in motorist's lane, was inadmissible as too remote); Hakkers v. Hansen, 60 N.W.2d 487, 337 Mich. 620 (no connection made between skid marks and accident); Billingsley v. Gulick, 233 N.W. 225, 252 Mich. 235 (pool of blood and impression in gravel on morning following accident erroneously admitted, where no affirmative proof that there had been no change).

N.C.—Vanhoy v. Phillips, 1972, 189 S.E.2d 557, 15 N.C.App. 102 (there was no abuse of discretion in failing to permit defendant's witness to testify that he had gone to scene on the day after the accident and observed glass all over the place and spots of blood around white line, where highway patrolman's testimony that he had found no glass on pavement when he investigated accident indicated that there had been change of conditions if there was glass "all over the place" the next day, and where stipulation and color photograph admitted into evidence made evidence of blood spot of little substantial material value); McAbee v. Love, 78 S.E.2d 405, 238 N.C. 560 (testimony of patrolman, that ten or twelve days after accident he observed tire marks on shoulder of road near site of collision, was properly excluded in view of fact that he had testified that on night of collision he did not see any tire marks, and that he had seen some at a later date, but that he did not know what made them).

Ohio—Thompson v. Cooper, Ohio Com.Pl., 95 N.E.2d 796, 43 O.O.2d 182, 59 O.L.A. 365 (would not be permitted to testify that at some time after the accident the green light controlling movement of traffic in direction in which defendant was moving had burned out, since a condition could not be shown to exist at a given moment by proving that the condition existed at some subsequent time); In re Heile, 29 N.E.2d 175, 65 Ohio App. 45.

Pa.—Robinson v. Brown, 171 A.2d 865, 195 Pa.Super. 384 (where main point of controversy was whether there was ice on the street and the road conditions were changing with the passage of time, admitting testimony of officer as to the physical conditions existing at collision when he did not arrive until about two hours after the accident was error).

R.I.—Romano v. Caldarone, 79 A. 2d 763, 78 R.I. 107 (testimony as to traffic conditions existing at scene some time after the accident was properly excluded).

S.C.—Collins v. Atlantic Coast Line R. Co., 190 S.E. 817, 183 S.C. 284 (section master, who stated that he was familiar with operating make of automobile driven by motorist, was incompetent to testify whether ignition switch of motorist's automobile had been thrown off as result of collision of automobile and train, where section master did not reach scene until 25 minutes after collision, during which time automobile had been moved, and did not testify that he had examined electrical or automatic devices on switch, or that he was familiar with electrical arrangement of automobile).

Wis.—Neider v. Spoehr, 1969, 165 N.W.2d 171, 41 Wis.2d 610 (within discretion to exclude as to marks observed 3 days later).

§ 424.5   TRIAL EVIDENCE   Ch. 424

Generally a witness cannot testify as to visibility available where it is not shown that the conditions were the same as those on the occasion of the accident.[46] However, in some cases the evidence of visibility subsequently has been held admissible.[47]

Wash.—Cleasby v. Taylor, 28 P.2d 795, 176 Wash. 251.

Contra

Testimony of an investigating officer as to the position of the vehicles when he arrived at scene was admissible to show point at which accident occurred, even though it was not shown that the vehicles were in the same position when the witness arrived at the scene as they were immediately after the collision. Malone v. Hanna, 156 So.2d 626, 275 Ala. 534.

46. Mass.—Trask v. Boston & M. R. R., 106 N.E. 1022, 219 Mass. 410.

N.C.—Caldwell v. Southern Ry. Co., 10 S.E.2d 680, 218 N.C. 63.

Of traffic control signal

As there was no proof that photographer took any photographs from exact position defendant motorist testified he saw green light, as the photographer did not see the intersection accident, and as there was no testimony to show that traffic control signal light was in same position on day photographs were taken as on day of accident, court properly denied plaintiffs the right to prove by the photographer that it was impossible for defendant to see traffic light from position where he said he stopped his automobile and proceeded when light turned green. Rains v. Hutson, Tex. Civ.App., 1968, 426 S.W.2d 880.

47. Ga.—Fields v. Jackson, 115 S.E. 2d 877, 102 Ga.App. 117 (testimony of witness for plaintiff, that after she left scene she burned lights on her automobile, was admissible with respect to issue whether there was sufficient light at time of collision to enable automobiles to be operated safely without use of their headlights).

Mo.—West v. Jack Cooper Transport Co., App., 372 S.W.2d 642 (testimony as to visibility and sight, as shown by photographs, measurements and sightings taken at scene).

Or.—Loibl v. Niemi, 327 P.2d 786, 214 Or. 172 (testimony as to visibility on following day at about same hour was competent when weather conditions were substantially the same as on day of collision).

Chapter 425

RELEVANCY AND MATERIALITY—OPERATION OF VEHICLES

Table of Sections

Sec.
425.1 Operation of Vehicles—In General.
425.2 —— Speed.
425.3 —— Lookout.
425.4 —— Control.
425.5 —— Right of Way.
425.6 —— Lights.
425.7 —— Signals and Warnings.
425.8 —— Stopping and Parking.
425.9 —— Turning.

§ 425.1 Operation of Vehicles—In General

Library References:
C.J.S. Evidence §§ 300, 628 et seq.; Motor Vehicles § 514 et seq.
West's Key No. Digests, Automobiles ⚿243; Evidence ⚿207(4), 327 et seq.

Warnings and admonitions to a driver by other occupants of the offending car, and any direction or suggestion made shortly before an accident concerning the driver's conduct in the operation of the machine, are circumstances in the chain of evidence to be considered in weighing the evidence as to negligence.[1]

Evidence that the driver was engaging in illegal activity has been held admissible, as an aid in evaluating the driver's conduct.[2]

1. **Cal.**—Hastings v. Serleto, 143 P. 2d 956, 61 Cal.App.2d 672.

   Conn.—Harbison v. Barwinsky, 124 A. 223, 100 Conn. 602.

   Mass.—Mendler v. Town Taxi, 1936, 3 N.E.2d 15, 295 Mass. 90; Hiller v. De Sautels, 169 N.E. 494, 269 Mass. 437 (re slippery condition of highway).

   Mich.—Horton v. Fleser, 1954, 64 N. W.2d 605, 340 Mich. 68; Lucas v. Lindner, 1936, 269 N.W. 611, 276 Mich. 704 (indicative of state of mind, when fails to heed).

   N.C.—Tart v. Register, 125 S.E.2d 754, 257 N.C. 161; Teasley v. Burwell, 153 S.E. 607, 199 N.C. 18.

   Absence of protest

   N.M.—Carpenter v. Yates, 273 P.2d 373, 58 N.M. 513.

2. **Utah**—Ferguson v. Jongsma, 1960, 350 P.2d 404, 10 Utah 2d 179 (in action by plaintiff who was dragged nearly 200 feet dangling from door of automobile driven without lights by defendant who was attempting to avoid arrest by

§ 425.1   TRIAL EVIDENCE   Ch. 425

Extent of damage and injury

Proof of the nature and extent of the damage done is admissible, as tending to throw some light upon the manner in which the accident occurred.[3] The jury may also consider the nature and extent of personal injuries in determining defendant's negligence.[4]

plaintiff for alleged theft of gasoline committed or attempted in plaintiff's presence, rights and duties of parties were proper factor to be considered by jury in determining whether defendant was negligent and whether plaintiff was contributorily negligent or assumed risk and court's instruction charging that evidence concerning attempted theft of gasoline was wholly immaterial and should not be considered by jury at all was erroneous).

3. Same statement in prior edition **cited by the court** in Hodgkins v. Christopher, 274 P.2d 153, 159, 58 N.M. 637; Jacobsen v. Poland, 80 N.W.2d 891, 903, 163 Neb. 590.

Ark.—Dedmon v. Thalheimer, 290 S.W.2d 16, 226 Ark. 402.

La.—Towbridge v. Rackle & Schmid, 3 La.App. 368.

Mo.—Cox v. Reynolds, App., 18 S.W.2d 575.

N.Y.—Helder v. Wiesel, 296 N.Y.S. 65, 251 App.Div. 747.

Pa.—American Tube & Stamping Co. v. Erie Iron & Steel Co., 125 A. 304, 281 Pa. 10; Hain v. Ebersole, 49 Dauph. 122.

Contra

In action against bus company to recover for damages to store and residence property occasioned by an intersection collision, evidence that bus was heavier than an ordinary automobile, and evidence of extent of damage to store and contents of residence, did not constitute evidence of negligence on part of bus owner. Sonnenburg v. Monumental Motor Tours, 81 A.2d 617, 198 Md. 227.

Irrelevant and immaterial

Ga.—Garrison v. Garmon, 96 S.E.2d 550, 94 Ga.App. 868.

4. Cal.—Dike v. Golden State Co., 269 P.2d 619, 125 Cal.App.2d 6 (doctor's testimony of result of autopsy, allegedly tending to show that an injury resulted from contact with front bumper).

Idaho—Asumendi v. Ferguson, 65 P.2d 713, 57 Idaho 450 (in actions for death of mother and child, jury could properly consider that if they had run into side of truck instead of being struck by front thereof they would not have been thrown in direction that they were, and would not have been so badly mangled and injured).

Mo.—Ryan v. Burrow, 33 S.W.2d 928, 326 Mo. 896; Cox v. Reynolds, Mo.App., 18 S.W.2d 575 (where defendant and his wife testified that pedestrian walked against car, and that there was merely a light "thump," testimony as to severity of injuries as shown by autopsy was admissible).

Ohio—Meuer v. Doerflein, 5 N.E.2d 948, 53 Ohio App. 536.

Pa.—Cunningham v. Spangler, 186 A. 173, 123 Pa.Super. 151 (testimony of undertaker as to nature and extent of injuries to plaintiff's wife held properly admitted as tending to show force and location of impact and how accident may have happened).

Tex.—Davis Transport, Inc. v. Bolstad, Civ.App., 295 S.W.2d 941 (permitted to testify that there was a large hole in the back of the head of the deceased occupant, for purpose of showing that first truck

Evidence of similar occurrences or conduct by same driver

Under the federal rule,[5] and in most state jurisdictions,[6] evidence that either party to an automobile accident had prior

was struck while it was proceeding straight ahead along highway rather than while it was in the process of making a left turn as contended by owner of second truck).

But see

It was improper and prejudicial to plaintiff to permit wife of a defendant who was called as witness for him to relate in her testimony the nature and extent of her own injuries. Waugh v. Cender, 173 N.E. 2d 860, 29 Ill.App.2d 408.

In actions for wrongful death of passengers in automobile operated by defendant, evidence of injuries sustained by defendant in accident was inadmissible and should have been excluded. Sanders v. George, 129 S.E.2d 480, 258 N.C. 776; Testimony that witness had seen wound on motorist's left arm was inadmissible to show that motorist had his left hand outside automobile to signal turn. Woods v. Roadway Express, 25 S.E.2d 856, 223 N.C. 269.

5. Federal Rules of Evidence § 404 (b), 28 U.S.C.A.

6. **Ala.**—Alaga Coach Line v. McCarroll, 151 So. 834, 227 Ala. 686, 92 A.L.R. 470.

Ark.—Hall v. Young, 236 S.W.2d 431, 218 Ark. 348, 20 A.L.R.2d 1207 (reversible error to require defendant-driver, over objection, to answer question as to how many previous accidents he had).

Cal.—West's Ann.Calif.Evid.Code, § 1101(a); Downing v. Barrett Mobile Home Transport, Inc., 1974, 113 Cal.Rptr. 277, 38 C.A.3d 519 (suggestion of accident proneness in cross-examination); Browning v. King, 324 P.2d 14, 159 Cal.App.2d 326 (that plaintiff had been involved in other accidents and evidence that plaintiff had struck a deputy sheriff several times and had engaged in several fights was prejudicial for reason that prejudicial suggestions had been placed before jury that plaintiff was accident-prone, claims conscious, and a brawling and unrespectable citizen); Lowenthal v. Mortimer, 270 P.2d 942, 125 Cal.App.2d 636; White v. Shepardson, 3 P.2d 346, 116 Cal.App. 716; Lindsey v. Pacific Electric Ry. Co., 296 P. 131, 111 Cal.App. 482; People v. Crossan, 261 P. 531, 87 Cal.App. 5.

Fla.—Florida Evidence Code § 90.404 (2)(a); Short v. Allen, App.1971, 254 So.2d 34 (similar prior fall of passenger from lowered tail gate of station wagon).

Ga.—Gahring v. Barron, 133 S.E.2d 389, 108 Ga.App. 530 (lengthy cross-examination of plaintiff as to his subsequent collisions, to place before jury evidence of plaintiff's negligence in unrelated situations ceased to perform its original function of determining what part of his injuries resulted from defendant's alleged tort and what part from other causes and became irrelevant and prejudicial under "other tranactions" rule); Taylor v. Marsh, 130 S.E.2d 770, 107 Ga. App. 575 (that plaintiffs' deceased had been convicted of speeding); Cox v. Norris, 1944, 28 S.E.2d 888, 70 Ga.App. 580; Elliott v. Georgia Power Co., 197 S.E. 914, 58 Ga. App. 151.

Iowa—Glass v. Hutchinson Ice Cream Co., 243 N.W. 352, 214 Iowa 825 (court's discretion re evidence of prior speeding and racing); Darden v. Chicago Northwestern R. Co., 239 N.W. 531, 213 Iowa 583 (that engineer in crossing accident on other occasions was reading newspaper and approached crossing without sounding whistle); In

§ 425.1 TRIAL EVIDENCE Ch. 425

re Hill's Estate, 208 N.W. 334, 202 Iowa 1038, modified on other grounds 210 N.W. 241, 202 Iowa 1038.

Kan.—Kansas Code of Civil Procedure § 60–455.

Ky.—Massie v. Salmon, 277 S.W.2d 49 (that defendants permitted another calf to escape from undisclosed enclosure and roam at large for some time several months before).

Me.—Maine Rules of Evidence § 404 (b).

Md.—Cumberland & Westernport Transit Co. v. Metz, 149 A. 4, 158 Md. 424, reargument denied 149 A. 565, 158 Md. 424, and appeal dismissed American Oil Co. v. Metz, 51 S.Ct. 40, 282 U.S. 801, 75 L.Ed. 720 (evidence as to manner in which vehicle was driven some distance from scene and on another road too remote).

Mass.—Warren v. Hanson, 195 N.E. 121, 290 Mass. 286; Polmatier v. Newbury, 120 N.E. 850, 231 Mass. 307.

Mich.—Bixby v. Gallagher, 1972, 204 N.W.2d 295, 43 Mich.App. 328.

Minn.—Hector Const. Co. v. Butler, 260 N.W. 496, 194 Minn. 310 (testimony that he cleaned oil filter in same manner on prior occasions and that no injury resulted held not prejudicial error, but best procedure was to show common custom or usage and to judge driver's negligence by that standard).

Miss.—Baxter v. Rounsaville, 193 So. 2d 735 (other disconnected accidents).

Mo.—Lawson v. Cooper, App.1972, 475 S.W.2d 442 (speed over 100 mph. on prior occasion, but not "plain error", in absence of proper objection); McComb v. Vaughn, 1949, 218 S.W.2d 548, 358 Mo. 951.

Neb.—Nebraska Rules of Evidence § 404(2).

Nev.—N.R.S. 48.045(2).

N.H.—Stocker v. Boston & M. R. R., 143 A. 68, 83 N.H. 401.

N.M.—New Mexico Rules of Evidence § 404(b).

N.Y.—Robinson v. City of Albany, 218 N.Y.S.2d 421, 14 A.D.2d 626 (but error was effectually rectified by court's clear, positive instructions to disregard such evidence, conveyed to jury several trial days after evidence was received and again in charge); Zucker v. Whitridge, 98 N.E. 209, 205 N.Y. 50.

N.C.—Mason v. Gillikin, 124 S.E.2d 537, 256 N.C. 527; Heath v. Kirkman, 82 S.E.2d 104, 240 N.C. 303.

Ohio—Melville v. Greyhound Corp., 1954, 133 N.E.2d 436, 99 Ohio App. 411 (even where other evidence as to prior conduct); Bachman v. Ambos, 79 N.E.2d 177, 83 Ohio App. 141 (prior accidents of plaintiff).

Okl.—Barger v. Mizel, 424 P.2d 41; Gillette Motor Transport, Inc. v. Kirby, 253 P.2d 139, 208 Okl. 68; Oklahoma Ry. Co. v. Thomas, 1917, 164 P. 120, 63 Okl. 219 (riding on fire truck at similar speed).

Or.—Warner v. Maus, 304 P.2d 423, 209 Or. 529.

Pa.—Jamison v. Ardes, 182 A.2d 497, 408 Pa. 188; Sanders v. Stotesbury, 1930, 100 Pa.Super. 523.

S.C.—Neely v. Carolina & N. W. Ry. Co., 117 S.E. 55, 123 S.C. 449 (showing merely that train came very near striking another automobile at a near-by crossing).

Tex.—Mrs. Baird's Bakeries, Inc. v. Roberts, Civ.App., 360 S.W.2d 850, writ ref. n. r. e.; Patterson v. East Tex. Motor Freight Lines, Civ.App. 1961, 349 S.W.2d 634, ref. n. r. e.; Orchin v. Fort Worth Poultry & Egg Co., Civ.App., 43 S.W.2d 308, reformed on other grounds 53 S.W. 2d 103 (testimony whether motorist was generally bad driver irrelevant on issue as to speed at time of accident).

Vt.—Melford v. S. V. Rossi Const. Co., 1972, 287 A.2d 577, 130 Vt.

148, appeal after remand 303 A.2d 146, 131 Vt. 219 (about 1½ hours before).

W.Va.—Fleming v. McMillan, 26 S. E.2d 8, 125 W.Va. 356.

Wis.—Wisconsin Rules of Evidence § 904.04(2); Stanley v. Milwaukee Auto Ins. Co., Limited Mut., 1956, 79 N.W.2d 662, 274 Wis. 226.

As to prior permission to drive

Even though daughter, who had an exclusive possession of automobile which was in father's name because of daughter's age, claimed that father had instructed her not to permit others to use automobile and that she did not give permission to party who was driving at time of accident, it was not error for court to sustain relevancy objection to cross-examination of daughter as to defendant daughter's having given permission on other occasions. Durrett v. Farrar, 1973, 203 S.E.2d 265, 130 Ga.App. 298.

But see

Mo.—Lawson v. Cooper, App.1972, 475 S.W.2d 442 (testimony that defendant, charged by plaintiff with excessive speed, had at one time driven over a hundred miles an hour was not wholly incompetent for any purpose and was not unjustly inflammatory and prejudicial so as to justify consideration of claimed error, notwithstanding objection was insufficient for lack of specificity).

Contra

In action for injuries to driver of automobile which was struck in rear by defendant's automobile, trial court did not abuse its discretion in admitting testimony of defendant's witness that defendant's driving, which witness observed several times during day on which collision occurred, was as careful as one could drive and that there was nothing abnormal about it. Faulk v. McPherson, 182 S.W.2d 130, 27 Tenn.App. 506.

Defense of products liability suit

Wash.—Breimon v. General Motors Corp., 1973, 509 P.2d 398, 8 Wash. App. 747 (evidence of plaintiff's bad driving habits was appropriately excluded in products liability or prior accident action, where reason for its being offered, namely, to infer that cause of accident was recklessness or speed of plaintiff at time in issue, was not relevant to that issue, and danger of prejudice, consumption of time, and distraction outweighed its questionable probative value).

Even where proved fact licensed

Testimony which was elicited from motorist merely to show that he was a licensed driver and that he had completed the driver's education course necessary to obtain driver's license prior to attaining age 18 did not constitute evidence that motorist was a particularly skilled driver, so that it was not error to refuse to permit cross-examination as to motorist's driving record for the year preceding the accident. McKillip v. Union Pac. R. Co., 1974, 525 P.2d 842, 11 Wash.App. 829.

Prior charges

Ga.—Durrett v. Farrar, 1973, 203 S. E.2d 265, 130 Ga.App. 298 (not error for trial court to sustain objection to questions which were propounded to police officer and which related to officer having made prior charges against driver involved in fatal accident).

Sustaining objection sufficient

Cross-examination of plaintiff as to whether she had been arrested following previous accident not related to accident giving rise to suit was improper, but failure of trial court to admonish defense counsel or to grant mistrial was not prejudicial error or abuse of discretion. Brownridge v. Leslie, Mo.1970, 450 S.W.2d 214.

To show own prior experience

Trial court erred in allowing lengthy testimony concerning wit-

§ 425.1   TRIAL EVIDENCE   Ch. 425

thereto been a party to similar occurrences is inadmissible on the issue of negligence. Likewise, evidence of later conduct is inadmissible to prove negligence on the earlier occasion.[7]

However, it is within the discretion of the trial court to permit evidence of the driver's conduct at a distance from the scene of the accident.[8] In a variety of circumstances the court has found prior conduct of a party to be too remote to constitute evidence that the conduct continued to the time in question,[9] and in other cases to be admissible.[10]

ness' experience while driving on the same highway, where no similarity of condition was shown between witness' experience and the collision. Carlton Co. v. Poss, 1971, 183 S.E.2d 231, 124 Ga.App. 154, affirmed 185 S.E.2d 803, 228 Ga. 402.

Use of intoxicants

Evidence regarding use of intoxicants by driver at a different time is ordinarily not admissible. Radio Cab v. Houser, 128 F.2d 604, 76 App. D.C. 35.

7. Ky.—Daniels v. Tackett, 1967, 416 S.W.2d 749 (testimony of state trooper that approximately 12 hours after accident he was almost hit by an automobile driven by defendant had no relevance and was insufficient to establish a pattern of reckless and wanton driving, and jury should have been admonished to disregard it).

8. Ark.—Hooten v. DeJarnatt, 376 S.W.2d 272, 237 Ark. 792 (where sequence of events is not too remote in distance and time).

Ill.—Schneider v. Wedding, 213 N.E. 2d 624, 66 Ill.App.2d 7 (and it is not required that there be testimony that misconduct persisted during interval between time when witness observed the vehicle and time of the accident).

Only to show direction traveling

Admission of testimony as to direction in which decedent was traveling 10 to 30 minutes prior to collision, which evidence did not purport to relate to specific acts of negligence alleged to be cause of collision but did contradict or raise doubt as to administrator's theory that decedent's automobile was being driven a certain direction at time of collision, as to which there were no eyewitnesses, was not abuse of discretion. Brown v. Nale, 1969, 245 N.E. 2d 9, 106 Ill.App.2d 238.

9. For cases concerning speed just previous to the accident, see § 425.2 at fn. 49 et seq.

For cases concerning display of lights just previous to accident, see § 425.6, at fn. 88 et seq.

Cited by the court in Crane v. Woodbury, 1972, 199 N.W.2d 577, 581, 41 Mich.App. 11.

U.S.—DiGregorio v. Industrial Supply Corp. of Orlando, C.A.Fla.1971, 438 F.2d 303 (under Florida law, in action arising out of rear-end collision, testimony that driver of overtaking vehicle at a distance of a mile to one mile and a half from collision was seen to be standing still or to be traveling very slowly as though driver were looking for sign should have been excluded as remote).

Ala.—Coker v. Ryder Truck Lines, 1971, 249 So.2d 810, 287 Ala. 150 (as to witness' "attempt" to pass defendant's truck, in that question could have been addressed to time and place anywhere up to 30 miles prior to accident).

10. See note 10 on page 445.

444

Ill.—Kackley v. Central Illinois Traction Co., 1915, 201 Ill.App. 164 (intoxication 1½ to 2 hours before).

Md.—Bennett v. Bass, 1967, 235 A.2d 715, 248 Md. 260 (objections to questions asking defendant motorist how fast he was traveling on boulevard at various points ranging from one and a half miles to six blocks distant from scene were properly sustained).

Mo.—Sauer v. Winkler, 263 S.W.2d 370 (that deceased passed witness in no passing zone before reaching collision point is inadmissible).

N.C.—Reeves v. Hill, 1968, 158 S.E. 2d 529, 272 N.C. 352 (change of lane).

Okl.—Washita Val. Grain Co. v. McElroy, 262 P.2d 133 (that person sounded horn ¾ of mile from collision for another vehicle is not admissible).

Or.—Frangos v. Edmunds, 173 P.2d 596, 179 Or. 577 (where collision occurred after vehicles had passed traffic light, evidence concerning driver's action before he came to light was properly excluded).

Va.—Butler v. Greenwood, 1942, 23 S.E.2d 217, 180 Va. 456 (manner of driving 900–1000 feet away).

Admission of conduct 10 days before

Statement of defendant, at scene, to effect that he had had a near miss in similar situation 10 days previously was too remote, and its rejection was clearly within discretion of trial judge who was not informed that plaintiff claimed it was relevant to show state of mind prior to accident. Larson v. Solbakken, 34 Cal. Rptr. 450, 221 Cal.App.2d 410.

Crossing centerline

Ill.—Hanck v. Ruan Transport Corp., 1954, 122 N.E.2d 445, 3 Ill.App.2d 372 (over centerline); Flesberg v. Prince Warehouse Co., 184 N.E.2d 813, 37 Ill.App.2d 22 (even if crossed centerline, would not in itself tend to prove that the truck was being negligently operated just prior to and at the time of the actual collision).

Offered as proof of condition of roadway

Relevancy of proffered evidence concerning condition of roadway and construction taking place a substantial distance from site where telephone utility employee met his death when body of defendant's oncoming truck snagged on wire employees had stretched across public road was for trial court in wrongful death action. Stuart v. Consolidated Foods Corp., 1972, 496 P.2d 527, 6 Wash. App. 841.

Offered as proof of state of mind

Evidence of defendant's conviction for reckless driving on an occasion not connected with and 45 minutes prior to accident complained of was not admissible for purpose of showing state of mind. Lindley v. Oppegaard, 1971, 275 N.E.2d 825, 150 Ind. App. 209.

Place where pedestrians walking 1000 feet away

Testimony as to where pedestrian and her companions were walking 1,000 feet from place of accident properly excluded, since such testimony had no probative value upon where pedestrian was at time of accident. Janse v. Haywood, 259 N.W. 347, 270 Mich. 632.

10. Cal.—Mathews v. Dudley, 297 P. 544, 212 Cal. 58, opinion corrected, Sup., 298 P. 819 (showing course of defendants' truck short distance from place of and immediately preceding collision); Jennings v. Arata, 188 P.2d 298, 83 Cal.App.2d 143 (about half mile from scene defendant ignored speed sign, and almost struck workmen about one minute before accident).

Conn.—Sosnowski v. Lenox, 53 A.2d 388, 133 Conn. 624 (that automobile was being driven on wrong

§ 425.1   TRIAL EVIDENCE   Ch. 425

Testimony that a driver had never had an accident before is generally rejected because of the tendency to open the door to

side of road at about 40 miles per hour two blocks away from the collision was not inadmissible in view of other testimony).

Mass.—Vieira v. East Taunton St. Ry. Co., 70 N.E.2d 841, 320 Mass. 547 (questions respecting the matter of driver's conduct in talking to another passenger shortly before reaching curve were not too remote from the issues).

N.C.—McGrady v. Quality Motors of Elkin, Inc., 1974, 208 S.E.2d 911, 23 N.C.App. 256, certiorari denied 212 S.E.2d 656, 286 N.C. 545 (in center of road 500 feet away).

Okl.—Boyd v. Midland Co-ops., Inc., 364 P.2d 670 (evidence of witnesses who testified that, shortly before accident, they had seen automobile meeting description of plaintiff's automobile which was not being driven entirely on its proper side of road).

Tex.—Hernandez v. H. S. Anderson Trucking Co., Civ.App., 370 S.W.2d 909, ref. n. r. e. (witness' recollection of having just met two vehicles traveling fast).

Wis.—Shapiro v. Klinker, 44 N.W.2d 622, 257 Wis. 622 (testimony of a motorist who followed defendant for about five miles and about 15 minutes prior to collision, and who was first person to reach scene, was not too remote and irrelevant and was admissible to prove manner of defendant driving prior to accident).

Lane of travel 60 feet from place of accident

Admission of testimony of third party that motorist was driving in center of highway when passed third party at a point about 80 feet south of a junction, which jury could find was about 60 feet from place automobile struck bicyclist, was not error. Reardon v. Marston, 38 N.E.2d 644, 310 Mass. 461.

Proper to show pattern as bearing on wantonness

Evidence as to manner of person's driving at point some distance in time or space from that of accident is not admissible, but exception exists where evidence is designed to show pattern of reckless or wanton driving. Wilson v. Com., Ky.1969, 445 S.W.2d 446.

Host motorist's manner of driving on outbound portion of trip to picnic site was not inadmissible as too remote in time or place from accident which occurred on return trip. Anderson v. Lippes, 1969, 170 N.W.2d 908, 18 Mich.App. 281; Where gross negligence or willful and wanton misconduct of motorist are at issue, scope of relevant testimony necessary to ascertain the "sum total" of actions is broad and includes evidence tending to establish state of mind. Id.

Rule relaxed in absence of occurrence witnesses

Absent occurrence witnesses, it was discretionary to admit testimony of pre-occurrence witnesses to effect that, for approximately five miles, deceased motorist had been driving in erratic fashion. Ryan v. C & D Motor Delivery Co., 186 N.E.2d 156, 38 Ill.App.2d 18.

Running light 150 feet from place of accident

In action by pedestrian struck by taxicab as he was crossing street, evidence that taxicab went through red light at intersection was admissible, notwithstanding fact that accident occurred one hundred or even one hundred and fifty feet south of intersection. Tobin v. Van Orsdol, 45 N.W.2d 239, 241 Iowa 1331.

perplexing side issues.[11] However, evidence of former accidents may be competent to rebut testimony that an allegedly negligent driver was a good, careful, and safe driver.[12]

Evidence of similar occurrences involving others at other times

Evidence of the occurrence, at the same place, of accidents other than the one from which plaintiff's cause of action arose is generally held admissible, if it tends to show the existence of a dangerous, unsafe thing or condition, though it is not admissible for the purpose of showing negligence.[13] It is received for the

11. **Ga.**—United Motor Freight Terminal Co. v. Hixon, 47 S.E.2d 171, 76 Ga.App. 653.

Minn.—Ryan v. International Harvester Co. of America, 283 N.W. 129, 204 Minn. 177.

Mo.—Friedman v. United Rys. Co. of St. Louis, 238 S.W. 1074, 293 Mo. 235.

N.C.—Rouse v. Huffman, 1970, 174 S.E.2d 68, 8 N.C.App. 307.

N.D.—Trautman v. New Rockford-Fessenden Co-op Transport Ass'n, 1970, 181 N.W.2d 754 (but, under all of evidence, answer did not affect substantial rights of parties to action and was therefore harmless error).

12. **U.S.**—Atkinson v. Atkinson, T. & S. F. Ry. Co., C.A.N.M., 197 F. 2d 244.

Ohio.—Williamson v. Eclipse Motor Lines, 62 N.E.2d 339, 145 Ohio St. 467, 168 A.L.R. 1356 (incompetence and recklessness of defendant's driver).

Pa.—Diehl v. Reiss, 76 Pa.Super. 189.

13. **U.S.**—Fortunato v. Ford Motor Co., C.A.N.Y.1972, 464 F.2d 962, certiorari denied 93 S.Ct. 517, 409 U.S. 1038, 34 L.Ed.2d 487 (evidence of accident frequency on an "S" curve to show its "dangerous nature", as relevant to theory of defense); Small v. Pennsylvania R. Co., 1935, 80 F.2d 704, 65 App.D.C. 112, certiorari denied 56 S.Ct. 669, 297 U.S. 724, 80 L.Ed. 1008.

Cal.—Johnston v. Yolo County, 1969, 79 Cal.Rptr. 33, 274 Cal.App.2d 46 (court did not abuse its discretion, in suit brought by passenger against county when host automobile failed to successfully negotiate sharp double curve in county road, in admitting evidence of earlier one-car accidents at the same jog in the road).

Fla.—Atlantic Coast Line R. Co. v. Hendrickson, 190 So.2d 178 (failure of automatic signal at scene within two years prior to or more than one year after accident).

Ill.—Popadowski v. Bergaman, 26 N. E.2d 722, 304 Ill.App. 422 (where truck drivers testified they saw no boys in the street, evidence that truck nearly struck one of some boys who were playing hockey in the street was admissible).

Ky.—Louisville & N. R. Co. v. Howser's Adm'r, 257 S.W. 1010, 201 Ky. 548, 36 A.L.R. 327 (to prove could not hear train).

Me.—Nadeau v. Perkins, 193 A. 877, 135 Me. 215 (in collision in nighttime with parked unlighted truck, that other automobiles collided or nearly collided with truck was admissible as corroborating that truck was not clearly discernible).

Mass.—Ouillette v. Sheerin, 9 N.E.2d 713, 297 Mass. 536 (in automobile colliding with unlighted parked truck, which he failed to see because of rain on portion of windshield faced by him while sitting on front seat beside driver, that

§ 425.1   TRIAL EVIDENCE   Ch. 425

limited purpose of showing that the unsafe thing or condition causing the particular accident was the condition or cause common to such independent accidents, and that the frequency of such accidents tends to show knowledge of such condition or the existence of danger.[14]

witness first saw truck when police car, on front seat of which he was riding beside driver during rain, was slowing down about 25 feet from truck less than hour after accident, was admissible).

Mo.—Knorr v. Wells, App., 270 S.W. 391 (other vehicles skidding on wet street car rails).

N.H.—Lovett v. Manchester St. Ry., 159 A. 132, 85 N.H. 345.

N.Y.—Stern v. State, 224 N.Y.S.2d 126, 32 Misc.2d 357, judgment affirmed 239 N.Y.S.2d 322, 18 A.D. 1115 (proof of subsequent accidents in same locality, automobile slid on slippery highway); Smith v. State, 124 N.Y.S.2d 264, 204 Misc. 743 (subsequent accidents).

N.C.—Karpf v. Adams, 74 S.E.2d 325, 237 N.C. 106 (skidded out of control on wet asphalt primer coat which had been permitted to remain exposed, and allegedly insufficiently indicated by warning signs).

Or.—Clary v. Polk County, 372 P.2d 524, 231 Or. 148.

Wash.—Meabon v. State, 1970, 463 P.2d 789, 1 Wash.App. 824 (two prior accidents on same stretch of overlay, due to slippery condition).

Prior parts failure

Where vehicle abruptly left road, allegedly because of failure of aluminum gearbox, permitting expert witnesses to testify regarding an accident occurring prior to that involving plaintiff passenger, as well as to accident occurring subsequently, in which gearboxes made of aluminum had allegedly failed, was proper where, although purpose of the testimony was to communicate that all three accidents occurred because of failure of gearbox, the focus was not on the accidents themselves, but upon inherent similarity in the physical and mechanical properties of the three gearboxes, all of which purportedly contained similar defects. Ault v. International Harvester Co., 1974, 528 P.2d 1148, 117 Cal.Rptr. 812, 528 P.2d 1148, 13 Cal.3d 113.

Proof theory of action possible

U.S.—Alaska Freight Lines v. Harry, C.A., 220 F.2d 272, 15 Alaska 457 (that on one occasion saw a chunk of ice fall from one of the tractor-trailers onto traveled portion of road in front of automobile in which officer was driving was properly admitted on issue whether it was possible for ice to fall off under circumstances in which accident occurred).

N.Y.—Klein v. Burleson, 122 N.Y.S. 752, 138 App.Div. 405 (possibility of collision without visible evidence on vehicle).

To prove presence of defendant vehicle

Ohio.—Glass v. Miller, App., 51 N.E.2d 299 (that witness passed a truck standing on highway at or near point of collision between five and ten minutes before accident was competent on question whether defendant's truck was parked on highway at time of collision).

14. **U.S.**—Spreitler v. Louisville & N. R. Co., D.C.Ill., 36 F.Supp. 117, reversed on other grounds, C.C.A., 125 F.2d 115 (failure of crossing signal on prior occasions); Illinois Cent. R. Co. v. Sigler, C.C.A.Tenn., 122 F.2d 279; District of Columbia v. Chessin, 61 F.2d 523, 61 App.

D.C. 260 (held admissible, though circumstances were not shown to be identical, as tending to show notice).

Ala.—Birmingham Electric Co. v. Lawson, 194 So. 659, 239 Ala. 236 (admissible on question of the proximity of the pole to the traveled lane being dangerous, and as going to show notice to public utility corporation).

Alaska—State v. Phillips, 1970, 470 P.2d 266 (admission of testimony concerning fatal accident which occurred on roadway in question one week prior to plaintiff's decedent's crash and approximately one mile north of site of decedent's accident was not error where trial court did not use evidence of other accident in its determination of cause of plaintiff's decedent's collision and such evidence bore relevance only to issue of state's standards of maintenance on more heavily travelled portions of roadway on which both accidents took place and to question of whether state had notice that its standards of maintenance were insufficient for portion of roadway in question).

Cal.—George v. City of Los Angeles, 124 P.2d 872, 51 Cal.App.2d 311; People v. Lang Transp. Corporation, 110 P.2d 464, 43 Cal.App.2d 134 (admissible to prove existence of such condition, actionable negligence, and notice of such condition); Gerberich v. Southern California Edison Co., 79 P.2d 783, 26 Cal.App.2d 471 (admissible to show dangerous condition).

Ill.—Huyler v. City of Chicago, 62 N.E.2d 574, 326 Ill.App. 555; Linneen v. City of Chicago, 34 N.E. 2d 100, 310 Ill.App. 274 (were substantially the same when such prior collisions occurred).

Iowa.—Lindquist v. Des Moines Union Ry. Co., 30 N.W.2d 120, 239 Iowa 356 (boxcar blocking crossing at night, evidence as to similar accidents at night at same crossing was admissible to show hazardous condition due to obstruction of crossing and knowledge of hazard on part of railroad).

Mass.—Alden v. Norwood Arena, 124 N.E.2d 505, 332 Mass. 267 (when wheel from racing stock car flew into grand stand, testimony that wheels had come off on other occasions was admissible).

Mo.—Moses v. Kansas City Public Service Co., 188 S.W.2d 538, 239 Mo.App. 361 (hole in pavement); Metz v. Kansas City, 81 S.W.2d 462, 229 Mo.App. 402 (action by motorist injured on driving into unlighted island in intersection on dark night).

N.H.—Belanger v. Berube, 185 A. 898, 88 N.H. 191 (where guest remarked after sudden stop that host would throw somebody through the windshield).

N.J.—Dolan v. Newark Iron & Metal Co., 87 A.2d 444, 18 N.J.Super. 450.

N.Y.—Kaplan v. City of New York, 200 N.Y.S.2d 261, 10 A.D.2d 319 (if physical conditions at those times were substantially similar to those existing at the time of the collision complained of); Hynes v. Railway Express Agency, 46 N.Y. S.2d 18, 267 App.Div. 835 (skidding because of slimy condition of roadway); Koehler v. City of New York, 186 N.E. 208, 262 N.Y. 74 (notice of existing dangerous condition due to fire hydrant on the side of the street).

Okl.—City of Seminole v. Mooring, 91 P.2d 1091, 185 Okl. 359.

Or.—Rader v. Gibbons & Reed Co., 1972, 494 P.2d 412, 261 Or. 354 (where one witness testified that during month of June he frequently traveled section of highway in which motorist was killed when rock entered automobile windshield and that he often saw rocks on the highway at times when general contractor for construction of

§ 425.1 TRIAL EVIDENCE Ch. 425

To render evidence of other accidents competent, the evidence must reasonably tend to show that the circumstances were substantially the same as at the time of the accident complained of,[15] and, the condition or thing shown to be the common cause

new highway in the area was working, and another witness testified that rock struck his windshield in morning hours of a day early in May when there was equipment working on haul roads running parallel to the highway in area of the fatal accident which had occurred on June 11 during daylight hours, the time, place and circumstances of incidents related by such witnesses were sufficiently similar to those of fatal accident as to permit admission of such testimony, in action against general contractor, for purpose of showing continuing defect or course of negligent conduct); Sheard v. Oregon Electric Ry. Co., 1929, 282 P. 542, 131 Or. 415 (stalling of automobiles at same place on railroad track).

Pa.—Yordy v. Northumberland County, 1932, 158 A. 607, 104 Pa.Super. 237.

S.D.—Allen v. McLain, 69 N.W.2d 390, 75 S.D. 520 (wherein defendant denied knowledge that driving at very fast rate around curves and over sharp hills was dangerous, properly admitted evidence of three previous accidents which defendant had had and in which he either had run into ditch or had upset).

Tex.—Beaumont, Sour Lake & Western R. Co. v. Cluck, Civ.App., 95 S.W.2d 1033, error dismissed (collision with flatcar); Gifford-Hill & Co. v. Henderson, Civ.App., 81 S.W.2d 274, error dismissed (action against highway contractor on theory that dirt permitted to fall on pavement created dangerous condition).

Va.—City of Portsmouth v. Cilumbrello, 129 S.E.2d 31, 204 Va. 11 (notice of dangerous condition).

Wash.—Ewer v. Goodyear Tire & Rubber Co., 1970, 480 P.2d 260, 4 Wash.App. 152 (under theory of notice to manufacturer, to permit introduction of evidence of another tire explosion).

Another location but similar conditions

Where locations of two highway construction projects were substantially similar in that both involved placing of lane barrels so that they might not be seen until it was too late to avoid an unanticipated danger, bridges constructed on both projects were similar, as were methods of construction, width of roadways was nearly the same, terrain and physical characteristics of roadway and surroundings were similar, approaches were similar, barrels were similar and same arrow warning truck was used on both projects to warn traffic, it was not error to admit in suit against contractor for injuries arising out of collision at one location evidence of injuries occurring at the other location; contractor's knowledge of prior accident in similar situation was material in determining exercise of reasonable care at and near scene of subsequent collision. Morrison v. Ted Wilkerson, Inc., D.C.Mo.1971, 343 F.Supp. 1319.

But see

In action for damages sustained when bridge collapsed, testimony that three years before accident another truck went through bridge held not strictly relevant. Yordy v. Northumberland County, 158 A. 607, 104 Pa.Super. 237.

Subsequent accidents

Evidence of prior accidents is admissible to show dangerous condi-

---

15. See footnote 15 on page 451.

tion and notice but evidence of subsequent accidents only to show dangerous condition. Laitenberger v. State, Ct.Cl., 57 N.Y.S.2d 418.

15. U.S.—Knight v. Baltimore & O. R. Co., D.C.N.Y., 8 F.R.D. 261.

Cal.—Martindale v. Atchison, T. & S. F. Ry. Co., 201 P.2d 48, 89 Cal. App.2d 400.

Conn.—Witek v. Town of Southbury, 1945, 42 A.2d 843, 132 Conn. 104 (no objection as to dissimilarity); James v. City of Waterbury, 12 A.2d 770, 126 Conn. 525 (evidence of minor collisions between automobiles at the intersection, offered to show a dangerous condition, was inadmissible as not involving conditions substantially similar to those confronting pedestrian); Petrillo v. Kolbay, 165 A. 346, 116 Conn. 389 (testimony that witness one night almost hit girl where fatal accident occurred).

Ill.—Moore v. Bloomington, D. & C. R. Co., 128 N.E. 721, 295 Ill. 63.

Iowa.—Mead v. Scott, 130 N.W.2d 641, 256 Iowa 1285.

Ky.—O'Neil & Hearne v. Bray's Adm'x, 90 S.W.2d 353, 262 Ky. 377 (evidence of other cars skidding on hill held admissible to show dangerous character of highway, where shown that conditions and management of other cars were the same).

Md.—Charles v. Mayor and City Council of City of Baltimore, 114 A. 565, 138 Md. 523.

Mass.—Bannister v. Berkshire St. Ry. Co., 18 N.E.2d 342, 301 Mass. 598 (circumstances under which other bus passengers bumped their heads against luggage racks).

Mo.—Cunningham v. City of Springfield, 31 S.W.2d 123, 226 Mo.App. 23.

N.J.—Di Domenico v. Pennsylvania-Reading Seashore Lines, 178 A.2d 10, 36 N.J. 455 (evidence of prior accident at railroad crossing was properly excluded, in view of failure of party offering such evidence to show circumstances of accidents).

N.Y.—Jasinski v. New York Cent. R. R., 1964, 250 N.Y.S.2d 942, 21 A. D.2d 456 involving vehicles using other crossing approaches); Jonas v. City of New York, 231 N.Y.S.2d 136, 36 Misc.2d 56 (when from such evidence it appears that pillar and approach to pillar were so constructed or maintained that accidents occurred although drivers of vehicles involved were operating at reasonable rate of speed under physical conditions then existing).

Okl.—St. Louis-San Francisco Ry. Co. v. Powell, 385 P.2d 465 (railroad crossing).

Tex.—Missouri-Kansas-Texas R. Co. of Tex. v. McFerrin, 291 S.W.2d 931, 156 Tex. 69.

Va.—Spurlin v. Richardson, 128 S.E. 2d 273, 203 Va. 984 (where claim was that brakes were defective but it did not appear that rolling on prior occasions had been caused by defective brakes).

Wash.—Hinkel v. Weyerhaeuser Co., 1972, 494 P.2d 1008, 6 Wash.App. 548 (where plaintiffs, suing as result of collision of automobile with rear of vehicle on highway which had stopped in fog and smoke from burning slash on defendant's property, showed that conditions of smoke and fog three hours earlier were similar to those existing at the time of the accident but did not offer to prove that drivers involved in prior accident had received a similar warning of the type plaintiffs had received, plaintiffs' offer to show that similar accident had occurred about three hours earlier was correctly rejected).

Extent of damage not evidence whether vehicles stopped

It was not error to exclude photographs of other wrecked automobiles

of danger in such accidents must be the condition or thing contributing to the danger of the accident complained of.[16]

The question of the similarity of conditions is within the discretion of the trial court,[17] and its determination is conclusive, if there is evidence to support it.[18]

in suit arising from automobile-truck collision, notwithstanding claim that photographs had a direct bearing on issue whether plaintiffs' automobile was stopped on highway at moment of impact, where photographs were not relevant to any issue developed in suit, in that accidents that caused damage to vehicles in excluded photographs did not occur at same time and place and no evidence was introduced showing that unrelated accidents occurred under substantially similar circumstances, or by means of same instrumentality. Franco v. Graham, Tex.Civ.App.1971, 470 S.W. 2d 429, reformed 488 S.W.2d 390.

Other collisions with street obstruction

In action against city for injuries sustained in collision with concrete signal light abutment, evidence of prior similar accidents at that locality which passenger sought to introduce was not admissible where such evidence was limited to proposed evidence of a single witness residing in locality of the intersection who, because he was not present at time of accident at issue, could not give details of the actual occurrences but could only recite subsequent conditions as he observed them. Perry v. City of Oklahoma City, Okl., 1970, 470 P.2d 974.

Showing negligent design of road

Proof offered by plaintiff of several prior accidents on parkway was admissible in action against city for alleged negligent design of parkway, when automobile he was driving struck concrete base of light pole on the parkway, upon showing of substantial similarity of circumstances. Rainey v. City of New York, 1970, 318 N.Y.S.2d 113, 35 A.D.2d 1003.

That other unattended vehicles tampered with

In action for injuries incurred when plaintiff's automobile collided at night on farm-to-market unlighted road with defendants' runaway automobile which had been parked at head of driveway adjacent to home, proffered testimony of a near but not next door neighbor of defendants, who was asked whether he had any experience of an automobile being tampered with while in his driveway or on his premises, was properly excluded as irrelevant since it did not relate to premises of defendants or to the night involved. Shepherd v. U. S. Fidelity & Guaranty Co., 106 S.E.2d 381, 233 S.C. 536.

16. Cal.—Wilkerson v. City of El Monte, 62 P.2d 790, 17 Cal.App.2d 615 (depression in street).

Ill.—Moore v. Bloomington, D. & C. R. Co., 128 N.E. 721, 295 Ill. 63.

17. U.S.—Atlantic Coast Line R. Co. v. Hadlock, C.A.Fla., 180 F. 2d 105 (where there was a claim that crossing was invisible at night and that sign had no reflector, permitting inquiry as to other accidents at crossing within two years was not an abuse of discretion).

Cal.—Gerberich v. Southern California Edison Co., 79 P.2d 783, 26 Cal.App.2d 471 (action for damages sustained when automobile collided with power pole).

S.D.—Berlin v. Berens, 80 N.W.2d 79, 76 S.D. 429 (which should be exercised cautiously).

18. U.S.—Balchumas v. Palmer, C. C.A.N.Y., 151 F.2d 842 (excluding evidence of other accidents as "too

§ 425.1 OPERATION OF VEHICLES

But in some jurisdictions the courts have held inadmissible proof of similar occurrences in the same vicinity and at other times.[19]

indefinite," though "strict" was affirmed).

N.H.—Lovett v. Manchester St. Ry., 159 A. 132, 85 N.H. 345.

[19] **U.S.**—Plough v. Baltimore & O. R. Co., C.C.A.N.Y., 164 F.2d 254, certiorari denied, 68 S.Ct. 740, 333 U.S. 861, 92 L.Ed. 1140; Interstate Motor Lines v. Great Western Ry. Co., C.C.A.Colo., 161 F.2d 968 (railroad crossing collision).

Cal.—O'Brien v. Schellberg, 140 P.2d 159, 59 Cal.App.2d 764 (testimony regarding defendant's prior observation of pedestrians at the intersection); Bramble v. McEwan, 104 P.2d 1054, 40 Cal.App.2d 400 (in last clear chance case).

Fla.—Powell v. Horne, 5 So.2d 451, 149 Fla. 240 (operations of train over the crossing on occasions wholly unconnected).

Ga.—Bazemore v. Powell, 188 S.E. 282, 54 Ga.App. 444 (witness narrowly avoided a collision at the crossing).

Kan.—Bledsoe v. Missouri, K. & T. R. Co., 90 P.2d 9, 149 Kan. 741 (even on theory showed dangerous crossing, as could be fault of motorist).

Ky.—Hauser v. Public Service Co. of Indiana, 111 S.W.2d 657, 271 Ky. 206.

Me.—Johnson v. Maine Cent. R. Co., 38 A.2d 884, 141 Me. 38 (railroad crossing accident).

Md.—Mayor and Council of City of Cumberland v. Turney, 9 A.2d 561, 177 Md. 297.

Mass.—National Laundry Co. v. City of Newton, 14 N.E.2d 108, 300 Mass. 126.

N.Y.—Provo v. Morehouse, 207 N. Y.S.2d 536, 12 A.D.2d 668 (permitting questioning, for purpose of showing that the other accident started with argument over parking fee and suggesting that attendant had greater concern for fee than for his own safety, was prejudicial error).

Or.—Southern Pac. Co. v. Consolidated Freightways, 281 P.2d 693, 203 Or. 657 (evidence as to frequent and numerous prior accidents involving railroad at or near such intersection was properly excluded).

Pa.—Stormer v. Alberts Const. Co., 165 A.2d 87, 401 Pa. 461 (where automobile collided, at night, with disabled vehicle which had been left at edge of excavated material, which defendant had placed on half of roadway in course of installing sanitary sewer, after driver of disabled vehicle moved one or two of lights from place where defendant had installed them to position at rear of disabled automobile, court properly excluded evidence as to occurrence of prior accidents at different parts of highway within four or five days of accident).

Wash.—Tyler v. Pierce County, 62 P.2d 32, 188 Wash. 229 (proof of notice not necessary, and nature of condition provable by other evidence).

Wis.—Poneitowcki v. Harres, 1929, 228 N.W. 126, 200 Wis. 504 (injected collateral issues).

Admissible only in absence of eye-witness

In brakeman's action where truck struck freight car at railway crossing, numerous persons being present at time of collision, evidence of other accidents at same crossing, happening before and after one which gave rise to suit, inadmissible, since such evidence is admissible only when there are no eye-witnesses. Dunham v. Cantlay & Tanzola, 49 P.2d 332, 9 Cal.App.2d 274.

§ 425.1 TRIAL EVIDENCE Ch. 425

Under some circumstances, evidence of former experiences not resulting in accidents has been held admissible to show a lack of negligence at the time and place in question.[20]

Evidence that travelers other than the one whose negligence is alleged to have caused or contributed to the accident in question have had similar experiences at the same place is not admissible to prove defendant's conduct constituted due care,[21] with-

---

20. Cal.—Leighton v. Dodge, 45 Cal.Rptr. 820 (evidence of three other skidding occurrences by following or preceding automobiles, closely connected in time and place, was admissible in rear-end accident case for limited purpose of showing excessive slipperiness of a portion of highway to corroborate defendant's testimony that highway was slippery).

Minn.—Bergman v. Williams, 217 N. W. 127, 173 Minn. 250 (previous parking on a grade, without child interference).

But see

In suit against sales company, chassis maker, and wheel maker allegedly liable under products liability for sale to city of fire truck chassis with defective wheel, there was no abuse of discretion by trial court in upholding objection to introduction of evidence as to whether any of the other 79 to 99 wheels made by maker out of same "heat" or batch of metals had failed, on ground that it would raise too many side issues as to where such other wheels were sold and how they were used. City of Franklin v. Badger Ford Truck Sales, Inc., 1973, 207 N.W.2d 866, 58 Wis. 2d 641.

Contra

U.S.—District of Columbia v. Chessin, 1932, 61 F.2d 523, 61 App.D.C. 260 (where alleged street depression caused accident, non-eventful use of other streets similarly constructed tended to raise collateral issues).

Ariz.—City of Tucson v. Gallagher, 1972, 493 P.2d 1197, 108 Ariz. 140 (in absence of evidence of prior accidents on portion of future roadway traversed by ditch which defendant driver drove into, testimony of lack of other accidents sought to be introduced by codefendant city was properly refused, notwithstanding that photographs admitted at plaintiff passenger's request showed tire tracks in the area).

Va.—City of Radford v. Calhoun, 181 S.E. 345, 165 Va. 24, 100 A.L.R. 1378 (unguarded and unlighted pile of concrete slabs in street).

Showing range of visibility

Ga.—Patton v. Smith, 1969, 168 S.E. 2d 627, 119 Ga.App. 664 (excluding testimony that, on night of fatal collision at time very close to that of collision, witness was driving along same road and in same direction defendant had driven and that she had seen figure of man on the road, whom she could not identify, at a distance of one or two automobile lengths in front of her, was reversible error where excluded evidence was on the same point as plaintiff's experimental evidence, the distance at which a man could be seen at night at the place of the collision, and was relevant to vital issue of whether defendant exercised ordinary care).

21. Mass.—Farmer v. New York, N. H. & H. R. Co., 104 N.E. 492, 217 Mass. 158.

Or.—Schairer v. Johnson, 272 P. 1027, 128 Or. 409 (testimony that witness drove his car through intersection where accident occurred at speed at which defendant was driving properly excluded).

454

Ch. 425　　　OPERATION OF VEHICLES　　　§ 425.1

out proof that the conditions and management of the cars were the same.[22]

Evidence of criminal violations

Evidence of a plea of guilty to a criminal charge arising out of an automobile accident is generally admissible as relevant evidence of negligence,[23] but it is not conclusive, and may be explained.[24]

Wis.—Poneitowcki v. Harres, 228 N. W. 126, 200 Wis. 504.

22. Mass.—Mailhot v. New York, N. H. & H. R. Co., 173 N.E. 422, 273 Mass. 277; Williams v. Holbrook, 103 N.E. 633, 216 Mass. 239 (other vehicle previously skidded at same place).

Laying foundation

Where defendant in accident case caused by icy highway sought to show experience of witness when witness passed scene at an earlier hour, exclusion of question as to how condition of highway when witness saw it after accident compared with its condition when he had driven over it earlier was error and prejudicial to defendant as preventing defendant from laying necessary foundation for admissibility of desired testimony. Dobosz v. Nyren, 38 A 2d 684, 131 Conn. 270.

23. U.S.—Prichard v. Conley, D.C. Tenn.1969, 48 F.R.D. 138 (certified copy of admission of defendant in criminal case that he was guilty of assault and battery with an automobile and driving while intoxicated was conditionally admissible); Hawkins v. Gorea Motor Exp., Inc., C.A.N.Y., 360 F.2d 933 (to driving at excessive speed for existing conditions); Eschelbach v. William S. Scull Co , C.A.N.J., 293 F.2d 599; Levelle v. Powers, C.A. Okl., 248 F.2d 774; U. S. v. Standard Oil Co. of Cal., D.C.Cal., 60 F.Supp. 807, affirmed 153 F.2d 958, affirmed 67 S.Ct. 1604, 332 U.S. 301, 91 L.Ed. 2067.

Del.—Boyd v. Hammond, 187 A.2d 413, 5 Storey 336.

Fla.—Chimerakis v. Evans, 1969, 221 So.2d 735.

Ga.—Edwards v. Bullard, 1974, 205 S.E.2d 115, 131 Ga.App. 34; Harrison v. Lawhorne, 1973, 203 S.E.2d 292, 130 Ga.App. 314 (guilty plea to charge of being drunk on the street, entered after plea bargaining in which the original driving while under the influence of intoxicating liquor charge was stricken, was properly admitted as an admission against interest in guest passenger's action against motorist, since substitute charge to which plea was entered was the result of the incident which served as basis of action); Locklear v. Morgan, 1973, 201 S.E.2d 163, 129 Ga.App. 763 (even though sheriff disclaimed signature on warrant).

Ind.—Brattain v. Herron, 1974, 309 N.E.2d 150, —— Ind.App. ——; Moore v. Funk, 1973, 293 N.E.2d 534, 155 Ind.App. 545.

Kan.—Scogin v. Nugen, 1970, 464 P. 2d 166, 204 Kan. 568.

La.—Moore v. Skidmore, 1974, 301 So.2d 428 (but such plea was not conclusive); Gruber v. Beeson, App.1973, 284 So.2d 820; Joynes v. Toye Bros. Auto & Taxicab Co., 1960, 119 So. 446, 11 La.App. 124 (not as to gambling or loitering on issue of competency of driver).

Mass.—Morrissey v. Powell, 1939, 23 N.E.2d 411, 304 Mass. 268, 124 A.L.R. 522 (though plea withdrawn); Dzura v. Phillips, 1931, 175 N.E. 629, 275 Mass. 283.

24. See note 24 on page 457.

§ 425.1

Miss.—Seals v. St. Regis Paper Co., 1970, 236 So.2d 388.

Mo.—Ferguson v. Boyd, 1970, 448 S. W.2d 901 (pleaded guilty to careless driving charge).

Neb.—Remmenga v. Selk, 1948, 34 N. W.2d 757, 150 Neb. 401 (reckless driving).

N.M.—Valencia v. Dixon, 1971, 488 P.2d 120, 83 N.M. 70, certiorari denied 488 P.2d 107, 83 N.M. 57.

N.Y.—Knibbs v. Wagner, 222 N.Y.S. 2d 469, 14 A.D.2d 987.

Ohio.—Kossouth v. Bear, 114 N.E.2d 80, 96 Ohio App. 219, judgment reversed 119 N.E.2d 285, 161 Ohio St. 378 (careless driving charge).

Okl.—Dover v. Smith, 385 P.2d 287.

Or.—Hazard v. Salles, 1960, 353 P.2d 548, 222 Or. 559 (not as against owner).

Pa.—Jensen v. Com. Dept. of Transp. Bureau of Traffic Safety, 1973, 307 A.2d 476, 9 Pa.Cmwlth. 451 (pleaded guilty to that charge by paying the fine and costs); Com. Dept. of Transp., Bureau of Traffic Safety v. James, 1972, 296 A.2d 530, 6 Pa. Cmwlth. 493 (when operator pays a fine and costs in relation to a traffic offense, such payment amounts to a waiver of a hearing and a plea of guilty).

Tex.—Atkinson v. Rister, Civ.App. 1968, 422 S.W.2d 821, error refused n. r. e. (to show that defendant admitted he had illegally parked the truck and had failed to have a red light or flag on the projecting load); Plains Transport, Inc. v. Isaacs, Civ.App., 361 S.W. 2d 919.

Vt.—Steele v. Lackey, 177 A. 309, 107 Vt. 192 (admission by driver that he had pleaded guilty to careless and negligent operation).

Va.—Bagley v. Weaver, 1971, 180 S. E.2d 686, 211 Va. 779.

W.Va.—Moore v. Skyline Cab, 59 S. E.2d 437, 134 W.Va. 121.

Wyo.—Severin v. Hayes, 372 P.2d 1017 (reckless driving and driving under influence of intoxicating liquor).

But see

U.S.—Dunham v. Pannell, C.A.Tex., 263 F.2d 725 (evidence as to disposition of truck driver's traffic ticket was inadmissible, as a legal plea of guilty, to prove judgment of conviction or to establish truth of facts recited in the traffic charge).

Minn.—Warren v. Marsh, 11 N.W.2d 528, 215 Minn. 615.

Pa.—Miller v. Gutherie, 191 A. 61, 325 Pa. 495 (in action for injuries to child struck by truck while skating on highway which was under construction and which was partially shut off by barrier marked with word "detour," violation of act providing for punishment of any one who should drive over highway which had been closed by proper authority was material only if unlawful act of traversing closed highway was proximate cause of the collision).

Concerning conduct at nearby location

Record of defendant's conviction for operating a motor vehicle so as to endanger, founded upon defendant's driving at a certain intersection, was admissible in action against defendant for wrongful death of officer whose automobile skidded off the road at a second intersection where conviction was based on a plea of guilty, and such record was not inadmissible on theory the conviction was based upon an occurrence too remote distance-wise from the scene of the accident. MacDonald v. Hall, Me.1968, 244 A.2d 809.

Contra

Minn.—Warren v. Marsh, 1943, 11 N. W.2d 528, 215 Minn. 615 (by statute, even when plead guilty).

Ch. 425 OPERATION OF VEHICLES § 425.1

Under the federal rule and under the rule in certain states, a plea of guilty which was later withdrawn may not be proven.[25]

Not plea of nolo contendere

Cal.—Christensen v. Orr, App.1969, 79 Cal.Rptr. 656, 275 Cal.App.2d 12.

Ga.—Windsor Forest, Inc. v. Rocker, 1970, 175 S.E.2d 65, 121 Ga.App. 773.

Not evidence of wilful and wanton conduct

The plea by truck driver who struck rear of stopped automobile to traffic citation charging violation of ordinance prohibiting "careless, reckless or wanton" driving was not sufficiently specific to justify concluding that he was pleading guilty to willful or wanton conduct since plea was an admission against interest which may be explained as was done by driver when he stated that in pleading guilty he merely was looking for the shorter way out. Glaze v. Owens, 243 N.E.2d 13, 104 Ill.App.2d 172.

Questioning not adequate

Refusal to allow plaintiff's counsel, in cross-examining defendant, to ask whether defendant had not "admitted" in a criminal prosecution in district court arising out of same accident that he was guilty of operating an automobile negligently was not an abuse of discretion, in view of fact that question was dependent upon defendant's own conclusions both as to meaning of question and as to legal effect of anything he might have said in criminal prosecution. Baxter v. Bourget, 42 N.E.2d 2, 311 Mass. 490.

24. **U.S.**—Franklin Life Ins. Co. v. Strickland, D.C.Miss.1974, 376 F.Supp. 280; Prichard v. Conley, D.C.Tenn.1969, 48 F.R.D. 138; State Farm Mut. Auto. Ins. Co. v. Worthington, C.A.Mo., 405 F.2d 683.

Conn.—Baritot v. Viggiano, 245 A.2d 298, 5 Conn.Cir. 123; Moulin v. Bergeron, 1949, 65 A.2d 478, 135 Conn. 443.

Ga.—Roper v. Scott, 1948, 48 S.E.2d 118, 77 Ga.App. 120 (driving while intoxicated).

Iowa.—Farm & City Ins. Co. v. Hassel, 1972, 197 N.W.2d 360.

Kan.—Scogin v. Nugen, 1970, 464 P.2d 166, 204 Kan. 568 (that cost and inconvenience of defending against a traffic ticket are practical motivations for plea of guilty to traffic violation).

La.—Hutchins v. Westley, 1970, 235 So.2d 434.

Mass.—Morrissey v. Powell, 1939, 23 N.E.2d 411, 304 Mass. 268, 124 A.L.R. 1522.

Mo.—Parker v. Wallace, 431 S.W.2d 136, citing 31A C.J.S. Evidence § 381 (explanation of plea of guilty at prior criminal case may be made and reason for entering plea may be given by party himself in subsequent civil action).

N.C.—Teachey v. Woolard, 1972, 191 S.E.2d 903, 16 N.C.App. 249, certiorari denied 192 S.E.2d 840, 282 N.C. 430.

N.D.—Borstad v. La Roque, 98 N.W.2d 16.

Ohio.—Wilcox v. Gregory, 1960, 176 N.E.2d 523, 112 Ohio App. 516 (record unclear).

Wash.—Atkins v. Churchill, 194 P.2d 364, 30 Wash.2d 859 (charge of entrusting automobile to unlicensed minor).

W.Va.—Utt v. Herold, 34 S.E.2d 357, 127 W.Va. 719.

Wyo.—Severin v. Hayes, 372 P.2d 1017.

25. Federal Rules of Evidence § 410, 28 U.S.C.A.

Cal.—West's Ann.Calif.Evid.Code, § 1153.

Fla.—Florida Evidence Code § 90.410.

Me.—Maine Rules of Evidence § 410.

§ 425.1 TRIAL EVIDENCE Ch. 425

Evidence of an investigation,[26] or an arrest,[27] or the filing of charges and the prosecution of criminal proceedings,[28] or evidence of the non-issuance of any charges [29] is not admissible.

Neb.—Nebraska Rules of Evidence § 410.

Nev.—N.R.S. 48.125.

N.M.—New Mexico Rules of Evidence § 410.

Wis.—Wisconsin Rules of Evidence § 904.10.

26. Mich.—Mullaney v. Woodruff, 273 N.W. 395, 280 Mich. 66.

27. U.S.—Fidelity & Cas. Co. of N. Y. v. Talbot, C.A.La., 234 F.2d 425 (but as trial court instructed jury not to consider it, testimony was not prejudicial).

Ark.—Breitenberg v. Parker, 372 S. W.2d 828, 237 Ark. 261 (but not prejudicial, where trial court admonished jury to disregard question and answer, and defendant neither moved for mistrial nor otherwise evidenced disagreement with ruling).

Cal.—Rednall v. Thompson, 239 P.2d 693, 108 Cal.App.2d 662 (for illegal parking).

Ill.—Mryatovich v. Chicago Transit Authority, 1969, 25 N.E.2d 345, 112 Ill.App.2d 437.

Ky.—Lincoln Taxi Co. v. Rice, 251 S.W.2d 867.

Mich.—Moffatt v. Helmer, 75 N.W.2d 887, 345 Mich. 153.

Mo.—Smith v. Fine, 175 S.W.2d 761, 351 Mo. 1179.

N.Y.—Landt v. Kingsway Equipment Leasing Corp., Sup., 159 N.Y.S.2d 453, affirmed 165 N.Y.S.2d 715, 4 A.D.2d 785.

Ohio.—Character v. Henderson, 1964, 195 N.E.2d 21, 1 Ohio App.2d 14 (not cured by admonition); Wolfe v. Baskin, 1940, 28 N.E.2d 629, 137 Ohio St. 284.

Pa.—Eastern Exp., Inc. v. Food Haulers, Inc., 1971, 285 A.2d 152, 445 Pa. 432 (police officer's testimony, on direct examination in action involving tractor trailers, describing what he did and found upon his arrival at scene was factual description only, did not indicate operator was guilty of reckless driving, and did not "open the door" to objectionable cross-examination in which counsel for plaintiffs elicited testimony that the officer escorted defendant operator from scene to office of a justice of the peace and arrested him for reckless driving); Patton v. Franc, 172 A.2d 297, 404 Pa. 306.

R.I.—Foster v. De Andrade, 149 A. 2d 713, 88 R.I. 442 (asked by own counsel).

S.C.—Wynn v. Rood, 91 S.E.2d 276, 228 S.C. 577 (but, propounding of questions seeking to adduce such evidence did not require declaration of a mistrial, where overwhelming weight of evidence showed a case of liability and patrolman had previously testified that defendant-driver had violated law).

Tex.—Isaacs v. Plains Transport Co., 367 S.W.2d 152.

Utah.—Hales v. Peterson, 360 P.2d 822, 11 Utah 2d 411.

Vt.—Paul v. Drown, 189 A. 144, 108 Vt. 458, 109 A.L.R. 1085.

W.Va.—Thornsbury v. Thornsbury, 131 S.E.2d 713, 147 W.Va. 771 (except insofar as it embraces an admission).

Wis.—Anderson v. Saunders, 113 N. W.2d 831, 16 Wis.2d 55.

28. Ala.—R. C. Bottling Co. v. Sorrells, 1973, 275 So.2d 131, 290 Ala. 187 (where on direct and redirect examination, following motorist, seeking to recover for injuries sus-

29. See footnote 29 on page 459.

tained when preceding truck driver made left turn while motorist was in process of passing him, related what investigating state trooper had said about dirty turn signals being difficult to see in the sun, his driver's license, his insurance and things of that nature and concluded that outside of accident "that's all I recall him asking me specifically," recross examination as to whether motorist had heard trooper say that he was charging motorist with passing improperly, an ultimate issue of fact, was improper).

Ark.—Girard v. Kuklinski, 360 S.W. 2d 115, 235 Ark. 337.

Cal.—Laursen v. Tidewater Associated Oil Co., 268 P.2d 104, 123 Cal.App.2d 813.

Del.—Prettyman v. Topkis, 3 A.2d 708, 9 W.W.Harr. 568.

Dist.Col.—Bill's Auto Rental v. Bonded Taxi Co., Mun.App., 72 A.2d 254.

Ga.—Crossley v. Collins, 1973, 198 S.E.2d 428, 128 Ga.App. 889 (but cured); United Motor Freight Terminal Co. v. Hixon, 47 S.E.2d 171, 76 Ga.App. 653.

La.—Braud v. Carmouche, 1974, 303 So.2d 774.

Mass.—Karasek v. Bockus, 199 N.E. 726, 293 Mass. 371.

Mo.—Cotton v. Pyle, 400 S.W.2d 72.

Ohio.—Schaeffer v. Davis, App., 83 N.E.2d 651, 52 O.L.A. 454.

R.I.—Solomon v. Shepard Co., 200 A. 993, 61 R.I. 332.

Tex.—Peek v. Parker, Civ.App., 210 S.W.2d 619.

Absence of accusation by party

In action against racing motorists, one of whom collided with plaintiff's approaching vehicle, refusal to admit evidence that plaintiff had not caused arrest of racing motorist who did not hit plaintiff's vehicle although plaintiff had taken such action as to racing motorist who hit plaintiff's vehicle was not error. Bierczynski v. Rogers, 1968, Del., 239 A.2d 218.

But see

Asking patrolman who investigated collision question relating to issuance of ticket to truck driver was not error where court had previously determined that it was permissible for plaintiffs' counsel to establish that driver of truck had pleaded guilty to violating traffic law, provided plaintiffs' pleadings alleged breach of such law as negligence proximately causing the collision. Lillie Sales, Inc. v. Rieger, Tex.Civ.App.1969, 437 S.W.2d 872, error refused n. r. e.

29. **Fla.**—Volk v. Goetz, 1968, 206 So.2d 250; Eggers v. Phillips Hardware Co., 88 So.2d 507.

Ga.—Boatner v. Sims, 1967, 154 S.E. 2d 282, 115 Ga.App. 284.

Kan.—Allen v. Ellis, 380 P.2d 408, 191 Kan. 311.

Mich.—Ilins v. Burns, 1972, 201 N.W.2d 624, 388 Mich. 504; Link v. McCoy, 1972, 197 N.W.2d 278, 39 Mich.App. 120 (not prejudicial where court instructed that such evidence was not to be considered in determining whether defendant was negligent).

Minn.—Dosh v. Elioff, 1974, 222 N. W.2d 326, 301 Minn. 169 (inadmissible on theory that it would rebut possible inference of excessive speed from testimony concerning length of skid marks left by automobile, where testimony concerning skid marks was introduced only as evidence of point of impact).

Neb.—Danner v. Walters, 1951, 48 N.W.2d 635, 154 Neb. 506.

N.C.—Beanblossom v. Thomas, 1966, 146 S.E.2d 36, 226 N.C. 181 (not reversible error).

Tex.—Lillie Sales, Inc. v. Rieger, 1969, 437 S.W.2d 872, error refused n. r. e.

§ 425.1   TRIAL EVIDENCE   Ch. 425

Under the usual rule, evidence of a judgment of conviction or acquittal upon a plea of not guilty is inadmissible to establish truth of facts on which the judgment was rendered.[30]

But see

Statute prohibiting introduction of record of conviction of any person for a traffic violation did not prohibit showing that no tickets were issued at scene of an accident. LeClair v. Sickler, 146 N.W.2d 853, 275 Minn. 320.

30. For discussion of proof of convictions as impeachment, see section 421.5.

Ark.—Briley v. White, 193 S.W.2d 326, 209 Ark. 941 (but denial of mistrial was not abuse of discretion).

Ga.—Smith v. Goodwin, 119 S.E.2d 35, 103 Ga.App. 248.

Ind.—Black v. Wachs, 163 N.E.2d 894, 130 Ind.App. 293.

La.—Buras v. Peck, App., 83 So.2d 783.

Mich.—Obermiller v. Patow, 1973, 207 N.W.2d 152, 45 Mich.App. 606.

Mo.—Beezley v. Spiva, 313 S.W.2d 691.

Ohio—Chambers v. Robert, 166 N.E.2d 530, 110 Ohio App. 472 (prejudicial error which could not be cured by charge of court).

Tenn.—Mitchell v. Farr, 222 S.W.2d 218, 32 Tenn.App. 200.

Tex.—Bowie v. Harris, Civ.App., 351 S.W.2d 668.

Acquittal

Generally, judgment of acquittal in criminal trials is not admissible as evidence of fact that plaintiff in a civil action did not cause the loss. Shoup v. Mannino, 149 A.2d 678, 188 Pa.Super. 457.

Contra

N.Y.—De Marco v. Young, 192 N.Y.S.2d 387, 31 Misc.2d 514 (and was prima facie evidence of facts); Smith v. Minissale, 75 N.Y.S.2d 645, 190 Misc. 114.

Contra as to felony conviction

U.S.—Federal Rules of Evidence § 803(22).

Cal.—West's Ann.Calif.Evid.Code, § 1300.

Kan.—Kansas Code of Civil Procedure § 60–460(r).

Me.—Maine Rules of Evidence § 803(22).

Neb.—Nebraska Rules of Evidence § 803(20).

Nev.—N.R.S. 51.295(1).

N.J.—New Jersey Evidence Rule 63(20).

N.M.—New Mexico Rules of Evidence 803(22).

Utah—Utah Rules of Evidence § 63(20).

Wis.—Wisconsin Rules of Evidence 908.03(22).

Dismissal

It was not error to admit in evidence for defendant, over objection that it was hearsay, report of an accident made by policeman which showed that defendant had been arrested for traffic violation and that the charge had been dismissed, where the evidence did not disclose whether the charge was made in court and by the court dismissed or whether the officer simply booked the charge himself and dismissed it. Swanson v. Moore, 31 S.E.2d 463, 71 Ga.App. 573.

Where evidence was admitted tending to show that investigating police officer had listed defendant's careless driving and plaintiff's failure to grant right of way as causes of accident, evidence of dismissal of traffic charge against plaintiff was

Proof of statutes, ordinances and regulations

Statutes and ordinances, as well as other regulations governing the equipment of vehicles operating upon the street or highway, or prescribing the duties of automobile or street car drivers or engineers of locomotives, are admissible,[31] if their validity and effectiveness are established.[32]

properly rejected. Friesen v. Schmelzel, 318 P.2d 363, 78 Wyo. 1.

Exception as to coroner's findings

Trial court committed no error in admitting in evidence, in action under death and survival acts, fact that defendant had been exonerated from all charges of criminal responsibility by coroner's inquest, after admission in evidence of pretrial statement that inquest had been had before coroner and that coroner's physician indicated that certain injuries had caused death, where court went on to neutralize any possible prejudicial effect of such material by proper instruction. Jamison v. Ardes, 182 A.2d 497, 408 Pa. 188.

Forfeiture of bond inadmissible
Wash.—Reynolds v. Donoho, 236 P. 2d 552, 39 Wash.2d 451 (but not prejudicial error).

31. **U.S.**—Smith v. Atlantic Coast Line R. Co., C.C.A.Fla., 127 F.2d 798; Long Transp. Co. v. Domurat, C.C.A.Ill., 93 F.2d 23 (right of way of pedestrians at intersections).
Ala.—Yarbrough v. Carter, 60 So. 833, 179 Ala. 356 (ordinance regulating speed admissible in action for injuries wantonly or wilfully inflicted, although there was no count claiming damages as for its violation, and although such violation was only simple negligence).
Cal.—Armenta v. Churchill, 267 P.2d 303, 42 Cal.2d 448 (construction safety order providing that trucks used to haul dirt, rock, concrete or other construction materials shall be equipped with a horn, bell, or whistle on both front and rear ends, or with a horn capable of emitting a sound audible under normal operating conditions from distance of not less than two hundred feet in rear of truck, provided that warning will be sounded while truck is backing up); Cassell v. McGuire & Hester, 10 Cal.Rptr. 33, 187 Cal.App.2d 579 (municipal traffic code provision making it unlawful to operate vehicles within sidewalk area except at driveways was not limited to protecting persons but was for purpose of protecting property as well); Squires v. City of Los Angeles, 224 P.2d 774, 100 Cal.App.2d 708 (statute prohibiting sale or use of reflectors, except of type approved by Department of Motor Vehicles, is not evidence of actual condition of a reflector when in use); Dolton v. Green, 164 P.2d 795, 72 Cal. App.2d 427 (ordinance regulating "street cars" not applicable to "interurban cars"); Formosa v. Yellow Cab Co., 87 P.2d 716, 31 Cal. App.2d 77 (irrespective of ordinance, truck driver was required to observe markers and if no markers were stationed at particular intersection to comply with state law applicable thereto); Coursault v. Schwebel, 5 P.2d 77, 118 Cal. App. 259 (ordinance regulating automobile operation, when overtaking street car stopping and discharging passengers admissible, although street car had gone few feet into intersection).
Colo.—Bauserman v. White, 114 P. 2d 557, 108 Colo. 101 (city traffic code related to "driving to left of the center of the street and reckless driving" admissible upon ample evidence of recklessness alone).

32. See footnote 32 on p. 466.

§ 425.1 TRIAL EVIDENCE Ch. 425

Fla.—Dabney v. Yapa, App., 187 So. 2d 381 (ordinance prohibiting a person from riding bicycle on sidewalk in business district); Smith v. Cline, App., 158 So.2d 553 (municipal traffic ordinances which were enacted by governing body of Metropolitan Dade County relating to passing on right and making of left turn at intersection); Blue & Gray Cab Co. v. Lowe, 196 So. 425, 143 Fla. 129 (ordinance controlling traffic at intersection).

Ga.—Russell v. Corley, 91 S.E.2d 24, 212 Ga. 121, opinion conformed to 91 S.E.2d 320, 93 Ga.App. 267 (right of way where pedestrian not in marked crosswalk); Griffin v. Browning, 181 S.E. 801, 51 Ga.App. 743 (that failure to recognize right of way of driver on the right is "reckless driving"); Hirsch v. Plowden, 134 S.E. 833, 35 Ga.App. 763 (regulation of operation of automobiles in relation to street cars).

Ill.—Krohn v. O'Bara, 115 N.E.2d 569, 351 Ill.App. 476 (speed ordinance).

Ind.—Norwalk Truck Line Co. v. Kostka, 88 N.E.2d 799, 120 Ind. App. 383, rehearing denied 89 N.E. 2d 625, 120 Ind.App. 383 (improper admission corrected by court's instruction and withdrawal).

Ky.—Illinois Cent. R. Co. v. McGuire's Adm'r, 38 S.W.2d 913, 239 Ky. 1.

Mass.—Woodcock v. Trailways of New England, Inc., 162 N.E.2d 658, 340 Mass. 36 (permitting the district supervisor of interstate commerce commission to introduce the commission's regulation requiring driver of vehicle stopped in traveled portion of highway to put out lighted fusee or lighted red electric lantern or red emergency reflector, and regulation of state registry of motor vehicles that no person shall stop a bus on state highway at any place other than a bus stop when a nearby bus stop is available).

Mich.—Kocks v. Collins, 47 N.W.2d 676, 330 Mich. 423 (testimony as to speed limit on street on which accident occurred was a fact which jury could consider in determining whether conduct was sufficiently reprehensible to constitute gross negligence).

Miss.—Somerville v. Keeler, 145 So. 721, 165 Miss. 244 (ordinance prohibiting automobile driving by child under 15).

Mo.—Teters v. Kansas City Public Service Co., 1957, 300 S.W.2d 511 (ordinance prohibited plaintiff's parking in bus zone, where bus struck opened door); Floyd v. St. Louis Public Service Co., 280 S.W. 2d 74 (city ordinance, requiring operator of overtaking vehicle to sound signaling device when desiring to pass another vehicle); McCormick v. Kansas City, Sup., 262 S.W.2d 868 (city ordinance limiting speed within 50 feet of intersection to 20 miles per hour); Kenney v. J. A. Folger & Co., App., 192 S.W.2d 73 (ordinance requiring vehicle emerging from a private driveway to stop); Weisman v. Arrow Trucking Co., App., 176 S.W.2d 37 (statute relating to brakes); Brown v. Alton R. Co., 151 S.W.2d 727, 236 Mo.App. 26 (speed ordinance).

Neb.—Larsen v. Omaha Transit Co., 86 N.W.2d 564, 165 Neb. 530 (ordinance prohibiting bus drivers from moving vehicle while passengers are ahead of driver's seat); Stark v. Turner, 47 N.W.2d 569, 154 Neb. 268 (school zone).

Nev.—Scott v. Smith, 311 P.2d 731, 73 Nev. 158 (ordinance establishing town speed limit was admissible even though accident occurred at hour when town's streets were deserted and town traffic was in no way involved).

N.J.—Perry v. Public Service Coordinated Transport, 56 A.2d 617, 136 N.J.L. 398 (city ordinance regulating parking).

N.Y.—Ebling Brewing Co. v. Linch, 141 N.Y.S. 480, 80 Misc. 517.

N.C.—Hensley v. Wallen, 127 S.E.2d 277, 257 N.C. 675 (speed statute); C. C. T. Equipment Co. v. Hertz Corp., 123 S.E.2d 802, 25 N.C. 277 (statute dealing with closing of highways and posting of warnings by highway commission).

Ohio—Welch v. Canton City Lines, 50 N.E.2d 343, 142 Ohio St. 166 (ordinance as to rights where traffic controlled by signal); Matz v. J. L. Curtis Cartage Co., 7 N.E.2d 220, 132 Ohio St. 271 (regulation requiring truck parked at night to be protected by flares).

Okl.—Hisaw v. Atchison, T. & S. F. R. Co., 1946, 169 P.2d 281, 197 Okl. 228 (requiring stop at railroad).

R.I.—Brey v. Rosenfeld, 48 A.2d 177, 72 R.I. 28, adhered to on rehearing 50 A.2d 911, 72 R.I. 316 (evidence of violation of ordinance was admissible as evidence of negligence but violation was not of itself proof of negligence); Drewett v. United Electric Rys. Co., 188 A. 877, 57 R.I. 169.

S.C.—Smith v. Carolina Milling Co., 167 S.E. 553, 168 S.C. 355 (speed ordinance).

S.D.—Buboltz v. Chicago, M. & St. P. Ry. Co., 199 N.W. 782, 47 S.D. 512.

Tenn.—Shew v. Bailey, App.1951, 260 S.W.2d 362, 37 Tenn.App. 40.

Va.—Birtcherd Dairy, Inc. v. Edwards, 91 S.E.2d 421, 197 Va. 830 (ordinance which gave baker right to stop truck on street to deliver loaf of bread to home of customer should not have been admitted in evidence, where, at time of accident, baker had finished delivery of bread and was selling bread from truck); Purington v. Newton, 49 A.2d 98, 114 Vt. 490 (speed at intersection).

Wash.—Oliver v. Taylor, 205 P. 746, 119 Wash. 190 (right of way ordinance).

Application of statutes limited in municipalities

Statutory headlight requirements do not apply to traffic on municipal streets unless such streets are state maintained municipal connecting links. Rogers v. Myers, Fla.App. 1970, 240 So.2d 516.

Contra subsequent enactment

Traffic law enacted subsequent to time of happening complained of is not relevant. McCusker v. B. & N. Transportation Co., 148 A. 896, 106 N.J.L. 167.

County supervisor resolution

Resolution by which county supervisors designated through highways and stop intersections and vehicle pertained to intersection involved was properly admitted. Wander v. Brady, 105 N.W.2d 86, 252 Iowa 183.

Even where conceded violation not a proximate cause

Evidence of city ordinance requiring hand signal for stopping was properly admitted in action arising out of rear-end collision with plaintiff's stopped automobile, despite admission by defendant's driver that he saw plaintiff's brake lights and that failure to give hand signal made no difference. Jeskey v. Yellow Cab Co., Fla.App., 136 So.2d 376.

Held inapplicable

Dist.Col.—Coleman v. Chudnow, Mun.App.1944, 35 A.2d 925 (traffic regulation defining intersection not applicable where collision outside of intersection).

Ga.—Draffin v. Massey, 1956, 92 S.E.2d 38, 93 Ga.App. 329 (stock law as to animals at large not applicable where cow was in custody).

Kan.—Allen v. Pearce Dental Supply Co., 1939, 88 P.2d 1057, 149 Kan. 549 (violation not shown to be proximate cause).

Mich.—Uithoven v. Snyder, 1921, 182 N.W. 80, 213 Mich. 318 (ordinance as to speed at railroad crossing

§ 425.1 TRIAL EVIDENCE Ch. 425

not relevant where accident was 125 feet away).

Mo.—Riley v. Bi-State Transit System, App.1970, 459 S.W.2d 753 (ordinance as to speed and yielding at intersection not applicable, where other vehicle subject to flashing red light).

Okl.—Sheppard v. Scrivner-Stevens Co., 127 P.2d 159, 191 Okl. 112 (inadmissible against "stopped" driver where applicable only to "disabled" vehicle).

Pa.—West v. Morgan, 52 Dauph. 361, affirmed 27 A.2d 46, 345 Pa. 61 (Highway Department rules as to precautions to be taken by own employees for their own safety not applicable in action between employee and a third party, also was no evidence that defendant knew of these rules, or that his conduct was influenced thereby, nor is there any evidence that the injury would have been avoided by compliance with rules).

Tenn.—Long v. Tomlin, 1939, 125 S.W.2d 171, 22 Tenn.App. 607 (traffic regulation of Department of Finance and Taxation deemed not to be law).

Tex.—Eubanks v. Colbert, Civ.App., 327 S.W.2d 457, 83 A.L.R.2d 378, writ of error refused n. r. e. (evidence that speed limit at intersection where accident occurred was 30 miles per hour was inadmissible over objection that the speed limit did not apply to policemen on duty and answering calls, and admission of such evidence was highly prejudicial); Stedman Fruit Co. v. Smith, Civ.App., 28 S.W.2d 622, error dismissed (ordinance contrary to state law).

W.Va.—Muldoon v. Kepner, 91 S.E. 2d 727, 141 W.Va. 577 (where, in action by ambulance guest-passenger against ambulance owner for injuries received in collision between ambulance and an automobile, owner did not offer in evidence permit signed by city manager designating ambulance as an authorized emergency vehicle, ordinance, which required other automobiles to stop or drive to curb when emergency vehicle approached was properly excluded).

Hit and run statute

Evidence as to conduct of servant immediately after alleged collision was relevant, and evidence as to any violation of "hit and run" statute was relevant on question whether truck was being operated in a willful and wanton manner. Hallman v. Cushman, 13 S.E.2d 498, 196 S.C. 402.

Metropolitan District Commission regulation

In action for injuries sustained by minor when sled on which he was riding struck defendants' automobile, regulation of the Metropolitan District Commission prohibiting coasting on any reservation except at such times and places as may be designated by it were properly admitted; but, if improperly admitted, such admission was harmless error, where it was coasting on a street and not on a reservation which was a proximate cause of the accident. Le Blanc v. Welch, 129 N.E.2d 908, 333 Mass. 207.

Not proposed legislation

R.I.—McKay v. Zuckerman, 1968, 248 A.2d 319, 104 R.I. 667.

Part of ordinance admissible

Ordinance providing that car should not be propelled faster than 4 miles per hour within city unless attached to engine, as provided in another section, held admissible, although other section was not introduced, since other section did not apply to unattached cars. Baltimore & O. R. Co. v. State, for Use of Carbone, 181 A. 830, 169 Md. 345.

A city ordinance, requiring driver to yield right of way to pedestrian crossing roadway within marked crosswalk, was admissible in evi-

464

dence on question of defendant's negligence and plaintiff's contributory negligence in action for injuries to pedestrian, struck by automobile while crossing street within pedestrians' marked lane, though other parts of ordinance were inadmissible. White v. Hasburgh, Mo.App., 124 S. W.2d 560.

Policeman's instructions

Evidence that school policeman had instructed boys not to ride double on motor scooters and on numerous occasions had taken them off when they had attempted to do so was not admissible as showing contributory negligence of plaintiff in riding behind driver on single seat of scooter, since such evidence did not tend to show knowledge and appreciation of dangers incident to method of riding engaged in by plaintiff. Greenlease-Ledterman, Inc., v. Hawkins, 186 P.2d 318, 199 Okl. 331.

Public Utilities Commission Regulation

Ohio—Claypool v. Mohawk Motor, 97 N.E.2d 32, 155 Ohio St. 8 (rules and regulations of the Public Utilities Commission respecting rear lights, reflectors, etc., could be considered by the jury in determining the issue of negligence of defendant).

Public Service Commission regulation

W.Va.—Frampton v. Consolidated Bus Lines, 62 S.E.2d 126, 134 W. Va. 815 (admission of certain section of the motor carrier's safety regulations, promulgated by Public Service Commission which sections were in force and effect at time plaintiff was injured was not error).

Public Works Department regulations

Neb.—Trussell v. Ferguson, 239 N.W. 461, 122 Neb. 82 (rules and regulations of the public works department applicable to "vehicles" on highway).

Rules of Interstate Commerce Commission

Iowa—Wright v. Des Moines Ry. Co., 1 N.W.2d 259, 231 Iowa 410 (admission of a book containing regulations adopted by the Interstate Commerce Commission relating to the driving of motor vehicles was error, notwithstanding that truck was used in interstate commerce, since rules did not have effect of "laws," and a violation thereof by truck driver, if any, would not constitute negligence).

Rules of State Park Commission

N.Y.—Mitchell v. State, 85 N.Y.S.2d 80, 193 Misc. 507 (rule of State Park Commission as to speed limit of motor vehicles in park would be admitted).

Safety bulletin

Police department safety bulletins concerning operation of emergency vehicle should have been admitted, in action for wrongful death of motorist whose automobile collided at city street intersection with police car which was on an emergency run and was traveling through intersection against traffic signal, as evidence of motorist's lack of contributory negligence, in view of factual statements in bulletin relevant to whether person in motorist's automobile could have heard the siren. Dillenbeck v. City of Los Angeles, 1968, 446 P.2d 129, 72 Cal.Rptr. 321, 69 Cal.2d 472.

State manual on highway design

In action for injuries sustained in accident occurring in center or "passing" lane of three-lane highway, portions of state manual on uniform highway control devices containing instructions for design of three-lane highways and instructions for various lines and other traffic control devices placed on such highways were material to issue of whether defendant or plaintiff violated any statute in driving in center lane and were properly admitted over objection that information contained in document

§ 425.1 TRIAL EVIDENCE Ch. 425

was immaterial. Konnerup v. Baker, 1971, 488 P.2d 241, —— Colo.App. ——.

Training manual

Cal.—Dillenbeck v. City of Los Angeles, 1968, 446 P.2d 129, 72 Cal. Rptr. 321, 69 Cal.2d 472 (training bulletins of city police department which concerned operation of police vehicles under emergency conditions and which contained statements to effect that police officer was seldom justified in exceeding district limit and that he should decelerate to 15 miles per hour in proceeding against traffic control device through blind intersection should have been admitted).

Fla.—Fowler v. City of Gainesville, 1968, 213 So.2d 38 (exclusion of testimony by police officer to effect that police automobile's flasher light should have been turned on when stopping traffic offender and trial court's failure to admit in evidence police training manual which also advised that flasher light should be turned on was not error).

32. Ariz.—Mitchell v. Emblade, 298 P.2d 1034, 80 Ariz. 398, on rehearing opinion adhered to 301 P.2d 1032, 81 Ariz. 121 (admission in evidence of city ordinance and state highway commission's resolution contrary to later statute).

Ga.—Carroll v. Yearty, 117 S.E.2d 248, 102 Ga.App. 677 (did not err in rejecting oral testimony of city clerk that speed limit in city was 25 miles an hour when clerk testified that what he knew about speed limit was merely hearsay and that he did not know of his own knowledge that there was an ordinance fixing speed limit); Western & Atlantic R. R. v. Swigert, 195 S.E. 230, 57 Ga.App. 274 (a document purporting to be a certified copy of a city ordinance is inadmissible where it was taken from the minutes of a city ordinance book of acts and it does not appear that the book of acts was ever adopted by the city authorities); Brooks v. Carver, 190 S.E. 389, 55 Ga.App. 362 (held not error, although certificate attached to ordinance was dated eleven months before accident).

Ill.—Rutowicz v. United Motor Coach Co., 261 Ill.App. 377 (ordinance not in force at time of accident).

Ind.—Bartley v. Chicago & E. I. R. Co., 41 N.E.2d 805, 220 Ind. 354 (objection to the admission of penal ordinance was properly sustained where there was no showing that the ordinance had ever been published as required).

La.—Haynes v. Fluitt, App.1951, 54 So.2d 844 (speed signs not legal evidence of limit); Martin v. Yazoo & M. R. Co., App., 181 So. 571 (ordinance not signed by the mayor was inoperative, and hence inadmissible).

Mass.—Nickerson v. Boston Elevated Ry., 66 N.E.2d 193, 319 Mass. 220 (obscure meaning made ordinance inadmissible).

Mo.—Brown v. Alton R. Co., Mo. App., 132 S.W.2d 713, record quashed, 143 S.W.2d 233, 346 Mo. 681 (speed ordinance, duly certified by city clerk, under seal, as being a true copy of ordinance of record and on file in his office, was properly admitted).

N.Y.—Vinci v. Charney, 1948, 80 N.Y.S.2d 521, 192 Misc. 302 (ordinance in conflict with statute as to right of way).

Headgear requirements

In action for injuries to motorcyclist struck by automobile, the matter of head gear was properly excluded where at time of accident the statute requiring use of safety helmets had not been effective, and the

466

Evidence of safety policy publications of non-official bodies may be admissible.[33]

It has also been held that the defendant was entitled to the admission of the ordinance to disprove negligence.[34]

ordinance requiring motorcyclists to wear helmets while operating rented machines had no application to motorcycle which was not leased. Burgstahler v. Fox, 1971, 186 N.W. 2d 182, 290 Minn. 495.

Highway Patrol Department approval inconsistent with statute

Minn.—Johnson v. Sunshine Creamery Co., 274 N.W. 404, 200 Minn. 428 (department approval could not be related).

Lack of signposting

Cal.—Guerra v. Brooks, 236 P.2d 807, 38 Cal.2d 16 (where there was evidence that motorcyclist was traveling at a speed in excess of 25 miles an hour, trial court erred in excluding evidence of lack of signposting which would make the area in question a zone in which speed was limited to 25 miles an hour).

Fla.—World Wide Rent-A-Car, Inc. v. Boshnack, App., 184 So.2d 467 (proper foundation for introduction of testimony as to speed limit in unposted location required the introduction of speed law as established by governing authority followed by testimony showing the same to be applicable to the physical area concerned).

S.C.—Smith v. Carolina Milling Co., 167 S.E. 553, 168 S.C. 355 (speed ordinance held admissible as to exercise of due care, though it had not been posted as the statute required).

Not relevant pursuant to statute

Cal.—Richards v. Stanley, 271 P.2d 23, 43 Cal.2d 60 (properly excluded as irrelevant ordinance forbidding owner to leave automobile unlocked and unattended with keys in ignition but providing that violation thereof should not have any bearing in civil action).

Obsolete ordinances

Md.—Baltimore & O. R. Co. v. State, for Use of Carbone, 181 A. 830, 169 Md. 345 (ordinances relating to manner of driving carriages within city limits, and to speed at which car should be driven on railway, passed during days of horse-drawn vehicles, held inadmissible, since obsolete).

Unreasonableness

Ohio—Weiler v. Pennsylvania R. Co., 28 N.E.2d 792, 64 Ohio App. 411 (not error, after hearing evidence upon reasonableness of ordinance, to exclude from evidence an ordinance which provided for a six-mile speed limit for trains).

33. **Wash.**—Raybell v. State, 1972, 496 P.2d 559, 6 Wash.App. 795 (in action against state based on claim that state was negligent in maintaining an inherently dangerous highway with inadequate guardrails at point where decedent's automobile left road, it was not an abuse of discretion to allow in evidence publications which pertained to guardrail safety policies and which were published by the American Association of State Highway Officials, with cautionary instruction that provisions of publications did not have force of law, that evidence of noncompliance did not establish negligence as a matter of law, and that jury could consider publications only in connection with all other evidence).

34. **Ohio**—Weimer v. Rosen, 126 N. E. 307, 100 Ohio St. 361 (to show speed allowed by ordinance).

§ 425.1   TRIAL EVIDENCE   Ch. 425

Operation in violation of license requirements

Most courts hold that evidence of the failure to have a license is inadmissible unless the party seeking to introduce such evidence can establish that the failure to have a license contributed in some manner to the injury.[35] However, the Massachusetts rule is that the failure to have a license is evidence of negligence, and is therefore admissible, although it is not conclusive evidence unless such negligence contributed in some manner to the injury.[36]

It also has been held that the defendant's certificate of public convenience and necessity issued is not admissible to prove

But see

In action by pedestrian, refusal to permit an officer to testify as to what was permissible to be done under a city traffic ordinance with reference to left turn into restaurant was not error. Briscoe v. Jones, Miss.1970, 233 So.2d 125.

35. **Ala.**—Giles v. Gardner, 1971, 249 So.2d 824, 287 Ala. 166 (admission into evidence of failure of defendant to possess a driver's license was prejudicial error requiring reversal); Chattahoochee Val. Ry. Co. v. Williams, 103 So.2d 762, 267 Ala. 464 (revocation inadmissible).

Ariz.—Mutz v. Lucero, 365 P.2d 49, 90 Ariz. 38.

Fla.—Goldner v. Lentin, App., 96 So.2d 553.

Ga.—Wade v. Drinkard, 45 S.E.2d 231, 76 Ga.App. 159; Georgia Power Co. v. Jones, 188 S.E. 566, 54 Ga.App. 578.

Ill.—Petty v. Illinois Cent. R. Co., 132 N.E.2d 1, 8 Ill.App.2d 367, cause remanded 144 N.E.2d 601, 11 Ill. 485; Perry v. Richerson, 122 N.E.2d 75, 3 Ill.App.2d 338.

Mo.—Dillenschneider v. Campbell, App., 350 S.W.2d 260 (testimony that driver of taxicab lost his driver's license after accident because of lack of insurance was immaterial and overruling of objections to such testimony was error, but such error was not prejudicial, particularly in view of instruction that loss of license was no evidence of negligence and should not be considered by jury).

N.J.—Mattero v. Silverman, 176 A.2d 270, 71 N.J.Super. 1.

Tex.—McIntire v. Sellers, Civ.App., 311 S.W.2d 886, writ of error refused n. r. e.

Wis.—Groling v. Goltz, 66 N.W.2d 195, 267 Wis. 390.

Violation of limited license

In action against driver and owner of dump truck which weighed, unladen, 13,900 pounds, for death of workman on road paving job, who was fatally injured when truck backed over him, court did not err in refusing to admit into evidence certified copy of chauffeur's license, which authorized truck driver to operate motor vehicle of not over 6,000 pounds, where there was no causal relation between accident and fact that truck had unladen weight of 13,900 pounds. Armenta v. Churchill, 267 P.2d 303, 42 Cal.2d 448.

36. **Mass.**—Watson v. Forbes, 30 N.E.2d 228, 307 Mass. 383 (also holding that it was error to permit the defendant to explain his failure to renew his license, though not prejudicial error in view of instructions).

Not mere grounds for revocation

Mass.—Simon v. Berkshire Street Ry. Co., 11 N.E.2d 485, 298 Mass. 454.

that the defendant was operating beyond the scope of authority at the time of the accident;[37] and that evidence that the defendant was operating the vehicle without a permit from the Railroad Commission is not admissible.[38]

Proof of wantonness or wilfulness

Evidence tending to prove indifference to the consequences of one's conduct is admissible on the issue of wantonness.[39]

It has also been held that evidence of violation of "hit and run" statutes, along with evidence as to the conduct of a driver before and after the collision, is relevant on the question as to whether the driver was guilty of willful and wanton misconduct.[40]

Statements after the accident may be admissible as tending to show conscious indifference as to the consequences of the collision.[41]

Subsequent conduct as admission [42]

Conduct of the defendant subsequent to the accident may be circumstantial evidence admissible on the issue of fault.[43] Evidence of a driver's flight, or failure to stop, after an accident is admissible as showing an admission or consciousness of responsibility.[44]

37. **Ala.**—Ex parte Bahakel, 21 So. 2d 619, 246 Ala. 527.

38. **Tex.**—Evans v. Jacobs, Civ. App., 228 S.W.2d 545.

39. **Ala.**—Cedar Creek Store Co. v. Steadham, 65 So. 984, 187 Ala. 622 (running fast near children).

Ariz.—Forquer v. Pinal County, 1974, 526 P.2d 1064, 22 Ariz.App. 266 (generally failure of an operator to stop and render aid after accident, in connection with other evidence, may be considered by jury).

40. **S.C.**—Hallman v. Cushman, 13 S.E.2d 498, 196 S.C. 402.

41. **Ark.**—Loose-Wiles Biscuit Co. v. Jolly, 238 S.W. 613, 152 Ark. 442.

42. For discussion of the admissibility of evidence of subsequent precautions taken, see § 424.2 at fn. 56 et seq.

43. **Ala.**—Prestwood v. Ivey, 138 So. 2d 713, 273 Ala. 281 (evidence of deeds executed by defendant in negligence action shortly after accident).

Cal.—Brooks v. E. J. Willig Truck Transp. Co., 255 P.2d 802, 40 Cal. 2d 669 (truck driver was negligent as a matter of law because he failed to stop after accident).

Contra as to lack of solicitude toward injured

Admission of evidence to effect that deceased, who was not seriously injured, was concerned about injuries sustained by his dog and was completely indifferent to suffering of plaintiff, who was lying on pavement at scene grievously injured, was prejudicial error. Wiebe v. Seely, 335 P.2d 379, 215 Or. 331.

44. **Ala.**—Greenwood v. Bailey, 184 So. 285, 28 Ala.App. 362 (woman exclaimed in hearing of defendant and witness, when defendant drove

§ 425.2   TRIAL EVIDENCE   Ch. 425

§ 425.2   Operation of Vehicles—Speed [45]

Library References:
C.J.S. Motor Vehicles § 516.
West's Key No. Digests, Automobiles ⚿243(7).

The rate of speed of a motor vehicle involved in an accident usually bears directly on the question of negligence, and may be considered by the jury with other facts in determining liability if within the issues.[46] In some cases, however, evidence of speed

up to scene shortly thereafter, "there is the car that struck" deceased, whereupon defendant immediately drove away without making reply).

Ga.—Battle v. Kilcrease, 189 S.E. 573, 54 Ga.App. 808.

Idaho.—Shaddy v. Daley, 76 P.2d 279, 58 Idaho 536 (consciousness of responsibility shown).

Contra

Mass.—Reardon v. Marston, 38 N.E. 2d 644, 310 Mass. 461 (that when motorist stopped automobile immediately after it struck bicyclist, motorist got out of automobile, and after looking at the bicyclist ran back to automobile and started motor was relevant on issue of motorist's negligence).

Miss.—Clark v. Mask, 98 So.2d 467, 232 Miss. 65.

45.   Comparable section in prior edition **cited by the court** in McClure v. Latta, Wyo., 348 P.2d 1057, 1060.

46.   **Ala.**—Osborn v. Grizzard, 37 So. 2d 201, 251 Ala. 275 (speed through intersection).

Ill.—Ashby v. Irish, 118 N.E.2d 43, 2 Ill.App.2d 9 (wanton conduct under guest statute).

Ky.—Hogle's Guardian v. Wolfzorn, 58 S.W.2d 577, 248 Ky. 396.

Mich.—Davis v. Hollowell, 40 N.W. 2d 641, 326 Mich. 673, 15 A.L.R.2d 1160 (injury to guest).

Ohio.—Carl v. Shaffer, 50 N.E.2d 182, 71 Ohio App. 339.

Tenn.—Mason v. James, 89 S.W.2d 910, 19 Tenn.App. 479.

Tex.—Polasek v. Gaines Bros., Tex. Civ.App., 185 S.W.2d 609, error refused (fact that automobile sputtered and backfired, thereby decreasing its speed, while crossing highway intersection).

Foundation for "Tactograph" record

Ariz.—Villegas v. Bryson, 1972, 494 P.2d 61, 16 Ariz.App. 456 (test showed speedometer cable 98.7% accurate, and expert said was within normal limits of accuracy).

Ark.—Bell v. Kroger Co., 323 S.W.2d 424, 230 Ark. 384, 73 A.L.R.2d 1019 (insufficient proof of accuracy of Tactograph which had been placed on truck some three years prior to collision).

Not acceleration rate of vehicle

In view of previous testimony of police officer that three-wheeled motorcycle which plaintiff's deceased had been driving would go 55 miles per hour, sustaining of defendants' objections to plaintiffs' questioning of officer as to how long it would take to reach 55 was not error, in absence of proof showing relevancy of the answer. Trautman v. New Rockford-Fessenden Co-op Transport Ass'n, N.D.1970, 181 N.W.2d 754.

Prior speed where lose control and come to rest on highway

Conn.—Weinstein v. Hallas, 100 A. 2d 733, 140 Conn. 387 (when defendant's automobile ran into rear of plaintiff's automobile which had gone out of control on slippery

is inadmissible, such as where such speed was not a proximate cause.[47]

On the question of the proper rate of speed of an automobile, the surrounding circumstances are relevant matters.[48]

road and had come to rest with rear portion projecting into defendant's lane of traffic, court did not err in admitting evidence of high speed at which plaintiff was proceeding prior to his loss of control over his automobile, in view of road and weather conditions and visibility, and in submitting to jury the question whether plaintiff's negligence was too remote to be a contributory cause).

Rule limited in last clear chance case

Where plaintiff rested cause on last clear chance rule, speed at which defendant's truck was being driven at time pedestrian started to cross its pathway properly excluded, being matter of driver's antecedent negligence. Braden's Adm'x v. Liston, 79 S.W.2d 241, 258 Ky. 44.

47. **Ky.**—Lowe v. McMurray, 412 S.W.2d 571 (tendered evidence which would have raised inference of excessive speed on part of driver of tractor-trailer, which collided at intersection with automobile when automobile attempted to make left turn in path of tractor-trailer, was properly excluded as irrelevant in action for wrongful death of driver of automobile, where there was no showing that driver of automobile had no reasonable opportunity to realize speed of oncoming tractor-trailer); Thronton v. Phillips, 90 S.W.2d 347, 262 Ky. 346 (on wrong side of road).

Utah.—Larson v. Evans, 364 P.2d 1088, 12 Utah 2d 245 (plaintiff's speed at time of intersectional collision was irrelevant in absence of showing that such speed violated some duty which he might have had at time of collision with motorist who failed to stop for stop sign).

48. **U.S.**—Brinegar v. Green, C.C.A. Iowa, 117 F.2d 316 (the imminent approach of plaintiff's automobile, the slushy condition of the highway, the view ahead, and slippery highway).

Ala.—Hood & Wheeler Furniture Co. v. Royal, 76 So. 965, 200 Ala. 607 (traffic on street).

Cal.—Perry v. McLaughlin, 297 P. 554, 212 Cal. 1.

Me.—Smith v. Elliott, 119 A. 203, 122 Me. 126 (absence of following traffic and absence of intersecting road on right side of highway).

Mo.—Andrews v. Parker, App., 259 S.W. 807 (evidence concerning difficulty in shutting off power of car).

Or.—Rauw v. Huling, 259 P.2d 99, 199 Or. 48.

Tex.—McClelland v. Mounger, Civ. App., 107 S.W.2d 901, error dismissed.

Wash.—Carlson v. Herbert, 203 P. 30, 118 Wash. 82 (absence of chains on slippery street).

Highway commission directive re speed on road under construction

In death action arising out of collision between automobile and "Tournapull", introduction of highway commission minute order setting the maximum, reasonable and prudent speed limit at 45 miles per hour on section of highway under construction was proper, as against contention that introduction of such order told jury that maximum reasonable or safe speed was 45 miles per hour, where court did not assume as a matter of law that driving over that speed was negligence, such issue being submitted to jury for their decision. Rains v. Heldenfels Bros.,

§ 425.2   TRIAL EVIDENCE   Ch. 425

The speed of an automobile a short distance before and after reaching the place of an accident generally may be shown.[49]

Tex.Civ.App.1969, 443 S.W.2d 280, error refused n. r. e.

Speed limit existing

Ga.—Black v. Aultman, 1969, 172 S. E.2d 336, 120 Ga.App. 826.

49. U.S.—MacCurdy v. U. S., D.C. Fla., 143 F.Supp. 60, affirmed, C.A., 246 F.2d 67, certiorari denied 78 S.Ct. 415, 355 U.S. 933, 2 L.Ed.2d 416 (should be received with care and not considered unless a proper predicate has been laid for its introduction); Standard Oil Co. of N. J. v. Sheppard, 148 F.2d 363, 80 U.S.App.D.C. 71 (high speed immediately after accident).

Ala.—Shirley v. Shirley, 73 So.2d 77, 261 Ala. 100; Townsend v. Adair, 134 So. 637, 223 Ala. 150; Lessman v. West, 101 So. 515, 20 Ala.App. 289.

Cal.—Lundgren v. Converse, 93 P.2d 819, 34 Cal.App.2d 445.

Conn.—Sosnowski v. Lenox, 53 A.2d 388, 133 Conn. 624.

Ill.—Harper v. Malandrone, 48 N.E. 2d 789, 319 Ill.App. 247.

Ky.—Bohannon v. Buschmeyer, 291 S.W.2d 44; Wood v. Dennison's Adm'r, 273 S.W.2d 374; Clay v. Sammons, 239 S.W.2d 927.

Minn.—Spencer v. Johnson, 281 N.W. 879, 203 Minn. 402; Quinn v. Zimmer, 239 N.W. 902, 184 Minn. 589.

Mo.—Douglas v. Twenter, 259 S.W. 2d 353, 364 Mo. 71; La Duke v. Dexter, App., 202 S.W. 254.

Mont.—Jones v. Northwestern Auto Supply Co., 18 P.2d 305, 93 Mont. 224.

Neb.—Schwarting v. Ogram, 242 N. W. 273, 123 Neb. 76, 81 A.L.R. 769.

N.H.—Dimock v. Lussier, 163 A. 500, 86 N.H. 54.

N.M.—Dahl v. Turner, 1969, 458 P. 2d 816, 80 N.M. 564, 39 A.L.R.3d 207, certiorari denied 458 P.2d 860, 80 N.M. 608 (observations of speed of defendant's automobile during continuous movement from time of collision until it collided with third automobile were both relevant and material to issue of speed of defendant's automobile immediately before first collision).

N.Y.—Clay v. Monington, 1943, 40 N.Y.S.2d 108, 266 App.Div. 695; Owen v. Gruntz, 1926, 214 N.Y.S. 543, 216 App.Div. 19.

N.C.—Queen City Coach Co. v. Lee, 11 S.E.2d 341, 218 N.C. 320; Potter v. Dixie Transit Co., 146 S.E. 709, 196 N.C. 824.

Or.—Martin v. Oregon Stages, 277 P. 291, 129 Or. 435.

Pa.—Gerhart v. East Coast Coach Co., 166 A. 564, 310 Pa. 535.

Tenn.—Hamilton v. Moyers, 140 S. W.2d 799, 24 Tenn.App. 86.

Wash.—Husby v. Fiorata Bros., 297 P. 1075, 162 Wash. 135.

W.Va.—Wilson v. Fleming, 109 S.E. 810, 89 W.Va. 553.

Automobile identity questioned

Ill.—Walsh v. Murray, 43 N.E.2d 562, 31 Ill.App. 664 (where there was evidence that defendant's automobile, a green sedan, was traveling 70 or 80 miles an hour, testimony of officers that about a half mile from the accident a green sedan passed them at about 60 miles an hour, and that a few seconds later they arrived at the scene and did not see any green car other than that of defendant, was properly admitted).

S.D.—Burrington v. Heine, 1974, 215 N.W.2d 119, —— S.D. —— (in action in which one of the parties alleged that two others were drag racing, admission of testimony by two witnesses that, a short time

Ch. 425   OPERATION OF VEHICLES   § 425.2

Ordinarily, the speed material for consideration in an automobile accident case is that at the instant of, or immediately before, the accident in question.[50] However, whether time and distance render evidence of speed prior to the occurrence of an accident too remote depends upon the circumstances,[51] the competency of such evidence being determinable by "causal connection or contact with the accident," rather than by specific distance or time.[52]

Evidence of the speed of a vehicle at various distances from the place of the accident has been held admissible.[53] However, in

before the accident, they saw two automobiles traveling abreast at an excessive rate of speed a short distance from the accident was not error, even though one of the witnesses was unable to identify the automobiles by model or color and second witness was able only to identify the color of one of the automobiles).

Tenn.—Crunk v. Grooms, 1969, 450 S.W.2d 15, 60 Tenn.App. 611 (not fatal could not state make or color of vehicle seen).

Utah.—Fretz v. Anderson, 300 P.2d 642, 5 Utah 2d 290, opinion modified and rehearing denied 308 P.2d 948, 6 Utah 2d 169 (in action by motorist against the estate of deceased arising out of a collision with deceased's overturned automobile on the highway at night, admission of testimony of another motorist, who testified that he had observed automobile of same make and model as that owned by deceased traveling south out of another town and that automobile was speeding, but who could not positively identify deceased's automobile with the one that he had seen speeding, was not error).

But see

Mass.—Simon v. Berkshire Street Ry. Co., 11 N.E.2d 485, 298 Mass. 454 (not of nearby area where limit different).

50. Cal.—Larson v. Solbakken, 34 Cal.Rptr. 450, 221 Cal.App.2d 410 (if not too remote).

Iowa.—Thomas v. Charter, 278 N.W. 920, 224 Iowa 1278.

Miss.—Barrett v. Shirley, 95 So.2d 471, 231 Miss. 364.

51. Iowa.—Anderson v. Elliott, 57 N.W.2d 792, 244 Iowa 670.

Mass.—Smith v. Neibauer Bus Co., 1952, 105 N.E.2d 238, 328 Mass. 624; Brown v. Thayer, 99 N.E. 237, 212 Mass. 392.

Miss.—Bennett v. Hardwell, 59 So.2d 82, 214 Miss. 390 (two-fifths of a mile and four or five minutes before).

Neb.—Ambrozi v. Fry, 62 N.W.2d 259, 158 Neb. 18.

N.C.—Corum v. Comer, 123 S.E.2d 473, 256 N.C. 252 (generally, evidence of speed at former time and at different place from scene of accident must, in order to be admissible, be accompanied by evidence from which jury may reasonably infer that speed continued to scene).

Pa.—Finnerty v. Darby, 138 A.2d 117, 391 Pa. 300 (one-half mile).

Two and one-half miles away

Ky.—Clay v. Sammons, 239 S.W.2d 927.

52. Mich.—Bryant v. Brown, 271 N.W. 566, 278 Mich. 686.

53. U.S.—Comins v. Scrivener, C.A. N.M., 214 F.2d 810, 46 A.L.R.2d 1 (testimony of witness that three, five, or ten miles from point of

§ 425.2   TRIAL EVIDENCE   Ch. 425

collision plaintiff was driving ninety miles an hour was properly admitted as tending to show circumstances from which it could be inferred that such speed continued up to point of collision); U. S. v. Uarte, C.A.Cal., 175 F.2d 110 (speed at points from four to eleven miles from place of collision); Dromey v. Inter State Motor Freight Service, C.C.A.Ill., 121 F.2d 361 (until a point about 1½ miles from collision speed of following automobile during race was from 65 to 70 miles per hour, where corroborative evidence showed continuity of excessive speed of following automobile up to point of collision).

Ariz.—Brooks v. Neer, 47 P.2d 452, 46 Ariz. 144 (speed at which defendant's automobile was running 1,400 feet from point of collision properly admitted, where evidence disclosed that automobile was going from 55 to 60 miles per hour when driver lost control, and that it continued at high rate of speed up to point of accident).

Ark.—Wagnon v. Porchia, 361 S.W. 2d 749, 235 Ark. 731 (automobile was traveling 85 miles per hour, and that the collision occurred 175 yards further down the road, or about five seconds after the automobile was last observed); Schwam v. Reece, 1948, 210 S.W. 2d 903, 213 Ark. 431; Jelks v. Rogers, 165 S.W.2d 258, 204 Ark. 877 (three blocks away); Missouri Pac. Transp. Co. v. Mitchell, 137 S.W.2d 242, 199 Ark. 1045 (testimony that approximately four miles back from scene bus passed a witness who was traveling 75 miles per hour, and that the bus continued at a high rate of speed).

Cal.—McGuire v. Navarro, 332 P.2d 361, 165 Cal.App.2d 661 (speed at which witness estimated the defendant to be traveling when defendant overtook and passed witness' automobile at a point one and one half to two miles from point of collision); Pruitt v. Krovitz, 139 P.2d 992, 59 Cal.App.2d 666 (one block away); Traynor v. McGilvray, 200 P. 1056, 54 Cal. App. 31 (operation of an automobile within 500 or 600 feet of the point of collision with another car a few seconds later).

Fla.—Hill v. Sadler, App., 186 So.2d 52 (one quarter of a mile away).

Ga.—Lovejoy v. Tidwell, 95 S.E.2d 784, 212 Ga. 750, conformed to 96 S.E.2d 539, 94 Ga.App. 851 (testimony that while witnesses were traveling at speed of 50 to 55 miles per hour, plaintiff's automobile passed them at a speed of 85 to 95 miles per hour, and that ten or fifteen minutes later witnesses arrived at scene of collision, was admissible).

Ill.—Carr v. Blackstock, 49 N.E.2d 279, 319 Ill.App. 369.

Iowa.—Waldman v. Sanders Motor Co., 243 N.W. 555, 214 Iowa 1139 (speed 540 and 400 feet, respectively, from place of collision).

Kan.—In re Roth's Estate, 382 P.2d 320, 191 Kan. 493 (speed 150 yards from intersection where accident occurred); Siegrist v. Wheeler, 286 P.2d 169, 178 Kan. 286 (manner and speed at which plaintiff was driving on public highway at point when it was about quarter of mile from place where accident occurred); Gabel v. Hanby, 193 P.2d 239, 165 Kan. 116 (speed of bus when 1,500 feet away from scene).

Ky.—Tingle v. Foster, 399 S.W.2d 475; Rowe v. Gibson, 309 S.W.2d 73 (speed about one-fourth mile from the scene of the collision); Ewing-Von Allmen Dairy Co. v. Fowler's Ex'r, 228 S.W.2d 449, 312 Ky. 547 (testimony of witness standing on highway about 500 yards from place of collision, who had continued to watch the automobile from time it passed him until collision occurred, and that there was no slackening or change in speed); Home Laundry Co. v.

Cook, 125 S.W.2d 763, 277 Ky. 8 (1,800 feet away); Paducah Coca-Cola Bottling Co. v. Reeves, 88 S. W.2d 39, 261 Ky. 539 (speed of fifty miles per hour one mile distant from bridge was competent to contradict testimony that truck was so mechanically arranged that it could not exceed speed of thirty-eight miles per hour); Wigginton's Adm'r v. Rickert, 217 S.W. 933, 186 Ky. 650 (speed four squares away from the point of the accident); National Casket Co. v. Powar, 125 S.W. 279, 137 Ky. 156 (testimony of a witness that an automobile passed him about a quarter of a mile from the place of an accident and that the automobile did not slacken as it approached the intersecting road where the accident happened).

Md.—Acme Poultry Corp. v. Melville, 53 A.2d 1, 188 Md. 365 (was not entitled to great weight, but was not too remote); Taxicab Co. v. Hamburger, 125 A. 914, 146 Md. 122 (testimony that taxicab was going at great speed and nearly ran into witness as it passed him two blocks away).

Mich.—Crane v. Woodbury, 1972, 199 N.W.2d 577, 41 Mich.App. 11 (passing in a no-passing zone 3 miles away).

Minn.—Johnson v. Farrell, 298 N.W. 256, 210 Minn. 351 (speed about half a mile from the intersection, where witness watched the automobile almost until the collision); Spencer v. Johnson, 281 N.W. 879, 203 Minn. 402 (speed a second or two before the accident at a point a block from place of accident).

Mo.—Wood v. Ezell, App., 342 S.W. 2d 503 (about one-half mile from scene of head-on collision); Shepard v. Harris, 329 S.W.2d 1 (where driver testified that his speed, whatever it was, remained constant from shortly after he left point of departure until immediately prior to accident, permitting parties who lived at places along road to testify as to speed of automobile when it passed them was not improper); Long v. Mild, 149 S.W.2d 853, 347 Mo. 1002 (several miles from the point of collision and up to within 3½ blocks from the point of collision, traveled at a speed of 50 to 60 miles per hour, where there was evidence that such speed was continuous all the way to the place of the collision).

Neb.—Sandrock v. Taylor, 1969, 174 N.W.2d 186, 185 Neb. 106 (seen from ³⁄₁₀ of a mile away until within 575 feet); Shields v. Buffalo County, 71 N.W.2d 701, 161 Neb. 34 (admission of testimony that defendant had passed witness' automobile about one and one-half miles from scene, while witness was traveling 45 miles an hour at nighttime, was not abuse of discretion).

N.H.—Giroux v. Gagne, 1967, 236 A. 2d 695, 108 N.H. 394 (ten miles away).

N.J.—Miller v. Trans Oil Co., 109 A.2d 427, 33 N.J.Super. 53, affirmed 113 A.2d 777, 18 N.J. 407 (speed in excess of 45 miles per hour three-quarters of a mile away was relevant as having tendency to prove speed at place of accident and consequently admissible, although remote).

N.C.—Greene v. Meredith, 1965, 141 S.E.2d 287, 264 N.C. 178 (50–60 mph in fog, 3 miles away); Honeycutt v. Strube, 134 S.E.2d 110, 261 N.C. 59 (a little under a quarter of mile from bridge near which collision occurred); Adkins v. Dills, 132 S.E.2d 324, 260 N.C. 206 (in view of other evidence bearing upon speed of overtaking automobile between time it passed from view of witnesses in overtaken vehicle until time of its collision; Wilson v. Camp, 107 S.E.2d 743, 249 N.C. 754 (one-quarter of a mile from scene was admissible).

Ohio—Solomon v. Mote, App., 49 N.E.2d 703 (one quarter mile

§ 425.2   TRIAL EVIDENCE   Ch. 425

away); Van Agthoven v. Zumstein Taxicab Co., 18 Ohio App. 395 (speed when a mile distant from scene).

Or.—Shoopman v. Long, 1969, 449 P.2d 439, 252 Or. 341 (12 miles away, where probative continued to scene); Hanson v. Schrick, 85 P.2d 355, 160 Or. 397 (one-half mile away).

Pa.—Rooney v. Maczko, 172 A. 151, 315 Pa. 113 (150 or 200 feet away).

Tenn.—Hamilton v. Moyers, 140 S. W.2d 799, 24 Tenn.App. 86 (speed of truck at point 200 or 300 feet).

Tex.—Proctor v. R. T. Herrin Petroleum Transport Co., Civ.App., 322 S.W.2d 42, affirmed 338 S.W.2d 422, 161 Tex. 222 (at a point approximately one mile from the scene); Davis v. Younger Bros., Inc., Civ.App., 260 S.W.2d 637 (testimony of two witnesses that truck's speed at point one to one and one half miles from scene was relevant to show speed of truck at time of accident, in view of truck driver's statement that his speed at time of accident and at point where seen by witnesses had remained unchanged).

Vt.—Tyrrell v. Goslant, 106 A. 585, 93 Vt. 63 (one mile away).

Wash.—Olson v. Rose, 151 P.2d 454, 21 Wash.2d 464 (was admissible for limited purpose of affecting credibility and accuracy of testimony touching speed at time of collision).

W.Va.—Poe v. Pittman, 1965, 144 S. E.2d 671, 150 W.Va. 179, citing C.J.S. Motor Vehicles § 516r, 150 W.Va. 179 (3 miles away).

Wis.—Mackowski v. Milwaukee Auto. Mut. Ins. Co., 82 N.W.2d 906, 275 Wis. 545 (traveling at 95 miles per hour at point three miles from place of collision, that automobile gradually drew away from him, and that the last he saw of automobile was when it rounded curve three-quarters of mile from place of collision, where driver's testimony showed unreasonable and unlawful speed on open highway for preceding ten miles).

Wyo.—Ries v. Cheyenne Cab & Transfer Co., 79 P.2d 468, 53 Wyo. 104 (two blocks away).

Limitation on rule

Evidence of speed at other points is not admissible unless they are of such close proximity that reasonable inference could be drawn that it was continued to point of accident, or if more remote, there is evidence of circumstance from which a reasonable inference could be drawn that speed was continued at approximately the same rate over intervening distance. Prince v. Petersen, 12 N.W.2d 704, 144 Neb. 134.

Position to observe

Wis.—Fox v. Kaminsky, 2 N.W.2d 199, 239 Wis. 559 (testimony of disinterested witness who noted speed of plaintiff's automobile at some 2,000 feet south of the collision, and some 600 to 900 feet east when witness was approaching the road on which accident occurred at right angles and was facing the road from a somewhat elevated point of view, was improperly excluded).

Testimony of two witnesses at different distances

In testimony that truck was running around 60 miles an hour three-quarters of a mile from accident, supported by testimony of another witness that truck was going at that speed 400 yards from place of collision, was admissible. Interstate Veneer Co. v. Edwards, 60 S. E.2d 4, 191 Va. 107, 23 A.L.R.2d 532.

Thirty-three miles

In action under Wyoming guest statute, testimony of witness that automobile, which was driven by defendant, and in which plaintiff was riding, passed automobile of witness while automobile of witness was

476

other cases such evidence, or even evidence of speed shortly before the occurrence of the accident in question, has been rejected under the rule against remoteness, as not indicating the speed of the vehicle in question at the point of the accident and as having no causal relation to the occurrence.[54] The admissibility

going 90 miles an hour at a point some thirty-three miles from the accident, was properly admitted under the circumstances, though it was admitted that defendant stopped for gasoline after first passing the automobile of the witness. Fleming v. Lawson, C.A.Wyo., 240 F.2d 119.

To show racing

Mass.—Brown v. Thayer, 99 N.E. 237, 212 Mass. 392 (speed they were going at different points along the way was admissible to show that they were racing).

While pursued by police

N.Y.—Christie v. Mitchell, 197 N.Y.S. 2d 206, 10 A.D.2d 52 (in action for injuries sustained by State Police officer when police automobile, which had pursued defendant's automobile for about seven miles at high rates of speed, struck rear of defendant's automobile when the latter stopped at blinking red light at intersection, limiting proof to what had transpired within one-half mile of scene on theory that events which occurred before that limited distance were too remote was prejudicial error).

Pa.—Fugagli v. Camasi, 1967, 229 A.2d 735, 426 Pa. 1 (because of topography pursuing police officer momentarily lost sight of host's automobile for about three-tenths of a mile immediately prior to accident, but within seconds officer came upon wreck in roadway, evidence of speed at which host's automobile was operated three-tenths of a mile from accident site was admissible).

54. U.S.—Jamison v. Kline, D.C. Pa.1970, 319 F.Supp. 951, order affirmed C.A., 454 F.2d 1256 (three miles away); Euson v. Starrett, C.A.Ill., 277 F.2d 73 (that, at points one and one-half and three quarters of mile from collision, driver of automobile on preferential road was driving at a certain speed was inadmissible in absence of additional evidence showing continuity of speed as automobile approached point of collision); Fleming v. Lawson, C. A.Wyo., 240 F.2d 119; David Bilgore & Co. v. Ryder, C.A.Fla., 211 F.2d 855 (where it appeared that the terrain was rolling and road was obscured from time to time by hills, exclusion of offered evidence of speed of plaintiff's automobile about ¾ miles before reaching point of collision, admittedly not observed by witness, was not an abuse of discretion); Winn v. Consolidated Coach Corporation, C.C.A.Tenn., 65 F.2d 256, certiorari denied 54 S.Ct. 453, 291 U.S. 668, 78 L.Ed. 1059, rehearing denied 54 S.Ct. 557, 291 U.S. 651, 78 L.Ed. 1059.

Ala.—Coker v. Ryder Truck Lines, 1971, 249 So.2d 810, 287 Ala. 150 (could have been 30 miles away); Utility Trailer Works v. Phillips, 29 So.2d 289, 249 Ala. 61 (exclusion of evidence showing speed four-tenths of a mile away and prior to the collision was not an abuse of discretion); Hodges v. Wells, 147 So. 672, 226 Ala. 558; Whittaker v. Walker, 135 So. 185, 223 Ala. 167.

Ariz.—Morris v. Aero Mayflower Transit Co., 242 P.2d 279, 73 Ariz. 390 (inadmissible as to speed four or five blocks from impact); Young v. Campbell, 177 P. 19, 20 Ariz. 71, appeal dismissed on rehearing 181 P. 171, 20 Ariz. 355.

§ 425.2 TRIAL EVIDENCE Ch. 425

Ark.—Schwam v. Reece, 210 S.W.2d 903, 213 Ark. 431 (that bus was driven about 50 miles per hour on another trip about 30 minutes prior to collision and two or three miles from scene).

Cal.—Gritsch v. Pickwick Stages System, 81 P.2d 257, 27 Cal.App. 2d 494; Ackel v. American Creamery Co., 55 P.2d 1195, 12 Cal.App. 2d 672 (excluding testimony as to speed of truck and its position on highway when it passed witness about block and a half distant from intersection where collision occurred held not error); Grand v. Kasviner, 153 P. 243, 28 Cal.App. 530.

Conn.—Buonanno v. Cameron, 41 A. 2d 107, 131 Conn. 513 (speed three-quarters of a mile away too remote).

Idaho—Sanders v. Hamilton, 419 P. 2d 667, 91 Idaho 225 (probable speed of defendant's automobile by proof of average speed that defendant traveled between points of intersectional collision and municipality which were 290 miles apart).

Ill.—Guffey v. Gale, 74 N.E.2d 730, 332 Ill.App. 207 (three-fourths of a mile away); Rzeszewski v. Barth, 58 N.E.2d 269, 324 Ill.App. 345 (did not abuse discretion in excluding evidence of defendant's speed when traveling six blocks from scene); Denton v. Midwest Dairy Products Corporation, 1 N.E. 2d 807, 284 Ill.App. 279 (speed of truck six miles from accident held error, where truck thereafter and prior to collision stopped for appreciable period of time and again resumed its course).

Iowa—Cunningham v. Court, 82 N. W.2d 292, 248 Iowa 654 (admissibility of testimony that defendant passed witness eight miles from intersection where accident occurred, at 80 miles per hour, was largely within trial court's discretion and refusal to admit testimony was not an abuse of discretion); Neyens v. Gehl, 15 N.W.2d 888, 235 Iowa 115 (eight-tenths of a mile from scene).

Ky.—Gauze v. Horn, 253 S.W.2d 606 (one-quarter mile); Eads v. Stockdale, 220 S.W.2d 971, 310 Ky. 446 (speed of truck over 300 yards from scene); Stevens v. Potter, 273 S.W. 470, 209 Ky. 705 (high speed a quarter of a mile from scene not relevant evidence of that rate at point of accident).

Mass.—Hagerty v. Tyler, 4 N.E.2d 463, 295 Mass. 581 ("shortly before").

Minn.—Janssen v. Neal, 1974, 223 N.W.2d 804 (had intervening 90-degree turn).

Miss.—Gough v. Harrington, 141 So. 280, 163 Miss. 393 (speed several hundred yards away).

Mo.—Reifsteck v. Miller, 369 S.W. 2d 229 (testimony that about 1½ miles from scene an automobile passed witness going 70 to 75 miles per hour); Harter v. King, App., 259 S.W.2d 94; Wood v. Claussen, App., 207 S.W.2d 802 (speed 1.2 miles from accident); Stelmach v. Saul, App., 51 S.W.2d 886 (grant of new trial for admitting testimony regarding speed of truck crossing intersection three blocks away 15 minutes before the collision was not erroneous); Raybourn v. Phillips, 140 S.W. 977, 160 App. 534.

Neb.—Langford v. Ritz Taxicab Co., 109 N.W.2d 120, 172 Neb. 153 (speed as turned corner on city street one block distant from scene); Prince v. Petersen, 12 N. W.2d 704, 144 Neb. 134 (two and five miles from place of accident).

N.J.—Miller v. Trans Oil Co., 113 A. 2d 777, 18 N.J. 407 (testimony by another motorist that about a minute before the accident and three-quarters of a mile away he was passed by a black sedan, similar to one driven by plaintiff, going

478

quite a bit faster than 45 miles an hour).

N.Y.—Bashaw v. Bouvia, 218 N.Y.S. 2d 194, 14 A.D.2d 640 (evidence of defendant's speed and absence of headlight, from four to eight miles from scene, where charged only with failure to exercise due care on snowy highway, although evidence ostensibly was offered to impeach defendant by contradicting his testimony on cross-examination); Shaw v. Skopp, 190 N.Y.S. 859, 198 App.Div. 618.

N.C.—Corum v. Comer, 123 S.E.2d 473, 256 N.C. 252 (evidence that defendant drivers, at least 20 minutes prior to read-end collision in which passenger was killed, were engaged in racing contest was inadmissible as too remote); Barnes v. Teer, 10 S.E.2d 614, 218 N.C. 122, rehearing granted and judgment vacated on other grounds 15 S.E.2d 379, 219 N.C. 823 (three or four miles away).

N.D.—Thompson v. Nettum, N.D. 1968, 163 N.W.2d 91; Gleson v. Thompson, 1967, 154 N.W.2d 780 (speed of decedent's automobile from a point about one-eighth mile from scene to within two hundred to three hundred feet from scene); Miller v. Larson, 95 N.W.2d 569 (excluding testimony as to speed of one of the vehicles at a point between one and two miles from the scene was discretionary where the witness did not observe the vehicle in question as it traveled the last mile immediately preceding the accident and there was no other evidence of speed within that distance); Armann v. Caswell, 152 N.W. 813, 30 N.D. 406.

Ohio—Hartford Fire Ins. Co. v. Elliott, 160 N.E.2d 130 (200 miles); Booksbaum v. Cousins, 1 N.E.2d 150, 51 Ohio App. 385, error dismissed 199 N.E. 217, 130 Ohio St. 336 (evidence of speed and of conversations occurring three or four miles from scene held inadmissible to establish wanton misconduct, where host then had no knowledge of danger).

Or.—May v. Mack, 356 P.2d 1060, 225 Or. 278 (testimony as to speed and manner of driving about 11 miles from scene, some 20 or 30 minutes before accident); Phillips v. Creighton, 316 P.2d 302, 211 Or. 645; Ramp v. Osborne, 239 P. 112, 115 Or. 672 (speed four or five miles from place of collision).

Pa.—Kaercher v. Miller, 156 A.2d 368, 191 Pa.Super. 416 (observed two automobiles proceeding through an intersection approximately a block and a half away from the point where decedent was struck, at a speed estimated at 50 miles per hour); Kelly v. Veneziale, 35 A.2d 67, 348 Pa. 325 (where witness saw defendant's automobile only when it passed him at another street 597 feet away from point of accident); McCaulif v. Griffith, 168 A. 536, 110 Pa.Super. 522 (speed and operation of defendant's truck 1,400 feet from scene); Mader v. Atkins, 49 Dauph. 314 (1,000 to 1,200 feet away).

S.C.—Wright v. South Carolina Power Co., 31 S.E.2d 904, 205 S.C. 327 (block away from scene).

Wash.—Hutteball v. Montgomery, 60 P.2d 679, 187 Wash. 516 (rejection of testimony as to estimated speed at different points several miles from scene held not error, especially where speed was not cause of collision).

W.Va.—Smith v. Edward M. Rude Carrier Corp., 151 S.E.2d 738, 151 W.Va. 322 (evidence as to driver's time of travel between two points on route earlier in day).

Wis.—Neumann v. Evans, 76 N.W. 2d 322, 272 Wis. 579 (did not abuse discretion in rejecting offer to prove that automobile passed witness' home on town road about a quarter of a mile from intersection at speed of about 50 miles per

§ 425.2   TRIAL EVIDENCE   Ch. 425

of evidence as to the speed of a vehicle prior to the time of an accident in which it was involved rests largely within the discretion of the trial court.[55]

However, one's "understanding" as to the speed limit is not admissible on issue of proper speed.[56]

Where there is evidence of the speed at which a motor vehicle involved in an accident was traveling at the time thereof, speed at other times is immaterial,[57] as is evidence of the average speed of automobiles along the road at the scene of an accident.[58]

Circumstantial evidence of speed

The speed of an automobile may, like any other fact, be established by circumstantial evidence, and the court should admit any character of circumstances which would indicate the speed at which the automobile was traveling at the time of the accident.[59]

hour and that she heard crash a few seconds thereafter).

55. **Cal.**—Lundgren v. Converse, 93 P.2d 819, 34 Cal.App.2d 445.

Iowa—Tobin v. Van Orsdol, 45 N.W.2d 239, 241 Iowa 1331.

Md.—Reid v. Humphreys, 122 A.2d 756, 210 Md. 178.

Neb.—Sandrock v. Taylor, 1969, 174 N.W.2d 186, 185 Neb. 106; Buhrman v. Smollen, 83 N.W.2d 386, 164 Neb. 655.

N.M.—Garrett v. Howden, 387 P.2d 874, 73 N.M. 307.

Or.—Yates v. Stading, 347 P.2d 839, 219 Or. 464.

Va.—Slate v. Saul, 40 S.E.2d 171, 185 Va. 700 (admission not abuse of discretion, though there was some conflict in testimony as to identity of bus referred to).

Wis.—Neumann v. Evans, 76 N.W.2d 322, 272 Wis. 579.

56. **Ga.**—Tittle v. McCombs, 1973, 199 S.E.2d 363, 129 Ga.App. 148 (in light of posted speed limit for the road).

57. **Ark.**—Missouri Pac. Transp. Co. v. Brown, 99 S.W.2d 245, 193 Ark. 304.

Mass.—Simon v. Berkshire Street Ry. Co., 11 N.E.2d 485, 298 Mass. 454.

58. **Cal.**—Cucinella v. Weston Biscuit Co., App., 257 P.2d 454, subsequent opinion 265 P.2d 513, 42 Cal.2d 71.

N.Y.—Sanford v. Moreau, 292 N.Y.S. 595, 249 App.Div. 915.

Or.—Elliott v. Callan, 1970, 466 P.2d 600, 255 Or. 256 (where designated speed for area in which automobile struck child in school crossing was 20 miles per hour, admission of testimony by police officers that it was customary practice for motorists to travel in such area at speeds approaching 40 miles per hour constituted reversible error).

59. **U.S.**—Giffin v. Ensign, C.A.Pa., 234 F.2d 307 (where preceding vehicle actually limits speed of vehicle following close behind, testimony as to speed of preceding vehicle is admissible to show speed of following vehicle); Atlantic Coast Line R. Co. v. Pidd, C.A. Fla., 197 F.2d 153, certiorari denied 73 S.Ct. 166, 344 U.S. 874, 97 L.Ed. 677 (departure time of train compared to time of collision);

Ch. 425   OPERATION OF VEHICLES   § **425.2**

The physical effect of the impact of an automobile or other vehicle with another vehicle, a person, or an animal is usually a material circumstance to be considered on the question of whether it was going at a negligent rate of speed.[60] However, evidence

New York Transp. Co. v. Garside, N.Y., 157 F. 521, 85 C.C.A. 285 (noise emitted); Melville v. State of Md. to Use of Morris, C.C.A. Md., 155 F.2d 440 (witness heard tires of truck squeal as it rounded a curve).

Ga.—Hall v. Slaton, 144 S.E. 827, 38 Ga.App. 619, reversed on other grounds Slaton v. Hall, 148 S.E. 741, 168 Ga. 710, 73 A.L.R. 891, conformed to Hall v. Slaton, 149 S.E. 306, 40 Ga.App. 288 (machine ran off a bridge, broke through and tore down upright timbers placed on the side of the bridge at certain distances from each other).

Ky.—Park v. Schell, 295 S.W. 161, 220 Ky. 317 (speed of street car alongside automobile).

Mo.—Tucker v. Carter, App.., 211 S.W. 138 (speed of lead car in a procession).

Neb.—Andersen v. Omaha & C. B. St. R. Co., 218 N.W. 135, 116 Neb. 487 (distance traveled by street car after collision and before it could be stopped).

Ohio—Peltier v. Smith, 66 N.E.2d 117, 78 Ohio App. 171; Acker v. Columbus & Southern Ohio Elec. Co., App., 60 N.E.2d 932 (bus driver's schedule).

Pa.—Lorah v. Rinehart, 89 A. 967, 243 Pa. 231 (inability to stop quickly).

Tex.—St. Louis, B. & M. Ry. Co. v. Watkins, Civ.App., 245 S.W. 794 (exclamations of persons witnessing accident).

Vt.—Abel v. Salebra, 61 A.2d 605, 115 Vt. 336 (failure of guest to protest).

Wash.—Heg v. Mullen, 197 P. 51, 115 Wash. 252 (comment of passenger).

Fuel restrictor

Testimony of an automobile mechanic who applied a fuel restrictor to the automobile in question, that he had tested the automobile two days before the accident, at which time maximum speed of the automobile was approximately 40 miles per hour, and that upon removing the fuel restrictor sometime after the accident he discovered by markings which he had placed thereon that it had not been tampered with in any manner, had to be considered in assessing the speed that the automobile was capable of being driven at time of the accident. Tyson v. Jackson, La.App., 118 So.2d 503.

60. **Cited by the court** in Rakestraw v. Norris, Mo.App.1972, 478 S.W. 2d 409, 416; and same statement in prior edition **cited by the court** in Union Bus Lines v. Moulder, Tex.Civ.App., 180 S.W.2d 509, 511. See also § 425.1 at fn. 3, as proof of negligence generally.

Ala.—Alabama Great Southern R. Co. v. Molette, 93 So. 644, 207 Ala. 624 (as to speed of train).

Ariz.—Reichardt v. Albert, 361 P.2d 934, 89 Ariz. 322.

Cal.—Chadek v. Spira, 303 P.2d 879, 146 Cal.App.2d 360; Linde v. Emmick, 61 P.2d 338, 16 Cal.App.2d 676 (extent of injury); Kastel v. Stieber, 8 P.2d 474, 215 Cal. 37.

Conn.—Bruce v. Bitgood, 156 A. 859, 113 Conn. 783.

Ill.—Rapers v. Holmes, 10 N.E.2d 707, 292 Ill.App. 116; Johnson v. Gustafson, 233 Ill.App. 216 (condition of the body of the horse).

Ky.—Gartrell v. Harris' Co-adm'xs, 187 S.W.2d 1019, 300 Ky. 82 (gruesome details admissible in view of defendant's assertion that his car

481

§ 425.2 TRIAL EVIDENCE Ch. 425

of the extent of the injuries to occupants or their deaths has been held not admissible.[61]

had almost stopped when collision occurred and fact that verdict was not unreasonable); Parris' Adm'x v. Molter, 65 S.W.2d 52, 251 Ky. 432 (milk cans on truck thrown forward by impact).

La.—Wilkinson v. National Sur. Corp., App., 154 So.2d 485.

Minn.—Knuth v. Murphy, 54 N.W.2d 771, 237 Minn. 225 (extent of injuries to victim's body).

Miss.—Pickwick Greyhound Lines v. Silver, 125 So. 340, 155 Miss. 765 (that bus was practically demolished and that a passenger was badly mangled admissible to show speed of bus when it skidded and turned over).

Mo.—Feltz v. Terminal Railroad Ass'n of St. Louis, 81 S.W.2d 616, 336 Mo. 790 (extent of injury).

Neb.—Shields v. Buffalo County, 71 N.W.2d 701, 161 Neb. 34; Koutsky v. Grabowski, 1948, 34 N.W.2d 893, 150 Neb. 508 (damage to vehicle and manner pushed across highway).

N.Y.—Bennetti v. New York City Transit Authority, 292 N.Y.S.2d 122, 239 N.E.2d 215, 22 N.Y.2d 742 (exclusion of evidence of injuries to passengers was reversible error in that such evidence had direct bearing on force of impact and relative speed of bus and automobile, and evidence should have been allowed, accompanied by appropriate limiting instruction).

N.C.—Adcox v. Austin, 1952, 70 S.E. 2d 837, 235 N.C. 591.

Ohio—Elgin v. Heaton, App.1949, 84 N.E.2d 299 (damage to house porch).

Or.—Wood v. Meyer, 1972, 492 P.2d 468, 261 Or. 113 (extent of damage); Francis v. Burns, 1969, 458 P.2d 934, 255 Or. 156 (damage to vehicles); Cameron v. Goree, 189 P.2d 596, 182 Or. 581; Schairer v. Johnson, 272 P. 1027, 128 Or. 409 (collision with telephone pole).

S.D.—Kriens v. McMillan, 173 N.W. 731, 42 S.D. 285 (rolled completely over, and injured party thrown considerable distance).

Tex.—City of Temple v. Wilson, Civ. App., 365 S.W.2d 393, error ref. n. r. e.; Northern Texas Traction Co. v. Smith, Civ.App., 223 S.W. 1013 (distance car dragged by street car).

Vt.—Paul v. Drown, 189 A. 144, 108 Vt. 458, 109 A.L.R. 1085; Duprat v. Chesmore, 110 A. 305, 94 Vt. 218 (that the collision threw the man riding with him toward the windshield, but did not throw him out, was admissible).

Wash.—Shields v. Paarmann, 249 P. 2d 377, 41 Wash.2d 423; Paddock v. Tone, 172 P.2d 481, 25 Wash.2d 940; Copeland v. North Coast Transp. Co., 13 P.2d 65, 169 Wash. 84 (as result of impact, automobile colliding with bus was knocked backwards, causing it to turn around several times, plaintiff was thrown to pavement and shortly thereafter automobile broke into flames and was burned).

Not in form of repair bill

Mo.—Boland v. Jando, 1967, 414 S.W. 2d 560 (exclusion of automobile repair bill offered for purpose of showing violence of the collision was not error).

61. See also § 425.1 at fn. 4, as proof of negligence generally.

S.D.—Kriens v. McMillan, 173 N.W. 731, 42 S.D. 285 (unduly creating prejudice).

Where no dispute as to speed

Miss.—Robinson v. Sims, 86 So.2d 318, 227 Miss. 375 (detailed testimony of how many bones were

Since the test of control of a motor vehicle is the ability to stop it quickly and easily, scars or marks on the payment, caused by skidding, are admissible on the question of speed, when connected with the defendant's automobile,[62] and other evidence showing the distance a vehicle traveled after the accident or after the application of brakes.[63] The distance within which a vehicle was actually stopped after an accident is some evidence of the distance within which it could have been stopped.[64]

broken in deceased's body and how broken neck made a scraping noise in turning head of dead body was not admissible in evidence as a showing by force of the impact the speed of automobile which struck pedestrian, where there was no dispute in evidence as to speed).

62. U.S.—Swink v. Colcord, C.A. Okl., 239 F.2d 518.

Cal.—Stafford v. Alexander, 6 Cal. Rptr. 219, 182 Cal.App.2d 301 (not such conclusive or unanswerable evidence that it necessarily overcomes contrary oral testimony); Butticci v. Schindel Furniture Co., 313 P.2d 62, 152 Cal.App.2d 165; Vedder v. Bireley, 267 P. 724, 92 Cal.App. 52; Fong Lin v. Probert, 195 P. 437, 50 Cal.App. 339.

Kan.—Briley v. Nussbaum, 252 P. 223, 122 Kan. 438, modified on other grounds 254 P. 351, 123 Kan. 58.

Ky.—Ryan v. Payne, 1969, 446 S.W. 2d 273.

Neb.—Shields v. Buffalo County, 71 N.W.2d 701, 161 Neb. 34.

N.C.—State v. Ormond, 191 S.E. 22, 211 N.C. 437.

N.D.—Olson v. Wetzstein, 225 N.W. 459, 58 N.D. 263.

Or.—Wood v. Meyer, 1972, 492 P.2d 468, 261 Or. 113.

Wash.—Stubbs v. Allen, 10 P.2d 983, 168 Wash. 156.

Wis.—Neider v. Spoehr, 1969, 165 N.W.2d 171, 41 Wis.2d 610.

63. Cal.—Bennett v. Central California Traction Co., 1 P.2d 47, 115 Cal.App. 1 (street car); Vedder v. Bireley, 267 P. 724, 92 Cal.App. 52 (distance traveled after application of brakes).

La.—Bradford v. Wertz, La.App., 52 So.2d 47, followed in 52 So.2d 54 (that, after brakes had been applied more than 50 feet north of intersection and force of collision had been sufficient to cause truck to jack-knife, truck still had sufficient momentum to carry it some sixty or seventy feet beyond collision point).

Minn.—Kimpell v. Duluth St. R. Co., 211 N.W. 955, 170 Minn. 35 (street car).

Neb.—Koutsky v. Grabowski, 34 N.W.2d 893, 150 Neb. 508 (skid marks, distance traveled after impact, and force of impact are pertinent evidence in arriving at estimate of the rate of speed).

Pa.—Lorah v. Rinhart, 89 A. 967, 243 Pa. 231 (distance traveled after accident).

Tex.—Northern Texas Traction Co. v. Smith, Civ.App., 223 S.W. 1013 (distance street car dragged auto).

Wis.—Ortmann v. A. Leath & Co., 205 N.W. 397, 187 Wis. 616 (that a truck, striking the plaintiff's car, traveled a distance of 12 feet until stopped, notwithstanding the application by the truck driver of his emergency brake, might be taken into consideration in determining both the speed of the truck and the control which its driver exercised).

64. Mo.—Cox v. Reynolds, App., 18 S.W.2d 575.

§ 425.2　　　　TRIAL EVIDENCE　　　　Ch. 425

Evidence as to the indication of a speedometer after an accident has been held admissible,[65] but such evidence has also been held inadmissible.[66]

Evidence of the respective distances traveled by two vehicles within the same time prior to a collision between them is admissible on the issue of relative speed.[67]

However, a statement by a motorist, shortly before a collision, of an expectation to be at a certain distant place within a certain time has been held not relevant on the question of that motorist's speed at the place of the accident.[68]

Evidence bearing upon whether there was a reason for hurrying is admissible.[69]

Stopping distance evidence

The chart accompanying this section affords much useful information on the subject of the distances required to stop an automobile while traveling at various rates of speed.[70] Addi-

---

N.Y.—Rogers v. Burke, 241 N.Y.S. 414, 229 App.Div. 361 (street car).

65. Or.—Albrecht v. Safeway Stores, 80 P.2d 62, 159 Or. 331 (in spite of expert witness' testimony that position of speedometer did not indicate previous speed).

66. Ill.—Jones v. Traver, 275 Ill. App. 181 (in the absence of other proof).

Wis.—Geason v. Schaefer, 281 N.W. 681, 229 Wis. 8 (on motorcycle).

67. Vt.—Page v. McGovern, 3 A.2d 543, 110 Vt. 166.

68. Ky.—Stevens v. Potter, 273 S.W. 470, 209 Ky. 705.

Or.—Babcock v. Gray, 107 P.2d 846, 165 Or. 398 (testimony as to time at which defendant's testator said, in afternoon before accident, that he expected to arrive at place toward which he was driving, when accident occurred three hours or more after such time).

69. Ill.—Ciampa v. Salvaggione, 1974, 312 N.E.2d 677, 20 Ill.App. 3d 47 (where plaintiff attempted to show that defendant had been hurrying at time of accident because he was late in reporting to his job as air traffic controller, testimony of defendant that back-up procedures existed whereby others would perform his duties if he were late was not objectionable as being speculative or improper attempt to testify as to custom or usage without proper foundation and was relevant as rebuttal to plaintiff's contentions as to speed).

70. Statements footnoted here by numbers 70 through 74, contained in section 6237 of last prior edition, were **cited by the court** in Miller v. Abshire, La.App., 68 So.2d 143, 147; Breland v. Forbes, La.App., 81 So. 2d 441, 442; Leonard v. Holmes & Barnes, Limited, La.App., 84 So.2d 109, 115, affirmed 94 So.2d 241, 232 La. 229; Wilson v. Williams, La.App., 82 So.2d 71, 75; Lemons v. Holland, 286 P.2d 656, 660, 205 Or. 163; Smith v. Hardy, S.C., 88 S.E.2d 865, 870, 228 S.C. 112; Crosby v. Brown Oil Tools, Inc., La.App., 92 So.2d 115, 120; Ingouf v. U. S. Fidelity & Guaranty Co., La.App., 92 So.2d 794, 796; Yates v. Booty, La.App., 94 So.2d 44, 46;

Ch. 425   OPERATION OF VEHICLES   § 425.2

Hicks v. Gillespie, 78 N.W.2d 145, 148, 346 Mich. 593; Adkins v. Boss, 290 S.W.2d 139, 143; Cooksey v. Ace Cab Co., 289 S.W.2d 44; Biggers v. Continental Bus System, 298 S.W.2d 79, 88, 157 Tex. 351, judgment on rehearing set aside 303 S.W.2d 359, 157 Tex. 351; Murphy v. Whitehurst, 300 S.W.2d 758, 761, ref. n. r. e.; Frazier v. Muse, La.App., 98 So.2d 693, 695; Guillory v. Allstate Ins. Co., La. App., 96 So.2d 866, 869; Guillory v. Frank, La.App., 95 So.2d 197, 200; Hebert v. Spano, App., 101 So.2d 713, 715; Knight v. Borgan, 324 P.2d 797, 804, 52 Wash.2d 219; McCandless v. Southern Bell Telephone & Tel. Co., App., 101 So.2d 704, 709, affirmed 120 So.2d 501, 239 La. 983; Danner v. Weinreich, Mo., 323 S.W.2d 746, 752; Warner v. Millers Mutual Fire Ins. Co. of Texas, La.App., 98 So.2d 693, 695; Guillory v. Firemen's Ins. Co. of Newark, N.J., La.App., 127 So.2d 328, 334, judgment annulled 132 So.2d 892, 241 La. 1047; Sapir v. Sewerage & Water Bd. of City of New Orleans, App., 127 So.2d 283, 285; Sinclair v. Cook, La.App., 128 So.2d 247, 249; Appelhans v. Goldman, Mo., 349 S.W.2d 204, 207; Bergeron v. Hetherwick, La.App., 140 So.2d 440, 443; Dillenschneider v. Campbell, Mo., 350 S.W.2d 260, 267; Dixie Drive It Yourself System, New Orleans Co. v. American Beverage Co., 137 So.2d 298, 303, 242 La. 471; Fontenot v. Travelers Indemnity Co., La.App., 134 So. 330, 333; Great American Indem. Co. v. Wilson, La.App., 140 So.2d 477, 480; Jones v. Fritz, Mo. App., 353 S.W.2d 393, 397; Stone v. Engler, Mo., 349 S.W.2d 38, 41; Biggs v. Verbois, La.App., 151 So. 2d 172, 185, writ denied 152 So.2d 561, 244 La. 465; Bourgeois v. Francois, La.App., 152 So.2d 383, 387; Reeves v. State Farm Mutual Automobile Ins. Co., La.App., 149 So.2d 230, 232, writ refused 150 So.2d 767, 244 La. 142; Shipley v. Schittone, La.App., 148 So.2d 918, 921; State v. Arena, 379 P.2d 594, 609, 46 Hawaii 315; Dent v. Faivey, Tex.Civ.App., 371 S.W.2d 63, 67; Shoemaker v. American Fire & Cas. Co., La.App., 157 So.2d 900, 902.

This statement in prior edition **cited by the court** in Wall v. Great Am. Indem. Co., La.App., 46 So.2d 655, 661, as authority for the statement that the actual stopping distance, after discovery of peril, of a car with good brakes at a speed of 25 miles an hour is much less than 75 feet. "It is therefore obvious," the court concluded, "that defendant, * * * had he observed plaintiff and taken proper precautions, would have had ample time to avoid the accident;" in Dupre v. Union Producing Co., La.App., 49 So.2d 655, 657, in which the court, on the basis of the chart accompanying this section, concluded that the defendant's automobile was traveling more than 70 miles an hour. In that case Lottinger, J., writing for the Louisiana Court of Appeal, said: "In Blashfield's Cyclopedia of Automobile Law & Practice at Section No. 6237, we find a chart which indicates the distance within which vehicles can be stopped. It indicates that a vehicle travelling 70 miles per hour, that the vehicle is moving at a speed of 103 feet per second and that it takes at least ¾ of a second, travelling at that speed, 77 feet before the averaged driver reacts to a warning and that likewise travelling at that speed it takes at least 218 feet for actual stopping distance of car with brakes in excellent condition and that it required a total distance to stop at that speed of 295 feet. There is no indication but that the brakes of the Ferguson [defendant's] car were in excellent condition as the actual skid-marks found on the paved road extended for 220 feet in length. Since the chart referred to above indicated that it required 218 feet for actual stopping distance of a car with brakes in excellent condition, we find that the Ferguson car

485

§ 425.2   TRIAL EVIDENCE   Ch. 425

tional source material on stopping and braking distances is included in § 3.3 of Chapter 3, Investigation Sources.

DO YOU KNOW, THAT

If your car is traveling at a speed of	Then it is moving at a speed of	The average driver reacts to a warning in 3/4 of a second, during which time the distance traveled is	Actual stopping distance of car with brakes in excellent condition—equivalent to deceleration of 23.5 ft. per sec. or to stopping in 18 feet from 20 miles per hour	Total distance required to stop is	If car plus load weighs 3500 pounds horse power developed while stopping equals	Which is equivalent to lifting this car to a height of
10 Miles Per Hour	14.5 Feet Per Sec.	11 Feet	4.5 Feet	15.5 Feet	35 Horse Power	3 Feet	.4 Sec.
20 Miles Per Hour	29 Feet Per Sec.	22 Feet	18 Feet	40 Feet	69 Horse Power	13 Feet	1.2 Sec.
30 Miles Per Hour	44 Feet Per Sec.	33 Feet	40 Feet	73 Feet	104 Horse Power	30 Feet	1.8 Sec.
40 Miles Per Hour	59 Feet Per Sec.	44 Feet	71 Feet	115 Feet	138 Horse Power	54 Feet	2.4 Sec.
50 Miles Per Hour	74 Feet Per Sec.	55 Feet	111 Feet	166 Feet	173 Horse Power	85 Feet	3.0 Sec.
60 Miles Per Hour	88 Feet Per Sec.	66 Feet	160 Feet	226 Feet	208 Horse Power	120 Feet	3.6 Sec.
70 Miles Per Hour	103 Feet Per Sec.	77 Feet	218 Feet	295 Feet	243 Horse Power	165 Feet	4.2 Sec.

Published in the interest of Highway Safety
By
Bendix Products Corporation
"Bendix-Cowdrey Division"
South Bend, Ind., U. S. A.

[B4318]

Charts of stopping distances furnish useful standards for comparison, though the special circumstances of each case must also be considered.[71]

travelled 220 feet after he had applied his brakes and was skidding on the road. This further indicates that the Ferguson car must have been travelling at a greater rate of speed than 70 miles per hour. We think this speed amounted to negligent driving under the circumstances;" in Eggleston v. Louisiana & A. Ry. Co., La.App., 192 So. 774, in connection with the statement that a motor vehicle proceeding at 60 miles per hour, with good brakes, could be stopped within less than 352 feet; and was referred to by the court in Magnolia Petrol. Co. v. Saunders, 104 S.W.2d 1062, 193 Ark. 1080, and in Missouri Pac. R. Co. v. Hancock, 113 S.W.2d 489, 195 Ark. 414, as authority for the proposition that the average person reacts to a warning in three-quarters of a second.

71. **Ky.**—Parker v. Redden, 1967, 421 S.W.2d 586 (held inadmissible, where skidded 95 feet before striking parked vehicle).

La.—Picard v. Joffrion, App.1967, 202 So.2d 372; Davis v. Surebest Bakery, App., 38 So.2d 624.

Charts found admissible

La.—Bergeron v. Hetherwick, App., 140 So.2d 440 (charts contained in Blashfield's Cyclopedia of Automobile Law, Department of Public Safety Table and Lawyers' Motor Vehicle Chart are admissible).

Mich.—Winekoff v. Pospisil, 1970, 181 N.W.2d 897, 384 Mich. 260 (objection deemed insufficient, and judicial notice taken of authenticity).

Wis.—Mainz v. Lund, 119 N.W.2d 334, 18 Wis.2d 633 (table of aver-

Where a charge of negligence is based upon driving at a dangerous and excessive rate of speed, evidence is admissible to show the distances within which a car of the class to which the one in question belongs can be stopped while traveling at specified rates of speed.[72] Such evidence is not competent to show age stopping distances of vehicles operated at various speeds under normal driving conditions on dry level pavement, as set forth in manual for motorists, issued by motor vehicle department, was admissible); Steffes v. Farmers Mut. Auto. Ins. Co., 96 N.W.2d 501, 7 Wis.2d 321 (Wisconsin Manual for Motorists published by the Motor Vehicle Department is competent evidence to establish distances required to stop an automobile at specified speeds).

Contra

Statement from chart in Highway Department book, pertaining to stopping distance at 60 miles per hour was hearsay. Breshears v. Myers, Mo., 266 S.W.2d 638.

Driver's admissions noted

In view of defendant's own testimony as to distance traveled by her automobile before being brought to a stop, admission of a so-called motor vehicle speed chart which showed distances required to stop an automobile at different speeds was proper. Hultberg v. Phillippi, 220 P.2d 208, 169 Kan. 610.

Foundation required

Chart of speed and stopping distances of automobiles incorporated in pamphlet prepared and published by Department of Motor Vehicles was properly excluded in action against motorist by employee of State Roads Commission, who was struck by automobile, where chart was not offered through any witness connected with Department of Motor Vehicles, police officer, or anyone having expert knowledge of subject. Schutz v. Breeback, 178 A.2d 889, 228 Md. 179.

Inadmissible for purpose offered

Highway department handbook containing chart purporting to show minimum distances at which motor vehicles can be stopped at various rates of speed was properly excluded where offered merely as laying foundation for "later testimony". Smith v. Hardy, 88 S.E.2d 865, 228 S.C. 112.

Little probative value

Where road was upgrade and not approximately level, reaction time and distances provided in statutory tables had little probative value. Stimeling v. Goodman, 115 S.E.2d 923, 202 Va. 111.

72. **Conn.**—Friedler v. Hekeler, 1921, 112 A. 651, 96 Conn. 29.

Idaho.—Bell v. Joint School Dist. No. 241, 1972, 499 P.2d 323, 94 Idaho 837 (did not abuse discretion in admitting one page of driver's handbook showing chart of average stopping distances).

La.—Picard v. Joffrion, 1967, 202 So. 2d 372 (inadmissible unless accompanied by proof of accuracy).

Md.—Bozman v. State, to Use of Cronhardt, 9 A.2d 60, 177 Md. 151.

Mo.—Danner v. Weinreich, 323 S.W. 2d 746; Tucker v. Carter, App., 211 S.W. 138.

Coefficient of friction proof

Where evidence indicated that ice on bridge where accident occurred was in initial stage of forming, not melting, refusal to admit expert witness testimony concerning coefficient of friction of rubber on melting ice was not error. Braswell v. Owen of Georgia, Inc., 1973, 197 S.E.2d 463, 128 Ga.App. 528.

§ 425.2   TRIAL EVIDENCE   Ch. 425

the exact speed of the car, but to show whether or not a car of the same character, going at an authorized rate of speed, could be stopped within less space than was apparently required to stop the car in question.[73] However, before such evidence is admissible it must be relevant to the issues in controversy.[74]

§ 425.3   Operation of Vehicles—Lookout

Library References:
    C.J.S. Motor Vehicles §§ 248 et seq., 516.
    West's Key No. Digests, Automobiles ⚖150, 243(10).

On the question whether a motorist kept a proper lookout, the jury may consider the motorist's observation of the pathway ahead, and whether there were diverting conditions or circumstances.[75]

Testimony of other motorists or persons as to difficulty they experienced in seeing the same hazard may be relevant.[76]

Law of physics

Expert testimony concerning general law of physics as applied to sliding vehicles was not admissible where it did not appear that testimony was at any time connected to testimony or facts of case. Dendy v. Eagle Motor Lines, Inc., 1974, 289 So.2d 603, 292 Ala. 99.

73. **Ill.**—Young v. Patrick, 153 N.E. 623, 323 Ill. 200.
    Kan.—Leinbach v. Pickwick Greyhound Lines, 23 P.2d 449, 138 Kan. 50.

74. **Mich.**—Winekoff v. Pospisil, 1970, 181 N.W.2d 897, 384 Mich. 260 (relevant to issue of whether emergency which confronted driver when child ran into traveled portion of roadway was or was not due to actionable negligence as charged).
    Wis.—Kloss v. American Indem. Co., 34 N.W.2d 816, 253 Wis. 476 (where evidence clearly showed plaintiff made no effort to apply brakes).

Instructions refused

In action by owner of bus for damages from collision with automobile, where there was no evidence that condition of brakes was a cause of collision, refusal to give instruction offered by motorist in language of statute containing table of stopping distances, was not error. Fresno City Lines v. Herman, 217 P.2d 987, 97 Cal.App.2d 366.

75. **Fla.**—Byers v. Gunn, 81 So.2d 723 (with reference to driver's lack of awareness of presence of girl on automobile).
    Iowa—Robertson v. Carlgren, 234 N.W. 824, 211 Iowa 963.
    Mo.—Lee v. Holland, App., 258 S.W.2d 30 (in action by minor pedestrian who was allegedly walking along road shoulder and was struck from behind by automobile traveling from 60 to 65 miles per hour, fact that driver had failed to see persons walking along road was evidence that driver had failed to keep proper lookout).

76. **Iowa**—Rolfs v. Mullins, 162 N.W. 783, 179 Iowa 1223 (evidence that a person could see an automobile two blocks away).
    N.H.—Moulton v. Gaidmore Poultry Co., 120 A.2d 135, 100 N.H. 92 (action for death of motorcyclist

Proof of drinking by the operator has been held relevant on the issue of lookout.[77]

Obliviousness under last clear chance

As other parties are not competent to testify as to an injured person's state of mind at the time of an accident,[78] circumstantial evidence to establish the fact that the injured person, at the time, was oblivious to danger is admissible.[79]

§ 425.4 Operation of Vehicles—Control

Library References:
C.J.S. Motor Vehicles §§ 290 et seq., 516.
West's Key No. Digests, Automobiles ⚖168(1), 243(7).

Under some circumstances, it is proper to ask the driver of an automobile about the degree of control then being exercised over the vehicle.[80] Where the ground of negligence relied on is that a driver lost control of an automobile, evidence of the course and distance the automobile ran after the collision is properly admitted, even though the speed of the automobile is not in dispute.[81]

whose vehicle collided with rear end of truck, owned by defendant, and which had been parked, on dark and rainy evening in question, on public highway, experiences of three motorists, who testified that they had experienced difficulty in seeing truck at about time of accident).

N.J.—Gibson v. Pennsylvania R. Co., 82 A.2d 635, 14 N.J.Super. 425 (exclusion of testimony of witness for defendant as to his observations of distance he was able to see along the track to his right while riding in an automobile along the highway was not error, where there was no testimony to evidence any similarity in this respect between the opportunities for observation available to this witness and those available to motorist colliding with train).

Vt.—Duprat v. Chesmore, 110 A. 305, 94 Vt. 218 (passenger may relate distance saw the hazard).

77. For discussion of proof of drinking generally, see § 427.3.

Va.—Jackson v. Prestage, 132 S.E.2d 501, 204 Va. 481.

78. Mo.—Crockett v. Kansas City Rys. Co., Sup., 243 S.W. 902.

79. Mo.—Crockett v. Kansas City Rys. Co., Sup., 243 S.W. 902.

80. Ala.—Berry v. Dannelly, 145 So. 663, 226 Ala. 151 (if unaware of hazard, not pertinent whether had control which would enable stop); Penton v. Penton, 135 So. 481, 223 Ala. 282.

N.Y.—Nagel v. Paige, 10 N.Y.S.2d 470, 256 App.Div. 487 (that skidded, and cause).

Speed at which vehicle would skid

Question to the driver whether his truck at 5 or 10 miles an hour would skid was "relevant" and was properly admitted. Stafford v. Zake, 20 A.2d 144, 179 Md. 460.

81. Wis.—Thomas v. Lockwood Oil Co., 190 N.W. 559, 178 Wis. 599.

§ 425.4　　　　TRIAL EVIDENCE　　　　Ch. 425

Proof of drinking by the operator has been held relevant on the issue of proper control.[82]

§ 425.5　Operation of Vehicles—Right of Way

Library References:
C.J.S. Motor Vehicles §§ 362 et seq., 381, 515.
West's Key No. Digests, Automobiles ⟲171(4–7), 243(3).

The possession of the right of way by one of two motorists colliding at an intersection is a material factor in determining the relative degree of care required of each, and evidence tending to show the negligence or due care of one, in view of the right of way of the other, is admissible.[83]

Evidence is admissible to show which of the intersecting roads was most heavily traveled and of most importance, but it is not error for the trial court to refuse to admit evidence that traffic on one of the intersecting roads customarily stopped for traffic on the other.[84]

Prior conduct of the defendant in previously crossing the centerline may be relevant.[85]

82.　For discussion of proof of drinking generally, see § 427.3.

Va.—Jackson v. Prestage, 132 S.E.2d 501, 204 Va. 481.

83.　**Ala.**—Ray v. Brannan, 72 So. 16, 196 Ala. 113 (error to exclude statement of plaintiff that he couldn't estimate position of defendant's vehicle when first seen).

Colo.—Rigot v. Conda, 304 P.2d 629, 134 Colo. 375 (where it appeared that at one time a stop sign had been in place for traffic proceeding southerly along road where it intersected highway, trial court erred in sustaining objection to inquiry as to whether or not truck driver knew that highway was a through thoroughfare).

But see

S.D.—Roth v. Jelden, 118 N.W.2d 20, 80 S.D. 40 (that defendant motorist had previously been familiar with highway intersection and did not know that in the meantime arterial designation had been changed was insufficient to legally excuse his failure to heed stop sign, and hence such evidence was inadmissible).

84.　**La.**—Faul v. Miller, App., 55 So. 2d 593.

85.　**Iowa**—Brower v. Quick, 88 N.W.2d 120, 249 Iowa 569 (in head-on collision admitting evidence that plaintiff had forced another vehicle off highway about a mile and a half from scene of collision and a few minutes earlier was not an abuse of discretion).

§ 425.6 Operation of Vehicles—Lights

Library References:
C.J.S. Motor Vehicles §§ 263, 286, 516.
West's Key No. Digests, Automobiles ⚖149, 243(9).

When collisions or other accidents occur at night, or before sunrise or after sunset, the question of the condition and use of the lighting system of the offending vehicle may be material. Thus, it is proper to inquire into whether conditions of visibility were such as to require the use of lights,[86] and whether the offending vehicle was equipped with a proper lighting system and whether it had been properly inspected.[87]

---

86. **Mich.**—Schock v. Cooling, 141 N.W. 675, 175 Mich. 313 (other cars lighted and nearby premises lighted).

N.H.—Lepage v. Theberge, 89 A.2d 534, 97 N.H. 375 (layman, police officer or expert may testify as to visibility at time of accident).

N.D.—Thompson v. Nettum, 1968, 163 N.W.2d 91 (immaterial in view of testimony as to visibility at the intersection of 300 feet or more).

87. **U.S.**—McQueen v. Navajo Freight Lines, Inc., C.A.Neb., 293 F.2d 590 (evidence of tail light found with defective filament); Clark v. Remington, C.C.A.N.H., 55 F.2d 48.

Cal.—Williams v. Layne, 1942, 127 P.2d 582, 53 Cal.App.2d 81 (whether truck had clearance lights); Flynn v. Kumamoto, 72 P.2d 248, 22 Cal.App.2d 607 (contra as to headlight on bicycle struck from rear).

Ill.—Piper v. Speroni, 47 N.E.2d 120, 317 Ill.App. 540.

Iowa—Mundy v. Olds, 120 N.W.2d 469, 254 Iowa 1095 (sheriff's testimony that he would say that plaintiff's taillights would not have been visible at 500 feet, as required by statute).

Ky.—Conley v. Fannin, 215 S.W.2d 122, 308 Ky. 534 (testimony of witness that some 600 or 800 feet from the place of accident a vehicle without lights almost collided with witness is admissible though witnesses could not identify unlighted automobile as that of plaintiff); Swift & Co. v. Thompson's Adm'r, 214 S.W.2d 758, 308 Ky. 529 (testimony of highway patrolman that one of the lights of defendant's car was out 20 to 30 minutes before the accident was competent).

Mich.—Boyce v. Shtukas, 11 N.W.2d 206, 306 Mich. 467 (evidence that automobile was in accident and its lights damaged two days before collision was admissible on question whether such automobile was being driven without lights on introduction of testimony that lights had not been repaired when witness saw automobile during such two days).

N.H.—Everett v. Littleton Const. Co., 46 A.2d 317, 94 N.H. 43.

N.J.—Wilson v. G. R. Wood, Inc., 1 A.2d 416, 121 N.J.L. 41 (rear stoplight).

Tex.—Franco v. Graham, Civ.App. 1971, 470 S.W.2d 429, reformed 488 S.W.2d 390 (notwithstanding claim that bulbs were not shown to be in same condition immediately after collision as before, where bulbs were connected to plaintiffs' vehicle by direct testimony of person who had removed bulbs from vehicle when it was located in a storage yard, and where chain of possession of bulbs from

§ 425.6 TRIAL EVIDENCE Ch. 425

Evidence as to whether the lights of a vehicle were burning immediately before the accident is admissible.[88]

Evidence as to whether the lights of an automobile were burning immediately after an accident has been held admissible on the issue of whether they were burning at the time of the accident,[89] but it has also been held that evidence of the absence of lights after an accident was not evidence that they were not burning at the time of the accident.[90]

such person to a consulting engineer and to trial court was established).

Va.—Reid v. Boward, 1943, 26 S.E. 2d 27, 181 Va. 718.

Condition 14 mos. later

In absence of evidence that automobile, involved in fatal accident with bicyclist, was in the same condition as immediately before accident, propriety of testimony from expert as to condition of automobile headlights a year and two months after accident was doubtful. Mason v. Stengell, Ky.1969, 441 S.W.2d 412.

Condition several days before

In action for injuries sustained when defendant's truck collided with rear of truck operated by plaintiff shortly after plaintiff had brought it to a stop after using foot brake for some distance, evidence that plaintiff's truck was equipped with a stop light which was in working order two or three days before accident was admissible. Hawley v. Rivolta, 41 A.2d 104, 131 Conn. 540.

Inspection

Generally, testimony of automobile owner or his agents as to inspections and examinations of automobile at some time before injury, claimed to have resulted from owner's negligence, as in failing to see that taillight was functioning, is competent. Brotherton v. Day & Night Fuel Co., 73 P.2d 788, 192 Wash. 362.

Rebuttal of defect

After introduction of evidence to the effect that automobile involved in fatal accident had been involved in wreck about a year previously and had not been repaired, motorist could offer any evidence that headlights were not affected by the earlier wreck or that he struck another object after striking deceased to contradict any evidence or inference that his headlights were defective at time of accident. Mason v. Stengell, Ky. 1969, 441 S.W.2d 412.

88. **Ill.**—Howard v. Ind., 50 N.E.2d 769, 320 Ill.App. 338.

Ky.—Kennedy Transfer Co. v. Greenfield's Adm'x, 59 S.W.2d 978, 248 Ky. 708 (only one light burning at point three quarters of a mile away from collision).

Va.—Burton v. Oldfield, 72 S.E.2d 357, 194 Va. 43 (no lights).

89. **U.S.**—Spund v. Myers, 90 F.2d 380, 67 App.D.C. 135.

Ky.—Service Lines, Inc. v. Mitchell, 1967, 419 S.W.2d 525 (permitting highway patrolman, who arrived at scene 30 minutes after it occurred to testify that he observed that left front parking light of automobile was burning was not improper).

Va.—Hall v. Hockaday, 1966, 146 S. E.2d 215, 206 Va. 792.

90. **La.**—Beard v. Morris & Co., 101 So. 147, 156 La. 798 (one light unlighted).

N.C.—Morris v. Jenrette Transport Co., 70 S.E.2d 845, 235 N.C. 568 (no lights not admissible).

§ 425.7 Operation of Vehicles—Signals and Warnings

Library References:
C.J.S. Motor Vehicles §§ 288, 516.
West's Key No. Digests, Automobiles ⊱151, 243(1).

Evidence of giving or failure to give warning signals is relevant in automobile accident cases.[91] However, if the other party saw the approaching car, evidence of the failure to give a statutory warning becomes irrelevant and inadmissible.[92]

---

[91]. **Ala.**—Durham v. York, 112 So. 2d 472, 269 Ala. 304 (evidence that defendant did not sound the horn as he approached the curve was relevant to the question of defendant's "willful or wanton conduct").

Cal.—O'Donnell v. Market St. Ry. Co., 86 P.2d 1077, 30 Cal.App.2d 630 (street car motorman's failure to give signal on increasing speed could be shown).

Colo.—Denver Tramway Corporation v. Perisho, 97 P.2d 422, 105 Colo. 280 (street car).

Ga.—Eidson v. Felder, 25 S.E.2d 41, 69 Ga.App. 225.

Iowa.—Frideres v. Lowden, 17 N.W. 2d 396, 235 Iowa 640.

Minn.—Lovel v. Squirt Bottling Co. of Wisconsin, 1951, 48 N.W.2d 525, 234 Minn. 333 (knew of presence of child).

N.Y.—Hoffert v. Tisdale Lumber Co., 39 N.Y.S.2d 516, 265 App.Div. 1012.

N.C.—Tart v. Register, 125 S.E.2d 754, 257 N.C. 161; Queen City Coach Co. v. Fultz, 98 S.E.2d 860, 246 N.C. 523 (left-turn signal).

Wash.—Nelson v. Bjelland, 95 P.2d 784, 1 Wash.2d 268, 125 A.L.R. 641.

Wis.—Hanes v. Hermsen, 1931, 236 N.W. 646, 205 Wis. 16.

Prior state approval of signal device not necessary

N.C.—Queen City Coach Co. v. Fultz, 98 S.E.2d 860, 246 N.C. 523 (relevancy and competency of evidence relating to electrical turn signal device did not depend upon prior approval of device by department of motor vehicles).

Signal less than required by statute

Neb.—Petersen v. Schneider, 46 N.W. 2d 355, 153 Neb. 815, opinion supplemented 47 N.W.2d 863, 154 Neb. 303 (that truck driver gave signal of intention to turn to the left from some point within 200 feet to within 20 feet of the point of turning, though it did not show full compliance with statutory requirement, was competent as bearing on the degree of negligence or contributory negligence of the parties).

[92]. **Cal.**—McCune v. Pacific Elec. Ry. Co., 196 P.2d 634, 87 Cal.App. 2d 201.

Minn.—O'Neill v. Minneapolis St. Ry. Co., 7 N.W.2d 665, 213 Minn. 514.

Contra

Colo.—Denver Tramway Corporation v. Perisho, 97 P.2d 422, 105 Colo. 280 (testimony concerning motorman's failure to sound gong was admissible to show the conditions and conduct of the parties preceding the collision, though plaintiff admitted that he saw the street car approaching).

Va.—Bowman v. Monongahela West Penn. Service Co., 21 S.E.2d 148, 124 W.Va. 504 (evidence of street car motorman's failure to sound bell was admissible, though plaintiff admittedly became conscious

§ 425.7

Evidence as to whether or not a vehicle was lighted at the time is competent on the question of the reasonable sufficiency of signals and warnings at night.[93]

§ 425.8 Operation of Vehicles—Stopping and Parking

Library References:
C.J.S. Motor Vehicles §§ 300 et seq., 329 et seq., 515.
West's Key No. Digests, Automobiles ⚖169, 173, 243(3).

Evidence tending to show failure to exercise care in the stopping or parking of a vehicle may be shown.[94]

§ 425.9 Operation of Vehicles—Turning

Library References:
C.J.S. Motor Vehicles §§ 300 et seq., 515.
West's Key No. Digests, Automobiles ⚖169, 243(3).

Evidence bearing on the issue of due care in turning is admissible.[95]

---

of car's approach when it was a block away).

93. Ala.—White Swan Laundry Co. v. Wehrhan, 79 So. 479, 202 Ala. 87.

94. For discussion of proof of signals to warn of the act of slowing and stopping see § 425.7.

N.H.—Adams v. Severance, 41 A.2d 233, 93 N.H. 289 (failure to warn of presence of stalled vehicle).

N.J.—Melone v. Jersey Cent. Power & Light Co., 103 A.2d 615, 30 N.J. Super. 95, affirmed 113 A.2d 13, 18 N.J. 163 (failure of truck driver to put out flares).

Illegal parking not excused by official's permission

In action by motorist when her automobile collided with defendant's unlawfully-parked truck as it was being backed into a street from a diagonal parking place at a curb, admission of testimony that municipal chief of police had granted defendant permission to so park in violation of a city ordinance was prejudicial error. Fries v. Goldsby, 80 N.W. 2d 171, 163 Neb. 424.

Negligence in abandonment

Testimony concerning defendant's action after he abandoned his automobile on highway at night was properly admitted as bearing on whether defendant had taken reasonable steps to remove the vehicle, in action for injuries resulting when plaintiff's vehicle struck defendant's automobile. Crotty v. Bright, 1969, 167 N.W.2d 201, 42 Wis.2d 440.

95. For discussion of proof on the issue of signals for turn see § 425.7.

Ill.—Delach v. Schuberth, 45 N.E.2d 198, 316 Ill.App. 452 (rejection of proof of impracticability of turning a truck except from the second lane from curb held error).

Chapter 426

RELEVANCY AND MATERIALITY—PARTICULAR ACCIDENTS

Table of Sections

Sec.
426.1 Proof of Legal Fault—Railroad Crossing Collisions.
426.2 —— Favored Vehicle Accidents.
426.3 —— Collisions With Street Obstructions or Defects.
426.4 —— Collisions With Animals.
426.5 —— Pedestrian Accidents.
426.6 —— Injury to Passenger.
426.7 —— Defective Equipment.

§ 426.1 Proof of Legal Fault—Railroad Crossing Collisions

Library References:
C.J.S. Railroads § 842 et seq.
West's Key No. Digests, Railroads ⊕347.

Evidence as to the failure of a railroad to keep a highway crossing in proper condition is relevant to issues of the negligence of the railroad.[1]

Proof of prior incidents may be admissible to establish that the crossing was extra-hazardous, if the conditions then were similar,[2] but not as evidence that the train crew acted negligent-

---

1. **Tex.**—Chicago, R. I. & G. Ry. Co. v. Steele, Civ.App., 264 S.W. 503.

Not letters requesting changes

U.S.—Bailey v. Baltimore & O. R. Co., C.A.N.Y., 227 F.2d 344.

Ill.—Maltby v. Chicago Great Western Ry. Co., 106 N.E.2d 879, 347 Ill.App. 441.

2. **Cal.**—Martindale v. City of Mountain View, 25 Cal.Rptr. 148, 208 Cal.App.2d 109 (that two motorists in crossing grade crossing had the wheels of their vehicles become locked in the rails, was inadmissible to show dangerous condition, in view of fact motorists approached crossing from opposite direction of decedent).

Colo.—Buchholz v. Union Pac. R. Co., 311 P.2d 717, 135 Colo. 331 (not in error for excluding evidence as to alleged prior accidents where there was no evidence to show that alleged prior accidents had been under comparable conditions).

Del.—Jewell v. Pennsylvania R. Co., 183 A.2d 193, 5 Storey 6 (evidence of two prior accidents at grade crossing was inadmissible, in absence of allegation that injury complained of was caused by structural, or other defect, in crossing itself).

§ 426.1 TRIAL EVIDENCE Ch. 426

ly in the instant case.[3] But such evidence is unnecessary where the dangerous condition is open and apparent and the railroad company has knowledge of its extra-hazardous character.[4]

Other examples of evidence which has been held admissible include a railroad's rules of operation.[5]

Duty to signal

The failure to give crossing signals may be shown on the issue of negligence of the railroad.[6]

Witnesses who could have heard train signals had they been given may testify that they heard no such signals.[7]

---

3. **U.S.**—Small v. Pennsylvania R. Co., 80 F.2d 704, 65 App.D.C. 112, certiorari denied 56 S.Ct. 669, 297 U.S. 724, 80 L.Ed. 1008 (accident at same railway crossing eleven years before).

 N.Y.—Masciarelli v. Delaware & Hudson R. Co., 34 N.Y.S.2d 550, 178 Misc. 458 (inadmissible to show that defendant's watchman was incompetent).

4. **Tex.**—Texas Mexican R. Co. v. Bunn, Civ.App., 264 S.W.2d 518.

 Wash.—Porter v. Chicago, M., St. P. & P. R. Co., 252 P.2d 306, 41 Wash. 2d 836.

5. **Cal.**—Powell v. Pacific Elec. Ry. Co., 1950, 216 P.2d 448, 35 Cal.2d 40; Nelson v. Southern Pac. Co., 67 P.2d 682, 8 Cal.2d 648.

 Ga.—Callaway v. Pickard, 23 S.E.2d 564, 68 Ga.App. 637.

 Ind.—New York Cent. R. Co. v. Wyatt, Ind.App., 184 N.E.2d 657, 135 Ind.App. 205, transfer denied 193 N.E.2d 63, 244 Ind. 373 (railroad's regulations pertaining to speed).

But see

In action by railroad section foreman for injuries sustained in collision between gas motor car and defendant's truck, printed rules and regulations of railroad governing its employees were inadmissible. Lee v. Molter, 35 N.W.2d 801, 227 Minn. 557.

Uniform traffic manual

 Ga.—Isom v. Schettino, 1973, 199 S. E.2d 89, 129 Ga.App. 73 (exclusion of uniform traffic control manual showing required warnings for railroad crossings, and refusal to allow evidence which might reflect on whether railroad exercised ordinary care in running of engine over crossing, required new trial, and exclusion of such evidence was not justified merely because taxi driver testified that he had traveled road many times before and was familiar with presence of tracks crossing road at that point).

6. **S.C.**—Collins v. Atlantic Coast Line R. Co., 190 S.E. 817, 183 S. C. 284.

7. **U.S.**—Illinois Cent. R. Co. v. Sigler, C.C.A.Tenn., 122 F.2d 279.

 Ala.—Southern Ry. Co. v. Terry, 109 So.2d 913, 40 Ala.App. 186, reversed 109 So.2d 919, 268 Ala. 510.

 Ark.—Missouri Pac. R. Co. v. Yarbrough, 315 S.W.2d 897, 229 Ark. 308.

 Cal.—Lahey v. Southern Pac. Co., 61 P.2d 461, 16 Cal.App.2d 652, certiorari denied Southern Pac. Co. v. Lahey, 57 S.Ct. 508, 300 U.S. 665, 81 L.Ed. 873 (automobile struck on foggy day).

 Ky.—Louisville & N. R. Co. v. Ratliff's Adm'r, 85 S.W.2d 1006, 260 Ky. 380.

A witness may testify that, although no whistle or a bell was heard at the time of an accident, such a signal was heard on previous occasions at the place in question.[8]

Safety devices at crossings

On the question of whether a railroad company should have maintained a signal device at a crossing, evidence is admissible to show that there are practical devices of such character in general use.[9] However, evidence as to a custom of having a flagman at other crossings different in character from the one involved in the accident should not be received.[10]

That a regulatory body passed a resolution requiring the railroad to place a signal light at the crossing is admissible to show that the railroad had notice that the crossing was dangerous.[11]

Mass.—Weir v. New York, N. H. & H. R. Co., 162 N.E.2d 793, 340 Mass. 66.

Minn.—Polchow v. Chicago, St. P., M. & O. Ry. Co., 270 N.W. 673, 199 Minn. 1.

Mo.—Chamberlain v. Thompson, 256 S.W.2d 779; Dodd v. Terminal R. Ass'n of St. Louis, App., 108 S.W. 2d 982 (testimony of automobile driver, who was listening for bell, admissible).

N.C.—Kinlaw v. Norfolk Southern Ry. Co., 152 S.E.2d 329, 269 N.C. 110.

Okl.—Fleming v. Pattillo, 167 P.2d 40, 196 Okl. 557.

S.C.—Mishoe v. Atlantic Coast Line R. Co., 197 S.E. 97, 186 S.C. 402 (witnesses 100 feet and 35 yards from crossing).

Utah.—Clark v. Los Angeles & Salt Lake R. Co., 275 P. 582, 73 Utah 486.

Ability to hear signal

N.C.—K. B. Johnson & Sons v. Southern Ry. Co., 199 S.E. 704, 214 N.C. 484 (is competent only when it is first made to appear that the witness was in a position to hear and could have heard the signal had it been given).

8. **Vt.**—Webster v. Canadian Pac. Ry. Co., 156 A. 524, 103 Vt. 460.

Limiting effect of testimony

Cal.—Downing v. Southern Pac. Co., 59 P.2d 578, 15 Cal.App.2d 246 (held proper under ruling that testimony was admissible only to show witness' power of observation, and was not admitted as being material as to whether train whistled on night of collision).

9. **Iowa.**—Rupener v. Cedar Rapids & Iowa City Railway & Light Co., 159 N.W. 1048, 178 Iowa 615.

N.H.—Alden Speares Sons Co. v. Boston & M. R. R., 1921, 116 A. 343, 80 N.H. 243 (bells installed by defendant at other crossings).

But see

Ala.—Watson v. Birmingham Southern R. Co., 66 So.2d 903, 259 Ala. 364 (evidence of the use and existence of different types of warning signals used at other places was inadmissible).

Rule as to automatic signal not admissible

Cal.—Adams v. Southern Pac. Co., 186 P.2d 729, 82 Cal.App.2d 560.

10. **Or.**—Case v. Northern Pac. Terminal Co., 160 P.2d 313, 176 Or. 643.

11. **Tenn.**—Tennessee Cent. Ry. Co. v. Dunn, 145 S.W.2d 543, 24 Tenn. App. 383.

§ 426.1 TRIAL EVIDENCE Ch. 426

Evidence that the safety devices at the crossing were not operating at the time of the collision is admissible.[12] And evidence that a railroad crossing signal failed to work at various times before the accident was admissible.[13]

To rebut any inference of negligence arising from its failure to operate at the time and place in question, testimony of an inspector of having inspected it daily for many days previous to the accident and having reported that it was working properly is admissible.[14] Evidence that such a signal had worked properly for a long period of time before an accident was admissible, especially where the only evidence of negligence in its maintenance was that, at the time of the accident, it failed to work properly.[15] The amount of evidence, and the time before and after an accident which evidence of the operation of a railroad crossing signal may cover, must rest in the discretion of the court.[16]

Negligence of motorist

Whether those in charge of an automobile approaching a crossing of railroad or street railroad tracks have used due care

12. **Ill.**—Ryan v. Illinois Cent. R. Co., 75 N.E.2d 533, 332 Ill.App. 440 (truck collided with flat car blocking crossing at night).

13. **U.S.**—Small v. Pennsylvania R. Co., 80 F.2d 704, 65 App.D.C. 112, certiorari denied 56 S.Ct. 669, 297 U.S. 724, 80 L.Ed. 1008.

Ky.—Whitney v. Louisville & N. R. Co., 138 S.W.2d 503, 282 Ky. 392.

Utah.—Parker v. Bamberger, 116 P. 2d 425, 100 Utah 361.

But see

U.S.—Willis v. Pennsylvania R. Co., C.A.Va., 269 F.2d 549 (refusal to admit testimony of woman living near crossing that, on prior specified dates, she had seen train passing crossing while gates were up, was not error, in view of evidence that gates and signals had been inspected regularly and had been found to function properly eight days before accident and two hours after accident).

Mo.—Davis v. Illinois Terminal R. Co., 326 S.W.2d 78 (proffered testimony by plaintiff as to nonoperation of flasher signals on occasions other than night of the accident were so remote and lacking in probative value as to render such testimony inadmissible, and such testimony could not be deemed admissible on theory that it was to refute evidence offered by railroad to prove the signal system at the crossing was infallible, in view of fact that railroad only offered testimony to show the lights were flashing during period from a short time after the collision until its cars were removed from the area, and testimony as to the manner in which the signal system worked).

14. **U.S.**—Southern Pacfic Co. v. Kauffman, C.C.A.Cal., 50 F.2d 159.

15. **U.S.**—Southern Pac. Co. v. Kauffman, C.C.A.Cal., 50 F.2d 159.

16. **U.S.**—Southern Pac. Co. v. Kauffman, C.C.A.Cal., 50 F.2d 159.

in endeavoring to avoid a collision with a car or train depends upon their conduct in view of all the circumstances, and evidence of such circumstances as the speed of a train,[17] or that the train was being backed around a curve [18] may be shown on such issue.

The reliance of a motorist upon a railroad's duty or practice of giving warning on the approach of a train may also be shown.[19]

In determining whether a motorist who went on a railroad crossing at the signal of a flagman was negligent, it was competent to show whether it was customary to maintain a watchman or flagman at the crossing.[20]

§ 426.2 Proof of Legal Fault—Favored Vehicle Accidents

Library References:
C.J.S. Motor Vehicles §§ 371 et seq., 462 et seq., 514 et seq.
West's Key No. Digests, Automobiles ⚖175, 210, 243.

In deciding whether one vehicle is a "favored vehicle," the issue is what the favored vehicle driver reasonably believed as regards the existence of an emergency, and it is not necessary to establish the authenticity of the information the driver received.[21]

Evidence that various other emergency vehicles were available to meet the emergency has been held inadmissible.[22] And

17. Ky.—Illinois Cent. R. Co. v. Applegate's Adm'x, 105 S.W.2d 153, 268 Ky. 458.

18. S.C.—Carter v. Atlantic Coast Line R. Co., 7 S.E.2d 163, 192 S.C. 441.

19. Mo.—Chapman v. Terminal R. R. Ass'n of St. Louis, App., 137 S.W.2d 612.

Limitation in suit by railroad employee

Admission, in railroad fireman's action against truck owner, of evidence of expert to effect that other protective devices were available for use by railroad to protect motorists at crossings was error, where neither litigant had responsibility for condition of the crossing in question. Mills v. Dunn Bros., Inc., 1972, 503 P.2d 1250, 264 Or. 156.

20. Ala.—Cunningham Hardware Co. v. Louisville & N. R. Co., 96 So. 358, 209 Ala. 327.

21. Dist.Col.—Gurganas v. W. K. Huntemann and Son Funeral Home, D.C.App.1969, 252 A.2d 911 (to be competent there is no requirement that evidence as to nature of call requesting an ambulance be introduced through testimony of police officer who made call, through records, or through testimony of injured party, but rather person who receives the information is competent to relate whatever was told him which led him to believe that call was an emergency one).

22. Cal.—Gallup v. Sparks-Mundo Engineering Co., 271 P.2d 34, 43 Cal.2d 1 (properly rejected evidence to show that various emer-

evidence that an ambulance passenger was not operated on immediately after arrival at hospital was held inadmissible.[23]

Since other traffic should have known from the sound of the siren of an approaching police automobile that the automobile was one which had the right of way, for this purpose a city ordinance prohibiting any vehicle except police automobiles and certain other designated vehicles having the right of way from using a siren is admissible.[24]

Driving an automobile in attending a funeral does not absolve the driver from the consequences of negligent conduct. Hence it has been held not to be error to exclude evidence that the automobile causing an accident was part of a funeral procession.[25]

§ 426.3 Proof of Legal Fault—Collisions With Street Obstructions or Defects

Library References:
  C.J.S. Motor Vehicles §§ 168 et seq., 234; Municipal Corporations § 781 et seq.
  West's Key No. Digests, Automobiles ⟬252 et seq.; Municipal Corporations ⟬755 et seq.

Evidence tending to prove a roadway defect responsible for an accident is admissible,[26] as is evidence tending to prove notice of the existence of a dangerous condition.[27]

gency ambulance facilities were available at town where driver was making call, since such evidence was irrelevant on question whether driver of ambulance reasonably believed that he was making an emergency call).

23. **Cal.**—Head v. Wilson, 97 P.2d 509, 36 Cal.App.2d 244.

24. **Mo.**—Nolan v. Kansas City Rys. Co., App., 247 S.W. 429.

25. **Ill.**—Link v. Skeeles, 207 Ill. App. 48.

26. **Corps of engineers regulation**
U.S.—Quinn v. U. S., D.C.Ark.1970, 312 F.Supp. 999, affirmed C.A. 8, 439 F.2d 335 (vehicle left road constructed and maintained by corps of engineers, harm resulting from violation of regulations was of type they were designed to prevent, so that regulations were both relevant and material).

27. **Alaska**—State v. Phillips, 1970, 470 P.2d 266 (prior accidents showed maintenance of road inadequate).

Cal.—Bigelow v. City of Ontario, 99 P.2d 298, 37 Cal.App.2d 198 (claim against city for damages suffered by some other person).

N.Y.—Kaplan v. City of New York, 200 N.Y.S.2d 261, 10 A.D.2d 319 (that notice of claim had been sent and received and a complaint served, in connection with accident which occurred at pillar supporting elevated railroad overpass prior to accident at same pillar in which taxi passengers were injured, could be shown in action by passengers against city only after dangerous condition to which no-

Proof establishing a duty to warn of the presence of a defect or obstruction is admissible.[28]

Evidence tending to exonerate the defendant for the presence of an obstruction is also relevant.[29]

tice and complaint related had been shown).

Tex.—City of Port Arthur v. Wallace, Civ.App., 167 S.W.2d 549, affirmed 171 S.W.2d 480, 141 Tex. 201 (testimony of milk truck driver concerning his personal experiences in driving over the intersection for purpose of showing notice to city of condition of streets).

Wash.—Reil v. State, 1971, 484 P.2d 1150, 4 Wash.App. 976 (allowing evidence as to the entire 12-mile stretch, as relevant to issue of whether state had notice of the condition, where there was no showing that the condition of the particular area where the accident occurred was different from that which prevailed along the entire stretch).

Condition of trees along road

Ariz.—City of Phoenix v. Whiting, 1969, 457 P.2d 729, 10 Ariz.App. 189 (evidence of condition of adjoining trees of similar appearance was admissible to show knowledge or notice to city of dangerous condition of trees).

Safety measure initiated

Mo.—Metz v. Kansas City, 81 S.W. 2d 462, 229 Mo.App. 402 (placement of lights on island in intersection).

28. Ga.—State Const. Co. v. Johnson, 77 S.E.2d 240, 88 Ga.App. 651 (contract between company and state highway department, which contained an undertaking by company to exercise control over approaches for purpose of warning public of danger incident to construction work).

N.Y.—Schofer v. Davis & Stearns, 25 N.Y.S.2d 10, 261 App.Div. 881, followed in Gurry v. Davis & Stearns, 25 N.Y.S.2d 11, 261 App.Div. 881 (specification in defendant's contract relating to protection of traffic).

Ohio—Fannin v. Cubric, 1970, 255 N. E.2d 270, 21 Ohio App.2d 99 (agreement between contractor and the state was properly admitted to show what part of duties imposed by law upon the state with respect to provision and maintenance of warning signs or traffic control devices the contractor had assumed).

Misleading center line

Testimony concerning misleading effect of center line of highway at scene was material and relevant to basic issue of negligence of state. State v. Stone, 1969, 452 P.2d 513, 104 Ariz. 339.

State manual on signs

Manual on uniform traffic control devices was properly admitted in motorists' action against highway contractors for alleged negligence in failing to provide warning signs, where it was received without objection and referred to by both sides before objection was made and specifications which were part of highway contract directed that signs and markers should conform to manual. Smith v. Lafortune, 1970, 179 N.W.2d 136, 288 Minn. 135.

Rule limited

Ill.—Fricke v. St. Louis Bridge Co., 32 N.E.2d 1016, 309 Ill.App. 279 (abutment obvious to observant).

29. U.S.—Pool v. Leone, C.A.Colo. 1967, 374 F.2d 961, certiorari denied 88 S.Ct. 309, 389 U.S. 943, 19 L.Ed.2d 300 (evidence concerning construction contract between defendant and state highway com-

§ 426.4 TRIAL EVIDENCE Ch. 426

§ 426.4 Proof of Legal Fault—Collisions With Animals

Library References:
C.J.S. Motor Vehicles §§ 381, 407 et seq., 411 et seq., 516, 565.
West's Key No. Digests, Automobiles ⚖176–178, 243(13).

Evidence bearing on the issue of negligence of the animal owner or the motorist is admissible.[30]

Evidence of characteristics of frightened animal

Where a motorist is charged with negligence in causing an accident by frightening a horse, evidence as to the characteristics and habits of horses in general is admissible.[31] Likewise, evidence of the character of the particular horse which was alleged-

mission, indicating that defendant was precluded by contract from putting up signs along highway project, was admissible in action for injuries sustained when plaintiff's automobile struck defendant's machine parked along highway, wherein plaintiff attempted to fix legal duty on defendant to erect warning signs).

But see

Refusal to admit contract between oil company and independent contractor into evidence, in suit by motorist who was involved in accident while driving through black smoke from fire set by oil company and employee of independent contractor, was not error where plaintiff had brought suit sounding solely in tort and where introduction of contract would have created a contractual issue between oil company and independent contractor based on indemnity clause. Gulf Oil Corp. v. Turner, Miss.1970, 235 So.2d 464.

Not contract between company and state as to warning signs

In death action arising out of collision between automobile and "Tournapull", refusal to admit in evidence the contract between construction company and state in relation to highway project was proper, since standard of care or duty owed by contractor was that of an ordinarily prudent person, and provisions of such contract setting out certain terms with regard to barricades, danger, warning and detour signs, and furnishing of flagmen were not admissible to establish a guide in determination of negligence or proper conduct. Rains v. Heldenfels Bros., Tex.Civ.App.1969, 443 S.W.2d 280, error refused n. r. e.

30. **Vt.**—Wright v. Shedd, 177 A.2d 240, 122 Vt. 475 (horse owner's attempt to conceal ownership gave rise to inference of culpability).

But see

Ill.—Guffey v. Gale, 1947, 74 N.E.2d 730, 332 Ill.App. 207 (that hogs were unruly held inadmissible).

Deemed inadmissible

Idaho—Nottingham v. McCormick, 1973, 505 P.2d 1260, 95 Idaho 188 (absent any evidence of ownership of horse or of its breed or color, and absent any evidence that animal that witness examined on road near ranch belonging to her and her codefendant was at scene, witness' testimony as to horse she found on highway was irrelevant and inadmissible).

31. **Iowa**—Delfs v. Dunshee, 122 N. W. 236, 143 Iowa 381.

502

ly frightened by defendant's vehicle, is admissible on the issue of whether the proximate cause of the injuries was the negligence of defendant or the vice of the animal.[32] Evidence as to the disposition or reputation of the horse in question as safe or unsafe, or vicious, or as to its getting beyond control at the sight of automobiles, is admissible on the issue of the contributory negligence of the driver of the horse.[33]

But proof of the reputation or disposition of the frightened animal, offered by the defendant, is irrelevant where no issue of contributory negligence is involved [34] and there is no showing that the animal was frightened or unmanageable before the collision.[35]

Evidence of the reputation of a horse which was allegedly frightened by defendant's car, causing the injuries sued for, is inadmissible to show the disposition of the horse.[36]

§ 426.5 Proof of Legal Fault—Pedestrian Accidents

Library References:
C.J.S. Motor Vehicles §§ 302, 382 et seq., 389, 391–396, 468 et seq., 470 et seq., 481, 482, 484, 485, 514 et seq. 584.
West's Key No. Digests, Automobiles ⟐160–166, 216–223, 243.

In addition to proof of conduct by the motorist as discussed in §§ 425.1 through 425.9 and in § 427.3 (drinking), other evidence probative of failure of due care toward a pedestrian is admissible.[37]

32. **Mo.**—Cain v. Wintersteen, 128 S.W. 274, 144 Mo.App. 1.

33. **Mont.**—Bliss v. Wolcott, 107 P. 423, 40 Mont. 491.

34. **Mo.**—Cain v. Wintersteen, 128 S.W. 274, 144 Mo.App. 1.

35. **Cal.**—Oberholzer v. Hubbell, 171 P. 436, 36 Cal.App. 16.

36. **Mo.**—Cain v. Wintersteen, 128 S.W. 274, 144 Mo.App. 1.

37. **Cal.**—Martinovic v. Ferry, 34 Cal.Rptr. 692, 222 Cal.App.2d 30 (truck driver's testimony that he thought boy he had seen on street while working on truck had gone into nearby house).

Iowa—Scott v. McKelvey, 1940, 290 N.W. 729, 228 Iowa 264 (prior pedestrian use of road at same point).

Mo.—Scaggs v. Uetrecht, 244 S.W. 2d 17 (evidence that defendant knew that many people en route to shopping district on next street were accustomed to cross street in the vicinity of place of accident between intersections, which were two blocks apart, was admissible as a circumstance bearing on question of whether defendant should have sounded a warning).

Epilepsy and mental condition of pedestrian

Ohio—Feldman v. Howard, 214 N.E. 2d 235, 5 Ohio App.2d 65 (refusal to admit evidence of pedestrian's epilepsy and mental incompetency was prejudicial error, though motorist did not know of pedestrian's alleged incompetency).

§ 426.5 TRIAL EVIDENCE Ch. 426

That the front of an automobile passed a pedestrian who then came in contact with the vehicle is a circumstance tending to show lack of negligence on the part of a motorist.[38]

Evidence tending to prove the point of impact is admissible.[39]

Where no direct proof is available as to a motorist's having struck a deceased pedestrian, circumstantial evidence is admissible to show negligence and an impact.[40]

Contributory negligence of pedestrian

Evidence tending to prove lack of due care by the pedestrian is admissible,[41] as is evidence tending to prove due care.[42] Gen-

---

38. **N.Y.**—Brenner v. Goldstein, 171 N.Y.S. 579, 184 App.Div. 268.

39. **Pa.**—Dougherty v. Favata, Pa. Com.Pl., 14 Chest. 90 (that hat was found at a spot between intersections minutes after the accident, and that no other clothing was found in the vicinity, such evidence was relevant to the issue of plaintiff's position at the time struck).

40. **Pa.**—Pfendler v. Speer, 185 A. 618, 323 Pa. 443.

41. **Fla.**—Rodriguez v. Haller, App. 1965, 177 So.2d 519 (ordinances regarding pedestrian duties).
Mich.—Sweet v. Ringwelski, 1961, 106 N.W.2d 742, 362 Mich. 138, 90 A.L.R.2d 1434 (that other school children crossed street elsewhere).

Antecedent intemperate habits

Tex.—McCarty v. Gappelberg, Civ. App., 273 S.W.2d 943, 46 A.L.R.2d 93, writ of error refused n. r. e. (testimony of first aid man on ambulance in which plaintiff was taken from scene to hospital that witness smelled alcohol in ambulance did not amount to such proof of plaintiff's intoxication at time of accident as to establish predicate necessary for admission of testimony offered by defendant as to plaintiff's antecedent intemperate habits).

Drinking

U.S.—Parkins v. Brown, C.A.Miss., 241 F.2d 367 (to prove the extent of her drinking of beer or other intoxicants during, or prior to, her journey).

Ark.—Sylvester v. U-Drive-Em System, 90 S.W.2d 232, 192 Ark. 75 (that deceased appeared to be under influence of whisky).

Ill.—Randal v. Deka, 134 N.E.2d 36, 10 Ill.App.2d 10.

Neb.—Nichols v. Havlat, 1 N.W.2d 829, 140 Neb. 723, opinion set aside in part on other grounds, 7 N.W.2d 84, 142 Neb. 534 (evidence of deceased's intoxication).

N.C.—Moore v. Bezalla, 84 S.E.2d 817, 241 N.C. 190 (witness who saw pedestrian about an hour and a half prior to accident was properly permitted to testify that pedestrian was intoxicated).

Or.—Lynch v. Clark, 194 P.2d 416, 183 Or. 431 (inadmissible where no evidence of carelessness).

Fact pedestrian had accident immediately prior

In action for death of pedestrian who was crossing highway to return to his own automobile which he had parked on shoulder following collision with another vehicle, admission of evidence of details of the deceased's prior accident was error, but mere fact of the accident and testimony tending to show that decedent was emotionally upset when he

42. See note 42 on page 505.

erally, evidence that the pedestrian was warned of the danger is admissible.[43]

However, in a variety of circumstances, evidence has been held inadmissible on the issue of contributory negligence.[44]

started to cross highway would have been relevant on question of contributory negligence. Perrotti v. Sampson, 329 P.2d 310, 163 Cal.App.2d 280.

Knowledge of pedestrian of driver's obscured vision

N.H.—Stowe v. Hartford, 18 A.2d 382, 91 N.H. 261 (evidence that pedestrians knew that automobile radiators were steaming that morning and that windshields were likely to become frosted was admissible on issue of contributory negligence).

Prior erratic conduct

Cal.—Ungefug v. D'Ambrosia, 1967, 58 Cal.Rptr. 223, 250 Cal.App.2d 61 (ambulance driver's testimony describing deceased's earlier crossing of street on which fatal accident occurred some few minutes later, including testimony of vehicles coming to screeching and disorderly halt as deceased staggered across the street, was not inadmissible as being too remote and immaterial).

42. Mo.—Sullivan v. Kansas City Public Service Co., App., 231 S.W. 2d 822, opinion quashed in part 248 S.W.2d 605, 363 Mo. 68 (fact that vehicle gave no warning).

La.—Cooper v. Lane, App.1973, 286 So.2d 759, writ refused 288 So.2d 645 (testimony, objected to as hearsay, that university traffic regulations gave pedestrians in crosswalk the right-of-way was relevant to show why pedestrian thought that driver would yield to him while he was attempting to cross within crosswalk).

43. Ark.—Powell Bros. Truck Lines v. Barnett, 121 S.W.2d 116, 196 Ark. 1082 (person who was injured while sleeping on portable bandstand located several feet off right side of down grade highway had been warned against resting or sleeping upon stand).

Wash.—Nelson v. Bjelland, 95 P.2d 784, 1 Wash.2d 268, 125 A.L.R. 641 (testimony that sheriff warned plaintiff and others not to go out on the highway with a flash light and try to stop cars, because it was dangerous).

But see

Signs prohibiting pedestrians from crossing street at point where pedestrian-plaintiff was crossing other than at crosswalk were not material or relevant, and admission of photograph of such signs was reversible error. Quigley v. Snoddy, 1968, 242 N.E.2d 775, 102 Ill.App.2d 232.

Contra

Decedent's walking on road in face of repeated warnings from police chief was not relevant on whether he was contributorily negligent at time of death. Jamison v. Ardes, 182 A. 2d 497, 408 Pa. 188.

44. U.S.—Mann v. Anderson, C.A. Ind.1971, 447 F.2d 533 (offered testimony that six-year-old plaintiff-pedestrian, who under applicable Indiana law was incapable of contributing to accident, had, immediately before being struck, asked his mother to take him across street but she had told him to go by himself was properly excluded as irrelevant in child's action).

Cal.—Clark v. Vieroth, 296 P.2d 823, 141 Cal.App.2d 462 (evidence that pedestrian had been away from city for approximately two years and that when she formerly lived

§ 426.6 Proof of Legal Fault—Injury to Passenger

Library References:
C.J.S. Motor Vehicles §§ 386 et seq., 397 et seq., 514 et seq.
West's Key No. Digests, Automobiles ⚖=181, 224, 243.

In addition to proof of conduct by the host motorist as discussed in §§ 425.1 through 425.9 and in § 427.3 (drinking), other evidence may be admissible under the special issues of passenger cases.[45]

in city there had been a crosswalk at place of accident).

Ky.—Clark v. Smitson, 346 S.W.2d 780 (admission of evidence, tending to prove that portion of street where pedestrian was struck was unmarked crosswalk although location was at place other than at intersection).

Va.—Greear v. Noland Co., 89 S.E. 2d 49, 197 Va. 233 (when pedestrian was struck by truck while he was standing on shoulder of highway talking to occupants of automobile parked on such shoulder, admission of evidence as to how much further away from road surface automobile could have been parked was prejudicial error).

Custom of other pedestrians

Permitting pedestrian who, when struck, was standing in middle of street, not in crosswalk and not at intersection, to prove that other pedestrians crossed at point where he attempted to cross, for purpose of either negativing negligence on his own part or of showing negligence on part of driver, who denied any knowledge of custom or that he had seen people crossing in area where plaintiff was hit, was improper. Taylor v. Crawford, 1969, 167 S.E.2d 404, 119 Ga.App. 262.

45. **Pa.**—Gregg v. Fisher, 105 A.2d 105, 377 Pa. 445 (wrathful arguments between occupants of two vehicles involved and vengeful spirit).

Ky.—Louisville Transit Co. v. Sexton, 1971, 471 S.W.2d 20 (stopping bus suddenly due to traffic hazard).

Va.—Kennedy v. McElroy, 81 S.E.2d 436, 195 Va. 1078 (evidence as to whether conduct of host was deliberate).

Acceptance of later ride

Host was entitled to show that guest had ridden with host after the accident in order to convince jury that guest would not have done so if guest had believed host had been guilty of wilful misconduct in the accident. Ching v. Dy Foon, 299 P. 2d 668, 143 Cal.App.2d 129.

As to knowledge of passenger's position on vehicle

Testimony by defendant's friend to the effect that defendant had stated that accident was her fault and that she should not have driven so fast with plaintiff on the rear end, standing alone, did not necessarily constitute an admission of preaccident knowledge of plaintiff's position on trunk. Day v. Mayberry, Mo.App. 1967, 421 S.W.2d 34.

Not evidence of level of friendship between host and passenger

Ill.—Chmiel v. Pierce, 1973, 291 N.E. 2d 862, 9 Ill.App.3d 130 (refusal in guest passenger case to permit evidence showing a close relationship between defendant driver and plaintiff passenger was proper).

Ohio.—Rector v. Hyer, Ohio App., 41 N.E.2d 886, 35 O.L.A. 451 (that guest had a short time previously broken off her engagement with motorist was not admissible as tending to prove motorist's wanton misconduct).

However, in a collision with a parked truck, the exclusion of evidence of conduct of a third person in failing to display flares with which the truck was equipped was not erroneous as to the defendant host.[46]

Status of occupant

Evidence tending to prove the status of the occupant is admissible.[47]

Tex.—Edmondson v. Keller, Civ.App., 401 S.W.2d 718.

Prior occasions of children around vehicle

In action for injuries sustained by nine-year-old plaintiff when he fell from the rear of defendant's dairy delivery truck, question directed to driver of truck as to whether he had encountered difficulty with children around his truck at the location of the accident should have been allowed, as it had bearing on what the driver might reasonably have anticipated from youthful intruders in the vicinity of the accident. Lavallee v. Pratt, 166 A.2d 195, 122 Vt. 90.

46. **Va.**—Yonker v. Williams, 192 S.E. 753, 169 Va. 294 (flares were not required by statute, effectiveness of flares was questionable, and negligence of truck driver, host's codefendant, would not exonerate host).

47. **Cal.**—Hayes v. Harry, 6 Cal.Rptr. 671, 183 Cal.App.2d 412 (defendant's motive for taking passenger's money); Provost v. Worrall, 298 P.2d 726, 142 Cal.App.2d 367 (refusing to permit driver to testify as to why he had agreed to take passengers on trip was error, but harmless where driver otherwise testified to his reasons).

Ill.—Schachtrup v. Hensel, 14 N.E.2d 897, 295 Ill.App. 303.

Neb.—Bergendahl v. Rabeler, 268 N.W. 459, 131 Neb. 538.

N.J.—Egan v. Levay, 11 A.2d 22, 124 N.J.L. 125, affirming 7 A.2d 813, 123 N.J.L. 14.

Ohio.—Cloverdale Dairy Co. v. Briggs, 2 N.E.2d 592, 131 Ohio St. 261.

As to status of other occupants

Mass.—McDonough v. Horan, 130 N.E.2d 551, 333 Mass. 319 (in action for injuries sustained while passenger was riding to work in defendant's automobile, exclusion of testimony of two other passengers that they had no arrangement to pay for transportation and that defendant had not requested payment was not error, as such testimony was immaterial).

Benefit to host

Mass.—Crowley v. McCauley, 155 N.E.2d 407, 338 Mass. 418 (evidence, of intimacy between defendant and man riding in front seat with her at time of accident, that defendant had been surprised to find her husband at home when the group went to defendant's home, and that there had been telephone calls to plaintiff on day of accident from defendant's husband seeking to learn of her whereabouts, would not have established such benefit to defendant as would give plaintiff status of invitee, and there was therefore no error in exclusion of such evidence).

Mo.—Bartlett v. Green, 352 S.W.2d 17 (in Missouri action brought by passenger in motorist's automobile for injuries suffered in Kansas accident, evidence should have been allowed, on issue of whether passenger was a guest under Kansas guest statute, tending to show that passenger was being taken to mo-

§ 426.6　　　　TRIAL EVIDENCE　　　　Ch. 426

On the question of whether an occupant was a guest of the driver at the time of an automobile accident in which he received injuries, conversations between such occupant and the driver concerning the proposed trip on which the accident occurred are ordinarily admissible.[48]

Where a truck driver had no authority to carry passengers, testimony as to whether a child, who was injured while riding on the front fender of the truck, was on the truck against the driver's wishes was inadmissible.[49]

Contributory negligence of passenger

Evidence of the care exercised by a driver may be relevant in determining whether a passenger or guest personally was taking all necessary precautions.[50]

S.D.—Kleinhesselink v. Porterfield, 83 N.W.2d 191, 76 S.D. 577, citing 31 C.J.S. Evidence §§ 270, 272, ref. n. r. e. (testimony of witness, who had accompanied son and father on trip, that father had stated "Let's wait until Art (the son) can go" and "He said he wanted Art to help him look at some cattle" constituted an admission of father unfavorable to administrator's theory that son was a guest within guest statute, and hence such testimony should not have been excluded as hearsay).

Issue whether decedent was driver or passenger

Ill.—Howard v. Ind., 1943, 50 N.E.2d 769, 320 Ill.App. 338 (decedent seen as passenger just prior to accident).

Minn.—Nicol v. Geitler, 1933, 247 N. W. 8, 188 Minn. 69.

N.Y.—Rost v. Kessler, 49 N.Y.S.2d 97, 267 App.Div. 686 (where crucial question was as to whether defendant or plaintiff's decedent was driving at time of accident, officer's testimony that decedent was driving automobile when he saw them a few hours before the ac-

torist's home so that passenger's mother would be free to help care for motorist's mother-in-law who was ill).

cident was admissible in corroboration of defendant's testimony that he was not driving).

Not evidence of intimacy between driver and passenger

It was reversible error to permit administratrix of deceased driver in action by passenger for injuries sustained when automobile ran off the highway to introduce evidence that passenger, who was a married woman, was allegedly intimate with deceased driver who was married to administratrix. Pearce v. Barham, 149 S.E.2d 22, 222 N.C. 707.

48. **Ala.**—Strickland v. Davis, 128 So. 233, 221 Ala. 247.

Cal.—Rapolla v. Goulart, 287 P. 562, 105 Cal.App. 417.

Wash.—Keisel v. Bredick, 74 P.2d 473, 192 Wash. 665.

49. **Ala.**—Jewel Tea Co. v. Sklivis, 165 So. 824, 231 Ala. 590.

50. **Iowa.**—Carpenter v. Wolfe, 273 N.W. 169, 223 Iowa 417.

Mo.—Clooney v. Wells, 252 S.W. 72.

Tex.—Hicks v. Frost, Civ.App., 195 S.W.2d 606, ref. n. r. e.

Failure of signal by other driver

In action by passenger in husband's automobile against driver and owner of another automobile for in-

And evidence tending to prove care or the lack of due care by the passenger is admissible.[51] Evidence of a warning given

juries sustained in collision at intersection when husband accelerated his automobile to pass around other automobile which was proceeding in same direction, as driver of other automobile attempted to make U-turn without proper warning as required by statute, failure to give proper warning could be considered by jury in determining question of passenger's contributory negligence. Carpenter v. Wolfe, 273 N.W. 169, 223 Iowa 417.

51. Cited by the court in Young v. State, Alaska 1972, 491 P.2d 122, 125.

Ill.—Josel v. Rossi, 1972, 288 N.E.2d 677, 7 Ill.App.3d 1091.

Kan.—Hampton v. State Highway Commission, 1972, 498 P.2d 236, 209 Kan. 565.

N.C.—Hughes v. Lundstrum, 1969, 168 S.E.2d 686, 5 N.C.App. 345 (evidence elicited from plaintiff on cross-examination as to manner in which he had driven his own automobile previous to time he was injured while riding in defendant's automobile was admissible as being relevant and material to a determination of what had been going on between plaintiff and defendant with regard to testing and demonstrating automobiles and their respective speeds and ability to accelerate shortly before accident).

N.D.—Borstad v. La Roque, 98 N.W. 2d 16 (testimony showing guest's knowledge and experience with regard to operation of a motor vehicle, and driving habits and driving abilities of host and extent and nature of acquaintance between parties, was admissible on issue of assumption of risk by guest in entering host's automobile).

Or.—Koski v. Anderson, 71 P.2d 1009, 157 Or. 349 (guest had no place to stay night, so continued riding).

Pa.—McIntyre v. Pope, 191 A. 607, 326 Pa. 172 (driver not hindered in prior driving by three other adults in driver's seat); Quaintance v. Evans, 38 Berks 101 (evidence of right to control driver admissible).

Contra as to non-use of seat belts

Del.—Lipscomb v. Diamiani, Super., 226 A.2d 914 (not admissible).

Fla.—Brown v. Kendrick, App., 192 So.2d 49 (refusal to permit evidence of guest passenger's failure to use seat belts as constituting defense to gross negligence was not error).

Ill.—Atz v. Goss, 1974, 316 N.E.2d 29, 21 Ill.App. 878 (evidence as to passenger's use of a seat belt would not be relevant to issue of whether driver of automobile which struck automobile in which plaintiff was riding was liable for plaintiff's injuries, but would go to the issue of damages).

Ohio.—Roberts v. Bohn, 1971, 269 N. E.2d 53, 26 Ohio App.2d 50, reversed on other grounds 279 N.E. 2d 878, 29 Ohio St.2d 99 (not reversible error where not argued and court did not submit contributory negligence instruction).

Contra as to purpose of trip

Trial court did not abuse its discretion in forbidding introduction of testimony to effect that purpose of automobile trip was to allow guest, a married man, to have illicit sexual relations with another woman, since matter of attempted illicit relations was immaterial to case. Dutcher v. Phoenix Ins. Co., 1968, 155 N.W.2d 609, 37 Wis.2d 591.

Conviction record of host

Mich.—Paratore v. Furst, 1969, 167 N.W.2d 126, 15 Mich.App. 568

§ 426.6   TRIAL EVIDENCE   Ch. 426

by a passenger or guest to a driver is generally admissible.[52]

A passenger or guest may testify as to observing a driver's conduct on prior occasions, on the issue of whether the passenger or guest was negligent in entering the driver's car with knowledge that the driver did not operate it carefully.[53] Evidence of

(only evidence of so much of driver's record as was known to passenger might have been admissible against passenger).

Riding with drinking driver

Ga.—Stephenson v. Whiten, 85 S.E. 2d 165, 91 Ga.App. 110.

Nev.—Downing v. Marlia, 417 P.2d 150, 82 Nev. 294.

N.D.—Hogan v. Knoop, 1971, 191 N.W.2d 263 (procured beer for driver 5 hours earlier).

Pa.—Balla v. Sladek, 112 A.2d 156, 381 Pa. 85 (that passenger and host had been drinking prior to accident was properly excluded since that fact alone was not sufficient).

R.I.—Handy v. Geary, 1969, 252 A.2d 435, 105 R.I. 419 (in view of the representations of defense counsel, in suits brought against driver by passengers who sustained injuries when automobile left road and struck boulder, that they had no evidence that the driver was intoxicated at time plaintiffs entered the automobile, the question of intoxication was not in issue and, accordingly, court properly refused to permit defense counsel to introduce evidence, in support of their contributory negligence and assumption of risk defenses, that the driver had been drinking beer in plaintiffs' presence shortly before plaintiffs decided to accept a ride).

Va.—Major v. Hoppe, 1968, 163 S.E. 2d 164, 209 Va. 193 (placing of beer and champagne in automobile and consumption of a portion of it by them was irrelevant as an element tending to show that deceased passenger assumed a risk which would bar recovery, and inadmissible for that purpose as it tended to confuse and mislead jury).

Non-use of seat belts

Cal.—Horn v. General Motors Corp., 1973, 110 Cal.Rptr. 410, 34 Cal. App.3d 773 (in action against manufacturer and dealer for injuries sustained by motorist when, as she reached her hand across steering wheel in attempting to avoid another vehicle, horn cap flew off steering column and motorist's face hit steel prongs which were left exposed, wherein plaintiff claimed that defendants were liable for any aggravation of injuries which were due to manufacturing defect, refusal to allow evidence of plaintiff's failure to use seat belt constituted prejudicial error).

Ill.—Mount v. McClellan, 1968, 234 N.E.2d 329, 91 Ill.App.2d 1 (use or non-use of seat belts and expert testimony, if any, in relation thereto, is circumstance which trier of facts may consider, not only to avoid injury to himself, but to mitigate any injury).

52.   Cal.—Miller v. Peters, 230 P.2d 803, 37 Cal.2d 89.

Ill.—Wilmoth v. Clutts, 81 N.E.2d 654, 335 Ill.App. 339; Sullivan v. Heyer, 21 N.E.2d 776, 300 Ill.App. 599.

Iowa.—Bass v. Muenchow, 1966, 146 N.W.2d 923, 259 Iowa 1010 (had exclaimed about other driver's actions 3 seconds before).

Evidence of failure to warn

In action by administrator of deceased passenger in automobile against driver for death of passenger

---

53.   See note 53 on page 511.

a guest's knowledge that the host customarily drove at high speed was inadmissible, in absence of evidence that the guest had any reason to suspect that the host would so drive under hazardous conditions, as the host did when the guest was injured.[54]

§ 426.7 Proof of Legal Fault—Defective Equipment

Library References:
C.J.S. Motor Vehicles §§ 260 et seq., 515, 516.
West's Key No. Digests, Automobiles ⟜148, 243(6, 8).

As a general rule, it is proper to show the condition and equipment of a vehicle involved in an accident.[55] But, if the con-

as result of collision, wherein evidence as to negligence of driver was confined to curve on which collision occurred and a point about 80 yards beyond where collision occurred, court properly excluded driver's testimony that passenger did not complain of the way that he was driving. Hargrow v. Watson, 104 S.E.2d 37, 200 Va. 30.

53. Conn.—Fitzpatrick v. Cinitis, 139 A. 639, 107 Conn. 91.

N.Y.—Overbaugh v. Emory Transp. Co., 146 N.Y.S.2d 898, 1 A.D.2d 729 (that driver before accident had walked with firm step, had performed manual labor and had had firm, strong voice).

But see

Evidence as to whether plaintiff had known of defendant's prior traffic offense record was properly excluded as immaterial, although defendant contended that parties had been drinking together and that plaintiff rode along while knowing that defendant was under influence of beer. Whitman v. Whitman, 128 S.E.2d 249, 258 N.C. 201.

54. Ill.—Burke v. Molloy, 14 N.E. 2d 279, 294 Ill.App. 442.

55. For discussion of evidence concerning the condition found after the accident, see § 424.5.

U.S.—Weir v. Simmons, C.A.Neb., 357 F.2d 70 (description of turn signal on tractor-trailer was not inadmissible on basis that no foundation had been laid that signals were of type approved by state motor vehicle department); Siebrand v. Gossnell, C.A.Ariz., 234 F. 2d 81 (evidence that there was no safety chain between truck and trailer was properly admitted for purpose of completely describing condition of truck and trailer, regardless of whether a statute on safety chains existed).

Ill.—Gass v. Carducci, 185 N.E.2d 285, 37 Ill.App.2d 181 (in action for injuries to passenger who fell from front seat, questions asked motorist relating to "trouble" with door when automobile was first purchased and failure of sellers to remedy the situation were not improper where all parties assumed that "trouble" related to defect in controversy and, in any event, such testimony had at least some probative value).

Iowa.—Mathews v. Beyer, 1962, 116 N.W.2d 477, 254 Iowa 52 (taillight not working, in rearend collision).

La.—Shaw v. New Orleans Public Service, App., 188 So. 187 (folding doors on bus).

Md.—State for Use of Chairs, v. Norfolk & W. Ry. Co., 135 A. 827, 151 Md. 679.

Mo.—Rettlia v. Saloman, 274 S.W. 366, 308 Mo. 673.

§ 426.7   TRIAL EVIDENCE   Ch. 426

dition or equipment of a vehicle has no connection with the accident in question, such evidence is inadmissible.[56] Evidence of-

N.H.—Marcoux v. Collins, 1947, 53 A.2d 322, 94 N.H. 345 (absence of rear mirror required extra lookout effort).

N.J.—Layton v. Pennsylvania R. Co., 155 A. 268, 9 N.J.Misc. 640.

N.Y.—Robertson v. Giangrasso, 180 N.Y.S.2d 627, 7 A.D.2d 733.

Ohio.—Lacey v. Heisey, 1936, 5 N.E. 2d 699, 53 Ohio App. 451 (door latch).

Steering problems

Pa.—Griffith v. Clearfield Truck Rentals, Inc., 1967, 233 A.2d 896, 427 Pa. 30 (expert who stated that noise, vibration, and wandering of lessor's truck could have been caused by wheel alignment, looseness in tie rod ends, lack of balance in front tires, tire pressure, speed, and/or road conditions sufficiently tied in those symptoms, noticed some ten days before accident caused by locking of steering mechanism, with the accident which immediately followed similar symptoms, to permit admission of testimony as to the steering problems some ten days earlier); Benn v. Brown, 185 A.2d 326, 409 Pa. 22 (failure to use chains); Lute v. Ross, 190 A. 391, 125 Pa.Super. 584 (jury held authorized to consider absence of chains on truck as bearing on issue of truck driver's negligence though truck driver testified that he had had chains on and was compelled to stop where he did when one chain came off).

Condition at prior time

Ky.—Campbell v. McCoy, Ky., 306 S. W.2d 843 (in action for injuries when truck went off road at curve, statement of former driver of truck on avowal that truck had a shimmy one month to six weeks before accident was properly excluded because of the time element alone).

Testimony describing repair parts

Where it could be reasonably inferred that parts in repair kit used to repair brake mechanism in defendant's automobile replaced similar specific parts which were on defendant's automobile at time its brakes failed, testimony of expert witness with regard to parts in repair kit was relevant in action arising out of failure of brakes wherein defendant raised defense that normal braking unit for the model of his automobile could fail without any prior warning. Vandergrift v. Johnson, 1974, 206 S.E.2d 515, —— W.Va. ——.

56. U.S.—Fortunato v. Ford Motor Co., C.A.N.Y.1972, 464 F.2d 962, certiorari denied 93 S.Ct. 517, 409 U.S. 1038, 34 L.Ed.2d 487 (testimony of automobile manufacturer's design engineer as to thickness of metal in gas tank which caught fire was not relevant to issue whether or not there was a hole in the tank which allowed fumes to go into the passenger compartment).

Cal.—Thompson v. Held, 183 P.2d 711, 81 Cal.App.2d 275 (when accident happened when dim-out regulations were in effect, objection to question whether motorist had had lights tested was properly sustained).

Ill.—Lamar v. Toohey, 180 N.E.2d 511, 34 Ill.App.2d 202 (evidence that generator was incapable of producing charge, since did not exclude possibility of light from battery power).

Ky.—Consolidated Coach Corp. v. Hopkins' Adm'r, 37 S.W.2d 1, 238 Ky. 136 (evidence that speedometer was not working and thus bus had no clock); Braden's Adm'x v. Liston, 79 S.W.2d 241, 258 Ky. 44 (condition of brakes immaterial

fered in a products liability case to prove a defect must tend to prove that the vehicle in the instant case was defective.[57]

where last clear chance doctrine relied on).

Or.—Markle v. Mulholland's Inc., 1973, 509 P.2d 529, 265 Or. 259 (testimony by rubber chemist that he inspected tire after accident and found rubber of side walls to be so subject to ozone deterioration that casing was not suitable for recapping was properly excluded in action which arose when recapped tire blew out and plaintiff's car left highway, absent showing that ozone deterioration rendered tire dangerous); Spence v. Rasmussen, 1951, 226 P.2d 819, 190 Or. 662 (bicycle had no headlight, but struck in rear); Frangos v. Edmunds, 1946, 173 P.2d 596, 179 Or. 577 (evidence as to signalling device, where no signal given).

Wis.—Nordahl v. Farmers Mut. Auto. Ins. Co., 1947, 27 N.W.2d 707, 250 Wis. 609 (admission of bad brakes).

Condition of another tire

Ill.—Van Winkle v. Firestone Tire & Rubber Co., 1969, 253 N.E.2d 588, 117 Ill.App.2d 324 (in action against manufacturer and seller of retreaded tire which allegedly blew out and caused accident, admission of photograph of one of other tires purchased from defendant showing a bubble in the tire was improper where there was no showing that a bubble was cause or related to cause of blowout or that it existed prior to time automobile hit concrete abutment).

N.Y.—Lynes v. Debenedictus, 102 N.Y.S.2d 684, 278 App.Div. 674, reversed on other grounds 103 N.E.2d 734, 303 N.Y. 772 (in action by guest when blowout of right front tire was caused by loosening of blowout patch, and automobile crashed into culvert, admission of testimony as to condition of other tires on automobile and difficulties which defendant had experienced with them was prejudicial error).

Unrelated defect in manufacture

U.S.—Kane v. Ford Motor Co., C.A.Pa.1971, 450 F.2d 315 (where driver of motor vehicle advanced theory that improper installation of right front brake hose caused hose to become abraded and to blow out, causing vehicle to swerve into railing, service letter distributed by manufacturer to dealers warning that some front brake wheel supports may have been bent out of proper position was irrelevant and trial judge did not abuse his discretion in refusing to admit the letter).

57. **Ark.**—Gatlin v. Cooper Tire & Rubber Co., 1972, 481 S.W.2d 338, 252 Ark. 839 (failure, in action against tire manufacturer, to allow witness to testify concerning conversation he had with asserted agent of the manufacturer as to batch of defective tires was not error, in absence of sufficient showing that such conversation was connected with tire in question).

Similar mechanical design on other vehicles

In suit arising out of truck accident caused by manufacturer's use of clip to hold speedometer cable against truck frame in such manner as to create cable and brake line contact causing brake line to rupture and service brakes to fail, trial court was unduly restrictive in ruling that evidence as to presence of similar clips on other trucks had no probative value unless clips were found on same model truck of same year. Reader v. General Motors Corp., 1971, 483 P.2d 1388, 107 Ariz. 149.

Cal.—Marocco v. Ford Motor Co., 1970, 86 Cal.Rptr. 526, 7 Cal.App.

§ 426.7   TRIAL EVIDENCE   Ch. 426

Generally, a defendant may introduce evidence of repair of the vehicle before the accident to establish that it was in good mechanical condition at the time of the accident.[58]

Evidence as to the condition of brakes may be material in determining the relative degree of care exercised by a driver under the circumstances.[59] Such evidence is material to the charge of

3d 84 (in action for alleged defects in transmission selector mechanism, which allegedly caused unattended automobile to move and crush plaintiff's arm, evidence, from record of congressional hearing, of unrelated defects with respect to model of automobile in question was inadmissible on issue of whether manufacturer in fact used defective materials in the mechanism in question, or omitted vital part thereof, though some of the unrelated defects involved omissions of parts or insertion of improper parts at the plant where the automobile in question was assembled).

La.—Landry v. Adam, App.1973, 282 So.2d 590 (once defect in automobile is proved, fact that similar defects occurred in other vehicles made by same manufacturer at approximately same time is proper evidence to support inference that defect, proved by other evidence, existed when automobile left manufacturer's hands, but for reasons of public policy, evidence of or reference to recall program itself is improper method of proving similar defects).

58. N.Y.—Joart Cab Corp. v. Consolidated Edison Co. of N. Y., Sup., 89 N.Y.S.2d 789 (testing brakes).

But see

Ga.—Riggs v. Watson, 47 S.E.2d 900, 77 Ga.App. 62 (not repairs on fleet of trucks).

59. U.S.—Mid-Continent Pipe Line Co. v. Whiteley, C.C.A.Okl., 116 F.2d 871.

Cal.—Howard v. Triangle Freight Lines, 241 P.2d 35, 109 Cal.App. 2d 620 (air brake line).

Ky.—McDowell v. Bryden, 162 S.W. 2d 2, 290 Ky. 549.

Mo.—Biscoe v. Kowalski, 290 S.W.2d 133.

N.J.—Siegeler v. Neuweiler, 102 A. 349, 91 N.J.L. 273.

At remote time

U.S.—Walker v. Warehouse Transp. Co., C.A.N.H., 235 F.2d 125 (withdrawing from jury evidence that emergency brake on truck had jammed while vehicle was being operated by a different driver on a different road some two months prior to fatal accident was not abuse of discretion under New Hampshire law).

Driver's belief as to condition

In action by librarian against insurer of county bookmobile for injuries suffered when bookmobile overturned, admission in evidence of question asked librarian in regard to whether she assumed that vehicle had been repaired and of answer that plaintiff assumed that brakes were fixed, was not error, in light of evidence previously taken in regard to the taking of the vehicle to garage prior to the accident, purchase of new tires, and librarian's lack of knowledge about motor vehicles. Aetna Cas. & Sur. Co. of Hartford, Conn. v. Brashears, 297 S.W.2d 662, 226 Ark. 1017.

Held within pleadings

Allegations of complaint that motorist was negligent in getting out of automobile without setting brake to prevent automobile from rolling

failure to keep a machine under proper control.[60]

Evidence establishing notice of the defect is admissible.[61]

Evidence that the driver had complained to the defendant or the defendant's agent about the condition of the brakes was admissible to charge knowledge of the defect.[62]

The issue of the adequacy of the notice to others of a known danger may make admissible evidence of the warnings, if any, given by the defendant.[63]

downhill were broad enough to admit proof of defective brakes, and case was proper for third-party action by automobile owner against repairers for allegedly leaving brakes in defective condition. Glassman v. Goldman, 230 N.Y.S.2d 947, 35 Misc. 2d 429.

60. Me.—Keller v. Banks, 156 A. 817, 130 Me. 397 (four-wheel brakes disconnected from front wheels, thereby lengthening to some extent the distance required for stopping car).

Mich.—Kuchcinski v. Curtis, 231 N. W. 569, 251 Mich. 210.

N.Y.—Parker v. Helfert, 252 N.Y.S. 35, 140 Misc. 905.

Identifying car with defective brakes

Admission of mechanic's testimony that he had repaired truck for defendant which had defective brakes is error, where truck repaired was not identified as one causing damage. Golubic v. Rasnick, 39 S.W.2d 513, 239 Ky. 355.

61. U.S.—Southern Pac. Co. v. Kauffman, C.C.A.Cal., 50 F.2d 159.

Tex.—McGinty v. Motor Truck Equipment Corp., Tex.Civ.App., 397 S.W.2d 263 (printed instructions which corporation had received from manufacturer of dump truck bodies and which recommended that the bodies be installed by welding them to hinges at or near rear of chassis instead of bolting them).

Knowledge of attempted repair

In action for injuries to passenger who fell from front seat, mechanic's testimony as to what motorist's husband told mechanic about the door's coming open, as well as husband's directions to repair it, was circumstantial evidence of motorist's probable knowledge of condition of door. Gass v. Carducci, 185 N.E.2d 285, 37 Ill.App.2d 181.

Must have been communicated to defendant

Copies of complaints filed in various courts against manufacturer based upon steering problems with same model vehicle as vehicle involved in the collision were inadmissible to show notice of alleged defect to manufacturer, to impeach manufacturer's witness who had denied knowledge of legal or written complaints of steering problems or to show negligent design where it was not disclosed when manufacturer had been served with, or notified of, the complaints and witness had testified that he knew nothing of the complaints. Julander v. Ford Motor Co., C.A.Utah 1974, 488 F.2d 839; In products liability case arising from collision involving vehicle which was alleged to have design defect, for complaints filed in other cases also involving alleged defect to have been admissible to show notice to manufacturer, notice would have to have been given prior to date of accident in question and sufficiently so that manufacturer could have taken steps to remedy the alleged situation.

62. Pa.—Smith v. Snowden, Tp., 34 A.2d 515, 348 Pa. 187.

63. Utah.—Simpson v. General Motors Corp., 1970, 470 P.2d 399, 24

§ 426.7   TRIAL EVIDENCE   Ch. 426

Evidence probative of due care by the defendant is also admissible.[64]

Utah 2d 301 (admission in evidence of service manual showing procedure involved in removing tail gate was not error, in action against manufacturer by automobile body painter for injury sustained when torque tension rod released and struck painter in forehead while he was disassembling station wagon tail gate for painting, where facts of existence of service manual, its availability to painter if he had asked for it, and its contents, could be considered as having some bearing upon issue whether manufacturer had taken reasonable precautions for safety of those who would be concerned with that assembly).

64. Proof of later development of safer design

Where driver and passenger claimed that 1960 model vehicle was defectively designed in failing to be equipped with energy-absorbing steering mechanisms, court properly permitted manufacturer to show technological development which ultimately made feasible energy-absorbing steering columns several years after accident. Gray v. General Motors Corp., C.A.Minn.1970, 434 F.2d 110.

Chapter 427

RELEVANCY AND MATERIALITY—COMPETENCY AND CONDITION OF DRIVER

Table of Sections

Sec.
427.1 Proof of Legal Fault—Competency of Driver.
427.2 ——— Condition of Driver—In General.
427.3 ——— ——— Intoxication.

---

§ 427.1 Proof of Legal Fault—Competency of Driver

Library References:
C.J.S. Motor Vehicles §§ 264, 265, 273, 431 et seq., 514 et seq.
West's Key No. Digests, Automobiles ⟳157, 192(11), 193(13), 195(3), 243.

On the issue of whether a traffic accident was caused or contributed to by the negligence of the driver of an automobile, evidence as to the general competency of such driver is inadmissible.[1] Nor is the fact that the driver of a machine, colliding with

---

1. **U.S.**—Solomon Dehydrating Co. v. Guyton, C.A.Neb., 294 F.2d 439, certiorari denied 82 S.Ct. 366, 368 U.S. 929, 7 L.Ed.2d 192.

   Minn.—Sauke v. Bird, 1963, 125 N.W.2d 421, 267 Minn. 129 (mental or emotional aberation inadmissible).

   Mo.—Wilson v. Shumate, 296 S.W.2d 72 (age, intelligence, and discretion of motorist and possession of or lack of intelligence and discretion of an adult were not proper matters for jury's consideration).

   N.Y.—Parkinson v. Syracuse Transit Corp., 109 N.Y.S.2d 777, 279 App. Div. 848.

   N.C.—Hoke v. Atlantic Greyhound Corp., 42 S.E.2d 593, 277 N.C. 412.

   N.D.—Knoepfle v. Suko, 108 N.W.2d 456 (offer of proof of several previous convictions of plaintiff for drunken driving, revocation of driver's license, and failure to pass driver's license examination was properly refused).

   Admissible on separate issue
   Decedent's "army separation qualification record," showing that deceased was a qualified operator of special heavy equipment with 18 months' experience, and testimony as to wages paid such operators, were admissible over objections of immateriality and of speculative character. Geier v. Tjaden, 74 N.W.2d 361.

   But see
   Erroneous admission of evidence that on day of head-on collision decedent was seen by plaintiffs' witness to be driving in careful manner was not prejudicial to defendants who thereafter doggedly attempted to show that decedent's prior mental illness adversely affected his capacity to drive. Sauke v. Bird, 125 N.W.2d 421, 267 Minn. 129.

§ 427.1 TRIAL EVIDENCE Ch. 427

another motor vehicle, had never been licensed to operate such a vehicle admissible to show a lack of skill and fitness to manage the machine at the time of the accident,[2] nor can the suspension of the license of a driver involved in an automobile accident have any rational tendency to show want of due care with respect to a subsequent accident.[3]

Evidence of the general inexperience of a driver has been held inadmissible.[4]

Contra

In action for injuries sustained when plaintiff was making a U turn on street at night and was struck by defendant's automobile which was traveling in direction in which plaintiff intended to travel upon consummation of U turn, proof of defendant's driving skill and experience was competent. Borucki v. McLaughlin, 101 N.E.2d 624, 344 Ill.App. 550.

Stock car racing experience

In action by passengers against host for damages suffered when automobile skidded off pavement and struck a tree, testimony as to whether host engaged in stock car racing had no bearing on points at issue and tended to prejudice rights of host and error in admission of such testimony was not cured by court's striking evidence and instructing jury to disregard it. Bell v. Highland, 113 N.E.2d 79, 350 Ill.App. 501.

2. **Ala.**—Giles v. Gardner, 1971, 249 So.2d 824, 287 Ala. 166.

Cal.—People by and through Dept. of Public Works v. J. P. Loubet Co., 1957, 305 P.2d 651, 147 Cal. App.2d 566; Armenta v. Churchill, App., 258 P.2d 861, subsequent opinion 267 P.2d 303, 42 Cal.2d 448; Wysock v. Borchers Bros., 232 P.2d 531, 104 Cal.App.2d 571.

Ill.—Wilson v. Hobrock, 100 N.E.2d 412, 344 Ill.App. 147.

Mass.—Polmatier v. Newbury, 120 N.E. 850, 231 Mass. 307.

Mich.—Kalinowski v. Odlewany, 287 N.W. 344, 289 Mich. 684.

N.J.—Ross v. Pennsylvania R. Co., 148 A. 741, 106 N.J.L. 536.

N.Y.—Guy v. State, 269 N.Y.S.2d 504, 50 Misc.2d 29.

N.D.—Knoepfle v. Suko, 1961, 108 N. W.2d 456.

Wash.—Mills v. Park, 409 P.2d 646, 67 Wash.2d 717.

Admissible on separate issue

Exclusion of evidence that plaintiff had restricted license permitting him to drive only to and from his work was improper and warranted new trial, in action for rupture of aneurysm of blood vessel of plaintiff's brain allegedly resulting from anger caused by accident wherein defendant contended that plaintiff's anger might have been caused by fact that at time of accident plaintiff had not been driving to or from work and had thus been violating his restricted license. Episcopo v. Minch, Del., 203 A.2d 273.

Instruction permit

Minn.—Knutson v. Nielsen, 99 N.W. 2d 215, 256 Minn. 506 (whether the plaintiff's daughter was driving with a driver's or an instruction permit or no instruction at all was immaterial).

3. **Mass.**—Peskin v. Buckley, 168 N. E.2d 791, 269 Mass. 177.

Mich.—Obermiller v. Patow, 1973, 207 N.W.2d 152, 45 Mich.App. 606 (where there had been no claim at that point in trial that he was a careful driver).

4. **Ky.**—Illinois Cent. R. Co. v. McGuire's Adm'r, 38 S.W.2d 913, 239 Ky. 1.

Ch. 427   COMPETENCY AND CONDITION   § 427.1

The rejection of evidence of rules or instructions which have been made or given by an employer to regulate the manner of operation of vehicles by employees has been approved.[5]

Evidence that a bus driver was instructed by the employer, the defendant in the action, to remain on duty for a period longer than 10 hours in a single 24 hour period in violation of a statute, is relevant on the question of exemplary damages.[6]

Negligent entrustment

If the action is brought against the owner of a vehicle on the theory that the owner entrusted the vehicle to an incompetent driver, any evidence relevant and material to the issue of competency of the driver is admissible. Thus it is proper to introduce evidence of inexperience, intoxication, or failure of the driver to procure a driver's license.[7]

Mass.—Hunt v. Boston & M. R. Co., 146 N.E. 30, 250 Mass. 434; Polmatier v. Newbury, 120 N.E. 850, 231 Mass. 307; Lang v. Boston El. Ry. Co., 98 N.E. 580, 211 Mass. 492.

Tex.—Kasch v. Anton, Civ.App., 81 S.W.2d 1097 (failure to instruct driver as to law of road inadmissible).

But see

N.H.—Dixon v. Wood, 125 A. 261, 81 N.H. 325.

Contra

W.Va.—Yuncke v. Welker, 1945, 36 S.E.2d 410, 128 W.Va. 299.

5. Ky.—Lehr v. Fenton Dry Cleaning and Dyeing Co., 80 S.W.2d 831, 258 Ky. 663 (speed instruction).

S.C.—Eudy v. Atlantic Greyhound Lines, 191 S.E. 85, 183 S.C. 306.

6. Tex.—Manning v. Sunshine Bus Lines, Civ.App., 205 S.W.2d 636.

7. Cal.—Shifflette v. Walkup Drayage & Warehouse Co., 169 P.2d 996, 74 Cal.App.2d 903 (unlicensed).

Ga.—Jones v. Cloud, 1969, 168 S.E.2d 598, 119 Ga.App. 697 (prior drunkenness); Jones v. Dixie Drive It Yourself System, 104 S.E.2d 497, 97 Ga.App. 669 (that driver is untrained and has not been licensed to drive).

Ohio.—Sours v. Sours, Com.Pl., 73 N.E.2d 226, 35 O.O. 85, 48 O.L.A. 310 (absence of temporary instruction permit).

Tex.—Mundy v. Pirie-Slaughter Motor Co., 206 S.W.2d 587, 146 Tex. 314 (no driver's license).

But see

Dist.Col.—Bill's Auto Rental v. Bonded Taxi Co., D.C.Mun.App., 72 A.2d 254 (charges of traffic violations against driver of taxicab was improperly admitted as bearing on negligence of taxicab company in hiring driver).

Ga.—Brundage v. Wilkins, 1970, 175 S.E.2d 108, 121 Ga.App. 652 (where there was no evidence to disclose that driver of wrecker was employed by another for principal purpose of driving motor vehicle, and it was undisputed that in operating wrecker at time of collision, driver was not actually engaged in hauling persons or property for hire, mere fact that driver was not licensed public chauffeur, even if true, disclosed no statutory violation and was of no benefit to plain-

§ 427.1 TRIAL EVIDENCE Ch. 427

Likewise the defendant may rebut an allegation of negligent entrustment with proof of a good driving record.[8]

Though evidence of a single instance of careless driving has been held inadmissible,[9] several prior incidents may be shown.[10]

Evidence which shows both the occurrence of previous accidents caused by an employee's negligence, and the employer's knowledge thereof has been held admissible.[11] Evidence of the habits of the driver and the driver's reputation is admissible, not

tiff as basis for actual negligence against owner of wrecker).

8. **Mich.**—Olweean v. Wayne County Road Commission, 1970, 182 N.W.2d 58, 26 Mich.App. 121, affirmed 190 N.W.2d 108, 385 Mich. 698.

9. **U.S.**—Winchester v. Padgett, D.C.Ga., 167 F.Supp. 444.

Mass.—Flynn v. Lewis, 121 N.E. 493, 231 Mass. 550, 2 A.L.R. 896 (rapid driving on forenoon of day of accident).

But see

Although evidence as to speed at a time and place that is remote from point of collision is not admissible to show speed at which vehicle was being operated at time of collision, such evidence was admissible for purpose of showing negligence in permitting driver who was operating the vehicle on both occasions to operate it. Myrick v. Sievers, 121 S.E.2d 185, 104 Ga.App. 95.

10. **Ark.**—Ray v. Mays, 411 S.W.2d 865, 242 Ark. 79 (proof of habit of driving while intoxicated may be established by specific acts or by general reputation in community where driver resides); Ozan Lumber Co. v. McNeely, 217 S.W.2d 341, 214 Ark. 657, 8 A.L.R.2d 261 (though previous acts involved careless driving while negligence presently charged consisted of leaving disabled truck on highway).

Colo.—Appelhans v. Kirkwood, 365 P.2d 233, 148 Colo. 92.

Ga.—Willis v. Hill, 1967, 159 S.E.2d 145, 116 Ga.App. 848, reversed on other grounds 161 S.E.2d 281, 224 Ga. 263, conformed to 162 S.E.2d 299, 117 Ga.App. 855.

Mich.—Vanderah v. Olah, 1970, 183 N.W.2d 473, 27 Mich.App. 342, affirmed 199 N.W.2d 449, 387 Mich. 643.

N.D.—Geier v. Tjaden, 74 N.W.2d 361 (habitual carelessness could not be established by reputation but by evidence of specific acts of negligence).

Tenn.—Kennedy v. Crumley, 367 S.W.2d 797, 51 Tenn.App. 359.

Contra as to convictions

Evidence of employee's past driving record was not admissible as violating statute providing that no evidence of conviction of a person for violation of the statute or ordinance pertaining to use of motor vehicles shall be admissible in any civil action. Elliott v. A. J. Smith Contracting Co., 100 N.W.2d 257, 358 Mich. 398.

11. **Mich.**—Tanis v. Eding, 264 N.W. 375, 274 Mich. 288.

Prior accidents of train engineer unknown by employer

In action by railroad for damages to train arising out of grade crossing collision with defendants' truck, it was prejudicial error to allow deceased engineer's deposition as to his prior accidents as evidence in furtherance of defense of negligent entrustment. Grand Trunk Western R. Co. v. Pre-Fab Transit Co., 1968, 165 N.W.2d 281, 14 Mich.App. 26.

to prove negligence of the driver, but to show that the owner had notice that the driver was incompetent.[12]

It is proper to testify in denial of any knowledge of previous careless driving by the operator.[13] However, evidence of mere

12. U.S.—Winchester v. Padgett, D. C.Ga., 167 F.Supp. 444; Department of Water and Power of City of Los Angeles v. Anderson, C.C. A.Nev., 95 F.2d 577, certiorari denied 59 S.Ct. 67, 305 U.S. 607, 83 L.Ed. 386 (reputation in the community for drunkenness and for being a reckless driver).

Ala.—McGowin v. Howard, 36 So.2d 323, 251 Ala. 204 (general reputation for being a wild and reckless driver).

Ariz.—Powell v. Langford, 119 P.2d 230, 58 Ariz. 281 (driver alleged to be habitual drunkard).

Ark.—Waller v. Yarbrough, 337 S.W. 2d 641, 232 Ark. 258; Hall v. Young, 236 S.W.2d 431, 218 Ark. 348, 20 A.L.R.2d 1207; Ozan Lumber Co. v. McNeely, 217 S.W.2d 341, 214 Ark. 657, 8 A.L.R.2d 261 (specific previous acts of carelessness are admissible); Chaney v. Duncan, 110 S.W.2d 21, 194 Ark. 1076.

Mo.—Lix v. Gastian, 261 S.W.2d 497 (that he knew specific acts of carelessness or recklessness or that driver's incompetence was generally known in community).

Ohio.—Clark v. Stewart, 185 N.E. 71, 126 Ohio St. 263.

Inadmissible in absence of knowledge

U.S.—R. J. Reynolds Tobacco Co. v. Newby, C.C.A.Idaho, 145 F.2d 768 (admitting a judgment record showing driver's conviction for reckless driving three years previously, in support of plaintiffs' theory that defendant employer had knowledge of driver's recklessness and incompetence, was error where it was not shown that employer had any knowledge thereof and the name appearing upon record was not the same as name of driver).

Ark.—Rook v. Moseley, 365 S.W.2d 718, 236 Ark. 290 (general reputation of being a drunken driver should have been directed to and confined to his general reputation in regard to area where he and alleged owner resided, and error in allowing testimony as to general reputation in other county or area to be presented required reversal).

Tenn.—Kennedy v. Crumley, 367 S. W.2d 797, 51 Tenn. 359 (convictions which were five years, four years, and three and one-half years, respectively, prior to date of accident giving rise to action against automobile owners and operator were too remote to be of evidential value upon issue of owners' knowledge).

Tex.—Lands v. York Oil Corp., Civ. App., 280 S.W.2d 628, writ of error refused n. r. e. (proof of nature of operation of vehicle shortly before collision or evidence tending to rebut inference in inability properly to operate motor vehicle because of physical defect); Allen v. Bland, Tex.Civ.App., 168 S.W. 35, error refused.

Wis.—Dormeyer v. Hall, 212 N.W. 257, 192 Wis. 197 (admissible to show that parents, also joined as defendants, were negligent).

Not to prove incompetence

Mass.—Leone v. Doran, 1973, 292 N. E.2d 19, 363 Mass. 1, order vacated in part on procedural matter 297 N.E.2d 493, 363 Mass. 886.

13. Mo.—Ross v. Wilson, 163 S.W. 2d 342, 236 Mo.App. 1178.

§ 427.1 TRIAL EVIDENCE Ch. 427

opinion that the driver was a careful driver has been held inadmissible.[14]

If the owner admits responsibility for the negligence of the driver, the sole issue for determination is whether or not the operator was then negligent, and evidence as to competence, experience, or absence of a driver's license, becomes immaterial and inadmissible.[15]

§ 427.2 Proof of Legal Fault—Condition of Driver— In General

It is ordinarily proper to ascertain an employee's physical condition at the time of an accident, as bearing on negligent operation, and therefore inquiry may be made as to such condition.[16] Evidence as to eyesight deficiency is ordinarily admissible.[17]

Tenn.—Frank v. Wright, 205 S.W. 434, 140 Tenn. 535 (general inexperience).

14. **Mich.**—Olweean v. Wayne County Road Commission, 1970, 182 N.W.2d 58, 26 Mich.App. 121, affirmed 190 N.W.2d 108, 385 Mich. 698 (as well as improper opinion evidence, however, error did not require reversal as it was invited).

15. **Cal.**—Armenta v. Churchill, 267 P.2d 303, 42 Cal.2d 448.

Conn.—Prosser v. Richman, 50 A.2d 85, 133 Conn. 253.

Miss.—Nehi Bottling Co. v. Ellisville v. Jefferson, 84 So.2d 684, 226 Miss. 586.

Tex.—Rodgers v. McFarland, Civ. App., 402 S.W.2d 208; Luvual v. Henke & Pillot, Division of Kroger Co., Civ.App., 366 S.W.2d 831, error ref. n. r. e.

Prior drinking habits

Ga.—Tittle v. Johnson, 1971, 185 S. E.2d 627, 124 Ga.App. 706.

16. **Ind.**—Hancock Truck Lines v. Butcher, 94 N.E.2d 537, 229 Ind. 36 (evidence that motorist had crossed center line twice in 10 miles preceding collision when no vehicles were approaching or passing was inadmissible to show she was sleeping); C. I. & L. Ry. Co. v. Prohl, 115 N.E. 962, 64 Ind.App. 302.

Mich.—Williams v. Edmunds, 42 N. W. 534, 75 Mich. 92.

Minn.—Richie v. Elmquist, 1969, 168 N.W.2d 332, 283 Minn. 375 (driver with physical or mental infirmities is held to same standard of care as any other driver and, to extent his infirmities affect his ability to meet that standard as it relates to accident involved, evidence concerning them may be admitted).

Wash.—O'Neil v. Wilshire, 57 P.2d 1254, 186 Wash. 276 (one-armed driver).

But see

Ala.—Wayland Distributing Co. v. Gay, 1971, 252 So.2d 414, 287 Ala. 446 (evidence concerning any disability affecting decedent's use of his right foot along with hospital records tending to show that deceased had cancer, emphysema, and other ailments and had had his right heel excised was properly refused, where there was no evidence that decedent had at-

17. See note 17 on page 523.

§ 427.3 Proof of Legal Fault—Condition of Driver—Intoxication

Evidence probative of the condition of intoxication is admissible on the issue of negligence,[18] especially if the testimony

tempted to apply his brakes or take other evasive action or that he was unsuccessful in any such undertaking and there was no offer to show how decedent's physical condition influenced operation of his vehicle in any manner).

Minn.—Clifford v. Peterson, 1967, 149 N.W.2d 75, 276 Minn. 142 (not shown revelation of blindness in one eye would have precluded license, so couldn't show concealment on license application).

Wash.—Bearden v. Chisholm's Estate, 1970, 476 P.2d 127, 3 Wash. App. 454 (didn't show licensed driver in fact impaired by slow reactions).

Wis.—Theisen v. Milwaukee Auto. Mut. Ins. Co., 118 N.W.2d 140, 18 Wis.2d 91, rehearing denied 119 N.W.2d 393, 18 Wis.2d 91 (proof that driver, who was shown to have brought a fifth of liquor to a party earlier in evening, was not an habitual user of alcoholic beverages and that he was physically exhausted would have tended to show that driver should have known that he was likely to fall asleep, and it was not error for trial court, in guest-host action, to reject such evidence when offered to prove justification for driver's going to sleep).

Contra

Ill.—Trippel v. Lott, 1974, 312 N.E.2d 369 (condition of hands not shown to have affected driving ability).

Not mere possession of sleeping pills

Va.—Smith v. Smith, 97 S.E.2d 907, 199 Va. 55 (in action resulting from collision which allegedly occurred when defendant motorist drove onto wrong side of road and collided with approaching vehicles, wherein there was no proof or admissible inference that motorist had taken sleeping pills and merely statements of opinions in evidence that she must have fallen asleep, court properly rejected testimony as to sleeping pills in her possession).

17. **Minn.**—Richie v. Elmquist, 1969, 168 N.W.2d 332, 283 Minn. 375 (relevant to issue of whether driver saw children walking alongside of roadway and whether he could accurately gauge his position on the road relative to the shoulder).

Mont.—Knott v. Pepper, 239 P. 1037, 74 Mont. 236 (not detail as to nature of deficiency).

But see

Testimony that when driver was talking with witnesses after collision they asked him to sign a paper, and he stated that he would have to get his glasses from automobile in order to see properly, was inadmissible on issue whether driver was negligent for operating automobile without wearing adequate eyeglasses. Burrow v. Nash, 259 P.2d 106, 199 Or. 114.

Contra where had corrective eyeglasses

Minn.—O'Neill v. Mund, 49 N.W.2d 812, 235 Minn. 112.

18. Comparable text in previous edition **cited by the court** in Cheatham v. Chartrau, 176 S.W.2d 865, 868, 237 Mo.App. 793; Borstad v. LaRogue, 98 N.W.2d 16, 21.

Ala.—Davis v. Radney, 38 So.2d 867, 251 Ala. 629 (sideswiping); Landham v. Lloyd, 1931, 136 So. 815,

§ 427.3   TRIAL EVIDENCE   Ch. 427

223 Ala. 487 (sober after the accident).

Ariz.—Beals v. Quigg, 11 P.2d 354, 40 Ariz. 196 (that defendant had possessed empty liquor flask found near collision and was intoxicated).

Cal.—Purcell v. Goldberg, 1939, 93 P. 2d 578, 34 Cal.App.2d 344.

Colo.—Grandell v. Tyler, 1960, 355 P.2d 1091, 144 Colo. 233.

Fla.—Gates v. McKay, App.1966, 181 So.2d 740 (two drinks).

Ga.—Powell v. Berry, 1955, 89 S.E. 753, 145 Ga. 696.

Ill.—Murphy v. Wilkins, 86 N.E.2d 295, 337 Ill.App. 646 (evidence of defendant's behavior and activities throughout evening preceding accident at country club, where he had dinner and drank alcoholic beverages).

Iowa.—Pierce v. Heusinkveld, 14 N. W.2d 275, 234 Iowa 1348; Smith v. Pine, 12 N.W.2d 236, 234 Iowa 256.

Kan.—Ayres v. Kansas City Rys. Co., 193 P. 1069, 108 Kan. 49.

Ky.—Gream v. Miller, 1951, 243 S. W.2d 502 (sober after the accident); Louisville Taxicab & Transfer Co. v. Tungent's Adm'r, 229 S.W.2d 985, 313 Ky. 1; Eads' Adm'r v. Purciful, 1942, 158 S.W. 2d 645, 289 Ky. 350 (drinking from 4-5 p. m. to 8 p. m., where accident at 12 p. m.); Whitney v. Penick, 136 S.W.2d 570, 281 Ky. 474; Wigginton's Adm'r v. Rickert, 1920, 217 S.W. 933, 186 Ky. 650 (saloon hopping).

Mich.—Davis v. Hollowell, 40 N.W. 2d 641, 326 Mich. 673, 15 A.L.R.2d 1160 (guest statute).

Minn.—Kedrowski v. Czech, 69 N.W. 2d 337, 244 Minn. 111 (contributory negligence).

Neb.—Egenberger v. National Alfalfa Dehydrating & Milling Co., 83 N.W.2d 523, 164 Neb. 704; Cunning v. Knott, 1953, 59 N.W.2d 180, 157 Neb. 170; Montgomery v. Ross, 1953, 58 N.W.2d 340, 156 Neb. 875; Callahan v. Prewitt, 1944, 13 N.W. 2d 660, 143 Neb. 787.

N.J.—Roether v. Pearson, 116 A.2d 529, 36 N.J.Super. 465 (is not conclusive); Damchuk v. Public Service Ry. Co., 1927, 136 A. 604, 5 N.J. Misc. 365 (smelled liquor on driver and passenger).

N.Y.—Donahue v. Meagley, 221 N.Y. S. 707, 220 App.Div. 469; Clyde v. Grill, Sup.1918, 172 N.Y.S. 136 (breath smelled of liquor).

Ohio.—Zalewski v. Yancey, 140 N.E. 2d 592, 101 Ohio App. 501.

Or.—Williams v. Nelson, 366 P.2d 894, 229 Or. 200; Christianson v. Muller, 239 P.2d 835, 193 Or. 548.

Pa.—Jardine v. Upper Darby Lodge No. 1973, Inc., 198 A.2d 550, 413 Pa. 626; Reedy v. Brown, 1959, 150 A.2d 707, 395 Pa. 382; Gregg v. Fisher, 1954, 105 A.2d 105, 377 Pa. 445; Ropele v. Stewart, 137 A. 2d 895, 185 Pa.Super. 522; Critzer v. Donovan, 137 A. 665, 289 Pa. 381.

Tex.—Gunter v. Morgan, Civ.App. 1971, 473 S.W.2d 952; Hicks v. Frost, Civ.App., 195 S.W.2d 606, ref. n. r. e.; Southwestern Bell Telephone Co. v. Ferris, Civ.App., 89 S.W.2d 229.

Utah.—Watkins v. Utah Poultry & Farmers Co-op., 1952, 251 P.2d 663, 122 Utah 459.

Va.—Baker v. Marcus, 114 S.E.2d 617, 201 Va. 905.

Wash.—Nelson v. Fairfield, 244 P.2d 244, 40 Wash.2d 496 (skidding); Paddock v. Tone, 1946, 172 P.2d 481, 25 Wash.2d 940 (odor of liquor); Bates v. Tirk, 31 P.2d 525, 177 Wash. 286.

Wis.—Odya v. Quade, 1958, 90 N.W. 2d 96, 4 Wis.2d 63 (as relevant to whether dimmed headlights).

But see

Mich.—Madalinski v. Hill, 269 N.W. 147, 277 Mich. 219 (death action).

on that issue is conflicting or different inferences may be drawn from it, but such evidence may not be used to enhance the award of damages beyond that which will fairly compensate plaintiff for the injuries suffered.[19]

Evidence as to a driver's intoxication should be confined to a time near the accident.[20] Evidence of a conviction for being

Limited because of pleadings

Ky.—Spartman v. Rowlett, 1968, 312 S.W.2d 618.

La.—Grimes v. American Motorists Ins. Co., App., 145 So.2d 62 (testimony of police officers that owner-passenger and her driver had been drinking prior to accident was not admissible in action by owner-passenger against her liability insurer to show contributory negligence of owner-passenger or an assumption of risk in riding with her driver, in absence of allegation to that effect in petition or answer, but was admissible to impeach driver's testimony that he had not had a drink).

Mere presence in bar

In passenger's action for damages sustained in collision between vehicle and telephone pole, testimony that accident occurred after driver had left restaurant named "Bank Cafe," in which liquor was served, was not inadmissible as improperly carrying inference that driver had been intoxicated at time of accident. Pescatore v. MacIntosh, 1974, 319 A. 2d 21, 113 R.I. 139.

Not just peculiar actions

Del.—Law v. Gallegher, 197 A. 479, 9 W.W.Harr. 189.

One beer

U.S.—Socony Mobil Oil Co. v. Taylor, C.A.Tex.1968, 388 F.2d 586, appeal after remand Hughes v. Mobil Oil Corp., 1970, 421 F.2d 1248, certiorari denied 90 S.Ct. 1868, 398 U.S. 950, 26 L.Ed 2d 289 (evidence that employee had drunk one beer prior to accident was properly admitted as relevant to issue concerning his ability to judge distance.)

Refusal of alcohol test

In prosecution for driving while intoxicated, trial judge should have considered defendant's refusal to take the chemical alcoholic test as relevant evidence, and invoking what trial judge thought was a presumption of law against defendant constituted prejudicial error. (Per Hamlin, J., with two judges concurring and one judge concurring in result). City of Monroe v. High, 1969, 223 So.2d 834, 254 La. 362.

Rule limited

Va.—Eubank v. Spencer, 128 S.E.2d 299, 203 Va. 923 (if there is no proof of one or more of the elements necessary to justify an award for punitive damages, evidence of intoxication may not be used to increase award).

19. **Cal.**—Strauss v. Buckley, 65 P. 2d 1352, 20 Cal.App.2d 7.

Va.—Baker v. Marcus, 114 S.E.2d 617, 201 Va. 905.

20. **Ala.**—Chattahoochee Val. Ry. Co. v. Williams, 103 So.2d 762, 267 Ala. 464 (each case must depend on its circumstances in determining precisely how many hours must elapse before such proof becomes irrelevant because too remote).

Ga.—Swift & Co. v. Lawson, 97 S. E.2d 168, 95 Ga.App. 35.

Idaho.—Stuart v. McVey, 87 P.2d 446, 59 Idaho 740 (intoxicated during period ending about three hours before collision was admissible as not too remote).

§ 427.3   TRIAL EVIDENCE   Ch. 427

Ky.—Illinois Cent. R. Co. v. McGuire's Adm'r, 38 S.W.2d 913, 239 Ky. 1.

Mass.—Clark v. Beacon Oil Co., 170 N.E. 836, 271 Mass. 27.

Minn.—Greene v. Mathiowetz, 3 N. W.2d 97, 212 Minn. 171 (witness' testimony as to plaintiff's intoxicated condition some five hours before accident was admissible since jury could find that plaintiff was unfit to drive the automobile because of his drunken "hangover").

Neb.—O'Neill v. Henke, 94 N.W.2d 322, 167 Neb. 631 (evidence as to drinking intoxicants within a reasonable time prior to an accident is a circumstance to be considered in determining whether or not motorist is guilty of gross negligence under guest statute).

Tex.—Proctor v. R. T. Herrin Petroleum Transport Co., Civ.App., 322 S.W.2d 42, affirmed 338 S.W.2d 422, 161 Tex. 222.

Utah.—Watkins v. Utah Poultry & Farmers Coop., 251 P.2d 663, 122 Utah 459 (about an hour before the accident).

But see

Permitting plaintiff's counsel to question defendant driver regarding her ability to drive on prior occasions after having had several drinks was relevant on issue of whether driver had displayed inability to drive properly such as to require passenger to take protective action. Gates v. McKay, Fla.App., 181 So.2d 740.

Testimony of witnesses concerning manner in which deceased drove during the afternoon and evening of the day preceding the collision, during which time he drank beer and whisky, should have been admitted as material in determining whether the deceased was intoxicated at or immediately before the collision. Workman v. Wynne, 94 S.E.2d 665, 142 W.Va. 135.

Condition subsequent to accident

U.S.—Neider v. Chrysler Corp., D.C. Pa.1973, 361 F.Supp. 320, affirmed C.A., 491 F.2d 748, and 491 F.2d 750 (evidence in products liability and negligence action against manufacturer of car involved in collision with plaintiffs' car, wherein owner of former car was impleaded by manufacturer, including evidence that if third-party defendant had alcohol level in his blood of .06% three and one-half hours after accident it would be extremely dangerous for him to drive at 120 miles an hour, was sufficient to reasonably show degree of intoxication rendering him unfit to drive at time of accident; accordingly, evidence of his intoxication was admissible under Pennsylvania law).

Ark.—Hall v. Young, 236 S.W.2d 431, 218 Ark. 348, 20 A.L.R.2d 1207 (where at least two hours had elapsed after accident before officer talked with driver, circumstances did not afford proper basis for officer's testimony that driver had been drunk).

Ill.—Van Huss v. Allen, 133 N.E.2d 727, 9 Ill.App.2d 572 (two State Highway Patrolmen's testimony that defendant driver was under influence of intoxicating liquor in their opinion when they saw him about two or two and a half hours after accident was competent, and exclusion thereof was error requiring reversal of jury's verdict of "not guilty" as to a defendant in whose tavern three witnesses testified that they saw defendant driver drinking beer one or two hours before accident).

Ky.—Tingle v. Foster, 399 S.W.2d 475 (evidence of pattern of driving indicative of alcoholic indulgence and as to defendant's conduct immediately prior to accident, together with admitted fact that she was an alcoholic and sole occupant of automobile, rendered admissible testimony concerning bot-

526

drunk at the time of a collision, and of similar convictions for being drunk before and after the collision, has been held inadmissible on the question of intoxication at the time of the collision.[21]

Intoxication may be proved by scientific methods, such as toxicologist's report, blood test, and urinalysis.[22] Also it is proper

tles found in her automobile and as to her condition after accident); Randle v. Mitchell, 142 S.W.2d 124, 283 Ky. 501 (testimony of officers who arrived at scene shortly after accident); Tipton v. Estill Ice Co., 132 S.W.2d 347, 279 Ky. 793 (testimony that driver was under influence of liquor late in afternoon or evening of day of accident was incompetent, in absence of evidence that driver had been drinking prior to accident).

Pa.—Reedy v. Brown, 150 A.2d 707, 395 Pa. 382 (in case involving issue of whether defendant had been unfit to drive because of intoxication when he got into automobile at 8 o'clock, testimony of a physician, as to his condition, when he examined him at 10:45 o'clock, was admissible on issue, and the lapse of time before the examination affected only the weight to be given the physician's testimony).

Habit of drinking

Tex.—Compton v. Jay, Civ.App., 379 S.W.2d 933 (generally, habits of intemperance or sobriety are admissible to corroborate or rebut alleged fact of intoxication on particular occasion); Tripp v. Watson, Civ.App., 235 S.W.2d 677 (it is not ordinarily permissible to show that driver was in habit of drinking intoxicating liquor or was intoxicated at some time remote from date of accident).

Use of intoxicants generally

Inquiry as to whether so far as witness knew driver used intoxicating liquor at all was objectionable, though driver had previously been cross-examined concerning empty beer bottles and one full bottle found in automobile after collision. Gile v. Nielsen, 145 P.2d 288, 20 Wash. 2d 1.

21. Cal.—Stickel v. San Diego Elec. Ry. Co., Cal.App., 181 P.2d 745 subsequent opinion 195 P.2d 416, 32 Cal.2d 157 (four misdemeanors involving drunkenness in the period of eleven years prior to the accident).

Tex.—R. T. Herrin Petroleum Transport Co. v. Proctor, 338 S.W.2d 422, 161 Tex. 222; Tripp v. Watson, Civ.App., 235 S.W.2d 677 (conviction for driving while intoxicated on occasion several months prior to date of collision).

But see

Ga.—Hardeman v. Georgia Power Co., 156 S.E. 642, 42 Ga.App. 435.

Contra

Where evidence was offered that defendant was intoxicated at time of collision, and he denied charge, evidence was properly admitted that he pleaded guilty to subsequent offense of driving while intoxicated, a felony, and that he had two prior convictions for subsequent offense of driving while intoxicated less than six months prior to date of collision. Compton v. Jay, Tex.Civ.App., 379 S. W.2d 933.

22. For discussion of admissibility of scientific evidence generally, see Chapter 432.

U.S.—Bach v. Penn Central Transp. Co., C.A.Ohio1974, 502 F.2d 1117 (aside from statutory law in Ohio, evidence of blood alcohol concentration in appropriate cases should be received like any other expert testimony, and though test procedures need not necessarily conform to those described in statute, they must accord with good practice in field to assure reliable results; similarly, expert evidence would be admissible for interpreting results, namely, for describing physical and mental condition of a person with a given blood alcohol concentration); Barnes v. Smith, C.A.N.M., 305 F.2d 226 (but held foundation lacking); Ravellette v. Smith, C.A.Ind., 300 F.2d 854 (even though blood sample from which analysis was made was taken without consent of decedent's family).

Cal.—Wagner v. Osborn, 37 Cal. Rptr. 27, 225 Cal.App.2d 36.

Iowa.—Augusta v. Jensen, 42 N.W. 2d 383, 241 Iowa 697 (physician's testimony that blood test one hour and 20 minutes after accident showed that defendant was intoxicated at time of accident, was not inadmissible as too remote).

N.Y.—Durham v. Melly, 221 N.Y.S. 2d 366, 14 A.D.2d 389 (but held foundation lacking); Iovino v. Green Bus Lines, 100 N.Y.S.2d 148, 277 App.Div. 1002 (exclusion of report of toxicologist made pursuant to law and in regular course of business as to quantity of alcohol found in brain of deceased was error); Bovey v. State, 93 N. Y.S.2d 560, 197 Misc. 302 (urine specimen taken from motorist while unconscious was not a violation of rights against self-incrimination and illegal searches and seizures).

N.C.—Brewer v. Harris, 1971, 179 S.E.2d 160, 10 N.C.App. 515, affirmed 182 S.E.2d 345, 279 N.C. 288.

Tex.—Hartman v. Harder, Civ.App., 322 S.W.2d 555 (but held foundation lacking).

Utah.—Fretz v. Anderson, 300 P.2d 642, 5 Utah 2d 290, opinion modified and rehearing denied 308 P.2d 948, 6 Utah 2d 169 (testimony of doctor, who had made a blood test from blood extracted from deceased's body without deceased's parents' consent, that deceased was intoxicated to the extent of confusion).

Va.—Major v. Hoppe, 1968, 163 S.E. 2d 164, 209 Va. 193.

Authority for test implied

For result of test performed on blood sample drawn from body of deceased passenger to have been admissible in action for death of passenger, it was not necessary to have direct evidence that officer had directed or authorized physician, who had been requested to perform services of coroner's physician, to remove blood sample from passenger, as such authority could be implied from nature of events as they transpired after passenger had been brought to hospital. Gardner v. Meyers, C.A. Neb.1974, 491 F.2d 1184.

But see

N.C.—Gibson v. Montford, 1970, 175 S.E.2d 776, 9 N.C.App. 251 (admission discretionary).

Contra

Va.—Russell v. Hammond, 106 S.E. 2d 626, 200 Va. 600 (in a civil suit there is no "accused," within contemplation of statutes authorizing admission of certificate of results of analysis of blood of "accused").

Fact of test

Refusing to permit police officer to testify as to whether he had given driver certain tests was improper, where question was on material issue of driver's intoxication, although such error was not prejudicial. Cseri v. D'Amore, 43 Cal.Rptr. 36, 232 Cal.App.2d 622.

Non-consent factor limited to claim of presumption of intoxication from content

Testimony as to results of blood-sample tests was not rendered inad-

to permit a layman to state an opinion, based upon facts ascertained by the witness' own observations, as to whether a person was intoxicated.[23] Actions of a driver which may be proved to show intoxication include unreasonable speed,[24] and involvement in one accident and the narrow avoidance of others.[25]

Evidence that the odor of liquor was on the driver's breath after an accident is sometimes admissible.[26]

missible in dramshop action by motorist, whose vehicle collided with that of plaintiff's decedent, and to whom defendants allegedly sold intoxicating liquor, where he did not consent to taking of blood from his body and no law enforcement officer requested test to be made. Weaver v. Lovell, 1970, 262 N.E.2d 113, 128 Ill.App.2d 338.

Rebuttal evidence to test

Where there was testimony in death action that decedent's blood contained 0.13% alcohol and that all members of group including decedent's host driver drank about same amount of beer, expert should have been permitted to testify, on basis of well-known formula, that decedent would have had to drink seven or eight bottles of beer to produce such percentage, though there was also testimony that group drank four bottles of beer apiece. Baltimore County v. State, Use of Keenan, 193 A. 2d 30, 232 Md. 350.

Showing of consent procedures limited to criminal actions

Statutory procedure for presenting option of consent or refusal to an operator suspected of driving under the influence of intoxicants and resultant statutory presumptions relate to criminal prosecutions for the offense of driving under the influence of intoxicating liquor, and statute has no application to admissibility of results of blood samples in civil actions against operator. Quesnel v. Raleigh, 1969, 258 A.2d 840, 128 Vt. 95.

23. For discussion of lay opinion as to intoxication generally, see § 430.1 at fn. 20.

24. Cal.—Tracy v. Brecht, 39 P.2d 498, 3 Cal.App.2d 105.

Or.—Bailey v. Rhodes, 276 P.2d 713, 202 Or. 511.

25. Cal.—Tracy v. Brecht, 39 P.2d 498, 3 Cal.App.2d 105.

26. U.S.—Gaynor v. Atlantic Greyhound Corp., C.A.Pa., 183 F.2d 482.

Ala.—Ayers v. State, 1972, 267 So. 2d 533, 48 Ala.App. 743 (that first police officer arrived at scene about 15 minutes after accident had occurred, that defendant was injured and effectively trapped in automobile at time of first officer's arrival, and that no alcoholic beverages were found in or around defendant's automobile, justified inference that defendant could not have had access to alcohol during that period of time and admission of first police officer's testimony that defendant's breath smelled of alcohol was not error); Kingry v. McCardle, 1957, 98 So.2d 44, 266 Ala. 533.

Cal.—Lusardi v. Prukop, 2 P.2d 870, 116 Cal.App. 506 (but form of proof questioned); Barrett v. Harman, 1 P.2d 458, 115 Cal.App. 283.

Idaho.—Maier v. Minidoka County Motor Co., 105 P.2d 1076, 61 Idaho 642.

Kan.—Cox v. Kellogg's Sales Co., 95 P.2d 531, 150 Kan. 561 (fact that the trial court eventually ruled out the testimony and instructed jury to disregard it did not constitute error where there was no testimony leading to the belief that the use of intoxicating liquors in any way caused the accident).

§ 427.3   TRIAL EVIDENCE   Ch. 427

It has been held that evidence of the presence of liquor in an automobile is inadmissible [27] and that evidence of the finding

Ky.—Tingle v. Foster, 399 S.W.2d 475.

Minn.—Knutson v. Farmers' Co-op. Creamery of Jenkins, 230 N.W. 270, 180 Minn. 116.

Mo.—Cheatham v. Chartrau, 176 S. W.2d 865, 237 Mo.App. 793 (competent when coupled with evidence that automobile was zigzagging as it approached point of collision and driver had his head drooped over steering wheel).

N.C.—Smith v. Kilburn, 1973, 196 S.E.2d 588, 18 N.C.App. 204, certiorari denied 198 S.E.2d 723, 283 N.C. 754.

Neb.—Nisi v. Checker Cab Co., 105 N.W.2d 523, 171 Neb. 49.

Tenn.—Burkett v. Johnston, 282 S.W. 2d 647, 39 Tenn.App. 276.

Va.—Hughes v. Moore, 1973, 197 S. E.2d 214, 214 Va. 27; Myers v. Sutton, 1972, 189 S.E.2d 336, 213 Va. 59; Marshall v. Shaw, 1955, 85 S.E.2d 223, 196 Va. 678.

Wash.—Garcia v. Moran, 1938, 77 P. 2d 988, 194 Wash. 328.

W.Va.—Lawrence v. Nelson, 1960, 113 S.E.2d 241, 145 W.Va. 134.

Properly excluded

Ky.—Allen v. Gentry, 340 S.W.2d 452 (properly declined to let jury hear testimony that plaintiff smelled of alcohol while in automobile with one of the defendant drivers and others shortly after the accident, in view of fact such testimony was insufficient to disclose drinking on the part of her or those riding with her, and in view of fact none of the testimony sought to be introduced was indicative of wantonness or gross negligence).

Ohio.—Morris v. Stone, 1972, 292 N. E.2d 891, 33 Ohio App.2d 101 (no abuse of discretion in trial court's refusal to permit plaintiffs to present testimony that would relate only to an odor of alcohol on breath of defendant with no indication that witness would otherwise testify as to condition of defendant).

27. Similar statement in prior edition **quoted by the court** in Smith v. Pine, 12 N.W.2d 236, 242, 234 Iowa 256.

Ark.—Oliver v. Miller, 396 S.W.2d 288, 239 Ark. 1043 (broken vodka bottle was properly excluded, where no testimony or allegations in pleadings were offered to the effect that driver had been drinking or was intoxicated and bottle was not found in automobile at place of accident but some five hours later at salvage yard to which it had been removed by other parties).

Ky.—McCulloch's Adm'r v. Abell's Adm'r, 115 S.W.2d 386, 272 Ky. 756.

Va.—Myers v. Sutton, 1972, 189 S.E. 2d 336, 213 Va. 59 (partially consumed can of beer under driver's seat).

Wash.—Girardi v. Union High School Dist. No. 1, Skagit County, 93 P. 2d 298, 200 Wash. 21.

But see

Where defendant's vehicle had allegedly struck pedestrian near left-hand shoulder of two-lane public roadway, that officer found a bottle cork in defendant's automobile that fit alcoholic beverage bottle discovered at scene and that paper on the cork meshed with that on neck of bottle, there was a reasonable nexus between officer's testimony and defendant. Smith v. Kilburn, 1973, 196

of a liquor bottle near the scene of an accident is also inadmissible, where there is no evidence as to the ownership or possession of the bottle before the accident.[28]

However, there are other decisions to the effect that evidence relating to the presence of liquor at the scene of an accident,[29] as well as evidence of the presence of liquor in the automobile,[30] is admissible.

S.E.2d 588, 18 N.C.App. 204, certiorari denied 198 S.E.2d 723, 283 N.C. 754.

28. **Iowa**—Johnston v. Calvin, 5 N. W.2d 840, 232 Iowa 531 (discretionary).

Ky.—Whitney v. Penick, 136 S.W.2d 570, 281 Ky. 474.

N.Y.—Wurtzman v. Kalinowski, 251 N.Y.S. 328, 233 App.Div. 187.

Tex.—Proctor v. R. T. Herrin Petroleum Transport Co., Civ.App., 322 S.W.2d 42, judgment affirmed 338 S.W.2d 422, 161 Tex. 222.

Absence of other evidence
Rejection of testimony to effect that bottle about half full of whisky-colored liquid lay on ground beneath the plaintiff when he was picked up, and that plaintiff's wife picked up other bottles from ground, was not abuse of discretion in absence of other evidence that plaintiff had been drinking. Smith v. Pine, 12 N.W.2d 236, 234 Iowa 256.

29. **Cal.**—Fenstermacher v. Johnson, 32 P.2d 1106, 138 Cal.App. 691.

Tex.—Brown v. Kirksey, Civ.App., 145 S.W.2d 217 (a beer can from which beer was running).

30. **Idaho**—Rosenberg v. Toetly, 1971, 489 P.2d 446, 94 Idaho 413 (photograph of ice chest which contained beer and whiskey bottles and which was in trunk of automobile was relevant as showing amount of alcohol consumed by driver).

Ill.—Boeker v. Grigg, 137 N.E.2d 503, 11 Ill.App.2d 368.

Ky.—Tingle v. Foster, 399 S.W.2d 475; Gream v. Miller, 1951, 243 S. W.2d 502 (half full bottle in car and breath smelled of liquor).

Minn.—Kouri v. Olson-Keogh Produce Co., 253 N.W. 98, 191 Minn. 101.

Or.—Larson v. Heintz Const. Co., 345 P.2d 835, 219 Or. 25 (permitting witness to testify that he saw the husband remove liquor from the automobile and place it behind a nearby log after the accident); Walker v. Penner, 227 P.2d 316, 190 Or. 542.

Tenn.—Burkett v. Johnston, 282 S.W. 2d 647, 39 Tenn.App. 276.

Admitted for limited purpose
Generally speaking, whether driver of one of vehicles involved in antecedent collisions had been drinking was immaterial to issue of defendant's humanitarian negligence in failing to stop before colliding with decedent's vehicle, but trooper's testimony as to location and condition of various vehicles was proper, and it was not error to permit, for purpose of testing thoroughness of trooper's investigation and observation, inquiry eliciting testimony that trooper had found beer in one such driver's vehicle; and, in any event, no prejudice resulted to plaintiff who had read into evidence deposition containing statement that deponent had noticed beer bottle in such driver's vehicle. Eddings v. Keller, Mo., 400 S.W.2d 164.

§ 427.3 TRIAL EVIDENCE Ch. 427

Evidence that a passenger was intoxicated at the time of the accident can not be used as proof that the driver was intoxicated.[31]

While a drunken person has as much right to a safe street as a sober one, evidence of the intoxication of one at the time of being injured in an automobile collision is relevant on the issue of contributory negligence, tending to show heedless exposure of self to injury.[32]

If, however, an allegedly negligent driver was not intoxicated or driving while under the influence of liquor at the time of an accident, the fact of having taken a drink has been held to have no bearing on the question of negligence.[33]

31. **Cited by the court** in Crosby v. Sande, N.D.1970, 180 N.W.2d 164, 173.
Okl.—Jackson v. Veach, 237 P.2d 899, 205 Okl. 329.

32. Cal.—Brkljaca v. Ross, 213 P. 290, 60 Cal.App. 431.
Ky.—Whitney v. Penick, 136 S.W.2d 570, 281 Ky. 474.
Tex.—Southern Traction Co. v. Kirksey, Civ.App., 222 S.W. 702.

Not too remote
In action for death of pedestrian walking into side of defendants' truck, evidence of deceased's intoxication about 12 hours before accident was not inadmissible as too remote from time of accident. Drury v. Hagerstrom, 157 P.2d 878, 68 Cal. App.2d 742.

33. U.S.—Miles v. Ryan, C.A.Pa. 1973, 484 F.2d 1255 (under Pennsylvania law, while proof of intoxication is relevant where recklessness or careless driving is the matter at issue, the mere fact of drinking intoxicating liquor is not admissible unless it reasonably establishes a degree of intoxication which proves unfitness to drive); Gensemer v. Williams, C.A.Pa.1970, 419 F.2d 1361; Rosa v. City of Chester, Pa., C.A.Pa., 278 F.2d 876 (purchase of whiskey and consumption of 3 glasses of beer more than 5 hours earlier); Parker v. Reading Co., D.C.Pa., 1965, 244 F.Supp. 494, reversed on other grounds but also questioned 363 F.2d 608.

Ill.—Gilberto v. Nordtvedt, 1971, 274 N.E.2d 139, 1 Ill.App.3d 677 (that defendant's decedent had had one can of beer at party just prior to accident should have been stricken but introduction of such irrelevant evidence was insufficient cause for reversal in light of fact that there was no attempt to show, by innuendo or inference, that decedent had been intoxicated); Warp v. Whitmore, 1970, 260 N.E.2d 45, 123 Ill.App.2d 157.

Mo.—Doisy v. Edwards, 1966, 398 S.W.2d 846 (exclude testimony as to smell of liquor on breath).

N.J.—Maladowitz v. Coley, 219 A.2d 177, 47 N.J. 55 (reference to liquor allegedly drunk by motorist was relevant only if liquor allegedly affected ability of motorist to drive).

Pa.—Kriner v. McDonald, 1973, 302 A.2d 392, 223 Pa.Super. 531 (unless show "copious drinking" or intoxication); Brazel v. McMurray, 1961, 171 A.2d 151, 404 Pa. 188 (only if driving recklessly); Fisher v. Dye, 125 A.2d 472, 386 Pa. 141 (unless it reasonably establishes a degree of intoxication which proves unfitness to drive); Critzer v. Donovan, 137 A. 665, 289 Pa. 381.

Wash.—Cameron v. Boone, 383 P.2d 277, 62 Wash.2d 420 (where only offer of proof was that person who had talked to motorist at scene of accident would say that motorist had some liquor on his breath and had admitted having had a drink).

Not mere presence in bar

Admission of evidence that defendant had been in "after-hours" bar immediately prior to accident was erroneous and prejudicial in absence of evidence that defendant was intoxicated or had been drinking. Morreale v. Prince, 1969, 258 A.2d 508, 436 Pa. 51.

Where gross negligence at issue

If driver is not so intoxicated that his ability to drive is impaired, proof of his prior consumption of alcohol is not relevant to gross negligence under the guest statute. Jenson v. Spencer, 1974, 525 P.2d 153, 269 Or. 411.

Chapter 428

RELEVANCY AND MATERIALITY—PERSONS LIABLE

Table of Sections

Sec.
428.1 Proof of Ownership and Control.
428.2 Proof of Agency Relationship.
428.3 Proof of Operation Within Scope of Agency.
428.4 Family Purpose Doctrine.

§ 428.1 Proof of Ownership and Control

Library References:

C.J.S. Motor Vehicles § 516.
West's Key No. Digests, Automobiles ⟸243(2).

Evidence tending to prove the identity of the driver of a vehicle is admissible on that issue.[1]

Identity of car involved

Evidence probative in identifying the car involved is admissible.[2]

1. **Ala.**—Shirley v. Shirley, 73 So.2d 77, 261 Ala. 100 (evidence that defendant's intestate was driving when such intestate and such minor started on trip, a few minutes before accident, was admissible on question as to who was driving at time of accident).

   Fla.—Stettler v. Huggins, App., 134 So.2d 534 (evidence that driver's license found in wallet of driver was issued to person to whom defendants had entrusted their automobile for purpose of having it driven from Virginia to Florida, and that hospital records showed that driver treated was same person as one to whom automobile had been entrusted, should have been admitted on issue of identity of driver).

   Ga.—Jones v. Britt, 42 S.E.2d 648, 75 Ga.App. 142 (articles owned by defendant found at scene).

   Or.—Stuart v. Kelsay, 1972, 494 P.2d 249, 261 Or. 326 (in action wherein issue was whether plaintiff's decedent or defendant's decedent had been driving automobile belonging to plaintiff's decedent, evidence of alcoholic blood level in decedents' bodies was admissible as fact of alcohol in blood of one was consistent with contention he was the one who drove in an apparent reckless fashion).

   Tex.—Denham v. Smith, Civ.App. 1953, 258 S.W.2d 419 (papers bearing name of defendant found in vehicle).

   Va.—Breeding v. Johnson, 1968, 159 S.E.2d 836, 208 Va. 652 (that blood, blond hair, and flesh were found in area where decedent sat when last seen before death in accident was admissible).

2. **Ala.**—Cargall v. Riley, 95 So. 821, 209 Ala. 183.

A witness may be permitted to testify as to vehicles in the vicinity of an accident at the time thereof and that a vehicle so present answered to the general description of defendant's car.[3]

Evidence as to the condition of defendant's car, at dates prior to and after the accident, is admissible for the purpose of showing that it was impossible for the car to have been present at the time and place of the accident.[4]

Testimony that broken auto parts were found near the scene of the accident thereafter is properly admitted to show the identity of the automobile involved.[5]

Evidence concerning the pursuit and capture of a motorist may be admissible for the purpose of identifying the car as the one involved in a collision.[6]

Ownership of vehicle

As elsewhere stated,[7] the presumption of ownership of a motor vehicle involved in an accident may arise from certain proven facts. Hence any evidence of facts giving rise to such presumption, or from which any inference of ownership may be drawn, is admissible.

The plaintiff may introduce evidence as to remarks or admissions of the defendant relating to ownership,[8] evidence as to

---

Mass.—Perrott v. Leahy, 19 N.E.2d 10, 302 Mass. 318 (inquiry of witness having seen trucks bearing defendant's name improper, where not shown defendants' truck bore their name).

N.C.—Morgan v. Bell Bakeries, Inc., 98 S.E.2d 464, 246 N.C. 429 (where it was alleged that accident was caused by driver of bakery truck, evidence relating to delivery of bread by other bakeries, testimony of their drivers with respect to their times of delivery at store and description of trucks used in making deliveries, was properly admitted).

Tex.—Richardson v. Impey, Civ.App., 94 S.W.2d 490, error dismissed (testimony as to number of vehicles with blue tool boxes held inadmissible).

3. U.S.—Melville v. State of Md. to Use of Morris, C.C.A.Md., 155 F.2d 440.

Ill.—Walsh v. Murray, 43 N.E.2d 562, 315 Ill.App. 664.

N.J.—Reilly v. Lobdell, 1926, 134 A. 834, 103 N.J.L. 200.

Pa.—O'Malley v. Public Ledger Co., 101 A. 94, 257 Pa. 17.

4. N.Y.—Chrominsky v. Piehl, Sup., 171 N.Y.S. 36.

5. Mich.—Zolton v. Rotter, 32 N.W. 2d 30, 321 Mich. 1.

6. Ark.—Duckworth v. Stephens, 30 S.W.2d 840, 182 Ark. 161.

7. See § 417.5 on Presumptions.

8. Ala.—Feore v. Trammel, 104 So. 808, 213 Ala. 293 (no matter to whom they are made, and without regard to their connection with possession or other concrete act of ownership).

Cal.—Lowmiller v. Monroe, Lyon & Miller, Inc., 282 P. 537, 101 Cal.

§ 428.1   TRIAL EVIDENCE   Ch. 428

the name and insignia on the vehicle,[9] evidence that defendant has taken out insurance against damage to the vehicle or liability through its operation,[10] and any other proof manifesting proprietorship.[11]

App. 147; Hammond v. Hazard, 180 P. 46, 40 Cal.App. 45 (evidence that at the time of the accident the defendant remarked, "my car is hurt just as much as the other car,"); Henderson v. Northam, 168 P. 1044, 176 Cal. 493 (silence when in the presence of statements by another).

Mo.—Latham v. Hosch, 233 S.W. 84, 207 Mo.App. 381.

Ohio—Goz v. Tenney, 136 N.E. 215, 104 Ohio St. 500.

Tex.—Holton v. Hutchinson, Civ. App., 90 S.W.2d 1103.

9. Same statement in prior edition **cited by the court** in Dufresne v. Cooper, 11 A.2d 3, 64 R.I. 120, in connection with the question of whether evidence that defendant's name appeared on automobile prima facie proved ownership.

U.S.—Callas v. Independent Taxi Owners Ass'n, 66 F.2d 192, 62 App. D.C. 212, certiorari denied 54 S.Ct. 89, 290 U.S. 669, 78 L.Ed. 578.

Cal.—Henderson v. Northam, 168 P. 1044, 176 Cal. 493.

Ky.—Lever Bros. Co. v. Stapleton, 233 S.W.2d 1002, 313 Ky. 837.

10. **Ark.**—Pollock Stores Co. v. Chatwell, 90 S.W.2d 213, 192 Ark. 83.

Cal.—Perry v. A. Paladini, Inc., 264 P. 580, 89 Cal.App. 275.

Fla.—Barnett v. Butler, App., 112 So.2d 907.

Ill.—Rhoden v. Peoria Creamery Co., 278 Ill.App. 452 (testimony as to insurance competent to show party was operating truck); Watson v. Trinz, 274 Ill.App. 379.

Iowa—Bash v. Hade, 62 N.W.2d 180, 245 Iowa 332.

Mass.—Lekarczyk v. Dupre, 163 N.E. 642, 265 Mass. 33; Marsh v. Beraldi, 157 N.E. 347, 260 Mass. 225.

Mich.—Layton v. Cregan & Mallory Co., 248 N.W. 539, 263 Mich. 30.

Minn.—Frye v. Anderson, 80 N.W.2d 593, 248 Minn. 478.

Mo.—Paepke v. Stadelman, 300 S.W. 845, 222 Mo.App. 346; Vaughn v. William F. Davis & Sons, App., 221 S.W. 782.

Tex.—Harper v. Highway Motor Freight Lines, Civ.App., 89 S.W.2d 448.

11. **U.S.**—Newell v. Harold Shaffer Leasing Co., Inc., C.A.Miss.1974, 489 F.2d 103 (insurance draft bearing the name of defendant company "et al." was admissible); Colby v. Long, C.A.Ohio 1961, 289 F.2d 137; Bettinger v. Northwestern Nat. Cas. Co., C.A.Minn., 213 F.2d 200, certiorari denied 75 S.Ct. 80, 348 U.S. 856, 99 L.Ed. 674.

Idaho.—Franklin v. Wooters, 1935, 45 P.2d 804, 55 Idaho 619.

Md.—Brawner v. Hooper, 1926, 135 A. 420, 151 Md. 579.

Mass.—Roselli v. Riseman, 182 N.E. 567, 280 Mass. 338 (defendant was rightly required to answer whether he owned automobile).

Minn.—Carey v. Broadway Motors, Inc., 91 N.W.2d 753, 253 Minn. 333; Frye v. Anderson, 80 N.W.2d 593, 248 Minn. 478; Holmes v. Lilygren Motor Co., 1937, 275 N.W. 416, 201 Minn. 44 (giving bill of sale as security).

Mo.—Vaughn v. William F. Davis & Sons, App., 221 S.W. 782 (settled claim for prior accident involving same vehicle).

N.J.—Yohannan v. Benisch, 135 A. 876, 103 N.J.L. 462 (mortgaging vehicle).

A chattel mortgage,[12] or a bill of sale,[13] covering the automobile involved may be introduced as documentary proof of ownership.[14] The same is true as to public records which show that the license number issued to the defendant corresponds to the number observed on the car which caused an accident.[15] A copy of a certificate of title or license receipt,[16] or a certificate of registration,[17] which is taken from public records, and which designates the vehicle involved as belonging to defendant, is admissible.

When the accident occurs during the period of time in which the vehicle is being sold by one party to another, or is being repossessed by a lien holder, all evidence bearing upon the intentions of the parties, with particular reference to compliance with state laws regulating the transfer of title in motor vehicles, is admissible, unless precluded by statutory rules as to conclusiveness of vehicle title documents.[18]

Ohio.—Harmon v. Liberty Cabs, App. 1949, 96 N.E.2d 304, 58 O.L.A. 286 (admission in pleadings).

But see

Cal.—Walker v. Nelson, 53 P.2d 977, 11 Cal.App.2d 297.

Unloading vehicle after accident
Where it appeared that transport truck was owned by defendant's son, but that it was being used to haul hay for defendant at time of collision, admission of testimony of witness who had helped unload the hay on day following collision, that he had been employed by defendant to aid in unloading was proper. Highway Ins. Underwriters v. Nichols, 255 P.2d 263, 208 Okl. 244.

12. N.J.—Yohannan v. Benisch, 135 A. 876, 103 N.J.L. 462.

13. Ky.—Gayheart v. Smith, 42 S.W.2d 877, 240 Ky. 596.

14. Same statement in prior edition **cited by the court** in Sexton v. Lauman, 57 N.W.2d 200, 202, 244 Iowa 670, 37 A.L.R.2d 353.

15. Ky.—Lever Bros. Co. v. Stapleton, 233 S.W.2d 1002, 313 Ky. 837.

Md.—East Baltimore Transfer Co. v. Goeb, 118 A. 74, 140 Md. 534.

16. Ala.—Macon County Lumber Co. v. Jones, 110 So. 1, 215 Ala. 157.

Fla.—Wilson v. Burke, 53 So.2d 319.

17. Mass.—Trombley v. Stevens-Duryea Co., 92 N.E. 764, 206 Mass. 516.

N.J.—Bodner v. Phoenix Indemnity Co., 168 A. 442, 111 N.J.L. 264.

N.C.—Jyachosky v. Wensil, 81 S.E.2d 644, 240 N.C. 217.

18. U.S.—Mason v. Automobile Finance Co., 121 F.2d 32, 73 App. D.C. 284.

Cal.—Ferroni v. Pacific Finance Corp. of California, 135 P.2d 569, 21 Cal.2d 773 (in action involving question whether automobile dealers or finance corporation was owner of automobile involved, exclusion of evidence of course of business dealings between dealers and finance corporation tending to establish that finance corporation was authorized by dealers to execute conditional contracts of sale on behalf of such dealers was prejudicial error).

Iowa.—Bash v. Hade, 55 N.W.2d 278, 244 Iowa 272 (in determining whether dealer or alleged purchas-

§ 428.1   TRIAL EVIDENCE   Ch. 428

The fact that the defendant applied for a license to operate the particular vehicle which caused the accident in question is a circumstance tending to prove ownership.[19] Therefore the application, or the record thereof, is generally admissible.[20]

§ 428.2   Proof of Agency Relationship

Library References:
C.J.S. Agency § 315 et seq.; Motor Vehicles § 516.
West's Key No. Digests, Automobiles ⬳243(12); Principal and Agent ⬳18 et seq.

On the question of the agency of the driver of an automobile for another, all evidence bearing on the driver's status is gen-

er owned automobile, that automobile was registered in name of dealer, that if there had been a sale dealer had not complied with federal reserve bank regulation pertaining to limitation of extension of credit, and that dealer had mortgage on automobile were facts to be considered by jury).

Ohio.—Fredericks v. Birkett L. Williams Co., 40 N.E.2d 162, 68 Ohio App. 217 (in action against dealer for damages arising out of operation of an automobile by dealer's sales manager, evidence showing that sales manager, prior to driving automobile, had completed purchase of automobile, but had not received a certificate of title, was incompetent to show title in sales manager because of certificate of title laws, but was competent to rebut presumption that automobile was being driven under authority of and in business of dealer).

But see

Ga.—Brown v. Bridges, 71 S.E.2d 665, 86 Ga.App. 455.

Proof not owner

In absence of causal connection between defendant's violation of statute imposing penalty for misrepresenting a material fact on an application for a certificate of ownership of a motor vehicle and accident involving automobile to which defend-

ant was registered owner, defendant was not precluded, in action arising from such accident, from introducing evidence showing that he was not owner. Gams v. Oberholtzer, 310 P.2d 240, 50 Wash.2d 174.

19. Same statement in prior edition **cited by the court** in Easley v. Roberts, La.App., 25 So.2d 245, 247.

Ala.—Windham v. Newton, 76 So. 24, 200 Ala. 258.

20. **Mo.**—Hufft v. Daugherty, 171 S.W. 17, 184 Mo.App. 374 (application required by the statute for the license number borne by the car causing the injury is admissible, although it was for a different year and for a different car).

Effect of statute

Statute, providing that certified copies of records of registrar of motor vehicles were admissible as evidence to prove facts contained therein, covered application for registration of truck, including statement of fact therein relating to ownership of truck, even though such statement was not in nature of admission against interest of person making statement. G.L.(Ter.Ed.) c. 90, § 30. Burns v. Winchell, 25 N.E. 2d 752, 305 Mass. 276.

Not application for dealer plates

Or.—Ramp v. Osborne, 239 P. 112, 115 Or. 672.

erally admissible.[21] Any evidence showing under what circumstances and for what purpose the automobile in question was de-

21. For general discussion of the admissibility of statements of the agent, see Chapter 434, Hearsay, § 434.5.

Similar statements in prior edition **cited by the court** in Davison v. Farr, Mo.App., 273 S.W.2d 500, 504; Keitz v. National Paving & Contracting Co., 134 A.2d 296, 303, 214 Md. 479.

U.S.—Spillers v. Tri-State Glass Lined Storage, Inc., C.A.Ind., 325 F.2d 322 (nature of ownership, use and storage of equipment and methods of assigning work to be done, circumstances attending scene of accident when operator called on defendant's superintendent as his "boss man," observation of operator in and about defendant's premises, pay records, the fact that, contrary to contract terms, alleged independent contractor did not do all work called for by contract, and methods of payment used, which were not disclosed in contract).

Ala.—York v. Chandler, 109 So.2d 921, 40 Ala.App. 58, certiorari denied 109 So.2d 925, 268 Ala. 700 (testimony that defendant told plaintiff to get two estimates of his damage and that when estimates were presented to him he stated he thought they were too high); Lowe v. Poole, 179 So. 536, 235 Ala. 441 (evidence which tended to show that one who engaged truck, and that one who directed pickers where to sit were in farmer's employ).

Ariz.—Maynard v. Hall, 143 P.2d 884, 61 Ariz. 32, 150 A.L.R. 618 (payment of fine for driver).

Cal.—Taylor v. Oakland Scavenger Co., 110 P.2d 1044, 17 Cal.2d 594 (contract between alleged master and third party, on issue of independent contractor).

Conn.—Muraszki v. William L. Clifford, Inc., 26 A.2d 578, 129 Conn. 123 (letter written by defendant's secretary stating that agent was no longer in defendant's employ, and policy covering insured's liability from occasional and not frequent operation of automobile in insured's business and naming agent as employee, were admissible for such evidential value as they had); Chouinard v. Wooldridge, 1925, 127 A. 908, 102 Conn. 66 (subsequent business relationship).

Ga.—White v. Morris, 1966, 152 S.E. 2d 417, 114 Ga.App. 618 (evidence of indirect control of work); Braun v. Georgia Kaolin Co., 1939, 4 S.E. 2d 100, 60 Ga.App. 347 (authority over manner of work not relevant); American Fidelity & Casualty Co. v. McWilliams, 191 S.E. 191, 55 Ga. App. 658.

Ill.—Tarka v. Pratt, 257 Ill.App. 403.

Ind.—Jones v. Furlong, 97 N.E.2d 369, 121 Ind.App. 279 (lease of truck was properly admitted for purpose of determining relation of truck operator to defendant lessor).

Ky.—Wilson v. Deegan's Adm'r, 139 S.W.2d 58, 282 Ky. 547 (use of vehicle by employee to go to lunch saved time); Lever Bros. Co. v. Stapleton, 1950, 233 S.W.2d 1002, 313 Ky. 837.

Md.—Maryland Cas. Co. v. Sause, 57 A.2d 801, 190 Md. 135 (owned vehicle driven by alleged independent contractor).

Mass.—Garfield v. Smith, 59 N.E.2d 287, 317 Mass. 674, certiorari denied 65 S.Ct. 1568, 1569, 325 U.S. 879, 89 L.Ed. 1995 (not I.C.C. rulings as to form of vehicle lease).

Mich.—New York Cent. R. Co. v. Michigan Milk Producers Ass'n, 143 N.W.2d 590, 3 Mich.App. 648 (termination of its relationship with owner of truck after accident

§ 428.2

was material on issue of relationship); DeCorte v. New York Cent. R. Co., 140 N.W.2d 479, 377 Mich. 317 (evidence of terminating relationship).

Mo.—Davison v. Farr, App., 273 S.W. 2d 500 (contract relating to driving was executed by alleged principals).

Mont.—Welch v. Nepstad, 337 P.2d 14, 135 Mont. 65 (particulars covering entire periods of time that driver of truck had worked for or had been employed by defendants and also to inquire into his rate of wage or pay and as to whether he was employed by month or otherwise).

Neb.—Dirks v. Ensign Omnibus & Transfer Co., 1922, 186 N.W. 525, 107 Neb. 556 (driver recently in employ and acting in manner as before).

N.Y.—Locasto v. Manning, Bowman & Co., 295 N.Y.S. 317, 251 App. Div. 21.

Ohio.—Leonard v. Kreider, 1 N.E.2d 956, 51 Ohio App. 474 (evidence concerning identification card and placards on truck after accident).

Pa.—Middle Atlantic Transp. Co. v. Keiser, 57 Dauph. 172.

Tenn.—Pratt v. Duck, 191 S.W.2d 562, 28 Tenn.App. 502 (deed conveying cotton gin to defendant admissible on question of agency of driver of truck operated for cotton gin).

Tex.—Newspapers, Inc. v. Love, Civ. App., 397 S.W.2d 469, ref. n. r. e. (evidence as to control exercised); Christopher v. City of El Paso, Civ.App., 98 S.W.2d 394; Ochoa v. Winerich Motor Sales Co., 1936, 94 S.W.2d 416, 127 Tex. 542, reversing 58 S.W.2d 193, and remanding cause for further consideration, Civ.App., 98 S.W.2d 235; Wells v. Henderson, Civ.App., 78 S. W.2d 683 (employer had said employee was agent of company, and as to conversation had by superintendent with employer in which employer said company had nothing to worry about accident).

Effect of statute

Defendant was not entitled to show that defendant's consent to servant's operation of truck was limited to servant's normal working time and confined to truck's normal route in course of his employment, in view of statute providing that one operating another's motor vehicle with owner's consent shall be deemed owner's agent in case of accident. Baker v. Rhode Island Ice Co., 50 A.2d 618, 72 R.I. 262.

Held not probative

Where provisions of construction contract between State Highway Department and general contractor did not have any probative value on critical issue whether general contractor had vicarious liability for negligence of driver and owner of nonowned truck, it was error to admit such contract's provisions into evidence in action against general contractor and others. Ben M. Hogan Co., Inc. v. Nichols, 1973, 496 S.W.2d 404, 254 Ark. 771. In subcontractor's employee's action against general contractor, testimony tending to show that owner and possibly driver of allegedly offending truck did not on date of collision have certificate of authority as contract hauler from state transportation commission as required under Motor Carrier Act was properly admitted on issue whether general contractor had vicarious liability for negligence of driver of such truck, even though other operators neglected to obtain such certificates and notwithstanding evidence that such truck had been hired to different people at different times. Id.

May rebut presumption

Statute under which registration creates presumption of owner's responsibility did not preclude admission of testimony dealing with lack

livered to the driver should be admitted.[22] In the trial of the cause the alleged agent may be interrogated as to the name of the employer and the nature of the alleged agent's duties.[23]

On the issue of whether a driver was an agent or employee of an automobile owner, or an independent contractor, a written contract between the driver and the owner was admissible,[24] as of driver's agency. Segal v. Yates, 1969, 253 N.E.2d 841, 356 Mass. 449.

Not proof of common ownership of stock

Ala.—Brown v. Standard Casket Mfg. Co., 175 So. 358, 234 Ala. 512.

Right of control critical

Excluding questions on direct examination of driver whether he was to get any special instructions while on the job was not error where the controlling question was not whether the driver was subject to the defendant's instructions while on the job but whether the defendant had any right to control the driver while operating the automobile at the time of the accident. Shea v. Bryant Chucking & Grinder Co., 145 N.E.2d 692, 336 Mass. 312.

Self serving statements

Evidence as to instructions given servant by employer loaning servant to another was inadmissible as self-serving. Balcus v. Sterling Exp. Co., 51 A.2d 479, 94 N.H. 270.

Telephone conversation with defendant's manager

Testimony of plaintiff's husband, that man at defendant's office answering telephone on husband's request for manager told husband defendant had report of accident, held competent, as bearing on relation between driver and defendant, without further identification of manager. Ogland v. Detroit Edison Co., 246 N.W. 503, 261 Mich. 583.

22. **U.S.**—Callas v. Independent Taxi Owners' Ass'n, 66 F.2d 192, 62 App.D.C. 212, certiorari denied 54 S.Ct. 89, 290 U.S. 669, 78 L.Ed. 578; Rhone v. Try Me Cab Co., 65 F.2d 834, 62 App.D.C. 201.

Dist.Col.—Nash v. Holzbeierlein & Sons, Mun.App., 68 A.2d 403 (evidence as to details of claimed bailment relationship between owner and driver).

Ind.—McDonald v. Swanson, 1 N.E. 2d 684, 103 Ind.App. 171 (ordinance requiring taxicab owners to obtain licenses).

Ky.—Packard-Louisville Motor Co. v. O'Neal, 58 S.W.2d 630, 248 Ky. 438.

Tex.—Coca-Cola Bottling Co. v. Krueger, Civ.App., 239 S.W.2d 669.

23. **Cal.**—Kelley v. R. F. Jones Co., 1969, 77 Cal.Rptr. 170, 272 Cal. App.2d 113; Shields v. Oxnard Harbor Dist., 116 P.2d 121, 46 Cal. App.2d 477.

Ind.—Zoludow v. Keeshin Motor Express, 34 N.E.2d 980, 109 Ind.App. 575 (when called to testify as to nature and character of employment by defendant at time of accident).

24. **Ill.**—Hartley v. Red Ball Transit Co., 176 N.E. 751, 344 Ill. 534.

Iowa.—Sanford v. Goodridge, 13 N. W.2d 40, 234 Iowa 1036 (admissible to show amount of independence granted).

Contract with third party

In action against contractor, to recover for injuries sustained when a third party's truck, which was removing surplus soil, backed into children lawfully on street, contract with town was inadmissible except that part relating to contractor's duty to remove surplus soil in the event con-

§ 428.2 TRIAL EVIDENCE Ch. 428

well as the daily report sheets and pay rolls of the owner.[25]

An agent's license to do business may be pertinent to show the status.[26]

The payment of an expense account submitted by an employee may be offered in evidence to show authority to use a car in the furtherance of the employer's business, and such payment after an accident is evidence of ratification of the use of a car on the part of the employer.[27]

Where defendant contends that a third person who owned, or was driving, the vehicle in question was an independent contractor, the financial responsibility of such third person may be shown.[28]

The carrying of liability or indemnity insurance by defendant, or by some third person, may generally be proved as throwing light on the relationship between defendant and a negligent driver.[29]

tractor denied obligation to remove soil. Bucci v. Butler, 53 A.2d 705, 73 R.I. 60.

25. **Ark.**—Terry Dairy Co. v. Parker, 223 S.W. 6, 144 Ark. 401.

26. **Ky.**—American Sav. Life Ins. Co. v. Riplinger, 60 S.W.2d 115, 249 Ky. 8 (in action against insurance company for agent's operation of automobile, proof of agent's license is pertinent only to show relationship with company).

27. **Pa.**—Gallagher v. Fleetwood, 97 P.L.J. 111.

28. **U.S.**—Eldridge v. McGeorge, C.C.A.Ark., 99 F.2d 835.

29. **U.S.**—Lawrence v. Vail, D.C.S.D., 166 F.Supp. 777; Eldridge v. McGeorge, C.C.A.Ark., 99 F.2d 835 (truck being used in work done under government contract); McCoy v. Universal Carloading & Distributing Co., C.C.A.Ohio, 82 F.2d 342; Callas v. Independent Taxi Owners' Ass'n, 66 F.2d 192, 62 App.D.C. 212, certiorari denied 54 S.Ct. 89, 290 U.S. 669, 78 L.Ed. 578, see note 40.

Ark.—Ozan Lumber Co. v. McNeely, 217 S.W.2d 341, 214 Ark. 657, 8 A.L.R.2d 261 (workmen's compensation insurance on truck driver); Delamar & Allison v. Ward, 41 S.W.2d 760, 184 Ark. 82 (contractor carrying indemnity or liability insurance on account of truck but claiming driver was independent contractor).

Ind.—Van Drake v. Thomas, 38 N.E.2d 878, 110 Ind.App. 586 (where salesman was working on a salary and commission basis at time automobile liability policy containing "employer's Nonownership Liability Endorsement" was issued, but the policy was not canceled subsequent to time when salesman began working on a straight commission); McDonald v. Swanson, 1 N.E.2d 684, 103 Ind.App. 171 (agency of taxicab driver).

Md.—Snowhite v. State, Use of Tennant, 1966, 221 A.2d 342, 243 Md. 291.

Miss.—Luke Const. Co. v. Jernigan, 172 So.2d 392, 252 Miss. 9.

Mo.—McAboy v. Hulett, App., 112 S.W.2d 86.

Ohio.—Kraemer v. Bates Motor Transport Lines, 11 N.E.2d 105, 56 Ohio App. 427 (compensation policy); Leonard v. Kreider, 1 N.E.

Ch. 428   PERSONS LIABLE   § 428.3

In an action against an occupant of a vehicle alleging that such occupant had "joint control" over the vehicle so as to be liable for the driver's negligence, the jury may consider the occupant's testimony concerning the directions and suggestions given to the driver.[30]

The general rule of exclusion of evidence of past similar occurrences includes evidence of prior trips to show joint enterprise,[31] or agency.[32]

§ 428.3 Proof of Operation Within Scope of Agency

Library References:
C.J.S. Agency § 317 et seq.; Motor Vehicles § 516.
West's Key No. Digests, Automobiles ⟐243(12); Principal and Agent ⟐118 et seq.

Evidence of various types has been held admissible on the issue whether the driver was acting within the scope of employment at the time of the accident.[33]

2d 956, 51 Ohio App. 474 (admission of "hired car endorsement" of transportation company's liability policy).

S.D.—Biggins v. Wagner, 245 N.W. 385, 60 S.D. 581, 85 A.L.R. 776 (evidence that truck driver took out liability policy covering automobile, for protection of himself and employer).

Tex.—Gladewater Laundry & Dry Cleaners v. Newman, Civ.App., 141 S.W.2d 951, error dismissed, judgment correct (workman's compensation insurance).

But see

In action against owner and driver, the owner's minor son, for injuries to occupant of automobile, who was also a minor and made weekly payments, which driver delivered to owner, for transportation to summer school in another city, admission of owner's liability policy, containing omnibus clause, and rider, reciting that automobile would be used "to carry school children to a summer school," was erroneous and prejudicial to defendants, as against contention that policy and rider showed that driver was owner's agent. Mc-

Aboy v. Hulett, Mo.App., 112 S.W.2d 86.

Held not probative

Mo.—Reiling v. Missouri Ins. Co., 153 S.W.2d 79, 236 Mo.App. 164.

30. **Ind.**—Jones v. Kasper, 33 N.E. 2d 816, 109 Ind.App. 465.

31. **Or.**—Brigham v. Munden, 19 P. 2d 1096, 142 Or. 471.

32. **Cal.**—Duff v. Schaefer Ambulance Service, 283 P.2d 91, 132 Cal. App.2d 655.

Tex.—Newspapers, Inc. v. Love, 380 S.W.2d 582 (testimony showing exercise of control by newspaper over previous district managers was incompetent to show actual control over district manager involved in collision as to details of work).

But see

Cal.—Blank v. Coffin, 126 P.2d 868, 20 Cal.2d 457.

Iowa.—Jones v. Sioux City, 170 N.W. 445, 185 Iowa 1178, 10 A.L.R. 474.

33. **Conn.**—Smith v. Firestone Tire & Rubber Co., 177 A. 524, 119

§ 428.3   TRIAL EVIDENCE   Ch. 428

Evidence is generally admissible, in proof of the scope of employment, to show what instructions were given by the defendant prior to an accident.[34]

Conn. 483 (testimony showing that salesman worked in evening selling defendant's tires was admissible for purpose of showing time of salesman's employment, though inadmissible to show agency, and, if collision occurred within time of his employment, such circumstance should be considered in deciding whether act was within scope).

Minn.—Schultz v. Swift & Co., 299 N.W. 7, 210 Minn. 533 (correspondence between employer and employee was relevant to show employer's reaction upon discovery of the facts of employee's personal use of the automobile, in determining whether such use was with employer's consent).

Miss.—Colotta v. Phillips, 85 So.2d 574, 226 Miss. 870 (drunken condition of the driver shortly after the accident and that he was still driving a truck for the employer at the time of trial).

S.D.—Alberts v. Mutual Service Cas. Ins. Co., 123 N.W.2d 96, 80 S.D. 303, citing C.J.S. Evidence §§ 780, 782 (absence of showing of written decision or other higher evidence that decision was made that Highway Commission's employee had acted properly in using his automobile for Commission's business, oral testimony that that decision had been made was admissible to show ratification of employee's act by Commission).

Daily log

In action arising out of Fort Worth collision between plaintiffs' automobile and defendant's truck, corporate defendant's driver's "daily log" reflecting that Fort Worth was his "destination or turn around point or place", was admissible and, as a business record, raised an inference that driver had been acting within scope of his employment at time of collision; but, in view of fact that form had not been prepared until morning following collision, it could be accorded no weight. Mosqueda v. Albright Transfer & Storage Co., Tex. Civ.App., 320 S.W.2d 867, writ of error refused n. r. e.

Evidence of good moral character

Where owner testified that chauffeur did not have authority to use her automobile at time of accident, admission of testimony of good moral character of chauffeur was error. Beach v. Richtmyer, 90 N.Y.S.2d 332, 275 App.Div. 466.

Not fact employer did not limit extension of courtesy

Or.—Albrecht v. Safeway Stores, 80 P.2d 62, 159 Or. 331.

Rule limited

In action against company, which operated concessions at auditorium and race track and which allegedly directed employee to drive from auditorium to race track, for injuries sustained when such employee while driving his automobile on route that led both to race track and to employee's home collided with automobile driven by plaintiff, sustaining of plaintiff's objections to question put to employee as to whether, if he had not been requested to stop by the race track he would have driven his automobile at same time and at same place where accident happened was proper where there was no evidence to show what time employee usually went home or whether he was on road earlier or later than usual because of direction to go to race track. Massey v. Berlo Vending Co., Mo., 329 S.W.2d 772.

34. **Cal.**—Hicks v. Reis, 134 P.2d 788, 21 Cal.2d 654 (used car sales-

A finding of order blanks of a salesman's employer in the automobile after an accident is a circumstance tending to show that the car was being used in furtherance of the employer's business when the accident occurred.[35]

Testimony of a witness who saw defendant's products in the defendant's vehicle was competent.[36]

Testimony of a prospective customer, whose home was so situated that the salesman could have been en route there when the accident occurred, was admissible.[37]

A driver's previous use of a vehicle for the same purpose for which it was being used at the time of an accident may be shown, on the issue of use within the scope of employment at such time.[38]

§ 428.4 Family Purpose Doctrine

Library References:
C.J.S. Motor Vehicles §§ 432 et seq., 514 et seq.
West's Key No. Digests, Automobiles ⇨195, 243.

Under the family purpose doctrine theory, evidence tending to prove that the vehicle was a "family car" is admissible.[39]

man use of vehicle for personal use, and discussion re same with fellow employee as bearing on issue of existence of rule against such use); Gordoy v. Flaherty, 72 P.2d 538, 9 Cal.2d 716 (failure to instruct employee against certain use not admissible in absence of employer of practice); Adams v. Wiesendanger, 150 P. 1016, 27 Cal. App. 590.

Ky.—Saunders' Ex'rs v. Armour & Co., 295 S.W. 1014, 220 Ky. 719 (forbidding use of car for private purpose).

Md.—Brawner v. Hooper, 135 A. 420, 151 Md. 579.

Minn.—Patterson-Stocking v. Dunn Bros. Storage Warehouses, 276 N. W. 737, 201 Minn. 308.

N.M.—Silva v. Haake, 245 P.2d 835, 56 N.M. 497.

N.Y.—Kelly v. Laundry Trucking Co., 79 N.Y.S.2d 771, 274 App.Div. 812; Baum v. Breslauer, Sup., 182 N.Y. S. 906.

Ohio.—Rad v. Gamble, 13 Ohio App. 488.

Tex.—Harris v. Levy, Civ.App., 217 S.W.2d 154.

35. **Ark.**—Mullins v. Ritchie Grocer Co., 35 S.W.2d 1010, 183 Ark. 218.

36. **Tenn.**—McMahan v. Tucker, 216 S.W.2d 356, 31 Tenn.App. 429.

37. **Mo.**—Mattan v. Hoover Co., 166 S.W.2d 557, 350 Mo. 506 (and that salesman had made appointment with unidentified prospect for about same time).

38. **Ind.**—Vincennes Packing Corporation v. Trosper, 23 N.E.2d 624, 108 Ind.App. 7.

Or.—Albrecht v. Safeway Stores, 80 P.2d 62, 159 Or. 331 (as tending to show that company knew or should have known of such practice).

39. **Conn.**—Nichols v. Nichols, 13 A.2d 591, 126 Conn. 614 (family member's not being licensed in state in which vehicle licensed).

§ **428.4**   TRIAL EVIDENCE   Ch. 428

Ga.—Belch v. Sprayberry, 101 S.E.2d 870, 97 Ga.App. 47 (that defendant-owner had made his truck available in some way to other members of his family was relevant on issue as to applicability of family car doctrine, as was fact that such vehicle had replaced a family purpose automobile).

Not fact of prior use of other owned vehicles

Minn.—Nicol v. Geitler, 247 N.W. 8, 188 Minn. 69.

N.C.—Eaves v. Coxe, 165 S.E. 345, 203 N.C. 173.

Chapter 429

RELEVANCY AND MATERIALITY—DAMAGES

Table of Sections

Sec.
429.1 Proof of Damages—Personal Injury.
429.2 ———— Property Damage.

§ 429.1 Proof of Damages—Personal Injury

Library References:
C.J.S. Damages § 146 et seq.; Evidence §§ 447, 546(9), 546(21) et seq., 546(91) et seq.
West's Key No. Digests, Damages ⚖︎166 et seq.; Evidence ⚖︎471(35), 477(3), 509 et seq.

In an action for personal injuries evidence of the force of the impact is admissible to indicate the extent of plaintiff's injuries, even if liability is admitted and the only issue to be tried is the amount of damages.[1]

1. **Cited by the court** in Kinney v. Smith, 1973, 508 P.2d 1234, 1236, 95 Idaho 328; and in Baltus v. Von der Lippe, 1972, 196 N.W.2d 922, 923, 293 Minn. 99.

Ala.—East Alabama Exp. Co. v. Dupes, 124 So.2d 809, 271 Ala. 504 (properly permitted to introduce evidence as to type of damage to automobile as result of the collision and that automobile could not be driven away after the collision, in order to show the force of the impact resulting in whiplash injury of passenger and fracture).

Cal.—Fuentes v. Tucker, 187 P.2d 752, 31 Cal.2d 1; Johnson v. McRee, 152 P.2d 526, 66 Cal.App.2d 524 (that she was struck in crosswalk and was either knocked or dragged for the distance which evidence indicated).

Colo.—Gourdin v. Waller, 1972, 495 P.2d 1142, 30 Colo.App. 498 (photographs of damaged vehicle and testimony regarding speed).

Fla.—Traud v. Waller, App.1973, 272 So.2d 19 (refusal to admit photographs and testimony, which related to force of impact, was reversible error).

Ill.—Phillips v. Lawrence, 1967, 230 N.E.2d 505, 87 Ill.App.2d 60 (although defendant admitted liability for injuries sustained by plaintiff whose automobile had been struck from behind, evidence that defendant had been traveling at speed in excess of 65 miles per hour when it struck plaintiff's automobile was admissible as having some bearing on extent of injuries suffered by plaintiff, and, in view of award of only $750 to plaintiff who had lost $200 in wages and incurred $170 in medical expenses, exclusion of such evidence required reversal).

Kan.—Howard v. Stoughton, 1967, 433 P.2d 567, 199 Kan. 787 (police

§ 429.1   TRIAL EVIDENCE   Ch. 429

officer's testimony which identified portion of motion picture showing only vehicles involved in collision, exhibits describing location of vehicles and distances they traveled after impact, and diagram and chart made from measurements at the scene, and which concerned skidmarks, braking speeds, reaction time, and opinion about speeds of the vehicles prior to collision was admissible to show nature and extent of damage to the vehicles and to establish foundation for consulting engineer's testimony describing the forces which he believed had been applied to plaintiff's body, in case wherein defendants admitted liability but vigorously contended that plaintiff's injury was not serious).

N.J.—Gambrell v. Zengel, 1970, 265 A.2d 823, 110 N.J.Super. 377 (court did not abuse discretion in admitting into evidence photographs of intersection and of the automobiles following the collision, and did not err in admitting testimony of investigating police officer as to location of debris at scene and as to distance traveled from alleged point of impact).

N.Y.—Rodriguez v. Zampella, 1973, 346 N.Y.S.2d 558, 42 A.D.2d 805.

Ohio.—Mikula v. Balogh, 1965, 224 N.E.2d 148, 9 Ohio App.2d 250 (expert opinion of speed based upon physical facts, even though speed violation not alleged as negligence; Camerlin v. Starr, App., 200 N.E.2d 817, 31 O.O.2d 39, 94 O.L.A. 225.

Tex.—Wright v. Alms, Civ.App., 368 S.W.2d 34.

Va.—Eubank v. Spencer, 128 S.E.2d 299, 203 Va. 923.

Wis.—Millay v. Milwaukee Auto. Mut. Ins. Co., 120 N.W.2d 103, 19 Wis.2d 330 (speed of vehicle).

Injuries of another

Mo.—Day v. Banks, App.1940, 143 S.W.2d 68 (two others).

Neb.—Jacobsen v. Poland, 80 N.W.2d 891, 163 Neb. 590 (testimony of wife of driver that when collision occurred she was thrown against and through windshield, and testimony of driver that he was shaken up and bruised on his side and knees, was proper).

Not injuries of another

Ill.—Waugh v. Cender, 173 N.E.2d 860, 29 Ill.App.2d 408 (improper and prejudicial to plaintiff to permit wife of a defendant who was called as witness for him to relate the nature and extent of her own injuries).

N.C.—Sanders v. George, 129 S.E.2d 480, 258 N.C. 776 (in actions for wrongful death of passengers, evidence of injuries sustained by defendant in accident was inadmissible).

Not market value difference

Evidence of difference in market value of automobile before and after collision was not admissible for purpose of showing force of impact, but introduction of such evidence did not constitute prejudicial error, where there was detailed testimony as to parts of vehicle damaged and parts repaired and also an admission on part of witness through whom testimony was offered that vehicle could have been repaired more cheaply than his statement as to difference in market value. Bower v. Murphy, 1969, 444 S.W.2d 883, 247 Ark. 238.

Rule limited

Force of collision is material fact to consider in determining whether any injury was sustained, but if it is established that some injury was sustained, force of collision should not be considered as a measure of damages. Jenkins v. Greyhound Lines, Inc., La.App.1968, 210 So.2d 390, writ refused 214 So.2d 161, 252 La. 837.

Ch. 429 DAMAGES § **429.1**

Evidence of the plaintiff's prior health and physical condition is admissible to determine the extent of the injury,[2] as is evidence

2. **U.S.**—Gee v. Owens-Illinois, Inc., C.A.Ga.1967, 384 F.2d 704 (testimony of doctor concerning visits to him by plaintiff prior to accident was admissible as relevant on issue whether plaintiff was in fact pregnant when injury occurred, notwithstanding fact that the testimony might have had prejudicial effect because of imputations of possible premarital pregnancy).

Cal.—Hall v. Superior Court In and For Alameda County, 1971, 97 Cal. Rptr. 879, 20 Cal.App.3d 652, hearing dismissed (in assaying contribution of collision to present state); Carney v. RKO Radio Pictures, 178 P.2d 482, 78 Cal.App.2d 659 (to determine cause of death).

Dist.Col.—Bill's Auto Rental v. Bonded Taxi Co., D.C.Mun.App., 72 A.2d 254.

Ill.—Kocimski v. Yellow Cab Co., 195 N.E.2d 745, 45 Ill.App.2d 288 (plaintiff's testimony that after release from hospital he "made 16 missions over Germany" was not prejudicial in action for injuries received subsequent to Air Force service referred to, where defendant had questioned plaintiff concerning facial scars and cheek bone depression resulting from prior injury for which he had been treated in hospital, and testimony was intended to rehabilitate plaintiff by showing that after hospital stay his health was such that he could actively participate as Air Force member).

Miss.—Walker v. Lamberson, 1971, 243 F.2d 410 (question whether people accused plaintiff of use of alcohol because she often fell due to dizziness was relevant).

Mo.—Rice v. Spindler, App.1973, 495 S.W.2d 688 (prior medical history was relevant in rear-end case in that it related to problems of the spine which was portion of the body also involved in case at trial, and fact that plaintiff was complaining of a neck injury at trial and history related to back problems did not make it sufficiently remote as to be nonadmissible); Stoeppelman v. Hays-Fendler Const. Co., 1968, 437 S.W.2d 143 (where extent of plaintiff's injuries was put in issue by defendants' answers filed to plaintiff's petition, plaintiff's testimony that he had been in Air Force, had been in good physical condition and had taken physical examinations for Air Force and Air National Guard was admissible to show his good physical condition prior to injury and was not inadmissible on basis that its only purpose was to create sympathy or prejudice for plaintiff because of his military service).

N.C.—Potts v. Howser, 161 S.E.2d 737, 274 N.C. 49 (testimony of injured party's former wife concerning his physical condition and complaints prior to accident was competent, where plaintiff's medical evidence tended to show a history of pain due to arthritis and rheumatism, and his complaints since accident related to pain in fingers, wrists, shoulder, neck and back).

Ohio.—Thompson v. Hauer, 1971, 283 N.E.2d 180, 30 Ohio App.2d 110 (records of the Bureau of Workmen's Compensation).

Or.—Marsh v. Davidson, 1973, 510 P.2d 558, 265 Or. 532 (where plaintiff testified that she had not suffered permanent injuries in previous accident, contrary allegations in complaint in action arising from previous accident were admissible to show that injuries complained of in instant case were not result of subsequent accident).

Pa.—McCay v. Philadelphia Elec. Co., 1972, 291 A.2d 759, 447 Pa. 490

(confusing evidence as to prior back disability).

Tex.—Texas Steel Co. v. Recer, 1974, 508 S.W.2d 889, ref. n. r. e. (service records of plaintiff, who had 14 years of military service, which showed absence of disability during course of plaintiff's service).

Wis.—Felde v. Kohnke, 1971, 184 N.W.2d 433, 50 Wis.2d 168 (where physician testified that only a direct, severe blow could have caused plaintiff's eye injury and there was nothing in record pertaining to plaintiff's prior hospitalization for nose fracture to indicate any injury to eye and defendant did not offer testimony of any other medical expert, trial court did not abuse its discretion in excluding record of such hospitalization and all testimony regarding the fight in which plaintiff's nose was fractured); Helleckson v. Loiselle, 155 N.W.2d 45, 37 Wis. 2d 423 (testimony concerning preexisting physical condition is proper on issue of pain and suffering because it tends to show that a plaintiff's suffering might not be entirely due to defendant's negligent conduct).

Circumstance of when suit filed

In view of related facts and circumstances in wife's suit for loss of consortium, time of filing of wife's suit in relation to trial of her husband's suit against same defendant tended to throw some light upon question of wife's damages, and in view of general objection of plaintiff trial court did not err in overruling objection to testimony that wife's petition had been filed approximately nine months after her husband's suit had been tried. Nichols v. Blake, Mo.1967, 418 S.W.2d 188.

Contra as to unrelated condition

Cal.—Downing v. Barrett Mobile Home Transport, Inc., 1974, 113 Cal.Rptr. 277, 38 C.A.3d 519 (where plaintiff did not claim kidney damage as result of accident in question and never actually denied having had any prior kidney problems, court erred in allowing defense counsel to cross-examine plaintiff on prior accident in which she had allegedly suffered kidney injury).

Latent prior condition

In response to plaintiffs' theory that accident was precipitating cause of infant plaintiff's schizophrenia defendants were entitled to show that child, because of latent psychotic tendencies, might have developed schizophrenia in any event, as bearing on amount of damages, even though exact prediction of infant plaintiff's future apart from the accident might be difficult or even impossible. Steinhauser v. Hertz Corp., C.A.N.Y.1970, 421 F.2d 1169.

Limited to significant prior condition

Evidence as to premarital pregnancies of pedestrian should not have been admitted in action for damages unless there was medical testimony giving it significance in relation to pedestrian's claimed injuries. Payne v. Zapp, Ky.1968, 431 S.W.2d 890.

Medical opinion excluded

Where there were no pleadings that plaintiff, who brought suit for injuries allegedly sustained when automobile in which she was riding was struck in rear by jeep driven by defendant, had ulcers prior to accident and that accident aggravated any ulcers she may have had, and where plaintiff's doctor could not testify one way or the other as to whether plaintiff had ulcer before accident, doctor's testimony concerning plaintiff's ulcer condition was properly excluded. Monk v. Cooper, Tex.Civ. App.1970, 454 S.W.2d 244, error refused n. r. e.

Not settlement for prior injury

S.C.—Young v. Martin, 1970, 173 S. E.2d 361, 254 S.C. 50.

of loss of earnings [3] and future earnings,[4] and other evidence of

3. U.S.—Kent v. Smith, C.A.Vt.1968, 404 F.2d 241 (while disabled).

Cal.—Hansen v. Warco Steel Corp., 47 Cal.Rptr. 428, 237 Cal.App.2d 870, rehearing denied 48 Cal.Rptr. 164, 237 Cal.App.2d 870 (not objectionable as insulting and embarrassing but was permissible as inquiring into his physical condition, extent of recovery and ability to earn a living).

Ga.—Moore v. Green, 1973, 199 S.E. 2d 317, 129 Ga.App. 268 (corset designed to encircle lower part of motorist's back); Malcolm v. Cotton, 1973, 197 S.E.2d 760, 128 Ga. App. 699 (testimony of plaintiff's husband regarding plaintiff's inability to perform her usual activities in the private business operated by plaintiff and her husband was not error, where evidence was not admitted for purpose of recovering damages for lost wages or loss of profits, which were not claimed, but was admitted to show decreased ability to labor, an element of pain and suffering).

Idaho.—Blaine v. Byers, 1967, 429 P. 2d 397, 91 Idaho 665 (plaintiff's physical ability to perform labor was competent as tending to show extent of injury received, although plaintiff claimed no damages by reason of loss of earning capacity).

Minn.—Fifer v. Nelson, 1973, 204 N.W.2d 422, 295 Minn. 313 (evidence of life expectancy).

Miss.—Strickling v. McDaniel, 1971, 247 So.2d 840 (in view of positive testimony of plaintiff as to serious and disabling effects of her injuries, how her injuries confined her to her home, interfered with care of her children and performance of her household duties, testimony that her automobile was parked at a certain night spot was germane and of probative value for consideration by jury, just as was testimony of police officer that when he was on night patrol he would see on occasions plaintiff driving her automobile).

N.H.—Pepin v. Beaulieu, 1959, 151 A.2d 230, 102 N.H. 84 (earnings upon return to work as proof of loss during disability).

Or.—Ardueser v. Rahier, 1972, 495 P.2d 724, 261 Or. 521 (no error allowing defendant to elicit from plaintiff during cross-examination that prior to time of trial she had verified a complaint which arose out of a fall from a horse at a time subsequent to injuries she received in automobile accident and in which plaintiff contended that she had received injuries to the cervical area of the back and the neck, as such evidence was admissible to show similar injuries she received from horse accident).

But see

Trial court did not abuse its discretion in excluding from evidence in action arising out of automobile accident deposition of an undercover state trooper concerning alleged solicitation for prostitution where the probative value concerning plaintiff's postaccident ability to perform physical tasks without pain was outweighed by the prejudice that would have resulted from permitting the jury to hear details of plaintiff's sexual escapades. Davis v. Chism, Alaska 1973, 513 P.2d 475.

Wis.—Jorgenson v. Hillestad, 27 N. W.2d 709, 250 Wis. 592 (findings of industrial commission examiner that disabilities were not due to automobile accident were inadmissible when award was interlocutory).

Cost of hired substitute

Mo.—Tryon v. Casey, App.1967, 416 S.W.2d 252 (cost of hiring a sub-

---

4. See note 4 on page 552.

§ **429.1**   TRIAL EVIDENCE   Ch. 429

stitute during incapacity is admissible).

Exclusion discretionary

Fla.—Inter-American Transport Equipment Co. v. Frank, App.1969, 227 So.2d 699 (refusal to admit records from prior, unconnected lawsuit to show that large sums of money had been drawn by plaintiff from corporation during three-year period, thereby impeaching his testimony that injury he had received in accident was so serious as to have precluded his performing valuable services for corporation, was not an abuse of discretion).

Orthopedic shoes

Ind.—Schoeff v. McIntire, 1972, 287 N.E.2d 369, —— Ind.App. —— (which passenger had to wear as a result of injuries sustained).

Post-surgery disability

Orthopedic surgeon, who removed a herniated disc from plaintiff's spinal column, was properly permitted to testify as to the percentage of permanent disability which generally follows the type of surgery he performed upon plaintiff, since fact that the surgeon had not had an opportunity to consider whether plaintiff's permanent disability was more or less than that which generally follows such an operation affected only the weight, not the admissibility, of the surgeon's testimony. Martin v. Mobley, 1969, 169 S.E.2d 278, 253 S.C. 103.

Proof of tax return limited

S.D.—Byre v. Wieczorek, 1974, 217 N.W.2d 151, —— S.D. —— (on issue of past earnings loss, the trial court properly excluded plaintiff's income tax returns for a number of years where such returns were based on farm income and aviation income and were in the nature of business returns and took into account such matters as inventory and depreciation).

Relevancy of legal problems of child

Testimony pertaining to indictment of son of plaintiff was relevant on question of plaintiff's mental and physical disabilities, and medical testimony to establish causal connection between plaintiff's condition and indictment was not necessary. Jakoski v. Holland, Alaska 1974, 520 P.2d 569.

4. U.S.—Ballantine v. Central R. of New Jersey, C.A.Pa.1972, 460 F.2d 540, certiorari denied 93 S.Ct. 133, 409 U.S. 879, 34 L.Ed.2d 133 (entitled to evidence and appropriate mathematical guidance on method of reducing lost future earnings to their present worth).

Mo.—Thienes v. Harlin Fruit Co., App.1973, 499 S.W.2d 223 (where plaintiff claimed that as result of injuries sustained he was unable to attend officer candidate school and thereby suffered loss of income, evidence as to military medals received by plaintiff was admissible if receipt of such medals tended to show acclimation to or aptitude for military service but was not admissible where medals were automatically awarded).

Deemed speculative

Idaho.—Rindlisbaker v. Wilson, 1974, 519 P.2d 421, 95 Idaho 752 (testimony that plaintiff was going to purchase ranch from his father in two years, that they were going to convert hay ground into pasture ground and run approximately 400 head of cattle on ranch, that they would make approximately $35–$40 per head of cattle, was too speculative to be admissible as proof of lost future earnings where at time of accident plaintiff owned only 40 head of cattle himself and was marketing with his father only 187 head annually, plaintiff and his father had not entered into any lease arrangement for winter rangeland and had taken no action to convert hay ground into pasture ground and evidence concerning intent to purchase ranch, showed little more than a bare intent).

Not "lost profits"

Del.—Sears, Roebuck & Co. v. Facciolo, 1974, 320 A.2d 347 (question put to friendly competitor of plaintiff on direct examination, as to the effect of competitor losing an average of one day per week on his earning capacity as owner and manager of his business was impermissible in that it called for a response which could not be proved, lost profits).

Present value

Or.—Osborne v. Bessonette, 1973, 508 P.2d 185, 265 Or. 224 (testimony of economist-statistician proffered by plaintiff concerning present value of future earnings which plaintiff would lose was admissible; however, trial court's refusal to allow such testimony did not prejudice plaintiff as such evidence would only have served as basis for reduction of damages, plaintiff's counsel, in argument to jury, advised that any loss of future earnings should be discounted to present value and discussed in detail the manner of discounting and the argument contained substantially the same information as the proffered testimony).

Tex.—Atchison, T. & S. F. Ry. Co. v. Ham, Civ.App.1970, 454 S.W.2d 451, error refused n. r. e. (testimony concerning single premium annuity is admissible in determining award necessary to provide plaintiff with an income for specified period, notwithstanding that profits of insurer and commissions of agent are included).

Prior earning capacity

Ga.—Carroll v. Morrison, 1967, 158 S.E.2d 480, 116 Ga.App. 575 (waitress is entitled to prove average earnings, including tips, for recovery of lost earnings, as against contention tips are mere gratuities and not income).

Minn.—Josephson v. Fremont Industries, Inc., 163 N.W.2d 297, 282 Minn. 51 (past earnings is relevant in assessing amount of wages lost due to defendant's wrong).

Mo.—Swiastyn v. St. Joseph Light & Power Co., App.1970, 459 S.W.2d 24; Haley v. Byers Transp. Co., 1967, 414 S.W.2d 777 (where airman suffering disabling injury was allowed to show his actual pay and allowance in Air Force and what they would have been up to date of trial had he remained in the service, and was allowed to testify that he had qualified for proficiency pay in electronics, anything further, such as "trend" in Air Force pay and plaintiff's prospective pay in future, would rest in pure speculation).

Mont.—Keck v. Bairs, Inc., 1968, 437 P.2d 380, 150 Mont. 562, 32 A.L.R. 3d 1158 (must know prior physical condition to ascertain prior earning power).

N.D.—Linington v. McLean County, (N.D.1968, 161 N.W.2d 487 (properly allowed to testify regarding his schooling for purpose of establishing damages by reason of loss of earnings).

Ohio.—Mathews v. Mumey, 1968, 238 N.E.2d 825, 15 Ohio App.2d 5 (loss of profits resulting from investment of capital or from employment of services of others is not admissible to establish loss of earning power; but, where it appears that business of a self-employed individual is primarily dependent upon his own labor, ability and training and that investment of capital and labor of others are only incidental to the income of the self-employed individual, loss of such business income is admissible to establish loss of earning power).

Tenn.—Dingus v. Cain, 1966, 406 S. W.2d 169, 56 Tenn.App. 294 (in suit by corporation president, for

disability since the accident.[5] Also admissible is evidence of pain and suffering,[6] of disfigurement,[7] of future consequences,[8] and loss of earning capacity, profits and losses of corporation employing 8-15 people were inadmissible as speculative).

Tex.—Greyhound Lines, Inc. v. Craig, Civ.App., 1968, 430 S.W.2d 573, error refused n. r. e. (loss can best be shown under evidence by comparing actual earnings before and after injury); Clanahan Const. Co. v. Mills, Civ.App., 1968, 426 S.W.2d 265, error refused n. r. e. (that plaintiff's income tax return for last year of full time employment was ten years old did not render it inadmissible for remoteness); J. A. Robinson Sons, Inc. v. Wigart, Civ.App., 1967, 420 S.W.2d 474, reversed on other grounds 431 S.W. 2d 327 (income tax returns of plaintiff are relevant to prior earning capacity).

5. **Wash.**—Conklin v. City of Seattle, 361 P.2d 578, 58 Wash.2d 189 (cross-examination of plaintiff's wife whether some six months prior to accident to plaintiff she had had plaintiff thrown in jail was relevant on the issue of whether the plaintiff was working regularly and it was not misconduct to ask it).

Probative value outweighed by prejudice

Tex.—Austin Road Co. v. Ferris, Civ. App.1973, 492 S.W.2d 64 (trial court properly refused to allow defendant to cross-examine plaintiff, who was an attorney, as to whether newspaper articles stating that criminal complaint had been filed against plaintiff charging extortion on ground that it was relevant to question of whether plaintiff's loss of earnings was due to injuries or adverse publicity, where plaintiff was never convicted and was later nobilled on the charge by grand jury).

6. **Ga.**—Melaver v. Garis, 1964, 138 S.E.2d 435, 110 Ga.App. 267 (doctor's bill as relevant).

7. **Ga.**—Malcolm v. Cotton, 1973, 197 S.E.2d 760, 128 Ga.App. 699 (testimony of plaintiff's husband as to his observation of plaintiff's disfigurement as a result of collision).

8. **Pa.**—Walsh v. Brody, 1971, 286 A.2d 666, 220 Pa.Super. 293 (where doctor had testified as to causal connection between schisis or splitting of retina of eye and accident, medical witness should have been permitted to testify as to effect of injury to retina on cataract surgery to be performed on that eye and error in not allowing testimony harmed plaintiff not only with respect to damages she was entitled to as result of effects of injury on future surgery but also damaged her in her proof as to mental anxiety suffered because of increase in hazards of cataract surgery; and court erred when, after permitting medical witness to testify that as result of injury to plaintiff's only good eye plaintiff had approximately a one in twenty change of losing her sight entirely, it refused to permit doctor to answer further question as to what chance an average person had of going blind).

Future expenses

Exclusion of physician's testimony as to cost of future surgery on right knee was proper where foundation proof of reasonable probable future medical expense was weak, and the error, if any, was not prejudicial in any event since jury disposed of the case on liability grounds. Schall v. Lorenzen, Iowa 1969, 166 N.W.2d 795.

S.D.—Koenig v. Weber, 1970, 174 N. W.2d 218, 84 S.D. 558 (cost of

other evidence bearing generally on the plaintiff's post-accident condition and injury.[9] Family status of the plaintiff is generally inadmissible.[10]

future plastic surgery treatment on injured, minor plaintiff who had residual scarring).

Future pain

N.C.—Howell v. Nichols, 1974, 207 S.E.2d 768, 22 N.C.App. 741 (properly excluded where plaintiff did not establish a reasonably certain causal relationship between the cervical spinal sprain suffered in the collision, which may have aggravated a preexisting back condition, and possible pain and suffering in the future).

Not connected

N.Y.—Putnam v. Stout, 1974, 361 N.Y.S.2d 205, 46 A.D.2d 812 (error to permit jury to consider spinal fusion operations where the first operation took place some 16 months after plaintiff's injuries were sustained, force of collision in question was light, plaintiff had long suffered from cervical degeneration in area of neck, the specific condition necessitating operation was not present after the collision, and collision did not adversely affect result of a prior cervical spinal fusion operation which was performed three months prior to collision and was necessitated by plaintiff's cervical disk disease).

9. **U.S.**—McGuire v. Davis, C.A.Ga. 1971, 437 F.2d 570 (proper to permit examining physician to testify about a perception motor problem incurred by accident victim, over objection that testimony was conclusory and without any support in evidence that victim had any such problem, where there was testimony linking perception motor problem to collision and doctor's identification of perception motor difficulty was based on victim's performance on psycho-diagnostic battery and doctor's personal observations of victim, a minor, in a variety of play situations); Blackstone v. Osche, D.C.Pa., 192 F.Supp. 174 (that plaintiff, while in hospital three days after having been injured in accident, was discovered by his wife embracing a young woman in a compromising position, was proper to elucidate and explain hospital entry that plaintiff was depressed while in hospital).

Ala.—Prestwood v. Ivey, 1962, 138 So.2d 713, 273 Ala. 281 (testimony of licensed mortician as to condition of body, as proof that accident caused death).

Ariz.—Chavez v. Pima County, 1971, 488 P.2d 978, 107 Ariz. 358 (where motorist testified, during trial of his suit against county for injuries sustained when his automobile collided with concrete abutment erected and maintained by the county, that as a direct result of such injuries he was no longer able to participate to any extent in various recreational activities including dancing, testimony that plaintiff danced with several people at cocktail party was permissible rebuttal).

Cal.—Rousseau v. West Coast House Movers, 1967, 64 Cal.Rptr. 655, 256 Cal.App.2d 878 (arrest records of plaintiff were admissible to refute plaintiff's claim that his physical difficulties were of recent origin and had been caused by accident and to rebut plaintiff's claim that his motor difficulties subsequent to accident resulted from traumatic epilepsy, and to prove, instead, that such injuries resulted from excessive use of alcohol).

Ill.—Wimberley v. Material Service Corp., 1973, 299 N.E.2d 425, 12 Ill.

10. See note 10 on page 558.

§ 429.1

App.3d 1051 (evidence that plaintiff had suffered a relatively minor back injury of short duration subsequent to accident was properly excluded as irrelevant, where it could not be reasonably inferred from testimony of doctor who treated subsequent injury that such injury was related to injury for which plaintiff sought to recover); Rylko v. Katz, 1967, 228 N.E.2d 135, 84 Ill.App.2d 93 (allowing defense counsel to inquire into plaintiff's arrest and acquittal for extortion was not improper in view of fact that plaintiff's doctors had testified that a shock to plaintiff's nervous system could have caused the injuries for which he sought to recover and which plaintiff claimed were sustained as a result of automobile accidents).

Kan.—Tucker v. Lower, 1967, 434 P.2d 320, 200 Kan. 1 (while in jail plaintiff had complained of pain and suffering, requested physician on numerous occasions, and had been given medication on regular basis to ease his pain).

Mo.—Hoffman v. St. Louis Public Service Co., 255 S.W.2d 736 (evidence as to possibility of passenger losing her other ovary and thereby becoming sterile, and of humiliation she might suffer in telling potential husband of her condition).

N.D.—Holecek v. Janke, 1969, 171 N.W.2d 94 (as to options of treatment available to patient in order to show course of treatment normal to a known condition).

S.C.—Merrill v. Barton, 1967, 156 S. E.2d 862, 250 S.C. 193 (admission of evidence relating to recurrence of back trouble more than a year after plaintiff suffered a whiplash injury was not abuse of discretion).

Wash.—Allen v. Mattoon, 1972, 504 P.2d 316, 8 Wash.App. 220.

Availability of unused free medical care

Question asked plaintiff on cross-examination as to whether she was entitled as a veteran's widow to free hospital service was proper as relevant to question of why, if plaintiff was injured, she did not seek treatment when she was present at military hospital shortly after time of accident. Murrell v. Spillman, Ky. 1969, 442 S.W.2d 590.

Condition at scene

Vt.—Duval v. Diamondstone, 1974, 315 A.2d 498, 132 Vt. 176 (condition of passenger described as being hysterical, in state of shock, and apparently suffering great pain).

Lawyer role in arranging medical care

Ky.—Murrell v. Spillman, 1969, 442 S.W.2d 590 (referred to chiropractor).

Not non-taxable nature of judgment

La.—Edwards v. Sims, 1974, 294 So. 2d 611 (as long as only net income figures are considered, the fact that damages received are excluded from gross income for income tax purposes is irrelevant; but where actuary did not really employ either gross or net income for his computation of loss of future wages or impairment of earning capacity, but instead utilized the difference between the wages plaintiff probably would have earned had he not been injured and the wages he actually earned in that year, under those circumstances any consideration as to the tax consequences of an award was relatively immaterial).

Not proof of unrelated conditions

Colo.—Walton v. Kolb, 1972, 500 P. 2d 149, 31 Colo.App. 95.

Ill.—Greim v. Sharpe Motor Lines, 1968, 242 N.E.2d 282, 101 Ill.App. 2d 142 (refusal to admit copy of prior complaint as substantive evidence that plaintiff's neck injury had been caused by prior accident was proper where defendant did not produce competent medical proof that a reasonable connection existed between prior injury and injury for which recovery was sought in subsequent action); King v. Gilland, 1967, 228 N.E.2d 741, 85 Ill.App.2d 358 (properly refused to admit testimony of physician designed to show that diagnosis made by plaintiff's doctors on hospitalization after accident was presumably the same as that made on her hospitalization one week prior to accident, where hospitalization prior to accident related to complaints in the lumbar area while complaints made by plaintiff as result of accident involved cervical area and right shoulder).

N.C.—Brown v. Neal, 1973, 197 S.E. 2d 505, 283 N.C. 604 (it is a matter of common knowledge that one engaged in strenuous activity such as calisthenics or military combat flying duty may experience sudden, severe back strain and discomfort followed by stiffness lasting several days with no history of previous back injury and mere proof of such back strain two years after automobile collision may not properly be considered by jury in determining amount of damages to be awarded for earlier injury in absence of expert medical testimony or other competent and substantial evidence as to causal relation between the two).

Pa.—Smith v. German, 1969, 253 A. 2d 107, 434 Pa. 47 (causal connection between plaintiff's marital difficulties arising from suspicion that his wife was having affair with neighbor and alleged paranoia and schizophrenia was not so closely connected and readily apparent without expert medical opinion that jury would be allowed to reach such conclusion rather than that alleged personality disorder stemmed from anoxia, allegedly resulting from injuries sustained in collision; admitting nonmedical testimony, which plaintiff had presented at his divorce proceeding and which tended to show that knowledge of his wife's affair upset him greatly, was prejudicial).

Tex.—Texas & Pac. Ry. Co. v. Nabhan, Civ.App., 1967, 413 S.W.2d 432, error refused n. r. e. (admitting testimony of plaintiff, who sought to recover for injuries sustained when backing train struck rear of plaintiff's automobile, regarding second hospital confinement and terrible pains during that period constituted prejudicial error where confinement had no connection with collision but was caused by the flu).

Proof of separate accident

Hawaii.—Loui v. Oakley, 1968, 438 P.2d 393, 50 Haw. 260, 272 (even though not all alleged tortfeasors may be before the court in the same action).

Idaho.—Fawcett v. Irby, 1968, 436 P.2d 714, 92 Idaho 48.

N.C.—Potts v. Howser, 1968, 161 S. E.2d 737, 274 N.C. 49 (evidence of injury in accident subsequent to accident in suit, where no competent medical evidence was offered to show what injuries were sustained in subsequent accident or what disabilities were suffered by reason thereof, was inadmissible).

Wis.—Fitzwilliams v. O'Shaughnessy, 1968, 161 N.W.2d 242, 40 Wis.2d 123 (where automobile in which passenger was riding was involved in accident, passenger was injured and while being taken to hospital in ambulance, ambulance was struck by another automobile, parties to actions arising out of the separate accidents would be entitled to produce evidence arising out of either accident in either action that might be brought as proof of, or in mitigation of, damages).

§ 429.1   TRIAL EVIDENCE   Ch. 429

Evidence of life expectancy tables is relevant where there is proof that the injury is permanent;[11] or where it is shown that

Refusal of medical examination

N.J.—Levine v. Scaglione, 1967, 231 A.2d 229, 95 N.J.Super. 338 (that plaintiff seeking recovery for injuries sustained when struck by automobile had refused, without justifiable cause, to submit to physical examination was admissible since jury might infer that such refusal indicated that plaintiff had something to hide or a consciousness of the weakness of her cause).

Tex.—Philipski v. Johnson, Civ.App., 1968, 428 S.W.2d 830, error refused n. r. e. (refusal to have examination by doctor of defendant's choice was admissible).

Settlement for subsequent injury

Evidence concerning settlement of plaintiff's claim for injuries sustained in subsequent accident was admissible, though involving a different tortfeasor, where the subsequent accident occurred shortly after the accident at suit and resulted in similar injuries, involving the neck, and where plaintiff had attempted to minimize the injuries caused by the subsequent accident and to attribute her disability to the accident at suit. Hobbs v. Reed, Okl.App.1970, 465 P.2d 780.

10. U.S.—Lebrecht v. Bethlehem Steel Corp., C.A.N.Y., 1968, 402 F.2d 585, 37 A.L.R.3d 1072 (references to dependent children of litigant are inadmissible when they are wholly irrelevant, but where references serve a legitimate purpose they are admissible).

Ill.—Hedrich v. Borden Co., 1968, 241 N.E.2d 546, 100 Ill.App.2d 237 (inability to play with two small children following accident resulting in severe spinal injuries was a factor which could be considered by jury in assessing damages, as well as the fact that he had become irritable toward children as the result of accident).

S.C.—Gause v. Livingston, 1968, 159 S.E.2d 604, 251 S.C. 8 (testimony of mother of minor passenger suing for injury to effect that passenger's father had been blind for 25 years and that the mother had six children and was the sole support of minor passenger was immaterial and irrelevant).

11. U.S.—Flick v. James Monfredo, Inc., D.C.Pa.1973, 356 F.Supp. 1143, affirmed C.A., 487 F.2d 1394 (admissible if permanent impairment of earning power results, and plaintiff need not show that he is incapable of performing any kind of work in order to permit such tables to be admitted).

Fla.—Morrison v. Bohne, App.1973, 274 So.2d 896 (mortality table).

Ga.—Crowe v. Harrell, 1970, 176 S.E.2d 190, 122 Ga.App. 7.

Ind.—Cerra v. McClanahan, 1967, 229 N.E.2d 737, 141 Ind.App. 469.

Minn.—Sorenson v. Cargill, Inc., 1968, 163 N.W.2d 59, 281 Minn. 480 (have considerable evidentiary value, but they are neither decisive of injured person's life expectancy nor of number of years his earning capacity would have continued undiminished had he not been injured).

N.H.—Bromfield v. Seybolt Motors Inc., 1973, 309 A.2d 914, 113 N.H. 525.

N.M.—Maisel v. Wholesome Dairy, Inc., 1968, 442 P.2d 800, 79 N.M. 310 (that plaintiff's present disability to right hip had increased by 20% over pre-existing disability and that this increased disability was permanent warranted admission of mortality tables showing life expectancy of person of plaintiff's age).

Or.—Zimmerman v. Ausland, 1973, 513 P.2d 1167, 266 Or. 427.

Ch. 429 DAMAGES § 429.1

the plaintiff will suffer damage in the future.[12] However, such evidence may be excluded unless it is also shown that the victim previously enjoyed "good health".[13] Other evidence may be admissible to prove that the plaintiff would not live the time indicated by life expectancy tables.[14]

Also in death cases, evidence as to the victim's prior life expectancy is admissible.[15] However, in a death case, proof of pros-

But see

Although there was proof that accident caused a back condition that was permanent, in view of fact that there was a total lack of proof that any permanent disability or damage resulted therefrom, receipt in evidence of mortality tables and instruction as to their use constituted reversible error. Garcia v. Southern Pac. Co., 1968, 442 P.2d 581, 79 N.M. 269.

Partial disability

Mortality tables should be considered even when the permanent disability may be only partial. Koenig v. Weber, 1970, 174 N.W.2d 218, 84 S.D. 558.

12. **U.S.**—Russell v. City of Wildwood, C.A.N.J.1970, 428 F.2d 1176.

Idaho.—Bratton v. Slininger, 1969, 460 P.2d 383, 93 Idaho 248 (under evidence that plaintiff had repeated seizures on at least 50 occasions, suffered loss of memory and personality change as result of scar tissue formed as result of concussion suffered, it was not error to permit jury to consider mortality tables).

Mass.—Cuddy v. L & M Equipment Co., 1967, 225 N.E.2d 904, 352 Mass. 458 (pain and suffering).

Exclusion proper

Trial court was correct in excluding mortality tables tendered by plaintiff for consideration in assessing damage for future pain and suffering, where orthopedic surgeon, who removed plaintiff's displaced disc, stated that operation was a success, where plaintiff returned to work within six months after accident and within approximately three months after operation, and where evidence was uncontradicted that plaintiff's yearly earnings increased after accident. Danzico v. Kelly, 1969, 250 N.E.2d 801, 112 Ill.App.2d 14.

13. **U.S.**—Tabor v. Miller, 1967, D.C. Pa., 269 F.Supp. 647, affirmed C.A., 389 F.2d 645, certiorari denied 88 S.Ct. 1810, 391 U.S. 915, 20 L.Ed. 2d 654.

Mass.—Cuddy v. L & M Equipment Co., 1967, 225 N.E.2d 904, 352 Mass. 458 (proper in view of doctor's testimony that at about time of the accident plaintiff felt in good health, with a minor exception).

14. **U.S.**—Century "21" Shows v. Owens, C.A.Iowa, 1968, 400 F.2d 603 (where there was no question raised as to plaintiff's use of intoxicants at time of collision, and pursuit of point could only legitimately relate to possible effect use of intoxicants would have upon longevity of plaintiff, trial court exercised its discretion in limiting defendants' inquiry on plaintiff's personal habits to period of seven years immediately prior to trial date).

15. **U.S.**—Continental Cas. Co. v. Jackson, C.A.Iowa, 1968, 400 F.2d 285 (life tables are generally admissible on limited basis in wrongful death or damage action for consideration of probabilities of damage over period of years; but they in no way serve to show whether person will or will not die by natural causes or otherwise at any particular age, nor do they tend to prove probabilities of such).

§ 429.1   TRIAL EVIDENCE   Ch. 429

pective wage scales was held to be speculative.[16]

The incidence of income taxes on the earnings of the decedent has been held to be competent evidence.[17]

Proof of medical expenses as evidence of damage requires the foundation that such charges were reasonable and necessary.[18] Plaintiff's outlay for X-ray examinations and photo-

---

16. **U.S.**—Rideaux v. Lykes Bros. S. S. Co., D.C.Tex., 1968, 285 F.Supp. 153 (prospective wage scale raises and cost of living increases is speculative and of little help).

17. **Iowa.**—Adams v. Deur, 1969, 173 N.W.2d 100 (incidence of taxes, federal and state, upon decedent's past and probable future earnings or income as they relate to present value of decedent's estate).

18. **Miss.**—Dennis v. Prisock, 181 So.2d 125, 254 Miss. 574.

Tex.—City of Dallas v. Pierson, App. 1970, 450 S.W.2d 99 (in action by pedestrian for injuries, including a comminuted fracture of the hip, testimony of doctor, who recommended that pedestrian not undergo operation in future, that future medical and hospital expenses, including an operation, might range from $2,000 to $12,000 or $15,000 was not competent evidence to support finding for medical, hospital, doctors and drug expense which in reasonable probability might necessarily be incurred in the future).

But see

Admission of a bill plaintiff received from pharmacy for medication was not error on ground that required foundation would require testimony of the doctor, where plaintiff testified that pharmacy bill was for medicine received from pharmacy which was prescribed by his doctor for injuries he received. Munro v. Privratsky, N.D.1973, 209 N.W.2d 745.

Contra

Statute making layman competent to identify doctor, hospital, ambulance service, drug and similar bills incurred in treatment of patients was enacted to eliminate necessity of having an expert witness testify that medical expenses are reasonable and necessary. Glover v. Southern Bell Tel. & Tel. Co., 1974, 207 S.E.2d 584, 132 Ga.App. 74.

Under statute providing that member of family of injured party or person responsible for care of patient is competent witness to identify doctor bills, hospital bills, etc., for expenses incurred in treatment on showing that bills were received from licensed practicing physician, etc., batch of personal checks with several receipts offered as a whole as proof of "expenses" from time of accident to time of injured party's death was properly excluded in absence of identification required by statute or proof that payments were for treatment for injuries received in the accident involved. Parham v. Roach, 1974, 206 S.E.2d 686, 131 Ga. App. 728.

New York rule

By rule, a medical bill is prima facie evidence of treatment or services rendered and also that the amount paid is the reasonable value thereof, limited to a recovery of $300, and if any part of the offer of proof based on such bill goes beyond itemization of treatment, services and reasonable value thereof, it is inadmissible, since such evidence would then tend to prove damages exceeding $300 and be outside the purview of the prima facie rule. Henderson

graphs for use as evidence in personal injury action, and not incurred for medical treatment for alleged injuries, should not be allowed as an item of damages in jury's verdict.[19]

Evidence, otherwise inadmissible, may be admissible in mitigation of damages.[20]

A plaintiff suing for damages resulting from injury to another person may introduce evidence to establish such loss.[21]

Evidence as to probability of less injury with use of safety precautions by the plaintiff has been held inadmissible.[22]

v. Marden Const. Co., 1969, 297 N. Y.S.2d 180, 58 Misc.2d 975.

Unitemized bill

Admitting medical expense statements, over objection that statements were summaries of bills which did not sufficiently identify when and what services were performed, was proper where statements in question, hospital and doctors bills, were identified by plaintiff and each doctor testified as to services that he had rendered and as to hospitalization and each statement bore either signature of doctor or his secretary or letterhead or signature of hospital authority. McGuire v. Davis, C.A. Ga.1971, 437 F.2d 570.

19. Kan.—Packer v. Fairmont Creamery Co., 149 P.2d 629, 158 Kan. 580.

La.—Lambert v. Faucheux Chevrolet Co., App., 161 So.2d 344.

20. Cal.—Helling v. Lew, 1972, 104 Cal.Rptr. 789, 28 Cal.App.3d 434.

N.Y.—Friedman v. N. Y. City Omnibus Corp., 70 N.Y.S.2d 628, 272 App.Div. 265 (payment from another).

21. Loss of consortium

Ala.—Cook v. Sweatt, 1968, 209 So. 2d 891, 282 Ala. 177 (jury had right to consider that husband was above 50 years of age and that wife was 52 years of age at time of accident and also the state of wife's health, disassociated from injuries she received in accident on which action was based).

Ga.—Cody v. Peak, 1966, 149 S.E.2d 521, 113 Ga.App. 676 (age and life expectancy of each spouse admissible in assessing loss of consortium claim).

Loss of services

Mo.—Tryon v. Casey, 1967, App., 416 S.W.2d 252 (evidence of cost of replacement help was improperly excluded on ground that it was not a "proper measure of damage in this case" because it was "completely speculative", where evidence was not offered to establish a legal measure of husband's damages, but only to be considered, subject to proof of necessity and reasonableness of expenditures as an aid to arriving at the value of wife's services in connection with her helping in his employment).

Okl.—Maples v. Bryce, Okl., 1967, 434 P.2d 214 (compensation to a parent for loss of services of a child may be substantial and is to be measured by the experience and judgment of a jury enlightened only by knowledge of the age, sex and intelligence of the injured child).

22. Md.—Rogers v. Frush, 1970, 262 A.2d 549, 257 Md. 233, 40 A.L.R. 3d 847 (doctrine of avoidable consequences was not applicable to limit recovery on theory that motorcyclist could have avoided consequences of accident by reasonable conduct on his part, since fail-

§ 429.1   TRIAL EVIDENCE   Ch. 429

For discussion of admissibility of evidence tending to prove wantonness or willfulness as supporting a claim for punitive damages, see section 425.1, at fn. 39 et seq.

Collateral source rule

Evidence that the plaintiff has been compensated by a person other than a joint tortfeasor for all or part of the loss is inadmissible.[23]

ure of motorcyclist to wear protective helmet was an event occurring before rather than after injury; thus, proffered testimony relating to extent of injury had helmet been worn was properly rejected).

Issue as to use of seat belt

Cal.—Horn v. General Motors Corp., 1974, 110 Cal.Rptr. 410, 34 Cal. App.3d 773 (failure to use seat belt, alleged to have contributed to aggravation of injuries by contact with defectively designed horn).

Colo.—Fischer v. Moore, 1973, 517 P.2d 458, 183 Colo. 392 (under law existing prior to adoption of comparative negligence statute, failure of motorist to use seat belt at time his automobile was struck from behind was not an affirmative defense to action for defendant's negligence and evidence that the plaintiff failed to wear seat belt could not be brought before jury to reduce amount of plaintiff's damages).

Ill.—Yocco v. Barris, 1974, 305 N.E. 2d 584, 16 Ill.App.3d 113; Atz v. Goss, App.1974, 316 N.E.2d 29, 21 Ill.App.3d 878; Josel v. Rossi, 1972, 288 N.E.2d 677, 7 Ill.App.3d 1091.

Kan.—Hampton v. State Highway Commission, 1972, 498 P.2d 236, 209 Kan. 565.

Tex.—King Son Wong v. Carnation Co., 1974, 509 S.W.2d 385 (contribution to injury cannot be proven by evidence that particular injury suffered would not have been sustained had seat belts been used).

23. U.S.—Golden v. Sommers, D.C. Pa.1972, 56 F.R.D. 3, affirmed C.A. 3, 1973, 481 F.2d 1398 (amount of retirement benefits and their effect on work expectancy were completely conjectural, but evidence of such benefits would not be admissible even if their amount and effect were certain); Mahon v. Reading Co., C.A.Pa.1966, 367 F.2d 25.

Ill.—Cargnino v. Smith, 1973, 308 N. E.2d 853, 17 Ill.App.3d 831 (social security and black lung benefits).

La.—Lefevre v. Allstate Ins. Co., App.1972, 258 So.2d 397 (hospitalization insurance from which plaintiff collected $10,000 played no part in suit for damages for injuries to his son).

Ohio.—Pryor v. Webber, 1970, 263 N.E.2d 235, 23 Ohio St.2d 104 (either by impeachment of testimony that wages were lost or by affecting weight of such testimony by presenting motivation, other than injury, for not working).

Or.—Jenks v. Larimer, 1974, 518 P. 2d 1301, 268 Or. 37 (was excludable, when offered as foundation for proposed questioning of plaintiff's doctor as to whether plaintiff was remaining disabled because of opportunity to receive disability payments).

Pa.—Palandro v. Bollinger, 186 A.2d 11, 409 Pa. 296.

R.I.—Thornton v. Ferris, 1971, 276 A.2d 758, 108 R.I. 491 (refusal to permit cross-examination of plaintiff, with respect to issue of incentive to return to work, as to

Ch. 429   DAMAGES   § 429.1

fact that salary of plaintiff, who was not shown to be a malingerer, had been paid during period of his disability was not abuse of discretion).

Tex.—Montandon v. Colehour, Civ. App.1971, 469 S.W.2d 222 (evidence that plaintiff was receiving benefits from United States government because of his prior military service violated collateral source rule and was improperly admitted, as against defendant's contention that the evidence was admissible on question whether plaintiff sustained loss of earning capacity and on question whether plaintiff was going to school because of his alleged injuries).

But see

Colo.—Niccoli v. Ayala, 1972, 501 P.2d 138, —— Colo.App. —— (even though tort-feasor who caused first accident could not assert defense that plaintiff had received a complete total satisfaction for his injuries through prior judgment against another tort-feasor for injuries received in subsequent accident, first tort-feasor could introduce evidence of subsequent injuries to plaintiff insofar as such evidence might aid in determining what injuries if any resulted from original collision).

Ky.—Rankin v. Blue Grass Boys Ranch, Inc., 1971, 469 S.W.2d 767 (since payments made to plaintiff by his employer because of plaintiff's legal entitlement to them would reduce claim for lost wages while workmen's compensation or gratuitous payments would not, defendant should have been permitted to show the nature of the arrangement between the plaintiff and his employer and of the payments received and should not have been limited to showing only fact of receipt of weekly payments as that fact may have indicated malingering by plaintiff).

La.—Crayton v. State Farm Mut. Auto. Ins. Co., 1974, 293 So.2d 575 (that total monthly compensation benefits and payments under disability policy exceeded plaintiff's wages at time of accident and that plaintiff returned to work just about the time she stopped receiving disability insurance could have been weighed by trial judge, who awarded damages for six months loss of earnings although plaintiff did not return to work until one year following injury, in evaluating plaintiff's motivation to return to work).

Mich.—Blacha v. Gagnon, 1973, 209 N.W.2d 292, 47 Mich.App. 168 (where defense counsel established adequate foundation in support of contention that plaintiff's injury was not as incapacitating as alleged by plaintiff and plaintiff participated in bowling and softball activities following the accident, week following alleged injury plaintiff worked every day including overtime, and testimony of doctor revealed no evidence of objective symptoms of injury claimed, considered together with cautionary instructions of trial judge, there was no abuse of discretion in admitting evidence of plaintiff's wage continuation benefits to show plaintiff's reluctance to return to his regular employment).

R.I.—Bookbinder v. Rotondo, 1972, 285 A.2d 387, 109 R.I. 346 (where testimony on whether there had been an actual impact between the two automobiles was in conflict, nature of two plaintiffs' employment for a family business and fact that the other plaintiff had a pre-existing hernia condition presented unique problems, and the trial justice did not abuse discretion in admitting in evidence the payroll records of the family business and the W–2 form of the other defendant with cautionary instructions on the collateral source rules together with statement that evidence was

§ 429.2   TRIAL EVIDENCE   Ch. 429

§ 429.2   Proof of Damages—Property Damage

Library References:
C.J.S. Damages § 157; Eminent Domain § 273(6); Evidence §§ 181 et seq., 546(57), 546(114) et seq., 593.
West's Key No. Digests, Damages ⚖174; Evidence ⚖113, 142, 471(20) et seq.

In an action for damage to property, evidence of the original cost is admissible,[24] as is evidence of the cost of repair.[25] How-

relevant only to the question of whether plaintiffs were out of work during the period of claimed disability).

Tex.—Johnson v. Reed, Civ.App.1971, 464 S.W.2d 689, error refused n. r. e., certiorari denied 92 S.Ct. 1197, 405 U.S. 981, 31 L.Ed.2d 256 (permitting defense counsel in suit for injuries allegedly sustained in accident to cross-examine plaintiff as to child support payments she received from her divorced husband was permissible for purpose of developing and rebutting plaintiff's testimony that she was divorcee and needed to work, despite her claimed physical condition, to support her daughter).

California rule

Before trial court may admit as proof that plaintiff has been malingering evidence that plaintiff suing tortfeasor has received collateral insurance payments, court must examine all relevant facts in case: for example, amount of plaintiff's out-of-pocket medical expenses, past or future earning capacity, seriousness of injuries and prognosis, and length of absence from work; and then court must be satisfied that the evidence establishes strong inference that plaintiff was motivated by insurance receipts rather than by actual disabling extent of his injuries; but if defendant fails to make an adequate showing, prejudicial impact of collateral source evidence will render it inadmissible. Hrnjak v. Graymar, Inc., 1971, 94 Cal.Rptr. 623, 4 Cal.3d 725, 484 P.2d 599.

24. U.S.—Nunan v. Timberlake, 85 F.2d 407, 66 App.D.C. 150.

Cal.—Jones v. Kauffmann, 1968, 71 Cal.Rptr. 10, 264 Cal.App.2d 857.

Ga.—Nail v. Hiers, 1967, 157 S.E.2d 771, 116 Ga.App. 522.

La.—Johnson v. Williams, App., 1967, 201 So.2d 674 (price paid by plaintiff for automobile less than ten days before was demolished was best evidence of actual value).

Md.—Checkpoint Foreign Car Service, Inc. v. Sweeney, 1968, 242 A.2d 148, 250 Md. 251.

25. Ill.—Morrissey v. Ward, 1972, 292 N.E.2d 110, 9 Ill.App.3d 241 (uncontroverted testimony that repair bill has been paid is sufficient to establish payment and render repair bill admissible as proof of damages); Saunders v. Wilson, 1969, 253 N.E.2d 89, 114 Ill.App.2d 380 (offer of repair bill, bearing no notation indicating payment, together with plaintiff's uncontroverted testimony under oath that bill had been paid, was sufficient to render bill admissible).

R.I.—Krasnoff v. Flynn, 196 A.2d 158, 97 R.I. 129 (following testimony of expert witness as to extent of damage).

But see

La.—Johnson v. Williams, App.1967, 201 So.2d 674 (testimony of repairman who inspected plaintiff's nearly demolished automobile ten months after accident, and after engine and three wheels had been removed, would not be given any weight).

ever, evidence of cost of repair is not admissible unless it is shown that the repair was necessary to restore the property to its former condition.[26]

And evidence of market value of a vehicle at the time of the accident has been held admissible.[27]

Proof of "loss of use" may be by reasonable rental value of damaged vehicle for a period of time reasonably necessary for repairs.[28]

Method of proof improper

La.—Vezinat v. Marix, App.1968, 217 So.2d 416 (where no estimate appeared of record as to amount of damage to company owned automobile driven by plaintiff at time of accident and plaintiff failed to produce party that assessed damage, his testimony that his account was debited by his employer with specified amount for such damage did not warrant award).

No foundation required for "paid" bill

Ill.—Smith v. Champaign Urbana City Lines, Inc., 1969, 252 N.E.2d 381, 116 Ill.App.2d 289 (admissible without other foundation as prima facie evidence of the necessity and reasonableness of repairs but may be overcome by proper proof in those cases where the bill is not correct in one or more aspects).

Railroad car

Ill.—Chicago, B. & Q. R. R. v. Ommen, 1968, 235 N.E.2d 880, 93 Ill. App.2d 299, appeal after remand 264 N.E.2d 535, 130 Ill.App.2d 713 (erred in excluding plaintiff railroad's evidence as to cost of repairs to three derailed cars and as to value of two derailed cars, which were damaged in excess of cost of repairs, based on American Association of Railroads' Rules which had been used for many years by all major railroads).

Supporting proof required

N.Y.—Wachsman v. Hethering, 1968, 294 N.Y.S.2d 760, 31 A.D. 522 (repair estimate not admissible without proof of value of vehicle).

26. **N.J.**—Parisi v. Friedman, 46 A. 2d 808, 134 N.J.L. 273 (admission of witness' estimate of cost of building new truck body was error in absence of evidence that the body estimated upon by witness was necessary to restore truck to its former condition).

27. **Md.**—Walston v. Dobbins, 1970, 271 A.2d 367, 10 Md.App. 490 (fair market value of average vehicle of type driven by plaintiff and that such vehicle would be total loss if its frame was bent as result of accident was not objectionable as vague or indefinite, notwithstanding it was not connected by other testimony with vehicle in question).

28. **Fla.**—Meakin v. Dreier, 1968, 209 So.2d 252 (testimony of representative of automobile rental agency to effect that it would cost $100 per week for plaintiff to rent vehicle similar to her automobile which was being repaired was admissible, in action for loss of use of pleasure vehicle).

Ind.—New York Cent. R. Co. v. Churchill, 218 N.E.2d 372, 140 Ind. App. 426.

Chapter 430

LAY OPINION EVIDENCE

Table of Sections

Sec.
430.1 Lay Opinions—In General.
430.2 ——— Speed.

§ 430.1 Lay Opinions—In General

Library References:
C.J.S. Evidence §§ 438 et seq., 445 et seq.
West's Key No. Digests, Evidence ⚖470 et seq.

Testimony in the form of an opinion, properly supported, may be received if it aids the factfinder.[1] Under the federal rule and the rule of certain states, the test is stated as whether it is "helpful to a clear understanding of his testimony".[2]

Under the federal rule,[3] and some state rules,[4] it does not matter that a lay opinion embraces an ultimate issue to be de-

1. **Alaska.**—Meyst v. East Fifth Ave. Service, Inc., 1965, 401 P.2d 430.

   Neb.—Drahota v. Wieser, 1968, 157 N.W.2d 857, 183 Neb. 66.

   N.H.—Walker v. Walker, 210 A.2d 468, 106 N.H. 282 (where officers came upon scene shortly after automobile crashed, and testified that they did not believe defendant's statement to them that his wife was operating automobile, court's decision that officers' opinion testimony would aid jury in deciding who operated automobile was sustainable).

2. Federal Rules of Evidence § 701, 28 U.S.C.A. (or helpful "to the determination of a fact in issue").

   Cal.—West's Ann.Calif.Evid.Code § 800(b).

   Kan.—Kansas Code of Civil Procedure § 60–456(a).

   Me.—Maine Rules of Evidence § 701.

   Neb.—Nebraska Rules of Evidence § 701 (or is helpful to "the determination of a fact in issue").

   Nev.—N.R.S. 50.265 (or is helpful to "the determination of a fact in issue").

   N.J.—New Jersey Evidence Rule 56 (1) (or is helpful to "the determination of a fact in issue").

   N.M.—New Mexico Rules of Evidence § 701 (or is helpful to "the determination of a fact in issue").

   Utah.—Utah Rules of Evidence § 56 (1) (or is helpful to "the determination of a fact in issue").

   Wis.—Wisconsin Rules of Evidence § 907.01 (or is helpful to "the determination of a fact in issue").

3. Federal Rules of Evidence § 704, 28 U.S.C.A.

4. **Cal.**—West's Ann.Calif.Evid.Code § 805.

   Fla.—Florida Evidence Code § 90.-703.

Ch. 430 LAY OPINION EVIDENCE § 430.1

cided by the trier of fact. However, in state jurisdictions, the general rule is that conclusions of a lay witness which a jury or the court acting as such, with the facts before it, can as well make as the witness, are properly excluded.[5] A witness should

Kan.—Kansas Code of Civil Procedure § 60–456(d).

Me.—Maine Rules of Evidence § 704.

Neb.—Nebraska Rules of Evidence § 704.

Nev.—N.R.S. 50.295.

N.J.—New Jersey Evidence Rule 56 (3).

N.M.—New Mexico Rules of Evidence § 704.

Utah.—Utah Rules of Evidence § 56 (4).

Wis.—Wisconsin Rules of Evidence § 907.04.

5. Comparable statements in prior edition **cited by the court** in National Alfalfa Dehydrating & Milling Co. v. Sorensen, C.A.Neb., 220 F.2d 858, 862.

Ala.—Shores v. Terry, 1970, 232 So. 2d 657, 285 Ala. 417 (objection to question which asked witness to describe magnitude of impact was properly sustained, as question sought nothing more than a speculative and impressionistic opinion, and where witness had testified to facts from which jury could reasonably infer magnitude of impact); Hurn v. Reynolds, 36 So.2d 603, 34 Ala.App. 79 (whether brick on truck would have helped sway truck to the right); Arrick v. Fanning, 47 So.2d 708, 35 Ala.App. 409 (whether witness could have seen signal if given); Alabama Power Co. v. Armour & Co., 92 So. 111, 207 Ala. 15 (whether under certain conditions as to speed of the two colliding vehicles the accident could have been avoided had the driver of the truck delayed making a turn until he had reached a specified point).

Ariz.—Buehman v. Smelker, 68 P.2d 946, 50 Ariz. 18 (negligence or prudence).

Ark.—Hutcheson v. Clapp, 226 S.W. 2d 546, 216 Ark. 517 (objection to question as to whose business salesman was engaged in at time of collision properly sustained).

Conn.—Robinson v. Faulkner, 1972, 306 A.2d 857, 163 Conn. 365 (in light of availability of facts which could have been clearly described to jury); MacLaren v. Bishop, 1931, 155 A. 210, 113 Conn. 312.

Ga.—Wallis v. Odom, 1973, 203 S. E.2d 613, 130 Ga.App. 437 (cross-examination of defendant as to whether driver had pulled out from parking place in supermarket shopping center into path of defendant's car, causing defendant to hit the car, was improper.)

Ill.—Delany v. Badame, 1971, 274 N.E.2d 353, 49 Ill.2d 168 (where all charges of willful and wanton conduct related to speed at which defendant motorist was allegedly operating this automobile, whether the speed was too fast was ultimate fact to be determined by jury and restricting certain of plaintiff's questions of defendant's father and defendant concerning their opinion as to whether 30 miles per hour was in fact too fast a speed to drive on curve where accident happened was not improper); Perkins v. Culver, 1971, 269 N.E.2d 333, 131 Ill.App.2d 881 (host driver's statement that collision was fault of other motorist was incompetent and should have been stricken as being an improper expression of opinion on an ultimate issue but was not ground for reversal as jury could not have been misled, confused or improperly influenced by such statement); Allen v.

§ 430.1 TRIAL EVIDENCE Ch. 430

Yancy, 206 N.E.2d 452, 57 Ill.App. 2d 50 (opinion that a party's conduct was negligent); Biniakiewicz v. Wojtasik, 90 N.E.2d 568, 339 Ill.App. 574 (asking police officer what he determined from his investigation was cause of accident was improper as invading province of jury); Mortvedt v. Western Austin Co., 1943, 50 N.E. 2d 764, 320 Ill.App. 337 (that certain tire marks shown on photograph taken 5 days later were skid marks seen at scene); Stephens v. Railway Express Agency, 47 N.E. 2d 384, 318 Ill.App. 228 (evidence that proposed repairs would improve building over what building was on day of accident properly excluded as "conclusion" of witness).

Iowa.—Hayungs v. Falk, 27 N.W.2d 15, 238 Iowa 285 (testimony that witness would have seen flares if set out was conclusion); In re Hill's Estate, 208 N.W. 334, 202 Iowa 1038, modified on other grounds, 210 N.W. 241, 202 Iowa 1038 (testimony as to what sort of driver defendant was).

Ky.—Service Lines, Inc. v. Mitchell, 1967, 419 S.W.2d 525; Dixie Ice Cream Co. v. Ravenna Grocery Co., 1947, 206 S.W.2d 824, 306 Ky. 182 (statement by overtaking driver that he could have overtaken truck had not it turned to left).

Md.—Brown v. Rogers, 1974, 313 A. 2d 547, 19 Md.App. 562 (in action arising out of pedestrian accident, question posed on cross-examination to witness: "If you had been in the girl's position, you wouldn't have walked out in front of that car, if it was going fast; would you?" was objectionable as invading province of jury); State, for Use of Emerson v. Poe, 1937, 190 A. 231, 171 Md. 584.

Minn.—Ramfjord v. Sullivan, 1974, 222 N.W.2d 541, 301 Minn. 238 (clearly erroneous to admit into evidence opinion of an investigating officer as to which party is at fault); Carpenter v. Mattison, 1974, 219 N.W.2d 625, 300 Minn. 273 (normally opinions concerning fault and responsibility are inadmissible at trial, even when introduced for impeachment purposes); Schwartz v. Minneapolis Suburban Bus Co., 1960, 104 N.W.2d 301, 258 Minn. 325 (question "would it have taken much application of brakes by the bus to have avoided this accident").

Miss.—Shivel v. Ferguson, 1972, 259 So.2d 123 (question of whether defendant, traveling on the through highway, had entered intersection or was approaching so closely thereto as to constitute an immediate hazard when plaintiff started to cross the highway was for the jury, and witnesses, in giving their opinions as to right-of-way, invaded the province of the jury); Lynch v. Suthoff, 1969, 220 So.2d 593 (patrolman or police officer, not eyewitness to accident, who investigates an accident shortly after it happens, may properly testify as to matters and things that he finds at scene, but he is not allowed to invade province of jury by giving his opinion as to how accident happened); Coleman v. Ford Motor, 1970, 240 So.2d 607 (in products case, opinion what happened to steering mechanism of truck); Standard Oil Co. v. Crane, 23 So.2d 297, 199 Miss. 69.

Mo.—Clear v. Van Blarcum, App., 241 S.W. 81.

Mont.—Demarais v. Johnson, 3 P.2d 283, 90 Mont. 366, 77 A.L.R. 553.

N.Y.—Hartley v. Szadkowski, 1969, 300 N.Y.S.2d 82, 32 A.D. 550 (opinion that highway was dangerous).

N.C.—Johnson v. Brooks, 1974, 208 S.E.2d 875, 23 N.C.App. 321 (basic facts concerning such matters as posted speed limit, weather and mechanical condition of defendant's automobile could have been described with sufficient clarity to allow members of jury to draw their own conclusions regarding speed of defendant's car, and plaintiff guest testimony that he was driving "a little too fast" was properly refused); Kaczala v. Richardson, 1973, 197 S.E.2d 21, 18 N.C.App. 446, certiorari denied 198 S.E.2d 722, 283 N.C. 753 (trial court erred in allowing police officer to testify, over objection, that his investigation revealed that fire truck had run a red light); Peterson v. Taylor, 1971, 178 S.E.2d 227, 10 N.C.App. 297 (whether vehicle could be operated in safety at 25 mph. in particular lane of parking lot).

Ohio.—Character v. Henderson, 1964, 195 N.E.2d 821, 1 Ohio App.2d 14; Mynatt v. Drenik Beverage Distributing, Inc., 1963, 188 N.E.2d 612, 119 Ohio App. 28 (card completed after accident which stated defendant's driver was not at fault).

Or.—Tyler v. Moore, 1924, 226 P. 443, 111 Or. 499.

Pa.—Warruna v. Dick, 104 A. 749, 261 Pa. 602.

Tex.—Barber v. Anderson, Civ.App., 127 S.W.2d 358, error dismissed, judgment correct (whether an accident was unavoidable); Hubb Diggs Co. v. Bell, Civ.App., 297 S.W. 682, reversed on other grounds, Com.App., 1 S.W.2d 575 (opinion expressed out of court as to whether certain rate of speed was excessive).

Vt.—Goodwin v. Gaston, 154 A. 772, 103 Vt. 357.

W.Va.—State Road Commission v. Darrah, 153 S.E.2d 408, 151 W.Va. 509; Reall v. Deiriggi, 34 S.E.2d 253, 127 W.Va. 662.

Absence of traffic charge
See also Relevancy, at § 425.1, fn. 29.

Ill.—Giles v. Kuennen, 200 N.E.2d 143, 50 Ill.App.2d 389 (testimony of police officer that he had not arrested motorist who collided with infant bicyclist was error and prejudicial since it could be inferred from the officer's testimony that he was of opinion motorist was free of guilt, which was ultimate question).

N.C.—Beanblossom v. Thomas, 146 S.E.2d 36, 266 N.C. 181 (patrolman's testimony that truck driver was never charged with crime in connection with three-vehicle accident was incompetent, as opinion on negligence issue, either to corroborate truck driver or to exonerate him of negligence, but admission of such testimony was not prejudicial to plaintiffs where evidence disclosed that patrolman had, at time of investigation, no evidence which would have justified such charge and jury must have understood that his decision not to charge truck driver with any violation of law was based only on information available to him at that time).

But see

Ga.—Howard v. Hall, 145 S.E.2d 70, 112 Ga.App. 247 (questions as to what witness considered to be safe speed on certain portion of road, particularly while children were out of school and likely to be in such vicinity, and as to relative positions of motorist and bicyclist if bicyclist could see certain mailbox were sufficiently specific and adapted to evidence, and admission of answers by witness who was automobile driver himself and resident of particular neighborhood was proper); Black & White Cab Co. v. Clark, 19 S.E. 2d 570, 67 Ga.App. 170 (plaintiff could testify as to effect facial disfigurement would have on chances of employment).

Ind.—Bartley v. Chicago & E. I. R. Co., 41 N.E.2d 805, 220 Ind. 354 (question whether witness saw anything, at time plaintiff's truck came into view, to indicate that plaintiff could not stop before crossing railroad track).

§ 430.1   TRIAL EVIDENCE   Ch. 430

not be asked whether a car would have collided with the other car if the driver had tried to avoid it.[6]

N.C.—Blackwell v. Lee, 103 S.E.2d 703, 248 N.C. 354 (testimony to effect that there were no obstructions on highway or on either shoulder except signpost on one of the shoulders was properly admitted over objection that testimony was incompetent).

Even when asked of adverse party

Question which inquired of adverse party as to whether such party did not think the speed of his automobile was excessive under the circumstances was improper as it violated the opinion evidence rule. Starner v. Wirth, 1970, 269 A.2d 674, 440 Pa. 177.

Reasonableness of speed

Where testimony of defendant regarding the reasonableness of defendant's speed as he was attempting to pass was elicited during his cross-examination, and came as result of argument with the defendant which led to the unresponsiveness of answer, there was no error in refusing to strike such testimony and no prejudice was shown by ruling since jury answered issue of negligence in favor of plaintiff. Coppley v. Carter, 1971, 179 S.E.2d 118, 10 N.C. App. 512.

Rule limited

Ariz.—Southern Pac. Co. v. Barnes, 415 P.2d 579, 3 Ariz.App. 483 (not error to permit plaintiff to elicit testimony from fireman and head brakeman who were in cab of engine on the evening of fatal crossing accident that in their opinion the crossing was particularly dangerous and extrahazardous, since opinion indicated a knowledge of existence of danger which was a pertinent issue and railroad had an opportunity to cross-examine).

Mass.—Reardon v. Marston, 38 N.E. 2d 644, 310 Mass. 461 (where bicyclist testified that, when he observed automobile after bicyclist entered highway from gravel path, automobile was 50 feet away and approaching along center of highway, the bicyclist was properly permitted to testify that he did not think it was safe to cross to his right hand side of the highway in front of the automobile, so as to explain his presence on left hand side of highway).

Rule qualified

Jury decides ultimate issues of proximate cause and fault and is under no obligation to accept witness' opinion, and, therefore, witness does not usurp jury's function or invade its province by giving opinion testimony. Meyst v. East Fifth Ave. Service, Inc., Alaska, 401 P.2d 430.

6. **Ala.**—Alabama Power Co. v. Armour & Co., 92 So. 111, 207 Ala. 15; Taylor v. Lewis, 89 So. 581, 206 Ala. 338 (questions asked driver as to whether he could have stopped car sooner properly overruled as calling for conclusion).

Ariz.—Buehman v. Smelker, 68 P.2d 946, 50 Ariz. 18.

Ga.—Williams v. Williams, 1967, 154 S.E.2d 33, 115 Ga.App. 168 (after defendant had testified that he was on his side of the road and that plaintiff's vehicle was also on defendant's side of road, further testimony of defendant that collision would not have occurred if vehicle in which plaintiff was riding had not been on defendant's side of road was a conclusion which might properly have been excluded, but admission of testimony was not harmful as such conclusion was unavoidable if defense facts were to be believed); Hughes v. Brown, 1965, 143 S.E. 2d 30, 111 Ga.App. 676 (whether driver could have avoided hitting

Sufficient and proper basis for opinions and conclusions must be established, where the opinion is to be received.[7] The federal

bicyclist at time driver first saw him start in front of auto).

Ky.—Service Lines, Inc. v. Mitchell, 1967, 419 S.W.2d 525 (refusing officer to state whether collision avoided by partially on shoulder).

Mo.—Chawkley v. Wabash R. Co., 1927, 297 S.W. 20, 317 Mo. 782.

Tex.—Wilson v. Whitcher, Civ.App. 1972, 477 S.W.2d 344, error refused n. r. e. (question of eyewitness whether motorist, who had entered highway from service station and who was involved in rear-end collision when her automobile stalled, would have been able to accelerate and get into traffic so as to avoid collision had her car not stalled was improper).

But see

Ga.—Millhollan v. Watkins Motor Lines, Inc., 1967, 157 S.E.2d 901, 116 Ga.App. 452 (where plaintiff attempted to show that it would have been possible for defendant to avoid head-on collision by driving onto shoulder of road or turning into private driveway, it was not error to permit witness to testify that he saw no opportunity for defendant to do anything other than what he did).

Mich.—Stillwell v. Grubaugh, 98 N.W.2d 490, 357 Mich. 344 (court did not commit reversible error in permitting witness to testify that he did not think that defendant could have started into intersection before light turned green for plaintiff, where witness had previously given facts on which alleged conclusion was based).

Contra

Ga.—Hughes v. Brown, 143 S.E.2d 30, 111 Ga.App. 676 (testimony that he does not know of anything he could have done to avoid accident is construed to mean that his opinion was that there was nothing else he could have done, and is admissible when based upon facts concerning which he testified); Carter v. Hutchinson, 126 S.E.2d 458, 106 Ga.App. 68 (in response to question as to whether there was anything he could have done to avoid striking child, that he would have turned to the right or left if he could have but that he thought he could stop before he hit the child, was admissible, when such testimony was given after a protracted examination of defendant concerning events and surrounding conditions).

Tex.—John F. Buckner & Sons v. Allen, Civ.App., 289 S.W.2d 387 (in action against road contractors, arising out of accident which occurred when plaintiff's automobile entered upon detour which was slick with fresh oil, plaintiff was properly permitted to testify that she did not know of anything her driver could have done after automobile started skidding to keep it from colliding with truck, there having been testimony that plaintiff was experienced driver and her driver having been examined as to skill).

7. Ala.—Alabama Power Co. v. Brown, 1921, 87 So. 608, 205 Ala. 167 (witness without driving experience could not state whether an auto could turn in a specified space).

Ga.—Mullis v. Merit Finance Co. of Savannah, No. 1, 1967, 158 S.E.2d 415, 116 Ga.App. 582 (excluded opinion of officer that item found in vehicle was a delinquent account bill of the driver's employer); Preferred Risk Mut. Ins. Co. v. Commercial Union Ins. Co. of New York, 1970, 173 S.E.2d 730, 121 Ga.App. 367 (testimony by claims manager that document attached to

§ 430.1   TRIAL EVIDENCE   Ch. 430

complaint was exact copy of policy issued to insured was conclusory and of no probative value, where manager further testified that he first had knowledge of policy several years after accident and that his knowledge as to original policy was based upon his examination of records and his experience and association with transactions of this nature); Augusta Coach Co. v. Lee, 1967, 154 S.E.2d 689, 115 Ga.App. 511; Hughes v. Brown, 1965, 143 S.E.2d 30, 111 Ga.App. 676 (father could state cost of drugs for son's use, where had purchased such for years); Evans v. Kent, 1922, 110 S.E. 685, 28 Ga.App. 172 (opinion, based upon examination of tracks, that vehicle would not have been hit if it had not turned in certain manner).

Iowa—Oakes v. Peter Pan Bakers, Inc., 138 N.W.2d 93, 258 Iowa 447, 10 A.L.R.3d 247 (question put to witness, driver of vehicle struck from rear by plaintiff's automobile, which plaintiff alleged had been pushed into witness' vehicle by defendant's van, as to whether he would have been able to hear another collision called for an opinion, but opinion could be given by driver who had had full opportunity for observation).

Ky.—Louisville Ry. Co. v. Allen, 246 S.W.2d 443 (sister who attended and cared for plaintiff while plaintiff was bedridden could testify that plaintiff was badly hurt and suffered a great deal during such period, but could not testify concerning pain suffered by plaintiff at time of trial and plaintiff's physical condition and ability to work at such time since such matters were not facts within witness' knowledge).

Md.—Murphy v. Board of County Com'rs, 1971, 284 A.2d 261, 13 Md. App. 497 (properly excluded questioning as to time hole on shoulder had existed, where witness said she didn't know).

Mass.—Barresy v. James A. Freaney, Inc., 150 N.E.2d 921, 337 Mass. 643 (in actions for injuries when automobile in which plaintiffs were riding skidded and collided, in vehicular tunnel owned by city, with rear of taxicab and defendant's truck parked near catch basin, which defendant's employees were cleaning pursuant to contract with city, testimony of tunnel superintendent, offered by plaintiffs, that defendant should have placed flares not less than 200 feet beyond either end of truck and that failure to do so was a violation of obligation to protect safety of traveling public did not show any regulation or instruction governing truck and was properly excluded).

Mich.—Rypstra v. W. U. Tel. Co., 1965, 132 N.W.2d 140, 374 Mich. 166 (plaintiff allowed opinion as to extent of disability).

N.D.—Trautman v. New Rockford-Fessenden Co-op Transport Ass'n, 1970, 181 N.W.2d 754 (questioning of police chief whether there had been danger of plaintiff's deceased, an officer, being discharged and suffering income loss).

Okl.—Barnett v. Richardson, 415 P.2d 987 (plaintiff's testimony that a doctor treated his neck injuries with heat treatments and shots and that he was able to start working part time about three months after accident but that it was about four months after accident that his neck didn't hurt him at all times was admissible, despite contention that plaintiff's injuries were purely subjective and could only be made by a medical expert); Nash v. Hiller, 1965, 398 P.2d 817 (patrolman's opinion, based only on hearsay, as to place where motorist passed pickup inadmissible).

Pa.—Andrews v. Jackson, 1967, 235 A.2d 452, 211 Pa.Super. 166.

Tex.—Tyler Mirror & Glass Co. v. Simpkins, Civ.App.1966, 407 S.W. 2d 807, ref. n. r. e. (plaintiff's testimony of cause of own injuries of no probative value); Mooneyhan v. Benedict, Civ.App., 284 S.W.2d 741, writ of error refused n. r. e. (properly excluded testimony of officer that legal speed limit was forty-five miles an hour at place where collision occurred on state highway inside city limits, where no city ordinance was in evidence, and there was no evidence that highway where collision occurred was in either a business or residential district); Yellow Cab & Transfer Corporation v. Warren Co., Civ.App., 148 S.W.2d 209 (plaintiff's witness not competent to testify that repairs had merely restored automobile to its former condition immediately before accident where witness had not seen automobile for two months prior to collision and automobile had been used considerably during that time).

Wis.—Kenwood Equipment, Inc. v. Aetna Ins. Co., 1970, 180 N.W.2d 750, 48 Wis.2d 472, rehearing 182 N.W.2d 241, 48 Wis.2d 472 (testimony as to visibility of signal lights, offered by two witnesses and based on observations of truck after accident, was not admissible as to one witness because of damage to truck caused by the accident, and was not admissible as to other witness because he did not have personal knowledge of whether rear signal lights of plaintiff's truck were visible from defendant's truck).

Wyo.—State Highway Commission v. Newton, 1964, 395 P.2d 606.

But see

Ala.—Britton v. Doehring, 1970, 242 So.2d 666, 286 Ala. 498 (defendant motorist's testimony that to best of his knowledge he was on his own side of road at time of head-on collision was not inadmissible, even though he also testified that he did not know on which side of road the collision occurred).

Ark.—Arkansas State Highway Commission v. Russell, 398 S.W.2d 201, 240 Ark. 21 (expert or lay testimony is competent even though it is based wholly or partly on hearsay).

Opinion of investigating officer

Ala.—Arrick v. Fanning, 47 So.2d 708, 35 Ala.App. 409 (where tire marks were only at point of impact, patrolman could not say whether one vehicle started a turn prior to reaching centerline of crossroad).

Ariz.—Dobbertin v. Johnson, 390 P. 2d 849, 95 Ariz. 356 (testimony of officer that he found no evidence of improper driving or parking or any other driver's violation was prejudicial where he was the only impartial witness who examined the scene and there was a strong possibility that the jury was influenced by his testimony); Womack v. Banner Bakery, Inc., 297 P.2d 936, 80 Ariz. 353 (error to permit former highway patrolman, who had not been an eyewitness thereto, to give his opinion as to cause thereof based upon statements made by driver after accident).

Cal.—Stuart v. Dotts, 201 P.2d 820, 89 Cal.App.2d 683 (opinion that pedestrian was not in crosswalk when struck, based not on matters which officer had observed but on examination of motorist's vehicle, marks near the accident, conversation with motorist, with another witness and with pedestrian was error); Stickel v. San Diego Elec. Ry. Co., 195 P.2d 416, 32 Cal.2d 157 (evidence that police officer had made in his note book a notation that cause of the accident was that truck went through a stop sign, was inadmissible on ground that notation was but an opinion of the officer, arrived at after he

§ 430.1   TRIAL EVIDENCE   Ch. 430

rule statement, and of the rule in certain states, is that the opinion must be "rationally based on the perception of the witness".[8]

A witness, shown to have been properly situated, may state an opinion that no warning signal was sounded.[9] Similarly, a wit-

had interviewed unidentified persons at scene).

Conn.—Giamattei v. Di Cerbo, 62 A. 2d 519, 135 Conn. 159 (refusal to permit officer to state whether he arrived at a determination of who was at fault, was not error, since question required officer to pass on truth of statements of parties made to him at time of investigation and was obviously a question which the trial court alone could answer).

Md.—State, Use of Stickley v. Critzer, 1962, 186 A.2d 586, 230 Md. 286 (officer's conclusion as to identity of driver excluded, without proof of what he saw in the vehicle after its removal from scene to support opinion).

Miss.—Billups Petroleum Co. v. Entrekin, 1950, 46 So.2d 781, 209 Miss. 302 (question to police officer whether gravel on highway was of character as would cause loss of control of vehicle was improper).

Mo.—Chester v. Shockley, Sup., 304 S.W.2d 831 (permitting an officer to give opinion from the facts learned in his investigation as to the point of impact was error).

N.H.—Zellers v. Chase, 197 A.2d 206, 105 N.H. 266 (was not error to permit trooper who was on scene shortly after accident to give his non-expert opinion that wheel marks indicated that automobile had been accelerating for some distance before it went off road).

S.C.—Gentry v. Watkins-Carolina Trucking Co., 154 S.E.2d 112, 249 S.C. 316, 37 A.L.R.3d 766 (testimony by police officer that left rear wheel of plaintiff's truck had been knocked off in collision was incompetent, but, in light of all the evidence, error in its admission was trivial and afforded no ground for reversal).

Wis.—Jacobson v. Bryan, 12 N.W.2d 789, 244 Wis. 359 (required official report of a traffic officer, coming to place of collision between trucks a short time after the collision had occurred, was admissible in so far as report was based on officer's own acts or observations but was inadmissible so far as report was based on conclusions from what others told him, or was his conclusions from what he had observed as to how the collision had occurred as that collision was a "sideswipe" collision).

8. Federal Rules of Evidence § 701, 28 U.S.C.A.

Cal.—West's Ann.Calif.Evid.Code, § 800(a).

Kan.—Kansas Code of Civil Procedure § 60–456(a).

Me.—Maine Rules of Evidence § 701.

Neb.—Nebraska Rules of Evidence § 701.

Nev.—N.R.S. 50.265(1).

N.J.—New Jersey Evidence Rule 56 (1)(a).

N.M.—New Mexico Rules of Evidence § 701.

Utah.—Utah Rules of Evidence § 701 (1)(a).

Wis.—Wisconsin Rules of Evidence § 907.01(1).

9. **U.S.**—Illinois Cent. R. Co. v. Sigler, C.C.A.Tenn., 122 F.2d 279.

Ala.—Southern Ry. Co. v. Terry, 109 So.2d 913, 40 Ala.App. 186, reversed 109 So.2d 919, 268 Ala. 510; Jordan v. Capers, 131 So. 557, 222 Ala. 197 (horn).

Ch. 430 LAY OPINION EVIDENCE § 430.1

ness may testify that no signal was given and that had a signal been given it would have been seen or heard.[10]

It is often difficult to distinguish between "fact" and "conclusion" or "opinion." Various types of testimony have been deemed "facts",[11] and other types deemed "conclusions".[12] A wit-

Ark.—Missouri Pac. R. Co. v. Yarbrough, 315 S.W.2d 897, 229 Ark. 308.

Cal.—Lahey v. Southern Pac. Co., 61 P.2d 461, 16 Cal.App.2d 652, certiorari denied Southern Pac. Co. v. Lahey, 57 S.Ct. 508, 300 U.S. 665, 81 L.Ed. 873 (automobile struck on foggy day).

Ky.—Louisville & N. R. Co. v. Ratliff's Adm'r, 85 S.W.2d 1006, 260 Ky. 380.

Mass.—Weir v. New York, N. H. & H. R. Co., 162 N.E.2d 793, 340 Mass. 66.

Minn.—Polchow v. Chicago, St. P., M. & O. Ry. Co., 270 N.W. 673, 199 Minn. 1.

Mo.—Dodd v. Terminal R. Ass'n of St. Louis, App., 108 S.W.2d 982 (testimony of driver, who was listening for bell); Young v. Bacon, App., 183 S.W. 1079.

N.C.—K. B. Johnson & Sons v. Southern Ry. Co., 199 S.E. 704, 214 N.C. 484 (only when it is first made to appear that the witness was in a position to hear and could have heard the signal had it been given).

Okl.—McBroom v. Meyer, 303 P.2d 303; Fleming v. Pattillo, 167 P.2d 40, 196 Okl. 557.

Pa.—Waltosh v. Pennsylvania R. Co., 103 A. 55, 259 Pa. 372.

S.C.—Mishoe v. Atlantic Coast Line R. Co., 197 S.E. 97, 186 S.C. 402 (witnesses 100 feet and 35 yards from crossing).

Utah—Clark v. Los Angeles & Salt Lake R. Co., 275 P. 582, 73 Utah 486.

10. Ariz.—Doubek v. Greco, 1968, 436 P.2d 494, 7 Ariz.App. 102.

Miss.—Heafner v. Columbus & G. R. Co., 1939, 190 So. 1, 185 Miss. 773.

11. U.S.—Neider v. Chrysler Corp., D.C.Pa.1973, 361 F.Supp. 320, affirmed C.A., 491 F.2d 748, and 491 F.2d 750 (testimony of civil engineer, describing what he saw when he observed scene and with respect to drawing he had made to show scene and measurements which he had made of it, was not opinion testimony requiring witness to qualify as expert).

Ala.—Stegall v. Wylie, 1973, 277 So.2d 85, 291 Ala. 1 (question which was asked of investigating police officer whether from the officer's observations he had reason to suspect that defendant had taken drugs, related to a fact and not to a mental operation, and was therefore properly allowed); Britton v. Doehring, 1970, 242 So. 2d 666, 286 Ala. 498 (testimony of police officer who investigated head-on collision as to position of automobiles on street when he arrived at the scene was admissible over objection that his other testimony, indicating he could not ascertain position of center line or shoulders of street, demonstrated that his testimony was based upon an inadequate opportunity to observe and thus constituted opinion evidence).

Ariz.—Universal Underwriters Ins. Co. v. State Auto. and Cas. Underwriters, 1971, 493 P.2d 495, 108 Ariz. 113 (may testify to existence of a custom as a fact).

Ga.—Essig v. Cheves, 44 S.E.2d 712, 75 Ga.App. 870 (testimony of

12. See note 12 on page 576.

575

Ill.—Land v. Bachman, 223 Ill.App. 473 (that one car struck another).

Md.—Gordon v. Contractors Transport Corp., 1973, 306 A.2d 573, 18 Md.App. 284 (testimony using formula in calculating pressure per square inch of heavy machinery and supplying data as to weight carried on trailer and amount of tire surface on roadway was nonexpert testimony); E. F. Enoch Co. v. Johnson, 37 A.2d 901, 183 Md. 326 (where in part of answer witness stated that he saw "an automobile going east").

Mass.—Luz v. Stop & Shop, Inc. of Peabody, 202 N.E.2d 771, 348 Mass. 198 (statement of store customer, who lost control over her automobile and drove over ramp onto sidewalk, that she was confused was not opinion evidence but rather evidence of state of mind); Campbell v. Ashler, 70 N.E.2d 302, 320 Mass. 475 (that no traffic was coming within specified distance); Cushman v. Boston W. & N. Y. St. Ry. Co., 65 N.E.2d 6, 319 Mass. 177 (statement of witness that he had never heard bus start as one did at the time of accident).

N.D.—Myers v. Hagert Const. Co., 23 N.W.2d 29, 74 N.D. 435 (that vehicle stopped suddenly).

Tex.—Briggs v. Lloyd, 405 S.W.2d 865 (testimony of witness, who lived near scene and who was not experienced highway patrolman or engineer, as to location on highway of debris and tire marks which he had observed and as to tire marks which led from point on defendant's side of road a distance of 150 yards to location of defendant's truck after collision); El Paso City Lines v. Smith, Civ.App., 226 S.W.2d 498, error refused ("every day you hear cars sliding out there trying to miss a street car or another automobile").

As to injury

Statements that witness noticed that speech of passenger was impaired more after the collision than before it and that "physical complaints such as, well, having back trouble and jaw trouble, it seemed that kinda slowed her speed down some" were admissible as constituting observations rather than opinions. McNeeley v. Blain, Miss.1971, 255 So.2d 923.

12. Ariz.—Finn v. J. H. Rose Truck Lines, 398 P.2d 935, 1 Ariz.App. 27 (that defendant's truck was "congesting" traffic and that the road was "completely blocked").

Neb.—Pahl v. Sprague, 42 N.W.2d 367, 152 Neb. 681 (statement of plaintiff that he was first in the intersection); Howerter v. Olson, 1945, 19 N.W.2d 346, 145 Neb. 507 (statement of driver after accident that something was wrong with brakes, but not saying what).

Or.—Klever v. Elliott, 320 P.2d 263, 212 Or. 490, 70 A.L.R.2d 1094 (statement directed to logging truck driver by one who arrived on scene of collision of logging truck and pickup truck after accident that it looked like a case of too much speed and that logging truck driver had not been watching where he was going was not one of fact).

W.Va.—Mercer Funeral Home v. Addison Bros. & Smith, 163 S.E. 439, 111 W.Va. 616 (that motorist could have passed a truck at curve if going at right speed).

Mathematical conclusion of speed and distance

In case where northbound plaintiff motorist turned west at intersection into side street and southbound defendant motorist collided with him, question propounded on cross-examination of plaintiff's witness that if plaintiff had judged speed of other automobile accurately, could plaintiff have waited a matter of just a

Ch. 430   LAY OPINION EVIDENCE   § 430.1

ness was not permitted to state whether or not a complaint was made to the driver of the vehicle as to the manner in which the automobile was being driven, for the question called for an expression of opinion concerning the driver's conduct, not what was said or done.[13]

Commonly the owner of property may testify to the value of the property before and after the accident.[14]

In an action for personal injuries in which plaintiff has asserted loss of earning capacity due to the injury, one is competent to testify as to the value of the plaintiff's services and the prevailing rate of wages;[15] past and present condition and

second before other automobile would have proceeded along its way, called for mathematical conclusion and was properly excluded. Roy v. Levy, 79 A.2d 847, 97 N.H. 36.

13. **N.Y.**—Dougherty v. Braddock Automatic Music Corp., 98 N.Y.S. 2d 514, 277 App.Div. 923.

14. **U.S.**—Lee Shops, Inc. v. Schatten-Cypress Co., C.A.Tenn., 350 F. 2d 12, certiorari denied 382 U.S. 980, 86 S.Ct. 552, 15 L.Ed.2d 470.

Ga.—Bradley v. Sherwin, 139 S.E.2d 512, 110 Ga.App. 632; Grant v. Dannals, 74 S.E.2d 119, 87 Ga.App. 389 (that he "guessed" automobile would be worth "certainly $1700" immediately before collision with defendant's automobile and "around $1200" after collision, though qualified by statement that it was witness' "feeling that difference in value was $500.00").

Idaho—Riley v. Larson, 1967, 432 P.2d 775, 91 Idaho 831, 42 A.L.R. 3d 1274.

Ky.—Howard v. Adams, 246 S.W.2d 1002 (automobile).

Md.—Rogers Cartage Co. v. Peglow, 106 N.E.2d 235, 122 Ind.App. 481.

Mass.—Duran v. Union Freight R. Co., 221 N.E.2d 405, 351 Mass. 351; Willey v. Cafrella, 146 N.E.2d 895, 336 Mass. 623.

N.D.—Imus v. Huber, 71 N.W.2d 339.

Tex.—Classified Parking System v. Kirby, 1974, 507 S.W.2d 586 (value of the automobile at the time of the theft); Cortez v. Mascarro, 1967, 412 S.W.2d 342.

And see

Plaintiff in fraud action against used car dealer, as owner of automobile, was qualified to testify as to difference in value as of date of purchase if automobile had been driven only 22,836 miles as against the same automobile if it had been driven 86,000 miles. Sarwark Motor Sales, Inc. v. Husband, 1967, 426 P. 2d 404, 5 Ariz.App. 304.

Insufficient foundation

Ga.—Mills v. Mangum, 1965, 141 S. E.2d 773, 111 Ga.App. 396 (only knew amount paid for it).

Mo.—Langdon v. Koch, App., 393 S.W.2d 66 (owner who appeared only to know that automobile had not been previously involved in wreck and to know amount of repair bill was not qualified to testify concerning amount of damage).

Rule limited

Judicial liberality in permitting owner of personalty to testify as to its reasonable market value should not be treated as an unrestricted license to engage in sheer speculation and unbridled guesswork. Hood v. M. F. A. Mut. Ins. Co., Mo.App., 379 S.W.2d 806.

15. **Mass.**—Cushman v. Boston W. & N. Y. St. Ry. Co., 65 N.E.2d 6, 319 Mass. 177.

§ 430.1 TRIAL EVIDENCE Ch. 430

ability to work without being caused pain;[16] and as to earn-

Testimony of others

Iowa—Henneman v. McCalla, 148 N.W.2d 447 (testimony of housewives, mothers and a husband and father as to reasonable value of services of decedent as a wife and mother).

Tex.—Murphey v. Blankenship, Civ. App., 120 S.W.2d 309 (value of wife's household services).

16. **Iowa**—Daniels v. Bloomquist, 138 N.W.2d 868, 258 Iowa 301, citing 32 C.J.S. Evidence § 546(22) (may testify as to his own health or physical condition; may state simple inferences drawn by him from his own conscious subjective sensations as to his physical condition; may testify as to condition of his health and freedom from sickness at a particular time; and may state his prior condition).

Mich.—Rypstra v. W. U. Tel. Co., 132 N.W.2d 140, 374 Mich. 166 (plaintiff's testimony as to extent of disability resulting from her injury).

N.Y.—Vincent-Wilday, Inc. v. Strait, 79 N.Y.S.2d 811, 273 App.Div. 1054 (past and present bodily condition).

N.C.—Carter v. Bradford, 1962, 126 S.E.2d 158, 257 N.C. 481 (that had 90 per cent loss of use of hand, to show how handicapped in her work).

Or.—Mayor v. Dowsett, 400 P.2d 234, 240 Or. 196 (whether she had suffered loss of feeling).

Tex.—Travelers Ins. Co. v. Rose, 389 S.W.2d 317, ref. n. r. e. 392 S.W.2d 462 (concerning physical condition of himself or another); Maedgen v. Kolodny, 384 S.W.2d 410, ref. n. r. e. (questions of apparent conditions of body or mind).

Rule limited

Cal.—Beagle v. Vasold, 53 Cal.Rptr. 129, 417 P.2d 673, 65 Cal.2d 166 (no witness may express his subjective opinion on evaluation of damages for pain and suffering).

Ga.—Hardwick v. Price, 152 S.E.2d 905, 114 Ga.App. 817 (may not express his opinion as to monetary value of damages for pain and suffering).

Rule stated

Rule that cause of injury, which requires determination by skilled and professional men, is question of science and must be proved by their testimony does not prevent a layman from testifying to facts in connection with his injury, which as layman he is capable of observing. Shinn v. Francis, Okl., 404 P.2d 1017.

Testimony of others

Ga.—General Gas Corp. v. Whitner, 140 S.E.2d 227, 110 Ga.App. 878, citing 32 C.J.S. Evidence § 546(23) (testimony of plaintiff's wife that he was still in shock upon arrival at home following collision, over objection that it was medical conclusion which witness was not qualified to give, was proper where witness described plaintiff's appearance and symptoms).

Or.—Frangos v. Edmunds, 1946, 173 P.2d 596, 179 Or. 577 (wife testifying whether plaintiff's prior hearing was "all right").

Tenn.—Johnson Freight Lines, Inc. v. Tallent, 384 S.W.2d 46, 53 Tenn. App. 464 (was proper to show by lay witnesses that plaintiff after having been involved in an accident appeared to be upset, hostile and to withdraw from social contacts).

Va.—Phillips v. Stewart, 148 S.E.2d 784, 207 Va. 214 (are competent evidence on issues concerning general health, strength, and bodily vigor of such person, his feebleness or apparent illness, or change in his apparent state of health or physical condition from one time to another).

Ch. 430 LAY OPINION EVIDENCE § 430.1

ings prior to the injury as compared to present earnings.[17] However, such evidence is inadmissible if it is speculative.[18]

In a variety of other circumstances opinion type evidence has been held inadmissible,[19] and in other instances has been held admissible.[20]

---

17. **Tex.**—Grocers Supply Co. v. Stuckey, Civ.App., 152 S.W.2d 911, error refused for want of merit (evidence of past earnings admissible to furnish jury a predicate from which they could fairly determine the extent of impairment of earning capacity).

18. **Neb.**—Piechota v. Rapp, 27 N.W.2d 682, 148 Neb. 442.

19. **Ala.**—Burress v. Dupree, 1971, 253 So.2d 31, 287 Ala. 524 (as to distance between vehicles when witness allegedly blinded); Casualty Reciprocal Exchange v. Wallace, 189 So.2d 861, 280 Ala. 61 (in declaratory judgment action by insurer to determine coverage under liability policy, question as to whether they had done anything whereby insured would reasonably believe that he had permission to drive automobile entrusted to him for repairs); Watkins v. Reinhart, 9 So.2d 113, 243 Ala. 243 (whether patrolman saw anything that would indicate vehicle had whipped around).

Ariz.—Finn v. J. H. Rose Truck Lines, 398 P.2d 935, 1 Ariz.App. 27 (under circumstances, including fact that there was no certainty as to part automobile which witness thought was going to overtake defendant's truck played in situation, it was less than clear what witness meant when he stated that defendant's truck was "congesting" traffic and that road was "completely blocked", and it was not an abuse of discretion to reject such opinion evidence, which was close to ultimate fact at issue in case).

Cal.—Sepulveda v. Ayako Ishimaru, 308 P.2d 809, 149 Cal.App.2d 543 (testimony of plaintiff that "I thought all that was necessary was to put out my hand and make my turn"); Cerm v. City and County of San Francisco, 222 P.2d 122, 99 Cal.App.2d 404 (that skid marks were made when vehicle was pushed by collision and not from slowing down).

Colo.—Jones v. Blegen, 420 P.2d 404 (four lay witnesses who expressed their opinions as to whether defendant was an unfit driver due to being intoxicated).

Ga.—Granger v. National Convoy & Trucking Co., 7 S.E.2d 915, 62 Ga.App. 294 (that witness did not come to testify because he would have lost his job); Elliott v. Georgia Power Co., 197 S.E. 914, 58 Ga.App. 151 (that plaintiff was in a "pretty bad condition" after accident); Gay v. Smith, 181 S.E. 129, 51 Ga.App. 615 (opinion fog very thick because thought smoke had been coming down).

Idaho.—Flowerdew v. Warner, 1965, 409 P.2d 110, 90 Idaho 164, citing C.J.S. Evidence § 546(11) (cause of his physical condition).

Ill.—Cunningham v. Central & Southern Truck Lines, Inc., 1968, 244 N.E.2d 412, 104 Ill.App.2d 247 (question propounded to plaintiffs' witness, a state police trooper, as to whether he had formed opinion as to how truck driven by plaintiff's decedent and truck driven by defendant came to collide at intersection).

Kan.—Smith v. Blakey, 1973, 515 P.2d 1062, 213 Kan. 91 (cannot give an opinion as to the amount plain-

---

20. See note 20 on page 581.

§ 430.1   TRIAL EVIDENCE   Ch. 430

tiff should recover for personal injuries, since that is question for jury).

Minn.—Jackson v. Wyatt Bros. Cement Co., 1972, 203 N.W.2d 360, 295 Minn. 145 (statements by bicyclists who were with minor plaintiff to effect that it was dangerous to go alongside truck between it and curb were inadmissible for purpose of showing standard of care of minor).

Miss.—Holifield v. Nester Chevrolet Co., 1968, 207 So.2d 636 (police officers who arrive at scene after collision may not offer opinion testimony).

Neb.—Brown v. Kaar, 1965, 134 N.W.2d 60, 178 Neb. 524 (that patrolman told wrecker could pull auto off slope, where not limited as proof of notice of alternative (method).

N.J.—Biro v. Prudential Ins. Co. of America, 1970, 265 A.2d 830, 110 N.J.Super. 391, reversed on other grounds 271 A.2d 1, 57 N.J. 204 (state police officer's opinion as to whether death was suicide); Sas v. Strelecki, 1970, 264 A.2d 247, 110 N.J.Super. 14 (officer's statement that witness backed up information given him at scene by driver and passenger was objectionable as conclusion, in addition to being hearsay).

Okl.—Hodo v. Cox, 1967, 437 P.2d 249 (officer opinion that truck blinker lights had not been working invaded province of jury).

Or.—Johnson v. Underwood, 203 P. 879, 102 Or. 680 (whether appearance of vehicle in photo would necessarily indicate nature of impact).

Pa.—Strausser v. Strunk, 1972, 295 A.2d 168, 222 Pa.Super. 537 (question asked defendant why he did not see child); Wilson v. Pa. R. Co., 219 A.2d 666, 421 Pa. 419 (court did not abuse its discretion in excluding witness' conclusion that motorist's wheels were spinning on approach to railroad crossing and that automobile had stalled after reaching crossing, where question whether such conclusions were necessary was question upon which reasonable men could differ); Jamison v. Ardes, 182 A.2d 497, 408 Pa. 188 (testimony of township police chief that prior to accident, giving rise to death and survival acts action, he had often warned decedent to stay off road).

Tex.—Security Mut. Cas. Co. v. Turner, 1970, 457 S.W.2d 305 (plaintiff is given quite a wide latitude in describing his physical condition at time of injury; however, he cannot give opinion evidence concerning a diagnosis which in its nature could be given only by a qualified physician); American Central Ins. Co. v. Melton, Civ. App., 389 S.W.2d 177, ref. n. r. e. (injured husband and wife who attempted to prove by their testimony alone the reasonableness of expenses incurred for x-rays, orthopedic care and physiotherapy, were not qualified to express opinion relating to reasonableness of such items, as these were matters outside scope of knowledge of ordinary laymen and must be established by those who are cognizant with such matters); St. Louis S. F. & T. Ry. Co. v. Williams, Civ.App., 104 S.W.2d 103, error dismissed (testimony of railroad employees that a railroad crossing was unusually dangerous).

Utah.—Barker v. Savas, 172 P. 672, 52 Utah 262 (testimony that witness saw deceased and tracks of automobile "that had run over him").

As to competence of driver

Mich.—Olweean v. Wayne County Road Commission, 1970, 182 N.W. 2d 58, 26 Mich.App. 121, affirmed 190 N.W.2d 108, 385 Mich. 698 (in negligent entrustment case, opinion driver was "careful driver" held improper).

N.Y.—Show v. Skopp, 1921, 190 N.Y.S. 859, 198 App.Div. 618 (that motorist was incompetent driver).

Characterizing driver's conduct

Ariz.—Dobbertin v. Johnson, 1964, 390 P.2d 849, 95 Ariz. 356 ("negligence" not proper subject).

Ind.—Lee v. Dickerson, 1962, 183 N.E.2d 615, 133 Ind.App. 542 (error to permit police officer to state that there was no improper driving).

Future pain

Wis.—Ianni v. Grain Dealers Mut. Ins. Co., 1969, 166 N.W.2d 148, 42 Wis.2d 354 (nonmedical witness is incompetent to express an opinion as to how long the pain will be projected into the future where the future consequences of the injury cannot be objectively determined).

Permanency of injury

Minn.—Rehnke v. Jammes, 1969, 168 N.W.2d 494, 283 Minn. 431 (disc injury is not the type which a layman is qualified to prognosticate is permanent, as in the case of loss of a limb or other obvious disability).

Point of impact

Ga.—Robinson v. McClain, 1971, 182 S.E.2d 157, 123 Ga.App. 664.

Minn.—Montagne v. Stenvold, 1967, 148 N.W.2d 815, 276 Minn. 547.

Neb.—Shamburg v. Folkers, 1971, 188 N.W.2d 723, 187 Neb. 169 (but, where defendant failed to object to identical question later put to another witness and answered in same way, objection was waived).

Wash.—McBroom v. Orner, 1964, 395 P.2d 95, 64 Wash.2d 887.

Sound as blowout

Conn.—Johnson v. Newell, 1970, 278 A.2d 776, 260 Conn. 269 (in action arising out of alleged blowout of tire recapped by one defendant and sold and installed by another, court improperly excluded witness' characterization of sound as a "tire blowout").

20. Ala.—Tombrello v. McGhee, 1968, 211 So.2d 900, 282 Ala. 408 (better view was that rejected testimony by police officer as to why accident report was not made, which was asked for in anticipation of answer that there did not appear to be an injury, was admissible; what weight to give testimony was a matter for jury to decide); Alabama Power Co. v. Jackson, 1936, 166 So. 692, 232 Ala. 42 (that electric wire entangled in fallen limb was "dangerous"); Penton v. Penton, 1931, 135 So. 481, 223 Ala. 282 (driver may say had vehicle under control).

Ark.—Sunray Sanitation, Inc. v. Pet Inc., 1970, 461 S.W.2d 110, 249 Ark. 703 (where plaintiff's truck had overturned on highway on which rotten eggs had been spilled, statement of plaintiff's employee that defendant's truck had been constructed so that liquid debris could easily spill out).

Cal.—Windeler v. Scheers Jewelers, 1970, 88 Cal.Rptr. 39, 8 Cal.App.3d 844 (as to own injuries); Christensen v. Malkin, 45 Cal.Rptr. 836, 236 Cal.2d 114 (properly allowed to testify as to quantity of liquor he had been served where he was experienced in bar business and himself was manager of a bar).

Idaho.—Tendoy v. West, 9 P.2d 1026, 51 Idaho 679 (that own vision was interfered with by lights of an approaching automobile).

Ill.—Schoolfield v. Witkowski, 203 N.E.2d 460, 54 Ill.App.2d 111 (questioning automobile mechanic about the main stress or blow to defendant's automobile was not error, where witness was not asked to reconstruct the accident or to tell point of initial impact and only testified that main point of im-

§ 430.1 TRIAL EVIDENCE Ch. 430

pact was to right side of automobile).

Ky.—Clements v. Peyton, 1966, 398 S.W.2d 477 (opinion as to direction from which sound appeared to come).

Md.—Fletcher v. Dixon, 1910, 77 A. 326, 113 Md. 101 (character of auto as a noise producer).

Mich.—Dumon v. Sines, 1972, 199 N.W.2d 872, 41 Mich.App. 291 (officer's opinion that one vehicle "hit" the other did not state opinion as to cause).

Miss.—Dennis v. Prisock, 1969, 221 So.2d 706, quoting 32 C.J.S. Evidence § 546 (22) (may describe injuries).

Neb.—Baker v. Daly, 1973, 211 N.W.2d 123, 190 Neb. 618 (permitting witness to be asked if he knew what was meant by a crosswalk did not improperly allow a lay witness to give his definition of a crosswalk); Redman Industries, Inc. v. Morgan Drive Away, Inc. 1965, 138 N.W.2d 708, 179 Neb. 406 (wind velocity).

Okl.—Andrews v. Moery, 1952, 240 P.2d 447, 205 Okl. 635 (as to which vehicle made certain skids).

Pa.—Topelski v. Universal South Side Autos, Inc., 1962, 180 A.2d 414, 407 Pa. 339 (could say own brakes failed).

Tex.—Kingham Messenger & Delivery Service, Inc. v. Daniels, Civ. App.1968, 435 S.W.2d 270 (wife's testimony concerning condition, as she observed it, of husband was admissible).

Utah.—Hales v. Peterson, 1961, 360 P.2d 822, 11 Utah 2d 411 (school principal's opinion as to walking and running speed of girls in deceased's class).

Vt.—Duprat v. Chesmore, 1920, 110 A. 305, 94 Vt. 218 (that had own auto under control).

Va.—Holbert v. Evans, 1968, 163 S. E.2d 187, 209 Va. 210 (question asked of officer who examined scene of pedestrian accident was improper in that it inquired whether statement given to officer by defendant was compatible with his physical findings at scene, which jury was as competent to pass upon as the witness, but error in admitting such testimony was harmless since jury could not have been misled thereby, especially since defendant driver had already testified as to the manner in which accident occurred, and jury was free to decide whether her sworn testimony differed from her unsworn testimony to officer and from the physical facts).

As to one's own intent

Tex.—Medina v. Sherrod, Civ.App., 391 S.W.2d 66 (intent with which party does act is known to him, and he is competent witness to testify as to such fact; but person's state of mind cannot be established by direct testimony of others, and witness cannot be permitted to testify as to intent or motive of another).

As to ownership of vehicle

Ga.—Kingston v. State, 1972, 194 S.E.2d 675, 127 Ga.App. 660 (and admission of tag receipt, even if error, was harmless since it was merely cumulative).

Employee's belief as to permission for personal use of auto

Ga.—American Emp. Ins. Co. v. Johns, 1970, 178 S.E.2d 207, 122 Ga.App. 577 (in liability insurer's action for declaration of noncoverage with respect to use of automobile by owner's employee, employee could properly be cross-examined as to whether employer would have objected to employee's running personal errand).

Indefinite terms

While descriptions given by defendant and by one of passengers in defendant's car of manner in which plaintiff's automobile came to a stop

582

Stopping distance opinions

Ordinarily expert testimony as to the distance within which an automobile could have been stopped is unnecessary.[21] One who knows the relevant conditions need not be an expert to ex-

prior to rear-end collision were expressed only in relative terms "abrupt" and "very abrupt," they were nevertheless admissible and were probative evidence. Rash v. Whisennand, Tex.Civ.App.1970, 453 S.W.2d 353, error refused n. r. e.

Justification for own conduct

Question as to whether chuckholes near railroad crossing where rear-end collision occurred were such as to require witness to stop in order to avoid them was not error where it was addressed to witness personally and called for statement of his practice and not for conclusion on ultimate issue of whether it was necessary for all drivers to stop for them. Gonzales v. Guber, 1970, 476 P.2d 581, —— Colo.App. ——.

Opinion of intoxication

Ariz.—Morales v. Bencic, 1970, 467 P.2d 752, 12 Ariz.App. 40 (testimony of arresting officers with 13 and 5 years experience).

Ill.—Suppe v. Sako, 36 N.E.2d 603, 311 Ill.App. 459 (action against tavern keeper under Dram Shop Act).

Ind.—Buddenberg v. Morgan, 38 N.E. 2d 287, 110 Ind.App. 609.

N.J.—State v. Shiren, 88 A.2d 601, 9 N.J. 445.

Or.—Brown v. Bryant, 417 P.2d 1002, 244 Or. 321 (where police officer as witness for guest testified that he could detect smell of alcohol on driver's breath, that driver was unsteady on his feet, and that his speech was slurred, a ruling of the Circuit Court that neither party could ask any witness his opinion whether driver was intoxicated at time of accident, so that driver was precluded from asking such question of guest and another passenger in automobile, both of whom might have been reasonably expected to give answers favorable to driver, was error).

Tex.—Mozley v. State, 1956, 290 S. W.2d 518, 163 Tex.Cr.R. 250.

Va.—Oliphant v. Snyder, 1966, 147 S.E.2d 122, 206 Va. 932.

Point of impact

Ga.—Royal Crown Bottling Co. of Gainesville v. Stiles, 1950, 60 S.E. 2d 815, 82 Ga.App. 254.

Ill.—Franklin v. Randolph, 1971, 267 N.E.2d 337, 130 Ill.App.2d 801 (testimony identifying an exhibit showing intersection and stating that that was where accident happened related only to general scene and did not suggest that witness was defining and pinpointing the point of impact).

Status of driver as employee

Mich.—Cowles v. Erb-Restrick Lumber Co., 1970, 176 N.W.2d 412, 21 Mich.App. 642 (by officer of corporate truck owner).

21. **Mo.**—Benson v. Smith, App., 38 S.W.2d 743.

22. **Mass.**—Foley v. Lord, 122 N.E. 393, 232 Mass. 368 (having been owner of automobiles for 14 years, and acquainted with operation of trucks, was properly permitted to give opinion that, from mark on curbing from rear of defendant's car for 30 feet, wheels were locked by brake, so that car should have stopped within 12 feet, going at 8 or 15 miles an hour).

Mich.—Morris v. Montgomery, 201 N.W. 496, 229 Mich. 509 (mechanic who drove the car involved and observed the road conditions).

§ 430.1 TRIAL EVIDENCE Ch. 430

press such an opinion,[22] since practical experience prima facie qualifies a witness on such matters.[23]

An experienced locomotive or civil engineer, or a witness with similar training or experience, may testify as to the distances required for stopping trains moving at certain rates of speed, or may testify as to the distance within which a certain train, which was involved in an accident, could have been stopped,[24] and this

Mo.—Young v. Bacon, App., 183 S. W. 1079.

N.C.—Costin v. Tidewater Power Co., 106 S.E. 568, 181 N.C. 196.

Utah.—Bryant v. Bingham Stage Line, 208 P. 541, 60 Utah 299 (had operated similar vehicles, and had made tests of stopping distance at various speeds).

23. Same statement in prior edition **cited by the court** in Christian v. Jeter, Mo., 287 S.W.2d 768, 770.

Mo.—Young v. Bacon, App., 183 S. W. 1079.

Tex.—El Paso Electric Co. v. Whitenack, Civ.App., 297 S.W. 258, affirmed, Com.App., 1 S.W.2d 594 (testimony of motorman as to distance within which street car could be stopped).

Insufficient experience

Where there was no evidence that driver had ever made trial of his ability to stop within any distance from any speed or that he was aware of fact that 33 miles per hour is 44 feet per second, trial court should have rejected as impossible driver's estimate that he could have stopped his automobile, traveling at speed of 30 to 35 miles per hour, within a "car length or so". Martin Furniture Corp. v. Yost, 1967, 230 A. 2d 338, 247 Md. 42.

24. U.S.—Mittlieder v. Chicago & N. W. Ry. Co., C.A.Neb.1969, 413 F.2d 77, appeal after remand 441 F.2d 52 (where braking systems on all trains operated generally in same way and all trains were subject to similar principles of physics in coming to a stop, fact that witness, testifying to distance required to stop train, had operated only switching engines in stockyards and not over road affected weight but not admissibility of testimony).

Idaho.—Hobbs v. Union Pac. R. Co., 108 P.2d 841, 62 Idaho 58 (fireman).

Mo.—Fair v. Thompson, 212 S.W.2d 923, 240 App. 664; Fitzgerald v. Thompson, 184 S.W.2d 198, 238 App. 546; Anderson v. St. Louis-San Francisco Ry. Co., Mo.App., 63 S.W.2d 182 (testimony of experienced engineer that train moving from 4 to 6 miles per hour could have been stopped in 15 feet without air connected to cars or 10 feet with air connected held admissible, where defendant had not shown whether air was connected); Bebout v. Kurn, 154 S.W.2d 120, 348 Mo. 501 (brakeman).

Okl.—Kurn v. Margolin, Okl., 101 P. 2d 818, 187 Okl. 135 (a witness who had 29 years' experience as a railroad machinist foreman and general foreman and had practical experience in the operation of engines and stoppage devices, and had run engines with engineers in testing them for speed and stopping ability, and who testified that by use of data he could figure out approximately the amount of feet within which a train could be stopped under conditions).

Opinion based on information from textbooks

Fact that engineer who testified concerning action of air brakes and

testimony as to distances may be given provided the witness knows all the material circumstances.[25]

Descriptive facts rule

One well-known exception to the rule excluding testimony which amounts to a conclusion of the witness arises where a situation which an ordinary observer is attempting to describe to the jurors is such that the witness cannot adequately place before them the primary facts so as to enable them to form a complete mental picture of the situation. Under such circumstances, the witness may aid the jury by inferences drawn from superior knowledge.[26] Where one with such superior knowledge is per-

their effect in stopping train took his figures as to speed and distances from standard textbooks held not to render testimony inadmissible, since testimony based on statistics found in standard authorities is admissible. Carbone v. Boston & Maine R. R., 192 A. 858, 89 N.H. 12.

25. **Mo.**—Grotjan v. Thompson, App., 140 S.W.2d 706 (lacking knowledge of the equipment of a train, he should not have been permitted to express his opinion as to the distance within which particular train could have been stopped).

26. **Ala.**—Arrick v. Fanning, 47 So. 2d 708, 35 Ala.App. 409 (question asked plaintiff as to whether his left arm extended further to left than left edge of truck was not improper as calling for unauthorized conclusion).

Cal.—Dean v. Feld, 175 P. 278, 77 Cal.App.2d 327 (testimony of 11 year old girl that automobile was "pretty close" when her sister went into street was admissible).

Conn.—Maclaren v. Bishop, 155 A. 210, 113 Conn. 312.

Fla.—Florida Evidence Code § 90.701(1).

Ga.—Seaboard Air Line Ry. Co. v. Young, 148 S.E. 757, 40 Ga.App. 4.

Ill.—State Farm Mut. Auto. Ins. Co. v. Short, 1970, 260 N.E.2d 415, 125 Ill.App.2d 97 (whether the driver of the car insured was a resident in the policyholder's home, to prove coverage by the insurance company).

Iowa.—Brady v. McQuown, 1949, 40 N.W.2d 25, 241 Iowa 34 (may describe highway marks as "tire marks", "skid marks", or "tire burn marks").

Md.—E. F. Enoch Co. v. Johnson, 37 A.2d 901, 183 Md. 326 (testimony of horse rider struck by tractor-trailer that "It looked like that truck * * * when it got to me, it swung in, for an automobile was going east and it looked like to avoid or keep from hitting that automobile that he swung over and hit me" was not inadmissible as a conclusion); Baltimore v. Turner, 136 A. 609, 152 Md. 216 (no signals given at crossing).

Mass.—Correira v. Boston Motor Tours, Inc., 169 N.E. 775, 270 Mass. 88 (statement that bus was skidding); Austin v. Eastern Massachusetts St. Ry. Co., 169 N.E. 484, 269 Mass. 420.

Neb.—Redman Industries, Inc. v. Morgan Drive Away, Inc., 138 N. W.2d 708, 179 Neb. 406 (unless it is based on pure speculation).

N.H.—Kelsea v. Town of Stratford, 118 A. 9, 80 N.H. 148 (why an automobile tipped over in a certain position).

§ 4301.1   TRIAL EVIDENCE   Ch. 430

mitted to state an opinion, facts upon which the opinion is based must be stated.[27]

When all the material facts are detailed, or are too numerous for a detailed statement, a witness may be permitted to give an estimate of the distance within which an automobile,[28] or of the dis-

N.C.—Myers v. Southern Public Utilities Co., 180 S.E. 694, 208 N.C. 293.

Pa.—Rice v. Shenk, 143 A. 231, 293 Pa. 524 (inference from condition of road that automobile skidded).

Wash.—Baird v. Webb, 294 P. 1000, 160 Wash. 157 (testimony as to measurements).

Wis.—Olson v. Hermansen, 220 N.W. 203, 196 Wis. 614, 61 A.L.R. 1243.

As "complex facts" exception

Testimony that witness thought defendant's truck was traveling "awfully slow", that as witness got "bumper to bumper" with such truck he saw that "it was stopped" and even testimony that small automobile had been pulled up as if to pass truck might have been admitted under complex facts exception. Finn v. J. H. Rose Truck Lines, 398 P.2d 935, 1 Ariz.App. 27.

"As shorthand" statement of fact

Opinion of motorist that if street car had remained stopped he could have passed through street intersection and averted colliding with street car held admissible as shorthand statement of fact, especially where witness was permitted to testify without objection to substantially same effect at other times during his examination. Myers v. Southern Public Utilities Co., 180 S.E. 694, 208 N.C. 293.

Visibility of object

Whether an object is rendered visible by light is a question of ordinary judgment based on common observation and an opinion may be given by witnesses having full opportunity for observation as to whether it was dark or daylight. Marr v. Olson, 40 N.W.2d 475, 241 Iowa 203.

27. **Ga.**—Gay v. Smith, 181 S.E. 129, 51 Ga.App. 615; Central of Georgia Ry. Co. v. Keating, 165 S.E. 873, 45 Ga.App. 811, reversed on other grounds 170 S.E. 493, 177 Ga. 345, conformed to 170 S.E. 497, 47 Ga.App. 336.

Status as employee

Testimony that white man dressed in overalls, carrying lantern and in charge of things and apparently train employee, made certain statement to witness as to how long train had been standing on crossing at time of collision, held properly admitted, since witness stated facts upon which he assumed that person referred to was railroad employee. Gay v. Smith, 181 S.E. 129, 51 Ga. App. 615.

28. **Ala.**—Great Atlantic & Pacific Tea Co. v. Donaldson, 156 So. 859, certiorari denied 156 So. 865, 229 Ala. 276 (burden of proving similarity of feel of brakes at time of examination as at time of collision must be met).

Ill.—Goldblatt v. Brocklebank, 166 Ill.App. 315.

Neb.—Blado v. Draper, 132 N.W. 410, 89 Neb. 787.

Auto mechanic

An automobile mechanic's opinion as to how long it would take an automobile to stop after brakes were applied going at a rate of 25 or 30 miles per hour was admissible, where mechanic had been engaged in automobile repair business for 20 years during which he had worked on automobiles, including brakes, and mechanic testified that he owned automobiles of same make and model as station wagon in which deceased was riding and had given them road tests.

tance within which a truck,[29] or a railroad train,[30] could have been stopped; but such an estimate, when based on memory or casual observation, must yield to one supported by unchallenged measurements or by reference to definite data on an accurate map.[31]

Another exception to the general rule may be stated as follows: an inference necessarily involving certain facts is the equivalent of a specification of such facts, and may be stated without a statement of them.[32] Hence, evidence is admissible to show the state of mind of one involved in an automobile accident, or the existence or absence of the emotions of fear, anger, joy, excitement, nervousness, earnestness, anxiety, disgust, curiosity, surprise, embarrassment, sympathy, despondency, displeasure, and satisfaction.[33]

Conclusions of law

One fundamental rule which should always be observed in automobile accident cases is that the testimony should be confined to facts, and that neither a party nor any other witness should be permitted to give an opinion on questions of law involved.[34] Therefore a witness should not be permitted to give

Zepeda v. Moore, Tex.Civ.App., 153 S.W.2d 212, error dismissed.

Contra

Pa.—Kummerlen v. Pustilnik, 45 A. 2d 27, 353 Pa. 327.

29. U.S.—Hoagland v. Canfield, C. C.N.Y., 160 F. 146.

30. S.C.—Harmon v. Columbia & G. R. R. Co., 10 S.E. 877, 32 S.C. 127, 17 Am.St.Rep. 843.

31. Md.—Storrs v. Hink, 173 A. 66, 167 Md. 194.

Wis.—Serkowski v. Wolf, 30 N.W. 2d 223, 251 Wis. 595.

32. Ala.—Pollard v. Rogers, 173 So. 881, 234 Ala. 92.

33. Ala.—Pollard v. Rogers, 173 So. 881, 234 Ala. 92.

Or.—Goebel v. Vaught, 269 P. 491, 126 Or. 332.

Excited and scared

Refusal to admit testimony that minor appeared to be excited or scared as he swerved to the left in front of automobile was error. Carmichael v. Harrison, Tex.Civ.App., 165 S.W.2d 510.

Frame of mind

In action by guest when blowout of right front tire was caused by loosening of blowout patch, and automobile crashed into culvert, since one of essential elements of plaintiff's right to recovery was a realization on part of defendant that use of defective tire involved an unreasonable risk, exclusion of testimony as to what was defendant's frame of mind was error, even though answer might be termed a conclusion. Lynes v. Debenedictus, 102 N.Y.S.2d 684, 278 App.Div. 674, reversed on other grounds 103 N.E.2d 734, 303 N.Y. 772.

34. U.S.—American Indem. Co. v. Richland Oil Co., D.C.S.C.1967, 273 F.Supp. 702.

Cal.—Hom v. Clark, 1963, 35 Cal. Rptr. 11, 221 Cal.App.2d 622 (rejection of officer's testimony as to

§ 430.1   **TRIAL EVIDENCE**   Ch. 430

purpose of department's "do not cross" signs at intersection, and whether crosswalk and alley existed).

Colo.—Kellogg v. Dillon, 1970, 472 P.2d 172, —— Colo.App. —— (cross-examination of defendant regarding his employment status and scope of the status with respect to passenger called for legal conclusions).

Ga.—General Ins. Co. of America v. Camden Const. Co., 1967, 154 S.E. 2d 26, 115 Ga.App. 189 (driver's testimony that during unloading operations tractor-trailer was under his "exclusive control" was a conclusion of law).

Idaho.—Hawkins v. Chandler, 396 P.2d 123, 88 Idaho 20.

Mo.—Hammond v. Emery-Bird-Thayer Dry Goods Co., Sup., 240 S.W. 170.

Tex.—Dallas Railway & Terminal Co. v. Gossett, 294 S.W.2d 377, 156 Tex. 252 (statements that street was a one-way street for northbound traffic were simply conclusions of witnesses, and did not constitute evidence that street had been duly and legally designated as a one-way street).

Wis.—Pagel v. Kees, 127 N.W.2d 816, 23 Wis.2d 462 (testimony as to opinion of insurance adjuster).

Conclusions of law defined

Whether a statement is an ultimate fact or a conclusion of law depends upon whether it is reached by natural reasoning or by an application of fixed rules of law. Brown v. Charlotte-Mecklenburg Bd. of Ed., 153 S.E.2d 335, 269 N.C. 667.

Meaning of warning sign held improper

Court did not err in sustaining objection to questions of a police officer as to meaning of a "No Turn" sign which was located on highway ramp where record did not disclose that police officer was qualified in any manner to express such an opinion, and if question did not call for an expression of opinion but only for the meaning of such a sign, that was something that was comprehensible to any ordinary person. Bedrosian v. O'Keefe, 215 A.2d 423, 100 R.I. 331.

Meaning of warning signs held proper

Testimony of highway engineer that white lines across lanes of traffic marked "school" "Xing" were warnings of school crossings ahead did not constitute lay opinion as to either a question of law or ultimate fact to be determined by jury and was admissible to assist jury in determining whether accident occurred within marked crosswalk. Pierce v. Barenberg, 421 P.2d 149, 91 Idaho 354.

Reasonable speed

Testimony of daughter of plaintiff motorist that at about five minutes prior to accident she saw two automobiles, one of them defendant's, going north and traveling at a speed in excess of that which was reasonable and prudent under circumstances, was inadmissible. Townsend v. Whatton, 1974, 521 P.2d 1014, 21 Ariz. App. 556.

Status as partnership

In action against alleged partners, where trial judge asked one of the codefendants if liability insurance in the partnership name was in force at time of accident, answer in affirmative was responsive evidence of continued existence of partnership and not objectionable as a conclusion of law of the witness. Bachand v. Vidal, 101 N.E.2d 884, 328 Mass. 97.

Fact that motorist stated on cross-examination that he and his passenger shared the profits and were partners was of no relevancy in action for damages by the passenger, since what the parties call themselves is a legal conclusion and not a fact. Bach

an opinion that vehicles on a certain street or approaching from a certain direction have the right of way.[35] An employee should not be permitted to testify that the trip did not concern the employers or their business, since such testimony relates to a question of law and not a question of fact.[36]

§ 430.2 Lay Opinions—Speed

Library References:
C.J.S. Evidence §§ 546(51) et seq., 546(52), 546(88).
West's Key No. Digests, Evidence ⇔471(23), 474(8), 492.

The rate of speed at which an automobile was moving at the time of an accident is not a matter exclusively for expert testimony.[37] A person who is of ordinary intelligence,[38] who has some

v. Liberty Mut. Fire Ins. Co., 1967, 152 N.W.2d 911, 36 Wis.2d 72.

35. U.S.—Bramley v. Dilworth, C.C.A.Ohio, 274 F. 267.

Ga.—Akin v. Randolph Motors, Inc., 99 S.E.2d 358, 95 Ga.App. 841.

Mo.—Hammond v. Emery-Bird-Thayer Dry Goods Co., Sup., 240 S.W. 170.

36. N.H.—Tuttle v. Dodge, 116 A. 627, 80 N.H. 304.

But see

Relation of principal and agent is legal one, depending upon existence of certain facts, and statement that it exists may be in nature of conclusion, yet relation is also condition of which anyone having personal knowledge of it may testify. Remmick v. Mills, N.D.1968, 165 N.W.2d 61, citing 3 C.J.S. Agency § 322.

37. U.S.—Denver Omnibus & Cab Co. v. Krebs, Colo., 255 F. 543, 166 C.C.A. 611.

Ariz.—Southwestern Freight Lines v. Floyd, 119 P.2d 120, 58 Ariz. 249.

Cal.—Sommer v. Martin, 204 P. 33, 55 Cal.App. 603 (14 year old boy).

Ga.—Central of Georgia Ry. Co. v. Luther, 1973, 196 S.E.2d 149, 128 Ga.App. 178.

Ill.—Sullivan v. Heyer, 21 N.E.2d 776, 300 Ill.App. 599; Koch v. Pearson, 219 Ill.App. 468 (policeman near scene).

Iowa.—Wilflin v. Des Moines City Ry. Co., 156 N.W. 842, 176 Iowa 642.

Mass.—Smith v. Neibauer Bus Co., 105 N.E.2d 238, 328 Mass. 624 (admissible where witness followed course of bus with his eyes for distance of 180 feet).

Mich.—Luttenton v. Detroit, J. & C. Ry. Co., 176 N.W. 558, 209 Mich. 20.

Minn.—Greenberg v. Holfeltz, 69 N.W.2d 369, 244 Minn. 175.

Mo.—Thornton v. Stewart, App., 240 S.W. 502 (boy thirteen years old); Flach v. Ball, 240 S.W. 465, 209 Mo.App. 389.

Md.—United Rys. & Elec. Co. v. State, 163 A. 90, 163 Md. 313.

N.M.—Bunton v. Hull, 177 P.2d 168, 51 N.M. 5.

N.C.—Harris v. Draper, 63 S.E.2d 209, 233 N.C. 221 (weight and credibility for jury); Hicks v. Love, 161 S.E. 394, 201 N.C. 773 (admissible without antecedent qualification).

Pa.—Gilmore v. Marsh, 1967, 227 A.2d 881, 424 Pa. 361; Fulkerson v. Wasserott, 53 Luz.L.Reg. 241.

38. See note 38 on page 590.

§ 430.2

Tenn.—Crunk v. Grooms, 1969, 450 S.W.2d 15, 60 Tenn.App. 611.

Tex.—Zepeda v. Moore, Civ.App., 153 S.W.2d 212, error dismissed.

W.Va.—Leftwich v. Wesco Corp., 119 S.E.2d 401, 146 W.Va. 196.

But see

Md.—State v. United Rys. & Electric Co. of Baltimore, 115 A. 109, 139 Md. 306.

Lay opinion favored

Minn.—LeMieux v. Bishop, 1973, 209 N.W.2d 379, 296 Minn. 372 (party having nonexpert opinion testimony as to automobile speed, foundationally based upon easily established facts, susceptible of specific contradiction and reasonably related to the perception of the lay witness, has not only right but perhaps duty to present such testimony; such testimony is preferable to opinion testimony of so-called accident reconstruction experts).

Speed of interurban car

Mich.—Luttenton v. Detroit, J. & C. Ry., 176 N.W. 558, 209 Mich. 20 (where driver of automobile had driven for several years and had ridden on interurban cars several times and formed a judgment of the speed at which they were running, there was no error in permitting him to testify as to the speed an interurban car was running).

Speed of snowmobile

Minn.—Carpenter v. Mattison, 1974, 219 N.W.2d 625, 300 Minn. 273.

Speed of street car

Md.—United Rys. & Electric Co. of Baltimore v. State, 163 A. 90, 163 Md. 313 (though motorist's inexpert estimate of speed of street car just before collision is worth but little, his testimony that it was coming at "an awful rate of speed" has probative force on issue whether it was coming fast or slow).

Speed of train

Mo.—Nicholas v. Chicago, B. & Q. R. Co., 188 S.W.2d 511, 329 Mo. App. 421 (truck driver's testimony that train was traveling at speed of at least 55 miles per hour was not inadmissible as speculative and unsupported by proven facts, in view of positive evidence that train was not within 750 feet from crossing when truck driver stopped and looked at point within 30 feet therefrom).

N.C.—Southern Ry. Co. v. Hutton & Bourbonnais Co., 1970, 177 S.E.2d 901, 10 N.C.App. 1 (if had reasonable opportunity to observe train in motion and did observe it).

38. Ala.—Vredenburgh Saw Mill Co. v. Black, 37 So.2d 212, 251 Ala. 302 (fact that witness had never driven a truck or automobile did not disqualify him from testifying as to speed of truck which struck pedestrian).

Neb.—Patterson v. Kerr, 254 N.W. 704, 127 Neb. 73 (one with knowledge of time and distance is competent to give testimony thereon; his opportunity and extent of observation being matters affecting weight of testimony).

Or.—Johnson v. Underwood, 203 P. 879, 102 Or. 680 (passenger in vehicle without speedometer).

Tex.—Merchants' Transfer Co. v. Wilkinson, Civ.App., 219 S.W. 891.

Even non-driver

Ariz.—Townsend v. Whatton, 1974, 521 P.2d 1014, 21 Ariz.App. 556; Southwestern Freight Lines v. Floyd, 119 P.2d 120, 58 Ariz. 249 (permitting girl bicyclist 12 years old to testify as to speed of the truck, where before she was permitted to give her estimate of such speed, she testified that her father had an automobile, that she rode

knowledge of the speed generally of the class of vehicles to which the one involved in an accident belongs,[39] and who actually witnessed the speed of the vehicle in question at or near the time of the accident in which it was involved,[40] or heard the noise made

with him often, that she watched the speedometer, and that she could look at a moving automobile and estimate close to its speed, although she had never driven an automobile).

Ark.—Eisele v. Beaudoin, 1966, 398 S.W.2d 676, 240 Ark. 227.

Nev.—Patton v. Henrikson, 1963, 380 P.2d 916, 79 Nev. 197 (15 years old).

N.C.—Murchison v. Powell, 1967, 153 S.E.2d 352, 269 N.C. 656.

Prior experience estimating speed
Witness who had observed traveling automobiles with view of estimating their speed, and testified that he could estimate speed of automobiles, is sufficiently qualified to testify as to rate of speed of defendant's car at time of collision. Becvar v. Batesole, 256 N.W. 297, 218 Iowa 858.

39. Ala.—Taylor v. Lewis, 89 So. 581, 206 Ala. 338.

Mass.—Davidson v. Beacon Hill Taxi Service, Inc., 278 Mass. 540, 180 N.E. 503.

Mo.—Brown v. Alton R. Co., 151 S.W.2d 727, 236 Mo.App. 26 (estimated speed of train from experience as train passenger).

Neb.—Tews v. Bamrick, 26 N.W.2d 499, 148 Neb. 59 (experienced driver who was following defendant could give opinion).

Okl.—Thompson v. Cooper, 135 P.2d 49, 192 Okl. 237; Thompson v. Cooper, 135 P.2d 52, 192 Okl. 240 (witness who had lived near railroad for many years, and had made observations of speed of trains, was qualified to testify as to speed of train).

W.Va.—Leftwich v. Wesco Corp., 119 S.E.2d 401, 146 W.Va. 196.

Wyo.—Potts v. Brown, 1969, 452 P.2d 975, quoting C.J.S. Evidence § 546(53).

Insufficient knowledge
Testimony as to speed of train estimated by witness on the basis of comparison with speed of automobile driven by witness, which he knew by reason of observation of speedometer, was incompetent, since experience of witness in judging speed was based only on his experience in driving automobile. Conrad v. Baltimore & O. R. Co., D.C.Pa., 146 F.Supp. 151, affirmed, C.A., 238 F.2d 624.

40. U.S.—Canadian Pac. Ry. Co. v. Slayton, C.C.A.Vt., 29 F.2d 687.

Ala.—Vredenburgh Saw Mill Co. v. Black, 37 So.2d 212, 251 Ala. 302; Davis v. Smitherman, 96 So. 208, 209 Ala. 244; Cargall v. Riley, 95 So. 821, 209 Ala. 183; Galloway v. Perkins, 73 So. 956, 198 Ala. 658.

Cal.—Hastings v. Serleto, 143 P.2d 956, 61 Cal.App.2d 672 (though testified had paid no attention to speed until just before the accident).

Colo.—Oglesby v. Conger, 1972, 507 P.2d 883, 31 Colo.App. 504 (includes opinion of own speed).

Conn.—Shea v. Hemming, 1921, 115 A. 686, 97 Conn. 149.

Ga.—Gunter v. Willingham, 1967, 158 S.E.2d 255, 116 Ga.App. 700 (ordinarily, where witness does not actually observe vehicle in motion, he must qualify as expert in order to give his opinion as to speed based on various external data); Eastern Dehydrating Co. v. Brown, 145 S.E.2d 274, 112 Ga.App. 349

§ 430.2 TRIAL EVIDENCE Ch. 430

(opinion with respect to speed of defendant's truck at time truck struck object on highway, where plaintiff gave facts on which his opinion was based, that is, distance traveled by truck after collision with object, and force with which truck subsequently struck plaintiff's home).

Ill.—Breslin v. Bates, 1973, 303 N.E. 2d 807, 14 Ill.App.3d 941; Shennan v. Chrispens Truck Lines, 44 N.E. 2d 339, 316 Ill.App. 160.

Iowa—Hayungs v. Falk, 27 N.W.2d 15, 238 Iowa 285; Schultz v. Starr, 164 N.W. 163, 180 Iowa 1313.

Kan.—Hampton v. State Highway Commission, 1972, 498 P.2d 236, 209 Kan. 565; Kelly v. Vucklich, 206 P. 894, 111 Kan. 199.

Ky.—Lundy v. Brown's Adm'x, 205 S.W.2d 498, 305 Ky. 721 (boy who saw vehicle strike companion and travel on nearly 100 feet).

La.—Fidelity & Cas. Co. of New York v. Aetna Life & Cas. Co., App.1971, 244 So.2d 255 (showed prior driving and observation of speeds).

Md.—Mulligan v. Pruitt, 223 A.2d 574, 244 Md. 338 (witness who was almost directly opposite from where accident occurred had sufficient period of time in which to observe automobile); Washington B. & A. Electric Ry. Co. v. William A. Fingles, Inc., 109 A. 431, 135 Md. 574.

Mass.—Smith v. Neibauer Bus Co., 105 N.E.2d 238, 328 Mass. 624 (admissible where witness followed course of bus with his eyes for distance of 180 feet).

Mich.—Hicks v. Bacon, 1970, 182 N.W.2d 620, 26 Mich.App. 487 (observed one car length or less); Mills v. Michigan Electric R. Co., 212 N.W. 75, 237 Mich. 393; Faulkner v. Payne, 157 N.W. 565, 191 Mich. 263 (saw vehicle "some rods away").

Minn.—Sanchez v. Waldrup, 136 N.W.2d 61, 271 Minn. 419; Dunkelbeck v. Meyer, 167 N.W. 1034, 140 Minn. 283.

Miss.—Ideal Cement Co. v. Killingsworth, 1967, 198 So.2d 248.

Mo.—Grotjan v. Thompson, App., 140 S.W.2d 706 (witness drove alongside of train and formed estimate of train's speed); Burke v. Shaw Transfer Co., 243 S.W. 449, 211 Mo.App. 353; Varley v. Columbia Taxicab Co., Sup., 240 S.W. 218.

Neb.—Kraft v. Wert, 35 N.W.2d 786, 150 Neb. 719; Lewis v. Miller, 230 N.W. 769, 119 Neb. 765, 70 A.L.R. 532; Anderson v. Omaha & C. B. St. R. Co., 218 N.W. 135, 116 Neb. 487.

N.M.—Bunton v. Hall, 177 P.2d 168, 51 N.M. 5.

Nev.—Patton v. Henrikson, 380 P.2d 916, 79 Nev. 197 (observed motor scooter in motion for 15 to 20 seconds immediately prior to collision with automobile, was competent to express opinion as to speed of scooter immediately before collision, though she was only 15 years of age at time of collision and not then licensed to drive).

N.C.—Davis v. Imes, 1972, 186 S.E. 2d 641, 13 N.C.App. 521 (seen 200 feet or more); Emanuel v. Clewis, 1968, 158 S.E.2d 587, 272 N.C. 505 (while standing in truck bed, as to speed of the truck); Honeycutt v. Strube, 134 S.E.2d 110, 261 N.C. 59; Loomis v. Torrence, 130 S.E.2d 540, 259 N.C. 381 (observed automobile when it was 85 feet away and who again saw automobile when it was 50 feet from intersection and who observed it afterwards through the intersection and for 90 feet beyond).

Ohio—Ohio Cas. Ins. Co. v. Landon, 204 N.E.2d 566, 1 Ohio App.2d 317.

Pa.—Shaffer v. Coleman, 35 Pa. Super. 386.

Tex.—Hanks v. LaQuey, 425 S.W.2d 396, error refused n. r. e. (no error in permitting witness to testify as

by the vehicle,[41] or one who actually experienced the physical effects of the speed of a vehicle, through having been struck by it,[42]

to his estimate of speed of automobile as it passed witness shortly prior to accident, although it was asserted that witness, a school administrator, was not qualified to judge the speed); Bee Line Coaches v. Folterman, Civ.App.1948, 207 S.W.2d 986 (minor passenger, as to speed of bus).

Wash.—Froemming v. Spokane City Lines, 427 P.2d 1003, 71 Wash.2d 265 (estimates of speed could be challenged on witnesses' limited opportunities to make careful judgment of driver's speed); Stubbs v. Allen, 1932, 10 P.2d 983, 168 Wash. 156.

Wyo.—Colwell v. Anderson, 438 P.2d 448.

Ill.—Conway v. Tamborini, 215 N.E. 2d 303, 68 Ill.App.2d 190 (admissible although bicyclist had only momentary opportunity to observe automobile, as fact that observation was momentary affected weight and not admissibility).

Observation of light beams

Iowa—Thornbury v. Maley, 45 N.W. 2d 576, 242 Iowa 70 (probative value of his testimony on such question is for jury).

N.C.—Jones v. Horton, 142 S.E.2d 351, 264 N.C. 549 (observed 400–500 feet).

41. **Cal.**—Bennett v. Central California Traction Co., 1931, 1 P.2d 47, 115 Cal.App. 1 (street car).

Mo.—Murphy v. Cole, 1935, 88 S.W. 2d 1023, 338 Mo. 13, 103 A.L.R. 505 (auto mechanic).

N.J.—Pierson v. Frederickson, 1968, 245 A.2d 524, 102 N.J.Super. 156 (weight to be given evidence of speed based on auditory perception is matter for determination by jury).

Contra

Nev.—Bernardini v. Salas, 1969, 448 P.2d 43, 84 Nev. 702, 33 A.L.R.3d 1397.

Ohio—Johnson v. Eastern Ohio Transport Corporation, 1942, 50 N. E.2d 1003, 72 Ohio App. 172 (exclusion not prejudicial error).

Va.—Meade v. Meade, 1966, 147 S. E.2d 171, 206 Va. 823 (incompetent to give opinion over 80 mph.).

Even from distance

Wash.—Hauswirth v. Pom-Arleau, 119 P.2d 674, 11 Wash.2d 354 (testimony of witnesses, who resided along highway and who heard roar made by automobile and sound of collision immediately thereafter, was admissible on question of speed, although distance from witnesses' homes to intersection was approximately a quarter of a mile, in view of brief interval between roar of passing automobile and sound of crash and the fact that no automobile other than automobiles involved was in vicinity at the time).

Rule limited

Or.—Thomas v. Dad's Root Beer & Canada Dry Bottling Co. of Portland, 356 P.2d 418, 225 Or. 166, rehearing denied 357 P.2d 418, 225 Or. 166 (may testify whether its movement was rapid or slow, but may not testify as to the rate of speed in miles per hour).

42. **Ga.**—Hill v. Kirk, 50 S.E.2d 785, 78 Ga.App. 310.

Mass.—Barney v. Magenis, 135 N.E. 142, 241 Mass. 268.

Mo.—Ottofy v. Mississippi Valley Trust Co., 196 S.W. 428, 197 Mo. App. 473.

N.C.—Harris v. Draper, 63 S.E.2d 209, 233 N.C. 221.

§ 430.2 TRIAL EVIDENCE Ch. 430

or otherwise,[43] is a competent witness on the issue of speed, since the requisite knowledge is derived from the exercise of the witness' own senses.[44]

Or.—Turner v. McCready, 222 P.2d 1010, 190 Or. 28; Cameron v. Goree, 189 P.2d 596, 182 Or. 581 (driver of car in which plaintiff was riding); Weygandt v. Bartle, 1918, 171 P. 587, 88 Or. 310.

Tex.—Merchants' Transfer Co. v. Wilkinson, Civ.App., 219 S.W. 891.

But see

Where plaintiff had had no view of defendant's truck prior to collision, he had been immediately knocked unconscious by the blow and he neither saw his automobile nor any photographs of it after collision, no foundation was laid for admission of testimony by plaintiff as to speed of defendant's truck. Boatner v. Sims, 1967, 154 S.E.2d 282, 115 Ga.App. 284.

43. **Mass.**—Barney v. Magenis, 135 N.E. 142, 241 Mass. 268.

44. **Ky.**—Bowling Green - Hopkinsville Bus Co. v. Edwards, 59 S.W. 2d 584, 248 Ky. 684.

Md.—Shaneybrook v. Blizzard, 121 A.2d 218, 209 Md. 304.

Mass.—Barney v. Magenis, 135 N.E. 142, 241 Mass. 268.

Minn.—LeMieux v. Bishop, 1973, 209 N.W.2d 379, 296 Minn. 372 (preferable to testimony of so-called accident reconstruction experts).

Tex.—Zetsche v. Lawler, Civ.App., 25 S.W.2d 907.

Could estimate approximately

Admission of testimony of witness was not error, though witness first testified that he could not estimate speed of automobile, where he later stated that he could estimate speed approximately. Smith v. Musgrove, 125 N.W.2d 869, 372 Mich. 329.

Rule restricted

Refusing to admit opinion of witness was not error, where, on cross-examination, witness indicated she could not accurately judge speed of vehicles under conditions stated. Clark v. Smith, 149 N.W.2d 425, 181 Neb. 461.

Speed of train

Ala.—Payne v. Roy, 90 So. 605, 206 Ala. 432 (worked on section several months).

Md.—Baltimore & O. R. Co. v. Wright, 84 A.2d 851, 198 Md. 555 (in actions against railroad for injuries sustained by pedestrian when train struck automobile at crossing in town and hurled automobile against pedestrian, pedestrian's husband was properly permitted to testify as to the speed of the train, over objection that he did not have sufficient opportunity for observation, where husband had been employed by the railroad for 26 years as a trackman, and he testified that he went across crossing ahead of pedestrian, that as he crossed track he saw light in watch box indicating that train was coming and that when he got across the tracks he heard the train coming, and that he walked over to his parked automobile about 125 feet south of crossing and saw the train when it came on the crossing).

"Swearing" to speed not required

Ga.—Ellison v. Evans, 69 S.E.2d 94, 85 Ga.App. 292 (nonexpert witness who sees a vehicle in motion may testify as to his estimate of speed and facts upon which he bases estimate, though he refuses to swear positively that his estimate is absolutely accurate, and where estimate is substantially

Ch. 430 LAY OPINION EVIDENCE § 430.2

However, the admission of a guess is erroneous.[45]

Preliminary to the admission of the testimony of a nonexpert on the question of speed, the witness' qualifications and opportunity for adequate observation as to speed should be established.[46] However, courts ordinarily do not adhere to strict rules on the question.[47]

correct); Thornton v. King, 58 S. E.2d 227, 81 Ga.App. 122 (couldn't swear how fast it was going but only how fast he thought it was going).

45. Fla.—Tranter v. Wible, App., 191 So.2d 595 (testimony by witness, who initially stated that he could not estimate speed of automobile which was struck by bicycle and that any estimate he made would be pure speculation and who subsequently stated that automobile was traveling at speed of 25 to 40 miles per hour, was given without any reasonable foundation).

Mo.—Gorman v. Franklin, Sup., 117 S.W.2d 289.

46. U.S.—Carpino v. Kuehnle, D.C. Pa.1971, 54 F.R.D. 28, affirmed, C.A., 474 F.2d 1339 (where eyewitness testified that it was only for split second that he caught any glimpse of automobile and just saw it flash by him, and that he had no idea how long he observed it, court properly refused to let witness estimate speed).

Colo.—Chancellor v. Sippel, 1972, 495 P.2d 556, —— Colo.App. ——.

Ga.—Gunter v. Willingham, 1967, 158 S.E.2d 255, 116 Ga.App. 700 (police officer who, although not qualified as expert, recited facts on which he predicated his opinion).

Mich.—Hinderer v. Ann Arbor R. Co., 211 N.W. 734, 237 Mich. 232 (opinion of a motorist as to the speed of a train which struck him, based upon his observation when the engine was upon him 2 feet away, has been excluded).

Mo.—Vaeth v. Gegg, 1972, 486 S.W. 2d 625 (brevity of defendant's observation of plaintiff's car prior to collision would not destroy credibility of his evidence as to plaintiff's speed but would only go to its weight).

N.H.—Cedergren v. Hadaway, 18 A. 2d 380, 91 N.H. 270 (that witness who testified to motorist's excessive speed had only a brief time to observe it affects only the weight of his testimony, not its competence).

N.C.—Miller v. Kennedy, 1974, 205 S.E.2d 741, 22 N.C.App. 163 (passenger in vehicle saw bicycle for only 100 feet, as to speed of auto and bicycle).

Okl.—Smith v. Hill, 381 P.2d 868 (where witnesses stated that they had driven vehicles and had observed other vehicles passing down the same section of highway, even though witnesses stated they had observed progress of defendant's vehicle for only about 15 feet).

Pa.—Chanin v. Master, 27 A.2d 40, 345 Pa. 268 (testimony of mechanic that truck was traveling from 45 to 50 miles an hour just before collision was not inadmissible as a matter of law, on ground that conditions for observation were not sufficiently favorable, where there was evidence that mechanic was standing on highway about 150 feet from place where collision occurred, that he observed truck continuously from

47. See note 47 on page 597.

595

§ 430.2 TRIAL EVIDENCE Ch. 430

time it came around curve 300 feet from place of collision until moment of impact, and that truck was visible).

Wis.—City of Milwaukee v. Berry, 1969, 171 N.W.2d 305, 44 Wis.2d 321.

Wyo.—Potts v. Brown, 1969, 452 P. 2d 975 (that witnesses who gave opinion as to speed of automobiles involved in collision at uncontrolled 90-degree intersection may have had only slight opportunities for observation could affect weight but not competency of their testimony); Cederburg v. Carter, 448 P.2d 608 (whether an eyewitness has had sufficient opportunity to observe and is sufficiently qualified to express an opinion are matters affecting weight and not admissibility); Taylor v. MacDonald, 409 P.2d 762 (testimony of approaching motorist as to speed of vehicle driven by defendant motorist at time it left road although witness indicated he had seen vehicle on road prior to time it started off for only "a half a block or such a matter" and that he had not observed it "too much").

Glimpse only

Ga.—Presley v. Griffith, 145 S.E.2d 384, 112 Ga.App. 377 (properly permitted).

Held inadequate

Pa.—Guzman v. Bloom, 198 A.2d 499, 413 Pa. 576 (properly refused to allow defendant to testify as to speed of plaintiff's automobile, where defendant testified that he did not see plaintiff's automobile until it was five or six feet from him, almost at split second of impact, particularly in view of his further testimony that, at impact, he was too nervous to observe anything); Heacox v. Polce, 141 A.2d 229, 392 Pa. 415 (properly refused to permit pedestrian to testify where, aside from fact that it is difficult to determine speed by speed of an approaching headlight, it was evident from pedestrian's testimony that if he had been permitted to testify it would not have been an opinion but a mere guess on his part); Kelly v. Veneziale, 1944, 35 A.2d 67, 348 Pa. 325 (saw 5–10 feet before accident).

Wis.—Pagel v. Kees, 127 N.W.2d 816, 23 Wis.2d 462 (where witness is unable to judge rate of speed because of his position, shortness of observation, lack of reference points, or other reasons, opinion is of no probative value).

Identity of vehicle insufficient

Ky.—Shields v. Goins, 1968, 426 S.W.2d 139 (testimony of witness that he saw black automobile traveling about 45 miles per hour and that he heard its tires scream as it rapidly turned corner just prior to accident was properly excluded because of lack of proper identification warranting admission when witness was unable to say that automobile he saw was one driven by defendant).

Momentary view

Ala.—Godwin v. Jerkins, 1968, 208 So.2d 210, 282 Ala. 11 (testimony is admissible even though witness giving testimony had only brief opportunity to observe speed, the momentary observation going to weight).

La.—Fidelity & Cas. Co. of New York v. McCasland, 1967, 203 So. 2d 756 (where witness stated that she did not see the automobile until the instant of impact, and had no personal experience in estimating speed of other moving automobiles).

Md.—Raines v. Boltes, 1970, 265 A. 2d 741, 258 Md. 325 (for 2 seconds, in rear view mirror).

Ch. 430   LAY OPINION EVIDENCE   § 430.2

If, however, a witness' estimate of speed is based solely upon an opinion of the force of an impact, it should not be admitted.[48] A lay witness can not give an opinion as to speed based solely

N.C.—Hall v. Kimber, 1969, 171 S.E. 2d 99, 6 N.C.App. 669 (passenger's opinion testimony as to speed of defendant's automobile prior to intersection collision was inadmissible where could not have had more than three seconds within which to estimate speed, and where defendant's vehicle could not have been stopped within distance and in manner established by physical evidence if it had been moving 80 to 90 miles per hour as estimated).

W.Va.—Lewis v. Mosorjak, 104 S.E. 2d 294, 143 W.Va. 648 (not inadmissible even though plaintiff observed it for only a brief moment before it collided with his automobile, in view of fact plaintiff did see the automobile long enough to be able to describe it, and in view of fact that as an eyewitness of its direction and the rapidity of its approach, he possessed more knowledge of those facts than did the jurors).

Observation at earlier time

Me.—Parker v. Hohman, Me.1969, 250 A.2d 698 (allowing witnesses who drove at rate of 45 to 50 miles per hour and who last saw decedent's automobile a couple of minutes before they arrived at scene to estimate that speed of decedent's automobile was 45 to 50 miles per hour was error).

Several hundred yards from automobile

Testimony of one, several hundred yards directly in front of an automobile in the nighttime, as to the speed thereof, might be of little value, but should not be excluded on that account. Owens v. Iowa County, 169 N.W. 388, 186 Iowa 408.

Train 1080 feet away

Sound basis existed for allowing lay witness, who observed train out of living room window as it approached crossing 1,080 feet from house and who had been a motor vehicle driver for 30 years, a town councilman, deputy constable, part-time policeman, and member of fire department, to testify as to speed of train and its comparison with speed of other vehicles with which he was familiar. Attal v. Pennsylvania R. Co., D.C.Pa., 212 F.Supp. 306, judgment affirmed, C.A., 323 F.2d 363.

47. **Mich.**—Jones v. Detroit Taxicab & Transfer Co., 188 N.W. 394, 218 Mich. 673 (ridden in automobiles and observed speed).

N.H.—Ware v. Boston & M. R. R., 31 A.2d 58, 92 N.H. 373 (opinion too fast for road conditions).

Tex.—Zepeda v. Moore, Civ.App., 153 S.W.2d 212, error dismissed (ordinary laymen with practical experience and observation with movements of automobiles may give opinion as to rate of speed).

Exclusion held error

Cal.—Rash v. City and County of San Francisco, 19 Cal.Rptr. 266, 200 Cal.App.2d 199 (refusal to allow pedestrian and bus passenger to testify as to speed of bus prior to accident was prejudicially erroneous even though neither witness drove an automobile).

48. Same statement in prior edition **Cited by the court** in Union Bus Lines v. Moulder, Tex.Civ.App., 180 S.W.2d 509, 511.

Mich.—Hicks v. Bacon, 1970, 182 N. W.2d 620, 26 Mich.App. 487; Hinderer v. Ann Arbor R. Co., 1927, 211 N.W. 734, 237 Mich. 232.

§ 430.2   TRIAL EVIDENCE   Ch. 430

upon the damage done to vehicles,[49] or from observations at the scene.[50]

That the witness formed an opinion from a mental review of the circumstances does not support an opinion formed from insufficient observations.[51] That a vehicle may have been going directly toward a witness does not affect the witness' competency, but rather the weight to be given the testimony.[52]

49. Tex.—Reaves v. Brooks, 1968, 430 S.W.2d 926, error dismissed (where officer's opinion as to speed and distance separating vehicles at time truck entered intersection was based solely on damage resulting); Morales v. Roddy, Civ.App., 250 S.W.2d 225.

50. U.S.—Carpino v. Kuehnle, D.C.Pa.1971, 54 F.R.D. 28, affirmed, C.A., 474 F.2d 1339.

Ala.—Birmingham Elec. Co. v. Thompson, 37 So.2d 633, 251 Ala. 465 (asking policeman, who investigated the accident after it happened, as to whether location of bus and other facts discovered by him indicated that bus had been hit a heavy or light blow by automobile was improper as calling for an unauthorized conclusion and invading jury's province).

Minn.—Schlukebier v. La Clair, 1964, 127 N.W.2d 693, 268 Minn. 64 (such as point of rest).

N.C.—Glenn v. Smith, 142 S.E.2d 596, 264 N.C. 706; Carruthers v. Southern Ry. Co., 59 S.E.2d 782, 232 N.C. 183.

Wash.—Allen v. Porter, 143 P.2d 328, 19 Wash.2d 503.

W.Va.—Reall v. Deiriggi, 34 S.E.2d 253, 127 W.Va. 662.

Police officer

Minn.—Pierson v. Edstrom, 1968, 160 N.W.2d 563, 281 Minn. 102, appeal after remand 174 N.W.2d 712, 286 Minn. 164 (police officer, who was not eyewitness to accident, was not qualified to give opinion).

51. Similar statement in prior edition **cited by the court** in Fisher v. Leach, Tex.Civ.App., 221 S.W.2d 384, 389.

Mich.—Hinderer v. Ann Arbor R. Co., 211 N.W. 734, 237 Mich. 232.

N.C.—Key v. Woodlief, 128 S.E.2d 567, 258 N.C. 291 (when witness testified that he saw the lights when automobile was 100–150 feet away but when he did not say that he observed them for any distance).

But see

Tex.—Humphries v. Louisiana Ry. & Irr. Co. of Texas, Com.App., 291 S.W. 1094 (opinion formed in calmness ought to be given more weight than one formed in excitement or when the matter about which the opinion is expressed arises suddenly and unexpectedly).

52. U.S.—Ford v. Southwestern Greyhound Lines, C.A.Tex., 180 F.2d 934 (occupants of automobile could testify as to speed of oncoming bus).

Ill.—Birnbaum v. Kirchner, 85 N.E.2d 191, 337 Ill.App. 25 (rainy night).

Mich.—Gibbons v. Delta Contracting Co., 4 N.W.2d 39, 301 Mich. 638.

Mo.—Johnson v. Cox, Sup., 262 S.W.2d 13 (speed of motorcycle).

Neb.—Koutsky v. Grabowski, 34 N.W.2d 893, 150 Neb. 508 (an overtaking automobile seen in rearview mirror); Lewis v. Miller, 230 N.W. 769, 119 Neb. 765, 70 A.L.R. 532.

Wis.—Pagel v. Kees, 127 N.W.2d 816, 23 Wis.2d 462 (testimony by witness, who was traveling in op-

598

Indefinite description

In some jurisdictions, it has been held that an indefinite description of speed, or a "mere epithet," as by the mere use of the words "fast" or "slow," is inadmissible, or that such evidence has no evidentiary force.[53] However, in other jurisdictions it has been held that a witness may use such expressions as "pretty fast" or "real fast,"[54] rapidly or slowly,[55] or other personal expressions of the witness.[56]

---

posite direction, as to estimated speed of truck about one-fourth mile from point of collision).

53. Ariz.—Rivera v. Hancock, 286 P.2d 199, 79 Ariz. 199 (where deponent eye witness, in answering question concerning speed of motorist stated the speed and added "Awful fast to be coming into an intersection," the quoted portion of answer was a conclusion and a gratuitous observation and was inadmissible despite plaintiff's lack of objection at the time of taking the deposition, and was properly deleted before being read to the jury although deponent did not consent to such deletion, in view of the making of an objection at first reasonable opportunity).

Ga.—Tittle v. McCombs, 1973, 199 S.E.2d 363, 129 Ga.App. 148 (where witness testified concerning the conditions at the time of the accident and gave his opinion of the speed of motorcycle, any opinion on "excessiveness" would have been a conclusion intimately related to the ultimate question of negligence and therefore invasive of the province of the jury).

Mass.—Sax v. Horn, 174 N.E. 673, 274 Mass. 428; Whalen v. Mutrie, 142 N.E. 45, 247 Mass. 316; Selibedea v. Worcester Consol. St. Ry., 111 N.E. 767, 223 Mass. 76.

Mo.—Migneco v. Eckenfels, Sup., 397 S.W.2d 682 (testimony that defendant's speed was "fast" did not constitute a statement of fact); Chance v. Atchison, T. & S. F. Ry. Co., Sup., 389 S.W.2d 774, certiorari denied 86 S.Ct. 389, 382 U.S. 939, 15 L.Ed.2d 349 ("excessive").

Neb.—Frasier v. Gilchrist, 1957, 86 N.W.2d 65, 165 Neb. 450.

Ohio.—Schackelford v. Commercial Motor Freight, App., 65 N.E.2d 879 ("seemed very fast to me").

Pa.—Starner v. Wirth, 1970, 269 A.2d 674, 440 Pa. 177 (such terms as "fast", "slow" or "excessive"); Warruna v. Dick, 1918, 104 A. 749, 261 Pa. 602.

54. Ind.—Vanosdol v. Henderson, 22 N.E.2d 812, 216 Ind. 240 ("pretty fast").

Ky.—Consolidated Coach Corporation v. Earls' Adm'r, 94 S.W.2d 6, 263 Ky. 814 ("real fast").

Wis.—Shaw v. Wuttke, 137 N.W.2d 649, 28 Wis.2d 448 (characterizations of speed of a seven and one-half-year-old boy on bicycle chasing another child down a somewhat inclined alley, as "fast" and "pretty fast").

55. Ala.—Davis v. Smitherman, 96 So. 208, 209 Ala. 244 (whether it was running fast or slow or the number of miles per hours as it appeared).

Cal.—Dean v. Feld, 175 P.2d 278, 77 Cal.App.2d 327.

Conn.—Shea v. Hemming, 115 A. 686, 97 Conn. 149.

Ky.—Consolidated Coach Corporation v. Earls' Adm'r, 94 S.W.2d 6, 263 Ky. 814.

---

56. See note 56 on page 600.

§ 430.2   TRIAL EVIDENCE   Ch. 430

Witnesses may be permitted to testify that a car was moving swiftly when it passed them shortly before the occurrence of a collision, although they are unable to estimate its speed in miles per hour.[57]

Md.—State v. United Rys. & Electric Co. of Baltimore, 115 A. 109, 139 Md. 306.

N.Y.—Marcucci v. Bird, 88 N.Y.S.2d 333, 275 App.Div. 127 (plaintiff's automobile was going fast and defendant's was going slow).

Pa.—Warruna v. Dick, 104 A. 749, 261 Pa. 602.

Contra

Ga.—Holloway v. City of Milledgeville, 132 S.E. 106, 35 Ga.App. 87 (evidence improperly admitted).

56.   **U.S.**—Moskowitz v. Peariso, C.A.Ky.1972, 458 F.2d 240 ("was flying").

Cal.—Rash v. City and County of San Francisco, 1962, 19 Cal.Rptr. 266, 200 Cal.App.2d 199.

Del.—Cornwell v. Ruhl, Del.1970, 262 A.2d 252 (testimony that automobile came "out of nowhere" was not objectionable).

Ill.—Ryan v. McEvoy, 1974, 315 N.E.2d 38, 20 Ill.App.3d 562 (a rather fast speed); Hester v. Goldsbury, 1965, 212 N.E.2d 316, 64 Ill.App.2d 66.

Iowa.—Hayungs v. Falk, 27 N.W.2d 15, 238 Iowa 285 ("it sounded like a car or something coming at a high rate of speed").

Md.—Charlton Bros. Transp. Co. v. Garrettson, 51 A.2d 642, 188 Md. 85 (though testified had not observed anything about the speed of street car, testified speed was moderate).

Mo.—Wineinger v. Logan, App.1973, 496 S.W.2d 275 (that plaintiff's motorcycle was going fast was not objectionable).

Mont.—Cross v. Trethewey, 1970, 471 P.2d 538, 155 Mont. 337 (faster than normal speed of others).

N.H.—Heath v. Joyce, 1974, 326 A.2d 260, 114 N.H. 620 ("sounded like an engine running at fairly high speed."); Stevens v. Polley, 1961, 168 A.2d 493, 103 N.H. 229.

Ohio—Elgin v. Heaton, App., 84 N.E.2d 299 ("like a bullet"); Acker v. Columbus & Southern Ohio Elec. Co., Ohio App., 60 N.E.2d 932 (that bus was moving as a "flash of yellow").

Stopped "gradually"

Ga.—Wilson v. Garrett, 90 S.E.2d 74, 92 Ga.App. 820 (court erred in refusing to permit witness for occupant of automobile to testify that driver of automobile stopped the automobile "gradually").

Supported by other testimony

Ga.—Granger v. National Convoy & Trucking Co., 7 S.E.2d 915, 62 Ga.App. 294 (permitting witness to testify that it was dangerous to drive automobiles on certain road at rapid speed and that it was dangerous to be there at all with anyone was not error, where witness had previously testified that there were two or three wrecks there, that they put tar on highway, and when it rained road was very, very slick).

S.C.—Ellenberg v. Arthur, 183 S.E. 306, 178 S.C. 490, 103 A.L.R. 437 (in action against motor vehicle carrier, admission of statement that driver of vehicle under circumstances had to be driving fast held not error, where witness had previously testified without objection that driver had said that he was driving fast to reach town ahead of cloud).

57.   **Conn.**—Shea v. Hemming, 115 A. 686, 97 Conn. 149.

Testimony describing the speed of a vehicle generally should not be a mere comparison with other moving objects, where no standard of the speed of the other objects is established. Thus, a witness may not be asked whether an automobile was going "as fast as a man running," there being no standard of running speed for a man, and the question not disclosing the gait contemplated.[58] Witnesses should not be permitted to give an opinion on the relative speed of two vehicles without a standard of rapidity.[59]

Ky.—Consolidated Coach Corporation v. Earls' Adm'r, 94 S.W.2d 6, 263 Ky. 814.

Specific estimate not required

Ga.—McBride v. Gill, La.App., 15 So. 2d 643 (witness was qualified to testify that an automobile was being driven at excessive speed, notwithstanding witness was unable to give the approximate speed).

58. **Iowa.**—Livingstone v. Dole, 167 N.W. 639, 184 Iowa 1340.

59. **Ala.**—Alabama Power Co. v. Armour & Co., 92 So. 111, 207 Ala. 15.

Neb.—In re Pott's Estate, 14 N.W.2d 323, 144 Neb. 1729 (testimony that vehicles hit "fast and hard" inadmissible as calling for conclusion and forming no basis from which jury could determine negligence as a result of excessive speed).

Exceeding customary speed

Evidence that defendant's car was being driven "ever so much faster" than cars were "commonly" driven on the street was improperly admitted, but, in view of the entire record, error was not ground for reversal. City of Grand Rapids v. Crocker, 189 N.W. 221, 219 Mich. 178.

Chapter 431

EXPERT OPINION EVIDENCE

Table of Sections

Sec.
431.1 Expert Opinion—In General.
431.2 Qualification of Expert.
431.3 Expert Opinion—Reconstruction of Occurrence.
431.4 —— Speed.
431.5 —— Bodily Injury.
431.6 —— Other Particular Matters.

§ 431.1 Expert Opinion—In General [1]

Library References:
C.J.S. Evidence § 546(60) et seq.
West's Key No. Digests, Evidence ⚖︎505 et seq.

Expert testimony should be received only where the subject-matter is complicated and embraces matters not elementary or of common knowledge.[2] Expert testimony is not desirable where

1. For cases concerning opinions as to how the accident occurred, see § 431.3.

   For cases concerning opinions as to speed of vehicles involved, see § 431.4.

   For cases concerning opinions as to bodily injury, see § 431.5.

   For cases concerning expert opinions as to other particular matters see § 431.6.

2. Comparable statements in prior edition **cited by the court** in Macy v. Billings, 289 P.2d 422, 424, 74 Wyo. 404; Carmody v. Aho, 86 N.W.2d 692, 697, 251 Minn. 19.

   Ala.—Kilcrease v. Harris, 1972, 259 So.2d 797, 288 Ala. 245.

   Cal.—Kastner v. Los Angeles Metropolitan Transit Authority, 45 Cal. Rptr. 129, 403 P.2d 385, 63 Cal.2d 52.

   Dist.Col.—Waggaman v. Forstmann, 217 A.2d 310.

   Ill.—Abramson v. Levinson, 1969, 250 N.E.2d 796, 112 Ill.App.2d 42, certiorari denied 90 S.Ct. 1868, 398 U.S. 950, 26 L.Ed.2d 290.

   Me.—Parker v. Hohman, Me.1969, 250 A.2d 698 (held inadmissible).

   Mich.—Washburn v. Lucas, 1964, 130 N.W.2d 406, 373 Mich. 610.

   Mo.—Baker v. Ford Motor Co., 1973, 501 S.W.2d 11 (issue presented by automobile manufacturer's effort to show by expert witness that tire marks appearing in photographs were made by rolling, not locked, wheels did not extend to matters so beyond knowledge and comprehension of average juror as to necessitate expert opinion testimony, and refusal of such testimony was not an abuse of discretion); De Lay v. Ward, 1953, 262 S.W.2d 628, 364 Mo. 431 (running speed of child is common knowledge).

Mont.—Jangula v. U. S. Rubber Co., 1966, 410 P.2d 462, 147 Mont. 98, appeal after remand 425 P.2d 319, 149 Mont. 241.

N.C.—Hughes v. Vestal, 1965, 142 S.E.2d 361, 264 N.C. 500.

Okl.—Hubbard v. Coates, 1968, 444 P.2d 204 (cause of motor vehicle collision); Barger v. Mizel, 424 P.2d 41 (excessive power of particular make of sports automobile was within knowledge and understanding of ordinary persons); Laffoon v. Kantor, 373 P.2d 252 (police officer's opinion as to maximum speed that automobile might be driven safely at intersection was properly excluded where intersection was completely described and condition appeared to have been well within experience and knowledge of persons of ordinary understanding).

Or.—Goodrich v. May, 255 P. 464, 121 Or. 418.

Pa.—Reardon v. Meehan, 227 A.2d 667, 424 Pa. 460; Costanzo v. Jim Belcher Buick, Inc., 149 A.2d 147, 189 Pa.Super. 136 (in action for loss of automobile as result of fire occurring while it was in defendant's place of business for servicing and inspection, jury were entitled to hear testimony of expert whose experience and knowledge in causes of fires was far superior to that of ordinary layman).

Va.—Grasty v. Tanner, 146 S.E.2d 252, 206 Va. 723; Portsmouth Transit Co. v. Brickhouse, 1959, 108 S.E.2d 385, 200 Va. 844, 78 A.L.R.2d 147 (whether bus driver could see below the elevation of a lower object).

Wash.—Thomas v. Inland Motor Freight, 81 P.2d 818, 195 Wash. 633.

Not prejudicial error to admit

In action in which main issue was whether defendant's automobile had run off hard surface of highway before it struck plaintiff, who alleged that he was standing on shoulder of highway, admission of testimony of officer, who was at scene after it had occurred, that defendant's automobile would have made tracks on shoulder of road had it gone off hard surface of road before striking plaintiff was improper inasmuch as it was expression of opinion on matter of common knowledge; however, admission of such testimony was not of sufficient import to constitute reversible error. Hill. v. Lee, 1969, 166 S.E.2d 274, 209 Va. 569.

Purpose served by lights

Admitting testimony of police officer who had investigated accident, which had occurred during daylight hours but at point at which visibility had allegedly been diminished by fog, to testify that primary purpose of using headlights in fog is to enable other people on roadway to see vehicle displaying its lights was not abuse of discretion as it is not common knowledge to all men that important purpose of using headlights in fog is to warn others. Church v. West, 1969, 452 P.2d 265, 75 Wash.2d 502.

Risks in operation of emergency vehicle

Nature of risks in driving emergency vehicle with a siren and feasibility of precautions to deal with these risks are subjects sufficiently beyond common experience of ordinary judge or juror to justify admission of expert testimony. Dillenbeck v. City of Los Angeles, 1968, 446 P.2d 129, 72 Cal.Rptr. 321, 69 Cal.2d 472.

Rule further defined

Trend is to permit expert testimony in matters which are complicated and outside knowledge or understanding of average person, and even as to matters of common knowledge and understanding where difficult of comprehension and explanation. Mack v. Davis, 221 N.E.2d 121, 76 Ill.App.2d 88.

§ **431.1** TRIAL EVIDENCE Ch. 431

the jury can get along without it, and it is admitted only when likely to be of aid to the jury.[3]

True test of admissibility of expert testimony is not whether subject matter is common or uncommon, or whether many persons or few have some knowledge of matter, but whether witnesses offered as experts have peculiar knowledge or experience, not common to the world, rendering their opinion founded on such knowledge or experience any aid in determining questions at issue. Wentzel v. Huebner, 104 N.W.2d 695, 78 S.D. 481.

Whether defendant could have acted alternatively

U.S.—Duff v. Page, C.A.Nev.1957, 249 F.2d 137 (that tow operator need not have blocked highway not admissible).

3. Alaska—Crawford v. Rogers, 406 P.2d 189; Meyst v. East Fifth Ave. Service, Inc., 401 P.2d 430.

Ariz.—City of Phoenix v. Schroeder, 405 P.2d 301, 1 Ariz.App. 510; City of Phoenix v. Camfield, 400 P.2d 115, 97 Ariz. 316 (opinion requested from expert, who had run series of automobile-crossing tests at intersection at which police vehicle had gone out of control and who had taken movie films of two of the tests, as to danger of intersection to motorists travelling at posted speed limit was properly excluded where jury had seen film and had facts described so as to be able to draw proper conclusions without expert opinion).

Ark.—Conway v. Hudspeth, 318 S.W.2d 137, 229 Ark. 735 (opinion on the basis of the position of the vehicles, the damage to them and other physical evidence found at the scene, and as to the order in which the collisions occurred, was inadmissible).

Ill.—Ray v. Cock Robin, Inc., 1973, 293 N.E.2d 483, 10 Ill.App.3d 276 (in view of photographic evidence clearly and accurately portraying location of drive-in picnic area in relation to nearby street intersection, from which alone the average person could know and comprehend that location of area could in some instances expose customers to dangers of traffic and that guard rails, barriers or blocks along or in front of north line of picnic area would have effect of slowing, stopping or deflecting vehicle coming onto premises from such direction, refusal of expert testimony on such matter was not error); McMahon v. Coronet Ins. Co., 1972, 286 N.E.2d 631, 6 Ill.App.3d 704 (where there were two eyewitnesses to accident, exclusion of opinion of alleged reconstruction expert as to whether or not decedent's automobile had collided with another vehicle immediately prior to mishap was proper); McGrath v. Rohde, 1970, 265 N.E.2d 511, 130 Ill.App.2d 596, affirmed 289 N.E.2d 619, 53 Ill.2d 56 (unless testimony of eyewitness to accident is incredible, unbelievable or contrary to accepted, natural or scientific laws, or unless testimony of an expert is found necessary, in addition to the testimony of an eyewitness, because it is essential to rely on the knowledge and application of principles of science beyond the ken of the average juror, expert testimony concerning the accident should be rejected).

Md.—Owens v. Creaser, 1972, 288 A.2d 394, 14 Md.App. 593, judgment reversed on other grounds 297 A.2d 235, 267 Md. 238 (refusal to allow police officer to answer question which stated, inter alia, that, assuming accuracy of testimony as to speed of favored driver, whether officer had an opinion as to whether or not favored vehicle would have been visible to unfavored driver at time she entered

Ch. 431   EXPERT OPINION EVIDENCE   § 431.1

The federal rule, and the rules of certain states, are stated in terms of whether the opinion "will assist the trier of fact".[4]

Under the federal rules of evidence,[5] and under the rules of evidence of certain states,[6] as under the case law generally,[7] an

intersection was not an abuse of discretion).

Minn.—LeMieux v. Bishop, 1973, 209 N.W.2d 379, 296 Minn. 372; Backman v. Fitch, 137 N.W.2d 574, 272 Minn. 143.

Mo.—Parlow v. Dan Hamm Drayage Co., Sup., 391 S.W.2d 315.

N.H.—Twardosky v. New England Tel. & Tel. Co., 62 A.2d 723, 95 N.H. 279 (whether pole obstructed public travel).

N.Y.—Pierce v. Great Lakes Forwarding Corp., 116 N.Y.S.2d 747, 280 App.Div. 1014 (results of certain tests made on vehicles similar to defendant's is inadmissible where there is no evidence that the defendant was negligent).

N.C.—Keith v. United Cities Gas Co., 146 S.E.2d 7, 266 N.C. 119.

Wash.—Thomas v. Inland Motor Freight, 68 P.2d 603, 190 Wash. 428.

But see

Or.—Groce v. Fidelity General Ins. Co., 1968, 448 P.2d 554, 252 Or. 296.

4. Federal Rules of Evidence § 702, 28 U.S.C.A. (to "understand the evidence or to determine a fact in issue").

Cal.—West's Ann.Calif.Evid.Code § 801(a).

Fla.—Florida Evidence Code § 90.702 ("in understanding the evidence or in determining a fact in issue").

Me.—Maine Rules of Evidence § 702 ("to understand the evidence or to determine a fact in issue").

Neb.—Nebraska Rules of Evidence § 702 ("to understand the evidence or to determine a fact in issue").

Nev.—N.R.S. 50.275 ("to understand the evidence or to determine a fact in issue").

N.J.—New Jersey Evidence Rule 56 (1) ("are helpful to a clear understanding of his testimony or to the determination of the fact in issue").

N.M.—New Mexico Rules of Evidence § 702 ("to understand the evidence or to determine a fact in issue").

Utah.—Utah Rules of Evidence § 56 (1)(b) ("are helpful to a clear understanding of his testimony or to the determination of the fact in issue").

Wis.—Wisconsin Rules of Evidence § 907.02 ("to understand the evidence or to determine a fact in issue").

5. Federal Rules of Evidence § 704, 28 U.S.C.A.

6. **Cal.**—West's Ann.Calif.Evid.Code, § 805.

Fla.—Florida Evidence Code § 90.703.

Kan.—Kansas Code of Civil Procedure § 60–456(d).

Me.—Maine Rules of Evidence § 704.

Neb.—Nebraska Rules of Evidence § 704.

Nev.—N.R.S. 50.295.

N.J.—New Jersey Evidence Rule 56 (3).

N.M.—New Mexico Rules of Evidence § 704.

Utah—Utah Rules of Evidence § 56 (4).

Wis.—Wisconsin Rules of Evidence § 907.04.

7. **Conn.**—Finch v. Weiner, 145 A. 31, 109 Conn. 616.

Mass.—Zandan v. Radner, 136 N.E. 387, 242 Mass. 503.

Mich.—Fraley v. City of Flint, 1974, 221 N.W.2d 394, 54 Mich.App. 570 (where two different elements of plaintiff's case were whether traffic light intervals were negligently set by defendant city and whether collision between truck and automobile of plaintiff's decedent was caused by the negligently set light, even though there were three eyewitnesses who testified that accident was caused by the inadequate notice of light changes to truck drivers, plaintiff was properly permitted to introduce expert testimony that traffic light cycle provided too short a notice for average truck with average driver to stop and the testimony of eyewitness and expert did not impermissibly overlap); In re Powers' Estate, 1965, 134 N.W.2d 148, 375 Mich. 150.

Mont.—De Marais v. Johnson, 1931, 3 P.2d 283, 90 Mont. 366, 77 A.L.R. 553.

N.Y.—General Acc. Fire & Life Assur. Corp., Ltd. v. Krieghbaum, 1974, 360 N.Y.S.2d 310, 46 A.D.2d 713 (conclusions of county coroner and chief of police were not objectionable on ground that they were testifying to the ultimate fact to be decided by trier of fact, that being whether decedent was killed in a hit-and-run accident).

Tex.—Payne v. Hartford Fire Ins. Co., Civ.App., 409 S.W.2d 591.

Wash.—Parris v. Johnson, 1970, 479 P.2d 91, 3 Wash.App. 853; Gerard v. Peasley, 1965, 403 P.2d 45, 66 Wash.2d 449.

Cause of vehicle failure

Expert witness' testimony, in response to hypothetical question as to what would cause axle shaft to become disengaged from cylinder in accident involving automobile in substantially the same circumstances as plaintiff's deceased's automobile, that disengagement would be due solely to undersized axle shaft was admissible over objection that it stated conclusion on very issue before jury in suit involving issue of whether automobile was negligently manufactured. Redman v. Ford Motor Co., 1969, 170 S.E.2d 207, 253 S.C. 266.

Computer study as to chance to avoid collision

Evidence was sufficient to support admission into evidence, for the purpose of establishing that defendant motorist had last clear chance, of computer study prepared by mathematics and computer expert to show that defendant motorist could have avoided the accident. Messex v. Louisiana Dept. of Highways, La. App.1974, 302 So.2d 40.

Effect of alcohol on driving

Expert witness, who was highly qualified expert in toxicology and pharmacology, was properly permitted to testify as to his opinion concerning relationship of amount of alcohol in driver's blood to driver's general ability to operate automobile, in suit arising out of collision at crossing. Mittlieder v. Chicago & N. W. Ry. Co., C.A.Neb.1969, 413 F. 2d 77, appeal after remand 441 F.2d 52.

Length of time highway defect existed

Testimony of chemical engineer, who dealt almost constantly with paving and construction materials for many years, at trial which took place eight years after accident that, based on clear and distinct pictures of hole in pavement, which truck driven by plaintiff hit prior to overturning, hole had been in existence not less than three or four weeks was admissible. Chambers v. Kansas City, Mo.1969, 446 S.W.2d 833.

On issue of "good faith" in excess-over-limits suit

In action against insurer by insured's judgment creditors who ob-

expert is ordinarily allowed to state an opinion on an ultimate issue of fact. A witness may state opinions or conclusions when in possession of special skill or knowledge of the subject-matter thereof, and if inexperienced persons are likely to prove incapable of forming a correct judgment without the witness' opinion.[8]

However, in certain cases, expert opinion on ultimate fact issues has been held inadmissible.[9] Expert testimony is not ad-

tained assignment of insured's cause of action against insurer for insurer's failure to settle, permitting expert witness to testify as to good faith of insurer was not error. Groce v. Fidelity General Ins. Co., 1968, 448 P.2d 554, 252 Or. 296.

Stopping distance

Mont.—Beebe v. Johnson, 1974, 526 P.2d 128, 165 Mont. 96 (in action arising out of accident to small foreign car which after passing one truck attempted to pass between such truck and left-turning truck further ahead, and rolled over, court did not err in allowing expert testimony relative to stopping distance of such foreign car traveling at 60 miles per hour, which testimony was introduced to show that driver of foreign car when confronted with the turning truck would not have stopped before striking truck if car driver had chosen to make full brake application).

8. **Cal.**—Weaver v. Shell Co. of California, 94 P.2d 364, 34 Cal. App.2d 713; Berkovitz v. American River Gravel Co., 215 P. 675, 191 Cal. 195 (whether damage could have resulted if other vehicle traveling only 20 miles per hour).

Mass.—Zandan v. Radner, 136 N.E. 387, 242 Mass. 503 (that unattended vehicle with engine stopped could not have moved without the intervention of some person).

Mont.—Demarais v. Johnson, 3 P.2d 283, 90 Mont. 366, 77 A.L.R. 553.

Neb.—Drahota v. Wieser, 1968, 157 N.W.2d 857, 183 Neb. 66 (vehicle dynamics).

S.C.—Collins v. Atlantic Coast Line R. Co., 190 S.E. 817, 183 S.C. 284.

Tex.—Texas & N. O. R. Co. v. Pettit, Civ.App., 290 S.W.2d 730 (not necessary that witness have had experience, knowledge and training in regard to particular signal device which was used at crossing involved, was competent to testify as to workings and operation of the signal lights).

Accident reconstruction

Ill.—Freehill v. DeWitt County Service Co., 1970, 261 N.E.2d 52, 125 Ill.App.2d 306, 43 A.L.R.3d 715.

Whether road "concealed"

U.S.—Dumas v. MacLean, C.A.N.H., 1968, 404 F.2d 1062 (admission of police officer's testimony that motel concealed road was within trial court's discretion, under New Hampshire law).

Where other evidence present

In view of eyewitness' testimony as to occurrence of accident between defendant's auto and plaintiff's motor scooter which was being overtaken by automobile, trial court did not err in rejecting testimony of expert as to how accident happened. Mayon v. Delta Well Logging Service, Inc., La.App., 167 So.2d 418, writ denied 168 So.2d 823.

9. Comparable statements in section of prior edition **cited by the court** in Macy v. Billings, 289 P.2d 422, 424, 74 Wyo. 404; Christ v. Wempe, 150 A.2d 918, 922, 219 Md. 627; Twidwell v. Davidson, 338 P.2d 326, 331, 54 Wash.2d 75.

§ 431.1　　　　　　TRIAL EVIDENCE　　　　　　Ch. 431

missible to prove that cars involved in a collision could not, if struck in the manner and under the circumstances testified to by other witnesses, have moved or come to rest in manner of the testimony in the case.[10]

An expert cannot give an opinion that, from the facts testified to by other witnesses, the driver was negligent, usually explained as being an instance where the factfinder is equally

Ky.—Hoover Motor Exp. Co. v. Edwards, 277 S.W.2d 475 (testimony of two witnesses, who were sought to be qualified as experts, concerning reasonable rate of speed for operation of loaded trailer-truck at night on icy roads); Thompson v. Kost, 181 S.W.2d 445, 298 Ky. 32 (whether blowout caused accident).

N.C.—Hubbard v. Quality Oil Co. of Statesville, Inc., 1966, 151 S.E.2d 71, 268 N.C. 489.

N.D.—Rettler v. Ebreck, 71 N.W.2d 759 (admission of highway patrolman's testimony, over objection, that speed was a factor in the accident).

Okl.—Barger v. Mizel, 424 P.2d 41 (that an inexperienced driver could not operate particular make of sports automobile without prior experience, instructions and warning or admonition as to its handling characteristics was properly excluded); Sandlin v. Freeman, 1964, 393 P.2d 816 (that decedent was in proper lane of travel).

Or.—Krause v. Southern Pac. Co., 295 P. 966, 135 Or. 310.

Right of control over roadway

Exclusion, in actions arising out of rear-end collisions of three automobiles as they were traveling in lime dust cloud which was created when road company spread lime on roadbed to prepare it for a freeway, of testimony of highway department inspector and road company official concerning right of control and right of direction by highway department over work in which road company was engaged was proper in that such testimony involved the province of jury. Austin Road Co. v. Evans, Tex.Civ.App.1973, 499 S.W.2d 194, ref. n. r. e.

10. **Ohio.**—Weigand v. Wenham Transp., Inc., 207 N.E.2d 254, 2 Ohio App.2d 131.

Okl.—Braggs v. Reese, 357 P.2d 997 (rebuttal of version vehicle was moving).

S.C.—Jenkins v. E. L. Long Motor Lines, Inc., 103 S.E.2d 523, 233 S.C. 87 (in action by motorist against motor truck carrier for injuries sustained by motorist in collision with oncoming tractor-trailer unit, which turned over on its side while rounding curve, trial court did not abuse its discretion in refusing to permit trailer repairman to give his opinion on question whether trailer had slid a considerable distance on its side as contended by motorist).

Wash.—Twidwell v. Davidson, 1959, 338 P.2d 326, 54 Wash.2d 75 (that one version was more worthy of belief).

Contra

Engineer was properly permitted to testify that bus, which struck rear of truck turning right into driveway, could not have been operating immediately to rear of truck as stated by truck driver, but that truck could have been operating to left and in front of bus and could have suddenly turned in front of bus as testified by bus driver. Yocum v. Kansas City Public Service Co., Mo., 349 S.W.2d 860.

capable to form the opinion.[11] Similarly the expert should not be allowed to state an opinion whether the conduct of a party was proper, under the case law of most jurisdictions;[12] whereas the

11. **Ariz.**—Dobbertin v. Johnson, 1964, 390 P.2d 849, 95 Ariz. 356.

Colo.—Thomas v. Pacheco, 1967, 429 P.2d 270, 163 Colo. 170.

Conn.—Kelly v. City of Waterbury, 114 A. 530, 96 Conn. 494.

Minn.—Moteberg v. Johnson, 1973, 210 N.W.2d 27, 297 Minn. 28.

Wash.—Poston v. Clinton, 406 P.2d 623, 66 Wash.2d 911 (discretionary rule concerned with determining limits on expert testimony should be used so that trials do not become contests between expert witnesses who, on examining exhibits and listening to testimony, tell jury which version of accident is more worthy of belief and advise as to which party should recover).

W.Va.—Underwood v. Goff, 1948, 49 S.E.2d 860, 131 W.Va. 662.

Proximate cause

S.D.—Jeitz v. Fleming, 1974, 217 N.W.2d 868, —— S.D. —— (question asked of highway patrolman as to whether he had an opinion as to sole proximate cause of collision was improper).

12. **Ariz.**—Dobbertin v. Johnson, 390 P.2d 849, 95 Ariz. 356 (testimony of police officer investigating scene that he found no evidence of improper driving or parking or any other driver's violation was inadmissible).

Colo.—Buchanan v. Brandt, 1969, 450 P.2d 324, 168 Colo. 138 (question attempting to obtain state highway patrolman's opinion as to whether collision was due to fault on part of defendant was improper).

Idaho.—Hawkins v. Chandler, 1964, 396 P.2d 123, 88 Idaho 20 (patrolman opinion that law did not require use of flares error, but not reversible).

Ill.—Gringer v. Dattilo, 1966, 225 N.E.2d 408, 81 Ill.App.2d 244 (testimony of an investigating police officer, in action by plaintiff against overtaking and overtaken motorists for injuries sustained when motorists collided and overtaking automobile careened into plaintiff's automobile in parallel lane, to the effect that overtaken motorist was to blame for accident was inadmissible); Giles v. Kuennen, 1964, 200 N.E.2d 143, 50 Ill.App.2d 389 (motorist's own opinion he could not avoid collision).

Ind.—Ohio Electric Co. v. Evans, 1922, 134 N.E. 519, 77 Ind.App. 669 (whether speed of train should have slackened).

Iowa.—Heth v. Iowa City, 1973, 206 N.W.2d 299 (whether to permit plaintiff's expert, who stated that he had visited T intersection both before and after single-vehicle accident but who effectuated no measurements and who admittedly did not use several factors ordinarily employed in evaluating a situation such as that at issue because it was not necessary to carry out a detailed investigation where there were obvious gross inadequacies, to express his opinion as to whether accident site street warning signs, lighting conditions and grading comported with accepted engineering standards was for trial court's discretion); Curry v. Jones, 138 N.W.2d 101, 258 Iowa 129 (admitting highway patrolman's testimony that his investigation of accident revealed no evidence of excessive speed on part of anyone and his testimony as to what he could see was not error, as such answers constituted statements of fact).

Ky.—Claycomb v. Howard, 1973, 493 S.W.2d 714 (the reasonableness of

§ 431.1 TRIAL EVIDENCE Ch. 431

speed); Barnes v. Pennsylvania Cas. Co., 208 S.W.2d 314, 306 Ky. 435.

Mass.—Griffin v. Hustis, 125 N.E. 387, 234 Mass. 95 (proper practice in operating a vehicle over grade crossing); Reed v. Edison Electric Illuminating Co. of Boston, 114 N.E. 289, 225 Mass. 163 (whether safe to operate vehicle under certain conditions).

Mich.—O'Dowd v. Linehan, 1971, 189 N.W.2d 333, 385 Mich. 491 (error to undertake to fix blame); Campbell v. Menze Const. Co., 1968, 166 N.W.2d 624, 15 Mich. App. 407 (permitting witness to testify with regard to what a reasonably prudent motorist driving in snowstorm would do upon seeing brake lights of lead vehicle go on and then seeing lead vehicle disappear in snow gust was improper as subject of inquiry was not sufficiently beyond common experience that opinion would assist trier of fact, but, under circumstances, ruling was harmless error.

Minn.—Pierson v. Edstrom, 1968, 160 N.W.2d 563, 281 Minn. 102, appeal after remand 174 N.W.2d 712, 286 Minn. 164 (admission of police officer's opinion that defendant driver was not at fault was improper invasion of jury's province).

Miss.—Pope v. Sanders, 1968, 217 So. 2d 1 (where patrolman and other witnesses at scene described position of disabled truck on other side of highway when cable was attached to truck and wrecker, jury had adequate basis for formulation of their own decision and opinion of patrolman as to whether truck was in a safe position when cable was released just prior to collision between cable and automobile in which plaintiff passenger was riding should not have been admitted); Hagan Storm Fence Co. v. Edwards, 1963, 148 So.2d 693, 245 Miss. 487 (accidentologist opinion as to responsibility was error).

Mont.—O'Brien v. Great Northern Ry. Co., 400 P.2d 634, 145 Mont. 13 (where highway patrolman admitted that he was not an eyewitness, that there was no way to determine speed of vehicle from skid marks and that he was not familiar with stopping distances in terms of speed, question asking him whether there was any evidence of motorist's violation of speed limit was without proper foundation and called for a conclusion, and his answer that "in my own mind I don't think the man was exceeding the speed limit" was pure speculation and conjecture, and admission thereof was reversible error).

Ohio.—Taylor v. Ross, App., 78 N.E. 2d 395, reversed on other grounds 83 N.E.2d 222, 150 Ohio St. 448, 10 A.L.R.2d 377 (that a car was traveling at a reasonable rate of speed).

Okl.—Hubbard v. Coates, 1968, 444 P.2d 204 (whether vehicle was properly operated); Jackson v. Brown, 361 P.2d 270 (that plaintiff was making improper turn at time of collision).

Tex.—Sanchez v. Billings, Civ.App. 1972, 481 S.W.2d 911, error refused n. r. e. (whether truck was in "normal" turning position).

Adequacy of warning

N.Y.—Colon v. Bridge Plaza Rental Corp., 1974, 360 N.Y.S.2d 896, 46 A.D.2d 13 (should not have been allowed to express an opinion over objection as to whether plaintiff's decedent had adequate warning prior to time his vehicle collided with rear of defendant's vehicle while latter was engaged in work of replacing burned out overhead light bulbs on city's highways, where circumstances were such that jury could have formed a conclusion as to issue of adequate warning).

Ch. 431   EXPERT OPINION EVIDENCE   § 431.1

more liberal rule of Federal Rules of Evidence and of the rules of certain states permits such opinions.[13]

Ohio—Fannin v. Cubric, 1970, 255 N.E.2d 270, 21 Ohio App.2d 99 (in action against highway construction contractor for alleged negligence in failing to warn westbound traffic that two-way traffic was being maintained in the northerly two lanes of four-lane highway, which negligence resulted in head-on collision, expert testimony as to what were proper procedures and custom and usage in providing signs or other traffic control devices in similar situations was properly excluded since such testimony went to ultimate issue to be determined by jury).

S.D.—Morin v. Chicago and Northwestern Ry. System, 1973, 209 N. W.2d 895, —— S.D. —— (trial court could reasonably have concluded that the adequacy of lights warning of backing of train cars across grade crossing was a subject within range of common knowledge and that the jury was capable of reaching their own conclusion from evidence available to them, and did not abuse discretion in refusing to permit testimony by highway patrolman that the white warning lights used at night were inadequate at the time of accident and that a red light was required to fairly apprise motorist of intrusion of train upon highway).

But see

Mont.—Demarais v. Johnson, 1931, 3 P.2d 283, 90 Mont. 366, 77 A.L.R. 553 (whether method of inspection for defects constituted reasonable diligence).

Dangerous character of road design

N.Y.—Rainey v. City of New York, 1970, 318 N.Y.S.2d 113, 35 A.D.2d 1003 (vehicle struck light pole).

Or.—Marshall v. Martinson, 1974, 518 P.2d 1312, 268 Or. 46 (in action for collision which occurred while defendants' automobile was overtaking and passing plaintiff's pickup truck, testimony of expert witness in response to hypothetical question as to whether, if accident happened as contended by defendants, there was "enough room" for defendants' automobile to proceed without hitting center guard rail would have been "speculative" in view of many varying factors involved in the problem and the expert witness' testimony was properly excluded).

13. **U.S.**—Frase v. Henry, C.A.Kan. 1971, 444 F.2d 1228 (testimony of patrolman, in response to question of plaintiff's counsel "Who do you find at fault in this accident?" that vehicle failed to yield right-of-way at intersection of road and highway did not cause jury to abdicate its function and was admissible as an aid to the jury insofar as testimony synthesized facts which jurors unaided could not have synthesized for themselves).

Cal.—Hart v. Wielt, 1970, 84 Cal. Rptr. 220, 4 Cal.App.3d 224 (permitting officer who had been in highway patrol for 13 years and who had extensive training and schooling in accident investigations to state his opinion as to what a reasonable rate of speed was in and about area of accident and whether driver's speed was excessive was not abuse of discretion).

Kan.—Ziegler v. Crofoot, 1974, 213 Kan. 480, 516 P.2d 954 (questions which asked highway patrolman, who had investigated the accident, which actions of the parties involved contributed to the accident, and which did not ask patrolman who was at fault, left the jury free to make the ultimate decisions as to faults, negligence or contributory negligence and were proper).

§ 431.1 TRIAL EVIDENCE Ch. 431

Under the federal rule, and under the rules of certain states, an expert may state an opinion based upon facts or data not admissible in evidence, if such fact or data is "of a type reasonably relied upon by experts in the particular field in forming opinions or inferences upon the subject".[14] Case law on the issue has varied, some cases holding such an opinion inadmissible,[15] other cases deeming it admissible.[16]

Ohio.—Beeson v. Criss, 1917, 7 Ohio App. 482 (that driver did not have vehicle under control).

14. Federal Rules of Evidence § 703, 28 U.S.C.A.

Cal.—West's Ann.Calif.Evid.Code, § 801(b).

Fla.—Florida Evidence Code § 90.-704.

Me.—Maine Rules of Evidence § 703.

Neb.—Nebraska Rules of Evidence § 703.

Nev.—N.R.S. 50.285(2).

N.M.—New Mexico Rules of Evidence § 703.

Wis.—Wisconsin Rules of Evidence § 907.03.

15. Ariz.—Killingsworth v. Nottingham, 1972, 501 P.2d 1197, 18 Ariz.App. 356 (can testify where opinion is based on investigation at scene and not founded upon statements made by other persons).

Ark.—Ben M. Hogan Co., Inc. v. Nichols, 1973, 496 S.W.2d 404, 254 Ark. 771 (where injured plaintiff's attorney had referred plaintiff to medical expert, not for treatment, and the expert's medical examination was conducted in presence of plaintiff's wife and his attorney, and expert's inquiries were answered in part by the wife and attorney, expert's opinion based in substantial part on such hearsay and self-serving information was inadmissible, and was specially prejudicial where treating physician did not testify).

Iowa.—Ruby v. Easton, 1973, 207 N.W.2d 10 (in action by pedestrian when he was struck by automobile, officer's opinion with respect to point of impact was inadmissible where opinion was based in part on out-of-court interviews with witnesses); Dougherty v. Boyken, 1968, 155 N.W.2d 488, 261 Iowa 602.

N.J.—Rogalsky v. Plymouth Homes, Inc., 1968, 242 A.2d 655, 100 N.J. Super. 501 (even if police chief had qualified as an expert, his opinion as to point of impact would have been inadmissible since it was based, in essential part, on what defendant had told him).

Okl.—Fidelity & Cas. Co. of New York v. Hendrix, 1968, 440 P.2d 735 (reversible error to allow jury to hear patrolman's testimony as to speed bus was traveling, when patrolman's opinion was based partially on statements made by bus driver and jury was not admonished to disregard these statements in assessing patrolman's opinion).

Tex.—Community Chapel Funeral Home v. Allen, Civ.App.1973, 499 S.W.2d 215 (failure to have present in court certain X-rays, which showed some spinal changes in plaintiffs following accident, was reversible error where, without such X-rays, plaintiffs' physician could not have given his testimony as to findings, causation and prognosis).

History received from patient by treating doctor

Ill.—King v. Gilland, 1967, 228 N.E.2d 741, 85 Ill.App.2d 358 (testimony regarding bleeding of preg-

16. See note 16 on page 613.

It also has been held that an expert may not base an opinion upon the opinion of another.[17]

nant plaintiff after her accident and her concern regarding possible injury to unborn child was properly admitted, since physician, who saw the bleeding only once and knew of other bleeding and brownish spotting through plaintiff's complaints, was treating physician and had formed an opinion based on actual observation as well as her complaints, notwithstanding defendant's complaint that testimony was not based on firsthand knowledge).

Mo.—Davies v. Carter Carburetor, Division ACF Industries, Inc., Mo., 1968, 429 S.W.2d 738 (may testify to what he personally observed and also to what patient said concerning his present existing symptoms and complaints; however, he may not base his opinion upon or testify to statements of patient with respect to past physical condition, circumstances surrounding injury, or manner in which injury was received).

Time elapsed in pedestrian crossing highway

Where speed at which boy crossed highway when he was struck by defendant's automobile was a vital issue in the case, testimony of engineer as to boy's crossing time which was not presented as opinion evidence but purported to establish the actual time, which must have been based primarily upon the boy's extrajudicial, self-serving statement to the witness that the boy was traveling at the same rate of speed as did another boy in the test conducted by the engineer was inadmissible as based upon hearsay. Skiles v. Schlake, Mo.1967, 421 S.W.2d 244.

16. Colo.—Houser v. Eckhardt, 1969, 450 P.2d 664, 168 Colo. 226, appeal after remand, 506 P.2d 751, —— Colo.App. —— (properly qualified medical expert who has examined a claimant for purpose of evaluating nature and extent of his injuries, and whose employment was for purpose of testifying in court and not for purposes of treatment, may testify to his opinion based upon reasonable medical probability as to nature and extent of claimant's injuries and disabilities and to other related matters when the expert's opinion is based upon claimant's statement of history and complaints and upon subjective symptoms and findings as well as objective symptoms and findings).

Ill.—Hastings v. Abernathy Taxi Ass'n, Inc., 1974, 16 Ill.App.3d 671, 306 N.E.2d 498 (testimony of physician who treated motorist that another physician concurred with testifying physician's own diagnosis and that motorist went to clinic for relief of same injury for which testifying physician treated him was admissible under exception to hearsay rule providing for physician's reliance upon outside sources).

Tex.—Central Power & Light Co. v. Martinez, 1973, 493 S.W.2d 903; Travelers Ins. Co. v. Hutchison, 1968, 425 S.W.2d 832.

Vt.—Vermont Terminal Corp. v. State Highway Bd., 1973, 313 A.2d 12, 132 Vt. 1.

17. Colo.—Herness v. Goodrich, 1971, 483 P.2d 412, 29 Colo.App. 322, appeal after remand 509 P.2d 1279, —— Colo.App. —— (portion of opinion testimony of accident reconstruction expert, which was based in part on opinion of another expert who had testified as to running speed of a four-year-old boy, was inadmissible).

Iowa.—Poweshiek County Nat. Bank v. Nationwide Mut. Ins. Co., 1968, 156 N.W.2d 671, 261 Iowa 844 (even though such opinions appear in evidence).

§ 431.1   TRIAL EVIDENCE   Ch. 431

Also there may be an issue whether the opinion should be refused as contrary to the physical facts.[18]

In general, an expert's opinion need only be an expression of professional opinion, and need not be considered to reach a level of "probability." [19]

Hypothetical Questions

Under the federal rule,[20] and under the rules of evidence of certain states,[21] the expert may be allowed to state an opinion

N.C.—Ingram v. McCuiston, 134 S.E.2d 705, 261 N.C. 392 (may not be predicated in whole or in part upon opinions, inferences, or conclusions of other witnesses, whether they be expert or lay, unless their testimony is put to him hypothetically as an assumed fact).

But see

Cal.—West's Ann.Calif.Evid.Code, § 804.

18. U.S.—Bitton v. International Transport, Inc., C.A.Wash.1970, 437 F.2d 817 (not abuse of discretion to strike ultimate opinions expressed by expert witnesses to effect that collision occurred on specified side of highway, where opinions were based on assumption that gouge marks found after collision were made at time of collision and such marks were not revealed by photographs taken of scene immediately following accident); Jackson v. Nelson, C.A.N.M.1967, 382 F.2d 1016 (where evidence in pedestrian accident case showed that there were 113 feet of continuous skidmarks which were not in a straight line, and plaintiffs' expert witness answered in the negative to court's inquiry as to whether he was assuming that there were continuous skidmarks, court properly concluded that expert's opinion was not based upon uncontroverted facts and did not err in striking the testimony and admonishing jury not to consider it).

N.D.—Stein v. Ohlhauser, 1973, 211 N.W.2d 737 (foundation for expert testimony as to speed, based on both skid marks and crash damage, must include proof that such determination of speed is scientifically possible).

Pa.—Heck v. Beryllium Corp., Com. Pl.1967, 58 Berks 12, reversed on other grounds 226 A.2d 87, 424 Pa. 140.

Vt.—Lambert v. Fuller, 1973, 303 A.2d 471, 131 Vt. 181.

19. Kan.—Ziegler v. Crofoot, 1974, 213 Kan. 480, 516 P.2d 954.

20. Federal Rules of Evidence § 705, 28 U.S.C.A.

21. Cal.—West's Ann.Calif.Evid. Code, § 802.

Fla.—Florida Evidence Code § 90.705.

Kan.—Kansas Code of Civil Procedure §§ 60-458; Ziegler v. Crofoot, 1974, 213 Kan. 480, 516 P.2d 954 (but upon cross-examination he may be required to specify all such basic data).

Me.—Maine Rules of Evidence § 705.

Neb.—Nebraska Rules of Evidence § 705.

Nev.—N.R.S. 50.305.

N.J.—New Jersey Evidence Rules 57, 58.

N.M.—New Mexico Rules of Evidence § 705.

Utah—Utah Rules of Evidence §§ 57, 58.

without prior disclosure of the underlying facts or data. In other jurisdictions, facts or data being relied upon, but not personally known by the witness, must be put to the witness in hypothetical question form.[22]

Where required, the hypothetical question asked of an expert must include all relevant facts shown by the evidence, and must not include any fact not shown.[23] However, considerable latitude

Wis.—Wisconsin Rules of Evidence § 907.05.

Not admissible

Kan.—Smith v. Hall's Estate, 1974, 524 P.2d 684, 215 Kan. 262 (investigating officer's opinion as to contributing factors to accident, which did not purport to be based either on personal knowledge or on anything introduced into evidence, but which was rather based on what plaintiff had told him at hospital after accident, was not within scope of statute on expert testimony, and was inadmissible).

22. Md.—Sun Cab Co. v. Walston, 1972, 289 A.2d 804, 15 Md.App. 113, affirmed 298 A.2d 391, 267 Md. 559 (operator of employment agency which placed domestic workers could not be barred from being called to testify as to value of domestic services performed by deceased on theory that his deposition showed that his only insight into the domestic circumstances of deceased's family was that there were six children, since proper procedure would be ruling under the applicable rules of evidence as to each question propounded, and since any opinion he might be asked to express would have to be based, not on any previous insight, but upon facts put to him in a hypothetical question or otherwise proper for him to consider).

N.C.—Lang v. Monger, 1973, 195 S.E.2d 347, 17 N.C.App. 724; Schafer v. Southern Ry. Co., 145 S.E.2d 887, 266 N.C. 285, modified on other grounds 148 S.E.2d 292, 267 N.C. 419.

23. Alaska.—Zerbinos v. Lewis, 394 P.2d 886 (whether sudden, complete loss of braking effect of defendant's foot brake might have been caused by a certain admitted loose brake connection on wheel was required to incorporate every fact in evidence in case wherein the material facts were undisputed as regarding amount of brake fluid observed on ground after accident).

Ariz.—American Honda Motor Co., Inc. v. Smith, 1974, 521 P.2d 1139, 110 Ariz. 593 (based upon material related outside of courtroom).

Conn.—Lowell v. Daly, 169 A.2d 888, 148 Conn. 266 (question asked of expert witness as to time it would take automobile to travel 350 feet at 25 miles per hour was properly excluded in absence of evidence that defendant operator traveled about that far at or about 25 miles an hour).

Hawaii—Kawamoto v. Yasutake, 1966, 410 P.2d 976, 49 Haw. 42.

Iowa—Karr v. Samuelson, Inc., Iowa 1970, 176 N.W.2d 204 (answer, in response to hypothetical question, that plaintiff's automobile was traveling at rate of 102 miles per hour immediately prior to impact was prejudicial error where hypothetical question asked witness to consider marks on pavement as shown by certain exhibits, where there was no indication that marks referred to were skid marks or tire marks, where witness, in answering question, mentioned picture showing scene of accident without referring to portions of such pictures considered or significance of such pictures, and where objection to testimony pointed out such inadequacies).

Ky.—Graefenhan v. Rakestraw, 130 S.W.2d 66, 279 Ky. 228.

Md.—Emery, to Use of Calvert Ins. Co. v. F. P. Asher, Jr. & Sons, 75 A.2d 333, 196 Md. 1.

Mont.—State Highway Commission v. Biastoch Meats, Inc., 1964, 400 P.2d 274, 145 Mont. 261.

N.Y.—Hunt v. Johnson, 19 N.Y.S.2d 191, 259 App.Div. 292.

N.C.—Johnson v. Johnson, 1974, 209 S.E.2d 420, 23 N.C.App. 449, certiorari denied 211 S.E.2d 212, 286 N.C. 335 (refusal of testimony based upon question which omitted fact truck was veering and decelerating was proper, as to opinion of its momentum); Bryant v. Russell, 146 S.E.2d 813, 266 N.C. 629 (where question included facts as to which there was no evidence then in the record); Ingram v. McCuiston, 134 S.E.2d 705, 261 N.C. 392 (improper to assume irrelevant facts).

Assumption too vague

Assumption of "regular concrete highway", in hypothetical question, was too vague to permit expert opinion as to speed based upon skid marks before collision. Grapentin v. Harvey, 114 N.W.2d 578, 262 Minn. 222.

Based upon inference

Md.—Baltimore County v. State, Use of Kennan, 193 A.2d 30, 232 Md. 350 (that one fact assumed to be true was shown through deduction made by expert himself by applying objective, scientific formula to other evidence did not render it a fact unsupported by evidence).

But see

Where professor of economics testifying as to projected wage loss and future medical expenses of plaintiff based his opinion in part on information supplied by plaintiff as to her educational and employment background and in part on official salary schedules of school district and data of Bureau of Labor Statistics, where there was no claim of surprise or that data was not equally available to all parties, and where trial court instructed jury that witness was merely giving his opinion, admission of witness' testimony was proper, even though testimony was based on data not in evidence. Williams v. General Motors Corp., Tex.Civ.App.1973, 501 S.W.2d 930.

Duty on objecting party

Pa.—Hartman v. Schmuck, Com.Pl., 78 York 181 (devolved upon defendant's counsel to object in such a manner to permit plaintiff's counsel to amend the question).

S.C.—Greer v. Greenville County, 141 S.E.2d 91, 245 S.C. 442 (should be excluded, provided the objection thereto specifically points out the imperfection).

Facts admitted by pleadings

Ohio—Barnett v. Hills, App., 79 N.E. 2d 691 (assuming that cab was traveling at speed of 35 miles per hour was not objectionable, where allegation in amended petition as to such speed was not denied).

In substantial accord with evidence

Where hypothetical question was in substantial accord with testimony and contentions of defendants, permitting answer was not error. Royal Crown Bottling Co. of Gainesville v. Stiles, 60 S.E.2d 815, 82 Ga.App. 254.

Insufficient basis

Where only description of plaintiff's injury was contained in a prior question asked medical expert which assumed that injury involved plaintiff's abdomen and chest, there was insufficient basis for hypothetical question whether, assuming that before accident plaintiff could lift

is generally to be accorded to the trial court.[24]

heavy objects and ordinary objects in doing farm work and after accident could not do so because of lack of strength, this was due to the injury plaintiff received. Pierce v. Heusinkveld, 14 N.W.2d 275, 234 Iowa 1348.

Admission in evidence of police detective's opinion concerning tendency of an automobile to swerve in a particular direction after a blowout, in response to hypothetical question not assuming facts sufficient to justify expression of opinion, was error and reversible. Hunt v. Johnson, 19 N.Y.S.2d 191, 259 App.Div. 292.

Not confined to undisputed facts

Evidence reasonably tending to prove facts relied upon in posing hypothetical question to expert is sufficient foundation, and question need not be confined to undisputed facts. Bogard GMC Co. v. Henley, 407 P.2d 412, 2 Ariz.App. 223.

Test stated

Ill.—Sherman v. City of Springfield, 222 N.E.2d 62, 77 Ill.App.2d 195 (alleged failure to consider all elements involved in evidence did not affect admissibility of opinion, based on personal observation, and any evidence which it was claimed was not considered, and effect of its consideration upon opinion expressed, were subjects for cross-examination); Graham v. St. Luke's Hospital, 196 N.E.2d 355, 46 Ill.App.2d 147 (where testimony is conflicting, counsel is entitled to base hypothetical questions on testimony supporting his own theory of case and any contrary testimony may be called to attention of expert on cross-examination by varying hypotheses).

Mo.—Davis v. Brezner, App., 380 S.W.2d 523 (proponent of hypothetical question is not required to cover all evidence but only to include such facts in evidence as will support his theory).

Mont.—Boehler v. Sanders, 404 P.2d 885, 146 Mont. 158, citing 32 C.J.S. Evidence § 446 (can give an opinion upon facts previously testified to by him, but not on facts known to him, but not communicated to court or jury; the witness must testify as to facts upon which he bases his opinion).

Okl.—C. T. Hughes Const. Co. v. Phillips, Okl., 401 P.2d 498 (is sufficient if it fairly states such facts in evidence as are relevant and material and sufficient to formation of accurate opinion by witness, and question is not improper because of omission of undisputed facts which are not material and essential to formation of intelligent opinion covering matter in question).

Vt.—Marsigli's Estate v. Granite City Auto Sales, Inc., 197 A.2d 799, 124 Vt. 95 (although inquiry by hypothetical question should include only data which there is fair possibility jury will accept, tendency of evidence is all that is required).

Unequivocal assumption required

Withholding of testimony of a doctor as to whether certain treatment would be proper treatment was discretionary where hypothetical question did not unequivocally assume the truth of the facts. Roberts v. Gale, 139 S.E.2d 272, 149 W.Va. 166.

24. **Colo.**—Hickman v. Hook, 1971, 486 P.2d 442, —— Colo.App. —— (asked as to speed of automobile at time it was struck from the rear).

Del.—Storey v. Castner, 1974, 314 A.2d 187 (there was no error in admitting in evidence deposition of plaintiff's treating physician despite claim of defendant that the diagnosis was not current and was based on inaccurate case history because physician did not know that plaintiff had suffered prior injuries to collar and neck

§ 431.1   TRIAL EVIDENCE   Ch. 431

In the instances where the hypothetical question is required, where some essential or basic fact is not shown, the opinion should not be received.[25]

bone and because opinion as to permanency of injury resulted from an examination seven and a half months before trial).

Ohio—Huffman v. Stone, 1971, 270 N.E.2d 347, 26 Ohio St.2d 159, certiorari denied 92 S.Ct. 339, 404 U.S. 978, 30 L.Ed.2d 293 (where appellant's counsel gave expert witness a description, supported by record, of circumstances surrounding collision, expert's opinion was based on that description, at no point in counsel's hypothesis was any mention made of locked wheels, and expert himself first mentioned locking of wheels and did so as part of his opinion regarding why vehicle went out of control, his opinion testimony was not inadmissible because opinion was based upon a circumstance not established by any testimony, viz., that wheels locked during braking process).

25. Ala.—Alabama Power Co. v. Johnson, 1967, 201 So.2d 514, 281 Ala. 259 (where there was no evidence of how much wires were stretched when struck by truck and expert's opinion was based in part on speculation by him as to how much wires were stretched, court properly sustained objection to question calling for opinion of expert regarding compliance of wires with safety requirements as to vertical clearance prior to accident).

Conn.—Gulia v. Ortowski, 1968, 238 A.2d 396, 156 Conn. 40 (court has discretion to determine whether hypothetical question is so lacking in essential facts as to be without value).

Ill.—White v. White Owl Express, Inc., 1974, 312 N.E.2d 411, 19 Ill. App.3d 868 (no testimony of vehicle defect referred to by expert).

Iowa—Bernal v. Bernhardt, Iowa 1970, 180 N.W.2d 437 (where it was not shown, in action by pedestrian, whether paving was wet or dry, rough or smooth, or clean or littered with dirt and rock, and highway patrolman did not say, for purposes of his estimation, on basis of skidmarks, of speed of defendant's vehicle, whether he considered such factors, sufficient factual basis had not been established for introduction of patrolman's estimate of vehicle's speed).

Mich.—O'Dowd v. Linehan, 1971, 189 N.W.2d 333, 385 Mich. 491 (opinion based upon extent of damage to vehicle not proven and only seen by expert 4 mos. after accident).

Ohio—State Auto Mut. Ins. Co. v. Chrysler Corp., 1973, 304 N.E.2d 891, 36 Ohio St.2d 151 (must first testify as to facts which are within own knowledge upon which opinion is based).

Okl.—Fuller v. Lemmons, 1967, 434 P.2d 145 (opinion is not admissible unless the facts on which it is based are admitted into evidence, and this rule applies when opinion is based on X-rays present in court but not offered in evidence).

Pa.—Murray v. Siegal, 1963, 195 A. 2d 790, 413 Pa. 23.

Tex.—Rogers v. Owens, 1968, 440 S. W.2d 406, reversed on other grounds 446 S.W.2d 865.

Wash.—Thomas v. Inland Motor Freight, 68 P.2d 603, 190 Wash. 428 (exclude opinion whether truck with sufficient braking power could have rounded curve, where speed unknown).

Basis for opinion regarding distance needed to stop or slacken

Evidence as to type of train brakes or their condition, load or tonnage

Ch. 431　　EXPERT OPINION EVIDENCE　　§ 431.2

§ 431.2　Qualification of Expert [26]

Library References:
C.J.S. Evidence §§ 454 et seq., 546(92) et seq.
West's Key No. Digests, Evidence ⚖=535 et seq.

Generally an expert witness must be shown to be qualified on the subject matter before the expert opinion will be admissible.[27]

in cars, whether train was operating on grade or otherwise, and type of locomotive and other equipment are matters that ordinarily have to be taken into consideration in forming an opinion regarding distance in which train can be stopped or its speed slackened. Bunch v. Missouri Pac. R. Co., Mo., 386 S.W.2d 40.

But see

In wrongful death action, there was no error in admission of testimony of expert as to projected earnings of decedent based on assumption that during year before death decedent earned $4,500 from school bus route and $2,700 from small farm, though there was no direct testimony stating that decedent did earn such amounts, where the summary of the testimony of all witnesses bearing on income would show that decedent was a hard working man whose income was increasing yearly and whose income in year preceding death closely approximated $7,200. Chicago, I. & L. R. R., Inc. v. Freeman, 1972, 284 N.E.2d 133, 152 Ind.App. 492.

26. Comparable section in prior edition **cited by the court** in Ellington v. Eley, Miss., 56 So.2d 796, 799; and **quoted by the court** in Macy v. Billings, 289 P.2d 422, 424, 74 Wyo. 404.

27. Ala.—State Farm Mut. Auto. Ins. Co. v. Humphres, 1974, 304 So.2d 573, 293 Ala. 413 (sustaining objections to questions as to whether horsepower of automobile was normal or extremely high and what horsepower had to do with speed of automobile was not error,

where witness had not yet been qualified as an expert, and was not prejudicial where he was allowed to testify without objection that when he saw the automobile it was traveling around 120 or 125 miles an hour).

Ariz.—City of Phoenix v. Mubarek Ali Khan, 1951, 229 P.2d 949, 72 Ariz. 1 (experience in driving small bus for an unstated period of time did not qualify witness as experienced bus driver).

Cal.—Kritser v. Kuttruff, 16 Cal. Rptr. 872, 197 Cal.App.2d 102 (testimony offered by plaintiff, through deposition of a highway patrol officer, to the effect that he had an opinion based entirely on examination of photographs at time of taking of the deposition that tire marks showed some application of brakes, was not admissible where witness was not asked about his qualifications to interpret photographic evidence, and no attempt was made to connect his attempted interpretation of the photographs with what he actually saw on the ground, and he did not testify that the photographs refreshed his memory or helped him understand what he had seen); Folger v. Richfield Oil Corp., 182 P.2d 337, 80 Cal.App.2d 655 (testimony as to propriety of driving truck in compound low gear was properly rejected when witness had never driven truck with capacity of that involved in compound low gear).

Ill.—Deaver v. Hickox, 224 N.E.2d 468, 81 Ill.App.2d 79.

§ **431.2**   TRIAL EVIDENCE   Ch. 431

It is said that one possessing specific knowledge or skills obtained either through a course of study or training, or by ex-

Ky.—J. C. Wells Bus Co. v. Kennard, 156 S.W.2d 873, 288 Ky. 507 (passenger who did not see speedometer, and who did not ride in car very much, and who on being asked how she knew what speed automobile was making replied, "I don't know" was not qualified to testify as to speed).

Mich.—Dark v. Fetzer, 149 N.W.2d 222, 6 Mich.App. 308.

N.J.—Di Domenico v. Pennsylvania-Reading Seashore Lines, 178 A.2d 10, 36 N.J. 455 (testimony of civil engineer as to whether he considered railroad crossing extrahazardous).

N.M.—Bunton v. Hull, 177 P.2d 168, 51 N.M. 5 (witness who did not see collision was not qualified to testify as to speed of truck at and immediately preceding the collision merely because of having driven automobiles for 37 years).

Tex.—Thomas v. Southern Lumber Co., Civ.App., 181 S.W.2d 111 (where witness had not seen particular attachment used to fasten trailer to truck, and had never had actual experience in operation of such connection, exclusion of opinion that method was dangerous and not approved was not error).

W.Va.—Gilbert v. American Casualty Co., 27 S.E.2d 431, 126 W.Va. 142.

Established in cross-examination

Ga.—Tifton Brick & Block Co. v. Meadow, 88 S.E.2d 569, 92 Ga.App. 328 (anything lacking in qualifying highway patrolman to testify, on direct examination by plaintiff's counsel, that one of truck's rear dual tires was flat when witness examined truck at scene and that witness did not think truck was safe to operate, was supplied by thorough interrogation of witness on cross-examination as to his experience in observing vehicles of type of such truck when traveling with flat tires).

Objection held sufficient

Objections that highway patrolman was not qualified to state opinion as to which vehicle had left skid mark, having arrived at scene approximately one hour afterwards, it having been raining, and there having been no attempt to qualify him as a skid mark expert, was sufficiently specific to challenge competence of expert testimony concerning relative position of automobiles to permit review of such question, and not merely question of patrolman's qualification as an expert. Padgett v. Buxton-Smith Mercantile Co., C.A. N.M., 262 F.2d 39.

Test stated

Alaska.—Crawford v. Rogers, Alaska, 406 P.2d 189 (true criterion for determining whether one qualifies as expert is not whether he employs his knowledge and skill professionally or commercially but whether jury can receive appreciable help from witness on particular subject involved).

Md.—Crews v. Director, Patuxent Institution, 225 A.2d 436, 245 Md. 174 (factors are actual experience of witness and the probable probative value of his opinion).

Mo.—Shelby County R-IV School Dist. v. Herman, 392 S.W.2d 609, citing C.J.S. Evidence § 457 (to be qualified it must appear that by reason of education or specialized experience he possesses superior knowledge respecting a subject about which persons having no particular training are incapable of forming an accurate opinion or of drawing correct conclusions).

Va.—Norfolk & W. Ry. Co. v. Anderson, 1966, 151 S.E.2d 628, 207 Va.

perience, is qualified to testify as an expert.[28] However, the testimony must be as to matters in which the witness is skilled.[29]

567 (may testify if shown to have sufficient knowledge to give value to opinion).

28. U.S.—Federal Rules of Evidence § 702, 28 U.S.C.A.

Fla.—Florida Evidence Code § 90.-702.

Ga.—Fried v. Richard, 1969, 168 S. E.2d 339, 119 Ga.App. 667 (police officer's lack of experience and training to form estimate of speed would affect credibility of his testimony but not its admissibility); Miller v. Travelers Ins. Co., 1965, 141 S.E.2d 223, 111 Ga.App. 245.

Ill.—Dauksch v. Chamness, 1973, 296 N.E.2d 592, 11 Ill.App.3d 346 (there is no distinction between testimony of an expert witness possessed of academic and scientific knowledge and testimony of an investigating police officer).

Kan.—Kansas Rules of Civil Procedure § 60–456(b)(2); Grohusky v. Atlas Assur. Co., 408 P.2d 697, 195 Kan. 626.

Me.—Maine Rules of Evidence § 702.

Mich.—Weeks v. Hyatt, 78 N.W.2d 260, 346 Mich. 479 (properly received testimony of witness as to manner of balancing automobile wheels, with tires on, where witness, though he did not have a technical education, had a great amount of practical experience with such type of work).

Minn.—Beckman v. Schroeder, 28 N.W.2d 629, 224 Minn. 370 (deputy sheriff and highway patrolman had necessary qualifications).

Miss.—Capital Transport Co. v. Segrest, 181 So.2d 111, 254 Miss. 168.

Mo.—North Kansas City Memorial Hospital v. Wiley, 385 S.W.2d 218.

Neb.—Nebraska Rules of Evidence § 702.

Nev.—N.R.S. 50.275.

N.J.—New Jersey Evidence Rule 56 (2)(b).

N.M.—New Mexico Rules of Evidence § 702.

Utah.—Utah Rules of Evidence § 56 (2)(b).

Va.—Norfolk & W. Ry. Co. v. Anderson, 151 S.E.2d 628, 207 Va. 567.

Wis.—Wisconsin Rules of Evidence § 907.02; Luke v. Northwestern Nat. Cas. Co., 143 N.W.2d 482, 31 Wis.2d 530.

But see

Educational and field experience are important in determining whether witness is an expert qualified to pass judgment in given case, but they alone are not sufficient to supply basis upon which to rest an opinion. State Dept. of Health v. Walker, 209 A.2d 555, 238 Md. 512.

Cross-examination of non-medical witness as to medical matter

Witness who was presented by defendant manufacturer and who had considerable expertise in dynamics of crashes and had examined several hundred x-rays in consultation with medical experts, was properly permitted to interpret x-ray in connection with his cross-examination. Gray v. General Motors Corp., C.A. Minn.1970, 434 F.2d 110.

Experience needed

Expert testifying about stopping distance of a train should have experience in testing or operation of trains of essentially similar size, construction, and equipment, under like circumstances. Gulf, M. & O. R. Co. v. Hollingshead, Miss.1970, 236 So.2d 393.

29. Cal.—Moore v. Norwood, 106 P.2d 939, 41 Cal.App.2d 359 (highway traffic engineer was not competent to give testimony as to the

§ **431.2** TRIAL EVIDENCE Ch. 431

The question of whether an expert witness is qualified rests largely in the judicial discretion of the trial court,[30] and its deter-

reaction time of the average driver as bearing on physical impossibility of plaintiff to avoid collision in emergency).

Kan.—Long v. Shafer, 174 P.2d 88, 162 Kan. 21 (proof that witness drove a truck for many years does not qualify him to testify as to cause of collision).

N.J.—Crager v. West Hoboken Transfer & Exp. Co., 41 A.2d 806, 132 N.J.L. 547 (physician may not testify as to suicidal tendency of deceased to jump in front of moving vehicles, where physician had not actually seen the deceased manifest such tendencies).

Interpretation of insurance policy

N.Y.—Suris v. Government Emp. Ins. Co., 1967, 278 N.Y.S.2d 708, 53 Misc.2d 454 (chiropractor was not qualified to testify that treatment rendered by him was such necessary medical expense arising from accident as to be within medical payments provision of policy).

Whether death was suicide

N.J.—Biro v. Prudential Ins. Co. of America, 1970, 265 A.2d 830, 110 N.J.Super. 391, reversed on other grounds 271 A.2d 1, 57 N.J. 204 (although investigating state police officer had had six years of police experience and his investigation of decedent's death was in performance of his official duties, he was not expert as to whether death was suicide).

30. U.S.—Carroll v. Seaboard Air Line R. Co., C.A.N.C., 371 F.2d 903.

Alaska—Ferrell v. Baxter, 1971, 484 P.2d 250.

Ariz.—Killingsworth v. Nottingham, 1972, 501 P.2d 1197, 18 Ariz.App. 356; Hinson v. Phoenix Pie Co., 416 P.2d 202, 3 Ariz.App. 523.

Colo.—Alcorn v. Erasmus, 1971, 484 P.2d 813, —— Colo.App. —— (to express opinion as to speed, based upon physical facts).

Conn.—Root v. Kakadelis, 212 A.2d 898, 3 Conn.Cir. 283.

Dist.Col.—Harvey's Inc. v. A. C. Elec. Co., 207 A.2d 660.

Fla.—Central Hardware Co. v. Stampler, 180 So.2d 205.

Hawaii—Bulatao v. Kauai Motors, Limited, 406 P.2d 887, 49 Haw. 1, rehearing denied 408 P.2d 396, 49 Haw. 42.

Idaho—Davis v. Nelson-Deppe, Inc., 424 P.2d 733, 91 Idaho 463.

Ill.—Abramson v. Levinson, 1969, 250 N.E.2d 796, 112 Ill.App.2d 42, certiorari denied 90 S.Ct. 1868, 398 U. S. 950, 26 L.Ed.2d 290; Pritchett v. Steinker Trucking Co., 1969, 247 N.E.2d 923, 108 Ill.App.2d 371.

Ind.—McCraney v. Kuechenberg, 1969, 248 N.E.2d 171, 144 Ind.App. 629 (deputy sheriff with eight years' law enforcement experience only three of which were devoted to accident investigation, was not, as a matter of law, qualified to testify as an expert on speeds under any and all circumstances); Kampo Transit, Inc. v. Powers, 1965, 211 N.E.2d 781, 138 Ind.App. 141.

Iowa—Hedges v. Conder, 1969, 166 N.W.2d 844; State ex rel. Schmidt v. Backus, 1966, 147 N.W.2d 9, 259 Iowa 1144.

Kan.—Ziegler v. Crofoot, 1973, 516 P.2d 954, 213 Kan. 480 (and unless the judge excludes the testimony, he shall be deemed to have made the findings requisite to its admission); Taylor v. Maxwell, 419 P. 2d 822, 197 Kan. 509.

La.—State Through Dept. of Highways v. Huson, 166 So.2d 3.

Me.—Parker v. Hohman, 1969, 250 A.2d 698.

mination will not be disturbed on appeal unless clearly erroneous.[31]

Md.—State Roads Commission v. Creswell, 201 A.2d 328, 235 Md. 220.

Mass.—Stevenson v. Hertz Corp., 1969, 252 N.E.2d 212, 356 Mass. 723.

Mich.—Krentz v. Union Carbide Corp., C.A.Mich., 365 F.2d 113.

Minn.—State by Mondale v. Mecklenburg, 140 N.W.2d 310, 273 Minn. 135.

Mo.—Brissette v. Milner Chevrolet Co., App.1972, 479 S.W.2d 176 (as to defect in tire); Union Elec. Co. v. Mount, 386 S.W.2d 126.

N.H.—Sigel v. Boston & M. R. R., 216 A.2d 794, 107 N.H. 8.

N.J.—Savoia v. F. W. Woolworth Co., 211 A.2d 214, 88 N.J.Super. 153, 14 A.L.R.3d 804.

N.M.—Bunton v. Hull, 177 P.2d 168, 51 N.M. 5.

Nev.—Levine v. Remolif, 390 P.2d 718, 80 Nev. 168.

Ohio—City of Akron v. Public Utilities Commission, 215 N.E.2d 366, 5 Ohio St.2d 237.

Okl.—Swyden v. State ex rel. Dept. of Highways, 387 P.2d 613.

S.C.—Collins v. Atlantic Coast Line R. Co., 190 S.E. 817, 183 S.C. 284.

Tex.—Standard Motor Co. v. Blood, 380 S.W.2d 651; Bass v. General Motors Corp., 1968, 447 S.W.2d 443, error refused n. r. e.; Kroger Food Co. v. Singletary, Civ.App. 1969, 438 S.W.2d 621 (rental value of vehicle).

Vt.—Campbell v. Beede, 1965, 207 A. 2d 236, 124 Vt. 434.

Wash.—Talley v. Fournier, 1970, 479 P.2d 96, 3 Wash.App. 808; Mason v. Bon Marche Corp., 1964, 390 P. 2d 997, 64 Wash.2d 177.

Wyo.—Logan v. Pacific Intermountain Exp. Co., 1965, 400 P.2d 488.

Degree of certainty required

Pa.—Moyer v. Ford Motor Co., 209 A.2d 43, 205 Pa.Super. 384 (expert who offers opinion about causes of accident must testify with some definiteness and must assert that it is his professional opinion that result in question actually came, not might have come, from cause alleged); Small v. Flock, 180 A.2d 59, 407 Pa. 148 (must state with some positiveness that a given state of affairs is the result of a given cause, and it is not enough merely to say that something could have happened from an alleged cause).

Witness disclaimer as expert

Ga.—Thornton v. Gaillard, 141 S.E. 2d 771, 111 Ga.App. 371 (fact that witness in his testimony may disclaim to be an expert is no reason for refusing to allow him to testify as one).

Iowa—Schmitt v. Jenkins Truck Lines, Inc., 1969, 170 N.W.2d 632, 46 A.L.R.3d 636 (that does not believe self qualified does not mean should not be accepted).

31. U.S.—Stancill v. McKenzie Tank Lines, Inc., C.A.Ga., 1974, 497 F.2d 529 (only if reviewing court determines that decision is "manifestly erroneous"); Jones v. Goodlove, C.A.Iowa 1964, 334 F. 2d 90.

Cal.—Goodman v. Community Sav. & Loan Ass'n, 1966, 54 Cal.Rptr. 456, 246 Cal.2d 13.

Colo.—National State Bank of Boulder, Colo. v. Brayman, 1972, 497 P.2d 710, 30 Colo.App. 554, judgment reversed 505 P.2d 11; Pomeroy v. Zeiler, 1970, 473 P.2d 988, —— Colo.App. —— (opinion as to the speed based upon the

§ 431.2 TRIAL EVIDENCE Ch. 431

In a variety of circumstances, witnesses have been deemed qualified to state opinions as to accident reconstruction,[32] as to

physical facts observed); Cullen v. Orback, 1970, 473 P.2d 177, —— Colo.App. —— (to express an opinion of speed based upon physical facts observed).

Ga.—American Fire & Cas. Co. v. Grizzle, 1963, 133 S.E.2d 400, 108 Ga.App. 496.

Ind.—McClure v. Austin, 1972, 283 N.E.2d 783, 152 Ind.App. 398 (refusal to permit opinion as to speed was not abuse of discretion, where reasonable men might differ as to whether or not the witness, who was a retired state trooper, and who testified that he investigated some 3000 accidents during his 30-year tenure as a police officer, and that he had attended certain traffic schools, was qualified to testify as an expert accident reconstructionist).

Md.—Spence v. Wiles, 1969, 257 A. 2d 164, 255 Md. 98; Nizer v. Phelps, 249 A.2d 112, 252 Md. 185.

Mich.—Anderson v. Lippes, 1969, 170 N.W.2d 908, 18 Mich.App. 281.

Miss.—Saucier v. Talkington, 170 So.2d 434, 251 Miss. 519 (exclusion of patrolman's evidence with regard to distance in which automobile could have been stopped was not abuse of discretion, in view of lack of requisite clarity of evidence as to patrolman's exceptional skill or expertness).

Mo.—State ex rel. State Highway Commission v. Bloomfield Tractor Sales, Inc., 381 S.W.2d 20.

Neb.—Flory v. Holtz, 126 N.W.2d 686, 176 Neb. 531 (speed of vehicles).

N.J.—Robbins v. Thies, 189 A. 67, 117 N.J.L. 389.

N.M.—Hayes v. Hagemeier, 400 P. 2d 945, 75 N.M. 70 (unless the ruling was manifestly wrong or trial court applied wrong standards in the determination).

N.Y.—Stevens v. Spring Valley Water Works & Supply Co., 247 N.Y.S.2d 503, 42 Misc.2d 86, affirmed 255 N.Y.S.2d 466, 22 A.D.2d 830 (not open to review in absence of serious mistake, error of law or abuse).

Okl.—City of Okmulgee v. Clark, 425 P.2d 457 (only where error is clear); Kurn v. Margolin, 101 P. 2d 818, 187 Okl. 135.

Pa.—Judy Ellyn, Inc. v. Hyde Park Fashions, Inc., 214 A.2d 296, 206 Pa.Super. 569.

Tenn.—Thomas v. Harper, 385 S.W. 2d 130, 53 Tenn.App. 549.

Tex.—Sharp v. Chrysler Corp., 1968, 432 S.W.2d 131, error refused n. r. e.

Vt.—Macauley v. Hyde, 42 A.2d 482, 114 Vt. 198.

Va.—Ames & Webb, Inc. v. Commercial Laundry Co., 133 S.E.2d 547, 204 Va. 616.

Wyo.—Taylor v. MacDonald, 409 P. 2d 762 (will not be disturbed except in extreme cases).

32. U.S.—Moss v. Associated Transport, Inc., D.C.Tenn., 33 F.R.D. 335 (witness who was director of university traffic institute and who was fully examined as to his qualifications in field of accident reconstruction was qualified to testify with regard to position of tractor-trailers at time and place of impact).

Ga.—Massee v. State Farm Mut. Auto. Ins. Co., 1973, 197 S.E.2d 459, 128 Ga.App. 439 (police officer with investigative training and experience in automobile collisions is an expert as to manner in which accident occurred); Bartow County School Dist. v.

angle of impact,[33] as to dangerous condition of roadway or railroad crossing,[34] as to employability of a plaintiff,[35] as to impact forces,[36] as to point of impact,[37] as to speed,[38] as to stopping dis-

Weaver, 1970, 175 S.E.2d 78, 121 Ga.App. 733 (professional degree in general safety, and familiar with literature).

Md.—Acme Poultry Corp. v. Melville, 1947, 53 A.2d 1, 188 Md. 365 (state police officer, opinion that tires would leave marks if pushed sideways).

As to indications from road gouge

Permitting witness, who had Ph. D. in chemistry, who had done previous analytical work for law enforcement agencies and was educated in physics, chemistry and geology, to state his conclusion that gouge marks made by steering knuckle of defendant's vehicle in asphalt lane of highway occupied by vehicle operated by plaintiff's decedents were made by removal of defendant's vehicle following collision rather than as result of collision was not abuse of discretion, notwithstanding that witness had no particular knowledge of asphalt and had not previously had occasion to determine direction of object moving on asphalt highway on analysis of marks it produced. Bitton v. International Transport, Inc., C.A.Wash. 1970, 437 F.2d 817.

33. **N.H.**—Jones v. Jones, 1973, 311 A.2d 522, 113 N.H. 553.

34. **Ill.**—Merchants Nat. Bank of Aurora v. Elgin, J. & E. Ry. Co., 1970, 257 N.E.2d 216, 121 Ill.App. 2d 445, affirmed 273 N.E.2d 809, 49 Ill.2d 118 (university professor, who had degree as civil engineer and had worked in state highway department for 21 years with background in study, practice and theoretical aspects of railroad grade crossing protection).

Minn.—Haukom v. Chicago Great Western Ry. Co., 132 N.W.2d 271, 269 Minn. 542 (witness who was chief engineer of railroad and warehouse commission and was its investigator as to adequacy of protection at grade railroad crossings was qualified to express opinion with respect to hazardous nature of crossing).

As to street illumination

Ill.—Baran v. City of Chicago Heights, 1968, 240 N.E.2d 381, 99 Ill.App.2d 221, judgment affirmed 251 N.E.2d 227, 43 Ill.2d 177 (did not abuse its discretion in suit against city involving alleged improper positioning of street light in denying city's request for voir dire examination of witness who testified that he held bachelor of science degree in electrical engineering with major in illumination and that he had worked for many years as electrical and illuminating engineer, or in permitting him to testify).

35. **Ala.**—Hagler v. Gilliland, 1974, 292 So.2d 647, 292 Ala. 262 (did not abuse discretion in permitting manager of local state employment service to testify concerning plaintiff's employability).

36. **Cal.**—Warren v. Pacific Intermountain Exp. Co., 1960, 6 Cal. Rptr. 824, 183 Cal.App.2d 155 (garageman who was at scene, as to whether possible that rear wheels of trailer would be knocked from under trailer by broadside blow).

N.D.—Holecek v. Janke, 1969, 171 N.W.2d 94 (where expert testimony as to determination of rearward force in accident on persons

37. See note 37 on page 626.

38. See note 38 on page 626.

§ **431.2** TRIAL EVIDENCE Ch. 431

in automobiles was based on expert's position as assistant professor of mechanical engineering and as a registered professional engineer and his education, background, special training and experience and not just his familiarity with studies conducted by University of California).

Wyo.—Logan v. Pacific Intermountain Exp. Co., 1965, 400 P.2d 488 (as to damage truck sustained in initial collision).

37. Ariz.—Goslin v. Bacome, 1971, 489 P.2d 242, 107 Ariz. 432 (as an expert concerning point of impact at intersection, where officer had been a police officer for two and one-half years, had received training with respect to investigating traffic accidents and had been trained as to procedures employed in establishing point of impact).

Cal.—Zelayeta v. Pacific Greyhound Lines, 1951, 232 P.2d 572, 104 Cal. App.2d 716 (7 years as traffic investigator).

Mich.—Link v. McCoy, 1972, 197 N. W.2d 278, 39 Mich.App. 120 (refusing opinions of officers, who had testified as to the physical facts, was not clearly erroneous where it was not clearly established that the officers were sufficiently qualified).

N.H.—Jones v. Jones, 1973, 311 A.2d 522, 113 N.H. 553 (police officer who had eight years experience, who had investigated about 100 accidents per year, and who had taken special courses in accident investigation).

Okl.—Graves v. Graves, 1970, 475 P.2d 171 (officer's testimony concerning his five years' experience on highway patrol as well as prior police experience and formal training).

Wyo.—Elite Cleaners & Tailors, Inc. v. Gentry, 1973, 510 P.2d 784 (professor who had conducted 500 tests in stability and stopping ability).

38. U.S.—Wise v. George C. Rothwell, Inc., C.A.Del.1974, 496 F.2d 384 (state trooper, who had been on police force for three and one-half years, during which time he was assigned to traffic division and had investigated four or five accidents a week, and who had 60 hours of advance accident training at Delaware State Police Training Academy and had been instructed about proper manner of examining damage to vehicles, location of damage to vehicles, determining points of impact, and length of skid marks, was qualified to testify with repect to speed at time of collision and to give an opinion based, not only on length of skid marks, but also on damage to vehicles involved, location of vehicles after impact, and areas of impact); Bonner v. Polacari, C.A.Okl., 350 F.2d 493 (patrolman who had 15 years experience as highway patrolman during which time he had investigated a considerable number of accidents and who had kept abreast of field of automobile investigations by attending various refresher courses at institutions was qualified).

Colo.—Cox v. Bonser, 1973, 507 P.2d 1128, —— Colo.App. —— (admission of opinions by three highway patrolmen, who had been on patrol for at least three and one-half years, had investigated large number of accidents, had attended accident investigation training school with periodic refresher courses, were assertedly trained to estimate speed from physical facts and required to determine speed in every accident investigated by them and were familiar with highway on which accident in question occurred, as to speed of defendant's automobile based on patrolmen's investigation was not abuse of discretion).

Fla.—Madden v. Killinger, App.1957, 97 So.2d 205 (improper to refuse opinion of captain of police academy).

Ch. 431   EXPERT OPINION EVIDENCE   § 431.2

Ga.—Reeves v. Morgan, 1970, 174 S.E.2d 460, 121 Ga.App. 481, reversed on other grounds 177 S.E. 2d 68, 226 Ga. 697, on remand 179 S.E.2d 648, 123 Ga.App. 64 (police officer who had three years of experience in investigation of accidents and had received training in such investigation).

Kan.—Hagood v. Hall, 1973, 505 P.2d 736, 211 Kan. 46 (notwithstanding existence of doubt as to qualifications of chief of police and basis upon which his opinion of speed rested, trial judge did not abuse his discretion in admitting such inconclusive opinion on speed since the credibility of the witness was adequately explored on cross-examination and since the testimony of speed was not a determinative factor in the case); Johnson v. Huskey, 350 P.2d 14, 186 Kan. 282 (state trooper who had had more than 16 years of service and experience in state highway patrol and who had investigated many accidents and had read and studied literature published by a university relative to arriving at speed of automobiles from observation of skid marks, distance traveled, damage to and locations of wrecked vehicles, was qualified to give his opinion as to speed based upon length of skid marks, etc).

Ky.—Kentucky Farm Bureau Mut. Ins. Co. v. Vanover, 1974, 506 S.W. 2d 517 (trooper who had investigated from 1,000 to 1,200 accidents over period of 16 years, had attended various schools relative to accident investigations, and had applied speed studies to accidents he had investigated was qualified to give expert opinion as to speed; and coroner who had investigated more than 200 accidents and had attended seminars on accident investigations was qualified as expert to testify as to speed of automobile at time of impact with farm equipment on highway).

Md.—Mulligan v. Pruitt, 1966, 223 A.2d 574, 244 Md. 338 (5 years driving experience).

Mich.—Anderson v. Lippes, 1969, 170 N.W.2d 908, 18 Mich.App. 281 (did not abuse its discretion in determining that witness who had been consulting engineer since 1920, had degrees in electrical and mechanical engineering with postgraduate work in civil engineering, who had been employed as traffic engineer and had made study of damage done to automobiles in accidents where speed was known, was qualified to testify as expert as to speed); Brummitt v. Chaney, 1969, 170 N.W.2d 481, 18 Mich. App. 59 (not abuse of discretion in finding that officer who had been investigating accidents for 15 years was qualified); Snyder v. New York Cent. Transport Co., 143 N. W.2d 791, 4 Mich.App. 38 (witness who, among other things, was a professor of mechanical engineering, whose educational accomplishments included a bachelor of science degree in aeronautical engineering and mathematics, a master of science and engineering mechanics and a doctorate in mechanical engineering, and who was also director of transport research institute studying various safety factors of automobiles was qualified).

S.D.—Smith v. Gunderson, 1971, 190 N.W.2d 841, 86 S.D. 38 (professor and licensed engineer, with experience investigating auto accidents).

Vt.—Cross v. Patch's Estate, 178 A. 2d 393, 123 Vt. 11 (state police lieutenant, who had 17 years experience and had investigated numerous accidents and had studied relationship between speed and damages resulting from automobiles striking immovable objects, with respect to speed of automobile which had collided successively with two guard rail posts and a cement bridge abutment).

§ 431.2   TRIAL EVIDENCE   Ch. 431

tances,[39] as to value of future loss,[40] as to value of a vehicle,[41] as

Wash.—Talley v. Fournier, 1970, 479 P.2d 96, 3 Wash.App. 808 (police officer, who had three years of experience in investigating traffic accidents at time of accident and about ten years at time of trial, was qualified to testify as an expert on speed based on skidmarks and other physical facts).

Wyo.—Elite Cleaners & Tailors, Inc. v. Gentry, 1973, 510 P.2d 784 (witness, who had a master's degree in mechanical engineering, who was a full professor at state university, who had a wide range of industrial experience, and who in last 12 years had conducted over 500 tests in stability and stopping ability of various vehicles).

Lack of prior experience not fatal

Fact that witness, a professional engineer, had no prior experience in reconstructing automobile accidents did not in itself disqualify him from giving opinion. Dahl v. Turner, 1969, 458 P.2d 816, 80 N.M. 564, 39 A.L.R.3d 207, certiorari denied 458 P.2d 860, 80 N.M. 608.

Train

Nev.—Los Angeles & S. L. R. Co. v. Umbaugh, 1942, 123 P.2d 224, 61 Nev. 214 (university professor of mechanical and aeronautical engineering).

39. **Fla.**—Madden v. Killinger, App. 1957, 97 So.2d 205 (improper to refuse opinion of captain of police academy).

Train

Nev.—Los Angeles & S. L. R. Co. v. Umbaugh, 1942, 123 P.2d 224, 61 Nev. 214 (university professor of mechanical and aeronautical engineering).

N.H.—Whipple v. Boston & Maine R. R., 7 A.2d 239, 90 N.H. 261 (qualified to testify regarding distances within which train could have been stopped at varying speeds, notwithstanding that on cross-examination as to his qualifications he admitted that at a previous trial he had advanced an erroneous theory as to principle on which air brakes operate, where witness stated that he had made extensive study of air brakes since such time, and witness was not called primarily as an expert on air brakes, but as a civil engineer who had long practical experience in observing actual effect of air brakes in stopping trains).

40. **Tex.**—Texas Steel Co. v. Recer, Civ.App.1974, 508 S.W.2d 889 (professor of economics and psychologist with 25 years experience in vocational disability determination were properly permitted to testify on issue of future earning capacity); Williams v. General Motors Corp., Civ.App.1973, 501 S. W.2d 930 (witness who held Ph.D. in Economics and was a professor of economics was qualified to testify on issues of projected wage loss and future medical costs); T & L Lease Service, Inc. v. Biddle, Civ.App.1973, 500 S.W.2d 186 (loss of earning capacity).

41. **Md.**—Kruvant v. Dickerman, 1973, 305 A.2d 227, 18 Md.App. 1 (where owner-operator of automobile repair shop had knowledge of and acquaintance with class of unique and classic automobiles and their values generally in the locality and had intimate knowledge of condition of automobile to be valued due to having repaired the automobile, such owner-operator was qualified to offer opinion as to value of the automobile after repairs, notwithstanding fact that he himself had neither purchased nor sold such type of automobile which was rare and unique, and notwithstanding fact that he failed to indicate knowledge of com-

to vehicle defects,[42] and as to various other issues.[43]

parable sales; rather, fact that he had neither purchased nor sold such an automobile merely affected weight accorded his opinion).

Mo.—Bader v. Hylarides, 1963, 374 S.W.2d 616.

Tex.—Allright Inc. v. Yeager, Civ. App.1974, 512 S.W.2d 731 (did not err in permitting plaintiff's witness to give his opinion as to reasonable market value of automobile damaged as result of theft from defendant's parking lot, notwithstanding claim that witness had never personally bought or sold damaged automobiles and that opinion dealt only with salvage or wholesale value which was less than reasonable market value, where witness had been a claims supervisor for five years and had served seven years as a field claims man and, in such capacity, had had occasion to evaluate automobiles in an undamaged condition and to fix salvage value of damaged cars); Caswell v. Satterwhite, Civ.App., 277 S.W.2d 237, ref. n. r. e. (as to value of ambulance before and after accident, where was an estimator of value of automobile wrecks and trade-ins and was familiar with market value of damaged and used ambulances in the county and knew their value as of date in question).

W.Va.—Adkins v. City of Hinton, 142 S.E.2d 889, 149 W.Va. 613 (owner of personalty destroyed or damaged beyond repair who made inquiries about selling price of items at various stores, who was a mechanic and who had bought, repaired and sold many such items and thereby had some knowledge of their fair market value).

42. U.S.—Proctor v. Colonial Refrigerated Transp. Inc., C.A.S.C. 1973, 494 F.2d 89 (on issue of alleged defective coupler assembly on trailer).

Ill.—Galluccio v. Hertz Corp., 1971, 274 N.E.2d 178, 1 Ill.App.3d 272 (an automotive service manager who had been in automotive service field for more than 20 years and in past 15 years had worked on or supervised work on an average of one brake system a day, including braking systems of type of van involved).

Mich.—Selmo v. Baratono, 1971, 184 N.W.2d 367, 28 Mich.App. 217 (witnesses in products liability case against manufacturer, respecting defects in design and manufacture of towing components which failed).

Miss.—Ford Motor Co. v. Dees, 1969, 223 So.2d 638 (witness who had 30 years' experience as part owner and manager of large automotive repair shop was qualified to testify on construction and working of steering mechanism of pickup truck and also as to manner in which cab was bolted to chassis).

S.C.—Redman v. Ford Motor Co., 1969, 170 S.E.2d 207, 253 S.C. 266 (witness, who had been actively engaged in field of automotive mechanics for more than 50 years, who had served as repair and maintenance manager for two large transportation services and under whose supervision many thousands of pressure fitted axles and bearings had been disengaged, was properly permitted to testify as expert on rear axle and bearings and braking systems and in particular automobile which was found with left rear axle shaft and wheel assembly loose and dangling from automobile outside fender well).

Brakes

U.S.—McSporran v. Ford Motor Co., D.C.Pa.1965, 238 F.Supp. 329

---

43. See note 43 on page 631.

§ 431.2

(brake engineer of manufacturer, as to whether defective air compressor belt in brake system caused accident).

Ariz.—Lowery v. Turner, 1973, 506 P.2d 1084, 19 Ariz.App. 299 (experience and background as a mechanic since 1930, a garage owner since 1939, a wrecking yard operator since 1939, and a race driver for 14 years was sufficient to support trial court's decision to permit him to give opinion concerning condition of the brakes of defendant's automobile and cause of accident, which occurred when defendant swerved to right to avoid hitting dog, braked his automobile when the two left wheels were on asphalt road surface while the two right wheels were on hard gravel surface of shoulder, and then spun to the right and across the road).

Ark.—Scott v. Jansson, 1974, 516 S.W.2d 589, 257 Ark. 410 (did not abuse its discretion in ruling that police officer, an experienced highway patrolman, was qualified to express opinion as to whether brakes were working properly, even though he was not a "brake expert").

Iowa.—Hahn v. Graham, 1964, 128 N.W.2d 886, 256 Iowa 713 (mechanic with many years experience in repairing damaged automobiles and appraising damage to them and who had two years training in trade schools on mechanical work in the United States Navy was qualified to testify as an expert as to condition of brakes).

Ky.—Willis v. Sherman, 1970, 464 S.W.2d 816 (automobile dealership service manager, specialized as mechanic).

Effect of dashboard design

U.S.—Stempel v. Chrysler Corp., C.A.Fla.1974, 495 F.2d 1247 (plastic surgeon, who was plaintiff's treating physician, who testified that he had treated several hundred persons injured by violent contact with dashboards and who had examined the dashboard in question, was qualified to give medical opinion to the effect that the dashboard's design contributed to the severity of plaintiff's injuries notwithstanding that surgeon had no practical experience in the actual design of dashboards).

Exhaust system

U.S.—Eastburn v. Ford Motor Co., C.A.Fla.1972, 471 F.2d 21 (permitting witness whose academic background was in chemical engineering and who had 20 years experience in industrial hygiene to testify about effects of lead poisoning upon humans was not an abuse of discretion, in products liability action for injuries allegedly caused by exposure to lead poisoning resulting from defect in exhaust system).

Steering

Ill.—Bollmeier v. Ford Motor Co., 1970, 265 N.E.2d 212, 130 Ill.App. 2d 844 (witness who had been in business of machinery for 25 years, spent 10 years as master mechanic, and was quite familiar with steering mechanism involved had sufficient experience and knowledge with respect to automobiles and other types of equipment to qualify as expert competent to testify as to cause of failure of steering mechanism).

Iowa.—Kleve v. General Motors Corp., 1973, 210 N.W.2d 568 (witness, who had been a mechanic for 33 years, was properly permitted to testify with respect to whether a defective steering mechanism was cause of accident).

Neb.—Kohler v. Ford Motor Co., 1971, 191 N.W.2d 601, 187 Neb. 428 (head of mechanical engineering of state college, two race drivers, and mechanics).

Tex.—Williams v. General Motors Corp., Civ.App.1973, 501 S.W.2d 930 (had worked on automobiles for 35 years and was familiar with design of steering system which allegedly caused accident and had personally examined the steering assembly in question).

Suspension system

U.S.—Moran v. Ford Motor Co., C.A. Neb.1973, 476 F.2d 289 (owner and operator of body and fender shop who had been in auto repair business for 18 years and who had frequently examined wrecked cars, including suspension systems, possessed sufficient knowledge and practical experience to make him well qualified to testify in action against manufacturer for breach of warranty concerning whether right front upper ball joint of the car's suspension system was defective).

Tire

U.S.—Smith v. Uniroyal, Inc., C.A. Ind.1970, 420 F.2d 438 (witness who had no experience in manufacture of tires but who had handled tires at service station for 22 years was competent even though he did not know whether defect in tire about which he testified was as to materials or workmanship).

Wheel

Mont.—Demarais v. Johnson, 1931, 3 P.2d 283, 90 Mont. 366, 77 A.L.R. 553 (that loose spokes caused wheel collapse, by garageman with 13 years experience).

N.Y.—Breese v. Hertz Corp., 1966, 267 N.Y.S.2d 703, 25 A.D.2d 621 (as to loosening and shimmying prior to disengagement).

43. Cal.—Poggetto v. Owen, 9 Cal. Rptr. 395, 187 Cal.App.2d 128 (a witness, who had training in physics of light and electricity and who had taken a course in optics and had done practical work in using physics of light refraction, was qualified to testify on photography and to interpret a photograph of motorcycle after collision); People v. Lang Transp. Corp., 110 P.2d 464, 43 Cal.App.2d 134 (structural engineer, who had studied stresses and strains, was qualified to testify on question whether bridge of given dimensions and materials could support given load, though his actual experience in building bridges was limited to two rather small structures).

Colo.—City of Pueblo v. Ratliff, 327 P.2d 270, 137 Colo. 468 (in action for injuries to motorist who drove into unguarded excavation, wherein a mechanic who repaired automobile after accident had described damage to right front wheel, engine, radiator and running board, opinion that damage to automobile was caused by a certain depth of a hole was properly admitted since experience was such as to enable him to state with reasonable accuracy the depth of a hole it would require to drop the automobile sufficiently to strike the running board).

Dist.Col.—McCrossin v. Hicks Chevrolet, Inc., Mun.App.1968, 248 A.2d 917 (opinion condition of carburetor caused fire).

Fla.—Seaboard Coast Line R. Co. v. Hill, App.1971, 250 So.2d 311, certiorari discharged, Fla., 270 So.2d 359 (determination that psychologist was sufficiently qualified to give a conclusion that an average driver would not have seen train in time to have avoided a collision).

Ill.—Noe v. Chicago Great Western Ry. Co., 219 N.E.2d 111, 71 Ill.App. 2d 347 (retired railroad fireman and engineer was qualified as to allegation that if railroad train brakes had been operating efficiently and properly the train would have stopped short of crossing).

Ind.—Walter v. Pence, 12 N.E.2d 367, 104 Ind.App. 532 (hospital su-

§ 431.2 TRIAL EVIDENCE Ch. 431

perintendent as to value of hospital care).

Kan.—Williams v. Esaw, 1974, 522 P.2d 950, 214 Kan. 658 (properly permitted to testify on the rated horsepower of motorcycle, where he was shown to have been in the business of selling and servicing motorcycles for a period of six years and where he was familiar with that particular machine and the manuals and the literature relating to the manufacturer's horsepower ratings).

La.—Shaw v. New Orleans Public Service, App., 188 So. 187 (description of mechanism and operation of bus doors by foreman of bus company garage).

Md.—Williams v. Dawidowicz, 120 A.2d 399, 209 Md. 77 (witness who had experience of 29 years, both as an operator and process engineer with certain machine, was properly permitted to answer hypothetical question whether a man with 20 per cent disability of left wrist, with limitation of motion in wrist and hand, with numbness in his fingers and who had lost the sense of touch in his fingers, was competent to operate such a machine).

Mass.—Wilborg v. Denzell, 1971, 268 N.E.2d 855, 359 Mass. 279 (experienced dealer who had driven stalled vehicle and 15 others similar to it, had sold automobile in question to driver's father and was familiar with scene, was sufficiently qualified to testify that before an automobile similar to the stalled automobile would stall for lack of gasoline there would be a warning of about 30 seconds during which time motor would skip, cough or sputter and that, at speed of 35 or 40 miles per hour, car would coast from 60 to 150 feet after motor had stopped).

Mont.—Knudson v. Edgewater Automotive Division, 1971, 486 P.2d 596, 157 Mont. 400 (though witness was not employed as engineer in field of lifting equipment and had examined the jack only a week prior to trial, witness was graduate mechanical engineer and had studied and had experience in design, stress analysis, and strength of materials, and his testimony related primarily to stresses upon pin designed to prevent overextension of arms of jack and not to the lifting mechanism).

N.Y.—General Acc. Fire & Life Assur. Corp., Ltd. v. Krieghbaum, 1974, 360 N.Y.S.2d 310, 46 A.D.2d 713 (town chief of police and county coroner who had seen many hit-and-run victims in the course of performing their duties were qualified to give opinion as to cause of death based on a comparison between those prior victims and the condition of deceased's body, and on the circumstances surrounding her death).

Okl.—Graham v. Banks, App.1969, 463 P.2d 1014 (eight years' experience in accident investigation, had completed traffic institute course, attended various seminars and lectures concerning accident investigation and who arrived at scene about 15 minutes after collisions).

Pa.—Flavin v. Aldrich, 1968, 250 A. 2d 185, 213 Pa.Super. 420 (admission of testimony of witness, who had attended general mechanics wheeled vehicle school in Army and had worked on civilian-type automobiles and had worked in a garage gas station, as an automotive expert was not an abuse of discretion).

Tex.—Keith v. Silver, Civ.App.1971, 476 S.W.2d 335, error refused n. r. e. (where witness testified that his business was that of automobile mechanic, that he specialized in repair of transmissions, and that he had worked on defendant's car before, trial court did not abuse its discretion in permitting witness to express opinions in passenger's ac-

Under other or similar circumstances, witnesses have been deemed not qualified to state opinions as to accident reconstruction,[44] as to point of impact,[45] as to speed,[46] as to value of a ve-

tion for injuries sustained when defendant's car repeatedly struck building while moving forward after having been put in reverse gear); Charles T. Picton Lumber Co. v. Redden, 1970, 452 S.W.2d 713, error refused n. r. e. (expert in field of accident analysis and scientific reconstruction was qualified to state opinions on basis of interrogatories, personal examination of scene, correlation of actual scene with photographs and studies, experience and calculations that truck driver involved in accident could have continued in his own right-hand lane and as to how much turn would cause a truck-trailer to jackknife).

As to wheel making skid mark

Trial court did not abuse discretion in excluding specific testimony of officer that skid mark was made by right rear tire of one of automobiles involved in head-on collision on ground that officer was not competent to render an opinion, and, in any event, the exclusion was not prejudicial, where two expert witnesses testified that the skid mark had been made by the right rear wheel. Felde v. Kohnke, 1971, 184 N.W.2d 433, 50 Wis.2d 168.

Chemist performing blood alcohol test

Chemist employed in laboratory of state bureau of criminal identification and investigation where he made numerous blood tests to determine alcohol content was qualified to make such a test and express an opinion on the results of such test. Barker v. California-Western States Life Ins. Co., 1967, 61 Cal.Rptr. 595, 252 Cal.App.2d 768, certiorari denied 88 S.Ct. 855, 390 U.S. 922, 19 L.Ed. 2d 982.

Significance of amount of alcohol

Mich.—O'Loughlin v. Detroit & M. Ry. Co., 1970, 177 N.W.2d 430, 22 Mich.App. 146.

44. Cal.—Fishman v. Silva, 1931, 2 P.2d 473, 116 Cal.App. 1 (operator of tow vehicle for 9 years, as to probable courses of travel after collision).

Colo.—National State Bank of Boulder, Colo. v. Brayman, 1972, 497 P.2d 710, 30 Colo.App. 554, reversed on other grounds 505 P.2d 11, 180 Colo. 304 (patrolman, as to identity of driver).

La.—Bonilla v. Arrow Food Distributors, Inc., 1967, 202 So.2d 438, writ refused 204 So.2d 577, 251 La. 399 (member state police for 25 years and experienced accident investigator, as to cause of 4-car collision and the time and occurrence of various impacts).

Mich.—Cook v. Kendrick, 1969, 167 N.W.2d 483, 16 Mich.App. 48 (police officer, as to cause of accident and automobiles' directions).

Tex.—Skelly v. King, Civ.App.1969, 443 S.W.2d 953, reversed on other grounds 452 S.W.2d 691, on remand 454 S.W.2d 775 (opinion vehicle skidded over centerline).

45. U.S.—Callander v. Hunter Motor Lines, Inc., C.A.Va.1963, 327 F.2d 754 (manager of auto repair business, as to whether certain marks indicated point of impact).

N.Y.—Stafford v. Mussers Potato Chips, Inc., 1972, 333 N.Y.S.2d 139, 39 A.D.2d 831; In re Sacco's Will, 1970, 312 N.Y.S.2d 259, 34 A.D.2d 885 (deputy sheriff).

46. U.S.—Flick v. James Monfredo, Inc., D.C.Pa.1973, 356 F.Supp. 1143, affirmed C.A., 487 F.2d 1394 (witness who had Bachelor of Science

§ 431.2 TRIAL EVIDENCE Ch. 431

degree in vocational teacher education and mechanical engineering, but who was not a registered professional engineer, was in no way qualified in accident reconstruction by his experience in family business selling ball bearings and automotive parts, and there was no error in prohibiting his testimony as to speed of motorcycle involved based on stopping distances set forth in owner's manual, in absence of any evidence as to how or where he became an expert in the stopping distance of motorcycles).

Cal.—Crooks v. Pirrone, 1964, 39 Cal. Rptr. 622, 228 Cal.2d 549 (never took course, and no showing knew sufficient facts or principles of physics).

Colo.—Oglesby v. Conger, 1972, 507 P.2d 883, 31 Colo.App. 504 (investigating police officer, who had spent one-half of his four years of police work in military service, who was a high school graduate and whose brief training school in accident investigation occurred after time of collision with respect to which he was offered as expert witness to give estimation of speed of the automobiles prior to impact, was not qualified).

Fla.—Seaboard Coast Line R. Co. v. Hill, App.1971, 250 So.2d 311, certiorari discharged Fla., 270 So.2d 359 (because of limited evidence of officer's qualifications in field of accident reconstruction and his own disclaimer of expertise, determination that officer was not qualified to give an opinion as to decedent's speed at impact in railroad crossing collision, based on appearance of vehicle after collision, was within trial judge's discretion).

Iowa.—Brown v. Guiter, 1964, 128 N.W.2d 896, 256 Iowa 671 (policeman for 9 yrs. and investigated accidents 5½ yrs.).

Kan.—Hampton v. State Highway Commission, 1972, 498 P.2d 236, 209 Kan. 565 (rejecting opinion testimony of investigating officer that plaintiff was going 80 miles per hour just before the accident was not an abuse of discretion, where the officer had had no special training in accident reconstruction and where his training in accident investigation had consisted of one week under the tutelage of a highway patrolman).

Ky.—Ryan v. Payne, 1969, 446 S.W. 2d 273 (to estimate speed from skids, must have had special training and experience); Lowe v. McMurray, 412 S.W.2d 571 (properly ruled that alleged expert did not have sufficient training, special knowledge, or skill to testify that tractor-trailer such as that involved in intersectional collision would not lay down skid marks when brakes were applied at 35 miles per hour, where he testified that he had made no experiments in the field and had never looked to see whether skid marks were laid down in such circumstances); Eldridge v. Pike, 396 S.W.2d 314 (opinion testimony on speed of truck by policeman who was not eyewitness but who merely investigated truck-automobile head-on collision on one-way bridge was inadmissible for lack of adequate qualifications of policeman who had not been shown to have observed similar accidents); E. P. Barnes & Bro. v. Eastin, 227 S.W. 578, 190 Ky. 392 (the driver of the truck was not qualified to give an opinion on how fast the automobile was traveling at the time of the collision; such collision being the only one which witness had ever seen).

Md.—Owens v. Creaser, 1972, 288 A. 2d 394, 14 Md.App. 593, judgment reversed on other grounds 297 A. 2d 235, 267 Md. 238 (refusal to permit police officer to answer questions which asked, inter alia, whether officer had an opinion in relation to speed of defendant's ve-

634

Ch. 431 EXPERT OPINION EVIDENCE § 431.2

hicle,[47] as to vehicle defects,[48] and as to various other issues.[49]

hicle at point of impact, and as to maximum and minimum rates of speed defendant lost in incurring 162 feet of skid marks, was not abuse of discretion where it appeared that officer was not specifically questioned as to his expertise in estimating speeds from his investigation of the physical facts).

Miss.—Gray v. Turner, 1962, 145 So. 2d 470, 245 Miss. 65 (police captain, basing testimony solely on mathematical chart received at police academy).

Tex.—Missouri Pac. R. Co. v. Rose, 1964, 385 S.W.2d 492, ref. n. r. e.

Opinion developed in cross-examination

Colo.—Simpson v. Anderson, 1974, 526 P.2d 298, —— Colo. —— (testimony of police officer on cross-examination that defendant was traveling at not more than 35 miles per hour when his automobile collided with motorcycle of plaintiff's decedent at intersection was not admissible, where plaintiff's counsel did not attempt on direct examination to qualify police officer as an expert capable of giving an opinion on speed and did not ask for such an opinion, and counsel for defendant made no attempt to lay a foundation for such an opinion on cross-examination).

47. Kan.—Lord v. State Auto. and Cas. Underwriters, Des Moines, Iowa, 1971, 491 P.2d 917, 208 Kan. 227 (buyer of new trucks, as to value of used truck, who stated lack of interest in used trucks).

48. U.S.—Butkowski v. General Motors Corp., C.A.N.Y.1974, 497 F. 2d 1158 (in action based on theory that fatal accident was caused by absence of external grease fitting on car's idler, trial court did not abuse discretion in determining that auto mechanic who was unfamiliar with the particular type of lubrication system employed on the model car involved in the accident was not qualified); Eves v. Ford Motor Co., C.A.Ind.1972, 466 F.2d 792 (in action when truck collided with culvert and cab separated from chassis, refusal to permit plaintiff's witness, a wrecking service operator, to testify as expert as to proper method of affixing cab to chassis of type of truck involved was not an abuse of discretion, where witness did not know weight of cab or size or tensile strength of bolts that had held cab to chassis, he initially displayed lack of firm knowledge on the mounting assemblies, and he had never seen the particular truck prior to the accident).

Colo.—Herrera v. Nakata, 1970, 478 P.2d 706, —— Colo.App. —— (where witness was an experienced exhaust systems mechanic but was not an engineer and did not have any special training in chemistry or metallurgy, trial court did not abuse its discretion in refusing to permit witness, who inspected subject vehicle in January, 1966, and who was asked for an opinion as to condition of exhaust system as of May, 1965, at time of inspection by defendant, to testify on subject of length of time exhaust system might have been in defective condition).

Nev.—Houlden v. Discount Motors, Inc., 1969, 451 P.2d 366, 85 Nev. 125 (refusal to allow witness to give his opinion, based on his examination of brake linings after accident approximately one month after sale, as to whether linings were worn out on date of sale of automobile was not abuse of discretion where witness was qualified to testify only regarding maintenance and repair of brakes and

---

49. See note 49 on page 636.

§ 431.2 TRIAL EVIDENCE Ch. 431

not as to expected life of brake linings).

R.I.—Redding v. Picard Motor Sales, Inc., 1967, 229 A.2d 762, 102 R.I. 239 (where defendant's prospective expert on disk brakes had worked as automobile mechanic for 12 years and had general experience with braking systems of automobiles, but had worked on disk brakes on only three or four occasions and on only two of those occasions did he work on make of automobile involved in suit, refusal to permit such witness to testify as expert on disk brakes was not improper).

Tex.—Sharp v. Chrysler Corp., Civ. App.1968, 432 S.W.2d 131, error refused n. r. e. (repairman, as to negligent design of brakes).

49. U.S.—Magill v. Westinghouse Elec. Corp., C.A.Pa.1972, 464 F.2d 294 (admission of testimony by actuary, who was not qualified as economist, in testifying to reduction of future earnings to present value, as to effect on present worth figures of earnings increase factor in accordance with practice in calculating sums necessary to fund pension plans was error); Carroll v. Seaboard Air Line R. Co., C.A.N.C.1967, 371 F.2d 903 (mortician, as to cause of death).

Alaska—City of Fairbanks v. Nesbett, 1967, 432 P.2d 607 (court did not abuse discretion in refusing to permit witness whose experience in the last few years with motorcycles had been just occasional and who had not maintained a technical interest in motorcycles to testify as an expert relating to the stopping characteristics of motorcycle and an automobile).

Cal.—Westbrooks v. Gordon H. Ball, Inc., 56 Cal.Rptr. 422, 248 Cal. App.2d 209 (failure of court to find that driver of defendant freeway contractor was qualified as to propriety of certain safety measures as contended by plaintiff suing for death of subcontractor's employee struck by track-type tractor of defendant general contractor was not an abuse of discretion).

Conn.—Siladi v. McNamara, 1973, 325 A.2d 277, 164 Conn. 510 (refusal to allow witness to testify did not constitute an abuse of discretion, where the witness was an administrator of a program designed to further highway safety in New Jersey, he had supervised and participated in accident analyses, but he made no claim to expertise with regard to the particular matter of composition of road surfaces, he did not know what an accident test was, and where it appeared that he was primarily an administrator rather than an investigator).

Ill.—Murphy v. Hook, 1974, 316 N.E. 2d 146, 21 Ill.App.3d 1006 (abused discretion in admitting testimony of engineering physicist who stated he had never done any work on automobile collision cases since he testified as a purported expert in areas in which he admittedly had no training or experience).

La.—Brumfield v. Fisher, La.1970, 235 So.2d 145, writ refused 239 So. 2d 346, 256 La. 822 (police officer who investigated accident, who had been on police force only three and a half months, who had worked with experienced officer for approximately eight weeks, and who admitted he had received no special training in accident investigation and that he was unfamiliar with effect of road conditions on stopping of automobiles, did not qualify as expert and was not entitled to expert witness fee); Ardoin v. Travelers Ins. Co., 1969, 229 So.2d 426 (testimony of pharmacists on cross-examination as to illnesses for which physician would or would not prescribe drugs obtained by plaintiff was objectionable as outside field of pharmacy).

Miss.—Bryan Bros. Packing Co. v. Grubbs, 168 So.2d 289, 251 Miss.

Ch. 431   EXPERT OPINION EVIDENCE   § 431.2

Medical Experts

Frequently, in automobile accident cases, the qualifications of medical expert witnesses are admitted, thereby dispensing with preliminary proof. Otherwise, a medical witness should establish the length of time of practice, the character of the witness' practice, the extent of experience in connection with the particular kind of injuries involved, and such similar facts.[50]

52 (admission of testimony of police officer who did not qualify as a mechanic as to amount of damages to the automobiles in terms of money was error even though officer was experienced in investigating accidents and it was part of his duty to fill out form giving amount of damages to each automobile).

Tenn.—Smith v. Bullington, App. 1973, 499 S.W.2d 649 (allowing witness to testify extensively about tires and tire safety but not permitting him to express opinion of what would happen under icy conditions in existence at time and place of collision, based upon inadequate experiential knowledge of witness regarding circumstances substantially identical to those involved, was within discretion of trial judge).

Tex.—Loyd v. Rumbaugh Trucking Co., Civ.App., 313 S.W.2d 542, ref. n. r. e. (did not err in not admitting testimony of operator and his helper as to whether from their experience with a truck they could tell whether it was about to stall, in view of fact each of such witnesses testified that he had some experience driving a truck but that neither had driven the type of truck involved).

Wyo.—Taylor v. MacDonald, 409 P. 2d 762 (admitting patrolman's testimony that if vehicle had left road at 80 miles per hour, as claimed by passenger, it would have gone into borrow pit in straight line, whereas it was not disputed that vehicle had not done so, was error absent proof of officer's qualification to give opinion).

Interpretation of safety rules

Railroad's witnesses, one of whom was an engineer formerly employed by railroad and the other of whom was county engineer in county in which automobile-train collision at crossing marked only by a cross-buck occurred, were not qualified to tell jury the interpretation which governmental agencies would place on automatic signal installation rules under a specific set of circumstances, and the trial court's rejection of their testimony was not abuse of discretion, even though one specification of negligence charged failing to provide an automatic signal at a dangerous crossing. Hoyt v. Chicago, R. I. & P. R. Co., Iowa 1973, 206 N.W.2d 115.

50. For discussion of sufficiency of basis for medical opinions on bodily injury conditions, see § 431.5.

Mass.—Nevanranta v. Koski, 138 N. E.2d 376, 335 Mass. 760 (general practitioner who attended plaintiff was qualified to give an opinion that accident was contributing cause of plaintiff's tuberculosis which subsequently developed).

Mo.—Sanguinett v. May Dept. Stores Co., 65 S.W.2d 162, 228 Mo.App. 1161 (physician with 9 yrs. experience competent, though referred patient to specialist).

Not qualified

Ohio.—Scarinze v. Farkas, 75 N.E. 2d 86, 80 Ohio App. 409.

Pa.—Gottlob v. Hillegas, 171 A.2d 868, 195 Pa.Super. 453 (no error in striking testimony of physician who had treated plaintiff who claimed heart condition resulted

§ 431.2   TRIAL EVIDENCE   Ch. 431

It has been held that a physician called as an expert must be licensed to practice in the state.[51] However, generally, a physician does not need to be a specialist in a particular school of medicine.[52]

from the accident, when he testified that he was not qualified to talk about heart itself).

Nurses

W.Va.—Gilbert v. American Casualty Co., 27 S.E.2d 431, 126 W.Va. 142.

51. **La.**—Herbert v. Travelers Indem. Co., 1970, 239 So.2d 367, writ refused 241 So.2d 253, 256 La. 1150 (statute prohibiting unlicensed physicians from testifying as medical or surgical experts is to deny unlicensed medical practitioners in state acceptance as medical experts in state's courts).

Tex.—Dallas Railway & Terminal Co. v. Brown, Civ.App.1936, 97 S.W.2d 335.

But see

Miss.—Mississippi Central R. R. Co. v. Alexander, 152 So. 653, 169 Miss. 620 (failure to record license not fatal).

Contra

U.S.—U. S. v. 60.14 Acres of Land, More or Less, in Warren County, Pa., D.C.Pa., 235 F.Supp. 401 (expert is one who qualifies as such by reason of special knowledge and experience, whether or not he is authorized to practice in his special field under licensing requirement imposed by statute, and inquiry by trial judge as to qualifications of such a witness should be whether or not witness possesses special knowledge or experience to qualify him, not whether he has complied with licensing requirements).

Pa.—Clark v. Horowitz, 143 A. 131, 293 Pa. 441 (hospital intern not incompetent as to mental condition).

Licensed in another state

La.—Brown v. Yellow Cab Co. of Shreveport, App., 94 So.2d 573 (deposition of doctor who treated passenger and was licensed to practice in another state was admissible as testimony of a medical expert even though he was not licensed to practice in Louisiana).

52. **U.S.**—Harris v. Smith, C.A. Neb., 372 F.2d 806.

Ark.—Swenson v. Hampton, 1968, 424 S.W.2d 165, 244 Ark. 104 (though referred patient to specialist).

Cal.—Rash v. City and County of San Francisco, 19 Cal.Rptr. 266, 200 Cal.App.2d 199.

Del.—Drucker v. Philadelphia Dairy Products Co., Inc., 166 A. 796, 5 W.W.Harr. 437.

Fla.—Hawkins v. Schofman, 1967, 204 So.2d 336, 46 A.L.R.3d 270.

Iowa.—State ex rel. Schmidt v. Backus, 147 N.W.2d 9, 259 Iowa 1144.

Ky.—Caudill v. Honeycutt, 1969, 437 S.W.2d 171 (testimony of doctor who examined plaintiff and based his finding of ruptured disc and permanent disability largely on x-rays was competent though doctor was not neurosurgeon and had not given plaintiff neurological examination); Rogers v. Sullivan, 1966, 410 S.W.2d 624.

Minn.—Koenigs v. Thome, 1948, 31 N.W.2d 534, 226 Minn. 14.

Mo.—Sanguinett v. May Dept. Stores Co., 1933, 65 S.W.2d 162, 228 Mo. App. 1161.

Mont.—Pachek v. Norton Concrete Co., 1972, 499 P.2d 766, —— Mont. —— (where physician treated plaintiff as soon as he arrived at the hospital and throughout his period

Ch. 431   EXPERT OPINION EVIDENCE   § 431.2

A chiropractor is competent to testify as an expert,[53] as

of recovery, physician diagnosed the subdural hematoma and called in neurologist for consultation, the physician kept all the hospital records except for the surgery and he examined those for postoperative treatment and he knew the surgical procedures used and, by the records, knew the size of the hematoma, physician's testimony concerning brain damage was properly admitted).

N.M.—Frederick v. Younger Van Lines, 1964, 393 P.2d 438, 74 N.M. 320.

N.C.—Brixey v. Cameron, 1970, 176 S.E.2d 7, 9 N.C.App. 339 (refusal to qualify, as a medical expert specializing in field of psychiatry, witness who was determined to be qualified to testify as a medical expert in field of general practice of medicine and who was allowed to testify fully as to his opinion concerning effects of collision on plaintiff's physical and mental health was not abuse of discretion); Spivey v. Newman, 1950, 59 S.E.2d 844, 232 N.C. 281.

R.I.—Morgan v. Washington Trust Co., 1969, 249 A.2d 48, 105 R.I. 13 (that doctor-witness was not specialist in field of radiology went only to weight and not admissibility of his testimony interpreting x-rays).

Tex.—Lantex Const. Co. v. Lejsal, Civ.App., 315 S.W.2d 177, writ of error refused n. r. e. (person, who was expert at making of electrical diagnostic test on an electroencephalogram, testified that he had made such a test on plaintiff and that the test reflected brain damage, even though expert was not a neurosurgeon and thus could not say what might have caused the brain damage).

X-rays

N.Y.—Honsberger v. Wilmot, 93 N.Y.S.2d 762, 276 App.Div. 884 (physician who had experience in taking X-rays and in reading them was qualified to testify as to opinion involving X-rays notwithstanding he was not a specialist).

53. Cited by the court in Corbin v. Hittle, 1972, 192 N.W.2d 38, 40, 34 Mich.App. 631.

Cal.—Johnston v. Pears, 3 P.2d 617, 117 Cal.App. 208.

Iowa.—Lowman v. Kuecker, 71 N.W.2d 586, 246 Iowa 1227, 52 A.L.R.2d 1380 (as to the future medical care required by plaintiff falling within his special field).

Kan.—Taylor v. Maxwell, 419 P.2d 822, 197 Kan. 509.

Md.—Elliott v. Patterson, 1971, 278 A.2d 431, 12 Md.App. 341; O'Dell v. Barrett, 163 A. 191, 163 Md. 342.

Mass.—Andrade v. Correia, 1971, 267 N.E.2d 503, 358 Mass. 786.

Minn.—Line v. Nourie, 1974, 215 N.W.2d 52, 298 Minn. 269 (as to percentage of permanent partial disability of mid and upper thoracic spine).

Mo.—Guiley v. Lowe, 1958, 314 S.W.2d 232 (to interpret x-ray); Harder v. Thrift Const. Co., App.1932, 53 S.W.2d 34.

Neb.—Fries v. Goldsby, 1956, 80 N.W.2d 171, 163 Neb. 424.

N.Y.—Badke v. Barnett, 1970, 316 N.Y.S.2d 177, 35 A.D.2d 347 (as to condition of subluxation, causation, and permanency); Jones v. National Biscuit Co., 1968, 289 N.Y.S.2d 588, 29 A.D.2d 1033 (chiropractor who had pursued courses of study in anatomy, structure of human body, and articulation of spine, among others, and who was licensed to practice chiropractic in New York and who had been in practice since 1949 was sufficiently skilled by reason of study and experience to warrant admission of his testimony as to condition he

§ 431.2 TRIAL EVIDENCE Ch. 431

is a chiropodist,[54] a physiotherapist,[55] or a psychologist.[56]

found in plaintiff's cervical column in area of second to fifth vertebra).

Or.—Carnine v. Tibbetts, 74 P.2d 974, 158 Or. 21.

Pa.—Falzone v. Grayce Farms Dairy, Inc., 65 Lack.Jur. 129 (within his field of competence and experience).

Tex.—Watson v. Ward, 1967, 423 S. W.2d 457, errors refused n. r. e.

Wis.—Green v. Rosenow, 1974, 217 N.W.2d 388, 63 Wis.2d 463 (licensed chiropractor who had treated plaintiffs was competent to testify as to his analysis and treatment, including his analysis of X rays he had taken, and as to causation of injuries he treated).

Beyond scope of profession

Fla.—Aiken v. Miller, 1974, 298 So. 2d 477 (properly sustained objection to question asked of chiropractor as to whether, based upon reasonable medical probability, a change in plaintiff's eyesight was result of accident, where proper predicate had not been laid, there had been no testimony as to qualifications of chiropractor to testify on problems related to eyes or vision and proffered answer to question was not responsive).

La.—Carvell v. Winn, App.1963, 154 So.2d 788, writ ref. 156 So.2d 603, 245 La. 61 (proper exclude as to causal connection to tonsilitis, vaginal bleeding, burning eyes, and stomach trouble).

Contra

La.—Tuger v. Audubon Ins. Co., App., 152 So.2d 354, citing C.J.S. Evidence § 458 (not entitled to give opinion as to injuries and, since his findings and diagnoses depended entirely upon specialized skills in fields of medicine, regarding which no lay witness may testify, his testimony could not be considered by courts).

N.C.—Allen v. Hinson, 1971, 183 S.E. 2d 852, 12 N.C.App. 515, certiorari denied 184 S.E.2d 883, 279 N.C. 726 (permitting chiropractor to give opinion as to whether accident caused conditions found in plaintiff and as to permanency of injuries was improper).

Contra as to mental condition

Tenn.—Lanius v. Donnell, 1968, 432 S.W.2d 659, 222 Tenn. 58.

Limited scope

Tenn.—Tom Still Transfer Co. v. Way, 1972, 482 S.W.2d 775 (only as to matters within limited scope of his profession).

Though unlicensed in state

La.—Ducote v. Allstate Ins. Co., App., 1970, 242 So.2d 103, writ refused 243 So.2d 532, 257 La. 618.

54. Okl.—City of Okmulgee v. Clark, 1967, 425 P.2d 457.

55. N.Y.—Gramza v. Gajewski, 258 N.Y.S.2d 469, 23 A.D.2d 817 (duly accredited physiotherapist, licensed by state, held bachelor's degree, and had done graduate work in neuro-anatomy, physiology and rehabilitation processes, refusal to permit his testimony as to his observations regarding muscle spasm and court's comments serving to depreciate the professional standing of witness were highly prejudicial and required granting new trial).

56. Cited by the court in Marshall v. Martinson, 1974, 518 P.2d 1312, 1316, 268 Or. 46.

Fla.—Reese v. Naylor, 1969, 222 So. 2d 487.

Md.—Spann v. Bees, 1974, 327 A.2d 801, 23 Md.App. 313 (testimony of qualified clinical psychologist as to his judgments and interpretations of various tests administered was admissible).

640

§ 431.3 Expert Opinion—Reconstruction of Occurrence

Library References:
C.J.S. Evidence §§ 546(70) et seq., 546(107) et seq.
West's Key No. Digests, Evidence ⚖️519.

Many courts look with disfavor on attempts to reconstruct how a traffic accident occurred.[57] In some cases, it has been held that such expert opinions should be excluded in the instances where direct proof on the subject exists;[58] and, in other cases, that such fact is not controlling.[59]

---

57. **U.S.**—Kapral v. Hartzelius, C.A. Md.1968, 392 F.2d 548 (refusal to permit plaintiff to call so-called "accident reconstruction expert" was not error).

Ariz.—Carrizoza v. Zahn, 1973, 515 P.2d 1192, 21 Ariz.App. 94 (caution should be exercised in admitting an expert's attempt to reconstruct accident solely on basis of such items as physical damage and skid marks).

Ark.—Wright v. Flagg, 508 S.W.2d 742, 256 Ark. 495 (while looked on with disfavor, there are exceptions to such rule); Woodward v. Blythe, 1971, 462 S.W.2d 205, 249 Ark. 793 (because of impossibility of establishing with certainty the many factors that must be taken into consideration); Waters v. Coleman, 1962, 361 S.W.2d 268, 235 Ark. 559 (where there were 5 eyewitnesses).

Ill.—Miller v. Pillsbury Co., 206 N. E.2d 272, 56 Ill.App.2d 403 (competent where there was no conflicting or contradictory evidence).

Miss.—Lynch v. Suthoff, 1969, 220 So.2d 593 (patrolman or police officer, not eyewitness to accident, who investigates an accident shortly after it happens, may properly testify as to matters and things that he finds at scene, but he is not allowed to invade province of jury by giving his opinion as to how accident happened).

N.C.—Hughes v. Vestal, 1965, 142 S.E.2d 361, 264 N.C. 500; Shaw v. Sylvester, 1960, 116 S.E.2d 351, 253 N.C. 176.

58. **Ill.**—Milton v. Britton, 312 N.E. 2d 303, 19 Ill.App.3d 922 (inadmissible in suit involving single vehicle accident where five eyewitnesses testified as to speed and path of decedent's automobile, investigating police officer testified as to vehicle's path as determined from measurements taken at scene, and jurors were not presented with questions which required scientific knowledge beyond that of typical jurors); Siltman v. Reeves, 1971, 269 N.E.2d 728, 131 Ill.App.2d 960 (as to whether taillight was lighted); Plank v. Holman, 1970, 264 N.E.2d 12, 46 Ill.2d 465.

N.D.—Bischoff v. Koenig, 100 N.W.2d 159 (where there was testimony showing where two automobiles came to rest, distance between them, distance of each from ditch, and condition and width of road, evidence was such that jury was as well qualified as patrolman to determine position of automobiles at or immediately before the collision and admission in evidence of exhibit consisting of drawing of patrolman illustrating his opinion as to positions of automobiles before collision and testimony of highway patrolman with respect to such positions was without foundation and constituted prejudicial error).

59. **U.S.**—Abranson v. Levinson, 1969, 250 N.E.2d 769, 112 Ill.App.

§ 431.3 TRIAL EVIDENCE Ch. 431

In some cases, it has been held that the question as to the probable courses the automobiles took after the impact is not the proper subject of expert testimony;[60] and, in other cases, held proper.[61] And a witness will not generally be permitted to give an opinion as to what instrumentality made certain tracks or marks observed;[62] but, in certain cases, such opinion evidence has been held proper.[63]

2d 42, certiorari denied 90 S.Ct. 1868, 398 U.S. 950, 26 L.Ed.2d 290.

60. Cal.—Fishman v. Silva, 1931, 2 P.2d 473, 116 Cal.App. 1 (decision prior to adoption of Evidence Code).

Wash.—Twidwell v. Davidson, 338 P.2d 326, 54 Wash.2d 75 (where truck collided with defendant's oncoming automobile, it was prejudicial error to permit expert to testify as to positions which vehicles would have taken if collision had occurred in manner related by truck driver).

61. Ill.—Tipsword v. Melrose, 1973, 301 N.E.2d 614, 13 Ill.App.3d 1009 (admissible in absence of adequate eyewitness testimony).

Iowa—Schmitt v. Jenkins Truck Lines, Inc., Iowa 1969, 170 N.W.2d 632, 46 A.L.R.3d 636 (where county sheriff as investigating officer had opportunity to observe vehicles at scene before they were removed and location of debris and gouge mark in pavement and tracks leading up to rear duals of trailer and was experienced in observing such accident scenes, sheriff was qualified to give opinion as to probable course vehicles took after impact and it was for jury to determine what weight to give such testimony); Robeson v. Dilts, Iowa 1969, 170 N.W.2d 408 (proper where based on personal examination made while scene remained unchanged and officer detailed his observations, including, inter alia, location of debris, location of vehicles when they came to rest, distance of the vehicles from purported point of impact and damage to vehicles).

N.H.—Beaudin v. Continental Baking Co., 50 A.2d 77, 94 N.H. 202 (that automobile struck on left front corner would pivot on left rear wheel was properly admitted).

Tex.—Mesa Trucking Co. v. King, 376 S.W.2d 863 (did not abuse discretion when permitted officer to testify as to course vehicles took after impact, where officer had been a deputy sheriff for eight years and had been in such work for 25 years and his duties involved patrolling of highways and he had investigated hundreds of accidents and his years of training permitted him to determine what happened from location of physical evidence as he found it at scene).

Wyo.—Krahn v. Pierce, 1971, 485 P. 2d 1021 (analysis of gouge mark on road).

62. Ariz.—Hinson v. Phoenix Pie Co., 1966, 416 P.2d 202, 3 Ariz.App. 523.

Ky.—Appalachian Stave Co. v. Pickard, 86 S.W.2d 685, 260 Ky. 720.

N.C.—Howard v. Wood, 139 S.E.2d 252, 263 N.C. 241 (investigating officer who testified to skid mark could not be permitted to draw conclusions, and it was for jury to determine whether mark was made by motorcycle).

S.C.—Smith v. Hardy, 88 S.E.2d 865, 228 S.C. 112 (a traffic consultant who derived his information solely from later examination of scene

63. See note 63 on page 643.

Qualified witnesses have been permitted to testify as to the portion of a vehicle at which the impact occurred,[64] and the direction of forces and angle of impact.[65]

---

and study of photographs, was properly prevented from answering questions as to what had happened on night in question and as to what had caused certain marks on highway).

63. U.S.—Burleson v. Champion, C.A.Ga.1960, 283 F.2d 653 (whether indentation in roadway caused by bumper).

Ala.—Alabama Power Co. v. Jackson, 166 So. 692, 232 Ala. 42; Alaga Coach Line v. McCarroll, 1963, 151 So. 834, 227 Ala. 686, 92 A.L.R. 470; Beatty v. Palmer, 1916, 71 So. 422, 196 Ala. 67.

Ky.—McCallum v. Harris, 379 S.W.2d 438 (testimony of trooper that he was able to identify marks on highway and trace them to respective vehicles was competent where there was no element of speculation present); Conley v. Jennings, 1944, 178 S.W.2d 185, 296 Ky. 652.

Mich.—LaFave v. Kroger Co., 146 N.W.2d 850, 5 Mich.App. 446 (may testify either from personal observation or from properly authenticated and admitted exhibits that certain marks are skid marks and that they were made by given vehicle, and may point out opinion as to point of impact); Dudek v. Popp, 1964, 129 N.W.2d 393, 373 Mich. 300.

Mo.—Silsby v. Hinchey, App.1937, 107 S.W.2d 812.

Utah—Batt v. State, 1972, 503 P.2d 855, 28 Utah 2d 417 (permitting police officer to testify as to what caused tire marks on highway).

Wis.—Jensen v. Rural Mut. Ins. Co., 1968, 163 N.W.2d 158, 41 Wis.2d 36 (that officer testifying as to tire marks north of center of highway and terminating at point near rear of plaintiff's eastbound vehicle had not measured width of tracks left in snow and had not measured width of plaintiff's automobile did not completely discredit officer's testimony linking tracks to plaintiff's vehicle).

64. Colo.—Ison v. Stewart, 94 P.2d 701, 105 Colo. 55 (from examination of vehicle and photographs).

Conn.—Finch v. Weiner, 145 A. 31, 109 Conn. 616 (even though second collision with fence occurred).

Contra

Ala.—Kilcrease v. Harris, 1972, 259 So.2d 797, 288 Ala. 245 (patrolman, who had gone to the scene after its occurrence and had observed the vehicles involved, and who was asked to look at picture of plaintiff's truck and pictures of intersection involved, but who was not shown a picture of defendants' truck, although he testified how it was damaged, was not entitled to testify as to what part of defendant's truck initially hit what part of plaintiff's truck where the jurors could have drawn their own inferences).

Fla.—Upchurch v. Barnes, App.1967, 197 So.2d 26 (decided prior to enactment of Florida Evidence Code).

65. U.S.—Campbell v. Clark, C.A. Kan., 283 F.2d 766 (did not abuse its discretion in admitting testimony of expert that automobile and truck came together at an angle, and that truck was angled to its right and automobile was angled to its left at instant of impact).

Ariz.—Bullard v. Stonebraker, 422 P.2d 700, 101 Ariz. 584.

Cal.—Hughes v. Kilgore, 43 Cal.Rptr. 820, 233 Cal.App.2d 541.

§ 431.3   TRIAL EVIDENCE   Ch. 431

It has also been held that an expert witness may testify as to the point of impact on the highway,[66] though other decisions have limited [67] or refused such opinions.[68]

Colo.—McNelley v. Smith, 368 P.2d 555, 149 Colo. 177.

Ohio—Dibert v. Ross Pattern & Foundry Development Co., 152 N.E.2d 369, 105 Ohio App. 264 (experienced mechanic who arrived at scene shortly after it occurred and examined positions of and damage to vehicles).

Wash.—McBroom v. Orner, 395 P.2d 95, 64 Wash.2d 887, 11 A.L.R.3d 914 (expert who had 30 years' experience in repairing automobiles and who, after seeing automobiles involved and examining pictures thereof, could testify as an expert as to direction of force exerted by each vehicle on the other).

But see

Mo.—Homan v. Missouri Pac. R. Co., 70 S.W.2d 869, 335 Mo. 30.

Exclusion not error

Pa.—Laubach v. Haigh, 1969, 252 A. 2d 682, 433 Pa. 487 (refusal to admit engineer's opinion, as expert witness, as to angle of impact and point of collision on highway was not error).

Insufficient basis

Ill.—National Bank of Bloomington v. Pickens, 1972, 289 N.E.2d 64, 8 Ill.App.3d 58 (where no observed facts impeached testimony of southbound experienced truck driver that vehicles were both headed north and that both were moving at the time of impact, his testimony that one vehicle struck the other in the rear was consistent with paint samples and metal bumper samples taken following collision and only other eyewitness gave similar testimony, it was reversible error to admit opinion testimony of accident reconstruction expert that collision occurred broadside).

Tex.—Jenkins v. Hennigan, Civ.App., 298 S.W.2d 905 (not error to strike testimony of expert as to angle at which automobile was turned at moment of impact, where testimony was not based on anything other than skid marks).

66. U.S.—Norton v. Gordon Foods, Inc., C.A.Ky.1972, 458 F.2d 1071 (not fatal that witness relied on facts outside record); Frank's Plastering Co. v. Koenig, C.A.Neb., 341 F.2d 257, citing C.J.S. Evidence § 520 (in view of physical evidence upon which opinion was based, notwithstanding that hypothetical question as to point of impact did not include testimony of witness who was sole survivor); Rhynard v. Filori, C.A.S.D., 315 F.2d 176 (expert testimony of police officer, who arrived at scene within one-half hour after its occurrence and who made close observations and measurements).

Ariz.—Bullard v. Stonebraker, 422 P. 2d 700, 101 Ariz. 584 (where his opinion was based on "splotch of dirt" found on highway, location of damage to automobiles, and absence of tire marks or other physical evidence on shoulder of highway); City of Phoenix v. Schroeder, 405 P.2d 301, 1 Ariz.App. 510 (that testimony of expert in field of accident investigation was not based on inspection of scene or vehicles involved but was based entirely on police photographs taken at scene after the accident went to weight rather than admissibility).

Ark.—Nelson v. Busby, 1969, 437 S. W.2d 799, 246 Ark. 247.

Colo.—Dolan v. Mitchell, 1972, 502 P.2d 72, —— Colo. —— (testimony

---

67. See note 67 on page 647.

68. See note 68 on page 648.

of officer who had conducted investigation of scene minutes after it had occurred and who was recognized as an expert as to point of impact was admissible even though there were no skid marks and automobiles had been moved slightly prior to officer's arrival, where extent of movement of vehicles was fully testified to by competent witness before counsel had attempted to elicit officer's opinion); McNelley v. Smith, 1962, 368 P.2d 555, 149 Colo. 177 (officer at scene).

Ga.—Finley v. Franklin Aluminum Co., 207 S.E.2d 543, 132 Ga.App. 70 (based upon trooper's own investigation).

Idaho—Grant v. Clarke, 305 P.2d 752, 78 Idaho 412 (where sheriff had testified that he had examined a great many accidents during his work, which extended over four years, that in his investigations he had tried to determine what had happened and particularly to locate the point of impact, and had testified as to the location of the automobiles when he arrived and that he had observed the debris on the road).

Ill.—Svrcek v. Kudlata, 320 N.E.2d 377, 23 Ill.App.3d 978 (police officer who had 19 years' experience on the force); Tipsword v. Melrose, 1973, 301 N.E.2d 614, 13 Ill.App.3d 1009 (in absence of adequate eyewitness testimony); Siebens v. Konicek, 1969, 247 N.E.2d 453, 108 Ill.App.2d 300 (based on location of debris).

Iowa—Ganrud v. Smith, 1973, 206 N.W.2d 311 (where evidence, including several photographs taken soon after collision in question, showed that both vehicles were demolished in the accident, and where parts of the vehicles and merchandise from one vehicle came to rest on all portions of pavement as well as both shoulders and in the ditches, trial court did not abuse its discretion in ruling that facts justified use of opinion); Rasmussen v. Thilges, Iowa 1970, 174 N.W.2d 384 (where expert testified he viewed scene, examined all exhibits relating to accident and based his opinion on speed and direction of travel of vehicles prior to accident, damaged areas of vehicles, width of traveled portion of highway and position of automobiles in relation to each other and highway after impact); Dougherty v. Boyken, 1968, 155 N.W.2d 488, 261 Iowa 602 (highway patrolman who had had special training in accident investigation and had investigated about 750 accidents was qualified); Lessenhop v. Norton, 1967, 153 N.W.2d 107, 261 Iowa 44 (testimony by expert in head-on collision case that he examined the scene within an hour after the accident or an hour or an hour and one-half and that his examination disclosed certain skid marks, "brights", and gouges, which he located by measurements, was sufficient foundation for admission of his opinion); Mickelson v. Forney, 1966, 143 N.W.2d 390, 259 Iowa 91; Nielsen v. Wessels, 1955, 73 N.W.2d 83, 247 Iowa 213 (based on debris).

Ky.—Mulberry v. Howard, 1970, 457 S.W.2d 827.

Md.—Nizer v. Phelps, 1969, 249 A.2d 112, 252 Md. 185 (police officer who had extensive training in accident investigation and was at scene immediately after accident and who observed and recorded physical facts had sufficient facts upon which to predicate opinion).

Mich.—Link v. McCoy, 1972, 197 N.W.2d 278, 39 Mich.App. 120 (may render opinion based on debris and skid marks); Howard v. Drew, 1970, 175 N.W.2d 351, 21 Mich. App. 146 (may render an opinion based merely upon debris and skid marks); Hoffman v. Rengo Oil Co., 1969, 174 N.W.2d 155, 20 Mich. App. 575 (such testimony contained no legal conclusions and did not determine fault); Brummitt v.

Chaney, 1969, 170 N.W.2d 481, 18 Mich.App. 59 (based merely upon debris and skid marks); O'Dowd v. Linehan, 1968, 165 N.W.2d 507, 14 Mich.App. 260, judgment reversed on other grounds 189 N.W. 2d 333, 385 Mich. 491.

N.M.—Tobeck v. United Nuclear-Homestake Partners, 1973, 512 P. 2d 1267, 85 N.M. 431 (where expert testified as to personal knowledge of handling characteristics of vehicles similar to tractor-trailer involved in accident, observed photographs of accident and vehicles involved, and measurements taken by investigating police officer).

Okl.—Jackson v. Brown, 361 P.2d 270 (when opinion is derived solely from examination of physical evidence at scene, and this testimony should be elicited in form of opinion rather than in terms of categorical facts); Miller v. Hickman, 359 P.2d 172 (fact that there were eyewitnesses to collision on curve of highway did not render inadmissible testimony of investigating officer); Tuck v. Buller, 311 P.2d 212, 66 A.L.R.2d 1043 (when opinion was derived from examination of physical evidence or indicia at scene).

Pa.—Peterman v. Neiswender, 57 Berks 14 (based upon specific facts observed at the scene).

S.D.—Koenig v. Weber, 1970, 174 N.W.2d 218, 84 S.D. 558.

Tex.—Kettle v. Smircich, 1967, 415 S.W.2d 935 (did not abuse discretion where he had investigated 240 to 250 accidents per year and on secondary schooling in the Department of Public Safety had experience with evaluating physical forces, applying kinetic energy formulas, dealing with test skills, and taking pictures); Hernandez v. H. S. Anderson Trucking Co., Civ. App.1963, 370 S.W.2d 909, ref. n. r. e. (6 yrs. as patrolman, with instruction in investigation).

Wash.—Parris v. Johnson, 1970, 479 P.2d 91, 3 Wash.App. 853 (officer's testimony as to position and condition of vehicles after accident and as to gouge marks on highway afforded sufficient factual foundation for officer's opinion); Poston v. Clinton, 1965, 406 P.2d 623, 66 Wash.2d 911 (were actively in charge of investigation).

Wis.—Felde v. Kohnke, 1971, 184 N. W.2d 433, 50 Wis.2d 168 (opinion based upon photographs, uncontradicted testimony as to trail of liquid debris and final resting place and position of automobile); Kamp v. Curtis, 1970, 175 N.W.2d 267, 46 Wis.2d 423 (where it was based on firsthand knowledge of physical facts concerning accident).

Assertion opinion not possible from debris location

Refusal, when plaintiff's eastbound truck collided with side of trailer towed by westbound automobile and then collided with westbound jeep, wherein it was conceded that resulting debris was nearly all on trailer's side of road, to permit expert testimony that point of impact could not be accurately determined from location of debris was error but was not prejudicial, in that it must have been apparent to jury that point of impact could not be determined with accuracy from location of wide variety of debris scattered over large area of highway. Carter v. Moberly, 1972, 501 P.2d 1276, 263 Or. 193.

Expert did not consider hearsay facts

Where investigating highway patrolman was asked as to whether he could give an opinion as to location of point of impact of automobiles without regard to what witness had told him and he said he could and then marked a diagram so as to indicate his opinion, his testimony was not inadmissible on theory that it was based in part on what an eyewitness had told him. Harris v. Reeves, Tex.Civ.App.1967, 421 S.W. 2d 689, error refused n. r. e.

Impact with pedestrian

Where point at which bus struck pedestrian was not so obvious that any person, trained or not, could infer from evidence where it was located, court properly admitted expert testimony of traffic officer who based his conclusions in part on statement given by bus driver to officer. Kastner v. Los Angeles Metropolitan Transit Authority, 45 Cal.Rptr. 129, 403 P.2d 385.

67. U.S.—Scott v. Fancher, C.A. Tex., 369 F.2d 842 (exclusion of testimony of lay witness who was offered as expert to give opinion as to point on highway where collision occurred and as to angle and manner in which trucks collided was not abuse of discretion); Parris v. Harris, C.A.Okl., 351 F.2d 52 (when opinion is based upon physical evidence observed at scene).

Ariz.—Gilbert v. Quinet, 369 P.2d 267, 91 Ariz. 29 (police officer, who admitted that he could not form an opinion as to point of impact of bus with boy solely from skid marks made by bus and dust marks on bus bumper, properly precluded from testifying).

Ark.—S & S Const. Co. v. Stacks, 411 S.W.2d 508, 241 Ark. 1096 (improper where there was no evidence to indicate that it was beyond jury's ability to understand facts and draw its own conclusions).

Ill.—Dobkowski v. Lowe's Inc., 1974, 314 N.E.2d 623, 20 Ill.App.3d 275 (it was error to admit opinion of state trooper that collision between northbound van and southbound tractor trailer unit occurred in the northbound lane where the jurors, using the physical evidence presented at trial, were no less competent to reach an opinion concerning the point of impact than was the trooper; in such case trooper's opinion testimony was not necessary; however, error was harmless where, under the physical evidence, the jury could not have logically reached any conclusion other than that the trucks collided in the northbound lane); Dauksch v. Chamness, 1973, 296 N.E.2d 592, 11 Ill.App.3d 346 (where the drivers gave eyewitness testimony as to location of the vehicles at time of collision and where investigating state trooper's opinion was based only upon his observation of physical facts and circumstances of collision, admission of trooper's opinion was error, but, where trooper's opinion that accident occurred in northbound lane stated only the obvious and was merely cumulative, the error was harmless); Freehill v. De Witt County Service Co., 1970, 261 N.E.2d 52, 125 Ill. App.2d 306, 43 A.L.R.3d 715 (exclusion proper where did not testify positively as to debris location or length and location of skids).

Ky.—Wells v. Conley, 384 S.W.2d 496 (state trooper could state opinion, from his examination of damage, that they struck at a certain angle, and could state opinion from examination of gouge marks in highway and tar or asphalt residue on bottoms of parts of vehicles that vehicles were moving in a certain direction when marks were made and that some marks were made by one vehicle and some by the other, but could not state opinion and offer diagram indicating that vehicles must have collided a few feet north of point where gouge marks appeared, based on assumption that vehicles moved only a few feet after collison).

Mich.—Link v. McCoy, 1972, 197 N. W.2d 278, 39 Mich.App. 120 (unless it can be established that testifying officers are so schooled and experienced that their measure of skill and special knowledge decidedly transcends the capabilities of

68. See note 68 on page 648.

§ 431.3   TRIAL EVIDENCE   Ch. 431

an average juror, who has been made fully aware of the physical facts, officers' opinions should not be received).

Neb.—Caves v. Barnes, 132 N.W.2d 310, 178 Neb. 103 (admissible where answers were limited to character of contact of vehicles and to results following contact and did not include statement as to point of impact).

Ohio.—Trebotich v. Broglio, 1973, 294 N.E.2d 669, 33 Ohio St.2d 57, 62 O.O.2d 410 (generally, question not one calling for skill or expert opinion, but is within experience, knowledge or comprehension of jury).

Pa.—Phillips v. Pickell, 57 Berks 107 (not error where the fact was not an issue for the jury).

Utah.—Day v. Lorenzo Smith & Son, Inc., 408 P.2d 186, 17 Utah 2d 221 (should not be admitted if it is based upon same evidence as is available to jury, and a layman of ordinary intelligence can equally determine what happened).

May place position of debris

Permitting patrolman to draw circle on plaintiff's exhibit, the plat of the area in which head-on collision occurred, to mark point to indicate where heaviest concentration of debris and shakedown was located as observed by patrolman was not improper on ground that it constituted an opinion from patrolman that it was the point of impact. Schneider v. Prentzler, Mo., 391 S.W.2d 307.

Not founded on statements of others

Ariz.—Bullard v. Stonebraker, 422 P.2d 700, 101 Ariz. 584 (patrolman or other officer, when shown to have proper training and experience in investigation of traffic accidents, may properly give opinion as to point of impact in traffic accident where his opinion is based on marks on highway, damage to vehicles involved, and location of debris on highway or other indicia at scene, but not when such opinion is founded on statements made to him by other persons).

Cal.—Kalfus v. Fraze, 288 P.2d 967, 136 Cal.App.2d 415 (police officer with proper training and experience in investigation of traffic accidents and submission of reports on facts and causes of such accidents may give expert testimony as to point of impact when his opinion derives from examination of physical evidence or indicia at the scene, but not when such opinion is founded on statements made to him by other persons); Hodges v. Severns, 20 Cal.Rptr. 129, 201 Cal.App.2d 99.

Iowa—Brooks v. Gilbert, 1959, 98 N. W.2d 309, 250 Iowa 1164.

68. **Ark.**—Reed v. Humphreys, 1963, 373 S.W.2d 580, 237 Ark. 315.

Fla.—Upchurch v. Barnes, App.1967, 197 So.2d 26 (decision prior to enactment of Evidence Code).

Ill.—Geisberger v. Quincy, 1972, 278 N.E.2d 404, 3 Ill.App.3d 437.

Minn.—Schoeb v. Cowles, 1968, 156 N.W.2d 895, 279 Minn. 331 (exclusion of police officers' opinion was proper, even if based on an incorrect reason); Montagne v. Stenvold, 148 N.W.2d 815, 276 Minn. 547 (admission, in action arising out of collision which occurred when plaintiff's eastbound automobile attempted to pass defendants' eastbound truck which began to execute left turn, of testimony by police officer that point of impact was 40 feet west of intersection was prejudicial error, where vital issue was whether point of impact occurred within intersection, as defendant claimed, or some distance west of it, as plaintiff driver claimed, testimony of each driver as to point of impact directly conflicted, officer was the only disinterested witness, and there was no instruction as to evaluating expert opinion).

Ch. 431 EXPERT OPINION EVIDENCE § 431.3

Opinions as to whether a vehicle was over the centerline of the highway have been held inadmissible,[69] and at other times admissible.[70]

Miss.—Jones v. Welford, 1968, 215 So.2d 240.

Mo.—Watts v. Handley, App.1968, 427 S.W.2d 272; Hamre v. Conger, 1948, 209 S.W.2d 242, 357 Mo. 497 (by highway patrolman).

Neb.—Sheets v. Davenport, 1967, 150 N.W.2d 224, 181 Neb. 62 (refusal to permit opinion based upon observation of marks on roadway 13 days after accident, which marks were identified by other witnesses as having been made when vehicles were dragged from scene of collision, was proper).

N.J.—Rogalsky v. Plymouth Homes, Inc., 1968, 242 A.2d 655, 100 N.J. Super. 501 (based in part upon statement of driver).

N.Y.—Stafford v. Mussers Potato Chips, Inc., 1972, 333 N.Y.S.2d 139, 39 A.D.2d 831; In re Sacco's Will, 1970, 312 N.Y.S.2d 259, 34 A.D.2d 885 (based upon position of automobiles after accident and location of the debris).

Ohio.—Trebotich v. Broglio, 1973, 294 N.E.2d 669, 33 Ohio St.2d 57, 62 O.O.2d 410; Dickman v. Struble, 146 N.E.2d 636, 104 Ohio App. 44 (question as to which side of center line of highway accident occurred did not involve interpretation of a scientific fact beyond knowledge, experience and comprehension of jury); Ross v. Stricker, 88 N.E.2d 80, 85 Ohio App. 56, reversed on other grounds 91 N.E.2d 18, 153 Ohio St. 153.

Or.—Thomas v. Dad's Root Beer & Canada Dry Bottling Co. of Portland, 356 P.2d 418, 225 Or. 166, rehearing denied 357 P.2d 418, 225 Or. 166.

Pa.—Laubach v. Haigh, 1969, 252 A. 2d 682, 433 Pa. 487 (exclusion not error).

S.D.—Kleinsasser v. Gross, 1964, 129 N.W.2d 717, 80 S.D. 631 (particularly where there were eyewitnesses).

Utah.—Beardall v. Murray, 1972, 496 P.2d 260, 27 Utah 2d 340 (as determined by use of formula relating to physics of a hypothetical case based on weights, speed of vehicles, angles of travel, etc., which were not shown to be connected with those involved in action).

69. U.S.—Bitton v. International Transport, Inc., C.A.Wash.1970, 437 F.2d 817 (based upon questioned evidence); Ordner v. Reimold, C.A.Okl., 278 F.2d 532 (in action for wrongful death of passenger in automobile which skidded across highway into oncoming truck allegedly as a result of being struck by overtaking automobile driven by defendant, testimony of district commander of state highway patrol that, assuming that automobile in which decedent was riding sustained blow of sufficient force to produce crease shown on left rear fender, such blow would not be sufficient to cause automobile to change direction abruptly to the left and cross highway, assuming also that it was under proper control, was objectionable on grounds that factual background of accident would not support the premise of such hypothetical question and such opinion testimony did not serve to enlighten jury in respect to a matter outside its competence).

Alaska.—Ferrell v. Baxter, 1971, 484 P.2d 250 (refusal, in action arising out of collision on ice and snow-covered curve of highway, to permit towing and alignment service

70. See note 70 on page 650.

§ 431.3   TRIAL EVIDENCE   Ch. 431

owner, who had been engaged in such business for 20 years and had assisted at 100 to 125 accidents per year, 20 to 25 of which were serious, and had often driven tractor trailer combinations, to express his opinion as to speed from photograph of tire tracks or as to location of rear of trailer relative to center of road at time of impact on ground that owner did not possess sufficient knowledge to assist in determining issue was not abuse of discretion).

Ark.—Wright v. Flagg, 1974, 508 S.W.2d 742, 256 Ark. 495 (where facts were not complicated and boiled down to whether motorist drove across center line of highway and into the proper path of oncoming truck, or whether motorist had completed his exit from highway and was parked parallel thereto when collision occurred, proffered testimony of consulting engineer and expert on forensic engineering as to position of the vehicles based on photographs made of the two vehicles soon after the collision, on a diagram prepared by officer, and on survey map showing the elevations and contour lines of the roadways, was properly excluded as invading province of jury).

Ill.—Payne v. Noles, 1972, 283 N.E.2d 329, 5 Ill.App.3d 433 (jury had testimony of four eyewitnesses).

Me.—Parker v. Hohman, Me.1969, 250 A.2d 698 (was based on uncertain angle of impact and unfounded assumptions as to speed, center of balance and degree of friction of tires on road).

Mich.—Cook v. Kendrick, 1969, 167 N.W.2d 483, 16 Mich.App. 48 (refusal to allow police officer to answer questions which would have elicited an opinion as to cause of accident and automobiles' directions was not an abuse of discretion, where defendant did not lay a proper foundation of data concerning accident).

Mo.—Housman v. Fiddyment, 1967, 421 S.W.2d 284.

Mont.—Lamb v. Page, 1969, 455 P.2d 337, 153 Mont. 171.

Neb.—Barry v. Dvorak, 126 N.W.2d 226, 176 Neb. 375 (in absence of any evidence before witness from which point of contact of automobiles in road could reasonably be inferred); Stillwell v. Schmoker, 122 N.W.2d 538, 175 Neb. 595 (expert should not have been permitted to express opinion as to lane in which collision between plaintiff and oncoming left-turning defendant occurred since physical facts were all before jury and location of collision was ultimate fact for determination of jury).

N.D.—Fisher v. Suko, 98 N.W.2d 895 (on a lazy S curve).

S.D.—Kleinsasser v. Gross, 129 N.W.2d 717, 80 S.D. 631 (for lack of proper foundation).

Tex.—King v. Skelly, 1970, 452 S.W.2d 691, on remand 454 S.W.2d 775.

Va.—Venable v. Stockner, 108 S.E.2d 380, 200 Va. 900 (error to permit witness to express opinion, based on marks in road and photographs of damaged vehicles, that tractor-trailer had been encroaching on lane of automobile by "at least a foot and a half").

Jumped divider

Refusal to permit reconstruction expert to testify as to which motorist jumped divider and hit the other was not error where expert's opinion was based on premise that accident occurred immediately as vehicle crossed median, and testimony tending to show such fact was not believable. Abramson v. Levinson, 1969, 250 N.E.2d 796, 112 Ill.App.2d 42, certiorari denied 90 S.Ct. 1868, 398 U.S. 950, 26 L.Ed.2d 290.

70. U.S.—Clifton v. Mangum, C.A.N.M., 366 F.2d 250 (admission of testimony, that scrape mark on north side of highway was made

Ch. 431   EXPERT OPINION EVIDENCE   § 431.3

Opinions as to stopping distance are generally admissible.[71]

A variety of other accident reconstruction opinions have been held admissible,[72] and a variety of others inadmissible.[73]

by left dolly or parking wheel on plaintiffs' trailer and that plaintiffs' truck had therefore been on wrong side of highway, involved identification of truck by scientific analysis of the incriminating scrape, a matter not within knowledge or comprehension of jury); Ward v. Brown, C.A.Okl., 301 F.2d 445 (though improperly supported in this case).

Ga.—Fuels, Inc. v. Rutland, 1970, 179 S.E.2d 290, 123 Ga.App. 23 (it was for jury to determine whether to believe or disbelieve the trooper); Sikes v. Wilson, 1946, 39 S.E.2d 902, 74 Ga.App. 415.

Ill.—Diefenbach v. Pickett, 1969, 248 N.E.2d 840, 111 Ill.App.2d 80 (testimony of a corporal of the state police who investigated accident).

Iowa.—Lucas v. Duccini, 137 N.W.2d 634, 258 Iowa 77 (where skid marks of plaintiff's automobile which were completely on plaintiff's side of street were sufficient physical facts on which to base opinion called for).

N.H.—Lynch v. Bissell, 116 A.2d 121, 99 N.H. 473 (where it could be found that the officer's experience in investigating many accidents would be of aid).

Wash.—Gerard v. Peasley, 403 P.2d 45, 66 Wash.2d 449.

Wis.—Rabata v. Dohner, 1969, 172 N.W.2d 409, 45 Wis.2d 111 (knew personally points of rest, and condition and terrain of intersection).

71. Colo.—Herness v. Goodrich, 1971, 483 P.2d 412, 29 Colo.App. 322, appeal after remand 509 P.2d 1279, —— Colo.App. —— (distance required to stop, in pedestrian case).

Ind.—Shelby Nat. Bank v. Miller, 1970, 259 N.E.2d 450, 147 Ind.App. 203 (concerning maximum distance required for stopping).

Kan.—Beardsley v. Weber, 1973, 516 P.2d 936, 213 Kan. 427 (admission of testimony of police officer, who had experience and training in area of accident investigation, that motorcyclist if his brakes were passable according to state law could have stopped if he was driving within the speed limit which ranged from 0 to 35 miles per hour was proper, even though there was no evidence as to how fast motorcyclist was going and no evidence that his speed was 35 miles per hour which was the speed used by officer in making his computations and forming his opinion).

Train

U.S.—Hartzler v. Chesapeake & O. Ry. Co., C.A.Ind.1970, 433 F.2d 104).

72. Ariz.—Killingsworth v. Nottingham, 1972, 501 P.2d 1197, 18 Ariz. App. 356 (where highway patrolman arrived on scene shortly after accident and made extensive investigation, he made official report comprising approximately 100 pages, he had been highway patrolman for seven years, he had had special schooling, and his opinion concerning reconstruction of sequence of impact was not based on statements of any witnesses but on observations at scene, review of physical facts at scene, and all other available information, opinion was admissible); Peterson v. Salt River Project Agr. Imp. & Power Dist., 1964, 391 P.2d 567, 96 Ariz. 1.

73. See note 73 on page 657.

Ark.—Woodward v. Blythe, 1971, 462 S.W.2d 205, 249 Ark. 793 (in action for death of motorist who, in veering to left to avoid colliding with unlighted automobile stalled partially on pavement, sideswiped a second automobile and was struck by following automobile driven by defendant, admission of testimony of physicist regarding physical dynamics of the accident was proper); Nelson v. Busby, 1969, 437 S.W.2d 799, 246 Ark. 247 (officer who investigated accident which occurred when pedestrian entered street in path of automobile which was then leaving curb was properly permitted to state conclusion, based upon examination of skid marks, that defendant's automobile had made "a rather rapid start."); McCormick v. Sexton, 386 S.W.2d 930, 239 Ark. 29 (testimony of state policeman who had investigated traffic collisions for five years and had attended school that some skid marks involved in three-automobile collision on highway were made by flat tire and as to difference in mark made by flat tire and by inflated tire was admissible).

Cal.—Hastings v. Serleto, 143 P.2d 956, 61 Cal.App.2d 672 (where police officer had made experiments to determine how fast automobile could make turn and leave tire burns, opinion of officer based on brush marks found at scene and evidence of collision of automobile with tree was admissible); Hart v. Wielt, 1970, 84 Cal.Rptr. 220, 4 Cal.App.3d 224; Hughes v. Kilgore, 1965, 43 Cal.Rptr. 820, 233 Cal.App.2d 541 (that auto was moving at moment of impact).

Colo.—Dolan v. Mitchell, 1972, 502 P.2d 72, 179 Colo. 359 (testimony of accident reconstruction expert concerning absence of metal smearing and extreme penetration of defendant's vehicle into side of deceased's vehicle at time of impact and tending to show that collision could not have occurred in accordance with plaintiff's contention was relevant and admissible where opinion was based upon photographs which were properly admissible, even though expert had not examined scene and the two vehicles involved within a short time after the accident).

Fla.—Mathews v. Carison, App., 130 So.2d 625 (in action involving issue as to whether defendant had had last clear chance to avoid hitting pedestrian, who was crossing four-lane highway in dark when struck, it was error to reject proffered testimony of traffic expert as to time it took for plaintiff to cross range of defendant's vision and as to stopping time of automobile).

Ga.—Yale & Towne, Inc. v. Sharpe, 1968, 164 S.E.2d 318, 118 Ga.App. 480 (under allegations of petition charging negligence in failing to provide a forklift truck in good operating condition and suitable for purposes for which it was to be used, industrial engineer testimony of vehicle's general condition as revealed by inspection about a month after operator was injured was admissible).

Ill.—Murphy v. Hook, 1974, 316 N.E. 2d 146, 21 Ill.App.3d 1006 (from examination of photographs); Adkins v. Chicago, R. I. & P. R. Co., 1971, 274 N.E.2d 507, 2 Ill.App.3d 906, reversed on other grounds 301 N.E. 2d 729, 54 Ill.2d 511 (where testimony of plaintiff's reconstruction expert did not reconstruct the collision itself and, though there were three eyewitnesses to collision, none of the witnesses were able to assist jury as to time and distances involved, trial court properly permitted plaintiff's expert to testify as to time which expired when decedent first perceived his dangerous situation, comprehended the problem and decided on a course of action and as to time used by

Ch. 431   EXPERT OPINION EVIDENCE   § 431.3

decedent in applying his brakes and approximate speed of truck just prior to collision); Pritchett v. Steinker Trucking Co., 1969, 247 N.E.2d 923, 108 Ill.App.2d 371; Woodrick v. Smith Gas Service, Inc., 1967, 230 N.E.2d 508, 87 Ill. App. 88 (in view of showing that condition of automobile, which had failed to decelerate when plaintiff let up on the accelerator allegedly because of defendant's faulty installation of an "autostart" device, had not changed from time of accident until time when certain tests and experiments were made on the automobile, proper foundation was laid for expert testimony based on those tests and experiments); Goldblatt v. Brocklebank, 1911, 166 Ill.App. 315 (possibility of stopping vehicle upon observation of danger).

Kan.—Hildebrand v. Mueller, 1969, 449 P.2d 587, 202 Kan. 506 (admission of testimony of expert witness, who had been with city police department for 35 years and with traffic department for 22 years, as to speed and location of automobiles just before entering intersection wherein they collided was not an abuse of discretion).

Me.—Parker v. Hohman, Me.1969, 250 A.2d 698.

Mich.—Coles v. Galloway, 1967, 151 N.W.2d 229, 7 Mich.App. 93 (no abuse of discretion by trial court in allowing police officer, who had investigated accident and had had experience in training in accident investigation, to testify as to which automobile caused each pile of debris found at scene).

Mo.—Creager v. Chilson, 1970, 453 S.W.2d 941 (even if officer used questionable formula in determining time it took for defendant's automobile to arrive at given point and distance traveled during that time by plaintiff); West v. Jack Cooper Transport Co., 1963, 372 S.W.2d 642 (over contention failed to allow for road conditions).

Neb.—Drahota v. Wieser, 1968, 157 N.W.2d 857, 183 Neb. 66 (within trial court's discretion to receive opinion that motor vehicle which was making "U" turn was in fact moving at time of collision even though driver testified that automobile was stopped).

N.H.—Sigel v. Boston & M. R. R., 216 A.2d 794, 107 N.H. 8 (a civil engineer of long experience in highway layouts, intersections and similar subjects could have been found to be more than ordinarily skilled and experienced to give evidence bearing on views, angles, seconds required to travel certain distances at certain speeds, safe stopping distances and related matters affecting liability in railway crossing collision); Walker v. Walker, 210 A.2d 468, 106 N.H. 282 (where officers arrived on scene shortly after occurrence and were men of long experience in investigating accidents, their opinion testimony that husband rather than wife was driving automobile when it crashed was not improper).

Okl.—Deskins v. Woodward, 1971, 483 P.2d 1134 (that there were marks on pavement indicating that vehicle was making a left turn at time of impact).

Pa.—Griffith v. Clearfield Truck Rentals, Inc., 1967, 233 A.2d 896, 427 Pa. 30 (witness who had been consultant in matters involving accidents of trucks of various makes and manufacturers was qualified to testify that in his opinion the only condition which could cause vibration, wandering, and locking of steering wheel of lessor's truck was defective maintenance of wheel balance, tire pressure, and/or tie rods, that the vibrations caused something to break in the universal joint, and that failure of rear universal joint caused locking of steering).

§ 431.3   TRIAL EVIDENCE   Ch. 431

Tex.—O'Kelly v. Jackson, Civ.App. 1974, 516 S.W.2d 748 (analysis and reconstruction of accident based on physical facts, photographs, diagrams, and other evidence); Polasek v. Quinius, 1969, 438 S.W.2d 828, error refused n. r. e. (but this rule does not permit the formulation of evidence such as calculations based upon facts assumed and not in evidence).

Utah.—Batt v. State, 1972, 503 P.2d 855, 28 Utah 2d 417 (observations as to nature of tire marks found on highway).

Wash.—Ulmer v. Ford Motor Co., 1969, 452 P.2d 729, 75 Wash.2d 522 (opinion as to cause of collapse of A-frame); Moyer v. Clark, 1969, 454 P.2d 374, 75 Wash.2d 800.

As to absence of defect

U.S.—O'Brien v. Willys Motors, Inc., C.A.Mich.1967, 385 F.2d 163 (steering).

As to steering defect

U.S.—Haddigan v. Harkins, D.C.Pa. 1969, 304 F.Supp. 173, judgment vacated on other grounds, C.A., 441 F.2d 844 (testimony that tie rod of southbound automobile which went out of control and which was struck by northbound automobile was hanging down and that it was mechanic's opinion that driver's loss of control of automobile was due to defective steering was properly admitted).

Iowa.—Kleve v. General Motors Corp., 1973, 210 N.W.2d 568 (where expert predicated his opinion that accident was caused by defective steering mechanism upon a personal examination of internal working parts of steering assembly, and further produced them in open court and there demonstrated, in presence of jury, their respective operations, functional purposes, and to him the apparent accident-causing defect, jury was in a position to determine foundational facts upon which expert based his opinion testimony and to properly evaluate same, and it was improper to exclude expert's opinion testimony by sustaining blanket motion to strike).

Miss.—Ford Motor Co. v. Dees, 1969, 223 So.2d 638 (testimony of witness who had 30 years' experience as part owner and manager of large automotive repair shop relative to construction and working of steering mechanism of pickup trucks did not invade province of jury and furnish ultimate answer as to whether pickup truck, which left road when steering mechanism failed causing injury to owner and driver, left manufacturer's control in dangerously unsafe condition).

Mo.—Central & Southern Truck Lines, Inc. v. Westfall GMC Truck, Inc., App.1958, 317 S.W.2d 841, citing C.J.S. Evidence § 533b (that tie rod end came loose).

Neb.—Kohler v. Ford Motor Co., 1971, 191 N.W.2d 601, 187 Neb. 428 (nature and cause of breaking of gear tooth in steering sector gear).

N.C.—Mann v. Virginia Dare Transp. Co., Inc., 1973, 198 S.E.2d 558, 283 N.C. 734 (conclusion that defect in steering mechanism caused bus to leave highway and opinion that conditions found would have been visible to a competent mechanic prior to time bus was delivered to lessee bus company should have been admitted).

Va.—Walrod v. Matthews, 1969, 171 S.E.2d 180, 210 Va. 382 (where expert testified from his examination of broken control arm of steering mechanism and underside of defendant's automobile that control arm socket had previously been split from shock or blow, his testimony was direct testimony as to previous split in socket and was not incompetent and inadmissible on theory that it was based on assumption of facts as to which there was no evidence in record).

Cause of accident

U.S.—Wilkins v. Hogan, C.A.Kan. 1970, 425 F.2d 1022 (physicist's testimony about how head-on collision could have occurred was not inadmissible, where it appeared that it was based upon physical evidence, and, when considered together with other evidence relating to position of two automobiles before and after impact, it became substantially more than abstract speculation).

Alaska.—State v. Phillips, 1970, 470 P.2d 266 (police officer, as to rut along roadway as cause).

Ark.—Jones v. Turner, 1968, 426 S.W.2d 401, 244 Ark. 603 (mechanic's opinion that oil plug came out due to lack of tightening at time of oil change).

Ga.—Massee v. State Farm Mut. Auto. Ins. Co., 1973, 197 S.E.2d 459, 128 Ga.App. 439 (permitting highway patrolman who wrote accident report on three-car collision to give opinion as to how the collision occurred did not invade province of jury).

Mont.—Pachek v. Norton Concrete Co., 1972, 499 P.2d 766, 160 Mont. 16 (highway patrolman).

Neb.—Petracek v. Haas O. K. Rubber Welders, Inc., 126 N.W.2d 466, 176 Neb. 438 (that accident was caused by a failure to properly tighten nuts on automobile wheel).

Cause of erratic vehicle action

N.Y.—Weiss v. Alexander's Rent-A-Car, Inc., 1972, 337 N.Y.S.2d 930, 40 A.D.2d 879 (as to what had caused rented vehicle to behave as described by plaintiff, who testified that steering wheel was tight, that vehicle pulled to the left, and that shortly thereafter the vehicle hit a bump or rut in the road, steering wheel froze, the brakes failed and the vehicle plunged diagonally to the left into a tree).

Cause of disengagement of axle

S.C.—Redman v. Ford Motor Co., 1969, 170 S.E.2d 207, 253 S.C. 266 (testimony that it was extremely improbable that in automobile wreck forces of sufficient intensity could be generated and applied in the right places to effect disengagement of axle from its bearing without breaking either bearing or axle housing was not pure conjecture and speculation, despite disappearance of axle in question a couple of days after accident and despite contention that witness' examination was cursory at most, and the testimony was properly admitted in suit involving automobile found after accident with left rear wheel assembly and axle loose and dangling from automobile outside fender well and involving issue of whether automobile was negligently manufactured).

Defect in brakes

Ariz.—Lowery v. Turner, 1973, 506 P.2d 1084, 19 Ariz.App. 299 (examined two and one-half years later); Miracle Mile Bottling Distributing Co. v. Drake, 1970, 471 P.2d 741, 12 Ariz.App. 439 (did not abuse its discretion in permitting witness to express opinion on basis of his engineering training and his experience and familiarity with braking systems as to effect of a 1$\frac{1}{16}$ inch thickness in brake linings and of impact loading on anchor pin, loading that pin was designed to withstand, and design capabilities of braking system of defendant's truck).

Cal.—Vandermark v. Ford Motor Co., 37 Cal.Rptr. 896, 391 P.2d 168 (striking testimony of plaintiff's expert on operation of hydraulic automobile brakes as to possible causes of failure of brake master cylinder piston to retract was error, even in absence of direct evidence that one or more of such causes existed, where damage to automobile in collision precluded determination as to whether master cylinder assembly had been properly installed and adjusted before accident).

Ill.—Jines v. Greyhound Corp., 197 N.E.2d 58, 46 Ill.App.2d 364 (not abuse of discretion to permit experienced mechanic to testify as to his examination of brake drum two months after collision and give opinion that faulty brake drum could have locked after being pushed, preventing manual pushing of automobile).

Kan.—Lenhart v. Owens, 1973, 507 P.2d 318, 211 Kan. 534 (testimony of expert that defective piston cup, which he found in brake cylinder of vehicle which struck plaintiff, was cause of power brake failure was not inadmissible on theory that cup in cylinder was exchanged after the accident for defective cup found by witness, absent any evidence that defective cup had been substituted even though vehicle had been purchased by and was in possession of owner's insurer for period of time after accident and before witness had examined the brake assembly).

Ohio.—State Auto Mut. Ins. Co. v. Chrysler Corp., 1973, 304 N.E.2d 891, 36 Ohio St.2d 151 (where mechanic who examined truck damaged in collision caused by alleged brake failure had specialized in the inspection and repair of brake systems and had seen ruptured brake hoses on 30 similar occasions, exclusion of mechanic's testimony in action against truck manufacturer and dealer which had repaired brake drum and linings of the truck that brake hose had ruptured from internal pressure rather than from external forces caused by the accident and was defective was erroneous even though testimony went to an ultimate fact).

Pa.—Woods v. Pleasant Hills Motor Co., 1973, 309 A.2d 698, 454 Pa. 224 (that connection of air supply line which was part of truck's braking system broke loose at time swishing sound was heard constituted a definite opinion and was therefore proper testimony for jury's consideration with respect to accident which allegedly resulted from defect in truck's braking system); Flavin v. Aldrich, 1968, 250 A.2d 185, 213 Pa.Super. 420 (opinion brakes had failed due to loss of fluid was admissible after expert had had an opportunity to test the brakes, and expert's failure to fully investigate braking system was merely a matter for jury).

Tex.—Sharp v. Chrysler Corp., Tex. Civ.App.1968, 432 S.W.2d 131, error refused n. r. e. (testimony of brake repairman in products liability case against manufacturer as to defective installation of adjusting unit of brakes and as to how adjusting unit became detached from its normal position resulting in brake failure).

Wash.—Thomas v. Inland Motor Freight, 1938, 81 P.2d 818, 195 Wash. 633 (worn condition, causing wheel to stop).

Defect in drive shaft

Wash.—Tokarz v. Ford Motor Co., 1973, 508 P.2d 1370, 8 Wash.App. 645 (that there was a defect in missing piece of the drive shaft).

Defect in suspension

U.S.—Moran v. Ford Motor Co., C.A. Neb.1973, 476 F.2d 289 (where owner and operator of body and fender business possessed sufficient knowledge and practical experience to make him well qualified as expert witness and witness' testimony was necessary to prove causation between alleged defect in suspension system and accident, trial court's exclusion of the expert opinion testimony of the automobile repairman was prejudicial error).

Wyo.—Logan v. Pacific Intermountain Exp. Co., 400 P.2d 488 (evidence that spring hangers of truck were broken and that, after impact with automobile, driver turned left and right and got no response from steering mechanism, furnished adequate basis for hypothetical question as to whether truck-trailer could not be steered with four broken spring hangers and cracked steering worm box broken from frame).

May refer to photographs of vehicles and scene

Where there was adequate testimony to confirm that the damage to automobiles and skidmarks displayed in photographs were those resulting from the accident, the photographs were proper subjects to be used by witness as a partial basis for reconstruction of the accident. Plank v. Holman, 1969, 246 N.E.2d 694, 108 Ill.App.2d 216, reversed on other grounds 264 N.E.2d 12, 46 Ill. 2d 465.

Tire failure cause

U.S.—Smith v. Uniroyal, Inc., C.A. Ind.1970, 420 F.2d 438 (fact that tire manufactured by defendant was not presented in evidence or made available to defendant did not render inadmissible testimony of witness, who had examined tire, that tire failure prior to accident was caused by defect, where parties stipulated at trial that tire was not preserved and was unavailable for inspection by defendant or as evidence).

Ill.—Cribbs v. Daily, 1966, 214 N.E. 2d 588, 67 Ill.App.2d 441 (could find whether rupture to tire was from blowout or from cut).

N.C.—Apex Tire & Rubber Co. v. Merritt Tire Co., 1967, 153 S.E.2d 737, 270 N.C. 50 (ran tests as to recapped tire failure cause).

Visibility

U.S.—Hartzler v. Chesapeake & O. Ry. Co., C.A.Ind.1970, 433 F.2d 104 (of train).

Which vehicle entered intersection first

Where two police officers testified from diagram of scene of intersection collision, described physical evidence at the scene, and second officer located point of impact at intersection and told of location of debris off the vehicles and recounted where both vehicles were damaged, officer was qualified to express an opinion as to which vehicle entered intersection first. Boehler v. Sanders, 404 P.2d 885, 146 Mont. 158.

73. **U.S.**—Trans-Cold Exp. Inc. v. Arrow Motor Transit, Inc., C.A.Ill. 1971, 440 F.2d 1216 (refusal, in action arising out of accident in which tractor trailer, as it was turning off highway into truck stop, was struck from rear by another large unit, to admit testimony was not abuse of discretion, notwithstanding contention that shortcomings in eyewitnesses' testimony, together with characteristics of vehicles, their tire marks, consequences of relative speeds, and other physical facts, required explanation by professional witness).

Ariz.—Bogard G. M. C. Co. v. Henley, 374 P.2d 660, 92 Ariz. 107 (admission of testimony of witness for truck driver in action against company, which had checked truck brakes, that accident was due to defective brake on left rear wheel locking was error, where opinion was based solely on skid marks on pavement, and witness testified that there were but single skid marks, but truck had dual rear wheels, which were bolted together, so that skid would have been double).

Conn.—Floyd v. Fruit Industries, Inc., 136 A.2d 918, 144 Conn. 659, 63 A.

§ 431.3   TRIAL EVIDENCE   Ch. 431

L.R.2d 1378 (did not abuse discretion in excluding question asked of plaintiff's witness on cross-examination as to how far truck would skid with 10 of its 12 wheels locked in straight line skid without regard to any fact other than coefficient of friction on road where evidence established that automobile was dragged along with truck after impact).

Fla.—Upchurch v. Barnes, App.1967, 197 So.2d 26 (did not abuse its discretion in refusing to permit traffic officer, who had not been an eyewitness to accident but who had investigated the same and had gone to various schools to study traffic, to testify as an expert regarding his opinion as to vehicle which had entered intersection first).

Ill.—McGrath v. Rohde, 1972, 289 N.E.2d 619, 53 Ill.2d 56 (whether defendant's automobile struck rear of plaintiff's automobile did not require a scientific knowledge beyond that of typical juror); McGrath v. Rohde, 1970, 265 N.E.2d 511, 130 Ill.App.2d 596, affirmed 289 N.E.2d 619, 53 Ill.2d 56 (where following motorist who was called by lead motorist as an adverse party testified fully as to course followed by lead motorist and the sequence of events leading to collision and the facts were not such that they required the aid of expert testimony for comprehension, testimony of accident reconstruction expert was inadmissible); Pearson v. Sutterlin, 1968, 234 N.E.2d 101, 91 Ill.App.2d 99 (several years of "investigation" of traffic accidents did not qualify police officer to express a descriptive opinion concerning what transpired when such investigative experience was defined as observing position of vehicles, providing medical attention for injured parties, arranging to have damaged vehicles moved from traffic, interviewing witnesses, and preparing and filing reports of the event).

Ind.—Carson v. Associated Truck Lines, Inc., 1968, 241 N.E.2d 78, 143 Ind.App. 431 (properly excluded testimony of witness, an accident reconstruction expert who had not viewed scene at time of accident and had not seen vehicles involved or debris and who based testimony on photographs, to effect that truck into which plaintiff's automobile crashed was not moving at time of collision, since testimony was irrelevant to central issue of plaintiff's contributory negligence and his conclusions were highly speculative)

Ky.—Eldridge v. Pike, 1965, 396 S.W.2d 314 (belief auto on bridge before truck speculative).

Me.—Bowe v. Willis, 1974, 323 A.2d 593 (physics professor who had never seen the vehicles involved in accident, had never checked the road surface where the accident occurred, had never seen the tires on the vehicles, and did not know the type or condition of the tires, should not have been allowed to present opinion to the effect that the accident could not have occurred as alleged by defendant because of tire marks on the roadway).

Mich.—Belen v. Dawson, 1974, 217 N.W.2d 910, 52 Mich.App. 670 (officer did not provide a very substantial foundation in support of his testimony and, because of heavy snow at scene of accident, there were no tire marks, tracks or slide marks which might have enabled officer to reconstruct position of defendant's vehicle prior to accident); Blackwell's Estate v. Hare, 1974, 213 N.W.2d 201, 50 Mich.App. 204, reversed on other grounds, 216 N.W.2d 419 (where there was no objective evidence to show that automobile was involved except evidence of rubber mark found on curb, and point in time when mark became affixed to curb had not been ascertained, police officers, though experts in acci-

§ 431.3 EXPERT OPINION EVIDENCE Ch. 431

dent investigation, had no underlying facts to consider which would remove question as to what had struck decedent from area of knowledge to which members of jury had access, and trial court properly refused to admit police officers' opinions as to what object had collided with decedent); O'Dowd v. Linehan, 1971, 189 N.W. 2d 333, 385 Mich. 491 (testimony of expert that gouge marks were caused by buckled frame members of certain automobile was not expert testimony but assumption or conclusion of witness and was excludible on proper objection).

Mo.—Shields v. Keller, 1941, 153 S. W.2d 60, 348 Mo. 326 (physician cannot state opinion pedestrian was struck by front of auto).

N.C.—Farrow v. Baugham, 147 S.E. 2d 167, 266 N.C. 739 (exclusion of determination of police officer, who investigated but did not see accident, that automobile driven by plaintiff's intestate was either stopped or barely moving was proper); Shaw v. Sylvester, 116 N. E.2d 351, 253 N.C. 176 (even though a highway patrolman investigated more than 400 wrecks, and took certain accident reconstruction courses, such officer was not qualified, based on his observation of a wrecked automobile and location outside the automobile of the bodies of the two people who were riding therein, to give an opinion as to who was driving the automobile which, during the course of the accident, lost one door and had another door opened and folded forward against a front fender).

S.C.—Roumillat v. Keller, 1969, 167 S.E.2d 425, 252 S.C. 512 (experienced damage appraiser, as to what damage caused by each of two collisions).

Tex.—Anderson v. McDonald, Civ. App.1972, 486 S.W.2d 123 (where police officer who investigated accident did not witness accident and arrived at scene after automobiles had been removed, testimony of police officer that driver had to stop automobile suddenly because highway lane was blocked by accident was hearsay); Sanchez v. Billings, Civ.App.1972, 481 S.W.2d 911, error refused n. r. e. (where speed and turning path of plaintiffs' decedent's truck was already established by direct testimony, testimony of witness regarding a normal turning speed and as to traces left by abrupt high speed turns was immaterial and exclusion of such evidence was not abuse of discretion); Foundation Reserve Ins. Co. v. Starnes, Civ. App.1972, 479 S.W.2d 330 (in insured's action against insurer under collision policy, question of whether insured was in speed contest at time of collision was not proper subject); East Texas Motor Freight Lines, Inc. v. Neal, 1969, 443 S.W.2d 318, error refused n. r. e. (as to position of vehicles involved at time of impact).

Utah—Macshara v. Garfield, 1967, 434 P.2d 756, 20 Utah 2d 152 (court was correct in action arising out of intersectional collision in not permitting police officer to reconstruct accident and speed and direction of the vehicles on basis of such physical evidence as gouge marks on lawn and on curbing, damage to automobiles and the course he assumed vehicles took after impact).

Wyo.—Taylor v. MacDonald, 409 P. 2d 762 (admitting patrolman's testimony concerning reaction time for turning steering wheel to get back on road after leaving it, using certain charts relating to braking, was error, there being nothing in the record to show the charts provided any true basis for the evidence elicited).

As to existence of defect

Colo.—West v. Torbuc Corp., App. 1973, 517 P.2d 485 (admission of expert testimony on behalf of plaintiff, suing motorcycle dealer because of allegedly defective throttle mechanism on motorcycle he was taking for a test drive, that the cable was defective based on examination of cable at time of trial three years after the accident and the admission of the cable itself were both improper in absence of any evidence that the cable was in a condition similar to that at the time of accident).

Kan.—Lenhart v. Owens, 1973, 507 P.2d 318, 211 Kan. 534 (in action brought by driver of stationary automobile for injuries sustained when another automobile collided with her, allegedly because of power brake failure, testimony offered by manufacturer's witness relating to heating of brake fluid and possible braking failure resulting from driving habit of simultaneous pressure on brake pedal and accelerator was properly excluded absent evidence that driver had been guilty of such a driving practice).

Fla.—Smaglick v. Jersey Ins. Co. of New York, 1968, 209 So.2d 475 (in action arising when automobile struck utility pole on right side of highway which, at that point, curved to left, traffic accident analyst's opinion as to whether automobile had braking or steering defect was not expert testimony and, therefore, was properly excluded).

As to how incident occurred

Colo.—Brayman v. National State Bank of Boulder, 1973, 505 P.2d 11, 180 Colo. 304 (where deemed hearsay, when based on diagrams and photos).

As to proper operation

Ky.—Tri-City Van & Storage, Inc. v. Slone, 1969, 437 S.W.2d 211, appeal after remand 485 S.W.2d 889 (testimony, elicited over objection, as to proper operation of tractor-trailer truck while rounding curve and approaching bridge was incompetent where opinions were not based upon relevant facts proven at trial and related to ultimate issue of actions of truck driver on occasion in question when truck sideswiped oncoming vehicle and then collided with second vehicle).

As to visibility

Md.—Beckner v. Chalkley, 1973, 310 A.2d 569, 19 Md.App. 239 (in action arising from collision at intersection during nighttime hours, testimony of witness concerning when motorists first had ability to see each other was inadmissible where calculations of time, distances and speeds were based upon what would have happened had the accident occurred during daylight hours).

Or.—Owre v. Crown Zellerbach Corp., 1971, 490 P.2d 504, 260 Or. 454 (refusal to permit consulting engineer to testify as expert for plaintiff as to tendency of surrounding objects, terrain and sun to make it difficult to see traffic light at intersection was not error, where it appeared that decedent knew of light and proffered testimony related to usual hazards to good vision encountered by all).

How rock propelled

Or.—Rader v. Gibbons & Reed Co., 1972, 494 P.2d 412, 261 Or. 354 (no proper foundation was laid for opinion, on whether rock which entered automobile of deceased motorist through windshield had been between dual tires of passing truck, by witness, who while testifying that he knew from his experience on construction projects that rocks were occasionally picked up between dual tires, did not testify that he ever examined such rocks or that he had any special competence in determining from a rock's appearance whether it had, in fact, been between dual tires).

§ 431.4 Expert Opinion—Speed [74]

Library References:
C.J.S. Evidence §§ 546(87), 546(88).
West's Key No. Digests, Evidence ⚖=514(2).

Expert testimony usually may be used to aid in determining speed.[75]

Except where, by rule, a witness is allowed to state an opinion without first relating its basis, the witnesses giving estimates as to speed should show preliminarily their familiarity with automobiles, their makes, and their operation, as well as the extent of the observations made at the scene, if any.[76]

74. Similar section in prior edition **cited by the court** in Monday v. Millsaps, 264 S.W.2d 6, 17, 37 Tenn.App. 371; Huguley v. State, 96 So.2d 315, 318, 39 Ala.App. 104, certiorari denied 96 So.2d 319, 266 Ala. 697; Knight v. Borgan, 324 P. 2d 797, 803, 52 Wash.2d 219.

75. **Cal.**—Berkovitz v. American River Gravel Co., 215 P. 675, 191 Cal. 195 (stopping distance and whether certain damage likely caused by impact at certain speed not common knowledge).

Ga.—Isom v. Schettino, 1973, 199 S. E.2d 89, 129 Ga.App. 73 (stopping distance of vehicle); Central of Georgia Ry. Co. v. Luther, 1973, 196 S.E.2d 149, 128 Ga.App. 178; Cobb v. Coleman, 1956, 93 S.E.2d 801, 94 Ga.App. 86.

Ill.—Jamison v. Lambke, 1974, 316 N. E.2d 93, 21 Ill.App.3d 629 (minimum braking distance traveling 20 to 25 mph).

Mass.—Harrington v. Travers, 192 N.E. 495, 288 Mass. 156.

N.M.—Tobeck v. United Nuclear-Homestake Partners, 1973, 512 P. 2d 1267, 85 N.M. 431 (testimony concerning speed and computation of coefficient of friction between vehicles and pavement).

S.D.—Smith v. Gunderson, 1971, 190 N.W.2d 841, 86 S.D. 38 (did not abuse its discretion in allowing professor to testify, as to speed, where professor was licensed engineer with years of experience investigating accidents and, because of his special knowledge and experience, his opinion could be aid).

Tex.—Anderson v. McDonald, Civ. App.1972, 486 S.W.2d 123 (as to stopping distances and ability to stop within such distances, by police officer who had been an officer for four years, investigated many accidents, attended training schools which taught investigation of accidents and who had been over section of highway where accident occurred many times and in same weather conditions as existed at time of accident).

76. **Conn.**—Stephanofsky v. Hill, 71 A.2d 560, 136 Conn. 379 (insufficient hypothetical).

Ga.—Hall v. Slaton, 144 S.E. 827, 38 Ga.App. 619, reversed on other grounds Slaton v. Hall, 148 S.E. 741, 168 Ga. 710, 73 A.L.R. 891, conformed to Hall v. Slaton, 149 S. E. 306, 40 Ga.App. 288.

Iowa—Bernal v. Bernhardt, Iowa 1970, 180 N.W.2d 437 (must show whether officer knew and considered dryness, smoothness and cleanness of road surfaces, kind of tread, condition of wear and inflation of tires, weight of vehicle and percent of grade of highway, and if he did not know or consider such variables, he must relate details of his training, experience

§ **431.4** TRIAL EVIDENCE Ch. 431

It has been held that revelation on cross-examination that the expert had insufficient basis for the opinion stated did not render the opinion inadmissible, but only went to the weight of the evidence.[77]

Notwithstanding the general rule that an expert may not state an opinion as to whether certain conduct was proper,[78] it has been held that an expert may state an opinion as to what speed would have been "reasonable".[79]

In particular cases it has been held proper for an expert to state an opinion based upon evidence of skid marks,[80] upon evi-

and experimentation which justify him in disregarding such factors); Nelson v. Hedin, 1918, 169 N.W. 37, 184 Iowa 657.

Minn.—Carson v. Turrish, 1918, 168 N.W. 349, 140 Minn. 445, L.R.A. 1918F, 154.

77. **Colo.**—Cox v. Bonser, 1973, 507 P.2d 1128, —— Colo.App. ——.

78. For discussion of the general rule against testimony as to whether conduct was proper, see section 431.1 at fn. 12.

79. **Colo.**—Ferguson v. Hurford, 290 P.2d 229, 132 Colo. 507 (in action arising out of collision of automobile which went out of control and off highway while rounding mountain curve at apparent high speed, testimony of state patrolman, who had seven and one-half years of service in mountainous regions and four years in locality of accident, as to reasonableness of speed around that curve was competent and relevant).

Wash.—Talley v. Fournier, 1970, 479 P.2d 96, 3 Wash.App. 808 (jury could not have been misled by an opinion concerning a safe rate of speed where a proper foundation was laid for such evidence by an experienced state trooper who was not only familiar with curve in road, having traveled on it on many occasions, but who investigated accident minutes after it occurred).

Wyo.—Krahn v. Pierce, 1971, 485 P.2d 1021 (permitting three highway patrolmen to testify on cross-examination that a speed of 35 to 40 miles per hour when they encountered icy condition of highway some 2 to 4 miles from scene was a "safe speed" was not error, where, in view of unusual and extraordinary circumstances presented by icy condition of highway and fog, it could not be said that opinion was not of aid to jury).

Harmless error

Va.—Peters v. Shortt, 1973, 200 S.E.2d 547, 214 Va. 399 (admission, in action to recover for wrongful death of passenger killed when defendant's automobile overturned on narrow gravel road, of trooper's opinion as to maximum safe speed at crash scene under conditions existing at that time was error, but such error was harmless, in view of evidence leading to conclusion that defendant exceeded safe speed under such conditions).

80. Similar rule contained in statement in prior edition **cited by the court** in State v. Lingman, 91 P.2d 457, 97 Utah 180.

U.S.—Solomon Dehydrating Co. v. Guyton, C.A.Neb., 294 F.2d 439, certiorari denied 82 S.Ct. 366, 368 U.S. 929, 7 L.Ed.2d 192 (under Nebraska law).

Ala.—Maslankowski v. Beam, 1972, 259 So.2d 804, 288 Ala. 254 (skid marks before impact, point of impact and the damage to the vehicles are three factors upon which an expert can validly predicate his opinion).

Cal.—Ungefug v. D'Ambrosia, 1967, 58 Cal.Rptr. 223, 250 Cal.App.2d 61.

Colo.—Ferguson v. Hurford, 1955, 290 P.2d 229, 132 Colo. 507.

Ill.—Fannon v. Morton, 1923, 228 Ill. App. 415.

Ky.—Ryan v. Payne, 1969, 446 S.W. 2d 273 (cannot be solely based upon use of skid-speed tables, especially where witness has no personal knowledge of mathematical and physical factors involved in compiling tables, but once witness is qualified as expert he may employ tables along with all other pertinent material in giving opinion).

Mich.—Brummitt v. Chaney, 1969, 170 N.W.2d 481, 18 Mich.App. 59 (though officer did not know coefficient of friction on street, efficiency of defendant's brake lining and tires, weight of automobile or whether skid marks were made by front or rear tires).

Mo.—Edwards v. Rudowicz, App., 368 S.W.2d 503 (lack of knowledge by police officer, who gave opinion as to stopping distance of an automobile traveling 30 miles an hour, as to braking distance of automobile traveling 25 miles per hour may have affected weight of his testimony but not his competency in view of other facts developed by the testimony; and admission of testimony of police officer as to speed based on skid marks was not an abuse of discretion when officer was present at scene shortly after the accident and personally observed the street and surroundings as well as defendant's vehicle).

Neb.—Brugh v. Peterson, 1968, 159 N.W.2d 321, 183 Neb. 190, 29 A.L. R.3d 236; Flory v. Holtz, 126 N. W.2d 686, 176 Neb. 531.

N.J.—DiNizio v. Burzynski, 195 A. 2d 470, 81 N.J.Super. 267.

N.Y.—Saladow v. Keystone Transp. Co., 271 N.Y.S. 293, 241 App.Div. 161.

N.M.—Alford v. Drum, 361 P.2d 451, 68 N.M. 298.

Okl.—Graham v. Banks, App.1969, 463 P.2d 1014.

S.D.—Heidner v. Germschied, 171 N. W. 208, 41 S.D. 430 (with other evidence).

Tenn.—Thomas v. Harper, 385 S.W. 2d 130, 53 Tenn.App. 549; Monday v. Millsaps, 264 S.W.2d 6, 37 Tenn. App. 371.

Tex.—Beynon v. Cutberth, 390 S.W. 2d 352.

Utah.—Batt v. State, 1972, 503 P.2d 855, 28 Utah 2d 417 (based on tire marks and other data).

Wash.—Talley v. Fournier, 1970, 479 P.2d 96, 3 Wash.App. 808; Still v. Swanson, 27 P.2d 704, 175 Wash. 553.

Wis.—Kloss v. American Indem. Co., 34 N.W.2d 816, 253 Wis. 476; Luethe v. Schmidt-Gaertner Co., 176 N.W. 63, 170 Wis. 590.

Approximation of skid mark

Complaint as to permitting expert to base opinion on approximate skid mark measurements did not go to the admissibility of such testimony but rather to weight to be given such testimony by the jury. Wegley v. Funk, 1968, 443 P.2d 323, 201 Kan. 719.

Indefinite terms

Testimony of police officer, who was an expert on forming an opinion as to speed from skid marks, that it was his opinion after examining skid marks that there was "no speed indication" according to skid marks was admissible over objection of plaintiff that opinion failed to prove that defendant was not exceeding speed limit, and it was for jury to interpret what witness meant by

§ 431.4 TRIAL EVIDENCE Ch. 431

dence of other physical facts at the scene,[81] and where the expert conducted experimentation,[82] as well as in a variety of other cases.[83]

phrase "no speed indication." Reeves v. Morgan, 1970, 174 S.E.2d 460, 121 Ga.App. 481, reversed on other grounds 177 S.E.2d 68, 226 Ga. 697, on remand 179 S.E.2d 648, 123 Ga. App. 64.

Limited to skids before impact

Ala.—Maslankowski v. Beam, 1972, 259 So.2d 804, 288 Ala. 254; Holuska v. Moore, 1972, 239 So.2d 192, 286 Ala. 268; Rosen v. Lawson, 1967, 202 So.2d 716, 281 Ala. 351.

81. Colo.—Cullen v. Orback, 1970, 473 P.2d 177, — Colo.App. — (highway patrolman opinion based upon physical facts observed at scene, that plaintiff was traveling in vicinity of 70 miles per hour immediately prior to accident); Starkey v. Bryan, 441 P.2d 314, 166 Colo. 43 (no error in admitting testimony of police officers who had investigated scene as to their opinion that northbound automobile, traveling on through street at time of collision in intersection with westbound automobile, had not been traveling in excess of speed limit).

Ga.—Massey v. Stephens, 147 S.E. 2d 53, 113 Ga.App. 10 (damage to vehicles and debris).

Kan.—Hubbard v. Havlik's Estate, 1974, 518 P.2d 352, 213 Kan. 594 (police officers who had been at scene and described damage and had investigated number of accidents involving vehicles traveling at known speeds were properly permitted to testify to opinions of speed of vehicle which struck tree, although each indicated that his opinion was partly guess and speculation).

N.H.—Barton v. Plaisted, 1969, 256 A.2d 642, 109 N.H. 428, 38 A.L.R. 3d 799 (based in part on condition of automobile).

Tex.—Bates v. Barclay, Civ.App. 1972, 484 S.W.2d 955.

82. Tenn.—Thomas v. Harper, 385 S.W.2d 130, 53 Tenn.App. 549, citing 32 C.J.S. Evidence § 533 (although road surface had not been shown to be same at time of tests as at time of accident and temperatures at those times had been different).

Tex.—Brown v. Herring, Civ.App. 1971, 466 S.W.2d 664, error refused n. r. e. (tests near and at scene, and observation of photos of vehicles).

83. U.S.—Bonner v. Polacari, C.A. Okl., 350 F.2d 493.

Cal.—Davis v. Ward, 32 Cal.Rptr. 796, 219 Cal.App.2d 144 (based upon statement of witnesses as well as upon personal observation where statements considered were of insignificant weight and were not essential to opinion).

Ga.—American Home Assur. Co. v. Stephens, 1970, 174 S.E.2d 186, 121 Ga.App. 306 (notwithstanding facts that safety expert never went to scene, never saw vehicles involved, and based opinion as to speed and as to grade of highway on an examination of photographs); Shelton v. Rose, 1967, 156 S.E.2d 659, 116 Ga.App. 37 (not error to allow a state patrolman who had participated in test relating to speed and stopping distances to testify on basis of result of such tests).

Ind.—Shelby Nat. Bank v. Miller, 1970, 259 N.E.2d 450, 147 Ind.App. 203.

Kan.—Hildebrand v. Mueller, 1969, 449 P.2d 587, 202 Kan. 506; Howard v. Stoughton, 1967, 433 P.2d 567, 199 Kan. 787 (police officer's testimony which identified portion

Ch. 431 EXPERT OPINION EVIDENCE § 431.4

of motion picture showing only vehicles involved in collision, exhibits describing location of vehicles and distances they traveled after impact, and diagram and chart made from measurements at the scene, and which concerned skidmarks, braking speeds, reaction time, and opinion about speeds of the vehicles prior to collision was admissible to show nature and extent of damage to the vehicles and to establish foundation for consulting engineer's testimony describing the forces which he believed had been applied to plaintiff's body, in case wherein defendants admitted liability but vigorously contended that plaintiff's injury was not serious); Taylor v. Maxwell, 419 P.2d 822 (in absence of a showing of any material exaggeration or perversion of facts assumed by witness, testimony of highway patrol officer based on facts assumed in hypothetical question plus information contained in diagram drawn by officer, who had investigated the accident, as well as pictures of the intersection and the automobiles, was admissible within the discretion of trial court).

Ky.—Ryan v. Payne, 1969, 446 S.W. 2d 273 (testimony as to speed from length of skid marks, force of impact, type of vehicle, condition of road and all surrounding factors is competent); Moore v. Wheeler, 1968, 425 S.W.2d 541 (officer who had investigated more than 450 accidents and who had received special schooling on various techniques and procedures involved in investigating accidents was qualified to give opinion as to speed of automobile which left road when attempting to pass truck, based upon skid marks on highway and berm and position and damage to the automobile).

Md.—Uhlik v. Kopec, 1974, 314 A.2d 732, 20 Md.App. 216 (where witness called to testify as to speed of defendant's car which struck pedestrian testified that, in the hundreds of scientifc experiments he had performed on dry blacktop macadam road surfaces such as that on which accident occurred, the coefficient of friction had been less than 70%, he arbitrarily lowered minimum coefficient for road on which accident occurred to 60% and he explained fully how he arrived at his determination that a dry, hard surface, clear of any defects, would not have lower coefficient than 60%, his failure personally to inspect road surface would have gone, at most, to weight of his testimony and exclusion of his offered testimony was improper).

Mich.—Anderson v. Lippes, 1969, 170 N.W.2d 908, 18 Mich.App. 281 (although based solely upon conditions existing after the accident); Snyder v. New York Cent. Transport Co., 1966, 143 N.W.2d 791, 4 Mich.App. 38.

Minn.—Storbakken v. Soderberg, 1956, 75 N.W.2d 496, 246 Minn. 434 (based upon application of conservation of momentum theory).

Mont.—Graham v. Rolandson, 1967, 435 P.2d 263, 150 Mont. 270 (that ex-highway patrolman who testified as to speed of automobile which struck boy on bicycle had retired from patrol some six years previously, that he did not measure any drag factor or coefficient of friction on particular road surface involved, and that as highway patrolman he would not have been permitted to testify in case where investigation was made year and a half after accident, were matters affecting weight rather than admissibility).

N.M.—Tobeck v. United Nuclear-Homestake Partners, 1973, 512 P. 2d 1267, 85 N.M. 431 (had knowledge of handling characteristics of similar tractor-trailers, and observed photographs of accident and vehicles involved); Dahl v. Turner,

§ 431.4   TRIAL EVIDENCE   Ch. 431

In other particular cases an expert's opinion as to speed has been held inadmissible where based upon evidence of skid marks,[84]

1969, 458 P.2d 816, 80 N.M. 564, 39 A.L.R.3d 207, certiorari denied 458 P.2d 860, 80 N.M. 608; Lewis v. Knott, 405 P.2d 662, 75 N.M. 422 (where speed of automobile, which went out of control as tire blew on slight curve, was critical to question of negligence, if any, of nonowner driver and the evidence was in conflict, refusal to admit testimony as to speed of automobile when it went into the curve radius based on expert's view of scene and evidence in case was error).

S.D.—Wentzel v. Huebner, 104 N.W.2d 695, 78 S.D. 481 (computation made by witness as to a minimum speed indicated by the free flight of the automobile was admissible inasmuch as it was helpful, if accepted by jury as accurate, in arriving at conclusion as to excessiveness of speed in assessing degree of risk to which host intentionally exposed his guests).

Tex.—Adams v. Smith, Civ.App.1972, 479 S.W.2d 390 (city traffic engineer who was experienced in investigating and reconstructing accidents and who had degree in civil engineering and had considered road conditions, various photographs, terrain, law of conservation of momentum, weather conditions, direction of travel and other pertinent factors was qualified); Buchanan v. Central Freight Lines, Inc., Civ.App.1970, 462 S.W.2d 391, error refused n. r. e. (not objectionable on basis that witness was permitted to make calculation of speed without knowing, but merely assuming, what the coefficient of friction witness utilized was).

Wash.—Martin v. Huston, 1974, 522 P.2d 192, 11 Wash.App. 294 (permitting accident reconstruction expert, who had investigated at least 750 accidents, who was familiar with controlled crash studies and had observed training films on controlled experiments regarding crashes, who had inspected main frame of plaintiff's car after engine had been removed, the radiator taken out, and the wheels likewise removed, and who had also examined two photographs of damage sustained by plaintiff's car, but who had not examined defendants' car, to testify as to speed differential between plaintiff's and defendants' cars).

84. Ala.—Giles v. Gardner, 1971, 249 So.2d 824, 287 Ala. 166 (where skid marks were not measured and state trooper who stated on direct examination that skid marks' length was from 50 to 75 feet stated on cross-examination that they could have been as much as 100 feet long, permitting witness to give opinion was error as based on indefinite figures and speculation and conjecture).

Ind.—Pickett v. Kolb, App.1967, 231 N.E.2d 856, superseded on other grounds 237 N.E.2d 105, 250 Ind. 449 (court's determination that police officer was not qualified to testify on direct examination as to what speed was indicated by vehicle leaving skid marks of 120 feet was not abuse).

Ky.—B-Line Cab Co. v. Hampton, 1952, 247 S.W.2d 34.

Md.—Spence v. Wiles, 1969, 257 A.2d 164, 255 Md. 98 (where police officer had been member of accident investigation division for only two or three years, he possessed no special training, and police lieutenant testified that it was necessary to know coefficient of friction at scene to calculate speed solely from skidmarks, refusal to allow officer to testify as to speed as derived from skidmarks was not an abuse of discretion).

upon evidence of other physical facts at the scene,[85] and where

Minn.—Sanchez v. Waldrup, 1965, 136 N.W.2d 61, 271 Minn. 419 (opinion based upon coefficient of friction, but street was icy).

Mont.—O'Brien v. Great Northern Ry. Co., 400 P.2d 634, 145 Mont. 13 (where highway patrolman admitted that there was no way to determine speed from skid marks and that he was not familiar with stopping distances in terms of speed, question asking him whether there was any evidence of motorist's violation of speed limit was without proper foundation and called for a conclusion, and his answer that "in my own mind I don't think the man was exceeding the speed limit" was pure speculation and conjecture, and admission thereof was reversible error).

N.H.—Cormier v. Conduff, 1968, 241 A.2d 795, 109 N.H. 19 (estimation of speed from skid marks, which involved numerous factors including weight of vehicles, nature of road surface and slope, and coefficient of friction, was properly excluded, where trial court was not satisfied that all factors necessary to formulate a meaningful opinion had been taken into consideration).

N.J.—Nesta v. Meyer, 1968, 242 A.2d 386, 100 N.J.Super. 434 (exclusion not error, as to officer without special training).

Tex.—Terbay v. Pat Canion Excavating Co., 396 S.W.2d 482, ref. n. r. e. (where, although officer had considerable training in manner of investigating collisions, he had no knowledge qualifying him to estimate speed from amount of damage sustained by them or any knowledge or experience qualifying him to express opinion as to speed of truck based on skid marks left on steep, wet, muddy and slick pavement); Standard Motor Co. v. Blood, 380 S.W.2d 651 (rejection of proffered testimony estimating speed before it was involved in accident was not error in absence of showing, with possible exception of one witness, of any technical or scientific basis for stating opinion from skids).

W.Va.—Orndoff v. Rowan, 1972, 192 S.E.2d 220, —— W.Va. —— (factors which must be considered in determining speed from skid marks are: the material of the road surface, the material of the tires, tire tread, temperature, air pressure in the tires, and the weight of the car, and exclusion not an abuse of discretion).

Harmless error to admit

Ala.—Giles v. Gardner, 1971, 249 So. 2d 824, 287 Ala. 166 (admission of state trooper's opinion, based on skid marks made after impact, as to speed of plaintiff's pickup truck prior to intersectional collision was error but was harmless error in light of testimony by plaintiff that his speed was about 35 miles per hour prior to impact and trooper's opinion that plaintiff was traveling at about 30 miles per hour).

Miss.—Marsh v. Johnson, 1968, 209 So.2d 906.

85. Ala.—Jowers v. Dauphin, 143 So.2d 167, 273 Ala. 567 (based on his observation at the scene of the wrecked vehicles, and skid marks on the highway after point of impact).

Colo.—Baldwin v. Schipper, 393 P. 2d 363, 155 Colo. 197 (refusal to permit investigating officer who had not seen collision to express opinion as to speed on basis of damage to vehicles, their location after impact, and skid marks of vehicle was not error).

Idaho.—Jorstad v. City of Lewiston, 1969, 456 P.2d 766, 93 Idaho 122

§ 431.4   TRIAL EVIDENCE   Ch. 431

(officers may not give opinion as to speed based on observation of scene, physical damage done to vehicle, distance traversed, and tire marks left on pavement after collision).

Ind.—McCraney v. Kuechenberg, 1969, 248 N.E.2d 171, 144 Ind.App. 629 (even when coupled with prior testimony concerning weather and road conditions, question posed by plaintiff to deputy sheriff, as to whether, based on skid marks and other evidence at the scene, defendant was exceeding speed limit when her automobile struck plaintiff's ward lacked requisite physical elements or foundation to allow an opinion concerning speed, expert or otherwise).

Iowa.—Tiemeyer v. McIntosh, Iowa 1970, 176 N.W.2d 819, 49 A.L.R. 3d 285 (where undertook to estimate speed entirely from photographs of automobiles and scene).

Kan.—Staudinger v. Sooner Pipe & Supply Corp., 1971, 490 P.2d 619, 208 Kan. 100 (where officer based his calculations on conditions of road surface when he viewed it some three and a half years after accident, trial court did not abuse its discretion in requiring testimony from further witnesses that no resurfacing had occurred during period and that the only change in condition was from "traffic polishing" before allowing officer to testify concerning maximum range of speed); Howard v. Miller, 1971, 485 P.2d 199, 207 Kan. 246 (where accident reconstruction expert examined automobile only from photographs, he used repair estimates furnished by others, and the length of skidmarks was not wholly ascertainable).

La.—Skinner v. Poston, 71 So.2d 702 (wherein evidence revealed that there were no skid marks left on highway by gasoline truck and that there were few physical signs).

Mich.—Blackwell's Estate v. Hare, 1973, 213 N.W.2d 201, 50 Mich. App. 204, decision reversed on other grounds, 216 N.W.2d 419 (in Motor Vehicle Accident Claims Act case involving mortal injury allegedly resulting from negligence of hit-and-run driver whose identity was unknown, evidence as to position of coins after impact did not require expert analysis, and it was not error to exclude opinion, as to speed of object which collided with decedent based upon scattering of coins).

Minn.—Thole v. Noorlun, 1970, 177 N.W.2d 295, 287 Minn. 52 (court's finding that evidence at scene and testimony as to prevailing conditions was insufficient to serve as a basis for an opinion was within its discretion).

Neb.—Brugh v. Peterson, 1968, 159 N.W.2d 321, 183 Neb. 190, 29 A.L. R.3d 231 (as the opinion on speed of plaintiff's expert depended on resolution of many variables and certain assumptions, it was, in effect, a mere statement of possibility, and court thus erred in permitting the witness to state his opinion as to speed of defendant southbound motorist's automobile, including the impact, and court should have confined the witness' testimony to speed computed on basis of skidmarks only).

Nev.—Choat v. McDorman, 1970, 468 P.2d 354, 86 Nev. 332 (based solely upon damage to vehicles).

N.D.—Stein v. Ohlhauser, 1973, 211 N.W.2d 737 (testimony, based on skid marks and on damage to the vehicles, lacked sufficient foundation where there was no showing of scientific way to determine speed from crash damage other than gross estimation, based to some extent on experience and judgment).

Okl.—Wall v. Partridge, Okl.1970, 466 P.2d 628 (admission of testimony of highway trooper, who reached scene about 30 minutes after it happened, regarding speed

the expert conducted experimentation,[86] as well as in a variety of other cases.[87]

of defendant's dump truck was error, where truck left no skid marks and the trooper admitted in effect that his estimate would be little more than a mere guess); Fidelity & Cas. Co. of New York v. Hendrix, 1968, 440 P.2d 735 (where there were no skidmarks from which speed could be estimated by any mathematical calculation, patrolman did not conduct investigation until almost two hours after accident, and there had been other traffic which had partially obliterated tire tracks of vehicle involved in accident, opinion of patrolman was inadmissible as conjectural and as based on facts from which jury could have been expected to draw for themselves as accurate a conclusion as that of the patrolman).

Tex.—Reaves v. Brooks, 1968, 430 S.W.2d 926, error dismissed (officer's opinion testimony has no probative value on speed, when based alone on damage resulting from collision, in absence of skid marks and showing of his qualifications as expert to determine speed).

86. N.M.—Galvan v. City of Albuquerque, 1973, 508 P.2d 1339, 85 N.M. 42 (even if witness was competent to testify as to the speed at which the police car was traveling when it collided with bicycle, where witness' affidavit stating that he had performed tests for purpose of ascertaining speed did not identify the tests performed or explain how the tests were performed, there was no satisfactory explanation of witness' conclusion as to speed; thus, affidavit did not set forth facts admissible in evidence and was not entitled to consideration by court in determining whether to grant summary judgment in favor of police officer who was driving police car).

87. Ariz.—Carrizoza v. Zahn, 1973, 21 Ariz.App. 94, 515 P.2d 1192 (was not admissible where opinion was not based on a foundation of properly admitted evidence but was based on assumptions that plaintiff's car went into broadside skid immediately after impact and slid at least two-thirds of distance to its final point of rest, that wheels were turned at impact in the opposite direction of the alleged slide and that car travelled on certain course while in the skid).

Dist.Col.—Bell v. Myrtle, Mun.App., 153 A.2d 313 (where it was shown that automobile traveled 48 feet beyond point of impact laying skid marks for last 20 feet, opinion of police officer as to speed at point of impact, based on his experience in over 400 pedestrian cases and on fact that he had test skidded automobile and discovered that at speed of 15 miles per hour automobile would skid 20 feet, but unsupported by any other substantial facts, such as personal observation, was properly excluded on ground that it would have been speculative).

Fla.—Delta Rent-A-Car, Inc. v. Rihl, 1969, 218 So.2d 469 (even if police officer was qualified in field of accident reconstruction it was error to admit his testimony that speed was 50 miles per hour, where there was complete absence of accurate measurements and of numerous other factors and physical facts which would necessarily have to be known and be taken into consideration in order to arrive at scientific determination of speed, however, error was harmless where officer's testimony was merely cumulative of other competent evidence that speed was 50 miles per hour); Smith v. Frisch's Big Boy, Inc., 1968, 208 So.2d 310 (where inadmissible testimony of

§ 431.4 TRIAL EVIDENCE Ch. 431

police officer as to speed of test vehicle formed part of the foundation for opinion).

Ill.—Deaver v. Hickox, 1967, 224 N. E.2d 468, 81 Ill.App.2d 79.

Kan.—Riley v. Holcomb, 359 P.2d 849, 187 Kan. 711 (highway patrolman should not have been permitted to give opinion in death action that defendant was driving 70 miles an hour, where patrolman testified that he did not base opinion on evidence found at scene and did not remember how he formed opinion).

La.—Welch v. Hayes, App.1971, 246 So.2d 864 (did not abuse discretion in refusing to admit investigating officer's opinion testimony where officer had not measured length of skidmarks left by vehicle from time brakes were applied until time of impact).

Nev.—Levine v. Remolif, 390 P.2d 718, 80 Nev. 168 (testimony as to speed was inadmissible where based on photographs which did not disclose damage to frames thereof and on diagram which was drawn by police officer inexperienced and untrained in reconstructing accidents and on some information furnished by another officer).

N.Y.—Lewis v. Wright, 1969, 303 N. Y.S.2d 718, 32 A.D.2d 950 (at moment of impact with guard rail); Lopez v. Yannotti, 263 N.Y.S.2d 523, 24 A.D.2d 758; Lombard v. Dobson, 230 N.Y.S.2d 47, 16 A. D.2d 1031 (based on analysis of photographs of positions of automobiles after accident, damage to automobiles, and other scientific formulae, but admission of such testimony did not require reversal).

Tex.—City of Austin v. Hoffman, 379 S.W.2d 103 (police officer's opinion as to speed of motor scooter, based on skidmarks left by scooter and physical damage to the scooter and the other vehicle, was inadmissible, where officer had not had any special training to determine how fast a vehicle must have been going to bend metal so many inches or make a dent of a certain size and did not know how much force it takes to bend metal and had made no such tests and had made no skidmarks, and such tests would have to be made to make an accurate estimate).

Va.—White v. Hunt, 1968, 161 S.E.2d 809, 209 Va. 11; Grasty v. Tanner, 1966, 146 S.E.2d 252, 206 Va. 723.

Wash.—Crowe v. Prinzing, 1970, 468 P.2d 450, 77 Wash.2d 895 (refusal to admit testimony of expert was not abuse of discretion where expert, on voir dire, stated, after counsel related that there was no evidence as to exactly what purported skid marks found at scene were, that expert could not help counsel); Moyer v. Clark, 1969, 454 P.2d 374, 75 Wash.2d 800 (where witness admitted that he had no knowledge of weight of automobiles involved in intersection collision, witness' offered testimony as to his estimate of speed, which was derived from vehicle's deviation from straight line after collision); Wilkinson v. Martin, 349 P.2d 608, 56 Wash.2d 921, corrected opinion 353 P.2d 440 (where pictures showing damage to and position of automobiles were in evidence and there was testimony of independent eyewitnesses as to speed, refusal to allow state patrolman investigating accident to state his opinion, based on lack of skid marks, damages to automobiles, and their positions after impact, as to relative speeds of automobiles just prior to impact was not error); Montgomery v. Hyatt, 282 P.2d 277, 46 Wash.2d 468 (opinion testimony of state patrol officer who arrived at scene some 20 or 30 minutes after collision and who identified photographs taken after collision).

§ 431.5 Expert Opinion—Bodily Injury

Library References:
C.J.S. Evidence §§ 447, 457, 546(61) et seq., 546(68) et seq., 546 (91) et seq., 552 et seq.
West's Key No. Digests, Evidence ⟬509, 543½, 544, 548, 555.

Opinions on most matters related to bodily injury are naturally beyond the ken of the factfinder, and thus are properly stated by qualified medical experts.[88]

A person permitted to testify as a medical expert may state, on direct examination, the grounds and reasons for an opinion before being called upon to give the opinion to the jury,[89] although this is not always necessary.[90]

---

88. **Ala.**—New York Life Ins. Co. v. Torrance, 1933, 153 So. 458, 26 Ala.App. 38, certiorari denied 153 So. 463, 228 Ala. 286.

Basis questioned

Fla.—Rimmer v. Tesla, 1967, 201 So. 2d 573 (thoroughness or comprehensiveness of examination by doctor who attempted but failed to find carotid pulse in neck of one victim of accident but observed another victim breathing for approximately 15 minutes thereafter went only to weight of his testimony that their deaths were other than simultaneous and not to its competency or credibility).

Forces from impact

Amount of force exerted on a person at time of impact is relevant to severity of possible injuries sustained and since not within ordinary experience of jurors is proper subject for expert testimony. Holecek v. Janke, N.D.1969, 171 N.W.2d 94.

Opinion large amount of violence applied

Admission of medical witness' testimony that he thought there had been a large amount of violence applied held not prejudicial error, where witness had examined plaintiff for several years, and testified in detail concerning tilting of pelvis and curvature of spine, and witness based his opinion upon bruises and discolorations from smaller blood vessels allowing blood to pour into tissues around muscles and near nerves, and that there was hardening of tissues under skin caused by absorption of blood clots which left disturbance and made nerves more sensitive. Kelso v. W. A. Ross Const. Co., 85 S.W.2d 527, 337 Mo. 202.

Reasonable value of medical services

U.S.—McCrea v. Nonweiler, D.C.Pa., 58 F.Supp. 79, affirmed 146 F.2d 109.

Ga.—Callaway v. Miller, 1968, 163 S. E.2d 336, 118 Ga.App. 309.

Md.—Walston v. Dobbins, 1970, 271 A.2d 367, 10 Md.App. 490 (as to charges of X-ray specialists).

89. **Mass.**—Cronin v. Fitchburg & L. St. Ry. Co., 63 N.E. 335, 181 Mass. 202.

N.J.—Lamberton v. Consolidated Traction Co., 38 A. 683, 60 N.J.L. 452.

90. For discussion of eligibility, under the federal rule and certain state rules of evidence, to state an opinion without first stating the underlying facts, see section 431.1 at fn. 20 et seq.

Ga.—Paulk v. Thomas, 1967, 154 S. E.2d 872, 115 Ga.App. 436.

Md.—Mangione v. Snead, 195 A. 329, 173 Md. 33 (that witness thought boy had probably had brain con-

§ 431.5   TRIAL EVIDENCE   Ch. 431

It has been stated that medical expert opinion should be based upon an objective examination, and not on history of the patient.[91] However, it also has been held that such opinion may

cussion "at accident," without first stating predicate for such opinion).

Ohio.—Scarinzi v. Farkas, 75 N.E. 2d 86, 80 Ohio App. 409 (causal relation between injury and infection).

[91]. For discussion of eligibility, under the federal rules and the rules of certain states, to state an opinion based upon facts or data not admissible in evidence, see section 431.1 at fn. 14 et seq.

Ga.—Overnite Transp. Co. v. Hart, 1972, 191 S.E.2d 308, 126 Ga.App. 566 (where physician was asked for an opinion based on hypothetical question but physician gave opinion based primarily on what plaintiff had told him, court's refusal was not error).

Ill.—Korleski v. Needham, 222 N.E. 2d 334, 77 Ill.App.2d 328; Montgomery v. Checker Taxi Co., 57 N.E.2d 231, 324 Ill.App. 83 (held not based on history obtained from patient).

Mich.—Layton v. Cregan & Mallory Co., 257 N.W. 888, 269 Mich. 574.

Minn.—Faltico v. Minneapolis St. Ry. Co., 268 N.W. 857, 198 Minn. 88; Paulos v. Koelsch, 263 N.W. 913, 195 Minn. 603 (permitting doctor to give diagnosis held not error, there being nothing in record indicating whether doctor based diagnosis on history).

Mo.—Rickard v. Pratt, Mo.App.1970, 459 S.W.2d 13 (held not prejudicial error, where opinion not based upon hearsay); Davies v. Carter Carburetor, Division ACF Industries, Inc., 429 S.W.2d 738 (may testify to what he personally observed and also to what patient said concerning his present existing symptoms and complaints; however, he may not base his opinion upon or

testify to statements of patient with respect to past physical condition, circumstances surrounding injury, or manner in which injury was received).

Pa.—Roberts v. Pitt Pub. Co., 1938, 198 A. 668, 330 Pa. 44.

Tex.—Goodrich v. Tinker, 1969, 437 S.W.2d 882, error refused n. r. e.

History obtained from parent

Minn.—Gordon v. Engineering Const. Co., 135 N.W.2d 202, 271 Minn. 186 (may base opinion on history furnished by attending physician or nurse, more particularly when nurse is patient's parent, if the patient is incompetent to provide information by reason of infancy or other disability, especially where corroborated).

Miss.—Wild v. Bass, 173 So.2d 647, 252 Miss. 615 (allowing doctor to use information he had received from minor plaintiff's mother as part of basis for his opinion and to detail to jury what mother had told him in his office about a year before the trial, including statement that child had been run over by an automobile, an issue for jury to try in case, was improper).

Non-treating doctor

Ga.—Wolfson v. Rumble, 1970, 174 S.E.2d 469, 121 Ga.App. 549 (evidence of mere subjective complaints of pain by patient to examining physician are inadmissible as hearsay to prove fact of pain by testimony of physician, but such testimony may be admissible for other reasons, for example, to explain diagnosis or opinion).

Ill.—Williams v. Brown Mfg. Co., 1968, 236 N.E.2d 125, 93 Ill.App. 2d 334, judgment reversed on other grounds 261 N.E.2d 305, 45 Ill. 2d 418, 46 A.L.R.3d 226 (permitting

Ch. 431   **EXPERT OPINION EVIDENCE**   § **431.5**

be based in part on history obtained from the patient,[92] or in

physician to state prognosis was not error, as against contention that history was within physician's knowledge, where although admittedly the physician had taken and knew history, upon being asked in cross-examination whether in his testimony he had taken the history into consideration, physician stated, inter alia, that he had consciously attempted in his testimony to eliminate history); Korleski v. Needham, 222 N.E.2d 334, 77 Ill.App.2d 328.

Mich.—Layton v. Cregan & Mallory Co., 257 N.W. 888, 269 Mich. 574 (inadmissible as based on hearsay).

Minn.—Faltico v. Minneapolis St. Ry. Co., 268 N.W. 857, 198 Minn. 88 (inadmissible).

Tenn.—Johnson Freight Lines, Inc. v. Tallent, 384 S.W.2d 46, 53 Tenn.App. 464 (not be permitted to testify as to conclusions reached from such examination).

Tex.—Liberty Mut. Ins. Co. v. Taylor, Civ.App., 376 S.W.2d 406 (may not testify).

Wash.—Lyster v. Metzger, 412 P.2d 340, 68 Wash.2d 216 (is limited to objective findings and answering of hypothetical questions).

Referred to for purpose other than basis of opinion

Excluding testimony of competent ophthalmologist as to cause of impairment of vision because of the physician's reference to hospital records of some ten years previous to the accident in which plaintiff was surgically cured of a cross-eyed condition was error where ophthalmologist did not rely upon the history in forming his conclusion and his mention of the records was only to negate the relevance of the prior operation to the present condition. Angel v. Rand Exp. Lines, Inc., 168 A.2d 423, 66 N.J.Super. 77.

92. Ariz.—Spector v. Spector, 1972, 496 P.2d 864, 17 Ariz.App. 221 (physician may base his opinion entirely on personal examination and observation of a patient, or in part on history as related to him by the patient).

Conn.—Brown v. Blauvelt, 1964, 205 A.2d 773, 152 Conn. 272.

Fla.—Wilkinson v. Grover, 1965, 181 So.2d 591 (examining physician).

Ga.—Williams Bros. Grocery Co. v. Blanton, 1962, 124 S.E.2d 479, 105 Ga.App. 314.

Ind.—Briney v. Williams, 1968, 242 N.E.2d 132, 143 Ind.App. 691 (opinion of a physician or surgeon based wholly or partly on statements and subjective symptoms related to physician by patient is admissible, where examination was made for purpose of qualifying physician or surgeon to testify as a medical expert).

N.C.—Lockwood v. McCaskill, 138 S.E.2d 541, 262 N.C. 663.

Ohio.—Cusumano v. Pepsi-Cola Bottling Co., 223 N.E.2d 477, 9 Ohio App.2d 105.

Pa.—De Marco v. Frommyer Brick Co., 201 A.2d 234, 203 Pa.Super. 486.

Tex.—Travelers Ins. Co. v. Hutchison, 1968, 425 S.W.2d 832 (opinion of expert based upon personal knowledge from examination of patient and upon hearsay evidence is admissible).

Not in as substantive evidence

Even if physician was consulted for sole purpose of qualifying physician as a witness, his testimony as to patient's medical history as revealed to him by patient was admissible, not as substantive evidence of truth of patient's statements to him, but as information relied upon by him in arriving at his diagnosis and prognosis. Gentry v. Watkins-Caro-

part upon reports of other medical personnel.[93]

lina Trucking Co., 1967, 154 S.E.2d 112, 249 S.C. 316, 37 A.L.R.3d 766.

Obtained from parent

Ky.—Miller v. Watts, 1969, 436 S.W. 2d 515 (father's eyewitness testimony that his son was injured when defendant turned in front of father's automobile without warning, father stopped suddenly and son was thrown from seat into part of automobile in front of him, was sufficient to support doctors' testimony as to son's diagnosis, notwithstanding that account of accident which son's mother gave doctors was hearsay).

Rule qualified

To establish a diagnosis or prognosis, an examining doctor may rely on statements, pathologically germane, given to him by the patient, but if he is to testify as to a causal relationship he must do so in response to a hypothetical question. Riddle v. Dickens, 217 A.2d 304, 241 Md. 579.

Wisconsin rule modified

If trial court determines that consultation is made by claimant with physician for bona fide purpose of treatment, fact that claimant also desires to utilize physician as witness on trial will not preclude physician from testifying as to patient's report of his subjective symptoms or from predicating medical conclusions upon such reports; modifying Kath v. Wisconsin Central R. Co., 121 Wis. 503, 99 N.W. 217. Ritter v. Coca-Cola Co. (Kenosha-Racine) Inc., 128 N.W.2d 439, 24 Wis.2d 157.

93. **Ill.**—Borowicz v. Seuring Transit Co., 1968, 240 N.E.2d 314, 98 Ill.App.2d 326 (testimony of plaintiff's physician of plaintiff's alleged pathology shown on X-rays, interpreted for the physician in written report of unidentified roentgenologist, which report was not produced in evidence, was not incompetent as hearsay, in view of fact that plaintiff's physician concurred in roentgenologist's report and did not merely read the report, and in view of fact that defense counsel rejected offer to produce the report in evidence).

Iowa.—Miller v. McCoy Truck Lines, 1952, 52 N.W.2d 62, 243 Iowa 483.

Kan.—Van Welden v. Ramsay's Inc., 1967, 430 P.2d 298, 199 Kan. 417 (admissible notwithstanding contention that such conclusion was based on X-ray interpretations and information obtained from another doctor, where the X-ray interpretation to which objection was made was that of roentgenologist to effect that there was compressed fracture involving the T7 dorsal vertebra, which interpretation was contained in hospital report which had been introduced in evidence without objection).

Mo.—Conlon v. Roeder, 1967, 418 S. W.2d 152 (hospital record mentioning "unconscious"); Harris v. Goggins, 1963, 374 S.W.2d 6 (hospital records admitted in evidence); Snyder v. Jensen, 1955, 281 S.W. 2d 802 (based upon interpretation of graph of test made under witness' direction).

Mont.—Pachek v. Norton Concrete Co., 1972, 499 P.2d 766, 160 Mont. 16 (medical testimony must of necessity in many instances be based on information acquired from outside sources, examinations by other doctors, nurses, notes and observations, X-rays and other tools of profession used in making of a diagnosis and is not, because of that, hearsay); Klaus v. Hillberry, 1971, 485 P.2d 54, 157 Mont. 277 (reports of neurologist were part of case file of attending physician and were used by him in making his diagnosis but final conclusions made were those of attending physician).

Ch. 431   EXPERT OPINION EVIDENCE   § 431.5

A medical expert may give an opinion either from facts within the witness' own knowledge and observation, or from facts embodied in a hypothetical question, or from the two combined.[94]

Wash.—Engler v. Woodman, 340 P. 2d 563, 54 Wash.2d 360 (did not err in refusing request of plaintiff to strike testimony of doctor that visual fields of plaintiff were normal, based on doctor's analysis of his office record, which contained visual field charts prepared by doctor's technician in accordance with doctor's instructions, and checked by doctor during course of plaintiff's examination by technician, where challenge went only to credibility of office record, and its alleged inaccuracy was not established by plaintiff, who challenged it).

But see
Testimony as to nature and extent of infant's injuries was objectionable, where physician apparently relied on X-rays and reports from other doctors and X-rays were not in evidence and none of other doctors whose reports he considered had testified in the case. Wild v. Bass, Miss., 173 So.2d 647, 252 Miss. 615.

Contra
Ga.—Sapp v. Kitchens, 1971, 186 S.E. 2d 121, 124 Ga.App. 764.

Must produce source information
Ill.—Hickey v. Chicago Transit Authority, 1964, 201 N.E.2d 742, 52 Ill.App.2d 132 (must produce myelogram or X-ray upon which opinion based).
Iowa.—Lovely v. Ewing, Iowa 1971, 183 N.W.2d 682 (where doctor stated that study of records of examination by other doctors played part in his evaluation of disability and that without use of result of previous examinations he could not have made final conclusion on her impairment and where none of the records was in evidence and none of the other doctors testified, part of his deposition which dealt with permanent injuries was inadmissible as being based upon hearsay and its admission was reversible error).
N.Y.—Sirico v. Cotto, 1971, 324 N.Y. S.2d 483, 67 Misc.2d 636 (radiologist's opinion to effect that plaintiff was suffering from the consequences of a lumbar-sacral sprain, which was based wholly upon X-ray plates which were not offered into evidence, was inadmissible, where plaintiff's counsel did not explain his failure to produce the plates).
Pa.—Messino v. Employers' Fire Ins. Co., Com.Pl., 31 Leh.L.J. 158 (information provided by others upon which a doctor relies to formulate opinion must be presented by the informant under oath to the jury in order that it may consider what weight to give to the opinion).
Tex.—Aetna Cas. & Sur. Co. v. Depoister, Civ.App., 393 S.W.2d 822.

Not when merely conclusion of other
Admission in evidence of opinion testimony of orthopedic surgeon relating to plaintiff's head injury was prejudicial error where orthopedic surgeon was merely stating the conclusions of other doctors to whom he had sent the plaintiff, and where, had opinion evidence given by orthopedist been excluded, there would have been no evidence before the jury of brain damage. Dupona v. Benny, 1972, 291 A.2d 404, 130 Vt. 281.

94. **Md.**—Coastal Tank Lines v. Canoles, 113 A.2d 82, 207 Md. 37; Langenfelder v. Thompson, 20 A. 2d 491, 179 Md. 502, 136 A.L.R. 960.
Mo.—De Donato v. Rollo Wells, Rec'r, 41 S.W.2d 184, 328 Mo. 448, 82 A.L.R. 1331.

§ 431.5   TRIAL EVIDENCE   Ch. 431

Conclusions may be based on an examination of the injured party,[95] even an examination arranged solely to qualify the physician as a witness.[96] Involuntary manifestations of pain, together with external evidence of an injury, may be relied on by a physician.[97]

The testimony of a physician that an injured person suffered pain is not objectionable as a conclusion of the witness.[98] A physician who treats an injured person may also state whether or not the pain complained of by the injured party is real or simulated.[99]

Ohio.—Krenger v. Palmer, 222 N.E. 2d 651, 9 Ohio App.2d 9 (where expert is familiar with facts by personal observation and so testifies, he may be asked directly for his opinion without stating facts upon which it is based).

95. U.S.—McGuire v. Davis, C.A.Ga. 1971, 437 F.2d 570 (that victim suffered brain damage where physician related that his opinion that permanent neurological deficiency was result of accident was based on physician's observations and testing of victim).

Md.—Mangione v. Snead, 195 A. 329, 173 Md. 33 (family physician).

Mich.—Krzywosz v. Crummett, 282 N.W. 853, 286 Mich. 649 (physician specializing in mental diseases).

Minn.—Piche v. Halvorson, 272 N. W. 591, 199 Minn. 526 (sufficient foundation for opinion that disability was due to accident).

Limited where saw plaintiff night before trial

Ill.—Gaydos v. Peterson, 20 N.E.2d 837, 300 Ill.App. 219.

Observation on street

Attending physician was properly allowed to give his opinion as to condition based in part upon observations made in a chance meeting in the street when physician observed plaintiff's facial tic, and physician did not have to limit himself to giving opinion based only on facts obtained or observations made upon professional consultation in physician's office. Pomrenke v. Betzelberger, 190 N.E.2d 522, 41 Ill.App.2d 307.

96. Ill.—McMahon v. Opatkiewicz, 91 N.E.2d 735, 340 Ill.App. 337.

Neb.—Kennedy v. Woods, 267 N.W. 390, 131 Neb. 217.

Okl.—Yellow Cab Transit Co. v. Bethel, 81 P.2d 667, 183 Okl. 219.

Tex.—Powell v. Sanders, Civ.App., 324 S.W.2d 587.

97. Minn.—Van House v. Canadian Northern Ry. Co., 192 N.W. 493, 155 Minn. 57.

98. U.S.—McGuire v. Davis, C.A.Ga. 1971, 437 F.2d 570 (properly admitted where record revealed that when physician exerted a slight amount of pressure on coccygeal area of spine victim responded in a manner that clearly indicated pain).

Ga.—Paulk v. Thomas, 1967, 154 S.E. 2d 872, 115 Ga.App. 436.

Ind.—Indianapolis & M. R. T. Co. v. Reeder, 76 N.E. 816, 37 Ind.App. 262.

Pa.—City of Philadelphia v. Shapiro, 206 A.2d 308, 416 Pa. 308, 11 A. L.R.3d 1241.

99. Alaska.—Peters v. Benson, 425 P.2d 149 (testimony that plaintiff did not exaggerate her complaints at all but was very stable individual to examine was admissible as directly responsive to question whether doctor had had to take plaintiff's word for tenderness in

Ch. 431   EXPERT OPINION EVIDENCE   § 431.5

Opinion of causation

A physician generally may express an opinion as to the cause of an injury;[1] but there have been holdings to the contrary.[2]

neck and right shoulder, and this testimony was not objectionable on theory that the doctor had been allowed to vouch for patient's character and veracity).

Ill.—Hastings v. Abernathy Taxi Ass'n, Inc., 1974, 306 N.E.2d 498, 16 Ill.App.3d 671 (not a malingerer).

Minn.—Koehler v. Kline, 1971, 185 N.W.2d 539, 290 Minn. 485 (permitting testimony to effect that plaintiff was honest, truthful, and straightforward in relating his symptoms was not error or prejudicial as witness was doing no more than telling jury that plaintiff was not a malingerer and that his injuries were not feigned); Van House v. Canadian Northern Ry. Co., 1923, 192 N.W. 493, 155 Minn. 57.

N.Y.—Hickenbottom v. Delaware, L. & W. R. Co., 25 N.E. 279, 122 N.Y. 91 (testimony that victim of amputation may experience pain in an imaginary limb).

Tex.—Austin & N. W. Ry. Co. v. McElmurry, Civ.App., 33 S.W. 249.

But see

Statements in physician's diagnostic report indicating that plaintiff had a "gross adult maladjustment" and that she was "feigning her way through life" were objectionable as not being relevant and not having proper foundation in that they were not shown to be related to observations made by doctor during examination. Hytha v. Schwendeman, 1974, 320 N.E.2d 312, 40 Ohio App. 2d 478.

Similar related testimony

Testimony of plaintiff's treating physician that he had advised plaintiff to get the matter behind her and that, although he didn't think it was an intentional thing on part of many patients, their aches and pains continued many times until litigation was finally settled and then one could really tell how much was functional and how much was organic in nature was properly admitted since physician was giving his opinion on plaintiff's condition and factors he felt to be relevant thereto, based on his personal observation and examination of plaintiff, and since such testimony was within realm of permissible expert medical testimony. Drake v. Shurbutt, 1973, 201 S.E.2d 184, 129 Ga.App. 754.

1. **U.S.**—McGuire v. Davis, C.A.Ga. 1971, 437 F.2d 570 (cause of phlebitis in leg); Padgett v. Southern R. Co., C.A.Tenn.1968, 396 F.2d 303; Hill v. Pennsylvania Greyhound Lines, C.A.Pa., 174 F.2d 171 (connection between herniated intervertebral disc).

Cal.—Inskeep v. Busby, 24 Cal.Rptr. 819, 207 Cal.App.2d 848 (physicians, who performed surgery on spine of plaintiff and who had actually observed herniated disc, were properly permitted to testify concerning causal relationship between herniated disc).

Colo.—Riss & Co. v. Galloway, 114 P.2d 550, 108 Colo. 93, 135 A.L.R. 878.

Idaho.—Drury v. Palmer, 375 P.2d 125, 84 Idaho 558 (cause and effect of pulmonary embolism).

Ill.—Geaschel v. Rokita, 1967, 232 N.E.2d 204, 89 Ill.App.2d 161 (cause of headaches); O'Keefe v. Lithocolor Press, Inc., 199 N.E.2d 60, 49 Ill.App.2d 123.

Iowa.—Ingebretsen v. M. & St. L. R. Co., 155 N.W. 327, 176 Iowa 74 (shock).

2. See note 2 on page 679.

§ 431.5   TRIAL EVIDENCE   Ch. 431

Md.—Marshall v. Sellers, 53 A.2d 5, 188 Md. 508 (insufficient knowledge of facts by physician); Langenfelder v. Thompson, 20 A.2d 491, 179 Md. 502, 136 A.L.R. 960 (that the retroverted and retroflexed uterus was in all probability caused by the accident); Standard Oil Co. v. Stern, 173 A. 205, 167 Md. 211 (delayed onset of condition); Marine v. Stewart, 168 A. 891, 165 Md. 698 (cause of nervousness).

Mass.—Wallace v. Ludwig, 198 N.E. 159, 292 Mass. 251 (whether hemorrhages left vitality so lowered that she could not resist infection of germs held proper subject).

Minn.—Piche v. Halvorson, 272 N.W. 591, 199 Minn. 526.

Mo.—Franklin v. Kansas City Public Service Co., 186 S.W.2d 546, 239 Mo.App. 151 (between injuries and stroke ten months later); Fritz v. Manufacturers Ry. Co., Mo.App., 124 S.W.2d 603 (whether condition of pain in stomach and bowels, constipation, headaches, and sleeplessness could have been caused by accident); Floyd v. A. Y. McDonald Mfg. Co., 46 S.W.2d 251, 226 Mo.App. 444 (cause of septicemia).

N.Y.—Siefring v. Marion, 253 N.Y.S.2d 619, 22 A.D.2d 765.

N.C.—Duke v. Meisky, 1971, 183 S.E.2d 292, 12 N.C.App. 329 (causing growth on breast to enlarge and spread); Todd v. Watts, 152 S.E.2d 448, 269 N.C. 417 (opinion based either upon facts within his personal knowledge or upon assumed state of facts supported by evidence and recited in hypothetical question); Bullin v. Moore, 122 S.E.2d 765, 256 N.C. 82 (doctor who examined and treated); Hester v. Horton Motor Lines, 14 S.E.2d 794, 219 N.C. 743 (physician's testimony that injuries found by him on deceased's body were not caused by truck striking or passing over her was competent).

Ohio.—Baird v. Cincinnati Transit Co., 168 N.E.2d 413, 110 Ohio App. 94.

Or.—Ferrante v. August, 1967, 432 P.2d 167, 248 Or. 16 (error to exclude opinion back strain caused by injury); Personius v. Asbury Transp. Co. of Oregon, 53 P.2d 1065, 152 Or. 286 (whether conditions could result from a traumatized kidney).

Pa.—Zelinsky v. Chimics, 175 A.2d 351, 196 Pa.Super. 312 (doctor should have been permitted to testify that collision in which occupant was jostled was cause of occupant's depressive reaction although occupant was not cut or apparently physically injured).

S.D.—Engberg v. Ford Motor Co., 1973, 205 N.W.2d 104, —— S.D. —— (within discretion to admit testimony of licensed mortician, who had investigated accidents for five years incident to his work as county coroner, relative to fact that deceased died from injuries sustained after he had been ejected from manufacturer's automobile).

Tenn.—Crowe v. Provost, 374 S.W.2d 645, 52 Tenn.App. 397.

Wis.—Engstrom v. Dewitz, 118 N.W.2d 710, 18 Wis.2d 421 (whether accident caused particular back injury); Gray v. Chicago, etc., R. Co., 142 N.W. 505, 153 Wis. 637 (opinion of treating physician that a tubercular condition, discovered for the first time more than a year after the injury, was the result of the injury).

Aggravation or acceleration of cancer

S.C.—Gambrell v. Burleson, 1969, 165 S.E.2d 622, 252 S.C. 98 (admission of testimony of family doctor and neurosurgeon as to alleged causal connection between collision and aggravation or acceleration of cancer of decedent, not solely relied on to establish causal connection, was not shown to be error though such testimony was

Ch. 431 EXPERT OPINION EVIDENCE § 431.5

The opinion of causation must be adequately founded,[3] and generally must be stated in terms of reasonable medical cer-

insufficient to meet "most probably" rule).

Wash.—Vanderhoff v. Fitzgerald, 1967, 431 P.2d 969, 72 Wash.2d 103 (whether rear-end collision accelerated bladder cancer).

Cause of death

U.S.—New York Life Ins. Co. v. Doerksen, C.C.A.Kan., 64 F.2d 240 (contributing cause).

Ill.—Wargo v. Buske, 273 Ill.App. 28.

Minn.—Mattfeld v. Nester, 32 N.W. 2d 291, 226 Minn. 106; Milliren v. Federal Life Ins. Co., 242 N.W. 290, 185 Minn. 614 (cause of death following pneumonia and miscarriage).

Pa.—Swingle v. Mill Creek Coal Co., 176 A. 828, 116 Pa.Super. 97 (contributing cause).

Condition at point remote from point of trauma

Or.—Frangos v. Edmunds, 173 P.2d 596, 179 Or. 577 (injury to the brain).

2. **Mich.**—Kemp v. Aldrich, 286 N. W. 81, 286 Mich. 715, reversing 282 N.W. 833, 286 Mich. 591 (witness could not give opinion that arthritic condition of plaintiff was caused by accident); Hunter v. Ithica, 105 N.W. 9, 141 Mich. 539.

Mo.—Feltz v. Terminal Railroad Ass'n of St. Louis, 81 S.W.2d 616, 336 Mo. 790; Thomas v. Metropolitan St. Ry. Co., 100 S.W. 1121, 125 Mo.App. 131.

N.Y.—Broderick v. Brooklyn, Q. C. & S. R. R. Co., 174 N.Y.S. 571, 186 App.Div. 546.

Ohio.—Lafferty v. Benge, 1971, 287 N.E.2d 640, 31 Ohio App.2d 235.

Wash.—Weber v. Biddle, 1967, 431 P.2d 705, 72 Wash.2d 22 (trial judge did not abuse discretion in refusing to permit physician who rendered emergency care to driver to express an opinion that cuts were sustained by her head hitting the windshield, because jury was as able as he to determine cause of cuts from description of damage to windshield and condition of her head).

Tex.—Republic Underwriters v. Howard, Civ.App., 69 S.W.2d 584, error dismissed.

Negativing intervening causes

Where plaintiff's physician had testified to fact that he had attended plaintiff over a period of years and treated her for the injuries out of which action arose and in fact saw her in the hospital within a few minutes after accident and continued to see and examine her again until shortly before trial, he could properly testify that in his opinion there were no intervening factors which could have affected her condition. Wilson v. Sorge, 97 N.W.2d 477, 256 Minn. 125.

3. **Md.**—Baltimore Transit Co. v. Smith, 1969, 250 A.2d 228, 252 Md. 430.

Mich.—Lawrence v. Tippens, 1974, 219 N.W.2d 787, 53 Mich.App. 461 (court's determination that testimony of psychiatrist, who performed psychiatric evaluation approximately one and one half years after accident and who made no physical examination, regarding alleged causal connection between bruise on hip sustained in accident and vaginal bleeding ten days later was inadmissible and mere speculation was within discretion).

N.Y.—Franzese v. Mackay Trucking Corp., 199 N.Y.S.2d 514, 10 A.D. 2d 713 (opinion was legally incompetent since it was based on sev-

§ 431.5 TRIAL EVIDENCE Ch. 431

eral assumptions of facts which were not proved, such as the assumption that motorist was predisposed to ulcers and that he suffered a shock which might have affected his endocrine glands which in turn might have precipitated bleeding ulcer); Drollette v. Kelly, 146 N.Y.S.2d 55, 286 App. Div. 641 (question was whether injuries had been sustained in accident in issue or in subsequent accident but there was no evidence of any physical consequence of second accident or that plaintiff had been injured therein).

N.C.—Branch v. Dempsey, 145 S.E. 2d 395, 265 N.C. 733 (physician who made purely superficial examination of decedent's body and who had not seen decedent prior to his death was not qualified to express an opinion as to cause of death upon basis of his own findings).

Held adequate basis

Mass.—Mazukna v. Powers, 130 N.E. 2d 579, 333 Mass. 331 (admission of testimony of physician, who treated plaintiff for brain hemorrhage resulting from hypertension and high blood pressure six years before accident involved, that plaintiff suffered concussion of brain, with aggravated hypertension was not error, though no evidence had been introduced as to what happened to plaintiff, where she and another witness subsequently testified that she was thrown forward in automobile and struck her head, rendering her unconscious, and had headaches and dizziness thereafter; physician's knowledge of plaintiff's previous physical condition being adequate basis for opinion expressed).

Held unfounded

Ill.—Butler v. Palm, 184 N.E.2d 633, 36 Ill.App.2d 351 (testimony that plaintiff's meningoencephalitis could be causally related to injury, diagnosed as whiplash, sustained three months before, was improperly admitted, where testimony was based on assumption that brain or spinal cord had been injured, but there was no evidence of such injury).

Mo.—Butcher v. Main, 1968, 426 S. W.2d 356 (saw patient complaining of pain several years after accident).

Or.—Peterson v. Schlottman, 392 P. 2d 262, 237 Or. 484 (refusal to strike cross-examination as to cause of a spinal injury based upon hypothesis that plaintiff had lifted an automobile in an effort to disengage his automobile from defendant's automobile which had struck the rear of plaintiff's automobile was prejudicial error where there was no evidence to support hypothesis that plaintiff had in fact made an effort to lift one of the automobiles).

Witness disqualified own opinion

Neb.—Whittington v. Nebraska Natural Gas Co., 128 N.W.2d 795, 177 Neb. 264 (testified could not speak with reasonable medical certainty as to cause of plaintiff's dizziness and nausea).

N.H.—Archie v. Blair, 225 A.2d 383, 107 N.H. 471 (after treating doctor testified that he did not know whether plaintiff's complaint of lame back bore any relationship to accident, further testimony that there was a possible relationship was incompetent).

R.I.—Renault v. John Hancock Mut. Life Ins. Co., 200 A.2d 588, 98 R.I. 213 (refusal to permit doctor to give his opinion as to whether death of insured would have occurred on date that it did as result of insured's pre-existing kidney condition without intervention of accident was not error in view of doctor's prior testimony that answer to such question would amount to pure speculation).

tainty.[4] However, it has been held that such opinions may be

[4]. **Md.**—Kujawa v. Baltimore Transit Co., 167 A.2d 96, 224 Md. 195, 89 A.L.R.2d 1166 (testimony of doctor that he could not be definite about probability of cause of emotional and nervous condition was properly excluded).

Miss.—Scott County Co-op v. Brown, 187 So.2d 321 (that she revealed psychotic tendencies when witness examined her nearly two years after accident, and that trauma can cause such condition, should not have been admitted, as it showed merely a possibility that prepsychotic condition was caused by accident).

N.Y.—Normile v. Thomas P. Spagnoletti Const. Co., 277 N.Y.S.2d 155, 27 A.D.2d 169 (educated medical theory may support opinion of causal relationship).

Pa.—Schwartz v. Feldman, 1961, 175 A.2d 153, 196 Pa.Super. 492 (not that might have caused or even that probably did).

Wash.—Carlos v. Cain, 1971, 481 P.2d 945, 4 Wash.App. 475 (proffered testimony of treating dentist that exact cause of bruxism was not known and that condition may have many causes was properly rejected as not legally sufficient to establish causal relationship between accident and victim's subsequent habit of unconsciously gritting or grinding the teeth).

But see

Hawaii.—Bachran v. Morishige, 1970, 469 P.2d 808, 52 Haw. 61 (where plaintiff had been injured in accident two years before, trial court erred in restricting testimony of witnesses on issue of apportionment of damages between accidents within term of "reasonable medical certainty.").

W.Va.—Pygman v. Helton, 134 S.E.2d 717, 148 W.Va. 281 (surgeon who performed operation to repair moderately large inguinal hernia was not required to conclude with reasonable certainty that collision was proximate cause of hernia; all that was required was that testimony should warrant reasonable inference that injury was caused).

Held adequate

Mo.—Lemm v. Gould, 1968, 425 S.W.2d 190 (neurologist's testimony as to causation "to a reasonable medical certainty" was not rendered self-destructive by statement "obviously he could not be certain because no one can" and that condition could have developed without such causation "because anything can happen.")

Pa.—Koedel v. Johnston, Com.Pl., 114 P.L.J. 125 (words "I think" equivalent to "I believe").

Rule further stated

U.S.—Eubanks v. Piedmont Natural Gas Co., D.C.S.C., 198 F.Supp. 522 (necessary to testify that taking all data into consideration it was his professional opinion that result in question most probably came from cause alleged).

Ill.—Boose v. Digate, 1969, 246 N.E.2d 50, 107 Ill.App.2d 418 (when doctor is asked to base his opinion on "reasonable degree of medical certainty", the certainty referred to is not that some condition in future is certain to exist or not to exist but rather the phrase refers to general consensus of recognized medical thought and opinion concerning probabilities of conditions in the future based on present conditions).

Minn.—Daly v. Bergstedt, 1964, 126 N.W.2d 242, 267 Minn. 244 (need not be free from doubt).

Witness disqualified own opinion

N.D.—Grenz v. Werre, 1964, 129 N.W.2d 681 (admitted could not state probability or certainty).

§ 431.5

stated in terms such as "might have caused" or "could have caused",[5] where supported by other competent proof of causation.[6]

Opinion of existence of condition

Whether a certain alleged injury or condition did occur or exist generally is a proper subject for a qualified expert.[7]

Wash.—O'Donoghue v. Riggs, 1968, 440 P.2d 823, 73 Wash.2d 814 (improperly permitted to express opinion on proximate cause of plaintiff's urinary retention condition, where doctor had prefatorially indicated that, on basis of his one visit to patient, he was unable to reach a conclusion as to probable cause, and where, moreover, his opinion, in which he hypothesized three possible causes of the urinary retention, was such that jury was required to resort to speculation and conjecture in order to determine which of the three possible causes was in fact the actual cause).

5. **Fla.**—Nationwide Mut. Ins. Co. v. Griffin, App.1969, 222 So.2d 754.

Ill.—Healy v. Nordhous, 188 N.E.2d 227, 40 Ill.App.2d 320 (whether there "could or may be" a causal connection between neck injury and a rear-end collision).

Iowa.—Dickinson v. Mailliard, 1970, 175 N.W.2d 588, 36 A.L.R.3d 425.

Mo.—DeMoulin v. Kissir, App.1969, 446 S.W.2d 162 (that collision could have been cause of dislocated jaw); Immekus v. Quigg, App., 406 S.W.2d 298 (even if testimony indicates nothing more than that certain result is scientifically possible, it is admissible to aid jury in determining reasonable inferences to be drawn from facts).

N.C.—Lockwood v. McCaskill, 138 S.E.2d 541, 262 N.C. 663 (whether or not the particular hypothesis was a capable cause).

Okl.—Oklahoma Natural Gas Co. v. Kelly, 153 P.2d 1010, 194 Okl. 646.

Pa.—Backiel v. Rosewicz, 54 Luz.L. Reg. 31 (testimony that plaintiff's severe headaches and dizziness could be the result).

Tex.—Gibson v. Avery, Civ.App.1970, 463 S.W.2d 277.

6. **Ind.**—Herman v. Ferrell, 1971, 276 N.E.2d 858, 150 Ind.App. 384.

Mo.—Jackson v. Cherokee Drug Co., 1968, 434 S.W.2d 257.

N.Y.—McGrath v. Irving, 1965, 265 N.Y.S.2d 376, 24 A.D.2d 236 ("possible" and "probable" approved).

W.Va.—Pygman v. Helton, 134 S.E. 2d 717, 148 W.Va. 281 (in view of testimony of plaintiff that he had not experienced pain before collision in area where hernia occurred and of testimony of doctor who examined him prior to accident that plaintiff did not have hernia, testimony of surgeon, who repaired hernia, that it was possible that collision caused hernia was admissible).

7. **Wash.**—Vanderhoff v. Fitzgerald, 1967, 431 P.2d 969, 72 Wash. 103 (opinion of doctor who had initially been advised by second doctor that presence of blood cells in urine was caused by lupus erythematosis was not baseless because second doctor eventually discarded the diagnosis of lupus erythematosis as incorrect, in view of fact that first doctor's opinion was based on number of considerations including initial observation and treatment).

Condition as cause of accident

U.S.—Arnold v. Loose, C.A.Pa., 352 F.2d 959 (under Pennsylvania law,

Ch. 431   EXPERT OPINION EVIDENCE   § 431.5

Physical disability

A physician may describe the extent to which any particular portion of the body is affected by injuries and let the jury draw their own inference as to the resulting incapacity to work,[8] or may state the probable effects of the injuries upon the party's disability.[9]

striking of testimony of orthopedic surgeon that defendant's decedent had lapsed into diabetic coma which was cause of collision was not beyond trial court's discretion where witness admitted he had never read any text on diabetes or diabetic comas, he did not know who was leading authority on diabetes or which was leading treatise, and he revealed no other special knowledge in field of diabetes).

Degree of certainty in question

Ga.—Graham v. Clark, 152 S.E.2d 789, 114 Ga.App. 825 (qualifying statements that his opinion was "just off the cuff" but a somewhat "educated guess" went to weight of testimony but not to its admissibility).

Md.—Mangione v. Snead, 195 A. 329, 173 Md. 33 (testimony that boy had "possibly" had brain concussion too indefinite).

Mont.—Farris v. Clark, 1971, 487 P.2d 1307, 158 Mont. 33 (insufficient where used words "suspect," "possible," and "probable").

8. Iowa.—Lovely v. Ewing, 1971, 183 N.W.2d 682 (testimony that plaintiff had "20% whole body permanent physical impairment and loss of physical function" was not objectionable for use of wrong standard in determining extent of permanent injury where court properly instructed on question of permanency under the testimony given by the doctor and the doctor refused to make any estimate of extent to which injury would handicap the plaintiff in her employment).

Mich.—Matthews v. Lamberton, 165 N.W. 748, 198 Mich. 746; Holman v. Union St. Ry. Co., 72 N.W. 202, 114 Mich. 208.

Mo.—Moore v. Parks, 1970, 458 S.W.2d 344; Banks v. St. Louis Public Service Co., App., 249 S.W.2d 481 (result of concussion); Kirchof v. United Rys. Co., 135 S.W. 98, 155 Mo.App. 70.

Tenn.—Luallen v. Booher, 1970, 460 S.W.2d 24, 62 Tenn.App. 155 (percentage of permanent partial disability).

9. U.S.—Standard Oil Co. of N. J. v. Sewell, C.C.A.Md., 37 F.2d 230.

Ala.—Pope v. Ryals, 167 So. 721, 232 Ala. 260.

Cal.—Harrison v. De Young, 39 P.2d 866, 3 Cal.App.2d 662 (microscopical change in nerve cells resulting from concussion).

Ind.—Ott v. Perrin, 63 N.E.2d 163, 116 Ind.App. 315.

Md.—Straughan v. Tsouvalos, 1967, 228 A.2d 300, 246 Md. 242 (personal or economic disability); Shivers v. Carnaggio, 165 A.2d 898, 223 Md. 585 (as to the extent to which an anatomical disability will cause personal or economical disability); Isaac Benesch & Sons, Inc., v. Ferkler, 139 A. 557, 153 Md. 680 (ability to perform household duties).

N.H.—Roy v. Chalifoux, 63 A.2d 226, 95 N.H. 321 (neurologist and psychiatrist testifying as to 4 year old child).

N.C.—Butler v. Armour Fertilizer Works, 142 S.E. 483, 195 N.C. 409.

R.I.—Lantini v. Daniels, 1968, 247 A.2d 298, 104 R.I. 572 (physician,

§ 431.5   TRIAL EVIDENCE   Ch. 431

Permanency

Testimony of qualified physician that certain of the injuries were permanent is generally admissible.[10]

being qualified doctor of medicine in good standing in medical profession, was competent to testify on question of patrolman's capacity and ability to return to police work which patrolman claimed he was psychiatrically unable to do, notwithstanding that physician lacked training or experience in field of psychiatry).

Tex.—Murphy v. Blankenship, Civ. App.1938, 120 S.W.2d 309 (ability to perform housewife duties); Zurich Gen. Accident & Liability Ins. Co. v. Kerr, Civ.App.1932, 54 S.W.2d 349 (as to housewife duties).

Vt.—Lewes v. John Crane & Sons, 62 A. 60, 78 Vt. 216.

Wash.—Stone v. City of Seattle, 391 P.2d 179, 64 Wash.2d 166 (whether or not plaintiff is able to follow gainful work or occupation).

Wis.—Collins v. City of Janesville, 87 N.W. 241, 111 Wis. 348 (effect of weather on condition).

Loss of intellect

It was not abuse of discretion to permit expert in psychological testing to testify that tests given to 13-year-old boy before and after accident indicated that he had lost one-half of his intellect. City of Austin v. Hoffman, Tex.Civ.App., 379 S.W. 2d 103.

Not when based on history

Where physician was an examining physician rather than a treating physician, it was reversible error to admit his testimony relating to his estimate of plaintiff's disability when opinion was based on combination of personal observation and history of case as told to him by plaintiff. Bondy v. West, Fla.App.1969, 219 So.2d 117.

Ruled improper

Ill.—Lazzaro v. Garrett, 1968, 242 N.E.2d 59, 100 Ill.App.2d 452 (after doctor had specifically stated that he did not know what plaintiff's duties were as a policeman, excluding doctor's testimony that plaintiff's prior injuries would not inhibit him from doing his duties was not abuse of discretion).

10. **Ariz.**—Schmerfeld v. Hendry, 245 P.2d 420, 74 Ariz. 159.

Ill.—Greim v. Sharpe Motor Lines, 1968, 242 N.E.2d 282, 101 Ill.App. 2d 142 (testimony of doctor who had treated plaintiff three times in connection with prior injury and who immediately after describing examination concerning neck injuries plaintiff allegedly sustained in subsequent accident expressed opinion that "condition of the patient" might or could be permanent was, in light of entire record, an expression of opinion as to permanency of conditions observed as result of injuries sustained in subsequent accident and was properly admitted); Hoffman v. Jenard, 1948, 78 N.E.2d 322, 334 Ill.App. 74 (based on examination and x-rays).

Iowa.—Ingebretsen v. M. & St. L. R. Co., 155 N.W. 327, 176 Iowa 74.

Kan.—Federal Betterment Co. v. Reeves, 1906, 84 P. 560, 73 Kan. 107, 4 L.R.A.,N.S., 460.

Md.—Riddle v. Dickens, 217 A.2d 304, 241 Md. 579 (that plaintiff had a nerve root compression of the cervical spine as a result of a disc protrusion and that plaintiff had a fifty percent permanent partial disability of his entire body was admissible, where witness based his opinion solely on his own observation and objective findings).

Proof of future consequences

Expert testimony as to the future consequences of a subsisting injury, on the issue of prospective damages, must be in terms of the certain or probable, and not of the possible.[11] The proof should show such a degree of probability for the occurrence of apprehended future consequences as amounts to a reasonable certainty that they will result from the original injury.[12]

Minn.—Piche v. Halvorson, 272 N. W. 591, 199 Minn. 526.

Mo.—Nance v. Lansdell, App., 73 S.W.2d 346.

N.H.—Welch v. H. P. Hood & Sons, Inc., 182 A.2d 461, 104 N.H. 207 (that testimony of attending family physician as to permanent injury was general rather than specific and was not buttressed by independent substantiating proof of x-rays or other tests went to weight of evidence rather than to its admissibility).

N.Y.—Zipprich v. Smith Trucking Co., 157 N.Y.S.2d 966, 2 N.Y.2d 177, 139 N.E.2d 146 (as to rearward protrusion of the fifth lumbar disc and as to continuance of disability); Griswold v. New York Cent. & H. R. R. Co., 21 N.E. 726, 115 N.Y. 61, 12 Am.St.Rep. 775.

Ohio.—Bobbitt v. Maher Beverage Co., 89 N.E.2d 583, 152 Ohio St. 246.

Okl.—Denco Bus Lines v. Hargis, 229 P.2d 560, 204 Okl. 339.

Pa.—Lorch v. Eglin, 1952, 85 A.2d 841, 369 Pa. 314.

Tenn.—Gulf Refining Co. v. Frazier, 1934, 83 S.W.2d 285, 19 Tenn.App. 76 (irregular leg movement).

Wash.—Stone v. City of Seattle, 391 P.2d 179, 64 Wash.2d 166 (permanency of disability of music teacher to play musical instruments).

But see

Md.—Calder v. Levi, 177 A. 392, 168 Md. 260, 97 A.L.R. 880.

Limited where dependent on plaintiff demonstration

Tenn.—Gulf Refining Co. v. Frazier, 83 S.W.2d 285, 19 Tenn.App. 76 (walking under own control).

11. **Md.**—Calder v. Levi, 1935, 177 A. 392, 168 Md. 260, 97 A.L.R. 880.

Mo.—Miller v. Haynes, App.1970, 454 S.W.2d 293 (testimony as to a condition which could, but which he did not then know would develop, which he did not expect or anticipate occurring, and of which he could then, some two years and eight months after accident, see no evidence was purely speculative and was improperly admitted); Rogers v. Spain, 388 S.W. 2d 518 (testimony that plaintiff's pain most likely would be permanent but that she could get entirely well as far as he knew was not speculative, but was to a reasonable degree of medical certainty that the injuries would be permanent); Kenney v. J. A. Folger & Co., App., 192 S.W.2d 73 (that might have a chronic backache for a long time held inadmissible).

N.C.—Fisher v. Rogers, 112 S.E.2d 76, 251 N.C. 610.

Ohio.—Brush v. Eastern Motor Dispatch, App., 104 N.E.2d 700.

Pa.—Lorch v. Eglin, 85 A.2d 841, 369 Pa. 314.

12. **Neb.**—Borcherding v. Eklund, 1952, 55 N.W.2d 643, 156 Neb. 196.

N.Y.—Strohm v. New York, L. E. & W. R. Co., 1884, 96 N.Y. 305.

But see

U.S.—Trapp v. 4–10 Inv. Corp., C.A. N.D.1970, 424 F.2d 1261 (may

§ 431.5   TRIAL EVIDENCE   Ch. 431

A physician's testimony as to future pain and suffering has been held properly admitted,[13] and whether an operation may relieve such future pain and suffering.[14]

Expert opinion of various other future consequences has been held admissible,[15] and in other cases inadmissible.[16]

testify as to probability, even though it be slight, of future risk of injury or surgery based upon present disability involved).

Held inadmissible

Md.—Mangione v. Snead, 195 A. 329, 173 Md. 33 ("future prospects").

N.Y.—Griswold v. New York Cent. & H. R. R. Co., 21 N.E. 726, 115 N.Y. 61, 12 Am.St.Rep. 775.

13. Fla.—Tampa Transit Lines, Inc. v. Smith, App., 155 So.2d 557 (even though opinion was based largely on subjective symptoms attested by plaintiff as of time of trial).

Ohio.—Shackelford v. Commercial Motor Freight, App., 65 N.E.2d 879.

14. Minn.—Johnston v. Selfe, 251 N.W. 525, 190 Minn. 269.

N.H.—Douzanis v. Boston & Maine Transp. Co., 7 A.2d 393, 90 N.H. 558.

15. Ark.—Reed v. McGibboney, 1967, 422 S.W.2d 115, 243 Ark. 789 (psychological effect in general of facial scars upon young girls was properly admissible).

Ind.—Cerra v. McClanahan, 1967, 229 N.E.2d 737, 141 Ind.App. 469 (properly permitted to testify that chest injuries "could" have an indirect effect on hereditary cardiac disease because chest injuries would limit activities which might be beneficial to well-being and stave off early onset of cardiac disease).

Iowa.—Lowman v. Kuecker, 71 N.W. 2d 586, 246 Iowa 1227, 52 A.L.R.2d 1380 (testimony as to future medical treatment for latent injury is proper if not imperative).

Mo.—Granberg v. King Candy Co., App., 81 S.W.2d 981 (that head injuries might result in insanity, epilepsy, and paralysis).

N.H.—Ramsdell v. John B. Varrick Co., 170 A. 12, 86 N.H. 457 (susceptibility to future fractures after once broken).

Tex.—Presswood v Jones, 381 S.W. 2d 485 (that condition would not get better but would grow worse).

Wash.—Wilson v. Lund, 1971, 491 P.2d 1287, 80 Wash.2d 91 (parental grief, mental anguish, or suffering in cases involving wrongful death of or injury to a child, expert psychiatric testimony will often be useful and proper, if not absolutely necessary, to provide a reasonably reliable basis for considering an award of such damages, to prevent trier of fact from falling into realm of mere speculation and conjecture, and to prevent trier of fact from resorting out-of-hand to legal assumptions and conclusions which have little or no supporting medical or otherwise reasonably reliable data).

Arthritis in future

Mich.—Sarzynski v. Stern, 1968, 163 N.W.2d 641, 13 Mich.App. 158 (properly admitted testimony of orthopedic surgeon to the effect that plaintiff had suffered a transverse fracture of right femur and a complete disruption of two ligaments in left knee and that there was very definite possibility of a progressing traumatic arthritis together with proof of costs antici-

16. See note 16 on page 687.

Ch. 431   EXPERT OPINION EVIDENCE   § 431.6

§ 431.6 Expert Opinion—Other Particular Matters

Library References:
C.J.S. Evidence § 546(60) et seq.
West's Key No. Digests, Evidence ⇌505 et seq.

Expert opinion testimony has been held admissible in a variety of circumstances on the issue of liability in automobile accident cases,[17] in train-automobile collision cases,[18] and in a

pated for treatment and left it to jury to determine the apprehended future consequences of injury, if any).

Chances of convulsive seizure

Pa.—Schwegel v. Goldberg, 1967, 228 A.2d 405, 209 Pa.Super. 280 (one chance in twenty of developing seizures in 20 years).

Later work disability

U.S.—Moe Light, Inc. v. Foreman, C.A.Ohio, 238 F.2d 817 (loss of earning ability at some time in future when plaintiff would become unable to continue with present employment because of injury to first sacral nerve root, which would probably become worse and cause complete inability to work, was not inadmissible as mere speculation or conjecture).

16. La.—Roy v. Yarbrough, App., 167 So. 883 (damages for six months' loss of time while convalescing from operation, which plaintiff was required to undergo in future to restore function of his shoulder, held too speculative and uncertain).

Mo.—Hahn v. McDowell, App., 349 S.W.2d 479 (testimony that possibility existed of cancer developing at site of burn scar was incompetent).

Ohio.—Haase v. Ryan, 136 N.E.2d 406, 100 Ohio App. 285 (where evidence was not sufficient to support claim of permanent injury to child's brain, testimony that there was possibility that clot might form a cyst and produce pressure on brain with resultant headaches,

dizziness and even a change of personality was highly prejudicial).

Wash.—Coffman v. McFadden, 416 P.2d 99, 68 Wash.2d 954 (testimony that there was a rare possibility of skin cancer, massive infection or amputation as result of injuries sustained did not meet test of reasonable probability that such conditions will occur as result of accident and should not be admitted if timely objected to on retrial).

As to nature of future treatment

Ill.—Heil v. Kastengren, 65 N.E.2d 579, 328 Ill.App. 301.

17. Ala.—Alabama Power Co. v. Scholz, 1968, 215 So.2d 447, 283 Ala. 232 (fact that picture used to elicit opinion as to what would happen after automobile motor was knocked off its mounting showed that motor was only off one mounting did not render expert's opinion inadmissible where uncontradicted testimony showed that motor had been sheared from both mounts).

Ky.—Powers' Adm'r v. Wiley, 44 S.W.2d 591, 241 Ky. 645 (regarding where the lights of one car would strike the other at a curve).

Mich.—O'Loughlin v. Detroit & M. Ry. Co., 1970, 177 N.W.2d 430, 22 Mich.App. 146 (testimony on significance of amount of alcohol in blood of motorist where witness had degree in chemistry, had worked approximately 23 years in chemical, pharmaceutical field and had worked with 12 physicians

18. See note 18 on page 688.

§ 431.6   TRIAL EVIDENCE   Ch. 431

analyzing blood samples and observing various test situations involving alcohol experiments).

Mo.—Jones v. Smith, 372 S.W.2d 71 (testimony as to eye level of driver of make of car owned by plaintiff was admissible to establish measurements used in computation of sight ranges).

Pa.—Williams v. Flemington Transp. Co., 207 A.2d 762, 417 Pa. 26 (under circumstances, admission of ophthalmologist's testimony as to effect of headlights of oncoming vehicle being turned on and off on eyes of approaching driver was not reversible error in case in which witness, who had been oncoming driver, testified that he turned lights on and off in effort to warn plaintiff's driver of danger); Mervine v. Sley System Garages, Inc., 164 A.2d 59, 193 Pa. Super. 394 (in action against parking lot as result of alleged negligence of lot's employees, testimony of automobile repairman, who had examined transmission shortly before it was damaged in parking lot and who had thereafter repaired it, that cause of destruction of transmission was breaking of drum due to heavy load upon it and that the heavy load could be brought about when rear wheels are spun on ice and snow, was admissible).

S.D.—Koenig v. Weber, 1970, 174 N.W.2d 218, 84 S.D. 558 (no error in allowing experienced highway patrol officer, who investigated scene at night and who took pictures with aid of flashbulbs, to testify that there was more light from a flashbulb at 15 feet than there was from lights of an approaching automobile).

Tex.—Osborne v. English, Civ.App. 1970, 458 S.W.2d 209, error refused n. r. e. (court, in action for injuries sustained when defendant accidentally drove automobile through exterior wall and into restaurant, did not abuse discretion in permitting witness, who testified that he did not repair automobiles for a living but had done a lot of mechanic work on automobiles in last 25 years, had done maintenance repairs on trucks as part of his employment and was sometimes paid to do work on automobiles, to give opinion testimony that acceleration of engine could cause it to twist and catch linkage connecting accelerator to carburetor).

Consequences of non-use of seat belt

Expert, who was authority in reconstruction and analysis of automobile accidents with extensive experience as witness in field, was qualified to express opinion with respect to consequences of failure of passenger to use seat belt. Truman v. Vargas, 1969, 80 Cal.Rptr. 373, 275 Cal.App. 976.

Own consumption of liquor

Motorist was properly allowed to testify as to quantity of liquor he had been served where he was experienced in bar business and himself was manager of a bar. Christensen v. Malkin, 45 Cal.Rptr. 836, 236 Cal.App.2d 114.

18. Fla.—Seaboard Coast Line R. Co. v. Hill, App.1971, 250 So.2d 311, certiorari discharged Sup., 270 So.2d 359 (subject matter of psychologist's opinion that an average driver would not have seen train in time to have avoided a collision was appropriate for expression of opinion under evidence that opinion included not just visibility of train on crossing but also deceptive quality of various factors that were present in environment and the manner in which a person would react to those factors); Atlantic Coast Line R. Co. v. Hendrickson, 1966, 190 So.2d 178 (electrical engineer, as to circuitry and operation of crossing signal lights).

N.H.—Sigel v. Boston & M. R. R., 216 A.2d 794, 107 N.H. 8 (testi-

688

variety of other types of cases;[19] and also on the issue of damages.[20]

mony that railway crossing did not meet standards of good practice throughout the nation and state of New Hampshire was not improper as setting ideal standards of safety rather than those of a reasonably prudent man).

Tex.—Southern Pac. Co. v. Stanley, Civ.App.1971, 473 S.W.2d 52, refused n. r. e. (where firemen on train which struck automobile wherein plaintiff's decedent was riding had been employed by railroad for 25 years and had a duty to keep a lookout in front of train and to his side and had at his command emergency brake valve, he was no doubt an expert and under circumstances it was proper to allow him to testify on cross-examination over objection that, if train had been slowed enough, collision would have been avoided).

Dangerous character of railroad crossing

Ill.—Adkins v. Chicago, R. I. & P. R. Co., 1971, 274 N.E.2d 507, 2 Ill. App.3d 906, reversed on other grounds 301 N.E.2d 729, 54 Ill.2d 511 (properly permitted railroad crossing protection expert, in response to question propounded to him on direct examination in regard to railroad crossing in question, to testify that he considered railroad crossing one of the most dangerous he had ever seen); Merchants Nat. Bank of Aurora v. Elgin, J. & E. Ry. Co., 1971, 273 N. E.2d 809, 49 Ill.2d 118 (opinion crossing was "very inadequately protected" was admissible, even though there were five eyewitnesses, as testimony was directed to whether crossing was adequately protected, not to what occurred); Merchants Nat. Bank of Aurora v. Elgin, J. & E. Ry. Co., 1970, 257 N.E.2d 216, 121 Ill.App. 2d 445, affirmed 273 N.E.2d 809, 49 Ill.2d 118 (hazardous nature of railroad crossing should be permitted in sound discretion of trial court when witness has a peculiar knowledge or experience not common to the world in general and which may aid the finder of fact).

N.J.—Di Domenico v. Pennsylvania Seashore Lines, 1961, 178 A.2d 10, 36 N.J. 455 (whether "extra-hazardous," and adequacy of warnings).

Nev.—Southern Pac. Co. v. Watkins, 435 P.2d 498, 83 Nev. 471 (did not err in admitting opinion of expert that railroad crossing was very dangerous).

Stopping distance of train

U.S.—Mittlieder v. Chicago & N. W. Ry. Co., C.A.Neb.1969, 413 F.2d 77, appeal after remand 441 F.2d 52 (absent evidence supporting assumptions of witness who would use kinetic energy formula to attempt to mathematically determine stopping distance of train, trial court correctly ruled that there was insufficient foundation to permit witness, a former professor of mechanical engineering and specialist in accident reconstruction, to opine on stopping distance of train traveling at speed of 25 miles per hour).

Mich.—Bauman v. Grand Trunk Western R. R., 1969, 171 N.W.2d 468, 18 Mich.App. 450.

Who was driving auto

Cal.—Dragash v. Western Pac. R. Co., 326 P.2d 649, 161 Cal.App.2d 233 (should have permitted expert witness, who was employed by the State Bureau of Criminal Identification and Investigation, to express an opinion, based on bruise marks, as to whether motorist was driving or whether other person in automobile was driving).

19. Mass.—Melvin v. H. J. Nassar Motor Co., 1969, 246 N.E.2d 679,

20. See note 20 on page 690.

And in a variety of circumstances expert opinion has been held not to be competent evidence on various liability issues in

355 Mass. 692 (in suit brought against seller of automobile, which was alleged to be defective, for breach of warranty and for deceit, admission of testimony on condition of automobile which was first viewed by expert 18 months after its purchase was within discretion of trial judge, where testimony was limited to conditions observed, expert gave no opinion as to cause of defects he found, and there was ample testimony relating to history of automobile during the 18 months).

Expert's reference to published report

It was reversible error to forbid witness, testifying on behalf of automobile purchaser in products liability case involving injury to buyer who was ejected from the automobile during accident because of an allegedly defective design of door latch mechanism, from referring to Cornell Aeronautical Laboratory reports as a basis for his expert witness' opinion that the absence of particular type of latch in manufacturer's automobile was a negligent design and produced an inherently unsafe vehicle. Bair v. American Motors Corp., C.A.Pa.1973, 473 F.2d 740.

On issue of insurer's failure to settle

U.S.—Liberty Mut. Ins. Co. v. Davis, C.A.Fla.1969, 412 F.2d 475 (properly refused to allow insurer's experts to testify as to whether insurer had acted in bad faith in failing to settle liability claim against insured but court properly allowed them to testify that it was not unreasonable for insurer to refuse to settle, in action based on insurer's alleged bad faith in failing to settle claims within limits of insured's automobile liability policy); Worden v. Tri-State Ins. Co., C.A.Kan.1965, 347 F.2d 336.

Ala.—Hartford Acc. & Indem. Co. v. Cosby, 173 So.2d 585, 277 Ala. 596 (testimony of counsel for plaintiffs in wrongful death action that there was a reasonable probability that a jury verdict would exceed $25,000 was admissible, in insured's instant action for negligent or bad faith refusal of liability insurer to settle the wrongful death action against insured within $25,000 limits of policy).

Wash.—Weber v. Biddle, 1971, 483 P.2d 155, 4 Wash.App. 519 (admission of testimony on issue of conflict of interest did not constitute abuse of discretion).

20. For discussion of medical opinion generally as proof of future consequences, see section 431.5 at fn. 11 et seq.

Testimony as to value of earnings

U.S.—Plant v. Simmons Co., D.C. Md.1970, 321 F.Supp. 735 (economist could properly use tables in technical paper, as to present value of estimated lifetime earnings, submitted by officials of population division and systems division of Bureau of Census and published by Department of Commerce in testifying as to present value of economic loss); Scruggs v. Chesapeake & O. Ry. Co., D.C.Va.1970, 320 F.Supp. 1248 (permitting college economics professor, who testified for plaintiff-widow on question of damages, to consider future trends in the purchasing power of money was not improper); Barnes v. Smith, C.A.N.M., 305 F.2d 226 (on the question of compensation for the death of a 17-year-old boy showing probable earning capacity of boy).

Idaho—Meissner v. Smith, 1972, 494 P.2d 567, 94 Idaho 563 (in action for wrongful death of 16-year-old youth who would likely have completed high school and college, who was diligent and hardworking, intended to go to college and was accumulating savings therefor, and whose parents possessed limited income potential directly tied to their physical labor and might well have received financial support in the future from the decedent, admitting testimony by an economist indicating probable future income of decedent based on certain assumptions regarding high school and college education and finding of probable or average disposable income was not an abuse of discretion).

Miss.—Mississippi Power & Light Co. v. Shepard, 1973, 285 So.2d 725 (testimony as to reasonable economic probabilities of a white male similar to deceased in age, education, and situation was inadmissible in death action as being too speculative to be of any real value).

Mont.—Putman v. Pollei, 1969, 457 P.2d 776, 153 Mont. 406 (testimony by university economics professor that projected lifetime earnings, discounted to present value, of hypothetical female physical education teacher in decedent's home town would approximate $175,000 was admissible for consideration by jury in determining loss of earning capacity of 19-year-old college sophomore physical education major who was killed); Krohmer v. Dahl, 402 P.2d 979, 145 Mont. 491 (testimony by qualified economist in wrongful death action concerning possible lifetime earnings of decedent who at time of his death was engaged in general studies at college).

Or.—Plourd v. Southern Pacific Transp. Co., 1973, 513 P.2d 1140, 266 Or. 666 (present value of what plaintiff contends to be a proper award for plaintiff's future wage loss or impairment of earning capacity may be most reliable method of presenting issues to jury).

To show force of collision

Police officer's testimony which identified portion of motion picture showing only vehicles involved in collision, exhibits describing location of vehicles and distances they traveled after impact, and diagram and chart made from measurements at the scene, and which concerned skidmarks, braking speeds, reaction time, and opinion about speeds of the vehicles prior to collision was admissible to show nature and extent of damage to the vehicles and to establish foundation for consulting engineer's testimony describing the forces which he believed had been applied to plaintiff's body, in case wherein defendants admitted liability but vigorously contended that plaintiff's injury was not serious. Howard v. Stoughton, 1967, 433 P. 2d 567, 199 Kan. 787.

Value "as a mother"

Iowa—Schmitt v. Jenkins Truck Lines, Inc., 1969, 170 N.W.2d 632, 46 A.L.R.3d 636 (did not err in permitting witness, qualified in field of home economics and experienced as a mother and acquainted with deceased mother and surviving children, to testify that deceased's value as a mother apart from her capacity of performing housework would be something approximating $200 a week).

Value of household services

U.S.—Har-Pen Truck Lines, Inc. v. Mills, C.A.Ga., 1967, 378 F.2d 705 (testimony of economics professor, as an expert on value of life of hypothetical housewife, placing monetary value on household services of such housewife was admissible in action by children for wrongful death of their mother); Schuler v. Berger, D.C.Pa., 1967, 275 F.Supp. 120, affirmed C.A., 395 F.2d 212 (permitting proprietor of an employment agency to testify to economic value of services rendered by a wife and a mother was not

§ **431.6** TRIAL EVIDENCE Ch. 431

automobile accident cases,[21] and in train-automobile collision cases,[22] and as to the issue of damages.[23]

improper on grounds that such evidence was not a proper subject for expert testimony).

Fla.—Atlantic Coast Line R. Co. v. Braz, 1966, 182 So.2d 491.

Md.—Sun Cab Co. v. Walston, 1972, 289 A.2d 804, 15 Md.App. 113, affirmed 298 A.2d 391, 267 Md. 559 (by operator of employment agency which placed domestic workers).

Minn.—Muckler v. Buchl, 1967, 150 N.W.2d 689, 276 Minn. 490 (as to reasonable worth and value of household services of kind performed by decedent before accident was not error, in view of witness' general experience, although witness had no experience specifically related to type of home maintained by decedent for her husband).

Mont.—Beebe v. Johnson, 1974, 526 P.2d 128, 165 Mont. 96 (concerning possible lifetime earnings of decedent who before death was rendering services to her husband's business and services as housewife, was not abuse of discretion where it presented to jury reasonable basis upon which to estimate with some degree of certainty probable future earnings of deceased).

Vehicle damage or value

Cal.—Naples Restaurant, Inc. v. Coberly Ford, 1968, 66 Cal.Rptr. 835, 259 Cal.App.2d 881 (active, experienced automobile salesman, when divorced from any pecuniary interest of his own, may be reliable source of information on market price, not only of automobiles he sells, but also of those with which his line directly competes).

Ga.—Martin v. Newton, 1973, 201 S.E.2d 31, 129 Ga.App. 735 (facts upon which insurance adjuster's opinion of damage to automobile was based sufficiently appeared where he had been assigned to handle loss, had photographed damage, and had reviewed itemized estimate of repairs with repair personnel); Central of Georgia Ry. Co. v. Little, 1972, 191 S.E.2d 105, 126 Ga.App. 502 (estimate made from photo); Wilkins v. Hester, 1969, 167 S.E.2d 167, 119 Ga.App. 389 (rental value of vehicle); Johnson v. Rooks, 157 S.E.2d 527, 116 Ga.App. 394 (testimony of plaintiff that he had owned automobile for six months, that he had purchased around 20 automobiles during his life, that he had repaired automobiles himself, and that he had repaired the automobile for damage to which he had instituted action was sufficient to admit his testimony as to value of and damage to automobile).

La.—Plotkin v. Martino, App.1966, 192 So.2d 381.

N.D.—Intlehouse v. Rose, 1967, 153 N.W.2d 810 (court did not abuse discretion in allowing automobile owner, who had testified as to his previous experience in appraising automobiles and his experience in teaching problems related thereto but who was not a mechanic or otherwise experienced in repairing automobiles, to testify as to his opinion that his automobile could not be restored to condition it was in immediately before accident).

Tex.—Classified Parking System v. Kirby, Civ.App.1974, 507 S.W.2d 586 (properly permitted to testify as to value, after theft, of damaged automobile, even though it had not been specifically shown that witness was familiar with the value of damaged vehicles); Emmco Ins. Co. v. Waters, 1967, 413 S.W.2d 484, error refused n. r. e. (salesman, saw wrecked truck).

21. Cal.—Sozzi v. Gull, 32 Cal.Rptr. 221, 218 Cal.App.2d 231 (refusal to

22. See note 22 on page 694.

23. See note 23 on page 695.

692

allow testimony to corroborate defendants' contention that further turning to avoid collision would have caused automobile to tip over and go out of control was not an abuse of discretion); Hunton v. California Portland Cement Co., 123 P.2d 947, 50 Cal.App.2d 684 (whether shoulder of a roadway was fit to carry a truck).

Colo.—McNelley v. Smith, 368 P.2d 555, 149 Colo. 177 (opinion as to cause of three-vehicle collision was properly rejected where was to be based solely upon photographs of vehicles taken at scene).

Ill.—Payne v. Noles, 1972, 283 N.E. 2d 329, 5 Ill.App.3d 433 (driver's witness' academic discussion of stability of motorcycle was objectionable on ground of improper foundation where opinion was not based on any physical facts or on particular motorcycle involved); Geisberger v. Quincy, 1972, 278 N.E.2d 404, 3 Ill.App.3d 437 (testimony by police officer that he determined point of impact from center of debris in street and that, based on damage to the vehicles, he "figured it was safe to assume that after they collided in the intersection, that they slid off, and the rear ends came together" was inadmissible as constituting mere speculation rather than expert opinion based on scientific principles).

N.H.—Adams v. Severance, 41 A.2d 233, 93 N.H. 289 (how rays of headlights will deflect on a foggy night.)

N.C.—Glenn v. Smith, 142 S.E.2d 596, 264 N.C. 706 (as to propensities of standard 1959 automobile to fishtail under certain conditions was properly excluded).

Ohio—Reigelsperger v. Pond, 210 N.E.2d 150, 3 Ohio App.2d 266 (the opinion of physician that truck driver was probably unconscious prior to collision with oncoming vehicle was not based on medical probability, and admission of opinion was prejudicial error, where physician made the collision the basis of his belief of unconsciousness).

Pa.—Springer v. George, 170 A.2d 367, 403 Pa. 563 (testimony that deceased, negligent motorist, had suffered a dizzy spell several months before and that coroner, who did not perform an autopsy, felt that motorist had fallen asleep or suffered a heart attack was inadmissible as pure conjecture).

Wash.—Litts v. Pierce County, 1973, 515 P.2d 526, 9 Wash.App. 843 (not abuse of discretion to exclude testimony of highway engineer, electrical engineer, practicing ophthalmologist and optometrist as to construction and illumination of highway intersection and as to driver's myopic condition interfering with depth perception at time of darkness where driver, whose passenger sought to recover from county for injuries sustained in collision occurring when driver was attempting left turn at allegedly negligently designed and illuminated intersection, was familiar with intersection, stated that he saw lights of oncoming car at all times prior to accident and that he saw and was familiar with the painted traffic control lines).

Cause of fire

Tex.—Bass v. General Motors Corp., Civ.App.1968, 447 S.W.2d 443, error ref. n. r. e.

Effects of alcohol

Absent evidence that experience gained by police officer in accident investigation and in testing percentages of alcohol in the blood were sufficient to endow him with medical expertise on effects of alcohol on human body, trial court did not abuse its discretion in excluding testimony of officer on effects of alcohol on judgment, coordination and reaction time of drivers. Staudinger v. Sooner Pipe & Supply Corp., 1971, 490 P.2d 619, 208 Kan. 100.

§ **431.6** TRIAL EVIDENCE Ch. 431

Meaning of company regulations

Purpose and meaning of regulations promulgated by Board of Education to govern operation of school buses used for transportation of school children was a judicial question, and refusal to admit testimony of State Board's Supervisor of Pupil Transportation concerning the purpose and meaning of the regulations, in action against school bus owner and operator and automobile driver for injuries sustained when pupil, who had just alighted from school bus, was struck by automobile while crossing road, was not error. Sammons v. Ridgeway, Del.1972, 293 A.2d 547.

Meaning of traffic sign

Expert testimony was not admissible as to meaning of a "No Parking Any Time" traffic control sign. Consolidated Mut. Ins. Co. v. Ramy, Fla.App.1970, 238 So.2d 431.

Necessity for warning sign

In absence of proof as to date of last re-surfacing of highway or condition of texture of highway at or near date of accident, no proper foundation was laid for expert opinion that "slippery when wet" sign should have been erected. Barrett v. State, 256 N.Y.S.2d 261, 22 A.D.2d 347.

Opinion re reaction upon passenger from braking

In prosecution for criminal negligence in operation of automobile resulting in death of bicyclist, wherein defendant contended that he was asleep in rear seat of automobile at time of accident, possible movements of rear seat occupant resulting from "hard" braking action and sudden brake release were not properly subject to expert opinion, and court erred in permitting official, who had long experience in connection with traffic matters, to testify to physical reaction automobile's movement at time of accident would produce upon person asleep in rear seat thereof. State v. Brady, 70 N.W.2d 449, 244 Minn. 455.

Where all but ultimate opinion permitted

In action by pedestrian for injuries sustained when struck by broken glass falling from the top of a light pole maintained by defendant power company and allegedly struck by codefendant's bus, exclusion of opinion on the cause of the breaking of the light globe on top of the pole was not prejudicial error where the expert was permitted to testify as to the properties of the cast-iron of which the light pole was made and to give his opinion as to the amount of force necessary to break the glassware on top of the pole and to state the amount of force which could be transmitted to the pole by striking a "No parking" sign attached to it. Boutang v. Twin City Motor Bus Co., 80 N.W.2d 30, 248 Minn. 240.

22. Ala.—Pollard v. Rogers, 173 So. 881, 234 Ala. 92 (that impact would cause certain damage if box car was moving).

Cal.—Guyer v. Pacific Electric Ry. Co., 75 P.2d 550, 24 Cal.App.2d 499 (wind so strong a witness could not hear train signal).

Me.—Johnson v. Maine Cent. R. Co., 38 A.2d 884, 141 Me. 38 (that the method of precaution at a railroad crossing was inadequate).

Dangerous character of railroad crossing

Ark.—St. Louis Southwestern Ry. Co. v. Jackson, 1967, 416 S.W.2d 273, 242 Ark. 858, appeal after remand 438 S.W.2d 41, 246 Ark. 268 (testimony that railroad crossing was abnormally dangerous, based on submitted facts such as type of highway, volume of traffic, signs and obstructions to view, and position of sun, was inadmissible, and its admission was prejudicial error).

Fla.—Seaboard Coast Line R. Co. v. Hill, App.1971, 250 So.2d 311, certiorari discharged Sup., 270 So. 2d 359 (that crossing was dangerous because it lacked adequate warning devices to have alerted a driver in decedent's position was a conclusion as to a matter within realm of a jury's ordinary experience and understanding and, therefore, admission of such testimony was erroneous but such error was harmless where there was substantial nonopinion testimony in record which would support conclusion that train on crossing presented a dangerous condition).

Ky.—Hargadon v. Louisville & N. R. Co., 1963, 375 S.W.2d 834 (and more dangerous than normal).

Miss.—Columbus & G. R. Co. v. Robinson, 1967, 198 So. 749, 189 Miss. 675.

23. Reference to treatise

Where witness, in suit against driver and driver's insurer for damages relating to stillbirth of plaintiff's child allegedly caused by accident which occurred when defendant's automobile left highway, crossed shoulder of road and struck utility pole, causing wire on pole to snap, was not qualified to answer questions regarding effect of electric shock on fetus because he had no personal experience on the subject, exclusion of expert's reference to and explanation of medical article, which itself was inadmissible as hearsay, was not abuse of discretion. Jennings v. Allstate Ins. Co., La. App.1973, 273 So.2d 534.

Chapter 432

SCIENTIFIC EVIDENCE

Table of Sections

Sec.
432.1 Scientific Tests—In General.
432.2 ——— Blood Tests.

§ 432.1 Scientific Tests—In General

Library References:
C.J.S. Evidence §§ 550, 586 et seq.
West's Key No. Digests, Evidence ⊂⊃150, 557.

The results of a scientific test, which is generally accepted in the scientific community,[1] is competent evidence if the essential conditions are sufficiently controlled to render the results probative.[2]

1. **Mo.**—Berry v. Harmon, 329 S.W.2d 784 (introduction of electroencephalogram and use by doctor to illustrate his findings concerning abnormal brain condition).

   Drunkometer
   Statute providing that results of test given by Harger Drunkometer or other similar device approved by American Medical Association and National Safety Council shall be received in evidence when it is shown that test is fairly administered constitutes legislative approval of Harger Drunkometer as device for administration of breath tests in connection with determination of amount of alcohol in person's blood, and no other approval of such device is required. NDCC 39–20–06. McDonald v. Ferguson, N.D., 129 N.W.2d 348.

   Polygraph
   N.M.—In re Moyer, 421 P.2d 781, 77 N.M. 253 (that Legislature by statute saw fit to license and regulate polygraphy did not raise profession or occupation to such scientific dignity as would justify Supreme Court's recognition of results of polygraph tests as admissible evidence).

   Tex.—Skillern & Sons, Inc. v. Stewart, Civ.App., 379 S.W.2d 687 (results of lie detector test inadmissible in civil case).

2. **Ill.**—Mack v. Davis, 221 N.E.2d 121, 76 Ill.App. 88 (where after four years of use and repair to steering mechanism, steering and brakes of tractor from which inexperienced 17-year-old farm employee fell were tested, essential conditions were not same or sufficiently similar to render results of test of probative value).

   Mich.—Taylor v. Murphy, 149 N.W. 2d 210, 6 Mich.App. 398; Bauer v. Veith, 130 N.W.2d 897, 374 Mich. 1 (steps in keeping and transporting specimen were not shown, and presumptions that official duty was properly performed and that public records are correct will not supply missing links in chain of evidence).

Equipment used in such tests must be shown to be accurate,[3] and the person performing the test must be shown to be qualified to perform the test.[4]

Psychological tests

That boy who was fourteen years and four days old when injured might have purposely given wrong answers to intelligence tests administered by psychologist and that the lower the boy scored thereon the better was his chance of being found free from contributory negligence did not make the tests inadmissible but only went to their weight. Dickeson v. Baltimore & O. C. T. R. Co., 220 N.E.2d 43, 73 Ill.App.2d 5.

Urine test

Neb.—Raskey v. Hulewicz, 1970, 177 N.W.2d 744, 185 Neb. 608 (authenticity of sample must be unequivocally established).

3. Radar device

Ky.—Honeycutt v. Com., 408 S.W.2d 421 (will treat as sufficient evidence of accuracy of radar device for measuring speed uncontested testimony that instrument was tested within few hours of its specific use, and found to be accurate, by use of calibrated tuning fork and by comparison with speedometer of another vehicle driven through radar field).

Mo.—Kansas City v. Hill, 1969, 442 S.W.2d 89.

Speedometer accuracy

Pa.—Com. v. Spangler, Com.Pl., 47 West. 121 (certificate required as to timely testing of speedometer of patrol vehicle).

Tactograph

Ark.—Bell v. Kroger Co., 323 S.W. 2d 424, 230 Ark. 384, 73 A.L.R.2d 1019 (admission of a "Tactograph" was error where there was insufficient proof of accuracy of such Tactograph which had been placed on truck some three years prior to collision).

4. Ala.—Graves v. Wildsmith, 177 So.2d 448, 278 Ala. 228 (did not err in refusing to permit motorcyclist and his father to show inaccuracy of speedometer on motorbike by merely showing result of tests conducted by young boys, without some showing of boys' ability to properly conduct tests and of accuracy of automobile's speedometer used in test).

Breathalyzer

N.Y.—Roy v. Reid, 1972, 329 N.Y.S. 2d 417, 38 A.D.2d 717 (it should at least be established that test was given by qualified operator in proper manner, that machine was in good working order and that chemicals employed were of correct kind and in proper proportions).

Tire quality control tests

N.C.—Thompson Apex Co. v. Murray Tire Service, Inc., 1969, 166 S.E. 2d 864, 4 N.C.App. 402 (in view of lack of evidence as to who made quality control tests performed on rubber shipped by manufacturer to tire retreader, as to whether tests were made by a person authorized to make them, and as to how records of tests were made, adequate foundation for admission of records of tests was not laid).

§ 432.2 Scientific Tests—Blood Tests

After proper identification of the blood sample,[5] proof that the test operator was qualified,[6] and after showing sufficient con-

---

5. **Cal.**—McGowan v. City of Los Angeles, 223 P.2d 862, 100 Cal. App.2d 386, 21 A.L.R.2d 1206 (exclusion of record of coroner showing determination that blood, wholly unidentified, showed intoxication was proper).

La.—Foy v. Ed Taussig, Inc., App. 1969, 220 So.2d 229, application denied 222 So.2d 884, 254 La. 135, 222 So.2d 885, 254 La. 139, certiorari denied 90 S.Ct. 428, 396 U.S. 957, 24 L.Ed.2d 421.

Va.—Neblett v. Hunter, 150 S.E.2d 115, 207 Va. 335.

Identification held sufficient

Cal.—Wagner v. Osborn, 37 Cal. Rptr. 27, 225 Cal.App.2d 370 (even though deputy coroner who took blood specimen from deceased host's body lacked personal knowledge of host's identity, where host was only person killed, and chain of possession of specimen was substantially established).

Ga.—Interstate Life & Acc. Ins. Co. v. Whitlock, 144 S.E.2d 532, 112 Ga.App. 212 (showing that police officer identified body at morgue as that of insured by personal papers and driver's license, that medical examiner took sample from body and sealed, labeled and packaged sample, and that officer carried sealed package labeled with decedent's name to state crime laboratory where toxicologist ran routine alcohol test and issued routine report, provided sufficient foundation).

Ind.—Brattain v. Herron, 1974, 309 N.E.2d 150, —— Ind.App. —— (was in continuous custody of police); Orr v. Econo-Car of Indianapolis, Inc., 1971, 276 N.E.2d 524, 150 Ind. App. 411 (proper chain of identification was established with respect to samples which were sent by coroner to state police laboratory for analysis of alcohol content, despite contention that there was no evidence as to the whereabouts of the specimens for a period of four days, where the evidence showed that the specimens were in the possession of the United States mail during the four days in question and was sufficient to identify the specimens mailed as being the same ones received; it was not necessary to show and identify each mail handler who had possession of the specimens).

Iowa—Rigby v. Eastman, 1974, 217 N.W.2d 604 (where physician, lab technician and medical technologist related their custody of specimen and the trial court found that it was more reasonable on record to say that there was no reasonable possibility of tampering by switchboard operators who had access to keys to the locked box in which the specimen was kept, there was no gap in the chain of custody because the switchboard operators were not called as witnesses).

Okl.—Perry v. City of Oklahoma City, 1970, 470 P.2d 974 (accounted for from time drawn through constant possession by police officer upon his person or in refrigerator of his residence until he delivered it to chemist, and possession by chemist until he ran test and made his report).

Wis.—Luedtke v. Shedivy, 1971, 186 N.W.2d 220, 51 Wis.2d 110 (where coroner mailed vial containing sample and labeled with name and address of plaintiff's decedent to division of motor vehicles in

6. See note 6 on page 699.

trol of test conditions,[7] test results as to liquor content in blood are admissible.[8]

Madison and chemist from division of motor vehicles in Madison received sample the following day, foundation was not insufficient on theory that there was no evidence to show delivery of sample to Madison and no evidence as to where the sample was from the time it was taken until the time the chemist analyzed it).

Foundation lacking

R.I.—Bruyere v. Castellucci, 200 A. 2d 226, —— R.I. —— (that county medical examiner had ordered taking of specimen of deceased driver did not make testimony concerning alcoholic content of specimen which bore label with same last name as deceased but which was taken at same morgue as that to which body of deceased's wife had been taken admissible on theory that presumption of regularity had arisen).

S.C.—Benton v. Pellum, 1957, 100 S.E.2d 534, 232 S.C. 26.

Waiver

Evidence of alcohol test analysis was properly admitted, in suit to recover proceeds of accidental death life policy on motorist, even though there was no positive proof that sample used in test was taken from remains of deceased, where by questions put by counsel to pathologist, plaintiff conceded that sample was that of her deceased husband. Romero v. Volunteer State Life Ins. Co., 1970, 88 Cal.Rptr. 820, 10 Cal. App.3d 571.

6. **Tex.**—Hartman v. Harder, 322 S.W.2d 555 (where did not show that either Chief of Identification and Criminal Records Division of the State Department of Public Safety, or laboratory manager who signed his name to a letter stating that, based on their examination of a specimen of a decedent's blood, decedent was intoxicated at time specimen was taken, were chemists, or that either of them were specialists in determining percentage of alcohol in a sample).

As to implied consent procedures

Iowa—Severson v. Sueppel, 1967, 152 N.W.2d 281, 260 Iowa 1169 (deputy sheriff of 3 years, and attended State Sheriffs School each winter).

Mortician

Mich.—Gard v. Michigan Produce Haulers, 1970, 174 N.W.2d 73, 20 Mich.App. 402 (sample taken by mortician from plaintiff's decedent shortly after fatal collision at request of a police officer did not have inherent reliability essential, owing to mortician's lack of training and experience in properly taking and preserving blood components).

Physician or nurse to take sample

Ark.—Simolin v. Wilson, 1972, 487 S.W.2d 603, 253 Ark. 545 (statutory requirement that only physician or registered nurse may withdraw blood for purpose of determining alcoholic content).

7. **U.S.**—Kuklis v. Hancock, D.C. Fla.1969, 304 F.Supp. 336, affirmed C.A., 428 F.2d 608.

Foundation held sufficient

U.S.—Jacobsen v. International Transport Inc., C.A.Iowa 1968, 391 F.2d 49, certiorari denied 89 S.Ct. 105, 393 U.S. 833, 21 L.Ed.2d 104 (report of medical examiner, who withdrew sample from decedent's cadaver, was admissible, both under statute providing that reports of a medical examiner's autopsies shall be received as evidence in any court, and under implied con-

8. See note 8 on page 700.

sent statute, notwithstanding fact that, with respect to admissibility under latter statute, needle used to extract blood was not in factory wrapped package and sample was not taken at written request of a peace officer).

Ga.—Elliott v. Leavitt, 1970, 178 S.E.2d 268, 122 Ga.App. 622 (established chain of custody including observation of taking of sample by deputy sheriff and sheriff's mailing of sample to director of state crime laboratory for blood alcohol analysis, and sheriff's receipt, from state crime laboratory, of certified copies of reports of state crime laboratory); Interstate Life & Acc. Ins. Co. v. Whitlock, 1965, 144 S.E.2d 532, 112 Ga.App. 212 (stated did not recall ever departing from established routine).

La.—Young v. All Am. Assur. Co., App.1971, 243 So.2d 894, writ refused 246 So.2d 197, 258 La. 349.

N.D.—Wanna v. Miller, 136 N.W.2d 563 (sufficient foundation existed in view of voluntary permission for extraction of the blood and proper safeguards taken in extraction, marking, handling, mailing, receiving, and analyzing the blood).

Wash.—Hoffman v. Tracy, 406 P.2d 323, 67 Wash.2d 31 (under testimony showing that while instrument used to extract blood from deceased driver had been the same instrument as used in embalming procedures, involving use of formaldehyde, but that it had been cleaned in customary manner prior to extracting blood, there was a prima facie case that test was reliable, notwithstanding other testimony that manner of cleaning was not reliable and that high alcoholic content shown by test should have rendered subject unable to operate motor vehicle at all).

Foundation lacking

U.S.—Barnes v. Smith, C.A.N.M., 305 F.2d 226 (chemical analysis of sample withdrawn from deceased motorist indicating an alcohol content nearly three times that sufficient under accepted standards to produce drunkenness was properly excluded for lack of a proper foundation when blood was withdrawn by an embalmer under conditions indicating probability of lack of chemical purity); Thomas v. Martin, D.C.Va.1961, 202 F.Supp. 540.

Ill.—Watson v. Fischbach, 1972, 284 N.E.2d 720, 6 Ill.App.3d 166, reversed on other grounds 301 N.E. 2d 303, 54 Ill.2d 498 (results of state toxicology laboratory's postmortem analysis of blood was properly excluded, where plaintiff failed to show that all available records with regard to sample had been introduced and failed to prove that customary routines and procedures in laboratory were processes commonly accepted by the medical profession).

N.Y.—Durham v. Melly, 1961, 221 N.Y.S.2d 366, 14 A.D.2d 389.

8. Ariz.—Kemp v. Pinal County, 1968, 442 P.2d 864, 8 Ariz.App. 41, appeal after remand 474 P.2d 840, 13 Ariz.App. 121.

Ill.—French v. City of Springfield, 1972, 283 N.E.2d 18, 5 Ill.App.3d 368.

Iowa.—State v. Charlson, 1967, 154 N.W.2d 829, 261 Iowa 497 (party seeking to introduce such evidence must lay a foundation showing that the specimen was taken by a duly authorized person using proper sterile equipment, that it was properly labeled and preserved, that its care and transportation were proper, and also the identity of persons processing it); Lessenhop v. Norton, 1967, 153 N.W.2d 107, 261 Iowa 44 (blood test analysis may not be introduced in evidence until party seeking introduction shows (1) that blood was timely taken, (2) from particular identified body, (3) by authorized licensed physician, medical technologist, or registered nurse designated by licensed physician, (4) that instruments used were sterile, (5) that blood taken was properly preserved or kept, (6) and labeled, (7) and if transported or sent, the method and procedures used therein, (8) method and procedures used in conducting the test, and (9) identity of person or persons under whose supervision tests were conducted).

Mo.—Bean v. Riddle, 1968, 423 S.W. 2d 709, quoting 32 C.J.S. Evidence § 607 (that county coroner withdrew sample from body of decedent and specimen was placed in glass bottle that could be sealed and had nothing in it before and that sample was given to sheriff and in turn to highway patrol officers who transferred it to patrol headquarters where chemist tested the specimen for presence of formaldehyde, acetone and alcohol was sufficient basis for admission of chemist's analysis).

N.J.—Jones v. Strelecki, 1967, 231 A. 2d 558, 49 N.J. 513.

N.C.—Wood v. Brown, 1973, 201 S. E.2d 225, 20 N.C.App. 307, appeal after remand 212 S.E.2d 690 (properly admitted where the sample was taken approximately three hours after the collision, funeral director had sufficient skill to extract the sample and no substance was administered to the deceased at emergency room prior to death that would increase the blood alcohol content); McNeil v. Williams, 1972, 191 S.E.2d 916, 16 N.C.App. 322 (toxicologist testified that in his opinion a person whose blood showed .17% of alcohol was definitely under the influence of alcohol).

Wash.—Zenith Transport, Limited v. Bellingham Nat. Bank, 1964, 395 P.2d 498, 64 Wash.2d 967 (not limited to criminal cases, under statute permitting coroner to retain specimen).

Contra

Refusal to receive evidence, in action against town arising out of death of motorcyclist, of test results relating to alcoholic content of blood and urine of motorcyclist which were obtained during an autopsy, was proper under statute where, although at time the tests were made the results would have been admissible, at time of trial such was not the case, and where town had no vested right in the former rule of evidence. Cook v. Town of Nassau, Rensselaer County, 1972, 338 N.Y.S.2d 842, 40 A.D.2d 1050, order affirmed 347 N.Y.S.2d 165, 33 N.Y.2d 7, 300 N.E.2d 706.

Held inadmissible

Mont.—Benner v. B. F. Goodrich Co., 1967, 430 P.2d 648, 150 Mont. 97 (testimony disclosed that it was improper to admit results of sample tests, but such admission did not constitute reversible error where there was sufficient testimony concerning drinking to reduce effect of admission of test results).

Post-mortem sampling

U.S.—Ravellette v. Smith, C.A.Ind. 1962, 300 F.2d 854.

Ariz.—Fitzgerald v. Maricopa County, 1971, 480 P.2d 385, 14 Ariz.App. 48 (witness who had in past conducted numerous experiments with blood taken from deceased individuals and tested for period of time to determine if there was significant change in blood alcohol content following death was qualified to express an opinion on relationship between post-mortem and premortem blood alcohol content of deceased driver's blood).

Ky.—Webb v. Stone, 1969, 445 S.W. 2d 842 (not disqualified because taken within two hours after death, in absence of proof that content changes so as to render unreliable).

§ 432.2   TRIAL EVIDENCE   Ch. 432

Statute not applicable on issue of general acceptance

Statute dealing with chemical analysis to determine percentage of alcohol in blood of motorist charged with driving while under influence of intoxicating liquor was not applicable, in action for death of motorist, to laboratory report showing amounts of alcohol in blood and brain tissues of motorist. N.J.S.A. 39:4–50, 50.1. Carroll v. Houtz, 225 A.2d 584, 93 N.J.Super. 215.

Statutory consent beyond death

Even though a driver suspected of having been intoxicated is dead and beyond the pale of prosecution, it remains within legitimate scope of investigating law enforcement officer's inquiry to seek out the cause of death, and statute providing that operator of motor vehicle is deemed to have given consent to blood test if arrested and that consent is not withdrawn by death was not enacted with intention of conditioning the taking of a blood sample from a deceased person upon his having been placed under arrest before death. Woosley v. Central Uniform Rental, Ky.1971, 463 S.W.2d 345.

Chapter 433

PROOF OF WRITINGS

Table of Sections

Sec.
433.1 Authentication of Writings.
433.2 "Best Evidence" Rule.

§ 433.1 Authentication of Writings

Library References:
C.J.S. Evidence § 634 et seq.
West's Key No. Digests, Evidence ⚖︎366 et seq.

Documentary evidence, to be admissible, must be properly authenticated.[1]

1. U.S.—Hommel v. Jackson-Atlantic, Inc., C.A.Ala.1971, 438 F.2d 307 (a manual on uniform traffic control devices for streets and highways, which was published by United States Department of Commerce, Bureau of Public Roads, offered to show that it was the suggested and adopted regulation for traffic control signs in Alabama, was not properly authenticated); Masterson v. Pennsylvania R. Co., C.A.Pa., 182 F.2d 793 (letters written by physicians).

Alaska.—Zerbinos v. Lewis, 394 P.2d 886 (receipts which were identified by overtaking driver involved in rear-end collision allegedly caused by sudden mechanical brake failure and which purportedly were issued to her for money paid for services rendered on the automobile, including brake adjustment and brake fluid, about two months prior to accident were admissible over objection no proper foundation had been laid).

Cal.—Lewis v. Western Truck Line, 1941, 112 P.2d 747, 44 Cal.App.2d 455.

Ga.—Cobb v. State, 152 S.E.2d 403, 222 Ga. 733 (notes from which witness swore, concerning defendant's statements, were sufficiently authenticated where witness testified that notes were his own in his own handwriting and initialed by him and others, and another person traced whereabouts of notes from time they were made until they were returned to witness); Cotton States Mut. Ins. Co. v. Clark, 151 S.E.2d 780, 114 Ga.App. 439 (letter received by insured and purported endorsement to his policy were admissible in action against insurer where agent and adjuster testified that they were familiar with letter and agent testified to familiarity with purported endorsement, and letter was on insurer's letterhead and purported endorsement was on insurer's form).

Ill.—Gauger v. Mills, 90 N.E.2d 790, 340 Ill.App. 1 (time cards).

La.—Corkern v. Main Ins. Co., Chicago, Ill., 1972, 268 So.2d 138, writ not considered 268 So.2d 673, 263 La. 608 (copy of policy endorsement).

§ 433.1 TRIAL EVIDENCE Ch. 433

Mich.—Brydges v. Home for the Aged, 129 N.W.2d 869, 373 Mich. 408 (a letter identified as being in handwriting of woman was properly received by trial judge).

Mo.—Kern v. Danbury, 1971, 471 S.W.2d 489 (no proof as to signature on alleged statement).

Neb.—Gorman v. Bratka, 300 N.W. 807, 140 Neb. 575 (where a party to a suit makes a written statement which is prepared by a third person and the party denies the authenticity and correctness of the statement, the person preparing the statement or some one cognizant with the facts should be called to lay a proper foundation for its admission in evidence).

N.Y.—Jackson v. Dickman, 1939, 9 N.Y.S.2d 688, 256 App.Div. 925, reargument denied 11 N.Y.S.2d 557, 256 App.Div. 1003 (stenographer minutes).

N.C.—Walton v. Cagle, 152 S.E.2d 312, 269 N.C. 177.

Pa.—Lemmon v. Bufalino, 205 A.2d 680, 204 Pa.Super. 481 (defendants were properly required to call insurance adjuster as their witness before admission of plaintiff's written statement to adjuster, where plaintiff denied material portions of statement and testified that she had not read it before signing it).

Tex.—Hinrichs v. Texas & N. O. R. Co., Civ.App., 153 S.W.2d 859, error refused for want of merit (railroad could not corroborate testimony of its agent by introducing in evidence unsigned statement written by agent at time of conversation with motorist and wife); Standard Paving Co. v. Pyle, Civ. App., 131 S.W.2d 200.

Authenticity admitted

U.S.—Brown v. Edwards, D.C.Pa., 258 F.Supp. 696 (under Pennsylvania law it is unnecessary to call scrivener to stand where a party admits that document in question is his statement, that he signed it, and, initially, that it is correct).

Ind.—Miller v. Alvey, App., 194 N.E. 2d 747, superseded 207 N.E.2d 633 (passenger, by admitting that signature on statement was her own, but failing to recall when, or that she had signed the statement, sufficiently identified such statement to permit it to be introduced without laying a further foundation).

Pa.—Geelen v. Pennsylvania R. Co., 161 A.2d 595, 400 Pa. 240 (typewritten statement where widow testified that signature was hers and did not deny that facts included in statement were true or correct).

R.I.—Campbell v. Di Iorio, 156 A.2d 79, 90 R.I. 141 (typewritten statement admittedly signed by wife, who claimed that it was obtained by a man who arrived at her home at dinner hour when she was unable to pause from her work to read it thoroughly, was properly admitted and accuracy of statement and failure of defendant to produce the man who obtained the statement were matters to be considered by the jury in giving weight to the document).

Wis.—Mack v. Decker, 128 N.W.2d 455, 24 Wis.2d 219 (testimony of a witness that two signatures on a statement were signatures of the witness constituted sufficient authentication to entitle the statement to be admitted, and her testimony that she could not recall giving or reading statement, and conflicting evidence as to whether she was under sedatives at time she signed it, went to the weight to be accorded the statement, and not to its admissibility); Jensen v. Heritage Mut. Ins. Co., 127 N.W.2d 228, 23 Wis.2d 344 (sufficient authentication to justify its admission, and then witness may offer explanation as to why he should not be bound by statement).

Carbon copy of vehicle registration

Court properly refused to admit in evidence duplicate registration certificates for the tractor trailer purporting to show that tractor trailer was registered in foreign state in the name of the alleged owner, where duplicate registration certificates appeared to be carbon copies bearing no seal or owner's signature, and alleged owner was not called on to produce original instruments for admission. Hill v. Moore, Tex.Civ.App., 278 S.W.2d 472.

Circumstantial proof

Ga.—Cotton States Mut. Ins. Co. v. Clark, 151 S.E.2d 780, 114 Ga.App. 439 (letter received through mails is not admissible when offered by recipient, without proof of its authenticity, but proof of its execution may be shown by circumstantial evidence).

Judicial notice declined

Wash.—Sadler v. Wagner, 1971, 486 P.2d 330, 5 Wash.App. 77 (did not abuse discretion in refusing to admit or take judicial notice of mathematical table designated "Present Value of $1" for various future due dates where the court was not advised of the identity, validity or use of the table other than statement of counsel that such tables could be found in any standard textbook).

Letters received in reply

Dist.Col.—Namerdy v. Generalcar, App.1966, 217 A.2d 109.

Where letter which had been sent to owner and driver to inquire as to name of their public liability insurance carrier was identified and introduced in evidence in action under uninsured motorist provision of motorist's policy, attorney who sent letter identified reply letter which was written by owner of Southbound vehicle and which stated that there was no liability insurance and attorney testified that he had received reply letter through mails in response to his letter of inquiry, reply letter was properly authenticated. Campbell v. American Home Assur. Co., 1972, 258 So.2d 81, 260 La. 1047, on remand 264 So.2d 701.

Multiple page document

Signature on second page of document which was characterized as a continuous integrated two-page statement was insufficient to warrant admission of entire statement, where plaintiff denied that initials appearing on page one were his, defendant did not otherwise prove that such initials were plaintiff's and defendant failed to call the scrivener who was in court. Grossman v. U. S. Slicing Mach. Co., C.A.Pa., 365 F.2d 687.

Party produced document

Where a party at trial calls for a document from his opponent and in response to the call receives it and examines it, the document may be put in evidence by the opponent, even though it would have been incompetent if it had not been called for and examined and the application of the rule is not dependent upon notice to produce before trial. Leonard v. Taylor, 53 N.E.2d 705, 315 Mass. 580, 151 A.L.R. 1002.

Tape recording

Ind.—Gibbs v. Miller, App.1972, 283 N.E.2d 592 (alleged telephone call, not authenticated).

Or.—Kruse v. Coos Head Timber Co., 1967, 432 P.2d 1009, 248 Or. 294 (neither a purported electronic dictaphone recording of a telephone conversation nor a typewritten transcription of such recording was admissible where no proof was presented showing that the tape accurately recorded the conversation).

Transcript of testimony at prior hearing

Permitting defense counsel to read to jury court reporter's transcript of testimony plaintiff had previously

§ 433.1   TRIAL EVIDENCE   Ch. 433

However, the federal rules [2] and rules of evidence of certain states [3] have provisions intended to liberalize the proof requirements.

The federal rules [4] and the rules of certain states,[5] as to documents attested to by a subscribing witness, obviate the need to produce the subscribing witness.

Public records

Public records are admissible when properly certified,[6] or otherwise authenticated.[7]

given at workmen's compensation hearing was error in absence of showing that plaintiff's counsel had agreed that transcript was admissible without authentication, and error required reversal in view of verdict that plaintiff take nothing. DeLong v. Williams, Fla.App.1970, 232 So.2d 246.

Unverified certificate of title

Automobile certificate of title was properly admitted although purported signature of seller had not been sworn to before notary. Hardware Mut. Cas. Co. v. Baker, Okl.1968, 445 P.2d 800.

2.—Federal Rules of Evidence §§ 901, et seq., 1005, 28 U.S.C.A.

3. Cal.—West's Ann.Calif.Evid. Code, § 1400 et seq.; § 1530 et seq.

Fla.—Florida Evidence Code § 90.901 et seq.; § 90.955.

Kan.—Kansas Code of Civil Procedure § 60–464 et seq.

Me.—Maine Rules of Evidence § 901 et seq.; § 1005.

Neb.—Nebraska Rules of Evidence § 901 et seq.; § 1005.

Nev.—N.R.S. 52.015 et seq.; 52.625.

N.J.—New Jersey Evidence Rules 67 et seq.

N.M.—New Mexico Rules of Evidence § 901 et seq.; § 1005.

Utah.—Utah Rules of Evidence § 67 et seq.

Wis.—Wisconsin Rules of Evidence § 909.01 et seq.; § 910.05.

4.—Federal Rules of Evidence § 903, 28 U.S.C.A. (unless deemed required by the laws of a jurisdiction whose laws govern the validity of the writing).

5. Cal.—West's Ann.Calif.Evid. Code, § 1411.

Fla.—Florida Evidence Code § 90.903.

Kan.—Kansas Code of Civil Procedure § 60–468.

Me.—Maine Rules of Evidence § 903.

Neb.—Nebraska Rules of Evidence § 903.

Nev.—N.R.S. 52.175.

N.J.—New Jersey Evidence Rule 71.

N.M.—New Mexico Rules of Evidence § 903.

N.Y.—New York CPLR Rule 4537.

Wis.—Wisconsin Rules of Evidence § 909.03.

6. Ga.—Western & Atlantic R. R. v. Swigert, 195 S.E. 230, 57 Ga. App. 274 (certified copy of the minutes of the mayor and board of aldermen of a city showing the adoption of a motion to increase the speed limit for vehicles).

Mo.—Brown v. Alton R. Co., 151 S. W.2d 727, 236 Mo.App. 26 (speed ordinance, duly certified by city

7. See note 7 on page 707.

clerk, under seal, as being a true copy of ordinance of record and on file in his office).

Tex.—Blaugrund v. Gish, Civ.App., 179 S.W.2d 257, affirmed 179 S. W.2d 266, 142 Tex. 379 (certified copy of report of physical examination of plaintiff in connection with his induction into the army would be admissible).

Accident report

Idaho.—Kleinschmidt v. Scribner, 30 P.2d 362, 54 Idaho 185 (not certified by legal keeper of record, but by another).

Blood test report

Ga.—Elliott v. Leavitt, 1970, 178 S.E. 2d 268, 122 Ga.App. 622.

Highway contract

In suit for damages sustained while driving at night on a highway which defendant was under contract to repair, admission in evidence of an instrument purporting to be certified copy of contract between defendant and state highway commission for construction of that part of highway on which accident happened was error, where document was not certified to by any person or public officer and custodian of records as provided by statute. Standard Paving Co. v. Pyle, Tex. Civ.App., 131 S.W.2d 200.

7. U.S.—Minneshaha County, S. D. v. Kelley, C.C.A.S.D., 150 F.2d 356 (weather bureau records).

Fla.—Economy Cabs v. Kirkland, 174 So. 222, 127 Fla. 867, affirmed 176 So. 151, 129 Fla. 309 (copy of a certificate of incorporation).

Ga.—Smith v. Smith, 152 S.E.2d 560, 222 Ga. 694 (duly authenticated copies of tax records are admissible over the objection that there was no evidence that taxpayer signed them).

Mass.—Canney v. Carrier, 130 N.E. 2d 879, 333 Mass. 382 (where plaintiff's counsel sought to prove ownership of vehicle which struck plaintiff by letter which he purportedly received from State Registry of Motor Vehicles, answering his questions relating to ownership of certain vehicle, since the letter was not among records which registrar was required to keep by statute, the letter was not admissible as a public record).

Minn.—Hector Const. Co. v. Butler, 260 N.W. 496, 194 Minn. 310 (corporation's report to workmen's compensation insurer in which it stated that truck driver was employee of corporation).

N.Y.—Yeargans v. Yeargans, 265 N.Y.S.2d 562, 24 A.D.2d 280.

N.C.—McClamroch v. Colonial Ice Co., 6 S.E.2d 850, 217 N.C. 106.

Tex.—Texas Dept. of Public Safety v. Gentry, 386 S.W.2d 758 (authenticated copies of notices of conviction for moving traffic violations).

Va.—Hague v. Valentine, 28 S.E.2d 720, 182 Va. 256 (certificate of title properly excluded where it did not meet statutory requirements as to proper authentication).

Wash.—Tire Towne, Inc. v. G & L Service Co., 1973, 518 P.2d 240, 10 Wash.App. 184 (reliability of public record sought to be introduced as exception to hearsay rule is based upon assumption that it has been prepared by public official who had a duty to make it, and where the official has neither prepared the document nor from first-hand knowledge can authenticate signature of its preparer, a proper foundation for its admissibility has not been laid).

Accident report

U.S.—Magee v. McNany, D.C.Pa.1951, 95 F.Supp. 675 (driver admitted own signature).

Minn.—Beckman v. Schroeder, 1947, 28 N.W.2d 629, 224 Minn. 370.

§ 433.1   TRIAL EVIDENCE   Ch. 433

The federal rule, and the rule of certain states, permits proof of a public record, or a document authorized to be recorded or filed, by introduction of a copy certified to be correct by a witness who had compared it to the original; and also by still other evidence of the contents where the original or copy can not be produced by the exercise of due diligence.[8]

Business records [9]

Business or "shop" records are admissible after proper identification.[10] However, a greater amount of proof is necessary to

N.Y.—Welde v. Wolfson, 1969, 302 N.Y.S.2d 906, 32 A.D.2d 973 (motor vehicle accident report is "official record" within CPLR rule relating to authentication of official record of court or government office in United States); Yeargans v. Yeargans, 265 N.Y.S.2d 562, 24 A.D.2d 280 (receiving police report which was made by officer of another state and contained no indication, except by possible inference, as to source of information recorded was prejudicial error, where officer who made report was not called to testify and report was admitted prior to reading of that portion of defendant's deposition in which she stated that she had given information appearing in report).

W.Va.—Carnahan v. Monroe, 1936, 185 S.E. 234, 117 W.Va. 279.

8. Federal Rules of Evidence § 1005, 28 U.S.C.A.

Cal.—West's Ann.Calif.Evid.Code, §§ 1530 et seq.

Fla.—Florida Evidence Code § 90.955.

Me.—Maine Rules of Evidence § 1005.

Neb.—Nebraska Rules of Evidence § 1005.

Nev.—N.R.S. 52.625.

N.M.—New Mexico Rules of Evidence § 1005.

Wis.—Wisconsin Rules of Evidence § 910.05.

9. For discussion of status within an exception to the hearsay rule, see § 434.10, § 434.11.

10. Mo.—Rossomanno v. Laclede Cab Co., 328 S.W.2d 677 (doctor's records); LeGrand v. U-Drive-It Co., 247 S.W.2d 706 (records as to time rented cars were returned).

N.Y.—Jezowski v. Beach, 1968, 298 N.Y.S.2d 360, 59 Misc.2d 224 (doctor's widow identified handwriting).

Wash.—Choate v. Robertson, 195 P. 2d 630, 31 Wash.2d 118.

Army medical records

Army medical records which custodian testified from his personal experience consisted of entries that had been made by medical officer were admissible under Uniform Business Records as Evidence Act, but even if there was not sufficient proof of personal knowledge under such Act, the entries were admissible under the Federal Official Records Act on the testimony of custodian describing the manner in which the records were prepared. Fauceglia v. Harry, 185 A.2d 598, 409 Pa. 755.

But see

In action against city for accident which occurred at location of defective traffic signal, erroneous admission of extract from accident report, "The Mike Room received a call from Motor Unit 203–M at 7:23 a. m., regarding condition of this signal, which in turn relayed information to TSR unit" was sufficient to justify granting of new trial. Hoel v. City of Los Angeles, 288 P.2d 989, 136 Cal.App.2d 295.

Contra

Investigative file, which was made up of reports by various individuals who had participated in the investigation of accident, was not admissible, upon testimony of police officers who had refreshed their recollection from file, and its admission, as well as fact that investigative file found its way into jury room constituted prejudicial error. Dragash v. Western Pac. R. Co., 326 P.2d 649, 161 Cal.App.2d 233.

Employment record

U.S.—Landon v. U. S., C.A.N.Y., 197 F.2d 128 (plaintiff's treatment record kept by medical department of plaintiff's employer and identified by employer's doctor as record made in regular course of business was properly admitted).

Hospital records

Fla.—Chilton v. Dockstader, App., 126 So.2d 281 (statements of consulting physicians and others as to progress of patient, though prepared during hospital confinement, were not part of "hospital records" within pretrial order for admission of such records without identification by custodian thereof).

La.—Brown v. Collins, App.1969, 223 So.2d 453 (where hospital record showing that blood was drawn from defendant was certified by hospital administrator and where letter signed by executive director of hospital certifying hospital record was attached to hospital record of test as to alcohol content of blood sample, records were not inadmissible on ground that they were not properly certified).

Mich.—Snyder v. Oldsmobile Division of General Motors Corp., 1969, 171 N.W.2d 597, 18 Mich.App. 578 (in action for subarachnoidal hemorrhage which plaintiff alleged had been caused by trauma experienced when automobile manufactured by defendant went out of control and defendant asserted that condition had been caused by high blood pressure and hypertension, medical record could not prove itself and trial court erred in allowing doctor to testify, over objection, regarding plaintiff's prior medical history as set forth in medical records of hospital, where doctor was unable to say who took history and person who took it was not produced for cross-examination).

N.J.—Sullivan v. Coast Cities Coaches, 1941, 19 A.2d 442, 126 N.J.L. 300, affirmed 21 A.2d 736, 127 N.J.L. 226.

Pa.—Hamilton v. Fean, 1966, 221 A.2d 309, 422 Pa. 373.

Tex.—Hartman v. Maryland Cas. Co., Civ.App.1967, 417 S.W.2d 640 (admission of X-rays which were taken three years before the injury in issue and which were attached to deposition of records custodian of hospital was error and reversible where there was no proof of compliance with statutory requisites relating to records made in regular course of business, or evidence of who made X-rays, how they were made, or whether they correctly portrayed that which they purported to represent).

Insurance company record

Mo.—Allen v. St. Louis Public Service Co., 285 S.W.2d 663, 365 Mo. 677, 55 A.L.R.2d 1022 (files of an insurance company relating to person's insurance claim arising from previous fall in store building were properly admitted, under Uniform Business Records Act, against objections that witness did not know whether any part of record had been removed, and that, in view of plaintiff's admissions, concomitant medical report was repetitious).

§ 433.1 TRIAL EVIDENCE Ch. 433

identify and show admissibility of a shop record than is required to introduce and admit a public document of record, since by its nature the latter imports greater veracity than the former.[11]

§ 433.2 "Best Evidence" Rule

Library References:
C.J.S. Evidence § 777 et seq.
West's Key No. Digests, Evidence ⇔157 et seq.

The "best evidence rule" is sometimes invoked in automobile accident cases;[12] but usually it does not apply to admissions of

Telephone company record

Iowa—Olesen v. Henningsen, 77 N.W. 2d 40, 247 Iowa 883 (admission of long distance telephone ticket on which was shown time of placing of call, in order to show accident occurred after sunset and that statute providing that vehicle must be lighted after sunset was therefore applicable was proper, where telephone ticket was identified by one or more telephone company employees who either made or had supervision and charge of records and who knew ticket to be genuine part of records of company and who could testify it was made at or about time shown thereon).

11. **Wash.**—Kellerher v. Porter, 189 P.2d 223, 29 Wash.2d 650.

12. **U.S.**—Federal Rules of Evidence § 1002.

Cal.—West's Ann.Calif.Evid.Code, § 1500.

Fla.—Florida Evidence Code § 90.952; Douglass v. Sapotnick, 171 So. 765, 126 Fla. 753, followed in 173 So. 926, 131 Fla. 246.

Kan.—Kansas Code of Civil Procedure § 60–467.

Me.—Maine Rules of Evidence § 1002.

Neb.—Nebraska Rules of Evidence § 1002.

Nev.—N.R.S. 52.235.

N.J.—New Jersey Evidence Rule 70; Falcone v. New Jersey Bell Tel. Co., 1967, 236 A.2d 394, 98 N.J. Super. 138 (hospital record).

N.M.—New Mexico Rules of Evidence § 1002.

N.Y.—Gursslin v. Helenboldt, 1940, 21 N.Y.S.2d 269, 259 App.Div. 1064.

Pa.—Sanner v. U. S. Transfer Co., 193 A. 830, 127 Pa.Super. 191 (copy of letter or document not admissible without proof that original not obtainable).

Utah.—Utah Rules of Evidence § 70.

Wash.—Rowe v. Dixon, 196 P.2d 327, 31 Wash.2d 173 (where statute authorizing county commissioners to grant permit for operation of overweight and overwidth trucks required that agreement be in writing, the writing itself constituted best evidence of the terms of the agreement).

Wis.—Wisconsin Rules of Evidence § 910.02; Ernst v. Greenwald, 1967, 151 N.W.2d 706, 35 Wis. 763 (highway commissioner's letter stating traffic light sequence at intersection).

As to x-ray interpretation

U.S.—Chicago, R. I. & P. Ry. Co. v. Howell, C.A.Okl.1968, 401 F.2d 752 (testimony should not be admitted without the x-ray).

N.Y.—Richter v. Trailways of New England, Inc., 1967, 282 N.Y.S.2d 148, 28 A.D.2d 737 (testimony without x-rays was prejudicial error).

710

Tex.—Community Chapel Funeral Home v. Allen, Civ.App.1973, 499 S.W.2d 215 (although court was unable to say that an X-ray is the best evidence of what it reveals, since ordinarily it requires an expert to interpret one, the doctrine of fairness requires, where possible, presence of an X-ray in court during interpretation thereof); Kollmorgan v. Scott, Civ.App.1969, 447 S.W.2d 236 (best evidence was doctor's testimony concerning his interpretation of film and not the film itself).

Contra where original is public record

Where records are in official custody, open to inspection by all parties, secondary evidence is admissible, especially where records are outside jurisdiction of court. Moerman v. Zipco, Inc., 1969, 302 F.Supp. 439, affirmed, C.A., 422 F.2d 871, decision adhered to 430 F.2d 362.

Duplicate

U.S.—Federal Rules of Evidence § 1003.

Fla.—Florida Evidence Code § 90.953.

Ind.—Oberlin v. Pyle, 1943, 49 N.E. 2d 970, 114 Ind.App. 21 (carbon copy of physician's report was admissible, without showing original unavailable).

Neb.—Nebraska Rules of Evidence § 1003.

Nev.—N.R.S. 52.245.

N.M.—New Mexico Rules of Evidence § 1003.

Ohio.—Hine v. Dayton Speedway Corp., 1969, 252 N.E.2d 648, 20 Ohio App.2d 185 (photocopy of release from liability of race proprietor, exchanged for permission to enter premises).

Wis.—Wisconsin Rules of Evidence § 910.03.

Guilty plea

Ga.—Cambron v. Cogburn, 1968, 164 S.E.2d 350, 118 Ga.App. 454 (refusal to admit certified copy of recorder's court docket entry showing plea of guilty of violation of ordinance by defendant was improper on objection that original signed plea of guilty would be highest and best evidence of plea, inasmuch as it was not disclosed that such signed plea existed or that plea in writing was required by statute in that particular recorder's court).

Tex.—Atkinson v. Rister, 1967, 422 S.W.2d 821, error refused n. r. e. (if issue is whether there was valid judgment of conviction against defendant, court record would be best evidence of the judgment and testimony that witness heard defendant plead guilty would not be best evidence).

Ordinances

Permitting chief of police and others to testify as to ordinance containing regulation applicable to intersection held error, since ordinance containing regulation was best evidence. Douglass v. Sapotnick, 171 So. 765, 126 Fla. 753, followed in 173 So. 926, 131 Fla. 246.

Stenographic notes

Ill.—Vander Veen v. Yellow Cab Co., 1967, 233 N.E.2d 68, 89 Ill.App.2d 91 (transcript admissible).

Minn.—Cooper v. Hoeglund, 22 N.W. 2d 450, 221 Minn. 446 (notes of statement is not written instrument within best evidence rule).

Vehicle ownership

Ga.—Wilkins v. Hester, 1969, 167 S. E.2d 167, 119 Ga.App. 389 (admission of bailor's testimony as to his ownership of automobile that was allegedly damaged while in possession of bailee was not error on ground that certificate of title or tag slip would be highest and best evidence of ownership); Harper v. Green, 1967, 154 S.E.2d 762, 115 Ga.App. 525 (copy of application for certificate admissible same as original application).

§ 433.2 TRIAL EVIDENCE Ch. 433

parties,[13] or to instances where it is offered on a "collateral" issue [14] (stated in the federal rule and in the rules of certain states

Mo.—Schwarz v. Gage, Mo.App.1967, 417 S.W.2d 33, 31 A.L.R.3d 371 (certificate of ownership of automobile is best evidence of its contents).

13. U.S.—Federal Rules of Evidence § 1007, 28 U.S.C.A.

Fla.—Florida Evidence Code § 90.957.

Ga.—City of Atlanta v. Blackmon, 179 S.E. 842, 51 Ga.App. 165.

Me.—Maine Rules of Evidence § 1007.

Mass.—Morrissey v. Powell, 23 N.E. 2d 411, 304 Mass. 268, 124 A.L.R. 1522.

Neb.—Nebraska Rules of Evidence § 1007.

Nev.—N.R.S. 52.285.

N.J.—New Jersey Evidence Rule 70 (1)(h).

N.M.—New Mexico Rules of Evidence § 1007.

N.Y.—Votos v. Petrocelli, 1967, 284 N.Y.S.2d 725, 28 A.D.2d 1145 (rule would not have been violated by receipt of testimony as to alleged admissions made by defendant at hearing at Department of Motor Vehicles).

Tex.—Atkinson v. Rister, 1967, 422 S.W.2d 821, error refused n. r. e. (testimony of sheriff that he heard defendant plead guilty to criminal complaint charging him with illegal parking and failure to have red light or flag on projecting load, after sheriff was called to scene in which plaintiff while riding in rear of pickup truck was struck by pipe protruding from truck, was admissible as evidence of admission or declaration against interest and its admission did not violate best evidence rule).

Wis.—Wisconsin Rules of Evidence § 910.07.

But see

Trial court properly excluded from evidence in death action copy of letter by secretary of village street and alley committee containing admission that grade crossing was hazardous, where plaintiff did not first prove prior existence of original letter, its loss, destruction or unavailability. Gillson v. Gulf, M. & O. R. Co., 1969, 246 N.E.2d 269, 42 Ill.2d 193.

14. Ark.—Lin Mfg. Co. of Ark. v. Courson, 1969, 436 S.W.2d 472, 246 Ark. 5 (testimony of witness regarding policy of company against employing persons with back injury such as plaintiff had sustained was admissible over objection based on best evidence rule, even though company policy had been reduced to writing).

Ga.—Wilkins v. Hester, 1969, 167 S. E.2d 167, 119 Ga.App. 389 (admission, in bailee's action for damages to automobile allegedly sustained while in bailee's possession, of testimony of witness that he was used automobile dealer was not error on ground that county or state license would be highest and best evidence where question of whether witness was properly licensed was not in issue); Millhollan v. Watkins Motor Lines, Inc., 1967, 157 S.E.2d 901, 116 Ga.App. 452 (proof of commission regulation requiring driver's log, preliminary to introduction of log).

Minn.—Buffalo Ins. Co. v. United Parking Stations, Inc., 1967, 152 N.W.2d 81, 277 Minn. 134 (plaintiff insurer in attempt to prove payment of insured's loss from theft of automobile from defendant's parking lot and thus insurer's right to subrogation of claim against parking lot owner was not required to produce the most conclusive evidence, namely, the cancelled checks, or an assignment, in

as where the writing "is not closely related to a controlling issue").[15]

As under the usual rule, and pursuant to the federal rules of evidence and the rules of certain states,[16] secondary form proof is permissible where the original is shown to be unavailable.[17]

It also is the general rule that information or data personally known to a witness may be stated even though the same information exists in a writing,[18] or where it is only the existence of the writing which is being shown.[19]

order for case to be decided on the merits).

15. **U.S.**—Federal Rules of Evidence § 1004(4), 28 U.S.C.A.

Cal.—West's Ann.Calif.Evid.Code § 1504.

Fla.—Florida Evidence Code § 90.954 (4).

Kan.—Kansas Code of Civil Procedure § 60–467(a)(4).

Me.—Maine Rules of Evidence § 1004 (4).

Neb.—Nebraska Rules of Evidence § 1004(4).

Nev.—N.R.S. 52.255(4).

N.J.—New Jersey Evidence Rule 70 (1)(d).

N.M.—New Mexico Rules of Evidence § 1004(4).

Utah.—Utah Rules of Evidence § 70 (1)(d).

Wis.—Wisconsin Rules of Evidence § 910.04(4).

16. **U.S.**—Federal Rules of Evidence § 1004, 28 U.S.C.A.

Cal.—West's Ann.Calif.Evid.Code, §§ 1501 and 1502.

Fla.—Florida Evidence Code § 90.954.

Kan.—Kansas Code of Civil Procedure § 60–467.

Me.—Maine Rules of Evidence § 1004.

Neb.—Nebraska Rules of Evidence § 1004.

Nev.—N.R.S. 52.255.

N.J.—New Jersey Evidence Rule 70.

N.M.—New Mexico Rules of Evidence § 1004.

Utah.—Utah Rules of Evidence § 70.

Wis.—Wisconsin Rules of Evidence § 910.04.

17. **Ark.**—Edwards v. T. H. Epperson & Son House Moving Co., 1969, 437 S.W.2d 480, 246 Ark. 194 (before sheriff could properly testify that driver of truck used to move house had presented card at scene which would have identified capacity of driver with defendant house moving company, proof of why card could not be presented would be necessary).

18. **U.S.**—Sayen v. Rydzewski, C.A.Wis.1967, 387 F.2d 815 (own income personally known).

Ga.—City of Atlanta v. Blackmon, 179 S.E. 842, 51 Ga.App. 165 (admitting testimony that there were no stop signs at intersection where collision occurred, over objection that traffic stop could be created only by ordinance and erection of stop sign, and that ordinance would be best evidence, held not error, since testimony did not attempt to show contents of ordinance).

Mich.—Gonzalez v. Hoffman, 1968, 157 N.W.2d 475, 9 Mich.App. 522, quoting 32A C.J.S. Evidence § 802 (payment of money may be proved by parol without accounting for

19. See note 19 on page 714.

§ **433.2**   TRIAL EVIDENCE   Ch. 433

absence of receipt evidencing such fact where witness can testify to the fact positively and from his own independent knowledge, not founded on his having seen the receipt).

N.J.—Kellam v. Akers Motor Lines, 1945, 42 A.2d 261, 133 N.J.L. 1 (policeman who heard plea of guilty could testify thereto).

N.Y.—Campoli v. Grand Union Co., 1968, 294 N.Y.S.2d 295, 58 Misc.2d 7 (own payment to physician).

Wash.—McCoy v. Courtney, 1948, 190 P.2d 732, 30 Wash.2d 125 (testimony as to work done on vehicle, without attempt to state contents of motor company records used for refreshment).

Writing tendered in court

Permitting proof of average monthly earnings received by plaintiff from operation of his gas station, by testimony based on summary or statement prepared from original business records and used to refresh recollection was proper, as against objection that such testimony was not the best evidence, where original business records were produced at trial and had been available to defendant. Hotovec v. Howe, 111 N.W.2d 748, 79 S.D. 337.

19.   **S.C.**—Mickle v. Blackmon, 1969, 166 S.E.2d 173, 252 S.C. 202 (that several articles had been published in leading scientific journals on causes of crash injuries, but content was not offered).

714

Chapter 434

HEARSAY

Table of Sections

Sec.
434.1 Hearsay—In General.
434.2 Admissions—In General.
434.3 —— As to Negligent Conduct.
434.4 —— As to Status in Vehicle.
434.5 —— As to Status of Persons Alleged to be Vicariously Liable.
434.6 Testimony at a Prior Hearing.
434.7 Dying Declarations.
434.8 Spontaneous Declarations.
434.9 Statements of Bodily Condition.
434.10 Business Records—In General.
434.11 —— Police Reports.
434.12 Other Particular Exceptions.

§ 434.1 Hearsay—In General

Library References:
C.J.S. Evidence §§ 192 et seq., 242 et seq.
West's Key No. Digests, Evidence ⟐268, 314 et seq.

The general rules of evidence applied in other civil cases control in automobile accident cases in passing upon objections to testimony on the ground that it is hearsay.[1]

1. **U.S.**—Federal Rules of Evidence § 802, 28 U.S.C.A.; Green v. Benson, D.C.Pa.1967, 271 F.Supp. 90 (statements by neighbors of defendants in wrongful death action and in ancillary garnishment proceeding that particular automobile was regularly furnished to defendants' son as repeated in automobile liability insurer's counsel's affidavit in opposition to motion for summary judgment was hearsay and inadmissible in evidence in garnishment proceeding); Podolsky v. La Forge, C.C.A.Mass., 92 F.2d 954 (a deceased motorist's statement made in hospital concerning speed of truck was properly excluded as "hearsay" under Massachusetts statute admitting decedents' declarations where motorist's widow was the only witness in support of making statement, and hospital records showed that motorist was unconscious when brought to hospital and remained so almost continuously until he died).

Ala.—Nettles v. Bishop, 1972, 266 So. 2d 260, 289 Ala. 100 (admitting trooper's accident investigation report, after reconstruction expert testified that in forming his opinion as to what happened when collision occurred he considered facts appearing in report, was reversible error; instruction that jury should consider only the physical facts appearing in report and should not consider any opinions therein did not cure error); Rosen v. Lawson, 1967, 202 So.2d 716, 281 Ala. 351 (testimony of widow as to a conversation between physician and her husband about husband's physical condition while in the hospital was inadmissible as hearsay, but admission was not reversible error as there was other testimony to show his physical condition).

Ariz.—Arizona Refrigeration Supplies, Inc. v. Brookshire, 1970, 477 P.2d 767, 13 Ariz.App. 481 (evidence from investigating officer's report that someone thought light was green at time of impact was hearsay).

Ark.—Higgins v. General Motors Corp., 1971, 465 S.W.2d 898, 250 Ark. 551 (recall letters, from manufacturer to buyer, which related to possibly defective brake hoses were hearsay as between buyer and dealer, although admissions contained in letters were competent for limited purpose of dealer's third-party action against manufacturer).

Cal.—West's Ann.Calif.Evid.Code, § 1200.

Conn.—Dowling v. Kielak, 1970, 273 A.2d 716, 160 Conn. 14 (excerpts from testimony of various persons before coroner, although made under oath and statements of witnesses to police); Izzo v. Crowley, 1969, 254 A.2d 904, 157 Conn. 561 (written statement signed by absent witness who was passenger in plaintiff's automobile was properly excluded).

Fla.—Florida Evidence Code § 90.802; Smith v. Frisch's Big Boy, Inc., 1968, 208 So.2d 310 (reversible error to admit, over objections, testimony by officer as to what another officer orally relayed to him as to speed of test automobile, used in making experimental accidental test run).

Ga.—Malcolm v. Cotton, 1973, 197 S.E.2d 760, 128 Ga.App. 699 (testimony of plaintiff's husband who was driving automobile in which plaintiff was passenger, as to precise mechanical forces which caused damage to automobile and his statement that such information and explanation was given to him by the "adjusters" for the defendant); Blanchard v. Georgia S. & F. Ry. Co., 1968, 162 S.E.2d 442, 117 Ga.App. 858 (letter from insurance company to railroad in which insurance company stated that damages to plaintiff's automobile were stated amount and that right to recover had been assigned to insurance company was hearsay and the admission into evidence of such letter constituted reversible error in plaintiff's action against railroad for property damage).

Ill.—Hansel v. Chicago Transit Authority, 1971, 270 N.E.2d 553, 132 Ill.App.2d 402 (that plaintiff's wife had stated after accident that she knew "this was going to happen," offered to show that she actually knew or thought she knew that accident would occur and that this might be attributed to intoxication, came within rule).

Kan.—Kansas Code of Civil Procedure § 60–460.

Me.—Maine Rules of Evidence § 802.

Mass.—Jacobs v. Hertz Corp., 1970, 265 N.E.2d 588, 358 Mass. 541 (in absence of a showing that registration certificate of defendant's truck was either an admission or an official written statement, kept under and conforming to requirements of law, document, offered to prove truth of its contents, would be offensive to hearsay rule).

Mo.—Rogers v. Fiandaca, 1973, 491 S.W.2d 560 (prior inconsistent statements of parents of decedent, which indicated that their son was driving automobile later involved in fatal accident, were not admissible as substantive evidence that son was driving the vehicle, and such statements would be considered for impeachment purposes only, even where there was a lack of first-hand evidence as to who was the driver of automobile when it left bridge).

Neb.—Nebraska Rules of Evidence § 802.

Nev.—N.R.S. 51.065.

N.J.—New Jersey Evidence Rule 63.

N.M.—New Mexico Rules of Evidence § 802.

N.Y.—Empire Mut. Ins. Co. v. Stroud, 1974, 353 N.Y.S.2d 184, 343 A.D.2d 931 (reports which were made by independent investigating agency hired by insurer and which contained wholly conclusory assertion that "Your insured adamantly refuses to cooperate" were clearly hearsay and should not have been received in proceeding wherein insurer sought to disclaim its liability to injured party on ground of lack of cooperation by insured); Carlson v. Schade, 1971, 321 N.Y.S.2d 527, 36 A.D.2d 852 (where issue in closely contested case was whether one defendant's conviction of charge of reckless driving was result of plea of guilty or a finding of guilt after trial, admission of hearsay statement of justice to effect that court clerk had told him that she had altered court records to reflect defendant's conviction on guilty plea was prejudicial error).

N.D.—Leake v. Hagert, 1970, 175 N.W.2d 675 (that tractor driver's son told adjuster that red lens on small rear light of tractor had been out for some time was error since son's statement was hearsay, but error was not prejudicial where other witnesses testified as to condition of taillight and whether light had a red lens).

R.I.—Gilbert v. Girard, 1971, 279 A.2d 919, 109 R.I. 68 (rule barring use applies no less to out-of-court utterances which are offered to prove an owner's consent to operation than it does to those which are offered to establish agency relationship).

S.C.—Johnson v. Finney, 143 S.E.2d 722, 246 S.C. 366 (question to highway patrolman as to whether he was able to locate an "eye witness" was objectionable as answer would have been hearsay).

Tex.—Clift v. Dunn, Civ.App.1972, 477 S.W.2d 641 (at hearing on plea of privilege, testimony of plaintiff that she learned from police report at police station that driver of other automobile was defendant was hearsay and of no probative value); Colls v. Price's Creameries, Civ.App., 244 S.W.2d 900, ref. n. r. e. (questions asked police officers on cross-examination in action for injuries sustained by child when struck by defendant's truck as to whether a little girl at scene had requested them not to give truck driver a ticket because accident was not his fault).

Utah.—Utah Rules of Evidence § 63.

Va.—Facchina v. Richardson, 1972, 192 S.E.2d 791, 213 Va. 440 (document from plaintiff's employer showing a summary of the plaintiff's wage rate and her absence from work following accident was not admissible).

Wis.—Wisconsin Rules of Evidence § 908.02.

As to lack of insurance

La.—Bullock v. Perry, App.1970, 238 So.2d 796 (admission of statements made by motorist to investigating officers at scene, to plaintiff and his wife in plaintiff's hospital room, and to plaintiff's insurer's adjuster to effect that he had no liability insurance, was prejudicially erroneous).

N.Y.—Lumpkin v. Aetna Cas. & Sur. Co., 1964, 251 N.Y.S.2d 203, 21 A.D.2d 860 (letter from motorist in response to letter from claimant's attorney).

Tex.—United Services Auto. Ass'n v. Ratterree, Civ.App.1974, 512 S.W.

2d 30 (admission by uninsured motorist's attorney that uninsured motorist was such was hearsay as to insurer and did not constitute legally admissible evidence of proof of any fact against insurer); Members Mut. Ins. Co. v. Clancy, 1970, 455 S.W.2d 447.

Balance of declaration admissible

Pa.—Jones v. Spidle, 1971, 286 A.2d 366, 446 Pa. 103 (where portion of defendant driver's statement to police, made shortly after driver's delivery truck had struck small boy on one-way street in residential neighborhood, had first been used by plaintiff in cross-examination of driver, defendants were properly permitted to subsequently introduce the whole statement into evidence).

Books or treatises

N.H.—Guptill v. Bergman, 1968, 240 A.2d 55, 108 N.H. 507 (exclusion of evidence offered to show, by use of "Old Farmers' Almanac", that twilight on day of accident had a duration of one hour and 33 minutes after sunset, which occurred at 7:08 P.M. Eastern Daylight Saving Time, was discretionary where there was direct evidence that weather was "cloudy-clear" and that fog patches had been encountered beyond where accident happened, and there was also evidence that defendant driver operated with his lights on low beam from time he and passenger departed officers' club at approximately 7:20 P.M.).

N.C.—Koury v. Follo, 1968, 158 S.E.2d 548, 272 N.C. 366 (medical textbooks and similar publications are objectionable).

But see

Only assertive conduct is hearsay and automobile operating manuals were not hearsay. Clary · v. Fifth Ave. Chrysler Center, Inc., Alaska 1969, 454 P.2d 244.

Contra as to deceased declarant, under Massachusetts rule

Mass.—M.G.L.A. c. 233 § 65 (if court finds made in good faith and upon the personal knowledge of the declarant); Shamgochian v. Drigotas, 1961, 177 N.E.2d 580, 343 Mass. 139 (statement of pedestrian, as to own drinking and exonerating driver).

Diagram prepared by investigating officer

Conn.—Terminal Taxi Co. v. Flynn, 1968, 240 A.2d 881, 156 Conn. 313 (exhibit consisting of diagram prepared by investigating police officer depicting routes of travel of vehicles from point of impact to point at which they came to rest based on what he had heard from others at scene was hearsay evidence, but its admission was harmless error).

Even in affidavit

Statement in affidavit by juror's wife that she observed juror conduct an experiment of driving an automobile up to grocery loading conveyor to determine which way the wheels would be turned while stopped at conveyor was hearsay and inadmissible. Bradshaw v. Campbell, 1968, 237 A.2d 547, 103 R.I. 319.

Hearsay by conduct

U.S.—Federal Rules of Evidence § 801(a)(2), 28 U.S.C.A. (intended as an assertion).

Ariz.—State ex rel. Herman v. Wilson, 420 P.2d 992, 4 Ariz.App. 420 (may be by conduct).

Fla.—Florida Evidence § 90.801(1)(a)(2).

Kan.—Kansas Code of Civil Procedure § 60–459(a).

Me.—Maine Rules of Evidence § 801(a)(2).

Neb.—Nebraska Rules of Evidence § 801(1)(a).

Nev.—N.R.S. 51.045(2).

N.J.—New Jersey Evidence Rule 62 (1).

N.M.—New Mexico Rules of Evidence § 801(a)(2).

Utah.—Utah Rules of Evidence § 62 (1).

Wis.—Wisconsin Rules of Evidence § 908.01(b)(1).

Hearsay defined

U.S.—Federal Rules of Evidence § 801, 28 U.S.C.A.

Ill.—Northern Trust Co. v. Moscatelli, 203 N.E.2d 447, 54 Ill.App.2d 316 (out-of-court statement offered for truth of matter asserted).

Okl.—Shinn v. Francis, 404 P.2d 1017 (is "hearsay" when its probative force depends on competency and credibility of some person other than the witness).

Medical witness relating statement of another physician

Ala.—Prince v. Lowe, 82 So.2d 606, 263 Ala. 410 (testimony of physician as to opinions expressed in a diagnostic conference by doctors not testifying and as to what was the consensus of the conference).

Ark.—Southern Farm Bureau Cas. Ins. Co. v. Pumphrey, 1974, 510 S.W.2d 570, 256 Ark. 818 (properly excluded as hearsay testimony by plaintiff's treating doctor as to what report from specialist who had examined plaintiff "stated.")

Cal.—Frampton v. Hartzell, 4 Cal. Rptr. 427, 179 Cal.App.2d 771 (testimony of a doctor for plaintiff that it was the opinion of certain hospital staff doctors that the accident was a contributing factor in the patient's mental illness was hearsay).

Ga.—Attaway v. Morris, 1965, 140 S.E.2d 214, 110 Ga.App. 873 (x-ray report).

Ill.—Adamaitis v. Hesser, 206 N.E.2d 311, 56 Ill.App.2d 349 (cross-examining witness, who testified as to X rays and who gave his interpretation and opinion, as to whether witness' interpretation differed from that of roentgenologist who was identified by witness as a specialist in his field, was error).

Mo.—Pietrowski v. Mykins, App. 1973, 498 S.W.2d 572 (medical report, purportedly prepared by "company doctor" who examined plaintiff, which was contained in files of second doctor who also examined plaintiff and who testified at trial of personal injury case).

N.Y.—Harker v. Chase, 274 N.Y.S.2d 64, 26 A.D.2d 854 (testimony of plaintiff's doctor that his opinion that plaintiff had sustained whiplash injury to cervical spine had been confirmed by a neurosurgeon who did not testify was inadmissible hearsay, but prejudice, if any, was overcome by the extensive medical testimony).

Okl.—Shinn v. Francis, 404 P.2d 1017, quoting 31 C.J.S. Evidence § 194 (evidence elicited on cross-examination from plaintiff's physician, who on direct gave his opinion as to cause and extent of plaintiff's injury on basis of his own examination and medical history furnished by plaintiff, in regard to reports and opinions furnished him by other physicians who thought that plaintiff had sustained no injury, constituted hearsay).

Tenn.—Patterson v. Kroger Co., 389 S.W.2d 283, 54 Tenn.App. 243 (use of pronoun we volunteered by medical witness, thus indicating witness was relating another's opinion, made testimony hearsay).

Wis.—Lewandowski v. Preferred Risk Mut. Ins. Co., 146 N.W.2d 505, 33 Wis.2d 69 (letters written by medical specialist to plaintiff's medical witness).

Repair estimate

Ga.—Wallis v. Odom, 203 S.E.2d 613, 130 Ga.App. 437 (where party who

§ **434.1** TRIAL EVIDENCE Ch. 434

The general rules of evidence in civil cases also control the question of the admissibility of testimony as a self-serving declaration.[2] A litigant may not testify as to one's own self-serving

inspected automobile was not present and therefore not subject to cross-examination, opinion contained in his estimate of repairs of automobile was inadmissible).

La.—Smith v. Frederick, App.1969, 221 So.2d 306 (where no representative of company making estimate of cost of repairs to taxicab testified, estimate was inadmissible); Turner v. Ewing, App.1969, 220 So.2d 518, writ issued 223 So. 2d 406, 254 La. 277, affirmed 232 So.2d 468, 255 La. 659 (testimony of owner of automobile as to another's estimate of cost of repair was hearsay and had no probative value).

N.J.—Dwane v. West Am. Ins. Co., 1972, 297 A.2d 865, 121 N.J.Super. 470 (statements as to mileage and value of damage to car were inadmissible in action by insured under collision coverage).

Stopping distance charts

La.—Guidry v. Grain Dealers Mut. Ins. Co., App., 193 So.2d 873 (charts indicating stopping distances at various speeds are not so uniform, so well recognized or so scientifically precise, that they should be excepted from general rule that scientific treatises are not admissible as independent evidence).

Mo.—Rooney v. Lloyd Metal Products Co., 1970, 458 S.W.2d 561 (received without objection however).

2. U.S.—Carantzas v. Iowa Mut. Ins. Co., C.A.Fla., 235 F.2d 193 (in suit involving question of whether automobile liability insurance had been transferred from 1941 automobile to 1950 automobile, testimony of employee that insured had told him that he had transferred the insurance and testimony of insured's wife that insured said he had given notice to agent to transfer insurance was properly excluded as hearsay).

Ala.—Hurn v. Reynolds, 36 So.2d 603, 34 Ala.App. 79 (letter written by defendant to plaintiff).

Conn.—Pluhowsky v. City of New Haven, 197 A.2d 645, 151 Conn. 337 (a motorist's accident report filed almost four years after accident and less than a month before trial that automobile had struck a body of water on highway which caused him to lose control and strike a telephone pole was not, as against a proper objection, admissible in his favor in his case against city since it was a mere self-serving statement).

Del.—Connor v. Lyness, Sup.1971, 284 A.2d 473 (handwritten unsworn statement, which was given by bus driver to insurance adjuster and which driver signed shortly after bus had collided with automobile, constituted inadmissible hearsay).

Ga.—Tifton Brick & Block Co. v. Meadow, 1955, 88 S.E.2d 569, 92 Ga.App. 328 (unless waived, or offered as foundation for admission by silence).

Mich.—Burke v. Enders, 9 N.W.2d 537, 305 Mich. 270.

Mo.—Wilt v. Moody, Sup., 254 S.W. 2d 15 (written statement to officer).

N.Y.—Rupp v. Christofolo, 70 N.Y.S. 2d 383, 272 App.Div. 856.

Pa.—Andrews v. Jackson, 1967, 235 A.2d 452, 211 Pa.Super. 166 (testimony of officer that defendant driver was unable to stop due to brake failure was hearsay that was highly prejudicial).

declaration even when so closely connected with the event as to be a part of the res gestæ.[3]

However, some evidence, though hearsay in form, is nevertheless admissible. In some instances the declaration is not offered to prove the truth of what was said, but only to prove that it was said.[4] Though it sometimes is stated that statements of

3. **Minn.**—Fischer v. Chicago & N. W. Ry. Co., 258 N.W. 4, 193 Minn. 73.

N.Y.—Green v. Downs, 1970, 316 N. Y.S.2d 221, 27 N.Y.2d 205, 265 N. E.2d 68 (reception of defendant's accident report, in which defendant stated that pedestrian had misinterpreted officer's instruction to vehicle to back up as signal for her to cross street).

Contra

Iowa.—Bass v. Muenchow, 146 N.W. 2d 923, 259 Iowa 1010.

Ky.—Roland v. Beckham, 408 S.W.2d 628 (that statement was self-serving was not sufficient to destroy its quality as res gestae).

Shown as part of cross-examination of adverse witness

Testimony of wife of plaintiff that defendant had, approximately two hours after collision in her hospital room, stated to her that his brakes failed and he could not stop was objectionable on ground that it was hearsay and indirectly self-serving as introduced by defendant in behalf of his defense on cross-examination of plaintiff's wife, where defendant failed to personally appear and testify. Holmes v. Campsey, Tex. Civ.App.1967, 415 S.W.2d 25.

4. **U.S.**—Federal Rules of Evidence § 801(c), 28 U.S.C.A. (stated as being when "offered in evidence to prove the truth of the matter asserted"); Ikerd v. Lapworth, C.A. Ind.1970, 435 F.2d 197 (after testifying that he was at scene when police arrived, stated that he gave his name to police as being witness).

Ala.—Norris v. Presley, 1974, 290 So. 2d 643, 292 Ala. 155 (in action against truck driver and partnership, truck driver's statements showing that alleged conversation between plaintiff and truck driver took place in which plaintiff informed driver that he would not sue driver if driver testified that he was employee of partnership were admissible not as proof of driver's agency or lack of it but to show existence of such conversation which plaintiff denied on cross-examination).

Cal.—Head v. Wilson, 1939, 97 P.2d 509, 36 Cal.App.2d 244 (as to statement to ambulance driver on issue whether vehicle then responding to emergency).

Del.—State Highway Dept. of Buzzuto, Del.1970, 264 A.2d 347 (testimony of doctor, who dispatched ambulance which collided with truck killing ambulance driver, as to instructions which he gave ambulance crew).

Ga.—Cowart Trucking Co., Inc. v. Stone, 1973, 199 S.E.2d 608, 129 Ga.App. 327 (testimony of physician that plaintiff "complained of pain; he had muscle spasm," was admissible to explain physician's course of conduct); Home Indem. Co. v. Godley, 1970, 177 S.E.2d 105, 122 Ga.App. 356 (insured's testimony, which related to conversation with investigating adjuster with respect to what insured wanted done with claim against him and which was elicited in reference to conversation between adjuster and insured showing that insured, who sought to recover from insurer for judgment rendered against him, never signed non-

§ 434.1   TRIAL EVIDENCE   Ch. 434

waiver agreement, never was advised by insurer that insurer was not going to cover him in actions against him, was seeking information as to when case would be settled and that insured expected insurer to protect him in case).

Kan.—Hastings v. Ross, 1973, 508 P.2d 514, 211 Kan. 732 (not hearsay where witness relates what was said by self at the time of the event).

La.—Nolan v. Liuzza, 301 So.2d 892 (in action by owner to recover for the loss of use of the automobile damaged by tort-feasor, testimony of owner and of insurance adjuster concerning dealer's explanation that repair took six months because parts could not be obtained was not admissible to show the truth of that statement by the dealer but was admissible to show that the owner's allowing the dealer to continue to hold the automobile so long was reasonable and therefore not a breach of his obligation of proper diligence).

Md.—Sun Cab Co. v. Walston, 1972, 289 A.2d 804, 15 Md.App. 113, affirmed 298 A.2d 391, 267 Md. 559 (where question propounded to witness in actions arising from taxicab-truck collision went not to the ultimate fact of whether the cab had been struck from the rear but whether witness had heard such a statement made, and if so, when, neither answer was hearsay when the officer-witness first answered that he had heard such a statement at manslaughter trial and then corrected such testimony by saying that the information was related to him by his superior).

Mass.—Belleveau v. S. C. Lowe Supply Co., 86 N.E. 301, 200 Mass. 237 (evidence was admissible to show that a pedestrian and his companions, while on the street, took precautions against injury, that just before the accident one of the companions looked back and stated that two street cars were coming, and that, after looking back a second time, he said that, if they hurried, they could catch the second car).

R.I.—Allen v. D'Ercole Const. Co., 1968, 244 A.2d 864, 104 R.I. 362.

Tex.—Allstate Ins. Co. v. Godwin, Civ.App.1968, 426 S.W.2d 652 (where question is whether a party has acted prudently, wisely, or in good faith, the information on which he acted whether true or false, is original and material evidence, and not hearsay); White v. Lilley, Civ.App., 286 S.W.2d 296 (that his family doctor, who did not testify, referred him to another doctor was not hearsay and was not prejudicial).

Basis of expert opinion

U.S.—U. S. v. Sowards, C.A.Utah, 339 F.2d 401 (generally, expert may testify as to hearsay matters, not to establish substantive facts, but for sole purpose of giving information upon which he relied in reaching his conclusion; when evidence is given for this purpose, jury should be so instructed).

Ill.—Hastings v. Abernathy Taxi Ass'n, Inc., 1974, 306 N.E.2d 498, 16 Ill.App.3d 671 (testimony of physician regarding type of work performed by patient whom he treated was admissible in action by patient in that type of work performed by patient might be factor in physician's diagnosis).

But see

Admission, in action for injuries allegedly caused by defective hydraulic lift installed by defendant corporation on truck owned by codefendant corporation and leased to plaintiff's employer, of hearsay testimony of fellow employee of plaintiff as to telephone conversation between employer and officer of codefendant relating to codefendant's notice of claimed defective condition prior to accident was prejudicial error. Rosenzweig v. Arista Truck Renting

722

mental state or intent constitute an exception to the hearsay rule,[5] the declaration's relevance may be to show the declarant's mental state only and not to prove the truth of the declaration.[6]

Corp., 1970, 309 N.Y.S.2d 93, 34 A.D. 2d 542.

Comment on action of vehicle

Testimony relating to statement, made four miles before collision when automobile in which injured person was riding passed automobile in which witness was riding, that occupants of passing automobile must have been drunk and that they would be found on the road if speed was kept up, was not "hearsay", was not too remote in time, and was not merely cumulative, and admissibility thereof was determinable as matter of law and not in trial court's discretion. Houston Oxygen Co. v. Davis, 161 S.W.2d 474, 139 Tex. 1, 140 A.L.R. 868.

Declaration probative of agency

Where taxicab owner defended death action on ground that taxicab driver was a contractor and not owner's agent, conversation in which driver and owner participated by which driver procured use of taxicab was not hearsay. Ex parte Rowell, 26 So.2d 554, 248 Ala. 80.

Patient relating treatment prescribed

Plaintiff's testimony as to what treatment his doctor prescribed was admissible over objection that it was hearsay. Gosselin v. Letourneau, 1968, 237 N.E.2d 23, 354 Mass. 761.

Proof of report of insurance loss

Hearsay testimony of insurance broker as to conversation wherein owner said that he had left automobile disabled and inoperative in the street near the curb with the keys in it, and as to later conversation wherein owner said that finance company could not find the automobile, both conversations communicated to insurer, was inadmissible as proof of theft in action for loss of automobile covered by policy but admissible as proof a report had been made against loss by theft. Associated Discount Corp. v. Insurance Co. of North America, 1967, 283 N.Y.S.2d 1006, 54 Misc.2d 1027.

Proof of reporting trade to insurance agent

In suit involving question of whether automobile liability insurance had been transferred from 1941 automobile to 1950 automobile, testimony of salesman handling sale of 1950 automobile to corporation, of which insured was sole owner, that he had heard insured's part of telephone conversation in which insured stated that he had sold 1941 automobile and purchased 1950 automobile, gave its motor and serial number and requested transfer of insurance was admissible under res gestae exception to hearsay rule. Carantzas v. Iowa Mut. Ins. Co., C.A.Fla., 235 F.2d 193.

"Verbal facts"

Statements not introduced to prove truth of what was said but to establish nature of transaction were admissible as verbal facts and were not hearsay. Caudill v. Citizens Bank, Ky., 383 S.W.2d 350.

5. **Cal.**—In re Mosier's Estate, 54 Cal.Rptr. 447, 246 Cal.App.2d 164 (when intent is material element of disputed fact, declarations made after as well as before alleged act which indicate intent with which person performed act are admissible in evidence as exception).

6. **Ala.**—Pollard v. Rogers, 173 So. 881, 234 Ala. 92.

Cal.—Benwell v. Dean, Cal.App., 57 Cal.Rptr. 394, 249 Cal.App.2d 345 (statements or declarations of mental state of declarant which do not directly declare mental or emotional state but are merely circum-

Other declarations classed as "verbal acts" are not deemed to be hearsay.[7]

stantial evidence thereof are not hearsay, but if they are declarations of mental condition, which directly asserts it, they are hearsay); Ohlson v. Frazier, 39 P.2d 429, 2 Cal.App.2d 708 (animosity between drivers); Hatzakorzian v. Rucker-Fuller Desk Co., 239 P. 709, 197 Cal. 82, 41 A.L.R. 1027 (warning of danger).

Fla.—Allen Morris Co. v. McNally, 1974, 305 So.2d 79 (statements by plaintiff motorist out of the presence of defendants were admissible under state of mind exception to hearsay rule to show her emotional condition during her hospitalization and during her period of recuperation at home, though she was available as a witness).

N.H.—Dane v. MacGregor, 52 A.2d 290, 94 N.H. 294 (where there was evidence that pedestrian had attended a dinner at which liquor was served, permitting witness to testify to statement by pedestrian that he was going to leave early because he was going fishing in the morning was proper since the testimony showed pedestrian's state of mind and explained why he left as he did and had some bearing on the issue of intoxication); Hebert v. Boston & M. R. R., 8 A.2d 744, 90 N.H. 324 (in actions against railroad company, driver's testimony that, if he had heard train whistle while he was going up-grade toward crossing, he would have stopped was admissible as tending to show quality of his act in proceeding without stopping and his state of mind, which was relevant to question of his due care, so that his similar unresponsive answers to questions were not necessarily harmful to defendant).

Intent to report trade to insurance agent

In suit involving question of whether liability insurance had been transferred from 1941 automobile to 1950 automobile, insured's statement to salesman who handled sale of 1950 automobile that he would call his "insurance agent" was admissible. Carantzas v. Iowa Mut. Ins. Co., C.A. Fla., 235 F.2d 193.

On issue of willfulness or conscious indifference

Ark.—Loose-Wiles Biscuit Co. v. Jolly, 238 S.W. 613, 152 Ark. 442.

Cal.—Cope v. Davison, 180 P.2d 873, 30 Cal.2d 193, 171 A.L.R. 667 (questions asked motorist concerning his intention to cause injury to guest were admissible to prove motorist's state of mind notwithstanding that intent to injure was not a necessary element of "willful misconduct"); Hastings v. Serleto, 143 P.2d 956, 61 Cal.App.2d 672 (proper to interrogate motorist accused of willful misconduct relative to his mental attitude and knowledge of probable consequences of his act, but such inquiry must be confined to his state of mind prior to or contemporaneously with the accident and not subsequent thereto).

Iowa.—Schmitt v. Cutkomp, 81 N.W. 2d 662, 248 Iowa 575 (only condition under which remarks of a host driver might become pertinent in determining whether host driver was guilty of reckless driving within meaning of statute providing that a host driver is not liable to a guest passenger except in cases of intoxication or reckless driving, would be if the remark, coupled with actions of the driver, exhibited evidence of a frame of mind showing no care, and a complete disregard for consequences).

7. **Mass.**—Charette v. Burke, 15 N.E. 2d 194, 300 Mass. 278 (in action for injuries sustained by 22 months old child when struck by automobile, testimony that father told child to wait where he was in front

In more recent development of jurisdictional "rules of evidence" the trend has been to make admissible certain prior declarations of a testifying witness (aside from any consideration of such constituting admissions of a party), and as substantive proof of its content (as contrasted to limited use for impeachment purposes only). The rationale would be that the declarant is at the trial, under the sanctions of an oath, that the witness' demeanor is then subject to the view of the factfinder, and that interrogation can be had to draw out any elaboration or explanation necessary to properly assess the witness' means of knowledge of the pertinent facts.

The federal rule defines out of hearsay status a prior declaration inconsistent with testimony of the declarant at the trial, so as to permit introduction of such prior declaration if it was made "under oath subject to the penalty of perjury at a trial, hearing, or other proceeding, or in a deposition".[8]

State jurisdiction rules similarly have made prior declarations of a testifying witness admissible,[9] even declarations which were not made under oath or in official proceedings.[10]

of house while father got him a cookie was properly admitted as a verbal act and a pertinent circumstance relating to father's conduct as custodian of child).

W.Va.—Keller v. Wonn, 87 S.E.2d 453, 140 W.Va. 860 (where defendant's decedent was charged with negligence in having driven while suffering from hypertensive disease, doctor's testimony that he had secured knowledge of decedent's physical condition by virtue of a hospital staff conference and had given decedent certain warnings concerning his condition was admissible under the verbal act rule).

8. Federal Rules of Evidence § 801 (d)(1), 28 U.S.C.A.

9. **Cal.**—West's Ann.Calif.Evid.Code, § 1235.

Fla.—Florida Evidence Code § 90.801 (2)(a).

Kan.—Kansas Code of Civil Procedure § 60–460(a).

Me.—Maine Rules of Evidence § 801 (d)(1).

Neb.—Nebraska Rules of Evidence § 801(4)(a).

Nev.—N.R.S. 51.035(2)(a).

N.J.—New Jersey Evidence Rule 63 (1)(a).

N.M.—New Mexico Rules of Evidence § 801(d)(1).

Utah—Utah Rules of Evidence § 63 (1).

Wis.—Wisconsin Rules of Evidence § 908.01(4)(a).

10. **Ill.**—Breslin v. Bates, 1973, 303 N.E.2d 807, 14 Ill.App.3d 941 (conversations which passengers in automobile being driven by defendant had with her concerning the speed at which she was driving and requesting her to drive slower were admissible over objection that they were hearsay, since the passengers and driver were present in court to recount circumstances and nature of conversations).

Limited to testifying witness

Deponent who was not present at trial and who had not been confronted with his alleged extra-judicial

§ 434.1   TRIAL EVIDENCE   Ch. 434

Historically, declarations which constitute admissions of the declarant party-opponent, or vicariously admissions of a party-opponent, have been admissible under an exception to the hearsay rule. Under the federal rule,[11] and under certain state rules of evidence,[12] such declarations have been defined out of hearsay and thusly made admissible.

§ 434.2 Admissions—In General [13]

Library References:
C.J.S. Evidence § 270 et seq.
West's Key No. Digests, Evidence ⚖︎200 et seq.

Admissions against interest on a material matter are admissible as an exception to the hearsay rule.[14]

statement when litigant took his deposition was not a person present at trial subject to cross-examination because of the taking of his deposition, and his alleged extra-judicial statement was not admissible under statute as an exception to the hearsay rule. K.S.A. 60–460(a, j, l). Thompson v. Norman, 424 P.2d 593, 198 Kan. 436.

11. Federal Rules of Evidence § 801(d)(2), 28 U.S.C.A.

12. **Me.**—Maine Rules of Evidence § 801(d)(2).

Neb.—Nebraska Rules of Evidence § 801(4)(b).

Nev.—N.R.S. 51.035(3)(a).

N.M.—New Mexico Rules of Evidence § 801(d)(2).

Wis.—Wisconsin Rules of Evidence § 908.01(4)(b).

13. See § 434.1 at fn. 11 et seq. for rules by which admissions are defined out of classification of hearsay.

And see § 423.1 at fn. 6 et seq., for cases holding inadmissibility of statements taken from injured parties within a limited period of time after an accident.

And see following sections for admissions as to particular subject matter.

14. **Cal.**—Bonebrake v. McCormick, 215 P.2d 728, 35 Cal.2d 16.

Ill.—Woodruff v. Pennsylvania R. Co., 202 N.E.2d 113, 52 Ill.App.2d 341; Rose v. City of Chicago, 45 N.E.2d 717, 317 Ill.App. 1 (deposition).

Ky.—Ison v. Mullins, 336 S.W.2d 599 (a statement made by a driver that something went wrong with the car and that he could not control it was an admission against his interest, to which defendant should have been permitted to testify).

La.—Falgout v. Younger, App., 192 So. 706.

Md.—Smith v. Branscome, 1968, 248 A.2d 455, 251 Md. 582.

Mass.—Morrissey v. Powell, 23 N.E. 2d 411, 304 Mass. 268, 124 A.L.R. 1522; Cronin v. Fitchburg & L. St. Ry. Co., 63 N.E. 335, 181 Mass. 202 (statement to physician).

Mo.—Beckwith v. Standard Oil Co., 281 S.W.2d 852; McComb v. Vaughn, 218 S.W.2d 548, 358 Mo. 951.

N.J.—Miller v. Henderson, 1956, 124 A.2d 23, 41 N.J.Super. 15.

N.Y.—McDermott v. Barker, 245 N.Y.S.2d 135, 20 A.D.2d 546 (statement in hospital record as to manner in which accident happened);

Fitzgerald v. State, 96 N.Y.S.2d 452, 198 Misc. 39 (statement by driver to police officer); Friedman v. New York City Omnibus Corp., 70 N.Y.S.2d 628, 272 App.Div. 265 (written statement signed by decedent and by decedent's widow in which they stated that decedent had had another accident after one in issue).

N.C.—Wells v. Burton Lines, 45 S.E. 569, 228 N.C. 422; Hobbs v. Queen City Coach Co., 34 S.E.2d 211, 225 N.C. 323.

Ohio—Backman v. Ambos, 79 N.E.2d 177, 83 Ohio App. 141 (declaration that sun was shining in plaintiff's eyes); Anderson v. City Cab Co., App., 38 N.E.2d 214.

Or.—Davis v. Dean, 350 P.2d 910, 221 Or. 110 (proper to show that at the time plaintiff was pressing his claim he was also making a claim against another party for similar injuries suffered in a subsequent accident).

Pa.—Lemmon v. Bufalino, 1964, 205 A.2d 680, 204 Pa.Super. 481.

S.C.—Eberhardt v. Forrester, 128 S.E.2d 687, 241 S.C. 399 (statement of operator, 15 or 20 minutes after collision with another vehicle, that brakes were "hardest" he had "seen" on any automobile he had ever driven); Llewellyn v. Atlantic Greyhound Corp., 28 S.E.2d 673, 204 S.C. 156.

S.D.—Berlin v. Berens, 80 N.W.2d 79, 76 S.D. 429 (charge to which litigant pleaded guilty).

Tenn.—Puckett v. Laster, 1965, 405 S.W.2d 35, 56 Tenn.App. 66.

Tex.—Montgomery v. Vinzant, Civ. App., 297 S.W.2d 350 (defendant's statement to police officers was independently relevant and admissible despite fact that such proof necessarily disclosed that defendant was either under arrest or imminently threatened with a criminal prosecution growing out of collision); Hinrichs v. Texas & N. O. R. Co., Civ.App., 153 S.W.2d 859, error refused for want of error.

Vt.—Crawford v. Lumbermen's Mut. Cas. Co., 1966, 220 A.2d 480, 126 Vt. 12.

Wash.—Lujan v. Santoya, 250 P.2d 543, 41 Wash.2d 499; Gillum v. Pacific Coast R. Co., 279 P. 114, 152 Wash. 657 (bulletin of railroad company concerning particular crossing).

Absence of prior contention of fact when subject raised

Driver's prior statement, which related to her possession of automobile, but which contained no reference to her having been given permission of insured's son to operate automobile, constituted an admission by driver and as such driver, the owner of the automobile and the owner's insurer, as substantive evidence relative to question whether she had permission of insured's son to operate automobile. Goodney v. Smith, 1968, 242 N.E.2d 413, 354 Mass. 734, appeal after remand 269 N.E.2d 707, 359 Mass. 749.

As to ownership

Ala.—Feore v. Trammel, 1925, 104 So. 808, 213 Ala. 293.

Cal.—Lowmiller v. Monroe, Lyon & Miller, Inc., 1929, 282 P. 537, 101 Cal.App. 147; Hammond v. Hazard, 1919, 180 P. 46, 40 Cal.App. 45.

Mo.—Latham v. Hosch, 1921, 233 S.W. 84, 207 Mo.App. 381.

Ohio—Goz v. Tenney, 1922, 136 N.E. 215, 104 Ohio St. 500.

Tex.—Holton v. Hutchinson, Civ. App.1936, 90 S.W.2d 1103.

But see

Even if plaintiff's sworn answers to interrogatories propounded in Massachusetts action qualified as admissions against interest when considered in light of plaintiff's testimony in Rhode Island case arising out of the same accident, refusing

§ 434.2   TRIAL EVIDENCE   Ch. 434

requested instruction that the prior inconsistent statement could be considered by jury as evidence of admission against interest and giving instruction that prior statements contradicting testimony could be considered in determining credibility did not constitute error. Tringa v. Murphy, 1971, 276 A.2d 462, 108 R.I. 430.

Even though opinion

Mo.—Scherffius v. Orr, App.1969, 442 S.W.2d 120 (where party believes a fact on evidence sufficient to convince him of its existence, even though it relates to a fact concerning which he could have no personal knowledge, his declaration of existence of that fact, if against his interest, is competent evidence against him, and such evidence, though not conclusive and of a very unsatisfactory character, is for jury to weigh and accord such value as jury sees fit); Howell v. Dowell, App.1967, 419 S.W.2d 257 (even though in form of conclusions as to ultimate fact at issue).

Or.—Kraxberger v. Rogers, 373 P.2d 647, 231 Or. 440.

Foundation not required

Ariz.—Dykeman v. Ashton, 1968, 446 P.2d 26, 8 Ariz.App. 327 (properly admitted without foundation, on showing that defendant had signed the statement).

Va.—Goodwin v. Gilman, 1967, 157 S.E.2d 912, 208 Va. 422.

Mental state of declarant questioned

Statement containing admissions against interest is admissible unless it is shown that it was taken when person giving it was under such mental state that he was unable to narrate facts and events in a way to be relied on; and whether it should be excluded on that ground is matter of discretion. Deffendoll v. Stupp Bros. Bridge & Iron Co., Mo.App.1967, 415 S.W.2d 36.

No constitutional issues in civil action

Where plaintiff pedestrian was conscious and alert at time police officer interviewed him in hospital, failure of officer to advise plaintiff of his constitutional rights before interview did not preclude use of statement in plaintiff's suit against motorist. Azzaro v. Stupar, 1969, 169 N.W.2d 151, 17 Mich.App. 170.

Offer to confess judgment inadmissible

Under statute, an offer by defendant to confess judgment for part of amount claimed, or part of the causes involved in action, is not an admission of the cause of action, or amount to which plaintiff is entitled, nor to be given in evidence at trial. Tulsa Cab Co. v. Warfield, 112 P.2d 366, 188 Okl. 642.

Own safety rules

Safety rules of a defendant employer do constitute hearsay, but are admissible as an implied admission of a party opponent. Dillenbeck v. City of Los Angeles, 1968, 446 P.2d 129, 72 Cal.Rptr. 321, 69 Cal.2d 472.

Report of accident

N.Y.—Jacobs v. Gelb, 1946, 62 N.Y.S. 2d 782, 271 App.Div. 101 (containing diagram); Nagel v. Page, 1942, 35 N.Y.S.2d 321, 264 App. Div. 231, appeal denied 36 N.Y.S.2d 237, 264 App.Div. 918.

Rule limited

Testimony as to statements made by owner, following her arrival at scene of accident which occurred while her son was driving, to effect that she should not have let son have automobile, was not admissible, in garnishment proceeding by judgment creditor against owner's liability insurer, under declaration against interest exception to hearsay rule. Straughan v. Asher, Mo.App., 372 S.W.2d 489, citing C.J.S. Evidence § 217.

A written admission may be signed by mark.[15] Inability of one who has signed an admission to read English does not make the admission inadmissible.[16]

The admission of one who died after making it may be admissible,[17] notwithstanding medical testimony that such party could not talk intelligently, the medical testimony merely raising a jury question.[18]

Statement not sufficiently attributed to party

Police report of investigation of accident did not constitute an admission which could be basis of finding of fact where report was not shown to be a verbatim statement or to have been secured solely from motorist sought to be charged with admission, and, therefore, police officers' testimony from report was not admissible as substantive evidence of sequence of events in accident. Paull v. Meyers, 186 A.2d 849, 200 Pa.Super. 74.

Statement seeking to influence witness' testimony

In action for injuries by passenger against owner of taxicab, refusal of trial court to permit driver to testify that passenger told him he would give him $50 if he would help him in trial was prejudicial error. Dix v. Gross, 128 S.W.2d 753, 278 Ky. 348.

Statements obtained in violation of statute

That statement from injured person confined in a hospital was obtained in violation of statute would not render the statement inadmissible in evidence. Penal Law, § 270–b. Bloodgood v. Lynch, 56 N.E.2d 718, 293 N.Y. 308.

Testimony at prior proceeding

Testimony given by insured, in prior bankruptcy proceeding, as to his motives in insisting that action brought against him as result of accident go to trial was binding on insured and his assignee, in subsequent action by his assignee to recover from insurer amount of verdict recovered against insured in excess of policy limits. Peterson v. American Family Mut. Ins. Co., 1968, 160 N.W.2d 541, 280 Minn. 482.

Though technically not a party

Decedent's widow, while technically not a party of record in her individual capacity to survival action and wrongful death action by administrator against railroad whose train struck and killed decedent at public railroad crossing, was a party beneficially and directly interested in the case, and her prior admissions or statements concerning material facts constituted substantive evidence of the facts asserted, and its admission in evidence for limited purpose of impeachment was error, and trial court properly granted railroad new trial. Geelen v. Pennsylvania R. Co., 161 A.2d 595, 400 Pa. 240, 91 A.L.R.2d 1.

15. **Ind.**—Grossnickle v. Avery, 152 N.E. 288, 96 Ind.App. 479.

16. **Mass.**—Hovanesian v. Boyajian, 4 N.E.2d 1006, 296 Mass. 165.

17. **Ill.**—Thompson v. Cheatham, 71 N.E.2d 211, 330 Ill.App. 428.

La.—Dunigan v. Haynes, App., 26 So.2d 710.

N.J.—Dolan v. Chesler, 68 A.2d 885, 5 N.J.Super. 313.

Va.—Virginia Electric & Power Co. v. Decatur, 3 S.E.2d 172, 4 S.E.2d 294, 173 Va. 153 (statement by deceased that he was driving).

18. **Va.**—Virginia Electric & Power Co. v. Decatur, 3 S.E.2d 172, 4 S.E.2d 294, 173 Va. 153.

§ 434.2   TRIAL EVIDENCE   Ch. 434

Admission by silence

Generally, where a definite statement of a matter of fact, affecting the rights of a party, is made under circumstances indicating that it was heard, a failure to reply is admissible as evidence of a concession of the truth of the statement.[19] However,

19. **U.S.**—Federal Rules of Evidence § 801(d)(2)(B); Ishler v. Cook, C.A.Ind., 299 F.2d 507 (police officer's testimony, that one of group of three eyewitnesses stated at scene that defendant was traveling at about 50 miles per hour).

Ariz.—Ruth v. Rhodes, 1947, 185 P. 2d 304, 66 Ariz. 129.

Cal.—Southers v. Savage, 12 Cal. Rptr. 470, 191 Cal.App.2d 100 (testimony of investigating officer that host driver in guest's presence stated that he sideswiped other automobile and that guest did not comment, was admissible on theory of adoptive silence, where there was conflicting evidence whether passenger was in condition which would excuse failure to speak).

Ga.—Crafton v. Livingston, 150 S.E. 2d 371, 114 Ga.App. 161; Tifton Brick & Block Co. v. Meadow, 88 S.E.2d 569, 92 Ga.App. 328.

Me.—Maine Rules of Evidence § 801(d)(2)(B).

Md.—Ferry v. Cicero, 1971, 280 A. 2d 37, 12 Md.App. 502.

Neb.—Nebraska Rules of Evidence § 801(4)(b)(ii).

Nev.—N.R.S. 51.035(3)(b).

N.J.—Greenberg v. Stanley, 143 A. 2d 588, 51 N.J.Super. 90, affirmed in part and reversed in part 153 A.2d 833, 30 N.J. 485 (inapplicable in absence of showing that motorist sought to be charged was conversing with or in company of supposed declarant or known to declarant as operator).

N.M.—New Mexico Rules of Evidence § 801(d)(2)(B).

Or.—Walls v. Clark, 1969, 449 P.2d 141, 252 Or. 414 (acquiescence to her husband's statement to police officer relative to accident may be shown).

Tex.—Carrick v. Hedrick, Civ.App., 351 S.W.2d 659 (statement of investigating police officer in telephone conversation with son of driver that in officer's opinion driver of automobile was at fault was not inadmissible, on ground that it was hearsay, where telephone conversation was initiated by officer in behalf of driver of automobile, and statement that driver was at fault was made in response to direct question by driver's son, and driver was near by when officer placed telephone call).

Wis.—Wisconsin Rules of Evidence § 908.01(4)(b)(2).

But see

Ky.—Arnett v. Thompson, 1968, 433 S.W.2d 109 (pretrial statement of husband in which he set forth his version of accident placing all of the fault on another party, and which was endorsed by his wife, was self-serving extrajudicial statement which was inadmissible when offered by husband for purpose of supporting husband's trial testimony, and, on appeal, error in exclusion could not be predicated on theory that statement constituted an admission against interest by wife suing husband).

Effect of statute

A statute permitting admission of a declaration or act of another in the presence and within the observation of a party, and his conduct in relation thereto, permits admission of a third person's statement made in the presence of the adverse party if the adverse party possessed an opportu-

silence is significant only where the nature of the statement and the surrounding circumstances are such as to render a reply natural and proper.[20]

nity and a motive to deny the statement if deemed incorrect. O.C.L.A. § 2–228(3). Swain v. Oregon Motor Stages, 82 P.2d 1084, 160 Or. 1, 118 A.L.R. 1225.

Rule applied to silence in presence of demonstration

Conn.—Cashman v. Terminal Taxi Co., 37 A.2d 613, 131 Conn. 31 (testimony of police officer as to what driver did during demonstration of how driver had driven taxicab at time of accident was improperly excluded on ground that demonstration was an "experiment" requiring extraneous proof of similarity of conditions, since demonstration was an "admission by conduct" which was admissible to show inconsistency with driver's statement as to his conduct).

Silence not established

Conn.—Obermeier v. Nielsen, 1969, 255 A.2d 819, 158 Conn. 8 (testimony of police officer as to statements made by operator of one of the four automobiles involved in multiple collision while all the operators were in police car was not admissible on ground that defendant driver's alleged silence amounted to an admission of the truth of assertion, where police officer, in response to question, could not recall whether defendant driver had said anything about the damaging statement made in police car).

Ill.—Miyatovich v. Chicago Transit Authority, 1969, 251 N.E.2d 345, 112 Ill.App.2d 437 (officer's testimony, in action arising out of collision between plaintiff's automobile and a bus, as to what eyewitness, who was unavailable at trial, had told him in bus driver's presence was not admssible where only direct evidence of bus driver's reaction to statement was officer's testimony that he could not recall what driver had said).

20. Ind.—Sanders v. Ryan, 41 N.E. 2d 833, 112 Ind.App. 470 (the liability of defendants under law of "respondeat superior" for act of one driving automobile belonging to defendants could not be implied from silence of defendants when an attorney, acting in behalf of a person who might make claim against defendants, sought to question them in regard to the accident).

Minn.—Fischer v. Chicago & N. W. Ry. Co., 258 N.W. 4, 193 Minn. 73 (motorist's testimony that after being assisted from place of accident he stated to men in charge of train that they did not have lights, did not ring bell or blow whistle, and that statement was not denied, held improperly admitted).

N.Y.—McEnroe v. Taylor, 107 N.Y.S. 565, 56 Misc. 680 (silence upon service of summons).

Or.—Klever v. Elliott, 320 P.2d 263, 212 Or. 490, 70 A.L.R.2d 1094 (exclusion of testimony of witness who arrived on scene after accident, that he had directed statement to driver that it looked like a case of too much speed and that driver was not watching where he was going and that driver, who was five feet away, made no comment or reply thereto was not an abuse of discretion in view of fact that witness was a fellow employee of other driver and that driver was rendering aid).

Wash.—Baird v. Webb, 294 P. 1000, 160 Wash. 157.

Wis.—Kowalsky v. Whipkey, 2 N.W. 2d 704, 240 Wis. 59.

§ 434.2   TRIAL EVIDENCE   Ch. 434

Moreover, there must be an opportunity to reply.[21] Further, in order that any significance may attach to a party's failure to reply to a statement, it must ordinarily appear that the statement was actually heard.[22] Being within hearing distance is not sufficient,[23] unless the situation was such that it must necessarily have been heard.

Admissions in pleadings

Broadly speaking, allegations in pleadings are admissible in evidence.[24] More specifically, statements in pleadings which are

21. **N.Y.**—Lichtenstein v. Cascio, 83 N.Y.S.2d 195, 274 App.Div. 309 (one to be charged with admission suffering from shock).

22. **Ala.**—Robinson v. Morrison, 133 So.2d 230, 272 Ala. 552.

Ariz.—Ruth v. Rhodes, 185 P.2d 304, 66 Ariz. 129.

Cal.—Henderson v. Northam, 168 P. 1044, 176 Cal. 493.

23. **Ariz.**—Ruth v. Rhodes, 185 P. 2d 304, 66 Ariz. 129.

24. **Cal.**—Muth v. Urricelqui, 1967, 60 Cal.Rptr. 166, 251 Cal.App.2d 901.

Conn.—Frye v. Krasicky, 1968, 247 A.2d 439, 5 Conn.Cir. 164.

N.Y.—Blakney v. Gleam Cab Corp., 1973, 349 N.Y.S.2d 77, 43 A.D.2d 520 (in wrongful death action, against owner and driver of taxicab, it was reversible error to exclude testimony that such passenger witness had sued only the driver and owner of the following automobile).

Or.—Marsh v. Davidson, 1973, 510 P. 2d 558, 265 Or. 532 (where plaintiff testified that she had not suffered permanent injuries in previous accident, contrary allegations in complaint in action arising from previous accident were admissible to show that injuries complained of in instant case were not result of subsequent accident).

Tex.—Beseda v. Transamerica Ins. Co., Civ.App.1967, 414 S.W.2d 742;

Miller v. Hooper, Civ.App.1936, 94 S.W.2d 230.

But see

Allegations of plaintiff's petition in regard to two dismissed defendants should have been excluded as tending to confuse the issues, and such matter was not admissible as admissions against interest. Macheca v. Fowler, Mo., 412 S.W.2d 462.

Not deemed an admission

Cal.—Jayne, Occidental Indemnity Co., Intervenor v. Morck, 1941, 111 P.2d 696, 43 Cal.App.2d 743 (in death action, evidence that one defendant, who sustained injuries in accident involved and testified as to his freedom from negligence, but asserted no claim for damages, failed to file cross-complaints or counterclaims in previous suits against him by several people for injuries arising out of such accident, was inadmissible).

Mo.—Jimenez v. Broadway Motors, Inc., 1969, 445 S.W.2d 315 (statement in manufacturer's abandoned answer in breach of warranty action that "in operating or permitting the operation of the vehicle in its then mechanical condition" plaintiff was negligent did not constitute an admission that automobile it had sold plaintiff was defective); Sanfilippo v. Bolle, 1968, 432 S.W.2d 232 (allegation of father of child killed in accident, made in prior case against another defendant, that defendant in that case was negligent, was not

Ch. 434   HEARSAY   § 434.2

satisfactorily shown to be those of a party or to have been approved by the party are admissible against the party making them or a successor in the litigation, as proof of the facts admitted therein, on any trial of the case subsequent to the making of such statements, including a trial in an appellate court, and are equally competent whether the pleader is plaintiff or defendant. But if an attorney undertakes to state the client's cause of action and includes therein utterances never made or authorized by the client, the client is not bound thereby, and such erroneous statements are not admissible against the client.[25]

Even abandoned or superseded pleadings are admissible.[26]

an admission that defendant in present case was not negligent, particularly where there was only a general allegation of negligence made in prior case); Littell v. Bi-State Transit Develop. Agency, App.1967, 423 S.W.2d 34 (if plaintiff makes inconsistent claims against multiple defendants, such pleas do not possess characteristics inherent in admissions against interest and may not be used as admissions upon another issue in same case); Howell v. Dowell, App.1967, 419 S.W.2d 257 (host driver's answer which denied all charges of negligence against him in guest's petition, and also alleged contributory negligence of guest, was not admissible as admission against driver's interest notwithstanding guest's contention that failure to see other vehicle in time to warn of its approach was only negligence of which she could have been guilty and that if she should have seen he also should have seen).

Not pleadings in behalf of minors

Admissions by a next friend or guardian ad litem in pleadings filed for infant are not ordinarily admissible against infant. Johnson v. Riecken, 1970, 173 N.W.2d 511, 185 Neb. 78.

25. **U.S.**—Christensen v. Trotter, C.A.Ariz., 171 F.2d 66.

Ariz.—Buehman v. Smelker, 68 P.2d 946, 50 Ariz. 18.

Neb.—Johnson v. Griepenstroh, 33 N.W.2d 549, 150 Neb. 126 (where amended pleading is inconsistent with original pleading, the original is admissible as an admission).

Ohio.—Byrum v. Red Star Transit Co., App., 80 N.E.2d 616, 81 Ohio App. 495.

Tex.—Gillette Motor Transport Co., v. Whitfield, Civ.App., 186 S.W. 2d 90.

26. **U.S.**—Raulie v. U. S., C.A.N.M., 1968, 400 F.2d 487.

Pa.—Monaco v. Gula, 180 A.2d 893, 407 Pa. 522.

Wash.—Davis v. Browne, 147 P.2d 263, 20 Wash.2d 219 (admission in original verified answer may be considered even though amended answer denied such allegation).

Limited to abandoned pleadings

Trial pleadings are inadmissible because they would be confusing but such is not true of abandoned pleadings or pleadings in another lawsuit, and such may be used as admissions against party's interest or to impeach a witness. Littell v. Bi-State Transit Develop. Agency, Mo. App.1967, 423 S.W.2d 34.

733

§ 434.2 TRIAL EVIDENCE Ch. 434

Admissions of agents or others [27]

While the statements of a person are competent as admissions against the declarant, such statements are not competent as against a principal,[28] or one not in privity with the declarant.[29]

27. For discussion of specific admissions by agents as to status of a person alleged to be vicariously liable, see § 434.5.

For discussion of specific admissions by agents of negligent conduct, see § 434.3.

For discussion of declarations admissible under the separate exception of "spontaneous declarations" or "res gestae", see § 434.8.

28. **Ala.**—Alabama Power Co. v. Sellers, 1968, 214 So.2d 833, 283 Ala. 137.

Ark.—Home Ins. Co. v. Allied Tel. Co., 1969, 442 S.W.2d 211, 246 Ark. 1095 (in absence of evidence that driver of plaintiff's vehicle had actual or implied authority to make such admission).

Ga.—Augusta Coach Co. v. Lee, 1967, 154 S.E.2d 689, 115 Ga.App. 511 (testimony of police officer that two weeks after bus allegedly struck rear of automobile the bus driver informed officer that bus did not have good brakes was clearly hearsay testimony and had no probative value in action by widow of driver of automobile against bus company for alleged wrongful death of driver of automobile).

Mass.—Hayeck v. Raymond, 154 N.E.2d 80, 338 Mass. 116 (an admission of ownership by the son would not be admissible against the father).

N.Y.—Van Campen v. Cram, 1968, 291 N.Y.S.2d 22, 30 A.D.2d 541.

N.C.—D. L. H., Inc. v. Mack Trucks, Inc., 1968, 164 S.E.2d 532, 3 N.C. App. 290.

Tex.—Bryant v. Kimmons, 1968, 430 S.W.2d 73; Miles-Sierra Co. v. Castillo, 398 S.W.2d 948, ref. n. r. e. (written admissions by former employees almost two years after accident giving rise to action against former employees and former employer were hearsay and inadmissible insofar as former employer was concerned).

Contra where authorized

U.S.—Federal Rules of Evidence § 801(d)(2)(C).

Me.—Maine Rules of Evidence § 801(d)(2)(C).

Neb.—Nebraska Rules of Evidence § 801(4)(b)(iii).

Nev.—N.R.S. 51.035(3)(c).

N.M.—New Mexico Rules of Evidence § 801(d)(2)(C).

Ohio.—Chowning v. Ajax Motor Service, 1938, 21 N.E.2d 1021, 60 Ohio App. 470.

Wis.—Wisconsin Rules of Evidence § 908.01(4)(b)(3).

Contra where concerns matter within scope, made during relationship

U.S.—Federal Rules of Evidence § 801(d)(2)(D).

Me.—Maine Rules of Evidence § 801(d)(2)(D).

Neb.—Nebraska Rules of Evidence § 801(4)(b)(iv).

Nev.—N.R.S. 51.035(3)(d).

N.M.—New Mexico Rules of Evidence § 801(d)(2)(D).

Wis.—Wisconsin Rules of Evidence § 908.01(4)(b)(4).

Written statement signed by attorney

Written statement prepared and signed by plaintiff's attorney and filed with police department was inadmissible to contradict plaintiff's tes-

29. See note 29 on page 735.

The authority of agents to make representations or admissions may be implied from an express authority to do some act or to act in some capacity.[30]

timony or as an admission against interest, where such attorney was engaged to do whatever was necessary in plaintiff's behalf, and plaintiff had not discussed facts of accident with him prior to filing of such statement, and gave him no specific authorization to prepare the paper, sign client's name thereto, and file it with police department. Kanderer v. McAllister Coal Co., 40 A.2d 624, 132 N.J.L. 410.

29. **U.S.**—Sternberger v. U. S., 1968, 401 F.2d 1012, 185 Ct.Cl. 528 (purported admissions in course of compromise negotiations by unauthorized person, such as parent or wife, do not amount to admission of the party); Tudor v. Leslie, D.C. Mass., 1 F.R.D. 448 (whether statements would be admissible against codefendant depended upon whether circumstances showed that statements were made with codefendant's authority and other considerations).

Absence of privity

Driver and persons injured were not in "privity" in instant action by liability insurer against driver and injured persons for declaratory judgment that policy issued to driver's brother-in-law did not protect driver on ground of change of ownership of automobile prior to accident, and consequently driver's statement, in his deposition in injured persons' action against him, that he had purchased automobile from brother-in-law prior to accident, was not binding on injured persons. Newark Ins. Co. v. Bennett, Ky., 355 S.W.2d 303.

But see

Evidence that motorist pleaded guilty to accusation charging him with hitting and damaging plaintiff while on highway and unlawfully failing to stop was admissible, in John Doe action against uninsured motorist insurer, as voluntary admission and prima facie evidence of facts admitted even though motorist was not real party in interest in John Doe action. State Farm Mut. Auto. Ins. Co. v. Godfrey, 1969, 171 S.E.2d 735, 120 Ga.App. 560.

Father of infant victim

Father's statement that his infant daughter who ran into street and came into contact with truck should have been in backyard was incompetent as an admission against the infant and admission of policeman's testimony as to father's statement was error but was not prejudicial where mother testified, without objection, that she had told girl to play in backyard. Hermance v. Slopey, 1969, 299 N.Y.S.2d 38, 32 A.D.2d 573.

Not as against statutory beneficiary of wrongful death benefit

Admission of testimony of defendant truck driver, in widower's action for death of passenger resulting from intersectional collision, as to statement made to defendant by passenger to effect that accident was not defendant's fault was prejudicial error. Carpenter v. Davis, Mo.1968, 435 S.W.2d 382.

Real party in interest

Testimony concerning statement made by five-year-old boy's mother to defendant declaring death a result of an unavoidable accident was admissible as an admission or declaration against interest made by person who, although not a party of record, was a real party in interest to wrongful death action by administratrix of boy's estate. Sherman v. Mountaire Poultry Co., 1967, 419 S.W.2d 619, 243 Ark. 301, citing 31A C.J.S. Evidence § 320.

30. **Mass.**—McGenness v. Adriatic Mills, 116 Mass. 177.

§ 434.2 TRIAL EVIDENCE Ch. 434

Admission made by the driver of a vehicle, made immediately following the accident, are not binding upon the occupants of the vehicle in absence of showing that the statements were part of res gestae or that the driver was an agent empowered to bind the occupants.[31] Likewise, admissions of occupants are not binding against the owner.[32]

Admissions by a co-owner of an automobile, not a party to the action, are competent evidence against the other co-owner, the defendant in the action, as an admission.[33]

"Declarations against interest"

Declarations against interest, by one other than a party, may be admissible under the separate exception to hearsay rule

Tex.—West Texas Produce Co. v. Wilson, 34 S.W.2d 827, 120 Tex. 35 (related to identity of driver employee).

Declaration of adjuster

N.H.—U. S. Fidelity & Guaranty Co. v. Kancer, 1967, 238 A.2d 5, 108 N.H. 450 (adjuster's statements as to whether insurer would defend insured, admitted over insurer's exceptions in proceeding by insurer against insured and claimants for decree declaring insurer not liable for claims made under policy, were relevant on question of insurer's alleged waiver of right to deny liability because of late notice of accident, were within adjuster's apparent authority in dealing with an insured and therefore were properly admitted in evidence).

Declaration of insurance agent

Permitting insured to testify in action against automobile liability insurer that insurer's local recording agent, who had issued policy to insured and collected premiums from him, told him shortly after accident that other motorist was "uninsured" as far as automobile liability insurance was concerned was not error. State Farm Mut. Auto. Ins. Co. v. Matlock, Tex.Civ.App.1969, 446 S.W. 2d 81, error granted, affirmed in part, reversed in part on other grounds, Sup., 462 S.W.2d 277.

Declaration of office secretary

Testimony by insured that he had talked with secretary of agent of insurer after motor scooter was involved in accident and that secretary had confirmed coverage of motor scooter under liability policy, although hearsay, was admissible as an admission in declaratory judgment action against insurer to establish coverage under policy. Rent-A-Scooter, Inc. v. Universal Underwriters Ins. Co., 1969, 173 N.W.2d 9, 285 Minn. 264.

31. **U.S.**—Maddux v. Cox, C.A.Ark. 1967, 382 F.2d 119.

Mich.—Germiquet v. Hubbard, 41 N. W.2d 531, 327 Mich. 225.

32. **N.Y.**—Bloodgood v. Lynch, 45 N.Y.S.2d 530, 267 App.Div. 797, appeal denied 47 N.Y.S.2d 282, 267 App.Div. 853, reversed on other grounds 56 N.E.2d 718, 293 N.Y. 308.

33. **Cal.**—Wilcox v. Berry, 195 P.2d 414, 32 Cal.2d 189 (in suit against wife as co-owner for injuries caused by the negligent operation of car by husband, statement by husband after accident admissible).

Ch. 434 HEARSAY § 434.2

of "declarations against interest",[34] but it first must be shown that the declarant is unavailable as a witness.[35]

Judicial admissions

Certain admissions are merely items of evidence and are held available against a party on the same theory that a self-contradiction is held admissible. Judicial admissions, however, made

34. **Ill.**—Clifford v. Schaefer, 1969, 245 N.E.2d 49, 105 Ill.App.2d 233 (host motorist's statement to police officer that he saw oncoming automobile prior to making left turn in front of oncoming automobile but that he thought he "could make it" into restaurant driveway constituted an "admission against interest").

Mo.—Carpenter v. Davis, 1968, 435 S.W.2d 382 (statement attributed to passenger, who died subsequent to collision, even though constituting opinion as to fault for accident, as distinguished from statement of fact, would have been admissible as admission against interest had passenger survived and action been brought for damages for her injuries).

Pa.—Rudisill v. Cordes, 1939, 5 A.2d 217, 333 Pa. 544 (deceased's declaration of defendant's non-liability, 10–15 min. after accident).

Limited to "collateral" issues

Extrajudicial admission of third person showing that insured procured him to take and destroy automobile bore directly upon main issue of insured's right to recover from insurer and was not admissible. Lewis v. American Road Ins. Co., 1969, 167 S.E.2d 729, 119 Ga.App. 507. Whatever may be meant by language "collateral to the main issue but essential to the adjudication" as contained in rule relating to admissibility of admission by person not party to action, it is not applicable if statement bears directly upon main issue in case. Id.

35. **U.S.**—Federal Rules of Evidence § 804(b)(3).

Cal.—West's Ann.Calif.Evid.Code, § 1230; Arellano v. Moreno, 1973, 109 Cal.Rptr. 421, 33 Cal.App.3d 877 (statement of nonparty owner of one car involved to police officer that point of impact between his temporarily inoperable car, which had been pushed at least in part to southbound side of street, and defendant's car, which was traveling on northbound side of street, was on northbound side of street, was admissible where owner was not available).

Fla.—Florida Evidence Code § 90.804 (c).

Ill.—Swearinger v. Klinger, 1968, 234 N.E.2d 60, 91 Ill.App.2d 251 (plaintiff's driver who was absent from trial because she was tending a sick child was not "unavailable" and defendant driver was not entitled to admit her statements under declaration against interest exception to hearsay rule).

Kan.—Kansas Code of Civil Procedure § 60–460(j).

Me.—Maine Rules of Evidence § 804 (b)(3).

Neb.—Nebraska Rules of Evidence § 804(2)(c).

Nev.—N.R.S. 51.345.

N.J.—New Jersey Evidence Rule 63 (10).

N.M.—New Mexico Rules of Evidence § 804(b)(4).

Utah.—Utah Rules of Evidence 63 (10).

Wis.—Wisconsin Rules of Evidence § 908.045(4).

§ 434.2   TRIAL EVIDENCE   Ch. 434

by either a party or counsel, may preclude introduction of proof to the contrary.[36]

36. **Ark.**—Miller v. Blanton, 1948, 210 S.W.2d 293, 213 Ark. 246, 3 A.L.R.2d 203 (plea of guilty to charge of reckless driving).

Cal.—Miller v. Johnston, 1969, 75 Cal.Rptr. 699, 270 Cal.App.2d 289 (opening statement of counsel).

Conn.—Kanopka v. Kanopka, 1931, 154 A. 144, 113 Conn. 30, 80 A.L.R. 619.

Ky.—Samuels v. Spangler, 1969, 441 S.W.2d 129 (if plaintiff makes opening statement of facts showing contributory negligence as matter of law on his part, such would constitute admission fatal to his case); Bell v. Harmon, 1955, 284 S.W.2d 812 (pre-trial deposition).

Md.—McLhinney v. Lansdell Corp. of Md., 1969, 254 A.2d 177, 254 Md. 7 (rule that "an opening statement is not evidence" is correct insofar as statements made in attorney's opening comments cannot replace requirement of substantive evidence, but it does not mean that an attorney, acting as his client's agent within scope of his authority, should not be able to make admissions favorable to opposing side).

N.C.—Lewis v. Piggott, 1972, 192 S.E. 2d 128, 16 N.C.App. 395 (an inference of driver negligence cannot be made from an accident when plaintiff passenger's own testimony is that there was nothing wrong with defendant's driving).

Or.—Morey v. Redifer, 282 P.2d 1062, 204 Or. 194 (testimony tending to falsify stipulation was inadmissible).

Vt.—Choiniere v. Sulikowski, 1967, 229 A.2d 305, 126 Vt. 274 (statement by defendant's counsel who conceded in final argument that defendant's operation of automobile which skidded across road onto plaintiff's side of road was negligent, was a "judicial admission").

Bound to own theory of facts

Where plaintiff's testimony constituted positive statements of facts that collision occurred when automobile in which she was riding was in proper half of roadway and came in contact with an automobile being operated in the wrong half of the roadway, her testimony amounted to a judicial admission that the collision occurred in plaintiff's driver's half of the roadway, and she was conclusively bound to a theory of recovery based on such facts. Hecker v. Schwartz, Mo.1968, 426 S.W.2d 22.

Conversation between counsel

Where identity of defendant as driver or owner was speculative, admitting testimony of alleged conversation between plaintiff's counsel and defendant's counsel, wherein defendant's counsel allegedly said trial would be confined to issue of negligence, held reversible error. Carle v. Rainey, 83 F.2d 600, 65 App.D.C. 343.

Held not an unequivocal statement

Defense counsel's statement to jury that evidence was such that he thought jury was required to give affirmative answer to special issue inquiring as to whether plaintiff wife had been injured as result of collision was not a "judicial admission" since it was not an unequivocal statement in view of defense counsel's other remarks vigorously denying that plaintiff wife had sustained any injury. Hedge v. Bryan, Tex.Civ.App.1968, 425 S.W.2d 866, error refused n. r. e.

Not conclusive on retrial

Concession of counsel, representing city in first trial resulting in mistrial, that failure of city to have barrier erected between "T" intersection and ditch was negligence amounted to an opinion or conclusion which made any effort on his part to testify to such conclusion inadmissible but which did not preclude introduction of other evidence in second trial to show that city was not negligent in failing to erect barrier. Starks v. City of Houston, Tex.Civ.App.1970, 448 S.W.2d 698, error refused n. r. e.

Not contradiction in deposition

Rule concerning destructive contradictions applies only to contradictions between parts of a party's trial testimony, not to a trial statement which is inconsistent with a deposition. Atley v. Williams, Mo. App.1971, 472 S.W.2d 867.

Not deemed judicial admission

U.S.—Guenther v. Armstrong Rubber Co., C.A.Pa.1969, 406 F.2d 1315 (testimony of employee, suing tire manufacturer for injuries sustained when tire he was preparing to mount on automobile of customer burst, that the tire which burst was a blackwall tire did not constitute a judicial admission which would preclude submission of issue of negligence to jury where tire which defendant manufacturer admitted making which employer's service manager stated caused accident and which was in court was a whitewall tire of a size different than that described by plaintiff, and it was error to direct a verdict against plaintiff employee).

Ill.—Sabo v. T. W. Moore Feed & Grain Co., 1968, 239 N.E.2d 459, 97 Ill.App.2d 7 (statements by plaintiffs' counsel in closing argument that counsel was particularly impressed with truthfulness of truck driver but that automobile driver had consistently lied, that he could not, in good conscience, state that he felt truck driver was at fault, or that his vehicle, prior to collision, had been on wrong side of road, did not constitute judicial admissions serving to relieve truck driver or truck owner of liability); Vincent v. Wesolowski, 1967, 232 N.E.2d 120, 87 Ill. App.2d 477 (following motorist's equivocal deposition statement that he did not notice any damage to northbound automobile in which passenger was riding did not constitute a judicial admission where at trial he testified that her damage was on left side only, the damage being to the taillight, and where he apparently did not think that a broken taillight, in comparison to $350 repair bill for his own automobile, was serious enough to be called damage).

Iowa—Harlan v. Passot, 1967, 150 N. W.2d 87, 260 Iowa 501 (where truck owner offered repair bill and defense counsel stated that there was no objection to its admission with the understanding that it was the bill under which repairs were made and showed the actual cost to repair truck, there was no judicial admission of actual cost of repair to truck and of the right to recover that amount in event of verdict for owner).

La.—Treadway v. State Farm Ins. Co., La.App.1967, 204 So.2d 609.

Mo.—Richardson v. Moreland, 1968, 435 S.W.2d 335 (testimony that had not continued to watch automobile with which he collided as it came off bridge and thought that he had plenty of time to turn was not admission of liability by defendant); Baldwin v. Atchison, T. & S. F. Ry. Co., 1968, 425 S.W.2d 905 (passenger's testimony that he could see possibly 200 feet when approaching grade crossing did not constitute judicial admission that he could see that far in full context of his testimony to effect that he did not know distance one could see from any point, that he was uncertain about view as one drew closer to tracks, and that one could not see too far until he got right up to the tracks, in action against railroad for injuries sustained in grade crossing collision); Smith v. Siercks, 277 S.W.2d 521

§ 434.2   TRIAL EVIDENCE   Ch. 434

However, it has been stated that "judicial admissions" are to be limited to matters within the peculiar knowledge of the party,[37] and to matters understandingly and knowingly stated by the witness.[38]

(plaintiff's testimony, that he had returned to and was in his own proper lane when the collision occurred, did not amount to a judicial admission as to the position of his automobile at time of the collision and did not preclude him from deriving benefit from more favorable testimony).

Tex.—Garner Motors, Inc. v. Innes, Civ.App.1974, 503 S.W.2d 655, error refused n. r. e. (variance, in certain respects, between testimony given by plaintiff, who was experienced mechanic, and testimony of expert mechanic whom plaintiff called as his witness presented matter of weight and credibility for jury, and plaintiff was not bound by that portion of such witness' testimony which was at variance with his own).

Stipulations made at prior trial

Exclusion of defendants' stipulation made without limitation at prior trial, admitting liability, was error. Gonzales v. Pacific Greyhound Lines, 214 P.2d 809, 34 Cal.2d 749.

37. Ill.—Vincent v. Wesolowski, 1967, 232 N.E.2d 120, 87 Ill.App.2d 477 (following motorist's testimony relating to speed and position of northbound automobile in which passenger was riding at time of collision did not involve fact peculiarly within following motorist's own knowledge and it did not constitute a judicial admission).

Not mere estimates or opinions

Mich.—Ortega v. Lenderink, 1969, 169 N.W.2d 470, 382 Mich. 218 (testimony of truck driver that, according to his best judgment, front of his truck was parked between 17 and 18 feet from crosswalk prior to time 7-year-old pedestrian ran out into intersection from in front of truck and was struck, where pedestrian was not prevented from presenting testimony of other witnesses as to question of distance involved and, in fact, did present three other witnesses, did not constitute a judicial admission on part of driver that he was in fact illegally parked within 20 feet of crosswalk).

Mo.—Colby v. National General Ins. Co., App.1973, 490 S.W.2d 323 (estimates of visibility and distances); Vaeth v. Gegg, 1972, 486 S.W.2d 625 (of time, speed, or distance).

N.H.—Sindorf v. Dow, 1972, 289 A. 2d 394, 112 N.H. 114 (as to location of vehicle in highway).

38. Conn.—Kanopka v. Kanopka, 154 A. 144, 113 Conn. 30, 80 A.L.R. 619 (witness restrained by knowledge of English).

Mo.—Johnson v. Bush, 1967, 418 S.W.2d 601 (in determining whether testimony amounted to a binding admission that she was a non-oblivious plaintiff, court was required to consider her testimony as a whole, and it was required that testimony relied on as an admission be clear and unqualified and not the result of mistake, oversight, misunderstanding, or lack of definite recollection).

Ch. 434 HEARSAY § 434.3

§ 434.3 Admissions—As to Negligent Conduct

The general rules as to admissions, discussed in § 434.2, have been applied to specific admissions of negligent conduct. In a variety of circumstances such admissions have been held admissible as to pertinent existing conditions,[39] as to the declarant's own acts of omission,[40] or of commission,[41] as to an acknowledge-

---

39. Conn.—Pluhowsky v. City of New Haven, 197 A.2d 645, 151 Conn. 337 (a motorist's accident report wherein he stated that his automobile struck a body of water and caused him to lose control and strike telephone pole).

Fla.—Goodis v. Finkelstein, 174 So. 2d 600 (statement of host driver, made to police officer at scene, to effect that she must have passed out again before losing control and that she had thought this would happen).

Md.—Joppy v. Hopkins, 1963, 188 A.2d 545, 231 Md. 52 (not sure where her vehicle was parked on road).

Mo.—Kasper v. Helfrich, 1967, 421 S.W.2d 66 (portion of police report that drivers of three automobiles, including that of defendant, had told investigating officer that forward automobiles were stopped and that then they were struck from behind by defendant's automobile).

Nev.—Tracy v. Pollock, 1963, 385 P.2d 340, 79 Nev. 1 (statement to eye doctor of progressive loss of vision before accident).

Condition of tires

Mo.—Crupe v. Spicuzza, App., 86 S.W.2d 347 (that driver, in deposition, had admitted front tire was "a little bad" held admissible, though it was back tire that blew out, where all tires were same age and purchased at same time).

40. Neb.—Whitaker v. Keogh, 14 N.W.2d 596, 144 Neb. 790, followed in 14 N.W.2d 600, 144 Neb. 796 (evidence that defendant's chauf-

feur immediately after collision stated, "Lady, I am sorry, I just saw you the instant I collided with you").

Pa.—Perciavalle v. Smith, 1969, 252 A.2d 702, 434 Pa. 86 (statements made by defendant driver of following automobile, immediately after collision, to effect that if he had had his automobile under control he could have avoided collision).

Wis.—Hack v. State Farm Mut. Auto. Ins. Co., 1967, 154 N.W.2d 320, 37 Wis.2d 1 (statement which motorist made to an investigator admitting he was in intersection before he saw automobile with which his vehicle collided was admissible as an admission against interest, notwithstanding motorist's claim that he did not understand what was being said in statement).

41. Ga.—Pruitt v. Pierce, 1959, 112 S.E.2d 327, 100 Ga.App. 808 (as to speed, and as to own insurance).

Ill.—Isley v. McClandish, 20 N.E.2d 890, 299 Ill.App. 564 (in administrator's action for death of child who was struck by automobile, evidence that parents on whose behalf action was brought permitted the child to play in public road, and evidence of parents' admissions with respect to that subject, was admissible on issue of contributory negligence of the parents).

Kan.—Mann v. Good, 1969, 451 P.2d 233, 202 Kan. 631 (admissions which host motorist made following passenger's death as to speed and passenger's asking host

741

§ **434.3** TRIAL EVIDENCE Ch. 434

ment that an adverse party was free of fault,[42] and as to other particular admissions.[43]

motorist to slow down prior to fatal collision).

Ky.—Webb Transfer Lines, Inc. v. Taylor, 1968, 439 S.W.2d 88 (that defendant driver had told sheriff that he knew he was in 50-mile speed zone and that in answer to question as to whether he was going 60 miles per hour or more he had said "I don't know. I was pouring it on").

Tex.—Love v. Grizzaffi, 1968, 423 S.W.2d 164 (testimony of investigating officer that motorist, sued for damage she caused when hitting building, had said that she had gotten her foot on accelerator instead of brake was admissible as an admission).

Wash.—Paddock v. Tone, 1946, 172 P.2d 481, 25 Wash.2d 940 (speed).

Plea of guilty

Ark.—Cherry v. Vinson, 1968, 427 S.W.2d 17, 244 Ark. 742 (of improper parking); Midwest Bus Lines, Inc. v. Williams, 1968, 422 S.W.2d 869, 243 Ark. 854 (charge of driving automobile over center mark).

Conn.—Baritot v. Viggiano, 1968, 245 A.2d 298, 5 Conn.Cir. 123 (to charge of failure to drive in right-hand lane).

Me.—MacDonald v. Hall, 1968, 244 A.2d 809 (record of defendant's conviction for operating a vehicle so as to endanger).

Neb.—Piechota v. Rapp, 1947, 27 N.W.2d 682, 148 Neb. 442 (reckless driving).

N.Y.—Quay v. Hertz Corp., 1968, 286 N.Y.S.2d 42, 29 A.D.2d 713 (to charge of failure to yield right-of-way).

N.C.—Grant v. Shodrick, 1963, 133 S.E.2d 457, 260 N.C. 674 (to charge of failure to yield right of way).

Tex.—Atkinson v. Rister, Civ.App. 1968, 422 S.W.2d 821, quoting 31A C.J.S. Evidence § 300, error refused n. r. e. (to complaint charging him with illegal parking and failure to have red light or flag on projecting load).

42. **U.S.**—Nu Car Carriers v. Traynor, 1942, 125 F.2d 47, 75 U.S.App. D.C. 174.

Iowa—Olson v. Hodges, 19 N.W.2d 676, 236 Iowa 612 (statement signed by guest while in hospital that defendant host was not driving fast or carelessly).

Mass.—La Plante v. Maguire, 89 N. E.2d 1, 325 Mass. 96 (plaintiff's statement that he did not believe any of the motorists were going "too fast"); Langan v. Pianowski, 29 N.E.2d 700, 307 Mass. 149 (guest's signed statement to insurance investigator indicating that host was driving carefully).

Mo.—Cash v. Bolle, 1968, 423 S.W.2d 743 (deposition testimony).

N.Y.—Packer v. Allen, 1971, 322 N.Y.S.2d 945, 37 A.D.2d 664 (where statement was offered by defendant to contradict coplaintiff's testimony at trial as to speed of defendant's automobile, which testimony at trial was to effect that he could not estimate such speed, while in prior written statement admitted into evidence coplaintiff stated that defendant's vehicle was going 15 miles per hour); Jackson v. Dickman, 9 N.Y.S.2d 688, 256 App.Div. 925, reargument denied 11 N.Y.S.2d 557, 256 App.Div. 1003 (excluding evidence that plaintiff made statements that the accident was not due to fault of codefendant was error as to such codefendant).

---

43. See note 43 on page 743.

742

Or.—Swain v. Oregon Motor Stages, 82 P.2d 1084, 160 Or. 1, 118 A.L.R. 1225 (an accident report prepared by passenger immediately after the collision and before he left the bus, on a form furnished by the bus company, in which passenger stated that driver of automobile was to blame for the accident).

Tex.—Birch v. Howard, 1969, 435 S.W.2d 945, error refused n. r. e.

Wis.—Hoffman v. Labutzke, 298 N.W. 583, 238 Wis. 164 (testimony by an uninterested witness, that approximately an hour and a half after accident guest told witness that accident was caused by an approaching automobile which crowded motorist's automobile off highway, was admissible as relating to an "admission against interest").

Accusation against other driver only

Statements by plaintiff and her husband to police officer that accident was caused by defendant were hearsay, self-serving and inadmissible as to the defendant, but such statements were inconsistent with plaintiff's claim that codefendant was at fault and as such were admissible on behalf of codefendant as admissions of plaintiffs. Walls v. Clark, 1969, 449 P.2d 141, 252 Or. 414.

But see

N.D.—Klein v. Harper, 1971, 186 N.W.2d 426 (where plaintiff's statement at scene that he would not make a claim against defendant was mere expression of state of mind immediately following collision and did not tend to prove who was at fault, trial court properly refused to permit defendant to cross-examine plaintiff as to whether he made such statement).

Statement of another motorist accepting blame

Trial court's refusal, in action by bus passenger against carrier for injuries sustained when bus in which she was riding collided with motorist, to admit motorist's statement "I'm to blame for it" was within court's discretion since declarant was not a party to suit and evidence was merely cumulative and constituted an opinion of a lay witness and could not operate as shorthand rendering of the facts. Galveston Transit Co. v. Morgan, Tex.Civ.App., 408 S.W.2d 728.

43. Ga.—Wade v. Drinkard, 1947, 45 S.E.2d 231, 76 Ga.App. 159 (as to fault).

Mass.—Harton v. Winship, 1950, 94 N.E.2d 774, 326 Mass. 380 (as to fault).

Mo.—Pyles v. Bos Lines, Inc., App. 1968, 427 S.W.2d 790 (deposition and answers to interrogatories).

N.H.—L'Esperance v. Sherburne, 1931, 155 A. 203, 85 N.H. 103 (statement to physician, "I am responsible").

N.Y.—Scott v. State, 240 N.Y.S.2d 279, 19 A.D.2d 574 (injured passenger's statement, not part of res gestae, as to how fast his father was driving when automobile went off state highway, killing father and resulting in claims against state, was admissible as against interest of passenger claiming damages for injuries but should not have been considered in administratrix' death case).

Wash.—Feldmiller v. Olson, 1969, 450 P.2d 816.

Admissible against declarant's estate

Mo.—Brautigam v. Hoffman, App. 1969, 444 S.W.2d 528.

Plea of guilty

U.S.—Waldron v. Hardwick, C.A.Ill. 1969, 406 F.2d 86 (operator's plea of guilty to traffic violation); State Farm Mut. Auto. Ins. Co. v. Worthington, C.A.Mo.1968, 405 F.2d 683 (insured's plea of guilty to manslaughter in connection with death of boy was admissible in subsequent garnishment proceeding

§ **434.3**   TRIAL EVIDENCE   Ch. 434

In a variety of other cases, purported admissions of negligent conduct were found to be inadmissible.[44]

brought against insurer by boy's mother who had secured judgment against insured, but it was not conclusive and insured's explanation of plea and his version of occurrence that occasioned criminal charge were also admissible).

Alaska—Leavitt v. Gillaspie, 1968, 443 P.2d 61.

Fla.—Chimerakis v. Evans, 1969, 221 So.2d 735.

Ga.—Henderson v. Henderson, 93 S.E.2d 822, 94 Ga.App. 64 (evidence that host driver attempted a plea of guilty to a charge of reckless driving by having her husband appear before a deputy sheriff and pay a fine, although not admissible on the theory that such action constituted a plea of guilty on her part, was admissible on the theory that it constituted an admission against interest).

Idaho—Mattson v. Bryan, 1968, 448 P.2d 201, 92 Idaho 587 (to involuntary manslaughter).

Ill.—Miyatovich v. Chicago Transit Authority, App.1969, 251 N.E.2d 345, 112 Ill.App.2d 437; Barnes v. Croston, 1969, 247 N.E.2d 1, 108 Ill.App.2d 182.

Kan.—Scogin v. Nugen, 1970, 464 P. 2d 166, 204 Kan. 568 (contention that cost and inconvenience of defending against a traffic ticket are practical motivations for plea of guilty to traffic violation is one affecting weight of evidence of guilty plea and may properly be presented to jury but does not justify exclusion of plea).

La.—Gorman v. Duke, App.1969, 217 So.2d 503, citing C.J.S. Evidence § 300(b).

Md.—Campfield v. Crowther, 1969, 249 A.2d 168, 252 Md. 88.

Mass.—Morris's Case, 1968, 238 N.E. 2d 35, 354 Mass. 420.

44. Fla.—World Wide Rent-A-Car, Inc. v. Boshnack, App.1944, 184 So.2d 467; Brickley v. Atlantic Coast Line R. Co., 13 So.2d 300, 153 Fla. 1 (in action for railroad crossing death, plaintiff's declaration against alleged joint tortfeasor with railroad for the same death was improperly admitted).

Mo.—Franklin v. Friedrich, 1971, 470 S.W.2d 474 (plea of guilty to charge of failure to exercise highest degree of care).

Tex.—Barrios v. Davis, 1967, 415 S.W.2d 714 (where defendant had been previously charged with traffic offense and had sent wife to pay fine, there was no error in excluding testimony concerning alleged plea of guilty to traffic offense in civil suit arising out of same negligence which gave rise to traffic charge).

Vt.—Ryalls v. Smith, 1963, 196 A.2d 494, 124 Vt. 14 (what host driver told officer as to how accident happened).

Declaration re planned alterations

Ill.—Gillson v. Gulf, M. & O. R. Co., 1969, 246 N.E.2d 269, 42 Ill.2d 193 (where letter from railroad to public officials related to matter of who would pay for installation of automatic warning device at grade crossing, letter was not admission by railroad that crossing was in fact dangerous or that it had duty to erect such a device and letter was not relevant).

Deemed not an admission

Cal.—Grant v. Hipsher, 1967, 64 Cal. Rptr. 892, 257 Cal.App.2d 375 (alleged tortfeasor's statement after accident "Go ahead and sue me. I am insured up to $25,000, but I hope she will settle out of court. It will be better for Nancy." was an expression of hope that matter

Declarations of an agent [45]

In establishing an owner's or principal's vicarious liability, the general rule is that the admissions of a driver or agent cannot be considered against the owner or principal,[46] unless the hearsay character of such evidence is somehow remedied.[47]

would be compromised, not an admission of liability).

Insurance reference not an admission

U.S.—Church v. Cochran, C.A.Ga. 1973, 480 F.2d 155 (properly excluded defendant's remark at scene to effect that he was covered by insurance, inasmuch as remark was hardly an admission of negligence and potential prejudice flowing from the admission of such statement far outweighed whatever probative value, if any, it might have had).

Not available to co-defendant

In bus passenger's action against bus company and automobilist for injuries sustained when automobile collided with bus, as between passenger and bus company, exhibit containing admission of automobilist that he did not blame bus operator for occurrence was a hearsay statement of a third party favorable to his codefendant and as it was made by stranger to passenger, it was wholly incompetent as evidence in support of bus company's defense against his claim and it was proper for passenger to request court to direct jury that admission was not binding on passenger and could not be considered as against passenger. Elms v. Kansas City Public Service Co., 335 S.W.2d 26, citing C.J.S. Evidence § 321.

Not available to joint tortfeasor

N.C.—Driver v. Edwards, 112 S.E.2d 98, 251 N.C. 650.

Not plea of nolo contendere

Cal.—Christensen v. Orr, 1969, 79 Cal.Rptr. 656, 275 Cal.App.2d 12 (statute providing that plea of nolo contendere may not be used against defendant as an admission in civil suit based upon or growing out of act upon which criminal prosecution is based envisions a personal injury suit for damages against defendant drunk driver).

Settlement and dismissal of claim of adverse party

Where parties agreed that dismissal of defendant's action against plaintiff would not prejudice plaintiff's right to sue for injuries sustained in same accident, no inference of admission of negligence arose. Manning v. Wymer, 1969, 78 Cal.Rptr. 600, 273 Cal.App.2d 519.

45. For discussion of admissibility of agent's admissions generally, see § 434.2, at fn. 27 et seq.

46. Similar statement from prior printing **cited by the court** in Big Mack Trucking Co., Inc. v. Dickerson, Tex.1973, 497 S.W.2d 283, 288.

U.S.—U. S. v. Standard Oil Co. of Cal., D.C.Cal., 60 F.Supp. 807, affirmed 153 F.2d 958, affirmed 67 S.Ct. 1604, 332 U.S. 301, 91 L.Ed. 2067 (plea of guilty).

Ark.—Bullington v. Farmer's Tractor & Implement Co., 324 S.W.2d 517, 230 Ark. 783; Elmore v. Dillard, 298 S.W.2d 338, 227 Ark. 260.

Conn.—Fairbanks v. State, 124 A.2d 893, 143 Conn. 653 (investigating officer was not the agent of the state for the purpose of making the statements attributed to him and they were not within his express or implied authority).

Fla.—Kaplan v. Roth, 84 So.2d 559.

47. See note 47 on page 747.

§ **434.3** TRIAL EVIDENCE Ch. 434

Ga.—Great American Indemnity Co. v. Oxford, 27 S.E.2d 880, 70 Ga. App. 208.

Iowa.—Wilkinson v. Queal Lumber Co., 226 N.W. 43, 208 Iowa 933.

Ky.—Cook v. Hall, 214 S.W.2d 1017, 308 Ky. 500; Square Deal Cartage Co. v. Smith, Adm'r, 210 S.W.2d 340, 307 Ky. 135 (truck driver); Southeastern Greyhound Lines v. Donohue, 1944, 182 S.W.2d 328, 298 Ky. 139 (statement by bus driver of having seen other vehicle zigzagging before the collision).

Md.—Wilson v. Dailey, 62 A.2d 284, 191 Md. 472; Baltimore & O. R. Co. v. State, for Use of Carbone, 181 A. 830, 169 Md. 345 (conversation between railroad yard conductor and driver of automobile after accident).

Mass.—Sherman v. Metropolitan Transit Authority, 189 N.E.2d 526, 345 Mass. 777; Palm v. Kulesza, 131 N.E.2d 472, 333 Mass. 461; Liberatore v. Town of Framingham, 53 N.E.2d 561, 315 Mass. 538 (letter written by town engineer purporting to state the facts was inadmissible as he was not authorized to make admissions for town or for truck operator, though engineer was agent of town in making and performance of contract between town and WPA).

Mich.—Kloosterman v. Kalamazoo City Lines, Inc., 1971, 192 N.W.2d 258, 386 Mich. 430 (guilty plea of bus driver to charge of failing to exercise due care).

Mo.—Douglas v. St. Louis Public Service Co., 231 S.W.2d 157, 360 Mo. 869; Grotjan v. Thompson, App., 140 S.W.2d 706 (conclusions of witnesses as to statements made by railroad engineer 40 minutes after accident at a time when he was not investigating accident for purpose of reporting facts to railroad, nor acting or claiming to act for railroad); Murray v. De Luxe Motor Stages of Illinois, App., 133 S.W.2d 1074 deposition of bus driver); Shelton v. Wolf Cheese Co., 93 S.W.2d 947, 338 Mo. 1129 (agent's narration of certain alleged circumstances or conditions of past event, made long after happening thereof, not competent).

N.J.—Barcello v. Biel, 61 A.2d 42, 137 N.J.L. 606 (truck driver's statement as to defective brakes); Decker v. Consolidated Feed, Coal & Lumber Co., 59 A.2d 15, 137 N.J.L. 154 (statements made by corporate officer to persons when they reported accident, and later to lawyer when he inquired about the accident).

N.Y.—Stanley v. Surface Transit, Inc., 248 N.Y.S.2d 157, 20 A.D.2d 854 (allowing police officer to testify that bus driver had stated that he did not know what happened and that he did not see anybody was prejudicial error); Schoenfeld v. Long Island R. Co., 97 N.Y.S.2d 271, 277 App.Div. 780 (statements by locomotive engineer and fireman); Galbraith v. Galbraith, 290 N.Y.S. 739, 248 App. Div. 914 (statements by driver of negligent acts committed by him); Boltan v. Barrett, Sup., 172 N.Y.S. 457 (re condition of vehicle).

N.C.—Carter v. Thurston Motor Lines, 41 S.E.2d 586, 227 N.C. 193; Hester v. Horton Motor Lines, 14 S.E.2d 794, 219 N.C. 743.

Okl.—Lacy Chevrolet Co. v. McGinnis, 72 P.2d 785, 181 Okl. 97.

Pa.—Gibson v. Bruner, 178 A.2d 145, 406 Pa. 315; Kunkel v. Vogt, 47 A.2d 195, 354 Pa. 279.

Tenn.—Kendall Oil Co. v. Payne, 293 S.W.2d 40, 41 Tenn.App. 201, certiorari denied 293 S.W.2d 43, 200 Tenn. 600.

Tex.—Kelly v. Green, Civ.App., 296 S.W.2d 576.

Vt.—Yardley v. Rutland R. Co., 153 A. 195, 103 Vt. 182.

W.Va.—Bean v. Baltimore & O. R. Co., 1 S.E.2d 881, 121 W.Va. 105.

However, the declaration of an agent will be binding on the principal where the scope of the agency includes authority to make statements;[48] and, in some jurisdictions, where the declaration concerns a matter in the scope of the agency and was made during existence of the relationship.[49]

§ 434.4 Admissions—As to Status in Vehicle

Also under the general rules as to admissions, discussed in § 434.2, admissions as to one's status in the vehicle have been held admissible.[50]

§ 434.5 Admissions—As to Status of Persons Alleged to Be Vicariously Liable

Library References:
C.J.S. Agency §§ 322, 324; Evidence §§ 241 et seq., 314.
West's Key No. Digests, Evidence ⚿123(11); Principal & Agent ⚿22, 122.

Also within the general rules as to admissions, discussed in § 434.2, statements made by an alleged agent are generally held inadmissible to prove the fact of agency, or having acted within the scope of employment.[51]

Wis.—Uren v. Purity Dairy Co., 32 N.W.2d 615, 252 Wis. 446, denied rehearing 33 N.W.2d 213, 252 Wis. 446.

47. For discussion as to declarations defined not to be hearsay, see section 434.1 at fn. 8 et seq.

For discussion as to declarations deemed to be within an exception for "declarations against interest", see section 434.2 at 34 et seq.

For discussion as to declarations deemed to be within an exception for "spontaneous declarations," see section 434.8.

48. See § 434.2 at fn. 28 et seq.

49. See § 434.2 at fn. 28 et seq.

50. **Colo.**—Green v. Jones, 319 P.2d 1083, 136 Colo. 512 (driver's understanding of purpose of money, which occupant's mother had given to driver, and which allegedly removed occupant from inhibitions of guest statute as payment for transportation).

Md.—Smith v. Branscome, 248 A.2d 455, 251 Md. 582; Terry v. O'Neal, 1950, 72 A.2d 26, 194 Md. 680 (defendant's statement to officers identifying self as driver).

51. **Ariz.**—Otero v. Soto, 267 P. 947, 34 Ariz. 87.

Ark.—Wright v. Harris, 262 S.W.2d 142, 222 Ark. 661.

Cal.—Shehtanian v. Kenny, 319 P.2d 699, 156 Cal.App.2d 576.

Conn.—Baptist v. Shanen, 145 A.2d 592, 145 Conn. 605; Voegeli v. Waterbury Yellow Cab Co., 150 A. 303, 111 Conn. 407, 69 A.L.R. 902.

Ga.—Mullis v. Merit Finance Co. of Savannah, No. 1, 1967, 158 S.E.2d 415, 116 Ga.App. 582; Swift & Co. v. Lawson, 97 S.E.2d 168, 95 Ga. App. 35.

§ 434.5   TRIAL EVIDENCE   Ch. 434

However, certain statements of an alleged agent have been held admissible on such issues under some circumstances.[52]

Idaho.—Lallatin v. Terry, 340 P.2d 112, 81 Idaho 238; Hayward v. Yost, 242 P.2d 971, 72 Idaho 415.

Ind.—Frick v. Bickel, 54 N.E.2d 436, 115 Ind.App. 114, motion denied 57 N.E.2d 62, 222 Ind. 610.

La.—Patrick v. Patrick, App.1970, 230 So.2d 759.

Mo.—Rivas v. Glenn, App., 345 S.W.2d 397; Rosser v. Standard Mill Co., 312 S.W.2d 106.

N.H.—Alexander v. Todd, 199 A. 82, 89 N.H. 365 (telephone conversation).

N.J.—Van Genderen v. Paterson Wimsett Thrift Co., 24 A.2d 223, 128 N.J.L. 41.

N.Y.—Sokolof v. Donn, Sup., 194 N.Y.S. 580.

N.C.—Brothers v. Jernigan, 94 S.E.2d 316, 244 N.C. 441 (portion of defendant's answer admitting that he was driving truck with general knowledge and consent of codefendant was not admissible against codefendant who had denied agency); Salmon v. Pearce, 27 S.E.2d 647, 223 N.C. 587 (amounts to no more than a mere narrative of a past occurrence).

Ohio.—E. W. Bohren, Inc. v. Dangler, 124 N.E.2d 837, 97 Ohio App. 217.

Tenn.—Frank v. Wright, 205 S.W. 434, 140 Tenn. 535.

Tex.—Brown Exp. Co. v. Dieckman, Civ.App., 344 S.W.2d 501; R. G. Duke & Son v. Burk, Civ.App., 233 S.W.2d 617.

Wash.—Sullivan v. Associated Dealers, 103 P.2d 489, 4 Wash.2d 352 (considered only for impeachment purposes where there was no other evidence establishing agency at time of accident).

Wis.—Thomas v. Lockwood Oil Co., 182 N.W. 841, 174 Wis. 486.

Even though "spontaneous"

Md.—Tregellas v. American Oil Co., 188 A.2d 691, 231 Md. 95 (statement of defendant's salesman to the effect that he was "on company business," was not admissible in view of fact existence of agency cannot be proved by unsworn declarations of the agent in absence of other evidence of agency).

Neb.—Myers v. McMaken, 1937, 276 N.W. 167, 133 Neb. 524 (that he was making a pickup for defendant).

Tex.—Hill v. Moore, Civ.App., 278 S.W.2d 472 (erred in permitting state highway patrolman to testify that driver of tractor trailer told patrolman that alleged owner owned the tractor trailer, since employment of driver was not part of the res gestae).

Statement as to being uninsured, offered against indemnification corporation

N.Y.—Rosen v. Motor Vehicle Acc. Indemnification Corp., 247 N.Y.S.2d 205, 20 A.D.2d 704 (not admissible as part of the res gestae, as a declaration against interest, nor as an admission against interest by one in privity or authorized to speak for the Corporation).

52. For discussion of exceptions recognized, in instances where the statement is made during existence of the relationship, see § 434.2 at fn. 28.

U.S.—Garford Trucking Corp. v. Mann, 163 F.2d 71, C.C.A.Mass., certiorari denied 68 S.Ct. 112, 332 U.S. 810, 92 L.Ed. 388 (that he took certain route while in course of duties).

Ark.—Golenternek v. Kurth, 212 S.W.2d 14, 213 Ark. 643, 3 A.L.R.2d 593.

Cal.—Gardner v. Marshall, 132 P.2d 833, 56 Cal.App.2d 62.

Conn.—Bogart v. Tucker, 1973, 320 A.2d 803, 164 Conn. 277 (where issue was raised as to whether there was agency relationship between defendant driver and owner of one automobile involved, testimony given by such driver, who testified that he had been given permission to operate automobile, that he had admitted to police officer that driver had stolen car was admissible both for its probative value and for purpose of impeaching driver's credibility); Smith v. Firestone Tire & Rubber Co., 1935, 177 A. 524, 119 Conn. 483 (salesman had said territory was in area of accident).

Mo.—Smith v. Fine, 1943, 175 S.W.2d 761, 351 Mo. 1179.

R.I.—Pescosolido v. Crugnale, 171 A. 2d 443, 93 R.I. 82 (driver was competent to testify as to what conditions, if any, were attached to his use of truck, that might make driver truck owner's agent).

Tex.—Coca-Cola Bottling Co. v. Krueger, Tex.Civ.App., 239 S.W.2d 669 (testimony of truck driver that he was driving the truck involved, and had been driving for defendant corporation for several years and that at time of collision he was on regular routine work training a route man).

Agent's construction of contract

Testimony that defendant newspaper's city circulation manager had told witness, district manager, that written contract with newspaper was not worth the paper it was written on and was made to protect the newspaper was material on issue of whether written contract had been abandoned by newspaper insofar as controlling details of work of another district manager who newspaper alleged had been independent contractor when involved in accident and was admissible over objection that it was an attempt by city circulation manager to state his own understanding of written contract and its effectiveness. Newspapers, Inc. v. Love, Tex., 397 S.W.2d 469, ref. n. r. e.

Declaration admissible against one secondarily liable

Testimony of fourteen year old boy plaintiff that, while visiting him in hospital, person who had been loaned automobile by another, said that she, in turn, had loaned automobile to its operator, was admissible against person and, therefore, other, as evidence that operator was driving with permission of other at time of accident, under Code of Civil Procedure provision that where question in dispute between parties is obligation or duty of third person, whatever would be evidence for or against such person is prima facie evidence between parties. Ingram v. Bob Jaffe Co., 293 P.2d 132, 139 Cal. App.2d 193.

Prior declaration of intent to go on business trip

Statement by salesman just prior to taking a motor trip that he was leaving on business of employer was admissible to prove that, at time automobile driven by salesman collided with plaintiff's automobile, salesman was within scope of employment. Tsirlis v. Standard Oil Co. of California, 90 P.2d 128, 32 Cal.App.2d 469.

Proper where spontaneous

U.S.—Murphy Auto Parts Co. v. Ball, 249 F.2d 508, 101 U.S.App.D.C. 416, certiorari denied 78 S.Ct. 413, 355 U.S. 932, 2 L.Ed.2d 415 (out-of-court utterance of defendant's employee, who had been driving his own vehicle, after working hours, when accident occurred, to effect that he was on an errand for his employer, was admissible); Kas v. Gilkerson, 1952, 199 F.2d 398, 91 U.S.App.D.C. 153.

§ 434.5   TRIAL EVIDENCE   Ch. 434

Admission of the alleged principal generally may be used to establish agency or conduct within the agency.[53]

§ 434.6   Testimony at a Prior Hearing

Library References:
C.J.S. Evidence § 384 et seq.
West's Key No. Digests, Evidence ⚖=575 et seq.

Testimony at a prior trial or official hearing is usually found to be within an exception to the hearsay rule,[54] if it is established

Where fact of employment conceded

Okl.—Stover v. Mackie, 41 P.2d 474, 170 Okl. 574 (that at time of accident driver, upon being asked, said that codefendant had lent him money to buy the automobile, and that he worked for codefendant, held admissible, in view of codefendant's admission that the employment existed and evidence as to sale of the automobile to codefendant for driver).

S.C.—Stevens v. Moore, 1948, 46 S.E. 2d 73, 211 S.C. 498 (statement bearing on whether then in course of employment).

Va.—Turner v. Burford Buick Corp., 112 S.E.2d 911, 201 Va. 693 (statements that he was on business for corporate defendant and was a salesman).

Where testimony limited to narrating own conduct

A statement made by driver of defendant's truck at time of accident that he was driving to the garage was a statement of fact showing just what he was doing, and from such statement of fact the legal conclusion that the driver was acting as defendant's agent could be properly drawn. Mancuso v. Hurwitz-Mintz Furniture Co., La.App., 183 So. 461, denying rehearing, App., 181 So. 814.

53. Md.—Hynes v. Wilson, 128 A. 70, 147 Md. 360 (admission by defendant that the son was demonstrating the car for the purpose of selling it for her was admissible to show that son was acting as defendant's agent at the time).

Mass.—Kramer v. Massachusetts Gas & Electric Light Supply Co., 11 N.E.2d 497, 298 Mass. 457.

Mo.—Kilcoyne v. Metz, App., 258 S. W. 4; Scott v. McLennan, App., 242 S.W. 140.

N.Y.—Regan v. Bellows, 1960, 200 N. Y.S.2d 575, 11 A.D.2d 586 (employer's report in files of Workmen's Compensation Board).

Ohio.—Goz v. Tenney, 136 N.E. 215, 104 Ohio St. 500.

Not statement of principal's wife

U.S.—Gallo v. Crocker, C.A.Miss., 321 F.2d 876 (declaration of principal's wife and bookkeeper was not admissible to show agency of an alleged employee of principal where there was no showing that wife had authority to bind her husband by a statement touching on the relationship between him and alleged employee).

54. Mo.—Bartlett v. Kansas City Public Service Co., 160 S.W.2d 740, 349 Mo. 13, 142 A.L.R. 666 (testimony in another action arising out of same accident).

But see

Even though nonresident eyewitness was not available at trial, court properly refused to permit two-week delay to enable such witness to attend and properly excluded testimony given at prior hearing. Rohr-

750

that the declarant is unavailable to testify,[55] and if a party to the present action, or a prior party with common motives and interests, has had the opportunity to cross-examine the witness.[56]

mayr v. City of New York, 1970, 307 N.Y.S.2d 539, 33 A.D.2d 920.

Effect of stipulation of parties

Under stipulation that either party might use testimony of any witness given at former trial, in order to save cost of taking depositions to perpetuate testimony, counsel did not have unlimited right to introduce transcript of testimony at former trial, particularly in case of a witness who had testified in former trial and who was actually present in court room during subsequent trial. Gilkerson v. Baltimore & O. R. Co., 51 S.E.2d 767, 132 W.Va. 133.

Foundation required to authenticate transcript

Proper foundation for admission of transcript of another cause requires court reporter to testify that the witnesses involved had been sworn and had testified on one former occasion, that the reporter had taken down their testimony in shorthand notes and that the transcript was a correct and accurate reproduction of his notes. Vander Veen v. Yellow Cab Co., 1968, 233 N.E.2d 68, 89 Ill. App.2d 91. For admission at trial of testimony by attorney of one party at a former hearing as to testimony of witness at that hearing, the attorney need only be able to testify as to the substance of what the witness said on the former occasion and not the precise questions and answers given. Id.

Nature of prior hearing challenged

Hearing conducted by Bureau of Motor Vehicles to determine whether to suspend or revoke operator's license or certificate of registration of any of persons concerned in accident wherein decedent suffered injuries which resulted in his death 17 months later did not constitute "prosecution in a court of justice" and therefore did not fall within statutory definition of an "action" or a "special proceeding", and decedent's testimony at such hearing was not admissible in subsequent negligence action by administratrix. Fleury v. Edwards, 200 N.Y.S.2d 675, 11 A.D.2d 588.

Not proper to show declarant later disavowed prior testimony

Where testimony given on former trial by witness since deceased is properly introduced into evidence, it is incompetent to show that such witness stated, since trial, that such testimony was untrue. Kelly v. King, Miss., 196 So.2d 525.

Not transcript of coroner's inquest

Extract from certified copy of transcript of evidence taken at coroner's inquest containing testimony of eyewitness to accident asserted to be unavailable was inadmissible. Wells v. Alderman, 1968, 162 S.E.2d 18, 117 Ga.App. 724.

55. Cal.—Traxler v. Thompson, 1970, 84 Cal.Rptr. 211, 4 Cal.App. 3d 278.

Ky.—Louisville Taxicab & Transfer Co. v. Johnson, 1949, 224 S.W.2d 639, 311 Ky. 597, 27 A.L.R.2d 158 (affidavit as to attempt to serve order for attendance held sufficient).

Tex.—Acker v. Thompson, Civ.App., 128 S.W.2d 852, reversed by agreement.

Unavailability defined

Ala.—Williams v. Calloway, 1967, 201 So.2d 506, 281 Ala. 249 (if witness subsequently dies, or becomes insane, or after diligent search is not to be found in juris-

56. See note 56 on page 752.

§ 434.6   TRIAL EVIDENCE   Ch. 434

diction of court, or has left state permanently or for such indefinite time that his return is contingent and uncertain).

56. **U.S.**—Federal Rules of Evidence § 804(b)(1), 28 U.S.C.A.

Ala.—Employers Ins. Co. of Alabama v. Cross, 1969, 226 So.2d 161, 284 Ala. 505 (insurer's proffered evidence of a showing for a witness outside of state admitted in previous trial was properly excluded at trial to determine whether insurer was liable for injuries under family combination policy even though previous trial was for damages resulting from same collision and same policy was involved, where different provisions of policy were involved and there was no opportunity for cross-examination in connection with showing made in former trial).

Cal.—West's Ann.Calif.Evid.Code, § 1291.

Fla.—Florida Evidence Code § 90.804 (2)(a).

Kan.—Kansas Code of Civil Procedure § 60–460(c).

Me.—Maine Rules of Evidence § 804 (b)(1).

Neb.—Nebraska Rules of Evidence § 804(2)(a).

Nev.—N.R.S. 51.325.

N.J.—New Jersey Evidence Rule 63 (3).

N.M.—New Mexico Rules of Evidence § 804(b)(1).

N.Y.—Turner v. Sunshine Taxi Corp., 58 N.Y.S.2d 422, 269 App.Div. 997 (defendant not a party to former proceeding).

Okl.—State ex rel. Blankenship v. Freeman, Okl.1968, 440 P.2d 744 (testimony must have been given at a previous regular trial of the same action or at a former trial or proceeding directed to well-defined issues where parties and issues were substantially the same; and there must have been an opportunity to cross-examine the witness at former trial).

S.C.—Gaines v. Thomas, 128 S.E.2d 692, 241 S.C. 412 (when trial at which it is offered is between the same parties, or their privies, and involves the same issues; even though there is lack of identity of parties the testimony is admissible when the party against whom the testimony is offered, as a party to the former action, had full opportunity to cross-examine witness).

Tex.—Harris v. Reeves, Civ.App.1967, 421 S.W.2d 689, error refused n. r. e. (had been cross-examined on former trial where issues were substantially the same as in instant trial).

Utah.—Utah Rules of Evidence § 63 (3).

Wis.—Wisconsin Rules of Evidence § 908.045(1).

Held inadmissible

In action for wrongful death of driver whose automobile was struck by truck owned by trucker, who was hauling poles under contract with electric company providing that trucker's employees would be carried on electric company's payrolls, where partner in electric company was not a witness in action, testimony of such partner given in Industrial Accident Commission's hearing of claim of widow of driver of truck for compensation for driver's death in another accident was hearsay. Morey v. Redifer, 282 P.2d 1062, 204 Or. 194.

Ch. 434   HEARSAY   § 434.7

§ 434.7 Dying Declarations

Library References:
C.J.S. Evidence § 238.
West's Key No. Digests, Evidence ☞275½.

The rule authorizing the admission of dying declarations is a well-recognized exception to the hearsay rule. However, in some jurisdictions it is settled that such declarations are admissible only in cases of homicide and are not admissible in civil actions.[57]

But, in other jurisdictions, the dying declarations of one injured in an automobile accident, respecting the accident, are admissible.[58]

The statement of an injured person, subsequently dying, made in good faith and on personal knowledge before the commencement of an action, and relating to what occurred at an accident, may be rendered admissible by statute.[59]

---

57. **N.J.**—Anastasio v. Rast, 26 A.2d 493, 128 N.J.L. 426 (statements made by fatally injured motorcyclist to police officer about one-half hour after accident).

Okl.—Sanders v. McMichael, 197 P.2d 280, 200 Okl. 501 (no exception to rule, though evidence might provide a basis for prosecution on charge of homicide).

58. **U.S.**—Federal Rules of Evidence § 804(b)(2), 28 U.S.C.A.

Ark.—Miller v. Goodwin, 1969, 439 S.W.2d 308, 246 Ark. 552 (statement to nurse at hospital that "a butane truck ran them off the road" was admissible as dying declaration over objection that decedent was not under a sense of impending death where burns covered 85 to 90% of his body and owing to his condition he asked at hospital that his wife not be permitted to see him).

Cal.—West's Ann.Calif.Evid.Code, § 1242.

Fla.—Florida Evidence Code § 90.804 (2)(b).

Kan.—Kansas Code of Civil Procedure § 60–460(e).

Me.—Maine Rules of Evidence § 804 (b)(2).

Neb.—Nebraska Rules of Evidence § 804(2)(b).

Nev.—N.R.S. 51.335.

N.M.—New Mexico Rules of Evidence § 804(b)(3).

Pa.—Sadowski v. Eazor Exp., Inc., 1968, 249 A.2d 842, 213 Pa.Super. 471 (testimony of police officer as to statement made by dying driver, crushed inside of smashed cab of truck-tractor which had gone down embankment, that driver had to leave road to keep from getting hit by one of defendant's trucks was admissible).

Utah.—Utah Rules of Evidence § 63 (5).

Wis.—Wisconsin Rules of Evidence § 908.045(3).

59. **Mass.**—Barney v. Magenis, 135 N.E. 142, 241 Mass. 268.

Or.—McCarty v. Sirianni, 285 P. 825, 132 Or. 290 (statute held to have changed former rule).

Massachusetts rule elaborated

Statute to effect that in any judicial proceeding declaration of deceased person shall not be inadmissible as hearsay if court finds that it was made in good faith and upon personal knowledge of declarant does

§ 434.8 Spontaneous Declarations [60]

Library References:
C.J.S. Evidence § 403 et seq.
West's Key No. Digests, Evidence ⚖118 et seq.

Declarations made under circumstances indicating that they are the spontaneous utterances of thought created by or springing out of the transaction itself and so soon thereafter as to exclude belief that they are the result of premeditation or design, are admissible, and are often classed as "spontaneous declarations", "excited utterances", or "res gestae." [61] The general rule is that not remove any ground of objection except rule against hearsay, but it is remedial and is to be construed liberally. M.G.L.A. c. 233 § 65. Old Colony Trust Co. v. Shaw, 202 N.E.2d 785, 348 Mass. 212. Mere opinion based upon facts not known to deceased declarant through his own senses is inadmissible. Id.

Where declarant is dead, evidence should not be lost merely because he stated conclusion rather than details that might be required of witness. Id.

60. Comparable section in prior edition **cited by the court** in Kreuger v. Neumann, 154 N.E.2d 741, 745, 129 Ind.App. 300; Smith v. Pine, 12 N.W.2d 236, 242, 234 Iowa 256; Riley v. Weigand, 86 A.2d 698, 702, 18 N.J.Super. 66; Atmanik v. Real Estate Management, 91 A.2d 268, 271, 21 N.J.Super. 357.

61. **U.S.**—Federal Rules of Evidence § 803(2), 28 U.S.C.A.; Picker X-ray Corp. v. Frerker, C.A.Mo. 1969, 405 F.2d 916; Gaynor v. Atlantic Greyhound Corp., C.A.Pa., 183 F.2d 482 (statement of driver's wife after accident that driver was drunk).

Ala.—Cone v. Ragan, 1972, 261 So. 2d 28, 288 Ala. 352 (letter written by employee of owner of truck driven by employee's daughter, to plaintiff who was injured when truck driven by daughter struck plaintiff's truck, which letter was written two weeks after the accident and contained statement "I know it was our fault," was not admissible against interest of writer's employer nor was letter part of the res gestae); East Alabama Exp. Co. v. Dupes, 1960, 124 So.2d 809, 271 Ala. 504 (testimony of driver that immediately after the collision the truck driver stated that he had looked away just before the collision); Harrison v. Baker, 71 So.2d 284, 260 Ala. 488 (statement made by one party to witness who arrived at scene not more than two minutes after the collision, before either party or his automobile had been moved, which statement was testified to as being "for God's sake, lady, get that man's name and tag number. He was sweeping from one side of the road so, until I couldn't miss him"); Alabama Power Co. v. Adams, 1944, 18 So.2d 145, 31 Ala.App. 438 (statement of unidentified bus passenger to injury victim, "girl, I know that hurt you").

Ark.—Intercity Terminal Ry. Co. v. Worden, 6 S.W.2d 547, 177 Ark. 464 (motorman's statement that he did not see automobile until he was so close he could not stop quickly enough and that car had nothing but hand brakes).

Cal.—West's Ann.Calif.Evid.Code, § 1240; Wilcox v. Berry, App.1947, 184 P.2d 939, subsequent opinion 195 P.2d 414, 32 Cal.2d 189; Salvo v. Market St. Ry. Co., 1931, 2 P. 2d 585, 116 Cal.App. 339.

Fla.—Florida Evidence Code § 90.803 (2).

Ga.—McDuffie County v. Rogers, 1971, 184 S.E.2d 46, 124 Ga.App. 442 (that plaintiff should go to a doctor and that he had insurance to take care of it was admissible); Butler v. Stewart, 145 S.E.2d 47, 112 Ga.App. 293 (defendant's testimony as to his passenger's declaration indicating that plaintiff had released brakes and her automobile was rolling backwards toward defendant's vehicle); Seaboard Air Line Ry. Co. v. Benton, 159 S.E. 717, 43 Ga.App. 495, reversed on other grounds 165 S.E. 593, 175 Ga. 491, conformed to 166 S.E. 219, 45 Ga.App. 832.

Idaho—Mason v. Mootz, 253 P.2d 240, 73 Idaho 461 (testimony of hospital nurses' aid that decedent, on becoming partly conscious shortly after being brought into hospital, said "watch where you are going and don't drive so fast"); McIntire v. Oregon Short Line R. Co., 55 P.2d 148, 56 Idaho 392 (engineer's statement he could have stopped if his glove had not caught).

Ind.—Tenta v. Guraly, 221 N.E.2d 577, 140 Ind.App. 160; Kreuger v. Neumann, 154 N.E.2d 741, 129 Ind.App. 300 (testimony of a witness that she heard defendant state "I thought that he was going to hit me, and I got over just as far as I could get without taking the mailboxes down,"); Hiatt v. Trucking, Inc., 103 N.E.2d 915, 122 Ind.App. 411 (testimony that injured truck driver said a minute or two after collision that he wanted witness to let driver's wife and children know about accident and asked why automobile driver turned in front of truck).

Iowa—Bass v. Muenchow, 146 N.W. 2d 923, 259 Iowa 1010; Barrett v. Chicago, M. & St. P. Ry. Co., 175 N.W. 950, supplemental decision on other issue 180 N.W. 670, 190 Iowa 509 (declarations of train engineer as to observations and what he thought).

Kan.—Kansas Code of Civil Procedure § 60–460(d)(2).

Ky.—Roland v. Beckham, 408 S.W. 2d 628; Sparks Bus Line v. Spears, 124 S.W.2d 1031, 276 Ky. 600; Consolidated Coach Corporation v. Earls' Adm'r, 94 S.W.2d 6, 263 Ky. 814.

La.—Micheli v. Toye Bros. Yellow Cab Co., 174 So.2d 168.

Me.—Maine Rules of Evidence § 803(2).

Mich.—Sexton v. Balinski, 273 N.W. 335, 280 Mich. 28.

Minn.—Gave v. Pyrofax Gas Corp., 143 N.W.2d 242, 274 Minn. 210.

Miss.—Coleman v. Ford Motor Co., 1970, 240 So.2d 607 (testimony of witness who arrived at scene shortly after accident that decedent was lying in truck and told him, in response to witness' inquiry as to what happened, "I don't know. I couldn't cut back" was not admissible in view of fact that it was not shown that statement was part of accident or so closely connected therewith to constitute part of occurrence).

Mo.—Billingsley v. Kansas City Public Service Co., 191 S.W.2d 331, 239 Mo.App. 440 (that he did not see automobile); Tyson v. Bernhard, 17 S.W.2d 270, 322 Mo. 633.

Neb.—Nebraska Rules of Evidence § 803(1); Suhr v. Lindell, 1938, 277 N.W. 381, 133 Neb. 856.

Nev.—N.R.S. 51.095.

N.J.—New Jersey Evidence Code § 63 (4)(b).

N.M.—New Mexico Rules of Evidence § 803(2).

N.C.—Freeman v. Hamilton, 1972, 187 S.E.2d 485, 14 N.C.App. 142, certiorari denied 188 S.E.2d 897, 281 N.C. 314 (motorist stated that he looked at motorcycle passenger and told her that she was going

§ 434.8   TRIAL EVIDENCE   Ch. 434

to be all right, and that passenger looked at him and said that it wasn't motorist's fault); Holmes v. Wharton, 1927, 140 S.E. 93, 194 N.C. 470.

Ohio.—Motorist Mut. Ins. Co. v. Cook, 1971, 285 N.E.2d 389, 31 Ohio App.2d 1.

R.I.—Rivera v. United Electric Rys. Co., 151 A. 130 (testimony that witness overheard motorman, in an angry manner, a few moments after the accident, say that he could have prevented the thing).

S.D.—Stratton v. Sioux Falls Traction System, 226 N.W. 644, 55 S. D. 464.

Tex.—Revisore v. West, Civ.App. 1970, 450 S.W.2d 361 (at scene told other party involved that he had fallen asleep and run a red light); Galveston Transit Co. v. Morgan, 408 S.W.2d 728; St. Louis, B. & M. Ry. Co. v. Watkins, Civ.App., 245 S.W. 794 (statement of driver asking what hit him); Houston Electric Co. v. Schmidt, Civ.App., 233 S. W. 637 (motorman stated that he would not have hit automobile so hard if he had not thought it was a jitney).

Utah.—Utah Rules of Evidence § 63 (4)(b); Jackson v. Utah Rapid Transit Co., 290 P. 970, 77 Utah 21.

Va.—Umberger v. Koop, 72 S.E.2d 370, 194 Va. 123 (statements made by truck driver to witness, who arrived at scene before occupants were removed from automobile while truck driver and witness were attempting to determine extent of occupants' injuries, that truck driver had done everything he could to keep from hitting automobile, that automobile had come to a full stop, and that truck driver had blinked his lights to signal he was going through); Southern Passenger Motor Lines v. Burks, 46 S.E.2d 26, 187 Va. 53 (statement of cab passenger that oncoming car veered into path of cab).

Wash.—Britton v. Washington Water Power Co., 1910, 110 P. 20, 59 Wash. 440, 33 L.R.A.,N.S., 109, 140 Am.St.Rep. 858.

Wis.—Wisconsin Rules of Evidence § 908.03(2); John v. Pierce, 178 N.W. 297, 172 Wis. 44.

Even declaration of child

Minn.—Watts v. Erickson, 69 N.W. 2d 626, 244 Minn. 264 (exclusion of statement made by 4 yr. old boy to his mother within ten or fifteen minutes after accident, in absence of any showing that such statement was made in answer to question or by way of justification or excuse or that it was invited by boy's mother, was error).

Pa.—Chicots v. Borough of Sewickley and Stoval, Com.Pl., 112 P.L. J. 454 (where a four years and ten months old child, still crying and in pain, told his mother that his bicycle had struck something on the sidewalk, it was held to be error to exclude from evidence the mother's testimony as to this statement of her child).

Wash.—Johnston v. Ohls, 1969, 457 P.2d 194, 76 Wash.2d 398 (that girl making declaration was not quite four years old at time of accident, and thus presumably not competent to testify directly, did not prohibit use of declaration).

Held inadmissible

Under Arkansas law, statements of driver were not a part of res gestae and were not admissible as substantive evidence of negligence. Maddux v. Cox, C.A.Ark.1967, 382 F.2d 119.

Lack of insurance

Tex.—Members Mut. Ins. Co. v. Tapp, Civ.App.1971, 464 S.W.2d 377 (driver's spontaneous statement, made at scene of accident involving insured under uninsured motorist policy, that driver had no insurance was made in excitement produced by an exciting event, was a statement of fact

Ch. 434   HEARSAY   § 434.8

which might subject driver to penalty of suspension of his right to an operator's license, was relevant to question of whether insured had made all reasonable efforts to ascertain whether driver had insurance coverage).

Statement of bystander

Ill.—Carroll v. Guffey, 156 N.E.2d 267, 20 Ill.App.2d 470 (evidence of plaintiff, that some bystanders stated that they saw the accident and that defendant ignored the traffic light, was not admissible, where the declarations of the bystanders were not made concurrently with the collision or uttered contemporaneously therewith and were but a narrative of what had taken place).

Md.—Cluster v. Cole, 1974, 319 A. 2d 320, 21 Md.App. 242 (in action brought against motorist by parents of 12-year-old girl who was struck by defendant's car, it was error to admit motorist's testimony that, while she was kneeling over girl's body and screaming hysterically, an unidentified "colored man" came up to her and told her it wasn't her fault, since there was nothing in the alleged statement of the "colored man," or the circumstances under which it was given, that would make it so inherently trustworthy as to dispense with the oath requirement and the right to cross-examination).

Mich.—Blackwell's Estate v. Hare, 1974, 216 N.W.2d 419, —— Mich. —— (in action under Motor Vehicle Accident Claims Act involving mortal injury allegedly resulting from negligence of hit-and-run driver, it was reversible error not to allow police officer, who arrived shortly after accident, to testify to statement made by unidentified person that automobile had struck decedent).

Neb.—Gain v. Drennen, 69 N.W.2d 916, 160 Neb. 263 (admission of defendant's testimony as to what woman witness had told investigating police officer, after pedestrian had been taken away in ambulance, concerning color of traffic signals at time of accident, could not be sustained upon ground that it was part of res gestae).

Or.—Wright v. Swann, 1972, 493 P.2d 148, 261 Or. 440, 50 A.L.R.3d 707; Bosin v. Oak Lodge Sanitary Dist. No. 1, 1968, 447 P.2d 285, 251 Or. 554; Schneider v. Moe, 1935, 50 P.2d 577, 151 Or. 353 (exclamation at scene "the old man has been hit" held admissible).

Pa.—Carney v. Pennsylvania R. Co., 1968, 240 A.2d 71, 428 Pa. 489 (out-of-court assertions by unidentified bystanders who may or may not have actually witnessed event are not properly admissible as part of res gestae, and, to justify admission, it is incumbent upon proponent to persuasively and convincingly demonstrate, by use of other corroborating evidence, that declarant actually viewed event of which he speaks).

R.I.—Martin v. Estrella, 1970, 266 A.2d 41, 107 R.I. 247 (a declarant need not be a participant in the exciting event before any of his statements relating thereto are admissible when sought to be related by another, and may qualify as long as the declarations relate to the immediate facts of the startling occurrence).

Tex.—Nutter v. Dearing, Civ.App., 400 S.W.2d 346, ref. n. r. e. (statement made to police officer about ten minutes after head-on collision by eyewitness who was in state of high excitement was admissible, however, exclusion of testimony was harmless where officer considered statement in reaching a conclusion as to identity of the eastbound driver whose negligence caused the collision); Lusinger v. Philpott, Civ.App., 392 S.W.2d 217 (where deputy sheriff arrived at scene about five or ten minutes

§ 434.8 TRIAL EVIDENCE Ch. 434

after collision, and a few minutes later deputy sheriff asked bystander if he saw collision, and bystander replied that he had seen collision, and that motorist had slowed down before entering intersection, and that operator of motor scooter was driving too fast, testimony of deputy sheriff was properly admitted concerning statements made by bystander).

Utah.—Morton v. Hood, 143 P.2d 434, 105 Utah 484 (where immediately after accident plaintiff's granddaughter stated that her grandmother had been hit while running across highway to catch a bus, and that granddaughter tried in vain to stop her, the statement was admissible).

Wash.—May v. Wright, 381 P.2d 601, 62 Wash.2d 69 (statement by disinterested eye witness to police officer approximately 20 minutes after child was struck to effect that child had dashed into street was admissible); Bennett v. City of Seattle, 156 P.2d 685, 22 Wash. 2d 455, 157 A.L.R. 1153 (statement made by bus passenger immediately after the collision that pedestrian walked into the bus, was admissible).

Test stated

Ariz.—Yellow Cab Co. of Phoenix v. Green, 1972, 494 P.2d 385, 16 Ariz.App. 485 (it must be spontaneous utterance of mind while under influence of transaction, test being whether declaration was facts talking through party, or party talking about facts).

Colo.—Gushurst v. Benham, 1966, 417 P.2d 777, 160 Colo. 428 (had to be exclamation and not in narrative form, instinctive rather than deliberate).

Dist.Col.—Watts v. Smith, Mun.App., 226 A.2d 160 (statements not relating to a description of event must be carefully scrutinized to test their spontaneity and a substantial foundation for their introduction must be laid, encompassing elapsed time and action, state of mind and general demeanor of declarant).

Ill.—Darling v. Charleston Community Memorial Hospital, Ill.App., 200 N.E.2d 149, 50 Ill.App.2d 253, affirmed 33 Ill.2d 326, 211 N.E.2d 253, cert. denied 383 U.S. 946, 86 S.Ct. 1204, 16 L.Ed.2d 209 (factors necessary are an occurrence sufficiently startling to produce a spontaneous and unreflecting statement, absence of time to fabricate, and statement must relate to circumstances of the occurrence).

Ky.—Roland v. Beckham, 408 S.W. 2d 628 (spontaneity, as opposed to mere proximity in time, is most important consideration).

Mich.—Rice v. Jackson, 1965, 134 N. W.2d 366, 1 Mich.App. 105 (occasion startling enough to produce nervous excitement and render utterance spontaneous, and statement made before time to contrive and misrepresent, and statement relating to circumstances of occurrence).

N.J.—Lieberman v. Saley, 227 A.2d 339, 94 N.J.Super. 156 (court must consider element of time, circumstances of accident, mental and physical condition of declarant, shock produced, nature of utterance, whether against interest of declarant or not or made in response to questions or involuntary, and any other material facts in surrounding circumstances, and such matters are to be weighed in determining basic question of whether utterance was spontaneous and unreflective and made under such circumstances as to indicate absence of opportunity for contrivance and misrepresentation).

Okl.—Arkansas Louisiana Gas Co. v. Evans, 397 P.2d 505 (statement must be substantially contemporaneous with the transaction,

statements relevant to an accident are admissible if made almost immediately after the accident.[62] They need not be made imme-

spontaneous rather than deliberative, and induced by happenings of events concerning which the statement is made, and not a narrative statement of what occurred given in response to questions).

62. U.S.—Jones v. Harris, D.C. Minn., 224 F.Supp. 630 (exclusion of testimony by plaintiff as to what defendant's wife, who was a passenger, stated to plaintiff immediately after collision was prejudicial error where defendant's wife was not at trial and was beyond reach of the trial court's process); Navajo Freight Lines v. Mahaffy, C.A.N.M., 174 F.2d 305; William C. Barry, Inc. v. Baker, C.C.A.Me., 82 F.2d 79 (statement of driver of tractor as to how collision with truck occurred).

Ala.—Whiddon v. Malone, 124 So. 516, 220 Ala. 220 (statement of driver that he went to sleep); Ruffin Coal & Transfer Co. v. Rich, 108 So. 600, 214 Ala. 622; Standard Oil Co. v. Douglass, 93 So. 286, 18 Ala.App. 625.

Ariz.—Hines v. Gale, 213 P. 395, 25 Ariz. 65.

Ark.—Intercity Terminal Ry. Co. v. Worden, 6 S.W.2d 547, 177 Ark. 464.

Cal.—Baker v. Western Auto Stage Co., 192 P. 73, 48 Cal.App. 283.

Colo.—Iacino v. Brown, 217 P.2d 266, 121 Colo. 450 (statement that it was "all my fault," etc.).

Del.—Garrod v. Good, 203 A.2d 112, 7 Storey 556 (testimony by passenger in defendant's automobile that immediately after accident driver of automobile in which plaintiff was passenger stated that "she had seen us coming but she had tried to speed up in an effort to beat us across the intersection" was admissible).

Dist.Col.—Watts v. Smith, D.C.Mun. App., 226 A.2d 160 (crucial to admissibility is proximity in time to occurrence which brought forth statement and identity of declarant).

Ga.—Southeastern Express Co. v. Nightingale, 126 S.E. 915, 33 Ga. App. 515.

Kan.—Tannahill v. Depositors' Oil & Gas Co., 203 P. 909, 110 Kan. 254.

La.—Talazac v. Phoenix of Hartford Ins. Co., App.1972, 259 So.2d 636 (remanded to allow plaintiff to try to show that alleged uninsured motorist was nervous and aggravated, asked if anyone was hurt).

Md.—Feigley v. Baltimore Transit Co., 124 A.2d 822, 211 Md. 1 (where conversation between transit company representative, an injured passenger, and latter's daughter took place a day or two after accident, it was clearly not part of "res gestae").

Minn.—Fenton v. Minneapolis St. Ry. Co., 89 N.W.2d 404, 252 Minn. 75 (statement, made by plaintiff immediately after the accident while he was lying on the ground with a crushed foot and groaning in pain, that his arm had been caught in the doors).

Mo.—State ex rel. Smith v. Trimble, 285 S.W. 729, 315 Mo. 166; Beeson v. Fleming, 285 S.W. 708, 315 Mo. 177.

N.H.—MacDonald v. Appleyard, 53 A.2d 434, 94 N.H. 362 (statement of driver that he was trying to fix his lights).

N.Y.—Constantinides v. Manhattan Transit Co., 34 N.Y.S.2d 600, 264 App.Div. 147 (alleged conversations long after the accident formed no part of the "res gestae").

Ohio.—Melville v. Greyhound Corp., 133 N.E.2d 436, 99 Ohio App. 411

(bus operator's statement, made immediately after collision and while passengers were being assisted out of overturned bus by operator, "God being my judge, I could not have gotten out of the way. The Hudson car ran right in front of me"); Lockett v. Anchor Motor Freight Co., App.1950, 97 N.E.2d 46 (immediately and half hour later, both admissible).

Okl.—Sand Springs Ry. Co. v. Piggee, 163 P.2d 545, 196 Okl. 136.

Or.—Personius v. Asbury Transp. Co. of Oregon, 53 P.2d 1065, 152 Or. 286 (statement made as soon as reached other vehicle); Schneider v. Moe, 50 P.2d 577, 151 Or. 353.

R.I.—Rivera v. United Electric Rys. Co., 151 A. 130.

Tex.—Rowe v. Liles, Civ.App., 226 S.W.2d 253, error refused (truck driver's statement that he saw automobile in which plaintiff was a passenger, but not in time to stop); Lang Floral & Nursery Co. v. Sheridan, Civ.App., 245 S.W. 467; Coleman v. Cook, Civ.App., 195 S.W.2d 1020.

Va.—Washington-Virginia Ry. Co. v. Deahl, 100 S.E. 840, 126 Va. 141.

Wis.—Levandowski v. Studey, 25 N. W.2d 59, 249 Wis. 421 (admission of truck driver that wheel was defective); John v. Pierce, 178 N.W. 297, 172 Wis. 44.

0–5 minutes

U.S.—Burger Chef Systems, Inc. v. Govro, C.A.Mo.1969, 407 F.2d 921 (employee's statement within a minute or two after accident that he was "going after meat" was admissible under res gestae exception; even if employee's utterance was erroneously admitted, it could not have materially affected merits of the action such as to require reversal).

Ala.—Harrison v. Baker, 1954, 71 So. 2d 284, 260 Ala. 488.

Ga.—Shapiro Packing Co. v. Landrum, 1964, 136 S.E.2d 446, 109 Ga.App. 519 (was at fault and was insured, held not admissible).

Ind.—Hiatt v. Trucking, Inc., 1952, 103 N.E.2d 915, 122 Ind.App. 411.

Ky.—Roland v. Beckham, 1966, 408 S.W.2d 628; Sparks Bus Line v. Spears, 1939, 124 S.W.2d 1031, 276 Ky. 600.

Ohio.—Ashworth v. Morrison, 1933, 196 N.E.2d 465 (to effect pedestrian relatives need not worry as insured up to $50,000, held inadmissible).

Pa.—Campbell v. Gladden, 1955, 118 A.2d 133, 383 Pa. 144 (victim, in 5–10 seconds, struggled to feet, with bloody face; and, in answer to question, stated "they must have backed out in front of me").

Tex.—Jackson v. Feeler, 1964, 380 S.W.2d 161 (when asked if knew ran stop sign, answered was looking at boys on bicycles).

Utah.—Jackson v. Utah Rapid Transit Co., 1930, 290 P. 970, 77 Utah 21 (statement 3–4 minutes later admissible, but not report over telephone).

W.Va.—Lawrence v. Nelson, 113 S. E.2d 241, 145 W.Va. 134 (statement made by passenger's driver, as to how collision occurred, to bystander, approximately two to five minutes after collision while dust was settling around vehicles, steam was coming from them, passenger was lying in road and driver was visibly excited).

5–10 minutes

Cal.—Southers v. Savage, 1961, 12 Cal.Rptr. 470, 191 Cal.App.2d 100 (driver and guest still in car).

Ind.—Gary Rys. v. Cline, 1951, 97 N. E.2d 628, 121 Ind.App. 449 (spontaneously, as soon as capable of speech).

Ky.—Consolidated Coach Corporation v. Earls' Adm'r, 1936, 94 S.W. 2d 6, 263 Ky. 814.

diately after the accident, provided there has not been time for the exciting influence to lose its sway and to be dissipated,[63] and

Mo.—Huston v. Hanson, 1962, 353 S.W.2d 577 (repeatedly made).

Ohio.—Ebeling v. Harman, 1948, 80 N.E.2d 704, 83 Ohio App. 519, opinion adhered to 82 N.E.2d 425.

Tex.—Rosenthal Dry Goods v. Hillebrandt, Civ.App.1926, 280 S.W. 882 (after detained to be interrogated, not admissible).

10–15 minutes

Ga.—Cambron v. Cogburn, 1967, 157 S.E.2d 534, 116 Ga.App. 373 (truck driver's statement at scene some 10 to 15 minutes after collision that truck belonged to dealer and that driver was dealer's agent and was returning truck to dealer was not spontaneous and was not part of res gestae).

Mont.—Blevins v. Weaver Const. Co., 1967, 432 P.2d 378, 150 Mont. 158 (testimony of driver of road construction water truck that driver of pickup truck which collided with road grader told him, about ten minutes after accident, that he had been traveling about 45 to 50 miles per hour was admissible).

Ohio.—Lacey v. Heisey, 1936, 5 N.E. 2d 699, 53 Ohio App. 451 (inadmissible).

Tenn.—Frank v. Wright, 1918, 205 S.W. 434, 140 Tenn. 535 (statement as to being on mission for employer, not admissible).

15–25 minutes

La.—Montgomery v. City of New Orleans, App.1972, 266 So.2d 482, writ denied 268 So.2d 258, 263 La. 370 (where investigating officer did not arrive on scene until 20 minutes after accident and report included statements of parties made at that time or later, report could not form part of res gestae).

Mo.—Hamilton v. Missouri Petroleum Products Co., 1969, 438 S.W.2d 197; Jefferson v. Biggar, 1967, 416 S.W.2d 933 (where eyewitnesses' statements were made at least 15 minutes after the collision, and were not, in any sense, utterances initiated by shock, tension, or excitement).

Tex.—Houston Transit Co. v. Farrack, 1966, 403 S.W.2d 184 (in extreme pain); Guerro v. Wright, Civ.App.1949, 225 S.W.2d 609, ref. n. r. e.

Wash.—Robbins v. Greene, 1953, 261 P.2d 83, 43 Wash.2d 315 (15 minutes).

25–30 minutes

Tex.—Harris v. Allison, Civ.App. 1928, 11 S.W.2d 821 (admissible).

30–45 minutes

U.S.—Roth v. Swanson, C.C.A.Minn. 1944, 145 F.2d 262 (not admissible).

Mo.—Calvert v. Super Propane Corp., 1966, 400 S.W.2d 133 (inadmissible, 40 minutes later).

Tex.—Keystone-Fleming Transport Inc. v. City of Jahoka, 1958, 315 S.W.2d 656, ref. n. r. e. (admissible).

45–60 minutes

Mo.—Grotjan v. Thompson, App., 140 S.W.2d 706 (conclusions of witnesses as to statements made by railroad engineer 40 minutes after accident at a time when he was not investigating accident for purpose of reporting facts to railroad, nor acting or claiming to act for railroad).

N.D.—Trautman v. New Rockford-Fessenden Co-op Transport Ass'n, 1970, 181 N.W.2d 754 (officer's statement as to what defendant truck driver had said 45 minutes after accident was admissible).

63. U.S.—Continental Cas. Co. v. Jackson, C.A.Iowa, 1968, 400 F.2d

§ 434.8 TRIAL EVIDENCE Ch. 434

285 (doctor's hearsay testimony as to what he was told by decedent patient was admissible as part of the res gestae, since the conversation in question took place about one hour after decedent was stricken with heart attack and at time when decedent was ashen gray, cold and still in shock).

Ala.—Ruffin Coal & Transfer Co. v. Rich, 108 So. 596, 214 Ala. 633.

Conn.—Rockhill v. White Line Bus Co., 145 A. 504, 109 Conn. 706 (a statement of a bus driver to a truck driver, immediately after a crash, that the failure of the bus brakes caused the collision).

Ga.—Dowdney v. Shadix, 1970, 176 S.E.2d 512, 122 Ga.App. 119 (statement made by deceased motorist 17 hours after collision could not be considered such a part of the occurrence).

Ill.—Perzovsky v. Chicago Transit Authority, 1974, 320 N.E.2d 433, 23 Ill.App.3d 896 (ambulance attendant's testimony which revealed that, while being transported to hospital and while in a state of shock, deceased told the attendant that a vehicle had struck him, was properly admitted as it did not prejudice the bus company and was so closely connected with the accident).

Iowa—Gibbs v. Wilmeth, 1968, 157 N.W.2d 93, 261 Iowa 1015 (statement of driver involved in head-on collision was properly admissible where it was made within an hour after accident, at a time when driver was upset and distraught over condition of her husband, who was in emergency room at the time); Barrett v. Chicago, M. & St. P. Ry. Co., 1920, 175 N.W. 950, 190 Iowa 509, rehearing denied 180 N.W.2d 670, 190 Iowa 509.

Kan.—Smith v. Hall's Estate, 1974, 524 P.2d 684, 215 Kan. 262.

Ky.—Roland v. Beckham, 408 S.W.2d 628 (although statement of school bus driver was in response to inquiry of witness who approached driver while driver was still pinned to bus and inquired as to what had happened to him, it could hardly be said that there was such "interrogation" as would remove bus driver from mental attitude of expostulation influenced by excitement and stress of accident itself).

Md.—Honick v. Walden, 1971, 272 A.2d 406, 10 Md.App. 714 (statements made by driver of vehicle which had struck plaintiffs' automobile within half hour and between five to seven blocks from place where statements, which indicated that driver might have intentionally struck plaintiffs' vehicle to get help when stabbed by passenger, were made, and made while driver's physical and mental condition indicated lack of composure, disclosed requisite spontaneity, proximity, nervous excitement and inculpatory nature to constitute res gestae).

Mo.—Rosser v. Standard Mill. Co., 312 S.W.2d 106 (statements of truck driver, at scene and about five to ten minutes thereafter, to the effect that driver was acting within the scope of his employment were not admissible as part of the res gestae, since there was no showing that they were spontaneous or that driver was suffering from shock or pain at the time they were made); Sconce v. Jones, 121 S.W.2d 777 (evidence that plaintiff, approximately one hour after the accident but before he was extricated from the wreckage, stated to parties who came to his aid that defective brakes caused the accident, was not admissible, where plaintiff's evidence failed to show that he was under such influence of shock or pain as to be unable to reflect or reason after accident).

Neb.—Komma v. Kreifels, 14 N.W.2d 591, 144 Neb. 745; Suhr v. Lindell, 277 N.W. 381, 133 Neb. 856.

N.H.—Scahill v. Jabre, 1958, 140 A. 2d 586, 101 N.H. 263.

N.J.—Cestero v. Ferrara, 1971, 273 A.2d 761, 57 N.J. 497 (statement that she stopped for red light, started up on green light and got hit, which appeared in record of patient's hospitalization and treatment following accident, qualified for admission although exact elapsed time between accident and patient's recorded description of it was not stated, where patient's utterance about accident was made very shortly after her return to reality and while she was in severe pain); Kelley v. Hicks, 1950, 76 A. 2d 23, 9 N.J.Super. 266.

N.M.—Otero v. Physicians & Surgeons Ambulance Service, Inc., 336 P.2d 1070, 65 N.M. 319 (statement to a police officer that the traffic light was green and it changed to "yellow" as the motorist entered the intersection and, being unable to stop, he accelerated his vehicle, where officer stated that the statement was made while he was investigating the accident and that the motorist at the time appeared nervous, excited and upset).

N.Y.—Wells v. Sinning, 1969, 310 N. Y.S.2d 594, 63 Misc.2d 20, appeal dismissed 310 N.Y.S.2d 515, 34 A. D.2d 682, affirmed 323 N.Y.S.2d 168, 28 N.Y.2d 916, 271 N.E.2d 698 (where decedent had just been involved in a startling accident, he was seriously injured and in great pain, he was unconscious from time of happening of accident until he gave his statement, after giving his statement he again lapsed into unconsciousness, and his statement referred to a detail of the main bewildering event).

Okl.—Arkansas Louisiana Gas Co. v. Evans, 397 P.2d 505 (declarations made after receiving injuries and made spontaneously and instinctively, while under influence of pain and shock).

Pa.—Thompson v. City of Philadelphia, 1972, 294 A.2d 826, 222 Pa. Super. 417 (statement to officer by elderly man in hospital x-ray room one hour after sustaining severely fractured hip that "I was crossing from the West to the East side of 21st Street. I saw the truck. I saw it back up. I couldn't get out of the way. It hit me. My left hip hurts." was properly admitted).

S.D.—Allen v. McLain, 69 N.W.2d 390, 75 S.D. 520 (testimony of doctor who had attended guest in hospital on night of accident that guest, when she had begun to recover from state of shock, had repeated several times in substance, "slow down, please slow down," was admissible).

Tex.—Jones v. Hopper, 506 S.W.2d 768 (testimony that injured driver stated, a couple of minutes after accident, that it was her fault and that she was late and was going to pick up her mother concerned an excited utterance which explained why the accident occurred and which flowed from a traumatic or startling event); Hartford Acc. & Indem. Co. v. Hale, 1966, 400 S. W.2d 310 (statements themselves cannot be used to prove an exciting event); Davis Transport, Inc. v. Bolstad, Civ.App., 295 S.W.2d 941 (statement made to witness while leaving emergency room at hospital where he had been taken for treatment was made during a period of only a few seconds of consciousness).

Utah.—Jackson v. Utah Rapid Transit Co., 290 P. 970, 77 Utah 21.

Wash.—Sater v. Owens, 409 P.2d 660, 67 Wash.2d 699 (testimony of state patrol officer, that driver, while dazed and in state of shock, told him that she fell asleep and drove off road).

§ 434.8 TRIAL EVIDENCE Ch. 434

before there has been time for deliberation or reflection.[64] Statements are not admissible if it is not shown when or where they were made.[65]

---

64. U.S.—Williams v. Watson, D.C. Tenn.1972, 346 F.Supp. 1377 (under Tennessee law, statement that witness purportedly made to defendant some two minutes after the collision between witness's automobile and defendant's automobile, relating to witness's opinion as to the cause of the accident, was not within exception); Elek v. Boyce, D.C.S.C.1970, 308 F.Supp. 26; Giffin v. Ensign, C.A.Pa.1956, 234 F.2d 307 (solicited response); Wicker v. Scott, C.C.A.Ohio 1928, 29 F.2d 807 (silence when questioned, but acted deliberately).

Ala.—Norwood Transp. Co. v. Bickell, 1922, 92 So. 464, 207 Ala. 232 (too much retrospection).

Ark.—Granite State Ins. Co. v. Martin, 1972, 480 S.W.2d 326, 252 Ark. 613 (in insured's action under uninsured motorist provisions, state policeman's testimony that insured had said at scene that his neck and back were hurting was inadmissible where insured's statement did not appear to have been an involuntary exclamation indicating pain but was narration of what insured thought his condition was).

Cal.—Wiley v. Easter, App., 19 Cal. Rptr. 809, opinion vacated 21 Cal. Rptr. 905, 203 Cal.App.2d 845; Gouzea v. Pacific Greyhound Lines, 169 P.2d 398, 74 Cal.App.2d 794; Salvo v. Market St. Ry. Co., 1931, 2 P.2d 585, 116 Cal.App. 339.

Colo.—Alcorn v. Erasmus, 1971, 484 P.2d 813, —— Colo.App. —— (made by witness to state patrolman proximately 30 minutes after the accident, was not a spontaneous or instinctive exclamation uttered at least somewhat contemporaneously with the event concerning which the statement was made, and the exception was improperly applied in allowing officer's testimony); Stahl v. Cooper, 1948, 190 P.2d 891, 117 Colo. 468.

Ga.—Fender v. City of Jesup, 1971, 186 S.E.2d 348, 124 Ga.App. 833 (constituted a narrative of what happened rather than spontaneous exclamations).

Ill.—Perkins v. Culver, 1971, 269 N.E. 2d 333, 131 Ill.App.2d 881 (host driver's statements made while at hospital approximately one hour after collision that he had been drinking and that collision was his fault); Perkins v. Chicago Transit Authority, 208 N.E.2d 867, 60 Ill.App.2d 431 (the pertinent point is whether there was sufficient time to allow an opportunity for reflection and invention); Johnson v. Swords Co., 1936, 3 N. E.2d 705, 286 Ill.App. 377 (statement by driver to father, after father moved auto).

Ky.—Barker v. Danville Const. Co., 1965, 389 S.W.2d 931 (driver's statement 10-12 days later inadmissible, though fatal accident); Ison v. Mullins, 336 S.W.2d 599 (a statement made by driver following his extrication from automobile in which he was pinned and extinguishment of fire which broke out in other automobile, in response to accusation from other motorist, that something went wrong with his automobile and that he could not control it, was a spontaneous declaration intimately connected with collision and near enough in point of time to exclude presumption that it was result of premeditation or design); Moore v. Illinois Cent. R. Co., 183 S.W.2d 29, 298 Ky. 433 (statement allegedly made by engineer 30 or 45 minutes after crossing collision, that he did not see the approach-

---

65. See note 65 on page 767.

ing automobile, was too remote in point of time); Consolidated Coach Corporation v. Earls' Adm'r, 94 S.W.2d 6, 263 Ky. 814 (30-minute interval).

La.—Rodriguez v. Trebitz, 1974, 304 So.2d 396 (made well after accident by one driver, who died 21 days after accident, to others regarding the manner in which accident occurred); Bullock v. Perry, App.1970, 238 So.2d 796; Manuel v. American Emp. Ins. Co., 212 So. 2d 527 (in absence of showing that other driver made statement to passenger and his host driver, that he did not have insurance, spontaneously or impulsively and in absence of evidence to show time which elapsed between accident and that statement made at scene, passenger failed to lay proper foundation for admission of that declaration as part of res gestae); Micheli v. Toye Bros. Yellow Cab Co., 1965, 174 So.2d 168 (ample time to compose self and reflect).

Md.—Brown v. Rogers, 1974, 313 A. 2d 547, 19 Md.App. 562.

Mich.—Grassi v. Austerberry, 150 N.W.2d 529, 6 Mich.App. 690; McPeake v. Grand Trunk Western Ry. Co., 1928, 219 N.W. 734, 242 Mich. 676.

Mo.—Wren v. St. Louis Public Service Co., 333 S.W.2d 92 (where occurrence appeared to have been a relatively minor rear-end collision, and there was no showing that the bus driver was excited or under the influence of shock or tension when he stated, approximately three or four minutes after the accident, that the collision was caused by failure of brakes on the bus, such utterance was not admissible); Shirley v. Kansas City So. R. Co., 298 S.W. 125, 221 Mo.App. 1158 (testimony by plaintiff's witness as to conversation with the defendant's witness some time after the accident is not a part of the res gestae); Downing v. St. Louis-San F. Ry. Co., 285 S.W. 791, 220 Mo.App. 260 (railroad conductor's statement to injured motorist when he reached her after train had stopped was held too remote); Fore v. Rodgers, App., 216 S.W. 566.

N.Y.—Garmon v. Mordente, 1969, 299 N.Y.S.2d 689, 32 A.D.2d 532 (officer's testimony that defendant told officer three days after collision that defendant had entered intersection on green light and collided with codefendant's automobile was not part of res gestae); Gaudino v. New York City Housing Authority, 259 N.Y.S.2d 478, 23 A.D.2d 838 (testimony of intern as to what plaintiff told him about accident through interpreter was inadmissible); Friedman v. N. Y. City Omnibus Corp., 70 N.Y.S.2d 628, 272 App.Div. 265; Muessling v. Leisner, 224 N.Y.S. 689, 221 App. Div. 524; Sokolof v. Donn, Sup., 194 N.Y.S. 580 (driver of defendant's automobile, about half an hour after the accident, stated that, when the accident happened, he was going to get two friends for the defendant—not admissible in proof that driver was in course of employment).

Ohio.—Stormont v. New York Cent. R. Co., 205 N.E.2d 74, 1 Ohio App. 2d 414 (proffered evidence of witness to effect that crew members of train admitted to witness at time a telephone call was made immediately after accident that grade crossing was extremely hazardous and dangerous and was in fact a death trap was not admissible); Anderson v. City Cab Co., App. 1939, 38 N.E.2d 214.

Okl.—Wray v. Garrett, 1939, 90 P.2d 1050, 185 Okl. 138 (3 hours later, in reply to question); Lacy Chevrolet Co. v. McGinnis, 1937, 72 P.2d 785, 181 Okl. 97 (12 hours later).

Pa.—Thompson v. City of Philadelphia, 1972, 294 A.2d 826, 222 Pa.Super. 417 (it need not be an emotional or impulsive outburst, and there is no rule which prevents, per se, "a narration of his idea as to how the accident happened" from being part of the res gestae; test to be applied in determining admissibility of the statement is whether circumstances of case were such as to preclude possibility of a shrewd and self-calculating answer); Wilf v. Philadelphia Modeling & Charm School, Inc., 1965, 208 A.2d 294, 205 Pa.Super. 196 (must be no break in continuity); Cocivera v. Philadelphia Transp. Co., 152 A.2d 272, 190 Pa.Super. 50 (alleged statement of driver made 10 or 11 blocks from scene to effect that another vehicle was involved and passenger should see doctor, was not admissible in absence of showing that declaration was spontaneous or was made in connection with startling event, that driver was laboring under stress or nervous excitement, and that statement was made so near occurrence both as to time and place as to qualify statement under res gestae rule).

R.I.—Hamrick v. Yellow Cab Co. of Providence, 1973, 304 A.2d 666, 111 R.I. 515 (made by deceased driver to police at police station on night of accident, and statement made by him on following day to person, who assertedly was employed by defendant and investigated accident).

S.D.—Stratton v. Sioux Falls Traction System, 226 N.W. 644, 55 S.D. 464 (motorman's statement relating to brakes of street car made 15 minutes after collision of street car with truck at intersection, and made after motorman left scene, constitutes narrative of past occurrence and is not contemporaneous and connected with the accident).

Tex.—Big Mack Trucking Co., Inc. v. Dickerson, 1973, 497 S.W.2d 283 (injured party already removed from scene); Duncan v. Smith, 376 S.W.2d 877, quoting 32 C.J.S. Evidence § 417, error granted (exclusion of bus driver's statements, that driver was trying to pass automobile on right prior to hitting guardrail where highway narrowed for bridge and that bus then struck automobile and oncoming truck, was not an abuse of trial court's discretion, where driver "calmly" made statement at time which could have been 30 minutes after accident); Main Street Garage v. Eganhouse Optical Co., Civ.App., 223 S.W. 316.

Wash.—Day v. Goodwin, 1970, 478 P.2d 774, 3 Wash.App. 940 (admission of statements of decedent's companions concerning critical details of accident, made some time during 90 minutes following accident, was prejudicial error requiring new trial, in absence of showing that statements were excited utterances or that circumstances were such as to exclude presumption that statements were result of deliberation or were not product of premeditation, reflection, or design); McCandless v. Inland Northwest Film Service, Inc., 392 P.2d 613, 64 Wash.2d 523 (telephone conversation by truck driver whose vehicle had struck and killed two pedestrians, narrating accident, was not part of res gestae where statements were correlatively neither spontaneous nor instinctive utterances evoked or dominated by transaction or occurrence itself, but made, even though under great emotional shock, following inspection of truck body, after walking to service station and dialing number).

Wis.—Wilder v. Classified Risk Ins. Co., 1970, 177 N.W.2d 109, 47 Wis. 2d 286 (it must be shown that statement was made so spontaneously or under such psychological or physical pressure or excitement that rational mind could not interpose itself between spontaneous statement or utterance stimulated by event and the event itself).

In hospital

Mo.—Gough v. General Box Co., 302 S.W.2d 884 (where plaintiff was rendered unconscious and taken to a hospital, and doctor saw the plaintiff about one and one-half hours after the accident, testimony of doctor that plaintiff, in answer to question, stated that a truck had jackknifed into him was not admissible, where plaintiff had testified that he was unconscious at the time he made the statement).

Wis.—Cossette v. Lepp, 1968, 157 N.W.2d 629, 38 Wis.2d 932 (decedent's statement to son, while decedent was in hospital, was not admissible, but error in admission was not prejudicial where there was other admissible evidence to decedent's similar declarations).

Wyo.—Auflick v. Dickson, 1968, 439 P.2d 452 (did not err in refusing to admit what was represented as plaintiff's statements made in hospital while unconscious where plaintiff testified he had no recollection of accident, since if made they were entered so long after occurrence they were not part of res gestae and in absence of offer of proof as to their content court and counsel could not determine whether they were so self-serving in character as to be inadmissible).

Own accident report

N.Y.—Newcomb v. Frink, 105 N.Y.S.2d 704, 278 App.Div. 998, amendment denied 106 N.Y.S.2d 904, 278 App.Div. 1028, appeal dismissed 103 N.E.2d 830, 303 N.Y. 669 (error to permit defendant to place in evidence his own written report of the accident).

65. Conn.—Mei v. Alterman Transport Lines, Inc., 1970, 268 A.2d 639, 159 Conn. 307.

Fla.—St. Germain v. Carpenter, 1956, 84 So.2d 556.

Iowa.—Smith v. Pine, 12 N.W.2d 236, 234 Iowa 256 (refusal of offer to prove as res gestae that defendant upon arriving at hospital stated she was on her side of highway and plaintiff's car was on wrong side was not abuse of discretion, where it was not shown how soon after collision defendant was taken to hospital).

Mich.—Gorman v. McCleaf, 119 N.W.2d 636, 369 Mich. 237 (where time of officer's conversation was not sufficiently fixed and conversation with fellow employee occurred several days later).

Mo.—Straughan v. Asher, App.1963, 372 S.W.2d 489, quoting C.J.S. Evidence § 217; Roush v. Alkire Truck Lines, Inc., 1957, 299 S.W.2d 518.

R.I.—Ficocelli v. Yellow Cab Co., 3 A.2d 246, 62 R.I. 73 (question asked plaintiff's wife as to whether taxicab driver said anything when he and she were lifting plaintiff out of taxicab as to condition of cab or injury to plaintiff by fall on floor thereof when he started to get out was not proper under res gestae rule, where the time and place of the possible statement were not made definite).

Tex.—Logan v. Grady, Civ.App.1972, 482 S.W.2d 313 (in absence of evidence showing whether declarant was excited or showing his emotional state at time he made statement as to events surrounding accident, predicate was insufficient); Parking, Inc. v. Dalrymple, 375 S.W.2d 758 (testimony of officer who talked to person immediately after occurrence and again later, where it was not shown what officer learned in first conversation or what was learned later); Texas & P. Ry. Co. v. Porter, Civ.App., 360 S.W.2d 568 (exclusion of statement of passenger was not error, where there was no showing as to the amount of time that elapsed between time automobile became stuck on the crossing and time statement was made, and no show-

§ 434.8 TRIAL EVIDENCE Ch. 434

If made after the occurrence, no matter how shortly, and if there is an attempt to explain the event or defend one's self, they are inadmissible.[66]

ing the statement was volunteered, or that passenger knew the matters with reference to which the statement was made); Coyle v. Shailer, Civ.App., 91 S.W.2d 920.

66. **Cal.**—Salvo v. Market St. Ry. Co., 2 P.2d 585, 116 Cal.App. 339.

Colo.—Gushurst v. Benham, 417 P. 2d 777, 160 Colo. 428 (testimony of highway patrolmen and son of decedent as to conversations with decedent about one and one-half to three hours after accident in which decedent gave explanation for having stopped his automobile on highway, constituting self-serving hearsay, was not admissible).

Ga.—Berry v. Dinsmore, 1967, 154 S.E.2d 653, 115 Ga.App. 256 (statement of defendant to witness ten minutes after plaintiff was allegedly struck by defendant's automobile that "he didn't think he had hit her" was not admissible as part of res gestae and error in admitting testimony was not rendered harmless by verdict for plaintiff where it appeared jury might have concluded that plaintiff's injuries were partially her fault, thereby reducing her damages under comparative negligence rule).

La.—Lefevre v. Allstate Ins. Co., App.1972, 258 So.2d 397 (alleged statement of defendants' four-year-old daughter that plaintiff's son, who was injured when defendants' unattended vehicle, parked by defendant wife on incline, rolled down incline and struck child, had climbed into vehicle with defendants' daughter and moved lever of transmission was properly excluded, since explanation or excuse by child exonerating herself immediately after an accident is normal reaction, and since, because of age and stipulated inability on part of defendants' daughter to remember any details of accident, it was impossible to cross-examine her as to accuracy of statement).

N.C.—Johnson v. Meyer's Co., 98 S. E.2d 315, 246 N.C. 310 (in action by pedestrian against store operator for injuries sustained when operator's advertising sign fell on pedestrian after motorist, who was in operator's parking lot, backed into the sign, motorist's statement that he was not responsible but that the parking attendant had left his automobile in "reverse" was a narrative by him of a past occurrence, and, therefore, was not admissible).

Or.—Zeller v. Dahl, 1972, 499 P.2d 1316, 262 Or. 515 (excluding of statement "Why were they on the wrong side of the road; why were they driving so fast?", made by plaintiff to ambulance driver after accident, on ground that statement was not an "excited utterance," was not an abuse of discretion where the statement was self-serving, in that it directly accused defendant of responsibility for the accident, where the evidence was not entirely clear as to what interval of time elapsed between the accident and the statement, and where there was evidence that during the interval plaintiff had time not only to think of her children and their welfare, but also to reflect upon various additional chores her husband would be required to perform because of her injury).

Contra

Md.—Honick v. Walden, 1971, 272 A. 2d 406, 10 Md.App. 714.

N.J.—Cestero v. Ferrara, 1971, 273 A.2d 761, 57 N.J. 497.

Ch. 434 HEARSAY § 434.8

Statements made by a driver shortly after a collision in report to a police officer,[67] or declarations made in response to inquiry ordinarily are not admissible.[68]

67. **U.S.**—Bowman v. Kaufman, C.A. N.Y.1967, 387 F.2d 582 (officer who came to scene should have been permitted to testify as to whether or not any of witnesses or parties involved mentioned brake failure as cause of accident); McCurdy v. Greyhound Corp., C.A. Pa.1965, 346 F.2d 224 (made within 10–15 minutes while noticeably nervous, held admissible); Connors v. Schmidt, C.A.Ohio, 257 F. 2d 146 (where witness had testified that she had been sitting in middle of front seat, testimony of police officer that another person had stated that he was sitting in middle of front seat was admissible under res gestae rule but even if inadmissible, was not prejudicial where it did not appear whether witness could have seen what she testified to have seen if not seated in the middle).

Ala.—Alabama Power Co. v. Sellers, 1968, 214 So.2d 833, 283 Ala. 137 (about one hour later defendant's truck driver made admissions about collision to state trooper, statements were not part of res gestae).

Dist.Col.—Sawyer v. Miseli, Mun. App., 156 A.2d 141 (statements of driver about 10 or 15 minutes after the accident to an investigating officer that owner told driver that he could take the car, and statement of the driver to plaintiff that defendant would be angry with the driver because the defendant loaned the driver his car, were not admissible as excited utterances, since the driver had a motive for falsely representing his authority to have possession of the vehicle to avoid a criminal prosecution).

Ga.—Southern Ry. Co. v. Allen, 1968, 165 S.E.2d 194, 118 Ga.App. 645 (statement of railroad engineer, who remained in engine which had stopped some distance from point of collision between railroad's engine and plaintiff's automobile, to investigating police officer, who had arrived at scene 10 minutes after the collision, that engineer had entered intersection at 60 miles an hour was made at least as long after the collision as a narrative of past events and could not be admitted as part of the res gestae); Augusta Coach Co. v. Lee, 1967, 154 S.E.2d 689, 115 Ga.App. 511 (statements, which were made by bus driver to investigating officer who was called to scene of alleged collision between bus and automobile, which were not made by bus driver in course of any transaction with officer in relation to bus company's business, and which were not in the nature of an exclamation uttered contemporaneously with occurrence, and testimony thereof by officer in action against bus company for death of driver of automobile was hearsay and wholly without probative value).

Ill.—Petty v. Illinois Cent. R. Co., 1956, 132 N.E.2d 1, 8 Ill.App.2d 367, cause remanded 144 N.E.2d 601, 11 Ill.2d 485; Montgomery v. Checker Taxi Co., 1944, 57 N.E.2d 231, 324 Ill.App. 83.

Iowa—Brooks v. Gilbert, 1959, 98 N. W.2d 309, 250 Iowa 1164, citing C.J.S. Evidence § 417.

Kan.—Mulich v. Graham Ship by Truck Co., 1946, 174 P.2d 98, 162 Kan. 61 (admissible).

La.—Audubon Ins. Co. v. Guidry, App.1973, 289 So.2d 311 (evidence of statements made to investigating officer at scene by driver and passenger that driver did not have

68. See note 68 on page 771.

769

§ 434.8   TRIAL EVIDENCE   Ch. 434

permission to drive vehicle was inadmissible as part of res gestae absent any showing as to lapse of time between accident and the alleged statements); Montgomery v. City of New Orleans, 1972, 266 So. 2d 482, writ denied 268 So.2d 258, 263 La. 370 (accident report which was prepared by investigating officer who arrived at scene some 20 minutes after accident was offered in evidence as primary evidence to show facts of accident); Fontenot v. Pan Am. Fire & Cas. Co., 1968, 209 So.2d 105, writ refused 211 So.2d 328, 252 La. 460 (statements by truck driver to city police officer about 40 minutes after accident to the effect that he thought that preceding defendant motorist was going to turn right and that she suddenly turned left were not admissible as a part of res gestae, since they were not made in a moment of tenseness or under circumstances which would reasonably preclude possibility of design, deliberation and fabrication).

Md.—Brown v. Rogers, 1974, 313 A. 2d 547, 19 Md.App. 562 (information obtained by officer from witnesses at scene concerning point of impact was not res gestae where, when officer arrived at scene, his sergeant already had things under control and there was nothing to indicate that statements were anything other than narrations of past events).

Mich.—Metcalf v. Peerless Laundry & Dye Co., 1921, 184 N.W. 482, 215 Mich. 601.

Miss.—Tyler v. Powell, 1972, 262 So. 2d 645 (patrolman's testimony that he had been told by driver that defendant driver of pickup truck had made left turn directly in front of automobile was not admissible, but admission of such testimony was harmless error, in view of overwhelming evidence against defendant).

Mo.—Galovich v. Hertz Corp., 513 S. W.2d 325 (testimony elicited from policeman to the effect that, after accident in which plaintiff was injured due to alleged defect in right wheel assembly and before ambulance arrived, plaintiff stated that the truck he was driving went out of control was not admissible as a res gestae statement either to show what caused the accident or to show that plaintiff did not black out as it lacked the spontaneity necessary); Brautigam v. Hoffman, App.1969, 444 S.W.2d 528 (where it was not shown that plaintiff was under influence of shock or pain or excitement of occasion of intersection collision involving her vehicle, so as to be unable or unlikely to reflect or reason before speaking, plaintiff's statement to officer, who conducted on-site investigation, that she stopped at stop sign, went across street, and that her automobile was hit on right side, was not shown to be part of res gestae).

N.J.—Sas v. Strelecki, 1970, 264 A.2d 247, 110 N.J.Super. 14 (within five to ten minutes after receiving radio call); Rogalsky v. Plymouth Homes, Inc., 1968, 242 A.2d 655, 100 N.J.Super. 501 (police chief's testimony that defendant, when questioned at scene after plaintiff had been removed to hospital, had told him that plaintiff had crossed center line was not admissible).

Ohio—Salyer v. Oyler Bros., App. 1955, 132 N.E.2d 628 (inadmissible).

Tex.—Strickland v. Pioneer Bus Co., Civ.App.1968, 427 S.W.2d 347, error refused n. r. e. (written statement signed by defendant's driver at scene within 15 or 20 minutes after it occurred and given to police officer was res gestae); Missouri Pac. R. Co. v. Rose, Civ.App. 1964, 380 S.W.2d 41 (made to officer who arrived after 17 minutes, held admissible); Luvual v. Henke & Pillot Division of Kroger Co., Civ.App., 366 S.W.2d 831, ref. n. r. e. (refusal to allow plaintiff

Ch. 434 HEARSAY § 434.8

to prove by investigating officer that operator of defendant's truck told him that "air went out on his truck and the brakes failed" was proper, where court could have concluded that statement was narrative of what had occurred, not the event speaking); Main Street Garage v. Eganhouse Optical Co., Civ.App., 223 S.W. 316.

Va.—Portsmouth Transit Co. v. Brickhouse, 108 S.E.2d 385, 200 Va. 844, 78 A.L.R.2d 147.

Wash.—Singer v. Metz Co., 171 P. 1032, 101 Wash. 67.

Wis.—Cornwell v. Rohrer, 156 N.W. 2d 373, 38 Wis.2d 252 (refusal to admit a statement which had been taken by investigating officer from tractor-trailer unit driver about one and one-half hours after passenger train had struck the unit while it was stalled and which was signed when driver of the unit apparently felt very upset was not manifestly wrong and thus was to be treated as a verity on appeal); Johnson v. Smitz, 1956, 79 N.W.2d 337, 274 Wis. 96 (not admissible); Pocquette v. Carpiaux, 52 N.W.2d 787, 261 Wis. 340 (where plaintiff knew when he was interviewed by policeman at hospital that investigation in part was to determine whether plaintiff had entered arterial street without stopping, thereby violating law, and plaintiff would naturally and inevitably be aware that civil action, either by or against plaintiff, could grow out of collision, statement made to policeman at hospital to effect that plaintiff had stopped at stop sign at intersection, which was consistent with plaintiff's testimony at trial, was not admissible in evidence to rebut defendant's claim that plaintiff's testimony that plaintiff stopped at stop sign was a recent fabrication).

But see

La.—Shipman v. Tardo, App.1974, 304 So.2d 381 (statement made by fatally injured pedestrian to officer 20 minutes after accident was part of res gestae and officer's testimony concerning the statement was admissible).

N.D.—Dimond v. Kling, 1974, 221 N. W.2d 86 (did not abuse discretion in admitting, as res gestae, statements of investigating police officer as to remarks made to him by injured passenger on bicycle in emergency room some 40 minutes to one hour after accident).

Tex.—Revisore v. West, Civ.App. 1970, 450 S.W.2d 361.

Passenger's statement

Ill.—Murphy v. Hook, 316 N.E.2d 146, 21 Ill.App.3d 1006 (did not err in excluding substance of declarations by defendant motorist's wife at time state trooper arrived at scene, indicating that she saw decedent's station wagon in the wrong lane of the highway just prior to the collision).

68. Ill.—Swearinger v. Klinger, 1968, 234 N.E.2d 60, 91 Ill.App.2d 251 (elicited from plaintiff's driver in conversation with police officer five to fifteen minutes after collision).

Mich.—Sexton v. Balinski, 273 N.W. 335, 280 Mich. 28 (admission, over objection, of police officer's testimony that codefendant told him at police station approximately fifteen minutes after accident occurred that defendant owned automobile held error as to defendant).

Pa.—Nunamaker v. New Alexandria Bus Co., 88 A.2d 697, 371 Pa. 28 (testimony of state policeman concerning statement made by driver to police an hour and one-half after accident was properly excluded in that statement was not part of res gestae).

But see

Iowa—Gibbs v. Wilmeth, 1968, 157 N.W.2d 93, 261 Iowa 1015 (state-

§ 434.8   TRIAL EVIDENCE   Ch. 434

Such a statement must explain or bear upon the main transaction or upon facts in dispute.[69]

ment given in answer to a question does not necessarily violate the res gestae rule; the important consideration is the spontaneity of the statement, however elicited).

N.Y.—Weiss v. Daitch-Shopwell Superettes, Inc., N.Y.City Civ.Ct., 271 N.Y.S.2d 323, 50 Misc.2d 735, affirmed 279 N.Y.S.2d 633, 53 Misc. 2d 644 (is immaterial that statement was made in response to question, so long as it was not too far removed in time from event to be proved).

Okl.—Wray v. Garrett, 1939, 90 P.2d 1050, 185 Okl. 138.

Or.—Bosin v. Oak Lodge Sanitary Dist. No. 1, 1968, 447 P.2d 285, 251 Or. 554 (that nonlitigant's spontaneous declaration was elicited by an inquiry is not conclusive against admissibility but is a factor for consideration).

69. U.S.—Elek v. Boyce, D.C.S.C. 1970, 308 F.Supp. 26 (statement as to speed not admissible where case issue was centerline violation).

Ariz.—Hines v. Gale, 1923, 213 P. 395, 25 Ariz. 65.

Ill.—Forssen v. Rieke, 1973, 295 N.E. 2d 84, 10 Ill.App.3d 677 (where there was sudden collision and resulting fire which caused driver to make emergency exit through vehicle's window, driver's statements which were made shortly thereafter and which requested that another vehicle be stopped were admissible).

Mo.—McComb v. Vaughn, 218 S.W. 2d 548, 358 Mo. 951 (declaration as to absence of lights on own vehicle, made 40 minutes earlier); Smith v. East St. Louis Ry. Co., 123 S.W.2d 198, 234 Mo.App. 1220 (alleged statement by motorman after collision with taxicab, that "this is one damn good way to get rid of the cabs," held, under the evidence, made too long after the collision to be admissible as a part of the res gestae, and not of such character as to explain cause of accident).

Neb.—Komma v. Kreifels, 14 N.W.2d 591, 144 Neb. 745 (statement of intent to quit use of liquor, held inadmissible in absence of connection of drinking to accident); Suhr v. Lindell, 277 N.W. 381, 133 Neb. 856 (statement of own expectation of dying not admissible).

N.Y.—Butler v. Manhattan Ry. Co., 38 N.E. 454, 143 N.Y. 417, 26 L. R.A. 46, 42 Am.St.Rep. 738.

N.C.—Coley v. Phillips, 31 S.E.2d 757, 224 N.C. 618 (statement of mother who did not see accident as to telling child about crossing highway).

S.C.—Anders v. Nash, 1971, 180 S.E. 2d 878, 256 S.C. 102 (pedestrian's son's statement "Mama, I told you not to cross," made shortly after pedestrian was struck, was sufficiently close in point of time and place to form part of res gestae but was inadmissible as it failed to explain, elucidate or in some way characterize the nature of the accident).

Tex.—Marshall v. Weingarten, 406 S. W.2d 761 (statements by driver, who was owner's employee's maid, to police officer soon after accident to effect that driver had come to business establishment to purchase commodity for owner's employee and that brakes on automobile failed as she attempted to stop and she struck pedestrian did not relate to or explain cause of accident but only driver's employment and were not admissible).

Comment as to insurance

Even if defendant's alleged statement "Don't worry, if your insurance doesn't cover this, mine will"

Ch. 434 HEARSAY § 434.8

It has been held that the statements must be of fact, and not merely the expression of the opinion or conclusion of the declarant.[70]

The decision upon the preliminary question of whether the declarant had any opportunity for deliberation and reflection, or whether the utterance was a spontaneous one will be left to the judge's discretion,[71] which determination will not be subject to review unless such discretion is abused.[72]

---

was part of res gestae, it did not tend to explain or prove admission of fault on part of defendant and was not admissible. Menefee v. Williams, 1968, 66 Cal.Rptr. 108, 259 Cal.App.2d 56.

70. Cal.—Ungefug v. D'Ambrosia, 1967, 58 Cal.Rptr. 223, 250 Cal.App. 2d 61 (declarant must have witnessed event to which his utterance relates).

Conn.—Johnson v. Newell, 1970, 278 A.2d 776, 260 Conn. 269 (in action arising out of alleged blowout of tire recapped by one defendant and sold and installed by another, court properly excluded alleged spontaneous utterance by person, who did not see accident but only heard it, that "that sounds to me like a shot or blowout").

La.—Fasullo v. Columbia Cas Co., 195 So.2d 361.

Mo.—McKenzie Transport Leasing Co. v. St. Louis Public Service Co., App., 349 S.W.2d 370; Kenney v. J. A. Folger & Co., App., 192 S. W.2d 73 (statement of defendant's driver that accident was his fault was inadmissible as conclusion).

Ohio—Reed v. Detroit, T. & I. R. Co., App., 132 N.E.2d 776.

Tex.—Zepeda v. Moore, Civ.App., 153 S.W.2d 212, error dismissed (testimony of plaintiffs' witness that, shortly after accident, truck driver said that he would have to move truck because he did not want to be responsible for another accident, was properly excluded as a "conclusion" or "opinion" of driver).

Va.—Chappell v. White, 1944, 29 S. E.2d 858, 182 Va. 625.

But see
Rule excluding opinion evidence is not applicable when opinion is part of a "spontaneous statement" or "excited utterance," particularly when coupled with statement of facts which explain, characterize or throw light on the exciting occurrence. Wright v. Swann, 1972, 493 P.2d 148, 261 Or. 440, 50 A.L.R.3d 707.

71. U.S.—Kenosha Auto Transport Corp. v. Lowe Seed Co., C.A.Ill., 362 F.2d 765.

Cal.—Ungefug v. D'Ambrosia, 1967, 58 Cal.Rptr. 223, 250 Cal.App.2d 61.

Colo.—Stahl v. Cooper, 190 P.2d 891, 117 Colo. 468.

Conn.—Rockhill v. White Line Bus Co., 145 A. 504, 109 Conn. 706.

Ill.—Johnson v. Swords Co., 3 N.E. 2d 705, 286 Ill.App. 377.

Iowa—Bass v. Muenchow, 146 N.W. 2d 923, 259 Iowa 1010.

Kan.—Letcher v. Derricott, 383 P.2d 533, 191 Kan. 596.

Mo.—Blackburn v. Ready-Mixed Concrete Co., App.1945, 188 S.W.2d 526.

Mont.—Blevins v. Weaver Const. Co., 432 P.2d 378, 150 Mont. 158.

Neb.—Suhr v. Lindell, 1938, 277 N. W. 381, 133 Neb. 856.

---

72. See note 72 on page 774.

§ 434.8 "Contemporaneous statement"

A related circumstance deemed to be an exception to the hearsay rule is where the declaration is made contemporaneous to the event being perceived, or nearly contemporaneous to it,[73] sometimes classed as a "present sense impression".[74]

N.D.—Trautman v. New Rockford-Fessenden Co-op Transport Ass'n, 1970, 181 N.W.2d 754.

Okl.—Indian Oil Tool Co. v. Thompson, 405 P.2d 104; Wofford v. Lewis, 377 P.2d 37; Feenberg Supply Co. v. Pierce, 95 P.2d 640, 185 Okl. 662.

Pa.—Wilf v. Philadelphia Modeling & Charm School, Inc., 208 A.2d 294, 205 Pa.Super. 196.

S.C.—Gentry v. Watkins-Carolina Trucking Co., 1967, 154 S.E.2d 112, 249 S.C. 316, 37 A.L.R.3d 766.

Tex.—Duncan v. Smith, 376 S.W.2d 877, citing 32 C.J.S. Evidence §§ 403, 420, error granted.

Utah—Morton v. Hood, 143 P.2d 434, 105 Utah 484.

Wis.—Cossette v. Lepp, 157 N.W.2d 629, 38 Wis.2d 932; Cornwell v. Rohrer, 156 N.W.2d 373, 38 Wis.2d 252.

72. **Colo.**—Stahl v. Cooper, 190 P.2d 891, 117 Colo. 468 (the tendency is to broaden, rather than to restrict, the res gestae rule).

Dist.Col.—Watts v. Smith, D.C.App., 226 A.2d 160.

N.M.—Garrett v. Howden, 387 P.2d 874, 73 N.M. 307.

S.C.—Powers v. Temple, 1967, 156 S.E.2d 759, 250 S.C. 149 (admission of testimony as to statements made by unidentified party some minutes after accident occurred was not abuse of discretion).

73. **U.S.**—Kirkendoll v. Neustrom, C.A.Kan.1967, 379 F.2d 694 (statement made to investigating highway patrolman by witness as to speed of plaintiff's vehicle one mile before collision was properly admitted as a "contemporaneous statement" under exception to hearsay rule. K.S.A. 60–460(d)); Petroleum Carrier Corp. v. Snyder, C.C.A.Ga.1947, 161 F.2d 323 (occupant's statement "Look out! He's on your side of the road").

Ala.—Birmingham Elec. Co. v. Gilbert, 48 So.2d 1, 254 Ala. 208 (conversation of bus driver just prior to fall of passenger).

Ariz.—Southwestern Freight Lines v. Floyd, 119 P.2d 120, 58 Ariz. 249 (in actions by two girls for injuries sustained when bicycle on which they were riding collided with a truck, the statement that "that truck is going to hit us", testified to by one of girls as having been made by other girl just before the accident).

Ark.—Schwam v. Reece, 1948, 210 S.W.2d 903, 213 Ark. 431 (bus driver's reply "I have no brakes").

Cal.—West's Ann.Calif.Evid.Code, § 1241.

Ga.—Roberts v. Bryant, 1967, 157 S.E.2d 517, 116 Ga.App. 386 (conversation between deceased and driver immediately preceding accident to encourage driver in his reckless driving was of probative value and was a part of the res gestae and in the nature of original evidence).

Idaho.—McIntire v. Oregon Short Line R. Co., 1936, 55 P.2d 148, 56 Idaho 392 (brakeman's statement to engineer just before collision).

Ill.—Sullivan v. Heyer, 21 N.E.2d 776, 300 Ill.App. 599 (guest's statement to motorist just prior to col-

74. See note 74 on page 775.

lision, "My God, Alice, that car: we are going to hit that car," was competent).

Iowa.—Bass v. Muenchow, 1966, 146 N.W.2d 923, 259 Iowa 1010 (about three seconds before collision passenger exclaimed "What is that fool going to do").

Kan.—Kansas Code of Civil Procedure § 60–460(d)(1).

Ky.—Ewing-Von Allmen Dairy Co. v. Fowler's Ex'r, 1950, 228 S.W.2d 449, 312 Ky. 547 (driver's statement "He is on the wrong * *").

Mass.—Correira v. Boston Motor Tours, 169 N.E. 775, 270 Mass. 88 (conversation in vehicle re presence of danger).

Mich.—Escott v. Locke, 1970, 181 N. W.2d 279, 25 Mich.App. 344 (driver's statement before intersection collision with truck "Oh, my God, he is going through the red light").

Miss.—Houston Contracting Co. v. Atkinson, 168 So.2d 797, 251 Miss. 220 (outcry on part of host driver shortly before she collided with a preceding truck which allegedly stopped on a bridge to the effect of "what in the world are you going to do" was admissible).

N.J.—New Jersey Evidence Rule 63 (4)(a).

Tex.—Claybrook v. Acreman, Civ. App., 373 S.W.2d 287, ref. n. r. e. (statements of witnesses who were sitting in automobile at side of road about a mile from place collision occurred, assertedly upon seeing defendant racing another automobile down the highway, including remark that "they won't last long at that rate of speed" should have been admitted).

Utah.—Utah Rules of Evidence § 63 (4)(a).

Exclamations of independent witnesses to driving

Md.—Baltimore & O. R. Co. v. State, for Use of Carbone, 181 A. 830, 169 Md. 345 (exclamation of another motorist who observed irregular driving).

Miss.—Ideal Cement Co. v. Killingsworth, Miss.1967, 198 So.2d 248 (testimony as to remark he made before the accident about speed of defendant's automobile which had passed witness more than a quarter of a mile from scene was hearsay, and was not part of res gestae, and was inadmissible; but admission of testimony was not reversible error, where other witnesses testified to automobile's speed immediately prior to accident).

S.C.—Marks v. I. M. Pearlstine & Sons, 26 S.E.2d 835, 203 S.C. 318 (exclamation of another who saw irregular driving).

Tex.—Houston Oxygen Co. v. Davis, 161 S.W.2d 474, 139 Tex. 1 (statement of overtaken motorist that other driver must be drunk and would be found wrecked).

"Spontaneous" statement

Fla.—Florida Evidence Code § 90.803 (1).

74. U.S.—Federal Rules of Evidence § 803(1).

Me.—Maine Rules of Evidence § 803 (1).

Nev.—N.R.S. 51.085.

N.M.—New Mexico Rules of Evidence § 803(1).

Wis.—Wisconsin Rules of Evidence § 908.03(1).

§ 434.9 Statements of Bodily Condition

Library References:
C.J.S. Evidence §§ 241 et seq., 403, 421.
West's Key No. Digests, Evidence ⇌127, 128, 268.

Evidence of expressions of then existing pain or physical condition, whether such expressions or declarations have been made at the time of the injury or subsequent thereto, is admissible as a specially recognized form of a spontaneous declaration or statement of a present sense impression.[75]

75. **U.S.**—Federal Rules of Evidence § 803(3), 28 U.S.C.A.

Ala.—Fidelity Service Ins. Co. v. Jones, 191 So.2d 20, 280 Ala. 195 (representations by sick person, of the nature, symptoms, and effect of malady under which he is laboring at the time); Lowery v. Jones, 121 So. 704, 219 Ala. 201, 64 A.L.R. 553.

Cal.—West's Ann.Calif.Evid.Code, § 1250.

Fla.—Florida Evidence Code § 90.803 (3).

Ga.—Wolfson v. Rumble, 1970, 174 S.E.2d 469, 121 Ga.App. 549.

Hawaii.—Kometani v. Heath, 1967, 431 P.2d 931, 50 Hawaii 89 (where accident victim could not, because of her head injuries, remember anything about her condition from accident until third day after accident, testimony by her physicians as to her complaints of pain and suffering was admissible to show pain and suffering as damages, and refusal to give requested instruction that nature and extent of injuries may not be proved by evidence of statements as to aches, pains or injuries made to doctor was not error).

Ind.—Cleveland, C., C. & I. Ry. Co. v. Newell, 1885, 3 N.E. 836, 104 Ind. 264.

Kan.—Kansas Code of Civil Procedure § 60–460(*l*)(1); Thompson v. Norman, 1967, 424 P.2d 593, 198 Kan. 436.

Me.—Maine Rules of Evidence § 803 (3).

Md.—Robinson v. Lewis, 1974, 317 A.2d 854, 20 Md.App. 710 (complaints made by deceased as to pain in his legs during 19-day period between accident and his death).

Mo.—Tryon v. Casey, 1967, 416 S. W.2d 252; Kenney v. J. A. Folger & Co., App.1946, 192 S.W.2d 73 (inadmissible unless natural and spontaneous expressions).

Neb.—Nebraska Rules of Evidence § 803(2).

Nev.—N.R.S. 51.105.

N.J.—New Jersey Evidence Rule 63 (12)(a).

N.M.—New Mexico Rules of Evidence 803(3).

Okl.—Gulf Oil Corp. v. Harris, 1967, 425 P.2d 957; Arkansas Louisiana Gas Co. v. Evans, 397 P.2d 505; Dewitt v. Johnson, 41 P.2d 476, 170 Okl. 625 (parent's testimony as to natural and ordinary complaints of child as to pain being suffered).

Or.—Frangos v. Edmunds, 173 P.2d 596, 179 Or. 577 (hospital patient's complaints of present pain).

S.D.—Plank v. Heirigs, 1968, 156 N. W.2d 193, 83 S.D. 173 (nurses attending woman were qualified to testify to her health and physical condition, and also as to her expressions of pain and complaints).

Utah.—Utah Rules of Evidence § 63 (12)(a).

Wis.—Wisconsin Rules of Evidence § 908.03(3).

Statements as to present pain and suffering, made to a specialist consulting with the injured person's regular physician are admissible,[76] but should be admitted with great caution because of the self-serving character of the statements, the question being left largely to the discretion of the trial judge.[77]

Statements to physicians

Evidence of all declarations of a patient made to a treating physician is usually admitted on the theory that, although such evidence partakes of the nature of hearsay, it derives credibility from the fact that the patient has an incentive beyond the ordinary obligation to tell the truth.[78]

But see as to spontaneity requirement

Mich.—Layton v. Cregan & Mallory Co., 257 N.W. 888, 269 Mich. 574.

76. Minn.—Cooper v. St. Paul City R. Co., 56 N.W. 42, 54 Minn. 379.

77. Or.—Reid v. Yellow Cab Co., 279 P. 635, 131 Or. 27, 67 A.L.R. 1.

78. U.S.—Federal Rules of Evidence § 803(4).

Ariz.—Nash v. Kamrath, 1974, 521 P.2d 161, 21 Ariz.App. 530 (plaintiff's statement that "her knees were ruined" was admissible); Simpson v. Heiderich, 419 P.2d 362, 4 Ariz.App. 232 (fact had already retained an attorney was not controlling as to admissibility of recitals).

Cal.—West's Ann.Calif.Evid.Code, § 1251.

Conn.—State v. Orsini, 1967, 232 A.2d 907, 155 Conn. 367 (equally applicable in civil or criminal).

Fla.—Florida Evidence Code § 90.803 (4).

Idaho.—Gonzales v. Hodsdon, 420 P. 2d 813, 91 Idaho 330 (if such statements are necessary for an accurate diagnosis and treatment).

Ill.—Koenig v. 399 Corp., 1968, 240 N.E.2d 164, 97 Ill.App.2d 345; Geaschel v. Rokita, 1967, 232 N.E.2d 204, 89 Ill.App.2d 161.

Kan.—Kansas Code of Civil Procedure § 60–460(*l*)(2).

Ky.—Arnett v. Thompson, 1968, 433 S.W.2d 109.

La.—Becnel v. Ward, App.1973, 286 So.2d 731, writ denied Sup., 290 So.2d 900.

Me.—Maine Rules of Evidence § 803 (4).

Neb.—Nebraska Rules of Evidence § 803(3).

Nev.—N.R.S. 51.115.

N.J.—New Jersey Evidence Rule 63 (12)(b); Pinter v. Parsekian, 223 A.2d 635, 92 N.J.Super. 392 (but statements as to cause of symptoms or conditions are generally inadmissible). Lamberton v. Consolidated Traction Co., 38 A. 683, 60 N.J.L. 452.

N.M.—New Mexico Rules of Evidence § 803(4).

N.Y.—Regan v. National Postal Transport Ass'n, 1967, 280 N.Y.S. 2d 319, 53 Misc.2d 901 (facts disclosed by decedent to physician or ascertained by physician by observation or examination are not hearsay).

N.C.—Inman v. Harper, 1968, 162 S.E. 2d 629, 2 N.C.App. 103.

S.C.—Gentry v. Watkins-Carolina Trucking Co., 1967, 154 S.E.2d 112, 249 S.C. 316, 37 A.L.R.3d 766 (trial court's discretion).

§ 434.9   TRIAL EVIDENCE   Ch. 434

To be provable, statements made to a physician by an injured person must relate to symptoms, ills, or the locality and character of pain.[79]

However, declarations as to past conditions, made to a medical expert so that the expert may testify, are generally inadmissible.[80]

Tex.—Miller Mut. Fire Ins. Co. of Tex. v. Ochoa, 1968, 432 S.W.2d 118, error refused n. r. e.; Texas Emp. Ins. Ass'n v. Steadman, 1967, 415 S.W.2d 211, error refused n. r. e.

Utah.—Utah Rules of Evidence § 63 (12)(b).

Wash.—Kraettli v. North Coast Transportation Co., 1932, 6 P.2d 609, 166 Wash. 186, 80 A.L.R. 1520.

Wis.—Wisconsin Rules of Evidence § 908.03(4); Erdmann v. Frazin, 1968, 158 N.W.2d 281, 39 Wis.2d 1 (that consultation of plaintiff with doctor was made for bona fide purpose of treatment, fact that plaintiff or her attorney also desired to utilize doctor as witness at trial did not preclude doctor from testifying as to patient's report of subjective symptoms or from predicating medical conclusions on such reports); Cossette v. Lepp, 1968, 157 N.W.2d 629, 38 Wis.2d 932.

Contra

Ind.—Cerra v. McClanahan, 1967, 229 N.E.2d 737, 141 Ind.App. 469.

Even facts as to nature of accident

Tenn.—Interstate Life & Acc. Co. v. Cox, 1965, 396 S.W.2d 80, 55 Tenn. App. 40 (necessary to diagnosis).

Related by another

A treating doctor may testify to an infant's case history as related to doctor by a parent, custodian, guardian, or nurse. Miller v. Watts, Ky., 1969, 436 S.W.2d 515.

Rule limited

Ga.—Paulk v. Thomas, 1967, 154 S.E. 2d 872, 115 Ga.App. 436 (physician's testimony that the plaintiff was still complaining of pain on particular date was properly excluded as hearsay because not made under such circumstances as to be equivalent to a spontaneous and involuntary outcry resulting from manipulation of patient's body by the physician); Brewer v. Henson, 1957, 100 S.E.2d 661, 96 Ga.App. 501.

79. **Or.**—Wise v. State Industrial Accident Commission, 1934, 35 P.2d 242, 148 Or. 461.

But see

Tenn.—Interstate Life & Acc. Co. v. Cox, 1965, 396 S.W.2d 80, 55 Tenn. App. 40 (facts of accident proper if necessary to diagnosis).

Where there were other witnesses

Permitting deceased driver's physician to testify as to decedent's statements concerning how accident occurred was improper, where there were other witnesses to the accident, driver's statement was given to doctor eight days after the accident, no treatment was given and driver was discharged at end of that first and only visit to doctor. Pinter v. Parsekian, 1966, 223 A.2d 635, 92 N.J.Super. 392.

80. **Ala.**—Lowery v. Jones, 1929, 121 So. 704, 219 Ala. 201, 64 A.L.R. 553.

Ill.—Hastings v. Abernathy Taxi Ass'n, Inc., 1974, 306 N.E.2d 498, 16 Ill.App.3d 671 (permitting physician who examined motorist to review history taken and to respond to questions concerning motorist's statements of subjective symptoms

In some jurisdictions the statements of an injured person to a physician, expressive of a past physical condition, may be repeated by the physician as explanation for the physician's opinions.[81]

While it has been held that a physician may repeat statements made by an injured person as to past events and supposed causes, the holding has been qualified by the further ruling that such statements must not go into the question of responsibility for the injury.[82]

of pain, illnesses, occupations and visits to a medical clinic was error but not reversible error, where content of physician's objectionable testimony had been previously introduced into evidence by competent testimony); Korleski v. Needham, 222 N.E.2d 334, 77 Ill. App.2d 329 (but reversal was not required where all that physician testified to had been previously admitted into evidence by other competent testimony); Santiemmo v. Days Transfer, Inc., 133 N.E.2d 539, 9 Ill.App.2d 487; Shaughnessy v. Holt, 86 N.E. 256, 236 Ill. 485, 21 L.R.A.,N.S., 826.

Ky.—Southeastern Greyhound Lines v. Webb, 230 S.W.2d 99, 313 Ky. 71.

Md.—Fisher Body Division, General Motors Corp. v. Alston, 1969, 249 A.2d 130, 252 Md. 51; Wilhelm v. State Traffic Safety Commission, 1962, 185 A.2d 715, 230 Md. 91 (made to psychiatrist).

Minn.—Simchuck v. Fullerton, 1974, 216 N.W.2d 683, 299 Minn. 91.

Or.—Reid v. Yellow Cab Co., 279 P. 635, 131 Or. 27, 67 A.L.R. 1.

Wis.—Wegerer v. Koehler, 137 N.W. 2d 115, 28 Wis. 241.

Also "demonstrations"

Evidence of statements and physical demonstration capable of simulation are not admissible if made to physician examining for purpose of testifying, and he is limited to testifying to purely objective conditions. Dickeson v. Baltimore & O. C. T. R. Co., 1969, 245 N.E.2d 762, 42 Ill.2d 103, 35 A.L.R.3d 1.

Also doctor examining to determine need for further treatment

Neither physician to whom plaintiff had been referred for orthopedic evaluation nor physician who had examined plaintiff "to see if he needed any further treatment" were "treating physicians" for purpose of rule precluding nontreating physician from relating history given to him by litigant. Rossello v. Friedel, 220 A.2d 537, 243 Md. 234.

81. **N.Y.**—Jones v. National Biscuit Co., 1968, 289 N.Y.S.2d 588, 29 A.D.2d 1033.

Wash.—Floyd v. Department of Labor and Industries, 416 P.2d 355, 68 Wash.2d 938 (such testimony is not evidence which establishes the fact of plaintiff's condition).

Explanation for treatment given

Testimony by physician as to plaintiff's complaint of pain may be admissible where given merely as explanation of course of conduct of physician, provided such course of conduct is relevant and material. Cowart Trucking Co., Inc. v. Stone, 1973, 199 S.E.2d 608, 129 Ga.App. 327.

82. **U.S.**—Brown v. Seaboard Airline R. Co., C.A.Fla.1970, 434 F.2d 1101 (statement given to physician that plaintiff was walking alongside train and was struck by a projection from train which caused him to fall under the same).

§ 434.10 Business Records—In General

Library References:

C.J.S. Evidence §§ 682 et seq., 730(2); Federal Civil Procedure § 457.

West's Key No. Digests, Evidence ⚖351 et seq.; Federal Civil Procedure ⚖1191.

Records made in the regular course of any business or regularly conducted activity as a memorandum of any act, transaction, occurrence or event are usually held admissible.[83]

Ala.—Lowery v. Jones, 1929, 121 So. 704, 219 Ala. 201, 64 A.L.R. 553.

Mo.—Bauer v. Independent Stave Co., App.1967, 417 S.W.2d 693 (with respect to circumstances surrounding injury or manner in which injury was received).

Admission not reversible error

A physician should not be permitted to repeat the plaintiff's narration to him of the manner in which the injury was received or the cause thereof, but the admission of such evidence is not reversible error, where the plaintiff testified directly to the same facts and there is no dispute as to the manner in which the injuries were received. Reid v. Yellow Cab Co., 279 P. 635, 131 Or. 27, 67 A.L.R. 1.

But see

N.J.—Cestero v. Ferrara, 1970, 265 A.2d 387, 110 N.J.Super. 264, affirmed 273 A.2d 761, 57 N.J. 497 (portion of hospital record which allegedly recited defendant's version of intersectional collision, i. e., "Pt. stopped for red light, started up on green light and got hit," was admissible, where, under circumstances surrounding defendant's admittance to emergency room, there was some question of a brain concussion and thus her ability to recall what had happened was important to physician's diagnosis and his determination as to whether to proceed to operate).

[83]. **U.S.**—Federal Rules of Evidence § 803(6) et seq., 28 U.S.C.A.; Grummons v. Zollinger, D.C.Ind., 240 F.Supp. 63, affirmed 341 F.2d 464 (message sent by one employee of insurer to another concerning instructions about handling claim was within regular course of business of insurer within Business Records Act); Kissinger v. Frankhouser, C.A.Va., 308 F.2d 348 (a United States Naval hospital record, including an entry showing result of a Bogen's test for intoxication); Ostrov v. Metropolitan Life Ins. Co., D.C.Pa., 260 F.Supp. 152 (where doctor's reports were made in course of his practice and his letters to a colleague were based on those reports, they were written in course of his normal practice and therefore were admissible).

Alaska.—Zerbinos v. Lewis, 394 P. 2d 886 (records made in regular course of business at or about time of act recorded).

Ariz.—Lenslite Co. v. Zocher, 388 P.2d 421, 95 Ariz. 208 (was intended to liberalize rules of admitting records); Welch v. Medlock, 286 P.2d 756, 79 Ariz. 247 (a highway department "fatality sheet" was not a "business record" within purview of uniform business records as evidence act).

Cal.—West's Ann.Calif.Evid.Code, § 1271; Springer v. Reimers, 1970, 84 Cal.Rptr. 486, 4 Cal.App.3d 325 (insofar as they record personal observations of attending physician or pertinent statements of patient's history which physician has made use of in reaching his professional opinions).

Colo.—Bates & Sons, Inc. v. Great Western Ry. Co., 406 P.2d 98, 158 Colo. 259 (railroad's time book and daily time reports containing names of employees, number of hours worked by each, description of work performed and daily time records kept by plaintiff in regular course of its business were admissible).

Conn.—Ianni v. Daily, 217 A.2d 707, 153 Conn. 445 (only such parts of the hospital record as are generally admissible can be introduced).

Del.—Watts v. Delaware Coach Co., 58 A.2d 689, 5 Terry 283.

Dist.Col.—Christensen v. Gammons, Mun.App., 197 A.2d 450 (not inadmissible merely because the records contained expressions of diagnosis).

Fla.—Florida Evidence Code § 90.803 (6); Allstate Ins. Co. v. Doody, 193 So.2d 687; Exchange Nat. Bank of Tampa v. Hospital and Welfare Bd. of Hillsborough County, 181 So.2d 9 (is intended to liberalize rules as to allowance of shop book memoranda).

Idaho.—Kelson v. Ahlborn, 1964, 393 P.2d 578, 87 Idaho 519, 13 A.L.R. 3d 274.

Ill.—Smith v. Champaign Urbana City Lines, Inc., 1969, 252 N.E.2d 381, 116 Ill.App.2d 289 (ledger sheet concerning repairs made on automobile was an original entry made by the bookkeeper in the regular course of business).

Kan.—Kansas Code of Civil Procedure § 60–460(m).

Ky.—Whittaker v. Thornberry, 209 S.W.2d 498, 306 Ky. 830.

La.—Bolding v. Eason Oil Co., 170 So.2d 883 (that railroad's records were not kept in Louisiana did not make certified copies thereof inadmissible as business records).

Me.—Maine Rules of Evidence § 803 (6).

Mich.—Giddens v. Appeal Bd. of Michigan Employment Sec. Commission, 145 N.W.2d 294, 4 Mich. App. 526 (lack of personal knowledge by entrant or maker, may be shown to affect its weight); Gile v. Hudnutt, 272 N.W. 706, 279 Mich. 358; Schmidt v. Riemenschneider, 265 N.W. 816, 196 Minn. 612.

Miss.—City of Bay St. Louis v. Johnston, 1969, 222 So.2d 841 (hospital records).

Mo.—Thienes v. Harlin Fruit Co., App.1973, 499 S.W.2d 223 (admission of army personnel record which was identified by warrant officer and which contained statement that plaintiff, who claimed he was prevented from attending officer candidate school because of injuries sustained, was relieved from officer candidate school for physical reasons was not error even though warrant officer had no personal knowledge why plaintiff was relieved from officer candidate school or nature of physical reasons referred to in record); Gathright v. Pendegraft, 1968, 433 S.W. 2d 299 (records of a hospital); Tryon v. Casey, App.1967, 416 S. W.2d 252 (physician's records).

Neb.—Nebraska Rules of Evidence § 803(5).

Nev.—N.R.S. 51.135.

N.H.—Corey Steeplejacks, Inc. v. Cray, 206 A.2d 617, 106 N.H. 126.

N.J.—New Jersey Evidence Rule 63 (13); Carroll v. Houtz, 225 A.2d 584, 93 N.J.Super. 215 (where two assistant county physicians performed autopsy on body of motorist, and, as part of autopsy, specimens of blood and brain tissues were set aside for alcohol analysis and were forwarded to laboratory, and laboratory report was forwarded to county physician and was placed in autopsy file, report came within ambit of Uniform Business

§ 434.10 TRIAL EVIDENCE Ch. 434

Records as Evidence Act and was admissible as part of county physician's records in action for motorist's death, though laboratory director, who signed report, was not called as witness, and though report, when received by county physician was not brought to personal attention of assistant county physician who testified and was not examined by him); Petrosino v. Public Service Coordinated Transport, 61 A.2d 746, 1 N.J.Super. 19.

N.M.—New Mexico Rules of Evidence § 803(6).

N.Y.—Spoar v. Fudjack, 263 N.Y.S.2d 340, 24 A.D.2d 731 (nurses' notes contained in hospital records of patient); Kardas v. State, 253 N.Y.S.2d 470, 44 Misc.2d 243 (extends to recorded information in hospital record obtained by observation by all persons under duty so to report); Bishin v. New York Cent. R. Co., 249 N.Y.S.2d 778, 20 A.D.2d 921 (employee's report of railroad grade crossing accident was admissible, any self-serving aspect thereof going merely to its weight).

Ohio.—Heinemann v. Mitchell, 220 N.E.2d 616, 8 Ohio Misc. 390 (hospital records); Lacy v. Uganda Inv. Corp., 220 N.E.2d 130, 7 Ohio App. 2d 237.

Okl.—Horn v. Sturm, 408 P.2d 541 (generally, hospital records must have been kept in ordinary course of business as an essential part of the system of business).

Or.—D. N. & E. Walter & Co. v. Van Domelen, 425 P.2d 166, 246 Or. 275; Gallagher v. Portland Traction Co., 182 P.2d 354, 181 Or. 385 (admissible to show plaintiff's condition before accident).

S.D.—Plank v. Heirigs, 1968, 156 N.W.2d 193, 83 S.D. 173 (adequate foundation was laid for admission of nurses' notes under Uniform Business Records as Evidence Act, and proof that these were the regular charts of the patient, kept and used by the hospital, in her care and treatment was sufficient to warrant their admission).

Tex.—Loper v. Andrews, 404 S.W.2d 300; Ford v. Aetna Ins. Co., Civ.App., 394 S.W.2d 693 (vouchers are admissible); Goshorn v. Hattman, Civ.App., 387 S.W.2d 422 (records of physician who went into service after treating plaintiff's wife for her injuries were admissible); Weaver v. Swofford, Civ. App., 386 S.W.2d 624.

Utah.—Utah Rules of Evidence § 63 (13).

Va.—Dalton v. Johnson, 129 S.E.2d 647, 204 Va. 102 (hospital records).

Wash.—Allen v. Fish, 393 P.2d 621, 64 Wash.2d 655.

Wis.—Wisconsin Rules of Evidence § 908.03(6).

Accident report to own supervisor

Exclusion of accident reports, which were furnished by plaintiff bus driver and his immediate supervisor to transit authority, which employed plaintiff, in regular course of business was error. Bromberg v. City of New York, 270 N.Y.S.2d 425, 25 A.D.2d 885.

Communication from another held in file

Business record statute did not apply to sheet of printed instructions which corporation had received from manufacturer of truck bodies and which did not even purport to have been made by employee or representative of corporation with personal knowledge of such act, event, or condition. Vernon's Ann.Civ.St. art. 3737e. McGinty v. Motor Truck Equipment Corp., Tex.Civ.App., 397 S.W.2d 263.

Computer print-out

U.S.—U. S. v. De Georgia, C.A.Ariz. 1969, 420 F.2d 889 (that business record is maintained in computer rather than in company books is immaterial in determining its admissibility, provided opposing party is given same opportunity to inquire into accuracy of computer and input procedures used as he would have to inquire into accuracy of written business records, and provided that trial court requires party offering computer information to provide foundation therefor sufficient to warrant finding that such information is trustworthy).

Miss.—King v. State for Use and Benefit of Murdock Acceptance Corp., 1969, 222 So.2d 393 (in allowing into evidence printout sheets made from magnetic tape used in computer, was not departing from shop book rule, but only extending its application to electronic record keeping).

Including hearsay and opinions therein

Minn.—Boutang v. Twin City Motor Bus Co., 80 N.W.2d 30, 248 Minn. 240 (did not err in admitting hospital record without first having deleted the diagnosis).

Mo.—La Mantia v. Bobmeyer, App., 382 S.W.2d 455 (physical finding of specialist who examined patient at request of treating physician was not subject to complaint that it contained conclusions and opinions).

N.J.—Falcone v. New Jersey Bell Tel. Co., 1967, 236 A.2d 394, 98 N.J. Super. 138 (diagnosis made by treating physician approximates statement of fact, being in reality what physician observed when he viewed patient with trained eye of expert).

Ohio.—Dillow v. Young, App.1965, 209 N.E.2d 623, 3 Ohio App.2d 110.

Okl.—Nye v. Cox, 1968, 440 P.2d 683 (that hospital records contain hearsay evidence does not render them inadmissible).

Or.—Mayor v. Dowsett, Or., 400 P.2d 234, 240 Or. 196 (relevant medical history of patient in hospital, furnished by someone other than patient himself and recorded in hospital record in compliance with requirements may be received).

Tex.—Love v. Travelers Ins. Co., 395 S.W.2d 682.

Not "history record" of hospital

Ill.—Flesberg v. Prince Warehouse Co., 184 N.E.2d 813, 37 Ill.App.2d 22 (hospital history record of plaintiff consisting of 19 sheets of notes made by doctors and nurses when plaintiff was a patient in the hospital was not admissible on theory it constituted a "business entry" made in the ordinary course of business of a hospital).

Not secondary copies

Work records of employer were inadmissible where records custodian admitted that those records were made by her only from other records and reports which were made by others and were not in evidence. Austria v. Donovan, Fla.App., 169 So. 2d 377.

Not summary therefrom

Where exhibit was not record of original entry kept in usual course of defendant's business, but was just a summary of information apparently taken from books of original entry, and person who kept books and presumably prepared exhibit was not available for cross-examination when exhibit was offered in evidence, defendant failed to lay necessary foundation to bring exhibit within exception. Seib v. Standley, 1967, 435 P.2d 395, 164 Colo. 394.

Rationale stated

N.J.—Brown v. Mortimer, 1968, 242 A.2d 36, 100 N.J.Super. 395 (is that records which are properly shown to have been kept as required normally possess a circumstantial probability of trustworthi-

§ 434.10   TRIAL EVIDENCE   Ch. 434

ness, and therefore ought to be received in evidence unless trial court, after examining them and hearing manner of their preparation explained, entertains serious doubt as to whether they are dependable or worthy of confidence, and the Act confers considerable discretion upon trial judge).

Rule limited

U.S.—Barnes v. Norfolk Southern Ry. Co., C.A.Va., 333 F.2d 192 (letters written by railroad officials some six months before accident and dealing with flagman's allegedly poor safety record were properly excluded as not made in the regular course of business, as not written at the time of accident to flagman or within a reasonable time thereafter, and as not being introduced to establish existence of prior accidents, but to establish probability of his contributory negligence); Cromling v. Pittsburgh & L. E. R. Co., C.A.Pa., 327 F.2d 142 (letter from parent railroad's file, apparently dictated by plaintiff-employee's physician, signed by secretary, and stating that employee was totally disabled did not qualify under federal statute either as business record of railroad as it was addressed to it or a business record of physician, and accordingly admission of letter which tended to prove that plaintiff was previously totally disabled from back condition was prejudicial error); Dilley v. Chesapeake & O. Ry. Co., C.A.Ohio, 327 F.2d 249 (foreman's written report of accident in which railway employee was killed was not admissible).

Cal.—Rosener v. Larson, 1967, 63 Cal.Rptr. 782, 255 Cal.App.2d 871 (where hospital report which contained plaintiff's statement that he suffered three strokes was used only for purpose of showing that first doctor was aware that second doctor's report recorded plaintiff's statement as part of history that doctor obtained from plaintiff and that first doctor took that fact into consideration in reaching his opinion that plaintiff, who had previously been injured in accident, had suffered from a salt deficiency syndrome and not cerebral vascular accident, and jury was instructed that plaintiff's statement was not to be considered as evidence that plaintiff had suffered strokes, report was admissible).

Conn.—General Motors Acceptance Corp. v. Capitol Garage, Inc., 227 A.2d 548, 154 Conn. 593 (not be used for admitting statements which are collateral to essential purpose of the business entry nor should it be allowed as a vehicle for admitting statements of third parties who had no business duty in relation to entry made).

Dist Col.—Trinidad Rambler, Inc. v. Schneider, Mun.App., 203 A.2d 430 (medical reports in file of insurer which had processed prior claim of plaintiff for workmen's compensation were not admissible in subsequent action for back injury as business records of doctors, where they were not in such form and evidence was not presented to show that writing was actually made by or under direction of physician at earlier time of his examination or that it was his custom and regular course of his professional practice to make such a record).

Md.—Smith v. Jones, 203 A.2d 865, 236 Md. 305 (letter from general foreman of highway department sign shop given in response to inquiry as to what records showed, stating that signs directing pedestrians to use stated crosswalk were in place at stated date, as conveying conclusion based in part on unspecified data and not being a public record or document was not admissible).

Mo.—Voyles v. Columbia Terminals Co., App., 239 S.W.2d 559 (accident reports are not considered as records made in usual course of

784

By express provision in the Supreme Court Rule,[84] the Illinois business records exception is inapplicable to "medical records".[85]

A statute making any writing or record which has been made in the regular course of any business as a memorandum of any act, transaction, occurrence or event admissible in evidence is valid.[86]

Those portions of the business record which contain irrelevant or immaterial matters, statements based upon hearsay, or matters otherwise incompetent should be excluded.[87] Portions business and they constitute nothing more than a narration of past events strengthened in no way by fact that they are in writing and therefore would be hearsay and self-serving).

Tex.—Loper v. Andrews, 404 S.W.2d 300 (where controlling question was whether boy suffered skull fracture and attending physician stated that boy suffered a "papilledema of the left optic disc of about two diopters", medical opinion attributed to another physician that "he believes" that such condition resulted from "a fracture of the base of the skull, and some left optic nerve pressure" lacked requisite medical certainty to qualify under statute); Texas State Bd. of Registration for Professional Engineers v. Dalton, Hinds & O'Brien Engineering Co., Tex.Civ.App., 382 S.W.2d 130 (partial transcript of questions, answers and comments made at a meeting of a state board was not admissible as a business record).

Tape recorded records

No particular mode or form of record is required and record prepared by electronic equipment and stored on tape, if it complies with requirements of statute, is as admissible as book accounts or records recording same information and calculations. Transport Indem. Co. v. Seib, 132 N.W.2d 871, 178 Neb. 253, 11 A.L.R.3d 1368.

Time made held critical

U.S.—Kincaid & King Const. Co. v. U. S. for Use of Olday, C.A.Alaska 1964, 333 F.2d 561 (not made until after litigation began).

Ariz.—Kemp v. Pinal County, 1968, 442 P.2d 864, 8 Ariz.App. 41, appeal after remand 474 P.2d 840, 13 Ariz.App. 121 (where proffered entry in county autopsy surgeon's record allegedly showing result of blood alcohol test was one of many numerical test results, 59-day lapse between test and entry was too long to permit admission of entry).

Wis.—Smith v. Milwaukee & Suburban Transport Co., 147 N.W.2d 233, 33 Wis.2d 269 (recorded recollections of six bus drivers who denied to their supervisor any knowledge of claimed fall were not properly admissible under business records exception to hearsay rule where such recollections related to event which took place six months before recollections were recorded).

84. S.H.A. ch. 110A, § 236(b).

85. But proper as "Past Recollection Recorded"

Ill.—Wilson v. Parker, 1971, 269 N.E.2d 523, 132 Ill.App.2d 5.

86. **Mich.**—Gile v. Hudnutt, 272 N.W. 706, 279 Mich. 358 (due process clause not violated).

87. **Ariz.**—Snyder v. Beers, 1965, 405 P.2d 288, 1 Ariz.App. 497.

Conn.—Orzechowski v. Higgins, 152 A.2d 510, 146 Conn. 463 (where plaintiff's physician sent plaintiff to a hospital for diagnostic purposes and physician received from hospital a copy of record of plaintiff's case and placed it in his file which he kept as a record in regular course of his business, and physician on the witness stand produced file and plaintiff took from it the copy of the record, record was inadmissible).

Ga.—Kilgore v. National Life & Acc. Ins. Co., 138 S.E.2d 397, 110 Ga. App. 280 (portions of hospital record containing diagnoses, made by physicians who were not witnesses were inadmissible).

Md.—Scott v. James Gibbons Co., 64 A.2d 117, 192 Md. 319 (statement of particulars of accident in hospital record).

Mich.—Bauer v. Veith, 130 N.W.2d 897, 374 Mich. 1 (portions of hospital record which do not refer to acts, transactions, occurrences or events incident to hospital treatment are inadmissible).

Minn.—Boutang v. Twin City Motor Bus Co., 80 N.W.2d 30, 248 Minn. 240.

Mo.—Pietrowski v. Mykins, App.1973, 498 S.W.2d 572 (where no proper foundation was laid for admissibility of medical report of "company doctor" who treated plaintiff, report was not admissible); State ex rel. State Highway Commission v. Koberna, 396 S.W.2d 654; Boland v. Jando, 395 S.W.2d 206 (portion of hospital record interpreting X ray as showing small spur-like projection off anterior inferior surface of body of C3 which could be small chip fracture was inadmissible over objection that the interpretation was speculative); LaMantia v. Bobmeyer, 382 S.W.2d 455 (assuming that letter, written by specialist to referring physician and reporting that he was unable to say whether patient had herniated disc, was part of business record, recital therein that specialist had a "hunch" that patient would have further difficulty should have been excluded; but admission of such evidence did not require reversal since it could not have materially affected result of trial, at which referring physician testified that patient had herniated disc).

N.Y.—Ehrlich v. Marra, 1969, 300 N. Y.S.2d 81, 32 A.D.2d 638 (admission of history part of hospital record which contained description of accident furnished either by infant plaintiff's mother, who was not party to action or by his father, who did not see accident, was error).

Ohio—Hytha v. Schwendeman, 1974, 320 N.E.2d 312, 40 Ohio App.2d 478 (statements in physician's diagnostic report indicating that plaintiff had a "gross adult maladjustment" and that she was "feigning her way through life" were objectionable as not having proper foundation in that they were not shown to be related to observations made by doctor during examination).

Or.—Gallagher v. Portland Traction Co., 182 P.2d 354, 181 Or. 385 (statement in hospital record re indigency of patient).

S.C.—Powell v. Shore, 131 S.E.2d 155, 242 S.C. 403 (did not abuse discretion in excluding record because there were contained thereon some notations about insurance payments); Peagler v. Atlantic Coast Line R. Co., 107 S.E.2d 15, 234 S.C. 140, 84 A.L.R.2d 794 (excluding hospital records purporting to show that the plaintiff was suffering from a psychiatric disorder and delirium tremens to such an extent that he was not in fit condition to drive at the time of his injuries, and that he was actually drunk at the time of the collision, was proper).

Tex.—Coastal States Gas Producing Co. v. Locker, Civ.App.1968, 436

Ch. 434   HEARSAY   § 434.10

S.W.2d 592 (recital in history that patient gave to doctor that patient stated that automobile hit patient broadside due to faulty brakes was inadmissible in that patient had no personal knowledge that accident involved faulty brakes and that only basis for statement was self-serving declarations of automobile lessee's employees at scene).

Admissible portions of hospital record listed

Unless subject to specific objection, the following hospital record data are admissible: the physical examination findings, the patient's symptoms and complaints, the treatment and progress records, diagnoses by those qualified to make them, the results of analysis and laboratory tests, X-rays, the behavior of the patient, and those parts of the patient's history inherently necessary (or at least helpful) to the observation, diagnosis and treatment of the patient. Allen v. St. Louis Public Service Co., 285 S.W.2d 663, 365 Mo. 677, 55 A. L.R.2d 1022.

Medical statements made as routine entries in course of hospital business, consisting of reports of patient's temperature, blood pressure, pulse, medicines and treatment prescribed, external bruises, skin rash, alcoholic breath, lacerations or injuries observable to persons generally, routine laboratory tests, expressions of pain, noticeable external physical marks or defects, and similar facts not involving medical opinions, are admissible. Martinez v. Williams, Tex.Civ.App., 312 S.W.2d 742. Statement in hospital report "hit by car" was based on hearsay and was ordinarily to be excluded, unless admissible as res gestae or admission of a party to the suit. Id. Statement in hospital report "Small laceration (superficial). Left parietal area" was admissible, since such condition could be observed by anyone. Id. Statement in hospital report "no evidence of any fracture or other injuries" was a conclusion and opinion of the doctor and was properly excluded. Id.

Limited to record of "an act, event or condition"

Tex.—Smith v. Selz, 395 S.W.2d 692 (notation in hospital record on patient's admission in 1962 that "There is a question about the patient having a mild coronary thrombosis in 1956 however this is very questionable" did not qualify as evidence under statute because the notation would not be a record of an act, event, or condition contemplated by the statute. Vernon's Ann.Civ.St. art. 3737e).

Not including summary of antecedent record

Each record offered must stand on its own attributes, and copies or summaries of antecedent records are inadmissible unless prepared in accordance with specified requirements of Act. Kemp v. Pinal County, 1968, 442 P.2d 864, 8 Ariz.App. 41.

Not objectionable as "diagnosis"

The words "whip lash of neck" in plaintiff's hospital record were not classifiable as "diagnosis" for purpose of determining whether the record should be excluded as a means of introducing diagnosis per se, but the four words appeared to fall in classification of description of physical condition. Osberry v. Watters, 1967, 151 N.W.2d 372, 7 Mich. App. 258.

Not opinion in record

Cal.—Rosener v. Larson, 1967, 63 Cal.Rptr. 782, 255 Cal.App.2d 871 (portion of hospital report stating that emergency room doctor observed "apparent C.V.A. involvement of left eye, hand and leg" was random opinion of hospital doctor, was not part of patient's history and constituted inadmissible hearsay).

Ga.—Norman v. Allen, 1968, 163 S. E.2d 859, 118 Ga.App. 394 (autopsy report was properly in evidence as

787

§ 434.10 TRIAL EVIDENCE Ch. 434

of medical records which were not germane to the diagnosis or treatment of the patient are not admissible.[88] However, a state-

report prepared in regular course of business of medical department whose regular course of business was to prepare such reports, under supervision of witness who had made personal examination of organs involved, and any matter of fact in autopsy report was a proper subject for opinion evidence; however, this would not include statements of opinions or diagnoses of others); Cassano v. Pilgreen's, Inc., 1968, 160 S.E.2d 439, 117 Ga.App. 260 (if hospital record contains diagnostic opinions and conclusions it cannot, upon proper objection, be admitted unless proper foundation is laid, that is, the person who entered such diagnostic opinions and conclusions upon record must qualify as expert and relate facts upon which entry was based).

Mich.—City of Grand Rapids v. McGough, 1973, 205 N.W.2d 502, 44 Mich.App. 473 (medical record containing a diagnosis or opinion is not to be ipso facto excluded from evidence; however, such evidence may be excluded in the trial judge's discretion if the entry requires explanation or a detailed statement of judgmental factors upon which the diagnosis or opinion is based).

N.Y.—Jezowski v. Beach, 1968, 298 N.Y.S.2d 360, 59 Misc.2d 224 (deceased doctor's opinions and diagnosis which were written in his own handwriting on backs of electroencephalograms were not admissible).

N.C.—Watson v. Clutts, 1964, 136 S. E.2d 617, 262 N.C. 153.

Ohio—Dorsten v. Lawrence, 1969, 253 N.E.2d 804, 20 Ohio App.2d 297 (opinion evidence from lay person contained in history portion of patient's hospital report, which bears on fault of one party in collision); Lewis v. Woodland, 1955, 140 N.E.2d 322, 101 Ohio App. 442 (x-ray report in hospital record, with opinion fracture was recent).

Tex.—Coastal States Gas Producing Co. v. Locker, Civ.App.1968, 436 S.W.2d 592 (record disclosed that notation "Air in brake system—abnormal time to remove air to get brake pedal," made upon record by automobile dealer's service manager in course of later making warranty claim against manufacturer was not recitation of fact based on personal knowledge of anyone testing brakes but was conjecture on part of service manager, so that notation was inadmissible); Martinez v. Williams, Civ. App., 312 S.W.2d 742.

Not physician's "impression" in hospital record

Exclusion of hospital record which contained notation as to physician's impression of injury was proper, as doctor's impression, as distinguished from opinion or diagnosis. Tavernier v. Weyerhaeuser Co., D.C.Or., 34 F.R.D. 534.

Where portion admissible, objection to whole improper

Where parts of hospital record dealt with injury caused by defendant and other parts of record tended to show that pre-existing conditions made it impossible for plaintiff to work, substantial portions of the record were admissible and objection to record in its entirety was properly overruled. Walls v. Macy's, 37 Cal. Rptr. 745, 226 Cal.App.2d 29.

88. Ala.—Liberty Nat. Life Ins. Co. v. Reid, 1963, 158 So.2d 667, 276 Ala. 25.

Conn.—Kelly v. Sheehan, 1969, 259 A.2d 605, 158 Conn. 281 (recital in hospital report that minor plaintiff was driving vehicle in which

ment made by the patient concerning the cause of injury may be pathologically germane to the treatment thereof, and therefore admissible as a proper part of a hospital record.[89]

he sustained injury had no bearing on diagnosis or treatment and was not admissible).

Md.—Yellow Cab Co. v. Hicks, 168 A.2d 501, 224 Md. 563 (statement in clinic record that on morning after accident plaintiff had visited his lawyer, who had referred him to doctor, was properly excluded as not pathologically germane to physical condition which caused patient to go to clinic in first place).

Minn.—Lindstrom v. Yellow Taxi Co. of Minneapolis, 1974, 214 N.W. 2d 672, 298 Minn. 224.

Mo.—Kitchen v. Wilson, 335 S.W.2d 38 (where a narrative statement of an optometrist was based in part on original business entries, but also contained embellishments, conclusions and opinions added in regard to effect on plaintiff's sight of injuries he sustained in an accident, matters not necessary or helpful to the observation, diagnosis and treatment of the patient, such statement did not qualify).

N.J.—Smith v. First Nat. Stores, Inc., 1967, 228 A.2d 874, 94 N.J.Super. 462 (court erred in requiring plaintiff, if he wished to introduce hospital record in evidence, to introduce the whole thereof including cover page which contained notations to the effect that case might be a possible workmen's compensation matter and that plaintiff's lawyer would pay hospital bill).

N.Y.—Williams v. Alexander, 129 N. E.2d 417, 309 N.Y. 283 (narration of accident causing the injury, not germane to the diagnosis or treatment, not admissible).

Alcohol test not admissible

Making report of test, as to alcohol content of patient's blood was not incident to or part of hospital treatment, and neither preparation of instrument showing result of such test nor attachment of same to hospital record could render it an entry or record made in regular course of hospital business. Bauer v. Veith, 130 N.W.2d 897, 347 Mich. 1.

Letter to patient's employer

Letters from physician addressed to employer about physical condition of employee do not constitute "business records" of employer. Hussein v. Isthmian Lines, Inc., C.A. La.1968, 405 F.2d 946.

Statements relevant to liability

A practical construction of statute providing that nothing therein contained shall be admissible as evidence which has reference to question of liability requires that a record which relates directly and mainly to the treatment and medical history of the patient should be admitted, even though incidentally the facts recorded may have some bearing on question of liability. M.G.L. A. c. 233 § 79. Wadsworth v. Boston Gas Co., 223 N.E.2d 807, 352 Mass. 86.

89. **Del.**—Watts v. Delaware Coach Co., 58 A.2d 689, 5 Terry 283.

Md.—Honick v. Walden, 1971, 272 A. 2d 406, 10 Md.App. 714 (where driver was treated at hospital for stab wound, portion of hospital history indicating that she had been stabbed would be admissible as pathologically germane in plaintiffs' negligence suit in which defense was based upon defendant's claim that driver had intentionally hit plaintiffs' vehicle in order to obtain help because she was being stabbed by passenger in her automobile and that negligence theory did not apply).

§ 434.10 TRIAL EVIDENCE Ch. 434

Authentication of records [90]

The business record must be properly authenticated before it is admissible,[91] and whether a record is sufficiently authenti-

---

90. See next section, § 434.11, at fn. 4 et seq., for cases relating to authentication of police reports.

91. **U.S.**—Johnson v. U. S., C.A. Mass., 325 F.2d 709 (burden to render papers admissible did not go to extent of proving that they were accurate but only that they were prima facie regular and kept for management and operation of business); Ostrov v. Metropolitan Life Ins. Co., D.C.Pa., 260 F.Supp. 152 (fact that custodians had no personal knowledge of contents of records did not affect admissibility of records).

Cal.—Gee v. Timineri, 56 Cal.Rptr. 211, 248 Cal.App.2d 139 (must include evidence as to mode of preparation and identification of records as made in regular course of business).

Fla.—Harwell v. Blake, 180 So.2d 173 (traffic court docket sheet, on which there was printed "Plea of Defendant ——— Guilty." and on which only written notations were charges, name of defendant, dates and notation "sentence suspended", was ambiguous and did not comply with provisions of statute, and, at least in absence of testimony of someone with knowledge of record to explain method of entries, it would have been error to admit docket sheet).

Ga.—Hirsch's v. Adams, 1968, 162 S. E.2d 243, 117 Ga.App. 847 (did not present a witness to testify of his own knowledge that document had been made in regular course of business for purpose of making a memorandum or record at time of the act, transaction, occurrence or event or within a reasonable time thereafter); Henry v. Century Finance Co., 139 S.E.2d 123, 110 Ga. App. 498 (documents, which were not identified, were without probative value).

Iowa—Pierce v. Heusinkveld, 14 N. W.2d 275, 234 Iowa 1348 (a shop record showing work done on brakes of truck was properly excluded where garage mechanic who worked on brakes and who identified record did not make it up, and record was in handwriting of the parts man, where neither the parts man nor any one else with personal knowledge of record was called to identify it).

Ky.—Whittaker v. Thornberry, 209 S.W.2d 498, 306 Ky. 830.

La.—Pereira v. Herbert, App., 59 So. 2d 729 (letter written by attending physician to plaintiff's counsel and uncertified copy of hospital record).

Mo.—Griggs v. Riley, App.1972, 489 S.W.2d 469 (testimony by member of the Judge Advocate's office that air force hospital records were received by him in response to a subpoena which he had forwarded to base and that he concluded the records were made during the regular course of business because "It was sent for and it came down" was inadequate to qualify the records for admission under the Business Records Act, in absence of any personal knowledge of the witness as to the manner in which the records were kept and in absence of any testimony concerning regulations prescribing the method of keeping military hospital records or that the records in question appeared to have been kept in accord with such regulations); Whitehead v. Martin, App.1969, 446 S.W.2d 505 (admitting report sent to treating physician by physician to whom plaintiff had been sent for examination was error where no witness familiar with

790

preparation of report identified it or testified to its method of preparation, but in any event, error was not prejudicial as statement that at time of examination, some 14 months after accident, physician could not find any reason for continuation of plaintiff's complaints, did not establish that plaintiff had never been injured and matters contained in report were merely cumulative of sender's deposition testimony read to jury); LaMantia v. Bobmeyer, 382 S.W.2d 455 (testimony of specialist's secretary, as to manner of recording and preservation of records of specialist's examination of patient for purpose of consultation with treating physician, was sufficient).

N.H.—Williams v. Williams, 182 A. 172, 87 N.H. 430.

N.M.—Sapp v. Atlas Bldg. Products Co., 308 P.2d 213, 62 N.M. 239 (absence of proof that hospital records were made in regular course of business of hospital and that it was regular course of business of hospital to make such records).

N.Y.—Ward v. Thistleton, 1969, 302 N.Y.S.2d 339, 32 A.D.2d 846 (admission of "Radiographic Request Card" containing notation that plaintiff wife was "Drunk" was error where no proof was offered to show who had made the entry, whether he was under duty to do so, what the source of his information was and whether entry was made in regular course of business of hospital); Dipace v. Hertz Corp., 1968, 290 N.Y.S.2d 124, 30 A.D.2d 515 (admitting photocopy of mechanic's report in support of plaintiff's claim that defective door was proximate cause of death of her intestate, which exhibit was identified as "type" of record kept by defendant and offered without proof of source of exhibit and without compliance with statute pertaining to business records, was reversible error).

Tex.—Love v. Travelers Ins. Co., 1965, 395 S.W.2d 682 (regular course, at or near time of event).

Wis.—Rupp v. Travelers Indem. Co., 115 N.W.2d 612, 17 Wis.2d 16 (records of deceased physician were properly excluded where there was no custodian of his records who identified and verified the entries and where some of the entries were illegible and the parties were in dispute as to their meaning).

Cancellation of insurance notice

Purported notice of cancellation of automobile policy was properly excluded where no foundation had been laid for its reception by testimony of witness that it was the regular course of insurer's business to record cancellation notices and evidence of issuance and mailing thereof in form of proffered exhibit, at the time or within a reasonable time thereafter. Moodie v. American Cas. Co. of Reading, 1967, 281 N.Y. S.2d 709, 28 A.D.2d 946.

Hospital librarian not required

Ordinarily foundation is laid by hospital librarian testifying that such records were kept by hospital in regular course of business and upon completion continuously remained in librarian's custody, but such is not only way to place hospital records into evidence if sufficient other foundation is established. Harris v. Smith, C.A.Neb., 372 F.2d 806.

School health record

Foundation for admission of school health record of plaintiff was adequate where it was established that information contained in record was that given to nurse or student assistant and same was later transcribed from daily log of the nurse's office to student's health record card. Snyder v. Beers, 405 P.2d 288, 1 Ariz.App. 497.

cated to justify its admission is a preliminary question of fact for the trial court.[92]

§ 434.11 Business Records—Police Reports [93]

Library References:
C.J.S. Evidence § 637 et seq.; Witnesses § 264.
West's Key No. Digests, Evidence ⚖︎333(1); Witnesses ⚖︎216.

Police reports are commonly held admissible under the business record exception to the hearsay rule.[94] However, such proof

Waiver

General waiver of identity of hospital records, made without reservation of specific objection as to essential elements of identity, waived proof of their correctness in being kept in ordinary course of business, of making of entries at or reasonably near time of events to which they related, and of their status as original entries. Nye v. Cox, Okl.1968, 440 P.2d 683.

92. **Ariz.**—Gallagher v. Viking Supply Corp., 411 P.2d 814, 3 Ariz.App. 55, 15 A.L.R.3d 1 (great discretion).

Cal.—Gee v. Timineri, 56 Cal.Rptr. 211, 248 Cal.App.2d 139 (broad discretion).

Iowa—Ritland v. Security State Bank, Radcliffe, 131 N.W.2d 464, 257 Iowa 21 (considerable discretion).

Mo.—Beggs v. Universal C. I. T. Credit Corp., 409 S.W.2d 719 (wide discretion); Langdon v. Koch, 393 S.W.2d 66 (considerable discretion).

N.H.—Williams v. Williams, 182 A. 172, 87 N.H. 430.

Ohio—Dillow v. Young, 209 N.E.2d 623, 3 Ohio App.2d 110 (trial court has some authority to admit or exclude where sources of record are dubious).

Or.—Mayor v. Dowsett, 400 P.2d 234, 240 Or. 196.

Tenn.—Tullahoma Concrete Pipe Co. v. T. E. Gillespie Const. Co., 405 S.W.2d 657 (much discretion).

93. For discussion of admissibility of police records under the "Official Records" exception to the hearsay rule, see § 434.12, Other Particular Exceptions, at fn. 6 et seq.

94. For general discussion of business record exception, see section 434.10.

U.S.—Bridger v. Union Ry. Co., C.A. Tenn., 355 F.2d 382 (within contemplation of former Federal Business Records Act); Salsberg v. Modern Transfer Co., C.A.N.Y., 324 F.2d 737.

Ariz.—Killingsworth v. Nottingham, 1972, 501 P.2d 1197, 18 Ariz.App. 356; Rodriquez v. Williams, 1971, 489 P.2d 268, 107 Ariz. 458.

Cal.—Taylor v. Centennial Bowl, Inc., 52 Cal.Rptr. 561, 416 P.2d 793.

Kan.—McElhaney v. Rouse, 415 P. 2d 241, 197 Kan. 136.

Mich.—Garmo v. General Motors Corp., 1973, 207 N.W.2d 146, 45 Mich.App. 703 (where police officer who prepared accident report could not recall whether he or his partner tested the brakes but officer prepared the report from evidence he observed, trial court properly admitted report in action against manufacturer).

N.J.—Schneiderman v. Strelecki, 1969, 257 A.2d 130, 107 N.J.Super. 113 (in suit under provisions of Unsatisfied Claim and Judgment Fund Act, accident report of police officer was admissible, not only as establishing that truck

has been held inadmissible where the author of the report is present and testified,[95] where the author is deceased,[96] and under various other circumstances.[97]

driver had left scene before arrival of officer, but also as pointing to possibility that a witness whose name and address were contained therein had seen occurrence).

N.Y.—Kruger v. Nassau County, 1967, 278 N.Y.S.2d 28, 53 Misc.2d 166; Chemical Leaman Tank Lines, Inc. v. Stevens, 1964, 251 N.Y.S.2d 240, 21 A.D.2d 556.

Tex.—Switzer v. Johnson, Civ.App. 1968, 432 S.W.2d 164 (deceased officer's record, which contained statement that driver had said he was looking to his right and did not see deceased pedestrian until he hit him, was admissible under business records statute to prove admission was made by party where driver's statement referred to in officer's statement was inconsistent with driver's testimony); Blakney v. Panhandle & S. F. Ry. Co., 1964, 381 S.W.2d 143, ref. n. r. e.

Limited use

La.—Hughes v. Williams, App.1974, 291 So.2d 919 (report was not admissible as primary evidence, but was admissible to serve as basis on which plaintiff's attorney had previously asked defendant driver if she had made a statement to policemen investigating accident and if statement as written by policeman was correct).

Not officer's private records

U.S.—Bowman v. Kaufman, C.A.N.Y. 1967, 387 F.2d 582 (while there are cases in which business records statutes may properly be used to facilitate proof of negative facts, policeman's memo book should not have been admitted to prove that none of witnesses interviewed complained about brake failure where officer was unable to directly testify as to such fact).

Mo.—Ensminger v. Stout, App., 287 S.W.2d 400 (patrolman's report which was solely his own and was not required by any statute to be made or filed and which contained conclusions from sources other than his own knowledge as to the cause of the accident was inadmissible).

Part to be deleted

If it is desired by either side that a police report of accident would be introduced in evidence as "business entries", the report should not be offered unless all parts containing objectionable material are first deleted. Calhoun v. Chappell, 1968, 162 S.E.2d 300, 117 Ga.App. 865.

Re accident on privately owned property

Police report of collision was not inadmissible under Uniform Business Records as Evidence Act on ground that accident occurred on private property since, while privately owned, parking lot where accident occurred was clearly a quasi-public place and subject to applicable provisions of Motor Vehicle Act which require a police officer investigating accident in the regular course of duty to make a written report thereof for use of Division of Motor Vehicles. N.J.S. 2A:82–35, N.J.S.A.; N.J. S.A. 39:4–1 et seq. Brown v. Mortimer, 1968, 242 A.2d 36, 100 N.J.Super. 395.

95. **Ga.**—Calhoun v. Chappell, 1968, 162 S.E.2d 300, 117 Ga.App. 865.

N.J.—Rogalsky v. Plymouth Homes, Inc., 1968, 242 A.2d 655, 100 N.J. Super. 501 (in view of what "Police Report of Motor Vehicle Ac-

---

96. See note 96 on page 794.
97. See note 97 on page 794.

§ 434.11   TRIAL EVIDENCE   Ch. 434

A report of a police officer based solely upon hearsay [98] or which contains the personal opinion of the officer [99] is not admis-

cident" contained and fact that police chief had testified to what was set forth therein, the report was not admissible as a business record. N.J.S. 2A:82–34 et seq., N.J. S.A.; Rules of Evidence, rule 63 (13), N.J.S.A.).

96. La.—Robinson v. St. Paul Fire & Marine Ins. Co., App.1974, 298 So.2d 282.

Va.—Lee v. Artis, 1964, 136 S.E.2d 868, 205 Va. 343.

Wis.—Voigt v. Voigt, 126 N.W.2d 543, 22 Wis.2d 573 (report taken by deputy sheriff in interview of defendant driver about a half hour after accident was inadmissible under official records of public officers' statute or business entry statute where sheriff died before trial).

97. U.S.—Miller v. Weiner, D.C.S.C. 1969, 298 F.Supp. 1016; Joffe v. U. S., D.C.N.Y.1969, 296 F.Supp. 1368 (thirty reports of city police taken over period of two years before and after date of accident involved were not admissible).

Fla.—Smith v. Frisch's Big Boy, Inc., App.1968, 208 So.2d 310 (under statute which required drivers and law enforcement officers to make written reports of accident, police record of experimental accident test run and oral testimony as to its contents were inadmissible).

Ill.—Hall v. Checker Taxi Co., 1969, 248 N.E.2d 721, 109 Ill.App.2d 445; Hendler v. Wolozin, 1969, 245 N.E. 2d 74, 105 Ill.App.2d 132, certiorari denied 90 S.Ct. 264, 396 U.S. 929, 24 L.Ed.2d 227 (police accident report may not be introduced into evidence, and testimony read from such a report is improper).

Ky.—Campbell v. Markham, 1968, 426 S.W.2d 431 (refusal to permit state trooper's report of accident to be read to jury was not improper).

Mich.—Germiquet v. Hubbard, 1950, 41 N.W.2d 531, 327 Mich. 225 (where officer was not refreshed by reading the report, could not read statement allegedly made by driver).

Tex.—Allen v. Williams, Civ.App., 380 S.W.2d 718.

Wis.—Wilder v. Classified Risk Ins. Co., 1970, 177 N.W.2d 109, 47 Wis. 2d 286 (portions may be admissible under "official records" exception).

Not in license revocation proceeding

N.Y.—Jenson v. Fletcher, 1950, 101 N.Y.S.2d 75, 277 App.Div. 454, affirmed 101 N.E.2d 759, 303 N.Y. 639.

Offered against other than a driver or owner

In action against taxicab owner and operator, and others, for injuries sustained and medical expense and loss of services incurred in collision which involved taxicab, admission in evidence, as proof tending to establish negligence of defendants other than taxicab owner and operator of report to Motor Vehicle Bureau made by taxicab operator, was error. Morini v. Murphy, 140 N.Y.S.2d 294, 285 App.Div. 1154.

98. U.S.—Colvin v. U. S., C.A.Ariz. 1973, 479 F.2d 998; Lindberg v. Short Line, Inc., C.A.R.I.1968, 399 F.2d 482; Yates v. Bair Transport, Inc., D.C.N.Y., 249 F.Supp. 681 (police blotter report prepared by police officer in regular course of duties and filed with department in accordance with the regulations and regular procedure, stating details of accident to which officer

---

99. See note 99 on page 796.

794

Ch. 434   HEARSAY   § 434.11

was not an eyewitness and indicating that there were no eyewitnesses would not be admissible over hearsay objection without indication as to who made statements relied upon and under what circumstances they were made).

Cal.—Stickel v. San Diego Elec. Ry. Co., 1948, 195 P.2d 416, 32 Cal.2d 157.

Ga.—Calhoun v. Chappell, 1968, 162 S.E.2d 300, 117 Ga.App. 865 (hearsay statement of parties as to manner in which collision occurred is not made admissible because writen down by police officer in report); Stubbs v. Daughtry, 153 S. E.2d 633, 115 Ga.App. 22.

Ill.—Redding v. Schroeder, 203 N.E. 2d 616, 54 Ill.App.2d 306 (testimony of police officer read from a police report regarding what motorist told him at scene and as to what he had been told pedestrian was doing before and at time of occurrence was improper).

Md.—Holloway v. Eich, 1969, 258 A. 2d 585, 255 Md. 591.

Mo.—Hamilton v. Missouri Petroleum Products Co., 1969, 438 S.W. 2d 197 (statement of driver of tractor-trailer that automobile was over center line at time of accident as contained in patrolman's accident report was not admissible).

N.J.—Sas v. Strelecki, 1970, 264 A.2d 247, 110 N.J.Super. 14.

N.Y.—Prado v. Onor Oscar, Inc., 1974, 353 N.Y.S.2d 789, 44 A.D.2d 604 (police aided card should not have been received in evidence to prove fact that decedent was a passenger in defendant's cab); Rubin v. O'Donnell, 1971, 326 N.Y.S. 2d 25, 37 A.D.2d 858 (based on information given to him); Mahon v. Giordano, 1968, 291 N.Y.S.2d 854, 30 A.D.2d 792; Fitzgerald v. State, 1950, 96 N.Y.S.2d 452, 198 Misc. 39 (police blotter report).

Okl.—Oklahoma Dept. of Public Safety v. Robinson, 1973, 512 P. 2d 128 (report of a highway patrolman is not admissible on theory that hearsay evidence is incorporated into the report); Bison Transports v. Fraley, 238 P.2d 835, 205 Okl. 520 (report of highway patrolman which stated that it was apparent that gasoline transport truck, which had crashed when coming down incline at high rate of speed, did not have any brakes which statement was not based on direct evidence of condition of brakes immediately prior to or after accident was conclusion based on hearsay); Wagner v. McKernan, 177 P.2d 511, 198 Okl. 425 (report based upon statements made by parties involved in accident); Hadley v. Ross, 154 P.2d 939, 195 Okl. 89 (investigation made six days after collision and based upon information of undisclosed informants).

R.I.—DiMaio v. Del Sesto, 1967, 228 A.2d 861, 102 R.I. 116 (exclusion of unexplicated police officer's report was proper where parts of its contents were hearsay).

Tex.—Switzer v. Johnson, Civ.App. 1968, 432 S.W.2d 164 (record by deceased officer showing that driver had stated he was looking to his right and did not see deceased until he hit him was not admissible because officer did not have personal knowledge as to which way driver was looking); McClesky v. Smades, Civ.App., 245 S.W.2d 269 (accident reports of municipal police officers).

Wis.—Novakofski v. State Farm Mut. Auto. Ins. Co. of Bloomington, Ill., 148 N.W.2d 714, 34 Wis.2d 154 (statement in police report of one-vehicle-accident that driver "apparently died of a heart attack before collision. Dr. Forkin d. o. a." appeared to be grounded on information supplied by a doctor and was thus inadmissible); Shaw v. Wuttke, 137 N.W.2d 649, 28 Wis.

§ 434.11   TRIAL EVIDENCE   Ch. 434

2d 448 (police officer cannot testify to any facts in traffic report excepting those based upon his own personal knowledge).

But see

Party offering police report into evidence need not show the source of police officer's information for each one of the items contained in police report as a condition to admission into evidence. Mucci v. LeMonte, 1969, 254 A.2d 879, 157 Conn. 566.

99. Cal.—Stickel v. San Diego Elec. Ry. Co., 1948, 195 P.2d 416, 32 Cal.2d 157.

Colo.—Orth v. Bauer, 1967, 429 P.2d 279.

Ga.—Calhoun v. Chappell, 162 S.E. 2d 300, 117 Ga.App. 865 (Code, § 38–711).

Ill.—Ruppaner v. Waue, 1951, 96 N. E.2d 847, 342 Ill.App. 451.

Ind.—Dale v. Trent, 1970, 256 N.E. 2d 402, 146 Ind.App. 412; State v. St. Anne Brick & Tile Co., 1968, 234 N.E.2d 664, 142 Ind.App. 338.

Kan.—Smith v. Hall's Estate, 1974, 524 P.2d 684, 215 Kan. 262; Sulkis v. Zane, 1972, 494 P.2d 1233, 208 Kan. 800; Morlan v. Smith, 380 P.2d 312, 191 Kan. 218 (statement that no improper driving was indicated was conclusion of investigating officer).

La.—Veal v. Hutchinson, App.1973, 284 So.2d 60, writ denied 286 So. 2d 662 (accident report made by police officer who died prior to trial was inadmissible for reason that it contained his opinions or conclusions from observations at scene such as location of point of impact and fact that one driver fell asleep and was traveling at high speed); Deville v. Aetna Ins. Co., App., 191 So.2d 324 (written report of out-of-court statements made by police officers, neither of whom was in court under oath and available for cross-examination was inadmissible, and was particularly objectionable when it contained opinions of officers formed from talking to other witnesses).

Md.—Honick v. Walden, App.1971, 272 A.2d 406, 10 Md.App. 714; Holloway v. Eich, 1969, 258 A.2d 585, 255 Md. 591.

Miss.—Hall v. Boykin, Miss.1968, 207 So.2d 645 (admission, over objection, of highway patrolman's accident report including drawing depicting position of vehicles prior to and after accident was error, inasmuch as patrolman had not witnessed accident and admission of report alone was sufficient to warrant granting defendant's motion for new trial).

Mo.—Ryan v. Campbell "66" Exp., Inc., Sup.1957, 304 S.W.2d 825.

N.Y.—Penner v. Central School Dist. No. 1, Towns of Canajoharie, et al., Montgomery County, 1972, 337 N.Y.S.2d 30, 40 A.D.2d 883 (conclusion of sheriff's department investigator as to the point of impact was improperly admitted but such did not warrant reversal where there was sufficient other evidence, including photographs taken at the scene, to support verdict); Neill v. Jodum Cab Corp., 1971, 328 N.Y.S.2d 540, 38 A.D.2d 562 (expressed officer's opinion, based upon information received solely from driver, that infant ran from between parked cars); Mandzych v. Karl, 1969, 307 N.Y.S.2d 139, 33 A.D.2d 786 (error to receive in evidence diagrammed conclusion of officer in his accident report, based on observations after accident and statements by defendant, as to point of impact); Sinkevich v. Cenkus, 264 N.Y.S.2d 979, 24 A.D.2d 903 (recital in police report that plaintiff was guilty of failing to stop on signal and that driver of defendant's vehicle was guilty of no violation contributing to intersection collision constituted conclusions of officer

sible. It has been held that portions of the report relating statements of others are to be excluded when the other declarant is not a person under a duty to make observations or record them.[1]

as to cause of accident which were prejudicial).

R.I.—Major v. Grieg, 1967, 230 A.2d 846, 102 R.I. 379 (but this does not render them inadmissible for purposes of impeaching subsequent contradictory statements).

Tenn.—McBee v. Williams, 1966, 405 S.W.2d 668, 56 Tenn.App. 232 (and invades jury province).

Tex.—McDonough Bros., Inc. v. Lewis, Civ.App.1971, 464 S.W.2d 457, error refused n. r. e.

But see

N.Y.—Oliver v. Schreiber, 1969, 302 N.Y.S.2d 316, 32 A.D.2d 790, appeal dismissed 304 N.Y.S.2d 602, 25 N.Y.2d 910, 252 N.E.2d 135 (statement in police officer's report that condition of defendant driver was "apparently normal" was admissible on issue of passengers' contributory negligence by virtue of claimed intoxication of driver); Welde v. Wolfson, 1969, 302 N.Y. S.2d 906, 32 A.D.2d 973 (it was reversible error to exclude motor vehicle accident report that defendant's vehicle was making left turn).

Deemed admissible

Mo.—Stegall v. Wilson, App.1967, 416 S.W.2d 658 (portions of accident report of police department indicating that operator of motor scooter had been injured, and that driver of automobile had made a statement against his interest, and measurements made by investigating police officer at scene of collision, offered in evidence under Uniform Business Records as Evidence Law by operator of motor scooter, were improperly excluded on ground that they contained conclusions).

1. **Conn.**—Mucci v. LeMonte, 1969, 254 A.2d 879, 157 Conn. 566; State v. Masse, 186 A.2d 553, 24 Conn.Sup. 45 (statements of volunteers and of those outside of police department, who are under no duty to make observations or record them as members of police organization, although made part of police records or reports, do not come within the statute; this is particularly true of reports containing statements of witnesses as to their own observations, opinions or speculations).

Md.—Honick v. Walden, 1971, 272 A.2d 406, 10 Md.App. 714.

N.J.—Sas v. Strelecki, 1970, 264 A.2d 247, 110 N.J.Super. 14.

N.Y.—Wright v. McCoy, 1973, 343 N. Y.S.2d 143, 41 A.D.2d 873 (where testimony of police officer as to source of information upon which his entries on "Aided and Accident Card" were based was not only vague, but also failed to identify any person under a business duty to relate the facts as his informant, statements contained in the report were not admissible); Toll v. State, 1969, 299 N.Y.S.2d 589, 32 A.D.2d 47 (report by state trooper who investigated but did not witness accident was inadmissible to prove main facts where it did not appear that whoever gave officer facts had business duty to do so).

Tex.—Logan v. Grady, Civ.App.1972, 482 S.W.2d 313.

Driver's report filed with police

Mass.—Kelly v. O'Neil, 1973, 296 N. E.2d 223, —— Mass.App. —— (inasmuch as accident report prepared by driver was not in regular course of any business in which she was engaged, the report was not admissible as a writing made in regu-

§ 434.11 TRIAL EVIDENCE Ch. 434

By express provision in the Supreme Court Rule [2] the Illinois business records exception is inapplicable to police records.[3]

Consistent with the discussion in § 434.10, at fn. 90 et seq., the party offering the police report must make proper authentication of the report.[4]

Statutes requiring reports of automobile accidents may provide that such reports shall be admissible in evidence solely to

lar course of business and the fact that police department to which she submitted the report maintained such reports on file in regular course of its business was not material).

Not cured where offered to explain diagram

Wis.—Wilder v. Classified Risk Ins. Co., 1970, 177 N.W.2d 109, 47 Wis. 2d 286 (it was improper to get conclusion of how accident happened based upon such statement in evidence by framing question containing such information and then asking investigating officer whether he wrote that conclusion in his report to explain diagram contained therein).

2. S.H.A. ch. 110A, § 236(b).

3. Ill.—Hall v. Baum Corp., 1973, 299 N.E.2d 156, 12 Ill.App.3d 755 (may be used for limited purpose of impeachment as to inconsistency or to refresh a witness' recollection but they cannot be used to divulge substantive evidence to the jury); Douglas v. Chicago Transit Authority, 1972, 279 N.E. 2d 44, 3 Ill.App.3d 318.

Trooper's sketch not excluded

Diagram or sketch made by trooper at scene showing certain measurements was not within prohibition against introduction of police reports but was itself admissible as diagram explanatory in nature although it was part of a police report, where diagram contained physical observations and measurements made by officer and gave jury a clearer picture so that they could more intelligently consider his testimony. Walls v. Jul, 1969, 254 N.E.2d 173, 118 Ill.App.2d 242.

4. Mo.—Olsten v. Susman, 362 S. W.2d 612 (not entitled to introduce report to show alleged admission against interest made by defendant, where detective, by whom plaintiff sought to establish authenticity of report, testified that he had no personal knowledge of statements, took no part in making report and did not know that information was accurate).

N.Y.—In re Motor Vehicle Acc. Indemnification Corp. (Landau), 247 N.Y.S.2d 175, 20 A.D.2d 699 (police accident report from which it might be inferred that no other vehicle was involved and that accident was caused by respondent's vehicle skidding on wet pavement was properly excluded, in proceeding involving claim against Motor Vehicle Accident Indemnification Corporation where officer did not testify).

No proof of source of information

N.Y.—Yeargans v. Yeargans, 265 N. Y.S.2d 562, 24 A.D.2d 280 (receiving in evidence police report which was made by officer of another state and contained no indication, except by possible inference, as to source of information recorded, was prejudicial error, where officer who made report was not called to testify and report was admitted in evidence prior to reading of that portion of defendant's deposition in which she stated that she had given information appearing in report).

798

§ 434.12 Other Particular Exceptions

Library References:
C.J.S. Evidence §§ 626–629 et seq., 630–633, 637 et seq., 696; Municipal Corporations § 447; Statutes §§ 85, 90, 450, 451, 457.
West's Key No. Digests, Evidence ⟶325–337, 355(6).

Other particular exceptions to the hearsay rule have been recognized in many jurisdictions.

Official records

One such exception to the hearsay rule is for "official records" or "public records",[6] made by one charged with the duty to

---

5. For discussion of the privileged nature of statements made to investigating officers, see § 423.1, at fn. 10 et seq.

Mont.—Morrison v. City of Butte, 1967, 431 P.2d 79, 150 Mont. 106 (prejudicial error in court-tried case).

Pa.—Kane v. Pepsi-Cola Metropolitan Bottling Co., Com.Pl., 113 P.L.J. 509.

Wis.—Voight v. Voight, 126 N.W.2d 543, 22 Wis.2d 573; Smith v. Rural Mut. Ins. Co., 123 N.W.2d 496, 20 Wis.2d 592.

6. **Ariz.**—State v. Stone, 1969, 452 P.2d 513, 104 Ariz. 339 (accident report made on scene by patrolman and later typed up by another officer stating that collision was caused by faulty highway markings was properly admitted into evidence as a "public record").

Cal.—Love v. Wolf, 38 Cal.Rptr. 183, 226 Cal.App.2d 378 (but official character of document will not make admissible otherwise inadmissible material contained therein).

Fla.—Smith v. Mott, 100 So.2d 173 (testimony of medical examiner as to report received by his office from public health service on alcoholic content of blood sample, which had been taken from decedent and submitted by medical examiner, was admissible under "public record" exception to hearsay rule and such report was prima facie evidence of what report purported to show).

Mo.—Edwards v. Firemen's Retirement System of St. Louis, 410 S.W.2d 560 (reports of medical examiners constitute public records and as such they are competent to establish such facts as law requires to be kept and are admissible without the aid of any statute).

Nev.—Havas v. 105 Casino Corp., 417 P.2d 239, 82 Nev. 282 (records which a private person is required to make and file with the government may be admissible as public records).

Or.—Finchum v. Lyons, 1967, 428 P.2d 890, 247 Or. 255, quoting C.J.S. Evidence § 637.

Tex.—Moore v. Spencer, 399 S.W.2d 880, citing 32 C.J.S. Evidence § 633 (sheriff's return was probative evidence that witness was outside state and as public record was admissible); Texas Dept. of Public

§ 434.12   TRIAL EVIDENCE   Ch. 434

Safety v. Miller, 386 S.W.2d 760 (notices or abstracts of judgments are certificates or reports made by public officers or employees, and these certificates are evidence of matters stated therein, and fact that they do not contain certain information which is immaterial to point of inquiry will not render recitations in public report inadmissible in evidence); Mothershead v. Texas Dept. of Public Safety, 375 S.W.2d 788 (motorist's public driving record properly authenticated by supervisor of records division of public safety department was properly admissible in proceeding adjudging motorist to be an habitual traffic violator and ordering suspension of his operator's license).

Wis.—Wilder v. Classified Risk Ins. Co., 1970, 177 N.W.2d 109, 47 Wis. 2d 286 (as to facts of which traffic report maker has personal knowledge, i. e., measurements and observations, etc.); Ernst v. Greenwald, 1967, 151 N.W.2d 706, 35 Wis.2d 763 (state Highway Commission's electrical work order and service report form indicating that flashing lights had been installed at intersection to operate only from midnight to 6 a. m. were admissible in action arising out of collision at intersection at 11:35 p. m.).

Autopsy report

Report of medical examiner, who withdrew blood sample from decedent's cadaver, was admissible, in wrongful death action, both under statute providing that reports of a medical examiner's autopsies shall be received as evidence in any court, and under implied consent statute, notwithstanding fact that, with respect to admissibility under latter statute, needle used to extract blood was not in factory wrapped package and sample was not taken at written request of a peace officer. I.C.A. §§ 321.271, 321B.1 et seq., 339.9. Jacobsen v. International Transport, Inc.,

C.A.Iowa, 1968, 391 F.2d 49, certiorari denied 89 SCt 105, 393 U.S. 833, 21 L.Ed.2d 104.

But see

U.S.—Remer v. Flying Eagle Whiteway Lines, C.A.Conn., 172 F.2d 831 (in actions for injuries and death of bus passengers in collision caused by tire blow-out, exclusion of a certificate of inspection of the bus made by an observer for the Connecticut department of motor vehicles was not improper, in view of ambiguity as to what it "contained" within Connecticut statute making records of department admissible as evidence of the facts therein "contained").

N.J.—McComish v. DeSoi, N.J.Super. A.D., 200 A.2d 511, affirmed in part and reversed in part 200 A.2d 116, 42 N.J. 274 (rule providing that official record or entry therein, when admissible for any purpose, may be evidenced by document purporting to be official publication thereof merely governs procedure by which official records may be received and does not provide for their automatic admissibility).

N.Y.—Regan v. National Postal Transport Ass'n, 1967, 280 N.Y.S. 2d 319, 53 Misc.2d 901 (facts disclosed by decedent's physician or ascertained by physician by observation or examination, when recorded on document such as death certificates, are subject to privileged communication rule, and are further subject to hearsay rule if offered in evidence by a medium of document).

Wash.—Steel v. Johnson, 115 P.2d 145, 9 Wash.2d 347 (admission of mimeographed sheet of paper containing figures showing a budget for minimum requirements for care of children, as compiled by State Department of Social Security, was error as being "hearsay", notwithstanding that paper was prepared pursuant to statutory direction, where content of paper was result of exercise of judgment founded on personal computations and opinions made by officials or employees of department, and subject matter did not relate to facts of public interest, and report was not retained for public benefit, but was designed merely for use of department).

Death certificate

Ga.—Liberty Nat. Life Ins. Co. v. Power, 1965, 145 S.E.2d 801, 112 Ga.App. 547 (not where based on hearsay).

Minn.—Engel v. Starry, 1964, 128 N.W.2d 874, 268 Minn. 252 (proper as to cause of death, but not to prove circumstances).

N.Y.—Sherman v. Pullman, 1968, 289 N.Y.S.2d 802, 29 A.D.2d 1044 (certificate of death should have been received); Regan v. National Postal Transport Ass'n, 1967, 280 N.Y.S. 2d 319, 53 Misc.2d 901 (statute making death certificate prima facie evidence of facts stated therein was enacted for very purpose of providing exception to hearsay rule).

Tex.—National Life & Acc. Ins. Co. v. Salas, Civ.App.1968, 426 S.W. 2d 327, error refused n. r. e. (certificate which did not purport to show opinion of doctor or any person who presumably knew cause of death was inadmissible); Reserve Life Ins. Co. v. Shacklett's Estate, Civ.App.1967, 412 S.W.2d 920, error refused n. r. e. (are prima facie evidence of the facts therein stated, such as statement that death was an accident).

Va.—Edwards v. Jackson, 1970, 171 S.E.2d 854, 210 Va. 450 (opinion of cause of death not competent); Bailey v. C. V. Hunter, Inc., 1966, 148 S.E.2d 826, 207 Va. 123 (not where physician never saw decedent).

Wis.—Novakofski v. State Farm Mut. Auto. Ins. Co. of Bloomington, Ill., 1967, 148 N.W.2d 714, 34 Wis.2d 154.

Held not public record

Letter from general foreman of highway department sign shop given in response to inquiry as to what records showed, stating that signs directing pedestrians to use stated crosswalk were in place at stated date, as conveying conclusion based in part on unspecified data and not being a public record or document was not admissible under business record statute or any other relevant statute or at common law, and its reception against pedestrian was prejudicial error where only eyewitness who testified that sign was present was at first uncertain. Smith v. Jones, 203 A.2d 865, 236 Md. 305.

Hospital record as "public document"

Ark.—Wilkinson v. Grover, App.1966, 181 So.2d 591 (in view of statute requiring records).

Miss.—City of Bay St. Louis v. Johnston, 1969, 222 So.2d 841 (constitute "public document" within public document exception).

Rule limited

County autopsy surgeon's records offered to show result of blood alcohol test failed to satisfy requirement that sources of information, method and time of preparation were such as to justify their admission. Kemp v. Pinal County, 1968, 442 P.2d 864, 8 Ariz.App. 41, appeal after remand 474 P.2d 840, 13 Ariz.App. 121.

Rule qualified

Question whether death certificate may be admitted to show cause of death is dependent upon facts peculiar to particular case. Regan v. National Postal Transport Ass'n, 1967, 280 N.Y.S.2d 319, 53 Misc.2d 901.

Absence of record

U.S.—Federal Rules of Evidence § 803(10), 28 U.S.C.A.

complete the record.[7] In certain jurisdictions, the content of such records may be conclusions from an investigation made pursuant to lawful authority.[8]

Ark.—Blythe v. Blythe, 410 S.W.2d 379, 241 Ark. 768 (in absence of statute, party cannot prove by public officer's certificate that certain public record does not exist, because such statement is testimony that should be subject to cross-examination).

Cal.—West's Ann.Calif.Evid.Code, § § 1284.

Fla.—Florida Evidence Code § 90.803 (10).

Kan.—Kansas Code of Civil Procedure § 60–460(o)(2).

Me.—Maine Rules of Evidence § 803 (10).

Neb.—Nebraska Rules of Evidence § 803(9).

Nev.—N.R.S. 51.175.

N.J.—New Jersey Evidence Rule 63 (17).

N.M.—New Mexico Rules of Evidence § 803(10).

Utah.—Utah Rules of Evidence § 63 (17).

Wis.—Wisconsin Rules of Evidence § 908.03(10).

7. **U.S.**—Federal Rules of Evidence § 803(8), 28 U.S.C.A.

Cal.—West's Ann.Calif.Evid.Code, § 1280.

Fla.—Florida Evidence Code § 90.803 (8).

Ill.—In re Ersch's Estate, 195 N.E. 2d 149, 29 Ill.2d 572 (records kept by persons in public office which they are required either by statute or nature of their office to maintain in connection with performance of official duties).

Kan.—Kansas Code of Civil Procedure § 60–460(o)(1).

Me.—Maine Rules of Evidence § 803 (8).

Neb.—Nebraska Rules of Evidence § 803(7).

Nev.—N.R.S. 51.155.

N.J.—New Jersey Evidence Rule 63 (15), (16).

N.M.—New Mexico Rules of Evidence § 803(8).

Or.—Fletcher v. Walters, 425 P.2d 539, 246 Or. 362 (report of blood-alcohol test performed on host driver by police bureau was not admissible as an official document and was properly excluded where test was not performed by bureau as part of an official duty).

Pa.—Githens, Rexsamer & Co. v. Wildstein, 1968, 236 A.2d 792, 428 Pa. 201.

Utah.—Utah Rules of Evidence § 63 (15) (but not "traffic accident reports").

Wis.—Wisconsin Rules of Evidence § 908.03(8); Novakofski v. State Farm Mut. Auto. Ins. Co. of Bloomington, Ill., 148 N.W.2d 714, 34 Wis.2d 154 (police report of accident qualified as "official record" within statute making every official record, report, or certificate of public officer pursuant to law evidence of facts which are therein stated and which are required or permitted to be by such officer recorded, reported, or certified).

Not driver's report

Even if copy of motorist's report of accident required to be filed with local police department were considered a "public record" equally with original, which was required to be filed with registrar of motor vehicles, copy would not be admissible, in tort action arising out of the acci-

8. See note 8 on page 803.

Such a record, however, may violate some other rule of evidence and therefore be inadmissible,[9] such as where a written re-

dent, under the official written statement exception to hearsay rule, since it was not prepared by public officer or employee acting within scope of his duty. Kelly v. O'Neil, 1973, 296 N.E.2d 223, —— Mass.App. ——.

8. U.S.—Federal Rules of Evidence § 803(8)(C), 28 U.S.C.A.

Nev.—N.R.S. 51.155(3).

N.M.—New Mexico Rules of Evidence § 803(8)(C).

Utah.—Utah Rules of Evidence § 63 (15)(c) (but not "traffic accident reports").

Wis.—Wisconsin Rules of Evidence § 908.03(8)(c).

9. U.S.—Pulvari v. Greyhound Corp., 1967, 375 F.2d 322, 126 U.S.App.D.C. 146 (evidence consisting of reports as to weather conditions at an airport two miles from scene was not competent on issue of care required of bus driver).

La.—Deville v. Aetna Ins. Co., 191 So.2d 324 (provision of Public Records Act pertaining to admission of copies does not permit admission of copy although certified unless original would also be admissible; if original would be subject to objection under general rules of evidence then same objection would exclude copy).

Md.—Baltimore & O. R. Co. v. State, for Use of Carbone, 181 A. 830, 169 Md. 345 (information as to identity of driver not chargeable to party against whom the record was offered).

Mass.—Kelly v. O'Neil, 1973, 296 N.E.2d 223, —— Mass.App. —— (contained statements made to police officer by other persons during course of his investigation and contained expression of opinion on part of declarant that defendant was guilty of operating under influence of intoxicating liquor).

Wis.—Wilder v. Classified Risk Ins. Co., 1970, 177 N.W.2d 109, 47 Wis. 2d 286 (matters appearing therein founded upon hearsay are generally admissible, but rule is qualified for traffic accident reports).

Not officer who received information

Mass.—Killard v. Hohmann, 175 N.E. 743, 275 Mass. 344 (driver's report at police station).

Not opinions contained therein

U.S.—Charleston Nat. Bank v. Hennessy, C.A.Fla., 1968, 404 F.2d 539 (opinion of coroner, a layman without medical training, that decedent "apparently had heart attack," based in part on information given him by others at scene, plus his own observations of exterior condition of body, would have been inadmissible if proffered on oral examination and was not made admissible because included in official death certificate).

Colo.—Orth v. Bauer, 1967, 429 P.2d 279, 163 Colo. 136.

Ga.—Liberty Nat. Life Ins. Co. v. Power, 145 S.E.2d 801, 112 Ga.App. 547, citing 32 C.J.S. Evidence § 638 (death certificate is not admissible to prove particular matters stated in certificate where statement is based on hearsay and not upon personal knowledge of physician or official completing certificate or statement is opinion to which physician or official would not be qualified to testify personally).

Me.—Knox Lime Co. v. Maine State Highway Commission, 1967, 230 A. 2d 814 (report or document prepared by public official, in order to be admissible in evidence, must contain facts and not conclusions involving exercise of judgment or discretion or expression of opinion).

Minn.—Milliren v. Federal Life Ins. Co., 242 N.W. 290, 185 Minn. 614.

port to the motor vehicle bureau, by one of the defendants in a death case, constitutes a self-serving declaration.[10]

Past recollection recorded

Another exception to the hearsay rule is "past recollections recorded," [11] where it is shown the record was made at or near

Utah—Bridges v. Union Pac. R. Co., 1971, 488 P.2d 738, 26 Utah 2d 281 (not as to alleged inherent opinion railroad crossing was extrahazardous).

Va.—Edwards v. Jackson, 1970, 171 S.E.2d 854, 210 Va. 450 (statement of cause of death in death certificate was merely opinion of physician signing certificate and death certificate was not competent to show cause of decedent's death where, in absence of physician's testimony, bare statement in certificate that disease of technical nature was cause of death might have confused jury of laymen and misled them to believe that death resulted from accident); Bailey v. C. V. Hunter, Inc., 148 S.E.2d 826, 207 Va. 123 (statement in death certificate that death was due to accident was not admissible to prove cause of death where medical examiner, who signed certificate, never saw decedent prior to his death, and had no personal knowledge that decedent had been in accident).

Wis.—Novakofski v. State Farm Mut. Auto Ins. Co. of Bloomington, Ill., 148 N.W.2d 714, 34 Wis.2d 154 (conclusions are not admissible under statute providing that every official record made by any public officer pursuant to law is evidence of facts which are stated therein and which are required or permitted to be by such officer recorded, reported, or certified).

Only "facts" known by official admissible

Word "fact" contained in statute providing that official certificate of head officer of state executive department as to contents of records in his department shall be received in all civil cases as competent prima facie evidence of facts contained therein and of nonexistence of such facts as are duly certified to as not existing in the records of the department refers to facts within knowledge of reporting officer or agent and not to hearsay statements. Orth v. Bauer, 1967, 429 P.2d 279, 163 Colo. 136.

Statute excluded "extraneous matters"

Statute providing that reports of investigations made by county medical examiner shall be received as evidence except that conclusions upon extraneous matters are not made admissible does not attempt to pass on admissibility of reports containing extraneous matters. I.C.A. § 339.9. Lessenhop v. Norton, 1967, 153 N.W. 2d 107, 261 Iowa 44. Admission of statement on back of county medical examiner's report which showed 82.5 mg% of blood alcohol in specimen taken from driver was reversible error in that it was extraneous to report which did not find that death resulted from driving while intoxicated or while under the influence of intoxicating liquor. Id.

10. **N.Y.**—Clark v. Thompson, 15 N.Y.S.2d 291, 258 App.Div. 748; Trampusch v. Kastner, 274 N.Y.S. 771, 242 App.Div. 803.

11. **Ark.**—Self v. Dye, 516 S.W.2d 397, 257 Ark. 360 (where investigating police officer testified that he had prepared accident report which had been kept in files of police department, that, before being called as witness, he had reviewed

the time of the happening,[12] and the witness then knew it to be accurate and true.[13]

report at request of attorney and that it was his practice to take statement from each driver involved in collision and record statements on his report, even though he did not have any independent recollection of statements of drivers and his memory was not refreshed by reading his report, proper foundation was laid for his reciting statement made by one motorist as recorded on the report made at the time.

Mass.—Ellingsgard v. Silver, 223 N. E.2d 813, 352 Mass. 34 (rests in discretion of trial court).

Mo.—S & H Concrete Const. Co. v. Genova, 384 S.W.2d 816, citing 98 C.J.S. Witnesses § 358c.

N.Y.—McDermott v. Barker, Sup., 237 N.Y.S.2d 598, affirmed 245 N.Y.S.2d 135, 20 A.D.2d 546 (entry in hospital record as to manner in which accident happened).

Foundation insufficient

La.—Loicano v. Maryland Cas. Ins. Co., App.1974, 301 So.2d 897 (where officer testified that, although he regularly patrolled highway in question, he had no recollection of accident and his investigation into the circumstances of it, and where police report of accident was not signed by officer but contained only his typewritten name and badge number and where officer could not identify the report as his, a sufficient basis was not laid for the introduction of the police report to represent the past recollection recorded of officer, notwithstanding fact that judge took judicial cognizance of radio logs of sheriff's office to discover whether or not officer had actually been assigned to this traffic investigation).

Not shown present recollection not refreshed

Ill.—Noumoff v. Rotkvich, 1967, 232 N.E.2d 107, 88 Ill.App.2d 116 (where tavern proprietor being sued by passenger under Dram Shop Act failed to establish that investigating officer did not have independent recollection of facts relating to sobriety and physical condition of tavern patron who, after leaving proprietor's tavern, had accident in which passenger was injured, and where proprietor also failed to establish that the officer, after reviewing his police report, was unable to refresh his recollection, admitting under doctrine of past recollection recorded proprietor's exhibit of blocked out portion of police report indicating that tavern patron was sober was improper).

Mo.—Watson v. Meredith Development Co., App., 410 S.W.2d 338 (was not shown that, after he had referred to sheets, his memory of facts was not so stimulated that he was then able to testify independently of their use, but he was asked to read therefrom and he did so, plaintiff's use of sheets did not fall within rule).

12. Colo.—McCall v. Roper, 1973, 511 P.2d 541, 32 Colo.App. 352 (exclusion of unsworn statement given by witness approximately one and one-half months after accident had occurred as being too remote in time from date of accident to be admissible under past recollection recorded exception to hearsay rule did not constitute abuse of discretion).

Ill.—Wolf v. City of Chicago, 223 N. E.2d 231, 78 Ill.App.2d 337.

13. See note 13 on page 806.

N.Y.—Brown v. W. U. Tel. Co., 274 N.Y.S.2d 52, 26 A.D.2d 316.

Pa.—Com. v. Butts, 204 A.2d 481, 204 Pa.Super. 302 (had made notes in own handwriting at time of examination).

13. U.S.—Federal Rules of Evidence § 803(5), 28 U.S.C.A.

Cal.—West's Ann.Calif.Evid.Code, § 1237.

Fla.—Florida Evidence Code, § 90.803 (5).

Ill.—Rigor v. Howard Liquors, Inc., 1973, 295 N.E.2d 491, 10 Ill.App.3d 1004 (officer failed to testify that he knew his report to be accurate when made); Wolf v. City of Chicago, Ill.App., 223 N.E.2d 231, 78 Ill.App.2d 337; Koch v. Pearson, 219 Ill.App. 468 (police report of accident).

Kan.—Kansas Code of Civil Procedure § 60–450(a); McElhaney v. Rouse, 415 P.2d 241, 197 Kan. 136 (if he made entries and knew at time of making them they were correct).

La.—Primeaux v. Kinney, App.1971, 256 So.2d 140, writ not considered 258 So.2d 87, 260 La. 1065 (testimony of state trooper, who investigated collision between plaintiff's van and bull allegedly belonging to defendant but who had no independent recollection as to how he secured information concerning bull's brand but who was sure that information placed on his report, including mention of brand, was correct and that he would not have placed such information in his report unless he was satisfied of the correctness thereof, was properly allowed).

Me.—Maine Rules of Evidence § 803 (5).

Mich.—Garmo v. General Motors Corp., 1973, 207 N.W.2d 146, 45 Mich.App. 703 (original memorandum made by witness from personal observation).

Minn.—Walker v. Larson, 1969, 169 N.W.2d 737, 284 Minn. 99 (court had discretion to determine whether recorded, signed, and witnessed statement, made by decedent's passenger prior to litigation and to effect that vehicle driven by decedent entered intersection against red light, should be admitted, where passenger when subpoenaed stated he had no recollection of accident but stated he would not have signed if statement were not true or if he had not first read statement).

Neb.—Nebraska Rules of Evidence § 803(4).

Nev.—N.R.S. 51.125.

N.J.—New Jersey Evidence Rule 63 (1)(b).

N.M.—New Mexico Rules of Evidence § 803(5).

N.Y.—Brown v. Tel. Co., 1966, 274 N.Y.S.2d 52, 26 A.D.2d 316.

Utah—Utah Rules of Evidence § 63 (1)(b).

Wis.—Wisconsin Rules of Evidence § 908.03(5).

Foundation required

Kan.—Mathis v. Stricklind, 1968, 443 P.2d 673, 201 Kan. 655 (elements of past recollection recorded are that past recollection must have been written down, recollection must have been fairly fresh when recorded, recollection must have correctly represented maker's knowledge at time of making, witness must verify that record accurately represented his knowledge at time of making, and original must be submitted if available).

Mich.—Jaxon v. City of Detroit, Dept. of St. Railways, 1967, 151 N. W.2d 813, 379 Mich. 405 (consists of: (1) showing that witness has no present recollection of the facts, (2) showing that witness' memory is not refreshed upon reference to the document, (3) showing that the document is an original memo-

Police reports made under such circumstances are admissible as "past recollection recorded" evidence.[14]

Omnibus discretionary exceptions

If the evidence is otherwise unavailable, and there is basis for belief of trustworthiness, the court may have discretion to receive hearsay statements.[15]

randum made by witness from personal observation, (4) showing that document was prepared by witness contemporaneously with events and was an accurate recording of the occurrence, and (5) a showing that substance of proffered writing is otherwise admissible).

14. For discussion of police reports as within the separate exception to the hearsay rule of "business records", see section 434.11.

U.S.—Gencarella v. Fyfe, C.A.R.I., 171 F.2d 419.

Ill.—Koch v. Pearson, 219 Ill.App. 468.

Mich.—Wallace v. Skrzycki, 61 N.W. 2d 106, 338 Mich. 165.

15. U.S.—Federal Rules of Evidence §§ 803(24), 804(5), 28 U.S.C.A.

Neb.—Nebraska Rules of Evidence §§ 803(22), 804(2)(e).

Nev.—N.R.S. 51.315.

N.J.—New Jersey Evidence Rule 63 (32) (declaration one now deceased); Jastremski v. General Motors Corp., 1970, 262 A.2d 218, 109 N.J.Super. 31 (fact that plaintiffs did not depose decedent or perpetuate his testimony while he was still alive did not render inadmissible testimony of decedent's brother-in-law concerning statement allegedly made to him by decedent at hospital shortly after time automobile which decedent was driving and which was manufactured by defendant turned over).

N.M.—New Mexico Rules of Evidence §§ 803(24), 804(b)(6).

Wis.—Wisconsin Rules of Evidence §§ 908.03(24), 908.045(6).

END OF VOLUME